ALSO BY ANDREW SOLOMON

The Noonday Demon: An Atlas of Depression

A Stone Boat

The Irony Tower: Soviet Artists in a Time of Glasnost

FAR FROM THE TREE

Parents, Children, and the Search for Identity

Andrew Solomon

SCRIBNER

New York   London   Toronto   Sydney   New Delhi

SCRIBNER
A Division of Simon & Schuster, Inc.
1230 Avenue of the Americas
New York, NY 10020

First Scribner hardcover edition November 2012

SCRIBNER and design are registered trademarks of The Gale Group, Inc.,
used under license by Simon & Schuster, Inc., the publisher of this work.

For information about special discounts for bulk purchases,
please contact Simon & Schuster Special Sales at 1-866-506-1949
or business@simonandschuster.com.

The Simon & Schuster Speakers Bureau can bring authors to your live event.
For more information or to book an event, contact the Simon & Schuster Speakers Bureau
at 1-866-248-3049 or visit our website at www.simonspeakers.com.

Manufactured in the United States of America

5   7   9   10   8   6   4

Library of Congress Cataloging-in-Publication Data

Solomon, Andrew.
Far from the tree : parents, children and the search for identity / Andrew Solomon.
p.   cm.
1. Children with disabilities—United States—Psychology. 2. Exceptional children—
United States—Psychology. 3. Parents of children with disabilities—United States.
4. Parents of exceptional children—United States. 5. Identity (Psychology)—United States.
6. Parent and child—United States—Psychological aspects. I. Title.
HV888.5.S65 2012
362.4083'0973—dc23   2012020878

ISBN 978-0-7432-3671-3
ISBN 978-1-4391-8310-6 (ebook)

See p. 907 for a continuation of the copyright page.

for John,

for the sake of whose difference

I would gladly give up all the sameness in the world

The imperfect is our paradise.
Note that, in this bitterness, delight,
Since the imperfect is so hot in us,
Lies in flawed words and stubborn sounds.

—Wallace Stevens,
"The Poems of Our Climate"

Contents

FAR FROM THE TREE

I

Son

There is no such thing as reproduction. When two people decide to have a baby, they engage in an act of production, and the widespread use of the word *reproduction* for this activity, with its implication that two people are but braiding themselves together, is at best a euphemism to comfort prospective parents before they get in over their heads. In the subconscious fantasies that make conception look so alluring, it is often ourselves that we would like to see live forever, not someone with a personality of his own. Having anticipated the onward march of our selfish genes, many of us are unprepared for children who present unfamiliar needs. Parenthood abruptly catapults us into a permanent relationship with a stranger, and the more alien the stranger, the stronger the whiff of negativity. We depend on the guarantee in our children's faces that we will not die. Children whose defining quality annihilates that fantasy of immortality are a particular insult; we must love them for themselves, and not for the best of ourselves in them, and that is a great deal harder to do. Loving our own children is an exercise for the imagination.

Yet blood, in modern as in ancient societies, is thicker than water. Little is more gratifying than successful and devoted children, and few situations are worse than filial failure or rejection. Our children are not us: they carry throwback genes and recessive traits and are subject right from the start to environmental stimuli beyond our control. And yet we are our children; the reality of being a parent never leaves those who have braved the metamorphosis. The psychoanalyst D. W. Winnicott once said, "There is no such thing as a baby—meaning that if you set out to describe a baby, you will find you are describing a *baby and someone*. A baby cannot exist alone but is essentially part of a relationship." Insofar as our children resemble us, they are our most precious admirers, and insofar as they differ, they can be our most

1

vehement detractors. From the beginning, we tempt them into imitation of us and long for what may be life's most profound compliment: their choosing to live according to our own system of values. Though many of us take pride in how different we are from our parents, we are endlessly sad at how different our children are from us.

Because of the transmission of identity from one generation to the next, most children share at least some traits with their parents. These are *vertical* identities. Attributes and values are passed down from parent to child across the generations not only through strands of DNA, but also through shared cultural norms. Ethnicity, for example, is a vertical identity. Children of color are in general born to parents of color; the genetic fact of skin pigmentation is transmitted across generations along with a self-image as a person of color, even though that self-image may be subject to generational flux. Language is usually vertical, since most people who speak Greek raise their children to speak Greek, too, even if they inflect it differently or speak another language much of the time. Religion is moderately vertical: Catholic parents will tend to bring up Catholic children, though the children may turn irreligious or convert to another faith. Nationality is vertical, except for immigrants. Blondness and myopia are often transmitted from parent to child, but in most cases do not form a significant basis for identity—blondness because it is fairly insignificant, and myopia because it is easily corrected.

Often, however, someone has an inherent or acquired trait that is foreign to his or her parents and must therefore acquire identity from a peer group. This is a *horizontal* identity. Such horizontal identities may reflect recessive genes, random mutations, prenatal influences, or values and preferences that a child does not share with his progenitors. Being gay is a horizontal identity; most gay kids are born to straight parents, and while their sexuality is not determined by their peers, they learn gay identity by observing and participating in a subculture outside the family. Physical disability tends to be horizontal, as does genius. Psychopathy, too, is often horizontal; most criminals are not raised by mobsters and must invent their own treachery. So are conditions such as autism and intellectual disability. A child conceived in rape is born into emotional challenges that his own mother cannot know, even though they spring from her trauma.

In 1993, I was assigned to investigate Deaf culture for the *New York Times*. My assumption about deafness was that it was a deficit and nothing more. Over the months that followed, I found myself drawn into the Deaf world. Most deaf children are born to hearing parents, and those parents frequently prioritize functioning in the hearing world, expending enormous energy on oral speech and lipreading. Doing so, they can neglect other areas of their children's education. While some deaf people are good at lipreading and produce comprehensible speech, many do not have that skill, and years go by as they sit endlessly with audiologists and speech pathologists instead of learning history and mathematics and philosophy. Many stumble upon Deaf identity in adolescence, and it comes as a great liberation. They move into a world that validates Sign as a language and discover themselves. Some hearing parents accept this powerful new development; others struggle against it.

The whole situation felt arrestingly familiar to me because I am gay. Gay people usually grow up under the purview of straight parents who feel that their children would be better off straight and sometimes torment them by pressing them to conform. Those gay people often discover gay identity in adolescence or afterward, finding great relief there. When I started writing about the deaf, the cochlear implant, which can provide some facsimile of hearing, was a recent innovation. It had been hailed by its progenitors as a miraculous cure for a terrible defect and was deplored by the Deaf community as a genocidal attack on a vibrant community. Both sides have since moderated their rhetoric, but the issue is complicated by the fact that cochlear implants are most effective when they are surgically implanted early—in infants, ideally—so the decision is often made by parents before the child can possibly have or express an informed opinion. Watching the debate, I knew that my own parents would gamely have consented to a parallel early procedure to ensure that I would be straight, had one existed. I do not doubt that the advent of such a thing even now could wipe out most of gay culture. I am saddened by the idea of such a threat, and yet as my understanding of Deaf culture deepened, I realized that the attitudes I had found benighted in my parents resembled my own likely response to producing a deaf child. My first impulse would have been to do whatever I could to fix the abnormality.

Then a friend had a daughter who was a dwarf. She wondered whether she should bring up her daughter to consider herself just like everyone else, only shorter; whether she should make sure her daughter had dwarf role models; or whether she should investigate surgical limb-lengthening. As she narrated her bafflement, I saw a familiar pattern. I had been startled to note my common ground with the Deaf, and now I was identifying with a dwarf; I wondered who else was out there waiting to join our gladsome throng. I thought that if gayness, an identity, could grow out of homosexuality, an illness, and Deafness, an identity, could grow out of deafness, an illness, and if dwarfism as an identity could emerge from an apparent disability, then there must be many other categories in this awkward interstitial territory. It was a radicalizing insight. Having always imagined myself in a fairly slim minority, I suddenly saw that I was in a vast company. Difference unites us. While each of these experiences can isolate those who are affected, together they compose an aggregate of millions whose struggles connect them profoundly. The exceptional is ubiquitous; to be entirely typical is the rare and lonely state.

As my parents had misapprehended who I was, so other parents must be constantly misapprehending their own children. Many parents experience their child's horizontal identity as an affront. A child's marked difference from the rest of the family demands knowledge, competence, and actions that a typical mother and father are unqualified to supply, at least initially. The child is expressly different from most of his or her peers as well, and therefore broadly less understood or accepted. Abusive fathers visit less abuse on children who resemble them physically; if you are born to a bully, pray that you bear his features. Whereas families tend to reinforce vertical identities from earliest childhood, many will oppose horizontal ones. Vertical identities are usually respected as identities; horizontal ones are often treated as flaws.

One could argue that black people face many disadvantages in the United States today, but there is little research into how gene expression could be altered to make the next generation of children born to black parents come out with straight, flaxen hair and creamy complexions. In modern America, it is sometimes hard to be Asian or Jewish or female, yet no one suggests that Asians, Jews, or women would be foolish not to become white Christian men if they could. Many vertical identities make people uncomfortable, and yet we do not attempt to homogenize them. The disadvantages of being gay are arguably no greater than those of such vertical identities, but most parents have long sought to turn their gay children straight. Anomalous bodies are usually more frightening to people who witness them than to people who have them, yet parents rush to normalize physical exceptionalism, often at great psychic cost to themselves and their children. Labeling a child's mind as diseased—whether with autism, intellectual disabilities, or transgenderism—may reflect the discomfort that mind gives parents more than any discomfort it causes their child. Much gets corrected that might better have been left alone.

Defective is an adjective that has long been deemed too freighted for liberal discourse, but the medical terms that have supplanted it—*illness, syndrome, condition*—can be almost equally pejorative in their discreet way. We often use *illness* to disparage a way of being, and *identity* to validate that same way of being. This is a false dichotomy. In physics, the Copenhagen interpretation defines energy/matter as behaving sometimes like a wave and sometimes like a particle, which suggests that it is both, and posits that it is our human limitation to be unable to see both at the same time. The Nobel Prize–winning physicist Paul Dirac identified how light appears to be a particle if we ask a particle-like question, and a wave if we ask a wavelike question. A similar duality obtains in this matter of self. Many conditions are both illness and identity, but we can see one only when we obscure the other. Identity politics refutes the idea of illness, while medicine shortchanges identity. Both are diminished by this narrowness.

Physicists gain certain insights from understanding energy as a wave, and other insights from understanding it as a particle, and use quantum mechanics to reconcile the information they have gleaned. Similarly, we have to examine *illness* and *identity*, understand that observation will usually happen in one domain or the other, and come up with a syncretic mechanics. We need a vocabulary in which the two concepts are not opposites, but compatible aspects of a condition. The problem is to change how we assess the value of individuals and of lives, to reach for a more ecumenical take on *healthy*. Ludwig Wittgenstein said, "All I know is what I have words for." The absence of words is the absence of intimacy; these experiences are starved for language.

The children I describe here have horizontal conditions that are alien to their parents. They are deaf or dwarfs; they have Down syndrome, autism, schizophrenia, or multiple severe disabilities; they are prodigies; they are people conceived in rape or who commit crimes; they are transgender. The timeworn adage says that the apple doesn't fall far from the tree, meaning that a child resembles his or her parents; these children are apples that have fallen elsewhere—some a couple of orchards away, some on the other side of the world. Yet myriad families learn to tolerate, accept, and finally celebrate children who are not what they originally had in mind. This transformative process is often eased and sometimes confounded by identity politics and medical progress—both of which have infiltrated households to a degree that would have been inconceivable even twenty years ago.

All offspring are startling to their parents; these most dramatic situations are merely variations on a common theme. Much as we learn the properties of a medication by studying its effect at extremely high doses, or look at the viability of a construction material by exposing it to unearthly supertemperatures, so we can understand the universal phenomenon of difference within families by looking at these extreme cases. Having exceptional children exaggerates parental tendencies; those who would be bad parents become awful parents, but those who would be good parents often become extraordinary. I take the anti-Tolstoyan view that the unhappy families who reject their variant children have much in common, while the happy ones who strive to accept them are happy in a multitude of ways.

Because prospective parents have ever-increasing options to choose against having children with horizontal challenges, the experiences of those who have such children are critical to our larger understanding of difference. Parents' early responses to and interactions with a child determine how that child comes to view himself. These parents are also profoundly changed by their experiences. If you have a child with a disability, you are forever the parent of a disabled child; it is one of the primary facts about you, fundamental to the way other people perceive and decipher you. Such parents tend to view aberrance as illness until habituation and love enable them to cope with their odd new reality—often by introducing the language of identity. Intimacy with difference fosters its accommodation.

Broadcasting these parents' learned happiness is vital to sustaining identities that are now vulnerable to eradication. Their stories point a way for all of us to expand our definitions of the human family. It's important to know how autistic people feel about autism, or dwarfs about dwarfism. Self-acceptance is part of the ideal, but without familial and societal acceptance, it cannot ameliorate the relentless injustices to which many horizontal identity groups are subject and will not bring about adequate reform. We live in xenophobic times, when legislation with majority support abrogates the rights of women, LGBT people, illegal immigrants, and the poor. Despite this crisis in empathy, compassion thrives at home, and most of the parents I have profiled love across the divide. Understanding how they came to think well of their own children may give the rest of us motive and insight to do the same. To look deep into your child's eyes and see in him both yourself and something utterly strange, and then to develop a zealous attachment to every aspect of him, is to achieve parenthood's self-regarding, yet unselfish, abandon. It is astonishing how often such mutuality has been realized—how frequently parents who had supposed that they couldn't care for an exceptional child discover that they can. The parental predisposition to love prevails in the most harrowing of circumstances. There is more imagination in the world than one might think.

I had dyslexia as a child; indeed, I have it now. I still cannot write by hand without focusing on each letter as I form it, and even when I do so, some letters are out of order or omitted. My mother, who identified the dyslexia early, began to work on reading with me when I was two. I spent long afternoons in her lap, learning to sound out words, training like an Olympic athlete in phonetics; we practiced letters as though no shapes could ever be lovelier than theirs. To keep my attention, she gave me a notebook with a yellow felt cover on which Winnie-the-Pooh and Tigger were sewn; we made flash cards and played games with them in the car. I reveled in the attention, and my mother taught with a sense of fun, as though it was the best puzzle in the world, a private game between us. When I was six, my parents applied for my admission to eleven schools in New York City, and all eleven turned me down on grounds that I would never learn to read and write. A year later, I was enrolled in a school where the principal grudgingly allowed my advanced reading skills to overrule test scores that predicted I would never learn to read at all. The standards of perpetual triumph were high in our house, and that early victory over dyslexia was formative: with patience, love, intelligence, and will, we had trounced a neurological abnormality. Unfortunately, it set the stage for our later struggles by making it hard to believe that we couldn't reverse the creeping evidence of another perceived abnormality—my being gay.

People ask when I knew I was gay, and I wonder what that knowledge entails. It took some time for me to become aware of my sexual desires. The realization that what I wanted was exotic, and out of step with the majority, came so early that I cannot remember a time preceding it. Recent studies have shown that as early as age two, male children who will grow up to be gay are averse to certain types of rough-and-tumble play; by age six, most will behave in obviously gender-nonconforming ways. Because I could tell early on that many of my impulses were unmasculine, I embarked on further acts of self-invention. When, in first grade, each of us was asked to name his favorite food and everyone else said ice cream or hamburgers or French toast, I proudly chose *ekmek kadayiff* with *kaymak*, which I used to order at an Armenian restaurant on East Twenty-Seventh Street. I never traded a baseball card, but I did recount the plots of operas on the school bus. None of this made me popular.

I was popular at home, but I was subject to corrections. My mother, my brother, and I were at Indian Walk Shoes when I was seven, and as we were leaving, the salesman asked what color balloons we'd like. My brother wanted a red balloon. I wanted a pink one. My mother countered that I didn't want a pink balloon and reminded me that my favorite color was blue. I said I really wanted the pink, but under her glare, I took the blue one. That my favorite color is blue but I am still gay is evidence of both my mother's influence and its limits. She once said, "When you were little, you didn't like to do what other kids liked to do, and I encouraged you to be yourself." She added, only half-ironically, "I sometimes think I let things go too far." I have sometimes thought she didn't let them go far enough. But her encouragement of my individuality, although doubtless ambivalent, has shaped my life.

My new school had quasi-liberal ideas and was supposed to be integrated—which meant that our class included a few black and Latino kids on scholarship who mostly socialized with one another. My first year there, Debbie Camacho had a birthday party in Harlem, and her parents, unacquainted with the logic of New York private education, scheduled it for the same weekend as homecoming. My mother asked how I would feel if no one attended my birthday party, and insisted that I attend. I doubt many kids in my class would have gone to the party even if there hadn't been such a convenient excuse, but in fact, only two white kids went out of a class of forty. I was frankly terrified of being there. The birthday girl's cousins tried to get me to dance; everyone spoke Spanish; there were unfamiliar fried foods; and I had something of a panic attack and went home in tears.

I drew no parallels between everyone's avoidance of Debbie's party and my own unpopularity, even when, a few months later, Bobby Finkel had a birthday party and invited everyone in the class but me. My mother called his mother on the assumption that there had been a mistake; Mrs. Finkel said that her son didn't like me and didn't want me at his party. My mother picked me up at school on the day of the party and took me to the zoo, and for a hot fudge sundae at Old-Fashioned Mr. Jennings. It's only in retrospect that I imagine how hurt my mother was on my behalf—more hurt than I was, or let myself notice I was. I didn't guess then that her tenderness was a bid to compensate for the insults of the world. When I contemplate my parents' discomfort with my gayness, I can see how vulnerable my vulnerabilities made her, and how much she wanted to preempt my sadness with the assurance that we were our own good time. Forbidding the pink balloon must be held as partly a protective gesture.

I'm glad my mother made me go to Debbie Camacho's birthday party—because I think it was the right thing to do and because, though I couldn't see it at the time, it was the beginning of an attitude of tolerance that allowed me to stomach myself and find happiness in adulthood. It's tempting to paint myself and my family as beacons of liberal exceptionalism, but we weren't. I teased one African-American student in my elementary school by claiming he resembled a picture in our social studies book of a tribal child in an African *rondavel*. I didn't think that this was racist; I thought it was funny, and vaguely true. When I was older, I remembered my behavior with deep regret, and when the person in question found me on Facebook, I apologized profusely. I said that my only excuse was that it was not easy to be gay at the school, and that I'd acted out the prejudice I experienced in the form of prejudice toward others. He accepted my apology, and mentioned that he was also gay; I was humbled that he had survived, where so much of both kinds of bias were in play.

I floundered in the tricky waters of elementary school, but at home, where bias was never tinged with cruelty, my more intractable deficits were minimized and my quirks were mostly humored. When I was ten, I became fascinated by the tiny principality of Liechtenstein. A year later, my father took us along on a business trip to Zürich, and one morning my mother announced that she'd arranged for us all to drive to Liechtenstein's capital, Vaduz. I remember the thrill that the whole family was going along with what was clearly my wish and mine alone. In retrospect, the Liechtenstein preoccupation seems peculiar, but the same mother who forbade the pink balloon thought up and arranged that day: lunch in a charming café, a tour of the art museum, a visit to the printing office where they make the country's distinctive postage stamps. Although I did not always feel approved of, I always felt acknowledged and was given the latitude of my eccentricity. But there were limits, and pink balloons fell on the wrong side of them. Our family rule was to be interested in otherness from within a pact of sameness. I wanted to stop merely observing the wide world and inhabit its wideness: I wanted to dive for pearls, memorize Shakespeare, break the sound barrier, learn to knit. From one angle, the desire to transform myself can be seen as an attempt to unshackle myself from an undesirable way of being. From another, it was a gesture toward my essential self, a crucial pivot toward whom I was to become.

Even in kindergarten, I spent recess making conversation with my teachers because other children didn't get it; the teachers probably didn't get it, either, but they were old enough to be polite. By seventh grade, I ate lunch most days in the office of Mrs. Brier, secretary of the head of the lower school. I graduated from high school without visiting the cafeteria, where I would have sat with the girls and been laughed at for doing so, or with the boys and been laughed at for being the kind of boy who should really sit with the girls. The impulse to conformity that so often defines childhood never existed for me, and when I began to think about sexuality, the nonconformity of same-sex desires thrilled me—the realization that what I wanted was even more different and forbidden than all sex is to the young. Homosexuality felt to me like an

Armenian dessert or a day in Liechtenstein. I nonetheless thought that if anyone found out I was gay, I would have to die.

My mother didn't want me to be gay because she thought it wouldn't be the happiest course for me, but equally, she didn't like the image of herself as the mother of a gay son. The problem wasn't that she wanted to control *my* life—although she did, like most parents, genuinely believe that her way of being happy was the best way of being happy. The problem was that she wanted to control *her* life, and it was her life as the mother of a homosexual that she wished to alter. Unfortunately, there was no way for her to fix her problem without involving me.

I learned to hate this aspect of my identity profoundly and early because that crouching posture echoed a family response to a vertical identity. My mother thought it was undesirable to be Jewish. She had learned this view from my grandfather, who kept his religion secret so he could hold a high-level job in a company that did not employ Jews. He belonged to a suburban country club where Jews were not welcome. In her early twenties, my mother was briefly engaged to a Texan, but he broke it off when his family threatened to disinherit him if he married a Jew. For her, it was a trauma of self-recognition, because until then she had not thought of herself as a designated Jew; she had thought she could be whomever she appeared to be. Five years later, she chose to marry my Jewish father and live in a largely Jewish world, but she carried the anti-Semitism within her. She would see people who fit certain stereotypes and say, "Those are the people who give us a bad name." When I asked her what she thought of the much sought-after beauty of my ninth-grade class, she said, "She looks very Jewish." Her method of rueful self-doubt was organized for me around being gay: I inherited her gift for discomfort.

Long after childhood, I clung to childish things as a dam against sexuality. This willful immaturity was overlaid with an affected Victorian prudery, aimed not at masking but at obliterating desire. I had some farfetched idea that I would be Christopher Robin forever in the Hundred Acre Wood; indeed, the final chapter of the *Winnie-the-Pooh* books felt so much like my story that I couldn't bear to hear it, though I had my father read me all the other chapters hundreds of times. *The House at Pooh Corner* ends, "Wherever they go, and whatever happens to them on the way, in that enchanted place on top of the Forest, a little boy and his Bear will always be playing." I decided that I would be that boy and that bear, that I would freeze myself in puerility, because what growing up portended for me was too humiliating. At thirteen, I bought a copy of *Playboy* and spent hours studying it, trying to resolve my discomfort with female anatomy; it was much more grueling than my homework. By the time I reached high school, I knew I had to have sex with women sooner or later and felt that I couldn't do so, and thought often about dying. The half of me that wasn't planning to be Christopher Robin playing forever in an enchanted place was planning to be Anna Karenina throwing myself in front of a train. It was a ludicrous duality.

When I was in eighth grade at the Horace Mann School in New York, an older kid nicknamed me Percy as a shorthand for my demeanor. We were on the same school-bus route, and each day when I boarded, he and his cohort would chant, "Percy! Percy! Percy!" I sometimes sat with a Chinese-American student who was too shy to talk to anyone else (and turned out to be gay himself), and sometimes with a nearly blind girl who was also the object of considerable cruelty. Sometimes, everyone on the bus chanted that provocation the entire ride. "Per-cy! Per-cy! Per-cy! Per-cy!" at the top of their lungs for forty-five minutes: all the way up Third Avenue, along the FDR Drive, across the Willis Avenue Bridge, the length of the Major Deegan Expressway, and onto 246th Street in Riverdale. The blind girl kept repeating that I should "just ignore it," and so I sat there pretending unconvincingly that it wasn't happening.

Four months after it began, I came home one day and my mother asked, "Has something been happening on the school bus? Have other students been calling you Percy?" A classmate had told his mother, who in turn had called mine. When I admitted it, she hugged me for a long time, then asked why I hadn't told her. It had never occurred to me: partly because talking about something so degrading seemed only to reify it, partly because I thought there was nothing to be done, and partly because I felt that the qualities for which I was being tortured would be abhorrent to my mother, too, and I wanted to protect her from disappointment.

Thereafter, a chaperone rode on the school bus and the chanting stopped. I was merely called "faggot" on the bus and at school, often within hearing distance of teachers who raised no objections. That same year, my science teacher told us that homosexuals developed fecal incontinence because their anal sphincters were destroyed. Homophobia was ubiquitous in the 1970s, but the smug culture of my school delivered a sharply honed version of it.

In June of 2012, the *New York Times Magazine* published an article by Horace Mann alumnus Amos Kamil about some male faculty members' predatory abuse of boys at the school while I was a student there. The article quoted students who developed addiction issues and other self-destructive behavior in the wake of such episodes; one man had committed suicide in middle age as the culmination of despair that his family traced to the youthful exploitation. The article made me profoundly sad—and confused, because some teachers accused of such acts had been kinder to me than anyone else at my school during a desolate time. My beloved history teacher took me out to dinner, gave me a copy of the Jerusalem Bible, and talked with me during free periods when other students wanted nothing to do with me. The music teacher awarded me concert solos, let me call him by his first name and hang out in his office, and led the glee club trips that were among my happiest adventures. They seemed to recognize who I was and thought well of me anyway. Their implicit acknowledgment of my sexuality helped me not to become an addict or a suicide.

When I was in ninth grade the school's art teacher (who was also a football coach) kept trying to strike up a conversation with me about masturbation. I was paralyzed: I thought it might be a form of entrapment, and that if I responded, he'd tell everyone that I was gay, and I'd be even more of a laughingstock than I already was. No other faculty member ever made a move on me—perhaps because I was a skinny, socially awkward kid with glasses and braces, perhaps because my parents had a reputation for protective vigilance, perhaps because I assumed a self-insulating arrogance that made me less vulnerable than some others.

The art teacher was removed when allegations against him emerged soon after my conversations with him. The history teacher was let go and committed suicide a year later. The music teacher, who was married, survived the ensuing "reign of terror," as one gay faculty member later called it, when many gay teachers were ousted. Kamil wrote to me that the firings of nonpredatory gay teachers grew out of "a misguided attempt to root out pedophilia by falsely equating it with homosexuality." Students spoke monstrously of and even to gay teachers because their prejudice was so obviously endorsed by the school community.

The head of the theater department, Anne MacKay, was a lesbian who quietly survived the recriminations. Twenty years after I graduated, she and I began corresponding by e-mail. I drove to the east end of Long Island to visit her a decade later when I learned she was dying. We had both been contacted by Amos Kamil, who was then researching his article, and had both been unsettled by the allegations he shared. Miss MacKay had been the wise teacher who once explained gently that I was teased because of how I walked, and tried to show me a more confident stride. She staged *The Importance of Being Earnest* my senior year so that I could have a star turn as Algernon. I had come to thank her. But she had invited me to apologize.

At a previous job, she explained, word had got around that she lived with another woman, parents had complained, and she'd gone into a kind of hiding for the rest of her career. Now she regretted the formal distance she'd sustained and felt she had failed the gay students to whom she might have been a beacon—although I knew, and she did, too, that if she'd been more open, she'd have lost her job. When I was her student, I never thought to wonder about greater intimacy than we had, but talking decades later, I realized how forlorn we'd both been. I wish we could have been the same age for a while, because who I am at forty-eight would be a good friend for who she was when she was teaching young me. Off campus, Miss MacKay was a gay activist; now, I am, too. When I was in high school, I knew she was gay; she knew I was gay; yet each of us was imprisoned by our homosexuality in a way that made direct conversation impossible, leaving us with only kindness to give each other instead of truth. Seeing her after so many years stirred up my old loneliness, and I was reminded of how isolating an exceptional identity can be unless we resolve it into horizontal solidarity.

In the unsettling online reunion of Horace Mann alumni that followed the publication of Amos Kamil's story, one man wrote of his sadness for both the abuse victims and the perpetrators, saying of the latter, "They were wounded, confused people trying to figure out how to function in a world that taught them that their homosexual desire was sick. Schools mirror the world we live in. They can't be perfect places. Not every teacher will be an emotionally balanced person. We can condemn these teachers. But this deals with a symptom only, not the original problem, which is that an intolerant society creates self-hating people who act out inappropriately." Sexual contact between teachers and students is unacceptable because it exploits a power differential that clouds the demarcation between coercion and consent. It often causes irrecoverable trauma. It clearly did so for the students Kamil interviewed and described. Wondering how my teachers could have done this, I thought that someone whose core being is deemed a sickness and an illegality may struggle to parse the distinction between that and a much greater crime. Treating an identity as an illness invites real illness to make a braver stand.

Sexual opportunity comes often to young people, especially in New York. One of my chores was to walk our dog before bedtime, and when I was fourteen, I discovered two gay bars near our apartment: Uncle Charlie's Uptown and Camp David. I would walk Martha, our Kerry

Blue terrier, on a circuit that included these two emporiums of denimed flesh, watching the guys spill out into Lexington Avenue while Martha tugged gently on the leash. One man who said his name was Dwight followed me and pulled me into a doorway. I couldn't go home with Dwight or the others because if I did, I'd be turned into someone else. I don't remember what Dwight looked like, but his name makes me wistful. When I eventually had sex with a man, at seventeen, I felt that I was severing myself forever from the normal world. I went home and boiled my clothes, then took a scalding, hourlong shower, as though my transgression could be sterilized away.

When I was nineteen, I read an ad in the back of *New York* magazine that offered surrogate therapy for people who had issues with sex. I still believed that the problem of whom I wanted was subsidiary to the problem of whom I didn't want. I knew the back of a magazine was not a good place to find treatment, but my condition was too embarrassing to reveal to anyone who knew me. Taking my savings to a walk-up office in Hell's Kitchen, I subjected myself to long conversations about my sexual anxieties, unable to admit to myself or the so-called therapist that I was actually just not interested in women. I didn't mention the busy sexual life I had by this time with men. I began "counseling" with people I was encouraged to call "doctors," who would prescribe "exercises" with my "surrogates"—women who were not exactly prostitutes but who were also not exactly anything else. In one protocol, I had to crawl around naked on all fours pretending to be a dog while the surrogate pretended to be a cat; the metaphor of enacting intimacy between mutually averse species is more loaded than I noticed at the time. I became curiously fond of these women, one of whom, an attractive blonde from the Deep South, eventually told me that she was a necrophiliac and had taken this job after she got into trouble down at the morgue. You were supposed to keep switching girls so your ease was not limited to one sexual partner; I remember the first time a Puerto Rican woman climbed on top of me and began to bounce up and down, crying ecstatically, "You're in me! You're in me!" and how I lay there wondering with anxious boredom whether I had finally achieved the prize and become a qualified heterosexual.

Cures seldom work swiftly and completely for anything other than bacterial infections, but it can be hard to see that when social and medical realities are in rapid flux. My own recovery has been from the perception of illness. That office on Forty-Fifth Street shows up in my dreams: the necrophiliac who found my pale, sweaty form close enough to a corpse to float her boat; the mission-driven Latino woman who introduced me to her body with so much jubilation. My treatment took only two hours a week for about six months, and it gave me an ease with women's bodies that was vital to subsequent heterosexual experiences I'm glad to have had. I truly loved some of the women with whom I later had relationships, but when I was with them, I could never forget that my "cure" was a distilled manifestation of self-loathing, and I have never entirely forgiven the circumstances that disposed me to make the obscene effort. Stretching my psyche between Dwight and those cat-women made romantic love almost impossible for me during my early adulthood.

My interest in profound differences between parents and children arose from a need to investigate the locus of my regret. While I'd like to blame my parents, I have come to believe that a lot of my pain came from the larger world around me, and some of it came from me. In the heat of an argument, my mother once told me, "Someday you can go to a therapist and tell him all about how your terrible mother ruined your life. But it will be *your* ruined life you're talking about. So make a life for yourself in which you can feel happy, and in which you can love and be loved, because that's what's actually important." You can love someone but not accept him; you can accept someone but not love him. I wrongly felt the flaws in my parents' acceptance as deficits in their love. Now, I think their primary experience was of having a child who spoke a language they'd never thought of studying.

How is any parent to know whether to erase or celebrate a given characteristic? When I was born in 1963, homosexual activity was a crime; during my childhood, it was a symptom of illness. When I was two, *Time* magazine wrote, "Even in purely nonreligious terms, homosexuality represents a misuse of the sexual faculty. It is a pathetic little second-rate substitute for reality, a pitiable flight from life. As such it deserves fairness, compassion, understanding and, when possible, treatment. But it deserves no encouragement, no glamorization, no rationalization, no fake status as minority martyrdom, no sophistry about simple differences in taste—and, above all, no pretense that it is anything but a pernicious sickness."

When I was growing up, we nonetheless had close family friends who were gay—neighbors, and surrogate great-uncles to my brother and me, who spent holidays with us because their own families would not have them. I was always bewildered that Elmer had gone off to World War II halfway through medical school, fought on the Western Front, and then opened a gift shop when he came home. For years, I heard that the terrible things he saw in the war had changed him, and that he didn't have the stomach for medicine after his return. It was only after Elmer died that Willy, his partner of fifty years, explained to me that

15

no one would have considered going to an openly gay doctor in 1945. The horrors of war had propelled Elmer into integrity, and he paid its price by spending his adulthood painting amusing bar stools and selling crockery. Elmer and Willy were a great romance in many ways, but an undertone of sadness for what might have been informed their lives. The gift shop was an apology for medicine; Christmas with us was an apology for family. I am humbled by Elmer's choice; I do not know that I would have had the courage to choose likewise, nor the discipline to keep regret from undermining my love had I done so. Though Elmer and Willy would never have seen themselves as activists, their galvanizing sorrow and that of others like them was the precondition of my happiness and that of others like me. When I understood their story more richly, I recognized that my parents' fears for me were not simply the product of overactive imaginations.

In my adulthood, being gay is an identity; the tragic narrative my parents feared for me is no longer inevitable. The happy life I now lead was unimaginable when I was asking for pink balloons and *ekmek kadayiff*—even when I was being Algernon. Yet, the trifecta view of homosexuality as a crime, an illness, and a sin remains potent. I sometimes felt that it was easier for me to ask people about their disabled children, their children conceived in rape, their children who committed crimes, than it would have been to look squarely at how many parents still respond to having children like me. Ten years ago, a *New Yorker* poll asked parents whether they would prefer to see their child gay, happily partnered, fulfilled, and with children, or straight, single or unhappily partnered, and childless. One out of three chose the latter. You cannot hate a horizontal identity much more explicitly than to wish unhappiness and likeness for your children over happiness and difference. In the United States, new antigay laws emerge with monotonous regularity; in December 2011, Michigan enacted the Public Employee Domestic Partner Benefit Restriction Act, which bars gay employees' partners from health-care coverage, despite allowing city and county employers to provide health-care coverage to all other family members, including uncles, nieces, and cousins. Meanwhile, in much of the larger world, the identity I inhabit remains unimaginable. In 2011, Uganda came close to passing a bill that would have made some homosexual acts punishable by death. An article in *New York* magazine about gay people in Iraq includes this information: "The bodies of gay men, often mutilated, began turning up on the street. Hundreds of men are believed to have been killed. Gay men's rectums had been glued shut, and they had been force-fed laxatives and water until their insides exploded."

Much of the debate around sexual-orientation laws has turned on the idea that if you choose homosexuality, it should not be protected, but if you are born with it, perhaps it should. Members of minority religions are protected not because they are born that way and can't do anything about it, but because we affirm their right to discover, declare, and inhabit the faith with which they identify. Activists got homosexuality removed from the official list of mental illnesses in 1973, yet gay rights remain contingent on claims that the condition is involuntary and fixed. This cripple-like model of sexuality is depressing, but as soon as anyone posits that homosexuality is chosen or mutable, lawmakers and religious leaders try to cure and disenfranchise the gay people in their purview. Today, men and women continue to be "treated" for homosexuality at religious reform camps and in the offices of unscrupulous or misguided psychiatrists. The ex-gay movement in evangelical Christianity deranges gay people by the tens of thousands by seeking to persuade them, contrary to their experience, that desire is wholly volitional. The founder of the antihomosexual organization MassResistance has argued that gays should be made specific targets of discrimination, due to the supposedly voluntary nature of their ostensible perversion.

Those who think that a biological explanation of gayness will improve the sociopolitical position of gay people are also sadly mistaken, as the response to recent scientific findings makes clear. The sexologist Ray Blanchard has described a "fraternal birth order effect," which holds that the chance of producing gay sons goes up steadily with each male fetus a mother carries. Within weeks of publishing this data, he was called by a man who had decided against hiring a surrogate who had borne previous boys, saying to Blanchard, "That's not really what I want . . . especially if I'm paying for it." The arthritis drug dexamethasone is used off-label to treat women at risk for producing daughters with a condition that partially masculinizes their genitalia. Maria New, a researcher at Mount Sinai Hospital in New York, has suggested that dexamethasone given in early pregnancy will also reduce the chances that such babies will grow up to be lesbian; indeed, she has described the treatment as making girls more interested in childbearing and homemaking, less aggressive, and more shy. It has been posited that such therapy might curb lesbianism even in the general population. In animal studies, prenatal exposure to dexamethasone seems to cause many health problems, but if any medication can actually limit lesbianism, researchers will come up with a safer one. Medical findings such as these will continue to have serious social implications. If we develop prenatal markers for homosexuality, many couples will abort their gay children; if we come up with a viable preventative drug, many parents will be willing to try it.

I would no more insist that parents who don't want gay children must have them than I would that people who don't want children at all must have them. Nonetheless, I cannot think about Blanchard's and New's research without feeling like the last quagga. I am not evangelical. I don't need to verticalize my identity onto my children, but I would hate for my horizontal identity to vanish. I would hate it for those who share my identity, and for those who lie outside it. I hate the loss of diversity in the world, even though I sometimes get a little worn out by being that diversity. I don't wish for anyone in particular to be gay, but the idea of no one's being gay makes me miss myself already.

All people are both the objects and the perpetrators of prejudice. Our understanding of the prejudice directed against us informs our responses to others. Universalizing from the cruelties we have known, however, has its limits, and the parents of a child with a horizontal identity often fail at empathy. My mother's issues with Judaism didn't make her much better at dealing with my being gay; my being gay wouldn't have made me a good parent to a deaf child until I'd discerned the parallels between the Deaf experience and the gay one. A lesbian couple I interviewed who had a transgender child told me they approved of the murder of George Tiller, the abortion provider, because the Bible said that abortion was wrong, and yet they were astonished and frustrated at the intolerance they had encountered for their identity and their child's. We are overextended in the travails of our own situation, and making common cause with other groups is an exhausting prospect. Many gay people will react negatively to comparisons with the disabled, just as many African-Americans reject gay activists' use of the language of civil rights. But comparing people with disabilities to people who are gay implies no negativity about gayness or disability. Everyone is flawed and strange; most people are valiant, too. The reasonable corollary to the queer experience is that everyone has a defect, that everyone has an identity, and that they are often one and the same.

It's terrifying to me to think that without my mother's sustained intervention, I might never have learned fluency in letters; I am grateful every day for the sufficient resolution of my dyslexia. Conversely, while I might have had an easier life if I had been straight, I am now wedded to the idea that without my struggles, I would not be myself, and that I like being myself better than I like the idea of being someone else—someone I have neither the ability to imagine nor the option of being. Nevertheless, I have often wondered whether I could have ceased to hate my sexual orientation without Gay Pride's Technicolor fiesta, of which this writing is one manifestation. I used to think that I would be mature when I could simply be gay without emphasis. I have decided against this viewpoint, in part because there is almost nothing about which I feel neutral, but more because I perceive those years of self-loathing as a yawning void, and celebration needs to fill and over-flow it. Even if I adequately address my private debt of melancholy, there is an outer world of homophobia and prejudice to repair. Some-day, I hope this identity may devolve into a simple fact, free of both party hats and blame, but that's some ways off. A friend who thought Gay Pride was getting a bit carried away with itself once suggested we organize Gay Humility Week. It's a good idea, but its time has not yet come. Neutrality, which appears to lie halfway between shame and rejoicing, is in fact the endgame, reached only when activism becomes unnecessary.

It is a surprise to me to like myself; among all the elaborate possi-bilities I contemplated for my future, that never figured. My hard-won contentment reflects the simple truth that inner peace often hinges on outer peace. In the gnostic gospel of St. Thomas, Jesus says, "If you bring forth what is within you, what is within you will save you. If you do not bring forth what is within you, what is within you will destroy you." When I run up against the antigay positions of modern religious bodies, I often wish that St. Thomas's words were canonical because his message embraces many of us with horizontal identities. Keeping the homosexuality locked away within me nearly destroyed me, and bring-ing it forth has nearly saved me.

Although men who murder usually target people not related to them, nearly 40 percent of women who inflict death kill their own babies. Reports of human children discarded in Dumpsters and the overburdened foster-care network point to the ability of human beings to detach. Oddly, this seems to have at least as much to do with the infant's appearance as with its health or character. Parents will usually take home a child with a life-threatening internal defect, but not one with a minor visible defect; at a later stage, some parents will reject even children with severe burn scars. Manifest disabilities affront parents' pride and their need for privacy; everyone can see that this child isn't what you wanted, and you must either accept the world's pity or insist on your own pride. At least half of the children available for adoption in the United States have disabilities of some kind. Half of those available for adoption, however, still constitutes only a small proportion of disabled children.

Modern love comes with more and more options. For most of history, people married only members of the opposite sex, from their own class, race, denomination, and geographical location—all increasingly disputed boundaries. Similarly, people were supposed to accept the children given to them because one could do little to choose or change them. Birth control and fertility technologies have severed the bond between sex and procreation: intercourse does not necessarily engender babies, nor is it requisite to produce them. The analysis of embryos prior to implantation and the expanding domain of prenatal testing give parents access to a wealth of information to help them decide whether to initiate, continue, or terminate a pregnancy. The choices are broadening every day. People who believe in the right to opt for healthy, normative children refer to *selective abortion*; people to whom that idea is anathema refer to *commercial eugenics*, evoking a world stripped of variety and vulnerability. A vast industry of pediatric medicine implies that responsible parents should revamp their children in various ways, and parents expect doctors to correct their children's perceived defects: to administer human growth hormone to make the short ones taller, to fix a cleft lip, to normalize ambiguous genitalia. These optimizing interventions are not exactly cosmetic, but they are not necessary for survival. They have led social theorists such as Francis Fukuyama to speak of a "post-human future" in which we will eliminate the variety within mankind.

Yet while medicine promises to normalize us, our social reality remains a miscellany. If the cliché is that modernity makes people more similar, as tribal headdresses and frock coats alike give way to T-shirts and jeans, the reality is that modernity comforts us with trivial uniformities even as it allows us to become more far-flung in our desires and our ways of realizing them. Social mobility and the Internet allow anyone to find others who share his quiddities. No closed circle of French aristocrats or farm boys from Iowa has been tighter than these new clusters of the electronic age. As the line between illness and identity is challenged, the strength of these online supports is a vital setting for the emergence of true selves. Modern life is lonely in many ways, but the ability of everyone with access to a computer to find like-minded people has meant that no one need be excluded from social kinship. If the physical or psychic place to which you were born wants no more of you, an infinitude of locales of the spirit beckons. Vertical families are famously breaking down in divorce, but horizontal ones are proliferating. If you can figure out who you are, you can find other people who are the same. Social progress is making disabling conditions easier to live with just as medical progress is eliminating them. There is something tragic about this confluence, like those operas in which the hero realizes he loves the heroine just as she expires.

Parents willing to be interviewed are a self-selecting group; those who are bitter are less likely to tell their stories than those who have found value in their experience and want to help others in similar circumstances to do the same. No one loves without reservation, however, and everyone would be better off if we could destigmatize parental ambivalence. Freud posits that any declaration of love masks some degree of odium, any hatred at least a trace of adoration. All that children can properly require of their parents is that they tolerate their own muddled spectrum—that they neither insist on the lie of perfect happiness nor lapse into the slipshod brutality of giving up. One mother who lost a child with a serious disability worried in a letter to me that if she felt relieved, her grief was not real. There is no contradiction between loving someone and feeling burdened by that person; indeed, love tends to magnify the burden. These parents need space for their ambivalence, whether they can allow it for themselves or not. For those who love, there should be no shame in being exhausted—even in imagining another life.

Some marginalizing conditions, such as schizophrenia and Down syndrome, are thought to be entirely genetic; others, such as being transgender, are believed to be largely environmental. Nature and nurture get positioned as opposing influences, when it is more often, in the science writer Matt Ridley's phrase, "nature via nurture." We know that environmental factors can alter the brain, and conversely, that brain chemistry and structure partly determine how much we can be affected by external influences. Much as a word exists as a sound, a set of marks on a page, and a metaphor, nature and nurture are diverse conceptual frameworks for a single set of phenomena.

Nevertheless, it is easier for parents to tolerate the syndromes assigned to nature than those thought to result from nurture, because guilt is reduced for the former category. If your child has achondroplastic dwarfism, no one will accuse you of bad behavior for having produced such a child. However, an individual's success at accommodating his own dwarfism and valuing his own life may be largely a function of nurture. If you have a child conceived in rape, you may encounter some blame—either for the rape itself, or for your decision not to abort the pregnancy. If you have a child who has committed serious crimes, it is often assumed that you did something wrong as a parent, and people whose children do not commit crimes may condescend accordingly. But there is increasing evidence that some criminality may be hardwired, and that even the most admirable moral instruction may be ineffective in swaying a child who is so predisposed to gruesome acts that, in Clarence Darrow's phrase, his murderous crime "was inherent in his organism, and came from some ancestor." You can enable or discourage criminal tendencies, but the result in either direction is by no means guaranteed.

The social perception of whether any supposed deficit is the parents' fault is always a critical factor in the experience of both children and parents. The Nobel Prize–winning geneticist James D. Watson, who has a son with schizophrenia, once told me that Bruno Bettelheim, the midcentury psychologist who asserted that autism and schizophrenia were caused by poor parenting, was "after Hitler, the most evil person of the twentieth century." The attribution of responsibility to parents is often a function of ignorance, but it also reflects our anxious belief that we control our own destinies. Unfortunately, it does not save anyone's children; it only destroys some people's parents, who either crumble under the strain of undue censure or rush to blame themselves before anyone else has time to accuse them. The parents of a woman who had died of a genetic illness told me they felt terrible because they hadn't had prenatal genetic testing, which did not exist at the time their daughter was born. Many parents similarly organize their guilt around some fictitious misstep. I had lunch one afternoon with a highly educated activist whose son suffers from severe autism. "It's because I went skiing while I was pregnant," she said to me. "The altitude isn't good for the developing child." I felt so sad hearing this. The roots of autism are confusing, and there are questions as to what may dispose children toward the condition, but altitude is not on the list. This intelligent woman had so assimilated a narrative of self-blame that she didn't know that it had come out of her imagination.

There is something ironic in prejudice against the disabled and their families, because their plight might befall anybody. Straight men are unlikely to wake up gay one morning, and white children don't become black; but any of us could be disabled in an instant. People with disabilities make up the largest minority in America; they constitute 15 percent of the population, though only 15 percent of those were born with their disability and about a third are over sixty-five. Worldwide, some 550 million people are disabled. The disability-rights scholar Tobin Siebers has written, "The cycle of life runs in actuality from disability to temporary ability back to disability, and that only if you are among the most fortunate."

In typical circumstances, to have children who won't care for you in your dotage is to be King Lear. Disability changes the reciprocity equation; severely disabled adults may still require attention in midlife, when other grown children are attending to their own parents. The most effortful stages of dealing with a child with special needs are generally held to be his first decade, when the situation is still novel and confusing; the second decade, because cognizant disabled adolescents, like most teenagers, feel the need to defy their parents; and the decade when the parents become too impaired to continue to provide care and worry acutely about what will happen to their child after they are gone. This account fails, however, to reflect that the first decade does not vary so much from the norm as the subsequent ones do. Taking care of a helpless disabled infant is similar to caring for a helpless nondisabled infant, but continuing to tend to a dependent adult requires a special valor.

In an oft-cited 1962 article, the rehabilitation counselor Simon Olshansky bluntly wrote, "Most parents who have a mentally defective child suffer chronic sorrow throughout their lives regardless of whether the child is kept at home or 'put away.' The parents of a mentally defective child have little to look forward to; they will always be burdened by the child's unrelenting demands and unabated dependency. The woes, the trials, the moments of despair will continue until either their own deaths or the child's death. Release from this chronic sorrow may be obtainable only through death." One mother of a twenty-year-old with severe disabilities said to me, "It's as if I'd had a baby every year for the past twenty years—and who would choose to do that?"

The difficulties such families face have long been acknowledged by the outside world; only recently have the pleasures become a topic of general conversation. *Resilience* is the contemporary gloss on what used to be thought of as perseverance. It is both a way to reach larger objectives—functionality and happiness—and an objective in itself, inseparable from what Aaron Antonovsky, progenitor of the study of resilience, calls a "sense of coherence." Parents whose expectations are diverted by children with horizontal identities need resilience to rewrite their future without bitterness. Those children need resilience, too, and ideally parents foster it. Ann S. Masten wrote in *American Psychologist* in 2001, "The great surprise of resilience research is the ordinariness of the phenomenon." Resilience used to be posited as an extraordinary trait, seen in the Helen Kellers of the world, but cheery recent research suggests that most of us have the potential for it, and that cultivating it is a crucial part of development for everyone.

Even so, more than a third of parents of children with special needs report that caring for them has negative effects on their physical and mental health. Researchers designing a study of the effects of sustained stress on aging settled on bringing up a child with special needs as a universally acknowledged stressor. Comparing women who had had that experience with women who had not, they found the caretakers had shorter telomeres—the protection at the end of a chromosome—than the control group, which meant that they were aging more rapidly at the cellular level. Taking care of disabled children causes your biological age to outpace your chronological age, which is associated with premature rheumatic conditions, heart failure, reduced immune function, and earlier death through cell senescence. One study reported that fathers who described a significant caregiving burden died younger than fathers with a lighter caregiving burden.

This is true, and so is its opposite. One study found that 94 percent of parents with disabled kids said they "were getting along as well as most other families" without such children. Another said that most parents they surveyed believe "that this has brought them closer to their spouse, other family members, and friends; taught them what's important in life; increased their empathy for others; engendered personal growth; and made them cherish their child even more than if he or she had been born healthy." Yet another found that 88 percent of parents of children with disabilities felt happy when they thought about their child. Four out of five agreed that the disabled child had made their family closer; and a full 100 percent endorsed the statement "I have increased compassion for others due to my experience."

Buoyancy may bring about the results it would appear to reflect; the children of mothers initially rated as optimists had more advanced skills at two than did the children in similar condition of pessimistic mothers. The Spanish philosopher Miguel de Unamuno wrote, "It is not usually our ideas that make us optimists or pessimists, but it is our optimism or pessimism that makes our ideas." Disability is not predictive of the happiness of either the parent or the child, which reflects the larger puzzle that people who have won the lottery are, in the long run and on average, only marginally happier than amputees—people in each category having adjusted rather quickly to their new normal.

The popular life coach Martha Beck wrote a passionate book about the "lovely epiphanies" she experienced in tending to her son with Down syndrome. The writer Clara Claiborne Park said in the 1970s of her autistic daughter, "I write now what 15 years past I would still not have thought possible to write: that if today I were given the choice to accept the experience, with everything that it entails, or to refuse the bitter largesse, I would have to stretch out my hands—because out of it has come, for all of us, an unimagined life. And I will not change the last word of the story. It is still love." One of the mothers I interviewed said she had had no sense of purpose until her son was born with severe disabilities. "Suddenly, I had this object for all my energy," she explained. "He gave me a whole new reason to be alive." Such responses are not uncommon. One woman wrote, "This thought runs like a bright golden thread through the dark tapestry of our sorrow. We learn so much from our children—in patience, in humility, in gratitude for other blessings we had accepted before as a matter of course; so much in tolerance; so much in faith—believing and trusting where we cannot see; so much in compassion for our fellow man; and yes, even so much in wisdom about the eternal values in life." When I worked in a juvenile prison, a long-serving correctional officer there exhorted her bevy of felons, "You gotta take your mess and find yourself a message!"

While optimism can propel day-to-day life forward, realism allows parents to regain a feeling of control over what is happening and to come to see their trauma as smaller than it first seemed. The potential pitfalls are wishful thinking, self-blame, escapism, substance abuse, and avoidance; resources might include faith, humor, a strong marriage, and a supportive community, along with financial means, physical health, and higher education. There is no definitive roster of strategies, although words such as *transformation* and *enlightenment* occur. Studies are highly contradictory and seem often to reflect researcher bias. Numerous studies, for example, show that divorce is more frequent among parents of children with disabilities, and an equal number show the divorce rate is significantly lower among such parents; further research finds divorce rates consistent with those in the general population. Parents who cope poorly with a disabled child are worn down by the effort in the same way that parents who are coping successfully seem to grow strong, but all of them are both worn down and strengthened. Being part of a group seems consistently to have meaning; the redemptive power of intimacies born from struggle is immense. In our Internet age, when every challenge or disability has a community attached to it, the parents of people with any given challenge can find their horizontal community as well. Although most families do find meaning in their predicament, fewer than one in ten professionals who deal with them believes it. "I was determined *not* to be around folks who saw us as tragic," one exasperated mother wrote. "Unfortunately, that included my family, most professionals, and just about everyone else I knew." A doctor's or social worker's refusal to recognize such parents' reality because it is happier than anticipated is a kind of betrayal.

Perhaps the most difficult prospect facing parents of challenged children is institutionalization: a practice that is now more euphemistically—if cumbersomely—called *out-of-home placement*. Institutionalization used to be the norm, and parents who wanted to keep their disabled children at home had to fight a system designed to take them away. That all began to change in 1972, after the exposure of the horrific conditions at Willowbrook, a home for the mentally retarded in Staten Island, New York. Unethical medical research had been conducted on residents, and the place was grotesquely overcrowded, with deplorable sanitary facilities and physically abusive staff. "Untended, some smeared with their own feces, many of the children were unclothed and all were simply left to sit in the ward all day," according to the *New York Times*. "The only sound picked up by the technicians was something of an eerie communal wail." Patients at such facilities experienced "institutionalism," a condition marked by withdrawal, loss of interest, submissiveness, lack of initiative, impaired judgment, and reluctance to leave the hospital setting, which one researcher likened to "mental bedsores."

After Willowbrook, placing children became suspect. Now, parents whose children are impossible to cope with have a tough time finding an appropriate placement and must confront a system that can make them feel irresponsible for pursuing this option. The pendulum needs to swing to an appropriate middle. The question is never easy; as with abortion, people should be able to make the choice that is right for them without having to feel worse about it than they already do. Disabled children are now supposed to live in the "least restrictive environment," a laudable objective that should ideally apply to other family members as well. As one researcher has pointed out, "Placing many severely handicapped children and youth in the least restrictive environment of their families results in their family being required to live in a highly restrictive manner." The child, the parents, and the siblings are all deeply affected by placement decisions.

My study is of families who accept their children, and how that relates to those children's self-acceptance—a universal struggle we negotiate partly through the minds of others. In turn, it looks at how the acceptance of the larger society affects both these children and their families. A tolerant society softens parents and facilitates self-esteem, but that tolerance has evolved because individuals with good self-esteem have exposed the flawed nature of prejudice. Our parents are metaphors for ourselves: we struggle for their acceptance as a displaced way of struggling to accept ourselves. The culture is likewise a metaphor for our parents: our quest for high esteem in the larger world is only a sophisticated manifestation of our primal wish for parental love. The triangulation can be dizzying.

Social movements have debuted in sequence: first religious freedom, women's suffrage, and race rights, and then gay liberation and disability rights. That last category has become a catchall for difference of many kinds. The women's movement and the civil rights movement were focused on vertical identities, so they gained traction first; the horizontal identities could not emerge until the pattern had been set by those with greater strength. Each of these movements borrows unabashedly from the ones before, and now some borrow from those that followed them.

Preindustrial societies were cruel to those who were different, but did not segregate them; their care was the responsibility of their families. Postindustrial societies created benevolent institutions for the disabled, who were often whisked away at the first sign of anomaly. That dehumanizing tendency set the stage for eugenics. Hitler murdered more than 270,000 people with disabilities on the grounds that they were "travesties of human form and spirit." The presumption that disability could be extirpated was current worldwide. Laws to permit involuntary sterilization and abortion were passed in Finland, Denmark, Switzerland, and Japan, as well as in twenty-five American states. By 1958, over sixty thousand Americans had been forcibly neutered. Chicago passed an ordinance in 1911 that decreed, "No person who is diseased, maimed, mutilated, or in any way deformed so as to be an unsightly or disgusting object in or on the public ways or other public places in this city, shall therein or thereon expose himself to public view." It stayed on the books through 1973.

The disability rights movement seeks, at the most basic level, to find accommodation of difference rather than erasure of it. One of its signal successes is to understand that the interests of children, parents, and society do not necessarily coincide, and that the children are the least able to stand up for themselves. Many people with profound differences maintain that even well-run asylums, hospitals, and residences are analogous to the treatment of African-Americans under Jim Crow. Medical diagnosis is implicated in this separate-and-unequal response. Sharon Snyder and David Mitchell, both academics in disability studies, contend that those who seek cures and treatments often "subjugate the very populations they intend to rescue." Even today, American children with disabilities are four times more likely than nondisabled ones to have less than a ninth-grade education. Some 45 percent of Britons with disabilities and some 30 percent of working-age Americans with disabilities live below the poverty line. As recently as 2006, the Royal College of Obstetricians and Gynaecologists in London proposed that doctors consider killing infants with extreme disabilities.

In spite of these persisting challenges, the disability rights movement has made tremendous strides. The US Rehabilitation Act of 1973, passed by Congress over President Nixon's veto, prohibited discrimination against people with disabilities in any federally funded program. This was followed by the Americans with Disabilities Act, passed in 1990, and several subsequent acts that appeared to shore it up. In 2009, Vice President Joe Biden opened the Special Olympics by declaring special-needs advocacy a "civil rights movement" and announcing the new post of special assistant to the president for disability policy. The courts, however, have narrowed the scope of laws pertinent to disability, and local governments have often ignored them altogether.

Members of minorities who wish to preserve their self-definition need to define themselves in opposition to the majority. The more accepting the majority is of them, the more rigorously they need to do so, because their separate identity collapses if they countenance its integration into the majority world. Multiculturalism rejects the 1950s vision of a world in which everyone is subsumed by uniform Americanness, and chooses one in which we all inhabit our own treasured particularities. In his classic work *Stigma*, Erving Goffman argues that identity is formed when people assert pride in the thing that made them marginal, enabling them to achieve personal authenticity and political credibility. The social historian Susan Burch calls this "the irony of acculturation": society's attempts to assimilate a group often cause that group to become more pronounced in its singularity.

When I was in college in the mid-1980s, it was common practice to speak of the "differently abled" rather than the "disabled." We joked about the "differently gruntled" and the "differently agreeable." These days, if you talk about an autistic child, he differs from "typical" children, while a dwarf differs from "average" people. You are never to use the word *normal*, and you are certainly never to use the word *abnormal*. In the vast literature about disability rights, scholars stress the separation between *impairment*, the organic consequence of a condition, and *disability*, the result of social context. Being unable to move your legs, for example, is an impairment, but being unable to enter the public library is a disability.

An extreme version of the social model of disability is summarized by the British academic Michael Oliver: "Disability has nothing to do with the body, it is a consequence of social oppression." This is untrue, even specious, but it contains a valid challenge to revise the prevalent opposite assumption that disability resides entirely in the mind or body of the disabled person. Ability is a tyranny of the majority. If most people could flap their arms and fly, the inability to do so would be a disability. If most people were geniuses, those of moderate intelligence would be disastrously disadvantaged. There is no ontological truth enshrined in what we think of as good health; it is merely a convention, one that has been strikingly inflated in the past century. In 1912, an American who lived until the age of fifty-five had had a good, long life; now, death at fifty-five is considered a tragedy. Because most people can walk, being unable to walk is a disability; so is being unable to hear; and so is being unable to decipher social cues. It's a matter of votes, and the disabled question these majority decisions.

Medical advances allow parents to avoid producing certain kinds of disabled children; many disabilities may be ameliorated. It is not easy to determine when to exploit these options. Ruth Hubbard, an emerita professor of biology at Harvard, maintains that expectant parents who test for Huntington's because they have a family history of the disease are in a quandary: "If they decide on abortion, they are as much as saying that a life lived in the knowledge that one will eventually die of Huntington's disease is not worth living. What does that say about their own life and the lives of their family members who now know that they have the gene for Huntington's disease?" The philosopher Philip Kitcher has referred to genetic screening as "laissez-faire eugenics." Marsha Saxton, a lecturer at Berkeley who has spina bifida, writes, "Those of us with screenable conditions represent living adult fetuses that didn't get aborted. Our resistance to the systematic abortion of 'our young' is a challenge to the 'nonhumanness,' the nonstatus of the fetus." Snyder and Mitchell speak of how the elimination of disability marks "the completion of modernity as a cultural project."

Some in the disability rights camp urge acceptance of whatever child you conceive, as though it were immoral not to conform to reproductive destiny. This is what the bioethicist William Ruddick calls the "'hospitality' view of women," which finds anyone who terminates a pregnancy nonmaternal, ungenerous, and unwelcoming. In fact, prospective parents are dealing in the abstract with something that could become tangible, and that's never an informed way to make a choice: the idea of a child or a disability is extremely different from the reality.

There is a problematic collision between feminism's prioritizing of legal abortion and the disability rights movement's opposition to any social system that devalues difference. "The fears are genuine, rational, and terrifying," the disability activist Laura Hershey wrote. "We all face the prospect that what is supposed to be a private decision—the termination of a pregnancy—might become the first step in a campaign to eliminate people with disabilities." She may be naïve about the motive, but correct about the result. Most Chinese people don't hate girls, and no one in China is pursuing a campaign to eliminate women. But couples have been legally limited to one child since 1978, and because many prefer a boy, they give the girls up for adoption or abandon them. Although prospective parents may not be out to eliminate people with disabilities, medical advances giving them the ability to make radical decisions could undoubtedly reduce the disabled population considerably. "In this liberal and individualistic society, there may be no need for eugenic legislation," Hubbard wrote. "Physicians and scientists need merely provide the techniques that make individual women, and parents, responsible for implementing the society's prejudices by choice."

Some activists have argued against the entire Human Genome Project, maintaining that it implies the existence of a perfect genome. The Genome Project has been construed this way partly because its authors pitched it to funders as a way to cure maladies, without acknowledging that there is no universal standard of well-being. Disability advocates argue that in nature, variation is the only invariable. Donna Haraway, who teaches feminist and cultural studies, has described the project as an "act of canonization" that could be used to establish ever-narrower standards. Michel Foucault, writing before the mapping of the genome was feasible, described how "a technology of abnormal individuals appears precisely when a regular network of knowledge and power has been established." In other words, the spectrum of normality gets constrained when those in power consolidate their privilege. In Foucault's view, the idea of normality "claimed to ensure the physical vigor and the moral cleanliness of the social body; it promised to eliminate defective individuals, degenerate and bastardized populations. In the name of biological and historical urgency, it justified the racisms of the state." It thus encouraged people outside normality to perceive themselves as helpless and inadequate. If, as Foucault had also argued, "life is what is capable of error" and error itself is "at the root of what makes human thought and its history," then to prohibit error would be to end evolution. Error lifted us out of the primordial slime.

Deborah Kent is a congenitally blind woman who has written about the pain that society's prejudice against blindness has caused her. Describing a level of self-acceptance that was almost unheard of before the disability rights movement came into its own, Kent has said that her blindness is, to her, a neutral trait like her brown hair. "I didn't long for sight any more than I yearned for a pair of wings," she wrote in an essay in 2000. "Blindness presented occasional complications, but it seldom kept me from anything I wanted to do." Then she and her husband, Dick, decided to have a baby, and she was shocked that he wanted their child to be seeing. "I believed that my life could not have turned out any better if I had been fully sighted. If my child were blind, I would try to ensure it every chance to become a self-fulfilled, contributing member of society. Dick said he agreed with me completely. But he was more troubled than he wished me to know. If he could accept blindness in me, why would it be devastating to him, even for a moment, if our child were blind as well?" Deborah entered into conception with grave concern. "I did not know if I could bear his devastation if our baby turned out to be blind like me."

After their daughter was born, Deborah's mother also expressed fear that the baby might be blind. "I was stunned," Deborah wrote. "My parents raised all three of their children, including my blind brother and me, with sensitivity and unwavering love. In all of us they tried to nurture confidence, ambition, and self-respect. Yet blindness had never become neutral for them, any more than it had for Dick." The baby turned out to be seeing, as Dick discovered by getting her to track his movements. He called his in-laws to tell them the news; he has since reminisced about the day his daughter turned to watch his moving fingers. "In his voice, I hear an echo of the excitement and relief that were so vivid for him on that long-ago morning," Deborah wrote. "Each time I hear the story I feel a twinge of the old pain, and for a few moments I am very much alone again."

Her aloneness reflects a disjunction between her own perception—that being blind is an identity—and her husband's—that it is an illness. I am both sympathetic to her point of view and perturbed by it. I imagine how I would feel if my brother were to announce a fervent wish that my nephews be straight and call everyone to revel if it turned out to be true. It would hurt me. Being blind and being gay are different, but having a selfhood that others perceive as undesirable is identical. But our decisions to maximize health (however complicated a category that word may reference) and avoid illness (ditto) do not necessarily devalue those who are sick or otherwise different. My own battles with depression have contributed to a meaningful identity for me, but if I were choosing between a depression-prone child and one who would never suffer such ravages, I'd go with option B in a heartbeat. Even though the illness would probably become a locus of intimacy for us, I still wouldn't want it to happen.

Most adults with horizontal identities do not want to be pitied or admired; they simply want to get on with their lives without being stared at. Many dislike Jerry Lewis's use of pathetic children to get funds for genetic research. The NBC news correspondent John Hockenberry, who has a spinal injury, said, "'Jerry's kids' are people in wheelchairs on television raising money to find a way to prevent their ever having been born." The anger is pervasive. "Adults responded to my difference by helping me, but some of my schoolmates responded by calling me names," wrote Rod Michalko, who is blind. "Only much later did I realize that helping and name-calling amounted to the same thing." Arlene Mayerson, an expert in disability rights law, contends that benevolence and good intentions have been among disabled people's worst enemies throughout history. The able-bodied can be generous narcissists: they eagerly bestow what they feel good about giving without considering how it will be received.

Conversely, the social model of disability demands that society modify the way business is done to empower people with disabilities, and we make such adjustments only when lawmakers accept that life can be painful for those who live at the margins. Patronizing gestures can be justly scorned, but increased empathy is often a precondition of political acceptance and an engine of reform. Many disabled people say that the social disapprobation they experience is much more burdensome than the disability from which they suffer, maintaining simultaneously that they suffer only because society treats them badly, and that they have unique experiences that set them apart from the world—that they are eminently special and in no way different.

A study that sought to determine whether money correlated with happiness revealed that poverty is connected to despair, but that once one gets out of poverty, wealth has little effect on happiness. What does correlate is how much money a person has compared to his social group. There is much scope to thrive on downward comparisons. Wealth and ability are both relative concepts. There are broad spectra in all these areas, and wide, shadowy borderlands in mental and physical disability as there are in socioeconomic status. A broad range of people can feel rich—or able—in relation to the context they live in. When a condition is not stigmatized, the comparisons are less oppressive.

Nonetheless, at the far end of the disability spectrum is a zone that corresponds to poverty, a place of severe privation, where rhetoric cannot make things better. The disability poverty line varies from one community to another, but it does exist. To deny the medical realities such people negotiate is equivalent to denying the financial realities of the slum child. The body and the mind can be agonizingly broken. Many disabled people experience debilitating pain, struggle with intellectual incapacities, and live in permanent proximity to death.

Repairing the body and repairing entrenched social prejudice are objectives that dance a troubling waltz; either fix can have unwelcome consequences. A repaired body may have been achieved through brutal trauma and in response to unfair social pressures; a repaired prejudice can eliminate the rights that its existence had called into being. The question of what constitutes any protected difference carries enormous political weight. Disabled people are protected by fragile laws, and if they are judged to have an identity rather than an illness, they may forfeit those safeguards.

All kinds of attributes make one less able. Illiteracy and poverty are disabilities, and so are stupidity, obesity, and boringness. Extreme age and extreme youth are both disabilities. Faith is a disability insofar as it constrains you from self-interest; atheism is a disability inasmuch as it shields you from hope. One might see power as a disability, too, for the isolation in which it imprisons those who wield it. The disability scholar Steven R. Smith posited, "A completely painless existence could also quite plausibly be seen as deficient for most people." Likewise, any of these characteristics can embody strength, some more easily than others. We are all differently abled from one another, and context—which is socially constructed—often decides what will be protected and indulged. Being gay was a disability in the nineteenth century in a way that it isn't now; and it is now a disability in some locations in a way that it isn't in others; and it was a disability for me when I was young and it isn't one for me today. The whole matter is intensely unstable. No one has ever suggested legal protections for ugly people to make up for the misaligned features that will compromise their personal and professional lives. For people disabled by inherent moral perplexity, we offer not support but imprisonment.

Because there is not yet a coherent understanding of horizontal identities as a collective category, those who strive for horizontal rights often rely on the disability movement's methodical rejection of illness models. Insofar as these conceptualizations of rights are about identity, they draw on the model of Alcoholics Anonymous and other 12-step recovery groups. AA was the first to suggest managing a disease by claiming it as an identity and drawing on the support of peers with a similar condition—that according meaning to a problem was crucial to resolving it. In a way, this near-paradox can be reduced to the last clause of Reinhold Niebuhr's Serenity Prayer, which is a tenet of the recovery movement: "Father, give us courage to change what must be altered, serenity to accept what cannot be helped, and the insight to know the one from the other."

Although we have moved in recent decades away from illness models and toward identity models, such a shift is not always ethically defensible. After I had come to see deafness and dwarfism and autism and transgenderism as identities worthy of appreciation, I came up against the pro-ana and pro-mia movements, which seek to remove the negative associations around anorexia and bulimia, promoting them as lifestyle choices rather than illnesses. Pro-ana and pro-mia websites offer "thinspiration" tips on crash diets, review use of emetics and laxatives, and validate competitive weight-loss postings. People who follow the advice on such sites may die: Anorexia has the highest mortality rate of any mental illness. To propose that anorexics are merely exploring an identity is as morally lax as accepting the belief of gang members that they are merely pursuing an identity that happens to entail killing people. It's clear that identity is a finite concept. What's not clear is the location of its boundaries. In my own life, dyslexia is an illness, while being gay is an identity. I wonder, though, whether it would have been the other way around if my parents had failed to help me compensate for the dyslexia, but had achieved the goal of altering my sexuality.

The wish to fix people reflects pessimism about their condition and optimism about the method of repair. In *Autobiography of a Face*, Lucy Grealy describes the childhood cancer of the jaw that left her permanently disfigured—and, to her mind, grotesque. I knew Lucy, though not well, and I didn't find her ugly. I always wondered where the deep conviction of her own repulsiveness came from because it informed everything she did, no matter how her charm distracted from her missing jaw. She wrote about how she prepared for one of her innumerable unsuccessful reconstructive surgeries and thought, "Maybe this wasn't my actual face at all but the face of some interloper, some ugly intruder, and my 'real' face, the one I was meant to have all along, was within reach. I began to imagine my 'original' face, the one free from all deviation, all error. I believed that if none of this had happened to me, I would have been beautiful." Lucy's death of a drug overdose at thirty-nine testifies in part to the oppressive costs by which anomalous people make their way through endless processes of repair.

If the surgeries had worked, Lucy might have had a happy life, just as good as if she'd come to ease with her appearance. That her face turned out to be irremediable makes one wonder whether her mind would have been similarly beyond mending. What might have happened if her energy had been focused on the singular intelligence that produced such a chronicle of intractable despair? I, too, would have tried the things Lucy did—possibly with the same result; I have always tried to mend whatever can be fixed and tend to accept only the inevitable. Her dream of vanquishing her problem, which was for decades sustained by doctors, did her in. Recent academic work suggests that people who know their condition to be irreversible are happier than those who believe their condition may be ameliorated. In such cases, ironically, hope may be the cornerstone of misery.

In 2003, a suit was brought in England against a doctor who had performed a late-stage abortion on a woman who would have given birth to a child with a cleft palate. Such abortions are legal for women likely to produce a child with a severe genetic defect, and the question was whether this defect fit that definition. Court filings quoted another mother whose son had a congenital cleft palate attesting, "I definitely would not have had a termination even if this baby had a cleft palate or lip, these days it can be repaired to such a high standard. It is not a disability." An untreated severe cleft palate can have dire consequences and is undeniably a disability. But there is no simple equation whereby the existence of the fix means that the condition is no longer a disability; rectifying a condition is not the same thing as forestalling it. Bruce Bauer, chief of plastic surgery at Children's Memorial Hospital in Chicago, who corrects facial deformities, said the children on whom he operates deserve "the chance to look like what they truly are—no different from anyone else." But whether the surgical fix makes them "no different" or permanently disguises their difference is a loaded question with broad ramifications.

The press abounds with heartwarming stories of surgical interventions, such as that of Chris Wallace, the boy born with clubfeet who now plays pro football. "I love my feet," he has said. People who seek surgical interventions almost always speak in terms of correction. Transgender people speak of sex-reassignment procedures as a means of remedying a birth defect. Those who champion cochlear implants for deaf people use the same rhetoric. The line between cosmetic intervention—what some call "technoluxe"—and corrective procedures can be a fine one, as can the line between becoming one's best self and conforming to oppressive social norms. What about the mother who has her daughter's ears pinned because she is being teased at school, or the man who seeks a surgical antidote to his baldness? Such people may be eliminating a problem, or they may merely be caving to peers.

Insurance companies deny coverage for many corrective procedures on grounds that they are cosmetic. In fact, a cleft palate can cause disfiguration, difficulty eating, ear infections that lead to hearing loss, severe dental problems, speech and language impairments, and—perhaps as a consequence of all this—severe psychological problems. Lucy Grealy's lack of a jawbone might not have been considered a crucial loss by some people, but for her it was mortal. Conversely, even a positive surgical outcome can pose difficulty for parents. On a website for parents of children with cleft palates, Joanne Green writes, "The doctor tells you that everything went perfectly. So why, then, when you see the baby, does everything look anything but perfect? Your sweet, laughing, loving, trusting, happy baby of two hours ago is now sick and hurting. And then you will take a good look at the face. Not the suture line, not the swelling, but the face. And you will be shocked at the difference you will see in your baby's face. Very few parents are initially thrilled with the surgery. The baby will almost seem to be another baby. After all, you loved the old one!"

How urgent is any problem and how dire is the solution? That is the proportion that must be entertained. It is always both essential and impossible to tease apart the difference between the parents' wanting to spare the child suffering and the parents' wanting to spare themselves suffering. It is not pleasant to be suspended between two ways of being; when I asked a dwarf what she thought of limb-lengthening, a process undertaken in childhood that can give someone the normalized appearance of average height, she said that it would just make her "a tall dwarf." At best, medical interventions allow people to move from the margins toward a more accommodating center; at worst, they leave people feeling further compromised and no less alienated. Alice Domurat Dreger, who has written about transgenderism and about conjoined twins, averred, "Far from feeling like a rejection of the child, normalization surgery may feel to some parents like a manifestation of full love and unconditional love. But parents may also seek surgical fixes because they feel like they will know how to be a parent to that child, whereas they often feel uncertain how to be a parent to this one."

People of higher socioeconomic status tend toward perfectionism, and have a harder time living with perceived defects. One French study said baldly, "The lower classes show a higher tolerance for severely handicapped children." An American study bears out that conclusion, inasmuch as higher-income families are "more apt to stress independence and self-development," while lower-income families emphasize "interdependence among family members." Better-educated, more-affluent families are more likely to seek placement for children, and white families do so more often than minority families, though disturbingly high numbers of minority parents lose children to foster care. I did back-to-back interviews with a wealthy white woman who had a low-functioning autistic son, and an impoverished African-American woman whose autistic son had many of the same symptoms. The more privileged woman had spent years futilely trying to make her son better. The less advantaged woman never thought she could make her son better because she'd never been able to make her own life better, and she was not afflicted with feelings of failure. The first woman found it extremely difficult to deal with her son. "He breaks everything," she said unhappily. The other woman had a relatively happy life with her son. "Whatever could be broken got broken a long time ago," she said. Fixing is the illness model; acceptance is the identity model; which way any family goes reflects their assumptions and resources.

A child may interpret even well-intentioned efforts to fix him as sinister. Jim Sinclair, an intersex autistic person, wrote, "When parents say, 'I wish my child did not have autism,' what they're really saying is, 'I wish the autistic child I have did not exist, and I had a different (non-autistic) child instead.' Read that again. This is what we hear when you mourn over our existence. This is what we hear when you pray for a cure. This is what we know, when you tell us of your fondest hopes and dreams for us: that your greatest wish is that one day we will cease to be, and strangers you can love will move in behind our faces." There are both additive and subtractive models of most conditions: either the person has an invasive condition that can be removed, such as an infection, or the person has been diminished by the condition, as when an organ gives out. Layers of illness or variance may be piled on top of a persisting "normal" person, who is obscured by them—or the condition may be integral to the person. If we give a deaf person hearing, are we releasing him into fuller selfhood, or compromising his integrity? Does reforming a criminal's mind give him a more authentic self, or just one that suits the rest of us? Most parents suppose that an authentic nonautistic self is hidden inside autistic people, but Sinclair and many others with autism do not see anyone else inside them, any more than I would see a straight person—or a pro baseball player—locked away within me. It is not clear that we can set free the child planned through love within a child conceived in rape. Perhaps genius, too, can be seen as an invasive illness.

Aimee Mullins was born without fibula bones in her shins, and so her legs were amputated below the knee when she was a year old. Now she is a fashion model with prosthetic legs. "I want to be seen as beautiful because of my disability, not in spite of it," she said. "People kept asking me, 'Why do you want to get into this world that's so bitchy and so much about physical perfection?' That's why. That's why I want to do it." Bill Shannon, who was born with a degenerative hip condition, devised a break-dancing technique using crutches and a skateboard. He developed a cult following on the avant-garde dance scene for the work he described as a natural outgrowth of his efforts to retain mobility. He was courted by Cirque du Soleil, but since he didn't envision himself as a Vegas entertainer, he agreed to train someone else in his routines. He taught an able-bodied performer how to move around on crutches just as he had. Cirque du Soleil's act "Varekai," which uses Shannon's technique and choreography, has been a huge success. Shannon's disability is not a risible spectacle, but the wellspring of a provocative and original enterprise. More recently, Oscar Pistorius, the South African who has two prosthetic lower legs, was ranked among the top 400-meter racers in the world and competed in the London Olympics in 2012. *Time* magazine named him one of the hundred most influential people in the world, and he has endorsement contracts with Nike and Thierry Mugler. Some kinds of grace would not have entered the world if everyone's hips and legs worked the same way. Deformity has been brought into beauty's fold, a catalyst for justice rather than an affront to it, and society has changed enough to marvel at a dancer on crutches, a model with prosthetic legs, an athlete whose speed relies on carbon-fiber calves.

Flaunting the visible technologies that compensate for a disability, as Mullins, Shannon, and Pistorius do, can empower those who use them. For many people, however, such trumpeting of their reliance on robotics is inconceivable. I suffer from depression and spent ten years seeking effective treatment for it. As someone whose ability to function would be compromised without psychotropic medications, I know the weird discomfort of recognizing that without enhancements I'd be someone else. I've also felt ambivalence about upgrading my emotional life, and I sometimes feel that I'd be truer to myself if I were morose, withdrawn, and hiding in bed. I know why some people make the choice not to medicate. Bewildered doctors and uncomprehending parents often question disabled people who reject the latest procedures and devices. Those disabled people, however, may be angered by the prospect of interventions that would make them function more like nondisabled people without mitigating the hard reality of their disabling condition. Some may even curse the contraptions that keep them going: dialysis, medication, wheelchairs, prosthetics, voice-processing software. I began taking psychotropic medications well past the age of consent and feel some ownership of the decision. Many interventions, however, have to occur at a much earlier age. The parents and doctors who pursue surgical corrections and early intervention for infants initiate a life narrative that they deem morally and pragmatically right, but they can never fully anticipate what will come of their decisions.

The disability rights movement assumes that most people who are alive are glad to be alive, or would be if they had adequate supports—that the wish to be dead is as aberrant among the disabled as in anyone else. Nonetheless, individuals have been named as plaintiffs in successful suits against their own birth, complaints generally brought by their parents on their behalf. The principle extrapolates from *wrongful death*, which results from physician negligence, and *wrongful birth*, which can be claimed when a family has not received adequate prenatal counseling. Wrongful-birth suits are brought by parents in their own names and will compensate only for costs they incur as parents—usually for care and support until the child is eighteen. *Wrongful life* compensates the disabled person rather than his or her parents and may entail funds across a lifetime. A wrongful-life suit purports to cover not a loss but a gain: the fact of someone's existence.

In 2001, France's highest appeals court awarded a large sum to a child with Down syndrome for "the damage of being born." The court stipulated that "the child's handicap is the actual damage to be compensated, and not his loss of happiness"—meaning that he deserved financial compensation for the indignity of being alive. The same court later granted compensation to a seventeen-year-old born mentally disabled, deaf, and nearly blind, saying that if his mother's gynecologist had diagnosed rubella during pregnancy, she would have had an abortion and her son would not have experienced a lifetime of pain. Disabled French people went ballistic about the implication that being dead was better than being handicapped. One father said, "I do hope that is not the way the rest of society looks upon our children—since this would be unbearable." In response to extensive protests, the French legislature outlawed wrongful-life suits.

In the United States, the idea of wrongful life has been validated in four states, although twenty-seven others have explicitly rejected it. Nonetheless, wrongful-life suits have been brought in connection with Tay-Sachs disease, deafness, hydrocephalus, spina bifida, rubella syndrome, Down syndrome, and polycystic kidney disease, and the courts have given awards, most strikingly in *Curlender v. Bio-Science Laboratories*. A couple who underwent genetic screening were not told they were carriers for Tay-Sachs; they had a daughter with the condition who died at the age of four. They argued, "The reality of the 'wrongful-life' concept is that such a plaintiff both *exists* and *suffers*. Had defendants not been negligent, the plaintiff might not have come into existence at all." They received compensation for the cost of care, and damages for parental pain and suffering.

Although wrongful-life cases address an ontological question about what kind of life is worth living, this is hardly what prompts them. Being disabled entails colossal expense, and most parents who launch wrongful-life suits do so in an attempt to guarantee care for their children. In an ugly twist, mothers and fathers must discharge the obligations of responsible parenting by stating in legal documents that they wish their children had never been born.

Some people can bear a great deal of pain and still experience great happiness, while others are made unrelentingly miserable by less acute pain. There's no way to know how much pain any particular baby can cope with, and by the time the parents form accurate perceptions of this, social prohibitions, legal strictures, and hospital policies make it exceedingly difficult to discontinue treatment. Even among self-aware adults, many people with apparently barren existences cling to life, while others with enviable situations kill themselves.

Over ten years, I interviewed more than three hundred families for this book, some briefly and some in depth, producing nearly forty thousand pages of interview transcripts. I interviewed but did not write about irreligious parents of fundamentalist children; parents of children with dyslexia and other learning disabilities; parents of obese children and of addicted children; parents of giants with Marfan syndrome, of limbless children with phocomelia syndrome, and of adult "thalidomide babies"; parents of premature babies; parents of depressed and bipolar children, of children with AIDS or cancer. I talked to parents who had adopted disabled children or children of a different race from another country. I talked to parents of intersex children who couldn't decide in what gender to raise them. I talked to the parents of supermodels, of bullies, and of the blind.

It would have been easier to write a book about five conditions. I wanted, however, to explore the spectrum of difference, to show that raising a child of extraordinary abilities is in some ways like raising a child of reduced capacities, to show that a child's traumatic origin (rape) or traumatic acts (crime) can have surprising parallels to the condition of his mind (autistic, schizophrenic, prodigious) or of his body (dwarfism, deafness). Each of the ten categories I explored poses a unique but related set of questions, which together describe the spectrum of issues faced by parents of children with horizontal identities. I found excellent scholarship on each of my individual topics, and some on the smaller collective topics (general books on disability, on retardation, on genius), but nothing addressing this overarching issue of illness and identity.

Each of these chapters poses a particular set of questions, and taken together, they indicate a spectrum of issues faced by parents of children with horizontal identities, and by those children themselves. The six chapters that follow this one deal with categories long classified as illnesses, while the four that follow those describe categories that appear to be more socially constructed. I have relied primarily on American and British interview subjects, but investigated one non-Western context in which what we perceive as an aberrant illness is commonplace—by studying congenital deafness in a village in northern Bali—and one non-Western context in which what we perceive as an aberrant identity is commonplace—by interviewing Rwandan women who conceived children in rape during the 1994 genocide.

Though I have gathered statistics, I have relied primarily on anecdotes because numbers imply trends, while stories acknowledge chaos. If you talk to a family, you have to process conflicting narratives, trying to reconcile the genuine beliefs—or canny manipulations—of various parties. I worked on a psychodynamic model according to which people's interactions with me in the microcosm of journalistic neutrality indicated how they interact with the world. Throughout, I refer to members of the families I interviewed by first name. I do this not to create a gloss of intimacy, as self-help books often try to do, but because various members of families share last names, and this is the least cumbersome way to keep track of my subjects.

I had to learn a great deal to be able to hear these men and women and children. On my first day at my first dwarf convention, I went over to help an adolescent girl who was sobbing. "This is what I look like," she blurted between gasps, and it seemed she was half laughing. "These people look like me." Her mother, who was standing nearby, said, "You don't know what this means to my daughter. But it also means a lot to me, to meet these other parents who will know what I'm talking about." She assumed I, too, must be a parent of a child with dwarfism; when she learned that I was not, she chuckled, "For a few days, now, you can be the freakish one." Many of the worlds I visited were animated by such a fierce sense of community that I experienced pangs of jealousy. I would not wish to trivialize the difficulty of these identities, but I knew about that going in. The revelation was all the joy.

While denying the anger and tedium of parenting can be crushing, dwelling on it is also a mistake. Many of the people I interviewed said that they would never exchange their experiences for any other life—sound thinking, given that exchange is unavailable. Cleaving to our own lives, with all their challenges and limitations and particularities, is vital. And that should not be exclusively a horizontal principle; that should be handed down from generation to generation with the silver spoons and the folktales from the old country. The British critic Nigel Andrews once wrote, "If something or someone doesn't work, it's in a state of grace, progress, and evolution. It will attract love and empathy. If it does work, it has merely completed its job and is probably dead."

Having a severely challenging child intensifies life. The lows are almost always very low; the highs are sometimes very high. It takes an act of will to grow from loss: the disruption provides the opportunity for growth, not the growth itself. Constant high levels of stress may age parents of profoundly disabled children, making them crankier and more vulnerable, yet some cultivate a deep and abiding resilience. It turns out they have grown more skilled at handling other life stresses. Even as the downside wears you thin, the upside keeps on giving. The more difficult the problem, the more profound these positives may be. One study explains, "Mothers reporting higher levels of caregiving demands for their child with intellectual disability also reported more personal growth and maturity." The Canadian scholar Dick Sobsey, himself the father of a disabled child, and his colleague Kate Scorgie write, "Parents of children with relatively mild disabilities may be more likely to adjust or accommodate by making minor or superficial changes. Conversely, parents of children with more severe disabilities may find it more difficult or impossible to go on with their lives as before and, as a result, may be more likely to undergo transformations." Positive transformations are achieved when initial disequilibrium, which is traumatic and brief, gives way to psychic reorganization, which is gradual and enduring. It would appear to be true that what doesn't kill you makes you stronger.

Those men and women who believe that parenting a disabled child has given them knowledge or hope they wouldn't otherwise have had find worth in their lives, and those parents who don't see such possibilities often can't. Those who believe their suffering has been valuable love more readily than those who see no meaning in their pain. Suffering does not necessarily imply love, but love implies suffering, and what changes with these children and their extraordinary situations is the shape of suffering—and in consequence, the shape of love, forced into a more difficult form. It doesn't really matter whether the meaning is there; it matters only whether it is perceived. Delusions of physical health may be delusions; someone who has congestive heart failure will probably die from it whether he believes that he has it or not. Delusions of mental health are more robust. If you believe that your experiences have vitalized you, then they have; vitality is an interior state, and experiencing it is its own truth. In one study, mothers who construed advantages from having premature babies experienced less psychological pain and were more responsive to their children's needs, while those who saw no advantages in the experience had children who were doing less well at age two. A study that looked at children with various complications at birth found, simply, "The children of mothers who had tried harder to find meaning had a better developmental outcome."

The world is made more interesting by having every sort of person in it. That is a social vision. We should alleviate the suffering of each individual to the outer limits of our abilities. That is a humanist vision with medical overtones. Some think that without suffering the world would be boring; some, that without their *own* suffering the world would be boring. Life is enriched by difficulty; love is made more acute when it requires exertion. I used to think that the nature of the challenge was extremely important. In my last book, I wrote about how at some level I loved my depression because it had tested my mettle and made me into who I am. I now think I could have had the same enrichment from having a child with Down syndrome, or having cancer. It is not suffering that is precious, but the concentric pearlescence with which we contain it. The raw grit of anguish will never be in short supply. There is enough of it in the happiest life to serve these instructive purposes and there always will be. We are more sympathetic to Holocaust survivors than to malcontent children of privilege, but we all have our darkness, and the trick is making something exalted of it.

We say that our struggles have ennobled us, but we don't know who we would have been without them. We might have been equally wonderful; our best qualities might be inherent rather than circumstantial. Nonetheless, most people look back even on unhappiness with nostalgia. I once accompanied a Russian artist to visit his elderly mother in Moscow. When we arrived at her apartment, we found her watching a Soviet propaganda movie from the 1940s on TV. I said to her, "Nadezhda Konstantinova, you were sent to the Gulag in that exact time, on the basis of that exact philosophy. And now you sit around watching that for entertainment?" She smiled and shrugged her shoulders. "But it was my youth," she said.

The question I was most frequently asked about this project was which of these conditions was the worst. From my own perspective, some conditions seem tolerable; some, desirable; others, terribly difficult. Bias varies, and other people revel in ways of being that I find frightening. I understand, therefore, why my own way of being frightens some people. Difference and disability seem to invite people to step back and judge. Parents judge what lives are worth living, and worth their living with; activists judge them for doing so; legal scholars judge who should make such judgments; doctors judge which lives to save; politicians judge how much accommodation people with special needs deserve; insurance companies judge how much lives are worth. Negative judgments are not confined to people who perceive themselves to be in the mainstream. Almost everyone I interviewed was to some degree put off by the chapters in this book other than his or her own. Deaf people didn't want to be compared to people with schizophrenia; some parents of schizophrenics were creeped out by dwarfs; criminals couldn't abide the idea that they had anything in common with transgender people. The prodigies and their families objected to being in a book with the severely disabled, and some children of rape felt that their emotional struggle was trivialized when they were compared to gay activists. People with autism often pointed out that Down syndrome entailed a categorically lower intelligence than theirs.

The compulsion to build such hierarchies persists even among these people, all of whom have been harmed by them. Halfway through my writing of this, a mother who had spoken to me freely about her transgender teenager's autism agreed that I could refer to him as male; she had originally asked me to avoid the issue of his gender because the prejudice against trans people and potential for hostile scrutiny terrified her. As I got to the end of the writing, a woman I'd known well as the mother of a transman admitted that her son was on the autism spectrum; she had not mentioned this previously because she thought the stigma was too significant. There is no consensus on what can be talked about and what needs to be hidden. Tobin Siebers makes a moving case for horizontal solidarity by pointing out that our disdain for people who cannot care for themselves is rooted in a false proposition. He argues that inclusion of disabled people "exposes the widespread dependence of people and nations on one another, dispelling the dangerous myth that individuals or nations exist naturally in a state of autonomy and that those individuals or nations that fall into dependence are somehow inferior to others."

The beautiful mosaic of multiculturalism was a needed antidote to the melting pot of assimilationism. Now it's time for the little principalities to find their collective strength. *Intersectionality* is the theory that various kinds of oppression feed one another—that you cannot, for example, eliminate sexism without addressing racism. Benjamin Jealous, president of the NAACP, the nation's oldest civil rights organization, told me how galling it was to him, growing up in a white town, when he and his adoptive brother were taunted for being black—and how much more distressing it was when some of the people who didn't patronize them for their race went after his brother for being gay. "If we tolerate prejudice toward any group, we tolerate it toward all groups," he said. "I couldn't have relationships that were conditional on excluding my brother—or anyone else. We are all in one fight, and our freedom is all the same freedom."

In 2011, gay marriage became legal in New York State after several Republicans in the state Senate agreed to support it. One of them, Roy J. McDonald, said that he had changed his stance on gay marriage because he had two autistic grandchildren, which had caused him "to rethink several issues." Jared Spurbeck, an autistic adult, thought his own quirks were "a sign of sinfulness" when he was growing up in the Mormon faith; when he started reading about gay Mormons, he found their experience much the same as his. "I couldn't ignore the parallels between autism and homosexuality. Once I'd accepted the one, I couldn't not accept the other."

I encountered activists of every stripe while I did this research and admired them even when I occasionally found their rhetoric expedient. The changes they sought seemed, individually, restricted to their particular province and experience, but as a group, they represent a rethinking of humanity. Most parents who become activists do so because they want to spur social change, but that impulse is never unalloyed. Some find it a relief because it gets them out of the house and away from their child without their having to feel guilty about it. Some use activism to distract themselves from grief; parents often laud what they rue most about their children to defend against despair. But just as belief can result in action, action can result in belief. You can gradually fall in love with your child, and by extension with that child's disabilities, and by further extension with all the world's brave disadvantages. Many of the activists I met were determined to help other people because they couldn't help themselves. Activism successfully displaced their pain. By teaching their learned optimism or strength to parents reeling from a recent diagnosis, they fortified it in their own families.

I understand this strategy firsthand, because writing this book addressed a sadness within me and—somewhat to my surprise—has largely cured it. The best way to get through these horizontalities is to find coherence, and in the wake of these stories, I recast my own narrative. I have a horizontal experience of being gay and a vertical one of the family that produced me, and the fact that they are not fully integrated no longer seems to undermine either. Some impulse toward anger at my parents evaporated, leaving only trace residue. In absorbing stories of strangers' clemency, I realized that I had demanded that my parents accept me but had resisted accepting them. Once I did, I was glad to have their ubiquitous company. The playwright Doug

Wright once said that family inflicts the deepest wounds, then salves them the most tenderly. When I realized there was no refuge from my parents' meddling, I learned to value it over loneliness and call it love. I started my research aggrieved; I ended it forbearing. I set off to understand myself and ended up understanding my parents. Unhappiness is a constant grudging, and in these pages, happiness served as a spur to amnesty. Their love always forgave me; mine came to forgive them, too.

I know that who I was appalled my mother and concerned my father, and I used to be furious at them for not embracing this horizontal part of me, for not embracing the early evidence of it. Writing has been a lesson in absolution, because I have seen the valiance love takes. Acceptance was always easier for my father than it was for my mother, but that was not particular to me; he accepts himself more readily than she did herself. In her own mind, she always fell short; in my father's own mind, he is victorious. The interior daring of becoming myself was my mother's gift to me, while the outer audacity to express that self came from my father.

I wish I'd been accepted sooner and better. When I was younger, not being accepted made me enraged, but now, I am not inclined to dismantle my history. If you banish the dragons, you banish the heroes—and we become attached to the heroic strain in our personal history. We choose our own lives. It is not simply that we decide on the behaviors that construct our experience; when given our druthers, we elect to be ourselves. Most of us would like to be more successful or more beautiful or wealthier, and most people endure episodes of low self-esteem or even self-hatred. We despair a hundred times a day. But we retain the startling evolutionary imperative of affection for the fact of ourselves, and with that splinter of grandiosity we redeem our flaws. These parents have, by and large, chosen to love their children, and many of them have chosen to value their own lives, even though they carry what much of the world considers an intolerable burden. Children with horizontal identities alter your self painfully; they also illuminate it. They are receptacles for rage and joy—even for salvation. When we love them, we achieve above all else the rapture of privileging what exists over what we have merely imagined.

A follower of the Dalai Lama who had been imprisoned by the Chinese for decades was asked if he had ever been afraid in jail, and he said his fear was that he would lose compassion for his captors. Parents often think that they've captured something small and vulnerable, but the parents I've profiled have been captured, locked up with their children's madness or genius or deformity, and the quest is never to lose compassion. A Buddhist scholar once explained to me that most Westerners mistakenly think that nirvana is what you arrive at when your suffering is over and only an eternity of happiness stretches ahead. But such bliss would always be shadowed by the sorrow of the past and would therefore be imperfect. Nirvana occurs when you not only look forward to rapture, but also gaze back into the times of anguish and find in them the seeds of your joy. You may not have felt that happiness at the time, but in retrospect it is incontrovertible.

For some parents of children with horizontal identities, acceptance reaches its apogee when parents conclude that while they supposed that they were pinioned by a great and catastrophic loss of hope, they were in fact falling in love with someone they didn't yet know enough to want. As such parents look back, they see how every stage of loving their child has enriched them in ways they never would have conceived, ways that are incalculably precious. Rumi said that the light enters you at the bandaged place. This book's conundrum is that most of the families described here have ended up grateful for experiences they would have done anything to avoid.

I I

Deaf

On Friday, April 22, 1994, I received a phone call from a man I had never met who had read my writing on identity politics for the *New York Times* and had heard I was planning to write on the Deaf. "There's a situation brewing at Lexington," he said. "If it's not resolved, we're going to see something happening in front of the center on Monday." I got some further details. "Listen, this is a serious situation." He paused. "You never heard from me. And I've never heard of you." And he hung up.

The Lexington Center for the Deaf in Queens—New York City's foremost institution of Deaf culture, which incorporates the largest school for the deaf in New York State, with 350 students from preschool through high school—had just announced a new CEO, and students and alumni were unhappy with the choice. The center board members had worked with a search team that included representatives of every part of the Lexington community—many of them deaf—to select a candidate. A hearing board member who had just lost his position at Citibank, R. Max Gould, threw in his own name and was elected by a narrow margin. Many deaf constituents felt that their lives were once more being controlled by hearing people. A core committee of local Deaf activists, Lexington student leaders, faculty representatives, and alumni organized within minutes, requested a meeting with the chairman of the board to demand Gould's resignation, and were summarily brushed off.

When I arrived at Lexington on Monday, crowds of students were marching outside the school. Some wore sandwich boards that read THE BOARD CAN HEAR BUT THEY ARE DEAF TO US; others wore DEAF PRIDE T-shirts. MAX RESIGN placards could be seen everywhere. Groups of students climbed up onto the low wall in front of Lexington so their rallying cheers would be visible to the crowd below; others chanted back silently, many hands moving together in repeating words. I asked the sixteen-year-old, African-American student-body president whether she had also demonstrated for race rights. "I'm too busy being Deaf right now," she signed. "My brothers aren't deaf, so they're taking care of being black." A deaf woman standing nearby threw in another question: "If you could change being deaf or being black, which would you do?" The student was suddenly shy. "Both are hard," she signed back. Another student interceded. "I am black and Deaf and proud, and I don't want to be white or hearing or different in any way from who I am." Her signs were big and clear. The first student repeated the sign *proud*—her thumb rose up her chest—and then suddenly they were overcome with giggles and returned to the picket line.

Protesters had commandeered a room inside to discuss strategy. Someone asked Ray Kenney, director of the Empire State Association of the Deaf, whether he had any experience leading a protest. He shrugged and signed back, "It's the blind leading the deaf around here." Some faculty members took sick days to join the demonstration. Lexington's director of public affairs told me that the students just wanted an excuse to miss classes, but that was not my impression. The faculty representatives to the core committee were vigilant. "Do you think the protest will work?" I asked one teacher. Her signing was methodical and emphatic. "The pressure has been building—maybe since the school was founded in 1864. Now it's exploding. Nothing can stop it."

Schools play an unusually important part in the lives of deaf children. More than 90 percent of deaf children have two hearing parents. They enter families that do not understand their situation and are often ill-prepared to contend with it. In schools, they are first exposed to Deaf ways. For many, school is the end of terrible loneliness. "I didn't know that there were other people like me until I got here," one deaf girl said to me at Lexington. "I thought everyone in the world would rather talk to someone else, someone hearing." Every state but three has at least one center or residential school for the education of the deaf. A Deaf person's school is a primary mode of self-identification; *Lexington* and *Gallaudet* were among the first signs I learned.

When capitalized, *Deaf* refers to a culture, as distinct from *deaf*, which is a pathological term; this distinction echoes that between *gay* and *homosexual*. An increasing number of deaf people maintain they would not choose to be hearing. To them, *cure*—deafness as pathology—is anathema; *accommodation*—deafness as disability—is more palatable; and *celebration*—Deafness as culture—trumps all.

St. Paul's declaration in his letter to the Romans that "faith comes by hearing" was long misinterpreted to mean that those who could not hear were incapable of faith, and Rome would allow no one to inherit property or title if he could not give confession. For this reason, starting in the fifteenth century, some inbred noble families undertook oral education of their deaf children. Most of the deaf, however, had to rely on the basic sign languages they could formulate; in urban settings, these evolved into coherent systems. In the mid-eighteenth century, the Abbé de l'Épée pursued a vocation among the poor deaf of Paris and was one of the first hearing people ever to learn their language. Employing it as a means for explaining French, he taught the deaf to read and write. It was the dawn of emancipation: you did not need speech to learn the languages of the speaking world. The Abbé de l'Épée founded the Institute for the Instruction of Deaf-Mutes in 1755. In the early nineteenth century, the Reverend Thomas Gallaudet of Connecticut, who had become interested in the education of a deaf child, set off for England to get information on deaf pedagogy. The English told him that their oral method was a secret, so Gallaudet traveled on to France, where he was warmly received at the institute, and he invited a young deaf man, Laurent Clerc, to accompany him back to America to establish a school. In 1817, they set up the American Asylum for the Education and Instruction of the Deaf in Hartford, Connecticut. The fifty years that followed were a golden age. French sign language mixed with homespun American signs as well as the sign dialect on Martha's Vineyard (where there was a strain of hereditary deafness) to form American Sign Language (ASL). Deaf people wrote books, entered public life, achieved widely. Gallaudet College was founded in 1857 in Washington, DC, to provide advanced education to the deaf; Abraham Lincoln authorized the college to grant degrees.

Once the deaf became high-functioning, they were asked to use their voices. Alexander Graham Bell led the nineteenth-century oralist movement, which culminated with the first international meeting of educators of the deaf, the Congress of Milan, in 1880 and an edict to ban the use of manualism—a disparaging word for Sign—so that children might learn to speak instead. Bell, who had a deaf mother and a deaf wife, disparaged Sign as "pantomime." Appalled by the idea of "a Deaf variety of the human race," he founded the American Association to Promote the Teaching of Speech to the Deaf, which sought to forbid deaf people to marry each other, and to keep deaf students from mixing with other deaf students. He asked that deaf adults undergo sterilization and persuaded some hearing parents to sterilize their deaf children. Thomas Edison jumped on the bandwagon to promote an exclusive oralism. When Lexington was founded, hearing people wished to teach the deaf to speak and read lips so they could function in the "real world." How that dream went horribly wrong is the grand tragedy around which modern Deaf culture has constructed itself.

By World War I, some 80 percent of deaf children were being educated without Sign, a situation that was to prevail for half a century. Deaf teachers who had signed were suddenly unemployed. The oralists thought signing would distract children from learning English, and any pupil who signed at an oralist school had his hand struck with a ruler. George Veditz, former president of the National Association of the Deaf (NAD), protested in 1913, "'A new race of pharaohs that knew not Joseph' are taking over the land. Enemies of the sign language, they are enemies of the true welfare of the deaf. It is my hope that we all will love and guard our beautiful sign language as the noblest gift God has given to deaf people." Deaf people were considered moronic—hence our use of the word *dumb* to describe idiocy—but such limitations were the result of denying them their language. The activist Patrick Boudreault has compared oralism to the conversion therapies used to "normalize" gay people, a social Darwinism run hideously amok. Despite all these unhappy developments, the schools remained the cradle of Deaf culture.

Aristotle contended that "of persons destitute from birth of either sense, the blind are more intelligent than the deaf and dumb" because "rational discourse is a cause of instruction in virtue of its being audible." In fact, expressive and receptive communication serve this function, even when not organized around hearing. That Sign might be a full language eluded scholars until the linguist William Stokoe published his groundbreaking book *Sign Language Structure* in 1960. He demonstrated that what had been deemed a crude, gestural communication system had a complex and deep grammar of its own, with logical rules and systems. Sign depends predominantly on the left hemisphere of the brain (the language hemisphere, which in nonsigning people processes sound and written information) and to a much lesser degree on the right (which processes visual information and the emotional content of gestures); it employs the same essential faculties as English, French, or Chinese. A deaf person with a left-hemisphere lesion after a stroke will retain the ability to understand or produce gesture, but lose the ability to understand or produce Sign, much as a hearing person with a left-hemisphere lesion will lose the ability to speak and understand language, but will still understand and produce facial expressions. Neuroimaging shows that while people who acquire Sign early have almost all of it in the language regions, people who learn Sign in adulthood tend to use the visual part of their brain more, as though their neural physiology were still struggling with the idea of it as a language.

A twenty-six-week-old fetus can detect sound. Exposure in utero to specific sounds—in one study, the music from *Peter and the Wolf,* and in another, the flyover sound of Osaka airport—causes a newborn to show preference or tolerance for those sounds. Two-day-olds born to French-speaking mothers have responded to the phonemes of French, but not to those of Russian; two-day-old American children prefer the sound of American English to the sound of Italian. Recognition of phonemes begins several months before birth; refinement of that ability, which includes a narrowing of it, takes place during the first year of life. At six months, infants in one study could discriminate among phonemes of all languages; by the time they were a year old, those raised in an English-speaking environment had lost the ability to distinguish the phonemes of non-Western languages. These are astonishingly early processes.

The critical period for connecting meaning to those sorted phonemes is between eighteen and thirty-six months, with a gradually diminishing language-acquisition capacity that tails off at about age twelve—though some exceptional people have acquired language much later; the linguist Susan Schaller taught Sign to a twenty-seven-year-old deaf man who had had no language at all until then. During the critical period, the mind can internalize the principles of grammar and signification. Language can be learned only through exposure; in a vacuum, the language centers of the brain effectively atrophy. In the language-acquisition period, a child can learn any language; and once he has language itself, he can learn other languages much later in life. Deaf children acquire Sign exactly as hearing children acquire a first spoken language; most can learn aural language in its written form as a second language. For many, however, speech is a mystical gymnastics of the tongue and throat, while lipreading is a guessing game. Some deaf children acquire these skills gradually, but making speech and lipreading the prerequisite to communication may consign deaf children to permanent confusion. If they bypass the key age for language acquisition without fully acquiring any language, they cannot develop full cognitive skills and will suffer permanently from a preventable form of mental retardation.

One cannot imagine thought without language any more than one can imagine language without thought. An inability to communicate can result in psychosis and dysfunction; the hard of hearing often have inadequate language, and researchers have estimated that up to one-third of prisoners are deaf or hard of hearing. The average hearing two-year-old has a vocabulary of three hundred words; the average deaf child of hearing parents has a vocabulary of thirty words at two. If one eliminates families with high levels of parental involvement and families who are learning Sign, the numbers become even more alarming. Douglas Baynton, a cultural historian at the University of Iowa, wrote, "The difficulty of learning spoken English for a person profoundly deaf from an early age has been likened to a hearing American trying to learn spoken Japanese while locked within a soundproof glass cubicle." Forbidding Sign does not turn deaf children toward speech, but away from language.

An oralist focus does not simply exist within the parent-child relationship; it becomes that relationship. A mother must, as one team of psychologists wrote, "impose herself upon his natural play-learning patterns, often against his will." Many deaf children who ultimately managed to develop oral skills complain that their schooling was dominated by the effort to teach a single ability—thousands of hours of sitting with an audiologist who squeezed their faces into positions, made them move their tongues in certain patterns, repeated drill exercises day after day. "In my history class, we spent two weeks learning to say *guillotine*, and that was what we learned about the French Revolution," Jackie Roth, a Deaf activist, said to me of the oralist education she had had at Lexington. "Then you say *guillotine* to someone with your deaf voice, and they have no idea what you're talking about. Usually, they can't tell what you're trying to pronounce when you say *Coke* at McDonald's. We felt retarded. Everything depended on one completely boring skill, and we were all bad at it."

The 1990 Individuals with Disabilities Education Act (IDEA) has sometimes been interpreted to assert that separate is never equal, and that everyone should attend mainstream schools. For wheelchair users, now provided with ramps, this is splendid. For the deaf, who are constitutionally unable to learn the basic means of communication used by hearing people, mainstreaming is the worst disaster since the Congress of Milan. If oralism destroyed the quality of the deaf residential schools, mainstreaming killed the schools themselves. At the end of the nineteenth century, there were eighty-seven residential schools for the deaf in the United States; by the end of the twentieth century, a third had closed. In the mid-twentieth century, 80 percent of deaf children went to residential schools; in 2004, less than 14 percent did so. Judith Heumann, the highest-ranking person in the Clinton administration with a disability, declared that separate education for children with disabilities was "immoral." But Heumann erred in omitting a deaf exception to her diktat.

In its 1982 decision in *Board of Education v. Rowley*, the US Supreme Court maintained that a deaf girl was receiving an adequate education if she was passing her courses and held that there was no need to provide her with a translator, even though her primary language was Sign and even though through lipreading she understood less than half of what was being spoken. Justice William Rehnquist wrote, "The intent of the Act was more to open the door of public education to handicapped children on appropriate terms than to guarantee any particular level of education once inside. The requirement that a State provide specialized educational services to handicapped children generates no additional requirement that the services so provided be sufficient to maximize each child's potential." At deaf schools, the standard of education is often low; at mainstream schools, much of the education is inaccessible to deaf students. In neither instance are deaf people getting a good education. Only a third of deaf children complete high school, and of those who attend college, only a fifth complete their studies; deaf adults earn about a third less than their hearing peers.

The deaf children of deaf parents frequently have a higher level of achievement than the deaf children of hearing parents. Deaf of deaf, as they are colloquially called, learn Sign as a first language at home. They are more likely to develop fluent written English, even if there is no spoken language at home and they attend a school where teaching is in Sign, than are deaf children of hearing parents who use English at home and go to a mainstream school. Deaf of deaf also score higher in other academic areas, including arithmetic, and are ahead on maturity, responsibility, independence, sociability, and willingness to communicate with strangers.

Helen Keller is said to have observed, "Blindness cuts us off from things, but deafness cuts us off from people." Communicating in Sign is more meaningful to many deaf people than being unable to hear. Those who sign love their language, often even if they have access to the languages of the hearing world. The writer Lennard Davis, a "child of deaf adults" (CODA) who teaches disability studies, wrote, "To this day if I sign 'milk,' I feel more milky than if I say the word. Signing is like speech set to dance. There is a constant pas de deux between the fingers and the face. Those who do not know sign language can only see the movements as distant and unnuanced. But those who understand signing can see the finest shade of meaning in a gesture. Like the pleasure some hearing people take in the graded distinctions between words like 'dry,' 'arid,' 'parched,' 'desiccated,' or 'dehydrated,' so the deaf can enjoy equivalent distinctions in the gestures of sign language."

Jackie Roth said, "Socially or in secret, we always signed. No theory could kill our language."

Deafness is defined as a low-incidence disability. It is estimated that one in a thousand newborns is profoundly deaf, and that twice as many have less severe hearing impairment. Another two or three per thousand will lose hearing before age ten. The Deaf activists Carol Padden and Tom Humphries wrote, "Culture provides a way for Deaf people to reimagine themselves as not so much adapting to the present, but inheriting the past. It allows them to think of themselves not as unfinished hearing people but as cultural and linguistic beings in a collective world with one another. It gives them a reason for existing with others in the modern world."

After a week of protests outside the Lexington Center, the demonstrators went to the Queens Borough president's office. The demonstration, though still in deadly earnest, had that air of festivity that clings to anything for which people are skipping work or school. Greg Hlibok, perhaps Lexington's most famous alumnus, was going to speak.

Six years earlier, Gallaudet University had announced the appointment of a new president. Students had been rallying for the university to have its first Deaf CEO, but a hearing candidate was selected. In the week that followed, the Deaf community as a political force abruptly came into its own. The Deaf President Now (DPN) movement, led by student activists, among whom Hlibok was the apparent leader, was the Stonewall of Deaf culture; Hlibok was the Deaf Rosa Parks. In a week, demonstrations closed down the university; the protests received substantial coverage in the national media; Hlibok staged a march on the Capitol that included twenty-five hundred supporters; and they won. The board chairman resigned, and her place was taken by a Deaf man, Phil Bravin, who immediately named Gallaudet's first deaf president, the psychologist I. King Jordan.

At the borough president's office, Greg Hlibok was electrifying. ASL is relatively noniconic; only a small number of signs actually look like what they describe. But an articulate signer can create a picture by mixing signs and gesture. Greg Hlibok compared the Lexington board to adults playing with a dollhouse, moving around the deaf students like little toys. He seemed to be building the house in the air; you could see it in front of you and witness the interfering arms of the board reaching into it. The students cheered, waving their hands over their heads, fingers splayed, in Deaf applause.

A week later, there was a protest on Madison Avenue in front of the office of Lexington's board chairman. Several board members marched, including Phil Bravin. After Madison Avenue, members of the core committee finally met with the chairman and an external negotiator. An emergency board meeting was scheduled, but the day before it, Max Gould resigned; a few days later, the chairman of the board followed suit.

When they are excited, many deaf people make loud sounds, often at high or low pitch—wordless exclamations of delight. In the halls of Lexington, students cheered, and anyone hearing was transfixed by the sound. Phil Bravin, who took over as Lexington's board chair, would say to me a few months later, "It was the best thing that could have happened to those students, no matter how many classes they missed during the protests. Some are from families that said, 'You're deaf; don't shoot too high.' Now they know better." At the Lexington graduation, a week later, Greg Hlibok said, "From the time God made earth until today, this is probably the best time to be deaf."

Jackie Roth did not grow up at the best time to be deaf, but she grew up in better times than her parents had. Walter Roth, Jackie's father, was an unusually beautiful baby, and his mother was thrilled with her son until she found out he was deaf, at which point she wanted nothing more to do with him. "She was so ashamed," Jackie said. Walter was given to his grandmother to raise. "My great-grandmother had no understanding of deafness," Jackie said. "But she had a heart." Unsure what to do with Walter, she sent him to eleven different schools—deaf schools, hearing schools, special schools—but he never learned to read or write past a third-grade level. He was so handsome that he seemed to glide along despite these limitations. Then he fell in love with Rose, ten years his senior, whose first marriage had fallen apart because she was infertile. Walter said he didn't want to have children anyway, and they were married. Two months later, Rose was pregnant with Jackie. Walter's mother declared it an outrage.

Walter and Rose were not proud of their deafness; when they found out that their daughter, too, was deaf, they both cried. Walter's mother shunned her new grandchild in favor of the hearing daughter Walter's sister had produced. Walter's siblings had married well; they had expensive weddings and bar mitzvahs in New York. But because Walter, uneducated, was working as a manual laborer in a printing plant, he and Rose lived in relative poverty; they would sit at a table in the corner at those functions, shunned, desperately trying to look as though they belonged.

"You would have liked my dad," Jackie said. "Everybody loved him. But he cheated on my mom all the time. He was a gambler who would do anything to get money, but we never had any." Yet Walter had both warmth and imagination, which Rose did not. "My mother wrote beautifully," Jackie said. "My dad was nearly illiterate. But he would sit at dinner with a dictionary, pick a word, and throw it at me. 'What does that mean?' It was my dad, who had no skills, who pushed me. My mother just wanted me to get married, have kids, meet someone who would take care of me." Walter was the one who emphasized putting your best foot forward. "He always said to me, 'You're never going out of the house looking like a poor girl. If you feel crappy, you don't let anybody know that. You walk with your head up.'"

Jackie was never allowed to sign in public; her mother found it embarrassing. Yet neither of Jackie's parents ever had a hearing friend. "It's as if the deaf community were my extended family," Jackie said. "My mother always worried about how other deaf people perceived them. She would get upset about my dad's behavior because her deaf friends would look down on them. If I did something wrong, she worried about my image in front of other deaf people." Many deaf people have some residual hearing; they can hear loud noises, or they can hear certain registers of sound, perhaps the high or low part of a sound. Jackie had good residual hearing, and she was a genius at sound discrimination and lipreading. This meant that, with hearing aids, she could function in the larger world. With amplification devices, she could even use the phone. By the time she was seventeen, she had attended four different schools while she tried to figure out who she was. "Am I deaf? Am I hearing? Am I what? I have no idea. All I know is that I was lonely," she said. At Lexington, she found herself picked on for not being deaf enough. At other schools, she was picked on for being deaf. Her younger sister, Ellen, who was completely deaf, was a boarding student at Lexington; her path looked easier and more straightforward to Jackie. Jackie was always pulled between the two worlds, and thanks to her oral skills she became the family interpreter. "When it came time to meet with the doctor, it was 'Jackie! Come here!'" she recalled. "When it came time to meet with the lawyer, it was 'Jackie! Come here!' I saw too much. I grew up much, much too fast."

One evening when Jackie was thirteen, her aunt called and said, "Jackie, tell your dad to meet us at the hospital. His mother's dying." Weeping, Walter rushed off to the hospital. When he returned at five o'clock in the morning, he began flicking the lights on and off to wake up his wife and daughter. Walter was doing some kind of jig and signing, "Mom deaf! Mom deaf!" Walter's mother had been given powerful antibiotics to combat a life-threatening infection, and the medicine had destroyed her auditory nerves. In the weeks that followed, Walter was there every day to help her. "He wanted to earn her love,"

Jackie recalled. "He wanted for the first time to have a mother. Never happened. She never wanted his advice or insight or even his tenderness." Yet seven years later, when Jackie laughed at her funeral, Walter slapped her across the face. "Only time in my life he did that," Jackie said. "It finally occurred to me that he loved his mother, no matter what."

When Jackie was fifteen, Walter was hired as a printer at the *Washington Post*, commuting home to New York to spend the weekends with his family. He was in a terrible car accident just a few weeks short of getting his union card; he was in a coma for a week, hospitalized for months, and unable to work for a year. Because he had not yet joined the union, he had no health insurance. The family, already financially strained, was now forced into bankruptcy. Jackie falsified her age and found work as a cashier at a supermarket, where she began stealing food. When she was fired, she had to admit it and Rose was horrified. The next day, Rose swallowed her pride and asked Walter's family for money. "They made a mockery of her, and they didn't give her a dime," Jackie said. "Being alone in the world with all those relatives, it's much worse than just being alone. It eats away at you."

Living at school, Ellen was protected from the breakdown of the marriage, but Jackie lived through every dark moment. "Because I was their interpreter, I became their referee," she said. "I had so much power, too much power. When I talk about it, it sounds so sad. But I'm not sad about it. They were wonderful parents. Whatever money they had, they spent on my sister and me. They went the extra mile, and then they fought about it in front of my eyes, and I love them. My father was a dreamer. If I said I wanted to be a singer, he never said, 'Deaf girls can't.' He just told me to sing."

Jackie was accepted to college at UCLA in the early 1970s, at the beginning of Deaf pride. Rose couldn't believe there were interpreters at the university. "Why would hearing people sign?" she said to Jackie. Jackie used the physical distance to start fresh. "In college, I regressed," she said. "It took me a long time to grow up again."

Walter died in 1986, when Jackie was thirty; Rose mourned his death, but she was happier without him, and her relationship with Jackie improved; when her own health deteriorated, Jackie invited her to move in with her in lower Manhattan. "She still recollected humiliations from when she was a little girl, years and years of bitterness," Jackie said. "I never want to be like that." As her father had urged, Jackie has lived in a far larger world than her parents were able to—working as an actress, a real estate agent, an entrepreneur, a beauty queen, an activist, a filmmaker—and she has none of her mother's bitterness. Her sparkling grace and admirable toughness have emerged from a collaboration between her intelligence and will. The cost, however, has been considerable. Walter's mother rejected him for being deaf; Rose's deafness prevented her from making use of her mind; Ellen went away to school and became marginal within her own family; and Jackie's gift for sound discrimination forced her into a premature maturity. Being deaf was a curse in the family, but so was hearing.

I first met Jackie Roth in her late thirties, in 1993. In her fifties, she became involved in the communications industry, working on Internet relays to allow deaf and hearing people to communicate via interpreters. She joined the board of a foundation that taught parents Sign and taught them how to support children with cochlear implants that provide synthetic hearing. Her work focused on bridging the cultures—just what she'd done in her own family. When she turned fifty-five, she threw herself a birthday party. It was a bounteous event, generous to all the people she loved, and it brought out the best in everyone. "It was almost like I had lived in two very separate worlds all my life, Deaf and hearing," she said. "A lot of my hearing friends had never seen the Deaf side. The Deaf people had never seen my hearing side. It was very wonderful for me to see everybody in one place. I couldn't do without either, and I finally realized that that's who I was. Thinking about the anxiety these issues have generated, I'm my mother's daughter. But isn't it great that I figured that out at a party? I'm my father's daughter, too."

Like Jackie, Lewis Merkin, an actor and playwright, struggled with the legacy of shame that surrounded deafness during his childhood. "When I was growing up, I looked at these grassroots deaf people, who were marginal, unimportant, completely dependent on others, who had no education, saw themselves as second-rate," he said. "I recoiled within. I felt sick at the thought that I was deaf. It took a long time for me to understand what it meant to be Deaf, what a world was open to me." Lewis was also gay. "I saw limp-wristed drag queens and guys in leather, and again I thought, that's not me; it was only with time that I came into a real gay identity." MJ Bienvenu, professor of ASL and Deaf Studies at Gallaudet, told me, "What we have experienced is so similar: if you are Deaf, you know almost exactly what it is like to be gay, and vice versa."

More than a hundred genes for deafness have been identified, and another one seems to be picked up every month. Some kinds of deafness are caused by the interaction of multiple genes rather than by a single one, and much deafness that occurs later in life is also genetic. At least 10 percent of our genes can affect hearing or ear structure, and other genes and environmental factors can determine how profound the deafness will be. About a fifth of genetic deafness is connected to dominant genes; the rest emerges when two carriers of recessive genes produce children together. The first genetic breakthrough came in 1997, with the discovery of connexin 26 mutations on GJB2, which are responsible for a large proportion of nonacquired deafness. One in thirty-one Americans carries GJB2, with most carriers unaware of their status. A small amount of deafness is X-linked, which means it comes only from the father, and another small percentage is mitochondrial, which means it comes exclusively from the mother. One third of deafness is syndromal, meaning that it is a component of a condition with other physical consequences. Of the nonsyndromal forms of deafness, some are regulatory and based on a disruption of DNA message processing; some are directly involved in the development of the cochlea; and the most frequent interfere with the gap junctions in which potassium ions relay sound as an electrical impulse to the hair cells of the inner ear.

Geneticists long dismissed Alexander Graham Bell's anxiety about the creation of a deaf race, but it appears that the residential school system, which allowed deaf people to meet and marry one another, may have doubled the rate of the deafness-related DFNB1 gene in America over the past two hundred years. Indeed, the worldwide prevalence of deafness genes seems tied to historical situations in which deaf people reproduced together. Blind people have not necessarily married other blind people, but language issues have inclined deaf people to marry one another. The earliest example of this is the deaf community that thrived under the Hittite empire thirty-five hundred years ago, which is now believed to have concentrated and spread the 35delG mutation. When GJB2 was discovered, Nancy Bloch, executive director of the NAD, commented via e-mail for a *New York Times* article, "We applaud the great strides made through genetic identification research, however, we do not condone the use of such information for eugenics and related purposes." Prenatal screening can pick up certain kinds of genetic deafness, allowing some prospective parents to opt against having deaf children. Dirksen Bauman, a professor of Deaf Studies at Gallaudet, has written, "The question of what lives are worth living is now answered in doctors' offices instead of in the Nazis' T-4 program. The forces of normalization seem to be gaining ground."

At the same time, genetic information has provided comfort to some hearing parents of deaf children. The geneticist Christina Palmer described a woman who had come in racked with guilt, certain that her child was deaf because of the rock concerts she had attended while pregnant. The geneticist found connexin 26, and the woman sobbed with relief. I came across a personal ad that began, "SWM seeks mate with C26." It was his identity, and a map for a genetic future; all the children of a couple who both have C26 will be deaf.

Most hearing people assume that to be deaf is to lack hearing. Many Deaf people experience deafness not as an absence, but as a presence. Deafness is a culture and a life, a language and an aesthetic, a physicality and an intimacy different from all others. This culture inhabits a narrower mind-body split than the one that constrains the rest of us, because language is enmeshed with the major muscle groups, not just the limited architecture of the tongue and larynx. According to the Whorf-Sapir hypothesis, one of the cornerstones of sociolinguistics, your language determines the way you understand the world. "To establish the validity of Sign," William Stokoe said to me shortly before his death in 2000, "we had to spend a long time dwelling on how it resembles spoken language. Now that the validity of Sign has been broadly accepted, we can concentrate on what's interesting—the differences between Sign and spoken language, how the life perceptions of a native signer will vary from the perceptions of the hearing people around him."

The Deaf activist MJ Bienvenu said, "We do not want or need to become hearing in order to consider ourselves normal. For us, early intervention does not mean earphones, amplifiers, and training a child to appear as hearing as possible. Instead, a good early intervention program would offer deaf children and hearing parents early exposure to ASL and many opportunities to interact with signing Deaf people. We are a minority group with our own language, culture, and heritage." Barbara Kannapell, another Deaf activist, wrote, "I believe 'my language is me.' To reject ASL is to reject the deaf person." And Carol Padden and Tom Humphries wrote, "Deaf people's bodies have been labeled, segregated and controlled for most of their history, and this legacy is still very much present in the specter of future 'advances' in cochlear implants and genetic engineering." These implants, devices surgically placed in the ear and brain to provide a facsimile of hearing, are a hot-button issue among Deaf people.

There are impassioned opponents of this model of Deaf culture. Edgar L. Lowell, director of Los Angeles' staunchly oralist John Tracy Clinic, said, "Asking me to speak on the 'place of manual communication in the education of deaf children' is like asking the shepherd to speak on the place of the wolf in his flock." Tom Bertling's memoir, *A Child Sacrificed to the Deaf Culture*, tells the story of how he was shipped off to a boarding school where he was instructed in Sign well below his intellectual level. He felt that ASL, which he derides as "baby talk," was being rammed down his throat; he has chosen to use English instead as an adult. One Deaf person said to me, "We really are the Israelis and the Palestinians." The social critic Beryl Lieff Benderly described it as "a holy war." When the Smithsonian announced plans for an exhibition about Deaf culture in the late 1990s, outraged parents who believed that a celebration of ASL was a challenge to oralism protested that they should be free to choose oral education for their children—as if, deaf historian Kristen Harmon pointed out, the Deaf community were in the business of child-snatching.

Yet the fear of losing one's child to the Deaf world is more than a dark fantasy. I met many Deaf people who thought of the previous generation of Deaf people as their parents. The higher achievement levels of deaf of deaf were often used as an argument that deaf children should be adopted by deaf adults. Even a pro-Deaf hearing parent said, "Sometimes Deaf culture looks like the Moonies to me: 'Your child will be happy, just don't expect to see her anymore, she's too busy being happy.'" Cheryl Heppner, a Deaf woman who is executive director of the Northern Virginia Resource Center and who advises parents of deaf children, said, "Deaf people feel ownership of deaf children. I admit it. I feel it, too. I really struggle in not wanting to interfere with a parent's right to parent, at the same time knowing that they have to accept that the child can never be one hundred percent theirs."

People whose language is Sign have had to fight for acceptance from within the confines of a language that their opponents do not understand; they could not explain what they wanted until they got it. This has created an intense anger that subtends Deaf politics. The Deaf psychologist Neil Glickman has spoken of four stages of Deaf identity. People start out pretending to be hearing, with the discomfort of the only Jew in the country club or the only black family in the suburb. They progress to marginality, feeling they are not a part of either deaf or hearing life. Then they immerse themselves in Deaf culture, fall in love with it, and disparage hearing culture. Finally, they achieve a balanced view that there are strengths in both the deaf and the hearing experience.

For Caro Wilson, teaching a child to speak was not about politics but about love. When Caro's son, Tom, was two weeks old, Caro's mother noticed that he didn't react when she wheeled his carriage past a pneumatic drill. Caro observed the deficit at six weeks. Their doctor remained unconvinced until Tom was eight months old, and Tom's father, Richard, didn't believe it until the medical diagnosis was in. Richard's first move was to buy every book he could find on deafness, and Caro's was to get the explanations over with. The Wilsons lived in a small village in the south of England. "The postmistress said, 'Would you like me to tell everybody?'" Caro recounted. "I said, 'Yes, I would like everyone to know.' So I got allies very quickly."

Caro had been a teacher, but she and Richard soon agreed that he would henceforth earn all the money while she would take care of Tom and later their daughter, Amy. "Suddenly, your house isn't yours anymore, because professionals are marching in as if they owned you and the deaf child," Caro said. "I remember very, very strongly thinking, 'If I could just run away with you, Tom, to an island, I'd teach you to talk, and we'd be *fine*!'" When Tom was eleven months old, in 1980, he got his first hearing aids. The family had to choose an educational strategy. "We met somebody with a deaf child who said to me, 'Caro, it's extremely simple. If he's intelligent, he's going to learn to talk.'" At three, Tom was already beginning to develop aspects of oral speech. His consonants were largely incomprehensible to everyone except Caro and Richard, but he was using his voice, and they tried to reward every effort he made to do so. With hearing aids, he could get loud sound, and Caro spent day after day doing drills, saying a thousand times, as loudly as she could, "This is a cup," and handing him a cup.

At first, they watched cartoons, where simple narrative gave a structure for learning sentences; in the face of Tom's deafness, low culture temporarily became high culture. Soon, Tom emerged as an early and fluent reader. Richard liked a book on deafness by Mary Courtman-Davies, and he wrote and asked her to work with Tom. She was severe and a disciplinarian; at home, the Wilsons called her "Mrs. Ferocious." "She was very good at analyzing his language and saw, for example, that he hadn't any adverbs," Caro said. "We saw her about once a month, and she'd give him some work that he and I did together every evening." When he was five, Tom tried to tell her a story that included the sentence, "So the mum picked up a bit of wood." Caro couldn't understand what the mum had picked up; she asked Tom to repeat himself, to draw what he was saying, and finally he brought her a block of wood from the basement. "If he could work that hard, then so could I," Caro said. "I was always quite scared of being too soft on him—especially in social behavior, social niceties, because he was going to need them more than anyone."

The next problem was school. When Tom was six, he was placed in a mainstream class taught by a man with a heavy mustache and beard, and when the Wilsons asked that Tom be transferred into another class, they were told, "We think it's important he learns to lip-read somebody difficult." Caro and Richard said, "We think it's important he learns his nine times table." The situation was not happy, and it was socially alienating. Tom came home one day and said that for sports, he had been asked to be the goalpost. "So we sent him to a very odd little private school with only fifty children," Caro said, "because one of the difficulties is that Tom is intelligent."

Then came secondary school. They met with the head teacher of the local school, who said, "I know people like you. You're going to have too high expectations of this child. That's not fair to you or the child, so you must lower your expectations." Caro was indignant, but also shaken. "I remember," she said, "standing at home, leaning on an apothecary chest. I said to Richard, 'He'll never read *Hamlet* and he'll never say *apothecary chest*.'" They looked at all the schools for which they might qualify, including the Mary Hare School for the Deaf, a boarding school in Berkshire. Although all students there are deaf, they do better on standardized national tests than the average British child. Richard had been miserable at boarding school and had sworn never to send a child of his away; Caro was opposed to private secondary education and was also horrified about having Tom so far from home. In the end, however, he went; Caro joined the board of governors. She said, "Tom was hit by homesickness and cried for the first two terms. I was very, very Tom-sick. In the second, third, fourth year, he was very happy, and sixth form was one of the happiest times he's ever had. Adolescence needs to be when you start to make lots of decent friends, or you don't learn how. He had friends there." There was informal signing, but teaching was spoken, and people were encouraged to use their voice. "An interestingly high proportion are from deaf parents," Caro said, "including signing deaf parents who want their children brought up orally. It's a nice place. It's hated by a lot of the Deaf community."

When Tom started, Richard visited the speech therapist and said, "Don't tell my wife I came. But I need you to teach this boy to say *apothecary chest*." The speech therapist thought this was absurd and so did Tom. Caro laughed as she described it. "He said *apothecary chest*. And he also read *Hamlet*." Tom's love of reading and words has been his common ground with his mother. As she and I talked one afternoon, she flipped through photo albums. There were hundreds of pictures of Caro and Tom walking, sitting, playing, working. Tom's sister made only an occasional appearance. "Richard's taking the photographs, but where is Amy?" Caro said. "She will tell you that that's what it felt like an awful lot of the time. I think it was a very good thing that Tom went to boarding school at twelve, because it gave Amy and me a second chance."

When Tom went away, Caro was elected to the board of the Royal National Institute for Deaf People (RNID). She tried to get some signing board members, but the political Deaf movement in England dislikes the RNID (which some say stands for Really Not Interested in the Deaf), and Caro never got anyone to join. Caro found the hostility both mystifying and counterproductive. "I always felt there was something about the signing deaf community that encourages a prolonged adolescence. It's powerful as a way of experiencing yourself, but ultimately without power in the larger world." Tom, too, found the politicized Deaf community difficult, but he believed in some measure of pride in deafness—or at least pride in being oneself, with deafness as part of it. "I remember Tom telling me about a boy in his dormitory who prayed every night to be cured," Caro said, "and Tom saying, 'That's very sad, Mum, isn't it? I would never do that.' I thought, 'Well, we've done something right.'"

Tom graduated well from Mary Hare and went to Bath University to study graphic design. He got a first, the top degree category, worked for two years at a graphic design company, then decided he wanted to see the world. He took a year and traveled through Australia, New Zealand, Southeast Asia, and South America. He then traveled on his own through Africa. Still, during this period he was somewhat aimless and at times severely depressed. Caro felt both worried and helpless. "Then one day, I heard footsteps coming up the stairs and it was Richard and Tom," she recalled. "Richard said, 'Tom's got some news.' As a parent, you instantly think, 'Oh, he's being prosecuted,' or something. He said, 'I've been accepted by the Royal College of Art for an MA.' We didn't even know he'd applied."

The Royal College, London's preeminent art school, turned out to be full of kindred spirits. For Tom, reimagining himself as an artist conclusively ended his depression, and he gained in both poise and confidence. Tom is still a loner by nature. He once told Caro that he would make an excellent monk if it weren't for God. "He makes such huge progress, but I still want to help somehow, and it's hard not to be allowed to anymore," Caro said.

Having not engaged with Deaf politics, Tom has no particular affection for his condition; indeed, though he was happy for me to talk to his parents, he opted not to meet with me as he didn't want to talk to anyone whose primary concern was his "deficiency," asserting that he saw the deafness as only a small part of who he is. "I can see no benefit whatsoever in Tom being deaf—for *him*," Caro said. "But the benefits for me were absolutely huge. If I'd had to deal with a disability where you spend all your time in the swimming pool or a gym, I would have found it very difficult. But my field is literature. So, to have something about language was absolutely fascinating. I'd been brought up among very clever, high-pressure people. For the first time, through disability, I met people who were good. I'd always been taught to despise people who are just 'good.' I met a lot of friends. I do a lot of charity stuff now. I wouldn't have done any of that without Tom, would I? It would have been a quite different life."

Caro admires Tom's confidence, and, even more, his courage. "He's making his soul," she said. "We live in this society where people are mostly making money or status. Tom would love money, and he'd love status, but that's not what he's doing. He's taking a long, slow time growing up, but life is quite long."

Shortly after Lexington's graduation in 1994, I attended the NAD convention in Knoxville, Tennessee, with almost two thousand deaf participants. During the Lexington protests, I had visited deaf households. I had learned how deaf telecommunications work; I had met dogs who understood Sign; I had discussed mainstreaming and oralism and the integrity of visual language; I had become accustomed to doorbells that flashed lights instead of ringing. I had observed differences between British and American Deaf culture. I had stayed in a dorm at Gallaudet. Yet I was unprepared for the Deaf world of the NAD.

The NAD has been at the center of Deaf self-realization and power since it was founded in 1880, and the convention is where the most committed Deaf gather for political focus and social exchange. At the President's Reception, the lights were turned up high because deaf people lapse into speechlessness in semidarkness. Across the room, it seemed almost as though some strange human sea were breaking into waves and glinting in the light, as thousands of hands moved at stunning speed, describing a spatial grammar with sharply individual voices and accents. The crowd was nearly silent; you heard the claps that are part of the language, the clicks and puffing noises that the deaf make when they sign, and occasionally their big, uncontrolled laughter. Deaf people touch each other more than the hearing, but I had to be careful of the difference between a friendly and a forward embrace. I had to be careful of everything because I knew none of the etiquette of these new circumstances.

I discussed the deaf travel industry with Aaron Rudner, then of Deafstar Travel, and with Joyce Brubaker, then of Deaf Joy Travel, who was organizing the first Deaf gay cruise. I attended seminars on ASL usage, on AIDS, on domestic violence. I talked to Alan Barwiolek, who founded the New York Deaf Theatre, about the difference between plays translated for the deaf and Deaf plays. I guffawed at Deaf comedians. (Ken Glickman, aka Professor Glick: "My blind dates are always deaf dates. You ever been on a deaf date? You go out with someone and then you never hear from her again.") Over dinner, the acclaimed Deaf actor Bernard Bragg performed lyrical signed translations of William Blake while his pasta grew cold; signers can talk with their mouths full, but they can't cut up their food while speaking.

The NAD is the host of the Miss Deaf America pageant, and Friday night featured the competition. The young beauties, dressed to the nines and sporting state sashes, were objects of considerable attention. "Can you believe that blurry Southern signing?" someone said, pointing to Miss Deaf Missouri. "I didn't think anyone *really* signed like that!" (Regional variations of Sign can be dangerous: the sign that in New York slang means "cake" in some Southern states means "sanitary napkin"; my own poor articulation led me to invite someone to have not *lunch*, but *a lesbian*.) Genie Gertz, Miss Deaf New York, the daughter of Russian Jewish parents who emigrated when she was ten, delivered an eloquent monologue about finding freedom in the United States—which included, for her, the move from being a social misfit in a country that is not easy on disability to being Deaf and proud. It seemed like such a striking and radical idea that one might be deaf and glamorous: an American dream.

At 2:30 a.m. night after night, I was still up, conversing. One deaf sociologist I met was writing a thesis on deaf good-byes. Before the invention in the 1960s of teletypewriters, or TTYs, which allowed deaf people to type messages to one another pre-Internet, the deaf could communicate only by letters, telegrams, or personal appearances. You could take two days just inviting people to a small party. Saying good-bye was never easy; you would suddenly remember whatever you had forgotten to tell, and knowing it would be some time before you could make contact again, you would keep on not leaving.

Alec Naiman, a member of the Deaf Pilots Association, was a world traveler until a crash in 2005, occasioned by ground crew who forgot that they were communicating with a deaf pilot, left him seriously injured. When I met him, he was fresh from a trip to China. "I met some Deaf Chinese people my first day, and I went to stay with them," he said. "Deaf people never need hotels; you are always given a place to stay with other Deaf people. Though we used different signed languages, these Chinese Deaf people and I could make ourselves understood; and though we came from different countries, our mutual Deaf culture held us together. By the end of the evening we'd talked about

Deaf life in China, and about Chinese politics." I nodded. "*You* couldn't do that in China," he said. "No hearing person could. So who's disabled then?" Disconcerting though it may sound, it was impossible, at the NAD convention, not to wish you were Deaf. I had known that Deaf culture existed, but I had not guessed how heady it is.

How to reconcile this Deaf experience with the rest of the world? MJ Bienvenu laid the groundwork for the bilingual and bicultural approach, commonly referred to as Bi-Bi, used at both the elementary and secondary model schools on the Gallaudet campus. In a Bi-Bi curriculum, students are taught in Sign, then learn English as a second language. Written English is afforded high priority; many students perform on par with their hearing counterparts. On average, schools employing a solely oral approach graduate students at eighteen who read at a fourth-grade level; students from Bi-Bi schools often read at grade level. Spoken English is taught as a useful tool within the Bi-Bi system, but is not a primary focus.

MJ, in her early forties when we first met, has signing so swift, crisp, and perfectly controlled that she seems to be rearranging the air into a more acceptable shape. She has been one of the most vocal and articulate opponents of the language of disability. "I am Deaf," she said, drawing out the sign for "Deaf," the index finger moving from chin to ear, as though she were tracing a broad smile. "To see myself as Deaf is as much of a choice as it is for me to identify as a lesbian. I am living my cultures. I don't define myself in terms of 'not hearing' or of 'not' anything else. Those who learn forced English while being denied Sign emerge semilingual rather than bilingual, and they are disabled. But for the rest of us, it is no more a disability than being Japanese would be." Deaf of deaf, with deaf sisters, she manifests a pleasure in American Sign Language that only poets feel for English. "When our language was acknowledged," she said, "we gained our freedom." *Freedom*— clenched hands are crossed before the body, then swing apart and face out—was like an explosion as she signed it. "There are many things that I can experience for which you have no equivalent," she said.

This is tricky territory. Some argue that if being deaf is not a disability, deaf people should not be protected under the Americans with Disabilities Act (ADA) and should not have the right to various mandated accommodations: translators in public-service venues, relay interpreters on telephone exchanges, captions on television programs. None of these services is automatically available to people in the United States who speak only Japanese. If deafness is not a disability, then on what basis does the state provide for separate schools, and on what basis does it provide Social Security disability insurance? The writer Harlan

Lane, who teaches psychology at Northeastern, said, "The dilemma is that deaf people want access and as citizens in a democracy have a right to access—access to public events, government services, and education—but when they subscribe to the disability definition in order to gain access, they undermine their struggle for other rights—such as an education for deaf children using their best language, an end to implant surgery on those children, and an end to efforts to discourage deaf births in the first place."

I met many deaf individuals who said that being deaf is of course a disability. They were indignant at the thought of a politically correct group suggesting that their problems weren't problems. I also met deaf people who subscribed to the old deaf self-hatred, who were ashamed and saddened when they gave birth to deaf children, who felt they could never be anything more than second-class. Their unhappy voices cannot be forgotten; in some ways, it doesn't matter whether their ears are cured or their self-image is cured, but they are out there in numbers and they need help from someone.

Luke and Mary O'Hara, both hearing, married young, moved to a farm in Iowa, and started to have children immediately. Their first, Bridget, was born with Mondini malformation, a syndrome in which the cochlea is not fully formed. It is associated with degenerative deafness and other neurological impairments, including migraine headaches and, because it impinges on the vestibular system, poor balance. Bridget's hearing loss was diagnosed when she was two; the Mondini diagnosis came many years later. Luke and Mary were advised to raise her just like any other child, and she desperately tried to figure out oral communication and lipreading without any special education. "My mom labeled everything in the house so I could see what words went with what things, and she made me use full sentences, so I have good spoken English compared to other deaf people," Bridget said. "But I could never find confidence in myself. I never said anything that didn't get corrected." The difficulties in the means of communication intersected with family deficits in the content of communication. "I didn't know how to express my feelings," Bridget said, "because my parents and sisters didn't."

Bridget had three younger sisters. "My sisters would go 'Duh! You're so stupid!' My parents' body language made it clear they thought the same thing. At some point, I just stopped asking questions." Bridget was so roundly teased for her errors that she came to suspect even her most powerful intuitions, which left her profoundly vulnerable. "I was raised as a Catholic," Bridget said, "so I depended on whatever adults told me and took it at face value." We all live in accordance with the norms we pick up socially; stripped of such norms, we can regulate neither ourselves nor others. The only person whom Bridget trusted unconditionally was her sister Matilda, two years younger than she.

Bridget was the first deaf person to attend her school. Since she had never learned Sign, there was no point having an interpreter, and she had to lip-read all day. Bridget would come home from school exhausted from it, and because she was a good reader in written English, she would curl up with a book. Her mother would tell her to put down the book and play with her friends. When Bridget said she didn't have any friends, her mother would say, "Why are you so angry?" Bridget remembered, "I didn't realize that there was a Deaf culture out there. I just thought I was the stupidest person in the world."

Bridget and her three younger sisters were subject to their father's violent temper. He would whip the girls with a belt. Bridget preferred outdoor chores to indoor ones, and she often helped her father in the yard. One day, they came in from raking, and Bridget went upstairs to take a shower. A minute later, her father, naked, stepped into the shower with her. "I was naïve in many ways because I didn't really have communication with anyone," she recalled. "But I somehow knew this was not right. But I was afraid." In the months that followed, Luke began to touch her, then forced her into submissive sexual acts. "At the beginning, I would question my father. He would escalate the physical abuse, and I would get whipped. I blame my mother almost more, for not doing anything." About that time, Bridget walked in on her mother in the bathroom, holding a bottle of pills. When Mary saw Bridget, she poured the pills down the toilet. "After I got older," Bridget said, "I realized she was *that* close."

When Bridget was in ninth grade, her grandparents took all the grandkids except her to Disney World; she had gone previously, and it was the others' turn. Bridget's mother went along, so Bridget was left home with her father. "I now have no memory whatsoever of that week," Bridget said. "But I apparently told Matilda about it when she got back from Disney World, and she later said she couldn't have anything to do with Dad, because of what he did to me." I wondered whether the abuse was linked with her deafness. "I was the easier mark," Bridget said. A friend of Bridget's suggested, "Her father believed that she would never say a word because she was deaf. That simple."

Bridget's marks started to slip in tenth grade. More and more material was in lectures rather than in reading, and she couldn't follow what was going on and was being tortured by classmates. Every time she went to the bathroom, she'd get beaten up by a gang of girls; she came home one day with a gash on her face that required stitches. Soon, the girls started dragging her to the janitor's closet between classes, where boys would take advantage of her sexually. "What angered me the most was adults," she said. "I tried to tell them. They wouldn't believe me." When she came home with her shin cut open and needed stitches again, her father called the school, but Bridget couldn't hear what he said and no one told her.

Bridget began having attacks of vertigo. "I now know that is a symptom of Mondini malformation. But I can't help wondering how much was also because of all the fear." Someone asked Bridget if she wished she were hearing, and she said she really didn't; she wished she were dead. Finally, she came home from school one day and announced that she was never going back. That night, her parents told her that there was a deaf school just forty-five minutes away from their house, which they had never mentioned because they wanted her to be part of "the real world." Bridget enrolled at fifteen. "I learned to sign fluently in a month," she said. "I started blossoming." Like many other deaf schools, this one had a low standard of education, and Bridget was academically ahead of her peers. She had been unpopular at her previous school because she was seen as an idiot. She was unpopular at this one because of her academic prowess. "Nonetheless, I became outgoing and made friends for the first time," she recalled. "I started caring about myself and taking care of myself."

Bridget had tried to get her mother to leave her father, and her mother had always "played the Catholic card," but after Bridget went off to college at NYU, her parents announced plans to divorce. "My mother had felt that I needed to have both of them," Bridget said. "Once I left, I guess she felt free."

In the years that followed, Bridget's headaches escalated; several times, she blacked out and collapsed. When she finally went to a doctor, he told her she needed immediate surgery for her malformation. She told him her symptoms were probably psychosomatic, and he was the first person to say to her, "Don't be so hard on yourself." Bridget eventually finished her degree and got a job in finance, but five years later, the episodes intensified again. Her neurologist told her not to work more than twenty hours a week. She returned to school, qualified in hospital administration, and did an internship at Columbia Presbyterian Hospital in New York, but she soon collapsed again, and her neurologist told her it was too dangerous to continue working. "The doctor told me I was going to destroy myself."

In her thirties, Bridget began having vision problems. She was wearing extremely powerful hearing aids, and they were amplifying the sound so much that they were stimulating her ocular nerve, causing her vision to blur. Her doctor recommended a cochlear implant. He thought it might help her migraines as well. Bridget had the procedure and is now able to understand some speech. "I love my implant," she told me. Her daily headaches became weekly. Her vision returned to normal. She has taken volunteer jobs, but employers want consistency, and her symptoms are unpredictable. "I so much want that stimulating feeling of being productive," she said. "But I have a disability, and either I can let it destroy me, or I can learn to enjoy my life. I would have liked to have kids, but how can you have kids when you know you might just get symptoms and have to stop everything?"

In 1997, Bridget's mother, dying of cancer, was given ten weeks to live. She was too sick to be alone. The three hearing sisters had families and couldn't deal with her, so Mary came to New York, to Bridget's small apartment. She lived another eighteen months. The burden of what was unsaid became intolerable. "I didn't get into the sexual, but I did talk about the physical abuse," Bridget said. "She started crying, but she wasn't ready to admit her part." When the care got to be more than Bridget could handle, Matilda moved in to help. "Matilda and I would talk at night, and Matilda talked about the sexual abuse," Bridget recalled. "It had a real impact on her, even though it happened to me and not to her." Matilda's anger was terrifying to Bridget—even though much of it was on Bridget's behalf.

Shortly before Mary died, Bridget's aunt called Matilda, saying that Mary was imagining crazy things in the hospital, weeping desperately about how Bridget had been sexually abused by her father and Mary hadn't done anything about it. "So my mother never apologized to me," Bridget said. "But she knew what happened, and she apologized to someone."

A year later, Matilda got divorced. "I didn't hear from her for almost two months," Bridget said. "Then she came to town, and I knew she was depressed. She said, 'I should have been the one who died.'" A few weeks later, Bridget learned that Matilda had hanged herself. Bridget explained to me, "I feel that I let her down. That my problems and my deafness and my sexual abuse were a burden on her. I'd said so many times, 'Matilda, any problem you have, talk to me. I know I've got enough problems of my own, but I'm always there for you.'"

Bridget's two remaining sisters have both learned Sign and taught it to their children; they now have videophones so everyone can be in touch. When one lost her husband to leukemia, she made sure there were interpreters at the service. They organize a family trip every year, which includes Bridget's father and Bridget. I wondered how Bridget could tolerate it. "He's old now," she said, "and harmless. What he did to me is a long time ago." Then she began to weep quietly. "If I didn't go, my sisters would want to know why. They have no idea what happened; they were much younger than Matilda and me. What would happen if I told my sisters?" She stared out the window for a long, long time. "What happened when I told Matilda?" she finally asked me. She shrugged her narrow shoulders. "A week in Disneyland every year—it's really a small price to pay."

Shortly after Bridget shared her history with me, the *New York Times* broke the story of the Reverend Lawrence C. Murphy, who had admitted to sexually abusing deaf boys at a Catholic boarding school in Wisconsin for twenty-two years. "Victims tried for more than three decades to bring him to justice," the *Times* wrote. "They told other priests. They told three archbishops of Milwaukee. They told two police departments and the district attorney. They used sign language, written affidavits and graphic gestures to show what exactly Father Murphy had done to them. But their reports fell on the deaf ears of hearing people." This story, of deaf children being abused, is ubiquitous, and Bridget was rare only in being willing to tell me about it. It's an open secret that deaf kids have trouble telling their stories. When a Deaf theater group did a piece in Seattle about incest and sexual abuse, they sold out an eight-hundred-seat auditorium, and they hired counselors to wait outside the theater. Many women and men broke down in tears and ran out during the performance. "By the end of the show, half the audience was sobbing in the arms of those therapists," one person who attended said.

The story of Megan Williams and Michael Shamberg lies at the other end of the spectrum. At sixty, Megan has the windblown good looks and the liberal sensibilities of Annie Hall—she's an idealist for whom idealism seems to have worked out, a woman who has made meaningful documentaries even though she's lived in the thick of the Los Angeles commercial-movie world. Where she is pragmatic, Michael Shamberg, the film producer to whom she was long married, is fond of abstractions; where she is always energized, he is somewhat aloof; where she is sparkling and quick, he is meditative and intellectual. They are both take-charge people. As the Deaf activist Jackie Roth said, "Megan looked at the world and didn't like a lot of what she saw, so she took it in her hands and fixed it."

When their son, Jacob, born in 1979, was eight months old, Megan began to suspect that he was deaf. The pediatrician said he had blocked eustachian tubes. Megan started banging pots and pans that night, but Jacob did not respond. She brought him back to the doctor, who said, "Okay. I'm going to blow up some balloons, stand behind him, and pop them with a hypodermic needle. You watch Jacob's eyes and see if they blink." Megan said, "Every time he popped the balloon, *my* eyes blinked, and I said, 'There's got to be a more sophisticated test.'" At LA Children's Hospital, Jacob was officially diagnosed.

Megan found a class on deaf education at California State University, Northridge, a university with a large deaf population. "There was a panel of parents who had deaf children. These mothers would just weep; then I would learn that their child was thirty. I thought, I am not going to be unhappy about this. I wish it weren't this way, but it is, and I am going to figure it out." Megan and Michael began hunting down deaf adults. "We would have them over for brunch and say, 'How were you raised, what did you like, what didn't you like?'" Megan recalled. She invented a primitive home sign language to use with Jacob, and she offered one of the visitors some pancakes, making a circle with her two forefingers and thumbs. The guest said, "We need to get you some lessons. You just offered me some pussy."

Michael said, "We learned that successful deaf adults aren't self-pitying. We realized that we had to immerse ourselves in that culture because that was where our child was going to live." The most urgent question was what to do about giving Jacob language. When Jacob was a year old, Megan and Michael went to the John Tracy Clinic, an oral-only program founded by Spencer Tracy for his deaf son. It was considered the preeminent institution for deaf children on the West Coast. "It was painted in discarded hospital green," Megan said. "There were pictures of Mrs. Tracy with Richard Nixon on the wall." Michael described the place as "rabidly oral." Megan had picked up some Sign, and in a conference at the Tracy Clinic, she said to the instructor, "Let's just sign, since it's only you and me and Jacob." The instructor demurred, but told her that Jacob was smart and would be able to say *apple* in a year. Megan replied that her daughter at that age could say, "Mommy, I had a bad dream," and that she expected the same for her son. The instructor said, "Your expectations are too high." That was the end of Jacob and the Tracy Clinic.

Megan was struck by how many of the deaf people she invited to brunch had no real relationships with their parents because there had never been fluent communication at home. So Megan and Michael hired a woman to teach the whole family to sign, and she moved in with them so that they could all learn as quickly as possible. "You're always knocking glasses over at dinner," Megan said. "Then it clicks in.

It's linguistic, and also three-dimensional and physical." When Jacob was two and a half, Megan was trying to dress him and he was fighting her. He signed, "Scratchy and itchy," and she realized then how important it was for them to share a language; what had seemed like willfulness turned out to be perfectly rational behavior. Michael mastered finger spelling and a pidgin Sign that worked for him and for Jacob.

Megan set aside her work to focus on Jacob's education. She called Gallaudet for advice. "I got the switchboard operator and said, 'I'm just looking for someone I can talk to about educating little children out here in LA.'" The operator suggested Carl Kirchner, a CODA who signed fluently and had just moved to the West Coast. Megan took Jake up to Kirchner's house. "I walk in and hands are flying," Megan said. "Jacob is just wide-eyed." When Jacob saw Carl's two daughters, he made the sign for "girls," and Megan said, "We were off and running." Kirchner had done parent workshops in the seventies and called them Tripod. Megan suggested setting up an advice hotline under the Tripod name. In that pre-Internet time, someone would call the Tripod number and say, "My child is deaf, and I need a dentist, and I'm in Memphis." Megan and Kirchner would contact deaf people and their families in Memphis and find a dentist who knew Sign. Someone else would say, "My child is deaf and I'm afraid he can't read, and I'm in Des Moines." So they would find a deaf-friendly reading specialist in Des Moines. Around this time Jacob, age five, asked Megan, "Are you deaf?" and she said she was not; he asked, "Am I deaf?" and she said he was; then he signed, "I wish you were deaf." Megan said, "That was such a healthy response. Not 'I wish I were hearing,' but 'I wish you were deaf.'"

Megan went to look at deaf schools. At Riverside, students were learning how to shop for food. "It was vocational training or rehab training. It wasn't school." There was signed education for deaf children in the Los Angeles public school system, but when Megan visited a classroom, she was unimpressed. "The teacher was signing, but the content was horribly dull. I went back to Michael and Carl and I said, 'We not only need a hotline, we need a school.'" They found three other interested families and a little preschool building; then they found enough students to make up a class and needed a teacher. Megan wanted someone trained in both Montessori and Deaf education; only three people in the country qualified, and one of them became the first teacher in the Tripod school program.

Megan was constantly caught in the snares of Deaf politics. She was told that she couldn't do all this because she wasn't Deaf enough. "Well,

I wasn't deaf, period," she said. Jacob was considered not Deaf enough because he didn't have deaf parents. One activist said to Megan, "What you're trying to do is very noble, but the best thing would be to give your child to a Deaf family and let them raise him." Megan ignored these assaults. She invented reverse mainstreaming, in which nondisabled children are put in a classroom that is focused on the needs of disabled children and learn as the disabled students learn. At Tripod, every classroom had two teachers, one with deaf-education teaching credentials, for ten deaf and twenty hearing students. Everyone signed. Megan sought out deaf-of-deaf pupils because she wanted their signing level.

The project required enormous amounts of money, and Michael set himself the task of securing it. He had just finished producing *The Big Chill*, and the cast all went on to other movies, and he persuaded them to lobby the studios to give Tripod the premieres. "Michael worked on the finances and supported me, but he was building a career, and I gave my lifeblood to Tripod," Megan said. Megan wanted to place Tripod within the public school system. The Los Angeles school district was annoyed by the challenge to their deaf-education program, so she moved her project to Burbank. "Then people started moving to Burbank because we were there," she said. "Burbank became a hotbed of Deaf culture. Even today, you can go into a McDonald's signing and someone will start interpreting for you."

People who don't use spoken language are often slow to grasp appropriate usage in written language, which is transcribed from a system that is foreign to them. The academic program that Megan put together at Tripod was unprecedented in addressing this challenge. "The biggest curse of deafness is illiteracy," Megan said. "Jacob writes better than I do." The Tripod children consistently tested at grade level or better, and the social context was unique. "There's so many people signing—teachers, hearing students, siblings—that the kids are integrated on every level," Megan said. "They're on the student council, they're playing sports."

Jacob said, "Tripod is about a revolution. I had hearing friends, deaf friends, didn't matter. But Tripod treats the deaf students like we don't actually have special needs, and, really, we do. It was helpful to me, but at some level, it's about my mother, not about me. To be fair, deaf schools at that time were all bad. Tripod was better than most, but there were not enough teachers, not enough money, not enough interpreters. I was really lucky, I know that, with this amazing family, but I've still got a lot of complaints."

Megan sighed when I recounted this. "There were a couple times when I had to do what was right for the program over doing what was right for my son," she said. "That was tough."

Michael has an elegant philosophical resolution about the tensions that led to their 1991 divorce. "Megan became Tripod," he said. "One, she genuinely wanted to help our child. Two, it was a calling. A worthy calling, but a consuming one. Ultimately, our relationship would have fallen apart for a number of reasons. But she was so obsessed with this thing that it began to eat into our marriage. The institution sometimes seemed more important to her than Jacob's individual education. Instead of this gigantic, groundbreaking program, we could have put together a group of three or four parents who could have afforded the tuition at a really good private school with interpreters. I wish Jacob had gotten more intellectual stimulation, but that said, I think he tends to demonize it a little bit."

Jacob saw Tripod's greatest strengths as being for the hearing kids. Yet Jacob's hearing sister, Caitlin, who grew up in the program, envied the way her family's life revolved around her brother's language and culture. More fluent in Sign than Megan or Michael, she came home from school in fourth grade and said, "Our class project is for each of us to teach the first graders something." Megan said, "Really, what are you going to teach?" Caitlin said, "Not sign language!"

Jacob went to the National Technical Institute for the Deaf at Rochester Institute of Technology, then dropped out after a year and worked at a resort in Hawaii. Then he went to Gallaudet. "I was struggling with depression, and honestly, Gallaudet's a really bad school," Jacob said. "But something important happened. Before, I'd looked down on deafness; I had a lot of self-hatred. At Gallaudet, I started meeting a lot of great deaf people who had the same interests I do. I don't really have that capital-*D* Deaf Pride, but I cherish the Deaf culture, and it's a place where I am empowered." For the first time, Jacob said, he felt normal. Megan regretted this timetable: "He was in his mid-twenties by then. I see that as a failure on my part."

I met Jacob shortly after he graduated from the School of Visual Arts at twenty-eight. He had settled in New York, and both his parents came to see him frequently; despite speech therapy, he is unable to speak in a way that is consistently comprehensible. "I've been sorry for myself for a long time, for being deaf," Jacob said. "Last year I tried to kill myself. It was not that I wanted to die, but I felt like I had no control over my life. I had a really bad fight with my girlfriend, and I took a whole bottle of Klonopin. I just wanted to give up. I was in the hospital for three days, unconscious. When I woke up, the first thing I saw was my mom's face, and the first thing she said to me was 'Stop the world. I want to get off.'

That's exactly how I felt." He sees a psychiatrist for medication; they sit side by side and type back and forth. The real trick, however, is finding a signing therapist. Jacob may have inherited his edge of despair from his father, who has struggled with depression through most of his adult life. "Then you mix in the deafness," Michael said. "But Jacob is tough. If the Holocaust came, he'd get so pissed off, he'd figure out a way to get through it. I hope he figures a way through normal life."

Megan has none of Michael's or Jacob's depressiveness; she is a woman of action. But she still has a sadness about her. "I'm sixty years old," she said, "and I sometimes wonder what I would have done if he'd been hearing." Michael said he didn't allow himself that fantasy. "I think somehow Jacob's been selected to be deaf and fucking figure it out, and that's his path," he said. "I've wished he could hear things, but at another level, I never think about what it would be like if Jacob wasn't deaf. I don't know if he'd have been happier. I don't think I would. He's just my son."

I wondered why Jacob's sense of struggle persisted in the face of so much acceptance and love. Jacob said, "Three nights ago, I went out for drinks with the other people in a class I'm taking, and all of them are hearing, and we just wrote back and forth. But there is a point where they're all chatting, and I'm like, 'What's going on?' I'm lucky that they're open to being with me, but I'm still left out. I have a lot of hearing acquaintances. But, good friends? No. Deaf culture teaches me how to see the world, but it would make surviving the world a lot easier if I could hear. If I were going to have a Down syndrome child, I think I would abort. But what if my mom had found out I was deaf when she was pregnant and aborted me? I don't want to be racist, but walking alone at night, I see an unknown black person approaching, and I feel uncomfortable, even though I have black friends. I hate it. So it's the same when I make people uncomfortable because I'm deaf: I understand it, and I hate it. I just hate it."

Having a vision can be a lonely business, and no strategy can unfold in its full glory without other people to carry the banner. What Megan first imagined at Tripod was extended and refined by those who followed her. Chris and Barb Montan's younger son, Spencer, was born deaf a decade after Jacob. "I had never met a deaf person," Barb said, "so I can only describe it as free-falling." Chris is president of Walt Disney Music, and his whole life has been sound. When Spencer was diagnosed, he was "rocked, devastated." Chris said his mind went down blind alleys. "What's going to happen to him? How can I protect him? How much money should I set aside?" Barb contacted Tripod.

"They said they would mail me a package right away, but I couldn't get through the weekend," Barb said. "So I went to the Tripod offices. Michael and Megan had had to create a net; I had one swoop out underneath me."

Barb went on, "In the beginning it's all sadness and woe and horror. My mother said, 'He'll end up in an asylum.' In her generation, you were deaf and dumb, you were sent away. But I had this gorgeous, blue-eyed son who just beamed at me. It didn't take long for me to say, 'Who has the problem here?' Because he was perfectly fine." The Montans decided almost immediately that they would learn to sign. "Spencer would take speech therapy, but we would learn his language and culture," Barb said. "I've got to go where he's going. I can't let any cognitive delay happen." Chris worried that the language gap would undermine his ability to be a good father. "I was scared that Spencer wouldn't know who I was as a person at the level of his older brother, who could hear my inflections. I said to Barb, 'We can't have Spencer feel like he grew up in a hearing household and got left out.'"

Deaf students from Cal State, Northridge, came over to instruct Spencer and his family in ASL. "They pulled into my driveway and began signing. 'Spencer, how are you? I see you have a car!'" Barb recalled, signing as she spoke. "I don't know how he knew it was language. But he was totally attentive. Week after week after week. 'Hello, how are you, are you ready to work?'" Barb and Chris created such a strong signing environment that Spencer didn't know he had a disability until he was four or five.

Barb has a nearly photographic memory and turned out to be a natural at Sign. Chris's years playing the piano made him extremely dexterous, and he became a fluent finger-speller. Spencer could interpret and understand his parents' signing as well as full-fledged ASL. "When he was born," Chris said, "I was working like crazy, building a company with Jeffrey Katzenberg and Michael Eisner. I could have gone to work for twenty hours a day. Barb turned to me early on and said, 'I think you're doing an okay job as a dad, and I know you're building your career at Disney, but I need more. I need you to be more of a person—a deeper person, a less selfish person.'" Chris told his colleagues at work that he'd have to cut back. Nils, the Montans' elder son, has been diagnosed with both severe asthma and attention deficit disorder. "I would say Nils had a harder time growing up," Barb said. "Spencer was easier. Nils is very cerebral, and Spencer is much more visceral, there's so much more kidding around, a tremendous amount of humor, play on words, play on signs."

Because public education does not begin until age five, Tripod has a privately funded Montessori preschool program for deaf and hearing children. Spencer's development in ASL was rapid; the hearing kids in the class learned nearly as fast. "Most disabled kids are always on the receiving end of help," Barb said. "What does that do for someone's self-esteem? But if a little hearing girl didn't know what to do in math, Spencer could help her." In the general population, she observed, you are learning to read until fourth grade, and you are reading to learn thereafter. The switching comes later for deaf children. "But once Spencer got it, did he ever take off," Barb said.

In 1993, Barb and a friend started Tripod Captioned Films, the first outfit that routinely captioned films to include all the nonverbal information: indications of music, of gunshots, of a ringing telephone or doorbell. When Spencer was nine, Lou Marino, a local youth coach, gave him a pitching lesson. Lou said, "I've coached for thirty years, how come I've never seen a deaf kid?" Lou and Barb set up the Silent Knights, which became a Southern California regional deaf baseball league. "He has incredible hand-eye coordination," Chris said. "He saw the ball better than other kids." Chris and Spencer practiced baseball together. "That was a way we talked," Chris said. "I would occasionally sign, but mostly we were sharing this thing. He had quiet confidence, and when he was the pitcher, the team would settle around him."

The Montans did consider cochlear implants. Chris said, "In 1991, I wasn't sure what way the technology was going to advance. If Spencer were newly diagnosed and thirteen months old today, I probably would implant him, and I say that knowing all the great Deaf people we've met, and as a strong supporter of Deaf culture. It's a different question today, medically and politically." If Spencer were to get an implant as a young adult, however, he would have to do auditory training to interpret the data it would produce. "He would lose a year of high school, when he is so socially on track and effective in his language," Barb said. "I don't think it would be worth it."

Spencer was refreshingly ecumenical about language, saying, "I know that my voice is useful, and I am glad to develop it. Mom and Dad went to take ASL classes so we could communicate. If they could learn ASL, I can do this, too. My main language is ASL. But by practicing and practicing, I don't need tutors to help me with my English. I work on my voice, and the kids at my school and in my baseball league work on signing. We want to live in one world." Barb has been frustrated by the antispeech sentiment in the Deaf world. "Spencer is fine signing with me the way I sign, with Chris the way he signs, with his deaf friends in fluent ASL. He is fully bilingual between written English and Sign." At the same time, she recognizes the deep importance of Deaf society. "Every culture, you want critical mass, and he's got it with his deaf friends. We all need our people."

Barb eventually became president of Tripod. "Last night, this mom walked in whose son is four," Barb said. "She's got nothing but worries. Spencer was doing his chemistry homework—moles, fractals—and I held up the sheet and said, 'Your son will do this.'" Spencer said, "Parents of deaf kids should know not to be afraid, not to let their kid be afraid. My parents made sure I was never afraid."

Debates still rage about oralism versus manualism, and whether signed teaching should be conducted in American Sign Language or with techniques such as Total Communication or Simultaneous Communication, in which Sign and English are combined to allow teachers to sign while speaking. These methods seek to provide deaf children multiple avenues of communication; however, problems can arise when one attempts to merge unrelated grammars and syntaxes. English and ASL are different in structure; one can no more speak English while signing in ASL than one can speak English while writing Chinese. English is a sequential language, with words produced in defined order; the listener's short-term memory holds the words of a sentence, then takes meaning from their relationship. ASL is a simultaneous language in which individual signs are amalgamated into composite ones; one complex, fluid movement could mean, for example, "He moved from the East Coast to the West Coast." Each sign includes a hand shape, a location on or near the body where the shape is held, and a directional movement. Additionally, facial expressions serve not just to communicate emotions, but as structural components of individual signs. This compounding works well for short-term visual memory, which can hold fewer discrete images than auditory memory. If one needed to make first the sign for "he," then "moved," then "from," and so on, the mechanical effort would become tedious and the logic would disappear; the same unintelligible jumble would result if one needed to speak several different words simultaneously. Forms of manually coded English such as Signed Exact English, Pidgin Signed English, or Conceptually Accurate Signed English, which go word by word through a sentence as if it were being spoken in English, are usually preferred by those deafened postlingually, who often continue to think in spoken language; however, for children acquiring a first language, sign languages based on oral ones are cumbersome and confusing. A grammar inappropriate to the medium cannot be grasped intuitively.

Gary Mowl, former head of the ASL department at the National Technical Institute for the Deaf, in Rochester, often corrects his children's grammar and usage in ASL. "People ask why you need to teach ASL to people who are already native signers," Mowl said. "Why do you teach English to English-speaking students? So many people use the language badly." There is nonetheless great variety in ASL users' individual "voices": some move their hands and faces precisely, some extravagantly, some playfully, and some with great solemnity. ASL has evolved, too; films of people signing in the early twentieth century show a different and less nuanced use of language.

Benjamin Bahan, a professor of ASL and Deaf Studies at Gallaudet, is deaf of deaf. He has described poignantly how he grew up thinking that his mother, who had an oral education, was the smart one, while his father, who had grown up manual, was a bit dim-witted. When he returned home after studying ASL at college, he realized that his father "signed beautiful ASL with grammatical features and structure," while his mother's ASL was substantially less fluent. ASL grammar is a locus of both precision and pride. Many Sign translators miss half of what is said, mistranslate, and lose the thread of the conversation; I found this myself as I worked with translators, many of whom had been drawn to ASL more for its similarity to theater than for its status as language. The grammar is so conceptually different from oral grammar that it eludes even many people who study it closely. Fluent translators can find it difficult to rearrange ASL structures into English ones, and vice versa, and lose the patterns of meaning. Accent and intonation tend to disappear entirely.

Hearing people often mistakenly assume that there is one universal sign language, but there are many. Due to the work of Laurent Clerc, ASL is closely related to French Sign Language; in contrast, ASL is very different from British Sign Language, which many ASL users contend is less sophisticated. "We don't have so many puns; we don't play with the words the way you do," conceded Clark Denmark, a lecturer in Deaf Studies at the University of Central Lancashire. "It's a more literal language. But it has strengths of its own." Some are concerned that the spread of ASL as a kind of lingua franca for deaf people will lead to the loss of other sign languages. No one has been able to assess how many sign languages there are, but we know of at least seven in Thailand and Vietnam; Iran has both Tea House Sign Language and Persian Sign Language; Canadians use both ASL and Québécois Sign Language.

The issue of deafness in most societies is one of linguistic exclusion, and I was interested in the idea of a context in which Sign was universal. In the small village of Bengkala in northern Bali, a congenital form of deafness has persisted for some 250 years and at any time affects about

2 percent of the population. Everyone in Bengkala has grown up with deaf people, and everyone knows the unique sign language used in the village, so the gap between the experience of hearing and deaf people is narrower than perhaps anywhere else in the world.

Bengkala is also known as Desa Kolok, or Deaf Village. When I visited in 2008, forty-six of the village's approximately two thousand residents were deaf. Because this deafness springs from a recessive gene, no one knows when it will emerge in his family. I met hearing parents with deaf children, deaf parents with hearing children, deaf families with deaf parents and children, deaf or hearing parents with a mix of deaf and hearing children. It's a poor village, and the general education level is low, but it has been even lower among the deaf. Kanta, a hearing teacher in the village, introduced a program in 2007 to educate the deaf of Bengkala in their own sign language, Kata Kolok; the first deaf class had pupils from ages seven to fourteen, because none had had any formal education previously.

The life of villages in northern Bali is based on a clan system. The deaf can both participate in and transcend their clans; for their children's birthdays, for example, they invite their own clan as well as the deaf alliance in the village, while hearing people would not invite anyone outside their clan. The deaf have certain traditional jobs. They bury the dead and serve as the police, though there is almost no crime; they repair pipes in the often troubled water system. Most are also farmers, planting cassava, taro, and elephant grass, which is used to feed cows. Bengkala has a traditional chief, who presides over religious ceremonies; an administrative chief, chosen by the central Balinese government to oversee government functions; and a deaf chief, traditionally the oldest deaf person.

I arrived in Bengkala with the Balinese linguist I Gede Marsaja, born in a neighboring village, who has studied Kata Kolok in depth. We climbed down into a canyon where a river rushed under a two-hundred-foot, sheer rock wall. Several deaf villagers were waiting for us by the water, where they keep a farm with a grove of rambutan trees, some elephant grass, and a variety of extremely hot peppers. Over the next half hour, the rest of Bengkala's deaf arrived. I sat on a red blanket at one end of a large tarp, and the deaf arranged themselves around the edge. People were signing to me, confident that I could understand. Gede translated and Kanta, the schoolmaster, provided further assistance, but to my surprise, I could follow fairly well and quickly learned a few signs. Whenever I used them, the entire group would break out in smiles. They seemed to have multiple levels and kinds of signing, because when they were signing to me, they were like a bunch of mimes, and I could follow their narratives clearly, but when they were signing to one another, I couldn't figure out what they were saying at all, and when they were signing to Gede, they were somewhere in between.

The Kata Kolok sign for *sad* is the index and middle fingers at the inside corners of the eyes and then drawn down like tears. The sign for *father* is an index finger laid across the upper lip to suggest a mustache; the sign for *mother* is an upward-facing open hand at chest level supporting an imaginary breast. The sign for *deaf* is the index finger inserted into the ear and rotated; the sign for *hearing* is the whole hand held closed beside the ear and then opened while it is moved away from the head, sort of like an explosion coming out of the skull. In Kata Kolok, positive words usually involve pointing upward, while negative ones involve pointing downward; one villager who had traveled told the others that the raised third finger is a bad word in the West, so they flipped the sign and now use a third finger pointing down to indicate *horrendous*. The vocabulary is constantly evolving, while the grammar is fairly static.

Second-generation language is always more sophisticated and ordered than first-generation, and a language of many generations acquires a clear architecture. Spoken language among farmers in northern Bali does not feature a large vocabulary, and neither does Kata Kolok. About a thousand signs have been definitely identified by scholars, but the deaf of Bengkala clearly know more signs than this and can combine existing signs to communicate new meanings. For educated Westerners, intimacy requires the mutual knowledge achieved as language unlocks the secrets of two minds. But for some people the self is expressed largely in the preparation of food and the ministrations of erotic passion and shared labor, and for such people the meaning embedded in words is a garnish to love rather than its conduit. I had come into a society in which, for the hearing and the deaf, language was not the primary medium through which to negotiate the world.

When we finished lunch, fourteen men put on sarongs, and two women donned fancy, lacy nylon blouses. Like most deaf people, they could feel the vibrations of the drum, and their dance included movements that seemed to flow from their mimetic language. They offered to show us the martial arts they use as the village security agents. I was interested in the way they mixed signing and the deployment of their hands and feet as weapons; one young man, Suarayasa, resisted joining in the demonstration until he was shamed into it by his mother, and the whole time he was showing us his abilities, he was also signing repeatedly "Look at me!" It was fierce but playful. The women dancers came around and gave everyone a Sprite, and then the men proposed a dip in the river, so we went skinny-dipping. The rock wall rose steep above us and long vines hung down, and the deaf men swung on them. I did somersaults in the water, others did headstands, and we set bait to fish for eels. Sometimes, one would swim underwater until he was right beside me, then shoot up out of the current. They continued to sign to me, and there was something exuberant, even joyful, about the communication. It seemed possible to contemplate this as an idyll, despite the poverty and disability of the villagers.

The next day, Kanta translated from Kata Kolok into Balinese, occasionally addressing me in his limited English; Gede translated Kanta's Balinese into English, occasionally signing in his limited Kata Kolok; and the deaf Bengkala villagers addressed me directly in animated Sign. Communication in this linguistic jumble was established through sheer force of collective will. There were limits to what one could ask because many grammatical structures couldn't be translated. For example, there is no conditional tense in Kata Kolok; the language also has no categorical words (such as *animals* or the abstract notion of *name*), only specific ones (such as *cow* or someone's actual name); there was no way to ask *why* questions.

I met the family of Santia, the deaf son of hearing parents, and his wife, Cening Sukesti, the deaf daughter of deaf parents. The two had been childhood friends. Santia was somewhat slow, whereas Cening Sukesti was vibrant, lively, and intelligent. Sukesti chose to marry a deaf man whose hearing parents owned enough land for them to work. Sukesti said, "I've never been jealous of hearing people. Life is no easier for them. If we work hard, we will get money, too. I take care of the cows, sow the seeds, boil the cassava. I can communicate with everyone. If I lived in another village, I might want to be hearing, but I like it here."

Three of Santia and Sukesti's four children are deaf. When their son Suara Putra was nine months old, hearing friends of his parents said he was hearing. At eleven months, he began to sign and is now fluent, though he feels more fluent in speech. As a young adult, Suara Putra often translates for his parents. He'd never want to give up his hearing: "I have two where most people have one," he said. But he maintained he could have been equally happy being deaf. Nonetheless he said, "I think my parents like having one hearing child. Not that they love me more, but I drink less and don't ask for money all the time. Yet I'd have less tension with them if I were like them." Sukesti said that Suara Putra signed even better than his deaf siblings because spoken language had made him more comfortable expressing complex ideas.

Another couple, Sandi and his wife, Kebyar, lived with their two deaf sons, Ngarda and Sudarma. Ngarda's hearing wife, Molsami, came from another village, and Ngarda was glad to have four hearing children. "We already have many deaf people here," he said emphatically. "If all of us are deaf, it's not good." Sudarma, on the other hand, insisted that he never would have married a hearing woman. "Deaf people should stick together," he said. "I want to live among deaf people, and I wanted deaf children."

In this community, people talked about deafness and hearing much as people in more familiar societies might talk about height or race—as personal characteristics with advantages and disadvantages. They did not discount the significance of deafness nor underplay its role in their lives; they did not forget whether they were deaf or hearing and did not expect others to forget it, either. The deaf alliance in Bengkala is extremely free in every sense except geography; their freedom is predicated on a linguistic fluency shared only in their village. I had gone there to investigate the social constructionist model of disability, and I found that where deafness does not impair communication, it is not much of a handicap.

It is not possible to re-create in America a world of acceptance like that which greets deaf children in Bengkala, but parents such as Apryl and Raj Chauhan succeed in building community to an extraordinary degree, negotiating the diplomatic challenges of ingratiating themselves in a culture that regards them with suspicion. From a privileged African-American background, Apryl grew up among artists; expression comes readily to her. She radiates determination, purpose, and a winning toughness. Raj is of mixed Indian and Pakistani background, handsome and smooth; you can imagine that he will still seem this young when he is old. He works in Internet sales, and he speaks with confident ease. Many of the parents of deaf children whom I met seemed anxious, but the Chauhans were relaxed; their innate sense of hospitality had disarmed a Deaf world that other parents had found forbidding.

When Zahra Chauhan was born in 2000, Apryl and Raj were young and struggling and had little experience of babies. The LA hospital where their daughter was born didn't perform hearing screenings on newborns. When Zahra was three months old, a fire in the building where the Chauhans lived set off shrieking alarms; Apryl ran to the baby's room and found her sound asleep. The pediatrician told Apryl that newborns can sleep through anything. As Zahra reached the age at which other children babbled, she wasn't babbling; the only sounds she made were little grunts. Apryl and Raj would try to test her, clapping when she was turned away. "Sometimes she would respond and sometimes she wouldn't," Apryl said. "Looking back, she most likely saw us out of the corner of her eye." At twenty months, Zahra had produced some version of *mama* and *dada*, but no other words; the pediatrician said that many children don't talk until they are three.

When Apryl took Zahra in for her two-year checkup, their regular pediatrician was out sick, and the substitute immediately said that they should have a hearing test. "Those two years that we lost would have been time for us to educate ourselves, for Zahra to have exposure to language, and for getting her hearing aids," Apryl said with regret. When the news came, Apryl was saddened by it, but Raj was not. He explained, "Apryl wanted to go through the stages of emptiness, fear, sadness, pain, uncertainty, and I wasn't there. This was just something to add to the list of stuff we had to deal with."

Early intervention in Los Angeles County was available for children from birth to three, so Zahra would be eligible for only a year of free services. "I had to educate myself as quickly as possible to know what we wanted," Apryl said. The audiologist said Zahra had some meaningful residual hearing in low registers, so a cochlear implant was not an obvious choice. Apryl said, "I want her to be confident in who she is. If she decides one day that she wants an implant, that's great. But I couldn't make that decision for her." Zahra acquired transpositional aids that drop all the higher-pitched sounds down into the low register where her residual hearing lies. But Apryl knew that hearing aids weren't going to make Zahra hear. "I had lost two years of communicating with my daughter," she said. "We started off with the repetition of 'Apple. Apple.' We were told it takes a thousand times for a deaf child before they get it. So it was all day long drilling things. 'Water. Water. Book. Book. Shoe. Shoe.' She might repeat something occasionally, but it didn't take me long to think, 'This is not good enough.' So within a month, we decided to sign. I could literally feel that a different part of my brain was working because I would get splitting headaches." Raj, who already spoke English, Hindi, a little Spanish, and Italian, said, "I always say it's like a Google search: 'Malibu, want, store, juice,' all at once." At first, Apryl and Raj were learning faster than Zahra, which allowed them to teach her, but Zahra soon pulled ahead.

Even though ASL is Zahra's primary language, Apryl and Raj wanted her to have as much fluency in speech as she could reasonably achieve, and they arranged for her to have speech therapy. When she was still making no progress at five, they found a new therapist, who asked Apryl what Zahra liked to eat. Apryl said she ate four foods: cereal, peanut butter, bread, and oatmeal. The therapist observed that those were all soft foods. "She has an oral motor problem as well," she explained.

"Her tongue doesn't have the strength to control sounds." Apryl and Raj started doing tongue exercises with Zahra. The process was much like that for building up any other muscle—but the fibrous tongue is actually the strongest muscle per inch in the body; if it were the size of a biceps, you could pick up a car with it. The exercises often used a tongue depressor, pushing the tongue around, building it up. Zahra was also told to chew gum as much as possible. The change was rapid. Zahra had always refused to eat meat, but once she had strengthened her tongue and got used to chewing, she was all for it. Her ability to produce sounds increased dramatically.

All this progress has come with considerable effort. Apryl has been a stay-at-home mom so that she can focus more fully on Zahra. "Even to tell us, 'I need to go to the bathroom,' means she has to stop, turn around, get our attention," Apryl said. "It's a full-body language. We're always giving her access to sound. If there's a bird, Raj says, 'Did you hear the bird?' Or an airplane, or a helicopter. Some days, she can iden- tify instruments in music—a horn, flute, piano—with the hearing aids. She hears more than she's technically supposed to."

Every Deaf person I met in California seemed to have been to par- ties at Apryl and Raj's place. "We get invited to a lot of Deaf events and vice versa," Apryl said. "I heard about a deaf man who worked for NASA, a great scientist, and I invited him over. People in the Deaf community are almost always willing to meet with hearing parents. But you have to reach out to them. They're not going to come to you." I had met so many parents who were intimidated by Deaf adults, and I wondered what had given Apryl and Raj the courage to break into that world. Raj explained that he had grown up in a small town in Georgia where the KKK marched on the weekends, and black and white kids sat at different tables in the lunchroom. "Deaf culture and black culture and Indian—you get flexible," he said. Raised by a mother with a strong sense of African-American history, Apryl was an activist as a kid. "I had gay friends, so we set up gay organizations at school. When I had a deaf child, it was, like, here's another one for me to be involved in." She held out her hands. "My whole life prepared me to access the Deaf world, and I'm preparing her to be comfortable in all the non-Deaf worlds. We have wide citizenships in this family."

In 1790, Alessandro Volta discovered that electrical stimulation to the auditory system could mimic sound. He put metal rods in his ears and connected them to a circuit, giving himself a nasty shock and hearing what sounded like "boiling paste." In 1957, André Djourno and Charles Eyriès used an electric wire to stimulate the auditory nerve of a patient undergoing brain surgery, who heard a sound like crickets; during the 1960s, researchers began placing multiple electrodes in the cochlea. These devices, instead of amplifying sound as a hearing aid would, actually stimulated directly the brain areas where sound would be received by hearing people. This technology was gradually refined, and in 1984, the FDA approved a device for use by late-deafened adults. Because it transmitted on a single channel, it gave information on the loudness and timing of sounds, but did not convey the content of those sounds. By 1990, a multichannel device, which stimulated different areas of the cochlea, was on the market; today, some devices operate on twenty-four channels. A microphone picks up sounds from the environment and conveys them to a speech processor, which selects and arranges those sounds. A transmitter and receiver/ stimulator receive this information as signals and convert them into electric impulses. Passing through a device placed within the skull, an array of electrodes sends those impulses to different regions of the auditory nerve, bypassing damaged portions of the inner ear.

The cochlear implant does not allow you to hear, but rather allows you to do something that resembles hearing. It gives you a process that is (sometimes) rich in information and (usually) devoid of music. Implanted early, it can provide a basis for the development of oral language. It makes the hearing world easier. Is it sound? One might as well ask whether a tree falling in an empty forest makes a noise. Some 219,000 people worldwide, at least 50,000 of them children, had received implants as of the end of 2010. Up to 40 percent of American children diagnosed under three receive an implant, up from 25 percent just five years ago. Some 85 percent of the children who receive them are born to white families with higher-than-average income and education levels. After the device has been surgically implanted, an audiologist works on mapping it, making a series of adjustments to ensure that it is tuned to the brain of the recipient.

The chief executive of the Cochlear corporation, the leading manufacturer of implants, told *BusinessWeek* in 2005 that usage represented only 10 percent of the potential market. The implant is sold in more than seventy countries. Some implant opponents complain of the limitations and dangers of the implant itself; according to the FDA, one child in four who receives it experiences adverse reactions and complications, most of which resolve on their own; some require further surgery. Some people have suffered disfiguring facial paralysis, and the implant interferes with diagnostic tests such as magnetic resonance imaging. A wire coming out of your neck can make you look like an extra from *Star Trek*, though it is possible to grow hair so the wire is generally hidden. Much of the cant about the danger of implants is alarmist; some propaganda about their transformative power is embellished.

A late-deafened adult who "regained" his hearing with an implant quipped that they make everyone sound like R2-D2 with severe laryngitis. Their approximation of sound often allows people who are already functional in spoken language to make sense of much of what they hear; however, people who have always been deaf and who receive the implants as adults often find them ineffective or just irritating. Unaccustomed to interpreting auditory information, the latter group might find it difficult to do so even if they were given perfect hearing; the brain develops around input, and a brain that has gone through development without sound is not organized to process it. But the extent of any individual's brain plasticity is hard to predict. In a recent interview, a deaf woman who had received what she called "the bionic ear" in early adulthood described having vertigo at first, and then feeling as though golf balls were bouncing around in her head. "I felt like it was a huge mistake for about five hours," she said. The next morning, she went out for a walk. "I stepped on a twig and it cracked. Leaves rustled. It blew me away."

Deafness, which often used to go undetected until age three, is now regularly diagnosed within hours of birth, and almost always before three months. Screenings of newborns are now supported by the federal government. The NAD originally championed these screenings on grounds that deaf infants could get exposure to Sign as early as possible; now those infants often get cochlear implants instead. "That's hugely painful," said the activist Patrick Boudreault, who opposes the implants. "Genetic counselors and implant specialists are the first responders—not Deaf people." Though the device is approved only for children over the age of two, children under a year old have been implanted. Hearing children learn phonemes throughout the first year of life, and their neural plasticity begins to decrease even at a year. A recent Australian study showed improved results for people implanted at seven or eight months, though the advantages to implanting before age one may not be worth the risks associated with anesthesia in babies. In another study, almost half of children implanted at two developed spoken language equivalent to that of hearing children their age; among those implanted at four, only 16 percent did so. For children who become deaf later—from measles, meningitis, or a developmental genetic condition—efficacy is linked to how soon the devices are implanted. Without sound, the neural architecture of the auditory cortex is permanently compromised.

These statistics are muddied, however, by their newness. Will someone implanted at seven months have a linguistic advantage when he's twelve years old? No one has seen how these early cases turn out across the life span because they haven't been done for long enough. Further, the devices being implanted now are different from the ones used even a decade ago. This means that all decisions about how early to implant children are based on speculation rather than experience.

One unintended consequence of the rise in cochlear implants is that they can make the parents of deaf children careless about language acquisition—which the FDA unfortunately failed to establish as one of the criteria for implant success in pediatric populations. Almost all children who have the implants show useful perception of sound, but with older implants, the sound was often too garbled to interpret as language. That problem is reduced but not eliminated with the newer implants. One study showed that almost half of implanted children had greater than 70 percent open speech discrimination (comprehending sound without visual clues); two-thirds had greater than 50 percent; and nine out of ten had greater than 40 percent. In a Gallaudet survey, nearly half of parents of implanted children believed their children "could hear and understand most words," while only one in five said their children could "hear and understand few words."

Nonetheless, a review of the broad literature on this topic concluded that the implant provides only coarse and degraded versions of sound, and therefore children with the implant receive fewer fine distinctions of spoken language than their hearing peers. This means that some implanted children, not exposed to Sign because they are expected to develop speech, may fall into that frightening category of the needlessly impaired who have meager primary language. Cochlear Ltd. has shown that implanted children learn "more and better" oral language, but "more and better" is a little vague if this is to be your sole mode of communication. Parents too often want to believe that the implants make their children hearing and do not secure any special deaf education for them. "You should bring up these children bilingually until it becomes clear that the child can develop satisfactory oral language," Robert Ruben, former chairman of the Unified Department of Otolaryngology at Montefiore Medical Center, advised. "Language of any kind, no matter what kind, must somehow be got into the head of the child soon enough."

The implant destroys all residual hearing. Although accurate hearing tests can be performed on very young children, it is not possible to determine how well those children might be able to use their residual hearing. Anyone with a hearing loss over 90 decibels is classified as profoundly deaf, yet I have met profoundly deaf people who were able to make such good use of their residual hearing that I could talk to them almost as I would to a hearing person. Hearing loss is measured as an average of loss in various registers; most sounds operate at many frequencies, so someone with a 100 decibel hearing loss could still be able to perceive high-frequency sounds. Even Tom Waits and James Earl Jones produce some high-frequency sound waves when they speak. Further, detection of sound and discrimination of sound are two separate abilities. Some people are able to use intuitive abilities, high-frequency functions, and other natural gifts to discriminate sound well beyond their ability to detect it.

The NAD's original response to the implants condemned "invasive surgery on defenseless children, when the long-term physical, emotional, and social effects on children from this irreversible procedure—which will alter the lives of these children—have not been scientifically established." As the devices evolved and came into wider use, the NAD moderated its position somewhat, saying, "The surgery decision represents the beginning of a process that involves a long-term, and likely life-long commitment to auditory training, rehabilitation, acquisition of spoken and visual language skills, follow-up, and possibly additional surgeries," and, "Cochlear implantation is not a cure for deafness."

If you are not in a village in northern Bali where everyone knows Sign, and you opt against the implants for your child, you will find yourself trying to learn a new language at the same time your child is learning it, and children can learn language better than adults can. To choose Sign for your deaf child is, in some significant ways, to surrender him or her to Deaf culture. It is not so easy to give up your own children, and it does not always work out so well for parent or child. Christina Palmer said, "It's the Deaf ethnicity hypothesis. If you come from a hearing family, you don't get the cultural aspect unless you somehow connect with other Deaf people and learn about a Deaf community." Whereas oral communication places strain upon the deaf member of the family, the decision to sign shifts the power base, placing the greater strain of understanding upon the hearing members. In effect, parents can learn Sign and always speak awkwardly to their child, or they can push their child toward oralism and know that he will always speak awkwardly to them. It is a familiar adage of parenthood that the parent should sacrifice for the child rather than the other way around, but to anoint Sign as the righteous choice is to prioritize a specific vision of how the margins understand the mainstream and vice versa.

Nancy and Dan Hessey have fallen passionately on both sides of this debate since their daughter Emma became deaf, and their quest has been as much spiritual as medical. They had both converted to Buddhism in adulthood and met at a Buddhist center in Boulder, Colorado. Nancy had a hysterectomy a few years later and became terribly depressed. When a colleague announced that she and her husband had decided to adopt a baby from Asia, Nancy became determined to do the same thing. Dan was determined that they should not, he laughingly recalled, "because it might get out of control, come to dominate your life"—but Nancy ultimately prevailed.

On June 29, 1998, Dan and Nancy arrived in Hanoi and headed almost immediately for the orphanage. "It couldn't have been more alienating," Dan said. "Third-world brutalist architecture, big picture of Ho Chi Minh." The deputy head of the orphanage explained that the baby they were to receive had had pneumonia, had lost a quarter of her weight, and had to stay at the orphanage until she finished her course of antibiotics. Nancy asked to meet her. "They put her in my arms, and she looked right in my eyes and smiled," Nancy said. But the smiling baby looked incredibly drawn, and the daughter of the head of the orphanage suddenly said, "I think you should take her to the International Hospital right now."

At the International Hospital, somebody took a chest X-ray, said that the baby's pneumonia was clearing up, and provided a prescription for cephalosporin. When the baby's face flushed, Nancy realized she was having an allergic reaction; soon she was throwing up blood and had bloody diarrhea. For the next ten days, Dan and Nancy lived in the hospital; eventually, they moved back to the hotel. US adoptions of Vietnamese babies had to be processed through Bangkok, so Dan went to Thailand. Nancy took the baby to the hospital daily for nebulizing. Sitting in the waiting room, Nancy saw a card from an Israeli doctor, which said that his clinic serviced the US embassy. Nancy brought him all the medical records, and he did blood work and explained that the baby had both cytomegalovirus and HIV; he assured Nancy that people would take care of the baby until she died, and that they would get another kid they'd be happy with.

Dan was furious. "What were we going to do, throw her back like a fish that wasn't worth the trouble to clean and eat?" he said to me. But American law prohibited the immigration of HIV-positive children. Fortuitously, the Hesseys had once taken in a member of the local Buddhist community who was dying of AIDS, so Dan knew people at the Boulder County AIDS Project who could help them. Meanwhile, Nancy waited and waited for the Vietnamese government to approve the adoption. After two fraught months, both sides came through, and the family all flew home together.

The baby, whom they had named Emma, was admitted on arrival in the United States for a clinical evaluation at Children's Hospital Colorado in Denver. Four days later, a doctor called with news: Emma was not HIV-positive. "The ripples of joy spread everywhere," Nancy said. Two weeks later, Emma couldn't hear anything except a loud bang. She had most likely been exposed to cytomegalovirus in utero, which had caused her hearing to degenerate until it was almost entirely gone.

A deaf member of the Hesseys' community told them how much better life was for deaf children of deaf parents. Nancy and Dan decided to be like those deaf parents. Dan had read the Deaf invectives against cochlear implants, and he and Nancy decided "to respect Emma for who she was rather than to fix her." But there were no deaf schools in Boulder. Their audiologist told them that they should move to Boston, San Francisco, or Austin, where deaf education was strong. So when Emma was fourteen months old, they relocated to Austin and enrolled Emma in early-learning programs at the Texas School for the Deaf. Emma had started walking, but she stopped; her motor focus was entirely on signing. Dan and Nancy began lessons in ASL, but neither showed much of a gift for it. Dan said, "You'd hear these stories like 'This deaf person's parents never learned to sign, how could they have ever done that?' I couldn't learn to sign to save my goddamn life." Nancy said, "But then we visited the public school oral program, and we met kids who were not allowed to sign, and it was horrific. It was very clear to both of us that it was definitely child abuse to try to make a deaf kid oral."

In Texas, Emma developed severe asthma, and the family found themselves in the emergency room weekly. Dan and Nancy had trouble finding work, and the marriage fell apart. Dan said, "Nancy's attention was completely on Emma's survival, which was a genuine issue at that point. But I no longer felt like she could collaborate with me. I had been demoted to being a helper in the background." When Dan announced that he had to return to Colorado, Nancy refused to go with him—but neither did she want to live and die in Texas. She had checked out the Learning Center for the Deaf in Framingham, Massachusetts, and hit it off with the head of the school, who offered her a job. Dan, who didn't want to be half the country away from his daughter, moved to nearby Vermont.

Nancy started working full-time at the school and wanted Dan to take Emma on a schedule; Dan was resentful and also scared of looking after Emma alone. "Compassion is the ability to care unconditionally for another person, not based on fulfilling your expectations," Dan said. "I was good on the theory, and then the bar got raised way high and it was very humbling." Meanwhile, neither of them was good at

Sign. "I was failing miserably at ASL, and it was my job, too," Nancy said. She began talking to Dan about cochlear implants. They had both been hailed as heroes by their Deaf friends for moving around the country to ensure their child an optimal Sign education, and now they were getting ready, as they saw it, to betray Deaf values.

When Emma was four, she had one ear implanted in a seven-hour procedure. Nancy took her to postsurgical follow-up and was told that the wound was severely infected and that her daughter might die; Emma was put on IV antibiotics. Her asthma had been linked to allergies to dairy, soy, wheat, and several other foods, and she had been managing well on a restricted diet and inhaled steroids. After the surgery, she became asthmatic again and nothing seemed to help. Nancy quit her job. Though they were divorcing, Dan and Nancy both decided to move back to Boulder. "It's kind of a circle," Nancy said. "She came to Boulder with hearing; she left when she was deaf; she came back when she was starting to hear again."

Meanwhile, Emma was caught between two cultures and two languages—exactly where her parents had hoped she would never be. She went to cochlear implant camp four days a week that summer for audiological training. At Dan's insistence and despite Nancy's bad memories of the first implant surgery, Emma was implanted in her other ear. This time, it all went smoothly. By the time I met Emma, she was nine. Her grammar and usage were not quite at age level, but she was speaking fluidly and unself-consciously. Nancy said, "She's done better than any of the professionals we've worked with have ever seen. They think it's because she was fluent in a language, ASL, before this." With the second implant, Emma shot up from a 25 percent success rate on open-sound recognition to 75 percent.

Dan and Nancy had sworn to keep Emma in a bicultural environment, but that became increasingly difficult. They noticed that when she could sign or speak, she always spoke. Gradually, when Emma was seven or so, they allowed her signing to stop, and they settled into a largely amicable coparenting arrangement. Emma said to me, "We had a hard trip to go home, but we made it because we're all strong and gentle."

Dan said, "When you have a disabled child, you say either, 'I've got this new asset in my life who is going to make me happy and proud,' or, 'I'm enslaved by my child who is going to be full of needs until I get so old and exhausted that I fall over dead.' The truth about this situation always involves both. Buddhism is about nothing else than these dualities. But did that make it easy? No. I had to relearn my Buddhist practice from the point of view of playing for real. I lost my hobby."

Most medical insurance will now cover the implant, the surgery, and the recommended audiological training. The cost can run well over $60,000, but the surgery is still an economically good choice for insurers. Industry-funded studies at Johns Hopkins and the University of California at San Diego have shown that implantation saves an average of $53,000 per child over the cost of other accommodations to deafness. But the calculus here is complex. Many people who have trouble adjusting to implants run up bills; deaf people who develop good Sign early are not as expensive as those who need accommodations for traumatic childhoods. For most hearing parents, the choice seems straightforward. One mother said, "If your child needs glasses, you get glasses. If your child needs a leg, you get a prosthetic. It's the same thing." Another said, "If, at twenty, Dorothy Jane wants to turn off her voice, that's fine. I want her to have a choice." Those with the implants who are reclassed as hearing do not receive the accommodations they would get as disabled people. The problem is that those who do not get implants may be seen as having "chosen" their condition in the face of a "cure," at which point they do not "deserve" the "charity" of taxpayers. The existence of the implants may, therefore, take disability status from other deaf people.

Rory Osbrink was born hearing, an eager and athletic child. One December Friday in 1981, soon after his third birthday, Rory came down with what appeared to be the flu. His parents, Bob and Mary, packed him off to bed, gave him liquids, and kept a close eye on him. He was no better by Saturday, and on Sunday, he suddenly seemed to be much worse, so they brought him to the emergency room. Bob and Mary sat waiting while the doctors ran some tests; eventually, one came out and announced, "We think he'll make it." Stunned, Bob replied, "He's got the flu, right?" They said, "He has rapidly advancing meningitis, and he's gone into a coma." Rory was in an oxygen tent for the next five days; he was in and out of the hospital for forty days. "He was getting repeated spinal taps, and they couldn't give him anesthetic because it would mask the white cell count," Bob recalled. "I was the only one that could hold him while he's screaming through those spinal taps. I still go into shock if I hear a three-year-old cry."

Bob Osbrink was a professional musician, and it had long been his habit to play his guitar and sing to Rory in the evenings. In the hospital, Rory stopped responding to Bob's singing. In an effort to control the Osbrinks' trauma, everyone at the hospital said that Rory's hearing would come back, though the medical staff knew his deafness was permanent. "False hope is brutal," Bob said. They brought Rory home in time for New Year's, and when fireworks went off, they ran up to comfort him, but he slept right through them. When he was well enough to stand, he fell, because meningitis often affects the inner ear as well as the cochlea; he had no sense of balance.

Bob Osbrink has been haunted by guilt ever since. "What if I had gotten him in sooner?" he asked. "The experts told me, 'We probably would have diagnosed the flu and said he didn't belong in the hospital.'" Bob and Mary had very different reactions to the experience. Bob became almost manically active, trying to keep Rory engaged, while Mary became quietly protective of her son. "One time she said, 'Does this not bother you at all?'" Bob remembered. "I got mad and I said, 'Of course it bothers me. It's tearing me apart inside. You sit and cry. I can't just sit and not do something.'" Bob gave up music; he didn't even listen to the radio for a year.

Neither Bob nor Mary knew what to do with a deaf child. "He wasn't a real verbal little guy in the first place," Bob said. "His older brother spoke very articulately, specifically, eloquently. He had good speech before he was three. Rory was not as advanced." Bob's parents had an acquaintance who knew Dr. Howard House, founder of the House Ear Institute, and Dr. House told Bob about a brand-new technology, the cochlear implant, which had not been approved for children. "We met deaf adults who had had an implant and saw that they could hear sounds. We reviewed studies on the one little girl who had been implanted and saw her reacting to her parents' voices. Rory had already been through so much hospital time. Were we going to put him through more?" Bob was aware that the FDA had not approved the device for children because of concerns about how a developing brain would respond to a foreign object inserted in it. The device was still single-channel, and none of the adults who'd received it had become fully verbal. Then Rory walked into the street and was nearly hit by a fire truck that was speeding past with sirens blaring. At four, Rory became the second child ever to receive an implant. "We thought awareness of sound would improve Rory's safety and would help his lipreading. It was a very emotional day when Rory sat in the testing booth and reacted to a sound." But the sound Rory got was extremely primitive and ultimately not very useful.

His inner-ear damage meant he was still unsteady on his feet. Bob wanted to recapture Rory's athletic promise, a long-term negotiation. Rory was enrolled at mainstream schools and played on the school teams. Bob coached Rory's Little League team and gave him extra practice mornings and afternoons. By the time he was eight, Rory was a star player, had begun to sign, and had joined a deaf team. Bob coached that team as well. Rory would read his lips and then interpret to the players. "You can have an international soccer team where everybody on the field is speaking a different language and yet they will play the game the same," Bob said. "The game itself allows you to connect. It has its own language. It meant he was 'that great ballplayer,' not 'that deaf guy.'" Bob shares music with his older son; sports was his bond with Rory.

Bob was interested in Sign, but he didn't study it, and Rory asked him to continue to speak to him; he even asked him to keep his mustache. "You talk to me more than anybody, Dad, with the coaching. If I can lip-read you, that keeps me sharp." But later, Bob realized that this was all part of the frequent deaf habit of seeming to get more than you do. "I didn't realize until later how much he was missing all the time," Bob said. "I knew how smart he was and he was not making it in algebra. I said, 'Let me sit in the class.' The teacher was writing formulas on the board and speaking with his back to the room."

In junior high, Rory began working seriously on ASL, and in high school he learned about Deaf identity. He got a baseball scholarship to the University of Arizona and went to meet the coach. "I called him on the phone over and over again, telling him about Rory's situation," Bob said. "'Rory's a great lip-reader. You just need to look him straight in the eye.' So the coach comes in and he's looking down, and Rory says, 'Coach, if you look up, I can really read lips well. Speak a little slower and I'm going to get it.' The coach pulls out a pad, drops it on his desk, and starts writing out notes—with an attitude. Rory wadded up the paper, said, 'I can't play for you,' drove out that night, and went to Gallaudet."

Rory never really came back to the hearing world. At Gallaudet, he majored in Deaf studies and philosophy, was the resident assistant in his dorm, and played on the baseball team. When Rory graduated, the Dodgers offered him a tryout. He got in touch with Curtis Pride, who played pro baseball and is hard of hearing, and who said that no one in the pro sports world was going to help "the deaf guy." Rory turned down the Dodgers' offer and got a master's in education instead. "It all goes back to that experience in Arizona," Bob said. "Every now and then, we'll go to a ball game and watch a guy playing. He'll go, 'Hey, Dad, I was as good as that guy, huh?' And I'll go, 'Yeah, you sure were.'"

Rory later married a woman who was fifth-generation deaf. He turned off his implant and has never used it again; he said that with it he felt like "a duck in a world of chickens." The Deaf world became his home. Rory now teaches deaf children in the fifth and sixth grades. He gave up baseball, but he coaches a Deaf team that has made it to championship level, and he's become a fanatic bicyclist. He has rewritten the course curriculum for California deaf education. "He's told me that he remembers a little bit about sound," Bob said. "But it's not a real vivid memory." Rory has militated against parents implanting their young children. "As for pediatric cochlear implant, it should not be tolerated since it ignores the child's right to choice," he wrote.

Bob said of his own decision, "I did what I thought was right. It was not some big philosophical discussion between Deaf and hearing, because I had no clue about that." Rory understands why his parents made their decision, and Bob understands why his son reversed it. "I realize that when he was in an oral environment, he was getting about ninety percent," Bob said. "That sounds like a lot, but if you really care about people—and he's a very empathetic guy—then you want to get everything. I totally accept and respect who he is and what he wants. I used to tell people I've got one son who is deaf, and I've got three who won't listen to me. Selfishly, I'd love for him to be able to sing and play the guitar with me, and he'd like for me to be fluent in signing."

I wondered whether the child must always win in these debates, whether there is some writ in which a parent's job is rising to the occasion, while a child's job is simply being. Bob Osbrink seemed both prouder and more melancholic than many other people I had interviewed. Rory was deafened at three, and three years is a long time in a parent's life and in a child's. I wondered whether Bob's wistfulness perhaps stemmed from having lost a deep connection with his son not once but twice: first music, and then sports. "The things that hurt me are things I missed, like my not knowing when he acted like he got it when he wasn't getting it," Bob said. "Laughing when everybody laughed but not knowing what the joke was. I'm sad that he had to go through everything he's had to go through. A part of me will always be sad. But I don't think he's sad, and I'm certainly not sad about who he is."

The bioethicist Teresa Blankmeyer Burke said, "It is rare that one grieves for something that one has not lost. Consider gender as an analogy. A woman might wonder what it would be like to be a man, or vice versa; yet, this curiosity is not likely to be expressed in terms of loss." Paula Garfield, artistic director of the London-based Deafinitely Theatre company, and her partner, Tomato Lichy, were thrilled when they found out their daughter was deaf because it gave her "a passport to inclusion in a rich and varied culture." The general culture feels that deaf children are primarily children who *lack* something: they *lack* hearing. The Deaf culture feels that they *have* something: they *have* membership in a beautiful culture. Hearing parents are thrown back on their own dichotomy: do they have a deaf child, or do they lack a hearing one?

Like Bob Osbrink, Felix Feldman thought that the ability to function in the oral world was valuable—that acculturation was the natural and only goal. When he had a daughter who was deaf, there was no such thing as an implant; when he had grandchildren who were deaf, the implant was advanced and the kids were not interested. Felix has an old-style Jewishness that habitually seeks the cloud accompanying any silver lining. In his view, and despite his love for his progeny, little recommends the experience of having two deaf children, and the arrival of three deaf grandchildren has been no further blessing.

Felix and Rachel Feldman's younger daughter, Esther, was born with cerebral palsy; with a hearing aid, her sound discrimination was sufficient for language development. Just as the family was struggling with her diagnosis, the pediatrician told them that their older daughter, Miriam, was deaf. It was 1961, and Felix and Rachel opted for an oral education for Miriam, same as Esther. The orthodoxy was still that children learning orally should have no exposure to Sign, so it was forbidden in their house. "We would break Miriam's arms if she signed," Felix said. Felix and Rachel went to class themselves to learn how to reinforce the oral lessons at home. Having heard of a good speech therapist in Santa Monica, they moved there. Their lives were focused around deafness. "We had contact with deaf people, but all speaking people," Felix said.

Though Esther now functions relatively well for a person with CP, the path was long and difficult. Miriam, though much more deaf, was a model child. She had speech therapy every day at school, and private tutoring three days a week. Her passion was competitive figure skating. The coach was allowed to give her three signs: one to say when the music started; one at the halfway point to tell her to speed up or slow down; and one at the end to tell her the music was finished. "Competing to music without hearing one note," her father said. "At school, she was always at the top of the class. With all the hearing children. Completely from lipreading the teacher. She never saw herself as handicapped." When Miriam was fifteen, she competed in the 1975 World Winter Games for the Deaf in Lake Placid, New York, and was immersed for the first time in a context where the primary language was Sign. "She picked it up very fast," Felix recalled. "There was nothing we could do."

Miriam said to me, "It was hard, learning Sign. It took many years because I came to it so late, and with so many anxieties, my mom and dad always saying, 'Don't sign, don't sign.' At the Deaf Olympics, everyone else was signing, and I didn't know how. It was humiliating." Felix felt betrayed by Miriam's signing, though he admits that her verbal skills have remained strong. Miriam started and runs the Jewish Deaf Community Center in her California town; she issues publications, organizes social events around Jewish holidays, and is a leader within her community. She conducts about 80 percent of her communication in Sign and about 20 percent in speech. "But *all* my language would be better if I'd been allowed to sign as a child," she said.

When cochlear implants became viable, Felix tried to get Miriam, then in her twenties, to have one, but she was enamored of the Deaf culture and the idea was repugnant to her. "We discussed, we fought, we screamed," Felix said. "I lost. We know younger and older people who have had it. They hear you, they use the telephone. They listen to the news, they watch TV. Why wouldn't you have it? Unfortunately, she and her ex-husband feel that it's genocide."

All three of Miriam's children—ages seventeen, fifteen, and thirteen when we met—are deaf. Felix pushed for them to receive oral coaching, but it is hard for parents who cannot hear to support oral instruction in the intensive way it requires. "Miriam took the line of least resistance," Felix said. "If they didn't sign, they would speak. It's heartbreaking." Though Felix can communicate easily with Miriam, he is unable to have a conversation with his grandchildren. Miriam's eldest is now enrolled at the world's only Orthodox Deaf yeshiva and is learning Hebrew and Yiddish. Miriam said, "I had to follow people's lips all day long. I didn't want my kids to go through that. My kids are happy, they know how to spell, and they were signing at eight months old. They were able to tell me how they felt, and what they wanted." I wondered whether they had hearing friends at school. "When my daughter started school, there were no other deaf children in her year. What did she do? She taught the hearing kids to sign, and some of them are still her best friends."

Felix was desperate for the grandkids to have implants. Miriam said, "Any time we get together with the family, that's all we talk about." Felix had offered his grandchildren a million dollars each to have the procedure; he said to me, "I should do it the other way. If they don't have the implants, I will take a million dollars each and give it away." He made a show of lowering his voice and whispered extremely loudly, "The truth is, she doesn't want me to be happy." Miriam turned to me. "I didn't hope for deaf children," she said. "I didn't expect them. Now that I have deaf kids, I am very happy because they are a part of the world that I'm in and they understand where I'm coming from. If I had hearing kids, however, my family would like me more." Then they both started to laugh. Felix said, "Well, that's our story. I think your book should be called *Father Knows Best*."

It will be some time before implanted people can savor the nuance of a Verdi opera or discern the voice of a single turtledove in a forest full of crows, but implant developers are closing in on enabling the perception of sufficient auditory information for the consistent development of verbal fluency. The objections left standing are conceptual. As Felix Feldman bitterly noted, many Deaf activists contend that cochlear implants are part of a genocidal attempt to destroy and eliminate the Deaf community. Some have compared pediatric implantation to intrusive surgeries, comparing them to those used to "correct" intersex conditions; intersex adults have militated against such interventions. The British Deaf activist Paddy Ladd refers to implants as "the Final Solution," and Patrick Boudreault speaks of a cultural and linguistic extermination campaign. Northeastern's Harlan Lane wrote, "Could you imagine if somebody stood up and said, 'In a few years, we're going to be able to eliminate black culture'?" He sees the implant as representing just such an assault. "If hearing people saw the Deaf community as an ethnic group with its own language, as opposed to someone who is handicapped, then you wouldn't have such a deep misunderstanding." Is the underlying hearing person being liberated by the implant, or is the authentic Deaf person being obliterated? Hearing specialists and medical clinics have, unfortunately, tended to give little support to campaigns to ensure that parents meet deaf people before implanting their deaf children. Many physicians do not provide parents with Deaf community contacts, and few parents seek out the contacts that are provided to them. Only Sweden has a law that requires such parents to meet with representatives of the Deaf community and learn about their lives before making this major medical decision for their child.

The question, really, is how we define the relationship between parents and children. A hundred years ago, children were effectively property, and you could do almost anything to them short of killing them. Now, children are empowered. But parents still decide what their children should wear, what they should eat, when they should sleep, and so on. Are decisions about bodily integrity also properly the province of parents? Some opponents of implants have proposed that people make their own choice when they turn eighteen. Even putting aside the neural issues that make this impractical, it is a flawed proposition. At eighteen, you are choosing not simply between being deaf and being hearing, but between the culture you have known and the life you have not. By then, your experience of the world has been defined by being deaf, and to give it up is to reject whom you have become.

Children with implants have experienced social difficulties; if the objective of the implants is to make the children feel good about themselves, the results are mixed. Some become what William Evans of the University of California has called "culturally homeless," neither hearing nor Deaf. The population at large does not like threats to binaries; binaries drive homophobia and racism and xenophobia, the constant impulse to define an *us* and a *them*. The wall between hearing and deaf is being broken down by a broad range of technology: hearing aids and implants that create what some activists call the "cyborg mix," bodies that are physically enhanced in some way.

Though some implanted adolescents disconnect them in their teen years, most perceive them as extremely useful. In one study from 2002, two-thirds of parents reported that their children had never refused to use the implant; there is presumably more adolescent resistance to, for example, seat belts.

Barbara Matusky told her husband, Ralph Comenga, that she would have children if he insisted, and he insisted. She was still working—driving a forklift in a warehouse for Procter & Gamble in West Virginia—when she was nine months pregnant with her son, Nicholas. It was 1987, and she'd never even heard the word *audiology*. When Nicholas was six months old, she decided to see a specialist; she thought maybe the baby was having ear infections. She had to wait three months for an appointment. The specialist sent the family to Johns Hopkins for further assessment, and another three-month wait. When she finally got the diagnosis, Barbara was offended by everyone's expectation that she would be in despair. But she said to me, "When you asked to do this interview, I said, 'If you're looking for somebody who was devastated by this, don't come here, because I don't have that story.' But I can tell you now that I didn't sleep and I cried a lot at night. I would lay in bed and say, 'If he is deaf and he wants to play football, what?' I did this with everything in his future life, everything."

Barbara and Ralph first chose an oral education for Nick. "I ended up with a teacher who would talk to me about the fabulous therapy she'd done and how successful her kids are," Barbara said. "Every day I would think, 'Today she is going to unleash the wonder.' It never happened." Nick loved garbage trucks, so Barbara would take him out and follow a garbage truck for hours, trying to teach him words to go with what they were watching, hoping that if the words referred to things that interested him, the words themselves would interest him. "Being oral was horrible, everything was about them saying words. It was so intense, so totally unnatural. I was a maniac." Ralph wanted to look at a cochlear implant—at that time, still a new technology—and Barbara refused. "That was not a decision I could make, to cut my kid's head open. You're trying to make a decision for this future adult, but what you've got is a baby. It's about who they are as people, and you don't know that when they're infants."

Barbara saw that Nick was too isolated, so she decided to have another child—a hearing sibling who could help translate for him. The day she gave birth, Barbara told the hospital about the protocols for testing hearing in newborns. Brittany, they declared, was hearing. "She is in her crib crying in her room, and I am playing with Nick, and I can remember hollering, 'Brittany, you're okay, you can hear me. Nick needs me.' I didn't know that what I really wanted was another deaf kid. Once I realized she wasn't hearing, which was within the first two months, I called the audiologist and said, 'Order me hearing aids.' I called the school and said, 'She's deaf, she needs to be in a class.' So at three months, she's aided, she's seeing Sign, a whole different situation." When two teachers were assigned to come to the house and work on Barbara's signing and Brittany's language exposure, however, Barbara found their presence oppressive. "I kept saying, 'My kids are right where they need to be,'" she recalled. "So they would say to me, 'Think how much smarter they would be if you had started earlier.' They were right, and I didn't want to hear it."

Brittany produced a broad range of phonemes and was identified as a good candidate for oral education, which Nick was already receiving. Nick, on the other hand, couldn't make a comprehensible speech sound. "I could just see that it wasn't going to work for him. So then it was like 'Do I sacrifice him for her? Or her for him? Because we can't be oral and sign.' So I decided, we're going to start signing."

They lived two hours away from the residential Maryland School for the Deaf, and she enrolled both children there. The school was then doing a version of Bi-Bi, but the school day took place in Sign. Barbara enrolled in an ASL interpreter-training program near the school. Ralph had to settle for an ASL class at a local high school. But she couldn't bear to have them board—"From not wanting kids, I fell in love with my kids"—so she drove them both ways every day. The deaf educators resisted the arrangement, but Barbara was adamant. "That part of it I hated. Deaf of deaf are golden, and deaf of hearing are subservient and not so great. My kids really feel the negative weight of all that. I question the Deaf community every step of the way. I might have said, 'Here, take my kids. Let them live in the dorm. Have at it, you are the experts.' Would my kids have been any further along developmentally? I can tell you, those kids who effectively lose their parents are much further behind." Once she'd done her interpreter's training, Barbara took a volunteer position at the school; eventually, she got a job there as a secretary. Barbara struggled to give her children a feeling of confidence. "The whole time they were growing up, I said, 'You can do anything you want to do. This doesn't limit you.' Then it started to hit me. It's got nothing to do with them. It's got to do with that hearing person across from them at an interview."

In the end, Barbara became a champion of Deaf culture. "I didn't embrace it for a long time," she said. "Now, I meet parents, and I say, 'Look, learning ASL is the hardest thing you will ever do in your life. You will never be good enough. You will still not understand your kid, and you will still not always be able to communicate what you want to say.' That's the truth and it's not easy."

When I met her, Barbara had become the head of family services for the deaf at a local university. Nick and Brittany are much less interested in Deaf activism than she is. Nick had announced that the best thing he could do for deaf people was to go out into the world and work and become himself. This is just fine with Barbara, who worked hard to give her children that confidence. "The Deaf community fills them up with pride, and then they don't want to let them go," Barbara complained. "A kid will be raised in a deaf school. He will go to Gallaudet. Then he will come back to the deaf school and teach. So their knowledge of the world is this. They bring nothing new and nothing diverse." Barbara got her kids enrolled at Northridge instead, where there is a strong Deaf studies program and a large Deaf population.

Both children have made strong showings in written English. While Nick makes little use of vocal language, Brittany decided in college that she was going back to speech therapy and has been thinking about getting an implant. She wants to work in film production, and she wants to be comfortable in the hearing world. "She wants to make it as easy for hearing people as she can," Barbara said. "Brittany has a lot of speech. The problem is, she is embarrassed to use it. She has an interpreter at college, who said to her, 'You shouldn't talk, because deaf people sound horrible when they talk.' So she's sending my husband e-mails saying, 'Does my voice sound horrible?' This is an interpreter, her lifeline to communication. If I saw this woman, I would probably choke her." Brittany has been concerned about how her Deaf friends would react to her getting an implant. "So what does she do?" Barbara said. "Does she give up her dreams and settle? Or does she get this implant if it will make it easier to get her dream job? They're deaf in a hearing world, that's the reality."

Barbara worries about her children in that world, but she has no regrets. "If my kids were hearing, my daughter and I would not have gotten along," she said. "We are two strong personalities. My son would have gotten into so much trouble. If I'd had hearing kids, I would have worked and they would have gone to child care. Having deaf kids made me a much better mother. I like fighting for the cause. I like empowering people. We get along really great, the bunch of us, we really do. I hope they have deaf children. I want them to have kids who are just like them."

Deaf people in the hearing world are always going to be at a disadvantage. So the question is whether people prefer to be marginal in a mainstream world, or mainstream in a marginal world, and many people quite understandably prefer the latter. At the same time, those who oppose cochlear implants—and who, in some cases, oppose hearing aids and other technologies—are a noisy bunch, which has often led people to universalize from their views. In fact, these views can be constraining. "There seems to be subtle pressure from some Deaf people to give up hearing aids—sort of a Deaf-liberation equivalent to bra-burning," wrote Kathryn Woodcock, a Canadian deaf woman. "There is prejudice in the Deaf community against any form of listening. At this point in my progressive hearing loss, I can usually still hear a firm, multiple knock on the door of a quiet room. This has earned me suspicious glances and even overt queries as to why I am present in a deaf group. This is absurd." The commentator Irene Leigh has written, "While I perceive myself as sufficiently competent in Deaf ways and as capable of participating within Deaf culture, I can also communicate adequately with users of spoken English. Because of this, I have at times been labeled as 'hearing-mind,' not truly Deaf."

Josh Swiller, a deaf man raised in the hearing world and educated orally, came to Deaf identity late and has written about it beautifully. He used hearing aids and other devices. "Basically, with aids you're constantly translating every line of language into itself. Like the high school sophomore at the college bar with a great fake ID, I could fool everyone into believing I was who I pretended to be. It gnawed at me that this way of navigating the world was based on a fundamentally untenable position, a two-sided lie. To others: I can hear you; to myself: it doesn't matter how much I miss or how alone I feel as long as others think I can hear. It drove me crazy. I kept doing it, it was all I knew." Swiller made his way to Gallaudet. Soon after he arrived, a school newspaper poll asked whether students would take a pill that would give them hearing instantly, and the majority answered that they would not, because they were proud of who they were. Swiller wrote, "But who are we? I wanted to know. Who looks out from our eyes?" Years later, he posted a short biography of himself on his website with this description: "In 2005, Josh had surgery for a cochlear implant. The implant has been a remarkable success. He also, with great pride, uses American Sign Language. He rejects the defensiveness and distrust that divides the deaf community and believes that our similarities should—and will—overcome our divisions."

While the debate rages over cochlear implants, implantable hearing aids and other assistive devices for hearing loss continue to be refined and developed. In parallel, research into biological, nonprosthetic cures for deafness has blossomed. There are many kinds of hearing loss, but most come from the loss of the auditory hair cells in the cochlea. These cells, which receive sound in a form in which it can be conveyed along nerve pathways to the brain, are produced in the first three months of the fetal period and are incapable of regenerating—or so conventional wisdom long assumed. In the early 1980s, however, Jeffrey T. Corwin, now at the University of Virginia, noticed that adult sharks have a greater number of receptive hair cells than baby sharks, and subsequent research demonstrated that fish and amphibians produce hair cells throughout life to replace those that have been lost. A few years later, Douglas Cotanche, director of the Laboratory of Cellular and Molecular Hearing Research at Boston University, discovered that baby chicks whose hair cells were completely destroyed by ototoxic poisoning or sound trauma regenerated hair cells. Tests confirmed that these chicks had recovered hearing. These discoveries led researchers to investigate whether such processes could be achieved in human beings.

In 1992, researchers in Corwin's lab fed retinoic acid to embryonic mice; the mice were born with six or nine rows of hair cells, rather than the usual three. Building on this work, in 1993 a group working at Albert Einstein Medical Center published an article in *Science* in which they described their success at causing the regrowth of hair cells by treating the damaged inner ear of an adolescent rat with a mixture of retinoic acid and calf serum. Since most deafness is degenerative (even those born deaf have usually lost auditory hair cells in utero), the question remained whether the new hair cells would survive in the inner ear, or whether they would die off again as their predecessor cells had done.

Hinrich Staecker, a professor of otolaryngology at the University of

Kansas, is now trying to determine what is necessary for the neuritic stem to grasp on to a hair cell—the process through which the response of the cochlea is transmitted to the brain. In the late 1990s, burgeoning insight into stem cells inspired inquiry into how they might be made to differentiate into auditory hair cells and then be introduced into the inner ear. In 2003, Stefan Heller and his colleagues successfully cultivated auditory hair cells from mouse stem cells. Six years later, a team at the University of Sheffield demonstrated that human fetal auditory stem cells could be cultivated in vitro, and that they would develop into either functional auditory neurons or hair cells; treating the cells with retinoic acid helped this occur.

Genetic research into deafness, which has so angered the Deaf community because of its relevance to selective abortion, is not primarily focused on pregnancy termination. Scientists are hoping to develop gene therapies to promote the growth of auditory hair cells, both in utero and postnatally. With the identification of the ATOH1 gene as essential to the development of auditory hair cells, researchers have focused on developing therapies to introduce and induce the expression of ATOH1 in animals, and to inhibit processes that damage existing cells, including oxidative stress, which appears to be a major contributor to age-related hearing loss. Other currently targeted genes control the function of the transduction channel that conveys messages from the auditory hair cells to the brain.

Technologies now in the works include the implantation of electrodes that stimulate hearing nerve fibers, the miniaturization of implant technology, fully implantable cochlear devices, and implantable hearing aids.

In the early 1960s, a rubella epidemic in the United States resulted in a high incidence of deaf children; this generation, currently in midlife, is called the Rubella Bulge. Vaccines now protect most expectant American mothers from rubella, and most children from rubella and meningitis. The deaf population diminishes. Cochlear implants mean that a large proportion of deaf children are functioning in the hearing world. "From the time God made earth until today, this is probably the best time to be deaf," Greg Hlibok said at the Lexington graduation; yet this is also the moment when the deaf population is dwindling. As it gets better and better to be deaf, it also gets rarer and rarer. Parents cannot understand their deaf child's future by talking to deaf adults, because those adults grew up in a vanished context. Parents who do not implant their children today are choosing a shrinking world. The Deaf movement was born in its modern form only when Stokoe recognized the linguistic complexity of ASL in 1960; some say that its demise commenced when implant surgery received FDA approval in 1984. Patrick Boudreault said, "We are still looking for answers to our own questions. Who we are, for example. What does language mean to us. How does the world interact with deaf people. We're just making these discoveries, and now we're under pressure." Christina Palmer said, "Eugenics and multiculturalism are head-to-head."

In 2006, a group of Deaf people proposed the founding of a Deaf town, in South Dakota. It was to be called Laurent, after Laurent Clerc, and its anticipated initial population was twenty-five hundred. The man behind the plan, Marvin T. Miller, said, "Society isn't doing that great a job of quote-unquote 'integrating' us. My children don't see role models in their lives: mayors, factory managers, postal workers, business owners. So we're setting up a place to show our unique culture, our unique society." The local county planning commission refused to approve the proposal, and it eventually fell apart. The people of South Dakota reacted to the idea of a deaf town much as a white suburb of the 1950s might have reacted to news of a black one. But even the deaf had rather mixed feelings. Deafweekly.com wrote, "Some question the need for such a town, saying such 'isolation' has gone out of fashion."

It is difficult to imagine the same being said about Bengkala, because that community has developed intergenerationally. It may be perceived by mainstream society as a community of the deficient, a hereditary error writ large. But it is clearly not artificial, and that is because it is vertical. The vertical is deemed natural, and the horizontal, unnatural. Implants come to seem more "natural" than deafness to hearing people such as Felix Feldman; resisting them seems like the artifice. As that perception takes hold, more people get implanted, leaving fewer to make up the marginal culture, creating more pressure to get implants, and so on until few people are left to populate the Deaf world. The loss of Deaf culture would be a great sadness; preventing any individual child from getting implants could be considered cruel. By narrowing a child's options, parents define that child as an extension of themselves, rather than a person of his own. Yet implants may compromise the option of being content in the Deaf world. As any identity becomes a choice, it is irrevocably altered, even for the people who choose it.

For many years, the defining means of deaf life was in-person socializing at deaf social clubs—now largely vanished as deaf people are able to communicate online. The deaf used to congregate at the Deaf theater—but with the advent of captioned television and film, the imperative to do so has faded. Is Deaf culture to be defined simply as a function of a shared language used for in-person interactions?

Just as Deaf culture is being forced to assimilate to the mainstream, mainstream culture is assimilating the Deaf world. As many as two million Americans know ASL. The early years of the new millennium saw a 432 percent increase in ASL courses. This made ASL the fifth most taught language in college, and the fifteenth most taught in the general population; a broad population has been bewitched by the perceived poetry of a physical communication system. While teaching Sign to deaf babies is less common in the age of cochlear implants, hearing babies are being taught Sign because they can make use of it before they have the oral muscle control to speak. More hearing people are applying to Gallaudet. Deaf people are ambivalent about all this. They note that the language has separated from the culture, and that many of the students learning it know nothing about Deafhood, a fashionable word for the deep experience of Deaf values. Edna Edith Sayers, a professor of English at Gallaudet, referring to ASL classes taught outside the academic context, noted, "Somehow, ASL's popularity has come at the cost of demotion to some kind of craft or hobby, like quilting or aerobics, taught by volunteer enthusiasts in church basements."

I am fully persuaded that there is a Deaf culture; I am persuaded that it is a rich culture. What social obligations are attached to recognition of a culture? Can we confer on it a societal equivalent to the landmark status with which we mark buildings that are never to be destroyed? Talk of Deaf lineage is fine insofar as any given child and his parents accept it. But we will never have a society in which children are routinely taken from their parents and given to another group of people to raise. The 90 percent or so of deaf children who are born to hearing parents will continue to be brought up as those parents see fit. If the cochlear implant is improved, if gene therapies advance so that children can effectively be cured, then cures will triumph. Vertical identities will go on forever, and horizontal ones won't. Harlan Lane wrote in outrage, "The relation of the hearing parent to the young deaf child is a microcosm of the relation of hearing society to the deaf community; it is paternalistic, medicalizing, and ethnocentric." This is true, but Lane seems not to recognize that parents have definitional license to be paternalistic. While it may be difficult for deaf people to learn speech, it is also difficult for parents to learn Sign—not because they are lazy or smug, but because their own brains are organized around verbal expression, and by the time they are of parenting age, they have lost considerable neural plasticity. Parents implant their children in part so that they can communicate with them. They may be wise to do so; intimacy between parents and children is one of the cornerstones of mental health for both parties.

The cochlear implant debate is really a holding mechanism for a larger debate about assimilation versus alienation, about the extent to which standardizing human populations is a laudable mark of progress, and the extent to which it is a poorly whitewashed eugenics. Jack Wheeler, CEO of the Deafness Research Foundation, has said, "We can conquer newborn deafness in America. If we can test every baby born and organize the parents as a political force so every baby gets what it needs, regardless of how much money the parents have, then the twelve thousand babies born deaf every year become twelve thousand babies who self-identify as hearing kids." The question is whether this is desirable. A race is going on. One team consists of the doctors who will make the deaf hear. They are humanitarian miracle-workers. On the other team are the exponents of Deaf culture. They are visionary idealists. Yet each would render the other irrelevant. As Deaf culture grows stronger, it is dying. "Deafness is almost always one generation thick," declared Lawrence Hott and Diane Garey, directors of the film *Through Deaf Eyes*; some scholars have called Deafness a "culture of converts."

"In a world full of childhood cures," said Rob Roth, whom I met at the NAD, "I would be neither deaf nor gay. That doesn't make me feel unloved or bad about myself, but I know that it's true." If Deaf culture can be made as visible, powerful, and proud as gay culture now is *before* the cure is perfected, then perhaps the accomplishments of the Rubella Bulge activists will allow for a long history of Deaf culture. If the cure comes before that happens, then virtually all hearing parents and many grassroots deaf parents will cure their children, and the tremendous accomplishments that have followed the Gallaudet uprising will be the conclusion rather than the beginning of a story. Then the history recounted here will be as poignant and remote as a tale of Babylon. Jacob Shamberg, who had taken part in the Gallaudet protests, wrote to me, "While I'm pretty comfortable with my disability and don't see CI as an evil force intent on destroying the Deaf culture, I do get a sense of impending extinction. There'll always be deaf people worldwide, but there is a real possibility that it'll be near-eradicated in developed countries within 50 to 100 years. I say 'near' because there'll always be immigrants, untreatable conditions, cultural hold-outs and so on. But no more people like me."

Would the world be better with more cultures in it? I believe it would. In the same way that we mourn the loss of species, and fear that reduced biodiversity could have catastrophic effects on the planet, so we should fear the loss of cultures, because diversity of thought and language and opinion is part of what makes the world vibrant. Commenting on the death of tribal languages and traditional storytelling in West Africa, Amadou Hampâté Bâ, a Malian ethnologist, said, "When an old person dies, it's a library burning down." And yet what is happening to the Deaf has happened also to the Quakers, to Native Americans, to whole tribes and countries. We live in an incinerator of cultures. It is estimated that by the end of this century, fully half of the six thousand languages currently spoken on earth will have vanished. The Tower of Babel is collapsing. With those tongues will go many traditional ways of life. The Australian linguist Nicholas Evans wrote of the urgency of finding "a new approach to language and cognition that places diversity at centre stage," pointing out that we are "the only species with a communication system that is fundamentally variable at all levels." The Deaf will vanish along with many ethnicities, their languages along with many languages.

I think the only locus for hope in the face of these dismaying statistics is to recognize that new cultures are being born all the time. This book chronicles numerous communities that would never have emerged without the Internet and its potential to sort people according to one shared value, even when they are infinitely diverse in location, language, age, and income. Some of those communities are cultures. The computer code that is at this precise moment causing the movement of my fingers to create text on the screen I am gazing at is language, too, and such languages are being generated rapidly. Historic preservation is noble, but it should not forestall invention.

My own father's culture was impoverished; he grew up in a tenement in the Bronx, made his way into the professional class, and raised my brother and me with many advantages. He has sometimes expressed nostalgia for that world he left and has tried to explain it to us. It is not our reality; indeed, it is hardly anyone's reality. The world to which he was born, of recent Jewish immigrants from Eastern Europe doing manual labor and speaking Yiddish, has vanished. There is no question that something has been lost. Yet I prefer the prosperous, American way I grew up. Jackie Roth spoke to me about today's Hasidic Jews. "They feel safe amongst themselves," she said. "They have their Shabbos on Friday night, they go to synagogue. They have their own schools, they have their own traditions, they have their own everything. Why bother with the rest of the world? That's what's happening with the Deaf community. It's going to be smaller and smaller, and the outliers are going to be increasingly marginal. We've got to stop playing deaf."

My first book was about a group of Soviet artists who evinced courage and brilliance in the face of an oppressive and cruel system—and then the Cold War ended, and their tremendous accomplishments became historical, and while a few negotiated the Western art scene's commerce and museums, many never made a decent work of art again. Deaf culture has been a heroic enterprise all this time, a beautiful, ingenious marvel, and now, like Soviet dissidence and Yiddish theater, it is slipping out of relevance. Some things from it will be carried forward, but the occasion of its brave dignity is passing. Every bit of progress kills something, but also encodes its origins. I do not wish for the life my father left behind, but I know that some spirit forged in that particular adversity made me possible.

Looking at the vogue for ASL among hearing people, the activist Carol Padden asked, "How can two conflicting impulses exist at the same time—to eradicate deafness and yet to celebrate its most illustrious consequence, the creation and maintenance of a unique form of human language?" One thing has no bearing on the other. You can admire Deaf culture and still choose not to consign your children to it. The loss of diversity is terrible, but diversity for the sake of diversity is a lie. A Deaf culture kept pure when hearing is available to all would be the equivalent of those historical towns where everyone lives as though it were the eighteenth century. Will those born without hearing continue to have things in common? Will their language remain in use? Of course—just as candles have remained ubiquitous in the age of electricity, just as we wear cotton in a time of microfibers, just as people read books despite television. We will not lose what Deaf culture has given us, and it is a worthy cause to delineate what parts of Deaf culture are precious and why. But vertical demand for medical progress will inevitably outflank any horizontal social agenda.

III

Dwarfs

Until I attended my first dwarf convention—the 2003 Little People of America (LPA) meeting in Danvers, Massachusetts—I had no clue how many kinds of dwarfism there are, nor how many varieties of appearance are collected under the category. Dwarfism is a low-incidence condition, usually occurring because of a random genetic mutation. Since most dwarfs are born to average-height parents, they do not have vertical community. There has been occasional talk about building a town for little people (LPs); there are metropolises where activist LPs have settled; there are high concentrations of otherwise rare dwarfing conditions among the Amish; but there has never been a significant geographic concentration of people of short stature. This means that the national LPA gatherings are not simply occasions to attend lectures and consult medical experts; for some participants, they are the annual exception to a certain kind of loneliness. The gatherings are emotionally intense; one dwarf I met told me she was "happy for one week a year," although others emphasized that they love both of their lives—the one in the larger world, and the one among their LPA friends. More than 10 percent of Americans of short stature belong to LPA, and the organization has a role in the LP community that is greater than that of similar groups for comparable populations.

Arriving at the Sheraton Ferncroft Resort, where the convention was taking place, I was struck by how the concentration of LPs changed my perception of them. Instead of seeing, primarily, short stature, I saw that one was exceptionally beautiful, that one was unusually short even for a dwarf, that one laughed uproariously and often, that one had an especially intelligent face—and so I began to recognize how generically I had responded to little people until then. I understood what a relief it had to be for them that no one was focused on their height. Of course, the LPA convention was all about stature, but it was also the place where stature became blessedly irrelevant.

It would be difficult for an outsider to acknowledge this particularizing view of, for example, Latinos or Muslims. To say that a person's ethnicity or religion had overwhelmed, even temporarily, one's ability to appreciate his other personal characteristics would seem bigoted. But dwarfism has been the exception to these social rules. According to Betty Adelson, author of *The Lives of Dwarfs* and *Dwarfism*, "The only permissible prejudice in PC America is against dwarfs." Mary D'Alton, chair of Columbia University's Department of Obstetrics and Gynecology and a leader in the field of high-risk pregnancy, told me that dwarfism is the most difficult diagnosis to communicate to expectant parents. "You say that the baby has a hole in his heart," she said, "and they say, 'But you can fix that, right?' But when I tell someone that they will be having a dwarf, they often seem disgusted by the idea."

Many of the attendees I met my first day at LPA could identify instantly conditions that I had never heard of or imagined and had certainly never seen. When I went down to the conference disco the first night, I saw a brother and sister who had primordial dwarfism; they were full-grown, perfectly proportioned, and only about twenty-nine inches high. Their parents stood with them to make sure they weren't trampled—a danger even at the dwarf convention. I learned that the girl played percussion in her high school band; she had a classmate who pushed her tiny wheelchair, and she held the drum in her lap—looking, in the words of a dwarf who was herself just three foot eight, "like a marionette." The conference featured athletic competitions; a marathon-length talent show, including acts from Christian music to break dancing; and a fashion show, which revealed a broad range of dressy and casual styles, all tailored to little bodies. The conference also provided an eagerly awaited opportunity for dating. A dwarf comedian cracked, "You know you're a teenager at LPA if you've had more boyfriends this week than you've had in the last year."

When I met Mary Boggs on my second day at LPA, she told me that the organization had changed her life. When her daughter Sam was born in 1988, the obstetrician initially assumed that the baby's diminutive size was a result of her premature arrival. A month later, while she was still in the neonatal intensive care unit, he diagnosed her with achondroplasia. "We would have rather had a child that was deaf or blind," Mary told me. "Just anything besides a dwarf would have been better. When you're thinking about what could go wrong with a pregnancy, this doesn't cross your mind. We were thinking, 'Why did we have another child at all?'"

Sam came home to her parents' house in the suburbs of Washington, DC, on oxygen and a monitor. After six months, when Sam was declared physically healthy, Mary took her to her first local LPA meeting. When Sam was a year and a half old, she had a shunt inserted in her head to relieve her hydrocephalus (the accumulation of cerebrospinal fluid in the head); fortunately, she did not have the skeletal problems that in later life afflict so many people with achondroplasia. Mary and her husband got step stools and put them all over the house; they purchased light-switch extenders; they moved the faucet on the kitchen sink. These adjustments at home were easier to control than the challenges outside. "We've had people chase us down the grocery aisle to ask questions," Mary said. "We learned to stare back. It frightens them off. I'd watch Sam not playing with the other kids because she's too small to do what they do. You just feel sad."

Before Sam set off for kindergarten, her parents told her that other kids would call her names; they reviewed what some of those names might be and taught her appropriate responses. Mary went to the school and explained Sam's special needs, giving the teacher a book about dwarfs that she could read aloud to the class. The school lowered the sink and water fountain and installed a grab bar so Sam could pull herself up on the toilet. The kids in her class learned her story, but each year it was new to an incoming kindergarten class, and some would call her names. So Sam decided to make a presentation to each incoming class. She would explain, "I'm little, but I'm eight years old. I'm in third grade. I'm a dwarf, and I'm just like you all, but just short." She did that every year through elementary school, and the teasing stopped.

When Sam was five, the Boggs family attended their first national LPA convention. "We walked in and saw a thousand dwarfs," Mary said. "Sam was in shock. I thought my other daughter, who is average height, was going to cry. It took two or three days for us to take it in." Over the years that followed, the Boggs family persuaded extended family and friends to come to meetings, so that they would know dwarfs other than Sam. "The grandparents could see adult dwarfs and realize, 'Okay, this is what Sam's going to look like,'" Mary said. She considered for a minute. "We went for Sam, but also so *we* could be comfortable with her. To make it easier for us to love her right."

Middle school was more difficult than elementary school. "People who had been friends for years were suddenly not wanting to hang out with her anymore," Mary said. "She was not called to go roller skating or go to the movies on Friday night. They pretended that it wasn't because she was a dwarf. But she knew." The athletics department gave her a varsity letter for being manager of the track team; she participated in student council and was elected treasurer of her class. Despite this, she was down to a couple of friends. "She's a little lonely," Mary said. "She'd have crushes on the boys at school, but eventually realized that average-size guys were not interested in going out with her. It was a big turning point when she started looking more at the hot guys at LPA."

When I met Sam, she was in the throes of her first romance. She was fifteen going on sixteen, attractive and strikingly mature, and, at three feet nine inches, fairly short for a teenager with achondroplasia. Mary was optimistic about the future. "I would prefer for her to have an LP boyfriend or LP husband," she said to me. "I think it'll be easier for her. It's kind of neat. I mean, you have a dwarf child. But it doesn't just stop there; it goes on forever. We're going to have, probably, a dwarf son-in-law, and dwarf grandchildren. What used to be an average-size family then becomes, when we're gone, a dwarf family! And to think, if I'd known about this early in my pregnancy, I might have terminated."

Writing in 1754, William Hay, a dwarf and the first notable memoirist of disability, described visiting a general: "I never was more humbled, than when I walked with him among his tall Men, made still taller by their Caps. I seemed to my self a Worm and no Man: and could not but inwardly grieve, that when I had the same Inclination to the Service of my Country and Prince, I wanted their Strength to perform it." This feeling of inadequacy salted with the wish to transcend it has been a common narrative among dwarfs, but in the long pause between Hay's dignified early account and the modern literature on the experience of being an LP, a grossness of prejudice has often quelled that dignity.

Woody Allen once quipped that *dwarf* is one of the four funniest words in the English language. To be in your very essence perceived as comical is a significant burden. When I described the other categories included in this book, my listeners were hushed by the seriousness of the enterprise; at the mention of dwarfs, friends burst into laughter. I would describe, for example, the time during a convention when a miscreant dwarf had made a bomb threat at 8:00 a.m., so that all hotel guests, most recovering from a night of intense partying, had to evacuate the building. People found hilarity in the mere idea of some five hundred sleepy dwarfs, many of them hungover, standing in the hotel's forecourt. This had some resonance for me; I know that not so long ago, people might have found the idea of five hundred sleepy homosexuals similarly hilarious. But homosexuality can be hidden, and being among gay people is not a visual gag. Passersby who might avert their eyes tactfully from wheelchair users stare at dwarfs. A sighted woman who marries a blind man inspires admiration; an average-size woman who marries a dwarf inspires suspicion that she has a fetish. Dwarfs still appear in freak shows; in dwarf-tossing competitions; and in pornography, where a whole subgenre featuring dwarf sex exploits an objectifying voyeurism. This is testimony to a callousness beyond that shown to almost any other disabled group. Barbara Spiegel, now director of community outreach at LPA, described how her grandmother said, "You're a beautiful girl, but no one's going to marry you. You need to be able to do everything because you're going to be alone." Barbara's stepmother complained about having to be seen on the street with her.

More than 80 percent of people with skeletal dysplasias—the primary dwarfing conditions, the most common among which is achondroplasia, resulting in shortened limbs, a large head, and an average trunk—are born to average parents with no history of dwarfism in their families, either because of de novo mutations or because both parents carry a recessive gene. Other forms of dwarfism include pituitary dwarfism, based on lack of human growth hormone, and psychosocial dwarfism, caused by severe physical abuse.

Parents are still dealing with a legacy of blame assigned to mothers. From medieval times into the eighteenth century, "monstrous births" were said to indicate the unfulfilled desires of lascivious women, whose obscene longings supposedly produced deformity. This theory, called Imaginationism, was hotly debated for hundreds of years. The Princeton historian Marie-Hélène Huet describes how "in the nineteenth century, discoveries in the fields of embryology and heredity provided scientists with new ways of explaining resemblances. But if the mother's imagination was no longer perceived by the medical field to be a factor in resemblances, its role as the shaper of progeny was never totally forgotten." John Mulliken, a pediatric surgeon, writes that every parent wants to know what he or she did to cause the situation. "In most cases, the answer is nothing. But every mother is blamed."

Dwarfism is also often outside the experience of doctors with whom these parents initially interact, and parents frequently recall being told of the condition with particular insensitivity. Adelson recounts one doctor's pronouncement to the parents of a newly diagnosed child—"You have given birth to a circus dwarf"—and another's equally heartless recommendation that a child he had diagnosed should "be institutionalized or sent to live with a dwarf troupe in Florida." One mother reported that most doctors acted as though her daughter were defective and therefore didn't deserve to be treated like a "real" baby. Another described being in the delivery room with her dwarf husband when the doctor said to them both, "I regret to tell you that your child is a dwarf."

Such behavior from a doctor is not merely a breach of etiquette; the way the news of a dwarfing condition is communicated to parents may have a lasting effect on their ability to love and care for their child. Mothers and fathers are helped by knowing right away that the child will have a full life span, that they did not cause the dwarfism through acts during pregnancy, and that their child can lead a happy, healthy, and independent life. Parents, in turn, influence friends and family; embarrassed parents create awkward friends. In addition to LPA, organizations such as the MAGIC Foundation and the Human Growth Foundation have fact-filled websites and sponsor both online chat rooms and local support groups, providing average-size parents of dwarf children opportunities to meet dwarfs who are living positive, fulfilling lives.

Nonetheless, many parents begin in sadness, denial, and shock. One dwarf, Ginny Sargent, wrote online, "No matter what we (as dwarfs) feel about how great it is to be alive, I still can't help but wonder how much more pain (more than I) my mother was in when I was in discomfort . . . upset, hurt, or disheartened and beaten down by my uniqueness."

Matt Roloff, former president of LPA and father on the popular television program *Little People, Big World*, said, "My parents didn't wonder what I would like to do, what kind of woman I'd marry, or how many children I would have. They wondered what I could do for a living, if I could ever marry, and if I could have children." He is now married to Amy, also a dwarf, and they have four children. *Little People, Big World*, which ran for almost four years on the Learning Channel, documented the Roloffs' lives on their farm in Portland, Oregon. The show is somewhat voyeuristic but fairly clear of sensationalism, and it has helped to normalize perceptions of LPs.

Amy Roloff grew up in a household in which few accommodations were made for her. Friends who came to visit wondered why the phone was positioned where she needed to climb on a stool to reach it. "My mom said, 'If Amy has to learn to adapt outside of the home, she might as well feel comfortable and learn to adapt within the home.' Nothing was really tailored to my needs, and that was a good idea, 'cause I'm more independent." The Roloffs have three average-height children and one, Zach, with achondroplasia. Amy didn't want to set up a house that suited the LPs in the family and felt foreign to the average kids, so she kept things "regular." She encouraged Zach to be both proud of and nonchalant about his dwarfism. "He said one day, 'Mom, we were playing and the kids were a little too rough.' I said, 'Zach, why don't you be a little grateful that, perhaps, this was a moment where they don't even think of you as a little person; they're just hanging out and goofing around with you? That's a good thing.'"

This equalizing spirit is extended to all of her children. Jeremy is the eldest and the tallest. "I have to remind Matt that we can't take advantage of Jeremy because he's tall. I don't want him to think that he's only good in the family 'cause he's tall." But even the *New York Times*, commenting on her children as they appear on TV, described Jeremy as "a gorgeous young athlete who manages the soccer ball with lazy grace," and his brother Zachary as having "a clever and intense persona." There's nothing wrong with a clever and intense persona, but it's interesting what different vocabulary comes up when the writer is describing, with kind intent, someone with a body that is not beautiful within the conventions of our larger society.

Lisa Hedley hosts her own radio program on NPR and is chief executive of a group of spas. She used to be a ballerina and comes from a prominent New York family; she lives between the city and Connecticut. The film she produced and directed for HBO, *Dwarfs: Not a Fairy Tale*, is joyous, yet clear-eyed about the difficulties faced by the people whose lives it chronicles. Lisa did not have the wisdom of that film when her daughter, Rose, who has achondroplasia, was born. While Lisa was in the hospital after Rose's birth, "they gave me a little pamphlet called 'My Child Is a Dwarf' and some other materials that showed a photograph of a toothless man cleaning the street, and another photo of dwarfs tending sheep," she recalled. Lisa decided she would do whatever she could to keep Rose from such conceptions of dwarfism.

When Rose was two, Lisa wrote an article for the *New York Times Magazine*, in which she said, "With one word my husband and I became unwitting members of a community whose bonds are not only the natural elations and tribulations of parenthood but also deeply confusing sorrow—a new understanding of random events, a skewed sense of reality. It never occurred to me, not even in my wildest disaster scenarios, that I would have a child different enough to elicit stares and change the way I think about a trip to the store or a walk on the beach. Early on I learned that the way other people react to a child of difference becomes integral to your experience of the world. Perhaps the most important thing about people's reactions is that they take their cues from me: if I'm cheerful and positive, people are delighted to point out all of my daughter's special qualities—bright eyes, charming smile."

When Rose turned four and developed self-awareness about her condition, Lisa sent her to a child psychologist so she could have a relationship in place if she ran into bumps and challenges as she engaged with the world. "Rose went one day a week after school," Lisa said. "But she hated it from minute one. She didn't want to talk about herself. She was almost vicious about it. I realized that we were medicalizing her condition, turning it into something that required treatment, when, in fact, she doesn't require treatment at all."

Lisa has had to balance her relationship with Rose against her relationship with her other three children, two of them older than Rose and one younger. "I'm particularly sensitive to her needs. I neuroticize them," Lisa said. "Her school did a concert at Carnegie Hall, and she walks out with that funny dwarf gait, going to her seat. I look at my husband, like, 'Did we forget she's a dwarf?' I tend to be shocked all over again and very sad in such situations." Lisa feels it would be dishonest to pretend otherwise, to herself or to Rose or to the world. "I adore Rose and I can't imagine life without Rose. I wouldn't trade her for the world. But I'm very tall; I'm thin; I was a ballet dancer. I imagined those experiences for her. When you have a child who can't share those things, you mourn the loss of an imagined life. On the other hand, I have an almost violently passionate feeling of who she is."

Rose refuses to give audience to self-pity. "She's very heroic about it, very strong," Lisa said. "But her battle is so relentless. I'm a private person and I don't like it. It's like being a celebrity when you didn't mean to be. We walk down the street and people go, 'Hi, Rose.' She's always trying to escape it, and she never can."

Rose has not identified with other little people, so the family has not been involved in LPA. It's always difficult to know how much such decisions create an attitude and how much they reflect it. "Support groups and conferences: is this something our family would do under normal circumstances, join any group, go to any organization?" Lisa said. "The answer is decidedly not. I asked Rose, 'Do you think it would be better if you knew some other little people?' She said, 'No, I want to live here in the life I have. I have plenty of friends. I know who I am.'" Lisa has a friend with a short-statured daughter a year younger than Rose. The family is very involved with LPA and returns from conferences with pictures of "really cute teenage little people," but Rose shows no interest. "The underlying question is to what extent we are fostering denial," Lisa said.

There is a cliché that dwarfs are often "feisty" (a particularly noxious word), and myriad articles run under headlines such as "Little Person, Big Personality." Some of this is just patronizing. Some of it, however, reflects the personality consequences of living as an object of near-universal curiosity. "None of my other children is as tough as she is, nor is my husband, nor am I," Lisa said. "Rose is very angry. It comes from just having to *deal* with it all the time."

The family arranged life around Rose more than she realized. They had an opportunity to move to London but stayed in the United States because they didn't want to unsettle her. Rose is a serious athlete, and her passion is riding. "I would never have chosen that for her," Lisa said with pride. "But my oldest son was a very good horseman, nationally ranked, and she saw that glory. She can tolerate going out into a ring, in front of a judge. She's competing against average-stature kids, all these cute little girls with pigtails and long, lanky legs, and she still wins awards. She sits up straight and proud. People keep saying, 'Isn't that amazing?' She doesn't want to be amazing because she's a dwarf. What she wants is to be judged like the others."

Lisa has been called on frequently to be a mentor and has convinced many women to keep their pregnancies after learning they were carrying a dwarf. She has also recommended adoption; she described meeting a family who simply couldn't deal with the prospect of having a disabled child. "Their older daughter was a cheerleader, and they thought she would be devastated because her 'sister would be such a freak'; those were the words the mother used. She ended up giving the baby away. Her new baby was never going to be a cheerleader in West-chester, so she couldn't love her." Another family she met with already had a dwarf child. "That family was economically and demographically very close to us," Lisa said. "So I thought, 'This is perfect: the girls can grow up together.'" She was shocked when the parents decided to give their daughter limb-lengthening, a controversial procedure that involves repeatedly breaking bones and stretching muscles. "It was a tough lesson, that just because their daughter is little doesn't mean we're going to have anything in common spiritually or emotionally. Five years in and out of wheelchairs. Limb-lengthening really frightens me for medical reasons, and even more because kids are busy forming their identity and who they are at that age. How do people become their best self? Not by constantly trying to change details."

Lisa said that, in spite of all her questioning, what had frightened her at first had, at some level, become unquestioned. "I was at Johns Hop-kins Hospital for one of her treatments many years ago. I was carrying her on the elevator. This other mother got in with her child, who was drooling and had, clearly, a very profound case of Down syndrome. I was looking at her with total pity, like, 'Oh, I can deal with mine, but I would not know what to do with yours.' And that was exactly how she was looking at me."

Parents can establish a relationship with dwarfism as an identity: travel to dwarf conferences, involve dwarfs in their child's life, put light switches where they are easily reached by a person of short stature, and refit the kitchen to make it convenient for a little person to cook there. There is a danger, however, that a child who grows up with short stature as a primary identity may feel trapped in a context he never chose. Even if he does not, he will have to face the identity's inherent limitation. You can elect to associate primarily with people who share your religion, ethnicity, sexual orientation, political convictions, recreational preferences, or socioeconomic status, but there just aren't enough dwarfs to make an all-dwarf life feasible.

Parents may prefer to mainstream completely: to persuade their child that being short is not so different from being tall, to encourage him to make friends with other children without regard to height, to say that the tall world is the real world and he will just have to get used to it. But it can be a strain to be told constantly that you don't really have a disability. Barbara Spiegel described how she would ask her father to hand her a glass from the cabinet. Her mother would say, "You're quite capable of getting it yourself," and would insist that Barbara drag a stepladder across the room rather than have the glass handed to her. "Sometimes it was a little extreme," she said. The idea of being just like everyone else, only shorter, is normalizing, but social context does not always support that normalization, and avoidance of the LP world can come at the cost of considerable isolation. Life often gets tough in middle school and high school; few teenagers of average height will date someone who is three foot six. "Most of the people I found attractive, guy-wise, were exceptionally tall," Barbara said. "I really didn't picture myself with an LP. I never imagined that I would marry one—no, two!—LPs."

What is right for one dwarf and family may not be right for another dwarf and family, and most families combine elements of various approaches—providing some access to the LP world, making an attempt to put their child at ease in the non-LP world, and availing themselves of medical treatments that respond to their child's specific needs and desires. The exact nature of the balance differs from household to household. Research indicates that short-statured people generally outscore their parents on measures of overall contentedness, which is to say that parenting a dwarf seems to be emotionally harder than being a dwarf. Another study found that people with achondroplasia were four times as likely as relatives to view their condition as "not serious," as opposed to "serious" or "lethal." One's own identity, replete with problems though it may be, usually looks more tenable than someone else's identity. Of course disparities of income and education are factors, and it is obviously more of a challenge to support a short-statured child with intellectual handicaps or severe skeletal and health problems than it is to deal with someone who is, in effect, just little. It is interesting to note that those close relatives of dwarfs who perceived the dwarfism as more burdensome for the affected individual were likely themselves to rank lower on inventories of happiness.

We still fit people into the binary of *disabled* or *nondisabled*; we grant those who are officially disabled social assistance, legal protections, and special parking spaces. It's difficult, though, to delineate where *disability* sets in. A man who is five foot six might prefer to be six feet tall but is not disabled. A man who is four feet tall faces significant challenges. Many dwarfs experience serious physical disabilities, but even putting aside medical problems, being short has a price. Dwarfism is recognized under the Americans with Disabilities Act (ADA), under which dwarfs are classed as "orthopedically concerned," but LPA long resisted the classification of dwarfism as a disability, though their position has now changed. No law requires supermarkets to provide a means to retrieve merchandise from high shelves. Legislation does not consistently mandate that gas pumps or cash machines be installed at a height that makes them accessible to little people. The federal government will not pay for adaptive equipment for people who wish to drive but are disabled by virtue of their short stature. Paul Steven Miller, an achondroplastic dwarf who served as commissioner of the Equal Employment Opportunity Commission in the Clinton administration, said while in office, "It's fair to say that LPA as an organization is not really an active player in the broader disability movement at the national level. But I think that that's the direction we're headed in." That move reflects a shift at LPA, spearheaded by their advocacy chairs Joe Stramondo and Gary Arnold, a generation younger than Miller, to engage with an ever-broadening definition of *disability* and an ever-broader range of services associated with disability status.

Rosemarie Garland Thomson argues in her book *Extraordinary Bodies* that "the 'physically disabled' are produced by way of legal, medical, political, cultural, and literary narratives that comprise an exclusionary discourse." But much of what extremely short-statured people cannot do is determined less by social attitudes than by physical arrangements made by the majority of human beings to suit taller people; the high-minded rhetoric around disability can feel like unwelcome clutter to some dwarfs. One mother of a dwarf worried, "I couldn't decide whether or not to request a handicapped parking permit. Would our daughter feel stigmatized? At school, should we get special step stools at the toilets? There is a problem of constant accommodation, but should we call it a disability?" The LP actress Linda Hunt once wrote, "Dwarfism, after all, isn't like cancer or heart disease. It isn't fatal, and it isn't even an illness. It is physical, though, and inescapable. You don't get over it. It is you. But you aren't it, and that's an important distinction."

The public still lacks a nuanced understanding of the various words used to describe little people. The first meeting of LPA (convened in 1957 as a publicity stunt to benefit the town of Reno, Nevada) was called Midgets of America. The fledgling organization's name was changed in 1960 to Little People of America so that little people of every description might feel welcome. The word *midget*, first coined to describe LPs displayed as curiosities, and drawn from the *midge*, an annoying small insect, is now considered deeply offensive—the LP equivalent of *nigger* or *spic* or *faggot*—and many mothers told me how much they feared that their child would be subject to this appellation. But the general population doesn't know that *midget* is an insult, and most people who use the word do so without ill intent. Is the use of an inappropriate word evidence of prejudice if the user doesn't know that the word is stigmatizing? The most famous small stars of P. T. Barnum's sideshows were proportional dwarfs, whose bodies have the same relative scale as those of average-size people. The term has frequently been used to refer to those whose small stature results from a pituitary anomaly rather than a skeletal dysplasia. When the *New York Times* used *midget* in an article on its business pages in 2009, there was outcry from LPA, and the *Times* revised its stylebook. But the term *dwarf* has its own burdensome associations. Barbara Spiegel has two children with achondroplasia, and she tried to bring them up with a sense of pride in who they are. When her older daughter asked what she should say to the kids in her kindergarten class about her stature, Barbara said, "Say you're a dwarf." Her daughter put her hands on her hips and said, "But I'm not make-believe!"

Betty Adelson, recently asked by journalist Lynn Harris what people of short stature prefer to be called, said, "Most individuals prefer simply to be called by their given names."

When Rebecca Kennedy was born in Boston in 1992, her doctors feared that she had inhaled meconium (prenatal stool), so she was brought immediately to the special-care nursery. After noticing that her head was rather large and her limbs rather small, one of the doctors announced to Rebecca's parents, Dan and Barbara Kennedy, that their newborn child probably had "either dwarfism or brain damage." The prospect of brain damage was terrifying, and so the diagnosis of achondroplasia, made three days later on the basis of X-rays, was an immense relief. The people at the hospital were positive about Becky. "A generation earlier, parents were given a negative view of what to expect," Dan explained. "We were given a very positive view of what to expect—maybe too positive. We were pretty much told, 'Things are fine; enjoy her; take her home.'" Dan's doctors were expressing a shift in attitude that people with disabilities have fought to effect. Most disabilities, however, require accommodation, and doctors do parents no favor if they trivialize the challenges ahead.

For five months everything appeared to go well. Then Becky contracted a respiratory virus that overwhelmed her delicate system. She ended up in the intensive care unit for more than a month and was given a tracheotomy. For two years, she had to have supplemental oxygen, and the Kennedys lived with a parade of nurses. By the time Becky was two and a half, her airways were developed enough so that the tracheotomy could be closed, and she has since been a reasonably healthy child. "The dwarfism was not that big a deal, but all this other stuff was a big deal," Dan recalled. "We've always wondered what effect those two years—with the tracheotomy, the night nurse—had on the subsequent development of her personality, and I don't think we know yet."

When Becky fell sick, Dan found LPA, and he was put in touch with Ruth Ricker. "Ruth was employed in a good job, turned out to have gone to the same college that we did, and was a smart and funny person, and I would have been happy to see Becky turn out like her," he said. Through Ruth, the family started to attend regional LPA events. Dan and Ruth developed the LPA website in the early days of the Internet, and Dan continued to manage and edit it for many years.

Becky has had some learning issues, which Dan attributes to hearing loss, a not uncommon complication among people with achondroplasia. When I interviewed Dan, Becky was ten and a half, and her father was anticipating the difficult waters of adolescence. "Becky looks in the mirror and she likes what she sees," Dan said. "But I don't kid myself. I assume that her most bitter critique of dwarfism is yet to come. Every adult dwarf I've ever talked to, almost without exception, says by the time they hit their twenties, they're proud of who they are and wouldn't change anything. But their teen years were hell. She doesn't have many friends now, and it's only going to become more difficult."

Dan began writing *Little People: Learning to See the World Through My Daughter's Eyes*. "I look at dwarfism as a metaphor for difference," he said. "Whether we value it; whether we fear it; whether we would stamp it out if given the opportunity." The research he did gave Dan insights that have helped Becky. He got a handicapped placard for his car because he realized that walking long distances was bad for anyone with a compressed spine. "Lee Kitchens, former president of LPA, said to me, 'Better a handicapped placard now than a scooter when she's thirty,'" Dan said. In his book, Dan complains that the freedom people felt in approaching him with questions about his daughter communicated "the unspoken message that Becky is public property, and that her parents are obliged to explain her to the world." Whether they like it or not, parents of dwarf children often feel they must display their families as emblems of diversity. "I'd like to think grappling with this has made me a better person," Dan said, "but I still don't think I'm very patient. Frankly, your life is in the hands of outside forces, and you just have to go with it. This definitely made me better at that."

More than two hundred genetic conditions lead to exceptionally short stature. Approximately 70 percent of dwarfs have achondroplasia; other dwarfing conditions include pseudoachondroplasia, spondyloepiphyseal dysplasia congenita (or SED), and diastrophic dysplasia. Little People of America designates as a dwarf anyone who is four foot ten or under as the result of a medical condition. This description does not officially include people with dwarfing conditions who grow taller than four feet ten inches, nor would it apply to children with no genetic anomalies whose dwarfism results from malnutrition or parental abuse and neglect. Nonetheless, such people are in general welcomed at LPA. The average height of a female achondroplastic dwarf is four feet, and of a male, four foot three. There are more than two hundred thousand people of short stature in the United States, and Victor McKusick, a geneticist specializing in diseases of connective tissue, has estimated that there are several million worldwide. The distance such people must travel to find expert help can be considerable; medical costs can be staggering; insurance often covers only a fraction of the liability a family faces. More than two dozen physicians serve on LPA's Medical Advisory Board, and conferences allow dwarfs to avail themselves of expert advice.

The mechanism of achondroplasia is an overactive gene, the same one that causes the bones of average people to stop growing at the end of adolescence. This process is kicked into gear prematurely by a variation of a single nucleotide. *Achons* (slang for people with achondroplasia) have short limbs in proportion to a fairly average trunk, and a large head with a protuberant forehead. People with SED, a more disabling condition, tend to be shorter than those with achondroplasia; they often have clubfeet, cleft palate, wide-set eyes, a small mouth, and a barrel chest that develops when their ribs grow faster than their spine. Diastrophic dysplasia is distinguished by clubfeet and cleft palate; "hitchhiker's thumb," which is low on the hand and has little flexibility; and a "cauliflower ear" similar to the calcified-ear deformities that many professional boxers develop. Diastrophic dwarfs often become so bent that they are unable to walk. The condition results from a recessive gene, so both parents must be carriers—and are usually unaware of it. Though the numbers vary, it would appear that achondroplasia occurs in about one in twenty thousand births, while one in ten thousand has a dwarfing condition, some of them fatal.

Since newborns always have short limbs in relation to their heads and torsos, the revelation, as with deafness, may come immediately or may be gradual. Most dwarfs are diagnosed by the age of two. Because their chests are small, their airways may be dangerously narrow, leading to rapid breathing, obstructions, and sleep disturbances. Infants with achondroplasia are also at increased risk for life-threatening brain-stem compression, in which pressure on the lower brain impedes its function. A study of mortality in achondroplasia determined that the risk of dying within the first four years of life was more than one in fifty. The chance of dying in childhood, adolescence, or young adulthood is also vastly increased. The body temperature of newborn dwarfs is somewhat higher than that of average infants, and carbon dioxide retention causes them to sweat more. Hydrocephalus and recurrent, damaging ear infections caused by variations in craniofacial shape may also complicate matters. Several other, low-incidence conditions are associated with mental retardation, including dwarfism caused by inadequate iodine, intrauterine growth restrictions, or psychosocial deprivation. Although cognitive and intellectual development generally proceeds apace, little people may still be challenged at school because of early oxygen deprivation resulting from an underdeveloped pulmonary system; because of damage to their hearing, from the repeated ear infections to which they are prone; or because of the need to focus energy on compensating for social stigma.

Early diagnosis is critical; many serious complications can be avoided through appropriate prophylactic treatment. Children with achondroplasia should have X-rays and scans to monitor their neurological and skeletal development. They may need complex dental work if their jaw is too small for their teeth. Some children have spinal columns too thin for their nerves to fit in without being pinched. This can lead to weakness, numbness, and pain. Small airways make the risks of anesthesia higher for dwarfs. If a curvature of the spine is not corrected early on, a dwarf child may develop a hunchback. An infant with a skeletal dysplasia should not be left sitting up, as his head is too heavy for his spine to support. Additionally, he should not be placed in any seat that curves the back; car seats should be padded to prevent him from resting his chin on his chest.

Because their heads are too heavy for their necks, many young children with achondroplasia cannot hold them up when they are crouching; only a fifth of them learn to crawl. *Snowplowing* and *reverse snowplowing* entail resting the head on the floor as a balancing point while using the legs for propulsion; *spider crawling, log rolling, army crawling,* and *seat scooting* involve exactly the sorts of motion that their vivid names imply. When children with achondroplasia are ready to walk, they often stand by *jackknifing*, keeping their head on the floor while straightening their legs, then lifting the upper body to achieve a full upright posture; muscle tone may be low, and joints may be unusually stiff or loose. Short-statured children perform these and many other acts in a unique way or at a later developmental stage, and LPs are supposed to avoid gymnastics, high diving, acrobatics, and collision sports because of possible joint and skeletal issues. They are encouraged to do swimming, golf, and other lower-impact sports. Because LP children should properly eat only about half as much as their average counterparts, many struggle with weight, a problem that LPA attempts to address in educational materials and panel discussions.

In adulthood, LPs may suffer chronic back problems, allergies, sinus problems, arthritis, rheumatism, hearing impairments, spine deformities, sleeping difficulties, chronic neck pain, or paralysis or weakness of the upper or lower limbs; they are far more likely than their average counterparts to undergo surgeries throughout life. The defining issues for most adult dwarfs are skeletal. The dysplasias are often associated with spinal stenosis, joint deformity and degeneration, and disk problems. In adults with achondroplasia, the narrowed spine often needs to be decompressed surgically to alleviate symptoms such as shooting pains down the legs, weakness, numbness, tingling, and pins and needles. Curvature of the spine may result in mechanical and neurological complications that affect the heart and the lungs, as well as mobility. Surgeries often performed on dwarfs include lumbar surgery for spinal stenosis to prevent paralysis and pain, cervical-spine surgery that ameliorates limb weakness, surgical division or sectioning of bone for bowleggedness, the insertion of shunts for hydrocephalus, and interventions to resolve obstructive apnea.

Leslie Parks's parents were not pleased when she began hanging out with Chris Kelly during her senior year in high school in Huntsville, Alabama. The future they had imagined for their daughter had not included a romantic entanglement with a dwarf, even one who was a local celebrity, a DJ with his own radio show. "I was your typical middle kid, nothing special about me," Leslie said. "So I sort of fell into it with him. I was in student government, and he would DJ parties. From the beginning, my parents were like, 'Nip it in the bud. He's divorced, he's got kids, he's a dwarf, he's a DJ, and he's no good.'" Leslie felt she was dating a star, but her parents didn't see it that way, and they threw her out of the house her senior year. Within a few months, Leslie and Chris were married.

When Chris was young, his parents had tried every new "treatment" on the market, including injections of growth hormone made from the pituitary glands of monkeys. Because of or in spite of the shots, Chris had made it to four feet ten inches, which is tall for a person with achondroplasia, and firmly refused to regard his dwarfism as a medical condition to be cured. "He got into being a DJ and a stand-up comic because he needed the approval of the masses to feel good about himself," Leslie said. "What he didn't particularly need was a one-on-one relationship." Chris's two children from his previous relationship were both of average height. When Leslie became pregnant, a few months after marrying Chris, she had no thought that she might be carrying a dwarf. At seven months, she went for an ultrasound. "They said, 'His head is too big for seven months. But his femur is much too short for seven months. What's going on here?'" Leslie knew exactly what was going on. "I was devastated. I'm glad I found out ahead of time, because I had time to get the mourning over with by the time he was born." Leslie could not talk to her husband about her despair at the prospect of a child who resembled him.

A tomboy who went through precocious puberty, Leslie had always had a skewed self-image. "In third grade I was developing already, and people made fun of me. I was always ashamed that my body wasn't right." She was overweight when she met Chris, became bigger after they married, and grew enormous and somewhat depressed when she had Jake. "I remember bringing him home from the hospital, thinking, 'This is the worst babysitting job I've ever had. When is his mother coming for him?'" Leslie's parents were horrified to have a dwarf grandson, but over time their attitude softened. Leslie's mother was a pediatric nurse, and she sent Leslie to a neurologist at Birmingham Children's Hospital who had experience with LPs. Leslie's pediatrician had told her that Jake's frequent vomiting was normal and that she could straighten him out when he arched his back in his sleep. "Then this specialist said, 'Does he sleep with his head back and his neck arched? That's how they achieve the most free, unobstructed breathing. Don't move his head.' I didn't know."

Chris, like the local doctors, tended to minimize his son's condition, while Leslie's parents clearly regarded her life as a calamity. Leslie and Chris became increasingly alienated as they navigated these issues, eventually divorcing when Jake was two. As a child, Jake would sometimes weep, saying, "I don't want to be little." Leslie wanted to cry, too. "What would be wrong about letting him know that you hurt for him, too?" she said. "You don't want your child to perceive that you think his situation is hopeless, but also you don't want to deny his experience. A few times, I've said, 'Have you talked to your daddy about this?' 'No, I'm crying 'cause I don't want to be like me, which means I don't want to be like him. That would hurt his feelings.'"

Jake had some learning delays; his focus has been social rather than academic. By the time he finished third grade, Leslie was worried he was falling behind. Private testing revealed that he had a learning disability, so she transferred him to a magnet school for special education. He hated it. "Jake can act," Leslie said. "He's done stuff on TV; he's very outgoing. He can think it, he can speak it; but as far as putting it down on paper, he can't do that for shit. You are entitled to free occupational therapy for fine motor skills for young dwarfs, but your pediatrician has to refer you. I didn't know to ask."

When Jake was a few years old, Chris remarried. Soon his new wife, Donna, was pregnant. Like Leslie, Donna had assumed she was going to have an average child and was astonished when her newborn son was diagnosed with achondroplasia. Donna called Leslie to ask for advice, and Leslie was incensed. "It was like, 'You bitch. I've had to sue him for child support 'cause he's spending everything running around with you. Now you want me to make the road easy for you?'" But when Leslie actually saw the baby, Andy, she knew she had a role to play. "I started praying, 'This is the only brother that Jake is going to have, and I need to get past this.' And I did." Leslie took Donna under her wing, set her up with the doctor in Birmingham, and warned her about the orthopedic challenges that lay ahead. Leslie told me, "A year ago, Chris and Donna came to me and said, 'We're working on our will. Would you take Andy if something happened to the two of us? We would want you to have him.' I just cried. 'Oh, my God, yes. Yes, I would.'"

Leslie and Chris have very different takes on parenting. "Dad is the fear side," Jake told me. "Mom's like, 'Hell, yeah, you're gonna play T-ball; you're gonna play baseball; you're just like everybody else.'" Leslie said, "There's been a lot of clinging. 'Where you going, Mom?' 'I'm just going to the bathroom. In forty-five seconds I'm going to come out.' But he was almost having panic attacks. I said, 'Get out of the uterus! You were born! Go away!' But he needs someone going, 'It's okay, you can do it.'" Leslie described how she had traveled to a family event when Jake was twelve, and how everyone reprimanded her for letting him roam the hallways unsupervised. "I said, 'He's in seventh grade. You're not thinking what's age appropriate; you're thinking what's *size* appropriate.'"

Eventually, the typical problems of adolescence set in. "I don't look at myself as a little person until somebody brings it to my attention. Normally, people do," Jake said. Leslie explained, "Everybody loves Jake. He's very popular. 'Yeah, I'll go to the dance with you. We'll go as friends.' They all love him and Jake's the first one to get out and dance. Both of his counselors over the last two years said, 'I wish all kids had his self-esteem.' But I know that we're coming into that painful stage of wanting girlfriends."

Leslie decided to take Jake to an LPA convention when he was thirteen. "We didn't know a soul," she said. "He had planned, 'I'm gonna make all these friends; I'm gonna go to the dance; I'm gonna do this, that, and the other.' Now he was overwhelmed, and I was overwhelmed." Later Jake said to me, "In regular life, I use my stature to start conversations with people, to make friends. At that first conference, all I had was myself." Jake befriended only tall people that week, most of them siblings of dwarfs. "You're too mainstream!" Leslie told him. "Why don't you make some little friends?" But he wasn't ready yet. The next year was different. "He became a real teenager," Leslie said. "I sneaked into the dance and just sort of pasted myself to the wall. I saw, 'He's dancing! He's slow-dancing!'" Leslie also caught her son lying about his age to a much older girl; it can be hard to guess the age of short-statured people, and Jake is relatively tall. "I said, 'If I have to bust you myself, you're not eighteen,'" Leslie said. "But at the same time, I was so glad he could carry it off." Jake adores LPA, but it's important for Leslie that he's happy in his own world, as well. As Jake said to me, "It's not like it's the only thing about me."

The permanent question of cure versus acceptance that runs throughout this book had particular resonance for Leslie Parks. When I met her, she had recently undergone gastric bypass surgery. She had already lost thirty pounds and was aspiring to lose another hundred.

"Being fat was my cross to bear," she said. "Being short is Jake's cross to bear. I've had these terrible feelings of guilt that I'm abandoning him. How can I say to my child, 'You have to learn self-acceptance and be okay with who you are'—but yet, I'm not. It's not my agenda for him to be tall. But if the work on regulating that gene went to trials, I'd be right there. Feeling so bad about my body, I'm open to what could be done for him. But I don't want to put my issues onto him. Unfortunately, it's almost impossible to get both those messages across."

Although most dwarfs are plagued by public mockery and can face serious restrictions and health problems, the cliché that they are cheery children seems to hold. Recent work suggests that this is most probably a form of compensation to ease social situations rather than a trait biologically linked to their condition. Many LPs feel, however, that this view of them trivializes the difficulty of their lives. Initial emotional development appears to be reasonably positive; on measures of overall happiness, LPs fare rather well in childhood compared to the general population. Parents have a difficult time as their children start to ask why they are so different. Euphemizing the details can be as toxic as playing them up. In *Living with Difference*, the anthropologist Joan Ablon writes, "Overprotectiveness is a pitfall most parents see themselves falling prey to at one time or another." Dwarf children often complain of being infantilized. In his guide for parents of dwarfs, Richard Crandall, founder of the California-based Short Stature Foundation, recommends, "Don't give in to the temptation to use a stroller beyond the normal age of stroller riding. Yes, your child may have to take four steps for every one you take, and this may slow you down at the mall. But it is better to arrive one-half hour early and walk together with your child at his pace than to treat him like a baby in a stroller." The Restricted Growth Association (RGA), the British equivalent to LPA, summed up results from a 2007 survey by observing that those who were treated in a more normal fashion tended to become more self-confident, and in turn more accomplished as adults.

In adolescence, LPs start showing higher levels of depression, as well as lower levels of self-esteem, when compared with their average-height siblings. Levels of depression seem to be higher for LPs with average parents than for LPs with LP parents, which may imply that despite best efforts all around, parents who know firsthand the trials of being an LP may be able to respond with greater empathy or sensitivity to their child's experiences. More profoundly, it reflects the difference between growing up with a vertical identity and growing up with a horizontal one; dwarf children who grow up with adults built like them internalize a more self-affirming conception of *normal* than those who are surrounded by family members of average height and proportions. As teenagers reach their full height, the contrast between dwarfs and their peers is thrown into relief. At that point, many LPs who had been content to live in a world of average people begin to feel the acute need for contact with other LPs, for whom their appearance is not erotically aberrant. LPA and similar organizations can be a blessing, though they can, equally, be a trial; Ablon points out that attending LPA can traumatize people who have blamed all their problems on their dwarfism, and who must now come to terms with personal flaws.

Dwarfs are stared at more and more as they mature and cease to look simply younger than they actually are. One recent study observed that adults with achondroplasia have "lower self-esteem, less education, lower annual incomes, and are less likely to have a spouse." The income statistic bears witness to institutional discrimination against LPs; the study found that while three-quarters of the dwarfs' family members, presumably demographically similar to them in most regards, made more than $50,000 per year, less than a third of the dwarfs made that amount. The great majority of college-age LPA members attend college, but outside LPA, the numbers are probably much weaker. Michael Ain, who has achondroplasia and is now a pediatric orthopedic surgeon at Johns Hopkins Hospital, recalled his experience as a medical school applicant. "In the one field where you think people would be most understanding, they were the most bigoted. Doctors told me, 'You can't be a doctor. Don't even apply.' The first guy I interviewed with told me I couldn't hold the respect of my patients, because of my stature." The level of prejudice can be truly astonishing. Ruth Ricker, former president of LPA, took a tenant who rents space from her out to dinner, and the waiters kept addressing the tenant, asking, "What would *she* like to eat?" Ricker said, "*I'm* the one with the good job; *I'm* the one with the good education. *I* own the condo, she pays rent to *me*, and they're treating me as if I'm completely incapable."

Some dwarfs who are not members of LPA regard their nonmembership as a political stance. John Wolin, an LP sports writer at the *Miami Herald*, summed up his issues with LPA by saying, "When one is different, when what you are has the ability to determine who you are, there is an urge to resist." Another LP was quoted in *Newsday* saying, "Believe it or not, the hardest thing for a dwarf is to meet another dwarf for the first time. When you look into the mirror, you don't see a dwarf. You see what you want to see. But when you see another LP on the street, then you see the truth." Members of LPA often accuse such detractors of being self-loathers who have not come to terms with their dwarfism, and, indeed, Wolin describes being guided through an LPA conference by a younger woman who was a longtime member and said, "She was a lifetime of self-acceptance ahead of me."

The day Beverly Charles was born in 1973, the doctors told her mother, Janet, that her daughter was always going to be small. But Janet, who had little education and no previous experience of dwarfism, did not understand how small. When she relayed the news to her husband—a Vietnam vet permanently in a wheelchair—he replied, "Small or large, we'll love her just the same." In the months that followed, Janet brought Beverly to the pediatrician once a week to monitor her growth, but Beverly was a poor eater and her weight stayed relentlessly the same. "The doctor said we didn't need to worry unless she started losing weight, but that happened at about three months, and I was beside myself," Janet recalled. It later turned out that Beverly's nose was completely obstructed; she was unable to breathe and eat at the same time, so suckling was a constant challenge for her.

The doctors in Lancaster, Pennsylvania, where the Charleses live, referred her to specialists in Hershey. One of them recommended treatment at a clinic in Germany, and he said he would try to raise money to send Janet and Beverly there. "But I was afraid," Janet told me. "I thought they'd see how little my child had grown and take her away from me." Beverly's dwarfism is most likely the result of a pituitary shortage, since she lacks the dysmorphism characteristic of the dysplasias, but the doctors in Hershey said there was no more they could do. No one told them that Johns Hopkins, less than two hours away, was a center of excellence in dwarfism, nor that Beverly's form of dwarfism might well have responded to the timely use of injected growth hormone.

It soon became evident that Beverly had significant learning disabilities. Her mother accompanied her on the school bus every day so she wouldn't be alone. Elementary school was lonely; high school was horrible. "They teased me and teased me," Beverly told me. One boy bullied her relentlessly. "I don't believe in violence," Janet said. "But I told Beverly, 'Next time he bothers you, just punch him in the nose as hard as you can.'" The boy's parents visited Janet and asked, "Where is your daughter who gave our son a bloody nose?" Janet pointed at Beverly, three foot seven, sitting on the sofa. The teasing stopped.

After high school, Beverly continued to live at home, working first at a Salvation Army shop, then at a printing press. In 2001, when Beverly was twenty-seven, Janet saw a mention on TV of an organization called Little People of America. She had never heard of LPA or known that there existed any community of little people. The only other little people she and Beverly had ever encountered were an elderly couple who worked in a grocery store in downtown Lancaster. Janet called the head of the local LPA chapter, saying, "I have to talk to you about my daughter. Will you come have lunch with us at Friendly's?" This was the beginning of what Janet calls Beverly's "rebirth." "I wasn't lonely anymore," Beverly said. They attended local LPA chapter meetings, always together, and the following year went to their first national convention.

When I met the Charleses, Beverly was just a few days short of her thirtieth birthday and still lived at home. I was touched by her child-like affect: as we talked, Beverly sat curled in her mother's lap. Janet assured me that outside the workday, they were never apart. "I don't let her go anywhere alone," Janet said. "Look how Elizabeth Smart was abducted—I don't want to take any risks."

In New England in the late 1950s, dwarfism was considered shameful, and when Leslye Sneider's mother learned she had given birth to a dwarf, she had a nervous breakdown and spent three years in a psychiatric hospital. "My mother was thirty-eight," Leslye said. "She has a very fragile makeup to begin with, and she just could not accept it. So she never saw me; never held me. I was born and she plummeted." Leslye's father did not do much better. "When the doctors told him that I was going to be a dwarf, and my mother was shipped off to McLean, it was the last straw. So he moved back in with his parents, and I was raised all around the state of Maine, by my maternal grandmother and a couple of my aunts."

When Leslye's mother came home from the hospital, "she did her best with what she had," Leslye remembered. "But my mother never got to grips with my being a little person. When we would go out shopping, and somebody would make a comment or stare, my mother would say, 'Oh, God! Why do I have to deal with this?'" Leslye's father remained distant; her closest relationships were with her babysitters, mostly French Canadians who had migrated to Maine. "They were from really wonderful, loving French Catholic families. I used to go to church with them, even though my parents were Orthodox Jews. I hate to think what my life would have been like without them."

At eleven, Leslye had never met another little person. That year, her mother became aware of LPA and took Leslye to a regional conference. When Leslye was sixteen, she attended her first national conference. "We'd receive newsletters all the time from the national organization, and there'd always be pictures of these young adults having this wonderful time. They were always the same ones. Within LPA, there are people on the sidelines, and people who are involved quietly, and then there's the 'in' folks. Somehow, I fell in with that crowd." Leslye had been miserable in high school. "I think LPA was what high school would have been had I been average-size." Leslye pursued dating possibilities, but it was difficult to get to know someone well enough in a week for a long-term commitment. "Many of us end up in relationships that we would have maybe not ended up in had we had more time to think about it. I ended up with a wonderful person, but we were light-years apart in terms of interests," Leslye said.

For a long time, Leslye wasn't told what had pushed her mother over the edge and into those long hospitalizations, but at some level she always knew. Her understanding that she had caused her mother to go crazy weighed heavily on her. "As a result of that, I'm very interested in early child development and object relations theory," she said. "Probably also as a result of that, I have no children. I have a lot of unresolved anger instead."

Many of Leslye's closest friends from LPA were from California, so she applied to UCLA and was accepted. She found a therapist and went on antidepressant medication, which she has taken ever since. "It made me realize that for so long, I'd been operating not quite up to par. All of a sudden, whoa. Is this what normal feels like?"

Leslye was nearing fifty when we met and had made peace with her life. "I always come back to feeling that I wouldn't have wanted it different," she said. "I've had some amazing experiences as a result of being a dwarf." Leslye befriended Dustin Hoffman when he was working on a project that included a dwarf. She became romantically involved for nine years with Paul Steven Miller and got to know many of the people in the first Clinton administration. "I was exposed to another life," she said. "Paul was really instrumental in my going back to school." When we met, Leslye was running Albuquerque's Protection and Advocacy System, an important civil rights position within local government. "I sometimes wonder which has had a bigger effect on my life—my dwarfism or my depression and all the other depression around me," Leslye said. "The dwarfism was easier to overcome than the sadness."

Since she and Paul split up, Leslye has been romantically involved with Bruce Johnson, an artist who is also a dwarf. "I wouldn't be with Bruce if I weren't little," she said. "How can I regret being an LP when it led me here?" Bruce's family had been the opposite of Leslye's—open and accepting. When he was born, the doctor's advice to his parents was "Take him home and treat him like any other baby," and that is what they did. Despite this, he admitted, "Sometimes when I watch another dwarf, I feel like we're pretending to be adults. It's a life's project coming to grips with, really, how you look." Bruce is significantly disabled. "If I could do it over, I'd want not to be a dwarf. It's been too difficult. I've had many more health complications and surgeries than Leslye, and I'm worn out. She's the best thing about being a dwarf for me, but I'd have loved her anyway."

Many dwarfs have agitated against dwarf-tossing, a "sport" in which a dwarf is put into a harness and a person of average height, often drunk, hurls him as far as possible onto a mattress or other padded surface. So far, laws against dwarf-tossing exist only in France, Florida, Michigan, New York, and the city of Springfield, Illinois. Both the Florida and French bans have survived legal challenges. The New York ban has required occasional enforcement since it was enacted in 1990. In March 2002, police issued citations to participants in a dwarf-tossing competition at a Long Island tavern; a February 2008 "dwarf bowling" meet planned by a Staten Island bar owner was canceled after a local newspaper reported that this variant on dwarf-tossing (in which a dwarf on a skateboard is rolled down an alley to knock over a set of pins) was also illegal. A 2005 SEC investigation into excessive and inappropriate gifts to securities traders found dwarf-tossing among the festivities featured at a lavish, $160,000 stag party financed by Fidelity Investments for one of its star performers.

That such objectification still takes place today is shocking, but the practice seems particularly demonic given the skeletal problems that dwarfs commonly suffer, which can be exacerbated by impact. Dwarfs in dwarf-tossing competitions are often in difficult circumstances and can make a desirable nightly income from participating; some have protested that they should be allowed to earn their living however they want to and have pointed out that pro football also leads to damage to the body. Others believe that tolerating the practice injures not only those dwarfs who allow themselves to be tossed but also the rest of the dwarf community, creating a public perception of dwarfs as subhuman, and thereby perpetuating a climate of ridicule. Opponents of dwarf-tossing contend that the tossing of some dwarfs implies the tossability of all dwarfs and point out that woman-tossing or even dog-tossing would not be allowed.

Some within LPA argue that it's also humiliating for a dwarf to play an elf in the *Radio City Christmas Spectacular*. For many dwarfs, however, Radio City and similar venues are easy money, and dwarf actors point out that with few exceptions—most notably Peter Dinklage, who starred in *The Station Agent* and *Death at a Funeral* and won an Emmy for his role on the HBO series *Game of Thrones*—they are seldom hired for mainstream roles. One such actor said to me, "There's an old Spanish proverb: I don't care if people laugh at me as long as I keep warm." The LP actor Mark Povinelli said, "When I first get a script, I flip through to see where I'm going to bite someone's ankle or punch someone in the nethers or fight the tall guy." In 2009, LPA banned the recruiters for Radio City from the conference. "My daughter did Radio City and she loved it," one parent of a dwarf said. "She's a pediatric oncology nurse. At no point in her life did she think she had to be an elf to make a living." Joe Stramondo, chair of LPA's advocacy committee and a doctoral candidate in bioethics at Michigan State University, said, "When people with dwarfism are portrayed negatively, they are usually portrayed *by* people with dwarfism. This complicates the issue."

Stereotypes are persistent. On the NBC series *Celebrity Apprentice*, running back Herschel Walker was asked to make a viral ad about All detergent. "What about if we use little people and let them wash themselves in All detergent in the bathtub, and you hang them out to dry?" he said. Joan Rivers replied, "We can hang them out on my terrace." Jimmy Korpai, father of a dwarf, argued that these celebrities were encouraging people to point and laugh at his daughter—a common occurrence for dwarfs, and one they find exhausting. Korpai said, "Imagine if I said what Herschel Walker did about a black person"; he filed a complaint with the FCC.

When the skeletons of what appeared to be a race of dwarfs were found on the island of Flores in Indonesia, Alexander Chancellor wrote in the *Guardian* about the shockingly dismissive tone that was used to describe them. "The reports in the media began by describing these ancient dwarfs as belonging to a 'human' species, but then proceeded to distance them from us modern humans as comprehensively as they could, referring to them as 'things' and 'creatures,' despite the fact that they apparently knew how to make stone implements, could light fires without matches, and organised hunting expeditions. These are achievements beyond the capacity of most people you see at the checkout counter." Today, the Aka, Efé, and Mbuti of central Africa generally grow no taller than four feet ten inches. The word *Pygmies*, often used to describe them, has been designated an insult, but that may be the least of their problems: African Pygmies are often worked to death as slaves, have been the targets of attempted genocide, and have even been cannibalized by aggressors seeking "magical powers."

A 2009 article by Lynn Harris on *Salon* about eliminating the word *midget* attracted extraordinary responses from what is in general an educated and refined readership. One wrote, "Deal with it. Grow a thick skin. Oh wait, that's dwarves with the thick skin, isn't it? I guess midgets have thin skin. Too bad. Sucks to be you." Another said, "I wholly support any person or group of people informing me how they *prefer* to be referred to. However when those people tell me I *MUST* use only approved words my response is to tell them to kiss my ass."

Anna Adelson was born at Beth Israel Hospital in New York in 1974, and when her parents, Betty and Saul, first saw her, they were filled with joy. Betty was able to hold Anna for a few minutes before she was taken away to be cleaned up. The next morning and afternoon, Betty couldn't understand why the nurses wouldn't bring the baby to her. She kept asking, and a nurse finally brought Anna in, but seemed to do so grudgingly. That evening, after Saul had gone home to be with their four-year-old son, David, the obstetrician came in to talk to Betty. "He said to me, 'I think there's a fifty-fifty chance she has Hurler's syndrome, which results in retardation and early death,'" Betty recalled. "Then he left, and alone, I wept through the night."

The next day, just before Betty and Saul went home with Anna, the hospital neonatologist told them that Anna had "something called achondroplasia." He asked, "Are there any short people in your family?" Betty said, "Our grandparents came from Eastern Europe—we've got lots of short relatives." The neonatologist said, "Anybody with sort of a large head?" Betty said, "Me. I wear big hats." The neonatologist looked grim and said, "She will be short." Betty asked, "How short?" He answered, "Under five feet." He did not give any further information about the potential complications and neglected to mention that most women with achondroplasia are closer to four feet than five. Betty went to the medical library at NYU and read. She wrote to a second cousin who was a pediatric endocrinologist, who replied, "There are these organizations, the Human Growth Foundation and LPA. Many people in these groups have good lives. Your daughter will probably be less disturbed by this than you."

When Betty and Saul went for walks in their Brooklyn neighborhood, Betty would feel tears welling up every time she noticed a disabled person. "You fight your battles in the world, but you close your door and there's comfort," she said. "Now there was no door to close. I wanted to meet another family with a dwarf child, and I wanted to meet a happy adult. I kept in constant motion until I found them. Then I began to breathe again." When Anna was four months old, Betty and her family found their way to Johns Hopkins and to Dr. Steven Kopits. "He would pick up the baby and exclaim in his Hungarian accent, 'What a beautiful baby you have!' He told you everything you needed to know, and what you should look out for. He would write a long letter to your pediatrician at home and make an appointment for you to come back for a follow-up. When we went to Johns Hopkins, I knew the medical part could be dealt with." When Kopits died in 2002, one mother of a diastrophic dwarf wrote, "I cried more at his funeral than I did for my own father." The mother of an achondroplastic dwarf wrote, "Dr. Steven Kopits has to be the greatest man that I have met in my life."

In the 1970s, the Moore Clinic at Johns Hopkins had an annual symposium for LPs and their families. Betty went to her first one when Anna was ten months old. "There were all these people in the pool—many with deformities I'd never seen before—adults and children of every shape and size," she recalled. "In bathing suits! I would look anxiously, and stare, and embarrassed by my staring, I'd close my eyes. Then I'd look some more. Until it sunk in. By the end of the day they had names and they were people whom I knew. Thirty years later, a lot of them are my friends. I am deeper and better for it."

Betty Adelson's activist career began shortly thereafter. When Anna was five, a social worker at the Moore Clinic invited some parents of dwarf children to weekend seminars to prepare them to mentor other parents. Betty and Saul went and soon joined a couple of dozen other families who lived on the East Coast to form a group called Parents of Dwarf Children. Betty and three other mothers wrote to the hospitals and clinics in their areas so that as soon as a dwarf was born, they could invite the families to their homes and offer support. "We'd help with information and medical referrals—but perhaps most importantly, offered them relationships with others who'd traveled a similar path," Betty said.

Betty was able to help many parents, but some resisted what she had to offer. She described speaking with a woman who had just learned in her seventh month that she was carrying a dwarf. "I said, 'Look. It's not a garden of roses, but there's a great deal that's fine.' She didn't call. So I called her the next day. She said, 'We decided to have an abortion.'" Betty explained that some people in LPA were longing to adopt a dwarf child. The woman said, "It's a second marriage for both my husband and me. We're both very beautiful people. We like to ski; we've had troubles before; now our life with each other seems to be perfect. We don't want to deal with something like this." After Betty described this encounter to me, I asked, "Would you have considered an abortion if you had known early in your pregnancy that you were carrying a dwarf?" Her eyes filled with tears. "I hope not," she said. "I really hope not."

Betty was by then familiar with the impediments that parents of dwarf children encounter. But her Anna was lively and sociable. "I went to the local Montessori school," Betty said. "She did everything she was supposed to. She held the gerbil and played with it; she separated from her mother; she drew." The school said they couldn't accept Anna because she might fall on the stairs. After a protracted exchange of letters, the director backed down; by then, however, the Adelsons had decided to enroll her at a nursery school attached to their local synagogue, where the director had said at an orientation meeting, "If your child has any special needs, please let us know, so that we can help!" Anna prospered there.

Anna has been a vegetarian since the age of twelve; she's marched for reproductive rights, and she traveled to Pennsylvania to ring doorbells for Kerry and for Obama. In junior high, when her school didn't want her to go on a ski trip, Anna organized friends to picket the headmaster's office. Remembering the incident, Betty laughed. "So that's my Anna. How could I not be glad of her?"

During adolescence, despite overall high achievement, Anna found it hard to concentrate on her studies. She then announced that she was gay. "She came out by calling me from college," Betty said. "The next day I wrote her a long letter. I told her that what was most important to me was not whether she loved a man or a woman, but that she loved and was loved well—that she experience passion, and the wonderful surprise of finding that someone feels about you as strongly as you do about them, lucky and full-hearted. I knew how important my reaction would be to her and was glad that I could tell her honestly that I believed that same-sex love was just as true and legitimate as love between men and women." Anna's father and brother were equally affirming.

Anna's acceptance of her dwarfism took longer than her grappling with her sexuality. She had stopped going to LPA events in early adolescence, feeling that the world of her average-size family and friends was sufficient, but despite some hesitancy, she returned when she was twenty-five. She soon became president of her local chapter and organized a "Difference within Difference" workshop at national conferences for those short-statured individuals who are set apart from the majority of LPs by race, religion, disability, or gender preference. At the 2004 conference in San Francisco, she initiated the first workshop and reception for LGBT attendees, a breakthrough for LPA, which has many conservative members. She has hosted this group at most of the conferences since.

When Anna was still a teenager, Betty decided to write two books— one for a popular audience and one for an academic audience—as a way of paying tribute to and celebrating the dwarfs she had come to know and love. Anna said the project was fine as long as it wasn't a book about her. Several years later, after noticing the piles of folders all over her mother's study, Anna surprised her mother with the present of a file cabinet tied up with a red ribbon, and a note that said, *Get yourself organized, Mom!* By the time the final drafts were being written, Anna was almost thirty and she acceded to her mother's request to write about her. She is mentioned with great tact and love in the afterword of Betty's invaluable *The Lives of Dwarfs*.

That book and Betty's numerous academic articles have helped to organize dwarf history, identifying historical figures who may have been dwarfs and looking at evidence for the role of dwarfs from dynastic Egypt and ancient Greece up to the present. Much of this history is a narrative of suffering and abuse. Unusual bodies have been described throughout history as reflections of sin, as omens from the gods, as the basis for laughter or charity or punishment. Leviticus stipulates that only men with perfect bodies could become priests, a sign of the emphasis placed on the normative form from ancient times. "I looked for precedents for what I was doing," Betty said. "Most of the earlier books had titles like *Freaks* or *Victorian Grotesque* or *Human Oddities*. I thought, there have been dwarfs for as long as there have been people, and what were they like? What were their lives? Until LPA was formed, few dwarfs knew each other except for the ones in entertainment, or, in earlier times, the ones sometimes gathered by kings and queens at court."

For many years, Betty took a leadership role on LPA's advocacy committee. In 2009, impressed by the enthusiasm of the new generation of dwarfs, she decided that it was time for her to pass the torch, and at the LPA conference banquet, the Executive Board conferred upon her the group's 2009 Distinguished Service Award. Anna, who was by then living happily with her girlfriend a few blocks away from Betty and Saul, made a moving presentation.

"She loves and is loved well, as I had hoped," Betty said. "If Anna had been average, would my world have been narrower? Yes. I recognize the gift that's been given. If someone had said to me, 'Betty, how'd you like to give birth to a lesbian dwarf?' I wouldn't have checked that box. But she is Anna, cornerstone of the family. I wish the road had not been so steep for her, but I'm so glad she managed to climb it with grace."

Martha Undercoffer, an LP, wrote in an e-mail to the Parents of Little People and Dwarfism Yahoo! newsgroups: "I have developed a safe and easy system to use. It is a business card. On the front: 'Yes, I noticed your behavior towards me.' (For some reason the public seems to think we don't notice their treatment of us.) On the back: 'I realize that you probably mean no harm by your actions and/or comments; however they did cause harm and were not appreciated. If you would like to learn more about individuals with dwarfism please visit http:// www.lpaonline.org.'" One LP wrote online, "I've bought myself a little MP3 player and I listen to music so I can't hear what anybody says about me, and I'm sort of in my own little world and I can do what I want." The Internet has been invaluable for LPs. "The current generation of young dwarfs have an ability to interact that would have been my greatest fantasy," one older dwarf told me.

Harry Wieder was among the most vital activists in the dwarf community. He was physically disabled and walked on crutches; he was gay; he was nearly deaf; he was often incontinent; and he was the only child of Holocaust survivors. He could be overbearing and exhausting, and his activism was always tinged with anger, but he was also full of relentless life. At fifty-seven, he was hit by a New York taxi and killed. When I described his litany of challenges, people would make laughing references to Job. Yet, he had decided that his disadvantages would be his crown of honor, and he achieved a wild gallantry in his very openness. I can remember his saying that most gay dwarfs at LPA wouldn't identify themselves because of stigma, but that he didn't believe in the opinions of others. He added, "Gay people are called fairies, and if I'm a fairy and a dwarf, I'm a magical children's story of my own. Where Judy Garland fits in is anyone's guess."

Harry complained that most dwarfs were so set on the politics of inclusion that they refused to acknowledge they were disabled—"and if they won't acknowledge that they're disabled, do you think they're going to acknowledge that they're gay?" Harry had learned from his parents' experience during the war that ignoring your identity did not, in fact, afford you protection. He achieved a great dignity through that belief. At his funeral, his eighty-seven-year-old mother, Charlotte Wieder, was taken aback by the great outpouring of grief, and by the many public figures—including the Speaker of the New York City Council, a state senator, and numerous other dignitaries—who attended. Charlotte told a journalist that she could not take credit for his accomplishments; indeed, she had often tried to contain his excesses—partly out of concern for his health, and partly out of a distaste for all that stigma. "In spite of my very strong feeling to protect him," she said, "I could not hold back his good."

The relentless visibility of dwarfs is amplified by their iconic place in fairy tales as supernatural beings, a burden not shared with any other disability or special-needs group. An essay in the *New York Times* has spoken of the "cruel folklore" in which dwarfs are "ugly Rumpel-stiltskins." Joan Ablon wrote, "Dwarfs carry with them the historical and cultural baggage of special and even magical status. Persons in the general population thus exhibit great curiosity about dwarfs, stare at them often unbelievingly, and in some cases even try to photograph them in a chance encounter." This strange awe of dwarfs can be as unsettling to them as disparagement; it is, above all, an emphasis on difference. Anne Lamott, a British dwarf, said that she thought about being little about as much as she thought about having teeth—that it was simply part of who she was and not a focus of consciousness. But she had to acknowledge that it was the focus for most other people who met her.

Taylor van Putten has spondylometaphyseal dysplasia, Kozlowski type, a disease that affects slightly fewer than one in a million people. As is characteristic of the condition, he is relatively tall for a dwarf, at four feet six inches, and does not have the distinctive facial structure shared by people with achondroplasia. Taylor was born at twenty-one inches, eight pounds nine ounces—figures that did not suggest dwarfism. Until his second birthday, he was in the 90th percentile for height. Nonetheless, he had a litany of woes. When Taylor's mother, Tracey, would move his legs to change his diapers, he would scream in pain, and when he started to walk at about a year old, he was clearly experiencing intense discomfort. He always wanted to be picked up and carried. "Something just wasn't right," Taylor's father, Carlton, said. But neither endocrinologists nor orthopedists could find anything wrong, until, when Taylor was two and a half, his parents brought him to be evaluated by a geneticist at Stanford University, who referred the family to a dwarfism specialist at UCLA, where Taylor received his first real diagnosis.

When I met Taylor at sixteen, he had had four limb-straightening surgeries, he suffered severe back problems, his rib cage was press-ing on his lungs, and doctors had recommended that both his hips be replaced. "I've been in casts for a total of forty weeks, so that's almost a year of my life," he said. He described the gradual revelation that he would be in some measure of pain as long as he lived.

Carlton van Putten's mother was one of eleven children in a Chero-kee family in North Carolina. Her family chose not to join the reser-vation and were rejected by the Cherokee people. Because they were a family of color, they were ostracized by the white community. They grew up in a house with a dirt floor, which her mother would disin-fect with urine. In college, she met Carlton's father, a black man from the Caribbean. Right after their marriage, Carlton's father took a job in California. As they traveled across the country, many hotels would not allow them to stay in the same room because he was black and she wasn't. "My parents' story prepared me to be father to Taylor," Carlton said. "My mom walks into this hotel, and to the hotel guy, she's white. But in her mind, she's black. Sometimes there's a big discrepancy between how we see ourselves, and how the world sees us."

When they received Taylor's diagnosis, the van Puttens grappled with how to normalize his life. "We were filling our heads with positive-mental-attitude books," Tracey said. "My main concern was to build his self-esteem. We probably went a little overboard, because he's borderline cocky. Wherever he went, he would make friends that would really look out for him, like bodyguards. I'd imagined him being stuffed into lockers or garbage cans. It never materialized." Taylor laughed when he heard that. "The only time I was put in a locker was when I got paid ten dollars to do it," he said, "and it was worth it."

Carlton's work took them east again, and Taylor attended elementary school in the Boston area. He was, in his own words, "school-famous"; his brother Alex told me, "Taylor was a king." Taylor was strikingly good-looking, and his proportions were not noticeably dwarflike until he was ten or so. "That's when the staring began," he said. "It's the same natural curiosity that makes someone slow down to look at a traffic accident and see if anyone died. Is there any blood? We just have to glance." The van Putten family moved near San Diego just as Taylor was finishing fifth grade. The transition to middle school wasn't so bad, but then, when the family bought a place a few miles away, in Poway, they had to switch school districts again. "That was my angry, socially retarded period," Taylor said. "Everybody's made their friends by seventh grade. I was just, like, 'Why should I even try *again*?' That's when I started looking in the mirror and saying, 'I really don't like that. Legs: short, stocky, curved, out of proportion. Everything: arms, hands, toenails.'"

After one of his surgeries, Taylor was prescribed strong painkillers. "I realized that I was getting high and I enjoyed it," he said. "I smoked a lot of weed, took a lot of ecstasy, acid, mushrooms." Tracey was upset but not surprised. "He was angry at us and he decided he was going to punish us," she said.

The spiritual has always been emphasized in Taylor's life; Carlton is a devout Christian who sings in his church every week and has released an album of inspirational music under the name Carlton David. Carlton said, "I believe there's a God. I believe God doesn't make junk. It's unfortunate that Taylor carries such a heavy burden. But I don't believe you are given the heavy burdens unless you can handle them." Taylor explained, "I've been going to church since I was born, still do. In the middle of my angry period, I recognized that I don't fit with Christianity. I don't think there could be any kind of puppet master that could be both a hundred percent love and power and still allow civilizations to rot and fester, and individuals to be born with this kind of pain." Over time, though, his anger began to resolve. "You can't solve what I have, but you can come to accept it. I quit drugs, and after that, in eleventh grade, last year, surrounded by all the coolest people I could ever want, I enrolled in four AP classes."

Taylor later said that he always managed to get what he really wanted. "But it requires a step or two more than most people need. It's pretty painful physically, most intensely in my legs and ankles. I use weights and swim because I care about being healthy and how I look. Going to hike with friends, my back is breaking, my hips are about to fall off. I have to take a break. 'Taylor, dude, what's up? Let's go.' I'm dying. I don't think most people realize. I have to purposely laugh if somebody makes a midget joke. I don't find it funny, but they're not trying to hurt my feelings, and I'm not going to go on a jihad against Comedy Central. I did the class-clown thing in elementary school, the quiet-in-the-corner thing in middle school, and now I try to balance it. Other people have no idea what it's like to be me. But then, I have no concept of what it's like to be normal."

Taylor used to want to be alone for the rest of his life, but now he wants to find someone. As he reimagines his future, his grandfather is his inspiration. "Look at what he faced and stood up to," Taylor said. "So my enlightenment—I kind of like to think of it as my enlightenment—is that I can have dwarfism be a factor in everything I do, but not hate it, not have it limit more than what it limits."

Dwarfs have created dating sites such as datealittle.com, littlepeople meet.com, lpdate.org, and shortpassions.com. "Much of the dwarf population missed the years the basic ground rules were learned," one LP said. "We're naïve. We never leaned over in a movie and gently let a hand fall onto a breast. First, we likely don't have the date. Second, our arms aren't long enough." The challenges may extend beyond those posed by social norms. John Wolin elaborated, "Many of us have trouble coupling. Our limbs may be too short or too rigid to bend around our partner's. Because of the spinal-cord damage many of us suffer, we may have trouble with erections or may find orgasm a guest with a mind of its own." Dwarfs must decide how they feel about being involved with average people (APs) rather than LPs. On the LPA website, one woman complained about the difficulty of not being able to kiss an AP or look into his eyes while they were having sex. Harry Wieder said, "For people of equal height, what is mysterious is the lower body, which you have to reach for—that's what's sexualized. For me, it's the opposite. I look at people below the waist all day every day, and my idea of intimacy is the special occasion of looking someone in the face. The feeling when having sex with APs that I needed to relate to the bottom half of the body, and not relate so much to the top half, was problematic."

For many little people, the question of whether to partner with another little person or one of average height is political. Some have contended that dwarfs who marry people of average height fail to accept themselves as dwarfs and reduce the available pool of spouses for LPs who seek similar-size partners. Rates of depression seem to be slightly higher among little people in mixed-height marriages. Although almost all dwarfs in LPA who married used to choose other LPs, an increasing number are marrying APs; and while mixed marriages used to be stigmatized at LPA, they are now much more widely accepted. Outside LPA, however, most dwarfs who marry still marry other dwarfs.

Wolin wrote that before he met his wife, "I feared—and *fear* doesn't really do justice to the brutal emotion I felt—that I would never be married." In researching this chapter, I became friends with the mother of an attractive, short-statured young woman. One day, I suggested that I knew someone who might like to be fixed up with her. The mother, a person of emotional restraint, became tearful. "My daughter is over thirty," she said, "and in all these years, you are the first person who has ever made such a suggestion. My son, who is average, everyone on the planet wanted to introduce him to their daughter or friend. But no one ever thought of my daughter as a sexual being."

Childbearing presents other challenges. The pelvic opening in many short-statured women is not large enough to allow an infant to pass, so virtually all deliveries are performed by cesarean section—which requires anesthesia, a risk for LPs. Carrying a child may be physically stressful to dwarf parents. As part of the overarching theme of dwarfs' having no privacy at all, dwarf parents are frequently interrogated about their procreative and birthing experiences. "As usual, the most bizarre comments come from the adults," one such mother described online. "IS THIS BABY YOURS? This is a question I would never think to ask of anyone with a baby but one I am asked several times a week." Adelson wrote, "For each LP couple that decides to have a child, the decision is an affirmation of their own lives, and a leap of faith about the lives they may expect for their children." Indeed, for this very reason, many little people, some with biological children and some without, adopt dwarf children given up for adoption by their average-size parents.

Yet many average-size parents do not give up such children, even when strongly advised to do so. When Clinton Brown III was born, his father, Clinton Sr., remembered, "I could see right away his arms were straight out, his legs were straight out, and his body was small. I almost fainted." A curtain blocked the view for Clinton's mother, Cheryl, but it did not block her hearing; the baby didn't cry, and none of the doctors or nurses said anything. When Cheryl cried out, "What's wrong?" one of the doctors replied in a hushed voice, "We have a problem here." Although Cheryl wanted to see and hold her baby, he was whisked away. Later, a doctor explained that her son was terribly deformed and likely to die, the result of diastrophic dysplasia. Such profoundly affected children are usually institutionalized, he said, and offered to handle Clinton's placement without her involvement, since it was sometimes easier for parents to give up a child they'd never seen. Cheryl was indignant. "That's my baby," she said. "I want to see my baby." The doctors were vague about prognosis; only a few thousand people in the world were known to have diastrophic dwarfism. "The information they had on it was two paragraphs," Cheryl recalled. "Two paragraphs on what the rest of our lives were going to be."

Clinton was in an incubator when Cheryl finally saw him, and she was allowed only to touch his toe, but when she did, his eyes opened and she saw that they were blue and beautiful. She also saw everything she would come to know as signposts of diastrophic dwarfism: the unjointed hitchhiker thumb that springs from the bottom of the palm, the flat nose, the cauliflower ears, and the cleft palate. He had scoliosis and clubfeet, and his legs were bunched up under him like airplane landing gear. His head was gigantic. "Some kids have a mild version of this, but he had every symptom possible," Cheryl said. "I think of it as the deluxe package." Clinton Sr. said, "We came home without him. I remember pulling into our street, looking at Cheryl, and it was just empty, you know?" Clinton Sr. went back to work as an engineer for a cable TV company, and Cheryl to her job at a call center. Clinton had his first surgery when he was two weeks old to repair an umbilical hernia. When the Browns brought him home a month later, he was so tiny that Clinton Sr. could hold him in one hand.

Once they had him at home, Cheryl tried to treat him as she would have treated any baby. "When I was young, I thought life went on a schedule. You go to high school; you find a job; you get married. When you have a child like Clinton, it's 'What happened to all that stuff I always counted on?'" When Clinton was eleven months old, Cheryl found Steven Kopits. "From that moment on," Cheryl said, "he controlled everything that happened to Clinton. Without him, Clinton wouldn't have walked." Clinton Sr. said, "You went into his office depressed, and you came out enlightened and with new hope." Cheryl said, "They weren't patients to him; they were his children. Nobody else ever comes up to that level. And no one will, because there'll never again be an angel like that on this earth."

Kopits was famous for developing long-term surgical programs for his patients; rather than perform a single operation in the unlikely hope of correcting all of a patient's problems, he would perform one that promised to reap benefits down the road and facilitate subsequent operations. In the end, he performed twenty-nine surgeries on Clinton Brown III. "I had asked my pediatrician what Clinton was going to look like," Cheryl said. "So he gave me a book on people in the circus. I went to Dr. Kopits. He said, 'Let me tell you something. That's gonna be a handsome young man.'" The long waits in Kopits's waiting room were notorious; a routine visit often became an all-day affair. "No question in my mind I would wait ten hours," Cheryl said. "He would say, 'I'm sorry, I have to see this one.' We knew if our child needed him that he would say the same to another family."

When Clinton was almost three, after six months of constant surgery, Dr. Kopits assigned him to one of his staff physiotherapists, and Clinton began to walk. Kopits worked on Clinton's clubfeet, his tibiae, his fibulae, his knees, his hips. Clinton had eleven back surgeries, cleft palate surgery, surgery to correct an inguinal hernia. He spent six months in a body cast, flat on his back, with a circle of metal with four pins fixed in his skull to immobilize his neck and spine. "I lived in the hospital with him for one month, two months, whatever it took for him to be rehabbed," Cheryl said. The call center where Cheryl worked gave her extra time off. The Browns needed two parental insurance policies for Clinton's surgical program; even then, the uncovered expenses were catastrophic. "You've heard of the Six Million Dollar Man?" Cheryl said to me, pointing at her son. "This is the Million Dollar Dwarf you're talking to."

Since diastrophic dwarfism is a recessive genetic trait, any other child Cheryl and Clinton Sr. might produce would have a one-in-four chance of inheriting it, so they decided not to have more children. "In the beginning, you live in six-month increments," Clinton Sr. said. "With our kind of kid, you don't look long range." Cheryl said, "The hardest thing was going out in public, that first negative comment or stare. I always had it in the back of my head that it should be a learning experience for everybody that encountered Clinton and me. We made it a little joke: 'Okay, look at that one, Mom. They're staring at me!' Then Clinton would just do a nice little wave and smile." Clinton Sr. said, "We were in a store once, and this little kid was hovering. So Clinton, who was twelve, ran around the next aisle and, as the kid came by, jumped in front of him and spooked him. The kid freaked out and broke down crying. I said to Clinton, 'That wasn't the right thing to do.' He says, 'But it felt *so* good, Dad.' And I said, 'Yeah, okay. That one's for you.'"

Clinton said, "When I was a kid, I was bitter towards the fact that I was little. Angry that I didn't have the same opportunities as everybody else. You either face the war, or you falter. It was everyone else's problem, that they didn't know how to handle it, and it was my problem that I didn't know how to teach them how." Clinton Sr. added, "Once he said, 'If I was average-size, I'd be great, wouldn't I?' He was eleven, in that hospital room. So now I had to leave the room 'cause I was crying, and I felt so helpless. When I came back, he said, 'That's okay, Dad. I have the answer.'"

"I was such a sports fan, and I wanted to be an athlete," Clinton said. "We used to play hockey in the street, but everybody started getting huge, and running me over, so I couldn't play. It's just a big piece of childhood that I missed out on." During the long periods of immobility and surgery, Clinton was homeschooled. It was his primary distraction, and he worked hard. "I figured I had nothing else to do, so I got ahead of my class on most things. I decided to do really well academically, 'cause I just had to be the best at *something*." When he graduated, Clinton was accepted at Hofstra—the first member of his family to enroll in college. He decided to major in banking and finance, volunteered to be a peer counselor, and helped run orientation week for new students. "I wish all life was college. I'm in the big, macho fraternity; I'm friends with all the girls on campus. I've dated here and there. I have fun."

With his unjointed fingers, Clinton still needed help buttoning a shirt, but he became increasingly independent in other regards, and he got a driver's license and a specially fitted car. "I remember when he told us he was driving," Clinton Sr. said. "A friend of mine tells me he saw Clinton on the Long Island Expressway! I go, 'You saw *Clinton* in a *van*, driving on the *LIE*?!' So I found his schedule, and I snuck down to school. I didn't want him to know that I was there, so I parked in the back. I'm thinking the teacher's drunk or he's a saint. Because they had a makeshift seat and steering wheel for Clinton. He drove right out. I didn't say a word because—well, I couldn't talk. I was amazed."

"When he first went to Hofstra, he met this group of guys that he's been hanging out with for the last four years," Cheryl said. "They would go out to bars and stuff. I said, 'Well, how do you get on that bar stool?' He goes, 'They lift me up, Ma.' I said to him, 'Your body is three feet tall; your friends are six feet tall. If you drink two beers, that's them drinking four beers.' I was terrified about his drinking and driving. I went past a bar and I saw his car parked there—it's very easy to recognize with all those fittings. I didn't think I could march in there like I wanted, but I left him three messages and sat home by the phone waiting for him to call. So I told this to the mother of a child who had gone to school with Clinton. She said to me, 'You're so lucky that he is at a bar.' I thought, 'Okay, if you'd told me when he was born that my worry would be that he'd go out driving after drinking with his college buddies, I'd have been overjoyed.'"

Clinton has learned to set boundaries with a public that takes his size as a waiver of all social rules. "I used to become really upset," he said. "I would cry. Now I just go right up to the person. My mom's always, 'Be nice, be nice.' But sometimes you can't be nice. I walked by this guy's table, and he goes to his friend, 'Oh, my God, lookit that midget.' I said, 'Don't *ever* do that,' and I knocked his beer into his lap. You can't yell at kids. They don't know any better. So I go up to the parent: 'Listen. Why don't you teach your kid some manners and have some class about you?' And it's no better in classy places." I remembered this conversation when Clinton and I had lunch a year later in a nice restaurant in midtown Manhattan, a place he had chosen near his office. As we walked to our table, every person we passed stopped talking and stared, except a few who looked out of the corners of their eyes. If I had shown up with a ring-tailed lemur or with Madonna, there wouldn't have been more focused attention. It wasn't hostile, but it was certainly not relaxing—and it was completely different from the experience I had, for example, pushing a multiply disabled child down a pier in San Diego. Benign pity can wear thin, but it's still easier than astonished fascination.

At eighteen, Clinton found his first summer job in finance; five days a week, he made the solo commute by scooter, train, and subway, an hour and a half each way, to the Manhattan offices of Merrill Lynch. "I want to have everything I can in my arsenal of education. My parents worry about me too much, and my way for them to let that go is for me to be financially and physically independent. I was in the hospital so much, so my parents were my best friends. Now I have no boundaries; I have no inhibitions; I want to do so much."

The great question in Clinton's life is mobility. For longer distances, he rides his scooter. He is in pain whenever he walks any distance—much sooner than Taylor van Putten, for example. "My hips and knees and joints are real bad. There's a lack of cartilage between the bones. The cold makes it worse." Despite this, I was impressed at how gracefully Clinton could swing his body around. He could weave his unbending fingers around the handle of a fork or a knife. "I figured out a lot by myself. I used to pick up pizza or a sandwich and put it on the top of my hand. Writing, I use two fingers. If I could change one thing, I would love to walk like a normal person. But I'm dancing all night; I'm doing everything." In fact, when I first met Clinton at LPA, he was dancing; he stayed long after I'd gone to bed. The next day, he was hobbled with pain but also on cloud nine, and he teased me about being the only person of average height on the dance floor: "You stuck out like a little person."

The summer job Clinton had at Merrill Lynch was in their legal department, filling out forms, and he was determined to secure a promotion. After he graduated, he was hired by Mutual of America Capital Management Corporation, where he prepared income statements and reports for technical analysts, obtained real-time stock quotes, and helped brokers identify trends in certain Internet stocks. During his time there, he had a bad experience with inadequate access on the subway. He obtained permission to address the board of the New York Metropolitan Transportation Authority at their next public meeting. Arriving at the midtown conference room, I found a mob of his friends and relatives who had turned out to support him. "I am standing in front of you as a representative of all disabled citizens of New York," Clinton said, poised and confident. "My story is of a violation of the Americans with Disabilities Act, a violation of civil rights, and a blatantly dangerous situation presented to all wheelchair-bound citizens who use the MTA's subways and trains. The purpose of this speech is to illustrate what is going on out there in your transportation system, let you know what it means to the people it is affecting, and drill down to a resolution. I am asking you to be my teammates in a quest for equality, and to work to fix this issue." At breakfast afterward, Cheryl confided in me that she could never, ever have done such a thing.

Cheryl said she thinks often about whether she would have wanted things to go another way. "When he was born, one of the nurses started crying and said, 'Oh, I feel so terrible. Why you? You're such nice people.' I said, 'Why not us?' Would I trade it? I would never trade it now." Clinton Sr. agreed, "I have to work with new, young guys on the job, and when they're lazy or say they can't do certain things, I don't tell 'em it's my son, but I mention that I know someone that it takes half an hour to get dressed in the morning, just to get outside and breathe fresh air. 'You guys have two hands, two arms, and a head. You've got every God-given tool you could have, and you're wasting it.'" He paused. "And you know what? I used to waste it, too. I learned that lesson from Clinton myself."

Both Cheryl and Clinton Sr. are somewhat in awe of their son—his courage, his academic and professional achievements, his big heart. "I don't think we did anything to make him into him," Cheryl said. "What did I do? I loved him. That's all. The other day these people, much higher up than us socially, much more educated, called me up and said they couldn't handle this. They were in Texas politics and thought the stigma would be harmful to them, and they gave their baby up for adoption. That's just what they were going to do, and it's the opposite of what I was going to do right from the beginning. The other day Clinton came home, and he goes, 'Ma, I saw a blind man today with a stick, in Manhattan. There were people rushing back and forth, and he was all alone. I just felt like crying, I felt so sorry for him, so I offered to bring him to where he needed to go.' Clinton just always had that light in him, and we were lucky enough to be the first to see it there."

There are many infrequent kinds of short stature for which genes have yet to be found, but for the primary forms the genes are now located, and many turn out to be closely related. Achondroplasia, for example, is in most cases based on a dominant mutation on fibroblast growth factor receptor 3 (FGFR3). A different mutation of FGFR3 causes hypochondroplasia, a milder form of dwarfism; another mutation in the same spot causes thanatophoric dysplasia, which is a lethal skeletal dysplasia. Because achondroplasia is dominant, if two achondroplastic dwarfs conceive a child, they have a 50 percent chance of having a dwarf child, a 25 percent chance of having a full-height child, and a 25 percent chance of having a double-dominant child; double-dominant children die in infancy. Numerous other skeletal dysplasias lead to death at or shortly after birth. Finding the gene for achondroplasia offered a deeper understanding of the mechanisms of the condition and allowed prenatal diagnosis of double dominants, giving parents the option to terminate pregnancies that were certain to end in tragedy. The process also allows people to select against healthy achondroplastic children.

The gene was identified by John Wasmuth in 1994; since then, genes have been found for SED, pseudoachondroplasia, and diastrophic dwarfism. Wasmuth was concerned about potential uses of his discovery. At the press conference to announce it, he was accompanied by officers of LPA. Leslye Sneider, who was on the podium with Wasmuth that day, recalled that he "understood the implications, and he wanted the world to see us—happy, thriving, well—standing there on the stage with him at the same moment that they learned that news." He opined that the test should be used only to identify double dominants. Because dwarfism is infrequent, it is not screened for in standard genetic testing. It is, however, possible to request a review for achondroplasia, either preimplantation for people using IVF or in amniocentesis or CVS (chorionic villus sampling). In many cases, the condition will be picked up in ultrasound later in the pregnancy. A quarter of respondents in a recent survey would choose abortion if they found out they were expecting a dwarf. Even more strikingly, more than 50 percent of medical professionals surveyed would make that choice.

The question of testing has since been hotly debated among little people, with some couples expressing the desire to screen out average-size fetuses and ensure a dwarf child. Dr. Darshak Sanghavi at the University of Massachusetts supports the right of dwarfs to make this choice, writing, "Many parents share a touching faith that having children similar to them will strengthen family and social bonds." As chairs of the LPA Advocacy Committee, Betty Adelson and Joe Stramondo wrote in a letter to the *New York Times* that physicians who refuse such requests "are actively practicing coercive eugenics." One LP couple described going in for preimplantation genetic testing solely with the purpose of avoiding a double dominant, only to be told by multiple clinics that they supported "healthy" pregnancies and would implant only nondwarf embryos. Carol Gibson, who has achondroplasia, as does her husband, said, "You cannot tell me that I cannot have a child who's going to look like me. It's just unbelievably presumptuous." Many little people, worn out by all this, choose to adopt short-statured children, who are routinely rejected by their birth families, especially in the developing world.

Ginny Foos and her husband have two children with achondroplasia, one biological and one adopted. "My nightmare is that my biological son's going to say to me, 'It's your fault,'" Ginny said. "My husband and I couldn't say that to our parents because it was a fluke for them. But he could very well say, 'You knew the genetics, and you went ahead and made me a dwarf.'" When Ginny and her husband decided to adopt a dwarf child, it was because, she said, "I think dwarfism shapes the soul as well as the body. There's an immediate bond between two LPs, be it same-sex friends, lifelong partners, or any other variant. When I met my husband, there was something that we had in common that was more than a physical attribute; it was a life experience. My husband grew up in Beirut—during the civil war!—while I grew up in Boston, so our histories are very different. Yet, simply because we're dwarfs, we're similar."

Many dwarfs live full, rich lives, and often dwarfism seems more of an inconvenience than a disability. On the other hand, the medical challenges can be daunting. Observers of trends in prenatal diagnosis have expressed concern that wealthier parents will opt for expensive testing and that poorer ones will be consigned to bring dwarfs into the world, a troubling demographic shift. Achondroplastic disability activist Tom Shakespeare addressed these issues in a BBC radio interview, saying, "I'm ambivalent about impairment. I don't think it's a tragedy—that's the traditional view. But neither do I think that it's irrelevant—which is, in a way, the radical disability view. I think it's a predicament." He identified problems with both seeking and avoiding such pregnancies. The advantage to knowing early that you are going to bear a dwarf is that you can adjust to the idea and either finish the grieving in advance if grief is part of what you feel, or terminate the pregnancy. The advantage to not knowing is that you don't carry the burden of choice, which can be terrifying and overwhelming for expectant parents.

LPA has responded to the issue of genetic testing with a statement that reads in part, "We as short-statured individuals are productive members of society who must inform the world that, though we face challenges, most of them are environmental (as with people with other disabilities), and we value the opportunity to contribute a unique perspective to the diversity of our society. For LPA members there is a common feeling of self-acceptance, pride, community and culture." Ericka Peasley, a dwarf and a genetic counselor who has worked on the LPA position papers, emphasized the hope that genetic information will not be used to eliminate human variety. "Giving families the opportunity to make early decisions about lethal conditions, rather than having to go through an entire pregnancy for a baby that we know is essentially going to die, is great," she said. "But we feel that people with achondroplasia or other viable skeletal dysplasias are able to have healthy, productive lives, and while we don't question anyone's right to terminate a pregnancy, we want to create an awareness that this may not be a good reason to do so." For now, genetic testing is usually employed for diagnosis, allowing families to know what to expect and what to do. A child with Morquio syndrome, for example, will need to be monitored for degeneration of eyesight and hearing; such children sometimes have cervical instabilities, and fusing the upper vertebrae can prevent significant damage to the spinal cord. Some researchers are studying how to turn off the gene that is prematurely activated in achondroplasia and stops bones from growing. Their work would not eliminate the gene, but would alter its activity and could eradicate the phenotype.

Writing in the *New York Times*, Virginia Heffernan described dwarfism "as a cherished inheritance—a trait, like deafness, that is simultaneously a stigma, a handicap, a source of pride and a prerequisite for membership in a complex, charismatic and highly exclusive culture." Ericka Peasley said, "I didn't feel when I was growing up that I didn't want to be this way; I just couldn't understand why people needed to see me the way they did, and I kept on being hurt by that. As I've grown older, I've had neck issues that cause me chronic pain. We have information now that life span is decreased for people with achondroplasia. You try to figure out if adding this unique LP perspective to the world outweighs the real and true disability and pain that can go along with having a condition like this. Some of us might say if you take away the surgeries and the pain, but leave the shortness behind, we'd go for that—but it's all or nothing."

Monique Duras, a Frenchwoman living in New York, went with her Russian partner, Oleg Prigov, for a fifth-month sonogram, expecting everything to be fine, and assuming it would take five minutes. "We were waiting to find out if it was a boy or a girl, and we asked what was happening, and they said, 'You'll see in the doctor's report,'" Monique recalled. "When we finally saw the doctor, he mentioned that there was a disproportion between our child's limbs and the size of his head. But it was not a big warning." Monique's obstetrician suggested an additional ultrasound at a specialist lab, where the doctor confirmed that the fetus had a big head, but observed that Oleg, too, had a big head and encouraged them to go enjoy their summer holiday.

By the time they returned, Monique was in her seventh month. Her gynecologist suggested another ultrasound, which was performed by yet another doctor. That doctor referred them to a genetic counselor, who said there was a risk of skeletal dysplasia. "I found it a little bit cold, and too distant, the fact that she used the medical term," Monique said. "I suddenly felt a heavy load of worries on top of me." The genetic counselor said, "The bad news is that there is a problem, and the good news is that we know exactly what it is. Achondroplasia is the most common form of dwarfism, and it has fewer complications than other dwarfing conditions do. But there is a risk of hydrocephalus, cervicomedullary compression, spinal stenosis, restrictive and obstructive lung disease, otitis media, and tibial bowing." Monique almost fainted. "I didn't want to face this," she explained to me. "I was close to eight months at this point. I thought, 'I hate all these studies. I wish we didn't know anything.' I also thought, 'I wish we'd known sooner.' My ob-gyn didn't want to give any kind of advice, which meant she didn't give me any support. She told me to look up Little People of America. That was all she had to say about it."

Monique talked to doctors she knew in France. "They all said that you don't take on problems or issues or differences you can avoid. They all thought that we should abort." The genetic counselor in New York referred them to a psychologist with a background in genetics. "The psychologist was saying that either way, there's always going to be a moment when you regret your decision. That had a very strong negative impact on me. I thought, 'I don't want to make a decision I'm going to regret.' It's very simple and very basic."

Of the possibility of aborting, Oleg said, "For my family, it was out of the question. They converted from Russian Orthodox to Catholicism and they believe deeply. My mother sent me a fax from Moscow asking us to rethink it. But I didn't tell Monique; it was not for my mother to decide this." Monique said, "Oleg doesn't want to know what people are thinking. I like to know everybody's opinion. I go all over the place, and then I choose. But that's the way I do everything. So we finally decided to abort. In France you can abort at any stage of the pregnancy. I needed to be away from New York and closer to my family. They were against my having this child, and I wanted their support."

So Oleg and Monique went to France and visited a clinic in Monique's hometown, Lyon. They secured an appointment with the senior doctor who reviews all the complex prenatal genetic cases for east-central France. "She has vast experience, and the people she sees almost always abort," Monique said. "We sat down and started to speak to her, and this assistant comes in with all the paperwork to start the process. I thought, 'What am I doing here?' I was shaking. The doctor said, 'If you don't want to do it, don't do it.' I was terrified. Oleg said, 'If you keep this baby, it's going to be okay.' I needed to go to the point of almost doing it, to just see what I wanted to do. And suddenly it was clear that I would have this baby." Monique told me this story with tears running down her face, and at the end of it she began to smile. "It was suddenly very clear," she repeated.

Monique and Oleg headed home to New York. "Then it was a race against time to learn everything we could about achondroplasia." They met with Lisa Hedley, who was a friend of a friend, and her daughter, Rose. "Now that we were going into it deliberately, it wasn't frightening, even when we learned difficult things about the orthopedics and other complications," Monique said. "The psychologist was wrong; I never regretted it. I wished I didn't have the choice at that time. But now I'm so happy that I did—that it was my positive decision to have this baby, not just something that happened to me."

When I first met Monique and Oleg, Anatole was four. "We wanted to give Anatole a brother or a sister who is dwarf as well," she said. "We can't do that; his condition is happenstance. Somehow, we have to ensure that he doesn't feel alone, like the strange one. We'll organize some interaction with LPA, and if there's a connection, we'll continue." Monique is an ardent patriot for French medicine, but equally so for an American social environment. She and Oleg take Anatole to Michael Ain, the dwarf orthopedist at Johns Hopkins. "I think it's good for Anatole to see him as a role model," Monique said. She also likes that Ain's patients are almost exclusively little people, and that he is well versed in the surgeries they might require. She seeks opportunities for Anatole to mix with both disabled and nondisabled peers.

"I'm into cultivating difference," Monique said. "So that's what I will communicate to him. 'Okay, you're different. How can you benefit from that?' I'm starting to love Anatole's proportions, the way he's very compact. He said, 'I want to be tall and strong, like Spider-Man.' I said, 'Anatole, you're not going to be tall like Spider-Man and Mommy and Daddy. But you can be very strong and very small.' He said, 'I don't want to be different!' I thought, 'Okay, so now it begins.'" In much of Europe, valued identities are still collective and conforming: Catholic, French, white. Difference is avoided as much as possible; it's striking that limb-lengthening has been particularly popular in southern Europe. "I was looking at the literature from an excellent school, and they mention at the end, 'We welcome children with disabilities,'" Monique said. "You'd never see that in a French school. New York is definitely the best place to live and now is the best time, too. I wouldn't want to be dealing with this in my grandparents' generation."

Monique's relationship with family in France has remained layered. "Aesthetics are so much more important there," Monique said. "My mother still thinks in terms of 'poor Anatole,' and I know she loves him, but my whole life is so strange to her. She respects my choices, but she cannot understand them, and so the family I've created has pulled me away from the one that created me."

I talked with Anatole about life as an LP a few years later, when he was almost seven. By that time, he had a younger brother who had just grown taller than him. I wondered whether he was having a hard time with that. He thought about it, then said, "No—I'm glad he'll be able to reach things for me." But he showed me with considerable pride that he had the upper bunk in the room they shared and explained how much further ahead he was at school. "Anatole figures out how to do things, and he's pretty independent," Monique said. "The kids are more nice than you would think, though there is teasing." She laughed. "But he's a nice person, and, you see, he brings out niceness in other people, so maybe his life won't be too hard after all."

For dwarfs, function follows form. The shape of their bodies determines their physical capabilities. Dwarfs decry two issues: the problem of how they look to other people, and the problem of how the world is not set up for people of their dimensions. Nowhere are the two more confused than in the debate around extended limb-lengthening, or ELL. Treatment commences at the growth-spurt age, usually around eight or nine. The child is sedated, and metal screws are inserted into the lower leg bones at one-and-a-half-inch intervals, so that they stick out through the flesh of the leg. Each leg is then broken in about ten places. Because there is no longer a functional bone in the lower leg, a large brace is affixed to the outside of the leg and attached to the projecting screws. In a month or so, the bone begins to heal—the fragments, in effect, reaching toward one another. When they are nearly connected, the brace is adjusted to pull them apart again and stretch out the leg, maintaining the breaks in the bone. This is repeated regularly for about two years, with the bone kept perpetually broken, perpetually healing, the ligaments and muscles and nerves all constantly stretched. When the lower legs have fully healed, the process is repeated on the lower arms, then the upper legs, then the upper arms. Limb-lengthening surgery means spending the end of childhood and most of adolescence in considerable pain, the fiber of the body shattered. It means spending those years with enormous metal braces covering your body and metal screws projecting from your arms and legs. But it does work. It can add fourteen inches to a person's height—making the difference between being three foot eleven and being five foot one, which can be the difference between being seen as freakish and being seen as normal. The intervention runs between $80,000 and $130,000.

ELL is both a cosmetic and a functional intervention, though many who have chosen it avoid discussing the cosmetic piece. Skeptics contend that ELL is complicated, painful, and has many troubling side effects, and that the procedure is unwarranted given that little people can function quite well in society without it. Like those who militate against cochlear implants, ELL opponents object to the surgery's stigmatizing implication that their condition needs to be corrected.

It is often arduous to distinguish the political position from the medical one. People who have had ELL tend to speak well of it, and studies show that the procedure boosts self-esteem. "Looking up all the time is hard," one LP who had had ELL explained. "Not just hard on the neck, but hard on the spirit." The response has an aura of the self-fulfilling prophecy about it. People who have opted for the procedure presumably needed a boost in self-esteem before they began and would find it difficult to belittle a process to which they had devoted many years of life. Nonetheless, people who have experienced complications are among the procedure's most vehement opponents.

The tension around this issue within LPA was reified in its decision to invite Dror Paley, the leading surgeon for ELL in the United States, to the 2002 national convention, and then to uninvite him when members objected. Gillian Mueller, who underwent limb-lengthening as a child and who has become an outspoken proponent for it, has said, "The most important thing any new parent can do is accept their child and teach him to accept himself. No child should grow up believing he has a condition that his parents are going to 'fix' when he's older." However, she states that the procedure can help people to live without the disadvantages of short stature. She is thrilled that she had it. One LPA executive has said, "We need to wait to an age where you can have a real discussion with the individual who's going to have it done, and have it really, truly be their decision. We'd recommend that they meet with a psychologist, that there be a very open and extended dialogue about it before a decision is reached." But like the arguments for delaying cochlear implants, this one is deeply flawed. This process works only during the time of natural growth: late childhood and early adolescence. It's later than the period of language acquisition, but much earlier than full maturity.

Some doctors have claimed that limb-lengthening may help to prevent the spinal and other orthopedic problems associated with dwarfism, and this is a topic of urgent debate. Dan Kennedy, who has not pursued ELL for his daughter, candidly writes, "A dwarf gains considerable benefit from limb lengthening simply because his upper arms are made longer. 'What is the most important thing you can think of other than being able to wipe yourself?'" Every case of ELL is different, so the risks and rewards cannot be generalized, and because ELL is fairly new, the long-term outcome is unclear. The rate of complications—ranging from mild and transient to severe and permanent—is higher for ELL than for any other orthopedic surgery. The target population for the procedure faces many orthopedic problems even without surgery, which further muddies the swampy waters.

Some children seem to move easily toward a celebration of their difference. For others, difference is almost insufferable. Likewise, some parents can tolerate having a child who is different, and some can't. At nine, I'd have given anything not to be gay and would have gone through a procedure like this had there been one for my condition; now that I'm forty-eight, I'm glad that I didn't compromise my body. The trick is knowing which prejudices of a nine-year-old are nine-year-old prejudices that will change with time, and which ones are true readings of the heart that will last into adulthood. The attitude of parents frequently shapes the mind-set of children, and surgeons must try to penetrate that film so they can clearly see the interests of the person on whom such a procedure would be performed. "My daughter hated being a dwarf," one mother said to me. "She would point to the dwarfs we introduced into the house, lovely people, and say, 'I'd rather be dead than be like those people. Those people are freaks. I hate them.' She didn't want to be a part of their world. We tried so hard to make it nice for her." The daughter insisted on and is glad to have had the procedure. Writing about elective surgery on children, medical ethicist Arthur Frank observes in the *Hastings Center Report*, "The possibility of fixing renders inescapable the question of whether or not to fix."

Surgery originated as a process of excision; the augmentative model of surgery is a modern intervention. Though descriptions of orthopedic procedures date back to ancient Greece, the use of such procedures in a recognizable way came from the eighteenth-century French physician Nicholas Andry. Michel Foucault famously used an image from Andry's *Orthopaedia: or, the Art of Correcting and Preventing Deformities in Children* (1743) to open his own *Discipline and Punish*, where it was intended as a model of persecution. The image shows, simply, a bent tree tied to a straight stake. Foucault would have regarded ELL as a form of torture brought about by a society that insists on conformity. Yet, while it may be a high calling to make the world more welcoming of dwarfs, it is easier in any given case to make dwarfs fit the world. The question is whether dwarfs who accommodate the world facilitate the continuance of social injustice, whether there is a moral imperative for them to refuse such procedures to keep the pressure on for the world to accommodate other dwarfs. This may be a great deal to demand of an LP who is trying to live a life of some personal satisfaction.

While human growth hormone (HGH) does not confer greater height on people with skeletal dysplasias, its use has long been approved for people with pituitary dwarfism. In recent years, HGH has increasingly been used aesthetically for young people in the general population who are not tall and wish to be so, or whose parents seek to protect them from the social disadvantages of shortness. Like ELL, such hormone therapy must be undertaken during the growth years, usually in the early teens. Whether it is effective in people with adequately functioning pituitary systems is debatable, but some studies indicate that it can add up to four inches of additional height. The FDA recently approved Humatrope for "unexplained shortness"—that is, for men with a final height under five foot three and for women with a final height of under four foot eleven. Of course, it is impossible to know what someone's final height will be until he reaches it, at which point it's too late for Humatrope, so this whole process is based on statistics and guesswork. The cost of treating people with Humatrope through those critical growth years is between $12,000 and $40,000. Some wealthy parents have sought HGH for children of average height because they believe that making their children really tall is a favor to them.

The advantages of height have been broadly established. Tall people garner more votes in elections, and recent studies show that men over six feet earn on average a salary 12 percent higher than shorter men. Tall people are icons of beauty in films, in advertisements, and on fashion runways. Proportionality has been praised as the essence of beauty since ancient times. Vitruvius, writing in the time of Christ, said that the Greek sculptors had understood this perfectly and had expressed a universal ideal: "For the human body is so designed by nature that the face, from the chin to the top of the forehead and the lowest roots of the hair, is a tenth part of the whole height," he begins, proposing a very undwarflike body type. Our language is full of praising expressions such as *stand tall and proud*, and of disparaging terms such as *fall short of, comes up short, paltry*, and *puny*. The use of *dwarf* as a verb—a disparaging one in most instances—does not help matters. William Safire once wrote in the *New York Times* of how Pluto had been reclassified as "a new category called dwarf planet, and all textbooks in all languages are ordered to refer to it with that adjectival derogation." The journalist John Richardson, who has investigated the lives of LPs, wrote, "Dwarfs will never assimilate. As long as movie stars have full lips and oval faces, as long as women dream of 'tall, dark, and handsome,' dwarfs are the difference that stays different."

Kiki Peck was born with Kniest dysplasia, a random mutation that leads to a rare variant of dwarfism characterized by lack of type II collagen, which occurs in cartilage and in the clear gel that fills the eyeball. It results not only in diminutive stature, but also in enlarged joints, a flat nose, severe myopia, hearing loss, and distortions of all other areas of the body where cartilage plays an important role. Kiki has "Swiss cheese cartilage," which results in arthritis-like symptoms and joint stiffness, a barrel-shaped trunk, large hands and wide feet, hips described by one of her doctors as "like melting ice," and bones that are unnaturally thin, with ends that are unnaturally wide. Her illness was not observed at birth, but when her mother, Crissy Trapani, brought her to the doctor for her one-month visit, she had lost weight. The doctor told Crissy to stop breast-feeding and use bottles so she could keep a rigorous account of Kiki's feeding habits. The weeks that followed were frightening; Kiki was diagnosed with "failure to thrive," and her life hung in the balance. She was taken to the University of Michigan Hospital, within driving distance of the Pecks' house, and even though none of her doctors had ever seen a case of Kniest—at the time, there were only two hundred known cases worldwide—they arrived at a correct diagnosis from X-ray images of her unusually shaped bones.

The months that followed were occupied with visits to geneticists and other specialists. "I just wanted to talk to somebody who knew what it would be like for her," Crissy said. "There was nobody." Kiki was found to be severely myopic and was fitted for spectacles at two months. "I went to four different places to find glasses that would fit her tiny face," Crissy recalled. "The woman was adjusting the glasses and Kiki was screaming, screaming, screaming. All of a sudden she stopped and she just stared. You could tell from the look on her face that she was like, 'I can see!'" Because cartilage is a part of the inner structure of the ear, Kiki also had significant hearing deficits, and she was fitted for hearing aids at six months. "That was a whole other adventure," Crissy said. "Try keeping hearing aids on a six-month-old. We lost a lot, and they're not cheap things to lose." By that time, however, Kiki had started to grow, and while she didn't grow as much as an unaffected child, she was keeping pace for her condition.

Crissy's parents had been upset by the diagnosis. "When I told my dad, my mom said he went right out to the golfing range and just slammed a whole basketful of balls. Then he came inside and started researching, and he found a Kniest group in Minnesota." The whole family flew out to meet them. "I remember preparing myself for the shock of meeting an adult who was affected," Crissy said. "Then I met her. She was a great person, super-friendly and super-accommodating, with all kinds of answers. So it was really good for me and my parents."

Building a life was extremely challenging, and Crissy found an outlet in poetry; the form entails control and was a good one to pursue in a powerless situation. "We didn't know if Kiki would survive," Crissy said. "We didn't know what kind of surgeries she might need. We didn't know what would happen to her spine; disks are cartilage. She didn't begin to walk until she was two, and even when she was just learning to stand up, she'd look arthritic, like she's eighty." Crissy said people with Kniest are also sure of themselves and strong-willed. "And quite intelligent," she added, "perhaps because they have had to do problem-solving since day one. Even in preschool, Kiki's teachers said that she always knows what she wants, and she's always had a great self-image."

When I met Kiki, she was in fifth grade, almost eleven. She had crutches next to her in the living room where we sat to talk and had recently been fitted with a brace to keep her back straight. Crissy and I were in jeans, but Kiki was wearing a party dress and big boots for our meeting; something in her was incorrigibly festive. "When I wake up, I'm stiff," she said. "I can't make a fist, and when I go to school, my fingers aren't ready to write yet." She uses a tricycle to get around the building. She announced to me that she was planning to be a veterinarian and a rock star when she grew up. Crissy said, "I'm sure she will one day, if that's what she really wants to do." Kiki had asked for a pet Chihuahua because she thought they could be little together. Money being tight, she got a hamster.

While I was at the house, Kiki and her older brother, Josh, had an argument because Kiki had kicked something and it had hit Josh. "I needed to move it," she said. "Why couldn't you just lean over and do it?" he asked. Kiki said, "I don't want to, because then it would be hard to get up." Josh was righteously indignant, but Kiki had a faraway look I have come to recognize in disabled children who don't know to what extent they are exploiting their difference for their own benefit. "Sometimes my brother thinks I have too much attention, and I try to tell him that it's not my fault," she said. "Yeah, it is," Josh said. "Sometimes, we actually say we hate each other," Kiki said to me pointedly. She paused and crossed her arms, then said very definitively, "And the truth is that we really love each other."

Crissy divorced Kiki's father, Caleb, when Kiki was in second grade. "Her father thought that she needed less medical care than I thought she needed," Crissy said. "When she had her surgeries, Caleb didn't come to the hospital; I think he was scared. For the last ten years, I've been just barely above water, gasping for air. All my vacation time was spent at University of Michigan Hospital." Crissy described the relentless rounds: the orthopedist four to six times a year, the ophthalmologist one or two times a year, the audiologist and otolaryngologist each two times a year at least, the rheumatologist regularly. Kiki has constant physical therapy, and Crissy does stretching exercises with her daily. "So many decisions," Crissy said. "She's in pain and replacing her hips might help, but if we replace them too soon, that could disrupt other growth, so when do we want to do it? Because it's so rare, there isn't much information, and that's the worst part, really." Crissy sighed. "I used to run marathons, and someone told me once that if you smile the whole way, you won't feel the pain. It worked. So that's what I do with this, too."

Mothering Kiki has been nearly revelatory for Crissy. "I grew up painfully shy. I was a teenager who worried about whether I was a few pounds overweight, or if my hair and makeup were right. Then when she came into my life, it was just like, 'How can I say I have to be a certain way, when I know she'll never be that certain way?' Why was I ever obsessed about that? Even when we've had our tantrums and I'm at the edge, I realize her strength. I was always really shy and self-conscious about the way I looked or I didn't feel so good about myself. Here I have this child who is the epitome of self-esteem under the most extreme circumstances. It's just a source of wonder to me." Crissy later wrote, "I think of the word *brave*, how I have to say it as a mantra, one syllable, one beat. She is more *brave* than I."

A few years after Crissy and Caleb divorced, and a few months after Kiki had major leg surgery, Crissy was diagnosed with breast cancer, requiring surgery, chemotherapy, and radiation. "There was a point where Kiki and I were joking with each other about who goes to see doctors more," Crissy said. "Having had Kiki for so long made the cancer easier. Because I'm like, 'This is just another thing to deal with and overcome. Just keep moving.' I didn't hide it from the kids. Josh was more frightened by it. Kiki was just head-on, like she's always been. Her response was 'My mom is always taking me to the doctor and now I'm taking my mom.' When I went through my lumpectomy and I was lying on the couch recovering, she put a wet towel on my head and cut up oranges and fed them to me."

When Kiki learned that her mother needed to shave her head before starting chemo, she offered to do it for her. When they were finished, Kiki announced that she would shave her own head, too. Crissy tried to stop her, but she was absolutely adamant. "My mom got so involved with my surgery," she said. "I hope it didn't give her cancer. Since I've spent so much time feeling different, I know how hard it is. So I wanted my mother to have someone else and not be different all by herself."

IV

Down Syndrome

Anyone involved in any way with disability has come across "Welcome to Holland," a modern fable written by Emily Perl Kingsley in 1987. In fact, any such person has come across it repeatedly: several hundred people have forwarded it to me since I started writing this book. Google shows more than five thousand postings of it, in connection with everything from leukemia to cranial abnormalities. Dear Abby runs it every October. It is standard issue from doctors to parents of disabled newborns. It has been set to music as a folk song and as a cantata. It serves as a theme for conferences and has been published in one of the *Chicken Soup for the Soul* books. People have even named their disabled children after it: Holland Abigail, for example. It is as iconic to disability as "How do I love thee?" is to romance. Many told me that it gave them the hope and strength to be good parents; others told me that it was too rosy and set up false expectations; and yet others said that it didn't adequately acknowledge the special joy of special-needs children. Here is the piece in its entirety:

> I am often asked to describe the experience of raising a child with a disability—to try to help people who have not shared that unique experience to understand it, to imagine how it would feel. It's like this....
>
> When you're going to have a baby, it's like planning a fabulous vacation trip—to Italy. You buy a bunch of guidebooks and make your wonderful plans. The Colosseum. The Michelangelo *David*. The gondolas in Venice. You may learn some handy phrases in Italian. It's all very exciting.
>
> After months of eager anticipation, the day finally arrives. You pack your bags and off you go. Several hours later, the plane lands. The stewardess comes in and says, "Welcome to Holland."
>
> "Holland?!?" you say. "What do you mean Holland?? I signed up for

169

Italy! I'm supposed to be in Italy. All my life I've dreamed of going to Italy."

But there's been a change in the flight plan. They've landed in Holland and there you must stay.

The important thing is they haven't taken you to a horrible, disgusting, filthy place full of pestilence, famine, and disease. It's just a different place.

So you must go out and buy new guidebooks. And you must learn a whole new language. And you will meet a whole new group of people you would never have met.

It's just a different place. It's slower paced than Italy, less flashy than Italy. But after you've been there for a while and you catch your breath, you look around . . . and you begin to notice that Holland has windmills . . . and Holland has tulips. Holland even has Rembrandts.

But everyone you know is busy coming and going from Italy . . . and they're all bragging about what a wonderful time they had there. And for the rest of your life, you will say, "Yes, that's where I was supposed to go. That's what I had planned."

And the pain of that will never, ever, ever, ever go away . . . because the loss of that dream is a very, very significant loss.

But . . . if you spend the rest of your life mourning the fact that you didn't get to Italy, you may never be free to enjoy the very special, the very lovely things . . . about Holland.

Seven to eight million Americans have intellectual disabilities; one out of ten American families is directly affected by mental retardation. Down syndrome, the result of a triplication of the twenty-first chromosome, is the most common form of intellectual disability, occurring in about one of every eight hundred births in the United States, for a total American population of more than four hundred thousand people. Far more such pregnancies are created; more than 40 percent of fetuses with DS miscarry or are stillborn. In addition to mental retardation, Down syndrome may entail heart defects (occurring in about 40 percent of cases), loose joints, thyroid disorders, a malformed digestive tract, leukemia, early-onset Alzheimer's symptoms (in at least a quarter of cases, a far higher proportion for those who live past sixty), celiac disease, shortness, obesity, hearing and vision problems, infertility, immune deficiencies, epilepsy, a small mouth, and a protruding tongue. Poor muscle tone affects the development of mobility, coordination, and, because of low tone in the mouth, speech. None of these features, except for slowed mental development, occurs in all cases of DS. People with DS also show unusually low rates of most cancers and are not subject to hardening of the arteries. People with DS have smaller brains, with reductions in most areas and fewer neurons in the cortex. They also have reduced synaptic density, and delay of myelination, the developmental process through which nerves are sheathed. They are at increased risk for depression, psychosis, disruptive-behavior disorders, anxiety, and autism. Down syndrome appears to have existed in all human populations across the span of human history; it has been found in chimpanzees and gorillas, as well.

The original and most reliable form of prenatal testing for DS is amniocentesis. The physician uses a needle to withdraw an ounce or so of amniotic fluid, in which some fetal cells are adrift; these cells are then analyzed for various conditions. Some people wish to avoid amnio because it carries a risk of miscarriage and because it seems intrusive for the fetus. CVS can be performed earlier than amnio but carries a greater risk of miscarriage. The "triple screen," done in the second trimester, tests the mother's blood for proteins and hormones associated with DS. Introduced in 1988, it identifies about two-thirds to three-quarters of cases. A quadruple screening, which looks for another hormone, brings this success rate up to four-fifths.

Ultrasound has been used to look for birth defects since the 1970s, and as imaging technologies and our ability to interpret the scans become more sophisticated, this is an increasingly reliable way to diagnose DS. Early in pregnancy, about the same time as CVS, an ultrasound test, nuchal translucency, measures the fluid behind the fetus's neck, which is increased in DS and other anomalies. Later in pregnancy, 3-D ultrasound can provide more precise information. New noninvasive blood tests may replace these techniques if they prove similarly accurate; one detects placental messenger RNA in the mother's bloodstream, and another measures bloodstream fragments of chromosome 21. No technique can establish the severity of prospective impairments, mental or physical.

At the time Emily Perl Kingsley and her husband, Charles, were expecting, they decided to forgo amniocentesis because the risk of injuring the fetus seemed too great. "And if I had had amnio," Emily said, "I would have terminated, and I would have missed out on what has been not only the most difficult but also the most enriching experience of my life." Jason Kingsley was born in 1974, in Westchester County, north of New York City. The doctor told Charles that such a child belonged in an institution and discouraged the Kingsleys from seeing the baby. He said that "this mongoloid" would never learn to speak, think, walk, or talk. Emily was kept tranquilized and given pills to stop lactation, on the assumption that she would not take the baby home. "They said he'd never be able to distinguish us from other adults," Emily recalled. "He would never be creative; he would never have an imagination. I was collecting a first edition of Lewis Carroll and putting aside all this Gilbert and Sullivan stuff that I love; I had boxes of things that I was going to do with this kid, all of it sophisticated and terrific. I turn on the television. All of a sudden, there's nobody who looks like me. Everybody is so perfect! I had vanished. I cried for five days nonstop."

This was soon after the exposé of horrific conditions at Willowbrook, and Emily and Charles couldn't bear the idea of institutionalization. But it was also a moment in the 1970s when nurture arguments held ascendancy; people sought to bring about their children's remission from various grave conditions through insight and lavish kindness. A social worker at the hospital where Jason was born mentioned that a new, experimental program called *early intervention* might help kids with DS to learn some basic skills. "We had to give it a try," Emily said. "If it turned out to be heartbreaking and miserable, we could institutionalize him based on our own experience, not on hearsay." So Emily and Charles brought Jason home, and when he was ten days old, they went to the Mental Retardation Institute. "I stood in the parking lot, with my ten-day-old baby in my arms, and I couldn't make my feet walk through a door that had that name on it," Emily recalled. "I was paralyzed. Charles pulled up in his car, saw me there, grabbed me by the elbow, and dragged me into the building."

The doctor at the institute said almost the opposite of what they had been told in the birthing room: that they had to start with stimulation of every kind, especially engagement of Jason's senses, because no one knew what might be possible for a child who received enough positive input. Charles and Emily ripped apart the elegant, pastel baby's room they had created, painting it blinding red with stenciled green and purple flowers. Emily persuaded the local supermarket to give her the giant lacy snowflakes they had used as Christmas decorations, and those went up, too. They hung things from the ceiling on springs, so they were always moving and bobbing. "You could get nauseated just walking in there," Emily said. They put in a radio and a record player so there was music all the time. They talked to Jason day and night. They moved his limbs through stretches and exercises to improve his muscle tone. For six months, Emily would cry herself to sleep. "I almost drowned him in the tears I shed over him," she recalled. "I had this fantasy, that I would develop a very fine tweezers and go in and pick out every extra chromosome of every cell in his body."

One day when he was four months old, Emily was saying, "See the flower?" for the eight hundredth time, and Jason reached out and pointed to the flower. "He could have been stretching," she said. "But I experienced it as him saying, 'O-*kay*, Mom, I *got* it.' It was a message to me: 'I am not a lump of mashed potatoes. I am a person.'" Emily called Charles immediately. "He's in there!" she cheered. The phase that followed was almost ecstatic. Emily and Charles tried to come up with novel experiences for Jason almost daily. Emily sewed a quilt that had a different fabric every few inches—terry cloth, velvet, AstroTurf—so that every time Jason moved he would experience a new sensation. When he was six months old, they took a giant roasting pan and filled it with Jell-O, forty packages' worth, and lowered him into it so he could writhe around and experience the strange texture, and eat some of it, too. They used brushes on the soles of his feet to make his toes curl up. He learned better than Emily and Charles could have hoped. Though his speech had the blurred cadences typical of people with intellectual disability, he was able to communicate with it. Emily taught him the alphabet. He picked up numbers; he learned words in Spanish from watching *Sesame Street*, where Emily had been a writer since 1970.

Jason started reading at four, ahead of many typical peers, and one day put together alphabet blocks to spell a headline: "Son of Sam." At six, he had a fourth-grade reading level and could do basic math. The Kingsleys started counseling families who had just had babies with Down's. "It became a passionate crusade, that other people shouldn't be told that their kid had no potential. We would meet them in the first twenty-four hours and say, 'You're going to have to work harder. But don't let anybody tell you that it's impossible.'" By the time Jason was seven, he could count to ten in twelve languages. He had learned Sign as well as English and soon could tell Bach from Mozart from Stravinsky. Emily took Jason on the road; they addressed obstetricians, nurses, and psychologists, as well as parents of children with Down syndrome. The year Jason was seven, they gave 104 lectures. Emily felt that she had licked DS; she lived in triumph.

Emily arranged for Jason to appear as a regular guest on *Sesame Street*, and he normalized tolerance for a new generation, playing with other children in a way that acknowledged but did not stigmatize his condition. She wrote a screenplay based on their experience and insisted that the producers cast children with Down syndrome, even though actors with DS had never before been on TV. Jason provided the voice for the character modeled on him. Jane Pauley did a special about Jason and a friend who also had Down syndrome and had received early intervention. The two boys eventually wrote a book,

Count Us In, in which Jason described the obstetrician who told his parents that he would never learn to recognize them or talk. "Give a baby with a disability a chance to grow a full life, to experience a half-full glass instead of a half-empty glass," he wrote. "Think of your abilities, not your disability." Jason became the first DS celebrity; his renown marked the emergence of Down syndrome as a horizontal identity. Thirty years later, Emily received a special award from the US Department of Health and Human Services for her work showing people with disabilities in mainstream media.

Emily had been told her child was subhuman. When this proved untrue, it was logical to question every traditional assumption about DS, and Jason broke records and stymied expectations. Yet while he could learn more than anyone else with Down syndrome had ever learned, he had limitations. Nuance eluded him. He could read better than he could understand what he was reading. "I knew I couldn't remove the chromosomes," Emily said. "But I really thought that maybe nobody knew what these kids were capable of. No one had been able to do what he did. Then around the time he turned eight, the rest of the world caught up and went past, and I began to realize all the things he couldn't do and would never be able to do. All the trained-seal stuff was fantastic, but in the real world, the intelligence to count in many languages is not as important as social intelligence, and he didn't have it. I had not made the Down syndrome go away."

Jason would hug strangers and didn't understand that they weren't friends. He wanted to attend sleepaway camp, but after he'd been there a week, Emily got a call saying that the other kids didn't like him and didn't like how he kept hugging everyone. Some parents had said that if Jason didn't leave, they were going to pull their own kids. When he played soccer, he would forget or not understand which team he was on. The typical kids who had been his friends began to snigger. He continued to play with toys for small children, and he watched cartoons beamed at kids half his age. It seemed that the miracle was unraveling; he could be a TV star and a successful author, but he could not function in mundane settings. "It was an unbelievably horrible readjustment for me," Emily said. Jason, too, was in anguish. One night when Emily was tucking him into bed, he said, "I hate this face. Can you find a store where we can get me a new face, a normal face?" Another night he said, "I'm so sick and tired of this Down syndrome business. When is it going to go away?" Emily could only kiss him on the head and tell him to go to sleep.

Emily began to rework her lectures. She still wanted to encourage people not to institutionalize their children. She wanted to say that she loved her son and that he loved her. But she didn't want to sugarcoat her message. It was at this time that she wrote "Welcome to Holland." Bringing Jason up wasn't the hell she had been told about when he was born, but it was also not Italy. Jason had become famous for breaking the mold, and it was hard to figure out whether to keep dragging him to greater heights or to let him stay where he was comfortable being—whether he'd have a happier life with more achievement or whether that achievement was only a vanity project.

As Jason reached adolescence, his classmates began having parties, but he wasn't invited and spent Saturday nights at home, watching TV and moping. Emily called other parents of teenagers with Down syndrome, asking, "Is your kid as lonely on Saturday night as mine is?" So when Jason was fourteen, the Kingsleys began to host a monthly party at their home, with food, soda, and dancing. "They felt so normal," Emily said. "They loved it." The parents would sit upstairs and talk about their shared experiences, so it was really two parties. When I met Emily, the monthly parties had been going for fifteen years. She had bought a karaoke machine and the kids—many no longer really kids—were having a rollicking good time. "I always say to people, 'Invest in inclusion, but keep one foot firmly planted in the Down syndrome community,'" Emily said. "'This is where your kid's ultimate friendships are going to come from.'"

Jason had been in a special-needs classroom, but nonetheless passed the exams requisite for a high school diploma. Emily located a post-high-school program in Amenia, New York, where young people with learning disabilities, most without other challenges, were taught money management, time management, cooking, and housekeeping in addition to clerical and other job-related skills. Jason's credentials and test scores were way ahead of those of most of the other applicants. "The parents freaked out when they saw that Jason was applying to this school," Emily said. "They thought it was going to turn into a 'retard school.' So I went to the school president. 'What's the criterion for entering this school? Is it the shape of your eyes? Is it how cute you are? If so, let's go down the hall, and I'll show you a few kids you ought to expel.'" Only after Emily threatened a lawsuit was Jason finally admitted; he was later judged by the administration to be a "model student."

Nonetheless, many things remain elusive. Jason wanted to drive. "It's fun for boys and sexy for girls," he said in *Count Us In*. "You can get girls if you drive." He had announced that when he was old enough, he wanted a red Saab turbo convertible. Emily paused as she recounted this, deeply frustrated. "So how do you tell your kid that he's never going to drive? I said, 'Your reaction time is slower than other people's.' I made it something physical. He's no dope. He shouldn't drive because he doesn't have the judgment, but how to say so?" Jason lives in a lonely demographic. He is too bright for most others with Down syndrome; they can't keep up with his verbal abilities, his puns, his games. But he is not bright enough for people without disabilities. "He has no peers," Emily said with a mix of enormous pride and terrible regret.

Jason described a life for himself that included a family and a dog and a white picket fence; he has a sort-of girlfriend, who also has DS. Emily took him in for a vasectomy. Though many males with DS are infertile, some are not. "It only takes one sperm to do it," Emily said. "We did not want to leave the responsibility of birth control to a girl whose capacity we were unclear of. If he wants to set up housekeeping with somebody and have a marriage, I'll give him the wedding of the age. Being a good parent, though—I simply don't see how he could do it."

Charles's dream was that his son would live independently, so he set Jason up in an apartment of his own. Jason found his first job at Barnes & Noble, tearing the covers off magazines destined for recycling. He found it excruciatingly boring and kept making up ways to amuse himself. When his supervisor insisted that this was not his job, he replied, "I'm an independent adult person and I make my own decisions"— showing the very spirit that Charles and Emily had fostered, applied in exactly the wrong context. He was fired soon thereafter. His next job was at the White Plains Public Library. He developed his own idiosyncratic way of shelving videos, and unsurprisingly, the library staff wanted things done their way. Jason argued about it until they, too, had to let him go.

"He wants to open a store where he will tell people the inner messages of Disney movies," Emily explained. "You wait in line, he says, 'Next!' and you come up and say, 'Please, Jason, would you explain the inner meaning of *The Hunchback of Notre Dame*?' He would say, 'The inner meaning is that it's what's inside people that counts, whether they're a good person, and that's more important than whether they're beautiful. That'll be fifty dollars, please. Next!' You cannot explain to him that people already know this, that they don't find it out at a store anyway. In some very, very basic ways, he's clueless." Emily threw up her hands. She told me mournfully, "The primary job of most parents is to make their kids think they can do anything; my primary job is to take him down. Reduced to a sentence, it's 'You're not smart enough to do what you want to do.' Do you know how much I hate having to say that?"

When Jason was twenty, his father was diagnosed with cancer, and three years later, he died. Jason became deeply depressed. Emily became depressed, too. Emily found Jason a therapist, then turned to Westchester Arc (the organization's name was originally an acronym for Association for Retarded Citizens), where Charles had served as president of the board. She wanted to qualify for ResHab, or residential habilitation, in which support staff come to a person's home and provide services and instruction in independent-living skills. She was tossed around in the bureaucracy until she finally broke down in tears in front of a committee and said, "My kid is destroying himself. I can't do all of this myself." Jason was finally given a caseworker who came in twenty hours a week. "That was a great help," Emily said, "but I started realizing that it wasn't enough. I had to bite the bullet and acknowledge that as smart as he is, he needs more structure and supervision. He just is not eating healthy meals at a regular time each day, or getting himself up and to work on time."

Emily decided that Jason needed to be in a group home. "It was a feeling of failure," she said. "We had worked so hard to make him the Down syndrome guy who didn't need it. But I had to look at what was best for him, and not at some ideal we had built up for ourselves." When Emily put Jason on the waiting list for a local facility, she found out that the wait was an impossible eight years. "Raising a kid like Jason," she said, "the kid is the least of the challenges. Jason was there to put his arms around me when the bureaucracies had nearly killed me." Services are seldom available to anyone who does not have the wherewithal to battle agencies. Doing so often requires education, time, and money—which is a painful irony given that these services are intended to benefit people who may be short on all three.

One day, Emily spotted a house for sale in Hartsdale, New York, and realized it would be a perfect group home. It had three bedrooms, enough for Jason and a companionable two friends; it was near the main bus stop, and across the street from a supermarket, a bank, and a pharmacy. Emily bought the house, then asked Arc to run it. The New York State Office of Mental Retardation and Developmental Disabilities now rents the house from Emily for the amount of her mortgage payment. Jason moved in with two of his best friends from the parties Emily had been throwing. The three receive Social Security disability checks that go straight to Arc, which spends the money to maintain and staff the house.

"They love one another," Emily said. "They call themselves the Three Musketeers." Jason has a job working for the local radio station, where he is happy. "I'm stepping back a little," she said. "The ultimate job is to appreciate him for who he is—and who he is, is really terrific. Anything he's accomplished, he's accomplished because he really stuck to it. Nothing comes easy to him." She paused. "He's kept a lot of dignity in the face of that. I really, really admire him tremendously. I'm also sad for him, because he's smart enough to know that almost everybody is accomplishing things that he's not, smart enough to realize that his life is different."

Even if a child never acquires the skills needed for independent living, he accumulates experience and history. "He says to me that he wants this particular video," Emily said, "and I used to say to him, 'You are intelligent enough to watch something better than that.' I used to think that if I kept pushing, he would have a better life in the world. But now I think, 'Well, if that's what he enjoys, who am I to interfere?' So I don't buy things like *The Brave Little Toaster,* but I don't give him a hard time if he wants to buy it for himself. You can have tulips and windmills coming out your ears, but you don't *ever* get to the Uffizi, and that's it."

A couple of years later, Jason was depressed again, and Emily reflected with concern on her original attempt to make Jason the highest-functioning DS kid in history. She said, "With perfect hindsight would I have done it differently? His intelligence has enriched our relationship so much and I would never want to give that up, but I'll admit that lower-functioning Down's kids are happier, less obsessed with how unfair it is. They have an easier time in many ways, but is that better? He takes such pleasure in words, in using his mind." I went to a reading at Barnes & Noble that Jason and his friend did when their book was reissued. Jason answered the audience's questions with fluency and poise. Emily was aglow and Jason was aglow, their pleasure in his intelligence a mutual delight. The parents of children with DS who had come to hear him were aglow, too, with hope. During the book signing, people approached Jason reverently. He and Emily were heroes, and Jason loved being a hero; I could understand his loneliness, but I could not miss his pride.

Once when I was at Emily's house, she called Jason and offered to take him and his roommates to *The Pirates of Penzance.* After a pause, I heard her say wistfully, "Well, okay, I guess I'll go on my own." The cliché is that people with Down syndrome are incredibly sweet-natured, and they are, but they are unsubtle in their thinking, and Emily's nuanced disappointment had not registered with Jason as it might with a typical child of six or seven. "He's not very introspective," she said. "He doesn't understand the origins even of his own feelings. So it's pretty much impossible for him to be outrospective and guess what's going on inside of me." A few years later she said, "Actually, in some ways he is the first kid with Down syndrome who is really introspective. It's not a boon to have Down syndrome and be introspective, because what you see when you look inside yourself are inadequacies. That's how deep he can look into himself. Jason was talking the other day about what he might have done if he hadn't had Down syndrome. I have never allowed myself that fantasy. It's too dangerous for me."

For most of recorded history, DS has not been compared to a holiday among windmills and tulips. The idea that "idiots" were amenable to amelioration originated with Jean Marc Gaspard Itard's attempt to educate the Wild Boy of Aveyron in the early nineteenth century. His theories were then developed by his pupil Édouard Séguin, director of the Hospice des Incurables in Paris, who structured a system for assessing the intellectually disabled and was the first to recognize the merits of early treatment. "If the idiot cannot be reached by the first lessons of infancy," he wrote, "by what mysterious process will years open for him the golden doors of intelligence?" Séguin emigrated to the United States in the middle of the nineteenth century and established institutions for the care and education of the disabled, whom he enabled to participate in civic life, often through manual labor.

Yet even as Séguin was bringing about such transformation, others argued that the cognitively disabled were not merely stupid, but evil and corrupt. The language of accusing rectitude is reminiscent of the Imaginationist argument that women who bore dwarfs did so because of their lascivious nature: deformity and disability were interpreted as evidence of failure. Samuel G. Howe's 1848 *Report Made to the Legislature of Massachusetts* articulates this pre-eugenic, dehumanizing vision: "This class of persons is always a burden upon the public. Persons of this class are idle and often mischievous, and are dead weights upon the material prosperity of the state. They are even worse than useless. Every such person is like a Upas tree, that poisons the whole moral atmosphere about him."

The first person to describe Down syndrome was John Langdon Down, in 1866. He referred to his subjects as *Mongoloids* or *Mongoloid idiots* on the basis that their faces, with slightly slanted eyes, resembled those of people from Mongolia. Down proposed that human evolution had gone from black people to Asians to white people, and that white people born with Mongolism were actually a throwback to their primitive Asian antecedents—a position then considered rather progressive insofar as it acknowledged evolution.

By 1900, the jobs that had been done by Séguin's trained individuals with mental retardation were being claimed by the great influx of immigrants, who did them more efficiently, and the institutions originally intended to educate the intellectually disabled were used to exclude them from an efficiency-oriented industrial society. Medical texts delineated how to classify someone an "idiot," an "imbecile," or a "moron"; eugenicists provided a spurious validation of the link between mental retardation and criminality, and laws favoring sterilization were instituted.

As late as 1924, a British scientist published material saying that these children actually were biological members of the Mongol race; that view was finally challenged in the 1930s by Lionel Penrose, a British doctor who used blood tests to prove that white people with DS were genetically related to other white people and not to Asians. Penrose also established that the greatest risk factor for DS was maternal age, identifying thirty-five as the cutoff point at which risk escalated. Oliver Wendell Holmes wrote in a 1927 Supreme Court decision, "It is better for all the world, if instead of waiting to execute degenerate offspring for crime, or to let them starve for their imbecility, society can prevent those who are manifestly unfit from continuing their kind. Three generations of imbeciles are enough." The forced-sterilization law, applied to people with many disabilities and disadvantages but particularly focused on those with intellectual disabilities, was not repealed for almost fifty years. In 1958, a French geneticist, Jérôme Lejeune, presented to the International Congress of Genetics his evidence that the condition was the result of a triplication of the twenty-first chromosome, of which there should be only two copies; the scientific name for Down syndrome is *trisomy 21*.

The psychoanalyst Erik Erikson (inventor of the term *identity crisis*), at the urging of his friend Margaret Mead, had sent his newborn son Neil to an institution within days of his birth in 1944 and kept his existence secret even from his other children, fearful that if anyone knew he had produced an "idiot" his reputation would be damaged. He had been told that his son would live no more than two years; in fact, Neil lived two decades. The view that a child with a disability was an unmitigated tragedy reached an apotheosis in Simon Olshansky's oft-quoted description of parents' "chronic sorrow." His was not the only such voice. The psychoanalysts Albert Solnit and Mary Stark lobbied in 1961 for a new DS mother to have "physical rest; an opportunity to review her thoughts and feelings about the wished-for child; a realistic interpretation and investment of the feared, unwanted child by doctors and nurses; and an active role in planning for and caring for the newborn child as she is able. These are the measures through which the mother can minimize or overcome the trauma of giving birth to a retarded child."

In 1966, the playwright Arthur Miller and his wife, the photographer Inge Morath, institutionalized their child with DS and told almost no one of his existence. In 1968, the ethicist Joseph Fletcher wrote in the *Atlantic Monthly* that there was "no reason to feel guilty about putting a Down's syndrome baby away, whether it's 'put away' in the sense of hidden in a sanatorium or in a more responsible lethal sense. It is sad, yes. Dreadful. But it carries no guilt. True guilt arises only from an offense against a person, and a Down's is not a person." Willowbrook, that hell house of the 1960s and early 1970s, happened for a reason; parents who had been persuaded that their retarded children were not persons left them in repugnant conditions.

Yet even as prejudice against those with intellectual disabilities was escalating, a new movement to help the disabled was also unfolding. The argument that the disabled warranted benevolent treatment coincided with a larger post-Enlightenment shift in our conception of early education. Historically, this had been the province of mothers, and the notion that experts had something to add began only with the founding of the first kindergartens in early-nineteenth-century Germany. At the end of the nineteenth century, Maria Montessori applied lessons she had learned from her work among the intellectually disadvantaged in Rome to typical children. Soon nursery schools began to crop up in Europe. In the United States, they burgeoned when the New Deal subsidized teaching jobs, then spread further as the Second World War effort called mothers into the workforce. At the same time, attempts to curtail childhood mortality were also under way, directed especially at the poor. The new science of behaviorism rose up in opposition to eugenics and suggested that people are made, not born, and can be educated and shaped into anything. The emerging field of psychoanalysis was concurrently examining how early trauma could interfere with healthy development, and some of its adherents began to question whether the shortcomings of the poor and disabled might be the result of early deprivation rather than organic inadequacy.

The 1935 Social Security Act included a provision that the federal government would match state funds for treating the disabled. Investigators soon began to look at how a stimulating and enriching environment allowed poor children to transcend their apparent deficits. John Bowlby, the father of attachment theory, demonstrated that good maternal care was crucial to the development of the healthy child, an insight so obvious today that it is hard to remember how radical it was a mere sixty years ago.

Eugenics was finally discredited when it devolved into the Holocaust. Meanwhile, the influx of handicapped veterans at the end of

World War II softened social prejudice against disabled people in general. In 1946, the US Office of Education set up a Section for Exceptional Children, which led to better education programs for people with special needs, but those children remained segregated from the larger society. In 1949, Ann Greenberg, the mother of a child with Down syndrome, placed advertisements in the *New York Post* seeking other parents who shared her concerns. A year later, they founded the Association for Retarded Citizens, now known as the Arc, and still one of the most prominent organizations in the field. Most parents thought of DS entirely in terms of nature: the child has a genetic anomaly and nothing can be done about it. Greenberg was among the parent activists on the side of nurture: the child has a genetic anomaly and there is work to be done.

When John F. Kennedy became president, he established a commission to study mental retardation and its possible prevention. Reintegration of the disabled into the larger society was spearheaded in part by his sister, Eunice Kennedy Shriver, whose 1962 article in the *Saturday Evening Post* about their sister Rosemary emphasized that even families of prominence and intelligence can have retarded children. She observed with sadness the poor living conditions to which most people with mental retardation were consigned. Her vision of change took meaningful form in the wake of the civil rights movement's rethinking of social inequalities. Black people had for so long been described as constitutionally inferior, and when they rose up against that characterization, they opened the door for other marginalized people to do the same. Head Start, founded in 1965, was dedicated to the idea that people lived in poverty not because inherent deficits qualified them for nothing better, but because they had not received appropriate and constructive early stimulus. Head Start combined health, education, and social services and trained parents as active partners in the treatment of their children.

By the end of the 1960s, insights from Head Start were being applied to people with intellectual disabilities, and in particular to children with Down syndrome. It became clear that people with DS showed a wide range of functioning, and that it was absurd to predict a newborn's abilities simply from his diagnosis. It seemed to follow that writing such people off at birth was unfair, and that their capacities should be maximized, both to give them a better life and to avoid later costs. Early intervention was better value for money than remediation. In 1973, Congress passed, over President Nixon's veto, the Rehabilitation Act, which stated, "No otherwise qualified handicapped individual in the United States shall, solely by reason of his handicap, be excluded from the participation in, be denied the benefits of, or be subjected to discrimination under any program or activity receiving federal financial assistance." Even with the budget cuts of the Reagan years, programs for disabled children remained in force; this population had become entrenched and drew broad public sympathy. The cause reached a triumphal apogee with the passage of the Americans with Disabilities Act in 1990, which extended the 1973 protections beyond the confines of federally funded programs. Parents, with support from disabled people themselves, had capitalized on changing ideas about humanity. They had validated lives long considered worthless. If racial minorities and the poor deserved support and respect, then so did people with Down syndrome and related conditions. If help to these other groups was best given early, then so, too, was aid to people with intellectual disabilities.

Early intervention (EI) is now a federal program for infants with any of a broad range of complaints—low birth weight, cerebral palsy, Down syndrome, autism—and it has vastly raised levels of functioning in all these groups. EI services provided before a child turns three may include physical therapy, occupational therapy, nutrition counseling, audiology and vision services, nursing support, speech-language therapy, and instruction on assistive technology, as well as support and training for parents who are having trouble coping. It entails a strong focus on sensory stimulation of all kinds. Hospitals are required to tell parents about these services. EI is available to people at every socioeconomic level, sometimes through home visits and sometimes in special centers. These early services are also a form of parent training and may help families to feel optimistic about keeping their children at home. The quality of services for children with particular disabilities varies enormously from state to state; New York, for example, has especially good EI services for DS, and anecdotes tell of people moving to the state specifically to access them.

EI is the full expression of the nurture-over-nature argument—the ultimate triumph of psychoanalysis, civil rights, and empathy over eugenics, sterilization, and segregation. It grew out of a strange nexus of federal politics, parent activism, and psychology; it was a result of changing understandings of nondisabled children and new theories of general early education. It continues to evolve today, as many forms of engagement are grouped under that now-ubiquitous rubric.

Change in both treatment and acceptance of people with DS, however, continues to be driven by parents. By demanding that physicians treat their children's physical ailments as respectfully as they would those of nondisabled children, they have brought about an astonishing increase in life expectancy for people so diagnosed. If *early inter-*

vention is ultimately a vague and ever-evolving umbrella term for a broad range of protocols, it has nonetheless been the organizing phrase for a radical rethinking of the lives of disabled people. Where science and biological cure have been stalled, the social model of disability has achieved wild triumph. Many specific techniques are invaluable in addressing particular needs, but the long and short of it is that disabled children, like nondisabled children, thrive on attention, engagement, stimulation, and hope.

When Elaine Gregoli's daughter, Lynn, was born in 1970, a few years before Jason Kingsley, the obstetrician announced to the baby's father, "Your daughter is a Mongoloid idiot." Elaine, just twenty-three years old, already had a son, Joe, two and a half, and she decided not to have more children. She had never heard of EI. "Lynn was a baby a very long time," Elaine said. "She didn't sit up till she was twelve months old; she didn't walk till she was almost two." Elaine went to an agency, YAI, where a doctor gave her some little exercises to do with Lynn. When Elaine returned two years later, the agency asked her whether she'd like to work there part-time, because they had a severely handicapped little girl with seizures, and they wanted a nurse around. "So Lynn was in the first preschool program that Brooklyn ever had, for two hours, twice a week, and I was right there to learn what I could," Elaine said. She became increasingly interested in the brand-new field of early intervention, and Lynn's school asked her to run their program.

Like Jason Kingsley, Lynn was immensely nourished by the nascent EI movement. She competed in the Special Olympics as a gymnast and an ice-skater. Her motor skills were always better than her cognitive skills, so Elaine mainstreamed her in recreational programs, but not in educational ones. She was in a regular Girl Scout troop, and in a swimming program with typical kids. "But she always was with the younger kids," Elaine said. "She was ten, and she was with six-year-olds. You keep her where she can succeed."

Sometimes, Elaine recalled, she needed to be reminded that her son needed equal praise for his accomplishments. Lynn didn't walk until she was almost two, but she was so small that she looked much younger. "Everybody would come to our house and go, 'She's walking!'" Elaine recalled. "My son came up to me one day and said, 'Mom, look!' He walked back and forth in front of me. He said, 'I know how to walk, too.' After that, I told people, 'When you come into my house, you look at and you praise both my children.'"

Despite the attention Lynn's condition demanded, Joe's relationship to his sister was generally positive. Elaine remembers the story of a schoolmate who said to Joe that his sister was retarded. It was hurled as an insult, but Joe didn't notice that; he just said, "Yes, she is," and got into a conversation about what it meant. "I'd wanted Joe to know that word, so it wouldn't be a shock to him," Elaine said. "It really was an eye-opener, that he realized that. It was like saying she had brown hair and brown eyes." Many years later, when Joe and his wife were expecting each of their sons, their obstetrician suggested that they go to a geneticist. Joe agreed, but said each time that he wanted to have the baby even if he had Down syndrome. "I was surprised at that," Elaine said. "That was when I knew that Joe really didn't feel she was a negative."

As an adult, Lynn works in a cafeteria, earning minimum wage, and she lives in a community residence; when I met the Gregolis, she had been there about ten years. Lynn reads on a first-grade level; she can do basic math with a calculator. Elaine said that she often wonders how much higher Lynn's functioning might be if she had had early intervention as it is now practiced. When I met Elaine, she and Lynn were fresh from a trip to Disney World with Joe and his wife and two young children. "Lynn was the aunt," Elaine said. "She took them on every ride; she bought them shirts; she really did great. Her nephews just love her. They play with her; she plays with them; she really enjoys them. I would love for Lynn to be a teacher, or a doctor. And she's a cafeteria worker. But for her, it's perfect. She loves that paycheck, and she goes to the bank and cashes it and puts it in her checking account. Writes her own checks. That's a big thing for her. So I've learned to love it, too."

Until her retirement in 2008, Elaine Gregoli served as assistant director of YAI/National Institute for People with Disabilities—the same agency she visited when Lynn was two. At YAI, part of Elaine's job was to tell other parents about EI. "All parents want to help their kids," she said, "even if they're distracted by poverty or drug addiction. Since early intervention is free, they go for it, and they mostly end up repeating things with their kids after the social worker leaves." The organization offers psychological counseling and respite care for families of people with disabilities; it serves twenty thousand people a day. Elaine also counseled parents who had a prenatal diagnosis of DS. "They're four months pregnant and have to make a decision within a week or two about whether to abort," she said. "I'll tell them all the good things and some difficulties. The parents may never accept what happened to them and yet accept their child. They're two separate things, the parental loss, and the actual person they will almost always end up loving."

The two key movements in educating disabled children after they have graduated from EI are *mainstreaming* and *inclusion*. Unlike EI, these two approaches affect nondisabled children. In the 1970s and 1980s, parents advocated for mainstreaming, so that disabled students could be taught mostly in dedicated classrooms within ordinary public schools. The 1990s brought a shift to inclusion, which educates disabled children in the same classrooms as their nondisabled peers, often with a special assistant. The most recent major piece of legislation in this area is the Individuals with Disabilities Education Act of 1990 (IDEA), which requires that all children with disabilities receive a free, appropriate public education in the least restrictive possible environment. This integrating of disabled children into regular schools has changed the appearance of the American classroom. Children with intellectual disabilities are usually educated in some mix between special-ed and heterogeneous classrooms unless their disabilities are too extreme for that to be viable; they may go to special schools only after every attempt has been made at achieving the least restrictive environment.

There are two essential questions in the debate about these philosophies: what is better for the child with a diagnosis, and what is better for the typical children (those without such a diagnosis). Some parents complain that disabled children in the classroom are a distraction and slow down learning for the rest. Conversely, Michael Bérubé, codirector of the Disability Studies program at Penn State, whose son has DS, argues that inclusion's benefits are "truly universal"—because being in a classroom with people with disabilities breaches the widespread distrust of and discomfort with people who are unwell and makes those who are able-bodied more humane. Children with DS who are included have good models for language development, learn behavioral norms, and tend to realize more of their potential than they would in an environment predicated on their limitations. Integrated education prepares people with DS for supervised employment, freeing them from the sheltered workshops of times past; it helps more of them to live relatively independently. Public schools are often required to be inclusive; fights still occur to incorporate these policies in private schools.

The pitfall is that people with DS who are in inclusion programs are often cut off from their peers, and people without DS are willing to go only a certain distance in building relationships with people who have the condition. "If the school superintendent and the principal and the teachers all buy into it and educate themselves, I think inclusion works beautifully," said Arden Moulton, one of the founders of the National Down Syndrome Society (NDSS). "But it also depends on the child. Some children shouldn't be in inclusion programs, just like some kids shouldn't be at Yale." Betsy Goodwin, NDSS's cofounder, said, "The purists end up with lonely kids. Teen years are hard enough. You can't expect a normal teen to have his best friend have a disability. It just isn't the way it works."

Betsy Goodwin was young and fit and didn't expect complications when her daughter, Carson, was born with Down syndrome in 1978 in New York. At the time, patients in private practice were generally counseled to institutionalize, and patients in clinics were instructed to take the baby home. In Betsy's view, this is because doctors who had personal relationships with their patients were ashamed of what they saw as their failure. Her obstetrician said, "Why don't you have a healthy baby, and we'll forget about this one?" Barton Goodwin had been open to the possibility of leaving Carson behind; he feared that he would lose Betsy to the world of disability. Betsy was also frightened, but more frightened of the alternative. She called her childhood friend Arden Moulton, a social worker, and said that the doctors wanted her to institutionalize her child. Arden said that was the last thing Betsy should do. However, the lack of resources for DS babies and their families quickly became clear. A few months later, Betsy, until then an interior decorator, decided to start an organization for parents in her situation and asked Arden to help her. "I was a professional," Arden recalled, "and she had the perspective of a parent." That is how, in 1979, the National Down Syndrome Society was established.

The first project of the NDSS was to organize a conference for scientists working on any aspect of trisomy 21, as there had never before been such a gathering and the work was diffuse. At that time, total research in the United States on DS was about $2 million annually; it is now approaching $12 million, which is still low for a condition that affects so many people. Betsy went to Washington to meet with the head of the NIH, who told her that with amniocentesis, there would soon not be anyone born with Down syndrome. "I don't know whether he'd met anyone Catholic," she said drily, twenty-five years later.

Betsy became pregnant again when Carson was two, and she considered amniocentesis. She wasn't sure whether she'd have had an abortion if she'd known that Carson would be born with DS. "I wasn't sure why I was doing it," she said. "To terminate? I honestly can't say. I wanted, at least, to know. But for some reason, he kept getting in the way of the needle, so we never obtained a good read. The amnio goes into twenty-two weeks, and a baby can survive at twenty-four, so it was becoming very unpleasant for me. I finally said to Barton, 'You can divorce me tomorrow, but I'm not going to go on with this process.

I'm going to have what I have.'" Betsy's son was born typical, as was another son a few years later. "My three kids get along great," Betsy said. "That was another warning of the obstetrician: it's going to ruin your marriage, and any kids you have subsequently will suffer. I really think, almost to a one, the siblings of kids with Down's grow up to be more sensitive and thoughtful—maybe even more fulfilled—than the rest of the population."

The Goodwins loved New York City, but when Carson turned eleven, Betsy thought New York was not the place to foster independence in someone who couldn't form adult judgments. "So I came up with Greenwich, Connecticut, which has a policeman on every corner. It struck me as a very safe town for a young woman like her to be walking around." Carson has a warm personality and is socially comfortable. When her brothers were in high school, she loved to dance. "I used to see this arm come out of her bedroom, and she'd grab one of her brothers' friends and make them dance with her," Betsy said. "Some of them, to this day, as men, say, 'I never would have known that step if it weren't for Carson.'"

When I met Carson, she had recently lost her job at Whole Foods because she always seemed to put the tomatoes at the bottom of the bag. "She's never been a tomato fan," Betsy said. "I assure you that the doughnuts would be on top." Carson has trouble understanding that other people think or feel differently—her mother's preference for John Coltrane over Britney Spears, for example, baffles her. She knows that her Down syndrome makes her different, even though she doesn't grasp exactly how. That is why, Betsy explained, her dancing gives her so much joy: "She loves anything that makes her an equal."

In the last three decades, NDSS has grown up alongside the child who inspired it; since Carson was born, it has awarded millions of dollars in scientific grants and has also supported social scientists focused on better educational strategies for people with intellectual disabilities. Once a year, NDSS organizes a conference at which scientists present their work to parents. The society has set up an annual Buddy Walk, which takes place in two hundred locations around the United States. People with Down syndrome walk with a friend to raise money and awareness; Buddy Walk events now bring in about a half million dollars a year to the organization. They also build community for people with DS and their families.

The National Down Syndrome Society has had to steer its way through treacherous waters. Some parents are concerned that an organization that researches ways to cure or ameliorate the symptoms of DS is not providing the affirmation that people with the syndrome need. Antiabortion disability activists have long argued that selective termination devalues the lives of disabled people; some have tried to persuade the NDSS leadership to take a strong position against abortion. NDSS would like to see more people keeping children with DS, but not because they are forced to do so by law.

Until Ronald Reagan signed the Baby Doe Amendment in 1984, which classed the neglect or withholding of treatment for disabled infants as child abuse, parents and physicians could essentially let such infants die if they wished. The Princeton ethicist Peter Singer has espoused the right of women to choose abortion through the end of pregnancy and to commit infanticide on newborns if they so choose. He has defended this position with the utilitarian argument that most women who eliminate an unwanted child will produce a wanted one, and that the loss of happiness of the child who is killed (whose life would have been unsatisfactory) is outweighed by the happiness of the healthy child who follows. Although Singer's position is extreme, it reflects the pervasive devaluation of people with Down syndrome and the assumption that their lives are displeasing to others and to themselves. One mother described being asked by a psychiatrist how she got on with her son with Down syndrome; when she replied, "Terrific," he said that there was no need to be defensive. Marca Bristo, who chairs the National Council on Disability, said, "Singer's core vision amounts to a defense of genocide."

By 2000, the resistance to prenatal screening from the disability rights camp had crystallized. Disability scholars Adrienne Asch and Erik Parens, in their seminal discussion of the problem, wrote, "Prenatal diagnosis reinforces the medical model that disability itself, not societal discrimination against people with disabilities, is the problem to be solved. Prenatal genetic testing followed by selective abortion is morally problematic and it is driven by misinformation." A few years later, Asch wrote, "Researchers, professionals, and policymakers who uncritically endorse testing followed by abortion act from misinformation about disability, and express views that worsen the situation for all people who live with disabilities now and in the future." Leon Kass, chairman of the President's Council on Bioethics under George W. Bush, has argued that we "treat" prenatally diagnosed illnesses by "killing" rather than tending to those who would develop them.

Preventing births of any subclass of people devalues them. A society in which fetuses with Down syndrome are routinely aborted clearly believes that DS is a grave misfortune. This does not mean that anyone hates or wants to slaughter people with DS; indeed, many people who would choose to terminate a DS pregnancy would also go out of their way to be kind to a living person with the syndrome. But I know from personal experience how kind sympathy can be a noxious prejudice; I do not care to spend time with people who pity me for being gay, even if their sympathy reflects a generous heart and is offered with egregious politesse. Asch claims that women abort disabled fetuses because of the woeful lives that would come of their pregnancies; that such woe is the product of chauvinism; that such chauvinism could be resolved. Janice McLaughlin, at the University of Newcastle, wrote, "Mourning the choice the woman is compelled to make is not the same as saying she is wrong or an active participant in discrimination. Instead, it points to the ways in which she, too, is a victim." But the acts of those women do not merely reflect the society; they create it. The more such pregnancies are terminated, the greater the chance that more will be terminated. Accommodations are contingent on population; only the ubiquity of disability keeps the disability rights conversation alive at all. A dwindling population means dwindling accommodation.

Of the 5,500 children born with DS in the United States each year, about 625 are born to women who had prenatal diagnosis and chose not to terminate. One doctor assured Tierney Temple Fairchild, who had a prenatal diagnosis, "Almost everything you want to happen will happen. It's just going to happen at a different schedule." This is untrue. A great deal does not happen on any schedule for people with DS. The remark was nonetheless helpful to the family in deciding to keep their child, and they didn't have amnio in subsequent pregnancies. "I had a choice and I chose life," Fairchild wrote. "Does that make me pro-choice or pro-life? Our political parties tell us we can't have it both ways. I chose life, but I am thankful I had the choice."

Like deafness and dwarfism, Down syndrome may be an identity or a catastrophe or both; it may be something to cherish or something to eradicate; it may be rich and rewarding both for those whom it affects directly and for those who care for them; it may be a barren and exhausting enterprise; it may be a blend of all these. "I've never seen a family who chose to have the baby and then were really sorry," Elaine Gregoli said. There is a strong movement to connect expectant mothers with a prenatal Down's diagnosis with families bringing up children with DS. Many parents have written memoirs expressing the rewards of raising such children, contending that there is less to complain of in Down syndrome than in the attitudes of the world. Of course, people who dislike having children with DS don't tend to write memoirs; neither do those of low socioeconomic status, for whom the obstacles to good treatment may be daunting.

My own observation is that some parents manufacture an affirmative construction of their child's disability to disguise their despair, while others have a deep and genuine experience of joy in caring for disabled children, and that sometimes the first stance can generate the second. I met disability activists who insisted that everyone's joy was authentic, and I met psychologists who thought no one's experience was. The truth is that while some people fall at either end of this spectrum, most are scattered across its wide span.

Deirdre Featherstone didn't want children, so she was delighted to learn that she was infertile. When she became pregnant in 1998, however, she felt she was stuck, and she decided to let things unfold. She was thirty-eight but not inclined to seek amniocentesis. "I believe certain things are not your business," she said. "If that baby is supposed to be inside alone for nine months, then you need to leave it alone. You don't go sticking things into their environment." Her husband, Wilson Madden, wanted to do amnio. "I wanted to give him that because he likes to plan," she said. "But the night before, I said, 'What if we found out something?' He said, 'I don't think that would make any difference.' I said, 'Well, if I find out there's something wrong, this kid's out of here, because, as you well know, I don't want to be anyone's mother. I don't even have the courage to be the parent of a regular kid. I'm perfectly ready to have an abortion if there's anything wrong. You aren't. So you'd better stop pushing the amnio.'"

They didn't have the test. "Thank God, because it would have been the biggest mistake of my life," Deirdre said. "You can't assess what you don't know." The day before her daughter, Catherine, was born, Deirdre, who is a jeweler and stylist, was supposed to be accessorizing a fashion show. She worked that afternoon, reviewing the outfits, then went home and had Thai food. When she began to heave in the night, Wilson realized she was in labor; she insisted it was just the takeout. A midwife delivered Catherine at home at ten the next morning and told her to see a pediatrician straightaway. The pediatrician confirmed visually that Catherine had Down syndrome. "I already knew that Catherine was the nicest person I was ever going to meet," Deirdre said. "It was harder for Wilson. It's probably always harder for the father, because they haven't had a physical relationship with the child for nine months." The pediatrician sent them for genetic screening the next day to confirm the diagnosis. "I had tears coming down my face, and she reaches up," Deirdre said. "She has one tear coming out of her eye, and she wipes my face. Twenty-three hours old."

Catherine was born into a very different world from the pre-EI one Lynn Gregoli and Carson Goodwin had entered, and Wilson felt that they had to look into every available mode of treatment. Deirdre said, "One of the things that made the early period difficult was that she would have therapy three times a week for speech, then occupational therapy, then physical therapy, and also craniosacral therapy. Her schedule was so full, it was hard for me to leave the house. That was probably the only difficulty, besides adjusting to the fact that somebody else is depending on you to live. I said to Wilson, 'If this is more than you can handle, you're free to go. I won't hold it against you and I won't think you're a bad person. But you can't stay upset forever.'" Wilson explained, "It never occurred to me to leave. But I was slower to get into the whole thing than Deirdre."

Deirdre surprised even herself. "I was so sure I was the parent who was not going to be able to deal with a child who was in any way different," she said. "I was just relieved to love her. She was very lovable. All my friends had these children they thought were perfect, and then they've had to come to terms with their children's limitations and problems. I had this baby everyone thought was a disaster, and my journey has been to find all the things that are amazing about her. I started off knowing she was flawed, and all the surprises since then have been good ones. She's one of the nicest, kindest, most thoughtful, sensitive people that I've ever met. She's funny. She always highlights the positive; I don't know how much of that is personality or if that's Down syndrome. When she makes up her mind that she's not doing something, that is that, which is also typical of Down syndrome."

The mother of a child with special needs inevitably becomes a soothsayer. "Somebody I know called me up in tears, saying, 'I just found out my kid has DS; what should I do?' I said, 'What do you want to do?' She said, 'It's my baby, and I want to have it.' I said, 'I'll tell you what, it's the best thing that has ever happened to me. And had I had the information, I would have made this big, big mistake by not having her. You've met my kid, we have a really good time.'" Recounting this to me, Deirdre added, "Down syndrome is easy, or at least Catherine is easy. Autism is probably a different experience. Would I make her life easier? Any way I could. Would I blink and turn her normal? No, I wouldn't. She may, at some point, have a different opinion and want to get facial surgery or some other normalizing procedure, whatever's out there by the time she grows up. Would I endorse her doing so if that's what she chose? If it comes up, I will, but I hope that I'll have raised her with enough personal strength and self-esteem to be happy in who she is."

Deirdre never had to make her way through the gauntlet of prejudice that so determined Emily Perl Kingsley's early experiences. "People still give up their child. People still have abortions when they find out," Deirdre said. "I'm not here to judge it. You hate lima beans, I love lima beans. There's a lot of political correctness that I find ridiculous. But I'll take whatever's made it unacceptable to make fun of a child because she's different. I think we are less tolerant of prejudice than anywhere else or any other time." She described being at Catherine's public school in Tribeca one day when a five-year-old girl said, "I heard that when Catherine was inside you, you broke your egg, and that's why she came out funny." Deirdre said, "If you break your egg, then you don't have a baby at all." The little girl said, "You mean she's not broken?" Deirdre said, "No, she's not broken. She's a little different." Deirdre looked around the play area and said, "See that little girl over there? She has red, curly hair, and you have blonde hair. This little boy, he's black and his mom and dad are white, and they're Italian, and his sister is his sister, but they're not really related biologically." One of the parents nearby said, "I'm Korean and my husband's white." Another said, "I didn't marry a man, but my partner is a lady, so my child is also different." In this world of infinite variety, Catherine was just another variation on the idea that the only normality is nonnormality. "Sometimes I see somebody with a child with Down's, and I'll say, 'My daughter's in the same situation, she's eight,'" Deirdre said. "Nine times out of ten, people will say, 'Congratulations. Welcome to the club.' I think a lot of us feel lucky."

As a mother, Deirdre is astonishingly patient. I witnessed her negotiating Catherine down from resistance on more than one occasion, capably steering her way around direct confrontations. Catherine tends to want to wear inappropriate clothes; she sometimes insists on a sundress when it's cold out. "I say, 'Why don't you wear pants under your dress, or over your dress.' Sometimes, she looks like she has furnished herself from a homeless shelter. She's good with that. So what am I going to say? I'm supposed to be building self-esteem, not knocking it down." It has been harder to maintain a sense of humor about the inevitable battles with the system, however. Wilson said, "It's important that she not be the slowest kid in the room. Maybe a hundred percent inclusion all the way is not the best. We're looking at a camp that caters to special-needs kids." Deirdre has a tigress's instinct when it comes to her daughter's education. "Her first kindergarten was not a fit at all. I requested a transfer on day two. Her education is just so important, it's more important than breathing. I had been to the board of ed, back and forth, and finally one day I hired a babysitter for Catherine for a week, and I packed a bag with my computer, a power pack, electrical cords, my cell phone, chargers, several days' worth of clothes, books. I went to the board of ed and said, 'I need to meet with the special-needs coordinator for this board of ed.' 'I'm sorry, she's not in. Can you come back?' 'No. I'm just going to stay. It's no trouble whatsoever. I have enough things for seven days, and I will sit here until she has time, but I don't want to rush her in any way.' I sat there, taking different things out of my suitcase, and making sure that everyone knows, oh, underwear, underneath that's the charger, and I'll get it out now, then put the underwear back in. After four and a half hours, somebody came out and said, 'Can we help you?'" Catherine was in a new school by the end of February. "I'm never unpleasant," Deirdre said. "But I make it clear that I do need certain needs met."

Five years later, I asked Deirdre how Catherine's education was going. "I was asking her about vocabulary words for school, and she said her new words were *opportunity* and *deficient*. I asked her for the definition of *deficient*, and she thought about that and finally answered, 'You, Mom.'" Deirdre burst out laughing. "I don't have a fear that everyone's going to find out I don't know what I'm doing as a mother because I've already admitted that. The question is how you educate yourself. Sometimes I think I'm a great mother. Sometimes I think I suck. I've never once in a million years said that I know what I'm doing being somebody's mother. I barely know what I'm doing being somebody's wife."

People born with DS develop slowly and stop short of typical intellectual maturity, but their development usually runs on a steady course. Anyone who can relate to a typical child through various developmental stages can relate to a person with DS. DS babies are slow to make eye contact, slow to sustain it, and slow with imitative behaviors. They do not start to speak until they are two or three years old, and they do not make two- and three-word phrases until they are three or four years old. DS children often fail to grasp fundamental principles of grammar. I once asked someone who worked with people with DS why some are so much smarter than others, and she said, "Why are some people without DS so much smarter than others?" Though the parallel holds, some people do have "worse" DS than others. David Patterson, a geneticist working on trisomy 21, recently wrote, "It is virtually certain that genes on chromosome 21 do not work alone to cause the features we recognize as Down syndrome. They must work in concert with genes on other chromosomes. This is likely to be one of the reasons for the wide diversity seen in persons with Down syndrome."

People with Down syndrome are often warm and sociable, eager to please, and free of cynicism. Larger studies indicate that many people with Down syndrome are also stubborn, defiant, aggressive, and sometimes disturbed. In addition to the physical challenges that some people with DS face, many have behavioral issues, including ADHD and oppositional disorders; those with milder cases tend toward depression and pronounced anxiety. The popular image is not so much groundless as incomplete. The experience of living with DS is not easy. According to a large, recent study, these children generally have "less idealized views of themselves" and experience "repeated exposures to failure which contributes to uncertainty and 'learned helplessness,' which in turn has been linked to depression and other problems."

People with DS are relatively low-energy and consistent in their behavior, which means that they are less demanding of caregivers than people with high-energy, chaotic disorders, such as bipolar disorder and autism. Both children and adults with DS are at heightened risk for physical and sexual abuse. Those with behavioral problems are more often placed out of the home by their families; they are less likely to fit in well in those settings, either, however, because they wear out paid support staff and are harder to take out in public. All of this, of course, exacerbates the symptoms that underlie their behavior.

Many treatments exist for the symptoms of DS, but none alleviates the condition itself. The extra chromosome cannot be suppressed or removed, though there is preliminary work on gene therapy to achieve this. Vitamin regimens have been in use to treat people with DS since the 1940s, as have off-label antihistamines and diuretics, though none of these has been shown to have any benefit; some, indeed, have been shown to have minor adverse effects. In addition, plastic-surgery protocols can normalize the appearance of people with DS. Such procedures include a sometimes pragmatic shortening of the tongue—which is said to reduce drooling, improve speech, and help people with DS to breathe better—and a wide range of cosmetic interventions such as nose jobs, removal of excess fat from the neck, and reshaping of the eyes to eliminate their slant. The National Down Syndrome Society and other groups object to these measures as unnecessarily painful and even cruel, the DS version of limb-lengthening, and also take umbrage at the prejudice against people who look as if they have Down's. They would like to use public education to change responses to a DS face rather than change its appearance.

Michelle Smith, a financial adviser at Wachovia Bank, is a perfectionist, and it is not easy for perfectionists to have children with disabilities. She has displaced her perfectionism onto mothering; if there is a perfect way to handle having a child with a disability, Michelle Smith has found it. She has even done a perfect job of renouncing perfection.

About fifteen weeks into her pregnancy, Michelle went for an alpha-fetal protein blood test. Her obstetrician said her results placed her at elevated risk for DS and offered her amnio. "I didn't even tell my husband that was an option," she recalled. "I went into complete and total denial. The person I had always been would have been the supercompetitive New York mom: the right clothes; the right barber; the right job. I would see disabled people and be so freaked out that I would just not look. But weird things happened during my pregnancy. I turned the TV on and just randomly saw a *Touched by an Angel* episode with the guy with DS. I was in Home Depot, eight months pregnant, and this Down syndrome little girl walked right up to me, with no mother or father with her, and put her hand on my stomach. I thought, obviously, somebody's trusting me with this pregnancy."

At the delivery of Michelle's son, Dylan, the midwife thought his neck was a little thick. She looked up Michelle's blood test. An hour later, she told Michelle that her son had Down syndrome. "They put him on my stomach, and he gave me a spooky look, where I actually felt like he was the sage and I was the child," Michelle said. "I was intimidated by him, in this really beautiful way."

Michelle was determined not to look at things darkly, but at first it was hard; the baby stirred up all her own fears and insecurities. When she brought Dylan home from the hospital, she entered her apartment building through the back door because she was afraid of what the doorman might say. When she got in an elevator with Dylan, she would blurt out his diagnosis. "I felt everyone was staring," she said. "But it was just all about *my* judgments."

As Michelle recounted it, her husband, Jeff, couldn't handle having a DS baby. "You have a conversation before you get married about children," she said. "Sometimes about money; sometimes, about religion. You rarely discuss what you'd do with a pregnancy with a special-needs kid." Jeff said that none of this would have happened if Michelle had just had the amnio. "Yes, it would have," Michelle said. "He would still be here." Jeff went through eight months of depression, and by the time he began to emerge, she had decided she wanted a divorce.

Immediately after the birth, Michelle began doing research on treatment for infants with DS. She read "Welcome to Holland," which helped her. "I read eleven books in the first two weeks," she said. "Then I met some other moms, who have been my saving grace. We have a group of four and we call ourselves 'the Down's moms,' and they're all women that I would be friends with anyway." They taught her how to navigate EI and everything that followed.

Michelle found an EI program located in the World Trade Center. Three months after Dylan was born, 9/11 happened. That was the end of the center. As she tried to figure out what to do next, Michelle felt the fighter in her coming to the surface. "The service coordinator for your agency is walking that fine line between giving you what you deserve, legally, and saving the state money. One of the other mothers said, when I had a bad meeting, 'Oh, you poor little neophyte. Here, pick yourself up.' So I hired a special-ed attorney to go to the second meeting with me. I don't know what you do if you're poor or uneducated with a Down syndrome kid, and you don't even know what you don't know."

Dylan soon proved to have problems that EI could not address. He had recurrent intestinal crises that landed him in the hospital repeatedly—forty-one emergency room visits in his first eleven months. "I had a frequent-flier card in the ER," Michelle said. "I would call and admit myself." Dylan needed three major operations; physicians at Columbia gave him a 2 percent chance of survival. Jeff and Michelle lived in the intensive care unit with him for nine weeks straight. "He was on fourteen machines," Michelle recalled. "They brought in a fifteenth machine, the dialysis machine. I sat there, looking at him, thinking, 'Just go. It's okay. I can't do this, either.' I felt so guilty, saying that I couldn't handle watching my kid die. The priest comes in four times to read last rites. There were women on the second floor of that hospital who were so affected by my son, they came up daily and prayed over him, with rosary beads." As Dylan fought for his life, the Down syndrome became secondary. By this time, Jeff, also, had overcome his negative early response. His conversion came too late for the marriage, but not too late for his son. "It wasn't until we almost lost him that Jeff realized how much he loved him," Michelle said. "Now they're inseparable. Jeff adores this child."

Dylan emerged at a year old with twenty-two inches of his colon missing and a patched heart, but his physical health has been excellent since then. "He has a little gas problem; he's stinky, but who cares?" Michelle said. Dylan responded well to EI. "I was one of these people who would have been annoyed that my son's preschool had special-needs kids that might slow them down," Michelle said. "So I make myself perfectly charming to the other mothers. The woman who runs his nursery school believes in inclusion as a way of life. She called me the second week of school and said, 'He has a major gas problem. Make no mistake about it: he's already different. If he's now the smelly little kid with Down syndrome, people are not going to want to play with him.' That was brutally, beautifully honest. We found Beano, which is an enzyme that controls the gas." Michelle nonetheless expects Dylan's sweetness to carry the day. "My grandmother got this little puppy, and he was trying to figure this puppy out. He had his favorite puzzle piece in his hand, and he gave it to the puppy. He gives his favorite things away. He's heart-spontaneous."

Michelle has the zeal of a convert. "It was like I was trying to get FM on an AM radio in my old life. In a weird way, it was like this happened so I could see what I was capable of. Every single trait that I wasn't good at, I've had to develop because of him. I was living superficially and attached to my ego and my stuff and my image. I was very judgmental, critical—and how can I be judgmental of anything now? We're supposed to share all of our talents and gifts, but we have to know what they are first. Now, I have to help people, instead of just using my talents to make money."

Michelle consults with new parents, encouraging them to keep their children with DS. In the one case in which the couple gave up the child for adoption, she was devastated. I asked her about people who didn't share her dynamism, spirituality, and sense of purpose. "They all do," she said. "That's the wild thing with special-needs parents. This comes raging out of you. I feel such strength and courage in these women. I say to them all the time, 'I know you don't feel like you know what you're doing. Trust me. You are the perfect mother for this kid.'" She paused for a second and smiled. "You know, they probably want to smack me."

In about 95 percent of cases, Down syndrome is the result of a spontaneous mutation rather than a transmissible gene, and people who have DS seldom reproduce. Because DS was among the first major genetic anomalies for which prenatal testing existed, and because it is the most common genetic anomaly that can be detected in utero, it has been at the center of the abortion debate. Statistics range, but at present, about 70 percent of expectant mothers who receive a prenatal diagnosis of Down syndrome choose to abort. Ironically, outcomes for people with DS have improved more radically in the last forty years than have the outcomes for almost any other anomaly. People who would have languished in institutions and died at ten are now reading and writing and working. With adequate education and health care, many live more than sixty years; the national life expectancy for people with DS in the United States is around fifty, double the 1983 figure. People with Down syndrome are also interacting with a world that has many more accommodations for people with special needs. Supported employment means that many higher-functioning people with DS can find jobs; the general tolerance in society means that a person with DS arriving at a restaurant or a store with his family is more likely to be received graciously. In a recent study in Canada, parents of children with DS were asked whether they would pursue a cure if one were available. More than a quarter said they would not, and another third said they were not sure.

Targeted abortion had been expected to eliminate most of the population with Down syndrome, but the proportion of people born with the condition in any given year has increased or remained constant since testing was introduced. Such children are not evenly distributed across the population. Eighty percent of Down syndrome births are to women under thirty-five who have not had testing, and many of these are poor, as wealthier people are more likely to seek prenatal testing even if they are not in a risk category. Studies suggest that among people who carry to term, those with fewer material advantages may be less perfectionist and ambitious for their children, and therefore more readily accepting of the permanent dependence of children with DS. Some agencies specialize in arranging adoptions of children with DS; the head of one said to me, "I wish I could show you a list of the people who've given up their babies to me. It would read like *Who's Who in America*." More women choosing to have prenatal testing and abort fetuses diagnosed with DS brings the DS population down, while more women conceiving in later life brings it up. As people with DS who used to die at ten are living to sixty, the number of people on the planet with Down syndrome is increasing; the number in the United States may double between 2000 and 2025, to as much as eight hundred thousand.

The American College of Obstetricians and Gynecologists recommended in 2007 that all pregnant women undergo nuchal translucency in the first trimester, with the option of genetic counseling and amniocentesis or CVS in the second trimester for those with poor nuchal translucency results. Disability rights groups oppose this protocol; the conservative columnist George Will, who has a son with DS, called it "a search and destroy mission." Moderates have asked that people simply be better informed about the experience of parenting a child with Down syndrome. Stephen Quake, a Stanford professor who developed one of the new blood tests for DS, said, "It's a gross oversimplification to assume that these tests are going to lead to the wholesale elimination of Down syndrome births. My wife's cousin has Down syndrome. He's a wonderful person. It's not an obvious step that you would terminate an affected pregnancy." Nonetheless, activists worry that women who wish to keep a DS pregnancy may feel pressured to terminate as prenatal diagnosis gets easier. People without health insurance have a much harder time obtaining prenatal tests, and some worry that this will make DS into a poor man's condition.

In contrast, Michael Bérubé points out that having children with DS could become the province of the rich if prenatal screening becomes universal and insurance ceases to cover the medical and educational costs for those who keep such children. The existence of tests provides an imperative to use and act on them. One study said that women who do not use prenatal testing or who keep a pregnancy they know will lead to a child with a disability "were judged more responsible, more to blame, and less deserving of both sympathy and social aid subsequent to giving birth to a disabled child than were women to whom testing was not made available." These demographic suppositions seem to cancel each other out and point to the confusion around conditions such as DS, which can be considered both burden and luxury, sometimes by the same person. Michael Bérubé wrote, "So much depends on whether our technologies serve our social desires or our social desires are made to serve our technologies." In a newspaper interview, he added, "The fifteen million dollars spent on the new test for Down by the National Institute of Child Health and Human Development might have gone instead toward much-needed research on the biochemistry of people living with the condition."

Prenatal screening and support for people with DS should not be mutually exclusive, any more than cochlear implants have to engender the death of Sign, any more than a vaccine for an infectious disease should prevent our treating people who develop it. In the pragmatic economy of modern medicine, however, an ounce of prevention is usually held to be worth a ton of cure. As the techniques for prenatal diagnosis of DS have become more available, funding for research in the field has diminished. This seems particularly tragic because treatment for the major symptoms of DS, long considered impossible, is now a field full of promise. In 2006, Alberto Costa demonstrated that Prozac could normalize the compromised development of the hippocampus in mice that had a Down's-like condition. He later found that the Alzheimer's drug memantine boosted memory in similar mice, most likely by quieting neurotransmitter systems that he believes interfere with learning in DS. In 2009, William C. Mobley, chairman of neurosciences at the University of California, San Diego, showed that raising norepinephrine levels in the brains of these mice allowed them to learn at the level of typical mice. In 2010, Paul Greengard, of Rockefeller University, normalized learning and memory in such mice by lowering levels of β-amyloid, which is also implicated in Alzheimer's disease.

Mobley said, "There's been a sea change in our ability to understand

and treat Down syndrome. There's been an explosion of information. As recently as 2000, no drug company would possibly have thought about developing therapies for Down syndrome. I am now in contact with no less than four companies that are pursuing treatments." Commenting in the *New York Times*, Craig C. Garner, codirector of the Center for Research and Treatment of Down Syndrome at Stanford University, said, "This was a disorder for which it was believed there was no hope, no treatment, and people thought, 'Why waste your time?' The last ten years have seen a revolution in neuroscience, so that we now realize that the brain is amazingly plastic, very flexible, and systems can be repaired."

As with the deaf and their implants, and dwarfs and their ELL, this is another scramble—not so much for identity, this time, as for science. If people with DS can be normalized, should we think more carefully about terminating DS pregnancies? Costa said, "The geneticists expect Down syndrome to disappear, so why fund treatments? It's like we're in a race against the people who are promoting those early-screening methods. If we're not quick enough to offer alternatives, this field might collapse."

Angelica Roman-Jiminez was twenty-seven when her daughter Erica was born in 1992. Erica was a first child, and there had been no thought of doing amniocentesis. But when the baby was born, Angelica knew that something was wrong. "I remember holding the doctor's arm and saying, 'Please tell me.' My husband, I could see it in his eyes." The doctor told Angelica that her baby had "mild Down syndrome"— though there is no way to tell the severity of Down's symptoms in a newborn.

The doctors offered the possibility of adoption, but Angelica was not interested; still, she wondered how to tell people. "I called my parents. I said, 'The baby was born with . . . ,' and I couldn't finish the sentence. My father said, 'Well, does she have all her fingers? Does she have all her toes?' I said, 'Yes, yes.' He said, 'Whatever it is, we'll deal with it.' You always hear about unconditional love for your children no matter what. And there it was." Her priest said, "God gave you this child for a reason. Anything that I've seen come your way, you're able to tackle it, and this will be the same."

Not everyone had the grace to respond in kind. "A lot of our friends looked at it as a death," Angelica said. "I couldn't move from *why*. 'Why did this happen to us?' But then you realize, 'Wait a minute, she's alive. She needs our love and attention.' I still wanted to do birth announcements, and I sent along a letter describing what our lives were now."

Though she is Catholic, Angelica was working in a clerical job at Trinity Episcopal Church in lower Manhattan, and a coworker had a friend who had a child with Down syndrome. "She stayed on the phone with me for over an hour and told me which books to read. To stay away from anything earlier than the eighties. To join a parents support group. That was when I broke out of that 'Why?'" It helped that Erica was born the same year that Jane Pauley featured Jason Kingsley on her program. Images of people with DS were proliferating, as they had not even a few years earlier.

Within six weeks, Angelica had enrolled Erica in an early-intervention program. "When your child is born with a disability, all your high hopes and dreams are shattered. When she was one, I was always looking to see whether she was keeping up with the other children at the center. She was struggling with her grasp, her gross and fine motor skills. Then one day she had the coordination to pick up a Cheerio, and I wanted to jump for joy. A few years later, she needed ear tubes. Of course we wanted to do our best there, because if you can't hear, how is your language going to develop? So the doctor said, 'Well, she's not going to be perfect.' I felt, how dare he say that? He's never going to be perfect, either."

Speech development was ongoing. "She would point at what she wanted, and we would encourage her, 'Tell us what you want.' One time she had an evaluation for school, and the psychologist asked me whether Erica made her bed in the morning. I said, 'Well, no. We're in a rush. I'll just do it, and we'll go.' She checked off, 'Not given the opportunity.' Now I try always to give her the opportunity, whether it's zippering up her coat, tying her shoelace. She can write her name, address, and phone number."

Erica struggles with poor judgment, as do many people with DS. "We try to teach her, 'This is danger, this is not,'" Angelica said. "She's very trusting, without stranger anxiety. We've taught her that when she meets someone for the first time, she should shake hands. We have to explain, 'You can't hug everyone. Not everyone is nice.'" Angelica looked sober. "She doesn't get phone calls. She doesn't get a lot of party invitations. We've had her in programs with other children who have disabilities, ballet and music classes. I feel these other children with special needs are her peers. I want her to have that close friend who is going through the same things she is. I started a Girl Scout troop for exceptional girls. We have girls who are autistic, girls with Down syndrome, girls who are wheelchair-bound."

This work occupies a great deal of Angelica's time. "I also have a younger daughter, Leah, who is in those preteen years, and sometimes she's concerned about how she's seen by others. 'Will they accept me if I have a sister with special needs?' We tell Leah, 'There's nothing to be embarrassed about. This is how God gave her to us.'" Erica shows no sign of knowing that she could ever be perceived as an embarrassment. "She realizes that she can't run as fast as other kids. Or she can't jump rope the way other people do. But she's never asked me why. Erica is, 'If you're good to me, I'll be good to you.' Part of me wants her to be aware, and the other part is, well, if she's aware, she won't be happy."

Angelica had been deeply committed from the first to finding meaning in her experience, and she came to see Erica's disability as an occasion for her own moral growth. When Erica was nine, Angelica developed breast cancer. "Having Erica made me stronger to deal with that," Angelica said. "I became this stronger person because of her." Trinity Church is only a few blocks from Ground Zero, and Angelica was there on 9/11. She kept her cool in the midst of the chaos, and for that, too, she thanks Erica. "God makes these things happen to us sooner rather than later, because maybe our role will be to help others and to grow from this experience," she said. "That's what I feel my ministry is now, to let folks know and invite them to my home, to have conversations. I couldn't stop the planes from coming. I couldn't stop my illness or her condition. You can't stop the future."

In her memoir, *Expecting Adam*, Martha Beck writes, "If you'll cast your mind back to high school biology, you may remember that a species is defined, in part, by the number of chromosomes in every individual. Adam's extra chromosome makes him as dissimilar from me as a mule is from a donkey. Adam doesn't just do less than a 'normal' child his age might; he does different things. He has different priorities, different tastes, different insights." Beck writes of the transformations her son has wrought in her own life. "The immediacy and joy with which he lives his life make rapacious achievement, Harvard-style, look a lot like quiet desperation. Adam has slowed me down to the point where I notice what is in front of me, its mystery and beauty, instead of thrashing my way through a maze of difficult requirements toward labels and achievements that contain no joy in themselves."

Children with Down syndrome tend to retain what the experts call *babyfaceness*. These children have "a small, concave nose with a sunken bridge, smaller features, larger forehead and shorter chin, and fuller cheeks and rounder chin, resulting in a rounder face." A recent study found that both the register in which parents speak to their DS child and the variances in pitch resembled the voice patterns parents use to speak to infants and young children. So the infantilizing comes from parents who don't think they're doing it, in response to a biological facial structure that they may not consciously register as meaningful. Intellectual inequality places certain limits on intimacy for parents, yet studies show that fathers of DS children spend much more time with their affected children than most fathers spend with their typical children.

Other studies show that, on average, children act more kindly, more generously, and with less hostility toward siblings with Down syndrome than toward typically developing siblings. They are also more compassionate and mature. This is true even though siblings of mentally retarded children can suffer social ostracism and are at elevated risk of emotional and psychological problems. DS and non-DS sibling relationships are both warm and courteous, stripped of the volatility of relations between equals. Play between non-Down's siblings and their DS counterparts is more hierarchical and may contain less laughter. Yet writing in *Newsweek* about her brother with DS, Colgan Leaming said, "My brother is not his disability. He is a teenager who loves sports and PlayStation, who cares a little bit too much about his hair and is a little bit too confident, who is kind to every person he meets, who makes you laugh so hard your stomach hurts. He's a boy just like anyone else. Kevin does not have 'special needs.' All he needs is a chance."

Sibling responses can rely on minimizing the disability, or on celebrating it, or on some combination of the two. Which mode gets used has something to do with the dynamics of a given family, and something to do with the severity of the affected person's deficits. It is easy to focus on the tales of people with DS who are triumphantly high-functioning, whose parents take great pleasure in how smart and successful they are within the parameters of the illness. Given how much less these children are likely to attain than typical children, however, to universalize intelligence and achievement as a measure of worth is in some ways to deny who they are. They are not so bright and can't accomplish so much by general standards, but have real virtues and are capable of personal fulfillment. Many parents of people with DS began their conversations with me by saying how super-high-functioning their children were, and I began to wonder how it was that I saw only parents of such high-functioning kids. When I began talking to their children, I found that some of them were extraordinarily intelligent and advanced given their condition, and that many others had a few things at which they excelled, from which their parents cheerily generalized. The parents' perceptions of high functioning frequently outstripped the children's actual level of accomplishment.

Without exception, these parents reported that their children tried hard to please them. Stubborn, intractable when stuck on an idea, the children nonetheless had an eagerness, not as typical of the other disorders examined in this book, that was infinitely moving to their parents. Down syndrome kids are famously sweet-natured, but their less advertised characteristic is that they are troupers.

Adam Delli-Bovi is at the lower end of Down syndrome function and is also diagnosed on the autism spectrum. At twenty-six, he had a mental age of between four and five, and to meet him after seeing Jason Kingsley speaking at Barnes & Noble made it difficult to believe they had the same condition.

Adam's mother, Susan Arnsten-Russell, was twenty-two and living in Ithaca, New York, when she realized she was pregnant: "It was the late seventies, people were into alternative lives. I knew I wanted children, so since I wasn't doing anything else, I let it happen." Her parents hastily arranged a wedding for her. Her new husband, Jan Delli-Bovi, had a nephew with Down syndrome, but it never occurred to them to do genetic screening. Adam was diagnosed the day after he was born. "There wasn't a single solitary moment when I considered giving him up for adoption," Susan said. "I started looking, too quickly, at how I could use this challenge for something good. I didn't give myself time to grieve. My parents thought it was a tragedy, so I had to make it into just the opposite. I was a very young twenty-two." Susan applied for federal supplemental security income (SSI) for Adam. When the first check came, Susan used it to enroll in a graduate-level course at Cornell called Learning and Children. She started volunteering in a daycare center and became involved with EI.

Susan's research and learning were critical. "A regular kid will initiate. They'll learn in spite of anything you do," Susan said. "But with Adam you had to kind of bring it to him, and he'd meet you maybe a quarter of the way." Shortly after his first smile, a physical therapist noticed that he was having strange spasms, and Susan took him in for a brain scan, which showed constant myoclonic seizures, which can cause severe retardation. Susan and Jan gave Adam six weeks of shots of ACTH, a stress-related hormone. They went to see a neurologist because Adam seemed to be suffering so badly with the shots. The neurologist said, "If any healing is going to come, it's going to come from Adam, and really the best thing you can do is pray."

"There was a very strong commune in this town called the Family," Susan remembered. "They all had these names that their leader had given them, like Freedom and Grateful and Sought and Ocean and Sojourn. They started doing healing circles for us. They had this wonderful land with this wonderful pond where we would hang out naked with our babies and everybody would swim and talk. They came up with ideas about how his soul was trying to make up its mind whether to be in the world. Even as a newborn, you have to commit to engage in the world, and he didn't seem to have made up his mind when he first arrived here."

When Susan took Adam back to the doctor, the seizures were gone. However, Adam had persistent upper-respiratory infections, and he's largely deaf in his left ear. His vision was weak and one of his eyes wandered. For a while, he wore an eye patch, and later, strong glasses. When Adam reached his first birthday, Susan's mother bought him a dog puppet, and he loved it most of all his things. "Then he started developing all these weird behaviors," Susan said. "He really liked to hold things and stare at them. So I'd be really mean. I would take the puppet and put it across the hall. Boy, he would crawl, crawl, crawl, and he would grab it. I would take it away and he would go after it again. Then I started putting the puppet in clear boxes so he could see it in there and would have to figure out how to take it out."

Susan and Jan conceived another baby—"so Adam would have company," Susan said. Taciturn, suspicious, beautiful, and full of intensity, Teegan is fiercely loyal to her brother. Adam was in the public school system in his early years, and Teegan was constantly defending him. "If teachers didn't understand him, I would try to make them understand," she said. "I used to go into his classroom in the morning and spend time there until I was almost late for my own class. It was much more upsetting to me to see him teased than it was for him to be teased. A lot of the time, I don't think he even noticed." Teegan always brought her friends home to see her brother. "I used how they interacted with him as a measure of their character."

By this time, Susan and Jan had split up, and Susan was doing her best to place Adam in a new school. "The flip side of early intervention is, it sets up expectations and pressures," she said. "You see all these wonder kids, like Jason Kingsley, or that one who used to be on *Life Goes On*. Today, I think Adam has reached his maximum potential, but at that time, I felt maybe he wasn't doing as well as the others because I wasn't doing as much as other parents. In this little cohort of kids with Down's here in Ithaca, he was the slowest one." Susan had gone along with inclusion because it was what everyone else was doing, but Adam knew he didn't fit in; one day he removed all his clothes during math class. "Kids need to be in places where they feel successful, where they have peers," Susan said. "Yes, they need role models, but they also need to be role models." Her parents found a summer camp for children with moderate to severe mental retardation, where Adam has gone every year since, and where his relative level of functioning is sufficient that he can help others.

Susan had grown up in a largely nonobservant Jewish household. She had an affection for Judaism as a culture, but limited knowledge of the Jewish faith. One day, Teegan said she wanted to learn more about Judaism. Susan went to the nearest temple to sign Teegan up for Sunday school and began to bring Teegan and Adam to services. "He loves routine," Susan said. "He loves schedules, ritual, the singing. Judaism really works for us because it has struggling and mystical stuff built right into it." Of the many nuggets of Jewish philosophy she quotes, she rests particularly on the Talmudic notion, drawn from Exodus 37:9, that God exists in dialogue. "In the Torah, they describe building this huge tabernacle out in the wilderness," she said, "and on top of the vehicle that carries the tablets, they put two angels facing each other, because that is where God exists, between people. The day Adam was born, my life became purposeful, and it has kept purpose ever since. God exists between us. I knew that soon after he was born, but Judaism gave me a vocabulary for it."

Adam managed to memorize enough Hebrew for a bar mitzvah. Shortly thereafter, Susan met William Walker Russell III, a WASP sound engineer with a recording studio in an old church, and when he saw her interacting with Adam, he fell in love with her. He remembered, "Susan said, 'I'm a mother of two children; one has Down syndrome and is going to be with me forever. It's never going to be just the two of us.'" Susan and Will married six months later. "Adam started wanting to dress like me early on, and it was incredibly complimentary to me and incredibly embarrassing to go out in public," Will said. "It's like, I'm wearing jeans, a brown leather belt, and a white oxford button-down shirt from the Gap. He's wearing exactly the same thing. I figured I was in."

Susan and Will's marriage coincided with the onset of adolescence for Adam. Adolescence is a challenge when it hits any boy of fourteen, but it's even harder for someone who is in many ways four and a half. "Will experienced the testosterone stage," Susan said. "Adam would all of a sudden decide to wreck the place. He would pull the fire alarms." Will said, "Adam was doing some testing of personal power. When a four-year-old misbehaves, you pick the kid up and you take them to their room. Adam is not portable to Susan. So she developed a way of talking, showing unbelievable patience, and would spend whatever time it took negotiating. One time, he was kicking and spitting. I came behind him in a loving restraint, picked him up, and put him upstairs in his room. I remember the look on Adam's face—what just happened? That behavior stopped pretty quickly."

Susan loves to dance, and she took up contact improvisation, which grows from the belief that dance is a way of communicating. A collective called Dance New England puts on a weekly session where people can dance barefoot and freestyle in an alcohol-free, welcoming environment. Susan had long realized that most of her communication with Adam was nonverbal, so this community had particular resonance for her. "Other people with Down syndrome are very social, very outgoing," Susan said. "He is not so much. A lot of the reason that I like the dance forms that I do is it gives you a way of interacting and connecting with people without having to talk." Every summer, the collective would rent a place in Maine on a clothing-optional lake for two solid weeks of dancing, with a strong emphasis on community-building and volunteerism. Adam worked for two hours every day in the kitchen. "Everybody wears purple," Susan said. "It's a very nice, affirming place for us. It's a time when everything Adam has learned during the year coalesces, and it prepares him for the next year."

When Teegan was in ninth grade, she contracted mononucleosis and spent a long stretch at home, cared for by her mother. "One day, out of the blue, she said to me, 'You know that I'm always going to have a place for Adam wherever I live,'" Susan recalled. "When she said that, I started thinking about a team of support around Adam, that she is a willing part of that team. She came to that on her own." To Teegan, it had always been obvious. "In some ways, I was always the older sister," she said. "Sometimes I was annoyed about having to take care of him on a specific night. But I never wished for a life without him. His thanks is in the form of love, more than gratitude. I know he loves me, which is enough. I wouldn't trade it for the world."

Will struggled at times with existing family dynamics. "The primary duo is always Susan and Adam," he said. "If Susan and I are talking and Adam interrupts, our conversation stops, and there have been times when I have resented that." The biggest tension when Will joined the house was sound. Adam's greatest pleasure in life is Broadway show tunes. Shortly after I met Adam, he offered to sing for me. His sound is an enthusiastic monotone hum, like an amplified refrigerator. He usually sings along to his favorite recordings, to which he listens, over and over, at high volume. Will is a sound engineer whose life is in his ears. Adam eventually agreed not to sing in the car when Will was driving; Will figured out how to deal with sound in the house. When I asked Teegan to describe life with Adam, she said, "Slow." Will concurred. "It's about Adam time. Just like when you're hanging with a four-year-old, you give up your agenda. I've learned that no one says that nut has to be tightened in thirty seconds. If it's tightened in five minutes, it's all the same. Adam is my Zen master."

Adam completed vocational school, then entered a work program, affixing labels and stamps, and sealing envelopes; when that didn't work so well, he started volunteering in a soup kitchen, where he puts out the salt and pepper and rolls the silverware in napkins. "Being helpful is one of his values," Susan said. "In fact, one of the other Down's mothers said to me that she told her son that she would take him to something but he had to be like Adam. 'Adam's always smiling and he listens to his mother, and if you agree to be like Adam, I'll take you with me.' So whenever he started being a little disruptive, she said, 'Are you being like Adam?' It worked. Adam being a role model. For a kid who is way smarter than him."

Adam is not allowed any TV or videos on the Sabbath, so he listens to CDs of Broadway musicals on headphones. At dinner on Friday night, he blesses the bread. He does the ritual washing of hands as well. Then he takes a long mineral bath; he loves baths, but because he is prone to fungal conditions of the skin, he can't take them the rest of the week. "Toileting is still an issue, so we have him on a schedule," Susan said. "I would like to transition him to listening to his body more; he has accidents sometimes. We deal with his mental age."

I was curious about what *mental age* actually meant. "If you think about the level of supervision you might give a six-year-old, or what a six-year-old could do, that's about what Adam needs," Susan said. "It might be more like five, in some ways more like four. Because six-year-olds can generally read more than he can and make phone calls and know what to do in emergencies. If the house were on fire and he was watching TV, he wouldn't leave. Maybe when it got very, very hot. He knows about walking when the traffic light says 'walk,' but he doesn't know to look around and see that a car might be turning. If we're leaving Adam in someone's care, I say, 'Imagine someone who's been five years old for ten years.' He's Mr. Helpful around the house; he does all these things that a five-year-old would never be five long enough to learn." Teegan added, "If you gather a whole group of six-year-olds together, they'll have a much wider range of ability than any single six-year-old. So one might have grown up with professional parents in the city, so he knows about computers. Another grew up in the country and knows all kinds of wild plants, and how to find their way around in the woods. If you keep somebody at a six-year-old level for long enough, they'll expand laterally. That's what he's been doing."

Susan has stopped trying to resolve the contradictions that her life with Adam tosses up. "When he was born, my big thing was I wanted him to be able to communicate. Now I know that even people who don't talk can communicate." One birthday, Susan had bought Adam a black felt hat like the ones worn in *Fiddler on the Roof*. She had bought him a Broadway-compilation CD, and Adam's favorite song was "One," from *A Chorus Line*. At the end of a day in Ithaca, Adam said he had something to show me, and I sat down in the living room. He made Susan find her own hat, he put on the CD, and the two of them did a little Michael Bennett pastiche of the dance from *A Chorus Line*, lifting the hats, twirling around, kicking at the right moments. Somehow, Adam had learned the moves, and with only minimal prompting from Susan, he did the whole thing, a little awkwardly but with charm. Looking at this private cabaret, I was struck by Susan's insistence on dance as a means of communication, and I thought that what the whole household had achieved was intimacy. Susan's genuine belief that happiness was a fluid concept seemed to fill the room with love.

Some three-quarters of intellectually disabled people in the United States live with their parents. "The natural desire of parents to nurture their children during their growing years should be especially encouraged for children whose progress is measured in centimeters," one study notes. "Whenever families decide that they can no longer bear the burden of care, the transition to a residential placement should be facilitated. Empowerment of people with disabilities cannot ignore those who provide day-to-day care." The likelihood of placement of younger children with DS depends on the severity of their disability, the extent to which their behavior disrupts the household, and the capacity of the parents' relationship to withstand the stress of a disabled child. Siblings may need attention their parents cannot muster when someone needier occupies focus; those same siblings may be deeply distressed by the placement of a brother or sister, feeling vulnerable to exile themselves.

One study found that almost 75 percent of parents reported feelings of guilt after placement; half said they felt guilt "constantly" or "every day." Many feel that placement reflects their failure as parents. When the child who has been placed comes home to visit, families often feel glad and stressed; when the child goes back to his residence, they feel sad and relieved. They feel worse if their child is in a small facility, even though those are usually more humane; small facilities resemble home, and the similarity forces parents continually to reassess their decision to send their child away. When care is provided by a small staff, some parents become competitive with them. Parents most often report that placement has made their functional lives easier, but not their emotional lives. Nonetheless, they seldom bring back children whom they have placed; the tendency is to stick with whatever decision you have made. Investigators note parents' positive feelings toward placement after they have placed their child; they likewise note the positive feelings of parents who have decided to keep their children at home. To some degree, people who will be happier with a placement are more likely to place their children, and people who will be happier with their kids at home tend to keep them at home. Ultimately, this is also a matter of resolving cognitive dissonance: people adjust their attitudes to fit their decisions so as to avoid internal discord.

Placement is a process, not an overnight decision. Preliminary separations, through respite care and day or weekend programs, may allow parents to explore how placement will feel; they may, equally, allow parents to delay placement by alleviating some burden of care. In addition to their gradual psychological adjustment to placement, parents face pragmatic challenges in researching appropriate facilities and figuring out how to apply for the preferred ones. One person who has worked on this topic described how a mother told him, "I could never put my child in one of *those* places!" Two years later, she placed him in the exact setting that had so offended her. "Calling the Regional Center was the scariest phone call I ever made," one mother said. Many people with DS are placed between eighteen and twenty-one, at the age when typical children are moving out of their family houses; some experts feel that creating a life course that mimics the stages for typical people is advantageous.

The proportion of children and youth in institutions has gone down by about three-quarters, but the total number of people in institutions has gone up, because life spans have lengthened. Though big state institutions still exist in thirty-nine states, they have mostly given way to a vast array of smaller, more intimate, community-based care facilities. More than half of parents visit only one facility and place their children there, sometimes for geographic reasons, but often without regard to the range of quality of such facilities. In 2011, the *New York Times* reported hideous abuses at residential facilities throughout New York State. "Employees who sexually abused, beat or taunted residents were rarely fired, even after repeated offenses," the paper stated. "State records show that of some 13,000 allegations of abuse in 2009 within state-operated and licensed homes, fewer than five percent were referred to law enforcement. One obstacle complicates any effort to take action against employees accused of abusing those in their care: The victims often cannot talk or have extreme cognitive impairment.

Local law enforcement officials point to this to explain a lack of prosecution of cases. But another factor seems to be at work. In many cases, the developmentally disabled do not have families actively involved in their lives, and, hence, no advocates." These abuses cast a long shadow over the experience of families who are grappling with placement decisions. Though spending on housing and treatment for people with intellectual disabilities in the United States averages $380.81 per person per day, the actual amount fluctuates widely from state to state and even from county to county.

Where families used to be counseled to separate themselves emotionally from the children they placed, many now remain deeply involved; placement out of the home is not placement out of the family. Most visit monthly at least and speak on the phone more frequently. Many parents want to be present to effect a progressive transition to avoid "transfer trauma." "The time to have a young adult go into a group home is when you're still around," Elaine Gregoli advised. "I hear horror stories of parents who have forty- and fifty-year-olds at home. Then the parents die, and these forty-year-olds have to go into a new environment, where they're asked to do things that they were never trained to do." Many retired parents who still care for their DS children describe them as a comfort in a world where many older people are isolated and purposeless. Nevertheless, most people with DS will ultimately need some kind of outside care unless their parents outlive them, or siblings or friends take over; few are able to live fully independently. About three-quarters of people with DS who are still at home when their parents die are moved to residential placement.

Some people with DS thrive at home and others thrive away from home, which reflects the personalities of the people with DS and the nature of their families. Living at home means a familiar environment, and, ideally, more love. Adults with DS who live with their parents may, however, suffer lack of contact with peers and considerable loneliness. As they grow older, such people have fewer things to do outside the house, and they tend not to learn skills for building friendships. One father in rural Pennsylvania, a construction worker, talked about how happy his daughter had been through high school; she had been a cheerleader and a member of the homecoming court, surrounded by friends. Once she graduated, however, her classmates moved away to college or got on with their busy lives, and he ended up taking her with him on his truck every day. She worked at Walmart a few hours a week and had no social life at all. She lived for two Arc dances a year. In one recent study, only about a quarter of adults with DS who lived at home could name a friend who was not part of their parents' social network.

Alongside the memoirs written by parents are, increasingly, those written by people with Down syndrome, who constitute a vital self-advocacy movement. More than eight hundred self-advocacy groups now exist in the United States alone, and members address themselves to legislators, caseworkers, and parents. Many of them are organized under the banner of People First, an international self-advocacy organization that began in Sweden in 1968. In 1973, the first North American meeting took place in Vancouver, where "mentally handicapped" people gathered at a conference called May We Have a Choice. People First operates in forty-three countries and has an estimated membership of some seventeen thousand. Their website explains, "We believe that if we can learn to talk at our meetings and among ourselves, we can learn to talk to anyone about things that are important to us. We talk to our parents, our service providers, our caseworkers, to city councils and mayors. We talk to legislators and legislative committees, to governors and even the President. Even though it may be hard to understand us sometimes, people listen to us because they know that we know what we are talking about." For people with intellectual disabilities to have organized on this scale, even with helpers, is astonishing, especially when one considers the prognosis for the condition even a few decades ago.

Until the late 1960s, no one with DS had ever achieved prominence of any kind, but since that time, actors, activists, writers, and artists with the condition have emerged. The first major publication by someone with DS was *The World of Nigel Hunt: The Diary of a Mongoloid Youth*, published in the UK in 1967. Hunt was the son of a school headmaster who, with his wife, attempted to educate Nigel like any other child and included him in the regular classes at his school. Nigel's book recounts his day-to-day life, with touching references to his mother's illness and death. Jason Kingsley and Mitchell Levitz's *Count Us In* is an often joyful and occasionally humorous account of their lives, including knowing descriptions of the particular challenges they've faced. In 2000, Windy Smith, who has DS, addressed the Republican National Convention in Philadelphia, reading aloud a letter she had sent to George W. Bush; she went on to serve on the President's Committee for People with Intellectual Disabilities within the Department of Health and Human Services. Many debated whether this represented exploitative manipulation by the Bush campaign, with one critic describing it as "the most grotesque piece of political theater I've ever seen."

The highest-profile person with Down syndrome for a long time was the actor Chris Burke, who starred in the TV program *Life Goes On*, but there have been many others, including Judith Scott, a fiber artist who died in 2005, and Luke Zimmerman, a young actor in the TV series *The Secret Life of the American Teenager,* who was also a football player at Beverly Hills High. In Germany, Rolf "Bobby" Brederlow, an actor, has a considerable following. Lauren Potter appears on the Fox hit *Glee* as a cheerleader with DS and has her own Facebook fan page. Arden Moulton described being with Chris Burke and having strangers ask for his autograph. "It was a mind-boggling experience," she said. "He was a star first, and a person with a disability second." The trickle-down effect is incontrovertible. A poised young woman said to me by way of introduction, "I have Down syndrome, like Chris Burke."

Research suggests that people with DS may have different learning mechanisms from typical children, and new studies are looking at whether the strengths of people with DS—who have, for example, unusually good short-term visual memory—can be harnessed to allow them to learn more, better, and faster. Because they hold visual information more readily than auditory information, teaching them to read as early as possible is especially important and may play a larger role in their language development than it does for typical children. Many memoirists, including Michael Bérubé and Martha Beck, suggest that their children have forms of intelligence not to be found on IQ tests—islands of insight, ability, and even wisdom that come surprisingly readily to them.

In his memoir about his son Ned, Greg Palmer says that Ned enjoys interacting with nondisabled people and engaging in conversation with them; the idea of isolating him among other mentally retarded people is anathema to his father. For many years, the Palmers avoided telling their son that he had DS, and when they finally broke the news, he said, "I find that a little hard to believe." His inability to grasp his limitations was one of the indicators of his unpreparedness for life out in the world. Like many others with DS, he has a puzzling mix of strong abilities—he can play several musical instruments and writes good poetry—and sharp limitations—he is unable to take the bus across town without getting completely lost. Greg Palmer acknowledges that he has sometimes infantilized his son; he offers self-criticism on that front and is similarly critical of a larger world that continues to infantilize Ned. He complains of a view of Ned as adorable and funny by people with whom he would like to engage at a more complex level. Ned is the author of this poem, which reflects his verbal sophistication, his naïveté, and his longing:

Girls

Girls are neat. Girls are sweet.
They're the kind of people I love to meet.
Teenage girls are what I love.
They're like angels from above.
I'm crazy for girls, I'm crazy for love.
Girls are like the wings on a dove.
When I grow up and am feeling old,
I'll find all the girls I love to hold.
I'd like to give all the girls a kiss.
If there weren't any girls, it's girls I'd miss.

People with DS have both romantic and sexual feelings. Many men with Down syndrome are sterile, but women with DS are as fertile as those without disabilities. Parents frequently worry that their children's sexual activity will result in the birth of kids for whom they would be unable to care. The next frontier for people with DS, however, is marriage. On *Life Goes On*, Chris Burke's character married a woman with DS and they lived in an apartment over his parents' garage.

Tom and Karen Robards were hard-charging Wall Street types who met at Harvard Business School. Six years into their marriage, in the mid-1980s, they decided to start a family. Karen had an easy pregnancy, and they were totally unprepared for Down syndrome. Tom was crushed, but Karen said, "We're going to love David just like any other baby. When people don't know what to say, we're going to tell them to congratulate us."

"I had massive crying jags," Tom said. "Then someone we didn't even know called us at the hospital to say, 'You're not alone.' That was our first moment of hope." The woman who called was Barbara Chandler, head of Manhattan Parents Support Group. "I remember asking, 'Is there any joy at all in raising a child with Down syndrome?'" Karen said. "She said, 'Yes. There is joy. There's also heartbreak.'" That honest answer gave Karen the energy she needed. The Robardses went to see a pediatrician on the Upper West Side. "There's nothing you can do," he said. Tom and Karen were shocked. "Did that mean that there was nothing for us even to think about?" Tom asked. They found a doctor who specialized in genetic defects. She told them to provide every possible form of infant stimulation. The State of New York early-intervention program arranged for physical therapists to visit the family at home. Speech therapists worked on feeding and chewing to develop oral motor abilities. The Robardses joined a support group. "Some of our closest friends are from that original group," Karen said. "We decided to write a pamphlet about the options after EI. We're lawyers, we're investment bankers; we know how to do research. We'll just call up the public, private, and parochial schools and organize all the information. It wasn't that simple. We faced the staggering bureaucracy of the public schools. I remember calling up a private school and I said, 'I understand you take children with special needs.' They said, 'Oh, yes.' I said, 'Well, let me tell you about my child. He has Down syndrome.' She said, 'Oh, not that special.' Then we tried the parochial sector. Again, 'No.' What were we going to do?"

So Karen and the parents' group raised $40,000 to start the Cooke Foundation, now called the Cooke Center, one of the largest organizations in New York City focused on educational inclusion for disabled children. From its inception, it was open to children of all socioeconomic backgrounds. It was nonsectarian, but began in affiliation with the Archdiocese of New York after Karen Robards persuaded the archdiocese's director of special education to supply a space. That space turned out to be two large public lavatories; these were renovated into two classrooms by a member of the support group, a contractor who did the work at cost. "If anybody had told me that I was going to spend the next twenty years building the Cooke Center, I would have said they were crazy," Karen said. "But we met other people and we bonded and then we had a mission. Once you have that fire in the belly, you can process the emotional devastation, which we'd been denying. As for what we built from there—you get sucked in."

They hired two special-education teachers—"one for each lavatory," Karen said. The principle from the beginning was that their children should spend time with typically developing students, so they enrolled them in public schools for some subjects and taught others at Cooke. David continued to attend both Cooke and the public schools, becoming the first disabled child in New York City to be included in a regular classroom. "You have to have a place in both worlds," Karen said. "Jason Kingsley and his parents had thrown open a lot of doors. We were able to walk through those doors. When they're younger, our kids can be more fully included in classrooms because everybody's just learning colors and social skills. As you go on, the gap grows wider, and our kids really need to be focusing on life skills. How do you join a gym? How do you take money out of the ATM? Things that come naturally for other kids require effort from our kids. So we work on building those skills so that they can be included not only in education but also in life."

When David was seven, the Robardses' second child, Christopher, was born bright and bouncing. At thirteen months, he began having seizures and eventually developed status epilepticus, an often-fatal condition in which the seizures are going on almost constantly and cannot be stopped. "I kept thinking, 'Oh, well, if it's only seizures, we've done Down syndrome and we can deal with that,'" Karen said. "But it wasn't just seizures." Christopher has shown cognitive delays, mental retardation, speech delay, and motor issues. "I didn't cry about David," Karen said. "But I cried without stopping about Christopher. How could this be happening twice in one family?" Later in life, Christopher would be diagnosed with partial agenesis of the corpus callosum, which is the nerve connection between the left and right halves of the brain; a typical corpus callosum is about ten thousand times larger than Christopher's. The syndrome may have been caused by a virus Karen contracted during the first trimester of pregnancy.

"The thing about Down syndrome," Karen said, "is that there were so many kids who had gone before, there was at least a path." Christopher has some strong abilities and some noticeable deficits. When I met the Robardses, Christopher had just taught himself solitaire on the computer, which David couldn't possibly do. But David is extremely emotionally available; Christopher has never shown much interest in other people and could make it through Christmas without noticing that it was a special day. "For five years or so, he was seizing weekly," Karen said. "We couldn't leave the house without worrying what was going to happen. So it put a very different strain on us than having a child with Down syndrome."

Karen was pregnant again when Christopher's issues began to surface, and when he was eighteen months old, Kate was born, free of disabilities. When Kate was young, she found Christopher hard to relate to and became close to David despite their nine-year age gap. "When David noticed that she was surpassing him, he got very competitive with her and was not necessarily the nicest," Karen said. While the Robardses wrestled with these dynamics at home, the Cooke Center they continued to oversee grew and prospered; it had 186 employees when I visited, twenty years after it was set up. "You can't learn how to be in human society if you're separated from it," Tom said of inclusion. "You learn at least as much from your peers as you do from your teachers." Karen said, "Special education is a set of services that can be delivered in any number of places. But it has to be delivered. You can't just dump a kid in a regular classroom and not train the teacher or put in additional support. Our tagline at Cooke is 'When everyone is included, we all learn more.' The typical kids learn empathy; they learn to appreciate diversity." Cooke now helps charter schools with programs for children with special needs, educates in the public sector, and trains paraprofessionals for inclusion. Cooke works with corporations, too, to provide jobs for disabled kids.

David was twenty-three when I met the Robardses, and he had done fund-raising for the International Down Syndrome Society. He had completed internships at News Corporation and at *Sports Illustrated*. "They had him archive the magazine once they put it to bed," Tom said. "Nobody else wanted to do that job. And he loved it." He was living semi-independently in a supervised setting; like Jason Kingsley, he is in the lonely high end of the Down syndrome world. "Kids who are high-functioning have more of a sense that they are different," Karen said. "David has said, for a long time now, that he wants a job, an apartment, and a wife. We said we can help him with two of those, but he's on his own for the third."

David's personality has been his best selling point. Karen said, "I've always said David will go very far because he's just so charming. When he just looks at you with those blue eyes . . ." She shook her head and laughed with the wonder of it. "If he meets someone and he knows that a relative is sick, next time he'll say, 'How's your father?' If he's on the phone, he always wants to know 'How is so-and-so?' He'll ask my sister, 'How are the girls?' He's got a lot of love in him." Tom concurred, explaining, "IQ measures two dimensions, mathematical reasoning and linguistic capability. But then you have emotional and empathetic intelligence. David has always had an interpersonal sense of what other people are feeling. Maybe not what they're thinking, but what they're feeling. We all learn that we have strengths and weaknesses. I'm never going to be able to play basketball. Is it sad when you realize that you're different? Or is it just somehow coming to terms with your own identity?"

When David finished high school, public special-needs education stopped. "There are very few postsecondary programs," Karen said. They finally located a school in Pennsylvania that David could attend, and at twenty-one he lived away for the first time. It was not easy for David or his parents. When I met the Robardses, David had just begun to take Effexor after being deeply shaken by a romance gone awry. He liked a girl with Down syndrome at his school. She had encouraged his attentions, but already had a boyfriend who was a friend of David's. When David was closed out by both of them, he became paralyzed with anxiety. David has a plethora of friends, and "a Rolodex that he works every day," according to Tom. Karen said, "David is a master of the cell phone and he loves to keep in contact, but he's also a lover of structure. So you would probably be Tuesday nights. Every Tuesday night he'll call you. We're Sundays and Wednesdays. 'David, do you think you could call us a different night?' 'No. You're Sundays and Wednesdays.' I think the rigidity helps stabilize him. I like knowing what I'm going to do on any given day, and he's the same way."

We drifted to the question of cure. "If you talk to people very involved in the Down syndrome community," Tom said, "you'll find a range of perspectives on whether looking for a cure for Down syndrome is a legitimate objective. There are people who won't even talk about that, because to talk about a cure is to diminish the value of the people who are alive with Down syndrome. Some would even say that if they could wave a magic wand and make their child normal, they wouldn't do it." I asked Tom what he would do if he had the magic wand. "If I could have David who he is but not have Down syndrome?" he asked. "I would do it in a minute. I would do it because I think, for David, it's hard being in the world with Down syndrome, and I'd like to give him a happier, easier life. So for David, I'd do it. But the diversity of human beings makes the world a better place, and if everyone with Down syndrome were cured, it would be a real loss. The personal wish and the social wish are in opposition. The question is whether we collectively learn more than we hurt."

Karen shook her head. "I'm with Tom. If I could cure David, I would, for David. But I think that we've grown so much as a result of having to deal with this. We've had so much purpose. I'd never have believed twenty-three years ago when he was born that I could come to such a point, but I have. For David, I'd cure it in an instant; but for us, I wouldn't exchange these experiences for anything. They've made us who we are, and who we are is so much better than who we would have been otherwise."

V

Autism

The hallmark of progress is the retrenchment of diseases. Countless infectious illnesses are now prevented by vaccines or cured with antibiotics; HIV can be controlled for many people with antiretroviral therapy; deadly cancers can be forced into permanent remission. Understanding how maternal exposure to viruses may cause deafness has reduced the number of deaf children born to hearing parents, and cochlear implants reduce the number of people who are functionally deaf. Treatments for pituitary dwarfism have brought down the numbers of little people. Down syndrome is both detected earlier, leading some prospective parents to terminate pregnancies, and addressed far more effectively; schizophrenia is mitigated by neuroleptics. Genius and criminality continue to appear at a constant rate. But, mysteriously, autism seems to be on the rise.

Some experts argue that we are simply diagnosing it more frequently, but improved diagnosis can hardly be the full explanation for the escalation from a rate of 1 in 2,500 births in 1960 to 1 in 88 today. We don't know why autism is on the rise; indeed, we don't know what autism is. It is a *syndrome* rather than an *illness* because it is a collection of behaviors rather than a known biological entity. The syndrome encompasses a highly variable group of symptoms and behaviors, and we have little understanding of where it is located in the brain, why it occurs, or what triggers it. We have no way to measure it but by its external manifestations. The Nobel Laureate Eric Kandel said, "If we can understand autism, we can understand the brain." That is a generous way of saying that we will understand autism only when we understand the brain.

Autism parents are activist. Not since the height of the AIDS crisis has there been such an aggressive campaign for funding and research, with scores of organizations (many of them with snappy acronymic titles such as SafeMinds) pursuing theories of causality, the development of behavioral treatments, appropriate schooling, disability benefits, support services, and supervised housing. Cure Autism Now, a parent group, pushed Congress to pass the 2006 Combating Autism Act, which mandated a billion dollars of spending in five years for research on autism and related disorders. Thomas Insel, director of the National Institute of Mental Health, said, "We get more calls from the White House about autism than about everything else combined." Between 1997 and 2011, the number of books and articles published per year about autism increased more than sixfold.

Autism is deemed a *pervasive disorder* because it affects almost every aspect of behavior, as well as sensory experiences, motor functioning, balance, the physical sense of where your own body is, and inner consciousness. Intellectual disability is not part of autism per se; the syndrome is rooted in a disruption of social function. The primary symptoms, which may occur or not in any constellation in any individual with autism, are lack of or delay in speech; poor nonverbal communication; repetitive movement, including flapping arms and other self-stimulating behaviors; minimal eye contact; diminished interest in friendships; lack of spontaneous or imaginative play; compromised empathy, insight, and sociability; diminished capacity for emotional reciprocity; rigidity; highly focused interests; a fascination with objects such as spinning wheels and sparkling things. Autistic children and adults often think in an extremely concrete manner and may have difficulty understanding metaphor, humor, irony, and sarcasm. They are given to obsessive, stereotyped behavior, forming attachments to seemingly random objects, arranging toys by size or color rather than playing with them. Autistic people may engage in self-injurious behavior, including hand-biting and head-banging; they may have sensory-motor deficits. Many autistic children do not develop the ability to point to things and instead have to lead someone to what they wish to indicate. Some have echolalia, in which they repeat words or phrases, often without any apparent understanding of their meaning. The diction of autistic people who speak may lack intonation, and such people will often talk to others at great and repetitive length about the objects of their unbounded fascination. Food rituals and an extremely limited diet are common. People with autism may be exquisitely sensitive to sensory overload from crowded spaces, human touch, fluorescent or flickering lights, and noise. Many autistic people find minor irritants such as clothing tags unbearable. Autistic people are frequently confounded by things that please most other people. While most autistic children show early signs of the syndrome (whether recognized or not), about a third appear to develop normally and then regress, often between sixteen and twenty months. Because any of these symptoms may occur in any degree, autism is defined as a spectrum that includes varying severity of varying symptoms.

In a caustic reply to "Welcome to Holland," with its touching depiction of disability as a strange but beautiful place full of quiet joys, one mother of an autistic child penned "Welcome to Beirut," equating the experience of parenting an autistic child with being dumped unceremoniously into the middle of a war zone. This hell is partly a matter of the autistic child's extreme symptoms, which may include a tendency to spread feces on the walls, the ability to go many days without sleeping, in a state of manic high energy, an apparent inability to connect with or speak to another human being, and a propensity for random acts of violence. There is no treatment for the atypical neurological configuration that is autism, but one can educate an autistic child, administer medications, or make dietary or lifestyle modifications that may relieve a child's depression, anxiety, and physical and sensory problems. No one has figured out what makes one treatment more effective than others for a particular person. To add to the frustration, many children are unresponsive to any form of treatment, but the only way to figure that out is to treat them for a long time and then give up. The treatments that are reported most effective are incredibly labor-intensive and vastly expensive. Numerous tales of "emergence" drive parents to fight toward an elusive miracle. So the chances are good that a parent will drive himself or herself nearly crazy, come to the verge of bankruptcy, and still have a child whose disturbing behavior cannot be resolved. Most parents can ultimately accept conditions that are untreatable and will devote themselves to treating those that are treatable, but autism betrays such neat Serenity Prayer divisions.

The cliché about autism is that the syndrome impedes the ability to love, and I began this research interested in how much a parent could contrive to love a child who could not return that affection. Autistic children often seem to inhabit a world on which external cues have limited impact; they may seem to be neither comforted by nor engaged with their parents and are not motivated to gratify them. Tending to them can be gravely frustrating because the distinction between deficits of emotion and deficits of expression is often opaque. It is largely unknowable to what extent severely autistic people can hear and understand everything but cannot make themselves heard or understood, and to what extent they lack some domains of awareness entirely. The question of how we love people with autism is Pascalian. If they can receive affection yet are not given any, they doubtless suffer. If they cannot receive affection yet are given much of it, that affection may be squandered—presumably the lesser of two evils. The problem is that emotion is not gratis. To love a child who does not evidently mirror your love exacts a more terrible price than other love. Yet most autistic children, despite the syndrome's reputation, do develop at least partial attachments to others, at least eventually.

There is another way to look at autism. Under the banner of neurodiversity, some people, many on the autism spectrum, have declared that autism is a rich identity, even if it is also a disability. The tension between identity and illness is common to most of the conditions in this book, but in no other instance is the conflict so extreme. Confronting desperately frustrated parents with the idea that autism is not an adversity can seem insulting. Other parents, however, frame their children's difference in a more positive light. Neurodiversity activists lobby for their dignity; some believe they speak for the larger autistic community and reject treatments that might eradicate autism. Since such treatments do not exist, this is abstract philosophy, but the arguments bear on when and how to use the limited interventions we do have.

Betsy Burns and Jeff Hansen had planned to have just one child, but when their daughter Cece was almost two, Betsy decided she wanted another and became pregnant almost immediately. Going for amniocentesis, "I said to Jeff, 'What would we do if we found out something was wrong?'" Betsy recalled. "And he said, 'Just love the child.' So we made a commitment to love a child with special needs, without even knowing that we already had one."

Cece had been a good baby, happy to play by herself, though even as an infant she didn't sleep much; the new arrival, Molly, was more demanding—but also more engaged. Over time, Jeff and Betsy worried that Cece was not talking. She never said *milk*; she gave them a cup. Their doctor assured Betsy that she was just an anxious first-time mother. Then Jeff, an English teacher, found a job at a Minnesota high school, so the family moved to St. Louis Park, outside Minneapolis. Betsy joined a mothers group when Cece was three and listened to the other women talk about their children. "I went cold. Something was terribly wrong," she said. Betsy requested an early-intervention assessment from the local department of health. The evaluator said, "It's troubling that she's interested in my jewelry but not in my face." Then she said, "I don't want you to think that any of this has to do with anything you and your husband ever did. I don't want you to be frightened when I use the word *autism*." Jeff went to the public library to check out books on autism. "I'll never forget the stricken look of the librarian when I plopped down those books on the desk," he said.

Because early intervention is a key strategy for autism, Betsy took Cece almost immediately to a public nursery school, where a few special-needs kids were in classrooms with typical children. Cece received speech therapy, occupational therapy, physical therapy, and music therapy. Nonetheless, her air of disconnectedness intensified, and she was self-injurious and sleepless. When Cece was four, they visited a local neurologist, who said, "If she's not talking at all after this high-quality early intervention, she'll never talk, and you should get used to that. She has serious autism."

Cece has actually spoken four times in her life, and every time the words were appropriate to the situation. When Cece was three, Betsy gave her a cookie; she pushed it back at her, saying, "You eat it, Mommy." Jeff and Betsy exchanged glances and waited for their world to change. Cece said nothing more for a year. Then one day Betsy stood up to turn off the TV, and Cece said, "I want my TV." At school, three years later, she turned on the lights and said, "Who left the lights on?" Then one day a puppeteer visited Cece's class; when he asked, "Hey, kids! What color is the curtain?" Cece responded, "It's purple." The capacity to formulate and deliver these sentences suggests a tantalizing lucidity below the silence. "I think for her to speak is like a traffic jam," Betsy said. "The wiring keeps the idea from getting to the mouth." To have a child totally incapable of language is distressing but straightforward, but to have a child who has spoken four times is to labor in terrifying murkiness. If the traffic could clear enough for her to speak on those occasions, could the right intervention clear it altogether? You must remain agnostic while talking to Cece, aware that she may be picking up everything, or that your words may be gibberish to her.

"I think she might be preliterate," Betsy said. "I believe that she has a wild intelligence somewhere. I worry that her soul is trapped." In childhood, Cece was assessed with an IQ of 50; her most recent therapist thinks she has no intellectual disability. When I met Cece, she was ten, and her favorite thing was to hold a lot of crayons and go across a piece of table and a piece of paper so she could feel the change in sensation where the paper ended and the table began. But for a brief time, she had suddenly started drawing faces, oblong, with eyes, a mouth, and hats. Then she stopped. "Something was coming through," Betsy said. "Just like something comes through when she says words."

The first time Cece was administered anesthesia was for dental work, in early childhood. Betsy wondered whether it would be easier if she died from the anesthesia. "My mother said, 'You just want to put her out of her misery,'" Betsy recalled. "But Cece wasn't usually miserable. I was. I was insane. When she came out of the anesthesia, I looked at that pale coloring, and her white-blonde hair, and those high cheekbones. And I realized, on some level, that this was going to be a new relationship. Because she was here for good." It's unclear to what extent Cece recognizes people or cares about having them near. "Sometimes you feel like a piece of furniture," Betsy said. "Even when she's snuggling with you, it can be just because she needs some deep-pressure input. Not 'Oh, I love you,' but 'It's warm; I can push against it.' I don't know if she recognizes me."

Betsy wrote a novel, *Tilt*, about this period of her life; in it, she described typical days with Cece. "The behavior specialist has told us that if we give her food while she is tantrumming—and we know she wants food because she stands by the cabinet and bangs the heels of her hands against the wood—then we will be rewarding her for tantrumming and bribing her into acquiescence. But when the world is horribly disorienting, what woman doesn't want to eat? She's turning into a kind of luminescent orb of a child." In another passage, Betsy describes, "I return to her bath and she is happily floating in the tub, pushing small brown things around, little brown things that are disintegrating. Little brown things that are shit. Oh, Christ! Oh, God help me. I scream get out get out get out. But why do I think she can understand? She's still smiling. I yank her out and her heavy self falls and slips against the side of the tub and then there is shit in her hair and shit on my hands and she is laughing. I can't put her back in the tub because the shit has to go down the drain and I can't rinse her off in the sink because she's too big, so I put towels on the floor and soak washcloths in the sink and squeeze them over her head and watch the water run down her sides. And then I see the holes still open in her leg and think, Great, shit in an open wound."

Jeff and Betsy had to arrange their house around Cece's behavior. The shelves were six feet high so that she couldn't reach them; the refrigerator was padlocked because Cece would do strange things with the food. Cece was frequently hospitalized because she had stopped sleeping or because she was hurling herself around. Doctors repeatedly suggested placement for Cece. Betsy fell into a catastrophic depression, for which she was hospitalized. "I wish hell were other people, instead of me," she later said. Toward the end of Betsy's stay in the hospital, Jeff found Cece trying to strangle Molly. The social workers arranged a place for Cece to spend three months. "They didn't tell me it was going to be permanent, 'cause they knew I would die," Betsy said. "On January first, 2000, she left our house forever." She was seven.

The facility director suggested that Betsy and Jeff wait at least a month before visiting, to allow Cece to become acclimated. While Cece seemed to be doing well enough, Betsy couldn't bear it, and several weeks later, on Cece's birthday, Betsy was hospitalized again. "Throwing something away that was part of her feels like throwing her away," Betsy said. "We've kept the padlocks and the high shelves as a little memorial to the time when Cece lived with us." Betsy belonged to a support group for mothers of disabled children, and the members lobbied for establishment of a group home in their community. When I first went to see Cece, she had been there two years. One of the other girls in the group home has cerebral palsy, and whenever her mother leaves, she cries. "I was talking to my sister and I said, 'Cece doesn't cry when I leave,'" Betsy said. "And she said, 'Imagine what you'd feel like if she did.'" Parents of children such as Cece fear that their love is useless to their children, and they fear that their deficits of love are devastating to their children, and it's hard for them to say which fear is worse. Three years after Cece's placement, Betsy said, "I'm allowing myself to see that I hate visiting. I feel really guilty if I don't see her on one of the prescribed days. A woman in my mothers group said, 'Because you're afraid if you don't go one day, you'll never go.'"

When I met Betsy for lunch, she said apologetically, "I have to leave my cell phone on because Cece's in the hospital and they may need to reach me." I said how sorry I was to hear it, that such times must be trying. "On the contrary," she said. "This is the one time when I know that it does her some good that I'm her mother. Mostly, I could be exchanged for any object with the same basic curves."

Then Cece will show a break in her autism. "One day I was leaving and said, 'Give me a kiss!' and she rubbed her face up against mine. One of the workers said, 'Cece's kissing her mama!' I didn't know that she didn't do that with other people. Not that it was what we'd call a kiss, but the air around her is really soft, so it serves as a kiss. Kissing her cheek is like kissing something so soft and dear that it's almost not there. Kind of like her."

Betsy once explained, "For her, sounds and sensations might be like a radio set between dials. I mean how the world *gets in* on you, with its buzzes and demands and hangnails and phone calls and gasoline smells and underwear and plans and choices. Cece loves to put on shoes that grip her feet the right way. Sometimes, in the spring, she would put on her boots just to feel them. She loves playing with the hair of African people. And she loves french fries, that whole crunchy, salty sensation. Who doesn't? She loves salsa and things that wake up her mouth. It's very fun for her to snuggle under things. She loves motion, going for a ride and looking out the window. She used to like the soft skin on people's elbows, and she'd follow behind them and hold on to that. If I think about her sensory issues, all I have to do is pull them back a little, and they're mine. I love crunching leaves when I walk. The same is true when I walk on very thin ice, and it crackles. There are certain things that I'm afraid if I get too close to them, I'll touch them for too long. My mother used to have a beaver coat that was so nice and soft. Then there are so many other things that I wouldn't want to go near. Limousines give me the creeps, and the longer they are, the more they creep me out. But I was always trying to arrange words, and trying to understand how they marry each other; how they separate, how they allow each other to spill off. She defies it. She *forces* the intellect to let go. You retreat to an intuitive level because that's the only way to read her."

Though Cece does not have spoken language, she knows some signs and makes erratic use of *more, please, time to go, outside, water,* and *juice.* When Betsy arrives for a visit, Cece will bring out her coat and boots to indicate that she wants to go out. When she doesn't want to go out, she takes Betsy's coat and puts it firmly on the floor. "She does something; she knows it contains meaning," Betsy said. "We have to learn her language, which can be as confusing for us as ours is for her."

It's hard to find neutral territory for intimacy with Cece. Much of Betsy's favorite time with Cece takes place swimming. This does, however, involve going into the public space of a swimming pool, where Cece is not capable of modifying her behavior. Betsy and Cece went to the pool at the St. Louis Park recreation center one day just after I met them. They arrived an hour before closing, when many families were there. The minute she arrived, Cece pulled off the bottom half of her swimsuit, defecated in the water, played with her feces, then ran around naked so that no one could catch her. One of the mothers screamed, "Contamination! Contamination!" Then all of the others began to yank their children out of the water. Lifeguards blew whistles and screamed, and Cece stood amid the chaos, laughing uproariously.

I went with Jeff, Betsy, and Molly to visit Cece at the group home on her tenth birthday. We had brought a cake in with us, but for safety reasons, there were no candles. The presents were brought out of a shopping bag. Cece climbed into the shopping bag and stayed there. The only other thing she liked were the ribbons, which she kept twining and untwining. "This party, which so disrupts routine, is probably distressing to Cece," Jeff said. "I don't know who we're doing this for." Practically speaking, their purpose was to show the workers that Cece's parents loved her, and that the staff should take care of her. "What was going through her head when she saw us come in?" Jeff wondered. "'Oh, there are those people again.'"

Betsy described the constant assault of people proposing interventions. "They ask, 'Have you tried vitamin therapy?' 'Have you tried auditory training?' 'What if it's food allergies?' We tried audio-integration training. We got those horrible vitamins. We did sensory integration. We did the elimination diet: we dropped wheat and corn and we did gluten- and dairy-free; we eliminated casein; we eliminated peanut butter. You're hoping for change, but you're torturing the kid. I end up feeling I have abandoned her; I haven't done everything possible. If I went to Russia; if I chopped off my head. Flagellation, immolation. Go to Lourdes. I read about how some parents of kids with special needs have started a research center, done forty-hour-a-week therapy, and it's really hard for those who can't afford that, who wonder whether if we'd done all that, our kids might be normal. She is who she is, and I can recognize her parameters and try to know what's comfortable for her and what isn't. That's all I can do."

Cece periodically escalates into violence: throwing things at group-home staff, hurling herself on the ground, biting herself. Doctors have attempted to medicate away this misery; in the nine years I have known her, Cece has taken Abilify, Topamax, Seroquel, Prozac, Ativan, Depakote, trazodone, Risperdal, Anafranil, Lamictal, Benadryl, melatonin, and the homeopathic remedy Calms Forté. Every time I saw her, the meds were being adjusted again. A few years after we first met, Cece's destructive behaviors were inexplicably escalating to the point that the staff at the group home felt unable to handle them. Betsy and a staff member took Cece to the emergency room. The nurse explained that they had to wait for the attending psychiatrist to complete the admission. "Okay," Betsy said. "But she's not going to last out here." Ninety minutes later, Cece started hammering on the vending machines; another two hours after that, after Betsy was finally called in to speak to the therapist, their conversation was interrupted by the sound of desperate shrieking from the waiting room. Cece had tried to smash the window, and a security guard had carried her into a padded room. The nurse, an attendant, and the guard were all trying to keep her there as she hurled herself against the door; they called for two armed security guards to sit outside. "Wow, good," Betsy said. "That's just what we need here. Pistols." Cece stayed in the hospital for eight days while the doctors fiddled with her medications, but they had little to try that hadn't already been tried. They called the group home and said, "Is it okay if she has cereal? She seems to want ten bowls of it a day." When she left the hospital, she had gained ten pounds, and no meaningful improvement in her behavior had been achieved.

In the meanwhile, the family has also had to deal with Jeff's bipolar illness, which has weighed heavily on other members of the family. Betsy has had to warn group-home staff that they can't assume that Jeff will be sane at any given time. "I don't want to demean or embarrass him. I love him. But those are calls I have to make, for Cece and not for Jeff. He thinks that if Cece had not been diagnosed with autism, the bipolar might never have been brought on. That's naïve, but I think it about my depression, too. Loving Cece has done this to us." In the three years that followed Cece's placement, Jeff was hospitalized twice for mixed manic episodes; Betsy was hospitalized three times for depression. "Maybe some people out there with a different brain constitution could have handled all this," Jeff said. "But the two of us ended up in the psychiatric ward."

Betsy resisted dressing Cece in typical teenager clothes; overalls have been her uniform of many years now. At the group home, Cece and a severely autistic boy named Emmett became friends. Like Cece, Emmett was unremittingly distressed, sleepless, occasionally violent, and heavily medicated. Betsy walked into Cece's room one day and found Emmett with her, his pants and diaper off—"exploring, shall we say"—as Cece ran back and forth by the windows. The caretaker was not supposed to leave them alone, but opportunity knocked when she was called to a crisis elsewhere. "Cece and Emmett are never going to think romance, but they might think closeness and pleasure," Betsy said. "They have such hard lives, and maybe they could find a little happiness that way." The staff at the group home, however, is unlikely to tolerate such a thing, and the risk of pregnancy is alarming to all parties.

"People keep saying, 'I don't know how you do it!'" Betsy said. "It's not like I can wake up and say, 'I don't think I'll deal with it anymore.'" I replied that some people do just decide not to deal with it anymore and leave it up to the state. "Hearing that," Betsy said, "it's as if somebody took a rake and dragged it through my guts." Molly came home from school one night and said, "How come God doesn't take away Cece's autism if God can do everything?" Jeff said, "Maybe that's the way Cece's supposed to be." Molly declared, "Well, God is you and you, and God is this table, and God is everything." And Betsy continued, "And God is Cece, too." Later, Betsy said to me, "On good days I perceive God's light about her, and on bad days I beg for God's understanding. That's the thing about autism: it just is. Cece is the Zen lesson. Why does Cece have autism? Because Cece has autism. And what is it like to be Cece? Being Cece. Because no one else is, and we'll never know what it's like. It is what it is. It's not anything else. And maybe you'll never change it, and maybe you should stop trying."

The word *autism* was used by the Swiss psychiatrist Eugen Bleuler in 1912 to describe a state in which "thought is divorced both from logic and from reality." For many years, what we now class as autism was a part of "childhood schizophrenia." In 1943, Leo Kanner, an Austrian psychiatrist who had emigrated to the United States, identified autism as a distinct disorder. He chose *autistic* because it underscored the extreme aloneness of the children he had studied. Kanner believed that autism was instigated by "genuine lack of maternal warmth," an idea further explored by the influential psychoanalyst Margaret Mahler. Imaginationism—the idea that mothers with perverse desires produced deformed or troubled children—had been long abandoned in relation to dwarfs and others with physical deformities, but it persisted for those with psychiatric diagnoses and fit quite naturally into Freud's account of formative early experience. Kanner's theory that unaffectionate parents made their children autistic led to the concept of the "refrigerator mother"—though he later allowed that autism might be inborn. It was Bruno Bettelheim, the influential and controversial midcentury psychologist, who later said, "The precipitating factor in infantile autism is the parent's wish that his child should not exist."

The researcher Isabelle Rapin, who has worked on autism since 1954, said to me, "We learned that it was an esoteric, rare, psychiatric disorder of highly intelligent but disturbed children. It was caused by mothers and treated with psychoanalysis, the goal of which was to break the glass ball so the butterfly could fly out. No one believed there were high-functioning autistics." Bernard Rimland, father of an autistic son, wrote *Infantile Autism: The Syndrome and Its Implications for a Neural Theory of Behavior* in 1964, proposing a fully biological explanation for autism. In 1965, parents created the National Society for Autistic Children; at the first meeting, they are said to have worn name tags in the shape of little refrigerators. "We mothers would have liked an apology," said Eustacia Cutler, mother of the prominent autistic intellectual Temple Grandin. "We deserve it. And so do the fathers."

The Austrian pediatrician Hans Asperger published a case study in 1944 of four children similar to those monitored by Kanner. However, while Kanner became one of the most influential voices in psychiatry in the English-speaking world, Asperger's work remained obscure and was available only in German until 1981. Like Kanner, Asperger believed that his patients were capable of great improvement. He also recognized their strengths, which often included creativity, a highly developed taste in art, and insight beyond their years. Asperger believed that the condition he had documented was an affliction of upper-middle-class people who pressured their children and then withdrew when their children disappointed them.

Children with Asperger syndrome are highly verbal early in their childhood, though they often use language in idiosyncratic ways. They generally have normal cognitive development and are interested in, though somewhat incompetent at, human interaction; a website put up by a young man with Asperger's explained that empathy is "successfully guessing what another person is feeling." They often lack basic social skills; Asperger coined the term *little professors* to describe his patients. They tend to be more aware of their condition than are people with classic autism, and this leads many into clinical depression. They are often more comfortable responding to communication than initiating it. The American Psychiatric Association is currently moving to eliminate the diagnosis; people with Asperger's would simply have *autism spectrum disorder*, a category that would encompass people with severe autism and people with other related diagnoses, such as childhood disintegrative disorder. This shift acknowledges that it is almost impossible to draw clear dividing lines among these diagnoses.

Though some speak of those with language as having high-functioning autism, people with extreme social deficits are not always helped by having a large vocabulary. While many autistic people may seem disengaged, individuals with Asperger syndrome may seem hyperengaged; they may stand too close and talk incessantly about obscure subjects. One researcher described interviewing someone with Asperger's who seemed to her to be just fine—they had a lovely conversation. The following week, they had the same conversation. A week later, they had the conversation again. One clinician told me about a patient who at age ten ran into the street in the middle of traffic, nearly getting run over and causing an accident. His mother said, "But I told you to look both ways before you step into the street!" He said, "I did look both ways." A psychiatrist I met described a patient who was a math genius, IQ 140, fully verbal, but socially disabled. When the pretty woman at the counter at McDonald's asked what he'd like today, he said, "I'd like to touch your crotch, please." He was completely befuddled when the police were called; he had answered her question and said "please."

Prominent voices among adults on the spectrum—such as Temple Grandin, an author, professor, and designer of cattle-handling equipment, or Ari Ne'eman, founder of the Autistic Self Advocacy Network—function enormously well and are interpersonally competent. Still, both have told me that it is a learned skill, that the social interaction we enjoyed was based on endless study. Grandin has written, "My mind works just like an Internet search engine that has been set to access only images. The more pictures I have stored in the Internet inside my brain the more templates I have of how to act in a new situation." Many people on the autism spectrum first learn to smile and to cry as works of theater. John Elder Robison, author of the autobiography *Look Me in the Eye*, describes hours spent memorizing human expressions so he could interpret or produce them. "I didn't even understand what looking someone in the eye meant. And yet I felt ashamed, because people expected me to do it, and I knew it, and yet I didn't. As I've gotten older, I have taught myself to act 'normal.' I can do it well enough to fool the average person for a whole evening, maybe longer." Every autistic person has a unique pattern of weaknesses and strengths, and a person can be extremely competent in one area, but quite incompetent in others. At the same time, the most impaired end of the spectrum is so different from the least impaired that it is sometimes hard to accept the persistent metaphor of the spectrum structure.

When I was in my twenties, I befriended an autistic man. He had not spoken until he was seven, and he laughed at things that weren't funny and ignored social niceties. He was rational, methodical, and a lightning-fast mental calculator who earned a fortune in fast stock trades. He had a photographic memory and had assembled a wonderful art collection. When I visited him one weekend, he put a single Philip Glass recording in the CD player and—as though Philip Glass weren't repetitive enough—left it playing constantly over the entire weekend. On another occasion, when I mentioned that I was going to Los Angeles, he volunteered detailed directions for every place that I was going; he explained that he had become fascinated by the city and had spent four months driving around it for ten hours a day. We fell out after he refused to own up to something hurtful he had done. I had assumed that his failure to comply with social norms was an affectation; only later did I understand that our friendship had been undermined by a neurological condition that was not subject to being fixed.

The poet Jennifer Franklin found a muse to equal her powers of expression in her severely impaired autistic daughter, Anna Livia Nash. For her poems about Anna, Jenny draws on the Greek myth of Demeter losing Persephone, who half vanishes from her life, bringing winter to the world as an expression of outrageous loss. She wrote:

I was the last to hear you
Scream because I did not

Want it to be true. You cried
Out in torment and the sun

Kept shining through the leaves.
That wasn't right.
. . . . .

Everyone who wasn't your mother

Tried to comfort me. I vowed
To remain unlaughing.

Even in the stunned novelty
Of devastation, I didn't realize

How easy it would be
To keep this promise.

Anna played with her toys oddly: she'd study each one carefully when she got it, almost as though she were cataloging it, and then she'd put it behind her. She would wake up in her crib and make little chirping noises to herself. She never pointed. Jenny called the pediatrician repeatedly, and he kept telling her to stop worrying. Just before Anna turned two, Jenny joined a Mommy and Me class, and on the first day Jenny noticed that the other children were interacting with her more than Anna ever had. "I suddenly realized that I was constantly trying to put on a show for her to get her attention," Jenny said. She took Anna back to the pediatrician, who once again said that Anna seemed fine, but when Jenny said, "She's not talking as much as she used to," his demeanor changed and he sent her immediately to a pediatric neurologist. The clinician at Cornell University Medical Center diagnosed her with PDD-NOS—"pervasive developmental disorder not otherwise specified" (which critics claim stands for "physician didn't decide")—explaining that Anna showed too much affection to receive an autism diagnosis. "Do not leave this office today and look up *autism*. This is not what this is," the doctor said. Jenny describes this half-diagnosis as a "grave disservice."

Jenny's husband, Garrett, is an oncologist and was used to death and illness. Jenny, who had always assumed that everything would go according to plan, felt completely blindsided. As she wrote in one of her poems, "I did not / Only lose you in an instant; / I abandoned the infinite possibilities / Of what you might have become." She set about researching autism education and got Anna qualified for early-intervention services. In addition, Jenny and Garrett paid a consultant $200 an hour out of pocket for four hours of behavioral therapy every week; the consultant also trained local therapists who were paid by the state to work with Anna. Jenny and Garrett sold a vacation house they had in Massachusetts and gave every penny to therapists. Jenny learned with the therapists for twenty hours a week. Anna had tantrums that could last forty-five minutes, and Jenny's arms were covered in bruises and scratches.

Anna seemed to be responding to the structured, intensive behavioral intervention at home. New York City did not yet have schools that functioned on this system, but at four, Anna was accepted at Reed Academy, a school in Garfield, New Jersey, with just twenty-four students and twenty-six teachers. Garrett's work kept him in New York, but Jenny moved to New Jersey so that Anna could attend. Reed uses applied behavior analysis, or ABA, a system originally developed by the neuropsychologist O. Ivar Lovaas at UCLA. Lovaas used a mix of positive reinforcement and harsh physical punishment, much like animal training; most ABA programs now use only incentives. Whenever a child does something desirable, he is rewarded; when a child is doing something undesirable ("stereotypies," such as head-banging, arm-flapping, rocking, or producing high-pitched noises), he is interrupted and steered toward desired behaviors. For each positive act, the child receives a sticker on a token board, and when a certain number of stickers accumulate, the child gets to choose a treat. At seven, Anna had some language, but used it rarely. When she started babbling incoherently, her teacher interrupted her with commands—telling her to clap, turn around, or touch her head. When she responded appropriately, it seemed to break the inner mechanism of the babbling, and she got a sticker. Then she had to answer questions, such as "Where do you live?" "How old are you?" "Where do you go to school?" Sometimes her teacher would make her read, sing, or do a lesson, all also rewarded. When she reached a full complement of stickers, she had five minutes to do whatever she wanted, with the proviso that she not lapse into stereotypy again. Sometimes she asked for a snack; sometimes, a piggyback ride.

Jenny kept up the system at home. "The only time that I don't do it is when she is in her room before bed," she said. "After I've said goodnight and read her ten books, if she's babbling in there, she's babbling." When I met Jenny, Anna was completing her third year at Reed. The improvements had been huge. She no longer engaged in self-injury and could tolerate visiting the supermarket. She had previously scratched Jenny and pulled her hair daily, but now she did so about once a month. She used her speech more readily. Jenny was relieved that Anna seemed to enjoy these developments. "It was the hardest thing in the world for me to see her cry and tantrum with the subpar ABA at home in the early days," Jenny said. "But she never cries at school. When it's done properly, it's not mean."

Anna comes home at four, and Jenny works with her nonstop until nine, using the token boards and the rewards system. When Anna goes to bed, Jenny, too hyped up to sleep, soothes herself with reading, writing, and movies. "I stay up almost all night and do things I can do alone in the dark, where I don't have to see people going about normal activities that I can't really be a part of." Jenny wakes at 5:00 a.m. to make breakfast for her daughter and does drills with her until the school bus comes. Exhausted, Jenny climbs back into bed until four o'clock rolls around again. "I was so ashamed at first, but now I've come to accept that this is what I have to do in order to survive."

Jenny has been depressed, overwhelmed, even suicidal. "But I can't give up on my child. She didn't ask to be born; she didn't ask to have this problem; she's completely vulnerable. If I don't take care of her, who's going to do it?" At the beginning of Anna's time at Reed, Jenny hoped Anna would become "indistinguishable from her peers" and be mainstreamed, but that has come to seem unlikely; *indistinguishable* is the catchword held out to parents over and over and is seldom realistic. Anna is teased for her difference; ironically, her imperviousness to ridicule is what marks her as unready for regular schooling. "I'd love Anna Livia to get to the point where she even knows she's being made fun of," Jenny said.

Jenny had had terrible morning sickness in the early stages of her pregnancy and had considered having an abortion. "Difficult as it is to admit this," she said, "there are times when I've thought, 'Would everyone have been better off?'" She described a trip to France when she visited the Musée de Préhistoire in Les Eyzies-de-Tayac. "I saw these bones of a mother holding a baby. They'd been buried in that unusual pose, and archaeologists were supposed to have been confused by it, but I wasn't. I thought, 'It'd just be so nice for something to just happen, if Anna Livia and I could just disappear like that.' But I would never do anything to hurt her."

The incompetencies associated with autism sometimes cluster into a terrifying level of pain—pain for the person with autism, and pain for those who attempt to care for that person. Scott Sea, father of an autistic child, described this experience in *Slate*: "When you see the balled-up pants and diaper on the floor, you know you are too late. A bright red smear across the door, the molding, the wall. Turn the corner and the bedroom is a crime scene. An ax murder? In fact, it is only your daughter at her worst. Shit everywhere. Splashes of blood glistening like paint, black clots, yellow-brown feces, and a three-foot-in-diameter pond of vomit that your daughter stands in the middle of, a dog-eared copy of *Family Circle* in one hand, reaching for the TV with the other. She is naked except for stockinged feet, blood soaked up to her ankles. Hands dripping, face marked like a cannibal, she wears an expression of utter bewilderment. A bloody handprint on the square of your back as she balances herself when you roll down her sopping stockings. In the warm rain of the shower she proceeds to dig. She is excavating for what remains of the impacted stool, hard as a French roll. The behaviorists, the gastroenterologists, the living-skills experts, all suggest their strategies and therapies and videos and diets and oils and schedules. Certainly she knows what you want—appropriate toileting. And there are occasions when she does just that. Goes in, sits, finishes. This, maybe 5 percent of the time. Some huge, softball-size stool discovered in the toilet bowl. You shout for each other and gaze in wonder as at a rainbow or falling star. That's how excited you are."

Fred Volkmar, head of the Child Study Center at Yale, tells of one of his patients, a twenty-five-year-old math genius who had thrived largely because of his mother's exquisite care, who said to her, "Why do you need a mother? Why do you have to have a family? I don't understand." His mother later said, "He thinks of everything very intellectually. But he doesn't understand how it makes me feel." The British psychoanalyst Juliet Mitchell observed, "In extreme cases, the violence of one's own nonexistence makes one gasp—it's not that you're eradicated; you're not even there to be eradicated. There is no trace of psychic equivalence, in which your recognition of another correlates with that other's recognition of you."

Irish mythology holds that a child may be whisked away at birth, and a fairy changeling left in its place. The changeling will look just like the child, but will have no heart; it will want to be left alone, will hold on to a piece of wood that recalls its fairy home, and instead of speaking, it will croak and hum. If the mother tries to caress or love it, it will laugh and spit and take revenge with bizarre acts. The only solution is to throw it on a bonfire. Martin Luther wrote, "Such a changeling child is only a piece of flesh, a *massa carnis*, because it has no soul." Walter O. Spitzer, a professor of epidemiology at McGill, who has testified before Congress about autism, seemed to refer back to such mythology in 2001 when he described autistic people as having "a dead soul in a live body." Autism advocates have understandably taken exception to such analogies; the prominent autism advocate Amanda Baggs said, "Being seen in light of the ghost of who you were expected to be is a kind of emotional violence for many disabled people." Neurodiversity activists such as Baggs might argue that the child who seems "lost" in a different world may be content in that world. Of course, this position is put forward by people who are able to communicate, and since one of autism's core traits is lack of empathy, autistic self-advocates' statements on behalf of others can be suspect. Self-advocates do, however, accurately observe that parents choose treatments on the basis of guesswork about what their children must want. Parents may work hard to help their children emerge from autism and fail to do so; they may, equally, help their children lose traits of autism, then find out that their children hated being "treated" and were happier the way they were.

Nancy Corgi, mother of two autistic children, has not had a warm relationship with fate. She has been utterly responsible in her handling of her offspring, but she has kept her own cool at a considerable price. "Having advocated and fought for these kids now for nineteen years," she said, "my entire personality has changed. I'm quick to pick a fight; I'm argumentative. You don't cross me. I have to do what I have to do, and I'm going to get what I want. I never was like this at all." I'd met so many families who tried to look on the bright side of horrible situations that I found something bracing in Nancy's brash assertions of misery and disgust, her ability to say that if she'd known what kind of children she was going to have, she wouldn't have had children.

Nancy's mother noticed some oddness in eighteen-month-old Fiona, and one day at the hairdresser's she got into a conversation with a woman who had an autistic son. He sounded like her granddaughter. She called Nancy and said, "I made an appointment with this pediatric neurologist, and it would be really nice if you just took Fiona in." Nancy, eighteen weeks pregnant with her second child, decided to humor her mother. The doctor took one look at Fiona and said, "She's PDD." Nancy was shocked. "It wasn't something that was going to be done by next week, fixed," she recalled. Fiona has classic autistic traits, is completely disengaged from other human beings, and showed no signs of developing speech on her own. She hates to be touched and wouldn't keep her clothes on. "All my food is locked up in the basement or it would be thrown on the walls," Nancy said. "Also, she could set the house on fire." At thirty-two months, Fiona started going to early intervention at the University of Massachusetts. "About three o'clock, I would start to physically shake, knowing she would be back at three thirty-ish," Nancy said. "I didn't want her coming home. When I got child-care help, I would lock myself in my room. I just wanted to sit at the bottom of the dark closet, no sound, no light, nobody."

The summer after Nancy's second child, Luke, turned two, Nancy and her sister were sitting on the beach at Cape Cod, and Nancy's sister said, "You have another problem." Nancy was astounded. "My son seemed totally normal, after dealing with my daughter," she recalled. Unlike her sister, however, she had no experience of normal children. "All of a sudden my whole life was all about testing and testing and testing," Nancy said. Her husband, Marcus, is an accountant. "He deals with the IRS every day. He's used to stubborn, ridiculous bureaucracy. He has the patience and know-how to deal with insurance companies, claims, the school system's financial stuff. That was his part, my part being that I got the kids to deal with. How many years did we drive up and down the Mass Pike for evaluations at Boston Children's? My kids are seventeen and nineteen, and I'm still doing it."

Though both children are diagnosed on the spectrum, their respective autisms manifest differently. When Fiona was eight, she jumped out a second-floor window because she wanted to make mashed potatoes and knew that if she found the front-door key in the garage, she could get to the potatoes and cook them. With coaching, Fiona eventually developed language, but her syntax and affect are odd. "If I am having a conversation with someone while my daughter is at the table, she talks to herself," Nancy said. "I go to symphony, I go to opera, I do theater with girlfriends. I'll buy Fiona a ticket because she loves to dress up, and she loves music. She mumbles and she's weird, with no idea how to relate to other people, but she doesn't interrupt or bother you." Luke was a sweet-natured child, but adolescence hit him hard. He had been on clomipramine since kindergarten, but was switched to Risperdal and Paxil at puberty when his symptoms escalated. "He is basically anxiety-ridden and really not too swift," Nancy said. "He only talks about what interests him: videos, movies, and animals. Zero common sense. If a four-year-old calls him a bad word, he might knock him across the room. He's angry. Two minutes later he'll be cuddly. Really crummy." Fiona was mainstreamed with an aide from first through eighth grade. Luke's deficits of intelligence and his disruptive behavior disqualified him from mainstreaming.

Nancy tends to express rage, but also feels despair, and when her children were young, that despair was closer to the surface. "I would get up at three in the morning and realize again that it's not just a bad dream. Then I would look at Marcus in the morning and say, 'How dare you sleep last night?' What we have left, as us, is much less than when we got married." Marcus worked long days—longer, in Nancy's view, than was necessary. Her mother, who lived a few streets away, asked Nancy how it was going, but seldom saw her. Her mother-in-law disengaged completely. "Nobody ever rolled up their sleeves to help," Nancy said. "Nobody liked my kids. They weren't likable, but if somebody had acted like they were, maybe that would have helped."

Nancy and Marcus were on a supplementary form of insurance called Mass Health, which helped pay for a part-time caretaker for the children. Then Mass Health went through a budget shakedown and eliminated the Corgis from the system. In the end, Nancy and Marcus paid for help themselves, but the sums of money were large. Nancy decided to enroll Fiona in a residential school at fourteen; Nancy and Marcus fought tooth and nail to get her in. "My husband broke down and cried and said, 'I just don't know what more we can do to show you what she needs.' That was one of two times I ever saw him cry." They enrolled Luke at fifteen. "You are talking about two kids who need as much supervision as a toddler," Nancy said. "So they are in school 281 days a year."

Luke loves pretty girls, but his inept attentions usually meet with rejection. Nancy has to keep explaining away these painful experiences for him. He is also uncontrolled and frighteningly strong. When Nancy and Marcus went to a wedding and left the kids with a sitter who had cared for them before, Luke picked up the sitter's two-year-old son and hurled him across the room. "He hit my mother last year," Nancy said. "He told my father to shut up." The Corgis belong to a beach club on Cape Cod, where Nancy has been going since childhood. The year after I met them, Nancy was told that Luke had made lewd gestures to a girl by the pool and was no longer welcome—though it was in fact merely an inept attempt to strike up a conversation. Nancy drafted a letter explaining that Luke's self-control was undermined by his brain's biology. It made no difference, and Luke was not allowed back. "We're used to living in the leper colony, aren't we?" Nancy said.

In spite of her persistent outrage, Nancy can speak of her children with tenderness. "My kids are very affectionate and cuddly and sweet," she said. "Fiona wasn't so much when she was little. But now we'll sit on the couch and I will sort of pet her and hold her. I used to tuck her into bed and give her a kiss and tell her I loved her. I would say, 'Say, "I love you."' She would repeat with me, 'I love you.' Eventually she knew what it meant and would say it to me on her own. Once, I fell asleep on the couch. She got a blanket and tucked me in and gave me a kiss. Fiona is functioning way beyond what we ever expected. People say, 'You can pat yourself on the back,' and we do." But Nancy worried constantly that someone would take advantage of Fiona and was trying to get both children sterilized. "The best we can hope is that we never have grandchildren," Nancy said sadly. "My husband will sometimes say, 'Would you marry me again?' I say, 'Yeah, but not with the kids.' Had we known what we know now, we wouldn't have done it. Do I love my kids? Yes. Will I do everything for them? Yes. I have them and I do this and I love them. I wouldn't do it again. I think anybody who tells you they would is lying."

Some nonverbal people with autism appear to have no language, either receptive or expressive. Some have trouble with control over the oral-facial musculature involved in producing speech and may be helped by keyboards on which they can type. Some lack access to the unconscious process through which our thoughts emerge in a string of words. Some have intellectual disabilities so great that they do not develop linguistic capacities. The relationship between language and intellectual disability is confusing; no one really knows what may be hidden behind speechlessness. Alison Tepper Singer, former vice president of Autism Speaks and founder and president of the Autism Science Foundation, told me that her eleven-year-old daughter had language at last—"which means that she says, 'I want juice,' not that she says, 'I feel that you're not understanding how my mind works.'"

Micki Bresnahan spoke of the challenge of decoding her son's communications. Although as a child he had very little language, he would repeatedly say "robot" whenever he cried. She would buy him toy robots and brought him to movies about robots, yet he continued to cry out "robot" in his distress. After two years and several therapists, Micki figured out that her son thought he had been made into a robot during back surgery for kyphosis, when metal rods were placed along his spine. "He couldn't express it, and I couldn't figure it out," she said. "He tested in the normal intelligence range. But he's very low-functioning. If he can't dress himself and he is a genius, what does that mean? That means he can't dress himself." Her son has limited speech and only occasional access to it. "He has to get upset to talk," she said. "It's neurological. He gets more and more agitated, and it is as if he's doing it so that he can talk. It's sadder now than when he was little. He's not going to get married, have kids, become a grandfather, buy a house. All the things that a person does in an adult life give it texture. All the way out to the horizon, there's nothing." Another mother said of her thirteen-year-old son, "If he were deaf and needed to sign, I'd learn Sign. But there's no way for me to learn his language because he doesn't know it himself."

In 2008, a Canadian girl with autism named Carly Fleischmann, having never used language, began typing at age thirteen. Her parents didn't even know that she could read or understand their speech. "We were stunned," her father said. "We realized inside was an articulate, intelligent, emotive person whom we had never met. Even professionals labeled her as moderately to severely cognitively impaired." Among the first things she wrote was, "If I could tell people one thing about autism, it would be that I don't want to be this way but I am. So don't be mad. Be understanding." Later she wrote, "It is hard to be autistic because no one understands me. People assume I am dumb because I can't talk or I act differently. I think people get scared with things that look or seem different than them." When a father wrote to Carly to ask what his autistic child would want him to know, Carly wrote back, "I think he would want you to know that he knows more than you think he does." Asked by her parents about her unexpected emergence, she said, "I think behavior therapy helped me. I believe that it allows me to sort my thoughts. Unfortunately it can't make me normal. Believing helped. Then a miracle happened, you saw me type. Then you helped me forget that I'm autistic."

Harry and Laura Slatkin live in an elegant house on the Upper East Side of Manhattan. Harry is a fragrance executive and a gregarious man-about-town, a designer of scents for Elton John, Oprah Winfrey, and others. Laura runs a successful scented-candle business. The Slatkins' affluence has helped them to obtain services for which other families must battle, and they have emerged as prominent autism activists and philanthropists. The Slatkins had twins in 1999, and while Alexandra appeared to develop normally, David was, at fourteen months, given to running up and down the hallway and giggling in what struck his mother as a peculiar way. After a couple of useless medical referrals, he was eventually given a diagnosis of pervasive developmental delay. Doctors often use this diagnosis as a way of breaking the news gently, and Laura was heartened by it. "That didn't sound so awful," she recalled, "because *delay* to me meant it was still coming and would just take time." But then she called up another doctor and learned that David might in fact be autistic. "That was a dagger through my heart that changed our world forever."

Early intervention sent therapists to work with David at home, and Laura began reading obsessively. "We were in such high gear, we didn't know what was coming at us," Laura said. "One night, I was writing my

thoughts in a journal. Would he ever talk? Go to school? Mak
Get married? What's going to happen to David? I just burst int
and Harry said, 'Laura, stop crying, because that's not going to help
David. It is not going to do anything for us. You have to take all your
energy and do something constructive.' And the next morning, we got
to work."

They established the New York Center for Autism to provide education, community outreach, and medical research. They put to use every
good connection they had. After discovering that no schools in New
York provided ABA, they met with the city's schools chancellor and told
him they wanted to start one that would; because they believed in universal access, they wanted it to be part of the public school system. The
New York Center for Autism Charter School was established in Harlem in the same building as PS 50, a regular public school, in 2005, its
headmaster and faculty handpicked by the Slatkins and another autism
mom, Ilene Lanier. The city funds the school at a cost of $81,000 per
pupil per year. There is one teacher for each student. Cheerfully decorated and filled with light, it is an oasis in the public school system.
The headmaster, Jamie Pagliaro, started a program for eighth graders
at PS 50 to work with the kids at the charter school, and now more
of these kids are clamoring to participate than the charter school can
handle. More than one thousand families are languishing on the charter school's waiting list.

Laura and Harry donated half a million dollars to Hunter College
to establish a program that teaches educators how to work with autistic children. The Slatkins hope that with enough trained faculty, there
could be a network of similar schools, so that every autistic child in
New York would have the option of attending such a program. "The
difference between a lousy and a superior education is the difference
between being able to live independently or not," Laura said. Additionally, the Slatkins have worked with Cornell and Columbia Universities
to set up a state-of-the-art center to provide top-level early intervention and ongoing clinical care for autistic people. They have also established a think tank called Transitioning to Adulthood to figure out how
to improve residential facilities for adults with autism, and to provide
appropriate vocational training.

While the Slatkins were setting up these programs, they were also
helping David. "The first year is the year of hope," Laura said, "though
you don't know it at the time. That is the year when you can still imagine that your child is one of the least affected and that he will emerge."
At the end of that year, Laura said to David's therapist, "So I just wanted
to know where David stands with respect to the other children that you

have worked with." He replied, "I would say that your son is probably the most severely affected child I've ever seen." Laura explained to me, "He didn't realize that I didn't know that. That was the day I lost hope, the worst day of my life. I thought we were making progress, I thought that maybe he would talk, that maybe he would go to regular school, that I did everything right. I got him help early, I got the best doctors in the world, I got the best educational people, I got forty hours of treatment a week, which was the most anyone had ever gotten. Given a great educational program, most children can make amazing gains; we see it every day at the charter school. But David wasn't going to be one of them. I just folded. My old life was over for me. From that day on, I had to use the words *severely affected by autism*. I had to wrap my arms around this future and make a new peace with it."

The Slatkins tried every form of intervention. In one, the therapist told them to do whatever David liked to do. "David used to love to run around our dining room table," Laura said. "So she said, 'Run around with him.' They ask you to enter their world. I'd like to get them out of their world." The time that followed was bleak. David has never developed any language, and his comprehension appears to be virtually nil. He cannot communicate with signs or by using the picture-exchange methods that work for many autistic children. When Laura and Ilene founded the charter school, they assumed that their sons would go there, but the public school system required that students be admitted via lottery, and neither child was chosen. For Ilene, this was a significant loss, but the Slatkins knew that David could get little out of even the best school in the world.

David would wake every night at two thirty and jump around his room. "One night, he was bouncing off the walls, and I turned to my husband and said, 'There are places for children like David, and we need to consider them because we can't live like this,'" Laura recalled. "Harry responded so violently. He said, 'Don't you ever say that ever again; my son's not going anywhere.' I figured that one day Harry was going to get to the point where he couldn't take this anymore. So I told him, 'I'm going to explore.'" David was never still. "He's on Risperdal, which should cause heavy sedation," Laura said. "It doesn't affect his hyperactivity at all. I think it's helped to reduce his aggressive behaviors, but he's been on it for so long that I don't know what he'd be like if he didn't take it. We tried to take him off once, and it was like taking someone off heroin. Harry suggested we get one of those darts that they shoot into a wild boar and just shoot him in the behind."

As David grew larger, he became increasingly violent and destructive. In the documentary *Autism Every Day*, Harry describes, tearfully, putting locks on all the doors on their weekend house, "because we didn't want David possibly going into the pond. But there were times when you hoped he did, because you wouldn't want him to suffer like this all his life." David's twin sister reached the point at which she said, "I don't want to come home from school; I don't want to walk into that house; I can't listen to it anymore." Harry said, "We're talking about a little boy who was eating his own feces or smearing it on the walls, who would go six days without sleeping, who pinched Laura so hard she had to go to the doctor, who pulled out his sister's hair by the handful."

Laura began a serious search for a residential placement. "It's going to be hugely, hugely painful, but I know he's headed there," she said. "It's just a matter of when." Sitting in her living room just off Fifth Avenue, Laura described this inevitability with both equanimity and sorrow, her head bowed. "I make him breakfast and lunch every day," she said. "And I make him that breakfast with love. I worry about that institutional setting. Nobody's going to know that he loves his bacon crispy and that he likes his pasta with just a little butter, not a lot."

Activism can forestall self-examination, but Laura Slatkin chose activism clear-sightedly to displace some of her sadness. "I work on this school my son doesn't go to," she said, "and I sponsor research that probably won't help him, and I have a think tank to design institutions where he may never receive care, because there is so little I can do to help him, and it makes me feel better to know that at least I can make some families' hope come true, the same hope I once had, that never came true for us."

We have no way to describe autism except by symptoms so variable that some clinicians refer to *the autisms*. We don't know its cause or mechanism. The modifier *idiopathic*, often used to describe autism, is essentially an indication that it is currently inexplicable. Researchers have developed numerous hypotheses about a "core deficit" from which all other symptoms flow. One popular principle is *mindblindness*, an inability to recognize how another person's thoughts differ from one's own. A child is shown a candy package and asked what he thinks it contains. He thinks it contains candy. It is opened and he is shown that it contains a pencil instead. He is then asked what another child will think when shown the closed package. Nonautistic children expect the other child to be duped just as they were. Autistic children expect the child to know the package has a pencil in it. A number of recent imaging studies have demonstrated that mirror neurons, usually activated when a person either performs or observes an action, fire in autistic subjects only when they themselves are doing something and remain mute when they are observing someone else. This fits with mind blindness. Uta Frith of University College, London, has theorized that people with autism lack the drive for central coherence that allows humans to organize and learn from outside information. Others speak of a shortfall in flexibility. Others yet have posited that the central issue for people with autism is attentional overarousal and underarousal. All these accounts may be true, but none particularly explains the others.

In his memoir, *Send in the Idiots*, Kamran Nazeer, who has autism, writes, "The challenge for autistic individuals is that they are overwhelmed even by their own minds. Typically they notice more details than other people. I know someone who can sketch buildings in architectural detail, from memory—placing not just rooms but elevator shafts, corridors, stairwells—after walking around them only once." Another woman he describes could play a piece of music from start to finish after hearing it for the first time. "Simultaneously, the ability of autistic individuals to categorize or process this information is more limited," Nazeer writes. "With this combination of high input and low output, inevitably a sort of logjam occurs. Consequently, autistic individuals try to focus on simple tasks that don't involve other people." John Elder Robison, diagnosed with Asperger's, recalls, "Machines were never mean to me. They never tricked me, and they never hurt my feelings. I was in charge of the machines. I felt safe around them."

Though brain imaging has done little to reveal the mechanisms of autism, it has revealed the organic substrates of some of these phenomena. A study conducted at Yale found that in adults with autism or Asperger's, the region of the brain activated during face processing corresponded to the region activated in nonautistic subjects during object processing. Autistic people with fixations, however, may recognize those in the area where most people register faces. So one autistic boy had the same region in his brain light up for his mother as for a teacup. But he was enthralled by Japanese Digimon characters, and when he saw those, the area where most of us process our intimate connections suddenly flashed on.

Bob and Sue Lehr did not intend to adopt a disabled child. However, in 1973, when Bob was working as a guest professor in Utah, the couple learned of a mixed-race child whom no one in the area wanted. They decided to make him part of their family, which already included one Caucasian biological son and one adopted mixed-race daughter. Utah required couples to wait a year from petitioning to finalizing adoption, but the Lehrs' attorney said they could bypass that system. Sue said to me, "We should have put together the clues."

After the family returned home to Tully, in upstate New York, it became clear that something was wrong with Ben. "He was a blob," Bob said. "We would pick him up, and he didn't tense up for the lift." The Lehrs called the Utah Division of Child and Family Services and requested Ben's medical records. After a few months without a response, the Lehrs had an attorney write to the agency; the agency offered to bring Ben back to Utah. "Excuse me?" Sue said. "I couldn't imagine just saying, 'Well, gee, my son is damaged; I'm going to send him back,' like he was a sweater." Their pediatrician put Ben through a battery of tests. He finally recommended that Sue and Ben just take their son home and love him. Bob was an experimental psychologist and continued to work in that field, but Ben's care was to become his primary concern. Sue, who had been a gym teacher, returned to Syracuse University to earn a PhD in special ed.

The local school didn't want Ben and made his life miserable, and the Lehrs sued the district. Sue told authorities, "You can't keep him out of your building because he is brown. Tell me where it says you can keep him out because he has autism." The work at school was modified for him, but he had to do it, though he had little language and couldn't initiate speech. Some people who cannot produce oral words can communicate in writing, and some who don't have the muscle control for handwriting type instead, and some who don't have even the control for typing use other methods. Ben learned *facilitated communication*, or FC, a system in which someone helped him to use a keyboard by giving his arms nondirected physical support as he typed. There has been great debate about whether what is expressed using FC is really the language of the disabled person or of the facilitator; Ben's parents are sure that he is controlling his FC utterances.

As he grew up, Ben would often smash his head on the floor, use knives to cut himself, put his head through windows. "His behaviors were a way of communicating," Sue said. "Not the best way, but other kids communicate using drugs or driving snowmobiles drunk." When Ben was a teenager, Bob and Sue took him to RadioShack, his favorite store. He panicked on the escalator, and at the bottom he sat down cross-legged and began smashing himself in the head with his hands and screaming as a crowd gathered. Sue always carried an FC keyboard, and when she took it out, Ben typed, *Hit me.* "And I thought, 'Oh, yeah, in the middle of the mall with a security guard, and you're black and I'm white,'" Sue recalled. "And then he typed out, *Like a record player.*" Sue suddenly flashed on a stuck needle; she struck him on the edge of the shoulder with the heel of her hand and said, "Tilt." Ben stood up and they walked calmly on across the mall.

In high school, Ben began having horrendous behavior problems. "I didn't like his aide, Willie, an obese, slovenly guy who always wore sweatpants," Sue said. "But I thought maybe I was just being judgmental. Then he was arrested for raping his own three-year-old daughter. Meanwhile, Ben was typing out that Willie had been hurting him and gave enough details to his speech therapist that she had the principal call the cops. Willie would say, 'Ben's having a hard time, so we'll go up to the weight room and lift weights.' And that's where Willie was raping him, while this other guy would watch. So we brought Ben home for a while and nurtured him, to make sure he didn't think it was his fault." When he returned to school, Ben developed meaningful relationships with his classmates, assisted by a particularly well-attuned aide. In his senior year, he used FC to write a column for the school newspaper. He invited a nondisabled girl to the prom, and she accepted (somewhat to the chagrin of her boyfriend); at the prom, he was elected to the king's court. At graduation, when he walked down to get his diploma, the whole audience stood up. Both Sue and Bob began to cry as she described it. "Thousands of people at this graduation. And they all stood up and applauded for Ben."

I was struck by the Lehrs' early decision to help Ben but not to "fix" him. "His sister said to me, 'Do you ever wonder what it would be like if Ben were normal?'" Sue said. "And I said, 'Well, I think he's normal for himself.' Have I wished that he didn't have all of his behavior problems? Absolutely. Have I wished that he had better language? Absolutely." Much of what he types is Delphic. For a while he kept typing, *And you can cry.* No one ever understood what he meant. Another day he typed, *I want to stop those, jerky feelings, jerky hurting. I get upset, then look stupid.* Bob described going to conferences and being surrounded by parents desperate for a cure—"It's going to be all better next year, crap like that. We were avant-garde in saying, 'No. It's going to be better right now. Let's make it as good as possible for him.'"

After high school, Bob and Sue gave Ben the down payment for a house eight miles from their own. His Social Security check covered his mortgage and most of his utility bills. He earned money by making wooden tables to sell at craft fairs. Someone was with him constantly, either a trained aide or a lodger who shared the house in exchange for caretaking. Because water is Ben's passion, the Lehrs found him places to swim and bought him a hot tub. A decade later, Sue's mother died, and the Lehrs took their inheritance and went on a three-month family camping trip to Europe. "Each person in the family got to pick one thing they wanted to do," Sue said. "Ben picked swimming in every body of water he could find. So he's been in the Mediterranean, he's been in the Aegean, he's been in pools and lakes and streams. We have a picture of him in Athens, sitting on the top of a stone wall, the highest point in Athens. He's got his little drumsticks and he's tapping on the stones and he's got a look of sheer joy on his face."

When they returned from Europe, Bob was diagnosed with Alzheimer's, which had advanced considerably by the time I interviewed him for this book. For two years, Bob didn't want anyone but Sue to know, but Ben would type out, *Daddy's sick*. Observing that Sue was upset, he'd type, *Mommy is broken*. Finally, Bob sat down and explained that Ben was right, Daddy is sick, but he wasn't going to die right away. In the face of this diagnosis, the Lehrs woke up anew to the profound effect Ben had had on them. "I absolutely handled the news differently than I would have if we hadn't had Ben," Bob said. Sue said, "I think I'd learned a lot from Ben about reading people, trying to understand what they're thinking or feeling that they can't articulate. About treating someone as a human being even when his thoughts and feelings are mixed up. How do we make you feel safe, loved, okay? I learned the way it works by having Ben. And so I had it ready when Bob needed it."

Autism is associated with underconnectivity between hemispheres and an overabundance of local connections; the neuronal pruning that helps the average brain avoid overload does not appear to occur in autism. Many autistic children are born with smaller heads than the norm, but by six to fourteen months, many have larger heads than the norm. The brains of autistic children are often enlarged by 10 or 15 percent, a condition that appears to resolve as the children grow. The human brain consists of grey matter, where thought is generated, and white matter, which conveys that thought from one area to another. In autism, inflammation has been observed in areas of the brain that produce white matter; too much is produced too soon, creating terrible noise, much like what you might get if every time you picked up your telephone, you heard not only the voice of the person you were calling, but also a hundred other voices all on the line at the same time. The fact that you and the other person were both speaking clearly would get lost in the cacophony. In autism, neurological losses have been observed also in the cerebellum, the cerebral cortex, and the limbic system. Autism genes may alter brain levels of neurotransmitters at crucial stages of development.

It seems likely that *autism* is a blanket term. Autistic behavior may prove to be a symptom of a variety of causes, much as epilepsy can be caused by a genetic defect in brain structure, a head injury, an infection, a tumor, or a stroke; or as dementia may be the result of Alzheimer's, cerebrovascular degeneration, Huntington's, or Parkinson's. No single gene or consistent set of genes causes the syndrome, although many genes that have been identified are functionally connected to one another, forming a network in the brain. It is not yet clear whether autism-related genes always or sometimes require environmental triggers to become active, nor, if so, what the triggers may be. Researchers have studied many possible developmental influences: prenatal hormones; viruses such as rubella; environmental toxins such as plastics and insecticides; vaccines; metabolic imbalances; and drugs such as thalidomide and valproate. Autism may be genetic, determined by spontaneous new mutations or through inheritance; it is strongly correlated with paternal age, possibly because of germ line de novo mutations that occur spontaneously in the sperm of older fathers. In a recent study, the rate of autism increased fourfold when researchers compared fathers in their thirties to those in their twenties, and the situation appears to be more drastic for fathers in later stages of life. Researchers have also hypothesized that autism is caused by mother/child genetic incompatibilities that play out during gestation. Others have proposed a theory of *assortative mating*, suggesting that people with particular personality types find one another more readily in our mobile, Internet-enabled era, so that two people with mildly autistic tendencies—"hypersystemizers"—produce children together in whom those traits are concentrated.

If we knew what goes on in the brain during autism, it would help establish which genes are implicated. If we knew which genes were implicated, we might be able to figure out what is happening in the brain. If we have only fragmentary knowledge of each thing, both goals are elusive. Up to two hundred genes may be implicated in autism, and some evidence suggests that you need several to manifest the syndrome. Sometimes, epistatic, or modifier, genes influence the expression of primary genes; sometimes environmental factors influence the expression of these genes. The closer the relationship between genotype (what genes you have) and phenotype (what behavior or symptoms you manifest), the easier it is to discern. In autism, some people with a shared genotype don't share a phenotype, and some with a shared phenotype don't share a genotype. Genetic research has demonstrated "variable penetrance" in autism—that is, one can possess known risk genes and not be autistic, and conversely, one can be autistic without having any known risk genes.

If one identical twin has autism, the chances are 60 to 90 percent that the other twin will be autistic as well, though the second twin may have a much milder or a much more severe version of autism. This indicates a strong genetic basis for the disorder. While traits such as eye color or Down syndrome are always shared by identical twins, many other characteristics are not shared absolutely, and the correlation for autism is the highest for any cognitive disorder—higher than for schizophrenia, depression, or obsessive-compulsive disorder.

If one fraternal (nonidentical) twin has autism, the chances are 20 to 30 percent that the other twin will have autism. Fraternal twins do not have identical genetics, but they do have near-identical environments. Nontwin siblings of children with autism are some twenty times as likely to have the condition as members of the general population. Even unaffected close relatives of people with autism are likely to have some subclinical social difficulties. All this suggests that there are strong genetic factors in autism, but that genes alone do not explain all instances of the condition.

A common disorder may be caused by a single anomalous gene. So anyone who has Huntington's disease, for example, has the aberrant Huntington's gene. Autism is the opposite of Huntington's in this regard. Hundreds of different genetic anomalies can predispose someone to autism. No individual *rare gene variant* occurs in very many people, but much of the population has a variant of some kind. The genome is full of hot spots, areas that mutate more easily and frequently than others. Some diseases—breast cancer, for example—are linked to a small number of specific gene mutations, each of which occurs on a particular stretch of a particular chromosome, and they are easily traced because women who have them frequently reproduce. Autism genetics are harder to map because there seem to be many rare gene variants associated with autism that are not usually inherited. They are sprinkled all over the genome. As Matthew State, codirector of Yale's Program on Neurogenetics, has said, "Saying you have found an autism linkage peak on the part of the genome you are studying is like saying you live near Starbucks. Who doesn't live near Starbucks?"

NIMH director Thomas Insel said, "It takes five thousand genes to grow a normal brain, and conceptually, any of them could go wrong and cause autism." According to Michael Wigler at Cold Spring Harbor Laboratory, no single mutation is associated with more than 1 percent of instances of autism, and many of the genes implicated have yet to be discerned. It's not clear whether the complex symptoms of autism arise from a number of separate genetic effects—compromising language separately from social behaviors, for example—or whether one genetic effect, brought about by multiple genes, cascades to various brain regions to generate the characteristics of the syndrome. Most genes associated with autism are pleiotropic, which means that they have multiple effects. Some of these effects are linked with conditions that often co-occur with autism, such as ADHD, epilepsy, and gastrointestinal disorders. Most demonstrate small effect sizes, which means that a gene may boost your chance of developing autism by 10 or 20 percent—not boost it tenfold, as would happen for many disease-risk alleles.

Many genetic diseases occur because a particular gene is abnormal in its structure. In some others, however, a gene is missing entirely; in yet others, there are extra copies of a gene. So let's consider the sentence "I am happy" as a stand-in for a sequence on the genome. The most frequent model for a disease would be for the sentence to come out as "I am harpy" or "I ag happy" or some other such disruption. In a rare case, though, it might come out as "I m hpy" or, alternatively, as "I amamamamamam happpppy." Wigler and his colleague Jonathan Sebat have looked primarily at these copy-number variations. A basic principle of genetics is that we have two of each gene, one from our mother and one from our father. But sometimes, a person actually has three, four, or as many as twelve copies of a gene or group of genes; or in the case of deletions, only one copy of a gene or group of genes, or none at all. The average person has at least a dozen copy-number variations, generally benign. Certain locations on the genome appear to be linked with cognitive disorders. Repetitions in these locations are associated with vulnerability to schizophrenia, bipolar disorder, and autism. However, deletions in the same region are linked only to autism. Wigler has found that many of his autistic subjects possess large deletions, lacking as many as twenty-seven genes. Sebat is now studying whether people with autism and a repetition have the same syndrome as those with autism and a deletion. He has found some significant correlations—for example, that the people with a deletion consistently have larger heads than those with a duplication in the same spot.

The ultimate goal is to map these genes, describe their function, develop model systems, clarify molecular and cellular mechanisms, and then, finally, devise practical applications of findings. We are still identifying the rare variants; we are at the tip of the iceberg. Wigler pointed out that even when we've got all the information, we will have to contend with gene interactions that are not always subject to mathematical mapping. "There is probably an interplay between personality and the deficit," he said. "You and I could have similar deficiencies, but we would make different choices. It sounds odd that a two-year-old may be making a choice about what he can and can't handle, but they probably do. You could have two kids that grow up in the same impoverished environment, and one joins the priesthood and the other becomes a thief, right? I think that can happen internally."

"We are at the place now where we were twenty-five years ago with cancer genetics," said Daniel Geschwind, codirector of the Center for Neurobehavioral Genetics at UCLA. "We know about twenty percent of the genetics; given how late the work started compared with research on schizophrenia and depression, the progress is remarkable." *Autism* is a catchall category for an unexplained constellation of symptoms. Whenever a subtype of autism with a specific mechanism is discovered, it ceases to be called autism and is assigned its own diagnostic name. Rett syndrome produces autistic symptoms; so, often, do phenylketonuria (PKU), tuberous sclerosis, neurofibromatosis, cortical dysplasia-focal epilepsy, Timothy syndrome, fragile X syndrome, and Joubert syndrome. People with these diagnoses are usually described as having "autistic-type behaviors," but not autism per se. If autism is defined by behavior, however, it seems counterproductive to describe as "not autistic" those whose autistic behavior has a known origin.

Until recently, researchers devoted limited energy to these infrequent syndromes, but some have now turned their attention to them with the thought that if we could understand why such conditions cause autistic behavior, we might be able to access the larger mechanisms of autism.

Rapamycin, an immunosuppressant drug usually used in organ transplants, has suppressed seizures and reversed learning disabilities and memory problems in adult mice with tuberous sclerosis; it might have a similar effect on some human beings with the condition. Dr. Alcino Silva of UCLA said of that work, "Memory is as much about discarding trivial details as it is about storing useful information. Our findings suggest that mice with the mutation cannot distinguish between important and unimportant data. We suspect that their brains are filled with meaningless noise that interferes with learning." This evokes the sensory experiences described by many autistic people; "noise" may be a major mechanism of the syndrome.

Fragile X and Rett syndrome are both single-gene mutations. People with fragile X have a gene mutation that encodes a protein that in turn blocks an important brake on protein synthesis in the brain. While the mechanism by which the mutation causes intellectual and behavioral deficits is not known, a current theory is that these symptoms result from excessive protein production. Mice artificially bred with the fragile X mutation overproduce protein, and show learning problems and social deficits. One therapy for fragile X syndrome would be to block the mGluR5 receptor, which is a major stimulus for protein synthesis in the brain. Drugs that do so have reduced the excessive protein, suppressed seizures, and normalized behavior in fragile X mice. The genetics and mechanism of Rett syndrome differ from those associated with fragile X, but mice artificially bred with the Rett syndrome mutation have likewise responded to drugs that target a pathway affected by their mutation.

A surprising finding from studies of mice with either fragile X or Rett syndrome is that even adult mice have shown striking reversal of symptoms with medication. Drugs for fragile X and Rett syndrome are now in early-stage clinical trials in humans, and very preliminary data with at least one compound suggest positive effects on social engagement in children with fragile X. Recent biomedical research has been fraught with exciting findings in mice that cannot be replicated in humans. Nevertheless, these findings raise a significant challenge to the assumption that developmental disorders are hardwired into the brain and cannot be reversed. If they are a consequence of impaired function of cellular pathways, then it may be possible to resolve some symptoms of autism without altering genes. In other words, autism symptoms may reflect not brain development, which is usually irreversible, but brain function, which is often pliable. It is clear, however, that instigating normal brain function in someone whose brain has developed without it will not fully resolve symptoms. Geraldine Dawson, chief science officer of Autism Speaks, said, "You've fixed their car's broken engine, but you still have to teach them to drive."

In 2012, Wigler and other scientists at Cold Spring Harbor Laboratory discovered a link between genes affected by fragile X and genes that are disrupted in some children with idiopathic autism. This suggests that medications showing promise in fragile X may be helpful to a larger subset of autistic people. Wigler and Sebat believe that we'll eventually see what more of the rare gene variants do. Some probably disable or duplicate enzymes that a drug might mimic or inhibit. Others might affect neurotransmitter levels or change the pH or environment of the synapse, and it may be possible to reverse those effects. "I would be amazed if there aren't pharmacological treatments for more of this," Wigler said. "We'll never know all the genes, and we'll never have a treatment that works for everyone, but we should be able to find good treatments for a subset of patients."

The Cambridge autism researcher Simon Baron-Cohen postulates that women are empathizers, hardwired to understand others, while men are systemizers, hardwired to organize factual and mechanical information. Autism, in this view, is an overexpression of cognitive masculinity—short on empathy and long on systems. Baron-Cohen has investigated the extent to which unusually high levels of prenatal testosterone might alter brain structure and engender autism. Given that more androgens circulate in utero during pregnancy with a boy, a smaller excess would tip a male fetus into autism than would tip a female. This may be a partial explanation for why autism occurs twice as often in males as in females.

Autistic people are indeed often systemizers; many have uncanny technical abilities. Some are savants who do not function independently in many areas of life but have extraordinary abilities in one domain—sometimes a relatively trivial one, such as the ability immediately to list the dates of Easter for every year until the end of time, and sometimes a useful one, such as the competence to create meticulously accurate drawings, or to hold in mind a complex design, or to produce a perfect map of Rome after flying over the city once. Whether this has to do with prenatal testosterone is subject to debate, but there is a maleness to this way of being.

Extreme trauma can provoke behavior that resembles autism. Some people appear autistic following perinatal injury. Grossly neglected children taken from Ceauşescu-era Romanian orphanages often showed autistic-like behavior, though examination showed them disengaged not merely from other people, but also from the material world. Bruno Bettelheim was a Holocaust survivor who had seen autistic-style withdrawal in other inmates at Dachau, and on this basis he mistakenly concluded that all autism was linked to abuse. Certainly, however, abuse can exacerbate symptoms associated with the disorder.

Too often, the presence of autism confuses parents and doctors, so that other ailments may go undetected or untreated. Margaret Bauman of Harvard Medical School described how one of her autistic patients had for years suffered spasmodic twists and writhing. These had been presumed to be the symptoms of autism and therefore ran unchecked. Referral to a gastroenterologist revealed that the patient had esophageal ulcers; when these were treated, her gyrations stopped. Fred Volkmar at Yale described a nine-year-old boy who had such severe motor issues that he was unable to hold a pencil. When the boy entered third grade and the other students were learning cursive penmanship, Volkmar suggested giving the boy a laptop. The teacher objected to giving the boy a "crutch." Volkmar said, "If you didn't have a leg and I gave you a crutch, that would be a mitzvah."

Approximately one-third of autistic people have at least one psychiatric diagnosis in addition to autism, compared to 10 percent of the general population, but they frequently don't get treatment for these complicating factors. One in five suffers from clinical depression, and about 18 percent from anxiety. Kamran Nazeer's autistic friend Elizabeth had inherited a tendency toward depression from her nonautistic parents. "The doctors were reluctant to prescribe antidepressants or make any firm diagnosis of the malaise," he writes mournfully. "Wasn't it all really caused by her autism?" She eventually committed suicide.

John Shestack and Portia Iversen founded Cure Autism Now, which was the leading private funder of autism research until it merged with Autism Speaks; they started the Autism Genetic Research Exchange, the largest open-resource gene bank in the world; they drafted many leading autism geneticists. "The belief that poor parenting caused autism meant that no meaningful research was done for fifty years after it was described," Portia said. "When our son, Dov, was diagnosed, autism was under the radar, not under the microscope. I didn't think I was good at science. But the same way you learn to jump if your house is on fire and you're on the third floor, that's how I learned the science of autism." She wanted to increase researchers' contact with families affected by autism. "The most effective thing we could do was to become the data," she said.

Like Carly Fleischmann, Dov Shestack has emerged as having normal intelligence—a whole mind that had been immured in silence for many years. When he was nine, Portia asked him to point to the letter *s*, and he did so, and she soon realized that he could read. "It was really shocking," she said. "You don't think they can read when you don't know they can think." When she understood that Dov could express himself, she asked him what he'd been doing all these years. "Listening," he said. His education remains problematic; he needs one-on-one support, but he's cognitively normal. "There's a popular belief that you can't have someone who acts retarded and is intelligent," Portia said. "But you can."

Portia Iversen has investigated the deepest riddle of autism: the relationship between what can be observed and what is going on inside autistic people. "Some autistic people seem unmotivated to communicate. I can't be positive, but it appears that way. Then there are people who desperately want to be understood. I see a big split in my son between his disorder and his personality. He's mostly not doing what he wants to do and acting as he wants to act. Many mornings, he starts making whining noises, flipping his hands; it's like a chemical storm. It just drives him. Even with that, he's much happier than before I realized he was saying something. Even constrained communication is the difference between life and death."

Given the broad range of symptoms, all of which seldom coincide in a single case, diagnosis is an extremely subtle enterprise and is made more difficult by the idea of an autism spectrum that fades into normality at one end. "It's much like IQ, weight, or height," Geschwind points out. "There's optimal weight; there's a few extra pounds that some people may find unattractive; there's obesity that undermines everything else about your health." Everyone's mind is disordered in some measure sometimes, and how a spectrum contiguous with normality can also be categorical is a complicated question. "Classrooms," Isabelle Rapin said, "are dichotomous, which is the only reason for these classifications of children whose differences are not black-and-white: so they can be put in the right room or center. This is policy, not biology."

The innumerable questionnaires and inventories, seldom fully sufficient for diagnosis, include the Autism Behavior Checklist (ABC), the Childhood Autism Rating Scale (CARS), the popular Checklist for Autism in Toddlers (CHAT), the seven-hour-long Diagnostic Interview for Social and Communication Disorders (DISCO), the Autism Diagnostic Interview–Revised (ADI-R), and the highly regarded Autism Diagnostic Observation Scale–Generic (ADOS-G). It's hard to find a consistent instrument that applies to both people who speak and those who are nonverbal. Any of these tests can produce different results depending on who is conducting it. In the ADOS, for example, you are supposed to see if you can coax a child into imaginative play. Some examiners I observed had tremendous vitality and imagination; others were simpering or overbearing or tired and not imaginative themselves. Also, the examiner has to be able to distinguish between what kids can't do (autism) and what they won't do (personality or mood issues). The severity of autistic symptoms tends to fluctuate in any individual, so someone may perform differently one day from another. More adults are seeking diagnosis, so the tests have to work for people of variable ages. Because autism is a developmental disorder, however, it is not diagnosed unless symptoms began before age three; autistic-like symptoms that set in later are not considered developmental.

Medicine has been too eager in many cases to dismiss parents' insight. August Bier, a physician practicing in the early twentieth century, said, "A smart mother often makes a better diagnosis than a poor doctor." The closeness with which a parent observes can be as powerful as the expertise with which a physician observes, and setting them up in opposition to each other is a disaster for everyone. But medicine is often unprepared for parental perspectives that do not align with an illness model. For many parents, diagnosis is a crossing of the Styx into hell. For others, such as Kathleen Seidel—disability rights advocate, founder of the website Neurodiversity.com, and parent of a young adult diagnosed with Asperger syndrome at the age of ten—it can be a revelation. "I think of diagnoses as an aid to pattern recognition in our lives," she said. "We could make sense out of things that had previously been inexplicable to us; we felt validated. At the same time, I could feel this pull of lessened expectations by virtue of a diagnosis, and it didn't seem right or healthy to me to think that way. God has many different ways to build a brain. A Cray supercomputer is used for really complex, intense computing that involves the manipulation of massive amounts of data. It runs so hot it has to be kept in a liquid cooling bath. It requires a very specific kind of TLC. And is the Cray defective because it requires this kind of nurturing environment for its functioning? No! It kicks ass! That's what my kid is like. He needs support, needs attention, and is amazing."

Marvin Brown's mother, Icilda, has delineated what she can influence and what she cannot, and she does not rail against what is beyond amelioration. It is easy to patronize "simple wisdom" by honeying the rough circumstances from which it generally springs, or by representing it as simpler or wiser than it is, but Icilda Brown seemed more at peace with her son's condition than almost any other mother I met. A lifetime of nonchoices had given her a gift for acceptance. She demanded good services for her son, but did not expect those services to turn him into someone else. The story of middle-class and affluent parenting of autistic children is an interminable saga of tilting at windmills; in contrast, I admired both Icilda's acquiescence and the happiness that was its corollary.

Icilda grew up in South Carolina, one of ten children in a poor African-American farming family. She came to New York in the 1960s and found work cleaning houses. She married young, and by thirty she was mother to five children. Marvin was next to youngest. By two, Icilda said, he was different. "Three years old, he started to talk, and then he just stopped, and he didn't really try to talk anymore until he was five." The diagnosis of autism came when he was almost four, in 1976. "He never would cry," Icilda recalled. "He just would be happy, playing and running back and forth. He would get up early—two in the morning every day. When he gets up, I get up. He couldn't stay still. I just got used to it." Cleaning houses for a living is not light work, and Icilda did it for many years on the three to four hours of sleep that her life with Marvin allowed her. "I prayed not to be too tired," she said. "I prayed for guidance, to help me to do the right thing, and for strength, to put up with him, because that's what it takes every day."

Icilda enrolled Marvin in a program for autistic children at Jacobi Hospital in the north Bronx, an hour from her home. The program kids were mostly attending public schools near Jacobi, and since Marvin hated to travel, Icilda picked up her family and moved near the schools. Marvin was a hand-flapper and had many other repetitive behaviors. He had limited speech. Even though Icilda's husband left when Marvin was ten, he has had a constant, attentive mother, the same schools, the same apartment, as much continuity as Icilda was able to manage. "When he's sad, he'll tell you, 'I'm very sad,'" Icilda said. "When he's happy, he's happy. If he gets angry, he'll say, 'I'm angry!' And I'll talk him down and pat him. I'll say, 'You just sit down and relax.' I can calm him." As a devout Jehovah's Witness, Icilda has relied on the community of her religion. "Our church was the biggest comfort and still is. Everyone there was very, very supportive. All of them know him; he knows them."

Taking care of Marvin became easier in some ways as he grew older. He slept more; he was better able to be on his own. But he became more self-conscious about his condition. When Marvin entered his twenties, Icilda gave up cleaning houses and found work taking care of the elderly in Mt. Vernon, New York, and her hours were a bit lighter. She had been advised by professionals that Marvin might do well in a group home, and she secured a place for him. Before taking him there, she said, "This is only if you want to stay." She promised to bring him home every weekend. At first he said he didn't like it, but she insisted that he give it a fair chance. He was no happier at the end of the year, so she brought him home. Some five years later, while Marvin was attending a day program in the Bronx, he became upset; others who were present later claimed that he was provoked by one of his teachers. Although Marvin had no history of violence, the day-program worker called the police, who manacled him and brought him to a mental hospital. When Icilda learned that her son was locked up, she rushed to the hospital to retrieve him. Marvin was terrified and utterly confused. Icilda was outraged. "I sent a letter to the mayor, the commissioner—everybody. I got one of the people I used to clean for to help me write. They brought the whole state down on them. They put the program under investigation." Other frightened people had gone through the same experience, and the woman who was responsible was removed from her job. Icilda transferred Marvin to a new day program, where he has been prepared for employment; under supervision, he has worked in a bookstore and for a messenger service and has learned to perform janitorial duties.

Icilda was sixty-two when we met, and it had been forty-three years since she began the care of infants. "He takes a lot of supervision," she said. "But he calls me, you know, 'my friend.'" She said it with domestic bluster and contentment and a shy smile. Icilda has become a community resource; she has met with hundreds of other parents, and she made videos of Marvin that are shown at the centers where he has been helped. "I'll say, 'You see my son now. And now see your kid's running and not talking. That was him. If you give up, your child doesn't have a chance.'" She paused, with a big, open smile. "I looked back, and I said to the Lord, 'Oh, thank you for bringing me from such a *long* ways.'"

The Autism Society of America estimates that one and a half million Americans are on the spectrum; the CDC says 560,000 people under twenty-one have autism; the US Department of Education says that autism is growing at a rate of 10 to 17 percent per year, and that numbers in the United States could reach four million in the next decade. Recent work suggests that more than 1 percent of the world population may be on the spectrum. Part of the upsurge has to do with the broadening of categories: people who might once have been classed as schizotypal or mentally retarded are now on the spectrum, as are some who would once have been thought odd but not given a diagnosis. Aggressive advocacy by parents has helped to establish better services for kids with autism than for kids with other afflictions. If you attach better services to a diagnostic category, some doctors will apply that diagnosis to children for whom it is not entirely appropriate in order to access those services. Parents who might once have shunned an autism label to avoid being unjustly blamed for their child's disability are now willing to seek out that label so their children may qualify for special-education services. California, for example, has considerable diagnostic substitution; the state reported a decrease in mental retardation coincident with a twelvefold increase over twenty years in services for autism. Autism researcher Laura Schreibman estimates that the lifetime cost of autism is $5 million; even parents with full insurance incur tremendous annual costs. Many insurers refuse to pay for labor-intensive strategies such as ABA, which is an educational rather than a medical strategy, and many parents who have the wherewithal sue their insurance company, their school board, their local government, or all three. Having a severely impaired child is utterly draining; these legal proceedings often stretch parents to the breaking point.

Is autism itself also on the rise? Inconceivable time and energy have been poured into this question, and no consensus has emerged, but it seems reasonable to conclude that both diagnosis and incidence have increased. During the decade that I spent working on this book, people would hear my list of chapters and then offer to introduce me to friends who were dealing with autism at least ten times as often as they would offer introductions to people with any of the other conditions. NIMH director Thomas Insel recounted a time during the 1970s when an autistic child was admitted to Boston Children's Hospital; the chief of service called the residents together to observe him, reasoning that they might never see an autistic child again. On Insel's own street today, which has nine houses, two children have autism. Steven Hyman, former head of the NIMH and former provost of Harvard, said, "The growth in the diagnosis of the autism spectrum reflects destigmatization and broader education. Does that mean that there is no increase in incidence? No, but it confounds our ability to tell." Several studies applying current diagnostic criteria have shown that people who were once considered nonautistic would be considered autistic by current criteria, though such work is always somewhat speculative.

Many scientists have argued that regressive autism is not regressive at all—that children with a particular genotype simply begin to show symptoms at a stage in their development; the autism comes in at its time, like teeth or body hair. Many parents whose children have regressed, however, argue nearly the opposite: that regression is caused by a specific environmental trigger. Because regression often occurs at around the same age that children are immunized, many parents have attributed their children's autism to vaccines, particularly the measles-mumps-rubella (MMR) vaccine, and vaccines containing the mercury-based preservative thimerosal. MMR was introduced in the United States in the 1970s and by the 1980s was in widespread use. Because it is not effective during the first year of life, when maternal antibodies block its action, the first dose is administered at about thirteen months. In 1998, British gastroenterologist Andrew Wakefield of the Royal Free Hospital published a paper in the *Lancet* positing an association between the MMR vaccine and gastrointestinal problems in autistic children. Wakefield and his colleagues described only twelve cases; nonetheless, journalists seized upon the story, and many parents stopped vaccinating their children. In Britain, rates of immunization against measles dropped from 92 percent to less than 80 percent, and cases of the disease began to skyrocket. Whereas only 56 children in England and Wales contracted measles in 1998, and none died, in 2008, 5,088 cases were reported in the UK, resulting in the deaths of 2 children.

Numerous demographic studies have consistently failed to demonstrate a link between vaccines and autism. One study conducted by the Centers for Disease Control and Prevention followed 140,000 children and showed no connection; a Japanese study demonstrated that unvaccinated children actually had a higher rate of autism. After it became known that Wakefield was recruited by an attorney seeking to build a legal case against vaccine manufacturers, that eleven of the twelve study subjects were involved in this litigation, and that Wakefield had been paid for his services by the UK Legal Aid Corporation, ten of the study's thirteen authors officially retracted their names from it. The *Lancet's* editor subsequently apologized for publishing the paper, which he described as "fatally flawed"; in 2010, following an investigation by the UK General Medical Council, the journal retracted it altogether. With the advent of each new piece of evidence absolving vaccines, Wakefield's acolytes have alleged a cover-up and have shifted to new arguments that keep vaccines in the spotlight. Once thimerosal had been removed from all vaccines routinely administered to children without any decrease in the rate of autism diagnoses, some proposed that the problem arose from combination vaccines and their supposed assault on the immune system, or simply from too many vaccinations altogether.

Witnessing autistic regression seems to traumatize parents much more deeply than recognizing a disorder present from birth; parents are possessed by the idea that the child who once played and laughed with them can be rediscovered. Most of our understanding of autistic regression comes from speaking to parents about their children's development. Typically, parents of children who regress witness their child's loss of language at about sixteen months. I met one child who was evaluated because he had an autistic brother and was therefore considered high risk. At six months, he was chortling, playing, and enjoying his exchange with a diagnostician. At a little more than a year, the same child appeared oblivious to the same evaluator; he did not laugh, smile, or acknowledge the presence of others; he seemed flabby and glassy-eyed. It was difficult to believe that he was the same child. Some researchers have questioned whether such regression results from loss of function, or whether apparent early sociability in infancy may rely on different brain regions than more mature sociability. Researchers have estimated that between 20 and 50 percent of autism cases involve regression.

The journalist David Kirby's *Evidence of Harm* describes the evolution of the autism-vaccine hypothesis and reports on the divisions between parents convinced that vaccines harmed their children, and scientists and policymakers involved in vaccine development. Each side believes that the other is motivated by financial conflicts of interest and willfully distorted science. Citing failure of petitioners' attorneys to produce adequate scientific support for their causation arguments, the National Vaccine Injury Compensation Program is currently in the process of dismissing over five thousand claims alleging that vaccines are responsible for making children autistic. The debate is frequently acrimonious. Katie Wright, daughter of Autism Speaks cofounders Bob and Suzanne Wright, has claimed that her son began to display signs of autism immediately after being vaccinated, and that he has recovered in part through treatments that addressed the vaccine injury; she has urged her parents and the scientists they support to abandon "failed strategies" and embrace her perspective. The Wrights posted a statement on the Autism Speaks website clarifying that their daughter's "personal views differ from ours." The vaccine argument is championed by ex–*Playboy* centerfold and comedienne Jenny McCarthy. Critics have observed that McCarthy gains considerable publicity from her crusade and earns a tidy living from speaking engagements.

In March 2008, the Atlanta Court of Federal Claims conceded in the Hannah Poling case that a chicken-pox vaccine had probably aggravated an underlying mitochondrial disorder to create autistic-type symptoms in one child. The case has been treated by antivaccinationists as overdue justice. Some draw parallels between themselves and the early antitobacco movement. "We had an epidemic in lung cancer and heart disease in the fifties and sixties and the cigarette companies had all this science that showed cigarettes had nothing to do with it," said Lenny Schafer, progenitor of the *Schafer Autism Report* and adoptive father of a young man with autism.

Many neurodiversity and autism rights activists are, conversely, offended by the vaccine arguments, which they find scientifically groundless and insulting to people with autism. Kathleen Seidel said, "Juries and judges hear these stories, and people's hearts lead the way. But hearts leading the way don't always lead to justice."

Epidemiological studies have demonstrated no correlation between vaccination and autism. Does that mean that *no* children have a vulnerability triggered by vaccines? One mother whose child regressed told me, "The pediatrician gave him the vaccine, and within twenty-four hours he had a white count of thirty-one thousand. He was in the hospital and they said it was sepsis. After he came out, he was less socially engaged. A lot less socially engaged. It was like I went into the hospital with one kid and I came out with another." Portia Iversen said, "You can't confront someone's experience with a lot of evidence." Insel said, "It seems to me that the story is the increase in food allergies, asthma, diabetes, autism, pediatric bipolar disorder, which has gone up fortyfold in the last ten years. I wonder if there isn't something more general going on that explains all of this. I can't tell you what. But that sounds to me like an environmental factor." Unfortunately, modern life has too many environmental variables to catalog: cell phones, air travel, televisions, vitamin pills, food additives. Many people believe that environmental heavy metals have afflicted their children. Others blame a broad range of other substances, especially bisphenol-A, a man-made, estrogen-based polymer used in plastics, which has an annual production of more than three million tons. Most geneticists acknowledge that these questions have not been fully resolved, and that they may not be resolved for many years.

Reversing much accepted science, however, in 2011, Stanford psychiatrist Joachim Hallmayer and his colleagues checked identical and fraternal twins for autism and used mathematical modeling to show that genetics determined only 38 percent of the cases they studied, while shared environmental factors appeared to be primarily responsible in 58 percent of cases. The rate of concordance in identical twins was lower than anticipated, suggesting that genetics does not tell the whole story; the rate of concordance in fraternal twins was higher than expected, suggesting that environment—perhaps the uterine environment—plays a significant role. Neil Risch, the director of the UCSF Institute for Human Genetics and the designer of the study, said, "We're not trying to say there isn't a genetic component—quite the opposite. But for most individuals with autism spectrum disorder, it's not simply a genetic cause." The study was described as a "game-changer" by Joseph Coyle, editor of *Archives of General Psychiatry*. A separate group, in a study published at the same time and in the same journal, found that mothers who took SSRIs, a category of antidepressants, just before or during pregnancy had children with an increased risk of autism. These data are all preliminary, and the data showing that autism is 70 percent heritable are more robust, but mainstream science will have to reconsider the idea of significant environmental risk.

Mark Blaxill is a polished Princeton graduate, founder of a business consulting firm, and one of the most sophisticated proponents of the vaccine causation of autism. He and his wife, Elise, went through ten rounds of IVF, ten miscarriages, and two ectopic pregnancies. They finally produced two daughters. Their second, Michaela, seemed to develop normally for her first year, but before she turned two, Elise began to think something was wrong. When she was two years and nine months, they got a diagnosis. "I wasn't engaged," Mark said. "Work was a big deal. Michaela was an easy child. My way of dealing with the grief was to get really aggressive about learning everything I could, so I went almost to vocational school in neuroscience; I was consumed with it."

By the time I met Mark, Michaela was twelve and had made significant progress. Mark listed the ten people who took care of her—therapists, sitters, doctors who attended to her delicate physical health. He was well aware that few people could afford all this. Nonetheless, he was deeply frustrated. "Michaela had a full-syndrome autistic diagnosis when she started. She didn't speak. Now she's engaged, lovely, very social. The language is still not quite at an Asperger's level, but she's approaching that. But all she wants to talk about is Jiminy Cricket and Pinocchio. Our job is to move her off that. I just want her to talk about something other than Jiminy Cricket."

Mark is consumed with his activism. "I think autism is a brain rash," he said to me. "And if you have politically incorrect ideas, like the fact that autism originated in vaccines and mercury, then you get accused of obstructing scientific inquiry. We believe that it's the epidemic, stupid; it's environmental. I'm unsatisfied with the solutions, I'm unsatisfied with the science, I'm unsatisfied with the institutions. Genetics research has failed miserably. And the CDC's job is to manage vaccine safety, so they produce bullshit studies that give them the outcome they want." Mark talked about a study he coauthored that showed reduced mercury levels in the first haircuts of autistic children, which he took as evidence that they are not able to excrete mercury as efficiently as other babies. He has published peer-reviewed papers in respected journals such as *NeuroToxicology*. Encountering his passion, it's hard not to be converted—except that much of the science he cites has been soundly refuted, and much of the science he disparages appears to have a strong empirical basis. Of course, science is always subject to revision, but, as Bruce Stillman, president of Cold Spring Harbor Lab, has pointed out, science cannot have an agenda, and it appears that this science does.

Mark said, "I was the captain of the football team, the president of the student council, National Merit scholar. I was a pleasure for my parents to have as a child. The autism advocacy thing is about the mission, it's not about winning or making more money than the other guy, or getting better grades—you consign yourself to the margin of respectable society if you do what I've chosen to do. It's liberating. 'Cause I don't give a shit what the *New York Times* thinks; I just want to do the right thing and make a mark on the world."

American law provides guarantees of education that are not matched by guarantees of medical care. Education is a government responsibility; medical care is a personal responsibility, controlled in large measure by insurance companies. For that reason, some advocates have preferred to keep treatment for autism in the arena of education rather than of medicine; so far, the pedagogic interventions appear to work better than the medical ones, so most current treatments are school-based. As with Down syndrome and many other disabilities, autism is best identified and addressed as early as possible.

Early intervention requires early detection. Ami Klin and colleagues at Yale have conducted an experiment in which both autistic and non-autistic adults watched *Who's Afraid of Virginia Woolf?* Using computer tracking, the researchers found that autistic people do not switch their gaze back and forth between the arguing protagonists as nonautistic subjects do. Building on that work, they have infants watch videos of other children and mothers; the typically developing infants focus on eyes, while the ones at risk for autism focus on objects or mouths. Despite broad concurrence that early diagnosis is valuable because early treatment is effective, there is no consensus about what that early treatment should be. As Bryna Siegel, a psychologist at UCSF, has written in *Helping Children with Autism Learn*, "The picture of autism treatment is complicated by the fact that there are very different perspectives from which to view treatment: developmental, behavioral, educational, cognitive, and medical. Practitioners from these different perspectives often don't understand one another's vocabularies."

Charles Ferster, an American behavioral psychologist, was the first to propose that people could learn through conditioning just as animals do. This idea led, in the 1960s, to the behavioral interventions now used in treating autism, most particularly to applied behavior analysis (ABA). Such treatments are based on observing the child, pinpointing his negative or obsessive behaviors, and developing positive substitutes for them. Desirable acts receive positive reinforcement: if the child speaks, for example, he may get what he wants. Negative acts do not receive reinforcement: temper tantrums are never rewarded. Many behaviorist treatments are in circulation. Much of this teaching remains unnatural to the child and thus requires constant maintenance, yet many parents consider it vital—just as many hearing parents require a language in which they can communicate with their deaf children.

Other successful autism treatments involve learning from the behavior of the person with autism. Dr. Stanley Greenspan garnered an enormous amount of publicity for his Developmental, Individual Difference, Relationship-Based (DIR®/Floortime™) Model, which involves getting down on the floor with the autistic child to forge a connection. Auditory Integration Training and Sensory Integration Therapy attempt to address the particular hypersensitivities of autistic children. Speech therapy introduces them to the use of language and helps with articulation. Soma Mukhopadhyay, with no background in the field, developed the Rapid Prompting Method (RPM) in India to treat her own son, who was nonverbal and now types poetry.

Service dogs that resemble Seeing Eye dogs are often invaluable to autistic children and adults, helping to stave off panic attacks, provide physical orientation, and build an emotional bridge between autistic people and the social world. One mother exulted about the change in her son, Kaleb, after a service dog joined their family. "He seems so much more secure and more grounded than he ever has before. He seems to be handling things so much better. It's so important for Kaleb and Chewey to be together twenty-four hours a day. They both need to know that they are each other's constant." A legal brief about whether Kaleb should be allowed to take a dog to school said, "Since receiving Chewey, K.D. becomes upset for shorter periods of time, completes his homework, and sleeps between six to eight hours per night. He has less difficulty transitioning between home and other public places, including school."

Some parents modify their children's diets, as there are anecdotes of people with autism who are unable to tolerate gluten, casein, and other substances that occur in many foods. The SSRIs, the class of antidepressants that includes Prozac, Zoloft, and Paxil, have been used to control the anxiety to which some autistic people are subject; the results appear to be mixed. As many as a fifth to a third of autistic people develop epilepsy, and they are helped by antiseizure medications. The stimulant drugs commonly used for ADHD are sometimes prescribed to calm people with autism, as are various sedatives, and antipsychotics such as Haldol and Mellaril.

The results achieved with all of these treatments are inconsistent, and the effort and cost of initiating them is extreme. Even if an autistic person develops and sustains speech, functional skills, and a degree of social awareness, he will not become nonautistic; a distinctive cognitive profile will remain. Kamran Nazeer described how he discovered in adulthood what is obvious to most children: "I began to understand. A conversation is performance, merely a series of juxtapositions. I say something to you. A phrase in what I said, a topic, a point of view, or nothing at all connects with something that you contain. Then you say something. And like this, we proceed." Such insights solve some challenges associated with autism, but they do not eliminate it.

Bruce Spade was a professional photographer in London for some twenty-seven years, and his eye for strange beauty shows in his lifetime of photographs of his autistic son, Robin, pictures that look deeply at a person who is sometimes inexplicably tortured and sometimes exuberant, sometimes angry at the camera and sometimes besotted with it. Robin is capable of great sweetness. "He used to have this thing Harriet and I called grebing," Bruce said. "I don't know if you've seen the great crested grebe doing a mating dance. They stand out of the water, and they shake their heads and make a lot of high-pitched sounds. Robin would look you in the eyes and he would shake his head, and sometimes he'd say, 'Look, look.' And if he grebed at you, that was his sign; you were in." But Robin was also inexhaustible and exhausting; as he grew up and grew stronger, his explosions of rage became increasingly frightening. He'd have a tantrum in the street and Bruce or Harriet would sit on him until he calmed down. Bruce and Harriet would have liked to have another child—"someone who knew how to play," in Bruce's words—but they were too tired to contemplate that.

When Robin was nine, he went off to boarding school. "It was either that or I had to give up work and go on the dole and look after him," Bruce said. The following year, when Robin came home for the summer, he was always hungry and his mother couldn't say no. "She wouldn't stop feeding him," Bruce said. "The back of the car was littered with the packets." Robin enjoyed the eating, but he was gaining weight at a terrifying pace; he soon weighed nearly three hundred pounds. "It almost destroyed our marriage," Bruce said. Robin became anxious about walking because he was so huge; soon, all his toenails became ingrown. Harriet had an affair. "We've argued so much that it's gone beyond reconciliation," Bruce said. "Harriet is always saying, 'It's time we divorced,' but we never do it, because neither of us could handle this alone."

Then Robin's school was closed down because a child escaped and died, revealing inadequate supervision that would fill any parent with anxiety. Only two schools in the UK would take someone as violent as Robin. Bruce and Harriet selected Hesley Village and College in Yorkshire, a Victorian farm on fifty-four acres with its own little hotel, a village green, a pub, a bistro, a hairdresser, a post office, and a bakery, all for seventy autistic people. The day Robin arrived, one of his new caregivers suggested they go for a walk, and Robin flew at him with a head-butt, jumped on top of him, and knocked him unconscious. Months of self-injury followed. Robin banged his head so hard that he would break through doors, and so frequently that he needed a skull X-ray; he scratched his skin until it bled. Then he got into the rhythm of the place, and the violence abated.

Robin has a lively sexuality. "He masturbates a lot," Bruce said. "He tries to look up your nose; that turns him on. I suppose it's an orifice, he's got that much. He wants to look up mine, and sometimes I let him, just for a minute, so he can get off. I don't want to discourage him, and he has so little pleasure in life and this is something I can do for him, not too difficult if I don't let myself think about the fact that he's my son, and it's about sex. But I don't want to get him obsessed with nostrils, so I try not to do it too often. There is a girl at college—his pace quickens when he sees her. And although she is very noisy, and he is not really good with noise, he goes all coy when she is in the same room."

Robin seems happier at Hesley now, but his erratic behavior continues. A few months before I met Bruce, Robin had come home on a break and couldn't sleep. After he had been awake for four days straight, Bruce and Harriet got a doctor to prescribe some sleeping pills; these enabled him to sleep for about three hours. When he awoke, he was thrashing around and seemed distraught, so Harriet sat on his bed to try to calm him down. He grabbed her hand and bit through her tendon. "She had to go to hospital," Bruce said. "She was shaking, in shock, and nearly unconscious. It was a terrible night." They took Robin back to college and wondered whether the visits home were more than he could handle. "But then he came home again the week before last and he was just lovely, affectionate, and a joy to be with," Bruce said. "He put his dirty plates in the washer. That's huge progress. We become very proud, just as somebody else is if their child gets a first at Cambridge."

In *The Cherry Orchard*, Chekhov said, "When many remedies are proposed for a disease, that means the disease is incurable." Autism invites treatments that range from optimism to quackery. The list of such treatments of dubious efficacy is even longer than the list of treatments that bring about improvement, and parents with fantasies of perfect remission put themselves at the mercy of flamboyant visionaries who tout a range of bizarre procedures as breakthroughs. Barry Neil Kaufman and Samahria Lyte Kaufman developed Option Therapy and the associated Son-Rise Program in the 1980s to treat their own son, who they claim was completely cured of his autism; in fact, one commentator claims that doctors who treated the boy expressed doubt that he ever had autism at all. The program costs $2,000 for an initial consultation with parents and then $11,500 for a one-week program with the child. A New York psychiatrist hatched Holding Therapy, in which parents physically restrain children when they exhibit problematical behavior; this seems to exacerbate tension in both children and parents. Bookstores overflow with books such as *The Horse Boy*, about a child who was supposedly led out of his autism by shamans in Mongolia. It sometimes seems that every parent whose child is thriving feels compelled to write a hubristic volume effectively called *What I Did Right*. Many such parents generalize from strategies that may only by chance have coincided with their children's "emergence."

While considerable time and money have been poured into such minimally tested behavioral and conceptual methods, these do not in general pose actual physical danger to children. Chelation, however, has great potential to cause long-term harm, and even greater potential to cause unnecessary short-term suffering. This procedure was originally developed to remove heavy metals from the bodies of wounded soldiers during World War I. Synthetic compounds are administered—usually intravenously, but sometimes intramuscularly or orally—to bind to metals, which are then excreted into the blood, urine, and hair. Chelation is recommended by advocates of the theory that a mercury-based preservative used in some vaccines causes autism. Although extensive research has failed to support its efficacy, as many as one in twelve American autistic children is estimated to have undergone chelation. At least one autistic child has died from hypocalcemia—a fatal drop in calcium levels leading to heart failure—during the procedure. Many more have experienced headaches, nausea, and depression. Some parents claim to have observed miraculous improvements as a result of chelation, and those claims, made in sincerity, have led to a burgeoning, often underground, and largely unregulated business in the chemical "detoxification" of autistic children. A patent-pending "protocol" using Lupron—a castration drug that changes the body as profoundly as any medication can—conflates the possible effects of prenatal testosterone on the development of autism with normal puberty. It has been championed by a father-son team despite a lack of any verifiable evidence for its efficacy; finding that their practice constitutes "a danger to the patient community," the Maryland Board of Physicians and authorities in at least six other states have suspended the father's medical license, while the son, who is not a doctor, has been charged with practicing medicine without a license. Other physical interventions—putting children in hyperbaric oxygen chambers, putting them in tanks with dolphins, giving them blue-green algae, or megadosing them on vitamins—are usually neither harmful nor helpful, though they can have dangers, are certainly disorienting, and cost a lot.

The first time I met Amy Wolf, she said of her daughter, Angela, "She has no speech and is frequently incontinent; is in a full-time, round-the-clock-care facility; is beautiful and loves us; and can't be in the world without help for a minute. She walks and enjoys it. She can't button a button. She can sort silverware; can eat with a fork, a spoon is a little tricky; can't cut things; needs a straw a lot of the time. Has very little fear and awareness, so she would walk in the middle of the busy street if you took your eyes off her. She understands more than she can express, how much no one has figured out. She takes pleasure in things. Sometimes she's quite distant. Sometimes she's bright and makes a lot of contact. Sometimes when she sees me, she's overjoyed, which is fantastic. She likes people—just not too many at once. She hates the doctor; hates the dentist; hates the shoe store; hates the hairdresser; hates big parties; hates surprises; hates change in routine—and, generally, seems quite at peace with her life at this point. The first fourteen years were hellacious."

In 1972, age twenty, Amy decided to leave behind the life of urban sophistication in which she had been brought up in New York and moved to an alternative community in Taos, New Mexico. She married a healer and acupuncturist, and in 1979 became pregnant. When Angela was born, it was immediately clear that there were problems. She was put into a full-body brace to correct a contorted frame, a displaced hip, and what looked like a clubfoot. Angela's body was hypotonic, with loose, elastic muscles that didn't keep her limbs in place, like a rag doll. She didn't walk until she was almost two. Words came, but slowly, and she was pitifully thin. Taos offered few supports. "There were no antidepressants," Amy recalled. "There were no services; no Internet; no therapists. There were outhouses, apricots drying, Indian pueblos, yurts, hippies, Hispanic ancient culture, and Native American ritual. And Angela and me, somehow very far apart from this community that I had held very dear." Her husband, healer though he claimed to be, could not cope with a disabled child, and he fled.

When Angela was three, Amy divorced and brought her back to New York to start again. At that age, Angela had some speech and could recite "Twinkle, Twinkle, Little Star." She could pick out the family car in the street. She was beginning toilet training. Then, bit by bit, it all fell away. She lost speech and became incontinent. Her muscle tone didn't improve. Amy had a long history with substance abuse and she spun out of control. "I was driving, when she was about four, drunk, with her in the backseat, having poured vodka down her throat while she was in the car seat, thinking that I'd kill us both by driving down an embankment into the Long Island Sound," Amy recalled.

Instead, she joined Alcoholics Anonymous and has been sober ever since. With the support of her parents, she began looking for cures.

Angela was never aggressive to anyone else, but she was often self-injurious. Mostly, though, she was just "out of control, and sometimes deeply distressed, and generally incomprehensible." When Angela was seven, a colleague told Amy about a Japanese woman, Kiyo Kitahara, who had achieved astonishing improvements with autistic children. She had founded a school in Kichijoji, Japan, a suburb of Tokyo. Amy met with her in Boston. Her interpreter offered, "Mrs. Kitahara says, 'Put your burdens on our shoulders.' Mrs. Kitahara can have Angela speaking within six months, but you will have to bring her to Japan." So Amy and her mother took Angela to Tokyo and entered her in the Higashi School. Amy was then physically blocked from entering the grounds and could see Angela only during her athletic periods, through a barbwire fence. "I stayed in Tokyo and looked at her, every day, through this fence," Amy recalled. "She seemed okay; they had her rollerblading a lot. We subsequently discovered that she was being deprived of water to toilet-train her. It all got very dark and strange. It took five months, and then I just gathered my precious child and got the hell outta Dodge." A Higashi School was later established in Boston, but has been repeatedly dogged by allegations of physical cruelty and assault on its disabled students.

Amy held on to her dream of a healthy child. "Another baby I craved; another baby I had. Until I had Noah, I was in psychological pain continuously. And the decision to have him helped with the scars." She found pregnancy terrifying and was "tested to within an inch of my life," she recalled. Amy's parents paid to construct a group home to be managed by the Nassau County Mental Health Association, and eleven-year-old Angela moved there shortly before Noah was born. When I met Noah, he was in high school and doing volunteer work as a music therapist for autistic children. "From the age of six, he would see someone blind and cross the street to help them," Amy said. "He is opened up spiritually, yet free of all the rage that I still hold." Noah concurred, "It's just taught me a lot of tolerance and acceptance. Like if someone says 'retarded' around Mom—God, it's like unnecessarily stupid what she does. Even if she's known the person for five seconds, she just goes for it."

"In all my dreams of her, she talks to me still," Amy said. "Letting go of speech was terrible. And letting go of the toileting just happened this year. Letting go is a continuous experience: it never finishes. I have to keep my rage in check; I have to keep my sobriety in check. I've experienced close family members suggesting that I kill her, and they would help me. I've experienced people offering the most idiotic possible cures: stuff to put in the bathtub, and gripe water, and handing me copies of *When Bad Things Happen to Good People*, and bullshit galore. I've also experienced the great inequity in the way our pay scales are structured, since the people who do the hands-on clinical work with this population are so energetic, and so frequently expert, and inspired, and they're making what waiters and waitresses make. A good measure of a society is how well it takes care of its sick people. Our society is an outrage." Amy spoke with the passion of someone running for office. "My story includes a continuous heartache that transcends everything else. There's no sense of time; it's just the same and the same. I forget how old I am, because I can't measure it in these ways."

While the deficits of autism are famous, the general public is less aware that people with autism may also have major abilities that the rest of us lack. Autistic subjects tend to perform better than others on certain cognitive tests, such as spatial-thinking assessments. Joyce Chung, whose daughter has autism and who served as autism coordinator at the NIMH, said, "If you removed the capacity for someone to become autistic, would that also remove the things that make us interesting as human beings? Maybe the same genetic structures also produce creativity and diversity." Thorkil Sonne, an executive in a Danish telecommunications firm and the father of an autistic child, has set up a specialist agency in Copenhagen that places people with autism on corporate projects, presenting them not as deficient individuals to be hired out of charity, but as people with singular skills.

But the notion of uncanny genius can also be used to objectify autistic people. John Elder Robison writes, "Being a savant is a mixed blessing, because that laser-like focus often comes at a cost: very limited abilities in nonsavant areas. Some of my designs were true masterpieces of economy and functionality. Many people told me they were expressions of a creative genius. And today I can't understand them at all. My story isn't sad, though, because my mind didn't fade or die. It just rewired itself. I'm sure my mind has the same power it always did, but in a more broadly focused configuration." I have heard Temple Grandin say the same thing, and my friend who played the Philip Glass CD told me that as his social abilities improved, his pure mathematical thinking weakened. The cure can be its own disease: when you take away what's perceived as wrong, you may also take away the person's gift.

I first met Temple Grandin when she was sixty, and famous for her ability to narrate her own autistic consciousness to nonautistic people. A cattle handler and livestock-facilities designer whose equipment is now used in the majority of US slaughterhouses, Grandin claims that she experiences fear as her primary emotion and has an overdeveloped startle reflex of the kind that protects animals from predators. "I think in pictures," she said. "I realized that should be able to help me figure about animals, because I think more the way an animal does." The cattle industry struck her as both inefficient and inhumane. Her objective has always been to improve the treatment of animals, which she believes she can do most effectively by reforming the places where they are killed.

When she was diagnosed as a child in the early 1950s, Temple showed the full range of autistic symptoms, and her mother, Eustacia Cutler, was told that she was a refrigerator mother. Eustacia could cope with Temple's strange behavior, but not with the emotional chill. "Tantrums are hard to handle, and fecal smears are smelly, but exclusion breaks the heart," Eustacia wrote in a memoir. "'Be fruitful and multiply,' God whispers in our ear, and leaves us to deal with the mess." Temple recalled, "When I was two and a half, I would sit there smelling space, eating carpet fuzz, screaming, stereotypic behavior." Her mother invented her own behaviorist system to help Temple, and she and the nanny she hired kept Temple constantly interacting. When I met Eustacia, she explained, "You have to pull them out of the limbo of their self-absorption." Temple was given art lessons and showed a talent for perspective drawing. Her mother did all she could to encourage this skill. "You want to be appreciated for doing something other people want," Temple recalled. "When the kid is really little, you've got to get somebody to just spend thirty-eight hours a week working with that kid, keeping them engaged. I don't think the method matters that much."

She expresses considerable gratitude for the attentions she received. "They put kids like me in institutions then. I had fifteen years of nonstop panic attacks, which was hard on everyone. If I hadn't found antidepressants in my early thirties, I would have been ripped apart by stress-related health problems, like colitis. I was very lucky to get some really good mentors when I was in college." She paused and looked at me as though she had just surprised herself. "I mean, what would have happened to me if my mother had put me away instead? I hate to even think about it." Eustacia found that she had to invent everything. "Why didn't the doctors know as much as I did?" she wondered when we spoke. As an adolescent, Temple said to her mother, "I can't love." Eustacia wrote, "Adolescence is hard enough for any child, but autistic adolescence is something devised by the devil." But Temple's boarding school had a stable full of abused horses that the headmaster had bought cheaply, and Temple found her joy in caring for them.

Many years later, Eustacia could admire whom Temple had become. "Slowly, with no innate concept, no intuitive clue—conscious intelligence her only guide, and even then not sure—she's taught herself over the years 'to meet the faces that you meet.' How bright and brave of her to want to meet us anyway, armed with such a flimsy, homemade mask. Autism is an exaggeration of what lies in us all. And studying it has been my form of exorcism." This does not mean that it has been free of disappointments. "Despite her extraordinary accomplishments, she knows that some part of the dream that I call 'life' lies a little beyond her. It accounts for her hunger to have me understand *her* dream: that she won't be forgotten. Her longing for some kind of recognition is so palpably real. As if love were too shaky and mysterious to rely on."

Temple receives thousands of letters from parents and readily offers advice. "Some of these kids, you've got to jerk them out of it. If you're not somewhat intrusive, you're not going to get anywhere with them," she said. Temple advocates behavioral and medical treatments, and anything to engender literacy. "Your kid is throwing a fit in Walmart because he feels like he's inside the speaker at a rock concert. He's seeing like a kaleidoscope; hearing's fading in and out, and full of static. I think some of those kids are getting scrambled HBO, but every once in a while, you get a little bit of an image in that scrambled HBO." Temple believes firmly that the higher-functioning you can make someone, the happier he is likely to be. Autistic children should develop skills consistent with their capacities. "You've got a kid who loves geology. Well, instead of developing his interest into a career, parents and teachers and therapists get hung up on social-skills training. And social-skills training's really important. But don't get so hung up on that, that you neglect his gifts." Temple Grandin attributes her success to her autism; "Genius is an abnormality, too," she explained to me. Without being self-aggrandizing, Temple has made what the world calls illness the cornerstone of her brilliance.

Into all of this comes the neurodiversity movement, with its celebration of some aspects of autism. One of the leading autism charities was called Cure Autism Now, since merged with Autism Speaks. While opposing a cure for autism is a bit like opposing intergalactic travel, one of the battle cries of neurodiversity is "Don't cure autism now." Like the rest of identity politics, this is an attitude forged and burnished in opposition to prejudice, treading a fine line between revealing a fundamental truth and attempting to create that truth. Conservatives complain that asking the larger society to accept autistic people's atypical social logic undermines the very principles that make it a society; members of the neurodiversity movement take exception to the idea that autistic behavior lacks social coherence and maintain that it is a different and equally valid system. They fight for their own definition of civil justice.

Thomas Insel said, "It's really important that we recognize schizophrenia, bipolar disorder, or autism as something that's happened to someone, that there's still a someone there who can fight against the illness." Jim Sinclair, an autistic adult and the cofounder of Autism Network International, wrote, "Autism isn't something a person *has*, or a 'shell' that a person is trapped inside. There's no normal child hidden behind the autism. Autism is a way of being. It is *pervasive*; it colors every experience, every sensation, perception, thought, emotion, and encounter, every aspect of existence. It is not possible to separate the autism from the person—and if it were possible, the person you'd have left would not be the same person you started with." The politically correct terminology in most of the world of disability is to identify the person ahead of the condition: you speak of a "person with deafness" rather than a "deaf person," or a "person with dwarfism" rather than a "dwarf." Some autism advocates take issue with the idea that they are "a self with something added," preferring "autistic person" to "person with autism." Others favor *autistic* as a noun, as in, "Autistics should receive social accommodation." Sinclair has compared "person with autism" to describing a man as a "person with maleness" or a Catholic as a "person with Catholicism."

Many neurodiversity activists question whether existing treatments are for the benefit of autistic people or for the comfort of their parents. Idiosyncrasies may be unsettling, but how much torment should a child go through to relinquish them? Isabelle Rapin said of her adult patients, "We shouldn't impose our values of success onto people who really have very different needs." Joyce Chung, who has an autistic daughter, said, "Our struggle was not to let ourselves experience our child's condition as a narcissistic injury." In other words, the autism is something that has happened to the child rather than to the parents. Alex Plank, who has Asperger syndrome and whose Wrong Planet website, an affirming forum for people with autism and their families, has over forty-five thousand members, said, "The organizations that have the best connections are the ones founded by parents of people with autism, which aren't going to have the same priorities as the autistic people themselves, especially if those parents' idea of success is to make their kid the same as the parents were when they were kids." Ari Ne'eman, who has Asperger syndrome and became a prominent self-advocate while still in college, uses the colloquial *Aspie* to describe himself. He said, "Society has developed a tendency to examine things

from the point of view of a bell curve. How far away am I from ↓
mal? What can I do to fit in better? But what is on top of the ↓
curve? Mediocrity. That is the fate of American society if we insist
upon pathologizing difference."

In December 2007, the NYU Child Study Center produced a series
of advertisements for their treatment program in the form of ransom
notes. One ominously announced, "We have your son. We will make
sure he will not be able to care for himself or interact socially as long
as he lives. This is only the beginning." It was signed "Autism." Another
said, "We have your son. We are destroying his ability for social interaction and driving him into a life of complete isolation. It's up to you
now," and was signed "Asperger Syndrome." Harold Koplewicz, then
director of the center, hoped to propel children with untreated mental
health problems into the hands of competent professionals. But the ads
were judged demeaning and stigmatizing by many people, including
some with autism spectrum disorders. Autism activists spearheaded a
campaign against them; the chief organizer was Ne'eman. In a memo
to the members of his Autistic Self Advocacy Network, he wrote, "This
highly offensive ad campaign relies on some of the oldest and most
offensive disability stereotypes to frighten parents into making use of
the NYU Child Study Center's services. While people with diagnoses
of autism and Asperger's often have difficulty with some forms of social
interaction, we are not incapable of it and can succeed and thrive on
our own terms when supported, accepted and included for who we are."

Ne'eman initiated a letter-writing campaign and recruited major
American disability groups to support his position. The campaign rapidly escalated and was soon reported in the *New York Times*, the *Wall
Street Journal*, and the *Washington Post*. Koplewicz was stunned by the
protests. On December 17, he insisted the ads were there to stay, but
the revolt was escalating, and two days later they were pulled. It was a
signal triumph for the neurodiversity movement, and for the broader
community that endorses disability rights. In the aftermath of the
debacle, Koplewicz conducted an online town-hall meeting, and more
than four hundred people participated.

Ari Ne'eman is not without social graces, but you can feel the effort
in them. He said, "Neurotypical social interaction is like a second language. One can learn a second language with great fluency, but no
one will ever be as comfortable in it as in one's own tongue." When
Ne'eman was in high school, his intellectual skills, social deficits, and
unusual learning style meant that he was considered both disabled and
gifted, which made for trouble figuring out what classes he should
take. "There's this stereotype out there of the shiny Aspie, but you

have to recognize and respect human difference, and the diversity of human neurology, regardless of whether somebody's academically brilliant," Ne'eman said. "As a public relations point, it's nice to have Vernon Smith, who has Asperger's and won the Nobel in economics, or Tim Page, who has Asperger's and won a Pulitzer. It's *a* point in favor of respecting and recognizing the legitimacy of human neurological diversity. But it would be a deep mistake to say that people should have their differences respected *only* if they can deliver some special talent." In 2010, age twenty, Ne'eman was appointed by President Obama to the National Council on Disability. His selection met a firestorm of criticism from those who argued that his positive characterization of autism would reduce funds needed to treat their children.

The term *neurodiversity* was originally coined by Judy Singer, an Australian sociologist whose mother and daughter both have Asperger's and who is herself on the spectrum. "I was at a workshop at a synagogue where they were trying to get us to come up with a better set of Ten Commandments than God's," she said. "My first was 'Honor diversity.'" Singer and the American journalist Harvey Blume were thinking along parallel lines, and though she first used the word, he was the first to publish it, in 1998. "We both noticed that psychotherapy was waning and neurology was on the rise," Singer said. "I was interested in the liberatory activist aspects of it—to do for people who were neurologically different what feminism and gay rights had done for their constituencies." The movement accelerated with the broadening of the spectrum, and with increased communication among autistic people. "The Internet," Singer said, "is a prosthetic device for people who can't socialize without it." For anyone challenged by language and social rules, a communication system that does not operate in real time is a godsend.

Camille Clark, who blogged for some years as Autism Diva, is diagnosed with Asperger syndrome, has been an important voice for neurodiversity, and is mother to an adult child with autism and spina bifida. "Autistic children love their parents," she said. "You may have to learn to see how your child expresses affection and not take it personally if your child doesn't show affection as typical children do. Deaf children may never speak the words 'I love you,' and deaf parents may never hear those words, but that doesn't mean that deaf children don't love their parents. For many Asperger syndrome and autistic people, just being in the presence of others is as much work as it is for a normally social NT [neurotypical] person to host a big party." Many autistic people find eye contact unsettling; Kathleen Seidel, founder of Neurodiversity .com, said that she learned to avert her own gaze as a means of respecting her son's needs. He, in turn, knew that physical contact had value to her and would occasionally give her a hug.

Clark feels that the concept of neurodiversity extends well beyond autism. "People with bipolar, schizophrenia, dyslexia, Tourette's, and so forth ought to 'subscribe' to it," she wrote to me. "Parents of autistic kids should be reasonable about what they can or can't do, and they shouldn't expect that their kid is ever going to be 'normal.' Autistic people are valuable as they are. They don't have value only if they can be transformed into less obviously autistic people." Jim Sinclair wrote, "The ways we relate are *different*. Push for the things your expectations tell you are normal, and you'll find frustration, disappointment, resentment, maybe even rage and hatred. Approach respectfully, without preconceptions, and with openness to learning new things, and you'll find a world you could never have imagined." One activist commented to me that the attempts to "cure" autistic people are less like a cure for cancer than a cure for left-handedness.

Many neurodiversity activists fear that in the event of a genetic test, selective abortion would result in "genocide." "I don't want to get old and know that there will be no more people like me being born," said Gareth Nelson, a man with Asperger syndrome who cofounded the website Aspies For Freedom. As with most of the conditions in this book, the abortion question is emblematic of the tension between identity and illness models. Ne'eman said, "We have never said that autism does not represent a disability, but that it doesn't represent a disease. Give autistic individuals the educational opportunities and the opportunities to prosper and do well on our own terms." Seidel said, "I have never ruled out the possibility that genetic research might yield helpful therapies for problems often experienced by autistic people. I'm all for the development of antagonists that might, for example, correct impairments in oral-motor function or serotonin metabolism, alleviate chronic anxiety, reduce a tendency to overstimulation, or decrease aggression. But I am primarily concerned about how to make life positive for the people on the autism spectrum who are here now, a group that happens to include my own child."

Some parents of severely autistic children dismiss the articulate self-advocates as not really being autistic. There's a central irony here. The increased rate of diagnosis is crucial to the claim that there is an epidemic—critical in lobbying for resources for research. But the higher-functioning people whose inclusion has brought up the numbers are often the ones who advocate against some of that research. Roy Richard Grinker, husband of Joyce Chung and author of *Unstrange Minds*, a book arguing that there is no epidemic, said, "At both ends of that spectrum, there's an antiscience perspective. The neurodiversity people are furious that the scientists want to cure autism; the antivaccine people are furious that the scientists won't do the studies they know should be done. Their premises are so different that any true dialogue is impossible. They're unable to speak with each other because they have such different epistemological and philosophical foundations."

Thomas Insel said, "This is the most polarized, fragmented community I know of. I think those kids have something seriously wrong with them. And when you start to argue that they just need to be accepted for who they are, you're selling them and yourself terribly short. I don't think we would do that with most cancers, or with infectious diseases. I sure hope we don't do it for people who have a brain disorder like this. Most parents want their kids to live the fullest life possible, and that's not possible when you're not toilet-trained. And it's not possible when you don't have any language."

"Please don't write about them," Lenny Schafer, editor of the *Schafer Autism Report*, said to me when I mentioned neurodiversity. "They're a handful of noisy people who get a lot of media attention. They're trivializing what autism really is. It's like stealing money from the tin cup of a blind man when you say that it's not an illness; you are getting the people who should be making political and social change to think that it's not a problem. You are slowing down funding for research." Other critics are even more vehement. John Best, parent of a child with autism, is author of the *Hating Autism* blog. One recent post showed a monkey engaged in autofellatio labeled "A neurodiverse nitwit ponders the vaccine trial." The antineurodiversity, antigenetics *Age of Autism* blog featured a Thanksgiving card with a photoshopped image of Alison Singer, Thomas Insel, and others who don't support the vaccine hypothesis eating a baby for their holiday meal.

Seidel referred to Insel's assertion that autism "takes away the soul of the child" as a "histrionic and stigmatizing assertion." She explained, "I don't believe that he has ever cited any specific examples of parents whose 'overacceptance' has led them to neglect their children's medical needs, or to deprive their children of an appropriate education, or to allow their children to descend into a state of self-indulgent incontinence, or to prevent their children from learning to communicate as best they can, or to stymie research into the causes and treatment of specific problems associated with autism. People such as Lenny Schafer set up this straw man saying, 'Oh, the neurodiversity people just want to let autistic kids rot in the corner and never have anything that will help them.' That's bullshit. No parent in their right mind would let their kid rot in a corner."

On the other side, Kit Weintraub, who has two children with autism, wrote, "The fact that my children have an abnormality of development does not mean that I do not love my children for who they are. As with any other condition that would threaten their future and their happiness, I do as much as I can to help them be as functional and as normal as possible. And no, 'normal' to me does not mean 'a cookie-cutter robot-child, trained to do my will.' It means: 'able, like most people without autism, to lead an independent, purpose-filled life—able to speak, able to communicate, able to form and keep relationships.'"

Some autistic people resent the perception that the activists who celebrate aspects of autism are speaking on their behalf. Jonathan Mitchell, an autistic man who wars with the neurodiversity movement on his blog, said, "The neurodiverse reach a vulnerable audience as many persons on the spectrum have been disaffected from society. Autistic people feel worthless and have low self-esteem and neurodiversity provides a tempting escape valve. The same is true for parents of sometimes severely autistic children who want to see their offspring as something other than deficient or broken." Of course, the broader disability rights movement can be intolerant of science; Judy Singer said, "I fell out with the disability rights movement because they were so sociologically oriented; they were almost the same as creationists in their hatred of biology." Members of the neurodiversity movement, though, do not in most instances deny biology; the presence of the prefix *neuro* makes it clear that biology is part of the argument. What they probe is the meaning of that biology.

Much of the antipathy results from divergent ideas of love. Many people who champion ABA or support the vaccine hypothesis believe that families who don't accept their views are consigning their children to ruin. Many neurodiversity activists think that ABA is dehumanizing and the vaccine hypothesis is insulting. Clark has argued that ABA is suitable only for animals. Seidel believes that the parents who describe their autistic children as vaccine victims are disparaging their own progeny: "I am very concerned about the long-term, deep psychological impact on my child of the proliferation of the erroneous concept that people on the autism spectrum are poisoned. It's scientifically incorrect and symbolically offensive."

It's naïve to criticize some autism activists for being autistic—idiosyncratic, single-minded, detail-oriented, not predisposed to imagine how listeners might respond to their words, and reluctant to compromise on a position unless offered a rational, intellectually supportable reason to do so. These qualities make autistic people somewhat less persuasive activists than they might wish, activism being in general helped considerably by charm. It's harder to account for the aggression of the antineurodiversity movement. Schafer complains that neurodiversity activists "see us as being less than loving, as evil, and that's just not who we are." Yet it is the antineurodiversity people who, on the *Evidence of Harm* discussion list on Yahoo!, have accused their opponents of being "lazy," "vaccine barbarians," "cheap whores," "motivated only by a paycheck," and "high-minded Fascist germ freaks" disseminating "malicious public relations hyperbole."

Sarah Spence, a pediatric neurologist who worked at the NIMH, said, "When we mitigate some of the underlying symptoms for people with severe autism, they do seem happier. As a clinician, you don't feel that they love being 'in their world.' They want to break out. We'd like to accommodate the politics of neurodiversity, but science and clinical support have to go before politics." Simon Baron-Cohen said, "Autism is both a disability and a difference. We need to find ways of alleviating the disability while respecting and valuing the difference."

The attempt to dictate black-and-white policy about a spectrum condition is inherently flawed. Some people are frustrated by not being able to communicate well, and some seem not to mind; others accept that speech is difficult or impossible for them and communicate with keyboards and other assistive technologies; others yet, by careful observation, develop enough skills to get by. Some people are shattered by their social deficits, and others are largely uninterested in friendship, and others still make friends in their own way. Some people are devastated by their autism, some are proud of their autism, and some simply accept it as a fact of their life. There is social conditioning here: those who are regularly disparaged are less likely to feel good about themselves than those who receive supportive messages. But there is also a question of personality. Some autistic people are optimistic and buoyant, and some are withdrawn and depressed; autism coincides with the full personality range to be found in the neurotypical population.

Steven Hyman said, "Severity, of course, matters. A certain amount is your life goals and whether you can achieve them, and whether you're experiencing distress and disability as a result of how you think and feel or whether you are happy with the way you are." Insel said, "For those who are most disabled, the neurodiversity approach is threatening. On the other end of the spectrum, it will help people to accept themselves in the same way it encourages us to accept their uniqueness. What I'm hearing from some part of that community is that if you accept us for who we are, it also means that you'll help us to become everything we can be." Jennifer Franklin, mother of Anna, spoke with passion about such manifestos. "If Anna Livia were an adult who wanted to wear diapers and not be potty-trained, I'm down with anything. I'd like nothing more than for her to develop the kind of consciousness that would allow her to join the neurodiversity movement. If Anna got to the point where she could tell a therapist, 'My mom is a bitch for putting me through this,' I would feel like I did my job."

Grandin argues that both the autistic person and the society have to make accommodation. She described the suffering of people who couldn't communicate, had toileting challenges, and were injuring themselves regularly. "It would be nice if you could prevent the most severe forms of nonverbal autism," she said. "But if you got rid of all the autism genetics, you'd get rid of scientists, musicians, mathematicians, and all you'd have left is dried-up bureaucrats. I see a picture in my mind of the cavemen talking around the campfire, and off in the corner, there's the Aspie guy, and he's chipping the first stone spear, figuring out how to tie it to a stick, cutting some animal sinews to do it. Social people don't make technology."

In a rebuttal of the suggestion that only those with few of the problems experienced by severely impaired autistic people are active in the neurodiversity community, however, the three webmasters of autistics.org issued a statement affirming that none of them is fully toilet-trained, and that one has no speech. "We flap, finger-flick, rock, twist, rub, clap, bounce, squeal, hum, scream, hiss and tic," they wrote, asserting that such behaviors do not impede their happiness. In a video called *In My Language*, the neurodiversity activist Amanda Baggs described her perspective. Baggs has repetitive behaviors and no speech. "The way I think and respond to things looks and feels so different from standard concepts that some people do not consider it thought at all," she says. "It is only when I type something in your language that you refer to me as having communication. People like me are officially described as mysterious and puzzling, rather than anyone admitting that it is themselves who are confused. Only when the many shapes of personhood are recognized will justice and human rights be possible."

Jane Meyerding, who is diagnosed with Asperger syndrome and works at the University of Washington, wrote, "If people on the autism spectrum all 'came out' and worked towards increasing institutional flexibility to the point where our 'special needs' could be accommodated, the world would be a much more comfortable, less alienating place for everyone else as well. Such a world would be one where it would be as normal for children to have different learning styles as it is to have different colors and textures of hair. Where everyone would 'have an accent.'" Joyce Chung described how her daughter, when "struggling over something she can't quite articulate," finally explained, "I think that's because of my autism, Mama." Would such a statement have been possible twenty years ago, and is the capacity for such self-accepting self-awareness a hallmark of maturity, liberation, even of triumph over the illness? "When people pity me for my daughter, I don't understand the sentiment," Roy Richard Grinker wrote. "Autism is less a disease to be hidden than a disability to be accommodated; it is less a stigma, reflecting badly on her family, than a variation of human existence."

Kate Movius, mother of an autistic child, wrote, "Nothing yet has yielded a 'eureka!' moment for Aidan, unveiled some ideal child beneath the autism. Instead it is I who have been revealed, rebuilt, and given a new way of not just seeing Aidan for who he is, but of seeing myself." Kathleen Seidel said, "The word *incurable* is quite devastating-sounding, but you can also look at it as being that autism is durable. Looking at this jewel through different facets does not trivialize the challenges of people who have tremendous obstacles. I'm trying to look at the whole picture, including the beautiful part of it. Autism is as much a part of our humanity as the capacity to dream. God manifests all possibilities, and this is one of the possibilities in our world. It's a part of the human condition—or conditions, as the case may be."

For the Deaf, medicine and activism are both galloping; for autistic people, both are trudging. Unlike deafness, autism has not been established as a culture in the eyes of even the liberal outside world. There is no formal language of autism to be recognized by linguists. There is no university with a long history of educating autistic people (unless one counts MIT). Institutions parallel to those that subtend the Deaf claim to culture—Deaf theater, Deaf social habits, Deaf clubs—are not in place for autistics. The complexity of the science means that autism has time before medical progress trumps identity politics, but the Deaf model should make it clear to the neurodiversity crowd that they are in a race, in which their primary advantage is the other side's tortoiselike pace. The autistic have on their side as well, however, the very real achievements of autistic people; retrospective diagnosis, albeit shaky science, suggests that Mozart, Einstein, Hans Christian Andersen, Thomas Jefferson, Isaac Newton, and a great many other visionaries would now be diagnosed on the spectrum. Describe a world without Helen Keller and most people wouldn't miss her so much; describe a world without those particular geniuses, and everyone would be impoverished.

Bill Davis grew up in the Bronx, found his way into street gangs, and then graduated into organized crime. One day in 1979, a twenty-year-old would-be model walked into the nightclub he was managing. "She took a carnation out of a vase, put it in my lapel, and said, 'You're with me.' We've been together ever since," he said. After ten years, Bill and Jae moved to Lancaster, Pennsylvania, where their daughter, Jessie, was born. Five years later, their son, Christopher, followed. Jae stayed home with the children; Bill tended bar. At two, Chris stopped talking. By two and a half, he was rocking back and forth in a corner. Jae recognized that something was seriously wrong, and though she had no driver's license, she announced one morning that she was driving Chris to Philadelphia to visit the Seashore House, a children's hospital. She didn't get a satisfactory answer, so two days later she said, "I'm going to Kennedy Krieger in Baltimore, and if that doesn't work, we're heading down to Haddonfield, New Jersey, to the Bancroft School." Bill said, "You can't drive around without a license." The next week, she passed the test. "It turned out those places were the top in the country, but when and how did she figure that out?" Bill said. "And learn traffic laws at the same time?"

Chris didn't sleep. He flapped his hands. He injured himself. He smeared himself with feces and flung it at his parents. He bit himself. He gouged at his eyes. He stared at the ceiling fan for hours on end. Jae had intuited that Chris would need infinite patience, and a progressive approach to things he found difficult, including intimacy itself. She and Bill broke everything into small tasks. "It was like, 'Can I just touch you?' 'Oh, thank you so much. You're great,'" Bill said. "He wouldn't walk to the end of the block. So I would take him half a block and say, 'What a great walk!'"

Chris had difficulty understanding cause and effect. He liked the motion of the car and screamed every time it stopped for a red light. Jae made red and green cards, and whenever the car approached a red light, she would show him the red one, and when it was time to go, she would show him the green. Once he understood the correlation, the screaming stopped. Jae gathered that he could absorb visual information, and she came up with a system of flash cards and symbols. "I was always watching what he saw," Jae said. She had become interested in the work of Vincent Carbone, a behavior analyst, so she drove to Penn State and cornered him in his office. When he said, "Lady, I've got to go," she said, "You don't understand. I'm not letting you out of your office until you agree to help me." After resisting for an hour, he told her she could join his next course. She stayed for a week and over the next few years developed several useful variations on his methodology. Carbone became so interested in these modifications that he sent a team up to Lancaster to observe her work with Chris. When Chris was six, Jae started taking in other autistic children. She found that one nonverbal boy liked clocks, so she bought him clocks and praised his interest. One day, he suddenly said to himself, "Good job, Juan." It was the beginning of speech.

Jae recruited interns at Franklin and Marshall College and Rutgers University to help implement her techniques, tutoring and directing them in their work at the house. She set up cameras in Chris's room and filmed the students so that she could correct their errors. She brought them to conferences and training programs. She wrote recommendation letters for them as they applied to grad school. By the time Chris was grown, Jae had trained more than forty interns; as other families in the area became aware of her work, she placed interns with them, as well.

Jae refused to believe that if Chris wasn't speaking at five, he would never do so. By the time he was seven, Chris had begun to produce words; at ten, he could speak in short sentences. Chris learned to match pictures of the American presidents to their names, and Jae made numerical games so that Chris could learn math and how to count money. When I first saw Chris's room, it was overflowing with learning materials: the beads and marbles he was using to learn to count were falling out of shoe bags; a cabinet held some five hundred homemade flash cards; musical instruments were everywhere; shelves upon shelves held bowls of everything from coins to plastic *Sesame Street* monsters. In addition, perhaps four hundred videotapes were piled around the room, crammed into shelves, wedged underneath and next to things, an Alexandrian library of cassettes.

When a new intern started, Jae would say, "Here's two hundred dollars. You're going to come into the next room, where we've hidden something. And you'll try and guess what it is and where it is." The person would come into a darkened room, and all the other interns would be screaming and clicking and making nonsensical remarks. The new intern would get more and more frustrated and would finally say, "I don't understand what you're doing! What do you want?" And Jae would say, "Come on, find it, and I'll give you two hundred dollars!" When the person finally walked out, Jae would explain, "That's what life is like for autistic children."

Bill took Jae's devotion as a challenge and took over negotiating with the state to pay for treatment. "The local schools people had been confronted by emotional parents who'd say, 'My son needs forty hours of therapy,' and they'd say, 'Sorry—you lose,'" Bill recalled. "I would say, 'Now, in *Ethridge vs. Collins . . .*' They *hated* me. But I grew up in the heartland of Irish gangs in New York. I certainly wasn't afraid of a schoolteacher in Lancaster." If it could be established that what Bill and Jae were doing at home was more appropriate for Chris than what the school district was offering, the district had to underwrite the program. Bill came in with an annual budget: what materials cost; what workshops cost; what the interns cost. Meanwhile, the development of therapies had become a family project. Chris's sister, Jessie, would take two of some instrument—a triangle, say—play one under the table, and ask Chris to play the same one over it; Jae explained the mechanism of that training to Jessie. When the first district psychologist came to review the family's requests, he asked eight-year-old Jessie, "What are you doing?" She said, "Collecting sound discrimination data." The psychologist said to the district committee, "The Davises know more than I do. Just give them what they want."

Still, the Davises, who had no health insurance, had a lot to pay for on their own. Chris had gymnastics, speech classes, hospital assessments, and consultations with a variety of doctors who did not take Medicaid. "I was working four bartending jobs, bringing home sometimes twenty-five hundred dollars a week," Bill said. "But, I swear to God, we couldn't pay our rent. When things got really bad, I'd hold a bar fund-raiser: I'd solicit a baseball from the Phillies; I went to the Flyers and got hockey sticks. I'd sell it all at the bar and raise six thousand dollars at a clip."

Like many autistic people, Chris has intestinal issues. Going to the bathroom can be painful for him, and he tends to hold on for as long as possible. "So his movements build up, and then movements explode behind movements," Bill said. "He'll say, 'Bath,' and he'll hug me. I clean him and disinfect the room. My God, this is filthy. It's stacked with old movies, and he's stepping on them, and he just peed over there. It's horrible. But it's what works." The place felt at once squalid and love-imbued. Bill told me that for Jae, who had had a harsh childhood, the chance to raise her children in a perfect home had been a cherished dream. "For her to let her house go—it was a real decision," he said.

When Chris was nine, the Davises decided that it was time for him to enter the school system. The school district agreed to let Jae train his teachers. The one who would be in charge of his education came to their home the summer before Chris was to matriculate. "She was open and very willing to learn and had kindness to her. I knew I could work with her," Jae said. That autumn, Chris attended school in a classroom with two other boys, the teacher Jae had trained, and four assistant teachers.

Soon after Chris started school, Jae began to say she was tired. "She would get up at six a.m., go to bed at three a.m.," Bill said. "Always writing; always on the Internet; always calling; always traveling. So I was surprised when she started saying, 'Could you just take him?'" She finally went to a doctor and found that, at age forty-five, she had a malignant cervical tumor the size of a grapefruit that had metastasized to her lungs and spine; one of her kidneys had shut down; she had suffered a minor heart attack; and she had lost enough blood through internal bleeding to need an emergency five-hour transfusion.

When I met Jae, she had been given a few months to live. A nurse came to the house to administer the chemotherapy Jae hoped would eke out a little more time. Even without hair, and somewhat emaciated, she was beautiful, and she had a gentleness that contrasted with Bill's machismo. She had insisted that I visit despite her condition. "I'm so lucky," she said to me, "that Chris started school. He's ready to do things on his own. Bill will make sure he gets what he needs. I always saw what he saw, but Bill feels what he feels. I've done what I came to do." The closed-circuit television system she'd set up to monitor Chris's teachers was still in place, so she could watch what happened in his room upstairs without rising. "It's just been such a strange experience for me, everything going on at once, my dying, Chris going to school," Jae said. "I worry more about my daughter and husband than about Chris. Honestly, he's just a happy kid. But it's hard to get him to conceptualize emotions, so I'm struggling to help him understand that I won't be around."

Chris had become aggressive, mostly toward Bill, whom he kept biting and punching and head-butting. But he had brought a lot of his videos downstairs, and he started curling up with them and his mother in her hospital bed. I arrived to find Jae drugged and elegiac; Chris was demanding and noisy and kept hitting himself and other things. "Don't hit Daddy," Bill would say, smoothing Chris's irate brow with one hand and holding Jae's hand with the other. Then Chris suddenly said to Jae in his thick voice, "I love you," and lay his head down on her chest.

Ten days after I met her, on a quiet October afternoon, Jae died. She bequeathed her teaching materials to the universities where she had found help. "It won't do any good to write it all down," Bill said, "because the real thing of it is Jae herself, not anything that I could record." Shortly before Jae's death, the city of Lancaster gave her the Red Rose Award for her work. A few days later, the Intermediate Unit that had fought the Davises on their educational priorities announced the Jae Davis scholarships to pay for ten families a year to attend the National Conference on Autism. Franklin and Marshall College announced the

Jae Davis Internship Program; Penn State announced the Jae Davis Parent Scholarship; the Organization for Autism Research set up the Jae Davis Memorial Award.

Bill soldiered through his grief. "Our marriage changed completely the day Chris was diagnosed," he said. "We very rarely had sex; we very rarely had a close or romantic moment. If we went out to dinner, which was once a year, we would talk about Chris. Things just replaced other things. If Chris never works or marries, who cares? Let Chris be Chris. Chris taught us everything. He taught us how to deal with him; how he learned; how to let him live his life. We drove to a spot the other night that his mother and he used to go to, and he just started to cry. And I know it was because of that. My son is not a puzzle. I know exactly what he is." Bill, who had always had a taste for tattoos, started inscribing Chris's disability on his body. Bill has the word *autism* emblazoned across his chest; an extremely large autism puzzle ribbon, the symbol of the Autism Society of America; and the symbol for Unlocking Autism: a *U*, an *A*, and a key.

I fell out of touch with Bill for a little while. "Jae pushed Chris so hard, and when she died, he said, 'No school,'" Bill said when we met again. "I thought, 'Well, if what he really wants is to watch television all day, should we keep pushing him to do all these other things?'" Bill was charged for truancy; pushed over the edge by Jae's medical bills, the family became homeless and lived for a while on park benches in Lancaster. Eighteen months after Jae died, Chris was maturing. The smearing of feces had stopped. Chris had begun to understand that the world had other rules than his, and that he must bend to them. It was almost as though the coddling attention of his demanding mother was needed to bring him out into communication, while his father's harder exigencies were needed to help him see its purpose—as if his mother gave him language and his father made him use it.

I had always been skeptical of Bill's assertions about Chris's verbal abilities; he had demonstrated only occasional comprehension of a few dozen words and spoke mostly in nouns and memorized short phrases. During my last visit, I was astonished to find him typing complicated entries into a computer; while I sat there, he logged on to eBay and searched for videos. Chris actually knew many words, but did not show an inclination to use them to connect with other people. But his capacity for emotion had grown, too. When I walked in, he began flapping his hands and making high-pitched sounds; I thought that could just be alarm, but when I sat down on the sofa, he curled up next to me.

Temple Grandin once described herself as "an anthropologist on Mars," a description that the neurologist Oliver Sacks appropriated as the title for one of his books. But Chris was like a Martian in a room-ful of anthropologists. "In case he feels everything," Bill said, "I talk to him about it all and I love him totally and completely. Just in case." Is it neurotypical prejudice to posit that human nature entails an aspirational longing to be loved, applauded, accepted?

Two diametrically opposite fictions contribute to a single set of problems. The first comes from the autism parents' literature of miracles. In its most extreme form, it describes beautiful boys and girls emerging from their affliction as if it were a passing winter frost, and, after wild parental heroics, dancing off into springtime fields of violets, fully verbal, glowing with the fresh ecstasy of unself-conscious charm. Such narratives of false hope eviscerate families who are struggling with the diagnosis. The other plotline is that the child does not get better, but the parents grow enough to celebrate him rather than seek to improve him and are fully content with that shift. This whitewashes difficulties that many families face and can obfuscate autism's authentic deficits. While the lives of many people who have autism remain somewhat inscrutable, the lives of people whose children have autism are mostly avowedly hard—some, excruciatingly so. Social prejudice aggravates the difficulty, but it is naïve to propose that it's all social prejudice; having a child who does not express love in a comprehensible way is devastating, and having a child who is awake all night, who requires constant supervision, and who screams and tantrums but cannot communicate the reasons for or the nature of his upset—these experiences are confusing, overwhelming, exhausting, unrewarding. The problem can be mitigated by some combination of treatment and acceptance, specific to each case. It is important not to get carried away by either the impulse only to treat or the impulse only to accept.

The world of disability has seen a great deal of filicide. Those who kill their autistic children usually claim that they wanted to spare those children suffering, but anyone who questions the autism rights movement has only to look at these stories to see how urgent a cause it is to argue for the legitimacy of autistic lives.

In 1996, Charles-Antoine Blais, age six, was killed by his mother, who did no jail time but served one year in a halfway house and then was appointed as a public representative by Montreal's Société de l'autisme. In 1997, Casey Albury, age seventeen, was strangled by her mother with a bathrobe cord, after refusing to jump off a bridge. Her mother said to the police, "She was a misfit. People were scared of her because she was different. I wish it could have been quicker. I'd wanted to kill her for a long time." She received a sentence of eighteen months for manslaughter. In 1998, Pierre Pasquiou was drowned by his mother, who was given a three-year suspended sentence. In 1999, James Joseph Cummings Jr., at the age of forty-six, was stabbed to death by his father inside the residential facility where he lived. Cummings Sr. was sentenced to five years in prison. That same year, Daniel Leubner, age thirteen, was burned alive by his mother, who was sentenced to six years in prison. In 2001, Gabriel Britt, age six, was suffocated by his father, who dumped his body in a lake and then received a four-year sentence for pleading guilty to a lesser crime. Also in 2001, Jadwiga Miskiewicz strangled her thirteen-year-old son, Johnny Churchi, and was sentenced to time in a psychiatric hospital; a medical examiner said that she had "'a rigorous standard of excellence' she couldn't live up to anymore." In 2003, Angelica Auriemma, age twenty, was drowned by her mother, Ioanna, who had first attempted to electrocute her. Angelica's mother said, "I worried obsessively"; she served three years. Also that year, Terrance Cottrell died of asphyxiation when his mother and other churchgoers submitted him to an exorcism. A neighbor described the mother as explaining how "they held him down for almost two hours. He couldn't hardly breathe. Then she said the devil started to speak through Junior, though he can't really speak, saying, 'Kill me, take me.' She said the church told her it was the only way to heal him." She was not prosecuted; the minister who had led the exorcism was sentenced to two and a half years in prison and fined $1,200. In 2003, Daniela Dawes strangled her ten-year-old son, Jason, and was given five years of probation. Her grief-stricken husband testified, "Until that day she was the best mother anyone could want." In 2005, Patrick Markcrow, age thirty-six, was suffocated by his mother, who received a two-year suspended sentence; that same year, Jan Naylor shot her twenty-seven-year-old autistic daughter, Sarah, then set the house on fire, killing herself as well; the *Cincinnati Enquirer* wrote that they both "died of hopelessness." In 2006, Christopher DeGroot was burned to death when his parents locked him in the house and set it on fire. Each of them was sentenced to six months in jail. In 2006, Jose Stable slit the throat of his son, Ulysses. He called the police and said, "I just couldn't take it anymore." Jose Stable served a three-and-a-half-year sentence. In 2007, Diane Marsh killed her son, Brandon Williams, age five; the autopsy said he had died of multiple skull fractures and an overdose of Tylenol PM tablets; his legs were covered in burn scars because his mother used to discipline him by dipping him into scalding water. She was sentenced to ten years. In 2008, Jacob Grabe was shot by his father, who pleaded not guilty by reason of insanity.

As the vast majority of these sentences suggest, the habit of the courts has been to treat filicide as an understandable, if unfortunate, result of the strains of raising an autistic child. Sentences are light, and both the courtroom and the press frequently accept the murderer's profession of altruistic motives. After Zvia Lev poisoned her sixteen-year-old autistic son, she said, "I just could not see my boy grow up slowly into a brainless man." The judge, encouraging a lenient sentence, said, "Her true punishment is having to live under the shadow of her crime, the memory of which will pursue her as long as she lives." About the murder of Charles Blais, the president of the Montreal Autism Society said that the murder was "unacceptable but understandable." Laura Slatkin said, "We've spoken to many families who say, 'We all share that hidden, dark thought.'" In an op-ed in the *New York Times*, Cammie McGovern, herself the mother of an autistic child, wrote, "In mythologizing recovery, I fear we've set an impossibly high bar that's left the parents of a half-million autistic children feeling like failures." Autistic children can make great strides, McGovern continues, but to expect complete recovery—"the person your child might have been without autism"— is to enter "a dangerous emotional landscape," one with scope for murder.

Yet *altruism* is a problematic word to describe acts that leave dead children in their wake. A quantitative study has shown that almost half of parents who kill a disabled child do no jail time at all. "While you could kill a person who has a cold, and that would end their suffering due to their cold, a more appropriate method is to provide them medical assistance, rest, plenty of fluids, and compassion," Joel Smith, an autistic adult, has written on his blog. "When a drunk driver, who does not plan the result, is sent to jail for life after killing an innocent child, surely a parent who plans a murder of her child should also get the same sentence."

The dangers of seeing disability entirely as illness and not at all as identity are starkly evident in the explanation Dr. Karen McCarron gave for suffocating her three-year-old daughter, Katie, in 2008. She said, "Autism left me hollow. Maybe I could fix her this way, and in heaven she would be complete." One of McCarron's friends said, "Karen never took a night off. She read every book. She was trying so hard." Katie McCarron's paternal grandfather has responded to such rationalizations with indignation. "Some newspapers have reported that this was done to end Katie's pain; let me assure you that Katie was not in pain," he wrote. "She was a beautiful, precious and happy little girl. Each day she was showered with love and returned that love with hugs, kisses, and laughter. I am positively revolted when I read quotes that hint at condoning the taking of my granddaughter's life." On another occasion, he said, "If these people are 'advocates' for people with autism, I can't imagine what the 'opponents' must be like."

Stephen Drake, research analyst for the organization Not Dead Yet, wrote, "On June 9, the *Chicago Tribune* published an article about the McCarron case. The title was 'Daughter's murder puts focus on toll of autism,' making the thrust of the article all too clear. More space was devoted to sympathetic comments about Karen McCarron and negative comments about autism itself than to descriptions of the victim or comments from deeply grieving family members." Dave Reynolds, editor of *Inclusion Daily Express*, wrote of such coverage, "In every case, neighbors and family members described the murderer as a lovely, devoted mother. In each case the murderer was portrayed as a desperate victim of her child's disability and a victim of a social service system that failed to provide enough of the right supports." Reynolds complains that these murders are exploited to secure subsidies for treatment programs and worries that this "reinforces the idea that these children are horrible burdens to their parents and to society. In no way can anyone justify murdering a child, nor sympathize with the killer. Each of these women had infinite alternatives to murder."

Others would vehemently disagree that the alternatives available to parents coping with autistic children are infinite; in fact, many parents who eventually turn on their children have first struggled to secure placements that eluded them. Heidi Shelton, who attempted unsuccessfully to kill herself and her five-year-old son, said, "I can't let Zach live in this world where he is constantly rejected by everyone, including his family, education system, etc." John Victor Cronin, who attempted but failed to kill his twenty-six-year-old son, his wife, and himself, was able to get his son a placement only after his trial. His wife said, "There's nowhere to go until people are almost killed; then they've got a place for people like Richard." If we feel some measure of responsibility toward these parents—and the outpouring of sympathy that commonly greets these murders suggests that we do—we would serve them and their children far better with more endgame strategies. We need respite care, and free and satisfactory residential placements; we need positive narratives of autism that free parents from the compulsion to eliminate the syndrome, even at the cost of eliminating the child.

Parents of autistic children are often sleep-deprived. They are frequently impoverished by the cost of care. They are overwhelmed by the unrelenting needs of children who often require constant supervision. They may be divorced and isolated. They may spend endless hours fighting their insurance and health providers and the local education authority that determines what services their child will get. They may forfeit their jobs because they miss so many days to deal with crises; they often have poor relationships with their neighbors because their children destroy property or are violent. Stress leads people to extreme acts; extreme stress leads people beyond our most profound social taboo: the slaughter of one's own child. Some claim to kill their autistic children out of love, and some acknowledge hate or anger. Debra L. Whitson, who attempted to kill her son, told police by way of explanation, "I waited eleven years to hear him say, 'I love you, Mom.'" Passion is confusing, and most of these parents act out of emotion so overpowering that to identify it as either love or hate is to reduce it. They themselves do not know what they are feeling; they know only how much they feel it.

More than half of the children murdered in the United States are killed by their parents, and about half of those parents claim to have acted altruistically. Societal acceptance of that label, however, has been shown to have a toxic effect. Criminologists consistently report that the use of the word *altruism* by bioethicists increases not only the number of filicides but also the frequency of abuse, disinhibiting parents who are already inclined toward violence. Copycat episodes commonly follow high-profile cases in which the altruism motive is endorsed. FBI profilers have argued that in many such killings the real motive is the need for power and control. Courtroom leniency sends a message to the society at large, to other parents, and to people with autism that autistic lives are less valuable than other lives. This line of reasoning comes perilously close to eugenics.

VI

Schizophrenia

The trauma of Down syndrome is that it is present prenatally and can therefore undermine the early stages of bonding. The challenge of autism is that it sets in or is detected in the toddler years, and so transfigures the child to whom parents have already bonded. The shock of schizophrenia is that it manifests in late adolescence or early adulthood, and parents must accept that the child they have known and loved for more than a decade may be irrevocably lost, even as that child looks much the same as ever. Initially, parents almost universally believe that schizophrenia is invasive, an added layer masking their beloved child, who must somehow be liberated from its temporary conquest. The more likely reality is that schizophrenia, like Alzheimer's, is an illness not of accrual but of replacement and deletion; rather than obscuring the previously known person, this disease to some degree eliminates that person. Yet vestiges persist, most notably in the doggedness of personal history, for the person with schizophrenia will recall events of a childhood in which mental illness played no apparent role. He will tell his parents the things they did right and tried to do right, as well as any history of trauma. He will know his cousins by name and will preserve certain skills: a mean backhand at tennis, perhaps, or the ability to raise a single eyebrow in surprise or disdain. He may sustain other continuities—a sense of humor, a dislike of broccoli, a love of autumn sunlight, a preference for rollerball pens. He may retain his most basic aspects of character, including kindness.

The betrayal of schizophrenia is its irrational juxtaposition of things that vanish and things that don't. Schizophrenia can take away the ability to connect to or love or trust another person, the full use of rational intelligence, the capacity to function in any professional context, the basic faculty of physical self-care, and large areas of self-awareness and analytic clarity. Most famously, the schizophrenic disappears into an alternative world of voices that he erroneously perceives to be external; these internally generated relationships become far more real and important than any interaction with the authentically outside world. The voices are usually cruel and often encourage bizarre and inappropriate behavior. The person who hears them is commonly terrified and almost always paranoid. Sometimes, the hallucinations are visual and olfactory as well and make a world full of actual threats into a writhing hell of inescapable terrorization. Though many schizophrenics become curiously attached to their delusions, the fading of the nondelusional world puts them in loneliness beyond all reckoning, a fixed residence on a noxious private planet they can never leave, and where they can receive no visitors. Between 5 and 13 percent of people with schizophrenia commit suicide. In some sense, though, that is the least of it; a woman whose schizophrenic brother committed suicide said, "Eventually, Mama got over Roger's death, but she never got over his life."

Few things could be worse than perceiving your dreams as true. We all know that lovely relief of stretching out to welcome a new day, free of shadow horrors that came in slumber. Psychosis is a gross disturbance in an individual's ability to distinguish self from reality. For schizophrenics, the membrane between imagination and reality is so porous that having an idea and having an experience are not particularly different. In the earlier stages of illness, schizophrenics often have symptoms of depression, because psychosis itself is distressing and because of the desperate nature of schizophrenic thought. This is the time of greatest suicide risk. In later stages, emotional capacity altogether is reduced, and people may seem vacant and emotionless.

Interviewing schizophrenics, I was struck by the way those deep in the disease seemed not to feel self-pity, which contrasted sharply with my experience of people with depression and other psychiatric disorders—a frequently whiny group to which I myself belong. People in the early stages were horrified and sad, but those who had been sick a long time were not. They complained about particular delusions or felt guilty not to be functioning better, but there was surprisingly little railing at the disease itself. Many had once been headed for wonderful lives, but the woman who had been a great beauty seemed, unlike her parents, not to think about the adventures in love she would have had; a sweet-natured fellow who had been wildly popular in high school could not tell me, as his parents could, how much pleasure a lifetime of friendships might have given him; a man who excelled at Harvard at the time of his first psychotic break never talked, as his parents did, about the career he had so narrowly missed. It seemed that illness had cut these schizophrenics off from those lives so entirely that they were hardly conscious of them. They had stoic grace in relation to their illness, and I was consistently moved by it.

The first time I met Harry Watson, he undermined my perceptions of schizophrenia. Impossibly good-looking at age thirty-eight, he had such a pleasant and open expression and such an easy and amusing way of speaking that I would not have known anything was wrong if I hadn't been told ahead of time. He was at a party thrown by his accomplished half sister Pamela and had come with his naturally elegant, casually intelligent mother, Kitty, and the three of them seemed like they could have been extras in *The Philadelphia Story*. "I think he always hopes it will be more fun than it turns out to be for him," Kitty said to me later. "He starts sweating a lot. He could barely get out of bed the next day."

Pamela and Harry share Kitty as their mother; Harry has two other half sisters via his father, Bill. The only boy and the youngest of the four, Harry was born in 1969 in California, much indulged and doted on. "He was a wonderful baseball player," Kitty said. "When he was about ten, he said the coach had asked him to be pitcher; Harry said, 'I don't think I could handle that kind of pressure.' Doesn't that sound strange from a ten-year-old? He has told me that even at that age, he felt like there was something wrong." Pamela, a novelist and journalist, said, "You hear this story a lot, but he was a golden boy. He was a great athlete, charismatic, the one everyone copied. Then my mother and his father, my stepfather, divorced when he was twelve, the same year I left for college. The message he had heard all along from his father was that you don't show weakness. Instead of admitting that he felt weird, Harry just hid it." Until he finished high school, Harry still had friends and seemed like a normal teenager. "He presents as much better than he is, so even since his diagnosis, his therapists have picked up much less than they should have," Kitty said. "He still thinks that if he acts like he's normal, he'll be treated more normally by the world. All it means is that he doesn't get as much help as he needs."

"We had no idea what was going on for a long time, so we didn't take steps to find him proper treatment," Pamela said. "The results were catastrophic. He was in the hands of this greedy, incompetent, unethical shrink my stepfather had found, and none of us realized how bad that situation was. It broke Harry's heart to find that this guy was a charlatan—something he could see only many years and hospitalizations down the road—and he was never able to trust another therapist that way." Recognizing psychosis can be a gradual project. "For years, I would instantly forget things Harry said and did that were just not right," Pamela said. "The year I was twenty-four and he was eighteen,

...became very depressed and secretive, and my mother convinced me to come home for Christmas to talk to him. We shut the door to his room and didn't emerge for six hours. He told me that everyone thought he was gay. He was convinced that his girlfriend thought he was gay, that all of his friends thought he was gay, that my mother and his father thought he was gay. I said, 'That's ridiculous! No one thinks you're gay.' That was a revelation, and he seemed to be freed, and I felt very good about having helped him. Taking a step back, that was a very complicated, prolonged delusion. He really needed serious treatment."

Harry enrolled in Rollins College and majored in philosophy and studied psychology—"clearly trying to understand what was happening to him," Kitty said. The next Christmas, Pamela and Harry went to Palm Springs to join Harry's father and his other children. "Harry was incredibly hostile," Pamela said. "One night, he suddenly announced that he had taken acid with one of my stepsisters. He discovered on this LSD trip that his brain always is that way. That's, basically, a declaration of schizophrenia." Still, despite little episodes of weirdness through his college graduation in 1992, Harry seemed to be holding on.

Four years after graduation, he became full-on psychotic for the first time, terrified of his own thoughts; he went into Langley Porter Psychiatric Hospital in San Francisco in the spring of 1996. "We started playing Scrabble, because it's hard to know what to talk about with someone that crazy," Kitty said. "He was pointing to a van in the street, saying that's where the FBI had their equipment. He thought the nurses were trying to poison him, and he didn't want to take medication. I went to his apartment after he was hospitalized and it was in complete chaos, like a reflection of the inside of his head."

Harry was in Langley Porter for ten days. When he came out, he found a job in computer programming. "It went well for a while, and then he was saying his apartment was bugged," Kitty said. "He had stopped taking one of his medications. I said, 'Why don't you come over here for the night?' He said, 'Your house is bugged, too, I'll show you where the transmitters are.' So he takes me down to the laundry room and points to where he says the stuff is. I hauled him off to Langley Porter again, and this happened on and off for years. Within three days of his leaving the hospital each time, you could feel the self-deception growing thicker and thicker." The war was being lost. "Unfortunately, by then, the voices had a grip on him," Pamela said. "How can you compete when they're piping in there twenty-four hours a day? It is *so critical* that parents of kids with mental illness see it early. If we had realized when he was fifteen that something was wrong, who knows what we could have done? It wasn't until he was thirty that he was finally helpless enough, freaked-out enough, convinced enough, that he was back in our hands for treatment."

Kitty experienced that year as a descent into deepening hell. "His father had a place in Napa," she said. "Harry went there for a weekend in 1997 and never left. After almost a year, I showed up one day, and when he saw me, he screamed, 'What the hell are you doing here?' like he was possessed by some demon. I said, 'Your dad and I feel that you need to come back to the city, start seeing a doctor regularly, live at home with me, and get on medication.' He said, 'I'm not going to.' I said, 'If you don't, we're throwing you out and you're going to be on the streets.' I was terrified that he would take me up on that, and I had found a private eye to follow him around, so that nothing bad would happen to him. A private eye to shadow someone with a paranoid delusion that he was being tracked by the FBI. He screamed how he hated me. Forty-eight hours later he moved home." Pamela remembered, "Harry also has a drinking problem, and in Napa he just drank. I mean, bottles of tequila, until he blacked out. It's amazing he's alive. Then drinking would make him incredibly depressed. That's when he would drive to the Golden Gate Bridge and sometimes stand right on it, thinking about whether to jump. He says he came very close once. But he's not a risk-taker, so he's less suicidal than you would expect."

In the months that followed Napa, Kitty found it a great relief to have Harry back at home but also a constant stress to see him lost in his madness. "I would be bringing people in the house and I never knew when he might emerge," Kitty said. "He often went off his meds and had to be rehospitalized. I would look around his room. It was the reverse of people who are addicts. If I didn't see any bottles, I was really worried." He soon moved back to his own apartment. "I would go ring the bell and he wouldn't answer, so I'd let myself in," Kitty said. "I had to go up a very steep staircase, and he would loom at the top. I was pretty sure he wouldn't push me down the stairs, but he would scream and it was scary." Pamela said, "He was hugely fat, incredibly hostile and angry, and didn't believe a word anyone said. His disdain was so evident that it was terrible to talk to him. He was becoming like Jim Morrison in his later years, holed up in the house, filling salad bowls with pasta and eating them in front of the television set. It was hard to imagine him functioning in any way, shape, or form."

Three years after Napa, when Harry was thirty-two, Kitty wanted to give him a fresh start, and she chose McLean, the mental hospital affiliated with Harvard, as the place to do it. "Getting him out of San Francisco and to McLean was an amazing achievement," Pamela said. "I still don't quite know how my mother did that. He was so ensconced in his little hole in San Francisco, and she had to persuade him to go along with it because she didn't have any legal power to make him do it." Harry was admitted as a long-term inpatient. He began new meds and started working with the therapist he has seen ever since. Harry, who is not tall, weighed 220 pounds; the doctors convinced him that this was neither smart nor healthy, and after about six months, he put himself on a diet and started running. Other patients would hum the theme from *Rocky* as he went sprinting across McLean's grassy campus.

"It was hard lugging all that blubber around," Kitty said. "Suddenly it dawned on me, why isn't there a fitness center there?" Kitty raised the money to build one. Harry helped pick out the equipment. Kitty's motivation was partly that she believes in fitness, but it also gave her an excuse to be in and out of the hospital without Harry's perceiving that she was constantly checking up on him. The fitness center now receives some seven hundred visits a month. Harry has lost sixty pounds since he went to McLean. "He runs every day," Pamela said. "He talks of having an illness. Frankly, if you had presented me with this scenario before he left San Francisco, it would have seemed like an impossibly upbeat outcome." But the years between his first hints of psychosis and McLean have taken their toll. "Not only was there time lost, but also the brain's not what it was after fifteen years of psychosis," Pamela explained. "He's a very damaged guy, but you can see how smart, articulate, and amusing he is, and what an interesting and dynamic life he might have had. He's sick enough that he can't really do anything, but well enough that he understands how much he's missing. He's well enough to know that he shouldn't tell other people the voices are real, but not well enough to believe it himself. He told me he was worried that 'the board' was going to make these terrible decisions about him. I said, 'God, the thing about these voices that's so unimpressive is how boring and dumb they are. I mean, the *board*? The cheesiest TV show could do better.' Then we can laugh. He and I also discuss a real hurdle he has not overcome, which is that he doesn't really want to stop listening to them. Even though they scare him, they've been friends." Kitty said simply, "Harry is having a tough time deciding whether he wants to be in the real world or that other world."

Harry now lives on his own in an apartment in Cambridge. He runs every day for an hour, watches television, and goes to a lot of movies and coffee shops. He sees his therapist. He's interested in fish and has a saltwater and a freshwater tank. He also had a job working in a greenhouse that is part of McLean's vocational program. But in Harry's world, nothing is stable for long, and on one of my later visits with

Kitty, she revealed that he had stopped going to the greenhouse. "His world has plateaued at the smallness that it's at," she said.

Kitty wears herself down with the relentless quest to help Harry up, and though she has been more successful than anyone could have hoped, her restless frustration takes a toll. "Having my own children was very freeing," Pamela said, "because I just couldn't live and breathe this every day." While she was saying this to me, Pamela put her cell phone on the table between us. "I have this as much for him as for my kids. He calls me when he's feeling deluded and needs to be talked out of it. I know that if I'm not hearing from him, things are okay." Kitty recognizes the advantages to this situation, but is also frustrated by it. "I had hoped Pamela would be more involved," she said. At the same time, Kitty feels that she should shoulder as much of Harry's care as she can for as long as she can. "He's very lonely, but as soon as anybody tries to befriend him, he starts to have paranoid thoughts about them," she said. "He told me he went running, and this guy says, 'Harry, Harry.' It's the guy who makes pancakes in the diner where he goes. They talked for a while. 'I felt like I was a member of a community,' he said." But Harry and his mother also joke. Kitty has kept a hand in at McLean by redesigning inpatient rooms. Harry said to her, "Gee, Ma, it looks like I've brought you a whole new career opportunity."

Finding the balance between encouragement and pressure remains almost impossible. "He's really doing the most he can right now," Pamela said. "Somehow, I feel like we're twins. There's been almost nothing he's explained that I haven't felt I could extrapolate from my own experience. I'm a fiction writer, and he is also a fiction writer, in his way. He creates other worlds; at times he's *lived* in other worlds. There are characters; there are planets. He has a great aesthetic sense, and that infuses his delusions. It's a very dangerous, scary, lonely world, but it also has moments of beauty in it. My mother deserves huge credit—for just never giving up. My stepfather couldn't stay in there, fighting; it was too painful for him, but it brought out the warrior in my mother. It's my mother, the doctors—and, most of all, Harry. He turns out to have a lot of grit. He's a hero to me. He's someone who's been in Vietnam for fifteen years. He still gets up and finds things to be joyful about. Would I have the stomach for the life he has? I'm not sure I would."

Kitty led long stretches of a charmed life before Harry got sick. "I was a lot more frivolous before I was dragged kicking and screaming into the world of mental illness," she said. "Now, I'm always helping people out or offering advice or finding them doctors. I'm sure it's been character-building, but frankly, I preferred being happy and frivolous." She knows that Harry feels guilty about the effect he's had on her life, so she tries to minimize it. I asked her how much of her time and emotional energy Harry occupied, and her eyes filled with tears. She shrugged, and forced a smile. "All of it. All of it," she said, almost guiltily. "I can't help it."

Schizophrenia is broadly categorized as having positive symptoms—the presence of psychotic hallucinations—and negative and cognitive symptoms—psychic disorganization, absence of motivation, blunted affect, loss of language (called *alogia*), withdrawal, compromised memory, and general decrease in functionality. One expert described it to me as "autism plus delusions," which is an inadequate but not unilluminating description. Here is a patient's description of her positive symptoms: "I could find no rest, for horrible images assailed me, so vivid that I experienced actual physical sensation. I cannot say that I really saw images; they did not represent anything. Rather I felt them. It seemed that my mouth was full of birds which I crunched between my teeth, and their feathers, their blood and broken bones were choking me. Or I saw people whom I had entombed in milk bottles, putrefying, and I was consuming their rotten cadavers. Or I was devouring the head of a cat which meanwhile gnawed at my vitals. It was ghastly, intolerable."

Here, by contrast, is another patient describing the experience of the negative and cognitive symptoms: "I am all the time losing my emotional contact with everything, including myself. What remains is only an abstract knowledge of what goes on around me and of the internal happenings in myself. Even this illness which pierces to the centre of my whole life I can regard only objectively. I cannot picture anything more frightful than for a well-endowed cultivated human being to live through his own gradual deterioration fully aware of it all the time. But that is what is happening to me." The Nobel laureate Eric Kandel described how schizophrenia takes away the wanting of enjoyment. "Imagine someone who has a great time whenever he goes out to dinner, but who has absolutely no interest in doing it," he said. The pleasure principle says that we will always seek gratification and avoid suffering, but for people with schizophrenia, at least half of this is untrue.

Emily Dickinson described such a descent into psychosis with terrifying clarity:

> I felt a Cleaving in my Mind—
> As if my Brain had split—

I tried to match it—Seam by Seam—
But could not make it fit.

The thought behind, I strove to join
Unto the thought before—
But Sequence ravelled out of Sound
Like Balls—upon a Floor.

Though most people experience schizophrenia as just such a sudden cleaving, it appears in fact to be a developmental disorder that is inscribed in the brain even before birth. It is degenerative, unlike autism, which, albeit pervasive and persistent, does not generally become increasingly debilitating over time. There is a rare syndrome of schizophrenia in preadolescence and childhood. The usual course for the condition, however, is that it unfolds through five predictable stages. It is asymptomatic until puberty in the *premorbid phase*, though recent research points to delays in walking and talking, more isolated play, poor school performance, social anxiety, and poor verbal short-term memory. This is followed by a *prodromal phase*, which lasts for four years on average, in which positive symptoms begin gradually to appear. The adolescent or young adult in this phase experiences changes in cognition, perception, volition, and motor function; has strange thoughts flash across his mind; struggles to understand whether illogical beliefs are true; and becomes suspicious and wary. Some people who will develop schizophrenia seem curiously detached from the real world even in childhood and gradually slip into psychosis. Most appear to have a dramatic break, sometimes in reaction to trauma and sometimes with no obvious trigger, in which they are suddenly transformed beyond recognition. This marks entry into the *psychotic phase*, with the onset of hallucinations or bizarre delusions, including delusions of control, thought insertion, thought broadcasting, and thought withdrawal. This usually occurs between ages fifteen and thirty and lasts for about two years.

No one has yet been able to discover what maturational event triggers psychosis. There are three primary possibilities. One is that the teenage rush of hormones changes gene expression in the brain. The second is that myelination, the adolescent process in which the brain wraps neuronal cables in a sheath so that they become maximally functional, goes wrong. The third is that synaptic elimination, or pruning, malfunctions. During normal brain development in infancy, new cells migrate within the brain, position themselves, and establish synaptic connections. An excess of these connections is made; during adolescence, only those that have been strengthened through repetition—that appear useful in the particular person—become enduring neural structures. An unhealthy brain may prune too much, not enough, or in the wrong places.

After somebody becomes ill, further changes occur in the *progressive phase*, which leads to clinical deterioration except when effectively controlled with medication. As the patient has repeated psychotic episodes, the condition worsens, finding its level after five years or so and settling into the *chronic and residual phase*. By this time, there has been an irrecoverable loss of grey matter in the brain. Positive symptoms tend to fade somewhat, while negative ones become more pronounced. Patients remain disabled, and persistently symptomatic. While more than 80 percent of patients respond well to antipsychotics during a first episode, only half of those treated at this stage show a comparable response.

When Janice Lieber was born, in 1953, her mother, Connie, had preeclampsia, a potentially fatal rise in maternal blood pressure, and the birth was rough. Janice seemed disengaged from the start. Connie thought she might be autistic; the pediatricians said she was mentally retarded. As it became clear that she was gifted at mathematics, the autism diagnosis stuck. At twenty-two, she had a psychotic break during her final year of college. Her father, Steve, brought her home; when she got there, she threw everything she loved out the window because a voice told her to do so. Connie called her doctor, who prescribed Mellaril, an early antipsychotic, for the weekend. Monday, Janice saw a psychiatrist and received a diagnosis.

Connie decided to learn all about schizophrenia, but not much information was out there. Then she and Steve went to Columbia for a meeting on schizophrenia and heard about NARSAD, the National Alliance for Research on Schizophrenia and Depression. NARSAD had at that time raised a total of $50,000 to support scientific investigation. Connie soon became president, a post she held for nearly twenty years; when she stepped down, Steve, who runs an investment fund, took over as chairman. The Liebers built NARSAD into the world's largest private funder of psychiatric and brain research; by 2011, it had given more than three thousand grants totaling almost $300 million to scientists in thirty-one countries. The Liebers personally review over a thousand research applications every year. They focus on original proposals by young researchers who cannot secure other funds. Herbert Pardes, president of New York-Presbyterian Hospital, said, "Most Nobel Prize winners could learn science from the Liebers."

Connie and Steve were messianically busy with NARSAD. One of Janice's psychiatrists asked her if she minded her parents being so occupied, and Janice said, "I don't see my mother as much as I'd like, but I know what she's doing. She's giving of herself for me and others. For mankind." Steve felt that their dedication affirmed for Janice how central she was in their lives, while also relieving some of the pressure that goes along with being an ill child. "She was the emblem of the challenge, and that was healthier than being the entire challenge herself," he said. When they began, the Liebers thought it would take ten years to reach a scientific breakthrough that could change their daughter's life. As this did not occur, they wanted to help Janice directly, and in 2007 they opened the Lieber Clinic at Columbia, which provides rehabilitative services. Janice goes to a day program there that teaches interpersonal sensitivity and other practical skills to people with schizophrenia. She has done remarkably well given the ongoing psychosis she faces, and now lives independently.

Connie has advised thousands of parents. "My name was on a lot of materials," she said. "And we never had an unlisted phone number; I don't believe in that. Anyone could find us, and if I could help them, I would." She smiled. "Some people take advantage, but I listen to them."

Schizophrenia, like *autism*, is a blanket term. Eugen Bleuler, who coined the word in 1908, actually referred to *schizophrenias*. In 1972, the eminent neurologist Frederick Plum famously said, "Schizophrenia is the graveyard of neuropathologists," meaning that no one had understood or would understand its etiology. We now understand more of schizophrenia than we do of autism. It is unclear whether schizophrenia should be subtyped according to biology (genotype) or behavior (phenotype). Despite the variety of genotypes and phenotypes for schizophrenia, no particular form or course of the disease has been linked to a particular set of genetic markers. Some people without the gene defects have the illness, and some people with these mutations do not; they are markers for vulnerability rather than guarantees of disease. One member of a family with a defective gene can be schizophrenic, but another member with the same gene defect might be bipolar or severely depressed.

Schizophrenia clearly runs in families; the most reliable predictor of developing the condition is having a first-degree relative who has it. But most who develop schizophrenia don't have such a relative. "Fact one: most schizophrenics do not have a schizophrenic parent," Deborah Levy, a practicing psychologist and a professor at Harvard, said. "Fact two: the incidence of schizophrenia is not decreasing, and in some places it is actually increasing. Fact three: schizophrenics have a very low reproductive rate. So how do we account for the persistence of the genes that give rise to it? One possible explanation is that most carriers and transmitters of schizophrenia genes are not schizophrenic." Identical twins show only a slightly higher than 50 percent concordance rate—the shared vulnerability is enormous, but the consequences of that vulnerability are by no means predestined. The children of the well twin and those of the ill twin are at the same escalated risk for the disease. So a person can have the susceptibility genes, not express them as schizophrenia, then transmit them to his or her children, who may develop schizophrenia. Nobody knows what protects some gene carriers from the condition. One mechanism of psychosis is an imbalance in neurotransmitters, particularly dopamine. Schizophrenic brains show reduced volume in the frontal cortex and hippocampus, and dysregulation of the striatum. Genetics most likely mix with environment to cause a shift in biochemistry, which then has a degenerative effect on brain structures. New work suggests that a genetic vulnerability may be activated by a parasite.

Everyone has a blueprint of thirty thousand or so genes, but the way those are expressed depends on the way the chromosomes are configured and on how external processes suppress or enable gene expression. A great deal of biochemistry determines when, how, whether, and to what extent a gene will be activated, and schizophrenia genes may go unexpressed, while protective genes may be overexpressed. As in autism, instead of a single genetic anomaly accounting for a large proportion of cases, a multiplicity of so-called *private mutations*—many, copy-number variations—may each be sufficient to cause the illness. These occur more often in offspring of older parents, especially older fathers. Another mechanism is spontaneous genetic mutation, the same process responsible for most occurrences of Down syndrome. It is now emerging that some spontaneous genetic defects, be they changes in copy number or single gene mutations, are found in schizophrenia, autism, and bipolar disorder. Is mental illness on a single spectrum, rather than a set of discrete disease entities? "I'd say it's more like a grid," said John Krystal, chairman of Yale's Department of Psychiatry and editor of the preeminent journal *Biological Psychiatry*.

The best way to determine what the gene defects are actually doing is to insert them artificially into the genomes of lab mice. The animals are observed to see if they mimic aspects of the illness in humans; then researchers try to understand how the gene is affecting brain development. Of course we have no way to tell if mice are hallucinating. Some such transgenic mice, however, become reclusive, hyperaggressive, or asocial; some refuse to affiliate with animals of the opposite gender or recoil from strangers. Many refuse to do work rewarded with food, giving up on tasks that normal mice will gamely pursue—a startlingly good approximation of the demotivation of schizophrenic people. Eric Kandel, who conceived and is designing some of these vast research protocols, has come to what he terms a "paradigm shift for schizophrenia." Many illnesses arise from the way a gene expresses itself ongoing; turn off the gene, and the symptoms vanish. Schizophrenia may originate in genes, but turning them off will not mitigate the illness; once it's in play, it must play itself out.

In 2011, I was privy to a conversation between a biotech executive and James Watson, the Nobel Laureate who, with Francis Crick, discovered the structure of DNA, and who has a son with schizophrenia. The executive opined that schizophrenia research was diffuse and chaotic; he had a grand scheme for getting everyone to collaborate, so people could each benefit from the knowledge of others. He had hoped he could inspire a breakthrough if he raised $400 million to address the problem. Watson said, "We're nowhere near the stage where collaboration is useful. We don't know enough; there's nothing anyone has figured out for anyone else to build on. We need an insight, not a refinement. If I had your four hundred million dollars, I'd find a hundred bright young scientists and give each of them four million. If I chose right, one of them would come up with something."

Every family member of a person with schizophrenia whom I met was scared by these genetic vagaries. One man told me that his girlfriend had refused to marry him because his schizophrenic brother represented a risk to his future children. "The history of schizophrenia is the history of blame," Maryellen Walsh has written in her guidebook for families and friends of people with the condition. Mothers have borne the brunt of such blame. Freud never suggested that early trauma engenders schizophrenia and did not advocate psychoanalysis for psychotic disorders. The poisonous term *schizophrenogenic mother* was put forward by the Freudian analyst Frieda Fromm-Reichmann in 1948. In her wake came theories of schizophrenia in which the entire family was to blame. One author wrote, "The patient's function is similar to that of an unsuccessful mediator of the emotional differences between the parents." Another, Gregory Bateson, said that schizophrenia is likely to occur for "a child whose mother becomes anxious and withdraws if the child responds to her as a loving mother." Such thinking was an antecedent to systems-oriented family therapy, based on the idea that the psychopathology of an entire family was manifested in a single individual as psychosis.

Thomas Insel, director of the National Institute of Mental Health, said that the most notable progress since the 1950s has been the end of the "blame and shame" game, but in my experience of people dealing with schizophrenia, both blame and shame remain highly operative. In 1996, two decades after the family systems theory had slipped out of vogue in professional circles, a national survey found that 57 percent of respondents still believed that schizophrenia was caused by parental behavior. An epidemic of self-help books such as the runaway bestseller *The Secret* argue that mental health is simply a matter of positive thinking. William James called earlier versions of this philosophy, written into Christian Science and other American metaphysical movements of the nineteenth century, "the religion of the healthy minded," celebrating "the conquering efficacy of courage, hope, and trust, and a correlative contempt for doubt, fear, worry." This concept is popular for its suggestion that healthy people have earned their health through personal courage. For those who are unwell, however, the suggestion that flawed discipline and weak character are the source of their psychosis is torture.

When mothers internalize blame, it interferes with the very support that people with schizophrenia most need. "I sometimes felt as though I wore a scarlet letter 'S' emblazoned upon my chest," wrote the bioethicist Patricia Backlar, who has a schizophrenic son. "That 'S' might stand for schizophrenogenic, but is as likely to impute personal shame." Another mother wrote, "An entire generation of mental health professionals was educated to believe that families cause schizophrenia. Some are still treating our sons and daughters. And still mistreating us." The psychiatrist E. Fuller Torrey, founder of the Treatment Advocacy Center, finds the blame problem absurd. "Any parent who has raised a child knows that parents are not powerful enough to cause a disease like schizophrenia simply by favoring one child over another or giving the child inconsistent messages," he wrote.

When the doctors at Long Island Jewish Hospital wanted to recruit Philip and Bobby Smithers for a genetic study of schizophrenia in the 1990s, their mother fought to keep them out of it. "What's in it for us?" she asked. In the first decade of the new millennium, Philip, Bobby, and their unaffected older brother, Paul, were in their thirties, and Paul's wife, Freda, wanted to know how vulnerable her children might be. As Freda began investigating the extended family, she found illness everywhere: Paul's aunt had been institutionalized her entire adult life with "postpartum depression," an uncle was "sick in the head," and many "quirky" cousins could barely function. Although Paul and Freda were high school sweethearts, Freda had met Paul's father only once before their marriage, because Paul kept everyone away from him. "You'd think that when Paul's brothers both started acting strange," Freda said, "their mother would have told the doctor that there's a family history of schizophrenia. But that's not the way they do it, so it took years for them to be diagnosed."

Secrecy is a difficult habit to break. "Every year we have a Thanksgiving for Freda's family, and then we have one for mine," Paul said. "If we mix the two, I'm defensive, my mom is defensive of my brothers, and it's upsetting to Freda's family to see these sick people. I don't discuss this with even my closest friends. I'm not in denial, like the rest of my family. I just don't like talking about it. I have an emotional connection with my brothers. I think about them every day. But do I have a relationship with them? Not really. They're very highly medicated."

Paul and Freda, who now have two sons, live in terror of seeing them develop schizophrenia. They considered using a sperm donor, but couldn't bring themselves to do so. "We're making genetic rolls of the dice," Paul said. Freda described her fear as a constant mental drain. She added, "We torture them in some ways. I read an article saying that people who develop schizophrenia have particular traits. We strip them naked; we're going through their whole bodies looking for webbed toes. Someone said more schizophrenics are born in the winter, so we timed it to have summer babies. Nutty, I know. In some ways, it's very liberating. Everyone wants their kid to be the smartest and the most athletic. We really don't care. As long as they're healthy." In 2008, Paul and Freda agreed to participate in a survey on schizophrenia genetics. "We sit by the phone," Freda said, "waiting to find out what the gene is, so we can test the kids."

In 1668, John Bunyan wrote, "Let them . . . recover one to his wits that was mad . . . and he that can do thus . . . shall have the name and fame he desires; he may lay abed till noon." There was little progress between Bunyan's times and modernity; for centuries, treatments for schizophrenia were ineffectual, barbaric, or both. In the nineteenth century, they included pulling teeth; in the middle years of the twentieth, they included lobotomy.

The development of antipsychotic medications, beginning with Thorazine in 1950, has been a miraculous breakthrough in treating schizophrenia's positive symptoms. Unfortunately, these medications have negligible effects on negative symptoms. As Helen Mayberg, chair of neuroimaging at Emory, said, "It's as though you've got a house that's burning down; you come in with the fire trucks and pump the place full of water; you put out the conflagration. It's still charred, smoke-damaged, flooded, structurally unstable, and pretty much uninhabitable, even if flames are no longer licking the walls."

The damage done by the disease persists, and the techniques for mitigating that damage constitute their own ordeal. Thorazine flattens personalities much as lobotomy did, and while newer medications are somewhat better, the number of people with schizophrenia who go off their medications indicates how detested they are by the patients who must take them. In the 1970s, the Soviets administered antipsychotics for torture and subjugation and were able to induce symptoms of psychological disability with them. "One loses his individuality, his mind is dulled, his emotions destroyed, his memory lost as a result of the treatment, all the subtle distinctiveness of a person is wiped away," said one survivor of such treatment at a Senate hearing on Soviet abuses of psychopharmacology. "Although I am afraid of death, let them shoot me rather than this." A patient named Janet Gotkin described her contemporaneous treatment in the American psychiatric system in similar terms: "I became alienated from my self, my thoughts, my life, a prisoner of drugs and psychiatric mystification; my body, heavy as a bear's, lumbered and lurched as I tried to maneuver the curves of my outside world. These drugs are used not to heal or help, but to torture and control." Another patient said, "The muscles of your jawbone go berserk, so that you bite the inside of your mouth and your jaw locks and the pain throbs. Your spinal column stiffens so that you can hardly move your head or your neck, and sometimes your back bends like a bow and you cannot stand up. The pain *grinds* into your *fiber*. You ache with restlessness, so you feel you have to walk, to pace. Then as soon as you start pacing, the opposite occurs to you; you must sit and rest." These accounts relate to older antipsychotics and neuroleptics, but the side effects of modern medications differ more in degree than in nature.

By the time I began to meet members of his family, Malcolm Pease was dead at fifty-two, but it was not yet clear why he had died. The previous twelve years had been the best of his adult life. Then one day a nurse at his group home found him curled up in what looked like a comfortable position, cold and dead. "He was very overweight," his brother Doug said, "largely from the medication. He had a lifetime of heavy smoking behind him. Because he was young, there were police; pretty much on the spot they ruled out suicide."

Of seventeen children in Malcolm's generation, siblings and cousins, four have severe mental illness. Many prefer not to discuss it, a position for which Penny Pease, Malcolm's mother, eighty-five when he died, has disdain. "I talk about it all the time, with a lot of people," she said.

In high school Malcolm had no meaningful signs of illness. "He was a really good athlete," Penny recalled. "He was a fantastic bridge player, and cribbage, and, oh, boy, was he competitive. He loved skiing; he loved everything. We had no clue." During his freshman year at Franklin Pierce, in the winter of 1975, he began hearing voices and developing paranoid fantasies. In March, his roommate called to tell the Peases that something was horribly wrong, and Malcolm's parents brought him home. "We knew he was in trouble," Penny said. "He wasn't making much sense." His brother Doug said, "He was completely out of control, didn't know why, and we didn't, either." The following November, Malcolm assaulted his father. "My parents sent him to the Institute of Living in Hartford, Connecticut, which was among the better private mental hospitals," Doug said. "It was captivity, really. They were feeding him sedatives. Your brother is a ghost in his former body, whom you can't reach because he's so dulled down. The other patients look like *Night of the Living Dead*." Malcolm soon signed himself out against advice, and his parents initiated a proceeding to have him committed. Over the years, he had to be recommitted dozens of times.

When he was not hospitalized, Malcolm lived with his parents. "My parents tried to love him back to health," said Malcolm's other brother, Peter. But Malcolm wouldn't stay on his medication. Their sister, Polly, said, "Once he was feeling normal, he would think, 'I don't need to take these anymore.' Then you crash and burn again. And again. And again." When he wasn't taking his drugs, he would become paranoid. "Everybody who came near, he would think, 'Oh, you're just trying to put me in the hospital and force me to take antipsychotics,'" Peter said. "Of course, he was right."

Everyone tried to keep up as much normality as possible. "All you can do is tell him what reality is, in a loving way," Doug said. Polly remembered, "Some of it was just funny. I remember he asked my mother where she was when Martin Luther King was shot and whether she could prove she didn't do it." Sometimes poetry crept in, too. When asked at one of his admissions what he was thinking, he said, "I do not like sex or French kissing. There is gas outside of the Indian Ocean, and there are diamonds up in the North Pole." Despite the madness, he sustained a central coherence. "He didn't disappear," Penny said. "He still liked animals, and playing cards. He missed the friends he'd had before he became sick." Polly said, "The thing that made him himself was always there. It just wasn't where you could find it all the time."

The hospitalizations became increasingly frequent. "The ongoing discussion, year after year, was, 'You have to stay on medication,' and Malcolm refused," Doug said. "Off the meds, he felt freer, more alive. Sort of high. Also mostly distraught. Would you rather be awake and alive, or a walking zombie? He would try to find the sweet spot in the middle." When Malcolm's father developed cancer, Peter decided that it was time to step in. "I carried the essence of who Malcolm was with me and never let who he became take that over," Peter said.

One of the first antipsychotics, clozapine, had been taken off the market in 1975 because it can reduce the concentration of white blood cells, a condition called *agranulocytosis*. Researchers eventually realized that clozapine was the most effective treatment for schizophrenia, and that for many patients its efficacy outweighed the side-effect risk. Malcolm started on clozapine when it returned to the market in 1990. Peter said, "There was always enough of who he really was for me to love, but sometimes it got squeezed rather mightily. Then with clozapine, it came back. The smile, the laugh, the sense of humor. If you know who somebody is, you can lead them back to themselves." In his human relationships, Malcolm remained deeply caring. "He was always just worried about everybody else," Polly said. Doug expressed enormous sympathy for Malcolm's reality: "He always felt he had wronged people along the way. We found a letter dated 2002 from his original doctor. Thirty years later, it says, 'Dear Malcolm, To the best of my knowledge, no, you never hurt anyone. Hope you are well. Sincerely, Dr. Koff.'" Penny said, "He never changed that way. I never loved him less because he was sick; I never loved him more; I never even loved him differently."

At thirty-nine, Malcolm graduated to a supported home in Framingham and got a job bagging groceries at the Stop & Shop. "That's what he could handle, and it was awesome," Doug said. "We were dancing in the streets." Malcolm had done well on the clozapine for about five years, and then it all began to come apart again. "He was always tinkering with his medication," Doug said. "He had to be hospitalized again. I was in the hospital to visit him, and the doctor says, 'Well, Malcolm is heading home now. He'll be just fine.' So I take him back to Framingham. He makes a suicide attempt that evening, ingesting laundry detergent." Malcolm was rushed back to the hospital. "It's ridiculous to try to commit suicide by eating Tide," Peter said. "The imagery, though, is interesting. I'm gonna wash this disease right out of my body!"

Polly's first husband and Peter's first wife had been afraid of and intolerant of Malcolm, and it had created tension in those marriages, both of which ultimately dissolved. However, all of Malcolm's nieces and nephews loved him. "He's just his own particular strong essence," Peter said. "There was no other weirdness going on than his being crazy. When he was well, we had great times." Malcolm's years in Framingham were relatively happy. He had refused to drive for decades, but after he went on clozapine, that changed, and Peter bought him a Ford Ranger. "That was one of the best days of my whole life, to see him driving out of that dealership with this huge smile on his face," Peter said. Malcolm was beloved at the Framingham home. One of the other residents told Peter, "Every morning, Malcolm would come down to the common room and say, 'Maurice, where can I take you today?'" Peter said, "Part of his ministry was driving people in his red truck, like a taxi service."

No one expected Malcolm to die when he did. Peter said, "Of course the illness reduces your life expectancy, and the medication, even though it's helping you, reduces your life expectancy, too. But at least he got himself to the best place he could. We'll take this death because of the quality of life he had."

Malcolm had been part of a McLean study on the genetics of schizophrenia. After he died, researchers there said they'd like his brain to study. Penny endorsed the idea. Doug enjoys repeating his comment at the memorial service: "Malcolm didn't complete college because of his illness. But he finally got into Harvard, and he's teaching the neuroscientists." The coroner's office took blood samples, just to rule out the possibility of wrongdoing. A few months later, the family learned that clozapine ended the same life it had redeemed. "We didn't realize death by clozapine was even possible, but are gradually learning more about it," Peter wrote to me. "It seems that toxic levels of clozapine built up over time because his liver was not processing it. Some have suggested to us that liver function should be tested regularly to make sure there is not a buildup in toxicity, and that this is a matter of standard practice. So it is probably a malpractice issue, which we won't pursue. At high levels, apparently clozapine can cause heart arrhythmia, and coma/respiratory arrest. Now we are left with the final tragedy—the medications we forced him to take, which he railed against and fought with all his spirit for most of his life, killed him. It is probably good that we did not know the cause of death before we celebrated his life and had the memorial service. This news beats us down, and it is very hard to rise up singing."

The liberation movements of the 1960s questioned the very concept of mental illness. Michel Foucault mounted a systematic assault on the idea that insanity was anything more than a power play by self-declared sane people. Erving Goffman maintained that mental hospitals made people crazy. R. D. Laing said, "There is no such 'condition' as schizophrenia but the label is a social fact and political event," spoke of schizophrenia as a "special strategy that a person invents in order to live in an unlivable situation," and maintained, "Madness need not be all breakdown. It may also be breakthrough. It is potentially liberation and renewal, as well as enslavement and existential death." Thomas Szasz emerged as the great apologist for the idea that schizophrenia is always a fiction.

The last generation has witnessed a great social experiment called *deinstitutionalization*, which has removed people with acute mental illness from large state institutions, reducing the number of schizophrenics in long-term custodial care in the United States from more than half a million in 1950 to some forty thousand today. This movement draws on a curious mix of valid optimism, economic expediency, and ideological rigidity. While previous treatment of schizophrenics was inhumane, current treatment is often negligible. Money and personnel were never shifted to the community facilities that were supposed to provide services after the institutions were closed; federal guidelines are incredibly vague, and oversight is virtually nonexistent.

The vision of treatment as a mechanism of social control infuriates people who are trying to advance encompassing treatment policies. E. Fuller Torrey, perhaps the most prominent critic of the social realities around schizophrenia, has said, "Freedom to be insane is an illusory freedom, a cruel hoax perpetrated on those who cannot think clearly by those who will not think clearly." Judge Berel Caesar wrote bitingly in 1990, "The right to treatment has become the right to no treatment," with the result that "we have consigned many persons to lives of quiet desperation, have destroyed the mental and emotional health of those who love and care for them, and have destroyed families—to the ultimate detriment and even destruction of the disabled person."

The therapist Ann Braden Johnson, author of *Out of Bedlam: The Truth About Deinstitutionalization*, complains of "the myth that mental illness is a myth" and argues that deinstitutionalization was the result of a politics that emerged as ideas about deviants changed, which was in turn the result of the emergence of biological psychiatry, which made it logical to spend mental health dollars on something other than custodial care. Near-universal institutionalization was ruinous, but near-universal deinstitutionalization is equally bad. The schizophrenia researcher Nancy Andreasen points out that state hospitals were "small communities unto themselves, where patients lived together as a family and were given a chance to be productively employed by the hospital farm, kitchen, or laundry." One of the new system's fallacies is its ambition to order. "The patients I see don't fit readily into most existing programs, and programs they might fit in simply don't exist," Johnson wrote. "Bureaucrats who drew up programs often have never seen a patient, much less treated one." A vacuum of empathy exists in any system that returns people who don't know how to be in a community to communities that may not be prepared to handle them. The lack of support and erratic access to medication often result in rapid deterioration, but family members who attempt to arrest that are frustrated by the courts. The elderly father of one schizophrenic said, "The authorities say it is their choice and their right to live like stray animals. Why is rapid suicide illegal and gradual suicide a right?"

When Madeline Grammont's brother William began to act erratically, their father refused to acknowledge what was going on. William had earned a perfect score on his math SATs and had been admitted to Harvard as a sophomore. By the end of his junior year he had to leave. "My father was mortified," Madeline said. William went up to his family's country place in New Hampshire. "He was subsisting on raw garlic and had knives sitting everywhere," Madeline said. "He was sleeping on the floor. My father found a small house for him in the woods, away from the summer community, so no one would see him. In fact, my father saw him only three times in thirty years." Once a week, William walked down to the town general store, usually clothed in just a towel, talking to himself; local teenagers would taunt him. His father maintained that he was just a touch eccentric, but his sister worried, and as their domineering father grew feeble in old age, she went up to see William. "Mice and rat turds everywhere, mayonnaise jars opened and rotting," she said. "Broken dishes everywhere. His bedroom was truly disgusting. He looked at me curiously, but he had lost his language. He made little squeaking sounds, and that was it."

So Madeline took over the case. She sought legal guardianship, obtained a diagnosis of schizophrenia, and brought him to a residential care center. There he began using rudimentary speech again. "I brought him flowers once—some lilies—and he leaned over and smelled them," she said. "I brought them every single time thereafter and I still do. I take him out every two or three weeks. He can't initiate conversation and he talks very little, but he seems increasingly able to understand. He basically saw his first treatment at age fifty-two. That kind of denial, the way my father was—it ate him alive, and now he's just a hollow wreck. A whole life slipped away, that didn't have to."

The brain is composed of grey matter, made of cell bodies; white matter, the axons that connect the cell bodies and create synapses; and ventricles, fluid-containing spaces that allow for circulation of the cerebrospinal fluid. When you lose brain tissue, you have bigger ventricles, and a cardinal feature of schizophrenia is enlargement of the lateral ventricles. While autism is characterized by an overabundance of synaptic connectivity, schizophrenia is marked by a dearth of it. People with schizophrenia also have fewer dendritic spines, which form synapses, and fewer interneurons, a type of brain cell that regulates mental activity. The positive symptoms of schizophrenia appear to be tied to abnormalities in the temporal lobe, where auditory and emotional perception are located. The negative symptoms appear to be tied to damage to the frontal and prefrontal lobes, where cognition and attention are based.

Genetic vulnerability to schizophrenia is subject to precipitating traumas, including variations in the uterine environment. Obstetrical, labor, and delivery complications are bad for a developing fetal brain, and schizophrenia patients are more likely to have a history of them. Maternal infections such as rubella and influenza during pregnancy also increase risk; the high rate of winter births of people who develop schizophrenia is probably linked to increased second-trimester maternal viral infections. Stressful events during pregnancy have been correlated with schizophrenia; the rate is higher, for example, for children of women who lived through a military invasion while carrying, or whose spouses died during their pregnancies. Famine in Holland during World War II led to a dramatic increase in the incidence of schizophrenia twenty years later. Scientists have proposed that prenatal stress results in the release of hormones that disturb fetal neurodevelopment; stress can activate the mother's dopamine system, and that may dysregulate the fetus's.

Postnatal events such as a head trauma in early childhood increase the risk of developing schizophrenia. Lifetime stress plays a role, too; the risk is particularly high among immigrants who go from underdeveloped settings to cities—people confronting exponential unfamiliarity. The most consistent postuterine environmental factor associated with a worsening of psychotic symptoms is the abuse of recreational drugs, including alcohol, methamphetamines, hallucinogens, cocaine, and marijuana, particularly in adolescence. When the Japanese gave methamphetamines to workers to increase productivity during the postwar recovery, they provoked epidemic levels of psychosis; although many people recovered after they stopped using the drugs, others had transient recurrence, and some had prolonged and even permanent impairment. A seminal study done in the 1980s with some fifty thousand Swedish conscripts showed that those who had used marijuana more than fifty times were six times more likely to develop schizophrenia. "The relationship between drug abuse and psychosis is perhaps like that between smoking and lung cancer," said Cyril D'Souza, a psychiatrist at Yale. "It's a contributing, not a necessary, cause. But some studies suggest that if you were able to eliminate cannabis, you could reduce world rates of schizophrenia by at least ten percent."

In schizophrenia, some gene-environment combination causes the neurotransmitters dopamine, glutamate, norepinephrine, serotonin, and GABA to become dysregulated, leading to excess activity in one dopamine pathway. This induces psychosis and other positive symptoms. Artificially releasing too much dopamine can provoke the symptoms of schizophrenia even in healthy subjects; suppressing it can mitigate those symptoms. Underactivity in another dopamine pathway creates impaired cognition and other negative symptoms. Antipsychotic medications block the ability of the brain to process high levels of neurotransmitters in some areas; they mimic controlled levels of those neurotransmitters in others. All successful antipsychotics lower dopamine levels, but lowering dopamine is not by itself enough consistently to remit all of the symptoms of schizophrenia, and new research focuses on drugs that will affect particular receptors for glutamate and other transmitters. Anissa Abi-Dargham at Columbia University is delineating which dopamine receptors are overstimulated and which are understimulated, to map ever more specific goals for medications.

Nonchemical interventions can play a meaningful secondary role. Talk therapies can help in the management of symptoms that do not respond to medication. Though cognitive behavioral therapy (CBT), which teaches people to redirect their present thoughts and behaviors, has the strongest track record, many other talk therapies have powerful exponents, and the law professor Elyn Saks has written movingly of her redeeming experiences with psychoanalysis in her battle with schizophrenia. What you do with your brain changes it, and if you can get someone with schizophrenia into a rational mode for some time, the positive effects are substantive. The theory is that much as someone who loses speech in a stroke can relearn talking through speech therapy, someone with psychosis may be able to train his way partially out of it.

Since the disease is associated with a progressive loss of grey matter in the brain, it makes sense that if you identify people quickly, treat them, and keep them well, you can limit the morbidity of the illness and prevent people from becoming irreversibly impaired. "The therapeutic nihilism that pervaded the field for the better part of the twentieth century is really no longer warranted," said Jeffrey Lieberman, chairman of the Department of Psychiatry at Columbia and director of the New York State Psychiatric Institute. "There is no better time in the history of mankind to have a mental illness than now, as long as you know where and how to obtain good treatment fast." As with autism, early detection and intervention may be key, an idea that has now engendered an International Early Psychosis Association. Early behavioral intervention in autism can diminish the expression of symptoms; the training seems to affect the brain's actual development. Early intervention may be equally promising in schizophrenia, even if *early* means age eighteen years rather than age eighteen months. Thomas McGlashan, a professor of psychiatry at Yale, has proposed that earlier diagnosis and medication during someone's first dip into psychosis may actually truncate the brain degeneration that otherwise characterizes advancing schizophrenia.

Given the inadequacy of cures, the increasing focus is on getting in even earlier—on prevention at the prodromal (pre-psychotic) stage. Patients are in what Lieberman calls a "Humpty Dumpty situation," in which "with our current tools it's easier to prevent the morbidity of schizophrenia from occurring than to restore people after it's happened." As Jack Barchas, chairman of the Department of Psychiatry at Cornell, points out, the longer you can keep someone functioning, the more solid psychic history he has to fall back on—so even delaying the onset of schizophrenia would have value. Experts have devised a menu of symptoms that indicate the prodromal stage: suspiciousness; unusual, magical, or bizarre thinking; extreme changes in behavior patterns; decreased functioning; inability to go to school or function at a job. Confusingly, many of these are also symptoms of ordinary adolescence. In studies that have followed subjects identified as prodromal, only a third have actually developed schizophrenia, though many others will develop serious disturbances. Starting in 2003, McGlashan tried giving the antipsychotic olanzapine (Zyprexa) to apparently prodromal people and showed that the rate of developing schizophrenia was somewhat reduced; it also made many people who might not have gone on to develop the syndrome obese, sluggish, and glassy-eyed. "The positive result was only marginally significant, and the negative result was clear," he said. It's difficult to figure out what to do with these mathematics, because while powerful medications may block the onset of psychosis, those medications have too many undesirable effects to be used on people who may just be presently grumpy, and we cannot now tell the difference.

Studies in England and Australia show that cognitive-behavioral and other nonbiological therapies can diminish or delay the onset of symptoms. Antioxidants and other neuroprotectants such as omega-3 fatty acids may delay the onset of psychosis without side effects. "It doesn't seem to matter what the intervention is," McGlashan said. "The psychocognitive behavioral intervention was just as good as medication. If you can keep them engaged, and relating, and challenging their symptomatic experiences, you can delay this crescendo into an acute psychotic episode. It could be that you are helping to prevent loss of learned connections in the brain." The families of people at high risk of developing schizophrenia should learn what to watch for, and doctors should meet frequently with patients, since they can escalate to psychosis in a few days. While antipsychotics are not recommended until psychosis sets in, aggressive response to anxiety and depression is in order.

A strong movement to categorize the prodromal phase as its own illness in the *DSM-5*—the diagnostic and statistical manual that is psychiatry's bible—as "psychosis risk syndrome" or "attenuated psychosis syndrome" was abandoned in the spring of 2012. The diagnosis would have given doctors protections and compensation for treating patients aggressively—but because the degree of psychosis risk in any individual is so difficult to quantify, the framers of the new *DSM* eventually determined that there was too much potential for unnecessary, stigmatizing, and harmful treatment. It makes sense that someone at risk for developing schizophrenia be treated with benign interventions and close monitoring, but the issue of stigma cannot be ignored, as it pertains to both self-image and medical insurance. McGlashan wrote, "The bottom line for me is that the psychosis-risk syndrome should be treated as a bona fide psychiatric disorder; it is real, and it can be very dangerous if ignored." John Krystal, however, pointed out, "The earlier you are in any mental disease process, the less you know what you're dealing with. Earlier intervention is almost always preferable and harder—sometimes so hard that it's not preferable. What they do in the *DSM* is a fashion question, like skirt lengths. But we have a dichotomous medical system. Good clinicians will lie about their patients' symptoms to get them insurance coverage and treatment if they seem to be sick, while poor ones will punish patients on this checklist basis."

Even with early identification, it can be a challenge to sustain treatment over the life span. Lieberman tells of a patient he treated early in his career: "He was twenty-one years old, Ivy League school, top of his class, popular, athlete, seemed to be destined for greatness. He developed psychotic symptoms, and I diagnosed schizophrenia and gave him medication. He had almost complete remission. Then he wanted to go back to school, and he didn't like the medication, so he stopped taking it. He became sick again, came back, we treated him, he improved, went back to school, and relapsed again. We treated him, and he made progress. Repeated again. The next time, he didn't get better. He never recovered."

George Clark is a physicist at MIT who works on theoretical astrophysics; he is both kind and almost entirely occupied by intellect. His wife, Charlotte, is capable of toughness after a tough existence, at once judgmental and sympathetic, as though it were her habit to find weakness everywhere around her and then forgive it. She has bright blue eyes behind wire-rimmed spectacles, snow-white hair neatly kept, and capable hands that she uses for punctuation when she speaks. They were both in their eighties when we met, and I saw with what gratitude George handed difficulty over to Charlotte.

When George and Charlotte married in 1980, each had a problematic daughter. George had Jackie, then nineteen, diagnosed with schizophrenia four years earlier. Charlotte's daughter Electa Reischer, the same age as Jackie, was disjointed and bewildering, but would not receive a diagnosis for another eighteen years. Charlotte told me that George had had a harder time than she because Jackie had once been so promising, whereas Electa had been odd all along. "I knew the day I gave birth that she was different," Charlotte said. "She was limp, like a bag of sugar." Charlotte tried to be the same mother to this child that she had been to her other children, but the connection was effortful. "She was oblivious. Other children were afraid of her; they saw that something was strange there." The family was living in Pakistan because Electa's father was working for USAID. The older children thrived at the international schools, but at five, Electa couldn't follow what was going on. A year later, her father was transferred to Jordan. She went to the American school in Amman, had a remedial tutor, and was coached by Charlotte. "By eight, she could read," Charlotte said. "But she wasn't interested; in fact, she wasn't interested in anything."

When Electa was nine, her father died suddenly of a heart attack, and Charlotte moved the family to Washington, DC. Electa was bullied in the local fourth grade; Charlotte put her in a special school, which helped briefly. By fourteen, she was out of control. "She was fucking, if you'll excuse the expression, anybody who would, and she was flunking out," her mother recalled. "So I sent her to boarding school. She was very unhappy there. I said, 'I was unhappy when you were here. You have to graduate from high school.' So she earned her GED. Then she said she would be a hairdresser. I thought, 'Hairdresser?' But she loved it and did well at it. Those were her best days. But slowly, slowly, she was going crazy."

One bright October morning, Charlotte called Electa, then thirty-seven, and Electa said, "I can't talk on the phone." Charlotte said, "Come over and have a cup of coffee." When Electa arrived, she said, "I can't talk in the house." So Charlotte said, "Let's go for a walk." Electa explained that she couldn't talk on the pavement, either; she could talk only if they walked in the middle of the road. So they dodged cars while Electa explained that the Mafia at MIT was after George, and that he might be part of it. A few months later, Charlotte received a call: one of Electa's friends had found her at the gym curled up in the fetal position, crying. The friend took her to the emergency room, where the doctors tried to do an EKG. Electa began screaming and thrashing and ended up in the psychiatric ward, where she finally received a schizophrenia diagnosis; she was also an alcoholic.

Over the following years, Electa's psychosis was contained by medication, but she suffered endless side effects. Her weight ballooned to over three hundred pounds. "She can hardly walk," Charlotte said. "She used to be the beauty of the family." Her enunciation was slowed, and she slept long hours. She met another schizophrenic, Tammy, who became her romantic partner. Then after ten years on clozapine, Electa's condition began to deteriorate in early 2006. "I remember saying to her, 'You're not taking your meds, are you?'" Charlotte recalled. "She said, 'I don't need my meds,' in a very aggressive tone." By October, she wouldn't answer the door, and her phone was disconnected. Neither Tammy nor Charlotte could find out what was going on. "She had a credit card on my account," Charlotte said, "and I yearned for the bill so that I could see where she had been and know that she was still alive, but when the bill hit ten thousand dollars, I had to cancel it."

Charlotte finally convinced a judge to authorize the police to break in. "The sink was stopped up, and there was food all over the place and it was crawling with maggots. I had to go back to court twice to have her committed, and when she went to the hospital, they couldn't even get her into a shower. Two nurses had to hold her down when they were washing her. But gradually the medication took hold. She began washing herself, and then she began being happy to see us." Electa, now fifty, hasn't worked since the breakdown. "She still can cut hair, but not as well as she used to," Charlotte said. "I encourage her to cut my hair once in a while, and she cuts Tammy's. It keeps some part of her alive."

Charlotte and George were childhood friends long out of touch; when Charlotte was widowed and George was divorced, they were reintroduced. They deliberately bought a house that didn't have enough space for Jackie and Electa to live with them. "Jackie had been beautiful, highly energetic, and popular," Charlotte said. "She showed early signs of her father's intellect. She was a brilliant flautist, and a champion chess player." When Jackie was fifteen, the math that had come so easily to her a year earlier was suddenly incomprehensible, and George found that he could not explain to her the simple equations that she could once have explained to him. George went to see the chief therapist at MIT, who said that Jackie was schizophrenic. Jackie's mother walked out on them both, leaving a marriage that was already in disarray.

When Charlotte and George got together, Jackie was nineteen and had just been evicted from a group home. "This was when I was deciding whether I wanted to live with George myself," Charlotte said. "I decided I was up for it. Jackie was supposedly taking Thorazine. She was actually flushing it down the toilet. Over dinner the first night after I moved in, Jackie took a plate and threw it across the room. Nobody's ever done that before or since at my table." Charlotte began to lay down ground rules. Shortly after Jackie turned twenty, Charlotte told her to make her bed, and she blew up. George heard her shouting and came downstairs. "He's very strong," Charlotte said. "So is she. He took her by both wrists; she was spitting in his face. He kept holding her. Finally she said, 'Dad, I don't know what's wrong.'"

A few months later, Jackie hitchhiked from Massachusetts to New York to surprise her estranged mother. When her mother asked her how the trip was, she said she was "only raped five times." Charlotte said, "Of course, you never know what to believe. You don't know what happened and neither does she." In the years that followed, Jackie was in and out of mental hospitals, group homes, and other protective arrangements that varied with the fluctuations of her psychosis. Eventually, clozapine came along. "She's very sweet, now that she's medicated," Charlotte said.

By the time I met Jackie, she was forty-nine and had been on clozapine for fifteen years, and she was living in a group home with seven other women. She spent most of her waking time at a day program that she referred to as "the club." If her caseworker deemed it necessary, she was hospitalized for a few days or weeks. Unlike most schizophrenics, Jackie did not become obese on antipsychotic medications. She plays tennis, swims a mile every day, and does yoga. She is antithetical to Electa's melancholy sluggishness.

Every Saturday, Charlotte and George have Jackie and Electa over. Electa often brings Tammy; Jackie sometimes brings one of the other women from "the club" or the group home. "Thankfully, Jackie and Electa like each other as much as schizophrenics ever like anybody," Charlotte said. "I don't want to say I don't want to be their mother anymore. But there comes a point when you're eighty-one and should not have to be taking care of your children as if they were five-year-old tiddlywinkies. I'm not even convinced it's making them happy. Electa remembers how it was to be well, which gets in the way of her being happy. Jackie is too out of it to be happy."

I went to one of Charlotte's lunches. Jackie was instantly engaged, intense and full of questions, while Electa was a manatee, vast, slow-moving, benign. Jackie substituted words for no particular reason, calling her car "my visa," for example. She began lunch by reciting Rilke at a breakneck pace and without expression, but when Charlotte asked her to repeat the poems more clearly, she said, "I can't; it's too painful." She told me proudly how she memorized poetry in the bathtub: "I recite to myself in cold water." She talked persuasively about the importance of physical exercise in the treatment of mental illness, then added, "When I play tennis with my sister, I can tell when she's cheating. She has this way of planning for the future. That's cheating."

Then things lapsed into true chaos. When I asked Jackie about her medications, she explained that she couldn't take birth control pills because she didn't want to have varicose veins. "But I don't think any man except my dad's spirit could make me pregnant," she said. "It says so in the Bible that he wrote. I feel responsible, just like Jesus Christ felt responsible when he handed out two thousand cigarettes. They weren't pans of bread. They were cigarettes, in my opinion. That's why she keeps killing my daughters that I had with my dad's spirit. One of them is ten years older than me for some reason. The other one I gave a dollar and twenty-five cents for a soda. I much prefer to have babies off women. Most people don't admit that they're gay, and they are. They're all gay in my opinion."

Then she looked at me closely and suddenly said, "Would you like more cucumbers?" and offered me the dish. I took some more cucumbers. "I really like my day program," she said, "and I have a real connection to poetry, too. I love making art. It's a real pleasure in my life these days." As seamlessly as we had crossed into psychosis, we were back on solid ground. Jackie was clearly unaware of the shift. Charlotte later said, "It comes and goes. It doesn't seem to be much harm to anyone, including her, though it takes some getting used to."

Electa has few intrusive delusions. "If what Jackie has is schizophrenia," Charlotte said, "I am inclined to think Electa is being medicated for an illness she doesn't have. But of course she does, really; it's just such a diffuse condition." Electa's negative symptoms are far more pronounced. "I just feel lethargic," she said. "I have to really psych myself up for grocery shopping. I can only do it once a month. So I eat a lot of stale things." When I asked Electa about the time when she had gone off her meds and been so ill, tears welled up in her eyes. "I wanted to feel high again," she said.

"I'll help you!" Jackie interrupted. "Wait here," she ordered, and ran off to find copies of her own recent poems. One of them was nearly gibberish, but the other contained these lines:

> And when I tried to find the
> lover to show her how much I
> loved her, all I found was
> emptiness and frenzy
> with that loud sound in the
> background drowning out my
> voice every four seconds . . .

The "loud sound" is the intrusive voices, rising relentlessly and constantly over any attempt at a rational mind—and a rational mind wrote this poem, which seems startlingly full of self-knowledge for the work of someone who believed she had conceived four hundred babies with her father. I thought of the Erinyes in pursuit of Orestes, the senseless anguish of a ceaseless, externalized torture. I said to Charlotte, "You do have your hands full."

"Sometimes life isn't about choices," she replied.

When a patient's resolve to continue with a detested medication fails, family members are often the first to notice and intervene—despite the obstacles the patient may devise. The parents' affection always aspires to reawaken a comparable emotion in its object. Like those who have autism, people with schizophrenia are often described as incapable of emotional attachment, but this is seldom true. "The blunted affect or emotional vacancy that's become a stereotype of schizophrenia is not blunted all the time and in many cases is not blunted most of the time," Deborah Levy said. Schizophrenia experts Larry Davidson and David Stayner write, "While perhaps appearing as wooden and vacant to others, and perhaps also feeling at an extreme emotional distance even from themselves, people with schizophrenia continue to describe a fervent wish for love and relationships that contrasts starkly with the empty shell image." Parents would do well to know that to most schizophrenics, a penumbra of affection is reassuring, even if it does not seem to penetrate their isolation.

Patients who have a trusting relationship with someone—a parent, a friend, a doctor—are more likely to take their medication. "About forty to fifty percent of my patients are noncompliant," said Jeanne Frazier, who works primarily with younger patients at McLean. "Sometimes they will come to me and say, 'Dr. Frazier, I'm feeling better and I want to stop my medication.' It becomes very clear with some that if I don't join them in their wish, they are going to do it anyway. So I say, 'I don't think it's the wisest thing to do, because you will run the risk of recurrence. But maybe at this point in your treatment it's important to find out for sure.' Then we come up with a plan to taper their medication by about thirty percent every week. I'll say, 'I want to support you in what you feel needs to happen. But you have to promise that you and/or your parents will page me immediately if you start hallucinating. You need to agree that if that happens, you're going right back on your medication.' I tell the families about the potential for suicidal ideation. Almost all of them have recurrence of symptoms and realize that they really need the medication. It's a learning process. If you really are decompensated, you lose all self-knowledge, but when you are beginning to decompensate, you know that there's something wrong. They become scared. Then, hopefully, they tell me."

The mother of one schizophrenic told me that her son's therapist had him write out a motto and post it on his refrigerator. "It says, 'I am a good person and other people think I'm good, too,' and it has had an enormous effect on him," she said.

George Marcolo had a lot of friends in high school in New Jersey. He had been a pothead in his teens, and in his senior year he took LSD. A few weeks later, he decided to try it again, but instead of taking one tab, he took four. "After that, things sort of felt weird," he recalled. "I think the acid sped up the progress of the disease, which I guess was already in me." In college, George was a brilliant physicist. "He is the smartest person in our family," his father, Giuseppe, said. George remembered, "November first, 1991, when I was at Boston College, I woke up and I felt like I was on acid. I had not taken anything or done anything. That didn't go away for eight years." George went to a doctor on campus, who said that it would pass. At the time, George accepted that; now he is outraged. "If I heard somebody say, 'I feel like I'm on drugs, but I'm not on drugs,' I'd be like, 'We'd better get you checked out.'"

He was loath to tell his parents or friends what was going on. "I was afraid they'd think I was insane. I substituted alcohol and pot for medicine. Everything was amplified. Food tasted really bad. If I had taken meds back then, I could have avoided eight years of that." Despite his symptoms, he kept up a 3.7 average in physics. "But it is progressive," George said. "The voices became more and more prominent." He took a job with a dot-com start-up on Wall Street. After a few months, he stopped going to work, and nothing his parents could say or do would get him to go back. George's parents had divorced when he was in high school, and he was living with his mother, Bridget. She explained to me, "Young men get out of college and somebody has to kick-start them because they don't realize that they are supposed to make a life. I thought he was in an extreme form of that. I was concerned, sometimes exasperated. But I didn't see the real problem." Things grew stranger. "He said he knew what the neighbors were thinking about down the street," Giuseppe recalled. Bridget was bemused. "Still, I didn't think there was psychosis," she said.

The Marcolos insisted that George see a therapist, and after about four months he shared that he had been hearing voices. "I was so frightened that I didn't even think of the word *schizophrenia*," Bridget said. It took some months for the Marcolos to find their way to David Nathan, a Princeton psychiatrist who has worked with people with thought disorders; he instantly recognized the severity of George's illness and put him on medication. George has not had a job since that postcollege stint on Wall Street.

George used to hide pills in the side of his mouth and spit them out when his parents weren't looking. During a relapse, he crashed his car three times. He finally became medication-compliant after a decade. His voices are persistent, but somewhat banal. "Sometimes they say critical things, but I can ignore that," he said. "Some voices are jerks, you know? You end up having the same conversations sometimes, with a new voice that doesn't know what you told the old voices. At first, I thought the voices were people around me. Then I realized that they didn't even do what they said they were going to do. So now, I hear them, I talk to them, but I don't believe they're going to do anything. While I'm talking to you, I can ignore them. The medication has never made them go away, but it makes it easier for me to deal with them. There's some I like to talk to and some that I can't stand. Even though I hate the whole thing, there are some voices I would definitely miss if they went away."

George moved in some years ago with Giuseppe, who has focused his life almost entirely around his middle son. "I wouldn't date because I can't afford other distractions," Giuseppe said. "I have to do what I have to do for George." George's older brother has indicated that he will take care of George when Giuseppe is gone. George, thirty-five when we met, was on clozapine and had regular blood tests. "I'm better than I used to be," he said. "I still get a little paranoid when I'm in public, but I can function. My parents have been very vigilant on my medicines, and they pay good attention to my behavior. I don't do too much. I basically talk to the voices all day long. If Dad's home and I'm going to talk to them, I go in another room. I don't like it when people see me talking to myself, even my father." Giuseppe has found ways to deal with the voices. He said, "George is laughing with them and I say, 'George, cut me in, let me know what everyone's saying,' and we joke a bit about it." Bridget said, "It doesn't seem like a very high-level conversation. Like guys standing on a street corner. It upsets me to hear it, but I take a deep breath and I never tell him to stop."

George sees Dr. Nathan every week, and Giuseppe usually goes along and sits through the session. George likes the arrangement, which saves him the trouble of explaining everything twice, to his father and to his doctor. "There's not much I can do other than take the meds, see the doctor," George said. "Just hope that the bad events keep to a minimum. My situation is obviously stressful for both of my parents, and I know it's not my fault, but I feel bad about it."

Giuseppe said, "I don't care what it's done to me. But I sit in my room and cry because of what he's missing. What life ought to be about, could be about, and isn't about for him." Bridget said, "He's such a wonderful person—decent, kind, gentle. He deserves so much better. At the beginning, I thought, 'He'll never have a normal life.' You just think, 'What is a normal life? Who has a normal life? What are any of us doing here?' I am so proud of my three sons for what they've accomplished. My oldest son, he's so talented and determined. My youngest son, he's so good at what he does. But George is so decent. Look at all he does with this going on in his head. I might be proudest of him."

Emerging with the early-intervention movement is the recovery movement, which proposes biological treatment to address positive symptoms, and psychosocial methods to ameliorate negative and cognitive symptoms. The focus is on improving the quality of life even for those whose clinical condition is poor, emphasizing that impaired people still have capacities that should be maximized. Case management makes certain that even patients who suffer continued psychotic symptoms, erosion of cognitive ability, and social limitations have somebody to handle their health insurance, take them to doctors' appointments, ensure that they have a place to live. Patients are helped in finding a workplace where their deficits are tolerated and supported; some are given rehabilitation training to develop job skills. Social skills training teaches them how to interact with others in more acceptable ways. Patients do computer-based brain exercises that enhance memory, decision-making, and attention. Any way that people can be knitted into the social fabric is precious. One mother whose son had recently been diagnosed described pulling into a gas station and looking at the teenager working the pump. "Two years ago, I would have thought he was living a sad, wasted, pointless life," she said. "Now I thought, 'Oh, if only my son could be like him.'"

Marnie Callahan's sister Nora has long been in constant conversation with Eric Clapton. Nora lived with Marnie for some time, but then one day Marnie came out of her room, eight months pregnant, and found Nora, then twenty-four, standing at the door with scissors in her hands. "I said, 'What are you doing?'" Marnie recalled. "She said, 'I have no idea why I'm here. Who are you?' I picked up the phone, seven o'clock in the morning, and I said, 'Mom, Dad, I'm bringing her home right now.'" In the years that followed, Nora lived with her mother and went on and off her medications until they were no longer fully effective. "Finally my mother had a stroke," Marnie said. "I can't say Nora caused the stroke, because my mother had borderline high blood pressure, but it didn't help. Nora pushed my mother down and broke her shoulder. So I went to the State of Maine and applied for guardianship. I talk to Nora or do some Nora-related thing at least four or five times a day." At fifty-three, Nora is now in assisted housing, but keeps her sister abreast of her exchanges with Eric Clapton. Yet much of who Nora was survives within this troubled and troubling self. "She sees people so clearly," Marnie said. "It's almost as if in our social order we've learned to mask and hide. Schizophrenics cut right through that. For all of her contentiousness and discordant behavior, she's just trying to get by, like all of us. I can't abandon her. I'll visit her in her simple little apartment, and even with all this pain, she still has that fight in her. She still tries to have dignity in every day. A little flower arrangement over here, something pretty there. That little touch of something creative. It doesn't die."

Jeffrey Lieberman, at Columbia University, evinced considerable frustration around how little use is made of the tools we have. "The problem is that people become mental patients in their chronic wasteland, stuck away someplace in their rooms, smoking cigarettes, doing nothing, going to see a doctor for a prescription once a month," he said. "We now have medical and social means to help people. But because of limitations in resources, lack of awareness, and stigma, most people aren't helped." Only a small percentage of people with schizophrenia are refractory—unresponsive to medical treatment—and need permanent hospitalization, he explained. The rest could be managed with acute-care hospitals and adequate community services. "We have people in the hospital whose families don't want or can't take them back, and they can't live independently, and we can't find them a supervised residence. You discharge them to a homeless shelter." In the United States, 150,000 people with schizophrenia are homeless; one in five people with schizophrenia is homeless in any given year. Such people are soon off their meds and back at the hospital for acute care. This serves neither their medical advantage nor the state's economic interest.

The 2008 National Survey on Drug Use and Health reports that cost is the primary barrier to care for serious mental illness. Less than half of schizophrenics in the United States receive outpatient services; a little more than half receive prescription medication; and half of those who go untreated blame cost and insurance issues. When I asked Jean Frazier whether it had been emotionally draining to work with schizophrenic patients, she said, "The thing that makes me emotionally drained is managed care. When I have to fill out yet one more form just to increase the dose of an antipsychotic that's already approved, it really impacts the quality of service I can provide." Treating schizophrenia in the United States costs more than $80 billion a year, expenses that could be controlled with programs of active outreach to patients—most of whom, with supports to stay in appropriate treatment, could avoid both descents into raving hell and the ensuing expensive hospitalizations and incarcerations, largely underwritten by taxpayers. As things work now, it falls to families to organize support groups, construct community centers, create websites, and write memoirs full of advice.

A family member can commit a schizophrenic to institutional care only if he poses an "acute" danger to himself or someone else, and the burden of proof is difficult even though at least one in five schizophrenics will attempt suicide. A schizophrenic man jailed for a misdemeanor after quitting his medication was seen eating feces from the toilet bowl in his cell. On grounds that a person would not die from eating human waste, and that the man was therefore not a danger to himself, the judge refused to commit him. Kenneth Duckworth, a former medical director for the Massachusetts Department of Mental Health, said, "It's harder to get into a state hospital than into Harvard

Medical School." Families are routinely obliged to lie about their relatives' symptoms to obtain services.

Half to two-thirds of people with schizophrenia live with their families or have parents as primary caretakers, but according to a recent survey, only about 3 percent of those families deem it an appropriate arrangement. "The problem is that people burn out, especially because a family member with schizophrenia may not appear to appreciate the enormous amount you do for them," Lieberman explained. The family must be a treatment center, an outpatient unit, a constellation of eyes to watch over, a series of hands to cook or clean or soothe or restrain—in short, an interlocking and yet ceaselessly shifting system of organizations for the patient's discipline or haven. Family members frequently give up or compromise careers to do this work, resulting in economic hardship, and they face the stress of what people in the field call "unrelenting contact" with an ailing relative. Ezra Susser, an epidemiologist in the School of Public Health at Columbia who has worked with indigent schizophrenics, said, "You have to be really careful not to set up a situation where the family feels that they are being compelled, morally, to do more than they really can do." While family involvement improves the lives of schizophrenics, it does not transform them into who they might have been without the illness, and a family's costs in such attentions must be weighed against the benefits that can be achieved.

The World Health Organization recently undertook a vast study to see where the best outcomes were for people with schizophrenia. The best short-term results were in Nigeria and India—where medical treatment is often extremely basic. The reason appears to be the family support structures that are built into those societies. "It was very difficult for me, when I first trained here, to understand how a family could drop off their son or daughter and just leave," said Cyril D'Souza, who is Indian. "If you adjust for everything else—medication, dosages, access to care, socioeconomic status—the ones who are doing well tend to have meaningful family relationships." Whether the kinship structures of developing societies are preferable to Western ones for people in perfect health is debatable, but the division of labor within extended families clearly allows for a higher quality of care for people with mental illnesses. In Senegal, when someone is taken on as an inpatient at a mental hospital, a member of his family usually accompanies him there and stays for as long as he does. Such habits reassure psychotic people that they are permanently knitted into the social fabric.

In the West, conversely, families often disenfranchise schizophrenics. Some people with schizophrenia lack insight into their condition and have to be strong-handled, but others are the primary experts on their own condition, and some have offered their families suggestions on how to interact with them. Support groups for families of people with schizophrenia have proliferated in the last twenty years as the stigma around having produced a mentally ill child has diminished. Esso Leete, founder of the Denver Social Support Group, has schizophrenia and pleads, "Criticize only constructively. Do not write off all conflict as symptomatic of illness. Find a role for us in the family other than being the 'sick' member." One support-group website proposes, "Approach delusions in a spirit of shared inquiry. Don't push if the person starts to get upset."

While the positive symptoms of schizophrenia are most disturbing and striking to outsiders, the negative symptoms are frequently more burdensome for families coping with a son's or daughter's hostility, absence of personal hygiene, and listlessness. It is hard to remember that these are not flaws of character. The father of one schizophrenic said, "My loving, bright, amusing son was now not just very ill, but had also turned distant, cold, bitter, insultingly rude. It would have been easy to dislike him intensely." Twenty-five years later, the father was still struggling with this problem: "How do you keep on loving a son who can be an unpleasant stranger?" One mother said, "These kids die but they never get buried." An activist group called Families of the Mentally Ill Collective, formed by families of schizophrenics in Massachusetts in the early 1980s, stated, "The sick child inhabits a different world and that world, consciously or unconsciously, terrifies the parents." Schizophrenia cannot be cured with encouragement and love alone, but it can be hugely exacerbated by neglect.

Malcolm Tate, a man with severe paranoid schizophrenia, made murderous threats against his family for sixteen years while they tried persistently to find him treatment. He was repeatedly hospitalized, repeatedly released too soon, and would not take medication on his own. Finally, in December 1998, his mother and his sister drove him from their home in South Carolina, and his sister shot him to death by the road, then wept. "I was scared that one day Malcolm was going to lose his mind and harm me and my daughter, and I just didn't know what else to do," she said at her trial. She was sentenced to life in prison.

Rosemary Baglio's family is riddled with schizophrenia. Her uncle came home from World War II a little "touched." He lived with Rosemary's family in Malden, a working-class, Irish suburb of Boston, and as a girl, Rosemary loved to go up to his room. On good days, he would put rolls in the player piano and show the kids Irish step-dancing. On bad days, he would argue with his hallucinations. When Rosemary was in her late twenties, her brother Johnny became psychotic at age seventeen. Rosemary told her mother that something was wrong, but her mother refused to hear it. When Johnny started smashing things, Rosemary was the one who took him to Massachusetts General Hospital. "My mother wouldn't let anyone visit him, other than the family," Rosemary recalled. "We were never to tell anybody he was mental. So Johnny just completely lost contact with everybody."

Rosemary eventually had nine children. Her third, Joe, was the first boy in her family. "He had beautiful auburn hair and soft brown eyes and dimples, and he was just sweet," she said. "Everybody loved Joe." In high school, Joe began to have troubles. His parents thought he was getting into drugs. His grades dropped. He stayed up all night. "Finally when he was seventeen, I told him, 'Daddy and I are taking you to be examined. We have to find out what is going on.' He was terrified." That very day, he had his first real breakdown. "The kitchen had a long pantry with a window at the end of it, and the cabinets were all glass," Rosemary said. "I came home and it was all smashed, and there was blood all over the kitchen ceiling."

Rosemary found him checked into the hospital, with a severed artery in his arm. When she got there, Joey said, "I'm sorry, Ma, I'm sorry." When she wept, he reasoned, "It's better I'm here than any of my sisters." He stayed for a month.

Rosemary was determined not to repeat her mother's imposed isolation of Johnny. "I was very sad, but he was sick and that was it. I was up-front about exactly what was going on." Joey finished high school and found a job in a photography store. Then one day Rosemary got a call that he was running in traffic and screaming incoherently. When he emerged from that hospitalization, Rosemary decided to find him a halfway house, but within a year he was psychotic again. The Tri-City Authority, responsible for mental health services in Malden, insisted that he was not sick enough to be hospitalized because he knew his own name and address. He was living on a barren, rocky slope above Malden; Rosemary wouldn't let him come home because she was afraid he would harm his siblings. "Can you sacrifice the other eight for the one that's sick? He was so gentle underneath that if he ever did hurt somebody, how would he live with that afterwards? I had to protect him, too."

To keep contact, she promised to pay for Joe's cigarettes; she gave him enough money for only one pack at a time, so he had to come by her house every day. "I'd make sure he had something to eat and give him his money, and off he'd go," she said. Her husband, Sal, had been unable to cope with his son's illness; thirty years later, Rosemary insisted that I interview her at her daughter's house because she said her husband would fall apart if he heard her talking about it. "Thanksgiving was coming, and it was really cold," Rosemary told me. "I said to the court clerk, 'You have to get me in to see the judge today.'" Meanwhile, Rosemary told Joe that he'd have to pick up his cigarette allowance at the courthouse. She pulled him in front of the judge. "There were no soles on his sneakers. He was dirty from lying on the ground all night. I said to the judge, 'Could you serve Thanksgiving to anybody, knowing your son is living like this?' The judge committed him."

After his condition was stabilized, he was released to Sal's octogenarian parents in Somerville, five miles away. To maintain good mental health, Joe needed to have daily injections of Prolixin in Malden. "He went the first day by bus from Somerville to Malden," Rosemary said. "He waited, he waited, nobody there. Got on the bus, went back to Somerville. For three days he went, but the person was out sick, and nobody told us. Joey never got his shots. The fourth day he started hallucinating. He went in the backyard at Sal's father's, crawling on the ground like an animal. My father-in-law comes out on the back porch. He says, 'Joey, you come in and Grandpa will help you.'" Joey attacked his grandfather so savagely that he had to have brain surgery; if he'd died, Joey would have been charged with murder. Joey was committed to one year at Bridgewater State Hospital for the mentally ill.

"Oh, he was sick," Rosemary said. "Then they realized his days on insurance had run out. The very next day he was miraculously cured, and he was going to come home. I said, 'If any harm comes to anybody because of what you're doing today, I'm taking you to court and I'm going to sue you for every penny this place is worth.'" Joey was transferred to another hospital, and he eventually got well enough to leave. By this time, he was in his mid-twenties. Rosemary was open to having Joe at home again, but if she took him in, he would lose services given only to those with no place to go. She finally installed him in a halfway house with his uncle Johnny. In his later years, he devoted himself to taking pictures of the other residents, images striking both for the desolation they portray and for the kindness with which they portray it. He also drew, a skill he'd had since childhood. His primary psychiatrist still has a picture Joey drew hanging in her office, an ink sketch of himself. "You have to really look closely," she said when I saw it, "but there's another man in Joe's ear. That's the voices whispering to him."

On April 5, 2007, Johnny choked on a piece of meat and died. Two days later, Joey was diagnosed with lung cancer. "As soon as he was diagnosed, we moved him right home, consequences be damned,"

Rosemary said, weeping. "Every day he had chemo. They found it in his brain, started another kind of chemo. Then it was back in the lung. And he never complained. Joey said to me, 'Ma, it looks like I'm not going to make it.' He says, 'Ma, if I'm fighting, let me fight. But if I'm slipping away, please let me slip away.' That's what happened. He just slipped away right with me sitting there." Johnny and Joe are buried side by side.

When I met Sal, Joey had been dead for six months, and Sal was a shadow of a man. He was down to 112 pounds, gaunt and sorrowful. Rosemary was overflowing with her story, but Sal's sadness had turned him entirely inward. "Can I make Sal better?" Rosemary asked. "No. Can I make him want to live? No. I have been fighting for Joey for thirty-two years, I've been protecting him and fighting for him every inch of the way. And I couldn't save him. I couldn't save him."

Six months before Johnny choked, Rosemary had put her parents' house, where she had grown up, into an irrevocable trust. "I did it in case the halfway house didn't keep going, so that if those two were alive and we weren't, they would never be on the street. It's set up now so that if any of my grandchildren develop this, which is likely, they cannot become homeless. We're just waiting to see who's next."

Schizophrenic self-advocacy is different from Deaf rights or LPA politics or neurodiversity because members of those movements are presumed to have an accurate understanding of themselves. They are often accused of not appreciating mainstream reality; dwarfs cannot really know what it's like to be tall, and people with autism may not conceive of the pleasures of social intelligence. Their comprehension of their own circumstances, however, is usually sound. The defining quality of schizophrenia is that it entails delusion, which complicates its claims on identity. Are people who gain a sense of coherence from their schizophrenia achieving self-acceptance, or are they in a web of denial that is a symptom of their illness? Schizophrenics' own decisions are complicated by *anosognosia*: having as a symptom of your illness the belief that you don't have an illness. In the Jacobean play *The Honest Whore*, Thomas Dekker writes, "That proves you mad, because you know it not."

Schizophrenic self-advocacy raises awkward ontological questions. Is there a self that is more real than a patient's own current experience, a true self that can be teased apart from the symptomatic one? "We should not be in the business of choosing selves," Elyn Saks has written in her memoir of her schizophrenia. One father said, "I thought my son's getting better would mean that he didn't hear the voices. His getting better only means that he doesn't listen to them as much." I sometimes think that the emphasis on insight among psychotic people is like our focus on contrition among criminals. Self-awareness and remorse imply that aberrant people are more like us than their actions suggest, and that consoles us. But they serve little advantage unless they change behavior. Though intelligence is in general associated with better life outcomes for people with schizophrenia who survive it, schizophrenics with higher IQ are more likely to commit suicide than those with lower IQ; insight begets lower self-esteem and more depression, even for those who do better at some kinds of self-care. Further, those who are delusional are less likely to commit suicide than those whose delusions have gone away—even though some schizophrenics commit suicide because of command hallucinations. This insight that mainstream society wishes upon people with schizophrenia allows them to act in accordance with what the world expects. But it shouldn't be misconstrued. "You have no idea how many people you interact with who are hearing voices, but have the insight not to pay attention to them," John Krystal said. "I'm in awe of the patients I see, many of whom are functioning incredibly well despite constant hallucinations. Understanding what's going on saves them. But it doesn't make them happy."

A recent *New Yorker* article described Linda Bishop, a woman with psychosis whose hospital records said that she was "extremely bright" and "very pleasant," and "denies completely that she has an illness." She refused to sign any paperwork that said she was mentally ill. The article explains, "When psychotic, she saw herself as the heroine in a tale of terrible injustice, a role that gave her confidence and purpose." Linda eventually starved herself to death in an abandoned house, believing she was doing the Lord's will, and apparently at peace inside her own madness—happier, in many ways, than Krystal's wiser patients.

The Mad Pride movement believes that self-determination is a basic human right that should be extended to people with schizophrenia and other mental illnesses. Bringing together people who are afflicted with psychosis, it builds a feeling of horizontal identity among people who may have little other community. Members seek to minimize reliance on psychotropic medications and take control of their own healing; Judi Chamberlin, one of the first activists, said, "If it isn't voluntary, it isn't treatment." Gabrielle Glaser wrote in the *New York Times*, "Just as gay-rights activists reclaimed the word *queer* as a badge of honor rather than a slur, these advocates proudly call themselves mad; they say their conditions do not preclude them from productive lives." Mad Pride has inspired events all over the globe, including recent demonstrations in Australia, South Africa, and the USA that have drawn both supporters and voyeuristic members of the public. An organizer for the Asheville Radical Mental Health Collective, a Mad Pride group in North Carolina, said, "It used to be you were labeled with your diagnosis and if people found out, it was a death sentence, professionally and socially. We are hoping to change all that by talking."

Mad Pride proponents advocate a wide range of health-promoting practices. David W. Oaks, who heads MindFreedom International and who has a diagnosis of schizophrenia, treats his condition with exercise, peer counseling, diet, and treks in the wilderness; he has refused medication and exhorts others to defy the psychiatric establishment. Of the period when he was forcibly medicated as a young man, he said, "They took a wrecking ball to the cathedral of my mind." Of his work since then, he said, "The human spirit is eccentric and unique and unconquerable and bizarre and unstoppable and wonderful. So this is really about reclaiming what it is to be human in the face of so-called normality." Sally Zinman of the California Network of Mental Health Clients said, "David is like the Malcolm X of the psychiatric survivor movement. He's out there speaking the truth in all its rawness and purity."

Oaks has brought the eye of the establishment to his cause; when he organized a hunger strike to protest the biological model of mental illness, the American Psychiatric Association met with the strikers, but found no middle ground and ultimately released a statement that said, "It is unfortunate that in the face of remarkable scientific and clinical progress, a small number of individuals and groups persist in questioning the reality and clinical legitimacy of disorders that affect the mind, brain, and behavior." More recently the antipharmaceutical activist Peter Breggin has pursued a campaign against the use of antipsychotics, saying, "The apparent improvement that patients show is actually a disability, a loss of mental capacity."

It is preposterous, even sentimental, to deny the biological nature of mental illness—or, indeed, the biological nature of mental health, however such a state is defined. But it would be unfortunate to dismiss David Oaks and Sally Zinman as merely crazy. Their relationship to Foucault and Laing is like Thomas Jefferson's to Rousseau, or Lenin's to Karl Marx. Ideas are the precondition of action, but the philosophers who hatch new concepts rarely put them into practice. Mad Pride represents the literalization of the old saw about the lunatics taking over the asylum. These activists believe they are throwing off a yoke of oppression. They both have a serious illness and have suffered tyrannical subjugation; the question is whether they can address the subjugation without making false claims about the nature of mental health.

Although most Mad Pride advocates criticize the manner in which medical professionals promote drugs as a primary treatment for mental illness, many rely on these drugs to function and support the right of others to choose for themselves whether to take medication. They insist that more can be done to mitigate side effects for those who must take such medications. Other activists speak of being "pro-choice" about drugs. Pharmacological treatments for schizophrenia carry risk of neurological impairment, metabolic dysfunction, long-term toxicity, diabetes, blood disorders, and rapid weight gain. Many people who initially experience their mental illness as a cataclysmic loss may make private decisions about how much treatment is worth how much side effect. The activist Will Hall has written in his *Harm Reduction Guide to Coming off Psychiatric Drugs & Withdrawal*, "In a culture polarized between the pro-medication propaganda of pharmaceutical companies and the anti-medication agenda of some activists, we offer a harm reduction approach to help people make their own decisions."

The British novelist Clare Allan wrote, "There seems to be some sort of agreement, a contract you sign when you first break down, that should you ever emerge from your madness and re-enter the 'normal' world, you promise never to mention what took place. The stigma attached to mental ill-health robs people of their experience, effectively tells them that for months or for years, or recurrently (as is often the case), they didn't exist at all. Is it any wonder groups such as Mad Pride find a need to address the issue of self-esteem?" Like other pride movements chronicled in this book, this one supports people with an intractable condition in their feelings of wholeness and worth. It emphasizes the cultivation of good self-care practices to support physical and emotional well-being. Rather than harkening back to a prepsychotic state, Mad Pride activists focus on concrete steps that mentally ill people can take to build a present life that is both functional and truthful. Responding to Allan, one online commentator said, "According to my doctor, I'm mad. I'm also proud of who I am and it's daft to pretend that my madness isn't part of that." The Icarus Project website explains, "We are a network of people living with and/or affected by experiences that are often diagnosed and labeled as psychiatric conditions. We believe these experiences are mad gifts needing cultivation and care, rather than diseases or disorders."

Much can be said for accepting yourself with whatever conditions you carry, but the obstacles to doing so are particularly formidable for schizophrenics. Some whom I met had found meaning in the condition, but none seemed particularly exultant about it. Despite moving statements made by advocates, Mad Pride does not have anything like the reach of the autism rights movement. I suspect that is partly because the agony can be so relentless in schizophrenia, but even more because of the illness's late onset. People with autism cannot imagine themselves or be imagined without it; it is intrinsic to their character. People with schizophrenia can imagine themselves without it because most didn't have it for the first two decades of their lives. If they posit "wellness," they are conceptualizing not an inaccessible fiction, but a familiar past. Mad Pride is positive for those who subscribe to it, and it has robust philosophical implications, but most people who descend into psychosis experience it, until negative symptoms and antipsychotics numb them, as a torment.

Clare Allan, having recognized the need for Mad Pride, said, "People have to play the cards they're dealt, and they become who they are through doing so. But would anybody seriously wish for their child to develop mental health problems? Their partner? Their friends? The reality I recognize from my experience, and from that of my friends and what I've seen on the wards, is hopelessness and despair." Alison Jost, of Yale's Interdisciplinary Center for Bioethics, wrote that it seems easy to compare Mad Pride with disability rights. "But in fact," she went on, "no matter how destigmatized our society becomes, mental illnesses will always cause suffering."

Walter Forrest's son Peter lapsed into schizophrenia his junior year in high school, arguing with his siblings so aggressively that he had to be physically restrained. "It was like the top of his head blew off," Walter said. "He'd always been Mr. Popularity, and then he had some minor social adjustment problems, and now we were wrestling him to the ground." A few weeks later in the car, Peter said, "Dad, don't hold the steering wheel that way, or I'm getting out." Walter was perplexed. "Peter had an offbeat sense of humor, so I was groping," he said. "A few days later, Peter found his way to the shrink's office at his school and melted down into total helplessness."

Peter rapidly developed acute illness. His father noted a greater loss every day. One night, Peter ambushed his father and tried to push him through a window. Eventually, Peter attacked Walter with a kitchen knife, and Walter had to call the police. Peter was put in a secure ward for six months. Like most parents, Walter struggled with the gradual realization that his son's problems were not transient. Walter explained, "The therapist who helped the most said, 'You've had the star quarterback. He's run over by a truck, breaks every limb in his body. Your hope now is not that he'll be a star quarterback, but that he will walk again.'" Peter is now in a residential facility, and he comes to see his father four times a year. "I take him to dinner, and he has a sleepover and goes back," Walter said. "Is there any positive in the relationship? Does it have its pleasurable moments? No. I would love him to do a minimum-wage job, bag groceries or something, and feel that he's done something to give himself worth. But the better he gets, it's almost the worse he gets, the sadder it is—because the 'might have been' just breaks your heart. Frankly, it would have been better if he'd died. Better for him, better for everybody. That sounds like the most terrible thing in the world to say. But his life is very, very hard for him, and it's hard on everyone else. Why didn't the truck just crush him completely if it was going to do this kind of damage?"

Walter looked for a long minute out the window. "And now I'm going to cry. You know, it *is* a death. Joy is one of the few gifts we can give to our fellow human beings, especially our children, and I haven't been able to give any to Peter."

People with schizophrenia are avoided, mocked, and misunderstood. Little progress has been made to reduce the stigmatizing use of terms such as *crazy*, *lunatic*, and *nutty*. When *One Flew Over the Cuckoo's Nest*, the film that shaped a generation's perceptions of schizophrenia, was filmed at Oregon State Hospital in 1975, the producers had the opportunity to use actual mental patients as extras, but declined because they "did not look strange enough to match the public image of mentally ill people." Though the Americans with Disabilities Act is supposed to shield the mentally ill, few protections are available to them. The number of both outpatient programs and in-hospital facilities is woefully inadequate, yet circumstances under which people with schizophrenia can live independently are also scarce. An American study from 1990 showed that 40 percent of landlords immediately rejected applicants with a known psychiatric disorder. People who are open about their schizophrenia are essentially unemployable, even if they have been asymptomatic for years. Only about 10 to 15 percent of them sustain full-time employment, but the structures of work can prove enormously beneficial; one leading researcher has noted, "No treatment I have seen is as effective as a job." Homeowners fight hard to keep treatment and residential facilities out of their neighborhoods. James Beck of the NIMH put it bluntly: "Many people can't tolerate working with chronic schizophrenics. Doctors and nurses don't like to treat patients who don't recover."

Although they are erratic in their behavior, most people with schizophrenia are not dangerous to strangers. Schizophrenics are five to eighteen times as likely to commit homicide as are members of the general population, usually in connection with substance abuse; even including substance users, however, only 0.3 percent will commit homicide. A 1998 study found rates of violence in psychiatric patients who are not substance abusers consistent with those in the general population, and such violence is five times more likely to be directed at family members. Almost one in four families living with schizophrenic relatives experiences physical harm or the threat of it. Nonetheless, because schizophrenic violence may respond to hallucinations and be directed at random strangers, it has the same dark-hand-of-fate feeling as plane crashes, which frighten us so much more than fatal car accidents even though they are considerably rarer.

In 2011, two cases of homicide by people with schizophrenia made headlines: Deshawn James Chappell's murder of Stephanie Moulton, a social worker who was caring for him; and Jared L. Loughner's spree in Arizona, during which he killed six people and wounded thirteen others, including US Representative Gabrielle Giffords, who was severely injured. Both men were thought to be potentially violent before these incidents took place, and both stories give evidence of a failed system.

When Deshawn Chappell was growing up, his mother, Yvette, thought he would be a minister. At nineteen, he changed. "He would say the devil was telling him to do things," Yvette recalled. "He would talk about curses and hexes." By twenty-one, he was constantly showering because his skin was crawling; he couldn't sleep because voices kept him awake. He nonetheless refused medication because of its side effects. Not until after his fifth arrest for assault was he referred to the Department of Mental Health. That arrest, in November 2006, was occasioned after Deshawn's stepfather, who had raised him, let him go from a job. Deshawn fractured three bones in his stepfather's left eye socket. The police report said that when officers arrived, the stepfather was "holding his head with a cloth and had blood running from his mouth."

Despite Deshawn's violent criminal record, he was passed around the state from facility to facility and ultimately placed in a group home where no one on staff was fully informed of his history. Stephanie Moulton, a petite young woman, was left on her own to care for seven people with schizophrenia because the budget didn't allow for additional support. The system failed her and her assailant. On January 20, 2011, Deshawn Chappell beat Stephanie Moulton, stabbed her to death, and left her seminude body in the parking lot of a church. "It was totally unnecessary for her to get murdered on the job when all she was trying to do was help people," her mother said. Yvette Chappell expressed deep sympathy for Stephanie's family. She explained that she had tried to get treatment for her son for years.

Unlike Deshawn Chappell, Jared Loughner had never been in tutionalized. But before his rampage at a Tucson supermarket whe Representative Giffords was holding a meet and greet, dozens of peo ple knew of his instability. His behavior at Pima College the previous year had become increasingly bizarre and threatening; the police were called to deal with him on five occasions. In an e-mail months before the shoot-out, a fellow student said, "We have a mentally unstable person in the class that scares the living crap out of me. He is one of those whose picture you see on the news, after he has come into class with an automatic weapon."

In September 2010, Jared Loughner was suspended from school and told he could not return until he had a mental health clearance. "It seemed obvious that he had mental problems," one of his professors told the *Wall Street Journal*. "He was speaking language X and everyone else was speaking language Y." Two months after his suspension, Jared bought a gun. Two months after that, he rampaged. His parents, with whom he lived, said only, "We don't understand why this happened."

Larry A. Burns of federal district court judged Jared mentally unfit to stand trial in May 2011, four months after his attack. The *New York Times* reported, "Mr. Loughner, 22, rocked back and forth in his chair during the proceedings, buried his face in his hands midway through and interrupted the judge with an outburst. 'She died right in front of me. You're treasonous.'" The psychiatrist appointed by the court found that Jared "experienced delusions, bizarre thoughts, and hallucinations." Burns would eventually put him on forced medication; his lawyers argued, "Mr. Loughner has a due-process right to bodily integrity free of unwanted, forcible administration of psychiatric medication." An appeals court took him off medication; Jared went fifty hours without sleeping, paced until he had open sores on his feet, and stopped eating. The prison restarted medication on grounds that he was a danger to himself, and Burns upheld their right to do so.

Jared was put back on medication on grounds that he was a danger to himself, but if he could be rendered competent to stand trial, the judicial consequences could be lethal. Cynthia Hujar Orr, a past president of the National Association of Criminal Defense Lawyers, asked, "Is it ethical and proper to help someone regain competence just to go after them for a death penalty offense or a murder offense?" A prison psychologist said that Jared sobbed uncontrollably whenever she met with him and covered his face. He ultimately pleaded guilty to avoid the death penalty, but his crime and illness constitute a punishment greater than any achieved by the criminal justice system. Jared Loughner, like Deshawn Chappell, is undoubtedly in sustained agony.

The facility containing the largest number of schizophrenics in the United States is the Los Angeles County Jail. At least three times as many mentally ill people are in jail as are in hospitals. Nearly 300,000 people with mental illnesses are in jail in the United States, most convicted of crimes they would not have committed if they had been treated; another 550,000 are on probation. Few are in for violent crimes; most are there for the myriad small transgressions that are inevitable for people impervious to social reality. They are dealt with not by doctors, but by police officers—and then prison guards and other criminals. A quarter of Massachusetts inmates required mental health treatment in 2011, up from 15 percent in 1998, according to the Department of Correction.

If one weighs the savings to the mental health system against the added burdens to the penal system, the penny-wise, pound-foolish nature of such budgeting becomes ludicrously obvious. The cases against Deshawn Chappell and Jared Loughner will cost the taxpayers hundreds of thousands of dollars. One can't help but wonder whether, for a fraction of that cost, their victims might still be living. While accommodating people with physical disabilities must be undertaken out of moral conviction, adequately treating people with severe psychiatric illness is a win-win situation; if moral conviction fails, economic self-interest should prevail.

"When other little girls were trying on their mothers' high heels, I was wrapping myself with Ace bandages, 'cause I thought it looked cool," Susan Weinreich recalled. Susan had a compulsion to bite her lips, and they were usually scabbed or openly bleeding. Ashamed, she would say to her mother, Bobbe Evans, "Why can't I stop?" Bobbe would just say, "You'll grow out of it." But schizophrenia did not manifest fully until Susan entered the Rhode Island School of Design (RISD) in 1973.

"I knew there was something wrong all along," Susan said, "but it wasn't until my freshman year that it became obvious to other people." During Susan's freshman year, her father left her mother. "That jostled everything enough so that symptoms started to bubble to the surface," Susan said. Unable to do her classwork, she began seeing a Freudian psychoanalyst, whose treatment involved regression to childhood states. Unfortunately, regression was one of Susan's symptoms, and she needed to move away from it, not deeper into it. "I was horribly dependent on him," she said. "I basically stayed in during the day and came out only at night, when I walked the streets and studied the moon. I saw deformed bodies; bloody faces; devils; bodies hanging from trees.

The real people I saw all appeared distorted. They were missing arms, legs. I remember being very threatened by stains in the asphalt, and plastic bags caught in the bushes in January."

In her sophomore year, Susan entered RISD's glass-blowing department. "I had an intense need to be around fire," she said. In the first semester of her junior year, the school asked that she withdraw. "I just was imploding, burning myself with cigarettes and putting my fists through windows. In my better moments, I would go to the Brown medical library, looking, looking, looking for what was wrong with me." Susan had three separate hospitalizations that year. The doctors would explain that she needed to be on medication for the rest of her life, but wouldn't tell her what was wrong with her; she, in turn, refused to give the hospital the contact information for her parents. "Even though I had no understanding of what was happening, I had a very strong, *strong* desire to protect my family. I believed that I had baby breasts and adult breasts, and that the baby breasts were going to drop off, and the adult breasts would take their place. But I believed that if my mother came to my apartment and stayed overnight, these little men and women were going to come out of my breasts. The men were carrying scythes, and the women were carrying burlap bags. They would hurt her. I was afraid my mother would see them, which meant she would know about the devil in me. I couldn't tolerate that."

When she took in her brother's cat while he was traveling the summer following her sophomore year, the animal hid under an old, green vinyl reclining chair. "I thought the chair was infested with fleas, and then the fleas became sperm. I took out a bucket of paint and painted the whole chair white and took out a kitchen knife and started stabbing it." She didn't bathe for months on end and didn't brush her teeth for ten years. "I was like an animal, my hair knotted and greasy. I would cut myself and paint on the walls with my blood."

Bobbe had never heard the word *schizophrenia* until Susan's analyst called in 1979 to find out what kind of insurance Susan had, because he had finally decided that she needed to be hospitalized, perhaps for life. "That snapped my mother into something," Susan said, "and she came up to Rhode Island, threw me in the car, and tore me away from this guy." Bobbe took Susan to a doctor who said she should be hospitalized at once. Susan had developed facial hair, possibly in response to medication, and decided to let it grow. "When I saw this daughter, who I wanted to be this cute little thing, with hair on her face, it was just horrible," Bobbe said. Susan said, "I had all kinds of delusions about what that meant. It was down to my jawbone, and it was very thick, coarse, sexual hair." Bobbe decided to take Susan directly to Four inds Hospital in Katonah, the best mental facility within easy driving distance. Susan was interviewed by Sam Klagsbrun, who ran the hospital. "I can still remember sitting in his office that day, and I even remember the Stars of David I had carved into my boots and drawn on my green shirt," Susan said. "The cigarette burns in it. He told me what was wrong with me. He gave me my diagnosis." Susan was admitted to Four Winds.

Susan's father had by now disappeared from her life completely; soon, Bobbe remarried. "I wanted *my* life to go on," Bobbe said. "To my friends, I just said, 'Susan is having a problem, and the divorce kind of triggered it.' I really wanted her out of my life, and I felt relief because somebody was taking her off my hands. I'm not proud of saying that, but it's how I remember feeling. I wish I had known someone like present-day Susan when she was so sick, because it would have given me such hope. But there was nobody."

Susan was at Four Winds for four months, then out, then back for another six, and eventually at a halfway house where she stayed for nine months in 1980 before moving back home, age twenty-four. "I would come home from work," Bobbe said, "and she would be lurking somewhere, not answering when I called her. Sam Klagsbrun said, 'You have to tell her to leave.' I said, 'But how can I?' He said, 'Just tell her that you would do anything in the world for her if she were making progress, but that this isn't helping her.' So I told her she had to leave. That was probably the hardest thing I ever had to do in my life." Bobbe wept. "She left, after writing a note that she was going to kill herself. Then she called Sam and went back to Four Winds."

Susan's accounts of Four Winds are rhapsodic: "It was a psychiatric utopia. There were ducks running around, and a chicken coop. I would spend my days in the pine forest. If an insurance company heard that today, they'd freak. Sam's treatment was incredible. I was an infant. He cuddled me; he hugged me. He picked me up out of a pothole in the pouring rain." Klagsbrun had started a hospice program—for nonpsychiatric patients with terminal physical illness—in the lodge where the psychotic patients lived. "You take someone like myself, who was clearly psychotic and not living in reality, and you face them with the biggest reality, which is death," Susan said. "Even in my confusion, I understood it on some level, and it shocked reality back into me. Here I am, actively self-destructive, and yet these people wanted to live so desperately. It made me ask *the* question, which is, do you want to live or die? I realized I wanted to move towards life."

Susan's emotional life began to revive. "I remember the first time I felt love, after all that. I don't even remember who it was—probably

Sam. I just started feeling what it felt like to love someone. I don't remember it being ecstatic; I just remember it feeling like when I would go fishing as a young girl, and a sunfish would catch the hook. Just that tug on the other end of the line. After all those years of being so isolated within myself and so disconnected, the medication sucked out some of the symptoms, and as the psychosis receded, it left room for my heart to grow. There were other psychotic episodes that followed, and I wasn't experiencing love too much during those. But during each remission, my experience of empathy and connectedness just expanded." Susan had continued to make art, and Klagsbrun adapted a little outbuilding for her to use as a studio. "My work has a dark side," she said, "but it's about creativity, and creativity is about giving life."

When Susan graduated from her most intensive treatment phase, she accepted a job at the hospital, which came with benefits, and her insurance paid for electrolysis to remove her facial hair. She was twenty-six years old. "Preparing for the larger world was still a tall order," she said. "I didn't know who the president was. My ego was like Swiss cheese. I was still having a lot of catastrophic visions. I didn't know the first thing about taking care of myself physically." She began seeing a therapist, Xenia Rose, and stayed with her for twenty years. "She had me write up a schedule. It had 'get up' and 'brush teeth' because I had no idea what a day was supposed to look like." Rose agreed to see Bobbe as well. "That was enormously helpful to me," Bobbe said, "because I had to just cry and say what I thought. But Susan's illness was not me; it was her. When I started to let go, she started to emerge."

By the time she was in her late thirties, Susan was reasonably stable. Zyprexa had "revolutionized" her life. She slept thirteen hours a night, but was coherent. Eventually, she switched to Abilify, which was less sedating. "I grow like lightning," Susan said. "What you see here today is a completely different soul than I was five years ago: developmentally, physically, visually, verbally. I've worked very hard, on every level, at eradicating every remnant of the illness. Intermittently, I have little things trigger here and there, but they only last a day or two. Sensory overstimulation, a bit of paranoia, misperceptions and distortions in my thinking and visual world. Some people get stressed and their back goes out. I get stressed and my mind goes out. But then it comes back."

Of all the things that required catching up, perhaps the most challenging was romance. At the time I met Susan, she was nearly fifty and had not yet had a full sexual experience. "I'd like to experience love. But do I know what love is? So far, my mother's it." Susan laughed. "My poor mother. She signed me up for three different dating services, simultaneously. It was grueling. But I looked at it as a way to grow developmentally. The schizophrenia has given me the ability to find something inside of me, parts of myself that I might not have been able to reach otherwise."

Susan has also attempted to reconnect with her long-absent father. One day she told me she had just spoken to him on the phone, for the first time in decades. "I told him that I loved him," she said. "It felt right to say that, despite his abandonment of me. I had written him a letter because he was turning eighty, and I thought I would free him from some guilt. I wanted him to know that he gave me the one tool I needed to climb out, which is my art, because he nurtured my creativity. He called after a week. We had a very superficial conversation about clamming or whatever he does down there, and then he became a little weepy, and he blurted out, 'I'll never forgive myself for walking out on all of you.' It took all I had to hold me back from jumping in my car and driving down there. But I decided not to call again. We have too much in common."

Bobbe eventually came to accept, understand, and finally be proud of her daughter. She works in the travel industry and gives all her earnings to Susan. In turn, Susan has donated most of the proceeds of her sales of her rich, strange, beautiful art to Four Winds. She has taken up public speaking. Bobbe heard Susan address a mental health dinner at Grand Central Station. "I couldn't believe it. There were like three hundred people there—and this is *Susan*. I mean, how did this happen?" Bobbe said. Susan's relationship with Bobbe is almost completely resolved. "She's definitely a stronger person than I've ever been," Bobbe said. "What saved her? It was her art; it was Dr. Klagsbrun; it was the support from her brothers and me. But most of all, it was Susan. There was something in Susan that always wanted to come to the surface. I deserve a medal. I really do. But Susan deserves lots of medals. I feel really bad that she had to go through what she went through. But I also recognize that if she hadn't, she wouldn't be who she is today. And who she is today is the most wonderful, charming, beautiful woman. She used to say, 'It's the cards you have dealt to you, Mom.' I think what I've finally come to terms with is that if you learn to live with things that aren't pleasant, then, suddenly, sometimes, they are."

The delusions of people with schizophrenia are not always cruel. "My son was doing the crossword," one mother told me, "and he was really mad because the voices kept giving him the answers." A young Indian man described his unusually affirmative delusions to me: "I would hear the leaves whispering love poems to me." Another man said, "I wish I could find a medication that would make the horrible voices go away and leave the ones I love." The relationship to the voices can be mediated by affection or even just urgency. A San Francisco mother said, "Even though they're not nice, they are his friends. It's private, and he understands them. His psychiatrist told him to be friendly to the voices and talk to them as though they were children."

Though schizophrenia was described in the ancient world and named a century ago, its mysteries continue to facilitate misconceptions. Michael Foster Green, professor in the UCLA Department of Psychiatry, writes, "When an illness is viewed as inexplicable and impenetrable, people tend to react to it with one of two extremes: either they *stigmatize* it or they *romanticize* it. It's hard to know which is worse." Someone who has never had a third-degree burn may not know what one feels like, but having had a first-degree burn, he can somewhat conceive of that pain; depression is an extreme version of commonplace feelings. Schizophrenia is fundamentally different. The German existentialist psychiatrist Karl Jaspers has identified "an abyss of difference" between psychosis and normal thought. The schizophrenic often cannot retrieve the language he knows, but even if he could, there is no appropriate language for him to use. We can understand the horrors of psychosis only at the level of metaphor.

Anyone who loves his schizophrenic brother or son or daughter or friend knows that this person, though afflicted with a betraying genome, is also the sum of his experiences. In his book about his brother's illness, Jay Neugeboren writes, "For paid professionals to act as if Robert were merely a vessel of flesh in which (bad) chemicals somehow rose up once upon a time and made him ill, and in which other (good) chemicals must now be poured, deprives Robert of what he still possesses in abundance: his humanity. How not cry out against any and all attempts, when it comes to human beings with lives like Robert's, to reduce their humanity to their biology?" Andy Behrman, a writer with bipolar disorder, explained, "Mental illness cannot be treated separately from the person; they are inextricably linked. I've answered the question 'Where does mental illness end and where do I begin?' In my case, we are one. I've made friends with the enemy. My treatment is successful precisely because it takes both me and my disorder into account and doesn't delineate between the two of us."

Sometimes, we adduce retrospective wisdom from medication response. If you improved on Depakote, you must have had bipolar illness. If Zyprexa made you all better, you were probably schizophrenic. Useful though these agents are, however, work on them is still inconsistent, tangled in unproved theories, preoccupied with neurotransmitters that play an opaque role in illness. Reductive thinking about the nature of mental illness—the suggestion that it can be fully described by chemistry—satisfies those who fund research, and that research may help sufferers. It is also dishonest. Schizophrenia has no margins; it becomes what it invades.

Classic schizophrenia is a horrible illness, but knowing what you or your child has can be weirdly comforting; classification builds identity. There is a community of people who have or treat the illness. But this condition operates in fine and sometimes bewildering gradations. Psychoanalyst Richard C. Friedman, who worked on the drafting of the *DSM-III*, said, "The problem in psychiatric diagnosis is that we have gone from an analog to a digital model, in which things are matters not of complex degrees but of a lot of 'yes' and 'no' that are like '0' and '1.' There are many practical advantages to classifying people, but clinical experience shows that isn't how the mind works. You have to deal with many layers of continuous phenomena."

No one has ever been able to say quite what is wrong with Sam Fischer. I met him when he was thirty-three through a psychiatrist who was treating him for schizophrenia, but another clinician produced a diagnosis of Asperger's. Sam clearly has a mood disorder, with periods of intense depression and occasional bouts of hypomania, a nonpsychotic but excessive feeling of worth and power. His manipulative social interactions suggest borderline personality disorder. He has anxiety and phobias, signs of obsessive-compulsive and narcissistic personality disorders, and a long-running post-traumatic stress disorder. He presents, in short, a perfect multitude of psychiatric symptoms assembled in one brain as though for a gala reunion. "Nobody really understands me," he said. "I'm too weird for that."

Sam was born jaundiced at less than five pounds, even though he was at term. He wouldn't eat. The doctors worried that he was slipping away, and his parents, Patricia and Winston, spent Sam's early life at Children's Hospital of Philadelphia, where doctors looked for brain tumors and kidney diseases. Sam also had scoliosis and an undescended testicle that would have to be surgically removed. He never crawled and started walking late. On early standardized tests, he was, his mother recalled, "a linguistic genius, and practically retarded when it came to doing puzzles."

In kindergarten, Sam saw his first psychiatrist, who said he was "walking along the edge of an abyss." In elementary school, Sam couldn't do math, and he couldn't write or draw because coordination eluded him. Patricia remembered, "Winston and I said to each other, 'There are calculators now. What does it matter that he can't do sports or drawing?' Sam talked in complete and flowing paragraphs. At a florist shop, he'd name every really obscure plant. To us, that was wonderful; it should have been a sign that something was not wonderful. We were sure the strengths would outweigh the weaknesses, though the experts told us repeatedly that the deficits overpower the strengths for most people."

In fifth grade, some older boys tied Sam to a fence and left him screaming for twenty-five minutes before a teacher discovered him. He was kicked down the stairs on more than one occasion. His parents switched him into public special ed, but he didn't fit in there, either. "It was as if Sam had dyslexia in reverse; he could read and decode things without trouble, but he couldn't do anything else," Patricia said.

Sam had realized that he was gay, but was still intensely closeted in high school. Then something happened in the bathroom at school. Sam described it as "attempted rape" and said bitterly, "This bitch guidance counselor said, 'He's a senior and you are only a junior so we're not going to do anything about it.' That pretty much ruined my life." While Sam feels the episode was underplayed, his father feels it was overplayed. Winston explained that someone exposed himself and came on to Sam. Whatever happened, Sam was traumatized and began to hear voices. He said, "They were voices from my enemies at high school, and I actually went from being very peaceful to very warlike."

His family took him to a psychiatrist, but Sam did not have a flying start with medication. "Moban didn't do any good," Winston said. "Ativan helped. Risperdal, a disaster; it screwed up his coordination. Prolixin, a fiasco; he had the dry heaves all the time. Then Mellaril. The truth sunk in that this was going to be a long haul."

At the end of his senior year, Sam made his first halfhearted suicide attempt. "I pulled him out of the bathtub when he was trying to drown himself. He was probably holding his nose," Winston said. Sam seemed to function better for a little bit, but was hospitalized three years later, after a confrontation with law enforcement. "He was talking to himself and the police picked him up, and he either said, 'I want to kill somebody' or 'I want to kill myself,'" Winston said. "He was in protective custody and he exploded. Eight people descended on him, putting him in restraints, and gave him Haldol. I was helpless. He was saying, 'Give me something so I can die.' It was terrible." Then Sam entered what he calls "Fat Pig Sam Period." He explained, "I was very racist and I hated everybody. From twenty-one to twenty-four I ate nothing but junk food, about eight times a day. I was obsessed with ice hockey. I don't know what made me turn into such a horrible, disgusting, obnoxious pig, but that is what I turned into."

Winston and Patricia took Sam to visit Gould Farm, a rehabilitation facility in Massachusetts, and Sam stayed one night and then insisted on coming home, claiming the people there were "even fatter and sicker than me." The Fischers were at a loss. Sam is a one-man refutation of the Freudian tenet that understanding your behavior helps you change it; he understands what's wrong with him, which made him feel superior to the residents at Gould Farm, but he is incapable of addressing any of it, which is why he was sent there in the first place.

After his childhood focus on botany, and his pig-period fixation on hockey, Sam became obsessed with the heyday of rock and roll, a passion he shares with Winston. He hunts down vinyl versions of music long forgotten by almost everyone else and identifies the moment of receiving a record he's ordered as the only time he feels genuine happiness. But he has been banned from the Princeton Record Exchange since the day he punched one of its clerks. Winston is usually left to smooth things over. "I like our time together, but it's too much. I'm his only friend. We're reaching a state where I don't know how much longer it can go on. If we'd been able to leave Sam at Gould Farm, he might've come to an existential realization that he had to make a life or end up in a hospital, but we could never face the idea of forcing him."

Winston and Patricia try to support any interest Sam shows in other people. Sadly, this policy seems to enable some of his most troubling deficits. "We were in a record store," Winston said. "There was an album cover for *The Knife*, which scared him. I managed to track down the lead singer's number. Sam established a telephone relationship with him. Sam called too often, as he always does. Usually the wife or girlfriend says, 'You have to stop letting this kid call, it's driving me crazy.' So that turned from being a sort of ideal moment where you explore the record that scared you, find the guy, and make friends, to being a nightmare that made him feel terrible about himself."

Sam spends his time making up rock bands and producing their album covers—drawing the art, making lists of songs, writing liner notes and lyrics. "My lyrics deal with love, hate, revenge," Sam said. "They are all homosexually oriented." Sam and I spent hours looking at his album covers. "Oblivion in Orbit. Cold realities and occasional joys of life in the British Army, of outer space, of strange phenomena, and of sex," Sam wrote on one of them. He also plays the electric guitar and has three of them.

Sam's other obsession is soldiers. "They are the one group that understand me," he said. "They look me straight in the eyes and try to make me feel unfragile, like they believe in me. Unlike my parents, who make no effort whatsoever." To Winston, the obsession is not irrational: "His fantasy is to be protected, so he was after me to help him meet soldiers." One might question the wisdom of indulging these yearnings for people who will be irritated by them, but part of the folie à deux is that Winston joins Sam in his troubled reality. "I found a job on this newspaper and realized that I could report on Fort Dix," Winston said. "They gave us a tour; he got to take pictures of the soldiers, meet and talk to them." Sam has an interest in foreign armies, as well. "When we travel to England, say, we'll board the train to Bristol and just turn him loose," Winston said. "He ends up having a great conversation with somebody in the services." Patricia is highly ambivalent about all this, but defers to it since Winston spends every day with Sam while she is at work. "Sam's psychiatrist says I have to crack down," she said. "But how do I crack down on Winston's niceness?"

Sam calls soldiers. Winston has managed to obtain British army directories for him. "I know these soldiers are frightened, and I know that they think they are doing something important, too," Sam said. "English boys and English men are beautiful. Very nice rosy skin. The first time ever I was in love was with a British soldier. It was a very painful experience because it was love at first sight. We talked for an hour and I wanted to spend my life with him. We never saw each other again. His name was Sergeant Gibbs. I was twenty-seven and he was thirty-three. I wanted to kiss him, but he was holding a machine gun. My heart was broken after that. Our first cat died soon after that happened. It was a really difficult period." Winston explained, "There's a guy manning the gate in one of these big government buildings off Hyde Park. Sam had a twenty-minute conversation with this guy, and he only knows his last name, Gibbs. But this guy became his dream hero, as if they had an entire relationship."

"We know where Sam's military fixation comes from," Patricia said. "It is a sexual fixation and a very familiar one. But also, he thinks of himself as living in a war zone and feels these people understand what it's like to survive in war conditions. I can't believe they'll talk to him, but they do. What poisons it is that he calls again and again and again. I say, 'Write down every call and keep a schedule of when it's okay to call back.' I open a four-page phone bill, and I say, 'Don't you think you've been calling a little too often?' He explodes. 'No, I'm not, I'm not, they don't mind.'" Patricia finally put her foot down and said, "You just can't keep making these phone calls," and Sam hit her. Winston called the police. But they remain afraid that setting firmer limits will only aggravate things.

"Sam and I went to Montreal every year," Winston said. "I would take him to see the Black Watch guys play bagpipes. Six years ago, Sam asked, could he talk to somebody in the Black Watch? They sent down a guy who turned out to be gay. He and Sam kept in touch, and when we went back the next year, Sam was determined to lose his virginity. I gave him some prophylactics, and the guy was going to take him to a bathhouse. I was by the phone waiting: Will it be awful, wonderful? It wasn't anything. The guy realized he didn't want to be responsible. He's now an enemy, like everyone Sam's ever met."

I met Sam for the first time over lunch in Princeton. He and Patricia had cooked together; it's their most peaceable mutual activity, and they assembled a delicious meal. Sam announced, "This was the worst winter of my whole life. I attempted suicide about six times." Patricia, who was at the table, said, "You thought about it; you didn't try." Sam said, "I had a knife at my wrists. I suffered two nervous breakdowns. I'm very sensitive to medications." "And alcohol," Patricia said. "And drugs," Winston said. "And people. And life," Patricia said. Sam receives some SSI—disability benefits—as well as an allowance from his parents and is planning a move to the UK. "But Patricia has just been a bitch! She's been the bird of doom. 'You're not going to England! Forget it!' That's all I hear from her. I've told her it would ruin my life if I didn't go this year, and it doesn't matter how many times I tell her that."

In fact, a great deal of love and insight emanates from these bewildered parents. "I don't believe in normality," Winston said. "It's just an averaging of extremes." Patricia said, "He thinks when the right records come in the mail, his problems will be solved. Or maybe he can get unstuck by moving to England. It's the lack of filters, the lack of self-control, the lack of ability to stick at anything, that's the problem. The rest of it is reality. He has no friends. He has no occupation. We're just the evidence of his dependence. If we say no to something that he wants, then it's 'You're not letting me live my own life.' When we say, 'There's nothing we would like better than to enable you to live your own life,' then it's 'You want to throw me out on the street.' He can analyze the situation just as well as I can. But it's not remediable. The hallucinations are really the least of it."

Before I left Princeton that day, I went to say good-bye to Sam. "Hey, thanks," I said. "I know it can be hard to have a total stranger come into your house and ask you all these questions." To my surprise, Sam gave me a warm hug, then looked me in the eye and said, "You didn't seem like a stranger to me." A deeply touching capacity for connection flashed in the room, and some self beneath the illnesses he had been parading seemed to touch me. Then it was gone again, lost in a monologue about a record I'd never heard of and that may not exist.

One of Sam's doctors told me that he probably has a neurological syndrome based in part on fetal development, manifesting in ways we cannot chart. The topic of diagnosis provokes a noise from Patricia that is equal measures a laugh and a suppressed sob. "It's been very difficult lately, with a lot of shouting and slamming of doors, and rising blood pressure," she said. "I'm in fight-or-flight mode, and we shouldn't be fighting and I shouldn't be fleeing. I control myself most of the time, unless I'm very, very tired. Sam's latest psychiatrist presented the case at a meeting and came back and said, 'They all agreed he needs structure,' and I looked at him like, 'What do you think I am, an idiot?' I never thought of that—Sam and structure! Come on over to our house and see if you can create any structure! We've done everything known to human beings to create structure."

Their progress has been to stop anticipating progress; that is its own kind of peace. "The problem," Patricia said, "is that we're growing older, and we haven't even written a will, because we don't know what to put in it. There's no one to look after Sam. My fantasy is that we'll make it until he turns fifty-five and then he can go into assisted care. So I have to keep this up into my eighties. It's particularly hard on Winston, but it's very hard on me, too. But it's worse for Sam. He picks up on the ways that we've given up, he must. He's very, very sensitive. I wish I could protect him from our despair."

Families rise to the occasion of various difficulties, struggle to love across those divides, and find in almost any challenge a message of hope and an occasion for growth or wisdom. In some instances schizophrenia and related psychotic disorders may be put into this service. Nonetheless, schizophrenia may be in a class by itself for unrewarding trauma. The rich culture of Deafness, the LPA-centered empowerment of dwarfism, the extreme sweetness of many Down syndrome children, the self-actualization of the autism rights brigade—none of this is really present in the world of schizophrenia, Mad Pride notwithstanding. We may hesitate to cure some problematic illnesses because they are also rich identities, but schizophrenia cries out almost unconditionally for treatment. The remarkable parents I met during this research would be better off, as would their children, if schizophrenia didn't exist. To me, their suffering seemed unending, and singularly fruitless.

VII

Disability

TAKING THE TRAIN

Someone says things will be better for him
In the mountains
So we board the morning train,
Hoping to reach the bright, whitewashed city
In the blaze of afternoon.
I have everything he will need:
Magazines with pretty pictures,
The Christmas candy he wants all year,
His water bottle and specially shaped spoon.
Quiet and happy, my son dozes.
His half-grown chest rises and falls
In silent hosannas, his breath bubbles
Milky as a newborn calf's.
The train bores through rock and scrub oak
For hours until suddenly, off to the right,
Glints the fierce splintered eye of the ocean.
This is not the way to the mountains
And why is everyone speaking Spanish?
I knew Spanish once
A uniformed official mimes his need
To punch our tickets, but
My purse contains only two maps
Of coastal Texas.
The official stops the train. Something must be done with us.
A tall station of polished mahogany
Looms in the green shade of palms.
In our coach, three rows of seats have vanished.
Where they stood, sand dusts the floor.

I must find my suitcase.
In it are knives, and a camera
To record what is happening to us.
The row of seats in front of us
Vanishes.
The row of seats behind us
Is gone too, all its people gone.
The sand whispers higher, to my ankles.
I find my suitcase in the next car,
Catches sprung, knife blades crumbled to rust,
The camera full of sand.
Only five seats remain.
In our two, another dark-haired woman
Tucks a blanket about the knees
Of another retarded boy.
I recall a Spanish phrase:
¿Dónde está mi hijo?
A young woman answers:
They put him off the train.
The train is moving again, fast.
The sand in the coach has climbed to my knees.
Outside, a desert stretches to the horizon.
Somewhere along the endless dunes
My son crawls alone,
Without even his walker.
Every morning of our lives
We board this train
And ride to the point of our separation.

—Elaine Fowler Palencia

*D*isability describes the older person whose bad ankles make walking long distances a trial, and the returning veteran who has lost limbs. The word is also used for people who would once have been classed as mentally retarded, and for anyone whose sensory apparatus is severely compromised. *Multiple disability* refers to people who are impaired in more than one way or from more than one ailment. *Severe disability* indicates a considerable impairment. *Multiple severe disability* (MSD) refers to people with an overwhelming number of challenges. Some people with MSD are incapable of controlled movement, locomotion, verbal thought, and self-awareness. Shaped more or less like other people, they may not learn their name or express attachment or demonstrate basic emotions such as fear or happiness. They may not feed themselves. Yet, inexorably, they are human, and often, they are loved. The passion for such children contains no ego motive of anticipated reciprocity; one is choosing against, in the poet Richard Wilbur's phrase, "loving things for reasons." You find beauty or hope in the existence, rather than the achievements, of such a child. Most parenthood entails some struggle to change, educate, and improve one's children; people with multiple severe disabilities may not become anything else, and there is a compelling purity in parental engagement not with what might or should or will be, but with, simply, what is.

Although the vagueness of the criteria for MSD makes it much harder to collate the relevant statistics than it is for single, clearly defined conditions, about twenty thousand people with MSD are born in the United States each year. Many who would not have lived beyond infancy are now surviving much longer because of evolving medicine. People actively debate whether extending the lives of these children should always be given priority regardless of their perceived pain and regardless of the ramifications for those who will be responsible for them. Thirty years ago, parents were advised to relinquish severely disabled children, often to let them die. In the last twenty years or so, they have been told to keep and love them. Most states offer supplemental income for family members who have to give up work to take care of an MSD child, as well as respite, health-care, and in-home services. People with MSD who can absorb some schooling have access to a more inclusive system. These services are not provided out of mere kindness; higher-functioning people are less expensive across their life span. For every dollar spent on vocational rehabilitation for people with disabilities, the Social Security Administration saves seven dollars.

David and Sara Hadden married in their early twenties and prepared for a high-powered life in New York. David worked at Davis Polk, one of the city's finest law firms, and Sara soon became pregnant with their first son, Jamie. Three days after he was born in August 1980, an intern entered her hospital room and said, "Your son just turned blue, and we don't know what's going on." The doctors couldn't find anything wrong and sent the family home with an apnea monitor that would sound an alarm if Jamie's breathing stopped. It never sounded, and David and Sara thought he was fine. When he was about three months old, their pediatrician said Jamie's head size was not following the normal growth curve and suggested a skull X-ray to make sure his sutures—the elastic part of the infant skull—hadn't closed prematurely.

The sutures were fine. "We went, 'Whew!'" Sara recalled. "Ignoring the fact that his head wasn't growing."

A few weeks later, the doctor said they should visit a neurologist, and they duly went to Columbia-Presbyterian, where a neurologist said that Jamie had salt-and-pepper pigmentation of his retina, then explained, "You've got king-sized problems. If you're thinking of having more kids, put it on hold. This child is blind, and probably is going to be severely retarded, and may not live long." Then he took a telephone call and said into the receiver, "I'm seeing a couple now with king-sized problems. On a happier note"—as he said "happier," the couple leaned forward expectantly—"I wanted to talk to you about another case." David and Sara walked out of the office in silence.

The next morning, Sara said to David, "I don't know why I'm saying this, but I feel very strongly that we need to have Jamie baptized." They hadn't gone to church in many years, but they looked in the yellow pages and found one around the corner. "I didn't understand it then," Sara said, "but I think I was acknowledging that Jamie had a soul. I've bristled at someone patting me on the head and saying, 'God has his mysterious ways.' I believe that life is a mystery, but I don't think we were given this situation from a specific deity for a specific reason. Still, we found a comfort in the church." David said, "When Sara asked to baptize Jamie, that was the beginning for us."

All Sara had accepted at that point was that Jamie was blind; she thought that his delays were tied to his lack of vision, and she resisted knowing that his brain wasn't growing. A month after visiting the neurologist, she and David took Jamie for an EEG. The EEG technician was digging into Jamie's skull as she applied the electrodes. "That's when we became advocates," David explained. "That's when we said, 'No, goddammit! You're not going to do that with our child.' That was a first; I had always been a well-behaved person who followed the rules. Jamie has made me a far better lawyer. He has forced me to develop advocacy skills that have sprung from passion as opposed to intellectual arguments. We have consented to being interviewed despite being very private people because it's part of advocacy. And Jamie's been a pioneer in that arena, right from those first hospital visits, and we're very proud of him."

At two, Jamie could push himself up into a sitting position, but at three he lost that ability; he was able to roll over until he was eleven, but can no longer do so. He has never developed speech or fed himself. He could urinate at first, but the relevant neurological processes soon failed, and he had to be permanently catheterized. "When we learned that Jamie was retarded, I was afraid," Sara said. "I had this

Helen Keller vision that if I found the right key, if I could just do the signs in his hand long enough, he would learn to talk. All of his teachers were urging me, saying, 'Yes, yes, yes, that's what you need to do, the more the better; maximize his potential!' It was wonderful support in one way, and an amazing guilt trip in another way."

Jamie's doctors were fairly confident that his condition was anomalous, and when Jamie was four, the Haddens decided to have another child. Their daughter, Liza, was born in perfect health. Four years later, they decided that it would be good for Liza to have a sibling who could someday help her to care for Jamie, so they had Sam. When Sam was six weeks old, Sara was putting him to bed, and suddenly he started twitching, and Sara immediately knew it was a seizure.

"With diagnosis, you have prognosis," Sara explained, "and with prognosis, you have greater peace of mind." But diagnosis remained elusive, even though it was soon clear that the two boys shared a syndrome. The Haddens have run advertisements in hospital journals and in *Exceptional Parent* magazine, seeking other children with a similar condition. They've had workups done on the boys at NYU and Boston Children's and Mass Eye and Ear; they've corresponded with doctors at Johns Hopkins. The constellation of symptoms experienced by Jamie and Sam seems to be unique, so no one has been able to predict how the boys would best be treated, how much they might deteriorate, or how long they might live.

Sam was even more fragile than Jamie. He kept breaking his legs because he had brittle bones; he ultimately had total-spinal-fusion surgery. Fed through a tube from a much earlier age than Jamie, Sam vomited all the time. At two, he spent six weeks in the hospital for continuous seizures. When he was admitted, his cognitive abilities were greater than Jamie's, but after that six-week period, he lost them. David and Sara both became snowed under. "People kept saying, 'Why don't you get help?'" Sara said. "But the idea of help was as overwhelming as the things we needed help with." When she explained to Liza that Sam was going to be like Jamie, Liza said, "Give him back and get another baby." This was hard to hear because it was just what Sara was thinking herself. "That was about the depression; that wasn't about not loving him," Sara said. "My big goal for the day at that point was running a load of laundry, and I didn't always achieve the goal." A few months after Sam's diagnosis, Sara hit rock bottom. "I sat on the kitchen floor trying to convince myself to take both boys with me to the garage and turn on the car and let all of us go on the carbon monoxide," she said.

Yet there was joy there, too. "If we had known that the condition might be repeated, we would not have risked it," Sara said. "Having said that, if I were told, 'We can just wipe out that experience,' I wouldn't. Sam got the full benefit of being Jamie's younger brother. I had a lot less trepidation taking care of him; I knew how to do it. Sam was easier to love. Jamie's a fighter; Jamie will stand up for his rights. Sam would just curl into you. The image I always think of is that orb of love that Woody Allen had in one of his movies." David concurred, "There's a lovely picture we have somewhere of Sara dancing with him when he was little. He was actually standing. Sara was rocking with him. He might have collapsed at any moment. But Sara and Sam were Fred Astaire and Ginger Rogers. They were magic together. It absolutely blows my mind, the impact that a blind, retarded, nonverbal, nonambulatory person has had on people. He has a way of opening and touching people that we can't come near. That's part of our survival story—our marveling at how he has moved so many people."

When Jamie was almost nine, Sara tried to lift him out of the bathtub and herniated a disc. All three of the children had chicken pox. The boys were in diapers and difficult to change. "I think any stay-at-home mom deserves a medal," David said. "But Sara deserves sixteen Purple Hearts. We had Sam, rushing off to the hospital with seizures; we had our four-year-old; and then we had Jamie, with his unpredictability. It was more than we could do." They secured an emergency placement for Jamie in June 1989, in a facility for adults about forty minutes away from their house in northern Connecticut. David and Sara became members of a class-action suit against the State of Connecticut, aimed at replacing large institutions with community care. "Jamie embarrassed the Department of Mental Retardation with the notion that the best they could offer an eight-year-old child was a sixty-bed institution with adults," David said with pride. An article about the fight ran in the *Hartford Courant* Sunday magazine, with Jamie on the cover, and in 1991, the Hartford Association for Retarded Citizens (HARC) set up a group home. The Haddens decided Sam should live there as well. They visited daily. With Liza in first grade and both boys out of the house, Sara decided that since her best means of communication with her sons had always been touch, she would go to massage school; she worked as a massage therapist for fifteen years.

Two years after Sam moved into the group home, he was having a routine bath when the staff member in charge of his care went to get some medication for him, which she was not supposed to do. While bathing, he would sit in a chair that fit in the tub, with a safety belt across his hips. Perhaps the belt had been forgotten, or perhaps the Velcro gave way. She was gone less than three minutes, and when she returned, Sam was underwater. David received the call at his office and immediately called Sara, who was driving Liza to boarding school. The three of them converged in the emergency room. "The doctor came in," David said. "We could tell by the look on his face. Sara and I were off in our own numb shock, and Liza was just furious, knowing that somebody screwed up." Sara said, "We'd talked about wanting the children to die, and then panicked if it seemed to be happening. It was best for Sam. I miss him terribly, and for me it is a tragic loss—but he had been fighting a hard fight a long time, and I have no doubt that he has gone to a better place."

The Haddens went to the home that night to see Jamie. The caretaker who had left Sam in the bathtub was there. "She was on the couch, in shock and just sobbing," Sara said. "I gave her a hug, and I said, 'Marvika, it could have been any of us.' She shouldn't have left him alone in the bathtub, but it's so hard to be vigilant every minute. We fuck up. All the time. If he had been at home, I can't say that I wouldn't have left him in the bathtub to go get a towel. It's incredibly difficult to hire and retain qualified people to do this very difficult direct-care work, and the pay is terrible. If we start charging people with crimes for making mistakes, how is that going to help? I didn't want to do anything that would discourage other people from entering this relatively thankless field. What's more, we had to keep going back to that home because Jamie was there. These guys had all saved our lives—by taking care of our kids day in and day out."

The caretaker was charged with reckless manslaughter. "We said to the prosecutor, 'Our wish is that you don't pursue this,'" David recalled. "'This woman is going to lose her job. She'll never get another job like this. This problem has essentially corrected itself.' We both wanted the compassion and healing to set in as quickly as possible." Marvika was eventually sentenced to five years, suspended, and one of the terms of her probation was that she never again work in direct care. After the sentencing, David gave her one of the bandannas that Sam used to wear around his neck to help with his drooling. "She let out this anguished wail that echoed in the marble corridors of the courthouse," David said.

The videotape of Sam's funeral memorializes an outpouring of extraordinary love—much of it for David, Sara, Liza, and Jamie, as well as for Sam. "I'd imagined Sam would die," David said. "I thought that there would be a sense of relief. And there was. But there's also this acute sense of loss, the feeling that if I could turn back that clock and save him, I would give my right arm to do it. I didn't expect to feel that way." Four years later, when they finally interred Sam's ashes, Sara said, "Let me bury here the rage I feel to have been twice robbed: once of the child I wanted, and once of the son I loved."

When I visited Jamie for the first time, when he was in his early twenties, he seemed, at first glance, inert. I noticed how pretty his room was: framed pictures and posters adorned the walls, a nicely patterned duvet lay on the bed and attractive clothes hung in the closet. I thought that selecting pleasing visuals for a blind person was somewhat eccentric, but Sara said, "It's a gesture of respect, and it sends a message to the people who work with him that we take care of him and expect them to do so, too." Jamie, who is tall and large-boned, has to be lifted from and returned to his bed with a pulley. The effort needed to keep him comfortable is tremendous, but although he seems capable of discomfort, he at first struck me as incapable of pleasure. Yet to be in the room with Sara and David and their son is to witness a shimmering humanity. "Sam's death had a mellowing effect on Jamie," Sara said to me. "But maybe the change was in us."

On later visits, I found that Jamie sometimes opens his eyes and seems to stare at you; he cries, smiles, and occasionally breaks into a sort of laugh. I learned to place my hand on his shoulder, since touch is his primary means of communication. Liza took two weeks off work to read him *The Chronicles of Narnia*, just in case he could understand it. Something about the gesture was incongruous, but I saw that he might be soothed by his sister's voice and presence, and that it was good for her to acknowledge his essential self. "It's raw, just being a person without trying to impress or achieve or accomplish anything," David said. "It's pure being. In a totally unconscious way, he is what human is. I find thinking about that helpful in building enough energy to counteract the demands of it."

When the group home staff unionized and went on strike, Sara said, "I strongly support their hopes and wishes, but I feel sad at how easily they can leave. I want them to love Jamie, to find it as hard to walk out on him as I would. It's a job and they do it pretty well and they are fond of him, but they don't love him. That makes it difficult for me to trust them, especially with the specter of what happened to Sam." A few years later, when Jamie had been moved to a home slightly farther away, Sara wrote to me, "Our visits to Middletown are like going out on a whale watch. Often we make the trip to find Jamie snoozing and have to settle for reports of 'You should have been here an hour ago; he was having a great time!' Or worse, sometimes we are back on the pitching seas of concern as we watch him experience discomfort and try to sort out its cause. We hope for those wonderful moments, like one we had two weeks ago, when we are there for his 'surfacing' and can feel his pleasure in being alive."

Sara and David described a dynamic within their marriage in which one of them gets into a dark place, and then the other. They take turns supporting each other. "It's a lot of work to pull each other out, and that's part of the partnership," David said. When I met the Haddens, they had just started Gestalt therapy, and their first exercise was to make a timeline of their lives in crayon. "I was filling it in, and I got to drawing the birth of our three children," Sara said. "And I just didn't want to fill in any more, and I started to cry. There's a lot of grief that—in the crisis of living out the logistics of our lives—there really wasn't any room to feel; there was a lot that we swallowed to make our lives happen."

Alan O. Ross writes in *The Exceptional Child in the Family* that parents' expectations "invariably include that the child will be able to surpass, or at least attain, the parents' level of socio-cultural accomplishment." He continues, "When the child does not conform to this image, the parents often need help in adapting their behavior to the reality—they must learn to cope with the dissonance between their image of 'a child' and the reality of 'their child.'" The tension often has less to do with the severity of the child's disabilities than with the parents' coping skills, the dynamics among healthy members of the family, and the importance the parents place on how people outside the family perceive them. Income, time available to focus on the child, and support outside the family are all significant factors. Perhaps the most insidious stress is the social isolation that can ensue when friends retreat, or when parents withdraw from friends' pity or incomprehension. The birth of a healthy child usually expands the parents' social network; the birth of a child who is disabled often constricts that network.

Susan Allport, an authority on maternal attachment, writes that in nondisabled populations "it is not parent providing care to helpless young but parent and young, together, performing carefully synchronized, ruthlessly selected dances of reproduction and survival. The newborn is born knowing its steps, but, like all ballroom dancers, it must have a partner. Parents are primed for parental behavior by their hormones and the act of birth, but in order for their behavior to continue, they must have partners that are responding appropriately." This idea comes up repeatedly in attachment literature. "There is probably no mammal in which maternal commitment does not emerge piecemeal and chronically sensitive to external cues," writes the evolutionary biologist Sarah Hrdy. "Nurturing has to be teased out, reinforced, maintained. Nurturing itself needs to be nurtured." In the *Handbook of Attachment,* the preeminent medical anthology in the field, Carol George and Judith Solomon propose that maternal attachment is "transactional, rather than linear and unidirectional." What becomes of the transaction with an MSD child, who can often express only appetite or pain, then signal satisfaction when hunger and discomfort are assuaged?

Yet parental attachment to children with MSD occurs time and again; like all love, it is in some measure an act of projection. One thinks that one loves one's children because they are beguiling and one's parents because they have given care, but many children whose parents have neglected them go on loving such parents, and many mothers and fathers of disagreeable children are enchanted by them. Carrie Knoll, a pediatrician, described a couple whose daughter was diagnosed with holoprosencephaly, a condition in which a hollow shell of a brain sustains only the most primitive automatic functions of life. "The parents never wavered from the stance that she was a normal baby," Knoll wrote. The child died only a few weeks after being born. "When I called the family to offer my condolences," she continued, "I understood that they mourned her as fully as other parents would have. To them, she was simply their child."

Louis Winthrop and his wife, Greta, were delighted the day their daughter Maisie was born. The next evening, after Maisie's feeding, she seemed to fall asleep on her mother's breast. The nurse was prepared to leave her undisturbed, but Greta, uncomfortable after a difficult delivery, said, "Why don't you take her back." In the brightly lit hospital corridor, the nurse saw that the baby had turned blue. Maisie had seizures for the next twenty-four hours. It's not clear whether she was having seizures because of oxygen deprivation or whether she stopped breathing because of a seizure. By the time the seizures stopped, her brain stem was bleeding heavily; the bleeding might have been a symptom of the damage or its source. "There is an endless gray scale," Louis said to me, "between her being completely fine and her dying. If we'd noticed sooner that the baby wasn't just asleep—well, it's impossible to know."

Louis asked the doctor whether Maisie was going to be okay. "I wouldn't rush to endow a chair at Harvard for her," he said. Louis and Greta were outraged. "I couldn't believe that was how he'd tell me that my daughter was likely to be profoundly retarded," Louis said. They next saw an audiologist, who said Maisie was going to be partly deaf. "I am not very demonstrative, but a tear came out of my eye as he was talking," Louis said. "He said, 'You're going to have to be tough or you're not going to get through this, and neither is she. If you can't be tough for yourself, you'd better be tough for her.' I pulled myself together and stopped crying, and I thought, 'Yes, I have to be the strong one.'" Still, he felt bruised by the way other parents avoided him: "You go into Central Park with a special-needs child, and the other parents look straight through you. They would never think to come over and suggest that their child could play with your child. I know how they feel, because until Maisie was born, I was one of those people in the park."

Louis and Greta have gone on to have another daughter, Jeannine, who is healthy. "We are different with Jeannine because of Maisie," Louis said. "My fear is that we don't pay enough attention to Jeannine because Maisie uses up so much energy. But on the other hand, we are more in touch with how miraculous Jeannine is and are more excited about every little thing she does, because we know that healthy development is not an inevitability." Though the Winthrops have struggled, they have certain advantages. "We can see that there's someone there," Louis went on. "Other people meet Maisie briefly and they think we're crazy, but we get enough sparks. We love her so much more than I ever imagined I could love anything. I am still haunted by that shadow Maisie, the one who didn't stop breathing. The one we got to know for a day. Just once or twice I've thought it might be better for all of us if Maisie died. I can never tell how much that's sympathy for Maisie's frustration and pain, and how much it's something selfish. It happens in my daydreams. In my real dreams, Maisie is often well, and she's talking to me."

The philosopher Sophia Isako Wong, whose brother has Down syndrome, asked, "What makes life as a parent worth living—or, in other words, what rewards do parents expect in return for the sacrifices they make in raising children?" Through most of the twentieth century, the standard perception was that families of disabled children could expect nothing; their emotional reality was summed up in the rehabilitation counselor Simon Olshanky's famous notion of "chronic sorrow." Drawing on the emotional vocabulary of Freud's *Mourning and Melancholia*, the psychiatric world addressed such births with the vocabulary of death. Parents who reported positive emotions were seen as overcompensating to disguise rage and guilt and overpowering wishes to harm their child. A 1988 review of the field concluded, "Researchers and service providers in the field of developmental disabilities view the family as a whole as embroiled in a series of acute crises interspersed with chronic sorrow. Thus the task of family support is seen as ameliorating the deadly pall of tragedy that hangs over the family."

The answer to Wong's question changes not only from family to family, but also over time; like many other identity groups explored in this book, this one has made radical social progress, and the "deadly pall" has lifted somewhat. Studies have shown that people who observe parents of disabled children notice more stress than those parents themselves report. Like disability itself—which may appear inconceivably awful to those who can only imagine what it might be like but is much less daunting to many for whom it is a fact of life—the labor-intensive experience of parenting a severely disabled child can eventually become routine, though as with Down syndrome, autism, and schizophrenia, the issue of placement can loom large.

While some people with severe disabilities may experience acute health crises or frightening seizures, much of their care has a rhythm, and human nature adapts to anything with a rhythm. The care can be done competently. An extreme but stable stress is easier to handle than a less extreme but erratic one. This is one reason why parents of people with Down syndrome have an easier time than parents of schizophrenics or of people with autism; with Down syndrome, you know with whom you are dealing from day to day, and the demands on you change relatively little; with schizophrenia, you never know what weirdness is about to strike; with autism, what meltdown moment.

Unmanaged or uninformed parental expectations are a poison, and specific diagnosis of the disabilities any individual has are a huge help. Jerome Groopman wrote in the *New Yorker*, "Language is as vital to the physician's art as the stethoscope or the scalpel. Of all the words the doctor uses, the name he gives the illness has the greatest weight. The name of the illness becomes part of the identity of the sufferer." The sadness of a poor prognosis is vastly easier than the chaos of no prognosis. Once the course is clear, most people can accept it. Since knowledge is power, syndromes associated with dire prospects are borne more nobly than those of which little can be understood. Identity is a function of certitude.

Paul and Cris Donovan married in the mid-1990s and moved to the Bay Area so Paul could work in the tech sector. Cris became pregnant with Liam shortly thereafter. Childbirth was uneventful, and Liam weighed in at eight pounds. However, the doctors were concerned when he didn't open his eyes, and when they checked, they saw that his eyeballs were the size of peas. "That was the beginning of our downhill run," Cris recalled. Liam needed immediate surgery to open his blocked intestines. Within a week, he would need another operation to repair his heart. After that, he developed a blood clot that almost killed him. By the time Liam was six weeks old, he'd had six major surgeries and had run up hospital bills over a million dollars, paid for by Paul's good insurance.

"Except that he would be blind, we didn't know if he was going to get better, or be okay, or what was happening," Paul said. "One of the goals with a kid with special needs is how to help them reach their potential. So it's helpful to know what their potential actually is. We never did. In some regards, that stinks, because it's hard to set out and achieve goals. In some regards, it's great, because we don't ever stop trying." Liam was ultimately diagnosed with CHARGE syndrome, an umbrella diagnosis for many children with MSD. It's an acronym: *C* for *coloboma*, a hole in one of the structures of the eye; *H* for *heart* defects; *A* for *atresia* of the choanae (blockage of the passages that connect the nose to the throat); *R* for *retardation* of growth and/or development; *G* for *genital* and/or urinary abnormalities; and *E* for *ear* abnormalities and deafness. Although Liam is blind, this is not the result of a coloboma, and his hearing is perfect; nonetheless, he met most of the other criteria for a CHARGE syndrome diagnosis and also has other symptoms that are not included in the diagnostic criteria. Nonetheless, Paul said, "It's convenient to have a simple response to the question of what's wrong."

Liam either refused to eat or threw up. Accumulating liquid in his lungs led to pneumonia. Despite a nasal feeding tube, he wasn't gaining weight in his first year. When he was upset, he would hold his breath and pass out; this behavioral communication is a way to signal pain, and it occurred frequently. Paul and Cris had to give Liam CPR some fifty times. Paul said, "One of my best friends asked, 'When are you going to put him in a facility?' I respected him for asking me the question. It hurt, but it was great. Then you make a decision not to put him in a facility, and it's your decision. There's a natural course of life. When he's eighteen or twenty-two, he should be moving on to some kind of home. Our job is to give him the highest quality of life and to reach his potential, whatever that is."

At the end of his first year, Liam weighed only fourteen pounds; in the first three months after a direct feeding tube was surgically implanted, he gained eight more. He needed a permanent shunt to relieve his hydrocephalus. His brain stem was being compressed by his spinal cord, so surgeons shaved the cord down, allowing the brain stem to shift. He had heart surgery because one of his mitral valves had started to close. His shunt had to be removed. Liam was up to fifteen surgeries by the end of eighteen months. Paul went to work from the hospital, then returned; Cris simply lived there. She began to cry as she recounted it. "I don't remember doing a lot of crying at the time," she said apologetically. "It was a state of constant crisis."

At first, Paul and Cris hoped that Liam might someday walk and speak. By the time he was two, they knew he was going to have permanent problems but expected some improvement; over the year that followed, Paul realized that life with Liam might get harder rather than easier. "I only remember breaking down and crying in horror once, and it was the first night," he said. "Still, I think you shed a thousand singular tears, randomly on Tuesday when you see someone else's six-month-old child jumping." Cris said, "The early-intervention people keep you alive. Then, when they think you're ready, they want you to go into a play group. I wasn't ready to accept that this was my group." The first time the Donovans set goals for Liam, Paul recalled, the document was thirty pages: "By the second year, we were after three things. We want him to walk, talk, and eat."

When I first met Liam, he seemed to be gazing into the distance through beautiful eyes, one of which he promptly removed with a little, fidgety gouge to his eye socket. "The man who made them is an artist," Cris said as she replaced Liam's eyeball. "He studied Paul's eyes and mine and made eyes a child of ours might have. They're there not only for aesthetics, but also to promote healthy development of the socket bones." At seven, Liam was in a wheelchair, and how much he was responding to the stimuli around him was hard to tell. Paul put his mouth near Liam's ear and began singing softly, "It's Liam, wonderful Liam, I love you, Liam, Liam, Liam, Liam." Liam smiled. Whether that was an acknowledgment of the content of the song, a response to the intimacy of the communication, or just a reaction to air brushing against his somewhat deformed ears was impossible to tell, but Paul clearly could make his child smile, to the gratification of both.

No one knows that a given child will require twenty surgeries over four years; the question of what to do is resolved one procedure at a time. It can be hard for parents who haven't been down this route to understand the gradualism of it, and while the cumulative effect of all these interventions may become brutal, to deny any single one can seem murderous. Paul admitted that sometimes he'd wondered about the surgeries, but said that he always sensed that Liam could feel pleasure, and that he and Cris believe that a human being capable of positive experiences warrants medical support. "Liam's smile got me through those nights," Paul said, and showed me pictures of Liam at seventeen months, when he was nearly dying, with a feeding tube snaked through his nose. Liam was indeed smiling; he looked almost blissful.

A few years after Liam was born, Paul and Cris decided to have another child. They had prenatal imaging of the fetus's heart, because a defect would have been the clue that she had the same syndrome as Liam, but they had decided they would keep the child in any case; they just wanted to be prepared. Their first daughter, Clara, was born healthy; so, a few years later, was their youngest, Ella.

As Liam grew older and heavier, Paul needed to help out more at home, so he moved to a less challenging job that allowed him to be home by five o'clock every day to do two to three hours of physical therapy with Liam. The Donovans had to learn what they could expect from the system, from their families, from Liam, and from themselves. Paul and Cris made a deliberate decision not to orient their entire life around Liam's challenges. "There are parents who quit their jobs and go into special ed," Paul said. "The old world ends. We have a life, and this is a part of our life. Our marriage philosophy is that we come first. If we don't have a healthy marriage, our kids won't have a healthy life." Cris added, "Maybe some people would look at this as bad parenting, but I haven't researched everything. I don't have all the information. I'm not looking for another diagnosis. It is what it is."

At home, the Donovans often keep Liam under the coffee table. He slides in there, and they have mounted toys that dangle down to just where he can touch them. At a party, a newish acquaintance said, "Hey, your kid's under the coffee table. Is he okay?" In those circumstances, Paul and Cris are happy to explain. They always give information to children who ask. "You say, 'Well, he doesn't see,'" Paul said. "Kids are like, 'What?' I say, 'Okay, what do you see out of your nose?' They say, 'What do you mean?' I say, 'That's it. There's not even a sensation. He doesn't even have an orientation for the visual. So he's lost in space completely.' They go running off saying, 'Mommy, what do you see out of your nose?'" Paul spoke of seven-year-old Liam as having "a beautiful spirit, an adequate mind, and a frustratingly inadequate body." Liam was unable to crawl, but could sit with support and could even pull himself along on a shiny wooden floor. The Donovans therefore have no rugs. Most of Liam's muscles were too weak to be useful, but some tendons were so tight that his hands couldn't be uncurled or his legs extended; nonetheless, he could catch a large, gently thrown ball. He is unable to chew, so his food must be pureed. "I dream of getting as much chocolate pudding as he does," Paul said.

When, during our days together, Liam began to cry, Paul said, "If he's crying like that, it's because he's not the center of attention." Paul thinks that the sound of his name is enough to make Liam feel included; Cris maintains that he can tell just what's going on. "He shows signs of intelligence that you don't see unless you spend a lot of time with him," Cris said. "His teachers and aides like that he gets bratty like that; it shows he's thinking." Liam laughs at jokes; he appears to like certain

TV shows and will lie soundless and contented for *Sesame Street* and *American Idol*. Paul is trying to get him enthusiastic about hockey. "It's a learned trait," Paul said. Though Liam cannot dress himself, he has learned to hold out an arm when his parents are dressing him. "It's more intake than outtake," Paul said. "But he's there."

Liam was in a special day school when I met him. Paul and Cris wanted him in a more academic context. "Without the challenge, we won't know what he's capable of," Cris said. But the Donovans have not fought the system as much as many other parents of disabled children. After fighting for a year to get Liam a wheelchair, they just paid for it themselves. They had found a house they loved and wanted to buy, but the special-needs person in that district was unhelpful, so they chose the house they live in for the good social services in its area. "Liam's not going to run the Boston Marathon on Tuesday," Paul said. "He's not going to go to Harvard Law next Thursday. It doesn't mean we don't fight for his rights and try to get him what he needs, but it has been collaborative, not competitive or negative. By the dependency that one child has, I've learned a lot about the management of independence with the other kids. The girls can do whatever the hell they want and I'll be proud of them. It's very freeing."

Catholicism runs deep in the Donovan family. Paul goes to church every Sunday with the girls; sometimes, he takes Liam. During the worst early years with Liam, Paul and Cris went to mass together every day. "When Liam was in the hospital, that gave me something to grab on to, but it was more the ritual than the faith," he said. Cris said, "It's the structure. It was a calming way to face every day that was going to suck." Paul wrote up a list of the ten things that enabled him to persevere, and the first was "Keep the faith," which he said he meant in the broadest possible sense. "It doesn't have to be religion. But for me, it was. I think there's a plan. The cross fell a few times. We had to pick it up. It's made my faith more relevant; it's made it more authentic." Taking Liam to church is part of a social vision as well. "Every kid in our church is perfect," Paul said. "They need to know that some things don't conform to the norm. Liam's one of them."

Toward the end of the weekend I spent with the Donovans, Cris mentioned that she was feeling good about her New Year's resolutions. I asked what they were. "You are part of it, actually," she said. "I resolved to do things that I'm afraid of. Doing this—talking all about myself and the hardest parts of our life with you—is something I can give back to the world, and I decided just to do it, and I'm glad I did. It helped me to lay it all out like this; it helped me see how hard it all is, and how terribly much I love our son."

Having a disabled child can be both isolating and an introduction into new networks, and the means of coping with that experience have been systematized over the last few decades. Parenting such a child clarifies the dynamics of a marriage as it does friendships; for parents who do not have real intimacy with each other or with friends, the going can be tough. "Social isolation remained a correlate of less positive mood, more depression, less attachment," one study found. Participating in support groups, advocacy, and medical research can help parents reframe their experiences. Making social connections with their child's caregivers is also helpful. For people who must accept a fixed external reality, the only way forward is to adjust internal reality. Many coping strategies have a Zen simplicity. Instead of resolving chaos, find beauty and happiness amid chaos. I am reminded of a friend who said that when she found out her husband couldn't fill her needs, she changed her needs; they've had a long, good life together.

Empathy and compassion work best in concert with the belief that you are still capable of shaping a meaningful life for yourself and your family. The technical term for this is *internal locus of control*, wherein one determines one's own trajectory, rather than *external locus of control*, wherein one feels entirely subject to outside circumstances and events. To achieve an internal locus of control, people actively seek to match their lifestyles with their priorities; a mismatch occurs, for example, when a man works a hundred hours a week while most valuing his role as a husband or father. Paradoxically, however, parents of disabled children often achieve a feeling of control by making a firm and positive affirmation of their lack of control. The most important thing, often, is a belief in something bigger than one's own experience. The most common source of coherence is religion, but it has many other mechanisms. You can believe in God, in the human capacity for good, in justice, or simply in love.

There are many chicken-egg findings here. It's hard to know to what extent positive experiences generate positive perceptions, and to what extent it is the other way around. Aggrandizing the nobility of woe is a coping strategy, but some parents and some disability scholars exalt the catalog of wonders until having a disabled child seems not merely rich in meaning, but almost preferable to other experiences of parenting. The disabled child becomes a glowing family hearth around which all gather in shared song. Such sentimentality can be destructive; it makes parents who are having a rough time feel worse, adding layers of guilt and defeat to their general experience of trouble. It is easier to forgive, however, if one considers the history of intense prejudice against which it reacts.

371

When Max Singer was born, one of his eyes was fixed to the left, and the other had an enlarged pupil. The first neurologist to whom Susanna and Peter Singer took their son referred them to a leading pediatric neurologist in New York. He examined Max, then turned to Peter and said, "You should take your pretty wife home and make yourself another baby, because you're never going to get anything out of this one. I don't know if he'll ever be able to walk or talk or recognize you or function or even think." The neurologist said that Max had Dandy-Walker syndrome, a congenital brain malformation involving the cerebellum and the fluid-filled spaces around it. Other doctors refined the diagnosis: Max had Joubert syndrome, which is a subtype of Dandy-Walker. More recent testing has demonstrated that he does not actually have Joubert syndrome, so his current doctor has reverted to the broader Dandy-Walker diagnosis, "but at this point," Susanna observed, "it doesn't really make much difference."

Susanna described the day she got the diagnosis as one of the worst of her life. "I'm not sure that we benefited from knowing instantly that there was something wrong," she said. "That slowed down my attachment to him." The Singers next took Max to a neurological ophthalmologist to figure out what was wrong with his eyes. The doctor determined that Max could see. Everything else was open to question. "The first doctor told us he would be a vegetable," Susanna said. "The next one said he could be slightly delayed. We had these diagnoses but no predictions about what they meant and were told that we wouldn't know what was going on until autopsy. It's very hard to live without clear expectations."

Susanna chose not to discuss Max's problems publicly when he was little. "I didn't know what was going to happen, and I didn't want Max to feel like people knew something about him if, in fact, it wasn't going to be that obvious." Susanna is an art agent who has represented many prominent artists, including Sol LeWitt and Robert Mangold. "I didn't take him around to art-world events," she said. "I was keeping him hidden. I regret that secrecy. It was lonely for both of us." When Max was three months old, the Singers hired a Trinidadian nanny named Veronica, who stayed with them for the next twenty years. "She was like a third parent, and maybe more than that," Susanna said. "If he had had to choose between us and her, he would have chosen her. She was with him all the time. She never ran out of patience." True to advice, the Singers tried for another baby, but Susanna kept miscarrying. They decided to adopt; while Susanna and Peter were sitting at their chosen adoption agency, they got a call from Veronica, saying that Max had come home from school with a fever. Susanna left the meeting so she could take him to the doctor. "Max isn't often sick; aside from his disabilities, he's actually very healthy. But the agency told us that, really, Max took too much work, and we couldn't give what was needed to another child. They rejected us. Maybe it would have been difficult for another child to have Max as a brother—but I think both would have benefited a lot."

Max can walk if someone has an arm around him and is holding him up. "Unless he decides he doesn't want to," Susanna said, "in which case he will stop and cross his legs, and it is virtually impossible to move him. If he wants to go to a movie or get to a television, he can practically run." Max can use a bathroom, and he has good movement in his left arm and right leg. "He can do a lot more than he does," Susanna explained. "He'll wait you out." Max understands language, but is incapable of producing speech. In many ways, this might seem to be a vast improvement over having neither expressive nor receptive skills, but the mix comes with its own frustrations; to understand and be unable to respond is maddening. Max can nod or shake his head. In hopes that Max might learn to sign, Peter and Susanna went to the American Sign Language Institute for two years; it soon became clear that Max lacked the motor control he would need for Sign. He can sign "more," "finished," "music," and "I'm sorry." He does not like speaking devices, but when he's forced to use a talking machine, something that translates typing or other symbols into sound, he can make fairly complicated sentences. He can read short words; he can write his full name.

"Max gets a real kick out of almost everything," Susanna said. "He's full of curiosity. There's nothing that makes him scared, except very big dogs. He's well-adjusted and feels very loved. Because he goes to a special school, he's never been ostracized or teased. Also, Max doesn't have any physical deformities that make people shy away. That's helped him a lot. I, frankly, was never all that good-looking. But I think he really is. He's extremely affectionate. He doesn't have the muscle control to kiss, but he hugs hard and often. It used to happen all the time that we would sit around with Veronica, and Max would put his arm around her. If we were laughing, he'd look at her, to make sure she was laughing, too. He's very sweet that way."

Max went off to a special summer camp for the first time when he was nine, and Susanna phoned the camp every day to check on him. Finally, one of the other campers took the call and offered some friendly advice: "Mrs. Singer, Max is having the time of his life. My parents always go away when I'm at camp; maybe you should consider doing that." Later, Max attended a camp run by the Hebrew Academy for Special Children. The Singers are secular Jews, but summer camps for special-needs children are often run by religious organizations. "I don't like religion, but I've learned it's not about me," Susanna said. "Every year Max goes to that camp, he comes back more mature, and he learns incredible amounts."

Max is comparatively well socialized and psychologically independent. When he got on the bus to go to the Special Olympics for the first time, he pushed Susanna away. "I was proud of that," she said. "From the beginning, I wanted this child to feel like he was the greatest thing in the world. I succeeded in that. Sometimes I wish I hadn't because he can be so arrogant, but I did." She smiled. "It is not a joyful thing, by any means, to have a special-needs child. But Max, himself, has given us a lot of joy. I had to change my ideas when he was born, about what it means to be successful, for him and for me; his happiness is his success for him, and mine for me. I wish that he would work a little harder at school. I wish he were willing to accomplish more, rather than be satisfied with hanging out. But maybe he would have been that kind of kid anyway. His basic disposition is like mine. Maybe that's why I like it. Buoyant and even. Basically happy, and willing to adjust."

Max loves Jim Carrey movies, has a sense of humor, and is a classical-music enthusiast. "My father's a huge opera buff, and I was named Susanna after *The Marriage of Figaro*," Susanna said. "Somebody gave me a CD of Cecilia Bartoli, and I put it on, and Max was entranced." Susanna has taken Max to see Cecilia Bartoli at the Metropolitan Opera and at Carnegie Hall. They went to see her give an interview at Hunter College. He has gone to her record signings. "He's a groupie," Susanna said. "Cecilia Bartoli, who has a dog named Figaro, has, I have to say, been very nice to Max over the years." She's signed albums to him; she's even signed a photograph for him. Susanna herself had an old, mean dog who died when Max was twelve. "Nobody particularly liked him except for me, and Max, who loved him like a brother," she said. "Max was going off to camp, and I said, 'Max, I really want a new dog. Is that okay?' He kept saying, 'No, no, no, no.' Finally I said, 'Max, suppose we name it after Cecilia Bartoli? He said, 'Yes.' We got the dog, but it was a boy, so the name is Bartoli, and we call him Bart."

When I first met the Singers, Max was twenty. "Adolescence is not easy with children like this," Susanna said. "This little angel that I once had, I don't have anymore, at least not so much of the time. He loves girls, especially pretty girls, but he's not necessarily appropriate with them. He has friends in a way, but I wouldn't say that they're really bonded together. I know he knows the difference between people like us and himself; he's dependent on everybody."

Things had taken a sharp turn for the worse earlier that year, and Peter and Susanna couldn't understand why. Max's behavior became so bad that they took him to a neurologist, who put Max on medication that seemed only to make things worse. Eventually, they learned that Veronica had been telling Max that she was leaving after the summer. She hadn't yet mentioned this to Susanna or Peter. Max had no way to explain what was wrong. "That's one of the hardest things about having a child who can think, and react, and love, and have the feelings we have, but not be able to tell us. I can't even imagine not being able to express such incredible fear and sadness. Once we talked it through, he accepted it; by the time he got back from camp, we had a new person and he's very fond of her. He's adjusted better than I thought, and better than we have; I cried and cried."

Veronica's departure was occasioned by her being tired after twenty years, by Max's being so large that he was becoming physically difficult to move, by her wish to return to Trinidad, and by her horror at the thought that Max would someday be moved to a group home. "Every time we talked about it, she cried," Susanna said. "I kept saying, 'You know this is the best thing for him.' She *knew* that. I felt like Max should be out of the house around the time he would have been going to college. I find it sad to see kids in their forties living with aging parents. I'd like to be around while he's transitioning, to help him, so when something happens to Peter and me, he isn't suddenly thrown into chaos."

It can be hard to find a place that can deal with someone who is as physically disabled as Max, but where staff are prepared to talk to him even though he can't speak and to cope with the depth of his understanding. His parents eventually found a place that seemed right, but it was still under construction when I met them, and they were waiting. Susanna is matter-of-fact about the group home. "It's not going to feel like a big void when he goes. It doesn't when he's in camp. Peter and I get along better when Max is away. We don't have help on weekends, and if Peter plays golf all day one day, that means I have to be with Max all day. Peter has the same problem if I need to do something. I don't believe that we'll have an empty-nest problem. I think that would have been very different with a normal child, so I get sad about not being sad."

I have heard mothers of healthy children express a fantasy of the child who would be forever tender and vulnerable and dependent, who would not go through the rebellion of adolescence or the detachment of adulthood. Be careful what you wish for. Disabled children are forever the responsibility of their parents; 85 percent of people with mental retardation live with or under the supervision of their parents, an arrangement that remains common until the parent becomes disabled or dies. This can cause the parents terrible anxiety as they age; it can also give them a permanent sense of purpose. Some parents who begin with gusto become overwhelmed by children who require special attention and, in midlife or later, begin to despair. Others who had originally wanted to give up their children for adoption fall gradually in love with them.

The life expectancy for people with disabilities is increasing; in the 1930s, the average age at death for institutionalized mentally retarded males was about fifteen and for females about twenty-two; by 1980, the figure for males was fifty-eight and for females it was up to sixty, though people without mobility die younger. For the parents—before the routines are learned, the emotional bond is made, and the fantasy of the imagined healthy child has been lamented—the initial stress is often overwhelming. Within a diverse sample of aging parents of developmentally disabled adult children, however, one research group found that nearly two-thirds felt their continuing role as caregivers gave them a sense of purpose, while more than half felt less lonely with their child still at home.

In 1994, Bill Zirinsky and Ruth Schekter, owners of Crazy Wisdom bookstore in Ann Arbor, Michigan, welcomed their first child, a red-haired boy whom they named Sam. He had a healthy birth, but things fell off over the next few months. Sam had no appetite, poor muscle tone, and wasn't reaching normal developmental milestones. He couldn't sit or roll over. At first, his pediatrician thought he might have a virus, but at six months, neurological and endocrine testing showed that Sam had a grave disorder. The pediatrician said he had "a hunch" that Sam would have a short life span; that his illness might be degenerative; that he might have demyelination of his nervous system, which can damage sensation, cognition, and movement; and that he would probably be "vegetable-like." The information was dropped, as Ruth described it, "like a lead balloon."

Bill and Ruth devoted all of their energy to finding out what was wrong. "For six months, we had thought our son was just developing slowly," Bill said. "In one weekend we had to deal with learning he was on a completely different life path." They contacted pediatrician after pediatrician, only to be told that they were mistakenly reaching "well-baby doctors." Finally, Ruth called one of the pediatricians on her list and described her son to the nurse, who said, "Dr. Weinblatt *loves* these kind of cases." They next made their way to the neurologist who would be with them for the long haul, Darryl De Vivo, at Columbia-Presbyterian Hospital. Bill remembered, "When we asked him, 'Is Sam likely to have a normal life? Is it still possible?' Dr. De Vivo said gently, 'It would appear that that won't be the case.' I knew that we were dealing with something that was not going to be remedied."

Bill's older sister has cerebral palsy, so he felt he had been trained to take care of a disabled child. Ruth said, "It would have been different if he'd been diagnosed at birth. All the bonding in those first six months was critical. I was so committed to him by then. I remember very clearly, in those weeks right after, wondering whether I would ever feel joy again, and wanting to sacrifice my own life for his, knowing I would gladly give up everything if he would be okay. Those were two really profound and totally new feelings for me."

Sam would never walk, talk, eat, or hear. He received nutrition via a gastric feeding tube (G-tube), was in a wheelchair, and had a seizure disorder. At the age of nearly ten, he weighed only thirty-two pounds. He suffered from constant reflux and pain. His condition was determined to be an undiagnosable, degenerative neurometabolic disorder. "There were relatives who, over the years, might meet or hear about Sam," Bill said. "Their conception of Sam was, quote, 'vegetable,' kind of a 1950s idea. Many more friends and relatives didn't always get him, but understood that there was more than meets the eye to him. Then there's the twenty percent of our friends who really spent time with Sam and got to know him, who would look in his eyes, then play a game or read a book with him. Sam was a mirror for how people understood consciousness." People asked Ruth whether she thought he knew who she was, and she explained that he knew who many people were. Sam loved visual things; he loved being in the water; he loved therapeutic riding. "He puts a smile on his face when he's riding a horse," Bill said. "When he is feeling good, it's really rich." Among the family photos of Sam are the wedding photos of one of his child-care providers. She had asked Sam to be the ring-bearer in her wedding, and there he was, strapped into his wheelchair and holding the rings on a velvet cushion. "He had a horrible weekend," Ruth said. "He had a lot of seizures, and we had to really drug him. But when it came time for him to go down the aisle, he totally pulled himself together and looked radiant. I feel he understood that the ceremony was something special."

Because Sam's disorder was unknown, the risk of a recurrence could not be predicted. After he turned four, Bill and Ruth decided to try for a second child. Juliana seemed healthy at first, but at about four months, the not-eating-well pattern started. In her fifth month, Ruth and Bill brought her to Dr. Weinblatt. When I first met the family, Juliana was almost seven, and her disorder was somewhat milder than Sam's. She was severely hearing-impaired, not deaf. She could walk, though not far and with great difficulty. Instead of having a G-tube surgically inserted through the abdomen into the stomach, she received nourishment through a less invasive nasal-gastric tube, which Ruth had learned to insert whenever Juliana pulled it out. Juliana did not have a seizure disorder and her health seemed less tentative than Sam's. Like Sam, she was tiny: though she was seven when I met her, she looked perhaps two. "She is a faerie sprite," Bill said, "a delightful and funny little girl from another planet. Like Sam, she is very sensitive and has continued to develop emotionally, even while her cognitive development is limited. Their emotional response to many things is age-appropriate: love, jealousy, excitement, attachment, sadness, compassion, desire, hope."

Ruth had more of a sense that the children weren't going to live for long than Bill did. Though Juliana seemed stable, Sam's illness was clearly progressive, and his life became steadily more difficult. In an average week, he would be good two days; three days he would have some hours when his stomach hurt, or he had mild seizures, or he would need to throw up; and two days he'd be disconsolate and have to be held much of the day. "I really wanted people to understand that our lives weren't utterly miserable," Ruth said. "Sam was beautiful to me and continued to be beautiful to me. I can't fault somebody for giving up a child like Sam or Juliana; it's a very tall order. But I never wanted to." They had all spent summers on Long Island with Bill's parents in a house by the sea, and as Sam's condition deteriorated, they contacted a local pediatrician. The pediatrician mentioned that while it's easy to let a child go by refusing life support in New York, it's extremely difficult to disconnect a child once he has been connected. They were furious at her. "We felt violated by it," Bill said. "She didn't understand that we thought Sam wanted to be here in this world." Bill and Ruth went for a long walk, and Ruth said that she thought Sam would tell them what to do. "By anybody else's standards, he was already living an incredibly impaired life," Ruth said, "but we had spent nine years with him and knew he could have pleasure, feel love, enjoy his environment, get a kick out of going to school. If that was still true, then I felt it was unfair to let him go."

A few years earlier, Bill and Ruth had decided to adopt a child, and Sam's escalating illness coincided with the notification that a daughter had been found for them. One of them had to go to Guatemala when the adoption was finalized. They kept putting it off, but Sam had been in the hospital for thirty-five days and their new daughter was wait-ing. So Bill and Ruth agreed that Bill would wait at the hospital while Ruth went to Guatemala. "It was really hard to go," Ruth said. "But he waited. He died the day after I returned."

When I visited Bill and Ruth two years after Sam had died, they were on Long Island again. Age two, Leela, their adopted daughter, was already bigger than Juliana, who at seven weighed twenty-two pounds. Pre-adoption, social workers had expressed concern that a normal child would struggle in their household, but that did not appear to be the case. "The way we love Leela is just different," Ruth said. "I'm constantly juggling those two things, and feeling like Juliana is get-ting short shrift because Leela is such a magnet for people's attention: she's verbal, she's interactive, she's loads of fun. But then, am I paying too much attention to Juliana? There's no easy path." Bill said, "Many people pay a lot of attention to Leela. Juliana watches. She's constantly measuring and evaluating every bit of it. It's painful to us, sometimes, to watch her watching as people pay so much attention to her sister."

Unlike Sam, Juliana was not confined to a wheelchair, and her dimin-utive size seemed congruous with her cognitive deficits; what would have been odd in a girl who looked like a seven-year-old was less odd in a girl who appeared to be not yet two. Aside from the nasal feeding tube, she didn't look unusual. Bill and Ruth waited until she was out of earshot to say that they had no idea how long she would live. I asked whether she could understand speech. Bill recounted reading aloud his notes on Sam's death when the family visited a neurologist. Juliana suddenly began to cry. "Juliana's response wasn't necessarily receptive language, but it's receptive something," Bill said. "It's receptivity to her parents' feelings or the vibrational field. We're both sensitive to not talking in front of her about things that might upset her, just the way you wouldn't with a kid who is more obviously cognitively normal. Just in case."

Juliana died two years after my day in Long Island, at about the same age as Sam. Her condition had deteriorated, and before she died, she lost the ability to walk, then most of the rest of her motor control, and was eventually unable to sit up. "Yet one senses that Juliana is not entirely discontented about her path," Bill wrote in an e-mail. "She is frustrated at times, and she cries sometimes when she feels sorry for herself. Yet there has descended upon her a certain wisdom and medi-tative resignation, which is very becoming. Meanwhile, she does suffer physically, and that is painful for her and us." When I praised the qual-ity of care he was giving to her, he wrote, "I think most people I know, if a child had been given to them who was profoundly disabled, would have risen to the occasion. I need to believe that. It's how I construct a good world."

After she died, Bill said, "I would have chosen the easier path. But now, knowing what I know, I would want Sam again, and I would want Juliana again. How could I trade the love I experienced with these two human beings? I was closer to Sam than any human being in my life. I spent more time lying on a bed with him, looking in his eyes, than anyone I've ever been with. I've spent a huge amount of time with Juliana, just hanging out with her, just loving her. So that's like asking any parent whether they would trade the love that they know for some abstract 'better' child. I would do it all again." Ruth reached over and took Bill's hand, with a look of deep compassion. "I actually think it's not believing in God that has given us that perspective. People always regale us with these little sayings, like 'God doesn't give you any more than you can handle.' But children like ours are not preordained as a gift. They're a gift because that's what we have chosen."

Siblings of severely disabled children have been studied extensively, but with inconclusive results. One study mentions that persons with disabled siblings "felt that living with a disabled brother or sister helped them be more responsible, be more tolerant," better able to see "the good in others, develop a better sense of humor, and be more flexible." However, these siblings also reported "embarrassment, guilt, isolation, and concern about the future of their disabled sibling." Another study of siblings of disabled children pitted clinical diagnosis of depression against "plain-old feeling bad" and found that while siblings of those with disabilities were in general more unhappy, they did not suffer from more diagnosable psychiatric problems than their peers. Often, the more obvious or severe the handicap, the easier it is for the nondisabled sibling, because the child does not present in a way that causes people to anticipate normal behavior; children who seem normal at first and then turn out not to be require more explaining. The worst disabilities seem to be associated with the best sibling adjustment. "This result seemed closely tied to the entire family's greater clarity about, and comfort with, a visible defect in the child," one study noted. Another observed that a diagnosis made a huge difference to younger siblings, who could use a simple explanation with friends; those with a sibling with no clear diagnosis had to struggle more.

The reason most commonly given for institutionalizing children in the heyday of institutionalization was that keeping a disabled child at home was unfair to healthy siblings, because the disabled child would take too much of the parents' energy and focus and embarrass the nondisabled child. More recent work shows that healthy siblings are often disturbed when parents institutionalize; Allen Shawn's book *Twin* details the pain he experienced when his sister was sent away. The interests of the nondisabled sibling are now more often held to require keeping the disabled sibling at home. This may be better for the disabled child as well, but it's striking how the conversation continues to prioritize the interest of the nondisabled sibling over that of the disabled one.

John and Eve Morris were a love story from the moment they met at a party at Cornell, where they were both undergraduates. They married young and moved to San Diego. "I didn't want to be with anybody else, even children, because I loved him so much," Eve said. Not until Eve was thirty did she commit to pregnancy. "I also didn't want to give up my freedom," she said. "As it turned out, I liked being a mother much more than I ever liked freedom."

Eve and John chose as their obstetrician a devout Mormon who was appalled by the local hospital's cesarean rate of one in five births. Before Alix's delivery, he told John and Eve that he "didn't think nature screwed up that much." They warmed to his enthusiasm. When Eve went into labor, she was given an external fetal-heart monitor. Doctors who later reviewed her monitor strip said it suggested distress, and that Eve should have had an immediate cesarean, but their doctor seems not to have noticed. By the time Eve delivered, Alix was "essentially dead"; her Apgar scores were zero, and she was an alarming dark purple color. She was whisked away to the neonatal intensive care unit (NICU). "The dream of normal parenthood shattered there before my eyes," John said.

Immediately following the birth, the doctors were careful not to offer conclusions about Alix's condition—perhaps because dire news can interfere with parental bonding, perhaps due to liability concerns, perhaps because they could not predict the extent and severity of her problems. Although they may immediately have recognized cerebral palsy, the diagnosis was not communicated to Eve and John until many months later. Cerebral palsy is any disability caused by damage to the cerebrum before birth, just afterward, or in the first three years of life. It comes in many shapes and sizes, with a broad range of possible motor impairments. As an infant, Alix screamed whenever Eve tried to feed her, choking on the milk because her throat was constantly raw from reflux, but the Morrises did not yet understand the extent of Alix's disability. "It took us a long time to confront the idea that anything had gone wrong in a big way," John said. Eve said, "I'd been a cheerleader;

I'd done well at school and gotten into Cornell; I had parents who loved me and were never abusive; I'd had a life of things going right, and somehow it was hard to think that everything wasn't still going right. Those habits kept me in denial for a long, long time. By the time I faced what was wrong with Alix, I loved her more than anything in the world."

John is a lawyer with some background in liability. He and Eve initiated a lawsuit against the doctor and hospital when Alix was eighteen months old. After two years, they arrived at a settlement, which included a lump-sum payment and a court-supervised annuity. The annuity is closely monitored; John and Eve must file annual expense reports. They immediately bought a customized running stroller and a wheelchair van, then hired a young woman named Erika Lundeen as a part-time caretaker for Alix. "Erika was never exactly a daughter to us, and never just a friend, and never just someone who worked for us," John said. "She was all of the above." When I met Erika, she was newly married. Alix had been her bridesmaid, dressed up and wheeled down the aisle for the occasion. "We will do anything to keep her in our lives," Eve said. "I want her to have kids, and then I'll start taking care of her kids. Keep it going." Erika lives a mile away, in a house that John and Eve own. "You remember *It Takes a Village*?" John said. "I'm trying to build a village, so there will always be second and third layers of people who are familiar with Alix." When Alix was two, John and Eve had a son, Dylan, named for his father's favorite singer, and Dylan's genial, healthy, enthusiastic persona has mitigated his parents' pain somewhat. "My advice is to have another kid," Eve said. "So you know what it feels like to have it how it's supposed to be."

Their major undertaking, accomplished with their own savings and some of Alix's lump sum, was to build their own house in the Point Loma area of San Diego. Designed by Eve herself, the house sits on a hill with a view of the ocean. The corridors and turns are wide enough to accommodate a wheelchair. A big swing hangs at one end of the living room; the sensation of motion is among Alix's chief joys. A hot tub on the roof goes mostly unused now because it has become too difficult to lift Alix in and out of it, but when she was younger, she loved it. She has her own fully equipped bathroom, an ergonomic bedroom with a built-in bed she can't fall out of, and a "sensory area" full of fountains, lights, sounds, and vibrations she can trigger if she hits a button (which she does only by chance). The house is beautiful but not showy, capacious and welcoming and utilitarian, with an honest, handmade feel to it. The beams are exposed tree trunks, and the kitchen-cabinet doors are made from willow twigs Eve gathered near her mother's house.

The house also represents a resignation to hard facts. "By the time she was six, we acknowledged that this is who and what she is and what her condition is, and it's not going to change," Eve said. "We stopped doing specific physical therapies, trying to teach her new stuff."

Early on, Eve joined a mothers group of women with CP children, but she has never been to a therapist. "When we started the lawsuit, I sometimes wished she had died," Eve said. "So I was thinking about seeing a therapist. But when you initiate a lawsuit here, they can requisition your talks with your therapist, and I did not want anybody to know that I had felt those things. I grew up in a WASP neighborhood, and everyone was supposed to be the same and act in set ways. I have a really easy time at home with her. But we never go out to dinner as a family because of how unpredictable she is. When John has friends over, or when there's a birthday party, or when I see my parents, I want her to be her best. I wanted her to be her best for you, even." Eve looked doleful. "I feel so much sadness sometimes. When my friends are talking about their girls' being mean, I catch myself saying, 'I'm glad I don't have a girl.' I do have a girl, but she's almost this other being. No one understands what it's like; even I know what it's like right now, and that's all. When you came to interview us, I thought, 'Well, I'm very happy to talk to you so long as you promise not to ask about the past or the future, because the present is the only thing I've got down.'"

When I met the Morrises, they had recently drafted an estate plan naming Erika as guardian for both kids; at twenty-five, Dylan would assume primary legal responsibility for Alix, though the lawsuit annuity will always provide sufficient income to hire a caregiver. Eve has tremendous apprehension around Dylan's future role. "I don't want him to have to play the role that John plays now," she said. At sixteen, Dylan maintained that he loved his sister and would always be glad to care for her. "I don't think she's ever missed a baseball game," he told me. "I was born into this. It's affected me all my life." Dylan's coach said that he knew Dylan must have a connection to a disabled kid, because he had never seen such maturity in someone who hadn't done some difficult caretaking.

Eve has consistently opposed having a G-tube surgically implanted in Alix. Alix, eighteen when I met her, has managed without one, though she needs to be fed every four hours to prevent reflux. Alix's impairments are unusually severe for cerebral palsy. All of the other CP children of the women in Eve's mothers group can walk, and all have at least rudimentary speech. One is attending college, and another has a job bagging groceries at a local supermarket. "Blessings are frequently mixed," John said. "Those kids recognize how they don't fit, that they don't have boyfriends or girlfriends, that kids laugh at them. Nobody ever teased Alix. She is so profoundly disabled and helpless that even the worst little snotty four-year-old never snickered at her. As for us, we have to think about seizures but not about her smoking pot behind the school. The fundamental role of the parent is the same: to provide for, and love, and give the best opportunity you can to your kids on any given day. I think we do that with Alix the same as we do with Dylan."

John and Eve have become habituated to their daughter's needs; what was once self-conscious has become intuitive. Alix is medically more stable than she has ever been; at the same time, her growth has made it impossible for the family to do things they used to enjoy, to take her swimming or to carry her around the house. The work of getting her in and out of bed or on and off the toilet has become especially difficult as John and Eve have grown older. "It's emotionally gotten easier even while it's physically gotten harder," Eve said. The qualities of helplessness that read as innocence in an infant seem incongruous in someone whose body is adult-size: the uncontrolled tongue, the flailing limbs, the stretching and turning body, the bunched-up muscles. Involuntary movements notwithstanding, Alix is always impeccably groomed. "I put nail polish on her and keep her hair long and dress her in pretty clothes so people will have something to say," Eve explained. "They come over and say, 'Look how nice your fingernails are!' instead of having to talk about what's wrong with her." For Eve, the most burdensome thing is the sympathy that so often supersedes connection. "I hate the look of pity, the people who say, 'You're such a good mom.'"

Staying with the Morrises for a week, I was overwhelmed by how much they had to do and how little they let it get in their way. John is a habitual runner, and Alix loves the sensation of the wind in her face, so he pushes her in a lightweight stroller for five miles every day. Eve takes her for wheelchair outings on the wharf. Every year, Eve makes a Halloween costume for Alix that incorporates her wheelchair: one year she was an alien in a foreign spacecraft; another year, an ice cream truck; and most recently, a Krispy Kreme doughnut distribution center. Eve trained as an artist, and the costumes are marvelous. John and Eve have a fairly equitable distribution of parenting. John is more resilient, and Eve is more attuned. "It doesn't hurt him when she cries," Eve said one afternoon. "He can lie down next to her and she can be crying for fifteen minutes, and he's just keeping her company. And I'm trying to fix it." When it can be fixed, Eve explained, her anxiety is useful, but most of the time it can't, and John's serenity serves a more vital function. Eve takes care of Alix's personal hygiene, including bathing her every other day, while John feeds her most of her meals when he's home. Alix cannot chew solid food, and she cannot swallow liquids without a risk of choking. Five times a day, John gives her a high-protein nutritional supplement mixed with rice cereal and sometimes flavored with a dollop of baby food. Every morning, John and Eve rise at five thirty to get Alix ready for school. It takes about forty minutes to wake and dress her. Then she needs to be fed. The school bus arrives at six thirty; it would be easier for them to drive her, but they want her to experience the social atmosphere on the bus. When Alix turned eighteen, her HMO switched her out of the pediatric system, so when I visited, Eve was taking her to a new GP, a new neurologist, and so on. A few days later, a wheelchair outfitter came to visit, and there was a family session to look over Alix's current chair and decide how it needed to be modified to serve her better. It took just over three hours to order the new chair.

Eve kept a diary through Alix's early years, but she has never gone back to read it. John said, "We remember all the things we hoped she would do one day, all the hours of physical therapy teaching her to turn over voluntarily, to raise up her head." Eve recounted a recent conversation in which the orthopedist told her that in later life, swallowing gets difficult again, and Alix might eventually need a G-tube. Eve said, "I thought we were at the stage that Alix wouldn't really get better, wouldn't get worse. You never get to relax." John agreed. "I've been invited a number of times to be on the board of the local United Cerebral Palsy," he said. "You know how people say, 'I give at the office'? I give at home. But on the other hand, if any parent could ask for just one thing for their child, what would it be? Not that they go to Harvard, but that they be happy. Alix is happy most of the time. So if I'd had only one wish, that's what it would have been, and I'd have gotten it."

The field of profound disabilities does not often have breaking scandals, but the Ashley treatment rocked that world. Ashley X, whose last name has never been revealed, was born in 1997, an apparently healthy baby. When she seemed irritable at about three months, her parents thought it was colic. It turned out to be static encephalopathy, a diagnosis that, like CP, describes a stable brain injury of unknown origin. It has left Ashley with limited functioning: she will never talk, walk, or feed herself, and she cannot turn over. She can sleep, wake, and breathe—and she can smile.

In a bid to defend his own and his family's privacy, her father has refused to meet face-to-face with anyone from the media; he refers to himself as AD (Ashley's Dad). He explained to me over the phone that he and his wife had initially resisted giving Ashley a G-tube because they had a visceral negative response to the idea of surgery. "She cannot chew, and she was always struggling with the bottle," he said. "We would spend six to eight hours a day to get enough nutrition to her." Finally, they had a tube inserted. Despite compromised brain function, Ashley is not unresponsive. "Ashley enjoys our company and voices," her parents said in a written statement. "When we sweet talk to her, she often radiates with a big smile. She enjoys rich music, walks outdoors, a swim on a warm day, the swing, etc." Ashley's parents started to call her their "pillow angel" because she was generally lying on a pillow and never gave them trouble; they have proposed the term be used for other people with MSD.

As Ashley grew from infancy to childhood, her care became more challenging. Hourly, her parents change her position and prop her back on her pillow. "We make sure she is well covered and pull her shirt down to cover her tummy; we wipe her drool, etc.," AD explained to me. "Also there are diaper changes, tube feedings, dressing, bathing, teeth cleaning, stretching, entertainment." All of this became harder as Ashley grew larger. "You start having difficulty including her in activities," AD said to me. "You want to be able to carry her, but your body aches. The notion formed gradually that her added size and weight were her worst enemy, and the idea to do something about it was an epiphany." When Ashley was six, her mother (AM) was talking to her own mother, who reminded her of a neighbor who had had hormone treatments to prevent her becoming extremely tall; this procedure was not uncommon in the 1950s, when girls over five feet ten inches were considered unattractive.

Ashley's pediatrician suggested that AD and AM visit Dr. Daniel Gunther, an endocrinologist at Seattle Children's Hospital. At their appointment several weeks later, Gunther acknowledged that Ashley's growth could be attenuated by administering estrogen, which would close her growth plates. Since Ashley will cry for an hour when she sneezes because she is so upset by slight discomfort, AD thought she would have a hard time with menstruation and the cramping it can cause. He proposed a hysterectomy. He thought breasts would get in her way when she was turned on her pillow or strapped in a wheelchair and asked that his daughter's breast buds, the small, almond-shaped glands that enlarge into breasts at puberty, be removed. All this would result in a person who was easier to move—which, in turn, he argued, would mean better circulation, digestion, and muscle condition for her, and fewer sores and infections. Giving Ashley a permanent child's figure would leave her with what her father called "a body that more closely matched her stage of mental development."

AM and AD had to persuade the hospital ethics committee that this was a viable set of procedures, and AD put together a PowerPoint presentation for that purpose. The ethics committee devoted a great deal of time to the question. "There were two main aspects to the parents' requests," said Dr. Douglas Diekema, who led the ethics panel. "We looked at whether we should permit growth attenuation to occur and whether we should permit a hysterectomy. The first issue was, do these things have the potential to improve this little girl's quality of life? The second issue was, what's the potential for harm here and is it significant enough that even with the prospect of some benefit we shouldn't allow it to move forward? The ethics committee struggled with trying to understand what potential troubles might come to a little girl from this sort of thing. Would someone in Ashley's position ever really care if they were twelve inches shorter? The conclusion was, in Ashley's circumstances height had very little value." Gunther said, "In the end it was the obvious bond and love that exists between Ashley and her parents that convinced them this was the right thing to do."

In 2004, Seattle Children's Hospital doctors performed a hysterectomy and a bilateral mastectomy on Ashley, who was then six and a half. While Ashley's abdomen was opened for the hysterectomy, they also removed her appendix, anticipating that she would not be able to communicate the symptoms of appendicitis should she ever develop it. Ashley's adult height is four feet five inches, her weight is sixty-three pounds, and she will never menstruate, grow breasts, or have the breast cancer that runs in her family. "It has been successful in every expected way," her parents wrote.

AD encouraged Drs. Gunther and Diekema to publish the protocol, which appeared in October of that year in the *Archives of Pediatrics & Adolescent Medicine*. A firestorm ensued. Arthur Caplan, of the University of Pennsylvania Center for Bioethics, characterized it as "a pharmacological solution for a social failure—the fact that American society does not do what it should to help severely disabled children and their families." He suggested that with better support services, Ashley's parents wouldn't have been driven to their radical act. Feminist and disability activists protested at the American Medical Association's headquarters, asking them to issue an official condemnation. One blogger wrote, "If 'Ashley' were a 'normal' child and the parents decided to have her surgically mutilated, the parents would be thrown in prison where they rightly belong. The 'doctors' involved in this case should have their licenses revoked." Another wrote, "They might as well kill her as cut pieces off at a time. Much more convenient, I'd say." FRIDA (Feminist Response in Disability Activism) wrote that they were "not surprised that the initial recipient of the 'Ashley Treatment' was a little girl, given that girls, and girls with disabilities in particular, are perceived as easier subjects for mutilation and desexualization." The *Toronto Star* complained about "designer cripples."

Parents of other disabled children joined the fray. Julia Epstein, communications director for the Disability Rights Education and Defense Fund and the mother of a disabled child, called the term *pillow angel* "terminally infantilizing." Another wrote, "My son is eleven, doesn't walk, doesn't talk, etc., etc. He's not going to get easier to carry. And still, I don't understand removing healthy tissue and functioning organs." Yet another parent wrote, "Caring for a five feet something, 110-plus pound adult with physical disabilities is no walk in the park. I've got the trashed lumbar discs to prove that. But I am truly just sick to my stomach to imagine that it's acceptable medical practice to surgically stunt a child's growth. Using their logic, why not just perform quadruple amputations? I mean, really, she's not going to use her arms and legs." These comments about growth attenuation echo in some way attitudes toward limb-lengthening for people with dwarfism.

The backlash shocked the hospital administrators, as it did AD and AM. "It was so extreme, and violent," AD said. "There were threats in e-mails." Washington Protection & Advocacy System, a federally mandated watchdog agency, ruled that involuntary sterilization requires a court order, and that the hospital was therefore in violation of the law. Following their report, Seattle Children's has agreed to appoint a disinterested party to advocate for the interests of any disabled individual for whom growth-limiting treatment is proposed. The debate has gone on ever since, with many commentators opining that the whole question is beyond the scope of medical ethics. In late 2010, the Seattle Growth Attenuation and Ethics Working Group issued new guidelines based on an uneasy compromise: "Growth attenuation can be an ethically acceptable decision because the benefits and risks are similar to those associated with other decisions that parents make for their profoundly disabled children and about which reasonable people disagree. But clinicians and institutions should not provide growth attenuation simply because parents request it. It is important to have safeguards in place, such as eligibility criteria, a thorough decision-making process, and the involvement of ethics consultants or committees."

Writing in the *Hastings Center Report*, one member of the Working Group complained of the assault on the Ashley treatment, saying, "This remarkable intrusion into private medical decisions lacks any plausible claim of harm to third parties other than emotional distress on becoming aware that one's moral or political views are not shared by everyone. By this criterion, parents seeking cochlear implants for a deaf child, surgical correction of club feet or scoliosis, or a do-not-resuscitate order for a terminally ill child should be reminded that their decisions may be offensive to others." But in the same issue, another author argued, "If growth attenuation should not be done on children without these impairments, then it should not be done on any children. To do otherwise amounts to discrimination."

The moral questions enmeshed in cases such as Ashley's have become steadily more complex in the last fifty years. It's problematic to resolve identity conditions, and it's problematic to neglect medical or social imperatives. AD set up a webpage to tell his side of the story; it has since had nearly three million hits, and at the time we spoke, AD told me he spent about ten hours a week blogging. Describing the protesters as a loud minority, he said that about 95 percent of the e-mail he and AM received was supportive. An MSNBC survey with more than seven thousand respondents showed 59 percent in support of the treatment. "More than 1,100 caregivers and family members with direct experience with pillow angels took the time to e-mail us with their support," Ashley's parents wrote. "If parents of children like Ashley believe that this treatment will improve their children's quality of life, then they should be diligent and tenacious in providing it for them." In the wake of the controversy, however, the procedure is unavailable.

Gunther said, "The argument that a beneficial treatment should not be used because it might be misused is itself a slippery slope. If we did not use available therapies because they could be misused, we would be practicing very little medicine." Writing in the *New York Times*, the Princeton ethicist Peter Singer said, "What matters in Ashley's life is that she should not suffer, and that she should be able to enjoy whatever she is capable of enjoying. Beyond that, she is precious not so much for what she is, but because her parents and siblings love her and care about her. Lofty talk about human dignity should not stand in the way of children like her getting the treatment that is best both for them and their families."

My conversations with AD made it clear to me that he loved Ashley, and that he believed fervently in the Ashley treatment. While writing this book, I met family after family who didn't know what to do as their children grew up and became too big to handle. Disability activists often referred to Ashley's loss of dignity, but having seen a number of similarly disabled people lifted up in pulleys with chains to be removed from bed, put in metal standers to preserve muscle tone, conveyed on rope systems into showers, I cannot see much dignity there.

Arthur Caplan and others referred to the need for better social supports for families of people with disabilities, but AD and AM undertook the treatment not because they didn't have resources to get ropes and pulleys and even nurses, but because they felt a different intimacy in carrying their child themselves. Most human beings—children or adults, physically impaired or able-bodied—prefer human touch to mechanical support. Whether that intimacy warrants surgical intervention is open to discussion, but to discount the intimacy and say all that is needed is more access to assistive devices is to miss the point.

Some activists said that the procedure was not for Ashley's benefit but to make her parents' lives less stressful. These things cannot be separated. If the lives of Ashley's parents are made easier, then they will be able to devote more calm and positive attention to her, and her life will be better. If she is in less pain, her parents' lives will be improved. They are yin and yang, those lives, and far more important than the choice to undertake a procedure is that AD and AM have not separated from Ashley, nor indicated any wish to do so. Ashley likes rides in the car, and the sound of voices; she likes to be lifted and held; and this treatment appears to mean that she can have many years of these experiences instead of going to a group home. Parental care, which so often outclasses other forms of care, will also probably increase her longevity.

It is not true that "love is not love which alters when it alteration finds." Love alters all the time; it is fluid, in perpetual flux, an evolving business across a lifetime. We commit to love our children without knowing them, and knowing them changes how we love them, if not that we love them. Activists are outraged at the things Ashley has lost: being tall, being sexually mature. These attainments are all part of the natural life cycle, but they are not exalted simply because they happen to most people. It's a subtle moral calculus to weigh out what is lost and what is gained by growth and sexual maturity, what is lost and what is gained by growth attenuation and hysterectomy. No one has said that the Ashley treatment is appropriate for people with significant cognition.

The calculus is very much complicated, however, by stories such as Anne McDonald's. She, too, was a pillow angel, permanently unable to walk, talk, feed, or care for herself; she remained small because she was malnourished in the Australian hospital where she was placed in the 1960s. "Like Ashley, I have experienced growth attenuation. I may be the only person on Earth who can say, 'Been there. Done that. Didn't like it. Preferred to grow,'" she wrote in a column for the *Seattle Post-Intelligencer.* "My life changed when I was offered a means of communication. At the age of 16, I was taught to spell by pointing to letters on an alphabet board. Two years later, I used spelling to instruct the lawyers who fought the habeas corpus action that enabled me to leave the institution in which I'd lived for 14 years." Anne McDonald eventually graduated from a university with majors in philosophy of science and fine arts. She traveled around the world. "Ashley's condemned to be a Peter Pan and never grow, but it's not too late for her to learn to communicate," McDonald continued. "It's profoundly unethical to leave her on that pillow without making every effort to give her a voice of her own."

McDonald's story and writing point to the inscrutability of people who cannot express themselves. Nonetheless, her growth attenuation was caused by horrible neglect in the institution where her parents had abandoned her, while Ashley's was brought about by parents who love her, to keep her with them. McDonald's intelligence had no chance to emerge; Ashley's has been given every encouragement. "I hope she does not understand what has happened to her; but I'm afraid she probably does," McDonald wrote. AD is mistaken in suggesting that Ashley is definitively incapable of mental development; the plasticity of even the most basic parts of the brain means that most people develop with the simple passage of time. A letter in *Pediatrics* protested, "The idea that we can be certain about prognosis for 'nuanced' communication in a three-year-old is simply wrong; too much depends on how the child is raised and cared for and at three years many parents are still too confused and sad to grapple with the future." In commenting on the Ashley story, Alice Domurat Dreger wrote touchingly of her own mother's polishing her grandfather's glasses as he neared the end of his life—"just in case he could still see."

Higher-functioning disabled people of necessity speak for lower-functioning disabled people, and the insights of higher-functioning disabled people are precious; their situation is, after all, closer to that of low-functioning disabled people than is that of the general population. A higher-functioning person who used to be lower-functioning—such as Anne McDonald—has particular authority. Nonetheless, claims to common cause are often muddied by projection. McDonald seems to be retelling her own history rather than responding to Ashley's. Ashley is essentially unknowable both to her parents and to the vocal advocates who believe they have spoken on her behalf. Disability rights advocates complain of a world that refuses to accommodate their reality, but AD makes a similar complaint: that a tyrannical group of empowered people prevents accommodation of an individual and her specific needs.

"A collective agenda/ideology is being shoved down the throat of all individuals with disabilities, whether it serves them as individuals or not," AD wrote. "This is disturbing in a society that believes strongly in the well-being of children and in individual rights. We feel the benefits to Ashley on a daily basis. We care about how this might help other kids in her situation. A lot of the criticism came from people who themselves have disabilities and was based on their feeling about how inappropriate the treatment would be for them. Clearly Ashley is in a vastly different category of disability than someone who is able to blog and write e-mails and make decisions for themselves. A chasm separates the two, not a slippery slope like some fear or claim. Newtonian physics works well in most cases, but not in extreme cases. As Einstein pointed out, it fails at high speeds. Relativity explains that very well. So, this ideology of the disability community works well. We support it. In this extreme case, however, it fails miserably."

Our understanding of brain science is so advanced and yet so primitive. We still have much to learn about brain plasticity and neurogenesis, and the nature of anyone's silence is always a matter of speculation. We make mistakes both in doing too much and in doing too little. Norman Kunc, who was born with cerebral palsy and is now a consultant and speaker on disability issues, has described how much of a gap there can be between the benign intention and problematic consequences of treatment for people with disabilities. He characterized his own early experiences with physiotherapy as akin to rape. "From the age of three until the age of twelve, three times a week," he said, "women who were older than I was, who were more powerful than I was, who had more authority than I had, brought me into their room, their space, their turf. They took off some of my clothes. They invaded my personal space. They gripped me and touched me, manipulating my body in ways that were painful. I didn't know I had any other choice than to go along with it. To me it's a form of sexual assault even though it was completely asexual. It's the power and domination that is part of the abuse. Obviously the therapist does not have the same intent as a rapist, but there is a difference between caring and competence. Many human service professionals assume that, because they care for people, their actions are inevitably competent. As soon as you challenge the competence of their actions, you're seen as questioning their caring for the person."

Kunc argues that doing something with love does not necessarily make it good. Even outside the world of disability, we all perpetrate and are subject to loving yet damaging acts within our families. That damage is likely to be greater and more frequent with horizontal identities because the good intentions are less informed. Because I am gay, my parents hurt me in ways they wouldn't have if I'd been like them—not because they wanted to hurt me, but because they lacked sufficient insight into what it was like to be gay. Their essentially good intentions, though, are crucial to my adult identity. I can't be sure whether AD harmed his daughter or helped her, but I believe that he acted in good faith. Parents are broken and full of error. Intention does not obliterate that error, but I think, contrary to Kunc, that it does at least mitigate it. Being hurt by those you love is awful, but it's less awful if you know they meant to help.

The word *genocide* gets thrown around a lot in identity movements. Deaf people speak of a genocide because so many deaf children receive cochlear implants; people with Down syndrome and their families speak of a genocide achieved through selective termination of pregnancies. Few people, however, would propose that people who are deaf or who have DS should be killed or left to die. Though some parents murder their autistic children, the practice is commonly held to be shocking and wrong. In cases of multiple severe disability, however, far more people feel comfortable with such a solution. This is in part because these children often live only by way of extreme medical intervention; they are a modern invention, and the idea of letting them die can be held up as "letting nature take its course."

In *Rethinking Life and Death*, Peter Singer quotes an Australian pediatrician, Frank Shann, who described two children in his care. One had had massive bleeding in his brain and therefore had no cerebral cortex; he was capable only of automatic function. In the next bed was a child who was healthy except for a damaged heart, and who would die without a heart transplant. The vegetative boy was a blood-type match, and his heart could have saved the other child, but this would have required that his organs be harvested before he was legally dead. Since this was impossible, both children died within weeks. Shann said, "If the cortex of the brain is dead, the person is dead. I suggest it should be legal to use the organs from the body of the dead person for transplantation." Singer does not agree that obliteration of the cortex is equivalent to death, but he nonetheless feels that the death of both children was a tragic waste. Disability advocates would say it is as unthinkable to kill a severely disabled child to save a nondisabled child as it would be to kill one nondisabled child to save another. Dead people clearly have fewer rights than living people, and Shann held that the first child in his scenario was exempt from the rights of the living. There may be science in this, but it feels weird to describe as *dead* someone who is breathing, sneezing, yawning, even producing some form of reflex smile.

Peter Singer maintains that what is in question is *personhood*. He proposes that not all persons are human beings; sentient animals of higher awareness are also persons. He likewise opines that not all human beings are persons. In *Practical Ethics* he wrote, "Killing a disabled infant is not morally equivalent to killing a person. Very often it is not wrong at all." Elsewhere he has contended, "If we compare a severely defective human infant with a nonhuman animal, a dog or a pig, for example, we will often find the nonhuman to have superior capacities, both actual and potential, for rationality, self-consciousness, communication, and anything else that can plausibly be considered morally significant." Singer in effect reverses *cogito, ergo sum* and says that those who do not think do not exist.

Nearly all agree that one cannot kill disabled children against their parents' will, but whether they can be kept alive against their parents' will is a tougher question. In 1991, Karla Miller, five months pregnant, went into labor and was rushed to her local hospital in Houston. Doctors told her she was having a "tragic miscarriage" and asked whether she and her husband preferred to let nature follow its course, or to have an experimental procedure that would probably leave the child alive but severely brain-damaged. The couple prayed and decided to forgo heroic measures. The hospital administration then informed them that hospital policy was to resuscitate all babies born over five hundred grams, and that if they did not want the baby saved, they should leave the hospital immediately. As Karla was hemorrhaging and in danger of bleeding to death, they chose not to do so. Though in many states Karla could have aborted a fetus at this stage of development, she did not have the right to refuse life support once the child had come out of her. When the baby arrived at 630 grams, medical personnel inserted a tube into the newborn's throat to give oxygen to her undeveloped lungs. She is blind and has never walked or talked.

The Millers took care of her, but they brought a wrongful-life case against the hospital, claiming that the hospital had acted against their wishes and should therefore provide a financial settlement to finance the child's permanent care. A court awarded the Millers $43 million in damages and expenses, but that decision was overturned on appeal. Official policy had kept their child from dying; official policy said it was their problem to deal with her needs for the rest of their lives.

The Miller case prompted enormous protest and a coalition of seventeen disability organizations filed an amicus brief that stated, "Most adults with disabilities, including those who have had a disability since birth, choose life and have quality in their lives. Most parents of children with disabilities value and believe their children's lives have quality." The disability-focused *Inclusion Daily Express* wrote, "Many disability rights advocates believe that the Millers' suit promotes infanticide—

the murder of babies—particularly of those with disabilities." Among people outside the disability rights community, opinions were less decisive. "I think that it is really inappropriate to override the wishes of the parents, particularly with children like this," said Ellen Wright Clayton, a pediatrics expert at Vanderbilt University. George Annas, a health-law and bioethics expert at Boston University, said, "The truth is, no one really knows what's best for kids like this, and there should be no hard-and-fast rule."

For legal purposes, the referent was a 1978 decision made in New York, in which the judge wrote, "Whether it is better never to have been born at all than to have been born with even gross deficiencies is a mystery more properly to be left to the philosophers and the theologians. Surely the law can assert no competence to resolve the issue, particularly in view of the very nearly uniform high value which the law and mankind has placed on human life, rather than its absence. The implications of any such proposition are staggering."

Opera, an art form largely devoted to finding beauty in catastrophe, was not a bad preparation for life for Julia Hollander, a director who has worked at the English National Opera. Before her second daughter, Imogen, was even conceived, Julia had wanted to think deeply about illness and had volunteered in one of Mother Teresa's hospices in Calcutta. Julia's pregnancy with Imogen appeared to go well until she went into sudden labor in the small hours of the night at thirty-eight weeks, on June 19, 2002. The pain was excruciating. "I'd had a protracted labor before," Julia recalled, "and it was a rather fun twenty-four hours in comparison with this." She phoned her midwife, who advised her to go to A&E, the emergency room, in Oxford. An administrator at the hospital said they couldn't take her because she was registered with a midwifery center; as they were arguing, Julia's water broke, and he advised her to head to the center immediately. Jay Arden, Julia's partner and the baby's father, drove her forty minutes there, and the center called in a midwife. The baby's heart rate was half of what it should have been, and the midwife told them to go immediately to a nearby hospital. Julia was screaming in agony by this time, and, knowing the baby was in distress, making every effort to deliver even though she was only three centimeters dilated. She gave birth within minutes of arriving at the hospital. Two weeks earlier, Julia's placenta had hemorrhaged, but because Imogen was already engaged, her head had kept the blood from seeping out.

Blood in the womb is poison. Hemorrhaging occurs in one in a hundred pregnancies, and frequently infants come out fine. But Imogen seemed to be having epileptic fits. Julia and Jay transferred her to the Oxford hospital that had refused them earlier, where she was placed in the Special Care Baby Unit (SCBU), a step short of intensive care. Later, Julia wrote, "In Limbo, the babies have died and now float between life and the after-life. These ones had been born but had not yet entered life." At the end of a week, Imogen opened her eyes, and ten days later, she went home with her parents.

Imogen couldn't latch on to Julia's breast, and she screamed all the time. "There was no logic to her screaming," Julia recalled. "My other daughter cries, but I know that if I go to her, she'll stop; often she's crying distinctly for me. There was nothing of Imogen's needing me, and nothing I did comforted her in any way. Not to have that was hateful." The care of Imogen became more and more difficult. She seemed seldom to sleep, and never to be awake without bellowing. Jay was able to coax her into at least a temporary quiet by swinging her around wildly and exhaustingly, but after a few weeks, he had to go back to his job. When Imogen was six weeks old "I remember throwing her down on the bed and saying, 'I hate you! I hate you!'" Julia recalled. "It seemed, in retrospect, that nature was telling me to reject this baby." The doctors, gnomic and withholding, still indicated that Imogen might be fine. Julia and Jay tried massage therapies, lactation consultants, colic remedies, a crying-and-feeding diary. Imogen had occasional moments of quiet or sleep, but never an expression of happiness or delight. Then she started throwing up after every feeding. Julia found two statistics on the Internet that stuck with her: eight out of ten parents dealing with severely disabled children were "at the breaking point," and 16 percent of such families in Britain gave their children up to care.

One visitor sent by the National Health Service (NHS) to check on the situation called Julia a saint. "Of course it was her job to get me to bond, because the NHS isn't going to look after these babies if they can possibly help it," Julia said to me. "Imogen wouldn't stop screaming, so I qualified for sainthood." Coexistent with this heroism was hideous rage. "One night in the dark, no moon and no candle, rocking Immie's angry little body back and forth, I feel myself swing just a little bit further," she later wrote. "This is what it would feel like if I were to smash her head against the wall. It would be so simple—her soft skull would crush like a boiled egg, if I just swung that bit harder. I didn't tell anyone about my fantasy, but it disturbed me greatly—the ease with which I really, truly imagined destroying my child." Imogen's smile was now so delayed that its absence was a sure sign of brain damage. The despair Julia and Jay had held at bay stormed the fortress.

A few weeks later, Julia took a respite weekend paid by the state and left Imogen with a substitute caregiver. She had looked forward to such freedom, but found that turning her daughter over to someone "better at loving a person like that than I was" deeply humiliating. Imogen was prescribed a raft of drugs despite the absence of a diagnosis; the pediatrician's warning that "major problems" lay ahead was hardly a coherent road map. Jay began to withdraw. "I was furious with him for not loving his baby," Julia explained. "It reminded me how trapped I was in an impossible, unrequited love for her." This bond, rife with ambivalence, had absorbed all the love she might have given to Jay, and he began threatening to leave. "We were discovering how selfish grief can be," Julia wrote.

Jay proposed that they suffocate Imogen—to spare pain for her and them. It would look exactly like SIDS, or cot death. Julia was horrified, yet she, too, longed for Imogen to die. "I couldn't live with her, and I couldn't live without her," she said. "What was best for her? Did she have a right to live? The word *right* is so heavy, isn't it? I think we're very, very muddled about children and life." Julia decided that smothering the baby might be a good idea; now Jay dissuaded her on grounds that if she went to prison, it would devastate their older daughter, Elinor, who at age two was becoming withdrawn and unhappy. Julia tried to figure out how to gird herself for the next stages. "It's a very confusing business, mourning for someone who is alive," she wrote. "You feel you shouldn't really be doing it." There was talk of suing the NHS. Julia and Jay could have received £3 million to look after Imogen until she turned twenty, but to do so they would have had not only to prove that the person at the Oxford hospital who sent them to the midwife had been negligent, which was clearly the case, but also that Imogen would not have lost so much of her brain had Julia been admitted. The assessment would have taken six years. Julia was terrified of the long battle, and of being left financially bereft with full responsibility for a brain-damaged child.

Just short of five months, Imogen's eyes started flickering, and her parents took her to a pediatric neurologist. The neurologist tested her and said tentatively, "It's likely Imogen will never walk or talk." Julia felt that if SCBU was limbo, this was hell. Further testing would take several days. The staff assumed that Julia would stay the night at the hospital—the same hospital that had refused her admission when she was in labor—as most mothers do. "I did a very heinous thing on the first night," Julia said. "I said, 'I'm not staying.' This great institution had betrayed me, and I was saying, 'Fuck you.' As I walked past the other parents, I did not meet their eyes. I was hanging up my halo. I got in the car, and I drove home." Julia became obsessed with the idea that

Imogen be allowed to die. She asked that a do-not-resuscitate order be placed on Imogen's charts. That weekend, Julia took Imogen from the hospital and had her baptized. The baptism only confirmed her wish to let Imogen go; to Julia, the doctors' relentless focus on life seemed almost sadistic.

On Tuesday, the neurologist showed Imogen's CAT scans to Julia and Jay. As he moved up the head, "we could see that gradually the grey shape was shrinking inside its regular oval frame, replaced by blackness," she wrote. "By the time his finger reached the row where the eyes jutted out, the shape was entirely black, with a lacy edge that looked to me like the frills around a black doily. The neurologist explained that the blackness was the space where Imogen's cerebral cortex should be, the lacy edge its torn remains." The doctor said, "Strictly speaking, she has no intelligence."

Julia said she needed time to absorb all of it, and the neurologist agreed to keep Imogen in the hospital for a week. Julia was preoccupied with the idea that this child never would or could know her, never could feel more than hunger and perhaps hardness and softness. The verdict about what to do next was entirely Julia's. She and Jay were not married, and even though he was named as father on the birth certificate, antiquated British law (since modernized) left him with no jurisdiction. Jay kept asking the doctors if Imogen could be like Christopher Nolan, the locked-in boy, deprived of oxygen at birth, whose mother went on teaching him against all odds, until a drug gave him the use of one muscle, which he used to type beautiful poetry. "When the neurologist said, 'There's no way that she could possibly be like that,' it was a relief to some degree," Julia said. "After that, Jay was very firm that he wasn't going to look after her. Either I would stay with him and lose Imogen, or I would stay with Imogen and lose him. I thought she was the one who needed me. I had to see the evidence that she didn't need me, and that it was my ego that needed her to need me." Later, Julia wrote, "It could not be the unrequited love I had once imagined. Instead, my love existed in a vacuum."

Two days before Imogen was to come home from the hospital, Julia stopped her daily visits. It felt like a charade, going to see someone who could never tell whether she'd been visited or not. Julia stayed in bed, curled up in a dark room. A visitor from the NHS who had adopted a child with cerebral palsy came by. "She was a very philosophical, wise person," Julia said. "I remember saying to her, 'When do you think is the best time to abandon your child if that's what you decide to do?' Her answer was, 'It'll always be the most horrible thing that you ever do.' That helped; there was never going to be a perfect time."

The moment the NHS visitor left, Julia called a lawyer and asked if she would be at risk of losing Elinor if she abandoned Imogen to the system. Julia was assured that she would not be. She asked what she should say to the hospital, and she wrote down the words. On the day Imogen was supposed to come home, Julia did not go to the hospital; she and Jay sat by the telephone and waited for it to ring. The nurse who called said that Imogen was doing well and asked when Julia would be coming in. "I shan't be coming in," Julia said. An astonished silence followed. The nurse asked that Julia and Jay come in for a meeting the next day. At the hospital, Julia used the line the lawyer had given her. She said, "I'm not the right mother for this child." The consultant did not question her decision. "That was a very gentle meeting," Julia said. The doctor asked whether they had ever thought of harming her, his tone suggesting the necessary answer. Jay said, "I can't say I haven't." And the doctor said, "Then let us take the burden away from you." Before they left the hospital, they went to see Imogen, and Julia held her and said to the social worker, "I do love her, you know." Leaving the hospital, Julia wanted to turn back, but Jay stayed the course. "It's me or her," he said, and they drove on, Julia weeping silently. At home, they threw away the clothes, the rattles, the bottles and nipple shields, the crib, the sterilizer, the high chair.

A few days later, a foster mother came to the hospital for Imogen. Tania Beale was a strong Christian, a single mother who already had another disabled child. "Imogen is lying in her cot when I enter her room," Tania later wrote in an essay for the *Guardian*. "I sense bewilderment, loss, confusion. Her parents and I size each other up. Who are these people who can bear to part with this beautiful little scrap of humanity? There is something about Imogen. She is determined. She will not be ignored. I have a cloth sling, and this becomes Immie's home. She lies over my heart, suckling on my finger. For the next few months, I wear Immie whenever I am awake." That first day, Jay and Julia gave Tania the pram and the car seat. Julia was impressed by Tania; she found her strong and dignified. "I felt she didn't see me as the pathetic mum who'd failed. I was so grateful for that," Julia said. British social services take the position that a child who is taken into care early should be adopted. The ostensible reason for this is that adoption is more stable, but adoptive parents are not paid for their services as foster parents are, so the state's motives are mixed. For Julia, the ability of someone else to love her daughter was both a relief and an affront. Adoption would mean a complete and irreversible termination of Julia's maternal rights and was frightening; she wished to remain attached.

A few years later, Julia said to me, "I think Tania now feels that our involvement with Imogen is to Imogen's benefit. I, on the other hand, have reached a stage where I would like Tania to be her mother." Tania no longer wants to adopt Imogen. "I got my timing wrong," Julia said. She had hoped that she and Tania could become friends, but that did not happen. When Imogen comes to visit, Jay tickles her until she laughs; he will take her onto the piano bench and play music to her. "In response, Immie would cease her yelling and raise her heavy head as if she were concentrating on the sound, eyes wide and mouth opening in an expression that you might call awe," Julia wrote. Julia began organizing fund-raisers for disabled children and became active at the hospice where Imogen went when she was ill. Julia published a book about her experiences. The family cannot live with Imogen herself, but cannot keep her from the center of their consciousness.

"I am aware that I see a different Immie to the Immie her family knows," Tania wrote. "One day, she smiles. It is brief, but it is there. I discover that she will smile in response to a whistle. On Immie's first birthday she sits in her chair and kicks out at some bells, she smiles at the noise they make and opens her mouth wide for some mashed-up chocolate cake. Slowly, she is learning that life might be worth living." Julia said that the smile was a muscle reflex; she had doctors to back her up. The child she knew and the one Tania described seemed so dissimilar as to obliterate each other. When I first met Julia, Imogen could still take food orally and chew; a year later, she had lost what Julia called her "one skill" and was fed through a G-tube. Imogen currently takes baclofen, which many paroxysmal children take to loosen their muscles; three anticonvulsants; two drugs for her digestive system; and chloral hydrate for sleeping. She sleeps in a sleeping rack, a board with the shape of her legs and arms, into which she is strapped to prevent her convulsive limbs from growing mangled. She has physiotherapy three times a week. On this regimen, Imogen has been given twenty years to live.

"Severe epileptic fits should have been killing her," Julia said. "That was nature's way of destroying this person. But, no. There was a drug that could stop the spasms. It's a very hard thing to want your child to die. To some degree, my anger is about the invention of these children. Because when I was born, they didn't survive. These Imogens are on the increase as the sophistication and tyranny of intervention escalate." Tania, on the other hand, wrote, "Imogen remains profoundly disabled but she knows her family, birth and fostered, and gets excited by visits from any of her grandparents." Tania's aura of calm certainty contrasts with Julia's tendency toward muddled drama. Elinor once asked,

"Mummy, if I get brain damage, can I go and live with Tania as well?" At Tania's behest, Julia has had the do-not-resuscitate stamp removed from Imogen's files. Unless Tania decides to adopt Imogen, these decisions rest solely in Julia's hands. "But I won't make them on my own," Julia said. "That would be cruel."

Julia's writing about her experience—first in newspaper articles, and later in a book—was a cry for expiation that met mixed responses. Some readers called her brave; others called her self-serving. The day of our last interview, she said, "Yesterday, I pushed Imogen along the street. It's a nightmare getting six blocks with a wheelchair. All the large cars are parked on the pavement, so you go along two cars' worth, where there's a big enough gap, and then you go onto the road, with the oncoming traffic. By the time you get six blocks, you're a serious martyr. Every time she's around, I experiment with being the mother of the disabled child. People walking along the pavement get out of the way and smile at you, that smile that goes, 'You poor thing, I'm glad I'm not you!' I can imagine polishing my halo at the end of every day. At the very same time, I can imagine being the most furious person in the world."

In Peter Singer's definition, Imogen, Ashley, and others like them are not persons. Nonetheless, the parents I met who lived with and cared for such children often described a great deal of personhood in them. It's impossible to establish in any given case in what measure such personhood is observed and in what measure imagined or projected. Singer does not argue that parents who believe in the personhood of their children have to act toward them as they would toward nonpersons, but he opens the moral framework for someone to think that these children are expendable. I am not sure that, as activists claim, this will lead us into Hitlerian proposals to eliminate a much broader range of the disabled, but neither am I sure that Singer's arguments are as rational as he makes them out to be. His fallacy is his assumption, for himself and for science, of omniscience.

The Australian disability advocate Chris Borthwick has written that for ethicists pondering such a question, "the identification of a class of people who are 'humans' but not human, if any such could be found, would be central." Borthwick says that we accept someone's state as vegetative when that person fails to persuade a doctor that he is conscious—in other words, what is in question is not consciousness, but the legible manifestation of consciousness. Borthwick views consciousness as largely unknowable. He points to a study published in *Archives of Neurology* in which nearly two-thirds of a group of eighty-four people judged to be "in a vegetative state" had "recovered awareness" within three years. "One must ask," he writes, "in the light of the evidence, why it is that reasonable, moral, and ethical writers can extract these qualities of permanence and certainty from data that is, to put the matter no more strongly, clearly capable of other interpretations." Borthwick maintains that even if some human beings are nonpersons, we cannot identify them definitively. It's hard not to think of Anne McDonald and Christopher Nolan, who seemed to many professionals to be nonpersons, and who ultimately emerged into shimmering personhood. The same rationale that makes us deplore the death penalty in cases where the evidence is not entirely conclusive should give us pause in these supposedly clear-cut cases.

Contemplating Singer and Borthwick, I was reminded of Susan Arnsten, mother of Adam Delli-Bovi, who has Down syndrome, and her fascination with the Jewish idea that God exists between people rather than within them. I thought of the work on Deaf culture that shows how Sign emerges unbidden when there are two people to communicate in it, but lies dormant in children isolated from others who might employ it. I recalled the outrage Jay Neugeboren felt at the suggestion that his brother's schizophrenia could be defined in chemical rather than in spiritual and personal terms. I dislike both the conceited science behind Singer's position and the mawkish sentimentality of those who insist that we treat all human life equivalently, always. Of course, practical answers must be sought, but to think of those answers as better than approximate is foolishness. We assign personhood to one another, and we assign it to or withhold it from these disabled children. It is not discovered so much as it is introduced. The psychoanalyst Maggie Robbins once said, "Consciousness is not a noun; it's a verb. Trying to pin it down like a fixed object is a recipe for disaster." Tania sees something elemental, some quality that we might call grace, in Imogen, and Julia doesn't; we commit an arrogant injustice if we insist that either woman is dreaming.

The daughters of the ant queen take care of their mother and siblings; in some bird species, older fledglings help parents raise younger chicks; but overall, little reciprocity is attached to nonhuman parenting. Human parenting is an ultimately bilateral lifetime relationship rather than a unilateral temporary one. Even before the ultimate turnaround in which children in their prime care for incapacitated elderly parents, the manifestations of reciprocity may determine the parents' social status and self-regard. The prospect of such payback is often elided with the earlier reciprocity of the child's adoring gaze, the affection implicit in dependency, the words of adulation lisped by children first grasping language. For the parents of MSD children, early reciprocity may be infrequent and ultimate reciprocity impossible.

But the pleasure of caring for children does not lie only in reciprocity. The French writer Annie Leclerc has spoken of "the profound taste we have for children," and the feminist psychologist Daphne de Marneffe has said that a mother's skill in responding to her child contributes "not only to her recognition of her child, but to her own sense of pleasure, effectiveness, and self-expression as well." Psychoanalysis has long proposed that mothers' early caretaking is a form of self-care. Freud describes how "parental love, which is so moving and at bottom so childish, is nothing but parental narcissism born again."

This commonality of interest seems to have strengthened most of the parents I interviewed for this chapter, but not all parents can achieve it. Some disability activists, abortion opponents, and religious fundamentalists have argued that those who are unwilling to parent disabled children shouldn't allow themselves to become pregnant in the first place. The reality, however, is that most people embark on parenthood in optimism, and even those who soberly consider a worst-case scenario cannot adequately predict their response to such a situation until they are in it.

Ambivalence exists in all human relationships, including parent-child. Anna Freud maintained that a mother could never satisfy her infant's needs because those are infinite, but that eventually child and mother outgrow that dependence. Children with MSD have permanent needs far beyond that infinity. In *Torn in Two*, the British psycho-analyst Rozsika Parker complains that in our open, modern society, the extent of maternal ambivalence is a dark secret. Most mothers treat their occasional wish to be rid of their children as if it were the equivalent of murder itself. Parker proposes that mothering requires two impulses—the impulse to hold on, and the impulse to push away. To be a successful mother you must nurture and love your child, but cannot smother and cling to your child. Mothering involves sailing between what Parker calls "the Scylla of intrusiveness and the Charybdis of neglect." She proposes that the sentimental idea of perfect synchrony between mother and child "can cast a sort of sadness over motherhood—a constant state of mild regret that a delightful oneness seems always out of reach." Perfection is a horizon virtue, and our very approach to it reveals its immutable distance.

The dark portion of maternal ambivalence toward typical children is posited as crucial to the child's individuation. But severely disabled children who will never become independent will not benefit from their parents' negative feelings, and so their situation demands an impossible state of emotional purity. Asking the parents of severely disabled children to feel less negative emotion than the parents of healthy children is ludicrous. My experience of these parents was that they all felt both love and despair. You cannot decide whether to be ambivalent. All you can decide is what to do with your ambivalence. Most of these parents have chosen to act on one side of the ambivalence they feel, and Julia Hollander chose to act on another side, but I am not persuaded that the ambivalence itself was so different from one of these families to the next. I am enough of a creature of my times to admire most the parents who kept their children and made brave sacrifices for them. I nonetheless esteem Julia Hollander for being honest with herself, and for making what all those other families did look like a choice.

VIII

Prodigies

Being gifted and being disabled are surprisingly similar: isolating, mystifying, petrifying. One of the most startling patterns that emerged during my research was that many people come to value abnormalities that are ostensibly undesirable. Equally, ostensibly desirable variances are often daunting. Many prospective parents who dread the idea of a disabled child will long for an accomplished one. Such children may create beauty in the world; they may derive intense pleasure from their achievements; they may stretch their parents' lives into wonderful new alignments. Clever people often have clever sons and daughters, but dazzling brilliance is an aberration, as horizontal an identity as any in this study. Despite the past century's breakthroughs in psychology and neuroscience, prodigiousness and genius are as little understood as autism. Like parents of children who are severely challenged, parents of exceptionally talented children are custodians of children beyond their comprehension.

A *prodigy* is able to function at an advanced adult level in some domain before the age of twelve. I've used the word expansively to include anyone who develops a profound innate gift at an early age, even if he does so more gradually or less publicly than classic prodigies. *Prodigy* derives from the Latin *prodigium*, a monster that violates the natural order. These people have differences so evident as to resemble a birth defect. The anxiety of abnormality goes beyond etymology. Few people wish to be identified as prodigies, especially given the correlation between prodigiousness and burnout, prodigiousness and freakishness. Prodigies are, in the eyes of many prodigies, pathetic, uncanny weirdos with little chance of lifetime social or professional success, their performances more party tricks than art.

The designation *prodigy* usually reflects timing, while *genius* reflects the ability to add something of value to human consciousness. Many people have genius without precocity, or prodigiousness without brilliance. The French poet Raymond Radiguet said, "Child prodigies exist just as there are extraordinary men. But they are rarely the same." Here, however, I've been engaged by a continuum that embraces both phenomena and have allowed the words considerable overlap. The subjects of this chapter indicate how the emergence of disproportionate ability, at any stage, may alter family dynamics, much as the emergence of schizophrenia or disability will do, at any stage. Premature attainment and ultimate merit are, however, very different identities.

Like a disability, prodigiousness compels parents to redesign their lives around the special needs of their child. Once more, experts must be called in; once more, their primary strategies for dealing with the aberrance often undermine parental power. A child's prodigiousness requires his parents to seek out a new community of people with similar experience; they soon face the mainstreaming dilemma and must decide whether to place their children with intellectual peers too old to befriend them, or with age peers who will be bewildered and alienated by their achievements. Brilliance can be as much of an impediment to intimacy as any developmental anomaly, and the health and happiness of families of prodigies do not outstrip those of others in this book.

Prodigiousness manifests most often in athletics, mathematics, chess, and music; I have focused on musical prodigies here because my ability to understand music exceeds my comprehension of sports, math, or chess. A musical prodigy's development hinges on parental collaboration; without that support, the child would never gain access to an instrument or the training that even the most devout genius requires. As David Henry Feldman and Lynn T. Goldsmith, scholars in the field, have said, "A prodigy is a group enterprise."

A parent is the progenitor of much of a child's behavior, telling that child repeatedly who he has been, is, and could be, reconciling accomplishment and innocence. In constructing this narrative, parents often confuse the anomaly of developing fast with the objective of developing profoundly. There is no clear delineation between supporting and pressuring a child, between believing in your child and forcing your child to conform to what you imagine for him. You can damage prodigies by nurturing their talent at the expense of personal growth, or by cultivating general development at the expense of the special skill that might have given them the deepest fulfillment. You can make them feel that your love is contingent on their dazzling success, or that you don't care about their talent. Prodigies invite a sacrifice of the present to the putative future. If society's expectations for most children with profound differences are too low, expectations for prodigies are often perilously high.

Musicality does not appear to convey an evolutionary advantage, yet every human society has music. The archaeologist Steven Mithen, in *The Singing Neanderthals*, argues that music plays a crucial role in cognitive development. Recent work on infant-directed speech—the exaggerated tonalities that almost everyone uses in talking to babies—has shown that infants prefer these melodic enunciations. The scholar John Blacking has said that music "is there in the body, waiting to be brought out and developed." Members of one culture can differentiate the joyful and sorrowful music of another culture. This innate capacity for musical discernment notwithstanding, music is shaped by exposure, like any language; we absorb our culture's characteristic harmonic progressions and feel the fulfillment or reversal of learned musical expectations. The sociologist Robert Garfias contends that music and spoken language are a single system acquired in early infancy, and that music may be our "primary means of sustaining a process of socialization."

Just as deaf children will begin to communicate with physical gestures, musical prodigies may use musical tones to convey information from the outset. For them, music is speech itself. It is said that Handel sang before he talked. The pianist Arthur Rubinstein would sing a mazurka when he wanted cake. John Sloboda, a music psychologist who studies why we respond emotionally to patterns of notes and rhythms, wrote, "Musical idioms are not languages, and do not have referential meaning in the way that languages such as English do. They do, however, have complex multi-leveled structural features which resemble syntax or grammar." This means that, in the sense proposed by the linguist Noam Chomsky, a deep structure of music in the brain can be vitalized by exposure to sounds. Leon Botstein, president of Bard College and himself a former prodigy, said, "What makes for a great musician is the emotional gravitation to music as an alternative form of linguistic communication." As with spoken and signed language, there must be not only a means to express, but also people to receive, respond, and encourage, which is why parental involvement is crucial to the emergence of this faculty.

That music is a first language does not guarantee brilliant use of that language, however, any more than American children's fluency in English makes them all poets.

For Evgeny Kissin, called Zhenya by those who know him, music was without question a first language, and one that his parents understood. In the mid-1970s, friends would visit the piano teacher Emilia Kissina in Moscow, and they would hear her young son play the piano. Frustrated at her reluctance to enroll him in a special academy ("They lose their childhood, they struggle so hard in those places," she would say), a friend arranged an appointment with Anna Pavlovna Kantor, of the famed Gnessin School, in 1976, when Zhenya was five. Kantor, too, was initially reluctant. "It was September," she recalled. "I said the exams were long over. 'When you meet the little boy,' this friend replied, 'you will understand that nothing is over.' One week after, this mother came with her son, with curls all over his head like an angel. He opened his bottomless eyes, and I saw a light in him. Without knowing how to read music or the names of notes, he played everything. I asked him to translate a story into music. I said that we were coming into a dark forest, full of wild animals, very scary, and then step by step the sun rises, and the birds start singing. He began in the piano's lower register, in a dark and dangerous place, and then, lighter and lighter, the birds awakening, the first rays of the sun, and finally a delightful, almost ecstatic melody, his hands running along the keys. I didn't want to teach him. Such imagination can be very fragile. But his mother said, 'Clever and faithful helper, don't worry. He is interested in whatever is new to him. Try.'"

The Kissins lived the life of the Soviet Jewish intelligentsia: physically uncomfortable, constantly frustrating, the pleasures of the mind partially filling in for ordinary discomforts of the flesh and ideology's constant intrusions on the spirit. Their assumption was that Zhenya's sister, Alla, would play piano like her mother, while Zhenya would be an engineer like his father, Igor. At eleven months, Zhenya sang an entire Bach fugue that his sister had been practicing. He began to sing everything he heard. "It was rather embarrassing to take him out in the streets," Emilia recalled. "As it went on, relentless, nonstop—I became frightened by it."

At twenty-six months, Zhenya sat down at the piano and with one finger picked out some of the tunes he had been singing. The next day he did the same, and on the third day he played with both hands, using all his fingers. He would listen to LPs and immediately play back the music. "Chopin's ballades, he would play with those little hands, and Beethoven sonatas, Liszt's rhapsodies," his mother told me. At three, he began improvising. He especially liked to make musical portraits of people. "I would make the rest of the family guess whom I was playing," he recalled.

Kantor taught him in the Russian tradition that the imagination and spirit of the performer should be equal to that of the composer. "Anna Pavlovna's greatest triumph," Emilia explained, "is that she prescrved his gift. She knew how to supplement what was there, never replace it." When I asked Zhenya how he had managed to avoid the burnout of so many wunderkinder, he said, "Simply this: I was brought up well." By the time he was seven, Zhenya had begun to write down his compositions. He played as though it were a necessary emancipation. "When I would return from school, I would, without taking my coat off, go to the piano and play," he said. "I made my mother understand that this was just what I needed." Zhenya used to make lists for Anna Pavlovna of the things he wanted to learn: "If I was asking for a difficult piece, I would put in brackets, 'Lenin said that difficult doesn't mean impossible.'"

He played his first solo recital in May of 1983, at eleven. "I had such a feeling of relief," he recalled. "During intermission, I was impatient to return to the stage." After the concert, the wife of someone high up in the Composers Union congratulated teacher and pupil and promised an invitation to perform. This was a gateway to fame and comfort in the Soviet period of deprivation. Kantor, however, was uneasy. "He is still very young," she replied. "He shouldn't be overexposed." A stranger standing nearby interrupted and identified himself as a doctor. "When I saw in what a state of enthusiasm the boy returned to the stage for his encores, I realized it would be even more dangerous for him to become so overexcited inside, without release," he said. "He needs to perform." Zhenya played at the Union's House of Composers a month later.

When the preeminent conductor Daniel Barenboim came to Moscow the following January, he heard Zhenya play and arranged an invitation to Carnegie Hall. Musical performance enjoyed a special status among the arts in the Soviet Union because interpretive acts were less ideologically suspect than creative ones. But the government sought to keep its geniuses, so neither Zhenya nor his teacher was told about Carnegie Hall. A few months later, Zhenya played both of Chopin's piano concertos in Moscow. Afterward, Zhenya's parents told him that they had a surprise: a visit to a town in the country. Years later he learned that they had arranged the trip because they knew what a sensation the concert would create, and they didn't want him exposed to so much praise.

As Zhenya began to tour, he received private tutoring "in the usual subjects of history, literature, mathematics, dialectical materialism, Leninism, military science, and so on." He had never been very connected to other people his age, and the escape from ordinary schooling was a relief. In 1985, he left the USSR for the first time to play at a gala in East Berlin for leader Erich Honecker. "There were some circus performers, then I played the Schumann/Liszt *Widmung* and the Chopin E Minor Waltz, and then a magician did tricks," he recalled. Two years later, with travel restrictions easing under the new policy of glasnost, Zhenya played for the renowned conductor Herbert von Karajan, who pointed at him and said through tears, "Genius." Unlike many prodigies, he does not mourn his childhood. "Sometimes I regret that the course of my life was set so early," he told me. "There was never any way to resist it. But even if my career had begun later, music would always have been the only thing that was important to me." In 1990, at eighteen, he made his Carnegie Hall debut to astonishing reviews; in 1991 the family emigrated to New York. Anna Pavlovna Kantor came with them.

Zhenya had been described to me before we first met in 1995 as a moonchild—peculiar, closed, incomprehensible—and at that initial encounter, he explained clearly that he had little to say about himself beyond the facts. He has never much liked talking, or journalists, or the attention many celebrities find flattering. He is indifferent to his success, except insofar as it allows him to play more. Zhenya is too tall and too thin, with a strangely large head, enormous brown eyes, pale skin, and a mop of crazy brown hair in which you could mislay something. The overall effect is slightly gangly, and his bearing combines the tense and the beatific. Watching Zhenya sit down at the piano is like seeing a lamp plugged in: decorative though it may have seemed, only then does its real use become apparent. You feel less that he is pouring energy into the instrument than that he is receiving energy from it. "I don't know if I would be able to live if I suddenly became unable to play," he said. Zhenya plays as though it were a moral act that could redeem the world.

Throughout the nineties, Zhenya was always accompanied on tour by his mother and Kantor. The dynamic between the two women was both intimate and respectful; neither would critique Zhenya's performance without consulting the other. Upon arriving in any new venue, Zhenya would run through his program. Kantor would sit still to assess the performance, while Emilia would wander the hall to check acoustics. Zhenya was never given leeway to become arrogant. "They didn't want me seeing myself as a great prodigy," he said. "But when I deserved it, they always praised me, too." While his father and sister disappeared to the shadows, Zhenya stayed with his mother and piano teacher; one critic referred to them as a "three-headed beast."

If Zhenya plays the piano with the fluidity with which I talk, he talks with the awkwardness with which I play the piano. His profound intelligence and complex thoughts are indicated but not expressed by conversation. Zhenya has a slight speech impediment, a lingering on explosive consonants that burst forth like popping balloons. His utterances are saturated with pauses; nothing organic leads from one word to the next. When he was little, Kantor would explain something, then, when he didn't respond, would explain again, more elaborately. Finally she would say, "Have you understood?" Zhenya would say, "Yes, I understood a long time ago." It had not occurred to him to say so. When he was in his twenties, the concertmaster of an orchestra with which he was to perform noticed his practicing during the break and commented that she could not work without an occasional rest. Zhenya said, "That is why you are not a soloist." He is solicitous to a fault, but this ingenuous frankness pervades his communication; the critic Anne Midgette wrote in the *Washington Post*, "The performance was so compelling precisely because of the awkward poignancy that accompanied the technical mastery."

I had been toying with the idea of music as a first language for some time before I put it to Zhenya one day about a year after we met. We were sitting in his apartment on Manhattan's Upper West Side. Our meeting had been impromptu; I wanted to know something about the structure of a Rachmaninoff cadenza. "This one?" asked Zhenya, and played six bars. On the tape of our meeting, the emotional transition is more surprising than the shift from speech to music: the notes contain all the feeling absent from the words. I thought of a fish that flips around on the deck of a boat, then slips back into pure grace in the water. A yearning to be understood—the primary beauty of Zhenya's playing—distinguishes this from technical facility. Though he was playing only to indicate passages to which I had alluded, I felt for the first time that we were in full conversation; it was as intimate as a confidence or an embrace.

Zhenya told me, "Music conveys what I feel; I don't know how to convey through speech at all. I don't like to speak about the music, either: it speaks for itself." Music makes sense of the world for him, which is why it seems to make sense of the world for his audiences.

More than a decade after our first meeting, I asked him whether he had fully realized his own insights; Zhenya said simply, "Not yet." Later he added, "When I played as a child, it was simply that I loved music and was just playing the way I felt it. The better and the clearer my ideas become, the more I realize how difficult it is for me to achieve them. In the past I have been tempted to take up conducting, but now I don't want to, exactly because I realize how difficult it is to play the piano. That's why now I am more nervous before my concerts than I used to be." This is as fair a description as I've heard of how a prodigy grows up.

For Zhenya Kissin, music is the repository of intimacy; others deploy it to express what circumstances or temperament forbid them to utter. The pianist Yefim Bronfman, called Fima, a prototype for explosive genius, was born in Tashkent in 1958. His father, Naum Bronfman, had been drafted into the Soviet army and taken prisoner by the Germans; he escaped and managed to walk six hundred miles back to Moscow, where he was imprisoned and tortured by Stalin. Fima's mother, Polina, had been a Nazi prisoner in Poland. Naum was a violinist who taught in the Tashkent conservatory; Polina was a pianist who taught pupils at home. "We always suspected that somebody was listening to our conversations," Fima told me. "So the only way you could express yourself was through the music. That's what made us work so hard at it." Music became a realm of liberty, a medium in which it was possible for the Bronfmans to articulate everything they couldn't say in a bugged apartment. Part of the beauty of Fima's mature performance is that lingering urgency. If some musicians converse in music because their brains are not strongly wired for spoken language, Fima—who has never married and, like Zhenya Kissin, lives with his mother—remains in those original suppressed conversations and produces music with the exigency of having been denied speech for the most important of his early dialogues. Russian music of the twentieth century consistently exploited the expressive merits of ambiguity, of being able to say things that a bureaucrat cannot pin down and label subversive. Music can liberate people immured in almost any kind of silence.

The origin of genius has been a topic of philosophical debate for at least twenty-five hundred years. Plato believed that genius was bestowed by the gods upon passive human beings. Longinus proposed that it was something a person does—that the genius does not receive divinity, but creates it. John Locke (who, tellingly, had no children) thought that parents could engender genius; he said, "I imagine the minds of children as easily turn'd this or that way, as water itself." This idea from the Age of Reason, the period in which *genius* took on its current meaning, gave way to a Romantic image of ingenuity swathed in mystery. Immanuel Kant said, "If an author owes a product to his genius, he himself does not know how he came by the ideas for it." Arthur Schopenhauer said, "Talent hits a target no one else can hit; genius hits a target no one else can see."

In 1869, Francis Galton's *Hereditary Genius* announced that genius could not be achieved by anyone not born to it. Lewis M. Terman, a eugenicist and follower of Galton's, developed the Stanford-Binet

Intelligence Test, which measured IQ, to categorize army recruits during World War I; after the armistice, he pressed to have it used on preschool-age children as a predictor of academic success. Because such quantifiable intelligence tests have built-in biases, measurements of low IQ appeared to demonstrate the inferiority of "undesirable" groups.

The question of how high IQ correlates to genius has been in debate ever since the tests were introduced. Terman followed a group of about fifteen hundred children with very high IQs; seventy years later, his critics claimed, they had accomplished no more than their socioeconomic status would have predicted. One child Terman had excluded as not bright enough, William Shockley, had coinvented the transistor and won the Nobel Prize in Physics. Psychometrics were nonetheless championed by the eugenicists. Paul Popenoe, who advocated forced sterilization of the "inferior," asserted that "no son of an unskilled laborer has ever become an eminent man of science in the United States." Hitler was well versed in the work and ideas of Galton and Popenoe; indeed, Popenoe enthusiastically collaborated with his Nazi counterparts, and defended them until it was no longer advantageous to do so. The Holocaust had a dampening effect on the notion of inherent supremacy, and in 1944, the anthropologist Alfred Kroeber suggested that genius was contextual. Why did fifth-century Athens, or the Italian Renaissance, or the Song Dynasty produce clusters of genius? Shouldn't it have a fixed population frequency?

If genius springs from genetics, a meritocracy is hardly more just than the divine right of kings; it, too, mythologizes inherent superiority. If genius results from labor, then brilliant people deserve the kudos and wealth they reap. The communist perspective is that everyone can be a genius if he will only work at it; the fascist perspective is that born geniuses are a different species from the rest of humanity. Many people fall short of their potential through lack of discipline, but a visit to a coal mine will amply demonstrate that hard work on its own neither constitutes genius nor guarantees riches. The history of high intelligence is no less political than the history of intellectual disability or of mental illness.

Leon Fleisher was born in 1928 in San Francisco, where his immigrant father had become a milliner who made hats for Lucille Ball. Leon's brother was the reluctant recipient of piano lessons, and Leon used to listen. "When my brother went out to play ball, I would go to the piano and play as the teacher wanted," Leon recalled. His parents soon switched the lessons to Leon, and before long he was studying with a Russian named Lev Schorr, "who was the San Francisco prodigy-maker. He felt it wasn't a good lesson until he made me cry. But he would take me out to lunch afterwards and feed me lamb chops."

In 1937, the conductor of the San Francisco symphony heard one of Leon's first recitals and decided that the boy should study in Italy with the renowned pianist Artur Schnabel. Schnabel politely declined; he was not interested in nine-year-old pupils. A few months later, the conductor invited Schnabel to dinner, snuck Leon in, and obliged Schnabel to listen. Schnabel immediately took Leon as a student, on the condition that he give no further concerts; Schnabel understood that Leon's mother wanted merely fame, and that he had to keep the boy focused on music. Leon and his mother went to Como in 1938. Schnabel's lessons were different from anything Leon had known. "The prodigy-makers separate technique and music," Leon said. "Schnabel maintained that technique is the ability to do what you want. He advocated sitting in a comfortable chair and studying the music before you started to play—not drumming it out before you'd thought how you'd like it to sound." Schnabel never had more than a half dozen students, and he made each attend the others' lessons. "He would do a whole lesson on twelve bars, and we would stagger out like inebriates," Leon recalled, "filled not just with information, but with inspiration. Schnabel dealt in transcendence."

At the brink of World War II, Italy was hardly the place for a Jewish pupil to study with a Jewish pianist, and before long Schnabel sent Leon back home. Schnabel emigrated to New York soon thereafter, so Leon's father had to take a job in an East Coast factory. "That became a heavy responsibility for a kid to carry around," Leon said. But his mother was singularly determined. "She gave me a choice between being the first Jewish president or a great pianist," he added ruefully.

Leon Fleisher made his Carnegie Hall debut in 1944 at sixteen and quickly established himself. His career rise was meteoric, and three years later, Schnabel told him that his studies were over. "I was desolate when he dismissed me," Leon said. "Then, I remember hearing on the radio one of his Beethoven sonata recordings, and reveling in how extraordinarily beautiful it was. But I wasn't sure that I would have done it quite that way."

Leon had a twenty-year blaze of glory before he was struck, at thirty-six, with focal dystonia, a neurological condition that causes involuntary muscle contractions, which made it impossible for him to use the third and fourth fingers of his right hand. Focal dystonia is associated with relentless repetition of fine-motor-skill patterns despite the onset of pain. Leon's son, the jazz musician Julian Fleisher, explained, "He used his right hand relentlessly because his mother told him to; he used it until it broke." Leon went through a depression; his marriage fell apart. "It took a couple of years of despair before I realized that my connection was to music, not to being a two-handed piano player," he said. He reinvented himself as a conductor, a teacher, and a performer of the limited but pyrotechnic left-hand piano repertoire.

Leon's maturity is highly self-aware. "You can either perform a piece as though you're in the midst of what's happening, or as a narrator," he said. "You know, 'Once upon a time, there was . . .' That can be more expressive. It frees the listener's imagination. It doesn't dictate, 'This is what I feel, therefore you should feel this.' A prodigy can't do that, but a fully developed performer can." He described brilliant young students as being like people who want to build a house around a decorative object. "I teach them, 'The bedroom goes here, the kitchen, there, and the living room, there. You have to have that before you fill it with beautiful things. First is the structure.'" His son wryly pointed out that this tremendously nuanced way of thinking does not extend to human relations: "It's not a question of being nice, but of noticing the minds of the people he loves. But then in the music, it's all there."

I wondered whether Leon's dystonia had brought any rewards. "This forced me, and so enabled me, to go sideways, to expand my field of—what is the companion word to vision: *aurision*? Were I given the chance to relive it and not come down with focal dystonia, I'm not sure I would change anything." The dystonia proved what he had learned from Schnabel: that musicianship requires modesty. "Schnabel likened the performer to the Alpine mountain guide," Leon said. "His aim is to lead you to the top of the mountain so that you can enjoy the view. He isn't the goal. The view is."

When Leon was in his mid-seventies, Botox relaxed the permanently cramped muscles of his hand, and Rolfing further eased the movement of his soft tissue. He began to perform with both hands again, and his subsequent recordings earned him high honors. "The technique isn't what it was, and what's left is the musicality," Julian said. "He almost doesn't play notes; he plays the meaning in them." Leon said, "I am in no way cured. When I play, a good eighty to ninety percent of my concentration and awareness is how to deal with my hand. I've worn away the cartilage between my joints, so bone is rubbing on bone in my fingers, and it's a little bit like 'The Little Mermaid.' She fell in love with a man, and her wish was granted: she became a human. The price was that every step she took was like walking on knives. That's a fairy tale I remember very, very clearly."

Musical prodigies are sometimes compared to child actors, but child actors portray children; no one pays to watch a six-year-old playing Hamlet. No discipline has ever been permanently transformed by a child's revelations. Leon Botstein said, "Prodigies confirm conventional wisdom; they never change it." Musical performance can quickly be integrated because it is rule-driven, structured, and formal; profundity comes later. Mozart was the archetypal prodigy, but if he hadn't lived past twenty-five, we'd know nothing of him as a composer. After the English lawyer Daines Barrington examined the eight-year-old Mozart in 1764, he wrote, "He had a thorough knowledge of the fundamental principles of composition. He was also a master of modulation, and his transitions from one key to another were excessively natural and judicious." Yet, Mozart was also clearly a child. "Whilst he was playing to me, a favourite cat came in, upon which he immediately left his harpsichord, nor could we bring him back for a considerable time. He would also sometimes run about the room with a stick between his legs by way of horse." Every prodigy is a chimera of such mastery and childishness, and the contrast between musical sophistication and personal immaturity can be striking. One prodigy whom I interviewed had switched from the violin to the piano when she was seven. She offered to tell me why if I didn't tell her mother. "I wanted to sit down," she said.

Most people who receive rigorous early training do not become singular musicians. Juilliard's Veda Kaplinsky, who is perhaps the world's most highly esteemed piano teacher for younger students, explained, "Until the child reaches eighteen or nineteen, you don't know if he'll have the emotional capacity for expression." A mature childhood can be a recipe for an immature adulthood—a principle most publicly borne out by Michael Jackson. A Japanese proverb says that the ten-year-old prodigy becomes a talented fifteen-year-old on the way to mediocrity at twenty.

The sprinter unwisely indulges his arrogance against the marathon runner, and likewise, parents who encourage their children's narcissism do them no favors. It is best to accomplish something before becoming famous, because if the fame comes first, it often precludes accomplishment. The manager Charles Hamlen, who has nurtured the careers of many stellar musicians, wearily described the parents who want their children to make Carnegie Hall debuts at twelve. "You don't build a career by playing Carnegie Hall," he said. "You build a career, and then Carnegie Hall will invite you to play."

Schnabel saw Leon Fleisher as a child with remarkable skills rather than a set of skills inconveniently attached to a child, but many parents lack the sophistication to make such a distinction. Karen Monroe, a psychiatrist who works with prodigious children, said, "When you have a child whose gift is so overshadowing, it is easy for parents to be distracted and lose track of the child himself." Van Cliburn was among the preeminent prodigies of the twentieth century, although he was not catapulted to fame until he was twenty-three, when he won the Tchaikovsky piano competition at the height of the Cold War and was welcomed home with a ticker-tape parade. His mother was his piano teacher, and when she was teaching him, she would say, "You know I'm not your mother now." Of his childhood, Cliburn said, "There were other things I would like to have done besides practicing the piano, but I knew my mother was right about what I should do." Cliburn lived with his mother all her life. But he largely forsook his career after the death of his father, who was also his manager, because he could not bear the pressure, and he suffered from depression and alcoholism, becoming a revered fixture of Fort Worth society—kind, affable, piously reactionary, and the figurehead of an eponymous competition that has become as prestigious as the one that he won.

In 1945, there were five piano competitions worldwide; there are now seven hundred fifty. Robert Levin, professor of music at Harvard, said, "The favored repertoire is music of such technical challenges that, as recently as thirty years ago, less than one percent of pianists were playing it. Now, about eighty percent are. It isn't an improvement. It reflects a purely gladiatorial, physical behavior. You should not tell a young student to learn the notes and then add the expression. You might as well tell a chef, 'First you cook the food, then you add the flavor.'"

Sue and Joe Petersen always put their son Drew's personal needs before his talent, but the two often seemed to coincide. Drew didn't speak until he was three and a half, but Sue never believed he was slow. When he was eighteen months old, she was reading to him and skipped a word, whereupon Drew reached over and pointed to the missing word on the page. Drew didn't produce much sound at that stage, but he already cared about it deeply. "Church bells would elicit a big response," Sue said. "Birdsong would stop him in his tracks."

Sue, who had learned piano as a child, taught Drew the basics on an old upright, and he became fascinated by sheet music. "He needed to decode it," Sue said. "So I had to recall what little I remembered, which was the treble clef." Drew said, "It was like learning thirteen letters of the alphabet and then trying to read books." He figured out the bass clef on his own, and when he began formal lessons at five, his teacher said he could skip the first six months' worth of material. Within the year, Drew was performing Beethoven sonatas at the recital hall at Carnegie Hall and was flown to Italy to perform in a youth festival where the other youths were a decade older than he. Sue said, "I thought it was delightful, but I also thought we shouldn't take it too seriously. He was just a little boy."

The family had some differences with Drew's teacher, and Sue was advised to seek out a teacher named Miyoko Lotto, who warned that she didn't have time to teach Drew, but would listen to him play and then refer him to someone else. When he finished playing, Lotto said, "I have time Tuesdays at four." Years later, she recalled, "He could barely reach the pedals, but he played with every adult nuance you'd ever want. I thought, 'Oh my God, this really is a genius. He's not mimicking and not being spoon-fed. His musicality comes from within.'"

Her enthusiasm was not entirely welcome. Sue said, "It was so extreme, and it gave me the creeps." Joe said, "It just sounded ridiculous." Sue could not take Drew into Manhattan every week, but she enrolled him with a teacher in New Jersey whom Lotto recommended. Lotto e-mailed Sue every couple of weeks to ask how things were going. Every few months, she'd invite Drew to play for her. "It felt very casual, but in retrospect, it was regimented and purposeful," Sue said.

On his way to kindergarten one day, Drew asked his mother, "Can I just stay home so I can learn something?" Sue was at a loss. "He was reading textbooks this big, and they're in class holding up a blow-up *M*," she said. Drew said, "At first, it felt lonely. Then you accept that, yes, you're different from everyone else, but people will be your friends anyway." Drew's parents moved him to a Montessori school, then to a private school. They bought him a new piano because he had announced, at seven, that their upright lacked dynamic contrast. "It cost more money than we'd ever paid for anything except a down payment on a house," Sue said. By junior high, he was performing frequently and had taken up competitive swimming with a team that practiced nine hours a week. When Drew was fourteen, Sue found a homeschool program created by Harvard; when I met Drew, he was sixteen and halfway to a Harvard bachelor's degree.

Spending time with the Petersens, I was struck not only by their mutual devotion, but also by the easy way they avoided the snobberies that tend to cling to classical music. Sue is a school nurse; Joe works in the engineering department of Volkswagen. They never expected the life into which Drew has led them, but they were neither intimidated by it nor brash in pursuing it; it remained both a diligence and an art. Joe said, "How do you describe a normal family? The only way

I can describe a normal one is a happy one. What my kids do brings a lot of joy into this household." When I asked how Drew's talent had affected their parenting of his younger brother, Sue said, "It's distracting and different. It would be similar if Erik's brother had a disability or a wooden leg."

The gravitational pull of music is inexorable for Drew. He said, "I thought at Harvard I would find some subject that I was really interested in, maybe even more than music. I haven't, and I'm not sure I really want to." Since Lotto was at the Manhattan School of Music, Drew has pursued his musical education there. "He said, 'I don't want management and publicity now; I don't want a childhood in music; I want a life in music,'" Sue recalled. She had fielded invitations to put him on *Oprah*. "He was seven," Sue recalled, "and he said, 'I'm not a circus act.'" At sixteen, Drew still didn't want management. "You have to be able to fight back," he explained.

I asked Drew how he could express so much through music after so little life experience, and he said, "I can only express it through music, not through words. Maybe I can only experience it through music, too." We assume that certain intimacies are apportioned to speech, others to sex, others to sports—but why shouldn't music be the locus of intimacy, and speech the locus of formality? A year after I met him, Drew was selected for a master class with the Chinese pianist Lang Lang, then twenty-eight, and I went to watch them interact. Lang Lang, for whom speech is easy, coached six students. He said the least to Drew, and Drew the least to him, yet Drew's playing changed to incorporate Lang Lang's insights with a fluency none of the others could muster.

Sue said, "His talent is a magnifying glass on what I need to do. To be honest, I have no way to know what I'm doing right or wrong except to ask him." Drew said to her, "You're always questioning. As much as I am a nonconformist, you're a questioner." She said, "Fortunately, your answers are very convincing."

Musical talent can be divided into three components: the athletic, the mimetic, and the interpretive. It takes physical prowess to move your hands or lips with the precision most instruments require. To be a musician, the person has to have a mimetic capacity to reproduce others' techniques. "That should not be dismissed as simply replication," said Justin Davidson, music critic for *New York* magazine. "That's how we learn to speak, to write, to express ourselves. Musicians who have a tremendous gift for mimicry can produce very refined interpretations at a very young age. Are they producing those because they've learned them from a teacher, from a recording, or from hearing other pianists, or because it comes to them internally? Everybody does both." Robert Levin said, "It's hard to convey a message if you haven't learned how to pronounce the words. People who have amazing minds, but neglect their technical skills, will fail just as surely as people who are perfect at what they do but have no message. You have to take these apparently incompatible elements and make a vinaigrette of discipline and experience." As Pierre-Auguste Renoir said, craftsmanship has never stood in the way of genius.

Musical performance, like Sign, requires that manual dexterity become the seat of emotional and intellectual meaning. Sometimes that meaning is there from the beginning, as with Drew Petersen. Sometimes it comes later. The cellist and pedagogue Steven Isserlis complained to me that music is too often taught as a competitive sport. "It should be taught like a mixture of religion and science," he said. "Being able to move your fingers very fast is very impressive, but has nothing to do with music. Music does something to you; you don't do something to music."

Mikhail and Natalie Paremski held comfortable positions within the Soviet system: Mikhail with the Russian Atomic Agency, Natalie with the Physics Engineering Institute. Their daughter, Natasha, born in 1987, showed a precocious interest in the piano; her younger brother, Misha, did not. "I was in the kitchen, and I thought, 'Who is playing?'" Natalie recalled. "Then I saw, 'It's the baby, picking out nursery songs.' My husband said music was a terrible life; he begged me not to give her lessons." But Natalie thought a few lessons could do no harm. Six months later, Natasha played a Chopin mazurka in a children's concert. "She decided, 'I'm going to be a pianist,' at four years old," Natalie said. Natasha was always first in her class at school. "We didn't worry about music, because she was so good in math, physics, chemistry. She could have easily done something else if she ran out of talent for this."

When the Soviet Union collapsed, people with Soviet-era privilege were figures of considerable suspicion. In 1993, Mikhail was brutally beaten on his way home from work late one night. The doctors told Natalie that night, "Prepare to be a widow." A corporate recruiter had been pestering Mikhail for years to work in the United States, but the Paremskis didn't want to leave Russia. After the attack, Natalie changed her mind. "Three days later, I take the paperwork to the hospital. Mikhail's hand, I move it myself to make his signature. When he woke up from his almost coma, I tell him, 'You're going to California.'"

Mikhail went ahead; the family followed in 1995. Natasha entered fourth grade, where everyone else was two years older than she. Within a few months, she was speaking English without an accent and coming first on every school test. The family couldn't afford a good piano; they finally found a cheap one that "sounded like cabbage," Natasha recalled. Natalie persuaded the school to let Natasha do independent study so she could perform. "Everyone would say, 'You must be so proud of your daughter,'" Natalie said. "I used to say that it's not for me to be proud, it's Natasha who does this herself—but I learned that this is not the polite American way. So now I always say, 'I am so proud of my daughter,' and then maybe we can have a conversation." Natasha agreed that her own impulse drove her success. "What did they do to make me practice?" she asked. "What did they do to make me eat or sleep?"

At thirteen, Natasha was in a competition in Italy, and one of the judges saw that she was going to play Prokofiev's six sonatas. He said, "You can't play this piece, because it's about prison, and you didn't go to prison." Natasha was indignant. "I'm not going to prison to improve my playing," she said. Natasha sees nothing strange in a musician's ability to express emotions she has not experienced. "Had I experienced them, that wouldn't necessarily help me to express them better in my music. I'm an actress, not a character; my job is to represent something, not to live it. Chopin wrote a mazurka, person X in the audience wants to hear the mazurka, and so I have to decipher the score and make it apprehensible to person X, and it's really hard to do. But it has nothing to do with my life experience. We need to keep populating the world with sound. If you eliminated one thing—if you deprived the world of, say, Brahms's Second Concerto—there would be something wrong. This world, with that Brahms in it, is my world—and some of what makes up that world comes through me."

Natasha graduated with top honors from high school at fourteen and was offered a full scholarship by Mannes College for Music, in New York. She signed with management, moved East, and began full-time study there. She lived with a host family in New York City during the week and spent weekends with her manager in the suburbs. Her mother worried about the deficit of soul in New York. "There is no time for vision! People are just struggling to survive, like in Moscow," Natalie said—to which her daughter replied, "Vision is how I survive." In those early New York days, Natasha and her mother spoke by phone constantly. Nonetheless, Natalie said, "That was my present to her: I gave her her own life."

I met Natasha when she was fifteen, and I first interviewed her when she was sixteen. A year later, in 2004, I went to her Carnegie Hall debut, for which she played Rachmaninoff's Piano Concerto no.

2. She's a beautiful young woman, with cascades of hair and a sylphlike figure, and she wore a sleeveless, black velvet dress, so her arms would feel free, and a pair of insanely high heels that she said gave her better leverage on the pedals. Her playing was as virile as her clothing was feminine, and the audience gave her an ovation. Her parents were not there. "They're too supportive to come," Natasha told me just before the concert. Natalie explained, "If I am there, I am so worried about every single note that I can't even sit still. It's not helpful to Natasha."

At Mannes, Natasha rapidly emerged as a star. "My teacher wants me to be aware of exactly what I am doing," she told me when she was twenty. "That can destroy spontaneity. If you are aware that you are going to take a risk, and the risk is going to be this, then it is not a risk anymore. Playing should be a hundred percent intuition and a hundred percent logic." Her younger brother, sitting with us, said sarcastically, "What a logical statement!" Natasha rejoined, "But very intuitive at the same time. When I play, I use my brain and I breathe and everything like that. But I'm not—" Natasha was at a rare loss for words.

"—thinking of yourself," her mother finished. Natasha nodded. "That's why I worry, because she loses weight, she forgets to eat because she is playing the piano."

Natasha shook her head. "The rest of life is so distracting."

In 2005, she was invited to perform a benefit concert for the Prince of Wales with Sting. "She made friends with Madonna," her mother said. "I didn't make friends with her," Natasha protested. "She told me, 'You classical musicians are too stuck-up. You really should think about wearing hot pants.'" The *New York Times*, which had declined to review her debut, wrote of a subsequent performance, "Youth, in her case, denotes freshness but also the rawness of new-cut wood. She delved into the score and emerged with all kinds of new notes and passages one felt one hadn't heard before." Despite these successes, Natasha remains unpretentious. "Everybody is calling me and telling me, 'Your daughter is so down-to-earth,'" Natalie said. "First it was 'You must be proud of your daughter.' Now, 'Your daughter is so down-to-earth.' This is a very American compliment."

Some people can name any note they hear with the effortlessness with which most people can name a color. The phenomenon of *absolute pitch* has been identified in only about one in a thousand to one in ten thousand people. The rest of us function on relative pitch—the ability to hear the intervals between notes. So almost anyone can sing "Happy Birthday," but only a few people can say whether it is being sung in E-flat. In those who have absolute pitch, the exact identity of the notes is unmistakable. One researcher described how a woman played a scale on the piano for her three-year-old daughter and named the notes; a week later, their oven chimed, and the daughter said, "Does the microwave always sing an F?" Another child complained when one of his toys, its batteries running low, played a quarter tone flat.

Some people who don't have innate absolute pitch can train themselves to recognize notes. Study may teach them to produce a G, for example, and they may be able to calculate other notes from there. This ability appears to be latent in a much higher percentage of the population. Since the measure of absolute pitch was traditionally the ability to name notes, there was no way to detect the ability among people who had not been educated to know the names of the notes in the first place. David Ross, a psychiatrist at Yale, found that some people who didn't have the training to name notes could tell when a band performed a favorite song a half step lower. Daniel Levitin, a psychologist at McGill, found that a surprisingly large number of people can produce the first tone of their favorite pop song. Another researcher demonstrated that many people can pick out the correct dial tone.

Absolute pitch does not always enhance musical ability. A singer described her struggle when other singers in her choir go flat by a quarter tone. Her natural impulse is to sing what is written in dissonance with the others. Another musician described how his youth-orchestra conductor said, "You're so intent on playing an F-sharp that you're not paying attention to what else is going on. An F-sharp is a different note if you're playing in D major, where it's the third, than if you're playing in G, where it's the leading tone." The boy had to learn to suppress his absolute pitch to become a musician.

Like so many other aberrations, musicality can be mapped physiologically. People with absolute pitch have an enlarged planum temporale in the auditory cortex of the brain. Violinists have an enlargement of the area of the brain that controls movement of the left hand. The parts of the brain that control motor coordination and language are greater in volume or metabolism among many musicians, suggesting that music is both athletic and linguistic. It is unclear, however, whether these characteristics are the basis of music ability, or the result of repetitive practice.

Robert Greenberg is a professor of linguistics. His wife, Orna, is a painter. Though neither is particularly musical, their infant son Jay would listen with rapt attention to the tunes on a Mother Goose recording, and whenever it stopped, he would cry, and they would have to play it again. At two, he began playing the cello; at three, he invented his own form of musical notation. Within a few years, he had a scholarship at Juilliard. "What would you do if you met an eight-year-old boy who can compose and fully notate half a movement of a magnificent piano sonata in the style of Beethoven, before your very eyes and without a piano, in less than an hour?" wrote Samuel Zyman, who teaches composition at Juilliard.

At fourteen, Jay explained on *60 Minutes* that he has constant multiple channels running in his head and simply transcribes what he hears. "My brain is able to control two or three different musics at the same time, along with the channel of everyday life and everything else," he said. "The unconscious mind is giving orders at the speed of light. I just hear it as if it were a smooth performance of a work that is already written." Supporting such a prodigy is a full-time job. "We had to go into debt and make sacrifices in our careers, but not because we were stage parents," Robert said to me. "It's because those changes were essential for our son's well-being, mental health, self-confidence, and ability to find mentors and friends."

The neuroscientist Nancy Andreasen has proposed "that the creative process is similar in artists and scientists, that it is highly intuitive, and that it may arise from unconscious or dreamlike mental states during which new links are created in the association cortices of the brain." Jay's descriptions of his compositional process support such observations. When asked how he found a musical idea, Jay said, "It comes to me. Usually it chooses the most inconvenient moment to do so, when I'm miles from the nearest sheet of paper or pen, let alone a computer containing music software. For instance, I'm walking and I hear a certain cadence played by two oboes, a bassoon, and a didgeridoo. So I go home, and from that I take more ideas for other melodies that will eventually come together to form a complete piece."

By the time Jay was fourteen, he had a recording contract with Sony Classical. His liner notes for a recording of his Fifth Symphony and Quintet for Strings give some insight into his oblique mind: "The Fantasia was the last movement to be completed, excluding a few minor technical revisions to the Finale; it is also the most structurally perfect movement in the piece, as it follows a mathematical function, $y = 1/x^2$. The graph of this function is based around the asymptotes of the x- and y-axes; from very close to, but still not quite, zero, it ascends slowly but steadily between the integers of $x = 1$ and $x = 0$ to almost touch the y-axis, which it once again fails to reach; this is mirrored across the axis. The Quintet describes the three facets of the human psyche according to Freudian theory: the superego, or conscience that restrains the rest of the piece (the Adagio); the ego, in touch with reality, and fulfilling the old adage that 'to those who feel, life is a tragedy; to those who think, it's a comedy' (the scherzo); and the id—the impulsive and instinctual, unconscious and ultimately most gratifying (the Prestissimo)." You would never guess from this how lyrical his music is or how gripping it can be.

Jay's manner is diffident, often to the point of rudeness; if you say little, he appears bored; if you say much, he evinces disdain, as though to say that his energy and yours might be better spent in other pursuits. One journalist told me that interviewing him was "like dropping stones down a well." His father said, "He loves to hear the music performed live; it nourishes him. He hates the part where they want him to come up on the stage. Schubert doesn't have to go onstage; why should he?" Jay's misanthropy has an aura of triumph, as though it were proof of an authenticity that more socially adept musicians presumably lack. "He does better with adults, but many adults are afraid of that precociousness and feel threatened or upset or intimidated," Robert said. Jay clearly has a deeper humanity than he lets the public see, and he's more likable in his music and even on his blog than in person. In his mix of reflective aptitude and arrogant naïveté, he is not altogether unlike Ari Ne'eman, the autistic man who was classified as both gifted and disabled. "My music does express my feelings, even if I'm not conscious of it," Jay said. Many people rely on music to communicate their emotions to others; Jay relies on it to manifest his emotions to himself.

Throughout much of history, prodigies were thought to be possessed; Aristotle believed that there could be no genius without madness. Paganini was accused of putting himself in the hands of the devil. The Italian criminologist Cesare Lombroso said in 1891, "Genius is a true degenerative psychosis belonging to the group of moral insanity." Recent neuroscience demonstrates that the processes of creativity and psychosis map similarly in the brain, each contingent on a reduced number of dopamine D2 receptors in the thalamus. A continuum runs between the two conditions; there is no sharp line.

Norman Geschwind, the father of behavioral neurology, observed that prodigies often have a mix of abilities and challenges including dyslexia, delayed language acquisition, and asthma—"pathologies of superiority." These can be severe. One family told me that their son could identify more than fifty pieces of music when he was two. He would call out, "Mahler Fifth!" or "Brahms Quintet!" At five, the boy was diagnosed with borderline autism. Their pediatrician's instruction was to break the burgeoning obsession by taking away music completely, which they did. The autism symptoms abated, but he lost his affinity for music. Some researchers claim that musical predisposition is a function of an autistic-type hypersensitivity to sound. According to the Israeli psychiatrist Pinchas Noy, music is the organizing defense of such children against the clatter that assaults them. A number of the musicians described in this chapter likely meet clinical criteria for autism-spectrum disorders.

The association between genius and madness makes many parents wary of prodigious children. Miraca Gross, an Australian expert on gifted children, posits that they have more resilience than other children, while *extremely* gifted children have less resilience. Zarin Mehta, president of the New York Philharmonic, said that he and his wife say to each other, "Thank God we don't have such talented children." The prodigy pianist Elisha Abas, who burned out at fourteen but has made something of a comeback in his mid-thirties, said, "Sometimes the shoulders of a child are not big enough to handle his genius."

Anyone who has worked with prodigies has seen the wreckage that can ensue when someone is asynchronous, which is the condition of having intellectual, emotional, and physical ages that do not align. It is no easier to have an adultlike mind in a child's body than to have a childlike mind in a mature body. Joseph Polisi, president of Juilliard, said, "Normal young children pick up the fiddle or go to the keyboard, and they're transformed before your eyes. It's frightening." His colleague Veda Kaplinsky added, "Genius is an abnormality, and abnormalities do not come one at a time. Many gifted kids have ADD or OCD or Asperger's. When the parents are confronted with two sides of a kid, they're so quick to acknowledge the positive, the talented, the exceptional; they are in denial over everything else." Musical performance is a sustained exercise in sensitivity, and sensitivity is the tinder of fragility. The parents of so many exceptional children must be educated to see the identity within a perceived illness; the parents of prodigies are confronted with an identity and must be educated to recognize the prospect of illness within it. Even those without a sideline diagnosis need to mitigate the loneliness of having their primary emotional relationship with an inanimate object. The psychiatrist Karen Monroe explained, "If you're spending five hours a day practicing, and the other kids are out playing baseball, you're not doing the same things. Even if you love it and can't imagine yourself doing anything else, that doesn't mean you don't feel lonely." Leon Botstein said bluntly, "Aloneness is the key to creativity."

Suicide is an ever-present risk. Brandenn Bremmer had prodigious musical abilities, finished high school at ten, and told an interviewer flatly, "America is a society that demands perfection." When he was fourteen, his parents left the house to buy groceries and returned to find he had shot himself in the head, leaving no note. "He was born an adult," his mother said. "We just watched his body grow bigger." Terence Judd performed with the London Philharmonic Orchestra at twelve; won the Liszt Piano Competition at eighteen; and committed suicide at twenty-two by throwing himself off a cliff. The violinist Michael Rabin had a breakdown and "recovered," only to die from a fall at thirty-five, his blood full of barbiturates. Christiaan Kriens, a high-profile Dutch prodigy in violin, piano, conducting, and composing, shot himself in the head in later life, leaving a note saying he felt he could not sustain a career in music.

Although Julian Whybra, in his writings on the emotional needs of gifted children, described "the growing problem of suicide among intellectually gifted children," others maintain that there is no research to show that such children are less emotionally hardy than others. That is not to say that brilliance is irrelevant to suicide. Some people may be spurred to suicide by their abilities, while others resist suicide because of similar abilities. Genius is both a protection and a vulnerability, and geniuses commit both more and less suicide. That the numbers average out the same does not imply that such rates are ontologically identical. The nuances of this dialectic—what drives some people to suicide keeps others from it—have not been adequately explored.

When these suicides do occur, parents tend to get blamed—and some do push their children to the breaking point. The presence of the stage mother, or the demanding father who is never satisfied, runs through the professional literature. Some parents are focused on helping their kids, and others, on helping themselves; many don't recognize a gap between these objectives. Some parents see the dream so vividly that they lose sight of the child. Robert Sirota, president of the Manhattan School of Music, said, "Mothers had their little boys castrated in Renaissance Italy to give them a music career, and the psychological mutilation of today is equally brutal." Mental health, independence of thought, and intelligence become particularly important as buffers of extraordinary aptitude that has nothing to do with them. Failed prodigies must forever carry the poisonous memory of themselves as promising. The narrative of prodigies is constantly pushed toward triumph or tragedy, when most must find contentment somewhere in between. The violinist Jascha Heifetz once described prodigiousness as being "a disease which is generally fatal," and one that he "was among the few to have the good fortune to survive."

The crudest and most straightforward form of exploitation is financial. In "The Awakening," Isaac Babel describes the subculture of prodigies in prewar Russia, where they represented a possible path out of poverty for their families. "When a boy turned four or five, his mother took the tiny, frail creature to Mr. Zagursky. Zagursky ran a factory that churned out child prodigies, a factory of Jewish dwarfs in lace collars and patent leather shoes." The prodigy pianist Ruth Slenczynska wrote in *Forbidden Childhood* of the beatings she endured: "Every time I made a mistake, he leaned over and, very methodically, without a word, slapped me across the face." Her 1931 debut, when she was four, met rave reviews. She remembers Rachmaninoff saying to her, "In one year you will be magnificent. In two years you will be unbelievable. Would you like some cookies?" One day, she overheard her father say, "I teach Ruth to play Beethoven because it brings in the dollars." She crumpled; when she gave up piano, "I was 16, felt 50 and looked 12." Her father threw her out; his parting words were "You lousy little bitch! You'll never play two notes again without me."

The Hungarian pianist Ervin Nyiregyházi was closely studied throughout his childhood by a psychologist who documented his early life in detail. Ervin's parents never encouraged him to learn to dress himself or cut up his own food. He was given a diet superior to that enjoyed by the rest of the family. He did not attend school. His parents harnessed his genius to gain privilege; they were invited to present him to European royalty. Later, Ervin said, "I was like a calling card. By the time I was five, I realized I was in a world of strangers." His father had numerous affairs with Ervin's patrons; his mother squandered the money her son earned.

When Ervin was twelve, his father died, and his mother turned Ervin's chief joy into a gruesome chore. "My mother hated me," Ervin said. He hated his mother in return and once praised Hitler for exterminating her. Like many people whose early talent is overpraised, he showed the wounded narcissist's mix of arrogance and desperate insecurity. "Whatever obstacles were put in my way, I just gave up," he said. He married ten times and divorced nine. For a while he was homeless. Though he lived to old age, he performed only occasionally, with mixed results; without his mother to play for or against, he had no motive for authentic expression.

Lorin Hollander's father was associate concertmaster to the legendary conductor Arturo Toscanini and shared his boss's temper. "I was a battered child," Lorin said to me. "If I played something that wasn't how he wanted it, I'd be knocked or punched off the piano seat." After his triumphant debut in 1955 at eleven, Lorin's life began to accelerate. "I was already playing fifty concerts a year when I was fourteen, and making a recording a year. At sixteen, I started to have severe depressive episodes, and I also started to lose control of my right hand and arm." Fifty-two years after his first performance at Carnegie Hall, he said, "The stage fright, often stage terror, was debilitating. I didn't know that I had a choice, that there was anything else in life. Nothing I did was up to my standard. That standard was not only technical perfection, but that every note be imbued with the complete palette of human emotions, of spiritual questioning, of the search for beauty."

Lorin's personal life became confused. "I don't know whether you call it a sexual addiction. But I was not sexually faithful in my marriages. There's no excuse. It's just stupidity. There was nobody to speak to about the yearnings and thirsts and needs," he said. "The giftedness comes equipped with this hell. No one tells you this. The music starts racing faster and faster and faster, and you can't hold on to it. I'd hide after performances. I'd leave stages at the end of a concert with the audience standing and cheering. I'd go out a back door to drown in my shame." Lorin has worked with the parents of gifted children, warning them of the dangers. "It is not possible to understand the highly gifted by extending our understanding of the average," he said. "From understanding the highly gifted, we can go back down, but not vice versa." In other words, Tolstoy can teach us to understand a farmworker, but farmworkers cannot in general give us insight into the metaphoric complexities of *Anna Karenina*.

Cruel parental control is hardly a recent invention. Mozart's childhood mantra was "Next to God comes Papa." Paganini said of his father, "If he didn't think I was industrious enough, he compelled me to redouble my efforts by making me go without food." In the early nineteenth century, Clara Wieck's diary was examined every day by her father, who also wrote large sections of it, some in his own hand, some that he made her copy out, as he trained her to become one of the Romantic era's singular pianists. "He persisted in using the first person throughout, as though Clara were writing," according to her biographer. "He seemed to be taking over her personality." When he realized she was in love with the composer Robert Schumann, he said, "You will have to leave one, him or me." She married Schumann, and her father refused to hand over the diaries.

In the absence of adequate hotels in Cleveland in the 1960s and '70s, the renowned Cleveland Orchestra put up visiting artists at the homes of board members, and Scott Frankel's parents opened their house to Itzhak Perlman, Pinchas Zukerman, and Vladimir Ashkenazy. By five, Scott was taking piano lessons; he had perfect pitch and soon was able to improvise on any tune. "My mother used to write jingles and had plans for me to succeed in a larger way in the field," he said. "My father's work tapped neither his interest nor his aesthetic ability. So he was very attuned to how terrific it would be if I did something that interested me."

Scott's first piano teacher knew that Scott had a remarkable talent; Scott knew, too. "There's something palpable when your abilities fill you with a divine sense of fate," he said. "It instantly separates, even alienates, you from your schoolmates." Playing for his parents, "I began to think they liked me for what I could do, perhaps to the exclusion of who I was. The pressure made music an unsafe area. My partner and I had people over for lunch recently, and one asked me to play and I said, 'No,' and I sounded really rude, and I felt that rage again. I can't shake it."

Scott believes that his mother's need for control extended beyond his playing. "She wanted to be in charge of where I was going to go to school, who my friends were going to be, what career I was going to have, whom I was going to marry, what I was going to wear, and what I was going to say. When I started to veer from her notions, it enraged her. She was mercurial, carnivorous, and boundary-disrespecting and thought of me as an extension of herself. My father was unable, or unwilling, or both, to protect me from her."

Scott began to study at the Cleveland Institute of Music with a Russian piano teacher who disdained the Midwest. "We had these long, ferocious lessons," he said. "If something was bad, her ultimate insult was to say it sounded Spanish. She'd say, 'The way you're playing the Bach—why does it sound so Spanish?' But the Cleveland Orchestra had a concerto competition, and I entered, played my best, and won. She couldn't believe it." The prize entailed a debut with the Orchestra; before long, Scott was off to Yale, where he discovered his calling—composing musicals.

When he told his parents he was gay, they were livid. "I resented the parochial affection," he said. "You get the whole package. You can't pick the shiny bits from the other bits." In his twenties, Scott became so angry at his parents that he stopped writing music. "Their interest made me want to eat the baby," he said, "to deprive them of something to pimp and market for their own purposes. Of course, it had the side effect of shooting myself, career-wise and ethos-wise, in the foot. I was completely unmoored, and nothing made sense anymore. All I had was drugs, sex, and therapy." Scott went ten years without touching a piano. "Yet music kept encroaching. I would be near a piano and feel emotions I couldn't shut out." Finally, Scott began composing the musicals that propelled him to Broadway.

He described how inspiration comes fast when he finds the right lyrics, and I said it sounded like a joyful process. "The music has a topography of incredible highs and lows. But my writing in general is pain-based," Scott said. "The varnished colors of regret and despair and hopelessness come out of my life experience." He showed me a picture on his iPhone of himself at five, wreathed in smiles. "This is exhibit A." Then he gave me a list of the antidepressant medications he was taking. "Exhibit B. That smiling little boy, I think he's my natural, essential nature, and if he'd been allowed to grow up without being damaged, I'd be writing happy-go-lucky music instead of Sturm und Drang music." He shook his head and I heard more sadness than anger in his protest. "The tunes might have been just as good," he said.

The violinist Vanessa-Mae's mother controlled every aspect of her life: her bank accounts, her clothes, and the sexually provocative photo shoot for the cover of the album she released at seventeen. Vanessa-Mae was never allowed to slice bread lest she cut her hand; she was not allowed to have friends, lest they distract her. Her mother said, "I love you because you are my daughter, but you'll never be special to me unless you play the violin." Vanessa-Mae chose a new manager when she was twenty-one, "desperately hoping for a normal mother/daughter relationship." She wanted companionship instead of supervision. Her mother has not spoken to her since; when a BBC film crew asked to interview Vanessa-Mae's mother, she wrote, "My daughter is nearly 30. That part of my life is well and truly over." Vanessa-Mae has been wildly successful, with a personal fortune estimated at $60 million, but she said, "I felt older at twelve than I do now." She explained, "I carry the e-mail she sent to the BBC around with me, and if I ever have any pangs about what our relationship might have been like, I read that and realize it is never going to be."

Nicolas Hodges was born into music. His mother, an opera singer who performed at Covent Garden, gave up her career to have a family. Nic began piano lessons at six and had by nine started an opera on the theme of Perseus. At sixteen, he told his parents that he had decided to be a composer, not a pianist. "It was like I'd stabbed them," Nic said. "What I had thought was all for and because of me was actually all for and because of her. It became shockingly clear that my mother didn't care what I wanted at all."

As Nic got older and his relationship with music deepened, he realized that he could not keep up his skill as both a composer and a pianist, and playing paid better. He wanted "to focus on who I already was and become not less of that, but more." His mother was delighted. "So I wrote her a letter saying I never wanted to speak to her again, and I had no contact for a year." Today, he plays mostly contemporary repertoire, which his mother dislikes. Even twenty-five years later, he said, "It's almost like an infidelity, and the partner never manages to forget the loss of trust. When I play nineteenth-century music, she says, 'Oh, oh, that's good! Oh, you do like that! Oh, you do!' When I put on a CD of Chopin when she was at my flat once, she said, 'Oh, so you still like Chopin?' It was like, 'Oh, you like boys, but you still like girls, too?' She was hoping that I would do something that pointed to her, that fed her."

Nic's eventual decision to return to performing contains a strange mix of defiance and acquiescence. "I went back to what she originally wanted, but by then, it was my choice to do that," he explained. "Having disappointed her so much and so suddenly when I was sixteen made it much easier for me to find what I really wanted to do."

Developing a life in music takes tremendous will. When the pianist Rudolf Serkin was director of the Curtis Institute of Music, perhaps the most prestigious music school in the world, a student said to him, "I've been trying to decide whether I can be a pianist or whether I should go premed." Serkin said, "I'd advise you to become a doctor." The boy said, "But you haven't heard me play yet." Serkin said, "If you're asking the question, you're not going to make it as a pianist." But questioning the decision to be a musician can be pressingly important. Even as enduring a genius as the cellist Yo-Yo Ma considered other careers after his prodigious youth. "It seemed as if the course of my life had been predetermined and I very much wanted to be allowed a choice," he wrote. He has expressed gratitude that his parents understood "that an early physical facility has to be combined with a mature emotional development before a healthy musical voice emerges." The singer Thérèse Mahler, a descendant of the composer Gustav Mahler, is likewise grateful she wasn't pushed into music. "I might have accomplished more if I had been," she said to me. "But I might not have discovered how much I need music. Because I was never pushed, I know it's my choice."

Deciding *not* to develop a life in music after a prodigious beginning also takes will. Veda Kaplinsky said, "By the time they become adults, it's very difficult for them to differentiate the profession from themselves. They can't imagine themselves doing anything else, even if they really don't want to be musicians." Some wonderful musicians simply do not want the performer's life. As the piano prodigy Hoang Pham told me, "When you're young, you see success, but you can't really touch it. As you grow older, you swim a little closer to the thing that you want to touch, and you realize it's actually not quite what it seemed. There's trouble at sea, and everything is a little rougher than it looked, and the thing that you thought was so beautiful in the distance is actually quite jagged and a little fallen apart. But you've already swum so far by that time that you just keep going."

Ken Noda's mother, Takayo Noda, saw an ad for piano lessons in the *Village Voice* and enrolled Ken when he was five. Within two years, his teacher suggested that he audition for Juilliard's precollege division. Takayo had wanted to be a dancer, but she came from a prominent political family in Tokyo, and her father had forbidden it. She wanted to give her son the artistic opportunity she had been denied. "Suddenly my mother was sitting next to me, watching me practice, making sure I did two hours, punishing me when I made mistakes," Ken recalled. "I loved music, but I started to actually loathe the piano. It's a very recalcitrant, difficult instrument that doesn't vibrate; it's like a typewriter, basically."

As his parents' marriage disintegrated, his practice sessions became more grueling. "Violent yelling," Ken said. "It was nightmarish. You should have to pass a bar exam to qualify as a parent for talented children. I tried desperately to believe she was not the prototype of a stage mother, because she always used to tell everyone else she wasn't, but she was. She was very, very loving when I did well, and when I didn't do well, she was horrific." Meanwhile, Ken's father effectively abandoned him. "He often expressed contempt for what I was doing. It wasn't really for me; it was contempt for her. Since I didn't have time for friends, and since I needed someone to love me, I kept working so she'd love me, at least sometimes. You see, I was born with two umbilical cords: the physical one that everyone is born with, and another that was made of music."

What Ken refers to as his "first career" began when he was sixteen. After an auspicious 1979 debut concert, with Barenboim conducting, he was signed by Columbia Artists Management. Barenboim said to Takayo, "There's so much emotion, and so much going on inside him, but physically, he's so tense, so almost contorted when he plays, and I'm afraid he's going to hurt himself." Ken became Barenboim's pupil. Technical proficiency was hard for him, but he played with poignant insight. "I was an old soul," he said. Even an old soul needs some dalliance with youth, however. "Starting young, being groomed, being put on a certain track, meeting very powerful, important people who nine times out of ten see you in the image they want to make you, it's intoxicating, frightening, and ultimately can kill you," Ken said. When he was eighteen, Takayo left his father for an Italian painter. "That's when suddenly everything clicked, and I realized she herself was trapped, and that I had become her outlet."

At twenty-one he came out of the closet, which was necessary for both his mental health and his music. "Young people like romance stories and war stories and good-and-evil stories and old movies because their emotional life mostly is and should be fantasy, and they put that fantasized emotion into their playing, and it is very convincing. But as you grow older, fantasy emotion loses its freshness," he said. "For some time, I was able to draw on this fantasy life of what loss would mean, what a failed romance would mean, what death might mean, what sexual ecstasy might mean. I had an amazing capacity for imagining these feelings, and that's part of what talent is. But it dries up, in everyone. That's why so many prodigies have midlife crises in their late teens or early twenties. If our imagination is not replenished with experience, the ability to reproduce these feelings in one's playing gradually diminishes."

Ken had a run of concerts with formidable conductors; management had him scheduled years in advance. When he was twenty-seven, he had a crisis that brought him to the brink of suicide. "I was suffocating. My playing began to be careful, a little bit anal-retentive. I never miss notes; I've always been a very clean player, but the cleanness became almost hypochondriacal. I felt unable to express anything." He walked into the office of the head of Columbia Artists Management and announced that he was quitting. His manager said, "But you have concerts booked for the next five years." Ken said, "I want to cancel my whole life." Fifteen years later, he told me, "It was the single most thrilling experience I've ever had."

Ken had saved enough money to live comfortably for some time without working. "So I just walked around New York for a year. I sat in parks; I went to museums; I went to libraries—all these things I had never been able to do. People would ask, 'Where are you playing next?' and I'd say, 'Nowhere.' That was the best year of my life because my identity and self-worth had absolutely nothing to do with my talent."

Then James Levine, artistic director of the Metropolitan Opera, offered Ken a job as his deputy, and Ken's second life in music began. Ken coaches the singers; while Levine is somewhat socially disconnected, Ken's sparkle and warmth draw out the performers. "The musical life I'm having now is a dream," he said. "I love the theater. I love singers. I love the Met." He performs occasionally, usually as an accompanist, taking the unspotlit position he prefers. "I do it to prove to myself that I didn't stop because of stage fright," he said.

It took Ken years to recognize the ways in which his new career resembled the relentless grind of his previous one. He woke every morning before five, studied operas, headed to the Met at six thirty, practiced for a few hours, rehearsed, coached, stayed until ten or eleven at night, and went home. At forty-five, Ken developed a staph infection; when the ER doctor asked for an emergency contact and Ken realized there was no one he wanted to inform, he entered a depression. He felt his musicality drying up again. It has served him as a bellwether: only when it wanes does he notice his underlying psychic decay. "It's very, very easy to fall into the trap of thinking you've lived all these emotions, because you've been reproducing them all day long. With middle age, I started yearning for life—life that I'd always been reading about in books, or seeing in movies, or witnessing in other people's homes."

Ken began his first serious relationship at forty-seven. "I'd had many love affairs, and they'd all been somewhat theatrical, shooting-star kind of romances," he said. "When I finally started to live, I had this incredible fear that my ability to produce art would dissipate." Periodically, this fear would spur him to withdraw. "The first time I broke up with Wayne, he was heartbroken," Ken recalled. "The second time, after three weeks, he just came back to find me." Ken described, as well, a social incompetence that was the legacy of his isolation. In the middle of a Gay Pride party, he announced that he had to go practice at the Met. Wayne said, "You're my partner. You can't just leave. You can't just run back to the Met and hide in a practice room." Ken said to me, "I never played with other children, so why at forty-seven would I go out and play with my partner?" Soon thereafter, Ken donated his piano and sheet music to charity. "It's a wonderfully simple feeling to come home, not have a piano."

After a period of estrangement, Ken has a cordial relationship with his father; Takayo has expressed enormous regret over his childhood, and they, too, have reconciled. "I can have overwhelming feelings of love for her," he said. "I don't hate her, ever. But the connection is so powerful, and I have to fight to have another focus in life." He paused. "The drive and focus that I have came from the way my mother drove me. That took me very far. I will never forgive her for my first life in music, which I hated, but I will never be able to thank her enough for my second life in music, which I love."

Some who love applause confuse that fervor with a passion for music. "Unfortunately," Veda Kaplinsky said, "they're going to be miserable.

Because most of the time, it's you and your music, not you and your audience." The critic Justin Davidson said, "When you're fourteen, you do it because it's expected of you, you're good at it, and you're getting rewards. By the time you're seventeen or eighteen, if that's still why you're doing it, there's a good chance you're going to crash. If music is about expression, you have to be expressing yourself by that point, not somebody else."

Sometimes the adults a prodigy wants to please are competing with one another. Like deaf children who learn Sign at school, many musicians share with teachers a cherished language that their parents cannot master. The relationship between teacher and student often triangulates the parent-child bond as it did with Leon Fleisher, his mother, and Schnabel. It can be like a messy divorce, with the teacher and the parents giving different instructions, with different objectives, and the child caught awkwardly in the middle. One teacher told me about a student so anxious about the divergence between her mother's suggestions and the teacher's that she forsook a promising career and switched to mathematics.

The Texan prodigy Candy Bawcombe, her parents, and her teachers all recognized her potential, and they were all damaged in the effort to realize it. Candy was different in multiple ways from the other children in Cleburne, Texas, in the 1960s. She was adopted; her parents were Yankees; and they liked to listen to the Chicago Symphony on the radio. They put Candy in ballet classes. She hated ballet but was fascinated by the pianist who played for the lessons. She told her parents, "If you let me quit ballet, I'll practice the piano and I'll never stop." Their priest loaned Candy's father an 1893 Steinway upright piano that an erstwhile parishioner had brought to Texas in a covered wagon.

Candy's teacher used to tour Texas with the Dallas Male Chorus, and he started taking Candy along to perform when she was seven. "In Mineola, a lady said, 'I want your autograph,'" Candy remembered. "I said, 'I don't know how to write in cursive yet.' She said, 'Honey, it doesn't matter. You're going to be the next Van Cliburn.'" People started to call her Van Cleburne as an inside joke. "I began to feel like a circus act," Candy recalled. "I eventually went to my parents and said, 'I don't feel good. My tummy hurts.'"

Her parents pulled her from the shows when she was eight. Someone introduced them to Grace Ward Lankford, the Fort Worth grande dame who had effectively created the Cliburn Competition. Lankford offered to put Candy in private school in Fort Worth, board her during the week, and take over her musical education. Candy's parents declined, but they took the assessments of their daughter's ability seriously, and Lankford became Candy's teacher. Candy's mother insisted that Candy practice four hours a day, but Candy was determined to do so anyway. "I'd said when I was four, 'I'm going to be a concert pianist,'" she said. "There was no other option for me." That year, she won a competition in Fort Worth. When Candy was ten, Lankford was diagnosed with advanced colon cancer and lived only three months. No one wanted Candy to witness mortal illness, so she never saw her mentor again. She told her parents that she couldn't play without Lankford. Then they received a call. On her deathbed, Lankford had asked the renowned Hungarian pianist Lili Kraus, artist-in-residence at Texas Christian University, to take Candy as a pupil.

"I was overwhelmed by the glamour," Candy said. "Lili Kraus was a European queen. The brocade gowns. The triple strand of pearls around her neck that she wore every day of her life. The violinist Felix Galimir later told me, 'Every man in Europe was in love with Lili Kraus.'" Candy had learned the Mendelssohn Concerto in G Minor and thought her new teacher would be impressed. "She listened, and then said, 'Now, darling, I will teach you how to play the piano.' She took all my books off the piano, threw them on the floor, and said, 'Play a scale.' So I played a C-major scale. Then she started saying, 'Play G minor. Play B-flat major. Play in counter-motion. Play four octaves.' She was asking me to do things I'd never heard of before. My whole life caved in and crashed down."

Candy's mother had been somewhat intimidated by Lankford, but she was in awe of Lili Kraus; she took home the teacher's dresses to mend. Candy displaced a lot of feeling onto her new teacher. "If you have the strong personality of a world-famous concert artist in your life at the age of eleven, how can that not overshadow your mother?" she said. "I wanted to emulate Kraus in every way." Candy developed a rapport with Kraus beyond her mother's reach, but her mother became her drill sergeant, keeping her at the piano for hours every day. "Nothing came before that," Candy said. "Ever."

For a year and a half, Candy played nothing but exercises: arpeggios, trills, scales, Czerny, scales in thirds, scales in octaves. "I thought I was going to go insane. What happened to the concertos?" Finally, Kraus decided Candy was ready for a Mozart sonata. They established a routine: Kraus would tour in Europe all summer, during which time Candy would have music to learn by heart; when Madame returned in September, Candy would relearn those same pieces "the right way." Candy's father was offered promotions, but they involved moving, which was unthinkable as long as Candy was studying with Kraus.

It became a running joke to introduce Candy as "Lili Kraus's student who is the next winner of the Cliburn Competition," which for Candy would "ratchet that bolt and screw tighter and tighter." She wanted to go to Juilliard, but couldn't bear to leave Kraus. "I'm the only student who learned the real technique that Kraus had," she said. "I spent fourteen years with her to earn it." But Candy decided that she wanted to make her mark playing the concerto version of Schubert's *"Wanderer" Fantasy*, and Kraus said, "I'm the only pianist who plays that piece." It was the beginning of trouble. "Madame Kraus was fighting to continue her career as long as possible," Candy said. "She wanted my youth, and she couldn't have it."

Candy felt pressured by her mother's focus and her father's missed career opportunities. She felt pushed by Kraus to triumph in a way that would elevate but not overshadow Kraus's own reputation. She felt the lingering burden of Lankford's hopes, and of being an adopted child who needed to prove herself worthy enough not to be abandoned. She felt the terrible anxiety that had begun with her sideshow act around Texas. She enrolled at TCU, where she began to struggle more and more with her work and physical health. She was, at last, preparing to enter the Cliburn Competition, playing the Prokofiev Piano Concerto no. 2.

Shortly before the competition, she became terribly ill and lost thirty pounds in a month. Doctors diagnosed her with anorexia, and for the next five years she became weaker and weaker; eventually, she was down to eighty-five pounds, though she is five feet ten. Her kidneys were giving out, and she was put on life support. Kraus wrote in her diary that she was saying good-bye to Candy before she died. In the hospital, Candy pondered her despair. "I accused my mother many times, 'You don't love me because I didn't win the Cliburn Competition.' I thought she'd seen me only as the piano prodigy. Madame Kraus loved me; I was her baby, and she called me Candy Bandy. But it was always 'Candy Bawcombe, pianist.' Why can't it just be 'Candy Bawcombe, person?'" She finally learned that she had Crohn's disease; it took her a year to walk again.

When she was nearly thirty, she wrote to Lili Kraus, "I have to leave you, Madame Kraus. I have to leave Fort Worth, and my parents, and my world as I know it, and jump into New York City." Candy sold everything she had to pay for Juilliard. "My parents were in tears," she recalled. "They knew I needed to do something, but they really didn't know what was ahead."

What she discovered at Juilliard was people. "I was so tired of being alone, on the road, in my career, in my life, in every way all the time," she recalled. Candy became romantically involved with a violinist at Juilliard, Andrew Schast. Andy was offered a job with the Dallas Symphony, and Candy married him and returned to Texas. Not long afterward, the marriage started to fall apart. "He was the esteemed conductor, and I had nothing to do," Candy recalled. Her relationship to Kraus had been poisoned by Kraus's one-upmanship; now she found it difficult not to compete with her husband. "I was ready to leave him," she said. Then she discovered she was pregnant. Motherhood unexpectedly united them; it focused Candy's energies on someone other than herself. "As a prodigy, you're always the most important person in the room," she said. "Miss Perfect, that's who I'd always been, and now, it wasn't about me. As it turns out, that's what I really wanted all along."

Candy eventually became the organist and musical director at the local Episcopal church. When I attended services there, I asked some of the congregants what they made of the music. Everyone knew she was a fine musician, but many of them didn't listen to classical music outside church, and some had never liked it before joining St. Andrew's. Listening to Candy play there felt a little like *Babette's Feast*, as the congregation stood up and sat down and fumbled with their hymnals while perfectly sublime harmonies cascaded all around them.

The parents of a prodigy cannot know whether that child will have sufficient skill for a career in music, and equally cannot know whether that child will want such a life. The pressure can be overwhelming, and even those who like performing may not want to live with constant travel that makes sustained relationships nearly impossible. Are parents preparing their child for a life that he or she will actually enjoy in adulthood? Many such parents have a single-minded focus on a solo career and don't deign to explore other ways to have a life in music, such as orchestral and chamber performance.

David Waterman's aunt Fanny, who has been called "Britain's best-known piano teacher," founded the Leeds Piano Competition, and both his elder sisters were prodigies. His parents were too worn out to push their third child toward music, too. Instead, he was pressured to become an all-around excellent student, and he decided very definitely against being a prodigy, learning the cello at a recreational pace. As a teenager, he fell in love with chamber music and the sociability it entailed. He joined an amateur quartet while he was an undergraduate studying philosophy at Cambridge and undertook a PhD there so he could keep his campus housing while he decided whether to become a professional cellist.

In 1979, David founded the Endellion String Quartet with three other musicians who had all been prodigies; thirtysome years later, the group has had to replace only one member and is going strong. David described how liberating it was for him to have a broad education and know that he could function in many other areas. That is not to say that his late start did not come at a cost. "If the quartet doesn't play for a week, the level to which I sink in that time is alarming. That doesn't happen to them. I'm sure that's to do with how deeply ingrained their movements are." He acknowledged, however, that a broader education had helped his human relations. "Knowing how to articulate has been very valuable for the quartet," he said.

I wondered whether David regretted those lost years of early practice. "I'd most likely be a failed soloist, instead of a successful chamber musician," he said. "I might be a better cellist now if I had made that decision in my teens. But I think I'd be a much less happy person. And that would actually make me a lesser cellist."

Musicians such as Ken Noda, Candy Bawcombe, and David Waterman retain a quieter life in music than their parents fantasized for them; others decide to keep playing but give up the notion of being heard. I knew someone in college, Louise McCarron, who showed brilliant talent as a pianist. In her early twenties, she was to make her Kennedy Center debut. Her parents hired a bus to take friends and relatives to the performance. Two days before the concert, everyone received notice that Louise had had an injury and would be unable to play. I thought it might be repetitive stress from all the practicing, but it was simply that her pinkie hurt. In the twenty-five years since, Louise has never scheduled or made a public performance. She lives alone in an apartment with two pianos and practices eight hours a day. Dating and marrying are impossible because she must "give everything" to her art. When she occasionally comes to a party, she introduces herself as a concert pianist, even though she has never given a concert.

While a taste for wealth and fame can propel parents of prodigies into exploitation, most are not venal; they are unself-aware, and powerless to separate their wishes from their children's. Young children mirror back their parents' ambitions. If you dream of having a genius for a child, you will spot brilliance in your child, and if you believe that fame would have salved all your own unhappiness, you will see a longing for prominence in your son's or daughter's face. While many performers are self-involved, it is often the parents of prodigies who are most obviously narcissistic. They may invest their own hopes, ambitions, and identities in what their children do rather than who their children are. Instead of cultivating curiosity, they may sprint for fame. Though they sometimes seemed pitiless to me, they were seldom vindictive; the abuse they perpetrated reflected a tragic misunderstanding of where one human being ends and another begins. Absolute power corrupts absolutely, and no power is more absolute than parenthood. The children of these parents, despite being the subjects of obsessive attention, suffer from not being seen; their sorrow is organized not so much around the rigor of practicing as around invisibility. Accomplishment entails giving up the pleasures of the present moment in favor of anticipated triumphs, and that is an impulse that must be learned. Left to their own devices, children do not become world-class instrumentalists before they turn ten.

When I spoke to Marion Price on the telephone to set up our interview, I invited her to bring her violinist daughter, Solanda, for dinner, but she said, "We have a family of fussy eaters, so we'll eat before we come." The Prices arrived wearing coats, and I offered to hang them up. Marion, speaking for her husband and daughter as well, said, "That won't be necessary," and they sat through the interview holding their outerwear. I offered them something to drink, but Marion said, "We are so used to our schedule, and it's not time for a drink right now." In three hours, none of them had had a sip of water. I had put out homemade cookies, and Solanda kept glancing at them; every time she did, Marion shot her a look. When I asked Solanda a question, her mother constantly jumped in to answer on her behalf; when Solanda did reply, she did so with an anxious glance at her mother, as though worried whether she'd delivered the right response.

The Prices live around their musical talent. Sondra, ten years older than Solanda, is a pianist; Vikram, four years older than Solanda, is a cellist. When Solanda was five, her parents had all three children in a children's orchestra; they now perform as a trio. Marion is African-American; Solanda's father, Ravi, is Indian, and he writes and plays smooth jazz. "We're hearing the word *gifted*, we're hearing the word *musical*," Marion said. "We see three children who, when they practice together, it seems like one person." It's an oddity of English that the word *play* refers both to what children do for fun and what musicians do for a living, and it is misguided to infer from these homonyms that performance and practice are recreational activities.

"We had music going from the time Solanda was conceived," Marion said. Solanda started piano lessons at four. "But she fell in love with Itzhak Perlman and the violin. Solanda got that violin when she was almost five. The nurture has always been there, but when you have a child who within a moment of having received that violin, they are making music, there's something innate there as well." Solanda explained, "I chose the violin because I thought it sounded like my voice." She began studying at Juilliard just shy of six. But her instructor "was kind of scrambling to keep up with what Solanda really needed," Marion said. "Solanda was digesting everything on the spot. She wanted to play the Beethoven D Major Concerto, the Brahms D Major, the Mendelssohn E Minor. And music theory is just the air she breathes."

All three Price children have been homeschooled. Marion develops the curriculum, and Ravi does the actual teaching. I asked Solanda about having friends, and Marion said that Solanda's siblings were her best friends. I asked Solanda what she did for fun. "Basically, Juilliard," Solanda said.

Solanda had been asked to perform at an important ceremony in the nation's capital. "I was nervous," Solanda said. "It was very, very shocking to be there, but I played my best and I didn't mess up." Marion said that both Solanda and the trio had been invited to play all around the country. "She played in the Midori and Friends series, and Midori was there. We have the photos to prove it. We're looking for more opportunities." In a rare interpolation, Ravi said, "We need to take it up to the next level, where it would be, as necessary, profitable." Marion was clearly embarrassed by the mention of money. There had been a few paid performances, she said, but her children mostly played for joy—"and it just so happens that their joy is something that brings joy for others," she explained. "I don't consider us to be pushy parents. Involved parents. Supportive parents. But I don't think we're pushy. I know what that looks like. I think we're just able to respond to what our children are asking for."

In general, I don't ask musicians to perform when I interview them. Marion was holding a violin case in her lap, however, so I asked Solanda if she wanted to play. Marion said, "What do you think you'll play, Solanda?" Solanda said, "I think I'll just play the Bach Chaconne." Marion said, "How about the Rimsky-Korsakov?" Solanda said, "No, no, no, the Chaconne is better." I was struck that Solanda had chosen the instrument for its resemblance to her voice; now it provided her only chance to be heard over her mother. Solanda played the Chaconne. When she finished, Marion said, "Now you can play the Rimsky-Korsakov." Solanda launched into "Flight of the Bumblebee," the proof of every virtuoso. Marion said, "Vivaldi?" and Solanda played "Summer" from *The Four Seasons*. She played with a clear, bright tone, although not with such brilliance as to resolve the question of why a childhood had been sacrificed for this art. I had hoped Solanda would light up at her instrument, but instead she brought out the violin's searing melancholy.

While the behavior of parents can be damaging, those parents can be victimized along with their children by the classical music industry. Many managers seem to believe that the only way to keep a paying audience is to ensure a constant flow of young musicians. There has always been a market for prodigies, but in the past thirty years the tendency has been to find a new one every week. A machinery has been established by people with short-term interests in the people they are using, for whom even the child's mental health is only a mercenary concern. "It's like burning fossil fuels," Justin Davidson said. "Constantly replenishing the prodigy supply, you flood the market. These managers are creating an oversupply of people who can do a narrow range of things, many of which are no longer of great interest. They're preparing them for a future that's in the past."

"It's a bewildering preoccupation," the pianist Mitsuko Uchida said to me. "Ask those audiences how they'd like to be represented in court by a seven-year-old; let them try surgery with a very gifted eight-year-old." The critic Janice Nimura said, "The child prodigy is the polite version of the carny freak. Gawking at the dog-faced boy in the side-show is exploitative, but gawking at the six-year-old concert pianist on the *Today* show is somehow okay, even inspiring, demonstrating just how high human potential can soar." While etiquette demands that we not stare at dwarfs, it makes no such claim for the privacy of the prodigy.

Pushing talented children can backfire; not pushing them can backfire, too. Leonard Bernstein's father, when asked why he'd opposed his son's career, replied, "How did I know he was going to be Leonard Bernstein?" Doing the interviews for this chapter, I began to feel that half the parents of these children had coerced them into an uncongenial musical life, while the other half had unreasonably held their children back. Jonathan Floril has the dubious distinction of having lived both clichés.

As a child in Ecuador in the early 1990s, Jonathan yearned for music lessons, but his mother, Elizabeth, didn't think music important, while his father, Jaime Iván Floril, who had left the marriage before Jonathan was born, ran a music academy and didn't think his son warranted the training. Jaime finally relented and allowed Jonathan to take piano at eleven. Within three months, the piano teacher told Jaime that Jonathan had a talent too significant for Ecuador and needed to train in Europe.

Jonathan's mother was enraged at the thought of his going abroad and tried to hold on to him through a legal battle for custody. "She was killing me," Jonathan remembered, "because my passion for music was everything." Two months later, Jaime closed his academy to take his son to Europe. Elizabeth had notified the police that her husband was trying to kidnap Jonathan, so they drove by night across an unmanned border in the Andes to Colombia to board a plane to Madrid. Jonathan, who had studied piano for less than six months, was accepted into the fifth year at the Rodolfo Halffter Conservatory.

His mother persisted in trying to get him back, and Jonathan had to assert over and over to the Spanish police that he wanted to stay there. "With all the weight that I had from my mother, I didn't know whether what I had done was right or wrong, and my father couldn't tell me," Jonathan said. He started reading for moral guidance: Aristotle's *Ethics* and Plato's *Republic*, Saint Thomas, José Ortega y Gasset. When he was twenty, I asked him what he now thought about his departure to Spain. "My mother said that music would prevent me from living my childhood," he replied. "But I didn't want to live my childhood anymore." Between eleven and sixteen, Jonathan won more than twenty competitions; his father, who could not find work as a music teacher, took a clerical job instead. "My prodigy time was very, very stressful," Jonathan said. He returned to Ecuador for the first time when he was fifteen, four years after his departure, to play a major concert. Though his mother greeted him there joyously, an unbridgeable gap had opened.

The next year, he earned a full scholarship to the Manhattan School of Music; he soon made his debut in Valencia and was reviewed as "more than a prodigy, because of not only what he performs, but also how he performs." His studies were changing him. "I started to grow into different criteria of musicianship," he said. "My father was asking me to work on repertoire that I thought was senseless; he set himself against me, and I hated him for that. I needed to do something besides win another prize." Having fled his mother in Ecuador, he now left his father. "He wanted me to learn popular selections and make a CD. I thought I was going to get lost in that superficial way of doing music. So he kicked me out of my home in Madrid. I had to pack in two hours. It was that drastic." I asked what effect that second exile had had on him, and he said, "It seems to me almost a pilgrimage, the way that I walk as a musician through life. Sometimes I feel that my fingers moving on the keys, it's like how a blind person reads in Braille. There is so much meaning that you find only when you are touching the instrument. I search to bring something noble to the world, something as noble as the passion of Jesus Christ. I'm not actually a religious person, but I believe there's something higher than us, that makes music what it is. I can serve that thing, even if I cannot see or know it."

At twenty, Jonathan will not play a Chopin mazurka without knowing the folk mazurkas that inspired it, and he won't play a nocturne without studying the time of bel canto. "Recently, I have gone back to recordings from the 1930s of Ecuadorean music," he told me. "The way I think and am is still rooted in my country, so I need to keep this part of myself alive." I wondered how the traumas of leaving his mother, then his country, and then his father still echoed. "I do not think there was another way," he said. "I understand why my parents turned against me. We all hate what we don't understand."

Gore Vidal wrote, "Hatred of one parent or the other can make an Ivan the Terrible or a Hemingway: the protective love, however, of two devoted parents can absolutely destroy an artist." Early trauma and deprivation become the engines of some children's creativity. One researcher reviewed a list of eminent people and found that more than half had lost a parent before age twenty-six—triple the rate of the general population. A horrific upbringing can kill talent or bring it to life. It is a matter of having a match between how the parents act and what a particular child needs. Robert Sirota said, "It's very easy to destroy a talent; it's much less likely that nurture can create ability where none existed."

Lang Lang, often billed as the world's most famous pianist, is the embodiment of brilliance honed in punishment. His father, Lang Guoren, wanted to be a musician but was assigned to a factory during the Cultural Revolution. When his eighteen-month-old son showed signs of being a prodigy, Lang Guoren's longing reared up. From the age of three, Lang Lang woke up every morning at five to practice. "My passion was so huge that I wanted to eat the piano up," he said. His teacher was astonished by his memory; he could memorize four big pieces every week. "My teacher was always telling her students to learn more," he said, "but she was telling me to slow down." At seven, at China's first national children's competition in Taiyuan, he took an honorable mention for talent and rushed onto the stage, shouting, "I don't want the prize for talent, I don't want it!" When another contestant ran over to comfort him, saying that he, too, had won an honorable mention, Lang Lang said, "You think you can compete with me? What the hell can you play?" Lang Lang's prize was a stuffed-dog toy; he threw it in the mud and trampled it, but his father picked it up and kept it on the piano at home in Shenyang, so Lang Lang would never forget how much work he had to do.

Lang Guoren had become a member of the special police—a prestigious job. He decided, however, that he had to take Lang Lang to Beijing to seek a place at the Attached Primary School of the Conservatory of Music, while Lang Lang's mother, Zhou Xiulan, would stay behind to earn money to support her son and her husband. "I was nine, and it was really painful to leave home, and I realized that my father was quitting his job to be with me," Lang Lang said. "I felt such pressure." Lang Guoren taught Lang Lang his maxim: "Whatever other people have, I will definitely have; whatever I have, nobody else will have."

Lang Guoren described quitting his job as "a kind of amputation." He rented the cheapest apartment they could find, without heat or running water, and told his son that the rent was much higher than it actually was. "That much money?" Lang Lang replied, shocked. "I had better really practice." He missed his mother terribly, and he often cried. Lang Guoren, who had always scorned domestic work, had to cook and clean. The teacher they had come to see in Beijing assessed Lang Lang harshly. "She said I played like a potato farmer," he recalled, "that I should taste Coca-Cola and play Mozart like that; my playing was flavorless water. She said, 'You Northeasterners are big, coarse, and stupid.' Eventually she said, 'Go home. Don't be a pianist.' Then she fired me."

Shortly thereafter, Lang Lang stayed after school to play piano for the celebration of the founding of the People's Republic of China, and he was two hours late coming home. When he walked in, Lang Guoren beat him with a shoe, then proffered a handful of pills and said, "You're a liar and you're lazy! You have no reason to live. You can't go back to Shenyang in shame! Dying is the only way out. Take these pills!" When Lang Lang did not take the pills, Lang Guoren pushed the boy onto the apartment's balcony and told him to jump. Lang Guoren later explained his behavior with a Chinese proverb: "If you do not let go of your child, you cannot fight the wolves." In other words, coddling exposes everyone to disaster. But Lang Lang was furious and refused to touch the piano for months, until his father swallowed his pride and begged him.

Lang Guoren had also begged another teacher to work with his son and sat through the lessons so that he could reinforce the instruction at home. "He never smiled," Lang Lang said. "He was scaring me, sometimes beating me. We were like monks. The music monks." A family friend commented that Lang Guoren never showed affection or let his son know that he was pleased. "It was only when his son was sound asleep that he would sit by him silently and gaze at him, fix his quilt, and touch his small feet," the friend wrote.

When they went back to Shenyang for the summer, Lang Guoren treated the visit as a mere change of location for piano exercises. Zhou Xiulan fought with him, demanding, "What does it matter to be a 'grandmaster' or not a 'grandmaster'? What the hell are you doing, acting as if you are preparing for war every day? How does this resemble a family?" Lang Lang would try to distract them from their arguments with his music; a friend said, "Every time they fought, his playing progressed." He worked so hard that he collapsed and had to go to the hospital for intravenous fluids every day, but his practice schedule never changed. "My father is a real fascist," Lang Lang said. "A prodigy can be very lonely, locked out of the world."

He was finally accepted at the Attached Primary School and then, at eleven, he auditioned to represent China at the International Competition for Young Pianists in Germany. He was not selected. Lang Guoren told his wife that she had to raise enough money to enter Lang Lang privately, which was contrary to etiquette and potentially humiliating. Before the contest, Lang Guoren identified a blind pianist from Japan as Lang Lang's most serious opponent and told Lang Lang to draw out his competitor about technique. Lang Lang then attempted to integrate the same approach into his own playing. When Lang Lang won, Lang Guoren sobbed for joy; when others told Lang Lang of his father's response, Lang Lang countered that his father was incapable of tears.

In 1995, at thirteen, Lang Lang entered the second International Tchaikovsky Competition for Young Musicians. His father would eavesdrop on the other contestants practicing and urged Lang Lang to do the same if anyone was working on the same piece that he was. In Lang Guoren's view, if the pianist before you played with strength, you should play with delicacy; if he played softly, you should begin with strength. This tactic would make it easier for the judges to remember you and would capture the attention of the audience. When someone later asked Lang Guoren how a thirteen-year-old could play something as heartbreaking as Chopin's Second Piano Concerto for the finals, he said he'd told Lang Lang to think about his separation from his beloved mother and his beloved country. Lang Lang won.

Within months, Lang Guoren withdrew his son from the Central Conservatory. He had arranged an audition with Gary Graffman at Curtis. Lang Lang recalled, "My dad said, 'The Chopin should be as light as the wind; the Beethoven should be heavy; when you use your explosive strength, be firm, generous, and natural, as if you were a mix of the English and Brazilian football teams.'" Lang Lang was accepted on the spot, and he and his father moved to the United States. During his first lesson at Curtis, Lang Lang said, "I'd like to win every competition that exists." Graffman said, "Why?" Lang Lang said, "To be famous." Graffman just laughed, but the other students told Lang Lang he should focus instead on being a superb musician; he didn't understand the difference. Though he has since learned tact, he has never entirely renounced this Olympic model. Graffman said to me, "With most students, you want to get them excited about the emotional content of the music. With Lang Lang, it was just the opposite: I had to calm him down enough so he could learn."

At seventeen, Lang Lang acquired a manager, who got him his first big break at the Ravinia Festival, outside Chicago. The critics were enraptured, and for the next two years Lang Lang sold out every concert, made numerous recordings, graced the covers of glossy magazines. "The higher the expectations, the better I play," he told me. "Carnegie Hall makes me play best of all."

Every tremendous prodigy story, like every political career, contains a backlash sequence that shocks the protagonist; the listening world has to go through its own rejecting adolescence between its childish rhapsody and its adult respect. Schadenfreude often makes the backlash mean. Lang Lang is socially porous, with a sensitivity to pleasing his specific audience that often seems reminiscent more of Beyoncé than of Sviatoslav Richter. Though these qualities are not incompatible with profundity, his playing to the gallery offends some sophisticates. The extent of Lang Lang's self-branding is indicated by his having trademarked his name; he performs as "Lang Lang™." He has signed endorsement deals with Audi, Montblanc, Sony, Adidas, Rolex, and Steinway. John von Rhein of the *Chicago Tribune*, who had helped launch Lang Lang's career, said a few years later, "The music became an accessory to the soloist's acrobatic performance. All he needed was a white sequined suit and a candelabra and Ravinia could have sold him as the new Liberace." Anthony Tommasini, of the *New York Times*, wrote that Lang Lang's solo debut at Carnegie Hall in 2003 was "incoherent, self-indulgent and slam-bang crass."

The narrative tension between composers' masterworks and Lang Lang's reading of them is exaggerated by his having grown up in a non-Western culture. "Western classical music in China is usually like Chinese food in the West: familiar but not quite the real thing," Lang Lang said. He can do an impeccable rendition of a Mendelssohn concerto and follow it up with a self-indulgent Mozart sonata played with inflated dynamics and distended tempo. But then he'll play elegantly again and critics will have to acknowledge his mastery. Five years after condemning him so sharply, Tommasini wrote that Lang Lang played "with utter command and disarming joy." When I see Lang Lang in concert, I am always struck by how much fun he appears to be having. "I'm not just giving as a performer," he said to me. "I'm also taking. My father is an introvert, my mother is an extrovert, and I am both: my father's discipline and my mother's happiness."

I first sat down with Lang Lang in 2005, in Chicago, when he was twenty-three. I had gone that afternoon to a particularly lovely performance in which he played the Chopin Piano Sonata no. 3 in B Minor. Following the performance, a line of some four hundred people waited patiently to get his autograph on their CDs, and Lang Lang never flagged. Afterward, Lang Lang invited me to talk in his room. When we arrived, Lang Guoren was watching television. He shook my hand, we exchanged pleasantries, and then, with his characteristic mix of brusqueness and intimacy, he took off his clothes and lay down for a nap. In my experience, everyone likes Lang Lang, and no one likes Lang Guoren, but Lang Lang is not as warm as he seems, and his father is not as harsh as he seems; they are collaborators in a single phenomenon. "When I turned twenty and became a huge success, I started to love my father," Lang Lang told me. "He listens very well, and he helps me do the laundry, pack. I'm a spoiled kid. After a big recital, nobody else is going to do a little massage at two o'clock in the morning while talking about the performance."

I once told Lang Lang that by American standards his father's methods would count as child abuse, and that their present conviviality was startling to me. "If my father had pressured me like this and I had not done well, it would have been child abuse, and I would be traumatized, maybe destroyed," Lang Lang responded. "He could have been less extreme and we probably would have made it to the same place; you don't have to sacrifice everything to be a musician. But we had the same goal. So since all the pressure helped me become a world-famous star musician, which I love being, I would say that, for me, it was in the end a wonderful way to grow up."

Several recent books hark back to the adage that practice makes perfect, setting the workload for mastery at ten thousand hours. The number is extrapolated from the observation by the Swedish psychologist K. Anders Ericsson that by twenty, the top violinists at Berlin's Academy of Music had practiced an average of ten thousand hours over a decade, approximately twenty-five hundred hours more than the next most accomplished group. Skills and perhaps neurosystems develop through drilling. Recent surveys in which people were ranked for talent and then followed for practice time showed that practice time mattered more than talent. David Brooks wrote in the *New York Times*, "The primary trait is not some mysterious genius. It's the ability to develop a deliberate, strenuous and boring practice routine. We construct ourselves through behavior."

There is, without question, considerable truth in this idea; if this were not the case, education would be futile, and experience would be a waste of time. I'd much rather go up in a plane with a pilot who's been flying for a decade than with one who's on his maiden flight, and no one chooses to eat anyone's first soufflé. But the sanctification of ten thousand hours as the basis for achievement has a Horatio Alger–like sentimentality to it. Leopold Auer, the last century's great violin pedagogue, used to tell pupils, "Practice three hours a day if you are any good, four if you are a little stupid. If you need more than that—stop. You should try another profession."

The inclination to practice assiduously may itself be inborn, and nourishing it may be at least as important as nourishing basic talent. The Stanford psychologist Walter Mischel developed the so-called marshmallow test in the 1960s. A child between four and six years old was sequestered with a marshmallow and told that he could eat it right away, or he could wait fifteen minutes and get an extra marshmallow. The children who could wait went on to have SAT scores, on average, 210 points higher than those of the children who could not. More recently, Angela Lee Duckworth, a psychologist at the University of Pennsylvania, gave high schoolers the choice between a dollar right away and two dollars in a week, and once more, those who could delay gratification had much higher levels of academic achievement, regardless of IQ. "Intelligence is really important," she said, "but it's still not as important as self-control."

Ellen Winner, who studies genius, has delineated a struggle between the "commonsense myth" that giftedness is innate and the "psychologists' myth" that giftedness is accrued through labor and study. The critic Edward Rothstein wrote, "The contemporary attack on genius is itself a mythology, an attempt to grasp the ungraspable by diminishing it, reducing it." Rothstein suggests that those who emphasize the role of sheer labor listen to Bach and Beethoven and try on the idea that they could have composed such music with sufficient effort. Veda Kaplinsky jokingly compared the question to what she'd once heard a psychiatrist say about sex in a marriage: "If the sex is good, it's ten percent.

If it's bad, it's ninety percent." She explained, "If the talent is there, it's ten percent of the package. If the talent is not there, it becomes ninety percent, because they can't overcome the lack of it. But just having talent is really a very minor part of what is necessary in order to make it in music."

Musicians often talked to me about whether you achieve brilliance on the violin by practicing for hours every day, or by reading Shakespeare, learning physics, and falling in love. The violinist Yehudi Menuhin said, "Maturity, in music and in life, has to be earned by living." The composer and performer Gabriel Kahane said, "There is always a Korean girl who has been locked in the basement practicing for longer than you have. You can't win that game." But more profoundly, *normal life* in these contexts is a euphemism for a richer life. Single-minded devotion to an instrument builds proficiency—but music embraces experience.

When I said that I was writing about prodigies, people kept mentioning a seven-year-old pianist named Marc Yu, who had appeared on *Jay Leno*, *Ellen DeGeneres*, and *Oprah*. I was invited to his New York debut, a recital in the Park Avenue apartment of a Shanghai socialite. Marc had just turned eight, but his small stature made him look about six. He would solemnly lisp the name of his next selection, play it with incongruous power and musicality, then spin around to look at his dazzling mother, Chloe, to see how he'd done.

Because Marc's legs were short, a little platform had been set up with extenders that allowed him to control the pedals. As he was playing a Chopin nocturne, the contraption shifted, and the pedals ceased to respond. Chloe crawled into the tight space below her son's pumping legs and began trying to realign the device. Marc didn't miss a note. Chloe couldn't make the thing work, so she kept lifting it and slamming it back down. It was so incongruous: the little boy intent on his fingering, and the stunning woman in her gown crouched noisily at his feet, the melodies pouring forth. It was as though Marc and Chloe were in a dialogue that the rest of us had stumbled on, a private interaction that could, ironically, take place only with an audience.

Well after the recital had ended and long past the bedtime of most eight-year-olds, Marc announced that he had learned the Emperor Concerto, and he played it for a few of us, counting out long silences for the orchestral passages, so he could come in exactly on cue. He brimmed with impatient, eager bravado, much as my eight-year-old niece does when she wants me to admire her swimming. As Marc made conversation with adults who were fascinated by him but not much interested in what he had to say, I guessed that his relationship with his mother might be the only one in which he is not anomalous.

Chloe Yu was born in Macao and came to the United States to study when she was seventeen. She married at twenty-five, and Marc was born a year later, in Pasadena. From that day, Chloe played the piano to him. "He didn't start to speak until after he turned two," Chloe recalled. "I was worried. Then he started speaking, English, Cantonese, Mandarin, and a little bit of Shanghainese as well. I was so relieved!" When Marc was almost three, he picked out a few tunes on the piano with two fingers; in a year, he had surpassed Chloe's ability to teach him. At five, he added the cello to his regimen. "Soon he asked for more instruments," Chloe recalled. "I said, 'That's it, Marc. Be realistic. Two is enough.'"

Chloe gave up the master's degree she'd been working on. She had divorced Marc's father, but because she had no money, she and Marc ended up living with her ex-in-laws, who gave them a room over the garage. Marc's grandparents did not approve of his "excessive" devotion to the piano. "His grandmother loves him a lot," Chloe said. "But she just wanted him to be a normal five-year-old." When Marc was in preschool, Chloe felt he was ready to perform and contacted local retirement facilities and hospitals and offered free recitals so Marc could do so without pressure. Soon the papers were writing about this young genius. "When I began to understand how talented he is, I was so excited!" Chloe said. "And also so afraid!"

At six, Marc won a fellowship for gifted youth that covered the down payment on a Steinway. By the time Marc was eight, he and Chloe were flying to China bimonthly so that Marc could study with Dr. Minduo Li. Chloe explained that whereas her son's American teachers gave him broad interpretive ideas to explore freely, Dr. Li taught Marc measure by measure. "In the future, Marc will be telling people, 'I'm American-born, but trained in China.' China will love him for that." I asked Marc whether he found it difficult traveling so far for his lessons. "Well, fortunately, I don't have vestigial somnolence," he said. I raised my eyebrow. "You know—jet lag," he apologized.

Marc was being homeschooled to accommodate his performance and practice schedule. "After a huge breakfast, he's sleepy," Chloe said. "So, we schedule something less intense—work on technique, maybe do homework. In the late morning, he has a nap, and then he'll do something that will use his brain, learn new material. It's all about time management. He should be just in third grade, but he's ahead in all subjects." Marc was doing college prep work and taking an SAT class. Chloe serves as his manager and reviews concert invitations with him. "I consult my boss first," Chloe said. Marc looked at her with an expression of frank incredulity. "I'm your boss?" he asked. Later Chloe said, "If he changes his mind and wants to become a mathematician, I'd accept it. Maybe initially I would be upset because we have spent so much time on this—it would be just like breaking up with your boyfriend. It's not easy, right?" Marc said reassuringly, "I like piano. It's what I'm going to do." Chloe smiled. "Right now, yes. But you can never tell. You're only eight."

To play as Marc does requires an extraordinary level of concentration. Marc said, "How much I practice depends on my mood. Like if I really want to accomplish something or it's before a concert, I would say six to eight hours per day. But if I'm not really in the mood to practice, maybe four to five hours. I was interested in composing, but I've decided I need to focus." His playing has required equal discipline from Chloe. I asked her whether she thought about her old ambitions. She smiled and held out her arms to Marc. "This is my work," she said. When I visited them in LA, Chloe had just remarried, and Marc had played at the wedding banquet. Chloe refused to move into a house with her new husband, however, because she thought it would interfere with practicing with Marc; instead, they live a few streets apart. I was reminded of couples with disabled children who are split by the unusual needs of their sons and daughters.

Children like to have heroes, and Marc's is Lang Lang. After reading a story in the *Los Angeles Times* magazine in which Marc declared his admiration, Lang Lang got in touch. "I admire Lang Guoren a lot," Chloe said. "I don't want to hear the word *pushy* used about me. But I want to be strong for Marc the way he was strong for Lang Lang." A few years later, Lang Lang arranged for Marc to perform with him at the Royal Albert Hall. I attended the concert, and when we all met afterward, I was struck by Lang Lang's avuncular gentleness with his protégé; I had never seen him so vulnerable.

I asked Chloe what she thought about the ten thousand hours. "It's more about nurture, I believe, than nature," Chloe said. "Marc's father had no interest in music, so the nature came from my side. The nurture came from me, too." She has strong views on American parenting. "In America, every kid has to be well rounded. They have ten different activities, and they never excel at any of them. Americans want everyone to have the same life; it's a cult of the average. This is wonderful for disabled children, who get things they would never have otherwise, but it's a disaster for gifted children. Why should Marc spend his life learning sports he's not interested in when he has this superb gift that gives him so much joy?"

Back in California, I asked Marc what he thought of a normal childhood. "I already have a normal childhood," he said. "Do you want to see my room? It's messy, but you can come anyway." So I went upstairs with him. He showed me a yellow, remote-controlled helicopter that his father had sent from China. The bookshelves were crammed with Dr. Seuss, *Jumanji*, and *The Wind in the Willows*, but also *Moby-Dick*; with *Sesame Street* videos and also a series of DVDs called *The Music of Prague*, *The Music of Venice*, and so on. We sat on the floor and he showed me his favorite Gary Larson cartoons, and then we played the board game Mouse Trap. He had a pair of rubber thumb-tips with lights inside, which he used for a magic trick that made it look as though the light he put in his mouth traveled right down to come out of his behind.

Then we went downstairs, and Marc sat on a phone book on the piano bench so his hands would be high enough to play comfortably. He squirmed for a minute, said, "No, it's not right," pulled one page from the phone book, sat down again, and launched into Chopin's *Fantasie-Impromptu*, which he imbued with a quality of nuanced yearning that seemed almost inconceivable in someone with a shelf of Cookie Monster videos. "You see?" Chloe said to me. "He's not a normal child. Why should he have a normal childhood?"

Classical music is largely a meritocracy, which makes it a fit route to social mobility for industrious people isolated by geography, nationality, or poverty. For many years, the prodigies were mostly Jews from Eastern Europe; now, the field is dominated by East Asians. Gary Graffman, himself one of the Jewish prodigies, has only six students, all of them Chinese. The general theory about the Asian dominance of classical music is that it reflects a sheer numbers game. "There are more than three hundred thousand children in China learning instruments," Graffman said. "If you see a child in Chengdu who is not carrying a violin case, it means he's studying the piano." Chinese and other tonal languages reinforce hearing acuity in infants and toddlers, and typical Chinese hands, with broad palms and generous spaces between the fingers, are especially well suited to the piano. Discipline and competitiveness are deeply valued and constantly reinforced in many Asian cultures. Because the study of Western music was not allowed in China during the Cultural Revolution, it took on the allure of a forbidden pleasure.

Many Westerners, meanwhile, are leery of "tiger mother" stereotypes. But the Hungarian psychologist Mihaly Csikszentmihalyi wrote, "One cannot be exceptional and normal at the same time." The question of when to specialize receives very different answers from place to place; European students narrow their fields of study much earlier than Americans, and Asians focus earlier still. If music is a language, then to have an intuitive hold on its grammar and produce it without an accent requires training from a tender age. Graffman said, "You can take up the piano or the violin at sixteen and learn to play rather well, but you'll be too late to become a first-rate soloist." Early specialization requires sacrifices. "Upper-class parents want their children to have arts, athletics, and community service," said Robert Blocker, dean of the Yale School of Music. "But it's very distracting for someone who really wants to be a musician. Profound achievement is usually the result of early identification and specialization."

If the gamble pays off, the sacrifices are easier to live with. When Lang Lang told me he was reconciled with his upbringing, I thought of the people who, long after the fact, were glad that their parents had encouraged them to undergo limb-lengthening—of how what looks like abuse in the present does not necessarily seem so once it's been completed successfully. On the other hand, how many children have loathed practicing the piano and then, as adults, bemoaned that their parents let them quit taking lessons? The danger is that being pushed toward early specialization can leave children believing that they have only one way to succeed. "It's irresponsible not to have a plan B," Karen Monroe said. Prodigies who don't make it will have worked insanely hard on something that can no longer sustain them, after having neglected skills needed to pursue any other kind of life. Blocker addressed a meeting in Korea for parents who hoped to send their children to Western music schools. After explaining the admissions process, he put down his notes and said, "I think it's really unfortunate that all of you came in here today. Many of you will send your children to another country at age twelve, thirteen, fourteen. One parent will come and the family will be divided. The students who go through this so young are vacant by the time they reach us. It's not that there's an absence of feeling and longing and intellect and music in there; it's that they could not be nurtured by touch or a family meal." There followed a stony silence.

If Chloe Yu scorned the idea of a normal childhood, May Armstrong simply had to bow to the reality that no such thing could be achieved with her son, Kit, born in 1992. Chloe, who believes in the dominance of nurture, may be said to have pushed her son toward his prowess; May, on the other hand, seems to have been compelled by hers into an alarming inevitability. Kit could count at fifteen months; May taught him addition and subtraction at two, and he worked out multiplication and division for himself. While digging in the garden, he explained the principle of leverage to his mother. By three, he was asking questions to which the answer was the theory of relativity. May, an economist, was frankly bemused. "A child of that ability can teach himself," she said. "A mother wants to be protective, but he was so capable that he didn't need protection. I can't say that was easy."

May had left Taiwan at twenty-two to study in the United States and spent holidays by herself; Kit's father was never in their lives. "I knew what loneliness was all about, and I thought he needed a hobby he could enjoy on his own," she said. So she started him on piano lessons when he was five, even though she had no interest in music. At his first lesson, Kit watched the teacher reading music, and when he came home, he made his own staff paper and began to compose without an instrument: the written language of music had come to him whole. May bought a used piano, and Kit sat at it all day. He could hear something once on the radio and play it back.

May enrolled him in school. "The other mothers said they wanted their kids to grow up in kindergarten," she said. "I wanted mine to grow down. His teachers said he let other children push him around, so I went in one day and saw another child snatch a toy away from him. I told him he should stand up for himself, and he said, 'That kid will be bored in two minutes, and then I can play with it again. Why start a fight?' So he was wise, already. What did I have to teach this kid? But he always seemed happy, and that was what I wanted most for him. He used to look in the mirror and burst out laughing."

By the end of second grade, Kit had completed high school math; at nine, he was ready to start college. May speculated that Utah would be a clean, safe place for a nine-year-old to start his undergraduate education, so they went there. "The other students often thought it was strange that he was there," May said, "but Kit never did." His piano skills, meanwhile, had advanced enough so that he had been taken on by management.

When Kit was ten, he toured the physics research facility at Los Alamos with his manager, Charles Hamlen. A physicist took Hamlen aside and said that, unlike the postdoctoral physicists who usually visited, Kit was so bright that no one could "find the bottom of this boy's knowledge." A few years later, Kit won a residency at MIT, where he helped edit papers in physics, chemistry, and mathematics. "He just understands all things," May said to me, almost resigned. "Someday, I want to work with parents of disabled children, because I know their bewilderment is like mine. I had no idea how to be a mother to Kit, and there was no place to find out."

May moved them to London to be with a piano teacher Kit liked, even though she had no working papers and couldn't secure a job there. "I wasn't happy about it," May said, "but I felt I had no choice." Kit soon met the revered pianist Alfred Brendel, and Brendel, who had never had a student, took Kit on. He refused payment for lessons, and when he learned that Kit was practicing at a piano showroom because May couldn't afford a decent piano, he had a Steinway delivered to their flat. When Kit was thirteen, an English journalist who was fervently opposed to the promotion of children as performers went to one of his concerts. "His playing was so cultured, his joy in performing so obvious, his commitment as he stretched his small frame to reach the low notes so total, that my objections seemed mean-spirited," the journalist wrote in the *Guardian*.

May credits Brendel for Kit's musicianship. "I still don't have a good enough ear to be any help to Kit," she said. "All I can do is remind him that he didn't do anything to deserve being who he is." May restricted Kit's schedule and media exposure through his adolescence, allowing him to do only a dozen concerts a year. "But now, Mr. Brendel has said he is ready for a full concert schedule, and he's eighteen, and it's not up to me. I'd have preferred that he be a professor of mathematics. It's a better life, without so much travel. But Kit has decided that mathematics is his hobby, and the piano is his work." Kit is pursuing an MA in pure mathematics in Paris; he says he does it "to unwind." I asked May if she ever worried that Kit, like many young people of remarkable ability, might have a nervous breakdown. She laughed. "If anyone's going to have a nervous breakdown in this setup," she said, "it's me!" Like many parents of exceptional children, May scaled back her own ambitions. She had hoped for an important job after she earned her PhD in economics—the PhD she never completed because Kit came along. "As a parent, and as a Chinese mother, sacrifice is part of the game," she said. "I would love to learn how to sacrifice joyfully, but so far I don't have that ability. Here I am, middle-aged and riding around Paris on a bike, panting and out of breath. What happened? But I admit he's given me a fascinating life."

Prodigies are not covered by the Americans with Disabilities Act; there is no federal mandate for gifted education. But if we recognize the importance of special programs for students whose atypical brains encode less accepted differences, we should extrapolate to create programs for those whose atypical brains encode remarkable abilities. Daniel Singal wrote in the *Atlantic Monthly*, "The problem is not the pursuit of equality but the bias against excellence that has accompanied it." Writing in *Time* in 2007, the educator John Cloud faulted the "radically egalitarian" values underlying the No Child Left Behind Act, which provides little support for gifted students. The 2004 *Templeton National Report on Acceleration* asserts that the school system is designed to hold back children of remarkable abilities. Once again, it falls to parents to advocate for their children's needs, often in the face of a hostile or indifferent educational system. Leon Botstein remarked drily, "If Beethoven were sent to nursery school today, they would medicate him, and he would be a postal clerk."

The rhetoric of antielitism that has fueled American politics and its culture wars over the past generation reflects a bias toward extraordinary people who can pass for ordinary. This bias is portrayed as democratic, when it is often dishonest; it smacks of dreary assimilationism, echoing misguided efforts to make gay kids act straight. Many gifted children choose between being ostracized and going underground; many disidentify, attempting to seem less accomplished for the sake of peer approval. One survey of super-high-IQ students showed that four out of five were constantly monitoring themselves in an attempt to conform to the norms of less gifted children; in another study, 90 percent were unwilling to be identified as part of the "brain" crowd.

It used to be believed that academically promoting prodigies damaged them socially—even though many were already ostracized for their abilities. Several parents joked about the fact that their children's friends were in their seventies; Robert Greenberg said that Jay socialized primarily online, where no one knew his age. The Internet has given prodigies a society, just as it has other identity communities—a place where they can connect with like-minded people and underplay potentially alienating differences.

In the 1990s, Miraca Gross studied children who were radically accelerated, starting college between eleven and sixteen. None regretted the acceleration, and most had made good and lasting friendships with older children. By contrast, gifted children stuck with age peers experienced rage, depression, and self-criticism. Today, most gifted programs keep children in an age-based setting some of the time and a skills-based setting the rest of the time. Neither affords a perfect fit. The mathematical prodigy Norbert Wiener wrote that the prodigy knows "the suffering which grows from belonging half to the adult world and half to the world of the children about him." He explained, "I was not so much a mixture of child and man as wholly a child for purposes of companionship and nearly completely a man for purposes of study."

Two distinct kinds of young people are grouped under the *prodigy* rubric: the driven, single-minded baby virtuoso, and the youth who loves music in his bones and therefore has a better shot at a sustained career. The latter kids are more broadly intelligent, curious, often articulate, and possessed of a sense of humor and perspective about themselves. They pursue some semblance of normal sociability during adolescence and end up going to college instead of conservatory. Being pragmatic, smart, poised, and healthy is in their makeup, just as their musical enthusiasm and aptitude are.

Joshua Bell is good at everything. He is the most prominent violinist of his generation; placed fourth in a national tennis tournament when he was ten; is the all-time high scorer on several video games; is one of the fastest solvers of the Rubik's Cube; holds an appointment in the MIT Media Lab; and is truly funny when he appears on the talk show circuit. He's handsome, charming, and seems riveted by whomever he's talking to, yet he also evinces the impenetrability of someone who wants privacy in the public eye. People meeting him for the first time are amazed at how accessible he is, and people who have known him forever, at how unknowable he is.

Josh's parents were not an obvious match; when they met, Shirley was fresh from a kibbutz, and Alan was an Episcopal priest. Alan left the ministry, earned a doctorate in psychology, and took a senior position at the Kinsey Institute for sex research in Bloomington, Indiana. "He was so nonjudgmental versus me," Shirley recalled. "I knew the answers to everything." Shirley is a strong presence with a disregard for boundaries. She wants to feed you, drink with you, play poker with you, sit up late talking. Dark, lithe, and pretty, she appears immensely powerful and touchingly vulnerable—willing to be honest with anyone else to the exact extent that she is honest with herself.

Alan had been a choirboy and Shirley played piano; their children would all learn music. Josh was born in 1967. At two, he stretched rubber bands from knob to knob on a dresser, pulling out the drawers to vary the tensions and create different sounds when he strummed them; as an adult he joked that he had progressed "from credenza to cadenza." He started violin at four, learning new music quickly. "It goes in one ear and it just stays there," Shirley said. Music became a world they shared intimately, but his creativity was always tinged with sadness. "He would wake up in the night crying," she went on. "My other kids, I could always hug and console. But with Josh, there was nothing I could do."

Josh became a local celebrity at seven, when he played the Bach Double Concerto alongside his teacher with the Bloomington Symphony Orchestra. His playing was elegiac, but lacked technical mastery. "My mother, even though she was invested and practiced with me, was not a great disciplinarian, and neither was my father," he said. "I crammed for tests the morning of the test, and crammed for concerts the day before, and lived by the seat of my pants. I sometimes went days without touching the violin at all, sneaking out the back door of the music building when I was supposed to be practicing, playing video games all afternoon, and rushing back for my mother to pick me up." In hindsight, he believes this lack of supervision was beneficial. "Doing nothing but music is not so good for your mental health," he said, "and it's not so good for the music, either."

The summer he was twelve, Josh attended Meadowmount, a summer intensive program for string players, where he had his first lessons with Josef Gingold, one of the twentieth century's greatest violin teachers. The Bells asked him to take on Josh as a full-time pupil. "They were always supporting my education," Josh said. "If my mother had been hands-off, I wouldn't have developed as a musician—at least not in the same way."

Shirley read about a competition sponsored by *Seventeen* magazine for high school musicians; having skipped a year of school, Josh just barely qualified. Shirley was too fretful to accompany him there. "When I got the phone call that he won, I screamed," she recalled. Then she sighed. "I loved having children. My kids became my life. But my youngest daughter was neglected. If Josh was performing on her birthday, we'd be at Josh's concert. I was on tour with Josh when she was growing up and didn't hear her screams inside. But gifted children have needs, too, and who's going to meet them?" The problem was not just time allocation. "I received such tremendous joy from Josh's music," Shirley said. "Every success he had gave me pleasure. The other kids could see that, and it hurt them." Josh has his own regrets about the effect his career had on his sisters, but feels that his mother's involvement was so crucial "that there was almost no way around it."

As Josh began performing extensively, his mother worried about how he could sustain his momentum with audiences. "When he's fourteen, it's less of a miracle than when he's twelve, even though he's playing much better," she said. Meanwhile, Josh's situation at school became increasingly uncomfortable. "I had that tall-poppy syndrome," he said. "Some teachers were threatened by anybody doing something out of the ordinary, and they made my life miserable." He graduated from high school at sixteen. "It was unthinkable for me to stay home after high school," Josh said. That meant Shirley's role had to change.

"It takes two for that kind of symbiotic relationship, and it takes two to handle the separation," she said. She was pained that Josh did not want her to manage his affairs. He moved into a condo in Bloomington that his parents had bought, and Shirley went over to do his laundry, "to stay involved." Josh recalled, "Managing my life had become my mother's world. We made a separation. Then it started to feel more like we were two different people, and I could tell her about my successes, and we could behave like adults." At twenty-two, he moved in with his first serious girlfriend, violinist Lisa Matricardi. "It lasted seven years," he said. "Some of my reliance on my mother was transferred to Lisa—probably in an unhealthy way."

Josh earned an artist's diploma at the University of Indiana in performance, music theory, piano proficiency, and German. He soon made his Carnegie Hall debut and at eighteen he won the prestigious Avery Fisher Career Grant; his corecipient that year was Ken Noda. He now headlines more than two hundred performances a year. Additionally, he leads the Saint Paul Chamber Orchestra. Josh was among the first classical musicians to do crossover, making a modish VH1 video of a Brahms Hungarian dance. He has bowed his fiddle with bluegrass bassist Edgar Meyer and has collaborated with jazzmen Chick Corea and Wynton Marsalis. He has recorded with Sting, Regina Spektor, and singer-songwriter Josh Groban. Every one of Josh Bell's albums has made *Billboard*'s Top 20; *Romance of the Violin* sold more than five million copies and was Classical Album of the Year. He has been nominated for several Grammys and has won one, and he owns a $4 million Stradivarius. "It allowed me to realize the colors I had imagined in the music I loved to play," he said. "It was like meeting the girl you're going to marry." He likes the high life and is classical music's equivalent of a rock star. But rock stars' lives don't look entirely glamorous up close. "Josh is so stressed, you can't get his attention on anything," his mother said, bemoaning that he started taking blood-pressure medication before he turned forty. I asked if the downside made her sad. "What gives me the greatest pleasure is when he calls me to ask my opinion about something, where I can still be a mother," she said. "We have a real musical connection. I have to be careful not to be too intrusive, which is my nature. I don't know him that well anymore."

When I related that conversation to Josh, he was indignant. "She knows me very well," he said. "Even now, I trust her opinion more than anyone's. When I'm planning a recital program, I still run it by her. I still want her approval after a concert. It really bums me out if I play what I thought was my best and she says she preferred the last time I did it." Josh had a son with his ex-girlfriend Lisa in 2007 and spoke about how Lisa and the baby were "basically one, which is normal with a mother and baby. When you're fifteen and your mother is still so enmeshed, it's unhealthy. When I was in my twenties, my mom was still doing my taxes." He did not consult her about his decision to father a child. "Her approval or disapproval still has such power," he said, "it's best not to let her in when it comes to some of the important things."

Like most parents of kids with horizontal identities, Shirley fears that her child is lonely. "He has an issue with intimacy," she said. "He doesn't want anybody on his back. I know, because he doesn't want me on his back. He's totally free, joking, and very funny in public. It's humbling to be in his presence. I mean, what's going to come out of his mouth? I'm always waiting to hear. But deep down, he's a little bit of an enigma. I think that's why people are drawn to him, because they can't know him. Neither can I. I couldn't comfort him when he was an infant, and in some ways, that's never changed. I think that's part of the nature of his genius, and it breaks my heart."

The advent of sound recording in 1877 had sweeping social consequences, making music ubiquitous even for those who could neither play it nor afford to hire performers. There is nothing exclusive about hearing music today; it requires no greater skill than the ability to turn on an iPod, and no more expense than the money to buy a radio. The magnificent performances once heard only at court may now be experienced in the supermarket, in a car, or at home. Like Sign before the cochlear implant and painting before photography, live performance had a different urgency before the phonograph. For musicians interested in live exposure, these technological changes can feel limiting; for those interested in wide distribution, they can be thrilling. Although the causal relationship is more oblique, new science is clouding the future prospects of musical prodigies as surely as it is threatening the Deaf and gay cultures and the neurodiversity perspective on the autism spectrum. The arguments about adaptation and extinction are as relevant here as to many so-called disabilities.

Despite the ever-increasing number of superlative musicians, audiences who know how to listen are dwindling—because of the jarringly alien qualities of much later-twentieth-century music, the surge in anti-elitism, the escalating cost of concert tickets, the elimination of childhood music-education programs, and the technology-spurred dispersal of media users into small, narrowly focused groups. This crossing of arcs echoes the experience of other identity groups that are gaining acceptance just as medicine threatens to eliminate them. We have disembodied music, as so much else, in modern life. The exploitation of prodigies is part of the reembodiment of music. If you see Marc Yu perform, for example, you see a miracle child, which is very different from merely hearing his capable playing online. Justin Davidson said, "An eight-year-old communicating something live in the concert hall is bringing everything he is to that moment. A big part of that is eight-year-oldness. That's what people are reacting to. There is no abstract performance beyond what the performer does. How can you tell the dancer from the dance? You can't. And it's artificial to try."

Conrad Tao, another American-born prodigy frequently identified as Chinese, is older than Marc Yu and younger than Kit Armstrong. His scientist parents emigrated from China in the early 1980s to do graduate study at Princeton. When the Tiananmen Square massacre occurred in 1989, shortly after their daughter was born, they decided to stay in the United States a little longer. Had they gone back, they would have had to conform to the one-child rule; "Conrad is a product of the fact that we stayed," his mother, Mingfang Ting, explained. She became a research scientist, creating predictive computer models of climate change at the University of Illinois, and his father, Sam Tao, worked as an engineer at Alcatel-Lucent. Both were focused on accomplishment, but neither of them on art. "Growing up during the Cultural Revolution, we sang patriotic songs, and that's all the music we had," Mingfang said. She and Sam perceived music as a luxury, one they wanted to offer their children. When Conrad was eighteen months old, a family friend set him on the piano bench and began playing; Conrad kept pushing him aside and finishing the tunes. The friend said, "If you can't make a musician out of this child, it's your fault." Conrad played so incessantly that his parents worried he might damage his fingers, and the teacher advised them to lock the piano.

Mingfang was not intimidated by her son's talent, but she was concerned about the ramifications of being called a prodigy and made him try other skills he couldn't master immediately. "I can't take credit for his talent," she said, "but I can take credit for his being humble." As his music progressed, she became concerned that he was missing the best opportunities to develop in his art. "A prodigy in Champaign, Illinois, might be not a prodigy somewhere else," she said. So when Conrad was nearly five, his mother took a sabbatical, and the family moved to Chicago; a year later, they moved again, to New York, where Conrad was accepted as a student by Veda Kaplinsky at Juilliard. The piano went into its own small, soundproof room. "People say he doesn't have the concert-hall feeling, but it's good if we can enjoy our life, too," Mingfang said.

They encouraged Conrad to forgo competitions "because they are sad," his mother said. "If you win, you feel sorry for your friends who lost, and if you lose, you feel sorry for yourself." Conrad explained it differently, though with a similar sensitivity to others: "I already have quite a few concerts to play. Many others don't, and if I enter, I'm taking the chance to perform away from them." Mingfang admits that theirs is not the typical Chinese attitude. "If I had stayed in China, I might have wanted my son in every competition, and I might have given him less love if he failed. But I've been Americanized. Now I believe that if you don't have calm in your heart, you can't really produce beauty." In her own view, Mingfang is a hybrid mother, too open-minded for the Chinese standard and too firm for the American model. Conrad is ambivalent. "I don't want to push the Asian label away because that feels really self-hating to me," he said. "But being classified as a Chinese-American child-prodigy pianist, that's already too many labels. My parents are actually much more appreciative of freedom than some Americans I know, because they didn't grow up with that. They're more appreciative of music because they didn't grow up with that. And I'm the beneficiary."

Conrad is doing independent study because his concert schedule became too complicated for regular school. He concedes that he doesn't have much of a social life, but school wasn't so great, either. "Everyone thought I was a smart-ass, and I can't dispute that," he said. Veda Kaplinsky worried that if he pursued a liberal-arts education, he might lose focus for his music, but Mingfang encouraged him to enroll at Columbia while continuing his studies at Juilliard. "Music is like the climate—it's a huge system with an infinite number of variables," Mingfang told me. "Conrad's work is very much like mine; it's about figuring out structures to make sense of what appears to be chaos."

One's own intelligence has novelty value when it is newly awakened, and at fifteen, Conrad was in that particular innocence. He said, "I think that the world has just as much to teach me as Veda, and so do people I don't know. Books have a lot to teach me. Films have a lot to teach me. Art, life, science, math, anything has a lot to offer. I'm a sponge. We live in a postmodern era, where kids hear every style of music and want to play it all at the same time while text messaging. I'm one of those kids." New audiences, he believes, must be cultivated. "I've always mourned the fact that indie rockers are more receptive to experimentation than the classical community is." He sighed. "My views on music change every week. I'm a teenager, prone to hormonal imbalances. I try to expose myself to as much as I can. Being a politician means that you can take any argument and turn it to your favor. I can't do that; I'm an artist, and I can only argue my point of view."

The gap between classical and popular music keeps widening, and the first approach to that problem has been for classical composers to try to move into that gap with music that speaks to both audiences. "There's always been a kind of DMZ between the pretentiousness of one and the amateurishness of the other," Justin Davidson said, "but no matter how aesthetics may have merged, you're dealing with a capitalist, commercial world on the one hand, and a not-for-profit world on the other. It's hard for two such different economic models to meet."

Fearful that their language appears to be dying and eager for widespread acclaim and the financial rewards that come with it, composers and performers have entered a mainstream they might once have disdained. Lang Lang appears in popular ads; Joshua Bell plays crossover music from movie themes to bluegrass; Conrad Tao sees part of his job as producing an audience for his music. Young composer-performers such as Christian Sands, Nico Muhly, and Gabriel Kahane strive for a music of wide appeal that soft-pedals the differences between classical and pop. They are fighting to save their own identity from erasure.

Christian Sands grew up on gospel, jazz, and pop. He won first place in the church talent show when he was three, after only a year of piano lessons; at four, he won a local composer's award in New Haven, Connecticut. His father, Sylvester, worked a night shift at Cargill, the behemoth agricultural company, so Chris was at home nights with his mother, Stephanie. "Music made me feel safe, so music was the way that he and I coped with having to be strong," she said. When Chris started kindergarten, the teacher told Stephanie that her son was incapable of sitting still and seemed to be on some other planet. Stephanie said, "He's not on another planet; he's just composing music in his head. He'll stop squirming if you let him play a lullaby or something for the other kids before naptime." Chris's room was next to his parents', and after he went to bed, when it was too late to play the piano, they would hear the clicking of his fingernails on the desk, as if it were a keyboard.

From the outset, Chris would improvise. "He could mix a little thing from Chopin right in the middle of his Bach," Sylvester said. When Chris was seven, his teacher said he should switch to a jazz teacher. "I could make things up, and nobody would say, 'Don't do that,'" Chris recalled. "I used to think my hands had their own brains. I call them 'the little people,' because each finger just does a different thing when it wants to do it."

Chris's teacher arranged a gig for him at Sprague Hall, the large concert venue at Yale. "It was a trio," Chris said. "The bass player is sixty-five, the drummer is maybe fifty-eight, and I'm nine, and I'm the leader. I didn't pay attention to the audience. It's almost, like, when you're a child and you're playing with a toy, and your parents have company; you don't even care if they're in the same room with you; you're just making your train go or finishing up your tower of blocks. The piano was my toy, and I was in my own world that I created." Chris received a standing ovation. His parents found him backstage, lying on the floor in his tuxedo and reading a book.

The invitations started to pour in. By the time he was eleven, Chris's music was airing on the radio, and he was selling homemade CDs. The next year, he played a special concert for all fifteen thousand sixth graders in the New Haven school district. He was asked to entertain at a cocktail party at Skull and Bones, a Yale secret society. One of the guests was Dave Brubeck's physician, who subsequently arranged for Chris to take lessons from Brubeck. At fifteen, Chris met Dr. Billy Taylor, who produced Chris's first major recording. In high school, Chris was playing as many as four gigs a week.

Chris's modesty slyly invites a little awe. He's handsome and affable and likes to pretend that even hard work is easy. When a friend complained that Chris was never available for socializing, he replied, "You are my friend, but music is my love, and it will always come first." Stephanie said, "He has to isolate himself, even from us. That could be painful. He's always been the one steering the boat, and we're just making sure it's not sinking." Sylvester said, "We told him, 'Pray before you play, and use your gift for the people, not for yourself.'" Stephanie described watching talk shows about young celebrities and trying to extrapolate how to be a parent to Chris. "I don't know if I ever understood the giftedness, but I understood that if you don't give him the piano, you might as well just not give him any air." All the same, his parents didn't want him to forfeit the usual pleasures of youth. During the breaks of his late-night concerts, they'd sneak out the stage door to play tag and roughhouse.

In 2006, at seventeen, Chris was invited to perform at the Grammy Awards for the legendary jazz pianist Oscar Peterson. He had been warned in advance that Peterson would be onstage in a wheelchair. Chris began to play Peterson's tune "Kelly's Blues." "Right in the middle of my second chorus, I hear some applause, and I'm thinking it's for me," Chris said, "and all of a sudden I heard a chord and I thought, 'Wait, I'm not playing that chord,' and I looked up." Peterson had pulled himself out of his wheelchair and made it over to the other piano onstage, and they began something halfway between a pianistic dialogue and a duel that ended the show exultantly.

Chris went on to the Manhattan School of Music, where, Sylvester said, he learned the names for what he was already doing. When I asked his parents what role each played in the development of his musical sensibility, Sylvester took credit for certain harmonies he favors, and Stephanie said she had shown him how to shape a story. When I visited the Sands family at home, Chris was twenty-one, and in the middle of writing an opera, half jazz, half classical, loosely based on his romance with a mezzo-soprano from Dubai. "Her story's as weird as mine," he said. "So my opera's about my doing jazz when everyone else was doing sports, and her doing opera when everyone else was doing shopping and Islam." He laughed. "Do I want to make operatic music, or do I want to do cutthroat, in-your-face jazz, or to be Afro-Cuban, or to use this new Latin style? From the dawn of time, man put sticks over here, berries over here. It's been like that forever, so everything is categorized, and that's why there's so many genres and subcategories. My music is a new beast, and it's untamed, and it's running rampant through the streets of New York."

Music education has been eliminated at most public schools, but people are not merely ignorant about classical music; they are often educated away from it. Paul Potts, pudgy and morose, sang Puccini's "Nessun dorma" on *Britain's Got Talent* in 2007 and received a staggering ovation; the YouTube clip of his performance has had nearly a hundred million views. His fans responded to the beauty of Puccini's music despite Potts's distinctly amateur, if poignant, performance. The same thing happened a few years later when eight-year-old Jackie Evancho sang Puccini's "O mio babbino caro" on a similar American program. Admittedly, Puccini was a populist; nonetheless, these phenomena suggest that many people who never contemplate listening to classical music are capable of being blown away by it.

Paradoxically, as general education about classical music is vanishing, the education of actual musicians remains ossified. "Conservatories, essentially, haven't changed since the Reign of Terror," Robert Sirota said. "You need iconoclasts who are willing to reexamine the repertoire, to reexamine what a concert is, to reexamine how people hear and listen."

Bunny Harvey and Frank Muhly married by default. Bunny's ex-boyfriend had been kicked out of Brown and asked his square buddy Frank to look after her. Bunny, who worked part-time as a go-go dancer, was in a relationship with a woman. "But something perverse in me decided to take him on as a project," she said, "and it backfired, because I fell in love." Frank dropped out of graduate school and has led a life untouched by career ambition, working on occasional films and other freelance projects. In 1974, Bunny won the Rome Prize in painting and they moved to Italy for two years.

When they returned home, she and Frank decided to have a child. "I didn't know what it took to be a parent," she said. "Now I think it's like art: you have the material and you deal with it in the most creative and loving way you can." Nico Muhly was born in Vermont; at nine months, he was mimicking bird sounds and soon identified a red-tailed hawk by its cry. During the winters, the family was based in Providence, where one of Nico's fourth-grade classmates sang in a choir. One day he invited Nico to come along. In Elizabethan choral music, Nico found himself immediately at home. "Downtown Providence was dead," he said. "Right in the middle of it was this old, grand High Anglican church, run by a bizarre, incomprehensible man, who programmed the most interesting music." A few months later, Bunny took Nico to Trinity Church in Boston, and the music director asked Nico whether he liked the organ; Nico sat down and played a Bach prelude and fugue from memory. Bunny burst into tears. "How could he even reach the pedals?" she said. "I knew he'd been singing, but I had no idea he'd learned the organ. This amazing thing had been hidden from me." Later that day, at a café in Harvard Square, Nico began composing a kyrie on a paper napkin. He had suddenly figured out what mattered to him.

"It was like birdsong—something triggers it and it comes out full-blown," Frank said. Bunny started bringing home CDs and scores from the Wellesley library, and Nico became seriously obsessed. "One day it was Messiaën," he said. "The next, I was like, 'I want to know everything about the marimba.' Nothing from the nineteenth century, ever. Early, early, modern, modern. That music just made me so insane and happy, like it was a narcotic."

Bunny returned to the American Academy in Rome as a guest artist when Nico was twelve. Nico attended Italian public school. A composer's studio was free at the academy, and one of the scholars agreed to take Nico as a piano student. "At home, he'd been an unusual child in a normal situation, but there, everybody was peculiar, and he could somehow be a normal child in this unusual situation," Bunny said. Nico said, "The whole thing felt very enchanted. Everyone humored me as much as they could stand to. And I became a musician."

Back in Providence, Nico directed all his high school musicals, inserting bits of Stravinsky and ABBA into *Bye Bye Birdie*. Meanwhile, the financial strains at home were considerable. Nico began to develop

OCD with a strong depressive undercurrent. When he was fourteen, he won a place at Tanglewood's summer music program, where he met young composers, many of them students in prestigious programs: for the first time, he was immersed in a completely musical environment. While Nico lacked their training, he had other experience that made him feel their equal. "I was worldly. I could book a train ticket to Naples. A lot of kids were on a very tight rein; their parents in Korea would call the dorm twice a day." Nico went on to enroll in both Columbia, for a double major in English and Arabic, and Juilliard. "I entered a manic fugue," he said. "I had all the self-destructive behavior that you would expect, except it was never going out and fucking guys in the park; it was writing music. I would get up in the middle of the night and hide, turn the monitor brightness to low. It felt like secret eating or something. Then I realized that I could stop obsessing if I drank too much. Which is the worst. So I went to this ridiculous shrink and sorted myself out."

Nico is aural and Bunny is visual, but they share the language of food. Bunny is a spectacular chef who grows her own vegetables and can slaughter and dress animals; shortly after I met Nico, he sent me a favorite photo of her holding half a pig carcass. Her French mother was an impeccable housekeeper who owned two duck presses and candied her own violets; when Nico moved into a Columbia dorm, his grandmother sent him a truffle mandolin. Nico claims that he didn't know you could buy mayonnaise in a store until he went to college. "I think I'm most proud of the fact that he likes that about me," Bunny said. "I always hoped he would find happiness in something. Music is that. But I've given him a sense of playfulness and security about making things and making mistakes and just playing in the kitchen, and it's good for him and his music." They resolve their occasional rifts by e-mailing about food, Nico said. "She'll write me twenty paragraphs about her Swiss chard, and it's all okay again."

You can feel in everything Bunny says an almost fanatical struggle for honesty, while Nico is a fabulist for whom truth is an unshiny thing. They like and grate on each other accordingly, but share a commitment to process. "Inside the music, even if you can't hear it, there's a little machine that does the thing it's meant to do," Nico said. "Some pieces, that's incredibly laid bare. Other pieces, it's buried, even erased." His second album, *Mothertongue*, includes a simple, pretty melody. "Even though it's a folk song, there's this huge piece of math that I figured out, structured my piece around, and then completely forgot about. There's a commitment to a subnarrative of creation in everything."

Nico has been commissioned to do ballet for American Ballet Theatre, an opera for the Metropolitan, arrangements for Björk. Some critics feel his music is too seductive. The composer John Adams, who has been an important influence on him, said, "I am not sure it is a good thing for someone so young to be so concerned with attractiveness of sound." In Nico's view, the idea that brilliance cannot be lovely is a vestige of the musical brutalism of post-tonality. "There exists a lingua franca of modern classical music that is indiscriminately ugly," he said. "*Speaks Volumes* is very pretty on purpose, just to say you can do this and still have it be meaningful and have emotional content. If there is emotional depth to my stuff, it is from repetitions lulling you into a sense of security and then taking it away, a perversion of what you expect; or something being so pretty and saccharine that you wonder if it's witch's candy."

Nico usually has two computers on and can compose while playing Scrabble and writing e-mail. "I have no ambition," he said. "I only have obsession. There's never a forward motion to it." He acknowledged that people conflate his exuberance with not yet having found a unique voice. "The whole conversation is made so much easier if you just confess to what you lifted. So if they say my work is derivative, I'm, like, 'I'll show you exactly the bar I'm copying from.'" Yet he is ambivalent about the role of language in describing music. "I know people who will not shut up about the nature of art. You're like, 'But your music's bad to listen to.' If you go to a concert, you shouldn't struggle to understand it. Honestly, I think part of it is, I'm not an asshole. I want to give people pleasure. Music is a food. You have to consume it. I love the phrase *preferable to silence*. Is this piece of music preferable to silence? We're in the business of art, but we're also in the business of entertainment, and spiritual and emotional nourishment. You have to carry that with you."

Parenting a prodigy entails being overshadowed, and being overshadowed comes more readily to some other parents than it does to Bunny Harvey. I did not ever feel that she begrudged Nico his gifts or success; she is obviously proud and delighted. But his success throws into sharp relief the shortcomings of an artistic vocation curtailed by the need to finance her son's life. It's a classic feminist bind: she could have had a richer career if she hadn't been a mother, and might have been a better mother if she hadn't had a career. Nico feels guilty, and therefore angry, about her having sacrificed for him, and she feels eclipsed by his independence. She intended to be a painter who had a child and ended up as a mother who also paints. Nico has carried the burden of her disappointment. They enact a kind of protracted *Liebestod* in which Nico has to keep murdering his mother to become her finest work of art. "I can't listen anymore to how she sacrificed her ability to be an artist so that I could be one," he said. "It sucks. Conversely, her joy in cooking has completely transferred. It is central to the way I think about everything." Bunny stands at a slight remove from Nico's triumphs. "People say, 'Congratulations, Nico is such a success,'" she said. "I didn't do any of it. But the task that Frank and I should be congratulated for is that he's a person who knows how to be happy. He chooses a controlled melancholy, but he has alternatives."

Nico is generous with his personal biography, but fiercely protective of his soul. It's an ostentation of privacy. "In early English church music, there are many screens between you and the heart of the matter," Nico said. "With Benjamin Britten's music, even if it's really exuberant, there's always this kind of obliqueness. But you can see the beating heart, the relic." The popular line on Nico Muhly is that he appears joyful but is actually sorrowful—that the beating heart is sad and the screens in front of it are lovely. That reduces him terribly. He has integrated the emotional spectrum so we can hear joy and sorrow both at once, but he never averages them. You may reach into his joy and pull out a surprising handful of sorrow, but when you examine that sorrow, you find it suffused with particles of joy.

Correcting a bias against genius is a social responsibility in part because most accomplishments are contingent on a social context: in some ways, this is the ultimate horizontal identity. A man with a natural aptitude for skiing who is born into poverty in Guatemala will most likely never discover it; someone whose primary talent is as a computer programmer would not have gone far in the fifteenth century. How would Leonardo have busied himself if he'd been born an Inuit? Would Galileo have advanced string theory if he'd been around in the 1990s? Ideally, a genius should have not only the necessary tools and conditions to realize his gifts, but also a receptive society of peers and admirers. As Alfred Kroeber noted in the 1940s, genius sparks genius. "If I have seen further," Sir Isaac Newton acknowledged, "it is by standing on ye shoulders of Giants." Like *sainthood*, *genius* is a label that cannot properly be affixed until considerable time and a few miracles have ensued. We help the disabled in a quest to make a more humane and better world; we might approach brilliance in the same spirit. Pity impedes the dignity of disabled people; resentment is a parallel obstacle for people with enormous talent. The pity and the resentment alike are manifestations of our fear of people who are radically different.

Juilliard president Joseph Polisi observed that devotion to classical music is predicated on "an acquired way of listening." As American pop culture became a global juggernaut in the late twentieth century, and multiculturalism became the key word on nonprofit grant applications, the perceived elitism of classical and experimental music eroded its audience at an alarming rate. It has been fashionable to dismiss classical and experimental music as exclusionary, which is a semantic argument. No one prevents the nonelite from entering classical music's hallowed halls, but such music is an acquired taste based largely on European aristocratic and liturgical traditions, and more affluent people are more likely to be comfortable and familiar with those traditions. The profound question is whether it is worth the effort. Lucretius defined the sublime as the art of exchanging easier for more difficult pleasures, and almost two thousand years later, Schopenhauer proclaimed that the opposite of suffering is boredom. Classical music, which may look dull to the uninitiated, contains complexities that can make it electrifying for those who study it. With a myriad of perceived flaws, people have learned to find meaning in difficulty, and while the challenges of deafness or Down syndrome may overshadow the rigors of learning to like Prokofiev, the quest for meaning via exertion is not altogether dissimilar. In both cases, earned pleasures supersede passive ones.

Better services for people with disabilities and disadvantages allow them to function better and thereby pay for themselves manifold. Educating the gifted is likewise in the public interest. If we credit scientific and cultural advances to this identity group, refusing them acknowledgment and support is costly to the population at large. We live in an anti-intellectual society in which people of extraordinary achievement are as likely to be considered freaks as to be lauded as heroes. Margaret Mead observed in 1954, "There is in America today an appalling waste of first-rate talents. Neither teachers, the parents of other children, nor the child's peers will tolerate the wunderkind." Voters want the president to be someone with whom they would feel comfortable having a beer rather than a singular leader with attributes they lack. Celebrities' talent is minimized soon after it has brought them to prominence. This phenomenon, which serves no useful end, is part of what the social critic Rhonda Garelick has called the "crisis in admiration."

I was struck by how many former prodigies who were critical of their own upbringings found themselves struggling with how to raise their own talented children. Candy Bawcombe's daughter, almost sixteen when I interviewed Candy, has perfect pitch, plays the piano, and studies voice. "When Katie first started piano, at three, I wanted to be extremely regimented," Candy said. "'It has to be three thirty every day, and we're going to do it this way.' It caused tremendous friction. I had to just let all of that go." I wondered why. Candy, who had been careful not to criticize her own mother, answered, "Because I didn't want her to blame me, someday, for a life that she didn't want." Nic Hodges has found himself similarly conflicted. "It would be very ungrateful to say that being given piano lessons at six is really pressure," he said. "I'm a musician, which wouldn't have happened if my mother hadn't been the way she was. I can't imagine being or even wanting to be anyone or anything else." Now he finds himself facing the quandaries of parenthood. "If you invest your whole life in a family business, you want your children to carry on investing in it," Nic said. "You want them to be artists who know everything you know and can benefit from everything that you've experienced. All parents want that, and it never works."

Jeffrey Kahane's father grew up in immigrant poverty, nine people living in two rooms; he became a highly regarded psychologist and was determined that his son traverse a similar distance. Jeffrey was frequently expected to perform at home: "I found real solace and joy in the piano, but it was tainted. I didn't want my love for music to be sucked up to feed my father's incredible need." Jeffrey met a girl named Martha at summer camp when they were ten; they wrote long letters, promising to marry young and have two kids—and they did. Martha was a music major at Berkeley and eventually became a psychotherapist; Jeffrey became a widely esteemed pianist and conductor.

Their son, Gabriel, was born in 1981. Martha noticed that he sang completely in tune at two; at four he asked her, "Do you hear the jazzy sound that train is making?" His talent, however, was not nourished with discipline, and his violin teacher eventually said there was no point going on. "My mom was the disciplinarian, and my dad, who was performing and gone a lot, stayed very much removed from my musical upbringing," Gabriel recalled. "They both had the right approach, and they both had the wrong approach."

Gabriel's musical influences were varied. He listened to rap CDs by Dr. Dre and Cypress Hill and House of Pain, but he also loved his parents' music: Paul Simon's *Graceland*, Joni Mitchell's *Blue*, the Beatles. He took up jazz piano, sang in a choir, became involved in musical theater. When he wanted to learn something, he learned it—"the speed with which he learned to play the piano in his teen years was mind-boggling," Martha said—but schoolwork didn't hold Gabriel's interest, which worried Martha constantly and worried Jeffrey not at all. "I thought he should do his homework," Martha said. "Jeff didn't really believe in the educational system. I remember Jeff said to me, 'Gabe is a huge talent.' I sort of got it, but I didn't get it like Jeff did."

Gabriel flunked out of high school. "It was mortifying to have this brilliant kid not graduate," Martha said. "Does the fact that I felt that make me a pushy parent?" Gabriel dropped in at the New England Conservatory of Music, took an ear-training test, and was accepted immediately; by the end of a year, though, he found it parochial. He was dating a young woman who went to Brown; he applied there and was accepted. "My hubris was helpful," he said. "I wrote some persuasive essay about why I was a fuckup at school." At Brown, he became attached to the idea of accomplishing something that would outlive him. "Being a creative rather than an interpretive artist was a way of dealing with the death drive," he said. He began composing, and his first musical won a prize from the Kennedy Center.

When Gabriel graduated, he moved to New York and began what would become the *Craigslistlieder*, a song cycle that took online personal ads as a libretto, which he premiered in 2006. He would perform the songs "in a dirty bar on a banged-up piano for a bunch of hipster kids from Brooklyn who knew nothing about classical music," he said, "and they would go crazy." But his work also appealed to classical musicians. In 2007, Natasha Paremski commissioned his first sonata. In 2008, he released an eponymous album and received a commission from the Los Angeles Philharmonic. I attended Gabriel's debut concert with Jazz at Lincoln Center. Even when the work was vaguely classical in mood and even when it was performed with a dozen other musicians, his centrality to it made it feel incredibly intimate.

He told me that he had to write his music to his own strengths because there was so much he couldn't do. I asked whether he regretted those gaps in his musical education. He said, "In every instance that I have witnessed someone whose childhood involved the push, there's arrested development, or there's a poisoned relationship to the art, and I just don't think it's worth it. My father and I have a deeply unambivalent relationship—and if there's any way in which I continue to try to be like him, it's in his appetite for knowledge as the basis and the foundation of why we do what we do."

His father wanted more than anything else not to replicate with his prodigious son the relationship he'd had with his own controlling parent. "I bent so far backwards to be disengaged from Gabe's successes that I went overboard," Jeff said. "Gabe said to me, 'I wish you had made me practice more.' I can't help thinking, though, that being allowed to find his own path resulted in a very unusual artistic presence." Martha said, "Gabe is such a kind person. And that's in his music. He's told me sometimes he thinks about the way I respond to music when he's writing, and he's thanked me for giving him that emotional honesty."

Gabriel has recorded or performed with pop musicians Rufus Wainwright, My Brightest Diamond, and Sufjan Stevens, as well as with classical stars such as cellist Alisa Weilerstein and baritone Thomas Quasthoff. The *New York Times* called Gabriel "a highbrow polymath." He told me that he "would like to reach a unified language." He explained, "The idea of being a genre-bending performer is tired, but I feel increasingly oppressed at the concert hall. I hate the institution's reactionary elitism, its lack of irony. In the classical world, people don't understand that Lennon and McCartney had as savvy a sense of harmony and melody as Schubert."

What few adults can do, even fewer children can do. In the grand scheme, however, genius is only marginally more astonishing than development itself. Small children go from nonverbal to verbal in two years, and to literate in five more. They can master several languages at the same time. They learn how the shapes of letters relate to both sound and meaning. They grasp the abstract idea of numbers and the means by which numbers characterize everything around us. They ace all this while they are learning to walk, chew, perhaps throw a ball, perhaps develop a sense of humor. Parents of prodigies are intimidated and awestruck at what their children can do—but so, fittingly, are parents of children who are not prodigies. Remembering that is the surest way to remain sane when parenting a child whose skills dramatically differ from or radically exceed one's own.

All parents of prodigies are making an enormous investment in a dubious outcome with huge risks: forsaken social development, crippling disappointment, chronic relocation, even permanent family rifts—all in the hope of an elusive lifestyle that may not be what the grown-up version of the prodigy turns out to want. While some parents push their kids too hard and give them breakdowns, others fail to support a child's passion for his own gift and deprive him of the only life that he would have enjoyed. You can err in either direction. The pushing error is more obvious and more present in our culture, but the other can be equally dire. Given the lack of consensus about how to raise ordinary children, it is unsurprising that none exists about how to raise remarkable children, and many parents of prodigies are flummoxed by children whose internal measure of happiness is radically alien.

Goethe's mother described telling stories to him: "Air, fire, water and earth I presented to him as beautiful princesses, and everything in all nature took on a deeper meaning. We invented roads between stars, and what great minds we would encounter. He devoured me with his eyes; and if the fate of one of his favorites did not go as he wished, this I could see from the anger in his face, or his efforts not to break out in tears. Occasionally he interfered by saying: 'Mother, the princess will not marry the miserable tailor, even if he slays the giant,' at which I stopped and postponed the catastrophe until the next evening. So my imagination was often replaced by his; and when the following morning I arranged fate according to his suggestions and said, 'You guessed it, that's how it came out,' he was all excited, and one could see his heart beating."

That one phrase, "my imagination was often replaced by his," bespeaks all that is most beautiful in the parenting of a remarkable child. In so replacing one's own imagination, one facilitates the growth of the child's. For the parents of prodigies, such wise self-effacement may exact a high price, but those who can set their own path by the light of their child's brilliance may find great solace in the ways that child remakes the world.

IX

Rape

A child conceived in rape gets as rough a start as a child with dwarfism or Down syndrome. The pregnancy is usually greeted as a calamity, upending family life that may already be riddled with strife. The mother not only doubts her ability to meet the challenges of child-rearing but is also uncertain whether she will ever get over the very fact of the child's existence. Rarely is a reliable partner on the scene to help. All new mothers are prone to ambivalence, but the hostility and revulsion often experienced by the mother of a rape-conceived child may be reinforced by her family. Society is likely to judge both mother and child unkindly.

With most disabilities, those who do not share a given condition struggle to find the humanity within it, while those who do share the condition gravitate toward one another for support, validation, and collective identity. With children of rape, however, the flaw is indiscernible to strangers, sometimes to family and friends, and often to the child, who must cope with its psychological shadow nonetheless. His horizontal identity is both profound and oblique. Often, his identity is a family secret, much as adoption can be, and who tells what, when, and to whom becomes a loaded give-and-take. You can keep your child's deafness or genius or autism secret only for a short time. Others are sure to notice; the child himself will usually notice. Children conceived in rape may go a lifetime without knowing their own identity. This means that who the mother is in the child's eyes and who the child is in the mother's are often in flux. Unlike adoption, however, which many experts believe should be shared with adopted children even before they can understand its full meaning, rape is too confusing and frightening to explain to a toddler; it's terrifying for any child to envision his parent as vulnerable, much less to feel complicit in that vulnerability.

Horizontal identities usually originate in the child, then spill over to the parents. Children conceived in rape, however, acquire their horizontal identity by way of their mother's trauma; here, the children are secondary, and they are much less likely to find others of similar exceptionality with whom to solidify that identity. The mother has the stronger horizontal identity, and the child has a resultant existential aloneness that follows from it. The mother of a schizophrenic may find herself in a club she never meant to join, but that association is defined by her child; the mother of a child conceived in rape has her own, separate, primary damage to negotiate. Her identity as a mother proceeds directly from her identity as a rape victim. Her child embodies the violence done against her and gives manifest permanence to what she may ache to forget. Instead of being unhinged by a startling discovery about her child, she knows what is wrong even before she learns that she's pregnant. Soon thereafter, like many other mothers of exceptional children, she must figure out whether she can love a child who is antithetical to anything she imagined or wanted.

Many people see children of rape as intrinsically defective—including, often, their mothers. Unlike other factions so perceived, this one has not coalesced into a thriving identity group; there is no obvious way to celebrate the part of oneself rejected by others. Even once a child knows his or her origins, he or she cannot easily locate others who share this identity. It is difficult to reckon with a visible disability and at least equally so to reckon with a defining difference that remains hidden. One of the few organizations founded to address this vacuum, Stigma Inc., took as its motto "Rape survivors are the victims . . . their children are the forgotten victims."

Historically, rape has been seen less as a violation of a woman than as a theft from a husband or father to whom that woman belonged, who suffered an insult and an economic loss (a woman's marriageability spoiled, for example). Hammurabi's Code described most rape victims as adulterers. A thousand years later, the Athenian state, prioritizing the protection of bloodlines, treated rape and adultery the same way; English law of the seventeenth century took a similar position.

Classical mythology abounds with rape, often by a licentious god. Zeus took Europa and Leda; Dionysus raped Aura; Poseidon, Aethra; Apollo, Euadne. It is noteworthy that every one of these rapes produces children, and that rather than being avatars of shame, they are half immortal. The rape of a vestal virgin by Mars produced Romulus and Remus, the twins who founded Rome. Romulus later organized the rape of the Sabine women to populate his new city. In the Renaissance, representations of that event often decorated marriage chests.

Yet the hostility such children's origins may inspire has also long been acknowledged. In ancient and medieval societies, women who bore children conceived in rape were permitted to let them die of exposure.

Misogyny is amply present in writings about rape throughout history. The great Roman physician Galen claimed that women could not conceive in rape—nor otherwise without an orgasm based in pleasure and consent. While Augustine promised women that "savage lust perpetuated against them will be punished," he also noted that rape keeps women humble, "whether previously they were arrogant with regard to their virginity or overfond of praise, or whether they would have become proud had they not suffered violation."

A woman in the American colonies could not make a claim of rape; her husband, her father, or, if she was a servant, her employer needed to present the cause to a magistrate. The understanding was that women were prone to bringing such charges to disguise illicit consensual sex. These women were considered guilty unless they could prove their innocence. In Puritan Massachusetts, a woman pregnant through rape was prosecuted for fornication. These habits of blaming the women began to change only with the social-justice movements of the early nineteenth century. The *Kingston British Whig* noted in 1835, "The bad character of a woman ought to be no reason that she should be without the protection of the law." Rape of black women in the United States was not acknowledged as rape; you could not violate your own property, and children conceived through such rapes were themselves slaves. Black men accused of rape were frequently found guilty if not killed without trial; white men often made cash settlements with their white victims to avoid prosecution. In the 1800s, the courts' primary concern was protecting white men who might be falsely accused. To prosecute for rape, a woman had to demonstrate that she had resisted, usually by showing evidence of bodily harm, and to somehow "prove" that the man had ejaculated inside her.

Rape remained underreported through the mid-twentieth century because women feared adverse consequences if they spoke out. One impregnated rape victim of the 1950s said, "If a certain male wanted to get out of being named the true father, he would get about five of his buddies to *swear* they had sex with the girl. Branded promiscuous, the female had little recourse against the fellow, and she already experienced shame galore for birthing a child out of marriage." The rise of psychoanalysis did not help matters. Though Freud wrote little about rape, his followers saw the rapist as someone suffering a perverse, uncontrolled sexual appetite who fed into women's "natural" masochism. As late as 1971, the criminologist Menachem Amir described how women have "a universal desire to be violently possessed and aggressively handled by men," and concluded, "The victim is always the cause of the crime."

Appalled, feminists of the 1970s began arguing that rape was an act of violence and aggression, not sexuality. Susan Brownmiller's 1975 landmark book, *Against Our Will: Men, Women, and Rape*, maintained that rape had little to do with desire and everything to do with domination. She proposed that rape occurred much more widely than acknowledged, a result of the power differential between men and women, and she called for "gender free, non-activity-specific" laws that would purge rape of its sexual content to moot the idea that both parties were implicated.

American law had defined rape as "an act of sexual intercourse undertaken by a man with a woman, not his wife, against her will and by force." Feminists attacked this definition, broadening it to include nonconsensual sex within relationships and marriages, extending it to include involuntary sexual contact other than penetrative penile-vaginal intercourse, removing the burden of proving that the encounter had been caused by irresistible force, and eliminating gender-specificity. The new view of rape encompassed sexual predation by a known assailant, and coerced contact even after consenting words had been spoken. Michel Foucault famously said of all sexual relations, "There is no difference, in principle, between sticking one's fist into someone's face or one's penis into their sex." A punch in the face is violence that employs the mechanisms of violence; rape is violence that tarnishes the apparatus of love. Rape violates the intimate, private self as well as the outer, social one. It is neither purely sexual nor purely violent; it is the humiliating expression of a power differential that aggressively unites these two motives and behaviors.

Both medical professionals and law enforcement officers are now widely trained to respond to evidence of rape. Legal definitions still vary from state to state and do not always accord with those used by the FBI and other federal agencies. Definitions vary even more widely internationally, and many countries classify forced sodomy as a much less serious crime than forced vaginal penetration. Because my focus is on women who bring up children conceived in rape, I did not speak to men, children, and postmenopausal women who have been raped, but no one is immune to rape's humiliating expression of a power differential.

As other social-awareness movements have transformed the experience of rearing a child with a disability, so feminism has changed the experience of rearing a child conceived in rape. The idea of a "proud victim" would have seemed laughable only a few decades ago; like all injury and abnormality, to be raped was ignominious. Because the crime was so rarely acknowledged or discussed, it was seldom prosecuted. Feminist definitions of rape have sought to quash the suggestion of victim culpability. Terms such as *sexual assault* and *criminal sexual conduct* address the primacy of violence and change our understanding of rape from something a woman experiences to something a man does.

Despite these enormous strides, rape often remains invisible. Our warnings to our daughters caution them against getting into a car with a stranger or going home with a man they meet in a bar, but 80 percent of rapes are committed by someone the victim knows. More than half of rape victims in the United States are under eighteen, and nearly a quarter of them—an eighth of the total—are under twelve. Rape is often habitual in abusive relationships and violent marriages. Impoverished women who depend on men for survival feel less volition over their own bodies. The Centers for Disease Control have asserted that rape is "one of the most underreported crimes" and estimate that only 10 to 20 percent of sexual assaults are reported.

There is not much writing about keeping children of rape, and the books that do exist mainly address genocidal conflicts abroad or are packaged in antichoice invective. The women I interviewed were eager to tell their stories in the hope that doing so might help others. It was painfully apparent, though, that they did so at considerable cost. Many would agree to meet only in extremely public situations because they felt they could not trust me enough to be in a more secluded location together. Others insisted on extremely private locations because the subject was so loaded that they couldn't bear to speak of it where someone might overhear them.

Marina James assured me that her neighborhood library in Baltimore was a good, quiet spot to talk, but when we got there, it was closed. It was a raw March day, but Marina guided us to a bench in a public park, where other people could see us, but not hear us. At twenty-six, she punctuated her most shocking thoughts with the word *obviously* and seemed to believe that anyone else of even moderate intelligence would have made the same decisions she did.

Marina had gone to Antioch College in 2000. "A lot of their philosophy is striving for the best and doing good for others," Marina explained. "These were always things that I held important." After freshman year, she took time off to live in New York with a boyfriend, became pregnant, and had an abortion that destroyed the relationship. Then she returned to Antioch. At a campus party when she was twenty, the student DJ slipped a disabling sedative into her drink and then violently raped her. "It's more of a physical memory than an intellectual memory," she said. "I don't have pictures in my head but I have feelings in my body."

She didn't press charges. "I know what defense attorneys do to rape victims," she said. "I drank, I did drugs, I had a good time. What justice would I get? It seemed like so much grief for nothing." When she talked about her experience to other women at the college, however, some confided that they'd been raped by the same man. None of them wanted to press charges, either, but they provided written statements that Marina presented to the dean, and the rapist was expelled. Because she didn't go to the police, Marina feels tragically culpable for the rapes she imagines him to have committed since.

When Marina learned that she was pregnant, she assumed she would have another abortion. But in her third month, she changed her mind; she didn't want to go through the process again. She would have the baby, then give it up for adoption. But as the months passed, she became disillusioned about adoption. She had used recreational drugs just before finding out that she was pregnant, and an adoption administrator told her not to say as much on the form because it might put off prospective parents. The deceit upset her. "The middleman was the only one benefiting, and all the people who had something at stake were being toyed with," she said. "My child was going to be biracial, and all the families were white and liked the fact that I was a well-educated white girl. The construction of her racial identity was going to be important, and I didn't think any of these people could help her with it."

So Marina decided to keep the baby. "Now that I have Amula and I have been really successful at being her mom, obviously I know I made the right decision. But at the time, I didn't know that. So it was torture." Marina gave birth later that year and chose the name, derived from *amulet*, because she wanted the baby to be a sign of good luck and a protection against the evil that had produced her. Marina was paralyzed with post-traumatic stress disorder (PTSD), perhaps mixed with postpartum depression. "I felt like I was a different person, and I couldn't even remember what the old person was," she said.

Marina went on to graduate school in social work, bringing her daughter to classes, but began to have frequent nightmares and had difficulty eating as well as sleeping. Amula started day care and saw other children dropped off and picked up by their fathers. Before she was two, she was asking, "Why don't I have a daddy?" It made Marina cry, and she didn't want to cry in front of her daughter, so she started getting counseling. "But they kept wanting me to talk about the rape," she said. "Everybody wants a play-by-play. I don't want to keep reliving a half hour of my life: I have all this other life that I would rather live."

At twenty-six, Marina is an idealist who lives to almost ostentatiously high standards, as if determined to outflank weakness and self-indulgence. She is attractive, poised, and somewhat severe. She talks about her own vulnerability easily, but she does not demonstrate it. It is hard to guess to what degree she was always like this, and in what measure being raped reshaped her. Like many of the women I met who had borne children through rape, Marina James sustained both revulsion at the origin of her pregnancy and profound joy in her child. "I thank God every day that I have my child. But I can't ignore the fact that it's a very painful thing, why she's here."

She didn't tell her mother about the rape until after Amula was born. Nonetheless, she and Amula moved to Baltimore because Marina's parents lived there and could help with child care; "That's where Amula is right now, obviously," she said. Marina's older sister, Nina, moved in with Marina and Amula. "My sister was like a mom to me since my mom was so absent, and now I'm like a mom to my sister because she prefers to regress," Marina explained. "I tell Amula, 'You don't have a dad, but we have Aunt Nini.' A lot of my Antioch friends are gay, and so I tell her lots of kids have two mommies or two daddies. I try to be proactive about how I frame it."

Marina eventually promised Amula that she would look for a daddy for her, but shows little interest in having a partner herself. "I don't consider myself a sexual person," she said. "I was before all this. I feel sad that Amula does not have a father—but not for me." Of course Amula does have a father, in the biological sense, and Marina knows his name. "Protecting her from him is the best thing I could do for her. My friends keep saying, 'You have to be able to forgive him in order to accept it and move on.' I want to punch people when they say that."

Although the rape and its aftermath tested Marina's belief, she has increasingly turned to God in a quest for greater insight. She was Christian, but her childhood friends were all Jewish, and after she returned to Baltimore, she reconnected with them and began to convert. "Studying Judaism has enabled me to feel emotion, which I haven't felt in years," she said. "It's enabled me to feel hope and to feel faith and it's definitely helped me to feel better. It's my way to not retreat from the world."

As a social worker, Marina frequently has to grapple with stories of sexual violence. "My personal pain is just a ripple in this huge ocean of pain that women feel every day," she said. Teaching other women about parenting "makes it even more meaningful for me to come home and give my kid a big hug and sit down and play with her on the floor—not just to enjoy it, but to be validated in knowing what a good job I am doing."

Marina has told her boss and several colleagues about Amula's origins. "People ask me and I don't like to lie," she said. "It makes people uncomfortable." For someone who deplores lying, it's all the more difficult to field Amula's increasingly complex and urgent questions. Marina says she doesn't feel ashamed, but remains concerned about how Amula would incorporate the rape into her own identity. "I just want her to know that she is always wanted, that I chose to keep her and feel that it was the right choice. Even when I was struggling every day with being a survivor, I never thought, 'I wish I didn't have this baby.'" When Marina is with Amula, she isn't remembering the rape. "I'm thinking, 'Oh, are your clothes clean for swimming tomorrow?' I'm being a mom. It's when I'm in bed at night that that stuff comes up." Marina said she related to veterans returning from Iraq. "They've seen horrific things that they could never express. They come home and they don't know how to use their bodies; they're different. Nobody understands, and they return to a community that has all these expectations that no longer make sense. That is exactly how I feel."

She surmises that having a baby soon after the rape may have curtailed her recovery. "I had to be a survivor and hit the ground running and take care of this kid," she said. But she admitted that without Amula, her method of recovery would simply have been to try to forget what had happened. "And then at some point later," she said, "it would have exploded." She worries that her bright, charming daughter might share personality traits with her rapist. "Half of her genes are evil," Marina said. "I can do whatever I should as her mom to make her this loving, wonderful, caring person. But in her is the DNA of a person who is really sick, and is that DNA stronger than what I can do?"

There is a war of statistics about the correlation of rape and pregnancy, and the confusion is only exacerbated by the adversarial agendas of the pro-choice and antiabortion movements. Some have argued that the biochemistry of fear promotes ovulation, concluding that one in ten coitally raped women gets pregnant; others have produced estimates as low as 3 percent. Women suffering ongoing abuse are particularly likely to conceive through that abuse, though violent abuse can cause damage, sometimes permanently, to a woman's reproductive capacity. Of course, pregnancy does not ensue when the victim is not of reproductive age, is using oral birth control or IUDs, or is a man. It is also precluded by nonvaginal rape.

Studies have found that between twenty-five thousand and thirty-two thousand rape-related pregnancies occur each year in the United States. In a 1996 study of rape-related pregnancy, half of the subjects terminated their pregnancies; of the rest, two-thirds kept the child, one-fourth miscarried, and the rest gave the children up for adoption. Extrapolating from those figures, at least eight thousand women in this country keep rape-conceived children every year.

Ready access to a safe abortion allows a woman who keeps a child conceived in rape to feel that she is making a decision rather than having the decision forced upon her. Even opponents of reproductive choice often allow for a "rape exception." Raped women require unfettered independence in this arena: to abort or carry to term; to keep the child or give him up for adoption. Women who opt to raise such children, like parents of disabled children, choose the child over his or her challenging identity. They and their children may struggle with societal condemnation.

Many women keep children conceived in rape because they have no access to abortion, because of religious beliefs, or because of a controlling partner, husband, or parent. I also met women who completed their pregnancies because deep self-examination led them to that decision. I met women who described keeping their pregnancies as a mute reenactment of the forced passivity they had experienced in rape. Some said their children felt like evidence—as if to abort them would be a denial of the event that produced them. Because the option to terminate any pregnancy is strongly associated with feminism, many of these women found their only support in the antiabortion movement and got saddled with a moral discourse to which they did not necessarily subscribe. Many women who wished to keep children conceived in rape said they felt intense social pressure to abort.

Pregnancy following rape is a double crisis. "Pregnancy after rape implies the nightmare not only of remembering the assault but also of giving it life inside her being," said Ana Milena Gil, a psychologist working in Bogotá, Colombia. "By violating her body as a place of identity and autonomy, pregnancy resulting from rape creates a circle of pain. If rape hurts, damages, breaks women, pregnancy traps them. Living with the violence in your womb means having the attacker inside you."

An infant conceived in rape unites the genetics of the mother with those of her assailant. For some women, the rape-engendered fetus represents the unwelcome conquest of her body by an alien being; for others, it seems to be an extension of herself. In an article in *U.S. News & World Report*, one otherwise antiabortion woman counsels her sister, pregnant through rape, "If someone shot you, would you walk around with a bullet inside of you?" But another woman in identical circumstances said, "The baby was innocent. A victim like I was." It is imperative to remove a "bullet" from your person; it is likewise essential not to deprive an "innocent child" of life. The language used in these contexts implies moral values. The antiabortion feminist Joan Kemp writes, "It is significant that a child conceived in rape is more often called 'the rapist's child' than 'the rape victim's child.' In what sense can a rapist possibly be considered the 'father of this child'?" Language can be spun to dictate the "reasonable" course of action. A woman raped by a military guard is said by Kemp to have "concluded that the child was hers; that to reject the baby was to succumb to patriarchal attitudes." In this framing, the figurative bullet lodged in the mother is transformed into her center of power.

Some women experience attachment and revulsion in rapid alternation. In other instances, an initial hatred can give way to love—sometimes when the movement of the fetus is first felt, sometimes not until the child has matured into an adult. Women who have grown to love such children are often outspoken critics of abortion. Kay Zibolsky, founder of the antiabortion Life After Assault League, explained of her own pregnancy at sixteen, "The baby was part of my healing process. When she started to move in me, I looked at her as part of me, not him." Similarly, Kathleen DeZeeuw tried to deny that she had become pregnant following her attack, wearing girdles to conceal the changes in her body and attempting to self-induce miscarriage, but once the fetus began to kick and move, she said, "I began to realize that this little life inside me was struggling, too. Somehow, my heart changed. I was no longer thinking of the baby as the rapist's." Sharon Bailey said, "Basically my feelings were 'It's just you and me, kid.' I considered us both to be victims."

Knowing that your child had no part in violating you, however, is different from feeling that your child is untainted. "The first time I held him," Kathleen DeZeeuw admitted, "I was instantly reminded of his conception. There were many times that I had terrible feelings of hatred toward him. The laughter of my little boy often reminded me of the hideous laughter of this guy as he had raped me. I took it out on my son." Another woman reported despairingly, "I had tried to convince myself that the rape never happened. Then I would look at her and realize, yes, it must have happened." Padmasayee Papineni, who has studied women pregnant through rape, wrote, "Rape survivors have a much greater fear about intimacy, less comfort with closeness, and more fear of abandonment. Feelings of rejection by the mother towards the infant can lead to a wide range of psychological consequences in the child. 'The children constantly reminded mothers of the horrors of rape, and that inevitably influenced mutual relations.'"

One August day in 1975, Brenda Henriques left her home in the projects in Queens to pick up her paycheck for working as an urban summer-camp counselor. She had tied the front tails of her shirt to show off her tanned belly in defiance of her mother, Lourdes. She got off the subway and was passing a parked cab when its door swung open and a man pulled her inside. "It was just so fast. I was on the floor. There was that hump in the middle of the car floor. So my butt was up on the hump and my face was down on the floor." The driver came into the backseat, and the two men raped her in sequence, then handed her jeans to her and pushed her back into the street with blood running down her legs.

Back home, she took a long shower and didn't say a word about what had happened. "Mom warned me about my shirt and I didn't listen, and look what happened," she said. "So I blamed myself. I felt like everybody knew. It was like I had a sign on me: 'Not a virgin anymore' or 'Rape victim: asked for it.'" When she missed her first period, she told her best friend, and they snuck out during recess and went to Planned Parenthood for a pregnancy test. When she called in for the result later and found it was positive, she collapsed in the phone booth, crying. At the time, abortion was legal for a sixteen-year-old without parental consent, but she "didn't think that an abortion would be a lie I could get away with." She told her boyfriend first, and he said he never wanted to see her again. Then she broke the news to her parents. Her father, Vicente, said, "Are you sure that's what happened? Why didn't you go to the police?" Years later, she shuddered. "Why, why, the whys came," she said. "I said, 'Mommy, I was wearing the shirt you told me not to wear.' And my mother says, 'You could be standing there naked on that corner, and no one would ever have a right to do that.' I cried with relief."

Still, they wanted to keep the pregnancy secret. Her Catholic father wanted her to go to stay with relatives in Puerto Rico and give the baby for adoption. Her grandmother told everybody that Brenda had secretly been married and her husband was in the military. The High School of Performing Arts wanted her to withdraw from classes; one of her friends circulated a petition, after which the school administration backed down, but moved her to a less visible place in the orchestra. Brenda felt she had to be her baby's champion.

Brenda gave birth the last week of her junior year. She wanted to name her daughter after her paternal grandmother, but her father said,

"I don't want my mother's name on that baby." She said, "I wanted her to have a crowning name that she wouldn't be ashamed of. I went through the Bible, and Rebecca means 'captivating,' and that just clicked." When Brenda's father saw the baby, he had a change of heart and wrote Brenda a card that said, "Thank you for giving me my first granddaughter."

Brenda slid into a postpartum depression. "Partly I guess it was biology," she said, "but partly it was that all my friends were off having a fun summer vacation and I was home with this baby." Her family doctor encouraged her to seek counseling. Even with a woman psychiatrist, it took Brenda a couple of months to describe the rape itself, upon which the therapist asked, "At any point, did it feel good? Did you enjoy it?" Brenda walked out and has never seen a therapist again. Vicente was a car mechanic and Lourdes was a nurse; Brenda's ambition was to be a doctor, but with an infant at home she couldn't reach so far. "So I volunteered for the ambulance corps," she said. "I would go into the training class dragging my daughter and put her in one of those little portable playpens, and that's how I got my EMT." Brenda loved working the ambulance and eventually became a qualified paramedic.

I asked Brenda whether her anger at the rapists had ever coalesced around Rebecca. "Never that," she said. "I look at her, I see me; I don't see the other person at all. I wasn't going to take her life away before she was born, and I sure as hell wasn't going to take her life away afterwards." But she was trying to process the rape. She became promiscuous for a few years, until she met a guy named Chip Hofstadter, who owned a fish store in Queens. They married eight months later, when Rebecca was four, because Brenda needed a way out of her parents' apartment, and Chip was willing to be a father to Rebecca. They had two more children, and all three grew up believing that Chip was their father.

Brenda and Chip separated when Rebecca was fifteen, and one of Brenda's subsequent boyfriends raped Rebecca. Brenda decided it was time to tell Rebecca about her own rape. "It wasn't good for her to live with lies anymore," she explained to me. Rebecca was furious and grew increasingly rebellious. She became pregnant by her first boyfriend, and Brenda became a grandmother at thirty-five. Two years later, Rebecca had another child by another father. When Rebecca became pregnant with her third, by yet another man, Brenda took her for an abortion, saying, "You're ruining your life, and I can't let you do this. I'll probably burn in hell for it, but there comes a time when I have to step in." Rebecca eventually joined the air force.

When I first met Brenda, Rebecca was stationed in Iraq, and Brenda was raising Rebecca's two children. "My grandchildren are my heartbeat," Brenda said. "I didn't think that I could love like that, and I didn't love like that with my own children—maybe I was too young, maybe the rape. But when I felt that love, I had to let the rape go. I've asked myself, 'If I ever saw my attackers in the street, would I recognize them?' The shadowy faces I visualize could be anyone. I depersonalized it. The rape was there, but it was an act, not people. All I know is I have something that these people will never know. Never know that they have a beautiful daughter. Never know that they have beautiful grandchildren. They'll never know. But I do. And so, as it turns out, I'm the lucky one."

American abortion law from the colonial period through the mid-nineteenth century was predicated on the English common-law principle that life begins with quickening—the moment when the expectant woman feels the fetus moving inside her, usually at four to five months. In 1857, the newly formed American Medical Association began a crusade against abortion even prior to quickening, and laws passed in 1860 and 1880 made abortion illegal at any stage unless the mother's life was at risk. In 1904, the journal of the AMA concluded that "pregnancy is rare after real rape," and that, regardless, the fetus's rights trumped the mother's as "the enormity of the crime of rape does not justify murder."

The 1930s saw a rise in illegal abortions as the Great Depression made large families harder to sustain. Many women died as a result of backroom operations by untrained practitioners. In 1936, Frederick J. Taussig, an influential physician, sought to make abortion available to women who "deserved" it without aiding those who might "abuse" the right, worrying that abortions for unmarried women or widows would result in a "lowering of the moral tone." He proposed a law, never implemented but highly influential, that would permit abortions for rape victims, mentally retarded women, girls under sixteen, and any "poorly nourished woman with a large family whose external conditions make the pregnancy and the subsequent care of the child a serious burden." In 1938, a physician was put on trial in England for performing an abortion on a fourteen-year-old rape victim, and his acquittal reflected a populist movement to liberalize the right to abortion, especially for rape victims. The trial was widely covered in the United States and led to open discussion of abortion.

In 1939, the first US Hospital Abortion Committee was formed to determine case-by-case eligibility, and by the 1950s, such committees were ubiquitous. They approved only "therapeutic" abortions: those intended to preserve the mother's health or to avoid the birth of a child with significant disabilities. Increasingly, however, they accepted the recommendations of psychiatrists who stated that a patient's pregnancy was endangering her mental health. Well-connected women could obtain psychiatric diagnoses fairly easily, but rape victims who could not pay a psychiatrist to vouch for their mental frailty had to show that they were nearly deranged. Some were diagnosed as licentious and had to consent to sterilization. So, contrary to Taussig's proposal, abortions became the province of the privileged. Here is a typical case-worker report about a woman raped in the postwar era: "She became a passive object and could not say 'no.' Here we see a girl who having lost parental love, continues to search for love and her primary motivation became centered in getting her dependent needs met." The clear implication is that mentally stable women do not get raped.

In 1959, the American Law Institute (ALI) proposed legalizing abortion if the pregnancy was the result of rape or incest, the fetus had severe abnormalities, or the mother's health was at risk. In 1960, Illinois made abortion legal in cases of rape, and over the next decade, a dozen states passed laws based on the ALI model. Nonetheless, the standard treatment in most states for unwed women who had been raped was to send them to maternity homes, where they were encouraged to surrender their children for adoption. They were told this would be better for the baby than a life of shame with an unwed mother. Women who wanted to abort were considered murderous; women who wanted to keep their children, selfish. Coerced relinquishments were common. Rickie Solinger, who has studied these surrenders, describes Kathleen Leahy Koch, date-raped in 1969, who complained that she was treated like a criminal, saying, "I was just someone who had to have a baby for some worthy family. It was completely dehumanizing." Another woman, Kay Ball, raped and pregnant in 1971, attempted suicide after surrendering her baby; she said, "I was so ashamed and beaten down emotionally and mentally that I just wanted to end it all."

In 1973, the Supreme Court affirmed a woman's right to an abortion in *Roe v. Wade*. In 1976, the Hyde Amendment cut off Medicaid funding for abortion except when the mother's health was at risk, and not until 1993 was a further exception made for women pregnant through rape or incest. Since 1973, the issue of rape has arisen in every legislative attempt to curtail or strengthen the freedoms established under *Roe v. Wade*. While abortion of fetuses with disabilities is often constructed as saving the putative child from suffering, the rape exception is held to be about saving the mother. By the late 1980s, polls showed that while half of Americans opposed abortions for most women, only a small percentage opposed abortion for rape and incest victims. A number of abortion bans without rape exceptions were struck down. In 1990, Idaho governor Cecil D. Andrus, who opposed abortion in most contexts, vetoed a ban because under it a rape survivor seeking an abortion "ceases to be the victim and becomes a criminal." In some instances, abortion opponents have agreed to rape exceptions on grounds that the pregnant women are "innocent"—unlike those who become pregnant because of their untrammeled passions.

The antiabortion movement argues that an unborn child is innocent even in cases of rape. One advocate wrote, "It would be wrong to deprive the child of his unalienable right to life and the due process of the law because of the sins of his father. Two wrongs do not make a right." The mother of a rape-conceived child said, "My child is not the exception that can be tossed away. There would be no one who could look her in the eyes and believe that she doesn't deserve life due to the choice of a man we never even knew." Some believe that pregnancy is a manifestation of God's will, quoting Jeremiah 1:5, which says, "Before I formed you in the womb I knew you, and before you were born I consecrated you." This passage is taken to mean that life exists even before conception. Many hard-line antiabortion activists claim to support the best interests of the mother, taking the position that there can be no feeling of empowerment in a decision to abort. J. C. Willke, founder of the International Right to Life Federation, said, "The woman has been subjected to an ugly trauma. Should we now ask her to be a party to a second violent act—that of abortion?" Rebecca Kiessling's pamphlet "Conceived in Rape: A Story of Hope" includes the assertion, "I am not a product of rape, but a child of God." A blogger wrote in sarcastic response, "Rape isn't abuse! It is another form of the immaculate conception!"

As with all contentious public issues, both sides look to selective statistics and dramatic personal stories to bolster their positions. The crucial difference is that the pro-choice movement is not, as Willke suggests, "asking" a woman to abort, but the "right-to-life" movement is attempting to force all pregnant rape victims to carry their fetuses to term. The British psychoanalyst Joan Raphael-Leff writes that a rape-conceived fetus may remain "an internal foreigner, barely tolerated or in constant danger of expulsion, and the baby will emerge part-stranger, likely to be ostracized or punished." One rape survivor, in testimony before the Louisiana Senate Committee on Health and Welfare, likened her son to "a living, breathing torture mechanism that replayed in my mind over and over the rape." Another described mothering a rape-conceived son as "entrapment beyond description" and felt that "the child was cursed from birth"; her son manifested severe psychological challenges and was ultimately removed from the family by social services.

Joan Kemp sees abortion as a solution "imposed by a society that places too much importance on male lineage and not enough on the value of each human being." In that regard, she categorizes the pro-choice movement as antifeminist. Some women who become pregnant after rape refer to the ensuing childbirth as a "second rape"; antiabortion feminists refer to the abortions that such women may choose to have as the "second rape." For some women, an abortion might be more traumatic than bearing a rape-conceived child. The pseudonymous Denise Kalasky writes of how she was put under involuntary anesthesia for the abortion of the pregnancy that began when her father raped her, so her parents could keep their reputations intact. Here, the abortion clearly constitutes another assault characterized by lack of choice.

Among those who would block the right of rape victims to choice, none is more determined than David C. Reardon, founder of the Elliott Institute. There is no eponymous Elliott; the institute's website explains that the name was selected to sound official and impartial. Starting in the early 1980s, some pro-life advocates opposed abortion even for rape victims on the basis that it could lead to a condition they named "postabortion syndrome," characterized by depression, regret, and suicidality—a condition formulated as evidence that the Supreme Court had been wrong, in *Roe v. Wade*, when it averred that abortion was a safe procedure. The ultimate goal of the Elliott Institute is to generate legislation that would allow a woman to seek civil damages against a physician who has "damaged her mental health" by providing her with an elective abortion. On the topic of impregnated survivors of rape and incest, Reardon states in his book *Victims and Victors*, "Many women report that their abortions felt like a degrading form of 'medical rape.' Abortion involves a painful intrusion into a woman's sexual organs by a masked stranger." He and other antiabortion partisans often quote the essay "Pregnancy and Sexual Assault" by Sandra K. Mahkorn, who suggests that the emotional and psychological burdens of pregnancy resulting from rape "can be lessened with proper support." Another activist, George E. Maloof, writes, "Incestuous pregnancy offers a ray of generosity to the world, a new life. To snuff it out by abortion is to compound the sexual child abuse with physical child abuse. We may expect a suicide to follow abortion as the quick and easy way to solving personal problems."

Younger women and girls, who don't have a clear idea of their own future, often decide to continue or end a rape-related pregnancy in rebellion against or compliance with the wishes of parents and other elders. Other women are in denial: one-third of pregnancies resulting from rape are not discovered until the second trimester. Any delay in detection or action reduces women's options, but many women are still recovering from being raped when they are called on to make up their minds whether to carry through their pregnancy. No matter which choice is ultimately made, pregnancy after rape can lead to depression, anxiety, insomnia, and PTSD. Rape is a permanent damage; it leaves not scars, but open wounds. As one woman I interviewed said, "You can abort the child, but not the experience."

The philosopher Susan Brison, herself a rape survivor, has said, "Trauma not only haunts the conscious and unconscious mind, but also remains in the body, in each of the senses, ready to resurface whenever something triggers a reliving of the traumatic event." A pregnancy literalizes this condition by staying in the body until abortion or delivery. In describing the problems of treating raped women, Croatian psychiatry professor Vera Folnegović-Šmalc said, "We frequently encounter a loss of vital instincts or even a death wish. Suicidal thoughts are evident above all."

Melinda Stephenson knew from childhood that she wanted to go into deaf education. Her father was deaf and her mother, hearing; as a hearing child, fluent in Sign, she served as her father's translator. He had completed only fifth grade, and her mother had graduated from high school; Melinda was determined to go to college. In her native Indiana, Ball State University was the only college that gave degrees in deaf education, so that's where Melinda went. In her sophomore year, she lived off-campus and commuted via the university-run shuttle service. The shuttles were driven by students, and Melinda occasionally chatted with them, including one, Ricky, who was a childhood-education major.

One evening on her way home, Melinda noticed a car idling in front of her building. She assumed it was someone dropping off her roommate, who usually returned from volleyball practice about that time, so she left the door unlocked. When she heard it close, she turned and saw Ricky. "He shoved me on the bed and said, 'If you scream, I will kill you.' I remember looking at my clock. It was eight forty-seven." The phone was ringing—she found out later that her mother was calling—but he cut the cord. "I was banging on the wall, I was kicking him, but then he showed me a knife, and I wanted to live. He left at eleven twenty-three."

Melinda sat on her bed without moving until five thirty the next morning, when she finally asked a friend to take her to the hospital.

The nurse expressed doubt that it had been a rape and did not offer emergency contraception. She did, however, summon the police, and Melinda made a report; the police asked if she wanted to press charges, and she said she couldn't. Melinda finished the fall semester with plummeting grades and dropped out halfway through the spring semester, paralyzed by anxiety. "I was petrified to leave my apartment," she recalled.

She moved back in with her parents and enrolled at Ivy Tech Community College, although it had no deaf-education program. When she realized she was pregnant and told her mother, it was already too late for an abortion; Melinda couldn't bear the thought of relinquishing the baby anyway. "I had to change and adapt, or be stuck in fear," she explained. "So I changed and I adapted." Many of the adaptations were painful. Anxious and deeply depressed, she was hospitalized twice—once on suicide watch. She was offered a job in deaf education out of state, but was terrified to live on her own.

When her son, Marcus, was born, Melinda's parents refused to treat him as their grandchild. "We have a secured area in the living room where we stay," Melinda explained. When her father is home, Marcus has to stay within five feet of her. "Marcus went to touch the TV the other day," she said, "and my dad went to hit him, and I yelled, 'You touch him, and you'll never see me again.'" When her sister adopted a daughter, Melinda's parents would take the little girl to the park and go to Grandparents Day at her school. But when a coworker asked Melinda's mother how her grandson was doing, she said, "What grandson? I don't have a grandson."

After college, Melinda got a job with Head Start. By then, she had developed compulsions, could not tolerate having different foods touch, began cutting herself, and couldn't go to a new place on her own, even a Starbucks. "If you get into my bubble," she warned, "I get angry." A child at Head Start wore a stocking cap one day that was identical to Ricky's, and she took it out of his cubby and threw it away. "He was four years old! I've got to fix this," she said.

Melinda started seeing a therapist who was a rape survivor herself. At first, Melinda couldn't talk about what had happened. When she did, she insisted that the door be locked first. Her therapist suggested that Melinda send anonymous postcards to Ricky laying out her accusations, as a way of getting it off her chest. She sent one every other day, from different towns. Sometimes she would print them out on a computer, other times she'd paste together words she'd cut out of magazines or imitate a child's handwriting. She mailed some to his job, others to his home.

After six months of postcards, Ricky brought charges against her for stalking, so she was fired from Head Start, where employees cannot be the subject of a criminal investigation. "I've worked at a job for two years, I've never been in trouble, I've never been late, I've never missed a day, nothing. And you're going to fire me over a postcard?" she said. Ricky then announced that he was going to sue for custody, and Melinda broke down. She took Marcus to Child Protective Services (CPS) and announced that she was signing him over. Her therapist met her there and convinced her to take Marcus home, but her mother offered to drive her back to CPS if she changed her mind again.

Melinda found another job in a toddler day-care center. Her mental state remained fragile, and the line between Marcus and Ricky seemed blurred for her. "I feel like they're connected, and there's no one-or-the-other," she said. "He'll touch me and say something, and I'll think, 'That's your dad.' What if I go to hurt him, thinking he's his dad? I'm petrified. Marcus is the spitting image of my rapist." She got a glazed look. "There's some things that he does, and I'll think, 'Oh, I'm so proud of you.' And then he'll talk to me and suddenly I can't even acknowledge him. Without him, what's going to make me get up in the morning? I guess I'm much less likely to kill myself if I've got him."

Within a year, Melinda wrote to me that she'd been dating a man for eight months and they were expecting a child. "Marcus is excited about being a big brother," she continued. "I am happy, therapy is going in a good path, and the best part, my parents can't tell us what to do anymore." Two months later, she wrote, "The guy I had been dating decided that I wasn't for him. He is now living in Michigan with his new wife. I named my daughter Eliza. Sad news is she was born dead. My pregnancy with her was so different than with Marcus. With Eliza I made sure that everything I did was in the best interest of Eliza. Kinda odd, huh? Wanted to ignore Marcus and hope it would go away and I have him, and then I do everything I can to take care of myself and my Eliza and I lose her." Six months later, she gave up Marcus; he was placed with a foster family that was considering adopting him. "I see him as much as I want," Melinda wrote, "which is not as much as I should. He is getting everything that I could not provide. I am not allowed to spend time alone with him, and I think that is very smart. I struggle a lot with losing Eliza. For Eliza's birthday I am having a cookout with some friends. I am so excited to make her 'gunk' cake. It's a 9 x 11 yellow cake with peanut butter icing covered in birdseed with whatever writing I decide to put on it. I will be putting this cake on her grave so that the wildlife can enjoy her presence and life as all of us do every day." So Melinda struggled on, in love with a child who was dead, and unable to love the one who was alive. Rape engenders both rage and sadness, and even as it had made Marcus the object of Melinda's displaced fury, it had made Eliza the safer receptacle of her despair.

Recent theorists have applied evolutionary theory to surmise that rape is primarily a reproductive strategy, the genes for which are likely to be selected. Jonathan and Tiffani Gottschall, who teach at Washington & Jefferson College, propose that rapists "target victims not only on the basis of age but based on a whole complement of physical and behavioral signals indicating a victim's capacity to become pregnant"— many of them the same signals that underlie nonrape attraction. Randy Thornhill and Craig T. Palmer, authors of *A Natural History of Rape*, argue that men who commit rape spread their seed far and wide, thus fulfilling the self-perpetuating drive of the selfish gene.

The idea that fantasies of forced reproduction often course through the minds of rapists accords with feminist theory. The scholar Catharine MacKinnon has emphasized this construct, writing, "Forced pregnancy is familiar, beginning in rape and proceeding through the denial of abortions; this occurred during slavery and still happens to women who cannot afford abortions." Susan Brownmiller has proposed that reproduction is the primary motive for many rapists. "Men began to rape women when they discovered that sexual intercourse led to pregnancy," she writes. In the developed world, rape may be an effective reproductive strategy within abusive relationships, but hardly otherwise: most victims do not become pregnant; most of those who do have abortions; and rapists are sometimes imprisoned, curtailing their reproductive potential. Mary P. Koss, a clinical psychologist at the Arizona College of Public Health who studies sexual violence, has said that rather than choosing between evolutionary and social explanations for rape, we must figure out how to integrate them.

Rapists are often repeat offenders; it is less well-known that women who have been raped before age eighteen are twice as likely as other women to be raped as adults. Sexual abuse perpetuates itself. The two statistics have an appalling symmetry. As aggression is rewarded in the rapist, the victim's ego becomes frayed and vulnerable. Then her understanding that the world is unsafe becomes a self-fulfilling prophecy.

Growing up in Milwaukee, Lori Michaels had a friendly relationship with Fred Hughes, who lived across the street with his wife and three kids. When Lori was twelve, Fred started buying her candy and taking her for rides in his car. After he'd built up some trust, he took her to a garage, put a 9 mm gun to her head, and made her perform oral sex on him. It happened four times over a couple of months; then Fred and his family moved to Chicago. She never told anyone.

When Lori was nineteen, Fred moved back to Milwaukee. Lori was staying with someone who knew him and sometimes she would wake up at night to find Fred in her room with his gun. He would take her back to the same garage, time and again for more than a year. Lori kept quiet about it; she feared what her mother, Clarabel, might say if she found out. One night her landlord's sister said, "Lori, Fred's been bragging about sleeping with you. Was that willingly?" Lori said it was not. "I didn't think so" came the response. "He did it to my daughter Ginger, too." Ginger was fourteen at the time. Ginger's mother called the police on Lori's behalf, and Lori took them to the garage. Ginger had already led them to the same place. "Who knows who else he was hitting up?" Lori remarked.

Not long afterward, Lori realized she was pregnant. She told her boyfriend, Bud, that either he or Fred could be the father. Fred was black, and Lori and Bud were white, so she figured she would find out when the child was born. When Clarabel got wind of what had happened, the harsh judgment Lori feared didn't materialize. "Are you going to get an abortion, put it up for adoption, keep it?" Clarabel asked. "If you keep the child, you can't take anything out on that child. And if you're not going to keep it, it's best to make a clean break and be done with it immediately." Clarabel listed the problems Lori would face, starting with racism if it was Fred's, and said it was hard work being a single mother. After a day of pondering, Lori told Clarabel she was going to keep the child, and her mother said, "I knew you would. I just wanted you to think before you made that choice."

Lori moved back home, but she sank into depression and slit her wrists when she was eight months pregnant. Bud found her and called 911. Lori insisted that the rape, not the pregnancy, had engendered her despair, that if she hadn't been pregnant, her suicide attempt would have been successful. "My son is what's kept me going," she said, echoing a frequent refrain among mothers of such children. That Lori had put up with years of rape without a suicide attempt and then made one during pregnancy called her logic into question. When the boy was born, he looked white. "And then when I went to change his diaper, his penis was black," Lori said. "So they told me, 'Mulatto babies come out white and their penises are black.'" Lori named him Bobby and took him home, where Clarabel did much of the caretaking.

Fred was prosecuted for his rapes of Lori and Ginger. Sentenced to two and a half years, he was released after two years for good behavior. Genetic analysis showed that Bobby was his son, and Fred requested custody, which he was not granted. Nevertheless, his wife repeatedly accosted Lori, demanding access to Bobby. Lori and Clarabel and Bobby eventually left Wisconsin and resettled in the Southwest. A few years later, Fred was in jail again, pending trial on charges that he had raped five girls and assaulted another so severely that she nearly died. The DA sought two life sentences plus fifteen years, but he filed paper-work incorrectly and the case was dismissed. Fred soon moved, and the system lost track of him. "Each time he rapes someone, it's more vio-lent," Lori said. "And now he's free."

When I met Lori and her family in the trailer park where they were living, Bobby was twelve. Lori said she rarely thought about Fred when she looked at Bobby. "My sister calls Fred 'the sperm donor,'" she related. "I believe Bobby's my miracle boy." The rest of her family have also been accepting. "My whole family was racist, the older gen-eration," Lori added, "but they treated Bobby very special. My great-grandma, she slipped once and called him a nigger. She looked at me and wanted to cry, and she never slipped again." Many of Lori's roman-tic relationships had been troubled, and Bobby had grown up defend-ing his mother in violent domestic situations. Her work history has also been spotty—in part because she has Social Security income on grounds of PTSD, and if she earns too much money, she'll lose those benefits. So she's worked at Burger King and Taco Bell, but she runs out of steam quickly and finds it hard to deal with other people on the job. The family mostly lives on the income Clarabel earns at Walmart.

Clarabel had thought the right time to discuss Bobby's origins with him was when he began to ask questions. So when he was seven, Lori told him she had been raped by his father, who'd put a gun to her head. "I don't want to know him," Bobby told me. Good-looking, friendly, and rather self-possessed at twelve, Bobby is also high-strung and moody. He has been diagnosed with ADHD and other learning disabilities—possibly inherited from Fred, who was illiterate. One cli-nician suggested that he may be bipolar as well. He has run into prob-lems with teachers and bounced from school to school. Bobby is the apple of his grandmother's eye. "Weekends or early in the morning," Clarabel said, "he comes and sits up on my bed, and I watch National Geographic and nature movies with him." Still, the emotional life of the family remains complicated. "I do a lot of hollering," Lori said. "I'm in anger management on Tuesday nights. We do family counsel-ing, and I'm on meds till I get back on track." Bobby loses his temper with his friends and once threw a TV while fighting with his mother.

"The counselor says he's not going to hit me," Lori said, "but he's seen so much violence."

Three days after Lori threw out one of her boyfriends at five in the morning for calling Bobby a nigger, she met Ringo Smythe via an online chat room where she was telling a friend about it. "Promise me you won't take this guy back," Ringo wrote. She and Bobby met him at the carnival where he worked the games. Bobby begged his mom to give Ringo a try; when I met Lori, they had been together almost a year, the longest either of them had ever lasted in a romantic relationship.

Still, Lori worries, given Ringo's background. "I come from a convict family," Ringo said. "My dad met my mom in a whorehouse, and she did drugs. And I've seen a lot worse stuff on the carnival circuit, so it's pretty hard to freak me out with anything." Ringo broke off midstream, then asked me to hit him hard. "I don't feel no pain in my arm because my dad used my arm as an ashtray." He rolled up his sleeve to show white scars from his shoulder to his wrist.

Although Ringo professed not to believe in psychotherapy, he agreed to join the family counseling sessions at which he discussed marrying Lori and adopting Bobby. First, he had to track down the woman to whom he was still married so he could file for a divorce. Both Lori and Ringo were burdened by massive debts. Still, Ringo had made major changes since he and Lori met. "I can't stand the heat. I hate trailers. I hate cats," he said. "I'm here in Arizona in a trailer park with five cats." I asked if that was all for Lori, and he said, "Yeah, Lori and Bobby both." When I visited, he had taken a leave from the carnival so he wouldn't have to be separated from them and was working the graveyard shift at Target, the discount retailer.

"I don't think about Fred a lot, but when Ringo does certain sexual things, I have flashbacks," Lori said. "I have bad days and good days. And sometimes the bad days last a week. But we do family things all the time. I would never think of going back to the past and changing anything—I'd have another kid, but not my Bobby. I got my boy."

"Where did I come from?" is one of the first urgent questions of childhood. A response that includes terror and powerlessness can undermine a child's feeling of safety. Many rape victims who bear children have to explain why they've had babies at an inappropriate age, in the absence of a stable romantic relationship, or despite lacking financial or emotional resources to provide care for the child. The extent to which a woman feels judged may determine the scope of her concealment or denial. Telling a secure child who isn't looking for answers the story of his or her conception can itself feel like an act of violence. Mothers who were unable to protect themselves are gratified by their ability to protect their children, and shielding them from such awful knowledge is part of that safeguarding. So one mother pledged online, "My son will never know the details of his conception. I don't want him thinking he wasn't wanted or conceived out of love."

The withholding of traumatic information is as loaded as the telling; often, the child gleans knowledge accidentally from people on whom it has no direct bearing, then feels betrayed by a lifetime's secrecy. In short, there is no good time or safe way to share the news, but concealing it can spell disaster. Holly van Gulden, an adoption counselor, explained, "Keeping secrets especially between generations within a family system implies the material withheld is shameful." To what extent is a mother's choice to spare her child the circumstances of his conception protection, and to what extent is it a dangerous form of denial? Even considered decisions about sharing or withholding fundamental information can have unintended consequences. One man who learned as an adult that he was conceived in rape said the knowledge freed him from seeing his mother as "the 'bad girl' or 'tramp' image that is sometimes associated with unwed mothers." The disapproval his mother had sought to evade by harboring her secret had blighted her son's view of her and, by extension, of himself. Children easily perceive and absorb humiliation, and if they are the nexus of a parent's shame, they bear it as a heavy weight.

To learn that you are the kind of person most mothers would prefer never even to imagine can produce an angry self-doubt similar to that of people with genetic anomalies who believe that selective abortion would invalidate their lives and eradicate their heirs. Some rape-conceived people have become antiabortion activists as a way of marking the fact that they were born. Lee Ezell, raped by her boss at eighteen, gave up her daughter Julie for adoption without ever seeing her. Twenty-one years later, Julie found her, and they shared a joyful reunion. "I'm so thankful that the choice was not available in 1963, when Lee could have been so tempted to easily end my life," Julie said. When Lee met her son-in-law, he said, "I want to shake your hand. I want to say thank you for not aborting Julie."

Some speak grandiosely about how they evaded abortion, as though they had been wily double agents in utero. They sometimes fail to empathize with the trauma to which they are connected. Sherrie Eldridge, conceived in rape and surrendered at birth for adoption, writes of being disappointed when she was reunited with her birth mother forty-seven years later. As her ten-day visit with her birth mother progressed, their incipient relationship grew strained. Her mother said that the reunion had brought a lot of pain to the surface. "*Am I so bad that I would cause her pain?* I kept asking myself," Eldridge writes. "At that time, I knew nothing of the horrendous pain a birth mother experiences both at relinquishment and reunion. I was dealing with my own pain and unresolved grief." Eldridge assigns her birth mother's grief solely to separation from her child, with no apparent awareness of the excruciating afterlife of her rape.

For years, Lisa Boynton thought her most important secret was that she had been abused by her grandfather since she was five. When Lisa was in seventh grade, she saw a census form on which her father had identified her as "stepdaughter." He had never wanted Lisa to know, her mother, Louise, told her, because he was afraid Lisa wouldn't love him anymore. Louise said she'd become pregnant at fifteen by a boy from school. "I was angry," Lisa said. "I'm still angry. My whole family knew that he wasn't my real dad, but no one told me."

The following year, Lisa and some friends were hanging out with a friend of theirs, Donny, who was "mentally retarded." Lisa was in eighth grade; Donny was twenty; they had made out a few times, but she never expected it to go further. She went upstairs with him to see something, and he raped her. She screamed, but nobody responded. When she came downstairs, shaking, and asked her best friend why she hadn't helped her, the friend said, "Oh, I thought you were just getting it, finally. It always hurts the first time."

Ironically, only after Lisa's rape—which she kept a secret—did her grandfather's habitual abuse come to light. Her mother overheard her telling a friend about it and prodded her into confessing the whole story. Lisa begged her mother not to tell her stepfather. "She said, 'Just go to bed. It will be all right.' And she must have gone downstairs and told my dad. I heard him throwing things, curses flying out of his mouth." They notified the police. Her stepfather's father pleaded guilty and was sentenced to five years on probation. Lisa received a letter of apology from him, but it sounded "as though a lawyer wrote it," she said. "To me, it meant nothing." Lisa's stepfather cut off relations with his own father.

The relationship between Lisa and Louise, despite this energetic support, remained bewilderingly strained. "My dad went above and beyond to make me feel like I was loved and part of the family," Lisa said. "It was my mother who always blamed me for things; my sister was always innocent." After the rape, Lisa became promiscuous. Like many victims of child sexual abuse, she had no sense of boundaries about physical intimacy. "I would sleep with anybody," she said. "Even though I'd been raped by Donny, I continued to have sex with him willingly, up until I was in eleventh grade." She added, almost in bewilderment, "I guess I'd confused sex with love ever since my grandfather began abusing me."

Then one day, when Lisa was twenty, Louise confessed that she herself had been raped and that she didn't know who Lisa's father was. The story was eerily similar to Lisa's own. Her mother and her best friend had gone out with two older men, and they'd stopped at the men's house. The best friend and one of the men disappeared together, and the other man invited Lisa's mother into another room, where he raped her. Then the first man came in and raped her, too. When she learned that she was pregnant, she didn't know which of them was the father. When Lisa pressed her mother for names, Louise gave obviously fictitious ones. "I don't think she's telling me the whole story," Lisa said. "Little things just didn't add up. I couldn't tell her I was angry that she never told me, because I could hear the sadness in her voice. And I never wanted to bring it up again. I'm going to die with a lot of unanswered questions."

All the secrets and lies have had a corrosive effect on Lisa, who, in her thirties, still doesn't feel like part of her own family. She has spent a good bit of time looking at online forums that have made her feel less alone. She eventually got a degree in social work, and as a group-therapy leader she counsels women who've experienced similar traumas. Her personal and professional lives are consecrated to recovery. "I minimize my issues and problems," she reflected. "But I'm the first to say, 'Don't minimize yours.'" She lives with a female partner and has a daughter from a previous relationship, to whom she is deeply attached. "I felt like I always had to look out for myself, because nobody else is going to look out for me," she said. "I want my daughter's life to be completely different from mine."

When we met, Lisa was seeing a therapist she liked, yet she had never discussed the rapes with her therapist. Instead of seeing them as connected, she viewed them as ludicrously coincidental. "I didn't think anyone would believe me," she said to me. "Even to myself, it seems far-fetched that someone could be sexually abused and raped—and then find out my mother was raped, too. The only people who know all the pieces are my mother and my partner. And now, you. I wanted to escape the trauma I experienced at my grandfather's hands and everything that came after that; however, I now know it is something that will always stay with me and I will not ever fully recover. What I can do is use my experiences to be a better social worker to my clients. I'm able to identify with and relate to them—but in a healthy way, without disclosing my own abuse."

Prejudice against rape victims and their children is as real as it is irrational. One blogger wrote, "Hmmm, so many children, born out of incest and rape. The CWS [child-welfare system] is overwhelmed and under-prepared. My suggestion? PUT THEM TO SLEEP LIKE UNWANTED PETS!" Even among people with less extreme points of view, prejudice is deeply ingrained. In disdaining and fearing rapists, as most people do, it is only too easy to disdain and fear their progeny. Liberal acquaintances who were all for Deaf politics and neurodiversity expressed unease about raising a child with "those genes." The innocence of the child is conditional in this domain. To the mother, he is an incarnation of the rape; to the world, he is the rapist's heir.

In the face of such bias, a mother may envision her parental relationship as euphoric—either through authentic religious ecstasy or to avoid acknowledging her ambivalence. Kathleen DeZeeuw, in *Victims and Victors*, says, "It was Patrick, my son, conceived in rape—whose life I had tried to snuff out—who taught me how to forgive. He was willing to forgive not only his biological father, but also me (for physically and verbally abusing him as a child)." Another mother speaking out in the same book said, "My daughter's identity is in being a child of God. She was the gift that brought me out of fear and darkness into the Light of authentic Love." The miracle is always twofold: of the child who overcomes his fearsome genes, and of the mother who trounces her initial dread. Rhapsody is helpful to both mother and child. One anti-abortionist wrote, "I am the product of rape, and not only rape, but of incest. My mother sacrificed her needs for mine, carried a shame that wasn't hers, and brought a baby into this world that in this day and age probably would not have made it. But she didn't stop there. Being unable to provide me with the things a child needs—like security, food, a roof over my head, schooling—she denied herself the right to keep me, her child. She selflessly let me go for adoption when I was seven." There's an element of will involved in understanding one's own relinquishment as an act of devotion.

When she was three, Tina Gordon called her mother "Mom" and was immediately rebuked. "Don't you ever call me that again," Donna said. "I'm not your mother." "But what am I supposed to call you?" Tina asked. "You can call me Donna," her mother replied. Tina's great-grandmother told her later, "It's not your fault. She was raped when she had you." Tina had no idea what her great-grandmother was talking about. "When I learned how to read, I looked it up in the dictionary and understood the violence part, but not the sex part," Tina said. "For a lot of my life, though, I felt damaged." Tina watched her older sister, Corinna, say "Mom" over and over and watched her receive at least sporadic flashes of love and attention. "I always had to remember that I was the stepchild, so to speak," Tina recalled. The only loving thing her mother ever did for her was to make her sweetened hot milk before bed. Ironically, however, Tina's estrangement from Donna may have afforded her a measure of protection from her mother's destructive tendencies.

Donna had had a nervous breakdown in college and was abusive to both Tina and Corinna when they were young. Donna was living in Florida when Tina was born, and a friend called Donna's mother to say that there was a new baby. "It might already be too late for the older daughter," the friend said, "but you've got to come and get these kids and maybe save this baby." So Tina's grandmother went to fetch the two girls. She found that Corinna was missing parts of her finger pads because Donna had put her hands on the stove as a punishment.

Tina and Corinna grew up in Mississippi under the far more loving care of their grandmother, who taught school by day and cleaned houses by night to keep the family going. Donna would visit and say that she was going to reclaim Corinna as soon as she got back on her feet. She made no such promises to Tina, who soon gave up seeking any kind of approval from her mother and focused on her grandmother and aunts, who proved far more reliable. As a result, Tina saw her mother's hypocrisies with greater clarity than her sister did. "If we were watching television, Corinna would sit on Donna's lap, and I was just on the floor by myself," Tina said.

When Tina was eight and Corinna was ten, their grandmother died at fifty-eight. Donna, close to forty, was clearly unable to handle them both. A great-uncle they barely knew felt they shouldn't be split up and agreed to take them both, so they moved to Connecticut. Aunt Susan and Uncle Thomas gave them material security, but ran an alienating, strict household, and the girls were unhappy. Donna would send care packages and Christmas presents to Corinna, but nothing to Tina. Uncle Thomas told Donna that if she couldn't send presents for both daughters, she shouldn't send anything. After that, there were just letters: cold and formal ones to Tina, effusive ones to Corinna promising to take her back. Two years after a fire at the house in Connecticut, Corinna was caught trying to set fire to it again, and she was sent to a juvenile facility. Another uncle took her in briefly after she was released, but then she wanted to move back in with Donna. Donna would have none of it, and Corinna was utterly devastated. Aunt Susan and Uncle Thomas weren't willing to have her back. So at fifteen, she ended up living on the streets in Mississippi.

Tina found it painful to be in her uncle's house when Corinna was not allowed to be there and decided to go to boarding school. "I've always just had maybe a little bit of a survivor instinct," Tina said. She was admitted to a girls' school, where she was one of seven black students in a population of one hundred and sixty. Her aunt and uncle cut her off after she was disciplined for smoking pot. "I started to be known at school as 'the orphan,'" Tina recalled. Meanwhile, Corinna was hustling and doing drugs; she had developed AIDS by the time Tina started college at New York University. "Donna contacted me to disparage Corinna," Tina remembered. "I said, 'I understand why she's made the choices she's made. Other people have had a huge part to play in that.' Donna said, 'What other people?' I said, 'You and others.' That was the end of her trying to reach out to me." The sisters, however, kept in touch, and Tina visited Corinna repeatedly in the last year of her life, when she was twenty-three.

"No matter what Donna said or did, Corinna would tell me that I should reach out to Donna, forgive Donna," Tina said. "Because I knew it would mean a lot to Corinna, I actually called Donna and asked her to call Corinna and say that she loved her and that she was in her prayers—just to reach out to her before she died. Donna said, 'I don't think I can do that.' Then she said, 'I know I haven't necessarily made good choices, but if I can make that up to you, tell me what I can do.' And I said, 'If you call Corinna, all is forgiven and forgotten.' She said, 'I've heard that she's prostituting, and I heard she was using drugs.' And I said, 'First of all, you don't know if that's true or not, and secondly, what does it matter? She's dying. You don't have to call and talk about her life or what she's done. It would just mean a lot to her if you would call and say that you're praying for her, thinking of her. Something. Anything.' She said, 'I don't know if I can do that.' And she didn't."

Tina enrolled in Columbia Law School, and as her accomplishments accrued, Donna began to seek her out. Donna called to ask whether she was going to be invited to see Tina graduate with honors. Tina said, "I haven't talked to you in years, and the last time I talked to you I made a request of you and you couldn't even do that. So why are you trying to be a part of my life now?"

Tina became a public defender. Having accepted injustice from birth, she found solace in defending other people. When I met her, she was seven months pregnant. I wondered whether she had fears about being a mother. "Despite all the things that happened, in a lot of ways I do feel very fortunate, very blessed," she said. "My grandmother was able to give us so much love. Even though I was only with her for eight years, she made such a huge impression." Tina was engaged to a man with a warm, supportive family, "the exact opposite of mine." Her fiancé is naturally affectionate, "and there are times when I'm suddenly, like, 'Every time you come in the room, you don't have to touch me.' He knows how I'm damaged." Tina has worked hard to build a life that can subsume the past. "I don't know what happened to Donna when I was conceived," she said, "but that curse has run its course, and it's going to stop here." She rested a hand on her pregnant belly, as though to indicate how love pushed away over and over again had finally found its object.

A woman who keeps a child conceived in rape has a permanent tie to her rapist. In some instances, hatred and fear keep the connection alive; in others, however, the mother is bracing herself for the possibility that either the rapist or the child might eventually seek out the other. Just as abused children cling to their abusive parents, driven by a biology beyond logic, so these women remain in thrall to their attackers, unable to break free of the terrible intensity of their connection. Unconditional rejection of the rapist, for them, feels too much like a rejection of the resultant child. If these women fail to experience the anger appropriate to being raped, they destroy themselves; if they evince such anger, they feel that they have failed their children. It's a more extreme version of a common challenge for people who have divorced. It can take a generation to transcend this ambivalence; one woman told me that when her child was born, she had the rapist's eyes. "Her beautiful baby daughter has *her* eyes," this woman said. "Now they're the family eyes, not the eyes of the man who raped me."

The grimmest challenge for many of these women comes if the rapist or his family tries to gain access to the child. Men who have gotten away with rape seldom retreat in shame or repentance; they sometimes play out their ghoulish exuberance by laying claim to their progeny. In instances where charges were never filed, the threat of joint custody is real. Stigma Inc., the online support group for people conceived in rape and incest, had a posting saying, "The father/rapist is thus deemed ineligible for visitation or custody of the minor child. However, as in the case of rape victims in general, the burden of proof that a rape took place is often placed upon the woman who has suffered the crime. Often it comes down to a 'he said/she said' issue."

When Emily Barrett would hug her mother, Flora, she was always pushed away. "But it took a minute for her to realize that she wanted to shoo me off," Emily told me, "and I miss those moments right before she did." Flora was a light-skinned Jamaican woman who had emigrated to New York for a better life. By the time Emily was twelve, Flora was on her fourth husband. "She was extremely charismatic, and beautiful, and she was funny," Emily said. "Other people loved her. She was a hypocrite, but it was still interesting to watch, almost like a science project." As an only child, Emily was lonely. Her father, Phil, did not live in the household, but Emily saw or spoke to him every day until she was eleven, when he suddenly disappeared. No one would tell her what had happened, so she assumed he was dead; before she turned thirteen, she developed a crush on a good-looking nineteen-year-old, Blake. He took to giving her rides to and from school, and one day in the car, he leaned over and kissed her. As the years passed, her attachment to him grew. When she was fifteen, Emily gave him her virginity, even though she knew he had a girlfriend.

That same year, Emily answered the phone one day, and it was her father, from whom she'd heard nothing for four long years. He told her to get together all the money she could and meet him at Grand Central Station. Emily headed for the station with $200. Phil appeared abruptly, yanked Emily behind a pillar, took the money from her, and jumped onto a train. Emily was shattered and tried to kill herself. "My mind went on some sort of carnival ride," she said. "And at the end of it was a whole medicine cabinet." Her mother took her to the emergency room. "I didn't know how to explain it other than to say, 'My dead father jumped out of Grand Central Station.' They really thought I was crazy." The resident psychiatrist kept Emily on the ward for twenty-three days, then advised Flora that Emily needed therapy. Three weeks after her release, Flora moved to Virginia, taking her reluctant daughter with her. "My mother dealt with problems by running away, and her idea of therapy was to buy a new house," Emily said.

In Virginia, Emily's mother found her a job doing bookkeeping for friends who owned a restaurant; Emily called them Uncle Eric and Aunt Suzette. Uncle Eric asked Emily to help out his brother, who owned a store, and the brother raped her after driving her to work. "It's not like on television," Emily said. "There's no black eye, and there's no knives and guns. It's five seconds. I was just stunned." She spent the next few days in a haze, then finally called the police, by which time the man had fled.

In the weeks that followed, Emily had severe headaches, and her breasts began to hurt. When Flora found out Emily was pregnant, she locked the doors and unplugged the phones while she decided what to do about it. "She told the school I had appendicitis," Emily said. "Every day she would come home and just scream. And then I'd hear her in her room crying and wailing in her shower. Then Uncle Eric and Aunt Suzette were coming over saying how I'm ruining their reputation. I was sixteen and I had no business having a child. But that whole experience was just insanity."

Flora finally took Emily to a clinic for an abortion. Emily had been educated in Catholic schools even though her family wasn't Catholic, because Flora thought it was a better education. Emily had been confirmed in the faith; now she was afraid she would burn in hell. She shared her regrets with the clinician, so he sent her home. "That ride home with my mother was one of the worst experiences of my life," she recalled. Flora said that if Emily had really been raped, she wouldn't care about losing the baby, and when they got home, she arranged an abortion at another clinic. Emily's pregnancy was terminated five days later. "For a long time, I would calculate in my mind and imagine how old that baby would be from when I was sixteen," Emily said. "I would see a baby and start to cry."

Aunt Suzette had assured Emily that the rapist had left the country, but Emily thought she saw him everywhere. "I was in a panic," Emily said. "And one day, I was walking from the bathroom to the kitchen, and my mother whispered in my ear, 'This never happened.' And that was it. It was like a switch went off in my head. I never talked about it again. I tried never to think about it again. And eventually, it just sort of dissolved into my mind."

As abruptly as Flora had relocated to Virginia, she moved back to New York. For a few years, life returned to normal. Emily resumed her friendship with Blake. She went off to college, but dropped out to take care of her mother after Flora was diagnosed with advanced colon cancer. Flora left Emily a small inheritance. In an eerie echo of Emily's final encounter with her father, she soon got a call from Blake asking for an urgent loan; she gave him $5,000, and he vanished.

Emily located him after a few years and asked about the loan; he said that he had some money to give her and told her to come over to collect it. "He gave me a drink with something in it," Emily said. "Next thing I know, I feel my clothes coming off. I'm seeing flashing lights and pictures. He was positioning my body, he was moving me around. I couldn't believe it. When I woke up, he was in the shower and I was shaking." Emily gathered her clothes and drove home. She was dating a policeman at the time, and when she told him what had happened, he took her to the precinct to report it. Blake was arrested, and the bringing of charges began. "They told me not to contact him, but I needed to know, I wanted to know *why*. I had known Blake for so long and he had been my best friend!" She called him, and he refused to talk because of the restraining order. Then he called her back and begged her not to go through with the charges.

Emily sensed that she was pregnant but couldn't face it: she took seven pregnancy tests, hoping that eventually one would be negative. She broke up with the policeman; her emotional life centered on Blake, the rape, and the pregnancy. At a hearing in her suit against him, when she realized that he might go to prison, she told the assistant district attorney during a recess that she couldn't see it through because she was pregnant by Blake. The attorney asked for a continuance, and Emily left the courthouse. "Blake ran after me and asked, 'What's going on?' And I told him, got in the car, made this crazy U-turn, and I drove."

Blake first convinced Emily not to have an abortion. "Then he said I didn't want my child to have its father in prison," she remembered. "'What are you going to tell it when it asks you where I am?' he said." That question brought up Emily's pain about her father's disappearance. "I couldn't sleep, I couldn't eat. I was losing it," she told me. Eventually, she told the ADA that she would not go forward with the rape case. She asked Blake to leave her alone. "But he just kept checking in with me, I guess to make sure that I didn't change my mind. When I was five months and a week pregnant, he told me that he was with another woman, that she was five months pregnant, and that she was moving in with him." Though Emily had not imagined building a life with him, she was crushed.

At the time, Emily was working at a day-care center. "I was a very happy, fun person," she said. "I was around kids all the time, and they were my life. But when I was at home, I turned off the lights, I came upstairs, and I just cried until six forty-five the next morning, when it was time to start work." Then Delia was born. "She was like a salve, like a panacea, which is a lot of responsibility for a newborn," Emily said. She began to think about the blank line on Delia's birth certificate, the one for the second parent, and she decided to add Blake's name in case Delia ever needed another close genetic relative for a medical emergency. What Emily hadn't considered was that Blake would be notified, and when she went to the courthouse to pick up the revised document, he was there. A judge granted him visitation rights. "I realized, 'He's going to be tied to me for the rest of my life,'" Emily said. "I didn't sleep for days before his first visit." So began an uneasy détente. Blake paid child support and saw Delia erratically for two years, then drifted away again. "I was so attached to Delia that I couldn't let go at all," Emily said. "When she was small, she was like a toy, so cute, all huge cheeks. But when she was about four, she started asking me questions about her father and where she came from, and it was like someone took a hammer and cracked me open and I spilled out all over the room."

By then, Emily was running a group of day-care centers. "And one day, I just stopped," she said, "like a clock stops working." She began having panic attacks, blackouts, olfactory hallucinations, and sudden flashes of disorientation. Her hair was falling out. Her doctor attributed the symptoms to stress and advised psychiatric counseling. "He said he wanted me to speak to somebody and he was going into his office to find some names of people he'd recommend," she said. "I don't remember anything after that, until I was in my office at school, and my phone was ringing, and my assistant was banging on my door. She said, 'Miss Emily, Miss Emily! Your doctor's been calling here for an hour. He said that you left your coat and shoes, and are you okay?'" Emily looked down and saw that she was in wet stockings; it was snowing outside.

Emily became intensely agoraphobic and lost her job. "I don't remember how Delia got food," she said. "It got done. I couldn't leave the house, except to go to therapy. Then I couldn't leave the room. I wasn't sleeping for days at a time. I was fragmenting." A psychiatrist put her on antidepressants, and she did constant talk therapy with him, and she gradually began to reemerge. "He saved me," she said. Just as she was getting it together, Blake turned up at the front door to say that he wanted to see Delia. The familiar cycle recurred. He would come occasionally to visit, then vanish, over and over. Emily decided she had to be strong for Delia and not keep her from her father, but Blake's motives always seemed unclear. "I didn't know what to do because he was her father, and she knew it," Emily said. "If something happened to me, he could get her. So I had to make sure he wouldn't hurt her, and the only way to do that was to let him know her so he would care about her."

Blake's attention was never reliable. "When he wasn't around, Delia sometimes said to me, 'I wish I had my daddy here,'" Emily recalled. "He'd be gone a year, and then he would show up. She would ask where he is, and I'd say, 'He's working, maybe,' or 'He'll come when he has time,' or 'Let's do something instead.' I redirected her for years and years, and every time she asked, I started cascading down a hill again." At seven, Delia broke her leg and began crying for her father, so Emily called Blake; he returned the call five months later and started coming over again. Emily had had a brief romance and given birth to a son, Gideon, seven years younger than Delia. Blake told Emily that she belonged to him and that her new child was a betrayal. The sexual brutality his argument implied frightened her, and she decided to flee, so she moved the kids back to Virginia.

When I met Emily, Delia was ten and had recently won a national academic award and matriculated in a magnet school for gifted children. "She's never asked about how she came to exist, and I know she wonders," her mother said. "She and I have had conversations about my prickliness, how I pull away. I would never, ever, ever tell her that it has anything to do with her. I always tell her it's because of me, and because my mom pulled away from me. But I don't do it with her brother." Emily had recently become engaged, and she told me that her fiancé, Jay, found this coldness toward Delia upsetting. Emily could not bring herself to tell him about Delia's origins in rape

"Fix me," Emily said to me as we sat on the floor of her office, late at night, doing this interview. "Why can't I hug my daughter? I love her, but when she touches me, it feels like hundreds of razor blades scraping across my skin, like I'm going to die. I understand that I just have to let her because she's a child, and so I do, but in my mind, I go someplace else, and I know that she knows it. So now she asks permission. I prepare myself. There are rules, like she can't come up behind me. Sometimes she forgets, and I'll jump, like a cat that you put water on, because her father had this stealth ability to just appear in front of you, and you don't know where he came from. She inherited that."

It has been hard working around so large a secret. "She wrote me a really sad letter, a year and a half ago," Emily said. "It said, 'This little girl misses New York. This little girl misses her father.'" When Jay accompanied Emily and her two kids to New York for the funeral of a family friend, he encouraged her to contact Blake for Delia's sake. So she did, arranging for them to spend an afternoon together. When he came to pick her up, he met Jay. The episode proved to be a turning point for Emily. "As soon as I got back to Virginia, my pregnancy, the incident, it all came into my brain and my body at the same time," Emily said. She finally told Jay the truth, and he was shocked.

"She looks like Blake in some ways, but not as much as she did when she was small," Emily added. "She reminds me of me, and I attempt to focus on that. Even if I don't always love myself, I can love myself in her. But there's that other part that makes me struggle every single day, because while most mothers just go with their natural instincts, my instincts are horrifying. It's a constant, conscious effort to keep my instincts from taking over."

The idea of rape within marriage was introduced in the late 1970s by Diana E. H. Russell, who maintained that 14 percent of married women had been raped by a husband. In the late eighties and early nineties, the marital exception to rape laws was gradually removed from the books in most states, despite spirited protests from the political Right, including some who claimed, echoing the misogyny of the colonial era, that accusations of rape within marriage would be used by vengeful wives to persecute innocent husbands. Instead, marital rape most commonly comes up in court within a larger pattern of domestic violence. Cases such as the 1989 Burnham case, in which a woman accused her husband of seventy counts of rape, were instrumental in this shift. Victor Burnham had over many years subjected his wife, Rebecca, to "beatings, being struck by gun butts, being held at gunpoint, being threatened with death, being tied up and raped, being forced to solicit strange men for sexual threesomes, being photographed in pornographic poses, being shocked with a cattle prod, and being forced to have sex with the family dog." The trial included both pictorial evidence and sworn testimony from men who had been "invited" by Burnham to have sex with his wife and declined, recognizing Rebecca's fear.

Louise McOrmond-Plummer, coauthor of *Real Rape, Real Pain* and herself a rape survivor, wrote, "The woman raped by her partner was routinely blamed and told that since her rapist was her partner, it wasn't 'real' rape. Women such as myself were being told that our pain was an overreaction; the fact of being in a relationship meant that any sexual rights were void."

Ashley Green is blonde, slender, and fragile as a reed. She radiates a longing for protection. Growing up with poor white parents in western Pennsylvania, where her father worked intermittently as a coal miner, she had little of it. Both parents were negligent, physically abusive drug users. When Ashley's father despaired of finding work, they moved to Florida. Ashley would often come home from school to find her depressed mother lying on the floor exactly where she had lain in the morning. Ashley was never sure whether there would be food to eat or when the electricity was going to be disconnected again. She had just turned sixteen when she met thirty-five-year-old Martin at a party. During the next year, he accompanied Ashley to church, paid for her to attend volleyball camp, suggested that he would get her a car. She already had a nineteen-year-old boyfriend, but she did not discourage Martin's friendship, which was nonsexual in a way characteristic of men who are grooming a victim.

Martin eventually said that he needed to hire someone to clean his apartment and suggested that Ashley take the job. "I cleaned for a couple of hours, thought I had done a good job, and he said, 'You need to do it again. This isn't clean enough,' and was very harsh with me." He offered her liquor; once she was drunk, he sodomized her twice anally.

In retrospect, the situation was clear to Ashley. "He knew what he had: a kid who wasn't being watched, who really wanted out of a very hostile and unpredictable home," she said. "He had food and transportation, these things my parents weren't going to provide. He had a nice apartment and a good job." Those advantages seemed like a step forward, so Ashley broke up with her boyfriend, dropped out of high school, and moved in with Martin. He turned out to be a drug user like her parents.

At seventeen, she became pregnant. Martin grew increasingly violent as the pregnancy progressed, beating Ashley so severely that she twice ran away to a shelter for battered women; once he stabbed her and she nearly died. "I was afraid he was either going to kill our child from beating me or take her from me when she was born," Ashley said. "I used to think if I could just take her from my stomach and hide her somewhere, maybe she would be born alive. I would pray, 'God, if you let my baby live, I'll be a good mother.'" In deference to her religious grandmother, Ashley married Martin just before their daughter was born. The beatings had put her repeatedly in preterm labor, a dangerous condition that can be brought on by stress; she held the pregnancy through multiple bouts, but when she felt the baby was really coming, she asked Martin to drive her to the hospital. He detoured to buy cocaine on the way, and Ashley arrived too late to receive licit drugs to blunt the pain of delivery.

Ashley instinctively loved her newborn girl, Sylvia, but had no idea what to do as a mother. "I was afraid of her. She was very colicky and very temperamental and cried day and night," Ashley remembered. The beatings continued, and sometimes Ashley could barely move. Ashley's aunt had persuaded her to report the abuse, so Martin moved them all to Alabama, beyond the reach of Florida law. When Sylvia was five months old, Ashley escaped with her to a shelter in Florida. They were allowed to stay for thirty days, and during that time Ashley got a driver's license, a car, and a job; arranged to stay with someone from her church until she found an apartment; and filed for divorce. When the baby would fall asleep, Ashley remembered, "I'd thank God I had her for one more day."

As the months passed, however, Ashley increasingly doubted her ability to take care of Sylvia on her own. When she worked, she lost food-stamp eligibility. Sylvia was getting sick frequently, so they needed better health insurance. So Ashley became a welfare mom, which meant better health care, but not enough money for rent. After a desperate year, she went back to Martin. "The day I packed my stuff, I still believed that he would get help and be okay," she said, "and we would be a family." Instead, Martin assaulted her sexually, then took Sylvia and sued for divorce. Ashley didn't see her daughter for three and a half months. Eventually she was granted joint custody, contingent on her continuing to live in Alabama. "It was like being held hostage," she said. Martin made a big show of his mistreatment of Sylvia. "He pulled up one day and there was marijuana smoke rolling out of the car. He actually tried to French-kiss her in front of me when she was three. She would come home with big bruises and knocks on her head."

Sylvia's underlying personality did not make things easier. "She was a very unhappy little baby, and I felt such guilt," Ashley said. "I was afraid to even bathe her, like her genital area. I was afraid I would do something because of the abuse I'd grown up with. She threw tantrums and pulled my hair out; she bloodied my nose one time. I got her a kitten when she was two. She would take that cat by the back legs and throw it on the couch, and she would sit on it and pull its whiskers out. I don't know if it's the violence that she's seen, the violence that's happening to her ongoing, what happened while she was still inside me and I was getting beat up, or if she was just born like him."

Ashley felt powerless. "When she was five, I was bathing her one day in the tub with me, and she told me that her dad and her did the same thing. I called a therapist, and she said, 'Don't ask her any more questions. Just bring her in.' It was worse than I had thought. The psychologist said that he was not only bathing with her, but he was having her wash his genitals, and doing things around her private area." Ashley filed for a protective order; Martin brought a countersuit seeking exclusive custody on grounds that Ashley was lying. Ashley had a clean record; Martin had previous convictions for drug possession and for beating Ashley and had been put in court-ordered therapy for violence. In the Alabama courts, however, he won. After the ruling, Ashley attempted suicide. Sylvia later complained to Ashley that Martin had walked in on her naked, climbed in the shower with her, hit her, and denied her food and medical care. Ashley returned to court and sued for custody again, appearing before the same judge. "I had tape-recorded phone conversations of her telling me about all this abuse, but he didn't allow me to play them. Instead, he ordered I would have to pay all of my husband's legal bills, fourteen thousand dollars. Now I'm terrified they're going to put me in jail."

She finally gave up on her daughter. "It's just too much trauma," Ashley said. "It's not that I don't love her. It's not that I don't want her to be free from that. It's that for whatever reason, God has seen fit for her to be there. God has seen fit for us not to have a relationship. And I've done everything I can do."

At twenty-six, Ashley decided to go to college. She graduated with a 3.8 average and became a qualified community counselor. Like Marina James, Brenda Henriques, Lisa Boynton, and Tina Gordon, Ashley has helped herself by helping others—but she has worked with offenders, not just with victims. "Most of them, the higher-functioning ones, were very socially skilled. They seemed like the nicest people you could ever meet, some of them; they're very socially skilled and they make people very comfortable, and that's how they accomplish what they do and that's how they keep their victims quiet. So, I learned a great deal when I was there and did a lot of healing of my own, and I think helped other people heal, offenders heal."

Eventually she met a man with whom she bore another daughter, in a "consensual, child-wanting, of-age, in-love relationship." Alicia was born with profound hearing loss in her left ear; her acquisition of speech was delayed and her articulation poor. After she was diagnosed with other delays, her father left, unable to cope. "She's a special-needs child, and that can be very trying at times, but I have very different feelings for Alicia versus Sylvia," Ashley said. "I think she's the reason I graduated with my bachelor's—and the reason I lived." Still, the shadow of Sylvia's deterioration loomed, especially when Alicia reached the age at which Sylvia had been taken away from her mother. "I looked at her last night. She was sleeping. And she looked a little bit like Sylvia, and I had to turn my head because I'm afraid she's going to die or I'm going to lose custody of her. I think this is the time to talk about statutory rape and how damaging it is: the injustice of having a child with an adult more than twice my age. I know that probably doesn't sound as serious as some stranger holding you down and forcibly raping you, but it has been for me and for our child, who will never be okay."

Statutory rape is a category that has often been abused. Someone I interviewed was arrested when he was found having sex with his girlfriend, who was six months younger than he, an underage seventeen to his legally adult eighteen, even though his girlfriend's parents approved of the relationship. The principle that no one over the age of eighteen should ever be allowed to have carnal relations with anyone under the age of eighteen can be hard to defend in such circumstances. It is nonetheless evident that in many situations statutory rape is rape. The influence men such as Martin can have over young girls who have been neglected or ill-treated by their own parents is difficult to exaggerate.

At fourteen, Sylvia appeared destroyed by her young lifetime of abuse. "She dresses like a boy," Ashley said. "You can't really tell that she's a girl. She's filthy and she smells horrible. She has psychotic-type symptoms." Talking about it, Ashley began to cry, then to stutter. Apologizing, she said, "The last visit I had with her, she told me she heard voices. One of the things that she talked about was her dad would come while she was changing clothes or showering, which is why now she doesn't shower and doesn't change her clothes."

Ashley is unable to work because she is taking care of Alicia full-time; she lives on less than $300 a month in an income-based apartment. Although she no longer sees Sylvia, she still pays child support to her onetime rapist out of the child support that she gets for Alicia. She has taken down all the pictures of Sylvia. "I have physical scars on my body from his abuse of me," Ashley said. "He's made her into another scar. I can't even stand to look at her. I would welcome her with open arms, I would go to therapy with her, but I would probably not let her in my home. I would be afraid she would abuse Alicia. I wish I had never had her. If I could go back, I would have aborted or I would have given her up for adoption. It hasn't been fair to me and it hasn't been fair to her."

A recent study has identified "coerced childbearing as a weapon in the arsenal of power and control." Numerous women who have been raped within relationships speak of the rape as a means used by a man to keep her under his thumb, the classic ploy of domination by keeping a wife "barefoot and pregnant." Women in surveys have variously said, "He raped me to keep me pregnant all the time because he knew I would never leave the kids," and "They own you when you have a child by him—part of the purpose in having a baby is to control you." As the mothers' children bear witness to ongoing sexual violence, they are more likely to be traumatized, and to be both victims of and perpetrators of sexual abuse themselves.

Although no one ever deserves to be raped, a woman's actions can have an enormous impact on her own safety. Yet some women repeatedly put themselves in situations of extreme vulnerability. Most of us anticipate bad things that could happen, but some are capable of reacting only to events that have already occurred. Talking to many women who had borne children of rape, I was struck by their inability to foresee the likelihood of danger inherent in their choices. Every bad thing that befell them, even at the hands of previous aggressors, came as a surprise. They could not tell the difference between people who warranted trust and those who didn't. They lacked guiding intuition and were blind to bad character until it manifested itself.

Nearly all such women I met had not been cherished or protected as children. At the most basic level, they did not know what caring behavior felt like, so they were unable to recognize it. Some were desperate for love and attention, which made them easy targets. Most were so familiar with neglect or abuse that they accepted it when it came their way; for many, abuse was synonymous with intimacy. Some who actively strove to improve their situation found themselves merely repeating their past; they kept falling back into the familiar muck.

It is difficult to imagine who Mindy Woods might be if her uncle had not started molesting her when she was ten. He lived next door in their small town in the Midwest. He molested her older sister for nine years, and Mindy every week or so for seven, sometimes while his own young daughters were in the room. He started in with their cousin when she was a small child, but she put a stop to it at thirteen, when she filed a police report. A detective came over to interview Mindy, but she clammed up. Her uncle negotiated a plea bargain, resulting in nothing more than community service and a fine. "My grandma saw it," Mindy recalled, "and she just used to call my sister and me sluts—ten-year-old sluts, quite a concept." In pictures of Mindy from third grade, she's a little slip of a girl. The next year, after the abuse began, she was twice as heavy, and by her senior year of high school, she weighed 275 pounds.

Mindy went off to college, but came home after three months. At twenty-one, she married "the first guy that ever let me cry all night and just held me." She tried to have children but was unable to conceive and could not find sexual satisfaction in her marriage. She divorced at twenty-five and traveled around the country with a truck driver she met on the Internet, eventually getting a trucker's license herself. Seeking to be subjugated by powerful "masters," she entered into the world of BDSM (bondage, discipline, sadomasochism). "My uncle made me that way. He molded me sexually," she said. "I don't think it's wanting to be a victim again. I think it's more analyzing. I want to figure out what I was feeling, what was going through my mind, and why the hell I let him do it."

BDSM relationships are supposed to be guided by mutuality; the slave consents to be led by her master, who putatively treats her with respect even as he commands her behavior. Seeking such a master, Mindy met a man from Michigan online; he turned out to be a psychopath. "You can be somebody who punishes somebody, who sets down rules and expects you to obey them, and still be a loving person," Mindy said. "There's a difference between punishment and abuse. A master is supposed to have love and respect for the submissive. It's called a gift of submission." The Michigander had erectile dysfunction owing to diabetes and never had intercourse with her; instead he raped her with objects, including a broomstick. He kept her locked in the house and told her that the neighbors were paid to call him if she tried to leave. It took her three months to escape. She was able to get online long enough to find "a place set up to rescue submissives who needed help," and the people there took her to a safe house.

When she left the safe house, she went to stay with a friend, Mamie, who was getting ready to be married and had asked Mindy to be her maid of honor. Mamie was pregnant and living with her fiancé, who was flirtatious in what Mindy took to be a friendly way. "It was in front of his wife-to-be, and she laughed," Mindy said, "so I thought it was okay." Mindy came down with a bad flu shortly after she arrived and started taking codeine cough syrup. She woke one night, groggy and confused, to find Mamie's fiancé having sex with her, whispering in her ear that he was going to make her pregnant. "I thought it was some weird nightmare from the codeine," she said. Mindy had learned with her uncle how to pretend that sexual assaults were not happening, and she woke up the next day and went about her business as usual. The second time, he put a pillow over her face to prevent her from crying out. The third time, Mamie walked in just as he was finishing up, and her fiancé said that he had been giving Mindy a massage for her back problems. Mindy remained mute and submissive. "I was just so afraid," Mindy said. "He knew I was extremely vulnerable and he knew that I didn't prosecute my uncle, that I didn't prosecute the idiot in Michigan—he knew my history of just letting things drop." Mindy stayed on at the house and was maid of honor at the wedding.

When she got home, Mindy went to her gynecologist and said she had been raped. She found out that she was pregnant. "I didn't have the money to get an abortion myself," she said. "I knew my parents would have shunned me if they'd found out. My mom is a born-again Christian. So if I still wanted to be in the family, I needed to keep the kid." Mindy went into a severe depression, and the fibromyalgia from which she had long suffered began to escalate, putting her in constant pain. "If I had not been pregnant, I probably would have killed myself," she recalled. "I've thought about suicide my whole life, ever since my uncle."

When she was four months along, Mindy met Larry Foster, and she was still with him four years later when I was introduced to her. "He knew everything before he decided to move in with me," Mindy told me. He was in the delivery room when she gave birth to Gretel and put his name on her birth certificate. Mindy was relieved when she had a girl. "I haven't had very good luck with males," she said. Mindy, who

weighs over three hundred pounds, wears both the collar of her submission to Larry and a pentacle that signifies her Wiccan belief system.
"I'm not Miss Betty Crocker or Martha Stewart or a neat freak who
bakes and has dresses, like his mom and grandma, but they're relatively
accepting," she said. Still, she feels unequal to motherhood. "Part of
being a mom is actually exerting a little authority over a kid. I'm submissive. I have no authority."

Having your mother in a dog collar, obeying orders, does not necessarily help build a little girl's self-esteem. Mindy sometimes calls Larry
"Master" around the house. Gretel calls him "Daddy." "I would get
upset with her if she called him Larry, just the same as I would get upset
with her if she called him Master, and to me that's just a normal parent
thing," Mindy said. She thinks she will eventually have to tell Gretel
about her biological father, "but for now, I want her to just know Larry
as Daddy."

Mindy takes medication for depression, diabetes, and fibromyalgia. "It's hard for me sometimes to get my mind clear enough to form
a sentence," she said. "There are times I can't pick Gretel up. I'll sit
down and she'll crawl up in my lap, but if she starts squirming around,
I can't take it. That's driving a wedge between her and me." The relationship with Gretel has some of the same quality of resignation that
typifies Mindy's submissive relationships with men. "She is a constant
reminder," Mindy said. "She's annoying, but what three-year-old isn't?
There have been a lot of times that I've wanted to drop her off at a
street corner somewhere and leave. I want to blame the fact that I don't
have a life on her. Then I think about it, and I do have a life. My life
is her. And once I get into that mentality, I love her to death." Then,
in the next breath, Mindy added, "I still wish I'd miscarried and didn't
have her."

Mindy writes poetry and fiction based in the BDSM world, almost
all of it about young girls being brutally ravaged by older men. For
Mindy Woods, there is always something beautiful in ruthlessness—it
repels and compels her and she writes of cruelty with hapless pleasure.
"I even cry about some of the stuff I write," Mindy said. It's hard not to
see elements of both Mindy and Gretel in the little girls who are tortured in these stories, hard not to see Mindy's anger and ambivalence
toward her daughter as anger at her own young self that allowed the
original abuse.

Mindy inhabits a world where choice and helplessness are impossibly blurred. Many of the women I interviewed who were raising children born as a result of rape have emerged from trauma into at least
superficially ordinary lives. Others, such as Mindy, remain at the outer

margins. Mindy represents the weirdness into which a woman can descend after childhood sexual abuse. Some women are damaged in ways that make them deeply alien. They manifest their scars by vanishing into netherworlds as sordid and disturbing as the events they have survived. Damage has lasting consequences.

Many parents and children I met who had coped with the obstacles associated with exceptional differences wanted to affirm their positive experiences and stand as models for others. Many had emerged from difficulty as better people and were eager to share their triumphs. By contrast, the mothers of children conceived in rape sought validation. Even if they had built fulfilling parental bonds, their child's identity had not transformed them. Most children of rape know that; they sense the festering penumbra of loss that shrouds them even before they slip into the world. Someone who does not share the defining condition might disavow the stigma attached to deafness or dwarfism without compunction, but it is almost inconceivable not to be repulsed by rape, and that taint haunts raped women and their rape-conceived children. Who, in this age of genetic determinism, could announce that his father was a rapist and not expect some degree of disquiet to ensue?

Even if being a child of rape may never become a celebrated identity, it may become a more socially accepted one, thanks to the improved educational, legal, and psychological handling of rape in recent decades. The less forbidden a topic rape is and the more easily its survivors can reach one another, the greater the likelihood that mothers and children will find the horizontal communities they need. Even without such support, some women manage to harness their trauma to good parenting—and a few even believe that reckoning with shocking violence has made them better parents than any less fearful history would have done.

Barbara Schmitz grew up on a farm in northern Nebraska in the 1970s. "My main memories of my childhood are being afraid and being very, very lonely," she said. Her brother, Jim, and sister, Elaine, were five and seven years older, respectively, and her school had only ten students, just one of them her age. Her mother was violent and unpredictable. "She used to beat Jim with a wooden hanger, and I'd be down at the end of the hallway, feeling helpless. When I got to the age where I could outrun her, she would torture my dog and cat in front of me to make me come back, because she knew that I would rather be beaten myself than have my animals hurt. Even my animals that I loved were used against me."

Her father was sexually abusive. She remembers his exposing his erect penis to her; other memories are hazier and more sinister. Once Elaine and Jim started high school, she and her father were often alone at home in the afternoons. "My dad had a room in the basement with this creaky, old cot, and I have memories of lying on that cot, knowing the door was locked, and my dad being there. There was a window above my head, and I would picture myself turning into a white bird and flying out through that window." Her vaginal area was chronically inflamed, and her mother told her to put Chap Stick on it. When Barbara was thirteen, her mother got her a spaghetti-strap dress for a wedding, and Barbara had put it on and was sitting on the kitchen counter, talking to her mother. "My dad got up and went into the bathroom down the hall, and when I looked, he was standing there with an erection. I turned to my mom, and she said, 'Cover yourself up.' So my mom knew."

Barbara recalled getting a particularly bad beating from her mother when she was nine or ten. "I was down on the floor, and she had these orthopedic shoes, and she was kicking my head. I bit her ankle and went running down to the basement, 'cause I knew where my dad kept the pistol. And she came after me. She had fists and this rage on her face. And then she saw the gun, and her face just went from rage to fear. I remember saying, 'If you come one step closer, I will shoot you.' She turned around and went back upstairs." After her mother would beat Barbara, she would make brownies. "That was her way of apologizing," Barbara remembered. "And if I didn't eat them, that meant that I didn't love her. So I got fat. Elaine is very pretty and thin and always had the new clothes, and I was always wearing the hand-me-downs. My mom dressed her up and let her be a cheerleader and in Girl Scouts. But Elaine was nice to me; the few times I remember being tucked into bed and hugged, it was Elaine who did it."

Barbara's best friend was her border collie, Pumpkin. Her father would make her beat the animal with a whip, and when Pumpkin had puppies, when Barbara was nine, he put them in a gunnysack with a brick and threw them in the creek. Barbara used to climb the hill behind the house and seek out tranquillity and peace. "I would talk to God a lot," she recalled. "I'd be like, 'Why are you letting this happen to me?' I was pissed at Him for a long time."

She remembers herself as "a mean little kid" who would cut off her dolls' heads and kick her older sister for no reason. "It was okay to be angry in my family. It was not okay to cry." When she started to weep after spraining her ankle as a teenager, her father slapped her repeatedly, telling her to shut up. Barbara longed for approval. "You know how a dog would rather be beaten, just to get attention that way, than be ignored?" So she started lifting fifty-pound bags of seed corn and doing other heavy farm chores; by way of reward, her father taught her how to play poker and how to fish.

Barbara finally escaped by going to college in Lincoln. During rush week for fraternity and sorority candidates, Barbara went to a big party, and a guy who seemed nice invited her over to see his frat house. He got her drunk on beer. "The next thing I remember, I was on the bed and being raped," she said. "I remember screaming, 'No!' and trying to fight. But I was still very drunk, and he was very strong. I still had my hymen, so there was lots of blood." As soon as he got off her, she crawled into the bathroom and locked the door; when she came out, he handed her $5. Back at her dorm, she took a three-hour hot shower and then stayed in bed for two days.

In the aftermath, her new life at college quickly began to fall apart. She became bulimic, using food to stifle her pain, just as she had been taught to do as a child. She began binge drinking and stopped going to classes. A few months later, she met Jeffrey, a friend of her room-mate's boyfriend. "Our relationship very quickly became about sex," she said. "It was not tender or emotional or even pleasurable for me." But it did help her begin to function again, and she and Jeffrey gradu-ated together. "It was like, 'Okay, what do you want to do now?'" So they got married. "I chose Jeffrey because he was emotionally distant," she said.

They moved to Omaha and threw themselves into their careers; Barbara worked seventy-five hours a week. "It was a great way to avoid going home, because there was nothing to go home for," she said. She told her doctor that her energy was flagging, and he prescribed an antidepressant. It helped her be more engaged and energetic, but she resumed binge drinking, which dulled her intense anxiety. Even though she was terrified of intimacy, she was also starved for affection, so she started casting about extramaritally. She met someone in an online sex chat room who was a born-again Christian. "He talked so much about love, and things that were very new to me," she recalled. "He opened the door for me to accepting Christ—which is odd, from a sex chat room. After that, there was always the sense that God was there some-where." One evening, she went into the bathroom and started to cry. "I got down on my knees, and I said, 'Please, before I die, just let me know what real love is.'"

When Dan O'Brien came into her life not long afterward, she thought he was the answer to that prayer. She had a new job for a big agricultural corporation, running support for a sales team in the Pacific

Northwest. She'd stay at work an extra hour to accommodate the time difference, and Dan, one of her long-distance clients, started calling her at the end of the day. He was fighting for custody of his three-year-old son and would send Barbara photos of the boy and ask for advice. "He was also asking me a lot of really personal questions. A lot of 'Why are you there so late? Why aren't you going home to your husband? Do you guys even sleep together anymore?'"

Barbara thought she had finally found her prince. She told Jeffrey all about him, and while her husband resented the new attachment, by then they were living such separate lives that he couldn't exercise much authority. Barbara and Dan would talk to each other for hours every night. "Dan was basically my dad, all over again," Barbara said, "but Dan was telling me how smart I was and feeding my ego. He loved me; he wanted to marry me; he wanted to have children with me. He would have moved to Omaha, but he had a little boy, so I needed to move to California. Now, keep in mind: we had never met each other."

She finally told Jeffrey that she was going out West to see Dan, and Jeffrey drove her to the airport. "The reality, of course, could not live up to my huge fantasy," she recalled. "I felt very much out of place, almost like I was watching myself in this play." They slept together right off the bat, using condoms, and although she still found no pleasure in sex, everything was relatively normal until they had an argument. "He grabbed me and threw me down, literally ripped off my clothes, and was inside of me before I even realized what was going on. What he was doing hurt. Afterwards, he said, 'Didn't you like that?' and went into the living room to watch TV."

Barbara didn't initially admit to herself that she'd been raped, but she felt as though her world were dissolving around her. She called Jeffrey and said she was coming home. In Omaha, she tried to pretend that nothing had happened, but when she found out that she was pregnant, she called Dan and told him, still half thinking that they might embark on a new life together. He accused her of getting pregnant so he would marry her. She didn't seriously consider an abortion: "I didn't think the child was real enough to even consider an abortion." Instead, she simply told her husband, "We're pregnant." They hadn't had sex in months, but Jeffrey was in denial as much as she was, and he accepted the fiction.

Barbara's life became increasingly surreal. Dan threatened her because he was worried that she would hound him for child support. Jeffrey played the role of the dutiful expectant father, going to Lamaze class and getting her Arby's in the middle of the night when she craved potato cakes. "But there was no love there," Barbara recalled. "I was working during the day, going through the motions. At night, I was lying on the bathroom floor crying and asking God to kill me." She didn't fully register that she was going to have a baby until she was in the delivery room. "And when I saw Pauline, it was just like 'Holy shit, there's a baby!'"

Maternal feelings did not set in. Barbara breast-fed and took care of her daughter, but she did so without love. "She was adorable, but when I looked at her, I saw Dan. I just wanted to die." One of her friends, who worked in a therapist's office, recognized that Barbara was in terrible shape and made a counseling appointment on her behalf; Barbara didn't have the energy to say no. Three months into therapy, Barbara read a book about boundaries. "There I am, right on page eight. This woman in her thirties was talking about things that her father would do. Such as come into the bathroom when she was in there naked, or urinate in front of her. And it said that was 'covert sexual abuse.' My entire life, I sensed that there was something really wrong with me. I suddenly saw that it was something that was done to me, that I couldn't help, and that's why I'm this way. I went and woke up Jeffrey and had him read that. He looked right at me and said, 'I always knew something had to have happened.'"

Barbara and her therapist began to talk about Barbara's childhood, and then about Dan, and Barbara finally identified what had happened to her as rape. She finally started to feel angry at Dan, and the angrier she grew, the more fiercely she began to love Pauline. "I'd be nursing her, and I'd just cry because she'd come from this horrible thing, but she was just so beautiful." The next step was to admit Pauline's parentage to Jeffrey. Jeffrey replied, "There's a part of me that wants to kick you out and never see you again, but that's not what I really want. So let's work this out." They entered marriage counseling, and later, he started individual therapy. Once he understood on an intellectual level how the relationship with Dan could have happened, he made peace with it and took responsibility for his part in their hollow marriage.

Jeffrey admitted to me that the outcome would have been different if he'd known from the start it was Dan's baby. "But Pauline was six months old before I found out," Jeffrey said, "and I already loved her. She was mine, whatever the biology was, and I couldn't give her up. That helped me to see that I really loved Barbara, too." Barbara, in turn, watching him snuggling with Pauline, "started to see the truth about Jeffrey—that he was so much better than I'd known—and the truth about Dan, that he was so much worse."

Barbara's parents found out that Dan was Pauline's father because

Dan had his girlfriend call them. At the farm for Christmas, Barbara and Jeffrey were sitting in the living room one night, holding Pauline, when Barbara's mother suddenly asked, "Was I good to you when you were growing up?" Barbara said, "No, you weren't." Her mother said, "I hit you once, and you deserved it." Then she told them to leave the farm and warned Barbara that if she ever returned she'd put a bullet through her head. A year later, Barbara's father sent her a card with a picture of her sitting on his lap. He wrote, "I'm really going to miss seeing Pauline grow up." Later, he called and said, "If you don't stop talking about how I sexually abused you, I'm going to kill you." But Barbara had already made the quiet passage to activism, which is incompatible with secrecy. She gave an interview to a local newspaper; she had her picture taken for inclusion in a project about women who have been raped and abused. Eventually, she testified in front of the Nebraska legislature and helped to get a law passed to abolish the statute of limitations for sex offenders.

When I visited Barbara and Jeffrey in Omaha, Pauline was six; she struck me as a cheerful little girl, easy to talk to, and cuddly with both parents. She wanted their attention, but seemed content to explore and return. "I never got the basics about love or even kindness," Barbara said. "It's like beginning a whole new language when you're forty: it's a lot harder than if you've heard people speaking it since you were a kid." She shuddered. "One time I gave her a hard swat, and the look on her face was devastating. That was enough to know, 'Okay, I'm never doing that again.' I don't want to turn into my parents."

Barbara has built a happy family on the ruins of a dysfunctional one. At the time of our initial conversation, she and Jeffrey had been married eighteen years. She was learning new social skills alongside her daughter. "I used to always wait for people to come up to me," she said. Then she started initiating contact, and teaching Pauline to do the same. "I'd say, 'What would be a good way to make a friend, do you think?' I'd take her to the park and practice. As we were parenting her, I was parenting myself. I had reached the point in my life where I had to start living as a real person, or I just didn't want to live. I mean, I gave Pauline life, but, in so many ways, she gave it to me. Pauline has the freedom to think for herself. I had some freedom, too, and I had a choice, too. I could have been my mother, and instead I decided to heal myself. My heart is very heavy for my whole family—even my dad. They're not bad people, really." She remembered the plea she'd made to God on her knees in the bathroom, years earlier, to know love before she died. "I thought that Dan was the answer to that prayer," she said. "But now I see that Pauline is the answer. Pauline was also the instrument. I opened my heart up to God first, then Pauline, then Jeffrey. Then I just thought, 'Okay, who's next?'"

Rape-derived pregnancy has come under specific scrutiny in the context of genocidal rape. If one's goal were to extirpate a race, one might imagine that the most appropriate tactic would be forced sterilization. In many armed conflicts, however, the conquerors impregnate the conquered race, who perforce deliver babies to the victors. This pervasive phenomenon is called *forced pregnancy*. A report from the War and Children Identity Project estimates some half a million people living now were so conceived. The British psychiatrist Ruth Seifert wrote, "The rape of women communicates from man to man, so to speak, that the men around the women in question are not able to protect 'their' women." Susan Brownmiller describes this full-scale invasion of women's bodies as "an extracurricular battlefield." There is a huge difference between these cases and the pregnancies through rape that occur in peacetime in the developed world, where being pregnant doesn't get you killed, doesn't mean you will be banned from your community, doesn't make you unmarriageable. In the West, one can hide a child's origins; one can give him up for adoption. Women who acknowledge and keep these children can often find men won't care where their child came from. The ethnic issues in many conflict zones, however, leave women pregnant from rape with no way to hide their story. The family knows; the community knows; there is no continuity with their previous life.

The genocide in Rwanda began on April 6, 1994, after the plane of President Juvénal Habyarimana was shot down. In the hundred days that followed, eight hundred thousand members of the minority Tutsi ethnic group were killed. Unlike the Nazi-perpetrated Holocaust, where the killings were clinical, systematic, and remote, the Rwandan mass butchery was a hands-on affair. The killings were committed by the Interahamwe—youth militias of the majority Hutu ethnicity—and farmers, mainly with farm implements, and persisted until Tutsi forces regained the capital city of Kigali. Now the Hutus again live under a largely Tutsi regime and feel enslaved by a hated minority, while the Tutsis loathe the Hutus for having murdered their families. In official interviews, Rwandans say, *"Plus jamais"* (Never again), but in private, most of the people I met said another eruption was only a matter of time.

A Rwandan proverb says, "A woman who is not yet battered is not a real woman." The culture's underlying misogyny was easily stoked by ethnic propaganda. By some estimates, as many as half a million women were raped during the paroxysm of terror, and subsequently they gave birth to as many as five thousand children. One woman recounted having a member of the murderous youth brigades back her up against a wall and then take his knife to her vagina, cutting out the entire lining of it, and hanging the gory tube of flesh from a stick outside her house. Many Hutus perceived Tutsi women—who tend to be tall, slender, and regal—as haughty and were determined to teach them a lesson. They raped not only to humiliate and shame their victims, but also as a way of killing; many of the men were HIV-positive and were encouraged by their leaders to infect as many Tutsi women as possible. About half of the Tutsi women who survived the genocide had been raped, and most of those contracted HIV.

The children produced through Rwanda's genocidal rapes are called *les enfants de mauvais souvenir*, or "the children of bad memories"; one writer called them the "living legacy of a time of death." Rwandan society blames the women, so these pregnancies were "rejected and concealed, often denied and discovered late," according to Dr. Catherine Bonnet, who studied the Rwandan rape problem. She observed that these women often self-induced abortion, attempted suicide, or committed infanticide. Some women left rape babies on church steps; the country is peppered with orphanages.

To understand how children of wartime rape differ from children conceived in less systematic rapes, I traveled to Rwanda in 2004, at the tenth anniversary of the genocide. I could not identify women who had abandoned or killed their children; the women I saw had kept their children. Many had been cast out by their families, who wanted nothing to do with "the child of an Interahamwe," and most were struggling to feed themselves and their children. The *enfants de mauvais souvenir* are accepted by neither Hutus nor Tutsis, and some Rwandan hospitals refuse to treat them. Jean Damascene Ndayambaje, head of the Department of Psychology at the National University of Rwanda, explained that it was considered a disgrace for the women to have allowed themselves to be raped rather than killed.

Espérance Mukamana, who works for AVEGA, the widows' organization in Rwanda, said that most of these castoff mothers "never find true love for their children. They love them enough to survive, but no more." Ndayambaje described how one woman had to be physically restrained while doctors performed a cesarean because she had clenched her vaginal muscles tightly in a last-ditch attempt to prevent the birth. When the doctors brought her the baby, she began ranting and was placed in a psychiatric hospital. Some mothers gave their children names such as War or Child of Hate or Little Killer. Mukamana said, "The children know that their mothers don't love them, but they don't know why. They speak and their mothers don't listen to them; they cry and their mothers don't comfort them. So they develop strange behaviors. They themselves are cold and restless."

Unlike most rape survivors, those in Rwanda have the solace and solidarity of a horizontal identity as members of an acknowledged group. Alphonsine Nyirahabimana, who works with wartime rape survivors and their children at AVEGA, said, "No one can forget what happened to them, so they might as well remember together." Some women who had conceived children in rape gained enough strength from this group identity to compensate for their loss of traditional social position. Professor Célestin Kalimba, head of the history department at the National University, said that a new Rwandan feminism has been among the accidental side effects of the genocide. "So much of the male population is either dead or in jail," he said, "and women have to step into major roles." The mothers who endured forced pregnancy emerged from the war as victims, entered a culture that further victimized them, and had to struggle toward a new society—if not for themselves, then for their castigated children.

At thirty-four, Marie Rose Matamura narrated the events of her life in an even monotone, with an air of complete resignation. When the genocide began, she fled to her church, but militias soon arrived and, with her priest's consent, killed almost all the people gathered there. She escaped, but was seized by a Hutu man who claimed her and her sister as his wives. This was not uncommon; many of the militia would force women into sexual slavery, cynically using the word *wife* to euphemize a multitude of sins. Marie Rose's acquiescence to her captor did not obviate her hatred of him. "In the road, hiding, you meet such a man," she said. "He would just go walking around the neighborhood raping the ladies. At any time this man could force me to accept his friends; I was raped by many others. He told me that he had given me HIV so he didn't have to waste time killing me."

Marie Rose's captor fled when the Tutsi forces approached; weak and desperate, Marie Rose and her sister remained in his house. After a medical exam, they learned that they both did, in fact, have HIV and were both pregnant. Marie Rose's sister died on Christmas Day 2001. Marie Rose took on her sister's son and has brought him up with her own daughter. "I am trying to forget what happened and concentrate on feeding them," she told me. "I can't hate my own child or my sister's child, though I never forget where they came from. The children ask me sometimes, 'Who is my father?' and I tell them that they don't have a father, that they never did."

Marie Rose had begun to develop skin lesions and feared that her neighbors recognized them as a symptom of AIDS. "I don't know who will take care of the children when I go," she said. "I go from door to door, asking people if they have dirty clothes to be washed; I braid hair for rich Hutu women with husbands. I feel so sad that I will die—not sad for myself, but for the children. Someday, I will have to tell them the truth. I think all the time about how I will do it and make up the speeches. I will tell them how to behave correctly, and what to do if someone tries to rape them. I fear what they will become with me; I fear what they will become after that, without me."

Rape has been used strategically since ancient times, and recently in at least thirty-six conflicts, including those in Bangladesh, Chechnya, Guatemala, several African nations, East Timor, and the former Yugoslavia. A Human Rights Watch report explained, "These incidents of rape are clearly aimed to subjugate, humiliate, and terrorize the entire community, not just the women and girls raped by the militias." Western observers reported mass suicides of pregnant Chinese women following the Rape of Nanking during the Sino-Japanese War in 1937, and many half-Japanese babies were objects of infanticide. After the Bangladeshi conflict, the prime minister called the women who had borne children of rape "national heroines," but many of them nonetheless left their babies in dustbins, and those who kept them were never accepted back into society. After the Kosovo war, a young man in Pristina told the *Observer*, "If I were normal, I would keep the kid, accept my wife. But in our culture, death is better than rape. I could not accept my wife. She would be dirty, evil, the castle of the enemy. A lot of women have been very sensible. They have kept quiet, they have given birth at home, and if they are even more sensible, they kill their scum babies." One of the victims of wartime rape in Sarajevo said, "It was a hard birth. It hurt a lot. But after what the Chetniks did to me, it wasn't anything." She never even looked at the baby. "If anyone had tried to show it to me after it was born, I'd have strangled them and the baby, too."

The journalist Helena Smith wrote about a woman named Mirveta who gave birth to a child conceived in rape in Kosovo. Mirveta was twenty and illiterate; her husband had abandoned her because of the pregnancy. "He was a healthy little boy and Mirveta had produced him," Smith writes. "But birth, the fifth in her short lifetime, had not brought joy, only dread. As the young Albanian mother took the child, she prepared to do the deed. She cradled him to her chest, she looked into her boy's eyes, she stroked his face, and she snapped his neck." She then handed the infant back to the nurses, in tears. "In her psychiatric detention cell," Smith noted, "she has been weeping ever since."

After the Interahamwe killed her husband, Marianne Mukamana went to the militia's base and offered herself, believing it was the only way to save her five-year-old daughter. She was raped countless times in the ensuing weeks and told that she would eventually be killed; instead, she was freed by the Tutsi forces. When Marianne delivered a second daughter nine months after the genocide, she felt a surge of loathing for the baby. Marianne was HIV-positive; her new daughter tested positive as well. "I wanted to throw her away," she recalled. "But then another heart came in me." She resolved that she would teach herself to love her two girls equally. She told me that she felt the same about both daughters, but when I asked whether she would still give the younger one away, she said that she would. The elder daughter is pure Tutsi and looks it; the younger has dark coloring and Hutu features. Neighbors say that they can't be full sisters, but Marianne tells them not to believe the lies of the street. "On my deathbed they will ask me why I am dying so young, and I will tell them everything."

The two girls are competitive for their mother's love. The tradition in Rwanda is that the youngest child is the most beloved, and for Marianne it has been hard to embody that cultural expectation. "I will die of AIDS, and my older daughter will be left alone," she said. "The reason is in the rape that made my younger daughter. How to know that without being angry? I try not to think of the past, because I am afraid of it, and I also don't think of the future, because now I know better than to have dreams."

Given the burdens associated with keeping such children in conflict zones—the loss of social status, the dimmed prospects of marriage—the number of mothers who do so regardless is astonishing. But though they often keep these children in good faith, they cannot necessarily provide them with adequate support. "I was used like a horse by the Indonesian soldiers who took me in turns and made me bear so many children," said a rape survivor in East Timor. "Now I no longer have the strength to push my children towards a better future."

A recent report noted that children of rape "become the symbol of the trauma the nation as a whole went through, and society prefers not to acknowledge their needs." Often, these children face legal problems. Nationality is commonly passed down paternally, so without a father, the child may be stateless. Zahra Ismail of the European

University Centre for Peace Studies explained, "This creates a problem for ensuring fundamental social benefits for children, as international law on children's human rights is based on an assumption of state
responsibility." In Vietnam, children of mixed race were called "dust of
life" after the war and denied education and medical care because they
had not been registered by their fathers; some mutilated themselves in
attempts to look more American or more Asian. Children of Bosnian
rape victims who sought refuge in Croatia were denied citizenship.
Children born to raped Kuwaiti women following the Iraqi occupation of 1990 still have no citizenship. Ismail argues that such children
are "also, albeit secondarily, victims of the rape, who are denied their
basic rights." She continues, "Forced pregnancy has so far been treated
solely as a women's issue, not giving children born of war any consideration. This not only led to their marginalization but also contributed
to their being overlooked as victims, and later being somehow cast into
the perpetrator camp."

The UN Convention on the Rights of the Child holds that children
should have the right of citizenship. It does not, however, separately
address the rights of children born of rape, nor contain any guarantee
of equal treatment for children born out of wedlock. Foreigners frequently wish to adopt these children, but embarrassed governments
ban or complicate that process for the sake of national identity. Governments in the countries where parents hope to adopt these children
often make policy that feeds into such shame. The UK, for example,
tried to facilitate the adoption of Balkan rape babies, but would not
grant rape victims the chance to immigrate to the UK.

Small, wide-eyed, mousy, and sad, Marcelline Niyonsenga maintains
the posture of an importuning child, looking up anxiously as if waiting
for someone's permission to go on living. She was nineteen when the
war began, visiting family in Kigali, and their house was attacked.
Shortly thereafter, she found another family with whom to hide. The
head of that household, an old man, threw out his wife and forced
Marcelline to become his sex slave. After two and a half months, he
announced that he was tired of her. She was gang-raped and reluctantly
found refuge with another rapist, a businessman who took her with
him to Congo. When she learned that the war was over, she begged
to go home, but she was pregnant, and her husband had decided to
keep her and the child. She waited months for a day when he was away
on business. She grabbed three thousand Congolese francs (about $5)
and persuaded a taxi driver to take her to Rwanda, where the United
Nations High Commission for Refugees took her in. Her damaged

uterus had to be removed after the birth of her daughter, whom she named Clémence Tuyisenge.

Since the war, Marcelline keeps house for her brother, a widower who has refused to let Clémence, who has AIDS, into his home. At least her brother did not abandon her, Marcelline said, even though she was raped and had HIV. Clémence stays with Marcelline's mother, where Marcelline visits her once a week. More worrisome to Marcelline than telling Clémence about her origins was the prospect of explaining to her that neither of them would live long. Clémence's body had already erupted in blisters her mother called "pimples." Whenever Clémence became acutely sick, her grandmother would bring her to Marcelline, who took her to the hospital. When they are both healthy, Clémence and Marcelline laugh together. When Marcelline is sick, Clémence curls up next to her to comfort her. Marcelline often ponders whether it would be better for her daughter to predecease her; on balance, she feels it would be preferable. "People pity me because I have this *enfant de mauvais souvenir*, but she is the light of my life," she said. "To be slowly dying like this without even the comfort of a child would be a thousand times worse. I am dying, but I am not alone."

One woman I met outside Gitarama explained that a man killed her family, including her husband and three children, took her in sexual slavery for the duration of the genocide, and then fled. She gave birth to a son, then developed AIDS; the son remained healthy. Knowing she would soon die, she worried that he would have no relatives to care for him. So she tracked down his father in jail—this man who had killed her husband and children—and decided to build a relationship with him. Every day she brought him homemade meals in prison. She could not speak of what she was doing without staring fixedly at the floor.

In discussing wartime rape, Bishop Carlos Belo of East Timor, who shared the 1996 Nobel Peace Prize, said, "Up to three thousand died in 1999, untold numbers of women were raped, and five hundred thousand persons displaced—one hundred thousand are yet to return." Susan Harris Rimmer of the Australian National University has pointed out that while other wartime atrocities are enumerated, the number of women subject to rape and forced pregnancy usually remains a mere impression. The word *untold*, in her view, is both literal and metaphoric.

Since 1869, the Geneva Convention has guaranteed the wounded and sick in battle medical care, and many would argue that abortion for rape victims falls within these parameters. The UN Human Rights

Council has indicated that denying a woman an abortion after rape may constitute cruel and inhuman treatment. But the United States continues to enforce the 1973 Helms Amendment, which states, "No foreign assistance funds may be used to pay for the performance of abortion as a method of family planning or to motivate or coerce any person to practice abortions." The current interpretation of that language is that any country or organization that receives US aid is prohibited from discussing or providing abortions even to women pregnant owing to wartime rape. "The truth is, almost all women pregnant from wartime rape would choose to abort," said Janet Benshoof, president of the Global Justice Center. "In Congo, forty percent of the rape victims are children. If you're thirteen, how can you bear a child? The mortality rates are incredible. The UN estimates that twenty percent of women who are raped in conflict and denied abortions will try to self-abort—which doesn't include the ones who have killed themselves instead." The US government pays for so-called cleanup kits to treat women who have botched their self-abortions, Benshoof said, "so we clearly know what's going on. These rapes are genocidally motivated, and we're facilitating genocide by making these women bear these children."

Alphonsine Mukamakuza is tall, dramatic, and expressive, with all the grace and chiseled beauty for which the Tutsi are known. The deadness that afflicted many of the women I interviewed had not touched her; she would be laughing one minute and wracked with sobs the next. She lived in a mud hut on the outskirts of Kigali, furnished incongruously with an airplane seat propped in a corner, and two broken wooden chairs. The only light came through a crack between the roof and the wall. In spite of this poverty, she was impeccably dressed in a long, cotton print dress and matching turban.

Alphonsine was twenty when the genocide began. She thought that the barbarism had broken out only in her village, so she fled to relatives in a neighboring village. The killing had started there, too, so she and her relatives decided to seek refuge across the border in Burundi. They were near their destination when shooting broke out. Alphonsine kept running as the rest of her family were gunned down behind her. She bolted into a house, where an old woman promised to hide her. That night, the old woman's son, an Interahamwe, came home. When he saw the elegant woman his mother had sheltered, he announced that he would make her his "wife." For three weeks he raped her repeatedly, and she did all she could to appease him, because without his protection she would probably be killed.

A month later Alphonsine realized that she was pregnant. After her son, Jean-de-Dieu Ngabonziza, was born, life became increasingly difficult. She moved in with a man who demanded that she "get rid of that child" or leave. Alphonsine made sure her son knew that he was a burden, beating him mercilessly and occasionally throwing him out of the house. If they went out in public, she would say, "Call me your aunt. Never call me your mother." Meanwhile, her consort beat her day and night. Finally, she summoned the courage to leave and moved to the slum where I found her. "And then," she recalled, "I saw that my boy was all I had. And sometimes he would laugh, despite everything, and it was when he laughed that I began to love him."

The 1998 Rome Statute, which established the International Criminal Court (commonly called the war-crimes tribunal), lists as a crime against humanity "the unlawful confinement of a woman forcibly made pregnant, with the intent of affecting the ethnic composition of any population or carrying out grave violations of international law." It does not stipulate that damages are due to the victims; it is concerned primarily with the punishment of the perpetrators, especially those of higher rank who have initiated rape campaigns. The International Criminal Tribunal for Rwanda achieved a breakthrough in 1998 when it found Jean-Paul Akayesu, a local mayor who had encouraged police to rape Tutsi women, guilty of crimes against humanity and torture. It was the first time that forced pregnancy was prosecuted as a form of genocide. But the statute and the legal precedent imply that the issue is genocidal intent, rather than mass rape. For women who are raped and become pregnant as a result, the parsing of motivation is irrelevant; to their children, it is meaningless. "Male victims of torture are received by their own society as heroes," Benshoof said. "Female victims of torture are considered prostitutes who have dishonored their families." In Iraq, more than half the women who reported being raped in the year after the American invasion were killed by their own families.

Legal scholars have worked toward establishing protections for women raped during war, but little work has been done toward providing for the resultant children, who are commonly abused, abandoned, or both. Rimmer has argued that such children should be reclassified as veterans, "publicly accepted as having valid claims on the Government, rather than seen as by-products of a crime or sin." This classification would give the children a pension; it would acknowledge the women's bravery and the children's challenges. Jeanne Muliri Kabekatyo, a regional manager for HEAL Africa who works with these mothers on building their relationships with their children, said, "We want to make out of these children artisans of peace."

Christine Uwamahoro's proud, erect carriage was not typical of the violated women I met in Rwanda. She was eighteen and living in Kigali when the killing started. One of the Interahamwe broke into her house and said, "Undress and lie down, or I'll kill you and your family." He came back repeatedly, and after each rape her father would give him money to go away. The family fled, but soon came to a bridge with a roadblock. They sat by the side of the road for two hours, waiting and watching as other people were slaughtered. As dusk fell, one of the Interahamwe approached with a murderous look, and they ran, but Christine's mother faltered. Christine's brother tried to help her. Over her shoulder, Christine saw them both being chopped up with machetes. Christine and her father walked sixty miles to the city of Gisenyi, hiding by day and stealing quietly along the road by night. By the time they arrived, however, the killing had spread there, too, so they walked another few miles into Congo, where they waited out the war. There, Christine realized she was pregnant.

She feared that she had become infected with HIV, but couldn't bear to find out and never did. She would pummel her infant daughter out of sheer loathing and gave the baby to her own father so she would not have to see her. Even ten years later, the child's existence filled Christine with sadness. She visited her sole surviving sister every day, but she visited her daughter once a month at most.

Unlike most women with *enfants de mauvais souvenir*, Christine remarried. Her new husband is a polygamous Congolese man who keeps another wife. "I couldn't marry a Rwandan after what had happened, not even a Tutsi," she said. "At first, I tried to hide my history from my new husband, but eventually I told him all about it, and he has been very kind. When I get sad, he takes me out for a walk. When I have flashbacks and bad dreams, which happens often, he reminds me that I could have been killed, and he comforts me." He even proposed that the rape-conceived child live with them, but Christine didn't want that.

I sometimes ask interviewees, especially those who seem profoundly disenfranchised, whether they have any questions for me. The invitation to reverse roles helps people feel less like experimental subjects. In Rwanda, these mothers' questions tended to be the same: How long are you spending in the country? How many people are you interviewing? When will your research be published? Who will read these stories? At the end of my interview with Christine, I asked whether she had any questions. "Well," she said a little hesitantly, "you write about this field of psychology." I nodded. She took a deep breath. "Can you tell me how to love my daughter more? I want to love her so much, and my best, but when I look at her, I see what happened to me and it interferes." A tear rolled down her cheek, but her tone was almost fiercely challenging when she repeated, "Can you tell me how to love my daughter more?"

Only afterward, too late to tell Christine, did I marvel that she did not know how much love was in that question itself. It is what anyone asks herself who lives with a child ignominiously conceived, who wishes to disentangle her own ambivalence. It calls starkly into question how much of any woman's love is inherent in mammalian DNA, how much it is a matter of social convention, and how much it is the result of personal determination.

More than any other parents coping with exceptional children, women with rape-conceived children are trying to quell the darkness within themselves in order to give their progeny light. For no other exceptional families is there less coherent support than for these. These mothers and their children need an identity community, a place to find more dignity than can be achieved in the piecemeal world of online supports. The children described in the rest of this book sustain injuries; these children, through no fault of their own, *are* injuries. But the ordeal that produces them does not shrink their mothers' hearts so much as those mothers themselves often fear. Maternal love can entrance these women even as they guard against it.

X

Crime

U nlike most of the conditions discussed in this book, criminality is the child's fault, something he has done deliberately and with choice. It is also the parents' fault, something they could have prevented with decent moral education and adequate vigilance. These, at least, are the popular conceptions, and so parents of criminals live in a territory of anger and guilt, struggling to forgive both their children and themselves. To be or to produce a schizophrenic or a child with DS is generally deemed a misfortune; to be or produce a criminal is often deemed a failure. While parents of children with disabilities receive state funding, parents of criminals are frequently prosecuted.

If you have a child who is a dwarf, you are not dwarfed yourself, and if your child is deaf, it does not impair your own hearing; but a child who is morally culpable seems like an indictment of mother and father. Parents whose kids do well take credit for it, and the obverse of their self-congratulation is that parents whose kids do badly must have erred. Unfortunately, virtuous parenting is no warranty against corrupt children. Yet these parents find themselves morally diminished, and the force of blame impedes their ability to help—sometimes even to love— their felonious progeny.

Having a child with physical or mental disabilities is usually a social experience, and you are embraced by other families facing the same challenges. Having a child who goes to prison frequently imposes iso- lation. Parents on visiting day at a juvenile facility may complain to one another in a friendly way, but aside from those communities in which illegality is the norm, this is a misery that doesn't love company. The parents of criminals have access to few resources. No colorful guides posit an upside to having a child who has broken the law; no charming version of "Welcome to Holland" has been adapted for this population. This deficit also has advantages: no one trivializes what you are going

...ough; no one uses learning centers with colorful crepe-paper decorations to try to turn your grief into a festivity. No one proselytizes that the only loving response to your child's crime is gladness or urges you to celebrate what you want to mourn.

Thousands of institutions have been designed to assuage the challenges attached to many horizontal identities: schools for the deaf, mainstreaming programs, hospitals for those afflicted with schizophrenic psychosis. Most juvenile criminals are institutionalized in state facilities intended more to punish than to rehabilitate. Many can't be turned around; the idea of near-universal rehabilitation is a liberal fantasy. But there are enough young convicts in whom the damage is situational that the moral imperative is to treat them all. An oncologist can tolerate the deaths of most of his patients because of the ones he saves; if we can redeem even 10 percent of would-be career criminals, we can reduce human suffering and economize on prosecution and prison. Jails draw on the popular belief that the more we punish people, the safer the country becomes. This resembles the assumption that the more you whip your children, the better they will turn out.

The three cardinal principles of imprisonment are deterrence, incapacitation, and retribution. Deterrence works to some degree; the prospect of jail can discourage those contemplating a crime, but it does so less than most of the general population thinks. Fight Crime: Invest in Kids, an organization led by more than twenty-five hundred police chiefs, sheriffs, prosecutors, and others in law enforcement, states, "Those on the front lines in the fight against crime know that it's impossible to arrest and imprison our way out of the crime problem." A meta-analysis that collated two hundred studies found that while the best rehabilitative programs—behavioral therapy, teaching family programs—achieved a 30 to 40 percent reduction in recidivism even for serious offenders, punitive therapies had null or negative effects. The National Institutes of Health advised, "Scare tactics don't work and may make the problem worse."

Incapacitation works insofar as people behind bars cannot easily commit further crimes. But unless one plans to keep offenders in jail for life, the problem remains of how they will behave when they get out. Prisons are often the locus of contagion, where first offenders learn criminal ways from more experienced peers. Joseph A. Califano Jr., chairman of the National Center on Addiction and Substance Abuse at Columbia University, recently said, "Juvenile justice systems have become colleges of criminality, paving the way to further crimes and adult incarceration." More than 80 percent of those incarcerated under age eighteen will be arrested again within three years of release. If you want your son to stay out of jail, then keep him out of jail, because once he's been in, he's likely to be in repeatedly.

Retribution is a fashionable euphemism for *revenge*, the schadenfreude a wronged person feels from seeing his tormentor disciplined. Retribution is a way of indulging the victims; they feel powerless, and seeing their adversaries jailed or executed sometimes makes them feel enfranchised. That has a limited merit; interviews with people who have fought to have others put to death reveal that execution did not afford them the satisfaction they had anticipated.

Cora Nelson was verbally and physically abused as a child in rural Minnesota. Her early marriage, which produced two daughters, Jennifer and Mandy Stiles, was a disaster; in her mid-twenties, she developed cervical cancer and was told she would never again conceive. When she fell in love with Luke Makya, a handsome, alcoholic Native American, he didn't mind that they would be unable to have a family. Then, to the astonishment of her doctors, Cora became pregnant and delivered what she called her "miracle baby," Pete. For Jennifer, Cora's eldest daughter, her new half brother was "my living doll that talked and walked." Luke, however, became increasingly alcoholic and vicious. "Something happened to him," Jennifer recalled. "The good man my mother had married, and that we all loved, ceased to exist."

When Luke went on a rampage, Jennifer would keep Pete in bed with her to protect him. Nonetheless, Pete witnessed his mother getting hit and choked, and he was walloped, too. "There were times when it was going to be a bad day—but there were times when it was good," Pete recalled. "The first time I ever shot a rifle, we were aiming at pop cans in the water, and the first one I shot at, I hit. He just scooped me up in his arms, like he was so proud of me." Once, Luke crawled into Jennifer's bed and put his hand on her thigh; Jennifer, who had already been the victim of sexual abuse from a male babysitter when she was six, fought him off. "I have more good memories of this man than I do bad," she said, "but the bad ones are *so* bad."

One evening when Luke was wasted, he beat Pete badly, then drove off to hit the bars. For Cora, this was the end; she packed their bags and left with Pete, then six, and Mandy, who was a teenager; Jennifer had already moved out. Cora had Luke evicted and moved back home. Luke broke into the house, cut up Cora's dresses, and took his guns. Cora obtained an order of protection and filed for divorce. In the months that followed, Pete would sometimes visit his father on weekends, but Luke would usually be wasted. Cora started seeing Ethan Heinz, a bus mechanic.

One week before Cora's no-fault divorce was supposed to come through, Mandy returned from school to find Luke at the kitchen table. She called Cora, who called the police, but Luke had fled before they arrived. Cora took the family to stay with Ethan. When they returned a few days later, they found the door open and called the police. Again, they found nothing unusual; Cora asked them to check the basement. "They go down, and he's in there," Pete remembered. "He's got a shotgun, a .22 rifle, and a .30-30 rifle. He comes out with the rifle in his hand, like he was going to shoot 'em. The gun was jammed, so he couldn't get a shot off—but they didn't know that. They shot him three times, and they killed him." Cora and her three children were upstairs.

Luke's plan had been to kill both Cora and himself. He had left his son a note, saying that what was to happen was not Pete's fault, and that if Pete should ever miss him, he need only "look at the constellation Orion, because that's me. Always the hunter, never the hunted." Pete said, "He had depression but wouldn't get help because he thought they'd make him give up his alcohol, and he loved his alcohol more than anything else. I wish so much he'd chosen me over alcohol. But he didn't."

After that, Cora would be fine some days, but on others, Pete recalled, "she just couldn't do much, and I'd have to take care of her a lot." That was a steep task for a grieving six-year-old—especially one who "felt like if I'd done something different, maybe he wouldn't have tried to kill my mom." Pete ached for the loss. "My father wasn't tall like me," he said to me. "But there's this jacket he had that fits perfectly. I wear it when I'm lonely."

The whole family went to live with Ethan. "Who wants to stay in a house where there's bullet holes in the appliances?" said Jennifer. She had gotten pregnant in high school and dropped out after her daughter, Sondra, was born. When her relationship with Sondra's father ended, she and Sondra moved back in with the family. Jennifer developed chronic migraines. "I retreated to my dark room, for years," she said. "If Sondra didn't share a room with me, I don't think I would have done anything for her." Just as Jennifer had been Pete's childhood companion, so six-year-old Pete was now Sondra's. "Pete picked up the slack, paid attention to her," Jennifer said.

But Pete was often sullen and withdrawn. In third grade, he got annoyed at a girl and stabbed her in the thigh, deeply, with a pencil. He developed attention-deficit/hyperactivity disorder and had trouble in school despite his obvious intelligence. The family moved to a pleasant working-class suburb, and the counselor at his new school tried to combat Pete's inattentiveness with Ritalin. But the ADHD was

mingled with serious depression, and Ritalin made him more agita
Antidepressants provoked hypomania in him. By then, his teachers had
labeled him a troublemaker.

Pete rejected Ethan as a father figure; as time passed, he began to
rebel against his mother as well. Cora found it difficult to discipline
him. "She loved him to the point of not seeing him," Jennifer said. At
thirteen, Pete broke into a store, stole some cigarettes, and was charged
with a gross misdemeanor. A year later, he tried to walk out of the Mall
of America with a shoplifted skateboard and went briefly to jail. By then,
he was also getting in trouble for truancy. Cora requested a psychiatric
consultation for him from her HMO, but Pete was denied treatment.

Soon thereafter, Marcella, the nine-year-old daughter of Jennifer's
best friend, Annie, told her mother that Pete had forcibly kissed her
and had rubbed her chest through her shirt; she insinuated that he had
done more to Sondra. Annie immediately called Jennifer. "I remember, vividly, throwing up right afterwards," Jennifer said. That night,
she asked Sondra about it. "Full-on sexual abuse, starting when she
was six," Jennifer said. "My baby brother, who I had taken care of, who
I would have died for, had done this to my daughter." She called the
police immediately.

Cora told Pete, "This is the absolute worst thing you could have
possibly done. I couldn't have imagined anything this bad, and I can't
imagine anything worse. But now I know. And I'm still your mother,
and I still love you. So you know what? Now you know for sure that
there's nothing you can't tell me." She also gave him an ultimatum: he
would have to get help and reform his behavior if he wanted to return
to her house. Jennifer said, "My mom did everything she could. He
wasn't able to say what he needed, and we couldn't read his mind."

The DA wanted Pete to be tried as an adult, even though he was
only fifteen. Jennifer wrote a letter on his behalf, noting, "My brother
needs to be punished, but even more, he needs help." Pete was sentenced to a program for sex offenders, where he was to serve almost
two years, and would then remain on extended juvenile jurisdiction
(EJJ), which meant that any future offense would earn him twelve
years in the penitentiary. While he was inside, he told his therapist
that Sondra's father had abused her sexually before he had done so; an
abuse expert who interviewed Sondra said her knowledge was "far too
detailed to be made up." Jennifer said, "Incest. I feel like I should be
in a trailer, married to my cousin, on *Jerry Springer*. It's weird—I was
abused by the babysitter, then Luke; and Sondra was abused by her
father, then Pete. They say lightning never strikes twice in the same
place, but that's just not true."

Pete worked hard at the euphemistically named Hennepin County Home School, a facility for juvenile offenders in Minnetonka, Minnesota. While he was there, he cried about his father's death for the first time. He also told Ethan that he loved him. "He would not have opened up like that if he hadn't been forced to," Cora said. Pete also became interested in creative writing and produced a collection of sonnets, a startling accomplishment for a boy with ADHD. Pete is physically intimidating, but in prison he achieved a gentle quietude. As his release date approached, Jennifer said, "I miss him so much. Yet I feel guilty for missing him, because it's like I'm betraying my daughter." She looked earnest. "My brother will never have the opportunity to be alone with any of my children. But I want him back—I do."

The Home School set up apology sessions for Pete to meet with his mother, Jennifer, and Mandy. He did not see the little girls because they were liable to be further traumatized by such an encounter; Annie chose to pass. "My daughter says if Jesus Christ can forgive the sinners on the cross next to him, she can forgive Pete," Jennifer wrote to me. "I said, 'Prove that my faith in you was justified.' And he's done everything I asked." She worried, however, that the full consequences of Pete's abuse might not surface until Sondra's adolescence.

A few weeks after Pete's release, the family celebrated Christmas together at Cora's, at Sondra's suggestion. By the time I returned to Minnesota the following May, new dynamics were in place. It was one of the first real spring days, a Saturday. Pete, Mandy's fiancé, and Sondra were playing football on the lawn, while the others cheered from the porch. Pete was seventeen; Sondra was eleven. I was momentarily shocked to see Pete tackle Sondra; one could sense no physical unease or emotional tension between them, which was unnerving. But the positive change in Pete was incontrovertible. "That sad kid who lived here is gone," Jennifer said.

Pete had made several visits to the Home School, and I asked why. "Inside, I got really close to this guy who vanished out of my life when he was released," he said. "That hurt me, and I was determined not to do that to the other guys. So I stop in once a month to see the people who helped me." Jennifer said, "He needed something more than we could give, and his way of crying out for help was through Sondra. It's almost like it had to happen—to save him, you know? Like poor Sondra was the sacrificial lamb." A year later, she wrote to me, "I was finally able to tell Pete this week that I forgive him. I couldn't do that until I was able to see for myself that he has changed. He is truly dedicated to living a productive life. My brother, for all of his weaknesses, is an amazing young man. I'm so grateful that I'm able to see that."

Two years after I met Pete, Jennifer married. At the rehearsal dinner, she wore a T-shirt with the lyrics LET IT BE, which seemed like a reflection of the family mood. After we ate, we watched Pete play baseball. At a change of innings, he came over and accepted hugs all around; as he returned to the field, Cora turned to me and said, "I finally have the son I always wanted."

Jennifer's matron of honor was Annie; Marcella and Sondra were the bridesmaids. Because Marcella was still uneasy about Pete, he had agreed to arrive at the reception late, when Marcella would be free to leave. But she chose not to do so. She and Sondra drew a chalk hopscotch court in the driveway, and after most of the guests had dispersed, the core group hopped through in wedding finery, including Pete. Pete had committed a crime of intimacy; his family had altered the nature of that closeness, but not its degree.

In a sweeping survey of over two million American teenagers, one in four had used, carried, or taken part in an episode involving a gun or a knife in the previous year. Other sources suggest that as many as one in ten has made a physical assault on at least one of his parents. About three million juveniles—a number greater than the entire population of Chicago—are taken into custody every year, and over two million of these are arrested. Juveniles are more likely to be caught than are adult criminals; like any beginners, they are somewhat incompetent. About 70 percent are referred to juvenile court; about a third receive probation, and 7 percent are incarcerated or placed outside their homes. Arrest has become what one critic called "an extension of the principal's office."

Despite these high numbers, the rate of violent juvenile crime has gone down fairly steadily since 1994; the per capita rate of arrest for violent juvenile crime is about half of what it was then, and the rate of arrest for murder in this population is down by about 75 percent. The many competing explanations for this shift include the economic growth through the earlier part of the new millennium; the end of the crack epidemic; the expansion of imprisonment, which keeps many would-be violent criminals off the streets; and changing methods of policing. It is impossible to amass reliable statistics on crime except inferentially from statistics on arrests. At times the police are under social pressure to arrest for every crime, with other periods of relative leniency. If people believe there is more crime, more police are hired, which leads to more arrests, which lead to statistics that seem to confirm that suspicion.

Kids who have committed crimes together reap different sentences according to the engagement of family. One judge told me that she would always give less time to an offender whose parents appeared to be positive influences, because "those kids might be able to learn, as opposed to destroying lives again." One young man I met was sentenced to ten months, while his cohort, at least in part because he had no family support, got five years. The thinking is sound, but the irony is inescapable: the deprivation that encouraged the child's criminality now lengthens his sentence. Juvenile crime results from the interplay of the genetics, personality, and inclinations of the juvenile himself; the behavior and attitudes of his family; and his larger social environment. The idea of the bad seed seems outmoded, but some people seem to be born without a moral center, much as some people are born without a thumb. The genetics of decency are well beyond our primitive science, but despite boundless love and support, some people are geared toward violence and destruction, lack all powers of empathy, or have a blurry sense of truth. In most people, though, the criminal potential requires external stimulus to be activated; the intense, internally determined psychopath of the movies is unusual.

Yet much of the law is organized around the notion that young criminals are intractably malign. Waivers, for example—which are issued by prosecutors or judges to allow a case to be moved from the juvenile system to an adult criminal court that can issue heavier sentences—have become increasingly popular. Ironically, most juveniles who are waived are not in for murder or assault; they have committed crimes against property or been picked up on drug charges. Judges in overburdened adult courts often dismiss these cases, but sometimes they use adult sentencing guidelines; punishment therefore tends to be either negligible or far too severe. Further, judges may be more likely to direct into adult courts the cases of juveniles who are members of racial minorities, who do not present themselves well, or who appear not to have supportive families. These circumstances do not justify heavier prosecution. In the 1990s, every state except Nebraska enacted legislation making it easier to try juveniles in adult criminal courts; the number of juveniles in adult prisons skyrocketed. In 2001, before the Supreme Court ruled that it is unconstitutional to sentence someone to death for a crime committed before the age of eighteen, some 12 percent of the population on death row were nineteen or younger.

The waiver problem is only the latest manifestation of our nation's confused attitude toward juvenile punishment and reform. The first American juvenile to be executed was Thomas Granger, killed in 1642 at sixteen for sodomizing a horse, a cow, and several other animals. Since then, more than three hundred juveniles have been executed;

the youngest was a ten-year-old, in 1850. An 1819 report from the Society for the Prevention of Pauperism lamented, "Here is one great school of vice and desperation with confirmed and unrepentant criminals. And is this the place for *reform*?" In 1825, that same organization sought to create an ideal rehabilitative environment where "simple labor" would equip inmates with skills so that the society at large would gladly receive them back. The first court specifically for juveniles was established in Illinois at the end of the nineteenth century, based on a subjective system of judging the character of young offenders. One of Chicago's earliest juvenile court judges said, "The problem for determination by the judge is not, Has this boy or girl committed a specific wrong, but, What is he, how has he become what he is, and what had best be done in his interest and in the interest of the state to save him from a downward career." In 1910, Judge Benjamin Lindsey wrote, "Our laws against crime are as inapplicable to children as they would be to idiots." Through the early twentieth century, the courts' discretion was a version of *parens patraie*—the government as parent—with an all-powerful state acting outside the adult system of checks and balances.

By the 1960s, reformers had begun to rise up against a capricious system. In 1967, in *In re Gault*, the Supreme Court examined the case of a young man convicted of making offensive sexual phone calls to a neighbor. The juvenile court judge committed the youth to a state school for up to six years—even though an adult found guilty of a similar offense would have gotten off with a fine of no more than $50 or two months in jail. In overturning the youth's sentence, the Supreme Court granted juvenile offenders the rights to a notice of charges, to counsel, to confront and cross-examine witnesses, and to invoke the privilege against self-incrimination; writing for the majority, Justice Abe Fortas declared, "The condition of being a boy does not justify a Kangaroo Court." The 1974 Juvenile Justice and Delinquency Prevention Act limited the time that juveniles could be detained without trial and stipulated that they should be separated from adult offenders by sight and sound. The Reagan administration pushed for a reversion to "get tough" policies; the head of delinquency prevention in the Justice Department complained that the courts had listened to the "psychobabble of social workers." States began using the waivers system, enforced the death penalty for some juveniles, and saw a significant increase in juveniles in jail; by the late 1990s, almost half of committed juveniles were locked up rather than in community or treatment programs.

Juvenile justice remains paternalistic. Police officers have discretion to dismiss detained youths, and many kids are remanded to their parents with a warning. Over the past twenty years or so, the Left, led by the ACLU and similar organizations, has sought more due process and better-defined rights for young offenders, but the resulting formalization has deprived the system of its leniency; one recent survey showed that only a third of juveniles felt their attorney had helped them. The Right has, meanwhile, pushed for harsher sentencing. The Left wants children to have the rights of adults but not the responsibilities; the Right pushes for exactly the opposite. The processing of cases is terribly slow, and juveniles may languish in detention for as much as a year pretrial, vastly upsetting their social and academic development. Though juveniles have their Miranda rights read to them, at least half have no idea what is being said. Sentences are harsher than they were pre-*Gault*. As juvenile justice scholars Thomas Grisso and Robert G. Schwartz have said in *Youth on Trial*, "The adult-like procedures introduced by the left worked in spiral-like tandem with punitive measures introduced by the right to create an ungainly, harsh, and internally contradictory juvenile court."

Maturity does not arrive with adolescence; statutory regulations long ago set a minimum age for drinking, voting, sex, and driving. Biological evidence now demonstrates that the adolescent brain is structurally different from the adult one, which supports making a distinction between adult and juvenile crime. In the prefrontal cortex of a fifteen-year-old, the areas responsible for self-control are undeveloped; many parts of the brain do not mature until about twenty-four. While the full implications of this variant physiognomy cannot yet be mapped, holding children to adult standards is biologically naïve. On the one hand, kids who commit crimes are likely to become adults who commit crimes; but on the other hand, kids who commit crimes act on impulses in part because they are kids.

More than half of juveniles who are arrested test positive for drugs, and more than three-quarters are under the influence of drugs or alcohol when committing their crimes. Arrested juveniles are twice as likely as age peers to have used alcohol, more than three times as likely to have used marijuana, more than seven times as likely to have used ecstasy, more than nine times as likely to have used cocaine, and twenty times as likely to have used heroin. These statistics do not elucidate whether substances actually influence juveniles to commit crime, whether substance abuse and criminality are symptoms of a single underlying personality disorder, or whether laws restricting access to substances compel abusers into criminal activities. They do suggest, however, that drug treatment for juveniles is important to fighting crime. Sadly, only slightly over 1 percent of those arrested receive substance abuse treatment.

Sophia and Josiah McFeely had no idea that their seventeen-year-old son, Chuck, was supporting a cocaine habit by dealing, nor that he was carrying a gun around south Boston. So they were completely bewildered when they heard a loud bang one night while Chuck and his friends were at the house. One of them had brandished a gun and mockingly proposed a game of Russian roulette. The others had tried to stop him, but he pulled the trigger once and shot himself in the head. Josiah ran upstairs just in time to hold him as he died. "When I go through recovery," Chuck said, more than twenty years later, "I relive that moment over and over again. That I could have stopped it, and didn't."

In college, Chuck was drinking and using heavily. He failed all his classes, and Josiah told him he wasn't going to pay tuition if Chuck wasn't going to study. Chuck went back to dealing and soon met a girl, Lauren, also a user; one night when they were high, they held up a gas station in Everett, Massachusetts, at gunpoint, wearing masks. Chuck bludgeoned the owner with a tire iron. Josiah found him a good lawyer, and the judge let him out on probation. "He'd already blown the money he stole up his nose," Josiah said, but he and Sophia repaid the injured party. To their dismay, Chuck and Lauren married—they were twenty-one—and soon had their first child, Mackenzie. When he was high, Chuck would hit Lauren; he went to jail twice for assault. Though they were both using heavily, mostly cocaine but also other substances, they had soon had two more children, Madison and Kayla; then, they divorced.

The kids stayed with Lauren, who disappeared on drug runs at night; eventually Social Services threatened to remove them. Chuck brought his three daughters to his parents' house and moved in with them as a stopgap to keep the girls out of foster care. Soon Chuck was using, and Sophia and Josiah told him he had to go. A year later, they applied for temporary custody; Sophia had to stop working, and she was resentful. "I used to be upset with myself," she told me. "For God's sake, they're your grandchildren. But it wasn't what I'd planned."

Since then, Chuck has been through major rehab fourteen times, as well as countless AA meetings and day programs; has lived in half-way houses; has gone through repeated detox. He has never managed more than nine months without a relapse. While cocaine and alcohol still figure large, he has also used heroin and OxyContin. He has been imprisoned for parole violations, driving under the influence, domestic violence, and petty theft. When he is clean, he is a different person, but he is seldom clean long enough for this other persona to be relevant. When I met Sophia and Josiah, Chuck was nearly forty, and their grandchildren had been living with them for a decade. Chuck is both reliant on and enraged by his parents' generosity. He was furious that they had told the kids about his heroin use. "That would be so upsetting for them," he said—seeming not to have assimilated that the use itself was upsetting.

Nine years after Josiah and Sophia made their sorry peace with taking care of the three girls, they were shocked at the news that Chuck's newest girlfriend, Eva, was pregnant, and that they were keeping the baby. "What the fuck are they thinking?" Josiah said. "She's a druggie, he's a druggie. They're three months clean and she gets pregnant?" When the baby was born, Sophia saw that the bassinet had Eva's name on it but not Chuck's. Eva said she did it that way to qualify for government aid for single mothers. "I thought, 'Oh, God, have we come to this?'" Sophia said. "I didn't want to hold the baby. I was thinking to myself, 'You poor thing, what have you got to look forward to?'" Yet Mackenzie, Madison, and Kayla keep holding out hope. "He's back in recovery," Sophia said. "They'll be angry, but the minute they see him, they just melt. It's sad to see how much loyalty they have." By Christmas, Eva had relapsed, and the baby was living with Eva's mother. "The kids were saying to me, 'Nana, are you going to take the baby? We'll take care of her!'" Sophia recalled. "How can I? Now?"

It is hard not to be struck by the mix of love and anguish Josiah and Sophia feel in relation to the three granddaughters who live with them. When I met the two younger girls, I was moved by the warmth between them and their grandparents—a warmth that belied the despair just beneath the surface. "The question is, are we doing it better this time around?" Josiah said. In early adolescence, Mackenzie started using drugs, and Sophia started calling the police. After a few arrests, Sophia went to court and said she couldn't keep going this way. The judge asked whether Sophia would take her home, and she said, "Absolutely not." Mackenzie said, "You never did this to my father!" And Sophia replied, "If I'd known more then, I would have, and maybe we wouldn't all be in this mess." Mackenzie went to a temporary shelter in Yarmouth, then to the only place in the state that treated addiction in teenagers. Sophia and Josiah now think that the second eldest, Madison, was born addicted. Kayla, the youngest, seems to be doing better, but since she's just eleven, it's hard to be sure.

"My mother worked as a scrubwoman, cleaning office floors at a buck thirty-five an hour," Josiah said. "We had to bring ourselves up. Then we brought our children up, and now we're bringing our grandchildren up." Sophia said, "For such a long time, I thought that everything was going to get better, and I told the kids that. I don't have any hope left now. We used to say, 'When is it going to end?' Now we say, 'We'll just take it as it comes.' The extent of alcoholism in the family makes me feel better, in a way; I can say that it's genetic. If I had known, I probably wouldn't have had children. Chuck could do better than he does, but I know he's not out having a good time. Once I was saying to him, 'Chuck, I'd like my life back.' And he said, 'Well, don't you think I would, too?'"

As many as three out of four incarcerated juveniles have a mental health diagnosis, as opposed to one of five in the general nine- to seventeen-year-old population. Some 50 to 80 percent of incarcerated juveniles have learning disabilities. Juvenile crime is also associated with low IQ, impulsivity, poor self-control, deficient social skills, conduct disorders, and emotional underdevelopment. These predisposing characteristics are manifest terribly early. In one study, parents were asked to describe their toddlers; they were reinterviewed ten years later. Those labeled "difficult" as small children were twice as likely to have committed crimes as those labeled "easy." Another longitudinal study looked at boys rated "troublesome" when they were eight to ten and found that they were three times as likely as controls to be adolescent offenders. Of course, for every simple equivalence (difficult babies become lawbreakers), there is a parallel possibility (mothers who find their children disturbing bring up criminals).

Those who swing into full-fledged delinquency before age twelve are highly likely to become chronic adult offenders and are much more likely to commit violent crimes than are those whose behaviors kick in later. This may reflect habit; the norms of your childhood are particularly hard to buck. It may also be that some children who are troublesome early have that missing moral thumb and are manifesting something so fundamental to their personality that it will be nearly impossible to ameliorate. If a child's delinquency stems from habit, then early interventions to break those habits might be effective; if it's genetic, then such interventions are much less likely to succeed. These possibilities are, of course, not mutually exclusive.

In the chapter on schizophrenia, I noted how many schizophrenics are in jail; in researching this one, I learned how many people in jail suffer from some vague mental health diagnosis. Incarcerating mentally unstable people with the larger prison population may exacerbate criminals' destructive behavior toward themselves and others. Carol Carothers, executive director of the National Alliance on Mental Illness Maine, has said, "It is hard to imagine a worse place to house a child that requires services for their mental illness."

Brianna Gandy, whose mother was a crack addict, was born with fetal alcohol syndrome and left in the charge of her grandmother. "I call my grandma 'Mom,' so she won't forget that she's taking care of me," Brianna said to me. Her father was entirely absent. "He has no job; he doesn't come to see me; he doesn't call up here; he doesn't write me," Brianna said. "And I don't know where he lives, so I don't write him, either."

At fifteen, Brianna had been in all sorts of trouble, but was especially given to truancy and lying. "I used to wake up in the middle of the night and steal food out of the refrigerator," she said. "And I would always tell my grandmother, 'It wasn't me, it wasn't me'—when there wasn't no one else it could be." At fourteen, Brianna started running away; she would sit in a park at night until someone came along and invited her home for a meal. "Just random people," she said. "Some of 'em couldn't have kids—and always wanted a kid. So I was their kid for that time." She also hung out with drug dealers and with homeless people. "I just don't like to be told to do something that I don't want to do."

Brianna was in for assault, and when she was angry, she was terrifying. "I had one assault here," she told me. "At Harbor Shelter, I assaulted their director. At St. Joe's, I assaulted staff. At St. Croix, I assaulted the director and staff there." There was something eerie about the calm way she listed these offenses. "I want to be a chef or a plumber," she went on, as though this sentence were contiguous with the last. "If I don't find a job right away, I'll be crocheting things to sell—instead of selling drugs, which I did, but it's too much drama. I crocheted two shirts already, and a hat, and I'm working on a purse."

Brianna's grandmother was at a loss over how to deal with her. "Since I got locked up, we talk more about personal things," Brianna said. "I've been telling her things that I wouldn't usually, like about getting raped—let's see—two different times. When I was three, by the neighbor; when I was thirteen, by my ex-boyfriend." Brianna's grandmother had suggested Brianna join Job Corps. Despite Brianna's disinclination to live with her grandmother, this proposal hurt her feelings. "I was wondering why she didn't want me home once I'm out of here—if she loved me anymore," Brianna said. But then she added, "I wish my grandma didn't love me so much and would just leave me alone and stop interfering." To wish for and resent parental love is a familiar adolescent paradox, but Brianna seemed completely unaware of any incongruity in her statements.

Clearly, a confused relationship to reality can enable criminal behavior—but so, too, can depression. Jackson Simpson shares his mother's depressive tendency, but whereas she has manifested the illness through withdrawal and drinking, he has manifested it through failure and aggression. Jackson told me that he'd always "had an interest for people who were depressed," and he thought a lot about his mother's diagnosis, but he couldn't seem to see that it might also apply to himself.

Jackson joined a gang when he was in the fifth grade and "ended up selling drugs, using drugs, carrying guns," he said, "stealing, robbing—everything you could pretty much name. I wasn't raised like that. I knew it was wrong, but after you do it for a while, you actually like it." He had committed the felony assault that landed him inside, however, only after he failed to make the basketball team at his school; his life's dream was to be a basketball star, but his school required that players have a minimum grade point average, and his was too low. He was so distraught that he dropped out; he eventually enrolled elsewhere, but he never bounced back. Earlier deeds had earned him probation, but following the basketball debacle, he fell into serious trouble. "He knew it was his fault and he was angry at himself about it," his mother, Alexa, said. "The self-esteem got real low. When you're in court every other month? And you're still doing things that you know are wrong? To me, that's a form of depression."

Six months after the basketball incident, Jackson was arrested on charges of assaulting someone. He was eighteen, and they planned to try him as an adult. Jackson finally gave a confession as a way to get a plea bargain, and he was sentenced to time in the Home School. "I knew it was making my mother's depression worse," he said. "In court she'd just be crying. Could barely even walk—had to have my dad help her in the courtroom. You could just see it in her face. They was so disappointed."

Alexa said, "I started drinking. I'm on antidepressants now." Jackson's depression likewise remained acute and carried with it an intense disaffection. His appetite and sleep were dysregulated; he was unable to imagine future plans. "I love my parents," he said. "But I've always thought I was adopted, because growing up, I felt like nobody could ever relate to me. I didn't even understand myself. That's how different I felt. And I still do." Jackson's error carried its own punishment. What he had done to his mother and how he had disappointed himself—these things caused him so much pain that his confinement to a jail cell was merely secondary. He was alone in ways more profound than any physical lock and key could enforce.

The public endlessly debates what children and teenagers who have broken the law deserve and don't deserve: drug treatment, adult sentencing, mental health care, etc. Yet juvenile justice in the United States is largely a story of gross abuses. In 2003, an article in the *New York Times* described Mississippi's juvenile detention system: "Boys and girls were routinely hogtied, shackled to poles or locked in restraint chairs for hours for minor infractions like talking in the cafeteria or not saying, 'Yes sir.'" A lawsuit brought against the operators of one center said, "Toilets and walls are covered with mold, rust, and excrement. Insects have infested the facility, and the smell of human excrement permeates the entire building. Children frequently have to sleep on thin mats that smell of urine and mold." Many children claimed to have been assaulted by guards; many were locked in their cells for twenty-three hours every day; infections caused by filthy conditions were rampant. Suicidal girls in Mississippi prisons have been stripped and put on lockdown in isolation cells with no light or window, and only a drain in the floor.

Another *Times* story reveals that in California's juvenile facilities "youths in solitary confinement are often fed what officials call 'blender meals,' in which a bologna sandwich, an apple, and a carton of milk are pulverized and fed to the inmate by straw through a slit in the cell door." A state review showed the California juvenile prison system to be "a dysfunctional jumble of antiquated facilities, undertrained employees, and endemic violence that fails even in its most fundamental task of providing safety." The US Attorney General's office found in Nevada that staffers were "punching boys in the chest, kicking their legs, shoving them against lockers and walls, slapping youths in the face, and smashing youths' heads in doors" and subjecting them to "verbal abuse in which their race, family, physical appearance and stature, intelligence, or perceived sexual orientation were aggressively attacked." A report by the Florida Inspectors General described how staff at a juvenile facility stood by as a seventeen-year-old begged for help and slowly died of a ruptured appendix. The list could go on and on. Joseph Califano has said, "We have fifty-one different systems of juvenile *in*justice with no national standards of practice or accountability." The abuse in the juvenile justice system is commensurate with the corrupting nature of its absolute power.

To immerse myself in the worldviews of juvenile prisoners, I took a position advising a theater project at the Hennepin County Home School. The school's ethos is not representative, which is why I chose it; Minnesota is known for its strong focus on rehabilitative programs.

With a population of mostly recidivist felons and a particularly strong program for underage sex offenders, the Home School presumes that punishment is accomplished by the lack of freedom accorded to inmates. The well-kept campus houses about 120 juvenile felons at a time, with 167 acres of grounds and a staff who help inmates understand their emotional lives as a means to contain their destructiveness. It offers full high school classroom work, with particularly strong arts and athletics programs; the name was chosen so that prospective employers would perceive the graduates without prejudice. It also provides intensive individual, group, and family therapy, as well as a special program for substance abusers. In some ways, it felt less like a prison than like a boot-camp boarding school; one inmate complained, "They want you to think all day. I'd rather be breaking up rocks or shit." Some of the kids keep up friendships with staff after they leave; some return to visit the place, nostalgic alumni of their own punishment. Many express ambitions to go to college; though few follow through, the desire reflects the optimism with which they have been treated. Let it not be supposed, however, that it is all talk therapy and crafts. Freedom of movement is constrained; even using the bathroom requires permission. When necessary, units are put on lockdown, and inmates are placed under harsh restraints. Outbreaks of violence, although usually quickly contained, are not uncommon.

The play I worked on with a group of twenty residents and several supervising adults was intended to awaken them to their capacity for accomplishment, and to teach them a better way to express their pain. Cynics decry such programs as incompatible with punishment, but giving wayward kids insight into how to build a better life benefits the society at large. Habits of ruthlessness had made the inmates' own hearts obscure to them. The director of the theater program, Stephen DiMenna, composed an affecting monologue for a broken chair and asked the kids which emotions he was expressing. The kids came up with "mad" and "resentful" and "weak" and "angry," but it took them twenty minutes to think of "sad," an alien concept to this roomful of sad people.

The Home School uses family therapy to resolve conflicts between inmates and their parents, to coach offenders on how to interact at home, and to train parents to exercise more effective control. Such methods may be crucial to breaking the kids out of a criminal identity, and to helping their parents see that their children's problems are not immutable. "I show these parents how to encourage their kids," said Terry Bach, one of the resident case managers. "These kids are just *thirsty* for praise. No matter how tough they seem, they need, they *want*, that."

The post-Freudian notion that all flaws are based in family relations is out of favor. It remains common, however, to blame an abusive childhood environment for the rate of juvenile crime, and certainly criminality can be the upshot of fear, loneliness, hatred, and neglect. I met parents of offenders who were preoccupied with their own problems or who seemed unacquainted with the usual rules of love, people who witnessed their children's pain without the slightest disturbance of their own mood. Some parents were criminal themselves and couldn't imagine or didn't value a different life. Some were hooked on substances. Others were so mired in poverty that they thought survival justified any means. Some were so angry at their children that affection seemed to have closed up shop, and some were acutely depressed. Many had given up on children they felt incompetent to help.

Some kids laughed when I asked how their parents felt about their incarceration. "Why the fuck would they even care? I'm in here, they don't gotta pay no bills for me," one inmate snarled. Others had no idea where their parents were. One said, "I'd love to have parents who hate me, like everyone here complains about, instead of just not having parents at all." Another said, "When I get outta here, I'm gonna find my mom and tell her I'm sorry for all the trouble I caused her, and then maybe she's gonna love me, if anyone can." When a female staff member addressed one inmate affectionately as "son," he said tartly, "I don't have no mama and no woman ever called me son and you ain't gonna be the one to start." One said, "I'm so homesick all the time—which is weird, 'cause I have no home."

But this popular narrative of abuse and neglect was not the most common one. Even if they couldn't cope or were narcissistic, most of the parents I met in researching this chapter loved their kids. Most knew that it would serve their children's interests to avoid crime—or at least to avoid punishment. Some were afraid of their own children. Many engaged in self-criticism and voiced a wish to make up for past deficits. Staff told me that some parents who seem attentive when their kids are in prison disengage once those kids are released; they can't act on love once a formal structure for it is removed. Even among those who loved well, affection often did not seem to keep regular company with insight. Nonetheless, love is among the good medicines for crime and anger. A broken family is still a family, and a broken home, still a home.

The relationship between kids in the justice system and their parents usually follows one of four tracks. The parents may abandon the child when he goes to prison, which may lead the child to feel lonely, lost, isolated, and desperate. The parents may abandon the child, which may prompt the child to take responsibility for himself or herself. The parents may remain or become deeply involved with the child, making the child feel that a bright future is possible. The parents may remain or become deeply involved with the child, reinforcing antisocial behavior by creating a permissive atmosphere of denial.

Dashonte Malcolm, known to his family and friends as Cool, was sixteen when we met, a good-looking, well-spoken African-American with manners that reflect both training and instinct, and a sense of humor about himself. He seems like a fellow you'd trust with your checkbook or your sister, so it was easy to believe that he was locked up because of someone else's bad behavior. "This is my first offense," he said, hanging his head, "and my last." While many of the kids at the Home School evinced embarrassment about the humiliation of being stripped of basic freedoms, Dashonte seemed genuinely remorseful about his crime.

Dashonte's father, a bus driver, had died of an alcohol-triggered stroke when Dashonte was five, and his mother, Audrey, had brought up her only son in the tough neighborhoods of south Minneapolis under the general patronage of her imposing father, the bishop of Minnesota of the Pentecostal Church of God in Christ, with forty-four churches under his aegis—a man by whose air of grand authority I was always slightly awed. Audrey Malcolm is large and beautiful, with soft eyes and an aura of quiet dignity. She enfolds you in good cheer, although closer observation reveals that she is somewhat reserved beneath her outgoing manner. Audrey and Dashonte live six blocks from her parents, and her brothers and sisters all live within a mile; they see one another almost every day. Dashonte describes his mom as his best friend; he told me he was thinking about having her face tattooed on his arm "so I'd always have her with me."

Audrey had moved a neighborhood away from the worst part of the ghetto to distance Dashonte from crime. "But there was always that thing picking at me, to go back to where the trouble was," Dashonte said. He described himself as "a badass" in school. According to Audrey, he got into scuffles, "always protecting somebody else." She added, "You want him to be compassionate, so some things you have to live with."

In third grade, a new kid arrived at Dashonte's school: Darius Stewart from Tallahassee. They got into a horrendous fight because Darius was allegedly harassing a smaller child. "They tore the classroom up," Audrey recalled. "Chairs flew, desks flew." The next day Dashonte and his opponent were best friends. Audrey didn't like Darius's influence, and she switched Dashonte to another school in sixth grade, to separate them. Two years later, Darius enrolled at the new school. When Dashonte was sixteen, Audrey bought him a car because public transportation was a prime setting for gang recruitment. Darius didn't have a car, and Dashonte took to giving him rides. After Dashonte crashed his car, Audrey told him to ride the public bus, but he complained that he was being drawn into gang life, so she bought him his second car.

Audrey was to buy Dashonte five cars before he turned eighteen. He wrecked three of them and maintained that each of those crashes was the other driver's fault. With the image of those wrecked cars in mind, I listened to the rest of his story. "Darius started getting more dependent, so I moved Cool out of his school, again," Audrey explained. Darius showed up at the new school's orientation. Soon thereafter, Dashonte came home from time on the town with Darius, and Audrey smelled alcohol on his breath. "I told him, 'Had your dad not been an alcoholic, he'd be living right here with you. Cool, you're going down. And I'm not going to let this happen, even if I have to lock your butt in the house for the rest of your life.'" To Dashonte, however, separation from Darius was almost inconceivable. "We were like brothers," he said.

The offense that landed Dashonte behind bars was aggravated assault. He and Darius had picked up a girl at a bus stop and wanted to go to a pool hall tournament that had a $7 admission fee. Darius proposed robbing someone. Dashonte had a gun and they found a boy alone, threatened him, and took $80 along with his jacket and sneakers. The news traveled around school after Darius wore the stolen clothing. Darius and Dashonte were arrested. "The detectives called and said, 'Aggravated robbery and assault.' I couldn't fathom it," Audrey said. She insisted that her son had never had guns—she searched his room from time to time and she knew. She walked into the Juvenile Detention Center, and Dashonte started crying. "I said, 'Cool, I might beat you half to death tomorrow—but I want to know tonight what happened,'" she recalled. "So he saw that I was more with him than against him."

At the trial, Darius blamed Dashonte; Dashonte blamed Darius. "Me and him both said that it was 'death before dishonor,' but when it came down to it, he got selfish," Dashonte said. I met them both and found Dashonte a great deal more likable than Darius, but Dashonte undeniably was the one with the gun. Following his arrest, Dashonte spent a week in detention and two months on house arrest, with an ankle bracelet that sent out an alarm signal if he went beyond the garage. He and Audrey sat up late talking, night after night. She kept asking for his motive, but he couldn't say.

Both boys were sentenced to eight months at the County Home School. "I felt like, you've already humiliated yourself," Audrey explained. "My mom used to tell us, 'I don't care if you killed somebody. I want you to come home and tell me.' That's what I wanted Cool to hear: whatever you do, you're my son. If it was murder, would I turn my back? No way. And I told him that." Audrey was known at the Home School for being the first visitor to arrive every visiting day, and the last to go. She wrote Dashonte a letter every day and closed each one, "Love you more than life itself, Mom." She was planning a celebration for Dashonte's release and had rented a penthouse in Las Vegas for their first weekend together. It was a mutual attachment. I had known Dashonte a month when he was granted his first off-premises time—four hours with his social worker. I asked what he was going to do, and he was definite: "I'm going to Bath & Body Works to buy my mom a birthday present."

There's a fine line between heroic love and willful blindness, and Audrey Malcolm has visited both sides of that line. "He said he didn't even think the boy they held up really took offense, because he was laughing at them through the whole thing," she told me. "Cool actually tried to give the money back, and Darius snatched it out of his hand." I wanted to believe what his mother believed, but both staff and other inmates told me that Dashonte was actually in the Bloods. It was easier to learn the hereditary titles of dynastic China than it was to get a handle on all the gangs in Minneapolis and how they overlapped. "I have older cousins that had their own little gang," Dashonte explained. That gang was the Fergusons—which sounded to me more like an indie band than like a sinister operation devoted to programmatic violence. "The Fergusons, their family is all Bloods," Dashonte added, "and we used to have little wars, in the school hallway after lunch, fun, fighting for real, but it was just all smiles." When I mentioned the gang to Audrey, she said that Dashonte had always had a need to be popular and pretended to be a gang member to get respect.

Dashonte admitted that acting out had been gratifying for him. "I had a lot of anger after I realized I didn't have a father," he said. I came to understand gangs as an answer to his hunger for male connection—a counterweight to his church heritage and the intense intimacy of his relationship with his mother. He explained his gang affiliation like this: "A lot of 'em are your blood family, or people married to my girl cousins, and people you're not related to at all, but you just feel like you're related. Having parties, just hanging out at the park, or just joking with each other—I liked that. Fighting for territory and just rivalries, that was secondary."

Shortly before Dashonte was released, I went with his mother to the Emmanuel Tabernacle Church of God in Christ. We arrived as people were streaming in, the women in bell-shaped hats that matched their dresses and handbags, their stiletto-heeled shoes adorned with diamanté butterflies and silk blossoms; the men in dandyish confections of suits, with pleats and gathered neckties. The atmosphere was warm and friendly. I greeted Dashonte's grandmother, the first lady of the church. A man was already in the pulpit, and soon a woman got up and started singing, and before long, everyone was singing, accompanied by a Hammond organ and a drum set. Periodically someone would say, "Praise the Lord!" or "I need you, Jesus." First-time visitors to the church were asked to stand and introduce ourselves. The first woman who spoke up said, "I am on business in the Twin Cities and it is Sunday, and I was not going to let this blessed day go by because without Jesus I am nothing!" A second made a similar speech that ended, "I am here today to be brought out of sin! Hallelujah!" Then the microphone was passed to me. Meekly I said, "I am here as a guest of Audrey Malcolm and Mother Forbes, and I am so moved by this congregation's faith." Everyone clapped.

The bishop was performing a consecration that day, so the head of the Sunday school preached. He began by talking about how parents didn't want to see what their kids were doing wrong, and referred to 2 Samuel and to 1 Corinthians as models for vigilance. "You've got to watch the company your kids is keeping," he said, "and when they start in with that wrong crowd, that wrong crowd is going to bring them down and they will do wrong." I was struck by this blaming of the "wrong crowd" that somehow compromised the natural purity of the kids of this church. Then began the enumeration of evil. The people of the church must rise against the "principality of homosexuality," and the modern moneylenders must be expelled from the holy places. The notion that the problems of black people in Minneapolis were the fault of gays and Jews or bankers reminded me of the excuses for Dashonte's three car crashes, or the notion that Darius had tricked Dashonte into malfeasance. The congregation's generosity braided with militancy and a hatred of otherness was oddly reminiscent of the gang ethos. The community saw this mix of harshness and kindness as an extension of a Christ who embodied both infinite love and the terrible verdicts of Judgment Day.

I called on the Malcolms six months later. Dashonte was out of the Home School; his grandmother came over, and the four of us had lemonade and carrot cake. "You know, as bad as I hate to say it," Audrey told me, "this was probably one of the better things that could have happened to Cool. It was overkill. But he needed a deterrent." I had heard that he still belonged to the Bloods, but with his mother in the room, he described the fine life he had imagined for himself, with a wife and an office job. It felt more like tact than deception. "Gang life is always going to be on my mind," Dashonte conceded when I later spoke with him alone. "When I'm at that desk job, it's going to be, 'What could I be doing right now if I was on the streets?' But if you're selling drugs, you've got to keep your guard up. Sometimes you can't even trust your cousin, your mom. And I'm through with that." You don't quit a gang in some grand ceremony; you let the affiliation peter out, often with ambivalence. I wanted to believe in Dashonte's resolve, but at that stage, his innocence felt like a flexible, daily decision.

Loyalty turned out to be Audrey's strong suit. Unlike most interview subjects, she always expected our conversation to be a two-way street. When I finally told her I was gay, she wrote me a letter that said in part, "Thank you so much for being open and honest with us. Nothing has changed as a result of you telling us that you are gay and have a part-ner. You never judged us because we were black, or because Cool was locked up, or because I'm a single parent raising a son alone and living in the inner city. Some don't get a chance at love and happiness, and now I know you to have that chance, and I'm happy. I choose friends because of their hearts. I'm sure God brought us together as friends for a greater purpose."

I came to love my visits with the Malcolms. Dashonte didn't quite get the white-collar job he'd talked about, but he managed to avoid serious trouble and did not return to prison. When he met a girl he really liked, he talked about her with joy; soon enough, they were engaged. In the end, his mother had believed him into becoming who he had sometimes pretended to be. Her gift for faith proved strong enough to achieve redemption not only in the next world, but also right here in this one.

I resolved to write about parents of criminals after seeing a television interview with Paul Van Houten, in 2002. His daughter Leslie was one of the Manson girls, members of a quasi-commune in the 1960s who committed vicious crimes under their charismatic leader's instruction. In August 1969, Leslie stabbed grocer Rosemary LaBianca fourteen times in the back. Thirty-three years later, Paul Van Houten appeared on *Larry King Live* to plead for parole for his daughter. "If Leslie had never smoked her first marijuana cigarette, this would never have happened," Paul Van Houten said. "You're blaming it on marijuana?" asked an incredulous King. "With marijuana and LSD, Manson was able to maneuver these people," Paul said. King rebutted, "Millions have smoked marijuana and didn't go kill people." An expert on the program added that Leslie hadn't been on drugs when she committed the crime. I was riveted by Paul's blindness to his daughter's free choice to murder. It reminded me of the parents of deaf children who couldn't understand that those children would never use spoken language happily or fluently, or the parents of people with schizophrenia who still fantasized that their intact children were only waiting to be revealed again.

Soon afterward, I read an interview with the mother of Zacarias Moussaoui, one of the perpetrators of the 9/11 attacks, in which she described how she became alienated from her son as he moved toward fundamentalist Islam, criticized her for not wearing a veil, and was inspired by a cousin to refuse womanly jobs such as making his bed. Still, his mother was unprepared for seeing her son's face on TV in connection with the attacks. "How could he be involved in such a thing?" she said. "I cannot eat. I cannot sleep. I keep saying to myself, 'Could this be?' All my children, they each had their own rooms. They had pocket money. They went on vacations. I could understand if he had grown up unhappy or poor. But they had everything." The quotations bespeak a relationship between a mother who had no idea who her son had become and a son who had no wish to tell her.

A young man from a middle-class family whom I met when he was serving in a juvenile prison told me he stole and crashed cars "because I can." Dan Patterson never cared about the things once he had them— he had proudly traded a $300 car stereo for a pack of cigarettes. When I asked about the cars' owners, he said, "What the fuck did they ever do for me?" At seventeen, he was on his tenth car-theft arrest. He talked about despair in his interactions with his parents. "When we tried to talk, it was always like there was a glass window in front of us. One time the cops picked me up and then let me go home. My dad was just like, 'Well, go to bed. I'll talk to you later.' So I went to bed, and about a half hour later I went out the window, and I took off again. And later, when he asked me why I did it, I told him, 'Because you didn't try talking to me.'" When Dan appeared in court, his mother said on the stand, "This is not my son. He's not that kind of person. Why can't I just take him home?" I asked Dan when he started lying to his parents. "When they stopped noticing who I am," he said.

Lionel Dahmer's book, *A Father's Story*, describes his relationship with his son Jeffrey, who killed seventeen young men in Milwaukee between 1978 and 1991. The memoir is both a celebrity biography and a cry for expiation. Jeffrey was clearly a disturbed child from a troubled family, but most boys from troubled families do not develop a obsession with murdering, dissecting, and eating their victim nel wrote, "My life became an exercise in avoidance and denial. Now, when I think of those final days, I see myself in some kind of mental crouch, half expecting some sudden blow, but hoping against hope that it would never hit. It was as if I had locked my son in a soundproof booth, then drawn the curtains so that I could neither hear nor see what he had become."

Such denial to the point of dissociation is not infrequent. In *Capital Consequences: Families of the Condemned Tell Their Stories*, Rachel King follows nine families as they struggle with death sentences. She includes the story of Esther Herman, whose son Dave committed a vicious murder, then came home for Christmas and refrained from mentioning his crime. "I had two very active businesses, and health issues, and was overseeing the care of people, and I was pretty much overburdened," Esther said. "Mother and my brother were in very bad health. It was an extremely difficult time. [Dave] was always a very kind person. He didn't want to overload me." In describing Dave's trial, Esther said, "We had not provided Dave with a healthy, loving environment growing up. We fought a lot and there was a lot of tension in our home. Even so, Dave had been a good person." The psychological conundrum for the child in Dave's position is that it is extremely alienating—even traumatic—to have parents who are in denial about who you are. A mother who would think you are "a very kind person" and "a good person" even after you've committed murder makes you feel you have to do yet wilder, more dramatic things to be credited with agency. Parental denial, ironically, may contribute to the unspeakable crimes that it later renders invisible.

As a child, Noel Marsh often saw his father, Tyrone, beating his mother, Felicity; Tyrone pushed Felicity down the stairs while she was pregnant with triplets, causing one fetus to die. Felicity's first job was to protect Noel, and her identification with him as a beleaguered victim would handicap all their future relations. She left Tyrone and married Steve Tompkins when Noel was six; of the five children she brought with her, Noel was her favorite. Steve found his new situation extremely difficult. "Anything Noel wanted, if she couldn't come up with it, then she felt like she was doing wrong," he said. Noel exploited these concerns relentlessly, trying to drive a wedge between Felicity and Steve when he thought he could profit by it.

Noel's transgressions began to accumulate. "The late hours; the lying; the stealing," Steve recalled. Felicity insisted that Noel couldn't be the one taking money from her purse. Steve would say, "Felicity, ain't nobody else here, baby. Why won't you wake up your eyes and see that Noel is not Noel anymore?" The situation inevitably created marital friction. Then Steve was diagnosed with pulmonary disease and was hospitalized for almost two months. After Steve returned home, Noel's erratic behavior escalated. Felicity recalled, "I used to ask him, 'Noel, do you hate me that much? I never would've dreamed that you would put the pressure and feelings you have on me.'" He asked her to tell the police he was home when he wasn't. "I stopped being me when I started to lie for him," she said.

Noel traces much of his pain to his deadbeat father. During one of Tyrone's infrequent visits, he asked Noel if he needed money. "I said, 'Yeah,'" Noel told me. "And he gave me some drugs and said, 'Here, sell these.'" Felicity said that Noel was just like Tyrone. "It really amazes me how that bloodline is in there," she explained. After Noel's brother was killed in a car crash, Noel's relationship with his mother deteriorated further. "She would sit in the house all day," Noel said. "I would leave and not come back. We was both depressed." By the time Noel turned sixteen, he had quit school; he was constantly stealing; he was dealing drugs; and his sister tipped off their parents that he was keeping guns.

Thugs started calling the house late at night, threatening Felicity. It was more than she and Steve could handle. "I had to call the police on him," Felicity recalled. "I think that's about the lowest, hardest thing a mother should have to do. But I knew, if I really loved my son, I had to." The police were rough during the arrest, and Noel ended up in the emergency room, but Felicity still felt that since Noel had made a name for himself resisting arrest, he was getting off light. She and Steve stood by him during his trial, and their united front influenced his sentencing; with such a good home, he seemed like a candidate for rehabilitation. He had been arrested with $3,000 in his pocket and had said it was Steve's. Steve reluctantly let the story go unchallenged, figuring that Noel would do enough time on the gun charge.

The prison time healed the silence that had set in between Noel and his mother. They didn't have much to say to each other at first, and she would often leave in tears. "He had me feeling so bad about *myself*," she said. Noel said, "She told me to strive for better. She don't be thinking I be listening, sometimes. But I listen. I remember everything." With more than a hundred pairs of stolen sneakers at home, Noel was a veritable Imelda of the ghetto. The Home School rule was that no inmate could have more than two pairs of shoes, but they could swap them out—so Felicity, unable to break the habit of indulgence, would bring two pairs every Sunday, taking away the previous, enabling Noel to reign as fashion prince even in jail.

The fathers who were missing from the lives of the boys I got to know seemed often to occupy more of their psychic energy than did other family members with whom they actually had daily interactions. No one else could substitute for the shortfall in paternal love; even Dashonte's strong grandfather and Pete's and Noel's upright stepfathers couldn't fill the aching absence in these boys. Their guilt-ridden mothers wanted to compensate for this underlying sadness, which they couldn't do; instead, they postponed making their sons take responsibility for their actions until the government stepped in to do it for them. Yet the relationship that was so traumatic for these young men was the first thing they set out to echo. I was shocked time and again by how these incarcerated kids reached for emotions far beyond their affective means, a reality often reflected in their having children of their own as early as possible. These children begetting children figured that maturity would be a consequence of parenthood, rather than viewing parenthood as an expression of an already established maturity. That conceptualization of parenting is appallingly naïve, but also touchingly optimistic, as though having children could provide a repair kit for damaged egos and fathomless despair.

Noel had two children before he was locked up at sixteen. "I buy all the Pampers my girl needs for my son," Noel told me proudly. He had grown up hearing the repeated parable of Tyrone's neglect of this particular matter, but apparently had not processed that his own drug dealing and resultant disappearances to jails and safe houses might be even more traumatic for his new family than their not having diapers readily at hand. Although he had experienced real love from his mother and meaningful support from his stepfather, Noel had it tattooed in his mind that Pampers, drugs, and sneakers were what fathers gave their sons.

Arguments about the nature-or-nurture origin of criminality are just as engaged as those about the origin of autism or genius. The National Institutes of Health's Maribeth Champoux and her colleagues have shown that newborn monkeys with a gene for extreme aggression will not grow up to be aggressive if they are cross-fostered to extremely gentle mothers, even though the aggression gene is still biologically active in them. In human beings, criminal behavior has been related to a genetic irregularity associated with changed function in a particular serotonin transporter. The neuroscientist Avshalom Caspi at Duke surveyed people with that polymorphism who had had a nonviolent childhood and found that they had the usual odds of developing antisocial behavior; among those people in his study who had that polymorphism *and* were beaten as children, 85 percent exhibited antisocial behavior. So the gene appears to confer not criminal behavior, but a vulnerability to develop such behavior under certain circumstances. While family can be a negative influence, it can also be constructive. One study concludes that "a positive family environment is the major reason youth do not engage in delinquent or unhealthy behaviors." A child who feels the lure of delinquency may resist it if he has a family characterized by intimacy. In a seminal collation of studies, Jill L. Rosenbaum declared, "The parental attachment factor explains delinquency better than any other factor."

Sometimes when poor family dynamics seem to have traumatized a child, it emerges that the child has actually instigated the poor dynamics. Single mothers have more delinquent children, though it is hard to say whether that is because growing up without a father is traumatic, or because single mothers are women who made poor choices of mate and make poor choices as parents, or because these women are forced to work overtime to take care of their families financially, with the inevitable consequence that intimacy suffers.

A child whose family relationships are troubled is more likely to seek out a negative peer group than a well-adjusted child is, and at that point it is hard to say whether the child has been influenced by his friends or has influenced them. Mothers often told me, "Jimmy just got in with the wrong crowd"—and then I talked to other mothers who claimed that Jimmy was the wrong crowd with whom their sons had fallen in. It seemed noteworthy to me that, with a few exceptions, the criminals I met were not enjoying their own crimes; they were trapped in behavior that often made them as miserable as it made their victims. Criminality felt in many cases more like an illness than many of the "illnesses" I had set out to study. We "cure" disabled people who would prefer not to be cured, but we fail to treat some people with this condition who could recover and would like to do so.

Karina Lopez came to the world in trouble and chaos. The third child of Emma Lopez, a Mexican-American teenage mother with a drug problem, Karina was born in St. Paul, Minnesota, and moved to Laredo, Texas, when she was a month old. Her father was already out of the picture, and all Karina knows about him is his name. Her mother was soon pregnant by Cesar Marengo, a drug dealer fresh from prison, and headed to San Antonio, where she gave birth to Karina's little sister, Angela. Whenever Cesar assaulted Emma, she would return to Minnesota with all four kids; then he'd come to take her back to Texas.

By the time Karina was twelve, she had attended thirteen schools. The FBI was a regular visitor to their house; Cesar was serving a ten-year federal sentence when I met Karina. "I'm glad Angela has a relationship with her father," Karina told me, "even if it's seeing him in jail. It's more than I ever had."

When Cesar was incarcerated, the family's primary source of income vanished. Before his arrest, however, he had helped Emma quit drugs; she found a job as a waitress, and Karina had to take care of Angela. She resented it. At thirteen, she began to rebel. "Most people that join gangs, it's because they have nobody who loves them, and that wasn't the problem," she said. "I had Mom, who loved me a lot. But we'd moved so much, and I never felt like I belonged anywhere, and a gang seemed like a solution."

Years of poverty and disruption have made no dent in Emma's stalwart character, and she carries herself with challenging self-assurance. For many years, she ran a cleaning service by day and waited tables by night, saving to buy a house. She mistrusts you until she decides to trust you, dislikes you until she decides to like you, and has no middle ground. When Emma discovered that Karina was in a gang, she learned where its members met. At the appointed time, she broke into an abandoned house opposite. "I look across, and these girls, with guns, are sitting in a circle," she said to me. "So I cross the street, bang on the front door, and say, 'Karina, you are coming home with me right now.' The whole gang is there; they could kill me. But I don't care. I wasn't having my baby in no gang."

"I didn't leave because of my mom, though that was a pretty weird scene," Karina said. "Gangs are pointless to me, period, but it's even more pathetic here in Minnesota. These people were riding the bus; they didn't even have money for drugs." Karina started hanging out with dealers, and the drugs were plentiful; soon she was using regularly, "high for two years straight, every day." She gradually moved from using to helping out dealers here and there without ever having a fixed position in their power structure.

On November 22, 2002, Karina went with her aunt's boyfriend, Xavier, to pick up a horse saddle stuffed with four pounds of cocaine. Karina's name was not on the package; she was just helping a "friend." As Xavier drove off, she saw that they were being followed. "I'm snorting coke and snorting coke, and I'm fearless when I'm high. So we get on the freeway, and there are at least ten cars behind us, with the lights and everything. He's like, 'We're probably just speeding.' I was going crazy. So we started panicking." They took a highway exit that turned out to be a dead end. "So it was meant to be," Karina said.

When Emma went to look for Karina, her first stop was the home of the "friend" to whom the package was addressed. When the police found Emma there, they connected her to the crime and arrested her. The police didn't believe a fifteen-year-old girl could have been operating independently at this level. Emma recalled, "I said to the cops, 'For ten years now I've had jobs, I've paid my taxes, I've sacrificed everything I knew how to give my kids a good life. You think I'd mess things up for them like this?'" She was angry for being wrongly accused, but she was mainly worried about her daughter. "I'm thinking, 'Okay, I'm in trouble for what I didn't do and I hope I can get off,'" she told me, "'but she's in trouble for what she did do and she's going to jail.'"

The police apprehended the "friend," who put all the blame on Karina. "I told them the truth, a hundred percent, and they didn't believe me," Karina said. "They said, 'You're doing forty-five years if you don't tell us what your mom has to do with it.' I was like, 'I guess I'll be doing forty-five years. My mom didn't have shit to do with it.'" Emma and Karina chose a lawyer from the yellow pages, unaware that they could have been represented by a public defender; meeting the lawyer's bills, Emma fell behind on her mortgage, and the bank foreclosed on the house she had worked a lifetime to buy.

The attorney was able to keep Karina's trial in juvenile court; if she violated the terms of her probation, however, she would be required to serve seven years in the state penitentiary. When she arrived at the Home School, her mother's case was still pending. "I didn't care about being in myself, but my mom, my mom I was so worried about. This is my fault. What is my little sister going to do? I mean, she was looking at a lot of years, and in federal."

Then one rainy day in May, a duty officer at the Home School told Karina to call her mother. "My mom never even told me about the court date, and she's like, 'Well, I went to court today . . . ,'" Karina explained. "My heart dropped. She's like, 'It was dismissed.' I started crying and laughing at the same time. I got on my knees and I thanked God. 'Cause I prayed every day for my mom's case to be dismissed. It was about a thousand times more important than what happened to me. I was locked up and thinking, 'I might not even come home to my mom,' and that was the sentence I couldn't face. Now I can't wait to go home."

Visiting anyone else at the Home School, I felt the heavy hand of authority and the oppressive shadow of sorrow. Karina acted as though she had invited me over for fun, and her laughter bounced off the grim prison architecture. She uses foul language easily, apologizes for it charmingly, and points out the comical side of her own anguish. She was put into the Home School's Odyssey program for substance abuse. "I'm a different person, honestly. I'll always have my love for cocaine and weed, 'cause I just do. I'll miss 'em. But I won't use 'em." The biggest change was her shifting consciousness of those who'd bought the drugs she'd helped to sell. "Shit, I never thought about the people who buy the little nickel. I don't meet the people that are prostituting, neglecting their kids, the people whose lives get destroyed."

When I first met Karina, she rhapsodized about being in love. "My boyfriend, Luis, he's been writing me every week since I've been locked up. And he went to all my courts." She'd met Luis Alberto Anaya when she was fourteen and he was twenty-one. "I know it's illegal, but mentally, I'm not a little girl." Our next visit was scheduled a few weeks later, but when I arrived at the Home School, the duty officer said she couldn't see me. I assumed she had violated some rule and was on lockdown, but she was actually in shock.

"On October fourth, I went on my home visit," she told me later. "Luis came with my mom to take me back on Sunday. I gave him a kiss on his hand because I couldn't climb into the back where he was, and that night I prayed, 'Take care of him.'" The next morning, when she was taking her high school equivalency (GED) tests at an official testing site, she learned that Luis had been shot on his way to work. Karina kept her face in her hands as she told me about it. "It was his first day of promotion that morning, to an office job. Sureños got him, the gang. My boyfriend was a gang member when he was fifteen; he was done with that."

Karina's counselors were scared that she was going to relapse, but the tragedy had a galvanizing effect on her. "I'm not going to mess up my life in his name," she said. "That's disrespectful for him." A few weeks later, Karina made arrangements to finish her GED tests, which she passed; the day she left the Home School, she had two job interviews and was offered two jobs. She remained close to Luis's family, and her probation officer, impressed by her hard work and clean urinalyses, let Karina go to Mexico with them a few months later. The police picked up the gang members who had allegedly shot Luis, and Karina attended every day of their trial, but the evidence was insufficient to convict them.

Karina moved on to a better-paying job at a bank. She was determined to buy her mother a house; to make her life a tribute to Luis; to make good. "I just want to be happy, even if I'm by myself. I want to have all the material things I need, but I want to be a respected person. I don't want to be just Karina who fucked up her life." Over the following two years, the girl who had never stayed in a school for more than a year stuck with her job at the bank and earned a promotion. She took some foolish risks—driving without a license, for example—but she kept off drugs and alcohol and never missed an appointment with her probation officer. A year after her release from the Home School, she developed a relationship with a man who could accept that she had Luis's name tattooed across her back.

We kept in sporadic touch, and five years after her release, she wrote to me in an e-mail, "My daughter just turned two, and I turned 22. This year was a roller-coaster. I separated from her father, then got back together. My stepfather, Angela's dad, was released after ten years, and went back to jail seven months later, so he's now looking at 25 years in prison at age 63. The government should put more money into rehabilitating criminals so that they have a chance to turn their lives around. Most of us want to, if we can just figure out how."

In addition to innate predisposition, three risk factors wield overwhelming significance in the making of a criminal. The first is the single-parent family. More than half of all American children will spend some time as a member of a single-parent family. While 18 percent of American families fall below the poverty level, 43 percent of single-mother households do. Kids from single-parent homes are more likely to drop out of school, less likely to go to college, and more likely to abuse substances. They will work at lower-status jobs for lower pay. They tend to marry earlier and divorce earlier and are more likely to be single parents themselves. They are also much more likely to become criminals.

Jamaal Carson's mother, Breechelle, had his older brother when she was fourteen and Jamaal a year later, by a different father. Jamaal grew up on the South Side of Chicago, an area of tremendous gang violence. The family moved to Minnesota when he was ten; when I met him, he was fifteen and on his third incarceration. Despite the word THUG tattooed on his upper arm, he had the clumsy manner of a child who had done something silly and got caught. Breechelle was a good-looking woman with an opinion about everything. When she came to see the kids' theater project, she spontaneously made a speech to the staff and other parents about how the kids' having "done made mistakes" didn't compromise their being "the most talented you could find," and deserving of "everything we can give 'em." This splendid announcement notwithstanding, Jamaal complained that she had not shown up for any of his court dates.

Jamaal acknowledged that his mother had been more supportive when he first had run-ins with the law. "I'm very thankful of my mom for keeping it real with me, and I understand where she's coming from. 'Cause she only thirty-two now, and she's just a child, just like me." Despite having four children, all by different men, Breechelle did seem childlike, bewildered by her responsibilities. "I kinda feel good that Jamaal's gonna spend his life in jail," she admitted. "Means someone else gonna give him food and put a roof over his head. No way he ever gonna take care of himself, I can see." She was less impressed by Jamaal's accomplishments as a small-time drug dealer than he was. "It such hard work," Jamaal said with a tinge of pride. "You gotta worry about people taking your life; about a junkie robbing you, shooting you. People messing with you, you gotta let 'em know, 'You can't fuck with me.' It's seven days a week, twenty-four hours a day." I asked whether he had contemplated other career options. "I don't know," he said. "I'll probably write. Probably do some counseling, deal with people like me. Something that ain't hard, you know?"

The second risk factor, often coincident with the first, is abuse or neglect, which affects more than three million American children each year. John Bowlby, the original theorist of attachment, described how abused and neglected children see the world as "comfortless and unpredictable, and they respond either by shrinking from it or doing battle with it"—through depression and self-pity, or through aggression and delinquency. These children commit nearly twice as many crimes as others.

Huaj Kyuhyun's mother pushed him into the Mekong River in a tire with other escaping relatives to save his life at the time of conflict in Laos. He was granted asylum in the United States at six. By the time he was twelve he had become active in the Asian gangs of rural Wisconsin; the following year, after keeping an eighteen-year-old girl in his community out all night, thereby dishonoring her, he was "married" to her in an illegal ceremony. Both a lover and a mother to him, she was the first person he'd ever felt close to, but he treated her badly and abandoned her with their two kids to go out partying with his friends. After repeated beatings, she left him, and his life became a downward spiral of heavy drug use; to make money he helped run a ring of underage prostitutes, paying girls with drugs to have sex with johns. This was the crime for which he'd been incarcerated.

When I interviewed him, he was fifteen, and he circled obsessively, relentlessly, around his remorse for the way he had treated his wife and his longing to have contact with his children. "It's like a needle poking deeper and deeper into my heart," he said. But he had no model in his past to look to for guidance, and he seemed utterly lost. His mother had recently materialized out of the jungle, and they had spoken twice

phone. "I don't know what to say to her," he said. His mother
during their conversation, suggesting that he had probably for-
her. "I didn't forget about you," he said. "It's just that I don't
know what it feels like to have parents."

The third giant risk factor, which often accompanies the first two, is
exposure to violence. One study found that children in its sample who
suffered physical maltreatment, witnessed interparental violence, and
encountered violence within their community were more than twice as
likely to become violent delinquents as those from peaceable homes; of
course, abused children also may carry their parents' genetic predisposition toward aggression. Taking them away from their families, however, seldom helps, because the child welfare system is also associated
with high rates of crime. Jess M. McDonald of the School of Social
Work at the University of Illinois has flatly stated, "The Child Welfare
System is a feeder system for the juvenile justice system."

Ryan Nordstrom, a white thirteen-year-old at the Home School,
told me with counterfeit bravado that he had always been on the wrong
side of the law. "They've put me on meds, which is why I look sweet
and innocent all the time," he said. I asked about his early transgressions. "When I was nine," he said solemnly, "I smoked! It's totally illegal when you're nine." At ten, Ryan threatened a kid at school with
a knife and was expelled. He was incarcerated for sexual abuse of his
little sister "on a daily basis, starting when I was eleven, but I didn't get
charged until my mom called the police when I was thirteen." His sister
was six when he started out. "I wanted what I wanted, and I didn't think
she'd be able to say no," he explained.

Despite psychotherapy, Ryan did not seem to recognize that smoking, even underage, was in an entirely different category from his treatment of his sister, who had been hospitalized with vaginal abrasions.
His parents liked S&M pornography and had played it regularly in
rooms through which their children passed; they would have sex while
Ryan was in the bed with them when he was eight years old. He may
have had inherent qualities that caused him to translate such unsettling
experiences into crimes, but those qualities were doubtless exacerbated
by the transgressions in his upbringing.

Troubled kids tend to be self-destructive. David P. Farrington,
professor of psychological criminology at Cambridge, notes that boys
convicted as minors drank more beer, got drunk more often, and took
more illicit drugs; they had started smoking earlier and were more
likely to gamble. They were likely to have had sex young, and with a
wider variety of partners, but less likely to use contraceptives. Many of

these behaviors are associated with poor impulse control, but they are also frequently expressions of low self-esteem—even self-hatred.

The social critic Judith Harris has proposed that the family environment is less determinative of criminality than the larger social milieu. Unlike adults, juveniles most often commit crimes in groups; less than 5 percent of early offenders act alone, and *groupness* often determines their criminal patterns, part of the youthful urges to fit in and impress. The likelihood of delinquency also relates to the availability of drugs and guns, the degree of poverty, the lack of attachment to one's neighborhood, and population density. Rates of female crime are higher than ever, though they still account for only about a quarter of juvenile arrests. Young women are more consistently driven to crime by traumatic experience than males are. According to one study, 75 percent of girls identified as juvenile delinquents by US courts have been sexually abused. About two-thirds of chronic juvenile offenders are gang members. In 2009, in the United States, there were 731,000 gang members, almost half of them juveniles, belonging to more than 28,000 gangs.

Tall, handsome, tough, with close-cropped hair, Krishna Mirador had a way of wearing prison clothes that made them look like fashion. His English was heavily accented and sometimes hard to understand, and he would frequently ask me, "How you say in English?" as he groped for vocabulary. Born in south Los Angeles, he told me, he had been abandoned at birth by a Latina mother whose name he never learned; he was raised by his father, Raul, who was only eighteen when Krishna was born, and who was a member of Sureños 13; the gang was the only family Krishna had ever known. When Krishna was eleven, his father was deported to Guatemala, but Krishna stayed in LA, hanging out with first one set of gangbangers, then another. One of his cousins was shot and died in his arms. "That made me snap out of it, 'cause that coulda been me," he said. Raul told him to get out of LA; he knew a woman in Minneapolis who owed him a favor, and when I met Krishna, he had been living in her house for four years. He'd never found out why she was in his father's debt, and he didn't want to ask.

The weekend after I met Krishna at the Home School, a rather beautiful Irish American woman in her mid-forties introduced herself as Carol and said, "My son Krishna wants to be in your research project." Then Krishna came into the room. "Hey, Mom, just give him your signature," he said in unaccented English. I stood there, astonished. Carol, who looked just like him, said how worried she was about Krishna, and I said that it seemed as if he'd had a rough time after the hard childhood in Los Angeles. She looked at me as though I were slightly unhinged. "Krishna was born and raised in Duluth," she said. Krishna subsequently insisted that his father had told him he was born in South Gate, California, a Latino ghetto outside LA, but when I met Raul a few years later, he just laughed.

Krishna remains the most convincing and unabashed liar I have ever met, and his lies are usually angry ones, such as this furious evisceration of his mother. When I called him on it the next day, he said, "I guess if she says she's my mother, probably she is." Krishna's parents related to each other with such abiding antipathy that it was impossible to construe the truth from either. Each expected me to hate the other, but in spite of myself, I liked them all. "It's so complicated, Andrew," Carol said, the first time we talked. "I'm just so afraid you won't be able to write it, because it's just too hard."

Carol Malloy and Raul Mirador met in the late 1980s through Ananda Marga, which is sometimes called a cult, sometimes a spiritual movement, and sometimes a discipline. The group preaches unity and love but has also been accused of weapons smuggling. One of Ananda Marga's doctrines is "revolutionary marriage"—originally a protest against the Indian caste system—in which people from completely different walks of life marry each other, thus breaking down bourgeois notions of class and nationality. Raul had visa problems, and Carol's marriage was failing. Raul agreed to pay for her divorce if she would marry him. "You were given points in the guru's eyes if you sought out the most difficult thing," Carol recalled. "I don't look ahead very well; in fact, I'm usually a move or two behind. So poor Krishna was born into that."

They lived in Duluth with Carol's two children from her first marriage. Carol owned a bakery where she and Raul worked together; she eventually handed the business over to Ananda Marga. Raul moved them all to Guatemala when Krishna was five. After nine months, Carol's two older children couldn't stand it and returned to the United States to live with their father, while Carol, in her own words, "chose ideology over love" and has never really reconnected with those children. It took her "five years of muddle" to learn the language and the culture in Guatemala, during which time, she said, "Raul became impossibly macho and bossy; he was probably always bossy, but in Duluth it was my house and my business, and it was less noticeable." She told him she was going to divorce him unless he returned to the United States with her; she was certain she could get custody of the children. Raul claims that she said, in earshot of the children, that she was ready to leave even without them, and that to spare them abandonment he agreed to try a return to Minnesota.

Krishna was ten; his sister, Ashoka, was eight; his brother, Basho, born in Guatemala, was four. Carol and Raul took jobs teaching Latino children in the Minneapolis public school system, and they entered couples counseling. "The kids were really happy," she recalled. "When Krishna was nine, I would sit on the floor by his bed and just read and read, and then we would talk and talk. We read *Don Quixote de la Mancha*. We read poetry; we read stories; history. We were so close. He doesn't remember it."

Nine months after their return, Carol came home one day to an empty house. Raul had taken all three children back to Guatemala. "I thought Raul was going to struggle with me," Carol said sadly, "and if we couldn't do it, we would divorce here, work through the history, and become friends. But he was a real coward." Though Carol was furious at Raul, she was also angry at Krishna, who was old enough to have made a choice. Krishna could never forgive his mother for having been willing to leave him behind in Guatemala; she could never forgive him for leaving her behind in the United States. For the first two years I knew him, Krishna maintained that he didn't remember his childhood. When I repeated this to Raul, all he could say was, "The children are very angry at Carol."

Carol served kidnapping charges on Raul through the American embassy. She went to Guatemala and tried to negotiate a settlement. "The visits were always in a locked room, at Raul's lawyer's office," she said. "There were two guards with machine guns, and I thought they were going to kill me. And the kids were so brainwashed." Carol eventually got custody in both countries. Raul went to jail, through Interpol, for kidnapping. "We presented the papers to Raul's parents. When we went in, the beds were still warm. The Mirador family had reabducted my kids." She left Guatemala in despair; two weeks later, Raul's parents paid someone off, and he was released.

Carol's separation from Raul seemed necessary to her, but she paid for it with her second set of children. "I was free, but I had lost everything," she said. "Raul wanted to punish me for wanting to be out of Ananda Marga, for wanting to go to grad school, for believing in myself." Many years later, Krishna wrote to me, "I know my father loves me even though he seldom says it, and I know my mom doesn't even though she says it all the time. I haven't seen my Dad have a girlfriend since my Mom. He says it's because he doesn't have time, but I know it's because she broke his heart."

While Carol had her kids' pictures appearing on milk cartons as missing children, his grandparents hid Krishna with cousins in LA for almost a year, and he joined Sureños. His first assignment, he told me, was to steal a car; then they gave him an Uzi with a full clip of ammunition and ordered him to take the car and "go get some rivals." He said, "I came back with no bullets left. When I felt that adrenaline pumping in my heart, I was like, 'Yeah, this is my shit. This is *my* drug.'"

After nine months, Raul called Krishna back to Guatemala. A year later, when Krishna was thirteen, he came to see Carol in Minneapolis. "I don't know how it happened," she said, "except that it was Christmas, and sometimes you can get a wish through. I invited him like nothing was wrong." Krishna had a good two-week visit, and Carol persuaded someone from Ananda Marga to negotiate for Ashoka and Krishna to come for Easter. When they arrived in Minnesota, she told them they weren't going back. "She didn't do it because she loved us," Krishna said. "She did it because she hates my father and it was revenge." Krishna was furious with his mother, but he liked America and didn't want to return to Guatemala; Ashoka was miserable and desperate to get home. Raul was beside himself, but couldn't enter the United States, because of a warrant for his arrest, so he asked a friend to retrieve Ashoka.

The day of the great escape, Ashoka was stuck at home with Carol's boyfriend. She called her father and explained in a whisper that she had no way to leave. He ordered Krishna to lure Carol's boyfriend out of the house, and as soon as they were gone, Ashoka bolted. "I helped my sister get out of the States illegally," Krishna said. "Which is kinda weird, 'cause most people are trying to get *into* the States illegally." Carol was devastated but took Krishna's staying as a compliment. To Krishna, it was payback. "She wanted a son so damn bad—I'm gonna show her how hard it is," he explained to me. "I had to make her life hell for a little bit." Carol, who had been a vegetarian, explained that she had started eating chicken with Krishna. She paused and held out her hands in desperation. "I'll do anything for a connection. But he doesn't, can't, share. Krishna will never really engage. His head is full of garbage; it's full of indoctrination; it's full of Guatemala."

This warped mother-son relationship, marked by rage and frustration on each side, changed dramatically one evening when Krishna went to buy some marijuana. He was fifteen. "We were kicking it right on Bloomington and Lake Street when a red Lincoln pulls up, and a dude starts blasting at us," he recalled. The police questioned everyone who was there, but detained Krishna in relation to the murder of a thirty-nine-year-old black man the preceding month. "I thought they were trying to scare me at first," he continued. "Black gangs fight black gangs and Chicano gangs fight Chicano gangs. We like killing each other, I guess. So no way was this me."

But the police soon filed charges against Krishna. When Carol learned that her son would be tried in the adult system, she organized friends to write letters, protest, and pack the courtroom. She explained that Krishna had previously been kidnapped and was traumatized. For the first time in Hennepin County, a murder case stayed in the juvenile system. Krishna faced an uphill battle. "My lawyer'd be like, 'Well, they offered us fifteen years.' *Us?* Motherfucker, you gonna do seven and a half, I'm gonna do seven and a half? I was like, 'I'm not gonna plead guilty to something I didn't do.'" Krishna was steely in his resolve, and the case was finally dismissed. By then he'd been in jail for seven and a half months.

"When they let him go, everyone thought, 'He'll really turn his life around,'" Carol said. "But he got right back into it." For once, Krishna agreed with his mother's version of events. "Being locked up made me think, 'Fuck everybody,'" he said to me. Things did not go well at home. Anyone who came to the house with a blue kerchief—a Sureños symbol—Carol kicked out. Krishna said, "I think a mother should be until the end. Even if I was doing life in prison, she'd still try to be there for me. I was testing her." She replied, "Krishna says he wanted to stay in Minnesota to make my life miserable, and that's why he kept himself in the gang. It's to see if I really love him. I don't think he planned it at all. The gang and the cult are the exact same: very hierarchical; rules; this small group of people dedicated to this pointless rigid structure and ready to die for it. He's re-creating the childhood he hated."

Two months after the charges against Krishna were dropped, he served a one-month sentence for having a gun. A few months later, he was picked up for parole violations, and at sixteen he was sent to a year at the County Home School, where I met him. Krishna told me that his girlfriend was pregnant—which she was not—and added, "I don't want Carol to even see the kid; I don't need her talking about 'Your first years were really something else.'" Krishna's ability to be angry at his mother for something she hadn't said to a baby who didn't exist was an impressive feat of projection. A little later, Krishna said, "I was just thinking how if my kid grew up to be like me, it would be my fault. That almost made me cry; I wanted to cry. My eyes kind of swelled up, but no tears." Anger had apparently crowded out all his other emotions.

"I could handle it if he were one of these kids all dressed in black, with blue hair and piercings," Carol said. "Even tattoos, if they're not gang-related, are fine. Even if he were gay, fine. I can never be fine with violence, and I wonder if that's why he chose it. They've got his back. Why do they have to have his back? Does anyone have your back? My medical insurance has my back. One thing he's proud of in the gang is that he tells other people what to do. He's always on that cell phone barking out orders in Spanish. I said to him, 'Look, I tell people all the time what to do, because I teach first grade. Would you consider it as an alternative?'" But Carol also admitted that she is in part responsible for who Krishna is. "You know me as who I am now, and I know you like me," she said sadly. "But believe me—I wasn't the same person then, and you wouldn't have liked me so much." She also thought that the complexities of being part white were too much for her son. "He's too scared to be himself. It's hard for mixed-race kids to stand up and say, 'I am neither here nor there; I am myself.'" In a letter Krishna wrote me, he said, "It would make sense to tell you who I am, even though sometimes *I* don't even know. Always classified as a 'spic' for my language, culture, looks, and demeanor, but always teased, ostracized and not fully accepted by my Latino brothers for being a 'half-breed.'"

Krishna loved giving tutorials about gang life. "The Hispanic gangs in California have been going since the 1900s," he told me one evening. "I'm not putting down black gangs, but there's more loyalty and honor with us. Gangs didn't really start as criminal organizations; they degenerated into that. But, look at the people in Enron, stealing old people's retirement funds. I, myself, or any of my homeboys, that's a rule, that you can't fuckin' jack old people. That's despicable." When I met Raul three years later, I saw that Krishna was echoing the tone of his father's earnest moral instruction. Most of the kids whom I interviewed for this chapter spoke correct English when they first met me and then relaxed into patois. Krishna spoke broken gang language, full of obscenities, until he relaxed, at which point he spoke perfectly grammatical English. Was his gang mode a defense to camouflage the sensitive person he really was? Or was he an incredibly hard guy who could manipulate people with his apparent softness? Krishna himself has no idea of the answers to these questions.

In the final month of his sentence, Krishna went out every day to a job and could leave the premises in the evenings with a responsible adult. I had applied for permission to take him to dinner. When we had sat up nights in the Home School, he would talk about how he wanted to go to college. Now as he tucked into a sirloin, his fixation was the gang. "Those are my people," he said. "I ain't gonna be sacrificing my loyalties just for living under Carol's roof." I mentioned that I had been interviewing Karina Lopez, and he laughed. "You heard her boyfriend died? My boys did that." He actually thumped his chest. "I saw her the day it happened, in the med unit, crying her ass off. I laughed." Karina later confirmed the episode: "He didn't have anything to do with the murder, but he sure enjoyed it."

I told him that it was hard to reconcile all this with the boy full of dreams with whom I'd played Scrabble a few weeks earlier. "They're all part of one person, though," he said. "My counselor just made me do an assignment on what a psychopath is. After reading twenty characteristics, I stopped, because it was scary. I love my hatred—it's so strong and sort of pure and real. And I kind of hate love, like I feel it's always false and disappointing, everyone saying they love me when they just want to control me. I love hatred and I hate love. So is that enough for me to be a psychopath? I don't think I'm evil. I hope not."

Three days later, Krishna went to his job and didn't come back. To run away when you have two weeks of transitional living remaining is ludicrous; instead of walking out with a clean record, he was on the lam. After three months, he was picked up in south Minneapolis and returned to the Home School. When I saw him there, I expressed mild surprise that he had stayed in a town where every policeman knew his face. "I went to the Greyhound station twice to buy a ticket to LA, but I was having too much fun here," he said. He complained that Carol had reservations about having him move back home. "Did my mom let me down?" he asked. "I don't think she let me up to begin with." Carol was sad. "He somehow missed the lesson on delayed gratification," she said to me. "I wish you could take over being his mother."

Krishna began what I was to recognize as a predictable cycle. As long as he was locked up, he was capable of optimism and hope, qualities that dissipated when he left his confinement. Now, he wanted to stay in gang life but not commit crimes, and he planned to do this by writing plays to be performed by gang members. He would beat their knives into scripts, their guns into production values. After describing to me the plot of one of his stories, he became abruptly ruminative. "I'm a banger. That's just the easy way out for me. That way I know where I stand. Whereas, when I'm trying to be positive, I don't really know where I stand—and I don't really know how committed I am to being positive."

I had heard a great deal about his father and wanted to see if Raul was the gentle sage of Krishna's raptures or the manipulative creep I'd heard about from Carol. Three years after I met Krishna, he was free and planning a trip to Guatemala. I proposed to his father that I visit at the same time. Raul wrote back, "You are welcome any time. You do not have to spend your money and time in a hotel. It will be our pleasure to have you with us so we can meet and talk freely."

Raul was warm and courtly and instantly likable, a small man with thick, black, wavy hair; he looked almost Asian and was dwarfed by his towering son. They met me at the airport; I threw my bags in the trunk of their elderly station wagon, and we headed to Krishna's grandparents' house, where I was given a room ordinarily reserved for visiting grandchildren, which had on the dresser, incongruously grouped, a light-up Santa Claus, a gigantic Mr. Potato Head, and a portrait of the pope.

Raul told me that he and Carol had loved each other. "Before we married, I said, 'I don't accept a marriage that leads to divorce, especially if there are children.' But she left anyway, and she wanted to have them with her, which she hadn't earned and couldn't do properly." We stayed up talking late that night, and Raul returned over and over to the language of morality. "I don't think this thing we see is the real Krishna," he said. "The real Krishna is that sweet boy who went up to visit America five years ago. The good side will come out on top, but whether it does so before he gets locked up for life or killed in a shootout I don't know." Later he said, "I can understand being willing to die, or to spend your life in prison, but not for a gang. Krishna needs a cause." Raul looked at me with sudden frankness. "Can you help him find one?" he asked.

In the morning, we went to an Ananda Marga school in an impoverished district called La Limonada. The children, three to six years old, were taught in two rooms, one above the other in a concrete bunker with a tin roof. Raul and Krishna were greeted with songs and a little dance, Krishna awkwardly receiving these salutations. The teacher asked if Krishna would give the kids English lessons, and he replied that his tattoos and gangster look would get him into trouble in the neighborhood—an excuse that clearly upset his father. Then Krishna said he had to bounce, so Raul and I drove to a small apartment on the outskirts of town and met a dozen Ananda Marga devotees from various countries. We meditated on faded prayer mats and talked about good and evil over a shared bowl of lentils.

That night, with bravado, Krishna took me to a gang-dominated part of the city, where he introduced me to the local Sureños. Everyone had guns and gang tattoos, and at one point we heard gunfire outside the room where we were gathered—and yet it felt weirdly like meeting someone's fraternity brothers on a college campus. I understood for the first time how Sureños could feel both utterly dangerous and uniquely safe. The gang was itself a horizontal identity, and crime served a function in Krishna's life not unlike the role that Deafness or dwarfism played in other lives I'd examined, not unlike the role that being gay played in my own life. I kept remembering the letter in which Krishna had said he couldn't tell me who he was because he didn't know. His mother had attributed the confusion to being biracial, but it also reflected the question of whether he was his mother's son or his father's, American or Guatemalan, good or evil—a catalog of dialectics too long to enumerate. In that ugly room in an ugly neighborhood he knew exactly who he was, which allowed him to relax as I had never seen him relax before.

I had been surprised to be drawn to the world of the Deaf, but it was much stranger to be seduced by this world. Yet from the inside, gangbanging was hospitable. I did not like hanging out with the Sureños any more than I'd liked my morning with the Ananda Margis and their lentils, but I did not like it any less, either. I knew that many of the people in that room had committed murder. They were kind to me, however, as a kindness to Krishna, a consideration for which he was clearly starved. That cordiality felt authentic and embracing. I had assumed that hanging out with the gang in the slums of Guatemala City would show me the toughest part of Krishna, but instead, it showed me the most vulnerable. Criminality is an identity, and like any other form of organized brutality—football, war, arbitrage—it can beget great intimacy. The social imperative is to suppress criminal behavior, but that should not preclude noticing the identity. I deplore violence, but I recognize the military intimacy it allows men who have no other occasion to bond. Indeed, I recognize that the conquests by which the map of the world is drawn derive from the loyalty and aggression of young men.

My last day in Guatemala, Raul had arranged for Krishna's grandfather to drive me to the airport. "Hey," said Krishna. "You want me to come with you?" A little gallantly, he picked up my suitcase to take to the car. During the drive, he told me about Guatemalan poetry, and I mentioned Elizabeth Bishop's poems from Brazil, which capture the displacement between the two Americas. I quoted some favorite lines, and he borrowed a pen to write them down. I had expected simply to be dropped off, but at the airport Krishna grabbed my suitcase out of my hand again, accompanied me inside, and picked a good line for me—good, he explained, because he could really be into the girl at the counter. He waited until I had checked in and escorted me to the security zone. I walked into the secured area, then turned around, and he was waving at me. "Thanks," he called out. "For what?" I asked. "For coming. For everything," he said. "I'll miss you, man." He coughed, looked embarrassed, and hurried away. That image of him, almost forlorn, printed itself on my heart; for a gleaming moment, I saw the sweet Krishna whom both Raul and Carol had described.

Krishna moved back to Minneapolis to live with his mother again, and the next I heard, he had been shot and was in critical condition; he'd lost a kidney and part of his gallbladder, and he had lacerations on his liver, a collapsed lung, and "catastrophic" bleeding. When he left the hospital, Carol asked him to find someplace else to live. "If they come to finish off the job," she said drily, "I don't want it happening in my house." After that, he was mostly on the run, but when I couldn't reach him on his ever-changing cell numbers, I was able to keep up because he returned to his mother's house to do his laundry and ironing. Five months later, Carol took him back. Then Krishna challenged some gang members, and they shot up the house. Ashoka, who had been on a long visit, returned to Guatemala the next day; in a letter she left for Krishna, she wrote, "I used to think you just needed focus, but now I feel like it's a slow form of suicide and I don't want to be part of it." Carol said, "So I'm losing both my children again."

A month later, Krishna got sixteen months for assault. This time, he went to the big house. When I visited, he apologized for the fictions he'd told me. The gang had disappointed him by then; one of the Sureños in the incident had turned state's witness. "I mean, don't join the gang if you can't understand; we have rules, we have bylaws, there is stuff you have to do and stuff you can't do." I proposed that if following rules were so attractive, he might as well follow the ones set by the US government, and he laughed. Krishna called Carol every week. "He calls me because he's allowed to," she said. "I have been so stupid to keep thinking that those speeches about doing better meant anything. I asked, 'What about that optimism you expressed in the play you were writing?' and he said, 'Those were just words.' Where's the reality? I'd give anything to be able to find it. Even if it's ugly, really, really ugly, I could accept it, if I could only see it, even for a few minutes. That's my dream." She looked at me sadly. "Andrew, I know you better than I know my son."

The next time Krishna was released from prison, he took his ACTs and sent the scores to several colleges, including UCLA, which was his first choice. But before his applications could be processed, he accompanied four fellow gang members on a drive that culminated in the shooting death of a member of the Vatos Locos gang. He was charged with aiding an offender for the benefit of a gang, pleaded guilty, and was sentenced to eight years in Minnesota's Stillwater maximum-security prison.

Krishna could have found community elsewhere if he hadn't been too petrified to try. He was certainly smart enough to go to UCLA; he hid behind bluster to avoid risks that scared him, and the guns he toted were only transitional objects, a flashier edition of Linus's security blanket. His freshman year shimmers on a dreamed horizon; to his "what is" there is a vast "what might have been," and he is haunted by it. Finding a horizontal identity can be life's greatest liberation, but it can also be crushing, and in this case, the figurative prison consigned Krishna to a literal one.

Stillwater has a vast grayness. Krishna looked spruce whenever he entered the visiting room, but his idealist streak had dimmed. "I don't hate Carol anymore," he said to me one afternoon there. "I used to think she was the one who had made me powerless, but now I think she loved me in whatever way she knows how. I just felt *so* powerless growing up, not getting to choose where to live, and I finally realized, I joined the gang so I could feel really powerful. And what's the upshot? I'm totally powerless again, right back where I started—only this time, I did it to myself."

Carol said to me, a few weeks later, "He wanted to work with the oppressed, to be with his people, with the disenfranchised Latinos. But what has he done? He gets them to kill each other. He lands them in prison. The people he says are his people—they'd be better off without him." I asked her if she thought she would be better off without him, and she said, "I've been without him the whole time. I don't really miss who he is at all. But who he was—I'm pretty sure I'm right about who he was, and I miss that person so much. And the person I thought that person would turn into, I miss him, too, with all my heart."

No other group of people has given me more confused information than these juvenile criminals. They didn't trust or like adult, white, male authority figures, and their knee-jerk dissembling was part of what had landed them in prison in the first place. More fundamentally, though, they didn't grasp their own reality. They didn't know for sure what had happened; their narratives were all conditional.

Jail concentrates human emotions because it confiscates so many normal human actions and robs the inmate of so many ordinary decisions: what to eat, when to eat it, when to shower, and on and on. When you are not on the street, fending for yourself, running from crime to crime, taking drugs that banish the world, you are compelled into reflection. In this pensive state, prisoners dwell on love and hate, on reunion and vengeance. They contemplate how to get back at whoever put them in the box; virtually all the prisoners I met blamed someone else for their incarceration if not for their crime. They also long for the people who offer them succor: a husband or wife, a boyfriend or girlfriend, the prisoner's children, parents whose relatively untempered love becomes a cherished souvenir of innocence.

The wrongs Krishna had endured were far more real to him than the ones he'd inflicted on others. I met other kids, though, who seemed to have become criminals to give some objective weight to a previous and crippling sense of guilt. One boy I befriended at the Home School, Tyndall Wilkie, had a fight with his mother, a preschool teacher, when he was six and told the school nurse that she had been abusing him, then repeated the story to the school social worker. She hadn't abused him; he just wanted to get her in trouble. Tyndall and his sister were put into permanent foster care; his mother was banned from teaching for five years. His whole life unfolded in the shadow of this error.

Mitt Ebbetts, a gang kid at another prison, described how, when he was eight, his mother would leave him in charge of his younger sisters, cautioning him never to answer the door. One day, the knocking was so insistent that he couldn't ignore it. It was the police, responding to a neighbor's complaint about the children being left home alone. They were taken from her care and caromed from foster home to foster home. Like Lord Jim, Mitt was haunted by one error; he felt he had ruined his mother's and sisters' lives and so eviscerated his own moral center. His later offenses, drug peddling and assault, fulfilled his need for self-punishment. The legend of crime is that it is spurred by parents who hurt their children. The legacy of crime is that children hurt their parents. Often, the pain attached to that transgression blots out all other remorse.

Love is not only an intuition but also a skill. Therapeutic prison programs such as the Home School's provide structure and momentum for reflection, via group sessions, diaries, and letter-writing. Having a child at the Home School also provides learning opportunities for the child's parents. Prison defines parameters for affection that are easier for some people than the unmapped, everyday world. You come on visiting day. You stay the whole time. You bring in those sneakers or help hold on to the girlfriend by treating her as part of your family. These obvious, concrete actions do not depend on sustaining a mood, which many people of short temper and shifting emotion find difficult. People who cannot achieve constancy from minute to minute can sometimes sustain it once a week. A valid trust—"my parents said they would come on visiting day and they did"—was nearly revelatory for many prisoners. In some cases, this support vanished when the child was released, but in others it functioned as training wheels: by the time the child's sentence was up, the parents were ready to perform their roles with new confidence and skill, unassisted.

Ideally, a juvenile's reintegration into the family can also be a mirroring of his or her pending reintegration into society at large. The first time I attended family visiting day at the Department of Community Corrections of Hennepin County, I was talking to two boys who seemed to be in much the same situation. They were the same age, had similar sentences, and were being released at about the same time. I soon learned, however, that the parents of one had traveled two hours to show up for every court date, every family counseling session, and every visiting hour; the boy's mother had already lined up a construction job for his release. The other boy halfheartedly joined in with his friend's family because his own middle-class, educated family, who lived less than two miles from the facility, never came. These two inmates were being released into different worlds.

I visited Castington, a high-security prison near Newcastle in the north of England, and found it more traditional and physically shabbier than the Home School. In Minnesota, staff would always tell the residents that they were under no obligation to talk to me. At Castington, I was invited to observe procedures and was present, for example, when new arrivals were strip-searched. The English inmates had not achieved the self-knowledge, or even the illusion of self-knowledge, that characterized their Home School counterparts. Frank Buckland, in prison for slashing the face of his cousin's boyfriend, seemed daunted by his approaching release date. "I've got the violence pretty well under control in here," Frank said; he had in fact been a model prisoner. "But I want to go out like the other blokes, have a drink, meet some girls. I don't know whether I'll go violent again." He spoke of his future character as though it were a mystery beyond his control. "We'll just have to wait and see," his mother echoed helplessly. The young people at the Home School were taught to begin thinking about, and planning for, what they were going to do on the outside; in contrast, I didn't meet a single Castington inmate who had any idea what he wanted to do with his life after his release.

Reflections on the future from inside a prison are fantasies of sorts, but the coherence and hopefulness of any particular fantasy has considerable bearing on the inmate's ability to turn his or her life around after prison. That Krishna spent his steak dinner with me extolling the virtues of gang life was a bad sign—just as Karina's using her boyfriend's murder as a reason to complete her GED was a promising one. The Home School provides a step-down program in which inmates are slowly returned to the world with supportive services. Terry Bach said, "I've had parents who feel comfortable calling me if something goes wrong after the kid gets out." Karina had remained close to her favorite correctional officer and had turned to her for advice from time to time. The injection of humanity into these relationships is enormously productive.

For most horizontal identities, the issue of collective innocence is central; the heart-tugging argument is that disabled children do not deserve to be castigated. Here, we deal with guilty children and, in some cases, with parents who have grossly erred. Yet many of these families have also been marginalized and brutalized, emotionally and economically isolated, depressed, and frustrated. I kept meeting parents who wanted to help their kids but didn't have the knowledge or means to do so effectively; like the parents of disabled children, they couldn't access the social services to which they were ostensibly entitled. Heaping opprobrium on these parents exacerbates a problem we could instead resolve. We deny the reality of their lives not only at the expense of our humanity but also at our personal peril.

Criminality appears to be more subject to resolve than many other conditions. No one can will his way out of Down syndrome, but some people can walk away from a criminal past. They usually require enormous supports to do so. Research on preventing crime has hatched a panoply of effective solutions, but we ignore most, writing off vast sectors of our society. While nearly three-quarters of people working with juvenile delinquents believe effective ways exist to treat the problem, only 3 to 6 percent believe that the juvenile courts are helping. Our lack of sympathy for these pariah children keeps successful treatment out of their reach. Aside from the common prejudice that therapeutic interventions are excessively soft on the criminal, the justification for withholding such treatments is often that they are ineffective and exorbitantly expensive. Neither justification has merit. The cost of jailing a minor ranges from about $20,000 to $65,000 per year. Prisons with more programs experience less violence, which reduces some expenses, but the major financial benefit lies in curtailed recidivism. A crime gives rise to enormous knock-on costs, including loss of property, trial expenses, health-care costs from injury, and psychological liabilities sustained by frightened victims. Joseph Califano, head of the National Center on Addiction and Substance Abuse, said, "Treatment and accountability are complementary rather than mutually exclusive objectives."

In a meta-analysis of 163 studies, William R. Shadish, professor of psychology at the University of California, Merced, demonstrated that family interventions are the most productive ones; another meta-analysis concluded, "The use of family and parenting interventions can result in a significant reduction in time spent in institutions such as prison and detention centers by juvenile delinquents." As with autism or Down syndrome, early intervention brings the best results. The 2001 US Surgeon General's report on youth violence confirmed that prenatal home visits to teach parenting skills to expectant mothers can reduce juvenile crime. Such programs are most effective when they are followed up; one researcher likened the approach to the dental model, in which regular maintenance is required to ensure good health—not the vaccination model, in which a single early-childhood action can prevent disease.

An impatient society wants treatment to be more targeted, so most family programs do not set in until at-risk children are older and address only the families of known offenders. These therapies are mostly known by abbreviations: BPT, FFT, MST, SFT, BSFT, MFGI, FAST, FET, TFC. Most draw on cognitive/behavioral models; parents learn how to be consistent, fair, and emotionally open; children learn how to identify their feelings, manage their anger, and communicate better. Together, kids and parents improve conflict-resolution skills. Some therapies also deal with practical matters such as helping families to get adequate housing, food, and clothing. Some put children into model foster-care environments and then bring the biological family to observe the foster family as a prelude to returning the child to them.

Alan Kazdin and his team at the Yale Parenting Center advocate disciplinary measures that are not associated with violence or fear; altering the home correctional system can steer young people clear of the state one. One study posited that a behavioral-communication approach could reduce recidivism by half. Another showed that kids on probation in a control group were almost ten times more likely to reoffend than similar kids who participated in family therapy. Another reported that institutionalized delinquents who received family therapy in prison had a recidivism rate of 60 percent, compared to a Sisyphean 93 percent rate for those who didn't. At-risk children whose families received no early therapy were 70 percent more likely to be arrested for a violent crime before they turned eighteen than those whose families had received such therapy. These statistics have had little effect on how we deal with juvenile crime. Only one of ten juvenile prisons uses family therapies, and only about a quarter of these do so consistently. We rail against the atrocities perpetrated by kids, but we consistently choose the satisfaction of retribution over the efficacy of prevention.

Basic family interventions, in approximate terms, can run anywhere from $2,000 to $30,000 per family served. The HighScope Perry Preschool Project showed that for new mothers deemed to be at risk, every $1 spent on treatment saved $7 in later costs—a number that didn't even take into account the positive economic contributions of this nonoffending population. While California's "three strikes" law has a cost per serious crime prevented of $16,000, and parole comes in at just under $14,000, parent training has a cost per serious crime prevented of just $6,351. Extremely good results have been shown for relatively inexpensive graduation incentives that keep kids in school. The Perry Project suggests that failing to intervene with at-risk low-income families with children under five in the United States may cost us as much as $400 billion. But while money spent on deterrence this year may vastly reduce prison expenses a decade down the line, it's hard to apply this equivalence to a line-item budget, especially one that needs to pay off within a political term.

Moral questions loom large in any discussion of such treatments. What message do we convey if we respond to violent crime with therapy? If we opt for less prison time, more crimes will be committed by people who would otherwise have been locked up. Three strikes was designed to reduce adult crime by 25 percent in California—a goal it may or may not have achieved. No preventive or therapeutic program has ever arrived at such ambitious goals. On the other hand, three strikes is scandalously expensive, and the state is on the verge of bankruptcy. We can't dismantle the justice system or knock out crime with kindness; fire is often needed to fight fire. At the same time, the overwhelming evidence is that punitive justice can be strengthened with therapeutic programs. To discard the prison system in favor of therapeutic interventions would be crazy; but a prison system that is used without therapeutic intervention, as in much of the country today, is at least equally crazy.

A peculiar arrogance accrues to people who cannot recognize the diversity of human impulses, and who feel superior because they do not lapse into behaviors that don't tempt them in the first place. People disgusted by sexual predators say smugly that they don't pursue the sexual favors of children, without acknowledging that they don't find children sexually attractive. Those who do not tend toward chemical dependency express disdain for addicts; people with small appetites patronize the morbidly obese. A hundred years ago, my homosexuality would have landed me in jail, and I am fortunate to live in a place and an era that allow me to be true to myself. If I'd had to deny my longings, it would have been a different experience from that of straight people who have no such longings to deny. Spending time with criminals, I have seen that while many have poor impulse control or are weak or stupid or destructive, many others are driven by a compulsion. Some manifest enormous courage by refraining from theft although the wish to steal burns in them every minute, and their restraint of demons they cannot eradicate is categorically different from the lawfulness of people who find the idea of thievery distasteful.

Families of criminals often struggle both to admit that their child has done something destructive, and to continue to love him anyway. Some give up the love; some blind themselves to the bad behavior. The ideal of doing neither of those things borrows from the idea of loving the sinner while hating the sin, but sinners and sins cannot so easily be separated; if human beings love sinners, we love them with their sin. People who see and acknowledge the darkness in those they love, but whose love is only strengthened by that knowledge, achieve that truest love that is eagle-eyed even when the views are bleak. I met one family whose own tragedy had led them to embrace these contradictions more than any other, one mother whose love seemed both infinitely deep and infinitely knowing of a blighted person. Hers was a love as dark and true, as embracing and self-abnegating, as Cordelia's.

On April 20, 1999, Eric Harris and Dylan Klebold, seniors at Columbine High School in Littleton, Colorado, placed bombs in the cafeteria, set to go off during first lunch period at 11:17 a.m., and planned to shoot anyone who tried to flee. Errors in the construction of the detonators prevented the bombs from exploding, but Klebold and Harris nevertheless held the whole school hostage, killing twelve students and one teacher before turning their guns on themselves. At the time, it was the worst episode of school violence in history. The American Right blamed the collapse of "family values," while the Left mounted assaults on violence in the movies and sought to tighten gun-control laws. Wholesale critiques of the larger culture were offered as explanation for these inexplicable events.

The number of people killed that day is generally listed as thirteen, and the Columbine Memorial commemorates only thirteen deaths, as though Klebold and Harris had not also died that day in that place. Contrary to wide speculation then and since, the boys did not come from broken homes and did not have records of criminal violence. The wishful thought of a world that witnessed this horror was that good parenting could prevent children from developing into Eric Harris or Dylan Klebold, but malevolence does not always grow in a predictable or accountable manner. As the families of autistics or schizophrenics wonder what happened to the apparently healthy people they knew, other families grapple with children who have turned to horrifying acts and wonder what happened to the innocent children they thought they understood.

I set out to interview Tom and Sue Klebold with the expectation that meeting them would help to illuminate their son's actions. The better I came to know the Klebolds, the more deeply mystified I became. Sue Klebold's kindness (before Dylan's death, she worked with people with disabilities) would be the answered prayer of many a neglected or abused child, and Tom's bullish enthusiasm would lift anyone's tired spirits. Among the many families I've met in writing this book, the Klebolds are among those I would be most game to join. Trapped in their own private *Oresteia*, they learned astonishing forgiveness and empathy. They are victims of the terrifying, profound unknowability of even the most intimate human relationship. It is easier to love a good person than a bad one, but it may be more difficult to lose a bad person you love than a good one. Sue Klebold once said to me, "I watched *Rosemary's Baby* the other night and my heart really went out to Rosemary." When Barbara Walters interviewed the father of one of Dylan's classmates after the events, he said of the Klebolds, "They're in a glass cage. And they have no more pieces to this puzzle than anybody else."

The last Sue Klebold heard from Dylan, the younger of her two children, was "Bye" as he let the front door slam on his way to school that April 20. In the middle of the day, Tom received a call about the shootings at school and learned that Dylan was a suspect. He called Sue. "I had a sudden vision of what he might be doing," Sue said. "And so while every other mother in Littleton was praying that her child was safe, I had to pray that mine would die before he hurt anyone else. I thought if this was really happening and he survived, he would go into the criminal justice system and be executed, and I couldn't bear to lose him twice. I gave the hardest prayer I ever made, that he would kill himself, because then at least I would know that he wanted to die and wouldn't be left with all the questions I'd have if he got caught by a police bullet. Maybe I was right, but I've spent so many hours regretting that prayer: I wished for my son to kill himself, and he did."

That night, police told the Klebolds to leave their house—both so the police could turn it inside out, and for their own safety. "I thought about Dylan being dead," Sue said, "and I thought, 'He was young and healthy and maybe he could be an organ donor.' And then I thought, 'Would anyone want the organs of a murderer?' That was my first taste of how the world would see my son." The Klebolds went to stay with Tom's sister for four days, returning home on the day of Dylan's funeral. "We didn't really know what had happened," Sue said. "We just knew Dylan was dead, that he'd killed himself, that he was involved with the shooting."

As Littleton's period of mourning began, a carpenter from Illinois erected fifteen crosses on a hillside near the school. "I was so buoyed by this," Tom said. "I wanted to be a part of the community. And I thought we could all grieve together." Sue remembered, "There were flowers, and Dylan's and Eric's crosses had as many as everyone else's."

Then the parents of some of the victims destroyed Dylan's and Eric's crosses. The youth group at a local church planted fifteen trees, only to have some of the victims' parents arrive with a press escort to chop down Dylan's and Eric's trees. At the high school graduation ceremony a week later, there were encomiums for the victims, but the head of the school told friends of Dylan and Eric to make themselves scarce. Before long, reports referring to the incident started using the number thirteen rather than fifteen. "The shorthand was this," Tom said. "Thirteen people died. Two Nazis killed them, and the parents were responsible. It was a lynch mob." Sue said reflectively, "I think the other parents believed they had experienced loss, and I had not, because their children were of value, and mine was not. My child died, too. He died after making a terrible decision and doing a terrible thing, but he was still my child, and he still died."

The Klebolds' lawyer had advised them not to talk to the press; their silence exacerbated local hostility. "You'd read something, and you couldn't respond to it," Tom said. "You knew that it was false, misleading, inflammatory." Sue said, "It was just like constantly being hit, and being hit again. And you couldn't fight back." In an act of agonizing catharsis, Sue handwrote notes to the parents of each child who had died or been injured. Though she did not feel responsible for what had happened, she wanted to mitigate the devastation. "To me, the only way to heal this community was to try to have a one-to-one relationship with each of the victims," she later explained. "My journey is not complete until I can say to these people, 'If you ever want to speak to me, I am available to you. I will meet in your home, a pastor's office, with a mediator if you want. If it would help you to talk to me, I'm here.'" She has never done it, because a counselor cautioned her that by contacting them, she might retraumatize them. "But I cried for their children just as I did for mine," she said. While the Klebolds faced a great deal of hostility, moments of unusual love also surfaced. "A few weeks after Columbine happened, I got a hug from the checkout clerk at Home Depot," Tom said. "Neighbors brought us food. And when I took my car in to have a bent wheel fixed, the mechanic said to me, 'At least you didn't change your name.' He respected that."

Investigations over the ensuing months revealed an atmosphere of bullying at Columbine. "Unless you were a part of the in crowd and had your athletic résumé, you had no status," Tom said. "So Dylan had to be resentful. The only thing that would certainly have prevented Columbine would have been to eliminate the chip on his shoulder, and the chip sprang from that school. He and Eric didn't shoot us, and they didn't shoot up Kmart or a gas station; they shot up the school. The whole social pattern at Columbine was unfair, and Dylan couldn't do anything about it. That would cause enough anger in a sensitive kid to make him retaliate."

Unbeknownst to the Klebolds, Dylan had experienced significant humiliation at school, though he was six feet four and not easy to push around. He had come home one day with ketchup spots all over his shirt, and when his mother asked what had happened, he said he'd had the worst day of his life and didn't want to talk about it. Months after his death, she learned of an incident in which Dylan and Eric had apparently been shoved and squirted with ketchup by kids calling them fags. "It hurt so much that I'd seen the remnants of that day and hadn't helped him," she said. When Tom went to pick up Dylan's car from the police station a few weeks after the event, one of the officers said to him, "My son came home from that school one day and they'd set his hair on fire right in the hall—his whole scalp was burned. I wanted to take that school apart brick by brick, but he said it would only make it worse."

A year after the massacre, the police turned over Dylan's journals to the Klebolds, who hadn't known of their existence. "Dylan's writing is full of 'I'm smarter than they are,'" Sue said. "He experienced disdain for the people who were mistreating him. He liked to think of himself as perfect, I think, and that grandiosity came through in the shootings. He started being more withdrawn and secretive in the last two years of high school, but that's not so unusual. The stereotype that he and Eric were these miserable little kids who were plotting because they were so isolated is false. He was bright. He was very shy. He had friends, and they liked him. I was as shocked hearing that my son was perceived as an outcast as I was hearing that he'd been involved in a shooting. He cared for other people." Tom demurred, "Or he seemed to."

"I can never decide whether it's worse to think your child was hardwired to be like this and that you couldn't have done anything, or to think he was a good person and something set this off in him," Sue said. "What I've learned from being an outcast since the tragedy has given me insight into what it must have felt like for my son to be marginalized. He created a version of his reality for us: to be pariahs, unpopular, with no means to defend ourselves against those who hate us." Their attorney filtered their piles of mail so they would not see the worst of it. "I could read three hundred letters where people were saying, 'I admire you,' 'I'm praying for you,' and I'd read one hate letter and be destroyed," Sue said. "When people devalue you, it far outweighs all the love."

Tom, like Dylan, had been painfully shy in high school and felt that because of their similarities he knew Dylan instinctively; he can identify with how Dylan may have felt, but not with what he did. Sue sees a terrible confluence of circumstances including depression, a school environment that caused rage, and an influential friend who had severe problems. "Dylan felt a little afraid of Eric, a little protective of him, and a little controlled by him," she said. "He was caught in something I don't understand that made him do this horrible thing. But I don't, can't, believe that that is who he was. Yes, he made a conscious choice and did this horrible thing, but what had happened to his consciousness that he would make such a choice? Something in him got broken. The same pathology that killed and hurt all the others also killed my son."

I was surprised that the Klebolds had stayed in the town where they had been party to so much anguish. "If we had moved and changed our names, the press would have figured it out," Sue said. "I would have been 'the mother of that killer' in the eyes of everyone I met. Here at least I had people who liked me as me, and people who had liked Dylan, and that was what I needed—especially people who had liked Dylan." Tom said bluntly, "If we'd left, they would have won. Staying was my defiance of the people who were trying to grind us into the ground." I ventured that it must have been hard to keep loving Dylan through the aftermath, and Sue replied, "No, it never was. That was the easy part. Trying to understand was hard, coping with the loss was hard, reconciling myself to the consequences of his actions was hard, but loving him—no, that was always easy for me."

It seemed to me, as I talked to the Klebolds, that Sue was Germany and Tom was Japan. Sue was intensely introspective and burdened with terrific guilt, while Tom proclaimed that it was horrible and then tried to move on. "What are you going to do?" he said. "He felt that he had a reason. He suffered the ultimate: he's no longer here. I'm sorry for the pain my son caused other people, but we had more than our share of pain in this, too. We lost our son; then we had to live with his memory being attacked." Like Japan, he also externalized the causes, but only to a point. "I imagined Eric telling him, 'If you don't do this, I will come and kill your parents,'" Tom later said. "But Dylan's willingness to participate is inescapable." Sue believes that Dylan would have been able to foil pressure from Eric if that had been the pivotal factor. She has wondered whether he might have endured some precipitating trauma, even if he'd been raped by someone, but has never found any evidence to that effect. In writings that go back to his sophomore year, she said, "He talks like a thoughtful, introspective, depressed kid, mostly about how he has a crush on somebody, and she doesn't know he's alive. Three months before the tragedy he's talking about how he wants to die, and he says, 'I might do an NBK with Eric.'" She learned that *NBK* stood for *Natural Born Killers*. "So as late as January, Dylan hadn't really decided that he was going to do this. He just wanted to die. But why blow up the school? I get in my car on a Monday morning, and I start thinking about Dylan, and I just cry all the way to work. I talk to him, or I sing songs. You have to be in touch with that sorrow."

An event of such enormity completely disrupts one's sense of reality. "I used to think I could understand people, relate, and read them pretty well," Sue said. "After this, I realized I don't have a clue what another human being is thinking. We read our children fairy tales and teach them that there are good guys and bad guys. I would never do that now. I would say that every one of us has the capacity to be good and the capacity to make poor choices. If you love someone, you have to love both the good and the bad in them." Sue worked in a building that also housed a parole office and had felt alienated and frightened getting on the elevator with ex-convicts. After Columbine, she saw them differently. "I felt that they were just like my son. That they were just people who, for some reason, had made an awful choice and were thrown into a terrible, despairing situation. When I hear about terrorists in the news, I think, 'That's somebody's kid.' Columbine made me feel more connected to mankind than anything else possibly could have."

The Klebolds had letters from kids who idealized Dylan, and from girls who were in love with him. "He has his own groupies," Tom said with an ironic half smile. They were heartened by unanticipated kindnesses. At a conference about suicide some years later, a man came up to Sue, knelt in front of her, and said, "I just want to tell you how much I admire you. I can't believe the way you have been treated. Every day I picked up the paper, and I expected to read that people were coming up your driveway with pitchforks." Sue has had strangers hug her. But the prospect of a normal life remains elusive. She recounted a recent trip to the supermarket when the checkout clerk had verified her name on her driver's license. "And then she says, 'Klebold . . . Did you know him?' And I say, 'He was my son.' And then she started in with 'It was the work of Satan.' And I'm thinking, 'Please, let's bag the groceries here.' As I leave the store, she's yelling out after me about how she's praying for me. It wears you down."

Before I went to meet Tom and Sue the first time, a friend asked me whether I was afraid of the Klebolds, as if I might succumb to some contagious evil in their house. Ultimately, what proved difficult to reckon with was their underlying normality. One of Dylan's friends said that he used to call them Ward and June, after the sunny couple on *Leave It to Beaver,* because their household seemed so pleasant and predictable. They showed me family photo albums and home videos. I was particularly struck by a video of Dylan on his way to his prom, three days before the massacre. He's a little churlish in the mode of adolescents, but also has a sweetness about him; he seems like a nice kid. It would never have occurred to me that he could be on the verge of wanton destruction. His long hair pulled back in a neat ponytail, he's adjusting his rented tuxedo and complaining that the arms are a little short, smiling while his date puts on his boutonniere. "Dad, why are you filming this?" he asks. Then he laughs and says, "Well, someday I'll watch it again, and I'll wonder what I was thinking." It was impressive dissembling, because he imparts the feeling of someone who will one day remember being dressed up, with a pretty girl, on the way to the biggest party of his life. Near the end of the video, he says, "I'll never have kids. Kids just mess up your life." The sudden angry moment comes out of nowhere and evaporates just as fast.

From the day of the bloodbath, April 20, until the following October, the Klebolds knew few details about what had transpired, except that Dylan was at the shooting and supposedly committed suicide. "We kept clinging to the belief that he hadn't really killed anybody," Sue said. Then came the police report. "It just launched my grief all over again, because I didn't have denial anymore. They could talk about which people he'd killed. Here's the little map of the school, with all the little bodies on it." Then they saw the "basement tapes," which Dylan and Eric had deliberately left behind, which reveal a Dylan unrelated to the young man in the prom video, someone spewing hatred, full of self-aggrandizing rage. "Seeing those videos was as traumatic as the original event," Sue said. "All the protective beliefs that we'd held on to were shattered. There wasn't hate talk in our house. I'm part Jewish, and yet the anti-Semitic stuff was there; they were going through every derogatory word: a nigger; a kike. I saw the end product of my life's work: I had created a monster. Everything I had refused to believe was true. Dylan was a willing participant, and the massacre was not a spontaneous impulse. He had purchased and created weapons that were designed to end the lives of as many people as possible. He shot to kill. For the first time, I understood how Dylan appeared to others. When I saw his disdain for the world, I almost hated my son. I wanted to destroy the video that preserved him in that twisted and fierce mistake. From then on, no matter how lovingly he would be remembered by those who knew him, the tapes would provide a lasting contradiction to anything positive that could be said about his character. For me, it's a smothering emptiness." On these tapes, like the hope at the bottom of Pandora's box, is one moment of kindness: when Eric mentions their parents, Dylan says, "My parents have been good to me. I don't want to browse there."

If you take Tom and Sue back to their prelapsarian memories, ease creeps into their voices. "Dylan was a marvel," Tom recalled of his son's early childhood. "Completely self-motivated. Curious." Every year on Dylan's birthday, Tom goes up to the place where the two used to hike and takes a Dr Pepper, because Dylan loved Dr Pepper, and the stuffed koala that was Dylan's childhood favorite. The Klebolds needed three years to clean out Dylan's room and to remake it into the pleasant guest room in which I slept on my visits. Sue said, "He was a wonderful, marvelous, pretty-close-to-perfect child. He made you feel like a great parent, because he did everything right. Dylan had this incredible sense of organization, and structure, and all this executive functioning." At three, he could already count to 110 and would use refrigerator magnets to make equations. He entered preschool a year early, earned top grades, and was accepted to the gifted-children program. "When he was very young, he would dump five or six puzzles into a pile, so he would have the thrill of working on them all at the same time. He liked mazes; he liked word searches. He played chess with Tom. He was just a delight." Sue looked at me sideways, then said quietly, "You can't imagine how long it's been since I had a chance to brag about my son." Later she said, "He was very malleable; you'd reason with him and say, 'This is why I think you should do something,' and you could almost always persuade him to change his mind. Which I used to see as a strength, from the perspective of a parent. But I see now that it might have been a terrible detriment."

Only one incident with Dylan, the year before the massacre, suggested something might be amiss. The spring of his junior year, Dylan had asked to spend the night at his friend Zack's place, and when Zack had to cancel, Dylan took advantage and went driving with Eric. On their way to set off fireworks on a canyon road, they stopped at a parking lot and noticed a van with video equipment in the front seat. They grabbed a rock, broke the window, stole the equipment, then turned on their interior lights to inspect their haul. When a policeman stopped to see what was going on, Dylan confessed to the theft almost immediately, and both boys were taken to be booked. "The phone rings," Sue said. "It was the sheriff's department—the darkest night of our lives to that point." They went down to the station to find Dylan and Eric in handcuffs. The police released the boys back to their parents' custody and put them in a diversion program, which aims to help juveniles avoid a criminal record by assigning them community service, educational directives, and restitution. With hindsight, Sue believes that this putative act of mercy was a mean trick of fate; had they gone to jail, the boys would have been separated and out of the school where they felt debased.

The family didn't get home until dawn, and Sue was so angry she couldn't speak to Dylan. When Tom went for a walk the next day with Dylan, he was startled by his son's fury about the arrest. "He felt so above it all, totally justified in what he'd done," Tom said. "The morality of the whole thing escaped him." Sue noticed a similar attitude, and the diversion record remarks that he didn't connect to the wrongness of what he did. "I said, 'Dylan, help me understand this,'" Sue said. "'How could you do something so morally wrong?' And he said, 'Well, I didn't do it to another human being; it was to a company. That's what they have insurance for.' And I said, 'Dylan! You're scaring me!' He said, 'Well, it scared me, too, because I don't know why I did it. Just, suddenly, we'd done it.' His mother chalked it up to teenage impulse and made him promise that he would never do anything of the sort again. "He said, 'I promise. But I'm scared, because I didn't know I was going to do it this time.' So I said, 'Well, now you know.'"

Sue asked the people in the diversion program whether Dylan needed counseling, and they administered standardized psychological tests and found no indication that he was suicidal, homicidal, or depressed. "If I could say something to a roomful of parents right now, I would say, 'Never trust what you see,'" Sue said. "Was he nice? Was he thoughtful? I was taking a walk not long before he died, and I'd asked him, 'Come and pick me up if it rains.' And he did. He was there for you, and he was the best listener I ever met. I realize now that that was because he didn't want to talk, and he was hiding. He and Eric worked together at the pizza parlor. A couple of weeks before Columbine, Eric's beloved dog was sick, and it looked like he wasn't going to make it, and so Dylan worked Eric's shift as well as his own so that Eric could have the time with his dog."

In the writing Dylan and Eric left behind, Eric comes off as homicidal; his anger is all directed outward. Dylan comes off as suicidal; his energy fuels self-abnegation and self-criticism. It's as though Dylan went along with the homicide for Eric's sake, and Eric with the suicide for Dylan's. Toward the end, Dylan was counting the hours he had left. "How could he keep it so secret," Sue wondered, "this pain he was in?"

When I asked the Klebolds what they would want to ask Dylan if he were in the room with us, Tom said, "I'd ask him what the hell he was thinking and what the hell he thought he was doing!" Sue looked down at the floor for a minute before saying quietly, "I would ask him to forgive me, for being his mother and never knowing what was going on inside his head, for not being able to help him, for not being the person that he could confide in." Later she said, "I've had *thousands* of dreams about Dylan where I'm talking to him and trying to get him to tell me how he feels. I dreamed that I was getting him ready for bed, and I lifted up his shirt, and he was covered with cuts. And he was in all this pain, and I didn't see it; it was hidden."

The Klebolds were caught in lawsuits brought by some victims' families. Four years after the tragedy, they were deposed—supposedly confidentially—in front of these parents. The next day, the Denver paper contended that the world had a right to know what they had said. "It was implying, after all that we'd been through, that they still believed we were at fault," Sue said. "It was, 'How could you not know? How could you not know?' And it's like, 'I can't answer that. I didn't know, I didn't know, I didn't know. How many times can you say that? Why would we have known and not gotten help, not told anyone?'"

In the wake of so many enormous stresses, Sue was diagnosed with breast cancer. "I don't believe in chakras," she said. "But you think about all this heart pain, and failed nurturing, and losing a child. I finally had an opportunity to meet some women who had lost children to suicide. There were six women, and three of us have had breast cancer. I used to laugh and say it was my version of comic relief. Because after all we'd been through, the breast cancer seemed like sort of a nice, normal thing." For two years after the maelstrom of Columbine, she thought that she wanted to die, but now she was jarred into a new sense of purpose. "It was like, 'Wait a minute! I have something I have to do first. I have to explain who Dylan was and what he was like.' I met a woman recently who had lost one son to suicide and whose other son was in jail, and I said to her, 'You can't appreciate or believe this now, but if you plunge deep into this, it will lead you to enlightenment. It's not the path you would have chosen, but it will make you a better and stronger person.'"

After Columbine, Sue had a client who was blind, had only one hand, had just lost her job, and was facing trouble at home. "She said, 'I may have my problems, but I wouldn't trade places with you for anything in the world.' I laughed. All those years I have worked with people with disabilities and thought, 'Thank God I can see; thank God I can walk; thank God I can scratch my head and feed myself.' And I'm thinking how funny it is how we all use one another to feel better."

Sue spoke of herself as a lucky person. "I was fortunate that Dylan did not turn on us. The worst thing he did to us was he took himself away from us. After Columbine, I felt that Dylan killed God. No god could have had anything to do with this, so there must not be one. When everything in your world is gone, all your belief systems, and your self-concepts—your beliefs in yourself, your child, your family—there is a process of trying to establish, who am I? Is there a person there, at all? A woman at work asked me recently how my weekend was, and it happened to be the anniversary of the shootings. So I said that I wasn't doing so well and I told her why, and she said, 'I always forget that about you.' I gave her a hug and said, 'That's the nicest thing anyone has said to me in years.'" But Sue does not forget. "I sat next to someone on a train a while ago and we had a really wonderful conversation, and then I could feel the questions coming—'So, how many kids do you have?' I had to forestall it. I had to tell him who I was. And who I am forever now is Dylan's mother."

When I mentioned to the Klebolds that I thought they spoke with an extraordinary clarity about their situation, in contrast to some of the other people I had interviewed for this chapter, Tom said, "We are able to be open and honest about those things because our son is dead. His story is complete. We can't hope for him to do something else, something better. You can tell a story a whole lot better when you know its ending." A few years after we first met, Sue said to me, "Way back when, we almost got a house in California, and our offer was turned down, and this house in Littleton came up, we made a low offer, and we were so thrilled when it was accepted. At the time we said how lucky we were that the house in California hadn't worked out. But if it had, Columbine wouldn't have happened. When it first happened, I used to wish that I had never had children, that I had never married. If Tom and I hadn't crossed paths at Ohio State, Dylan wouldn't have existed and this terrible thing wouldn't have happened. But over time, I've come to feel that, for myself, I am glad I had kids and glad I had the kids I did, because the love for them—even at the price of this pain—has been the single greatest joy of my life. When I say that, I am speaking of my own pain, and not of the pain of other people. But I accept my own pain; life is full of suffering, and this is mine. I know it would have been better for the world if Dylan had never been born. But I believe it would not have been better for me."

XI

Transgender

Western culture likes binaries: life feels less frightening when we can separate good and evil into tidy heaps, when we split off the mind from the body, when men are masculine and women are feminine. Threats to gender are threats to the social order. If rules are not maintained, everything seems to be up for grabs, and Joan of Arc must go to the stake. If we countenance people who want to chop off their penises and breasts, then what chance do we have of preserving the integrity of our own bodies? As the noted psychoanalyst Richard C. Friedman once joked, "It might help if they all wore T-shirts that said, 'Don't worry—it won't happen to you.'" Gender itself is a slippery concept. The author Amy Bloom says, "Male is not gay or straight; it's male. Neither the object of desire nor the drinking of beer nor the clenching of fists makes maleness. We don't know what does, and neither do transsexual men, and neither do the people who treat them, psychologically and surgically." But though gender is hard to define, it is not hard to know. Jan Morris, who wrote bravely of her transition—the process of switching gender—in the 1970s, has said, "Transsexualism is not a sexual mode or preference. It is not an act of sex at all. It is a passionate, lifelong, ineradicable conviction, and no true transsexual has ever been disabused of it." She explained, "My inner uncertainty could be represented in swirls and clouds of color, a haze inside me. I did not know exactly where it was—in my head, in my heart, in my loins, in my blood."

The term *transgender* is an encompassing term that includes anyone whose behavior departs significantly from the norms of the gender suggested by his or her anatomy at birth. The term *transsexual* usually refers to someone who has had surgery or hormones to align his or her body with a nonbirth gender. The term *transvestite* refers to someone who enjoys wearing clothing usually reserved for the other gender.

Though the terms get used in a variety of ways, *transgender* and its abbreviation as *trans* are the most widely accepted in the trans community. A *transman* was born female and became a man; a *transwoman* was born male and became a woman. *Intersex* describes people who are born with ambiguous genitalia or are in some other physical way both male and female from birth.

It is a poverty of our language that we use the word *sex* to refer both to gender and to carnal acts, and from that unfortunate conflation springs much of the disgust around the notion of transgender children. Being trans is taken to be a depravity, and depravities in children are anomalous and disturbing. But trans children are not manifesting sexuality; they are manifesting gender. The issue is not whom they wish to be with, but whom they wish to be. As Aiden Key, a trans activist, put it, "My gender is who I am; my sexuality is who I bounce it off of." This is an essential distinction. Yet teasing out the complexities of transgender identity reveals how often these things can be confused—in a child, by a parent, and across the larger community. *Gay* and *trans* are separate categories, but a grayscale runs between them. Making the distinction is especially hard in childhood. A butch little girl or a feminine little boy may want to switch genders immediately; may develop that wish later; or may never develop it at all. One mother described being asked by a male friend whether her boyish daughter was gay and saying, "She's four—I don't think she's got sexual desires yet." But such children may be demonstrating qualities associated with subsequent patterns of attraction; they may, in effect, be pre-gay even if they haven't yet conceptualized the erotic.

In 1987, Richard Green published his influential *The "Sissy Boy Syndrome" and the Development of Homosexuality*, in which he followed a cohort of forty-four feminine little boys for fifteen years. Only one transitioned; most turned out simply to be gay. Sexuality and gender are independent yet entwined variables. Because cross-gender expression is much more common among gay people than it is among straight people, prejudice against such expression is a gay issue. Despite Jan Morris's assertion, gay, too, is an identity—not something you do, but something you are. One can be gay despite never having had carnal relations with anyone of one's own gender; and one can be trans and have presented only in the gender one was assigned at birth. Those who are ignorant about homosexuality and transgender culture tend to confuse and conflate them with reason: homophobia has always targeted gender nonconformity. Immeasurable differences exist between the outré gay guy who likes fashion and decorating magazines, and the school football hero who happens to prefer sex with men. While the footballer may encounter legal challenges if he tries to marry a man, and may hear slurs from his teammates if they find out, he will not encounter the same day-to-day abuse that will likely make his class-mate's life a living hell.

The political liberty of transgender people has been ingrained in the battle for gay and lesbian rights. There are far more gay people than trans people, and the trans movement needs numbers behind it, but the conflation of the two issues nonetheless causes confusion. Some gay people think their trans brothers and sisters are in the same situation as themselves only more so and become passionate advocates on their behalf; others find the trans community embarrassing and attempt to dissociate themselves, a pattern especially common among gay men who want to assert their masculinity credentials. The split echoes, in some ways, the split among early feminists about lesbians, with some viewing lesbianism as the ultimate expression of their identity, and others believing gay women would undermine their battle to ingratiate their ideals with the mainstream. The Employment Non-Discrimination Act (ENDA), intended to protect gay people from job discrimination, came before Congress in 2008 without any protection for gender expression. When the National Gay and Lesbian Task Force fought for a gender-expression clause that would have prevented people from being denied employment or fired solely because they did not conform to gender type, they were told by Representative Barney Frank, who had introduced the bill, that they were asking for too much.

Gender dissonance can manifest extremely early. By age three or four, sometimes even younger, children may notice an incongruity between who they are told they are and who they sense they are. That discrepancy has been called gender identity disorder, or GID. In early childhood, gender nonconformity is often tolerated, but by seven or so, children are pushed hard into gender stereotypes. Trans children may respond to such pressure by becoming anxious and depressed. Telling their parents is usually terrifying for them. "If you don't let them transition, their internal energy is fully occupied with gender identity, and this keeps them from reaching their developmental markers," said Stephanie Brill, founder of the counseling entity Gender Spectrum, and author, with Rachel Pepper, of *The Transgender Child*. "Often with transition, children's learning disabilities and other diagnoses resolve themselves because the mind and heart are not so occupied with this central problem."

Even twenty years ago, most transsexuals sought to move completely from one gender to the other. Nowadays, the categories are blurred. Some live *stealth*, meaning that everyone around them believes that they were born into the gender they inhabit. They feel they have failed when they are identified as their natal sex. Others live openly as transmen or transwomen. Many spend some time stealth and some openly trans. Some people are *genderqueer*, identifying as neither male nor female. Others are *gender fluid*: male some days, female other days, and sometimes neither, or both. Some suffer from *gender dysphoria*— a deep misery about the body into which they were born—but others reject the darkness of that term. Some are exhibitionistic, and some, extremely private.

People in any of these categories may or may not have had surgery, be taking hormones, or have had a variety of other physical interventions; collectively, they form what one author has called a "gender chiaroscuro." The *DSM* says that one in thirty thousand genetic males and one in a hundred thousand genetic females will undergo actual sex reassignment surgery in their lifetime, but such statistics would suggest that there are only fifteen hundred postsurgical transmen and five thousand postsurgical transwomen in the United States. The figures are based on antiquated surveys and reflect an extreme view of what constitutes reassignment surgery, not acknowledging, for example, that creating or removing breasts is a reassignment surgery even in the absence of genital procedures. Lynn Conway, a computer engineer who has analyzed more recent data, has estimated that there are between thirty-two thousand and forty thousand postoperative transwomen in the United States, but said that only one in five or ten people who experiences intense discomfort with birth gender pursues genital surgery. The National Center for Transgender Equality estimates that for up to three million Americans, in Barbara Walters's phrase, "what's between their legs doesn't match what's between their ears."

Scientists, psychologists, clergy, and academics argue about whether bodies should be altered to accommodate minds, or minds to accommodate bodies. Some believe that all people who vary from gender norms can, with psychiatric treatment, live contentedly in their birth gender; they prescribe a broad range of reparative therapies to address the mind/body dissonance. Others presume that the role of medicine is to facilitate transition and believe in using hormones and surgery to do so. Parents are in a bind, familiar throughout this book, between cure and acceptance. Advocates for reparative therapy insist that people live better in unmutilated bodies and that medical corrections involving considerable pain, risk, and expense should be options of last resort. Opponents contend that strict gender rules are archaic and punitive, and that discouraging transgender people from inhabiting their real selves is a prescription for despair, often for suicide. Received wisdom is evolving at a breakneck pace. The social model of disability—that the problems trans people have are the result largely of the social attitudes they encounter—is argued here with particular ferocity.

Parents who support their child's transition—the shift away from a natal gender—must refer to that child by a new name; they must use new pronouns; and they must switch the words *son* and *daughter*. Linguistic chaos often ensues. "He's my daughter," one mother explained to me as she introduced her transgender son. Another said, "I use the word *child* because I cannot wrap my mind around *daughter*, even though I am fine calling my child Elaine." Sociologist Holly Devor writes, "In those cases where persons were living as men at the time of their interviews but were talking about events lived as girls or women, I have used feminine pronouns. For example, 'He remembered that as a girl, she had been a tomboy.'" How we name something determines how we perceive it.

Most of the trans people I met disliked *MTF* (for male to female) and *FTM* (female to male), feeling that these terms demean the people to whom they are applied. Many activists speak of people having been "declared male" or "declared female" at birth and later becoming "affirmed females" or "affirmed males." Trans people often refer to the nontrans population as *cisgender*, borrowing the idea from the cis-trans distinction in chemistry; the Latin prefix *cis* means "on the same side." I have chosen to refer to people by natal gender prior to transition and by affirmed gender after transition, and to impose this on my interviews with families as much as possible. In cases where people prefer that their pretransition name be forgotten, I have consistently used the post-transition name.

Twenty-seven weeks pregnant as a single mother, Venessia Romero was rushed to a Denver hospital, where she gave birth to a girl and a boy. The girl looked fairly strong, but the boy was less than a pound and a half and covered with fuzz, his organs visible through his unformed skin. Premature babies are given pulmonary surfactants, which help them to breathe. Because the girl was stronger, they treated her first; she had an adverse reaction and died within minutes. The boy survived.

Within a year, Venessia met and married Joseph Romero, an air force sergeant. The baby's father had never even seen him; Joseph adopted him and changed his name to Joseph Romero II, called Joey. When the baby was twenty months old, the family was posted to the US Air Force base in Okinawa. "The baby would cry all the time," Joseph recalled. "But not 'I want food,' 'I want to be changed.' It wasn't a physical need, and we had no way to console him. The temper tantrums were so bad that we couldn't take him out in public."

Over the next four years, Joey was diagnosed with ADHD, depression, anxiety, attachment disorder, and asthma. At three, he was on fourteen different medications. "We had a child who never smiled," Venessia said. "All the time we were cooing, 'Oh, you're such a good boy, such a beautiful boy.' Boy, boy, boy. Every time I put shoes on him, they were little boy's shoes. A little boy's jacket." Joey was already interested in wearing girlish outfits; Venessia thought he was probably gay and worried about how that would go with her military husband.

The Romeros had access only to military doctors, who were cautious of a diagnosis that the military does not welcome, but one finally told Venessia, when Joey was five, to look up GID online. "It was making him squirm just to say that, like his rank was going to fall off," Venessia said. "I had never even heard the word *transgender*. I was hugely relieved. Other people go through this?" The Internet introduces trans people and their families into instant networks that can provide information and support; it likewise offers misinformation. Online spaces created to shield and help trans children can easily become the locus of predators with disturbing erotic fantasies, or of transphobic people with murderous intentions. In this instance, however, Kim Pearson—herself the mother of a transgender child and one of the founders of TransYouth Family Allies (TYFA), a group that supports families addressing gender variance—found Venessia online. "She carried me to a forum with other parents," Venessia said. "I cried with gratitude."

The revelation threw Joseph into an abrupt and severe depression. Venessia started to call their child Josie. "Josie wouldn't go outside unless she could go in her girl clothes. I had to decide then, was I willing to leave my marriage to protect Josie? Well, to make Josie be a boy is asking her to commit suicide. I'm not that kind of parent." By this time, Venessia and Joseph had adopted a younger daughter, Jade, from China. "I'm willing to give Joseph up, and I'm willing to walk away from Jade, which was incredibly hard. But Josie was five and had already paid enough penance for ten lives." While Venessia was making these calculations, her husband gradually came around. "She had that sparkle," he said. "I just decided, Josie is here to stay."

When I first met Josie, she was eight, and she said, "I'm a girl and I have a penis. They thought I was a boy until I was six. I dressed like a girl. I said, 'I'm a girl.' They didn't understand for the longest time." Josie was increasingly assertive about her need to be a girl all the time, so one day Joseph agreed to take her to school on the base in a denim skirt with a pink rabbit on it, and pink leggings underneath.

The kids were mostly accepting, but their parents were another story. "The next day, there was a screaming crowd outside Josie's classroom door," Venessia said. "I was terrified." In Josie's own yard, someone snatched her bicycle from her and tossed it into the jungle. "People were throwing things at our house, calling us child molesters," Venessia said. "Little girls screaming, 'You're a fucking faggot.'" The wife of the judge advocate general on base started a petition to remove Josie from school. "It was awful when everyone found out I was a girl," Josie remembered. "My neighbor Isabelle said she was going to call the police and put me in jail. It made me sad. I thought she was my friend."

Venessia allowed Josie to choose her clothes, and every day she shunned the boy clothes. "She wouldn't go outside without a skirt on," Venessia said. "But she's got the biggest smile on her face. Well, I'm going to smile, too. So I did. I was holding her hand tighter than usual, but she just kept on marching." Before long, Venessia and Joseph had taken her off all her medications. Her asthma, depression, anxiety, and attachment disorder were all gone. But the military told the family to get out of Okinawa, claiming they could not protect Josie; they were reassigned to a base in the Arizona desert.

Venessia didn't want Josie at another military school. She located a public school in Tucson with a liberal-leaning principal and enrolled both daughters. But Josie's teacher refused to call her by a female name and told Josie that Venessia was a "mean mommy" who was forcing her to live as a girl when everyone could see she was a boy. "She was an awful, rude teacher, who didn't want me at her school," Josie said. "I got so angry and frustrated." Venessia said, "Josie's self-esteem was crushed. She was back to being gloomy." Josie complained of stomachaches and headaches and fought every day against going to the school, which began sending truancy notices.

The Romeros moved to another town. Fearing for Josie's safety, they installed alarm wiring on the windows and doors and bought a Great Dane to intimidate attackers. Venessia sent an e-mail to the principal of the local public school that began, "I'm the proud mother of an eight-year-old transgender daughter." His head of human resources said, "We follow state laws, and there are no antidiscrimination protections for your child here." In November, Venessia placed her daughters at a Waldorf school, but, at $20,000 per year, it was impossible on an air force salary. The only option left was homeschooling. Josie said, "I miss going out." Joseph said, "The isolation is the price we pay to shield her from a world that could harm her."

Isolation is not the only difficulty. "I always have the penis problem," Josie said. "I want to get rid of it. But I think it will hurt. They said I have to be a certain age to take my penis off, when I'm more like fifteen." Venessia said, "Eighteen. But you'll be able to take estrogen and grow boobs sooner than that." Josie explained, "When I'm a mommy, I'll adopt my babies, but I'll have boobies to feed them and I will wear a bra, dresses, skirts, and high-heeled shoes." She seemed equally definite when she told me that she wanted to marry someone with rainbow-colored hair who was beautiful on the inside and the outside. "We'll get a baby here in Arizona, and then go live in whatever state Jade is in so we can be next-door neighbors," Josie said. "We'll live in a tree house. I'll grow my hair all the way to California."

Later, Venessia said to me, "I wouldn't put Josie through surgery until she was emotionally ready for the physical pain, but if she were, I would absolutely do it right now." Venessia plans to give Josie puberty blockers, which stop the production of testosterone and estrogen. "She won't have testosterone ravaging her body," Venessia said. "So she'll never get an Adam's apple or facial hair. She'll never look like a man in a dress." Venessia found a doctor in Tucson who was willing to work on this protocol. Joseph persuaded the department of records to issue a new birth certificate for Josie, with her correct name and gender. But Venessia also deliberately kept toys for boys around the house, saying, "I don't want her to feel like she's proving she's a girl by playing with Barbies all the time."

Most trans children I encountered were living stealth. I was struck that many of these kids had gone from one discrepancy—living in an anatomical gender that was anathema to them—to another—living in a gender that did not match their body. Josie's openness had come at high cost, but she struck me as more truly free than many other trans children. Josie has become an activist. It's a hard role to imagine for someone who is eight and still thinks she may live in a tree house, but this strange jumble of hypermaturities and childishness was her core. When I met her, she had just been filmed by National Geographic for her second documentary; she has met with members of Congress and the governor of Arizona. I wondered to what degree Joseph and Venessia shared—or, indeed, manufactured—this activist bent, but Venessia, who had considered the wisdom of having her daughter stealth at least in some contexts, asked rhetorically, "What's the first thing Josie says? 'Hi, my name is Josie. I'm eight. I'm transgender. Who are you?'"

In 2009, Kim Pearson, by then a friend of the family, was chosen for a community service award but was unable to attend the ceremony; she asked Josie to accept the award on her behalf. Seven hundred people were in the audience. "She turns to me on the podium," Venessia remembered. "She whispered, 'Mommy, I have really big stage frightfulness right now.' But she whispered right into the microphone. Everyone laughed, and that relaxed her." Josie ad-libbed her speech and got a standing ovation. "Josie's very fragile, very emotional," Venessia said. "But Josie wants to change the world."

Venessia noted, "Little boys don't go around saying they're little girls without good reason. They're trusting you to listen, and we didn't know how. The other day she said, 'Mommy, why did you want me to be a boy?' That killed me. I told her, 'I didn't understand and I'm really sorry.' She said, 'It's okay, Mommy. I love you, and everything's so good now.'"

Gender is among the first elements of self-knowledge. This knowledge encompasses an internal sense of self, and, often, a preference for external behaviors, such as dress and type of play. Gender identity's etiology, however—posited to lie in genetics, in uterine androgen levels, in early social influences—remains obscure. Heino Meyer-Bahlburg, a professor of psychology at Columbia University who specializes in gender variance, has described numerous possible biological mechanisms, and said that as many as four hundred rare genes and epigenetic phenomena may be involved, genes associated not with hormone regulation, but with personality formation. "The view we have of the brain now is like those wonderful pictures of earth that the first astronauts took from the moon," said Norman Spack, associate professor of pediatrics at Harvard University and a leading endocrinologist in the field. "You can see the continents, the oceans, the weather systems. When you can read the license plates, we'll know what causes gender nonconformity." Like autism, gender nonconformity seems far more prevalent than ever before; as with autism, whether the condition is actually more frequent or simply more recognized is unclear.

The nongenetic biological arguments are confusing. The synthetic estrogen diethylstilbestrol (DES), developed in 1938 and used until the early 1970s to prevent miscarriage, has had many adverse effects on both males and females exposed to it in utero. A 2002 survey of members of the DES Sons Network found an extraordinary 50 percent rate of transgenderism; this supports the hypothesis that gestational hormone levels can trigger cross-gender identity. Scientists have also expressed concern about endocrine disruptors (EDCs), a class of chemicals found in everything from food to floor polish to packing materials. EDCs are known to be responsible for an increasing incidence of deformities in amphibian reproductive systems; researchers have speculated that they might be responsible for the increasing incidence of genital abnormalities and atypical gender identity in human beings.

In 1991, Georges Canguilhem, a historian of science who worked on the concept of mutation, wrote, "Diversity is not disease; the *anomalous* is not the pathological." Being trans is without question anomalous; the relentlessly debated question is whether it is also pathological. Gender identity disorder was introduced as a medical category in 1980. The *DSM-IV* requires that four of the following five symptoms be present for a diagnosis in children: strong and persistent cross-gender identification, defined as the desire to be, or the insistence that one is, of the other sex; persistent discomfort about one's assigned sex or a sense of inappropriateness in the gender role of that sex, often manifested in cross-dressing of some kind; an inclination toward cross-sex roles in make-believe play, with fantasies of being the other sex; a constant wish to participate in the stereotypical games and pastimes of the other sex; a preference for playmates of the other sex. Boys diagnosed with GID commonly prefer feminine clothing and hairstyles, often are mothers when they play house, avoid rough-and-tumble play and athletics, and are interested in female fantasy figures such as Snow White. Girls diagnosed with GID often have intensely negative responses to being asked to wear dresses, prefer short hair, are often mistaken for boys, seek out rough-and-tumble play, enjoy sports, and choose fantasy figures such as Batman. In an age when women can work in construction and men can marry other men, the notion of a medically enshrined, "Batman vs. Snow White" typology of gender identity seems reductive, yet it still has considerable currency in the medical literature. The diagnosis is specified as inapplicable to anyone with an intersex condition.

Whereas most children will play at an early age with toys suitable to either gender, trans kids often refuse the toys associated with their natal sex. Meyer-Bahlburg describes these children as "pervasively gender atypical from birth." A scale of gendered behavior ranks people as very masculine at one end and very feminine at the other. Typical boys are 3.5 to 5 standard deviations in the direction of masculinity, and the girls are the same number of deviations toward femininity. But trans kids will tend to be 7 to 12 deviations from the norm in the direction away from their birth gender. In other words, natal males become more female than most females, while natal females become more male than most males. "It's almost like their play is a political statement," Spack said. Adults with GID show clinically significant distress or impairment in social and occupational functioning. Some children who have gone undiagnosed will manifest the syndrome during puberty or afterward; conversely, only a quarter of children given a GID diagnosis will show full cross-gender identification in adolescence. In other words, sometimes their play means nothing about their future identity and sometimes it means everything. This is why decisions about how to raise them are so fraught.

Many professionals who work with trans children believe that the society at large is failing them. Kelly Winters, founder of GID Reform Advocates, has written, "Behaviors that would be ordinary or even exemplary for gender conforming boys and girls are presented as symptomatic of mental disorder for gender nonconforming children," meaning that what is deemed healthy in a girl is considered a symptom of psychiatric illness in a boy. Activists have spoken of the GID diagnosis being used not only to prevent natal boys from identifying as girls and natal girls from identifying as boys, but also to stigmatize or prevent effeminate homosexuality and butch lesbianism. Stephanie Brill added, "A male child who says, 'I must be a girl because only girls want to do these things,' is not showing evidence of being transgender; he's showing evidence of sexism." Gerald Mallon and Teresa DeCrescenzo, social workers with experience in this community, complain that natal boys are given "the sports corrective," and natal girls, "the etiquette corrective." At the 2009 meeting of the American Psychiatric Association, protestors gathered at a "Reform GID Now!" demonstration. Diane Ehrensaft, of the Child and Adolescent Gender Center in Berkeley, California, where she specializes in children with gender identity issues, said, "The mental health profession has been consistently doing harm to children who are not 'gender normal,' and they need to retrain."

Other activists, however, rail against the possibility of losing the diagnostic category. In *The Riddle of Gender*, Deborah Rudacille writes, "The diagnosis legitimizes the range of hormonal and surgical interventions that have provided relief to thousands of transsexual and transgendered people. Activists who argue that the 'medical model' of gender variance 'pathologizes human diversity' tend to miss this point. Without some sort of diagnosis, sex reassignment becomes nothing more than a kind of extreme cosmetic surgery/body enhancement, or in the view of critics, a fad, a fashion, a 'craze.'" GID's presence in the *DSM* facilitates insurance coverage for the psychological support transgender people may require; William Narrow, the research director for the *DSM-5*, has said, "The harm of retention is stigma, and the harm of removal is potential loss of access to care." The task at hand, he continued, is "to create a situation where access can be not only available but increased, and discrimination can be reduced." This quandary echoes the experience of deaf people and dwarfs, who may not care for the disability label yet need it to secure accommodations and services.

Surgical and endocrine interventions for transgender people, however, are seldom eligible for reimbursement and tax deductibility. Many transgender people would like to see their condition classified as a physical condition, which would resolve that problem. Michele Angello, a PhD therapist specializing in gender identity issues, has pointed out that if something can be fixed with a physical transformation, it shouldn't be categorized as a mental health condition. Some activists maintain that trans, like pregnancy, is a medical condition but not a disease. The AMA has issued a resolution that they "support health insurance coverage for treatment of gender identity disorder as recommended by a physician," which leaves the door open for bodily or psychological interventions. Reclassification as an endocrine or neurocognitive condition could be achieved by developing a new listing in the *ICD* (the *International Statistical Classification of Diseases*) of the World Health Organization.

As long as GID is classed as a mental illness, professionals will try to cure it, and parents will refuse to accept it. It is time to focus on the child rather than on the label. Edgardo Menvielle, a psychiatrist at Children's National Medical Center, said, "The goal is for the child to be well adjusted, healthy, and have good self-esteem. What's not important is molding their gender." It seems right to prioritize each child's mental health over a system that makes universal predictions about what should constitute happiness or what values are healthy. Menvielle does not see trans children as being automatically disordered; he does see them as being at risk. Peggy Cohen-Kettenis, a professor of gender development who works in Amsterdam, has likewise attempted "to diagnose and treat functional problems (such as separation anxiety, disorganized parenting, and depression), so regardless of which gender the child ultimately exhibits, the family is well." In other words, gender identity should not obscure underlying problems, and such problems should not interfere with addressing gender identity.

Most Deaf people don't take exception to being called *deaf*; most people with intellectual disabilities raise no objection to the term *Down syndrome*; yet *gender identity disorder* infuriates the people it ostensibly describes, to a degree and extent that transcends semantics. Most conditions in this book entail a positive model of identity and a negative model of disorder. While no one wants to be put in a stigmatized diagnostic category, most people fight the stigma rather than the category. Those who think of deafness or autism as identities can do so even if others call them disorders. *GID* suggests not simply that trans people have a disorder, but that their identity itself *is* the disorder. This is a dangerous standpoint. We all have multiple identities, and most of us regret some of them, but identity is who we are. The law of identity is among the first precepts of philosophy; it states that everything is the same as itself. Aristotle explained that "the single cause" as to "why the man is man or the musician musical" is simply "because each thing is inseparable from itself." Locke declares that our most fundamental knowledge is "a man is a man." Undermining anyone's personal tautology by suggesting that he should not, in fact, be himself sabotages whatever he might become. The GID designation bespeaks an agenda of terminating identity. You can seek better ways to manifest identity, but you can't ask any class of people to discard their identity itself. The twentieth century reached its nadir with attempts to free the world of Jewish identity, Tutsi identity, or the many identities that communism suppressed. The practice of obliterating identities does not work at this macro level; it does not work well at the micro level, either.

Bettina and Greg Verdi both come from traditional Italian Catholic families in the Northeast. Greg works as an airline ground mechanic and Bettina as a preschool teacher. When Greg was hired by Lockheed Martin, they moved south of Atlanta. Their second child, Paul, preferred pink toys at three months; at two, he would drape a shirt over his head to mimic long hair and wear one of Bettina's tank tops as a gown. When he was two and a half, Bettina agreed to get him a yellow, flowered dress at a garage sale. "I figured at home at playtime, what's the harm?" Bettina said. Greg was not entirely comfortable with the dress, but like Bettina, he assumed it was a phase. When their older son, Eric, was four, his preschool had a visiting day for siblings, and Bettina took Paul. "Families were coming in with girls in frilly dresses, and Paul gasps, 'Mom, I want that dress,'" Bettina recalled. "All the moms were giggling." Bettina told her pediatrician that Paul headed for the girls' section at every toy store. The doctor said, "Well, then, say no." Greg said, "Paul would say, 'If I can't have the girl toys, then let's get out of the toy store.'"

At five, Paul said to Bettina, "Mom, I want to go to school as a girl, dress like a girl, have a girl name, have girl toys. I want to be a girl." Bettina was terrified. They went back to their pediatrician and asked what he thought about GID; he told them "those children" mostly committed suicide, so they should go to the Christian bookstore, read up on it, and pray. Bettina found a therapist in Atlanta and made an appointment to go in with Greg. "I was prepared to make this happen without Greg," Bettina said. But on the drive home, Greg said to

Bettina, "Okay, let's do it." Bettina called a good friend whose kids were the same age as hers and suggested a playdate. "I told her, 'We want you to call her Paula.' She said, 'Oh, Bettina, I don't know. The kids are going to make fun of him.' I said, 'Can we try it?'" So they went. The older son said to Eric, "Uh, how come your brother is dressed like a girl?" Eric said, "It's called transgender. It means when a boy wants to be a girl or a girl wants to be a boy. I don't really want to talk about it." The boy said, "Okay, let's go play." The younger one never even noticed, probably because Paul had always acted like a girl.

Bettina went to see the religious education director at her Catholic church. "I was so emotional about it. She was like, 'Okay, do you want her to attend as Paula? We'll just change the paperwork.' So we transitioned at church." Next, Bettina told the school, and the principal said, "We provide a safe, friendly environment for all our children, and yours is no different." Paula would have to use the nurse's bathroom, but otherwise, she would just be Paula. Bettina's family was supportive from the start. Greg's parents, already in their eighties, accepted it the first time they saw Paula.

But Greg and Bettina did not reckon with their community. "Suddenly, we're in the Bible Belt," Greg said. Bettina notified the neighbors. "I had gone to the bus stop with this one guy every morning for two years, and I felt like he was my friend," she said. "The first week of school he would meet me at the end of his driveway with papers he downloaded about how evil this was." One brother and sister put their hands on Paula's head on the school bus and prayed to turn her back into a boy. Paula came home and said, "I didn't really mind, but does this mean they're not going to be my friends?" Bettina went to see the mother of the praying kids. "She's telling me, 'God doesn't make mistakes.' I'm telling her, 'Look, if God doesn't make mistakes, then your son doesn't have a vision problem and doesn't need glasses.' 'Well, that's not the same thing.' 'Why is it not the same thing? It's a body part. What's the difference?' I just said, 'Look, you're a really good mom, and I know in my heart of hearts, if you were in my shoes, you would do the same thing. You would listen to your child and make your child happy.'"

Bettina works at the preschool where her children were enrolled, and she informed everybody there about the situation. She warned her boss that there would be a backlash. A month later, her boss told her, "A parent questioned your ability to teach. I said, 'You cannot find a better teacher. What she does in her home life doesn't affect what she does at work. Your child is lucky to be in her class. Bettina would be willing to sit down with you and answer any questions. So I'm going to hang up. Why don't you write down your concerns and call me back?'" The parent never called back, and the parent's daughter remained enrolled.

I first met Greg and Bettina at a trans conference in Philadelphia. Soon, a beautiful little girl came over with Greg's courtly parents, who presented the deceptive air of having attended trans conferences for decades. Paula shook my hand, a little somberly, then skipped down the hallway, her grandparents in pursuit. Bettina said, "This conference is more for us than for her. She knows what she's doing. We're clueless." I asked whether they thought Paula's identity would, over time, be trans or simply female. Bettina said, "Greg doesn't see her as transgender anymore, but that's partly because he doesn't give her a bath every day."

Bettina and Greg showed me the "safe folder" they take with them at all times. Many parents of trans kids keep one: paperwork to be shown in the event of trouble, as law enforcement and the medical system can be unfamiliar with or hostile to gender variance. A folder may include letters from the child's pediatrician and a psychotherapist confirming the child's gender identity; letters from at least three friends or family members and, if possible, a pastor or minister or other prelate that testify to the parents' sound parenting skills; videos or snapshots of the child displaying atypical gender behaviors throughout life; copies of birth certificates, passports, and Social Security cards that reflect a change of gender or name; a home study documenting family stability, if available; and a Bureau of Criminal Information report that shows that the parents are not child abusers.

I asked whether Bettina's advocacy perspective made it easier for her than for Greg, or the other way around. Greg began crying. "I just struggled," he sobbed. "Because it was my little boy. I want my child to be happy. But I found the pictures of us as a family before all this, and I miss that little boy. Just once in a while, it still hurts." I asked Bettina whether she ever felt that way. "No," she said, after a minute's thought. "What I regret is that time with Paula that I didn't have. I missed my daughter's infancy, spending all my energy on someone else who never existed."

Many parents of trans kids described to me grieving for the child they had lost, even as they gained another. The mother of one transman observed, "The same-sex parent experiences a certain kind of rejection—a rejection by one's child of membership in a tribe—that the opposite-sex parent doesn't." I met one father at a trans conference who said, "I accept it intellectually, but I still have emotional prejudice against my son—and even saying *son* sticks in my throat." He had an autistic daughter and a deaf wife. "Autistic and deaf were easy. No one blamed me. But this—people laugh at me. Why can't he just come to terms with his handicap privately? We all have handicaps and disabilities, and we learn how to live with them." This father's son said to me, "I knew from the time I was an infant that I had something to hide, and for a long time I didn't even know what it was. But I immediately knew who I was not—and then who I am is what was left."

One father fought against using feminine pronouns for his trans daughter and ended up in counseling. "Finally our therapist asked—is it making him happy for you to insist on calling him a boy? Of course the answer was no. But when he asked me if it would make my son happy if I called him *she*—the answer was a clear yes. He then asked what was more important to me than my child's happiness. I started to cry. My fear of ridicule coupled with my fear of the ridicule he would suffer was causing me to deny him true happiness."

The Bettelheim-like notion that the child's gender-inappropriate behavior is symptomatic of the parents' gender transgressions determined treatment for most of the twentieth century. In the 1940s and '50s, the psychologist John Money posited that gender is a learned set of behaviors and attitudes. He believed that health required strong gender identification and favored giving girls every encouragement to be girlish, and boys every inducement to masculinity. Money's theory was explicitly tested on David Reimer, one of identical twins whose penis was burned off during a circumcision. Money proposed to Reimer's parents that they raise him as a girl, oversaw infant sex-reassignment surgery, and instructed them to give him only girlish clothes and toys. The parents were told that they must never tell David what had happened. For years, Money published fraudulent articles about the great success of this experiment, thereby encouraging others to attempt similar therapies, which damaged thousands of people. Only in the late 1990s did David Reimer give an interview to *Rolling Stone*, which eventually grew into the book *As Nature Made Him: The Boy Who Was Raised as a Girl*. Reimer's childhood was the antithesis of the one Money had portrayed, filled with rage and misery: he insisted on urinating standing up and despised Money and the dolls and frilly dresses that were forced on him. His behavior at school became so violent that his parents finally broke down and told him the real story when he was fourteen. Reimer had penile reconstruction and lived as a man in later life, but the damage done was enormous, and he committed suicide at thirty-eight.

Recent science suggests that successfully raising genetically programmed boys as girls is almost impossible. A study from Johns Hopkins looked at children born with cloacal exstrophy—a condition in which they have XY (male) chromosomes and testes, but no penis—who were castrated and assigned female gender at birth. Many chose to live as boys or men as they grew up, and all had "moderate-to-marked interests and attitudes that were considered typical of males." William G. Reiner, who authored the study, said, "These children demonstrate that normal male gender identity can develop not only in the absence of the penis, but even after the removal of testicles or castration at birth, and unequivocal rearing as female. Their identity and gender role seem to have developed despite a total environment telling them they were female."

Kirk Murphy was treated for childhood effeminacy at UCLA in the 1970s under the auspices of O. Ivar Lovaas, the theoretician who developed the reward-and-punishment behavioral treatments for autism to which some autistic people have vigorously objected. Kirk's mother was coached through a one-way mirror to reward him for masculine behavior and to ignore feminine behavior. Though he became so upset during these sessions that he would scream, his mother was reassured that she was doing the right thing. At home, a token system much like that used with autistic children was put into play. He was given blue chips for masculine behaviors; a certain number of these meant he got a treat. He received red chips for feminine behaviors and was beaten by his father with a belt when he had too many of them. The effeminate behavior eventually ceased, and for years the work was written up as a success.

The experimenters changed Kirk's name to Kraig for their publications and made him an avatar for the pliability of behavior. George Rekers, the therapist who had worked directly with Kirk, became a founding member of the Family Research Council, a religious organization that lobbies against gay rights; he was ultimately revealed to be gay himself. Kirk joined the air force and lived as a masculine man—until he hanged himself in 2003 at thirty-eight. His mother and siblings went public in 2011 to talk about how the therapy had destroyed him. His sister said, "The research has a postscript that needs to be added. Kirk Andrew Murphy was Kraig and he was gay, and he committed suicide. I want people to remember that this was a little boy who deserved protection, respect, and unconditional love. I don't want him to be remembered as a science experiment." Phyllis Burke's *Gender Shock*, published in 1996, documented with considerable horror that many of the techniques that destroyed Kirk Murphy were still in use—and still receiving government funding. Indeed, some are in use even as I write.

Tony Ferraiolo showed such pronounced masculinities all his life that doctors who examined him when he was still called Anne thought he must be intersex. When I met him, Tony was in his forties. His father had not spoken to him in five years; his mother saw him occasionally and continued to call him Anne. "They're missing out on a really cool guy," Tony said to me.

At five, Anne and her twin, Michelle, were playing football with their brothers, Frank and Felix, and Anne took her shirt off. Her mother said, "Girls don't take their shirts off." Anne began to cry and said she was a boy. "She never played with dolls," Tony's mother, big Anne, remembered. "She never wore a dress. She wouldn't carry a pocketbook. I surmised she was going to be a lesbian." Three early behaviors are often taken as indicators of fixed identity: what underwear the child selects; what swimsuits the child prefers; and how the child urinates. "I remember trying to stand up and pee as a little kid," Tony said. "I never wore girl underwear or bathing suits. I didn't even know that people had intercourse, but I knew that my gender was male." When Anne was in fifth grade in a New Haven elementary school, the teacher asked what each pupil wanted to be when he or she grew up, and Anne said she wanted to be a boy. The class erupted in laughter. By eleven, she was self-injurious. "You've got a little kid that's outside for recess, taking a piece of glass, cutting themselves," Tony said. "I'd gouge and gouge, then take dirt and try to get an infection, to hurt myself as much as I could. My parents knew it. No one did anything." Anne's sister, Michelle, identified as a lesbian early on, but she was a jock, as popular as Anne was marginalized.

Anne's father, Anthony, was abusive, and big Anne, addicted to Valium, was passive in the face of that. Adolescence is a trauma for most trans people, and for Anne, doubly so, as she had organic surges of both male and female hormones, despite showing no anatomical or genetic markers for intersex. "My facial hair and boobs are growing at the same time. What the hell's going on here?" By the time Anne was thirteen, she was shaving every day. "I took up drugs and drinking; I was suspended more than I was in school." From age thirteen, Anne was being sexually abused by a neighbor who was a good friend of her father's. The neighbor would call and ask Anne to help him with something. "If I didn't go, I got punished. If I went, I got raped." She finally told a neighbor what was happening, and the neighbor told her parents. "Two days later, my father had the guy over for a beer. From that day on, I didn't trust anybody," Tony said. Her father often refused to speak to her; when she was sixteen, he threw her out of the house. She walked fifteen miles into New Haven and moved in with a girlfriend;

when that arrangement failed, she was homeless for a month. "Then I called my mother and asked to go back home," Tony recalled, hanging his head. "I went back into the bullshit."

Through her twenties and thirties, Anne was a club promoter and threw huge parties for hundreds of lesbians; she started a band called Vertical Smile. But she never felt like a lesbian. She started using *Tony*, spelled *Toni* in a concession to the family. "I used to pray to God that I was a butch lesbian," Tony said. "But a butch lesbian wants breasts and a va-jay-jay. A transgender person wants a penis." In his mid-thirties, Tony was in a car accident and received an insurance settlement. His family suggested he buy a house. He spent the funds on a double mastectomy.

Tony was not interested in bottom surgery. "That part of my body isn't public, so it was never an issue. The boobs were public. When the doctor unbandaged me, my knees just buckled. When I took my girlfriend, Kirsten, to the beach, I said, 'I'm experiencing everything for the first time.' I haven't shaved since. I fuckin' love my goatee. When I look in the mirror, I see the person that was always supposed to be there. I used to take sleeping pills so I wouldn't have to live much of my life. Now all I want is to stay awake." When I saw Tony, he'd lost more than sixty pounds. "You can't love your body if you hate your body. Now, I eat healthy. I work out." Tony credits his therapist, Jim Collins, for much of his psychic transformation. "I was an angry lesbian," he said. "I didn't want to be an angry man."

Tony's younger brother, Felix, said, "My sister's my brother now, and I've never seen him happier in my life." Felix's kids switched naturally from "Aunt Toni" to "Uncle Tony." Tony's father and his brother Frank were not supportive. Big Anne was distraught, and they did not meet for a full year after the surgery. "Then she just said, 'Well, I'll come over,'" Tony said. "I thought, is she going to open the door and pass out? So, she came in and she was like, 'Oh, my God, you look just like my dentist.'" After Tony's surgery, Michelle began calling herself Nick. "At first, I was pissed," Tony said. "The first thing I do alone as a twin, he's got to stand on my fuckin' coattails. But I can see his sadness that he's not who I am yet. He still has breasts. He doesn't pass. People were like, 'You're sure he's not doing it because you did it?' I said, 'I need to support him no matter why he's doing it.'"

When I asked big Anne if she could see that Anne had become Tony, she said, "Once in a while, I say 'Tony,' but mostly it just comes out 'Anne.' Really down deep, it's my daughter. When I look at 'him,' I still see her." She turned to Tony. "You always had that angry something that was bothering you inside. But I didn't know anything about this back then. I was stupid, in a way." Tony put a hand on her arm. "I don't think you were stupid," he said. Big Anne said, "I watched things on television about it. I started understanding more. It's not that you wanted to be this way." She turned to me. "Her being unnatural, I was upset by it at first. But I understood more how they felt inside. Now she does all this activism. That's very good." Big Anne turned back and forth. "You're still my child," she said to Tony. "I still love her," she said to me. "You know what I mean. Him?" I asked Tony whether he minded being called "Anne" and "she." He said, "Andrew, she thinks I'm a straight girl going through a phase. But I had to realize that my mother's my mother. My mother can call me 'them,' and it wouldn't bother me. What bothers me is that I still see her just four or five times a year."

Big Anne's quiet acceptance of and palpable love for her child are in her mind subsidiary to the splintering of her family following Tony's transition. She responded to most of the questions I asked her about herself with information about her husband; her effacement of Tony echoed her self-effacement. When I asked how she had felt about Anne's being gay, she said, "My husband accepted her being a lesbian." She turned to Tony. "He knows that you should have been a boy, but he still says, 'Why couldn't she just stay a lesbian like everybody else?'" Tony said to his mother, "You have risen to the occasion. You come and see me. We talk." Big Anne sighed and turned to me. "My husband went to his mother's sister, who's ninety, and she started crying, 'She's still your child. You go see her. You'll get used to it.' Then the priest said, 'Go see him. He's your son. Tell him that it bothers you, but talk to him.' But he never did. When holidays come around, I'd like to have all my children with me, but he won't allow it. He worries that people will think he gave in." I was surprised that big Anne had agreed to talk to me. Tony had told her to watch an *Oprah* special about trans kids; she called him and said, "I'll meet with Andrew, if you like. That was you. I'm sorry. I didn't know." Tony explained, "Nobody fuckin' knew in the seventies. My mother's a nice lady. She has a good heart. But this is big. Her only two daughters weren't daughters." I asked big Anne what her husband would say when she arrived home. "He'll ask how she is," she said. "He misses her."

Tony's natural hormonal balance—whatever caused him to grow facial hair—has been sufficient, and he does not take testosterone. Like all trans people, Tony is often asked about his genitalia; he takes it as a question about his strap-ons. "A lot of people ask, 'Do you have a penis?' My answer is 'I have five.' I just go to the next question. 'Does your girlfriend know you're trans?' I'm like, 'Love is honesty. I'm not ashamed of who I am.'" Tony described being at a Stop & Shop and seeing a woman he used to work with. "She was, 'Oh, my God! Annie?' I said, 'Actually, it's Tony now.' She grabs my hand and says, 'It is not God's fault that you're a freak.' I just said, 'I've never been happier in my life.' I knew that if I lost it, it would have been, 'Oh, look at the transguy, what an asshole.' If you have a positive interaction with me as a trans person, you're going to think twice about jeering at a trans-woman, or doing a hate crime. There's a purpose to everybody's life. That's mine. I want to start a nonprofit to give two guys a year chest surgery. Screw Starbucks gift cards. You want to give somebody a present? Give them a chest, give them a penis."

A few months later, Tony started a foundation to do exactly that, and he named it after his beloved therapist, Jim Collins, who had died a few months earlier. "He inspired me to be an activist, as I hope to inspire people behind me to be activists, and hopefully the people behind them won't have to be activists, 'cause it won't be a fucking issue," Tony said. When big Anne had confessed, during our conversation with Tony, that she still worried everything was her fault, her son had responded, "It's nobody's fault. But I have to tell you that if it was your fault, I would thank you. Because my transition is the best thing that ever hap-pened to me." Then Tony laughed. He said, "Life isn't about finding yourself; life is about creating yourself."

Natal males who become females are often unconvincing as women when clothed because of their height and the thickness of their bones; however, their postoperative genitalia, sexual response, and urination patterns can be almost identical to those of genetic females. Natal females who transition can usually pass in public once they develop facial and body hair, deep voices, and, in many instances, male-pattern baldness, but their sex organs are noticeably different from the genuine article; most cannot urinate while standing up, and none can achieve a male orgasm. One preoperative transwoman I met said, "These body parts are nice but they're not mine, and it makes me feel better to know that I don't have to keep them going forever." A transman to whom I repeated this replied, "I'm like one of those IKEA sets of furniture that looks great until you realize you're missing a few parts."

It takes little injected testosterone to overwhelm a genetic female's estrogen—about the same amount that would be administered to a male whose body was not producing the hormone. To overwhelm a genetic male's testosterone is a bigger project. A female whose body is not producing estrogen requires one to two milligrams of estradiol per week to remain premenopausal. A genetic male requires twenty-eight to fifty-six milligrams of estradiol per week to feminize the body. Many endocrinologists recommend that genetic males undergo gonadectomy as early as possible, because such high levels of estradiol create health risks. After gonadectomy, estradiol is effective in much smaller doses.

Most professionals working with trans people follow the Harry Benjamin Standards, which require that the patient live in his or her preferred gender for at least a year and complete a full year of psychotherapy prior to surgery or hormone treatment, and that two clinicians, one a doctor, recommend medical procedures. These safeguards are intended to weed out people at risk of postoperative regret, though many complain that they eat up time when a despairing person could be achieving happiness through a speedy transition. They also protect health-care providers from liability.

For natal males being affirmed as female, procedures may include not only castration and vaginoplasty, but also electrolysis, which can take up to five thousand hours and cost over $100,000; feminizing facial surgeries to reduce the forehead, chin, and jaw; a nose job; a tracheal shave to reduce the Adam's apple; breast augmentation; hair transplants to conceal baldness; and tightening of the vocal cords. The construction of a vagina is most often achieved through penile inversion. After a space is cleared between the rectum and the urethra, the inverted skin of the penis is used to line the vagina, sometimes supplemented by skin grafted from the stomach, buttocks, or thigh. A second method, rectal sigmoid transfer, uses a segment of the large intestine to create a vaginal lining, which provides natural lubrication and unlimited vaginal depth. The procedure is more invasive, more costly, and can lead to mucus leaking into the vagina. In both methods, the scrotal skin is used to create the labia, and part of the glans, to create a clitoris.

Natal women being affirmed as male may remove breasts (double mastectomy), uterus (hysterectomy), ovaries (oophorectomy), fallopian tubes (salpingectomy), and vagina (vaginectomy), because regular gynecological exams are anathema to most transmen. Surgically constructed penises are expensive and often unsatisfactory, so many transmen opt not to have them, but for those who do, there are two primary methods. In a genitoplasty, the surgeon wraps skin around the hormonally enlarged clitoris to form a penis about the size of a thumb. It maintains orgasmic capability but is not generally large enough for intercourse. In a phalloplasty, a tube of skin is raised up out of the groin or mid-abdomen and attached to the pubis; it looks a bit like a suitcase handle. Secondary procedures augment the blood supply to this flap, and it is cut free after two to four months and sculpted to resemble a phallus. It lacks sexual feeling, but implanted silicone rods or a manual pump can allow an erection. In the most complicated procedure—running at least $100,000—flesh from the forearm, with the blood vessels and nerves that supply it, is fashioned into the shape of a penis, and then, using microsurgery, the blood vessels and nerves are attached to those in the pubis. Such a penis appears most natural and has sensation. In any procedure, a scrotum is constructed by sewing the labia majora together. Urethroplasty—urethral extension to the end of the newly made glans—is a further surgical undertaking. "Think what a complicated organ it is," Norman Spack said. "It's amazing it works at all, and the human species depends on it."

Prepubescent transgender children with supportive families may avoid some physical difficulties of transition through the use of hormone blockers, which suppress puberty. This therapy may start as early as age ten for girls and twelve for boys. Lupron, the most common of these GnRH inhibitors, was developed thirty years ago as an alternative to surgical castration in the treatment of androgen-dependent tumors; because it is associated with decreases in bone mineral density and compromised memory, it requires careful monitoring. The treatment effectively buys families time; if the child is indeed transgender, puberty blockers can save him or her from going through the "wrong puberty" and may obviate many surgeries in later life. Girls administered Lupron do not develop breasts, widened hips, female fat distribution, or active ovaries. The estrogen surge that limits female height does not occur for them, so they grow tall. Boys administered Lupron do not develop facial or body hair; their voice does not deepen and their Adam's apple doesn't grow; bones do not thicken, shoulders broaden, or hands and feet enlarge. Estrogen supplementation, which closes the growth plates, can be timed to limit their height.

The essential androgyny of childhood can be prolonged. If someone goes off Lupron without starting cross-sex hormones, the deferred puberty of his or her natal sex will begin within a few months and will follow its natural course. Cross-sex hormones will initiate the puberty of the person's affirmed gender. None of the children in the original, Dutch protocol to study this practice has chosen to revert to natal gender, and most have stayed on GnRH inhibitors until they obtain gender reassignment surgery between eighteen and twenty-one. Lupron delays certain events, but it is also an event itself, heralding a profound transformation. There is concern that starting children on blockers will cause some who are just going through a phase to make it permanent; they may be too embarrassed, scared, or confused to revert if they think that they've made a mistake.

In Britain, where reassignment surgery is covered by the National

Health Service, particularly conservative policies on hormone blockers prevail. The Gender Identity Development Service at the Tavistock Clinic requires patients to progress through most of their natural puberty before allowing them to transition. Domenico Di Ceglie, the team's child and adolescent psychiatrist, reports that 20 percent of adolescents treated at his clinic choose to forgo medical intervention after completion of puberty. The underlying modernist fallacy here is that doing nothing is not doing something—that slowing transition is cautious, and accelerating it is rash. Rushing a child into a transition in which he will psychically or medically be trapped for the rest of his life would be a terrible mistake; however, forcing a child who is firm about his own identity to develop a body that will never match who he knows himself to be, even after multiple, expensive, traumatic surgeries, is equally troubling. The Tavistock model of prudence contains marked cruelty.

In the United States, these are family problems rather than national policy. "Parents say, 'I'm not ready to deal with this yet,'" Stephanie Brill said. "But they are dealing with it. Badly." Spack said, "Those who oppose puberty blockers complain of the young age at which we make this 'intervention.' I would argue that puberty itself is the most noxious intervention possible." Use of Lupron for gender dysphoria is seldom covered by American insurance plans, and its prohibitive cost creates a class divide between transgender youth whose parents are willing and can afford it, and all others. Likewise, there is a generation gap. At trans conferences I attended, older people would weep openly when they met children who would never have to "walk this earth as their genetic sex," as one put it. Shannon Minter—civil rights attorney, legal director for the National Center for Lesbian Rights, and himself a transman who did not have the benefit of Lupron—spoke of these young people as "a kind of superclass."

What did transgender people experience in the past, when they could not alter their bodies to harmonize with their identity? What will transgender people experience in the future, when surgery becomes more refined? These questions are both technical and teleological. Minter acknowledged, "The idea that in order for a child to express his or her authentic identity there has to be a dramatic physiological intervention challenges our most foundational ideas about authenticity and self-identity. It can feel like a technological madness." One has to wonder whether it is more of a technological madness than the cochlear implant. Many people outside these horizontal identities class that intervention as a way to normalize an abnormality, and this as a way to indulge one. It is instructive to note, however, that whereas the protest *against* cochlear implants comes from the marginal identity group, the demand *for* trans surgeries comes from the marginal identity group.

Jennifer Finney Boylan has written two books that deal with her gender switch and has held forth about gender identity on *All My Children* and *Oprah*. When I asked whether she hoped to be perceived as female or as transgender, she said, "On a national stage in front of twenty million people, I'm happy to be trans. On a day-to-day basis, when I go into a store, restaurant, or gas station, I want to be read as a woman. I refer to myself as female, knowing that *female* includes Britney Spears and Barbara Bush. Look at Julia Child! I'm certainly as feminine as Julia Child."

I visited Jenny, then forty-nine, in her mother's house on the Philadelphia Main Line. Her old room looked like a boy's room—banged-up furnishings, rock-and-roll posters on the walls. She showed me an adjoining storage room. "Back in the day, there were girls' clothes in here, my mother's, my sister's," Jenny said. "I could grab whatever was on the back of that door." Jim Boylan always knew that he was female, but he also knew that his transition would be painful for others. "So, I thought, if I can make the guy thing work, let's go for that," Jenny said. "It took until I was almost forty before I saw that I'd gone as far as I could, forty-four before I had surgery. Rather than wishing I'd gone through transition earlier—if it's about wishing—I wish that I'd been born female. Here I am, a grown woman, but I have a boyhood. If I ever feel lost or melancholy, it's because I can't see my life as a whole, I can't figure out how I got here from there."

Becoming Jenny involved the usual surgeries, including vaginoplasty and a "tracheal shave," but she was quick to point out that surgery is not the most important aspect of transgender experience. "A life is about more than one trip to the hospital," she said. "The surgery turns out to be easy. Nothing is cut off. The neo-vagina looks like it's supposed to and does what it's supposed to; the plumbing works and so does the electricity. I've been to doctors who didn't know and couldn't tell."

Jim Boylan was married, and his wife, Deedie, chose to stay in the marriage, though she once said to Jenny, "Every success you have as a woman is a failure for me." They have two children together, fathered when Jenny was still a man. "Deedie is a straight woman who's the center of my life, and yet she's not attracted to me," Jenny said. "Everyone always says Deedie is this great saint. Does it betray a complete lack of humility to say that she's lucky to be married to me because I'm a nice person and I love her and I'm a good parent to our children? All kinds of things happen to families. Children get cancer. Parents have car accidents. Families have to move to Texas. This has involved some heartbreak, but life does that anyway." At six and eight, Jenny's two sons decided that they couldn't really call her *Daddy* anymore. They already had a *Mommy*. So they announced that they were going to call her *Maddy*. When Jenny last did *Oprah*, her older son wrote a letter that was read on the show. It said in part, "Sometimes it's true that I wish I had a regular father. Most of the time, though, I feel like I am the luckiest kid on earth. I cannot think of a way in which life could be better."

Transition is a change of identity for the person who goes through it, and also for all the people who surround that person. "I'm glad for my story to be a public narrative where things worked out," Jenny said. "You know, boy meets girl, boy is girl, girl meets girl, girl stays with girl. That age-old tale. The biggest change for me is not going from male to female: it's going from someone who has a secret to someone who doesn't really have secrets anymore. It's unimaginably difficult to know that other people consider your fondest of dreams and greatest of sorrows (a) incomprehensible and (b) hilarious. A double life is exhausting and ultimately tragic, because you can't ever be loved if you can never be known." People often question a trans person's authenticity in his or her affirmed gender. "I call myself a gender immigrant," Jenny said. "I'm a citizen of this land of women. But it is true that I was born somewhere else. I came here, and I got naturalized." Jenny laughed slyly. "Or unnaturalized, as the case may be."

In the summer of 2000, Jenny decided to tell her mother, who was then eighty-four years old. "I thought Mom was going to be resilient," Jenny said. "But *resilient* means that someone snaps back after a blow, and I was aware that it was going to be a blow. She was bewildered, so I started to explain it, and I began to cry." I met Hildegarde Boylan when she was ninety-one, and as we all sat together, she said to Jenny, "You waited until five o'clock when we were having a gin and tonic. Then you just said, 'I always wanted to be a girl, and I didn't know how to tell you, because I didn't think you'd love me anymore.' Then I broke down and said, 'I'll always love you.'" Hildegarde experienced considerable difficulty at the beginning. "He'd led a perfectly normal life," she assured me. Jenny protested, "I was never perfectly normal." Hildegarde laughed. "I was a Cub Scout leader and he was a Cub Scout." It took Hildegarde some time to be ready to tell her friends, but about a year after that conversation she had a party to introduce her daughter. She turned to Jenny. "You were surprised when all of *your* close friends accepted it so readily. So I thought it worth trying *my* friends. I hadn't even heard the word *transgender* so I just went with *Jenny*. It's impossible to hate anyone whose story you know." Hildegarde leaned forward as if to tell me a great confidence and said the only thing she could never accept was Jenny's shoulder-length blonde hair. Turning to Jenny, she said, "If I tell you this, you'll cut your hair tonight when you go to bed: Ann Coulter has your hair." Jenny said indignantly, "So does Laura Dern, and she's a movie star!"

Jenny had come out to her sister, who was living in England, six months after telling her mother. "She was the last major, important figure in my life that I came out to," Jenny said. "I mailed her this lengthy letter, and she wrote back basically, 'I don't want to get to know this Jennifer.' A year later I got a letter from her daughter Eliza, who's ten, saying, 'I don't understand this, I'm scared of this.' I wrote her back, 'I'm sorry you're scared. I know it's confusing. My love for you hasn't changed and I hope, in time, you'll get used to me.' My sister called a week later, furious. How dare I write her daughter a letter like that? Finally she said, 'What we would like is to be left alone.' I said, 'I'll always love you.' That was seven years ago now. I remember thinking, 'Well, now it's going to be as hard for Cyndy as it used to be for me.' She and all the people I loved would have to go through years of learning how to talk about this. That fear I carried all those years—the shame, the secrecy, the inability to tell someone else—is what I gave to my mother and sister."

In her Jim days, Jenny had hoped that she could fall in love with a woman and learn to be happy being a man. "We are who we are as a result of who we love," Jenny said. She smiled her bright smile. "I'd always prayed for love to save me, and in a weird way, it *was* love that saved me, although not in the way I expected. The love of Deedie as well as the love of my family didn't keep me a boy, but it gave me the courage to know that if I did come out, it would be okay. Love didn't enable me to stay a man. It was love that enabled me finally to tell the truth."

Responding to advocates for allowing children with persistent gender dysphoria to transition, the bioethicist Alice Domurat Dreger wrote, "Changing a kid's name and gender identification at the age of five or six? This approach takes gender claims of little children so seriously that it's actually beholden to a ridiculously strict notion of gender. The great majority of young children who declare they are a gender that doesn't match their birth sex grow out of the mismatch. Young girls who declare in word or behavior that they are boys end up all over the place, which at some level *proves* to me most really *are* females. Sex-changing interventions are nontrivial. They involve substantial physical risk, including major risk to sexual sensation, and a lifelong commitment to trying to manage hormone replacement. The problem is *us* and the way we demand certainty from *them*, the way we insist on conformation to a two-sex model as early as possible."

Josie Romero and Tony Ferraiolo were adamant about who they were almost from infancy; Jenny Boylan knew but tried to repress the knowledge; but many others are deeply confused. Parents must determine whether such children are in a transient obsession or expressing a fundamental identity; they must guess what will make their child happy when he or she is grown, and how best to accomplish this. These balances are hard for parents to achieve: to supervise without presiding over, to caution but not demand, to impel but not insist, to protect but not throttle. Parents must take care not to squash their child's identity, nor to build it up so much that they create the truth to which they intend to respond. In *Mom, I Need to Be a Girl*, Just Evelyn wrote of her child, "I knew his life would be difficult and sad. How could a mother help, and would a mother's love be enough?" Many parents are willing to do what it takes for their children to be happy, but it isn't always possible to know what it takes.

Abrupt, decisive transformation occurs regularly in fairy tales, fantasy literature, and comic books, but not in most real lives, where change tends to be gradual and incomplete. In her memoir *The Woman I Was Born to Be*, transwoman Aleshia Brevard writes, "I consciously tried to create a boy child who might be worthy of love. Painstakingly, I tried to mimic the acceptable traits of other males around me. I knew, and so did my daddy, that the mimicry was a sham." In her poignant book *Transparent*, Cris Beam writes about a Latino transgirl who named herself Ariel after the heroine of *The Little Mermaid*. "Ariel had to go talk to her father, who turned her into a human being for real," the girl explained. "I want to go through the story just the way Ariel did it, turning into a real girl and getting the guy." But struggling to become who you've always been and be loved anyway is a continuous process, usually marked with ambivalence.

Hendrik and Alexia Koos grew up in South Africa and emigrated to Canada shortly before the end of apartheid, choosing a fairly small community where Hendrik's abilities as a GP might prove valuable. Both parents knew that their eldest daughter, Sari, was unhappy; she'd been diagnosed with ADD, a learning disability, and an anxiety disorder. When she announced, at fourteen, that she had "the wrong body," Hendrik was terribly upset; it seemed like just another stab in the dark.

When we spoke, a little more than a year had passed since Sari had become Bill, and Hendrik seemed to be holding his feelings just in check. "We started reading, and we found out that there were guidelines and ages, and he was younger than these guidelines, and he was really pressuring us," Hendrik said. "I almost felt impotent as a parent. What was I supposed to do? I could say, 'You're a kid; you have to be patient.' Or I could listen to my child. I've never wanted to pressure my children; my best dream for them is to be themselves. But I was so worried, I was exhausted by it." Bill himself was anxious and ambivalent, and that made everything harder. I had become interested in interviewing Hendrik after hearing him question the adult trans people on a panel. "They were so self-confident, so full of 'I am who I am,'" he said to me. "People said, 'Once your child can be who he is, you'll see a new person.'" Hendrik laughed. "No. It was a few steps forward, a few back. Overall the steps forward are more, but it's an ongoing fight to gain good ground."

Hendrik said he derived resilience from being a doctor. "From medicine, I learned to understand that life has challenges without always understanding where they come from. I felt, 'I'm not going to try to *remedy* my child's mind.'" Hendrik's second source of strength was even more striking. "As a white person coming of age in apartheid, I wanted to get rid of racism in my life, and sexism, and genderism, too. My South African experience was a preparation for learning to say, 'I accept you for everything.'"

Although Hendrik Koos's kind openness was different from Rex and Karen Butt's visceral enthusiasm, their children experienced similar ambivalence. Rex and Karen didn't believe in gendering childhood; they brought up their two sons with a toy kitchen and read to them from Letty Cottin Pogrebin's *Stories for Free Children*. "When I had a baby shower, I didn't want blue or pink," Karen said. "We had yellow and green." They told their sons that women could do anything men could do.

Elementary school was lonely for their son Jared, high school was rocky, and Haverford College was not the revelation he had hoped for. One of his friends set him up on a blind date with a girl from Bryn Mawr, with whom he had his first kiss and his first relationship. The relationship entailed sexual expectations that were alien to Jared, and one night his girlfriend walked in on him wearing her clothes. He said, "I think life would be a lot easier for me if I was a girl." She replied, "Oh, honey, you can't be a girl. Not with that nose." It was said in a tone of fun, but Jared sank into a severe depression. He had won every academic prize at his high school and was valedictorian; now, he was flunking. He had no sex life, and almost no social life. He dropped out and moved home.

Three months later, he said to his parents, "I think I'm gay." He went out on his first date with a guy and he realized he wasn't gay. He nonetheless decided to attend an LGBT conference for high school kids, partly because he felt as though he had stopped growing up and was in effect still a high school student, even at twenty-two. He dropped into the Transgender 101 panel. Two days later, he and his mother were out shopping, and he asked her to pull over so he could tell her something. "It's something big, isn't it?" she said. He told her he was trans, that that was his life path. She said, "Oh, why would anybody want to be a woman? It can be so hard being a woman." Later that day, he asked his family to gather so he could tell them; he said he was willing to lose people in his life over it. His younger brother, Chad, said, "That's bullshit. Anybody who would leave your life over this never was really in your life in the first place." Rex said, "I've been so worried about your being depressed. I don't know what the hell *trans* means, but at least you're not irretrievable to me." Jared became Cadence Case. She explained to me, "It's a measure of how supportive my parents were that my father's first question was 'Are you going to be okay if we have to save up to pay for this?'"

When I met Cadence, eight years after she began transition, she was thirty, and lingering in an intermediate territory. She had long hair, male-typical fat distribution, a tall, lanky body, and no breasts. She wore earrings and gender-neutral clothes. She had endured months of electrolysis but had more to go. Her only surgery was a nose job. I asked how she had seemed before transition. "I was intelligent, compassionate, and not macho," she said. "I never came off as feminine, and I doubt I ever will. And I don't really have a problem with that. I've reached an accommodation where I don't hate myself. If you have a spectrum of gender, I'm sixty, maybe sixty-five percent towards female."

Outsiders tend to think of the urgent surgery as being genital, but that is often not the feeling of trans people. "Facial surgery is the gateway to living full-time," Cadence said. Rex and Karen had found surgeons for genital procedures, but Cadence didn't call them. Her parents interpreted her delay not as reluctance, but as unhappiness. "For a long time, she was too depressed to deal with it," her mother explained. Rex said wryly, "We're more in a hurry than she is sometimes."

Karen was reprimanded by the head of the school where she taught for talking about Cadence's transition where she could be overheard, and she was furious. "No one tells me not to talk about my kid," she said. Rex said, "I'm more activist about this than I've been about anything. It really is how I identify myself." Rex and Karen cofounded a local chapter of PFLAG—Parents, Families, and Friends of Lesbians and Gays, a group that now includes families of trans people. When I last saw them, they had just been invited to be grand marshals of the 2009 Mid-Hudson Gay Pride Parade. Rex asked the board president why they would want them in such a role, and she wrote back, "Because you love your child." Cadence said, "I think they're more comfortable with my being trans now than I am. They're just far left, while I'm radically farther left. But I don't do as much about it."

Parents such as Rex and Karen encourage their children to use therapy to explore gender issues; others, though, turn to therapy in the hope of deterring such exploration. The choice of approach will depend not only on the child's needs, but also on the parents'. Reparative therapies— psychological, religious, sometimes biological—remain ubiquitous, and the parents who seek such treatment for their children are generally motivated by sincere conviction. Stephanie Brill said, "Everybody loves their children, but they have different ideas of how to help them." She encourages parents to meet other parents and find a new normal that includes their experience. "They don't have to condone their child's wearing nail polish; it's not about arguing about what's appropriate in church," she said. "It's about expressing love, which is reassuring to the child, and also, actually, to the parent." People whose lives have been bound by strong gender conventions, however, often believe that hewing to social norms will protect their children from abuse in the world. That very notion can constitute abuse inside the family.

Jonah and Lily Marx live in New Jersey, within commuting distance of New York, but said that they did not know anyone who was gay, much less anyone who was trans. Nothing they said indicated that their son, Caleb, wanted to be a girl; he did not insist on wearing dresses, did not hate his body, had never said he was female. When I suggested a therapist who could help Caleb figure himself out, Lily said, "I need to find someone who persuades people not to have a sex change operation. That's all I can think about. Now it's third grade. The boys get tougher. The girls don't really want to play with boys anymore." But then Lily recounted, "One of the moms said, 'When we got the class list, my daughter put a thumbs-down for every boy except Caleb.' So he's not weird enough that no one likes him."

Occasional teasing seemed not to bother Caleb much; it bothered his parents, who were challenged imagining a happiness so different from their own. "He hates team sports," Lily said. "But he loves to boogieboard, ice-skate, and swim, and he dives competitively." Jonah said, "He's a very happy boy, very comfortable in his own skin. He likes ceramics and photography, but he won't do Little League or use a urinal." Lily said, "He has almost no male friendships. Middle school could only be worse. My daughter torments him: 'You're acting like a girl.' 'Stop acting weird.' Constantly." Lily and Jonah had decided to get their children a puppy and described how Caleb had responded by jumping up and down gleefully and "effeminately." Jonah said, "He's not familiar with how to be excited because he's never been in an environment with other boys who have won a game together."

Caleb went to sleepaway camp and loved it. He had starring roles in both musicals that summer. He loved the counselor who directed them. "When we met the counselor, he had on a tight, purple T-shirt, skinny jeans, and purple Converse sneakers," Lily said. "Definitely out-of-the-box. Caleb came home asking for these clothes. I was not buying him purple sneakers. I have to protect him." I wondered about enrolling him in a local theater program. "I will not play into that," Lily said. Jonah added, "He's got a tremendous physique. He could excel at whatever sport, but he just doesn't have the interest. There's only so much that Lily and I can do to shelter him from what will inevitably be broader ridicule for how he is."

Both parents showed considerable anxiety about a future that they viewed as nearly inevitable. "I mean, he likes one boy," Lily said, shortly after telling me that all his friends were girls. "If you looked at this kid, you would think football player. He's big and tall. But he's very much like Caleb, doesn't play sports. Then there's this one other boy that he's very good friends with. His name is Karl, and he's very athletic. But when's he going to ditch Caleb? Because he's a cool kid, Karl. We love him. So I'm just wondering when it's not going to be okay to be friends with the weird kid." Lily wondered if Caleb's unwillingness to play catch or shoot baskets with his father was connected to his awareness that he's not living up to Jonah's expectations. "I personally think that he knows he's disappointed Jonah," Lily said. "If I asked him to go have a catch, he would. If I asked him to shoot baskets, he would." Jonah said, "Which begs the question as to why you don't." Lily said, with the dignity of her gender and no touch of irony, "Because I don't shoot baskets and play catch."

Caleb had never been trans, but he was mildly gender variant. He came out as gay at thirteen, and almost immediately made a suicide attempt. Sometimes, one becomes fully visible only through catastrophe: Caleb's adolescent despair spurred his parents to renounce efforts to resolve his childhood aberrance. They acknowledged clearly that he was always lovable and loved, and began the steep climb toward rebuilding his battered ego—and their own.

Reparative therapies for gay people are now deemed unethical by most professionals, but whether reparative therapies for trans people should be regarded the same way is widely debated. Among the most controversial figures in the field is Kenneth J. Zucker, psychologist in chief and head of the Gender Identity Service at the Centre for Addiction and Mental Health in Toronto, who continues to hold considerable sway and was appointed in 2008 to lead the *DSM-5* task force on GID. Zucker contends that natal girls who are trans see their mothers as disenfranchised and therefore wish to be men, while natal boys wish to draw close to detached mothers by becoming girls. Activists believe that the high rate of depression in children denied the right to transition is the result of their struggle to conform; Zucker believes that the wish to switch genders is a symptom of underlying depression. The hypothesis that GID sometimes has social and family origins can be defended. Zucker's views on how to treat GID are much less robust. The conservative Catholic Education Resource Center and the National Association for Research and Therapy of Homosexuality (NARTH) are both indebted to Zucker's work, though they overlay it with Christian ideology.

Using techniques derived from the models Phyllis Burke criticizes in *Gender Shock*, Zucker instructs parents to model gender roles, pushing these mothers and fathers into behavior consistent with midcentury gender stereotypes. He then asks that they impound cross-gender toys and prevent cross-dressing. Friendships with members of the same gender are to be encouraged, and cross-gender friendships are to be halted. One mother described confiscating Barbies and unicorns from a child who, when given trucks, simply refused to play. When he reverted to drawing, his parents were to take away the pink and purple crayons and insist that he draw boys; in the end, his mother said, he was living a "double life," acting like a boy in front of her, and escaping into a girl world whenever he could.

Zucker claims that no patient who began seeing him by six has switched gender; he recently announced that a follow-up study of twenty-five girls he first saw in childhood showed only three with persistent gender dysphoria later in life. At the same time, because adolescents are less malleable than children, Zucker will sometimes recommend hormones and surgery for people who come to him later. He does so with regret. Many of Zucker's patients have determined to live in their birth gender at the end of his therapy, but a recent article in the *Atlantic Monthly* quoted the mother of a Zucker-treated child who doubted her adult daughter, an alcoholic and self-mutilator, would outlive her. It seems overreaching to call this a success. Stephanie Brill said, "In my experience with many people who come to us after seeing Zucker, his work can alter gender expression, but it does not touch gender identity."

The question is whether trans people, like most gay people, have a fixed identity that only a fool would try to alter—or whether a child born male who says he is really female is like, in Zucker's simile, a child born black who insists he is white, and needs to be eased into accepting himself. Zucker points to the rigid way many trans children adopt the stereotypes of the opposite gender. "There is no joy in their play," he said. "They're struggling, experiencing social ostracism and difficulty establishing friendships with children of their own gender." Zucker feels that the idea of GID as a natal condition not subject to repair is "simpleminded biological reductionism." The therapists who support early transition are, in his words, "liberal essentialists." He explained, "Liberals have always been critical of biological reductionism, but here they embrace it. I think that conceptual approach is astonishingly naïve and simplistic, and I think it's wrong."

Susan Coates, former head of the Childhood Gender Identity Project at Roosevelt Hospital in New York, agrees. She said, "I've seen about three hundred and fifty kids with gender issues. They are fundamentally creative, and part of the creativity allowed them to imagine solving their problems by switching gender. My experience is that no one becomes transgender who had treatment early. If you work on separation anxiety and aggression, the gender problem starts to fall away. Anxiety is what leads to gender dysphoria." Zucker and Coates are accomplished academics who have personal integrity, but—like some of the activists who attack them—they seem to imply that universals exist in a field of highly varied stories.

You can damage someone who is trans by preventing him or her from living in his or her true gender; you can damage someone who has GID but will not be trans by trapping him or her in an ill-fitting cross-gender identity. The trans-friendly therapist Michele Angello said, "Parents tell me often, and it's sort of PC, that they are following their child's lead. If your child is seven, you probably don't let them choose what they're going to eat for dinner, let alone if they're going to transition to a new gender. There is a very, very occasional phenomenon where the parents have their own mental health issues and their kid is not the most masculine male, so they've decided that their child is trans. The kid isn't transgender and is being talked into it." Stephanie Brill said, "It's important not to overdiagnose transgender children. That's a very small part of the gender variant population."

When Dolores Martinez was fourteen and still a boy named Diego, living in Massachusetts, his mother caught him with his first boyfriend. "I was in a miniskirt doing the dirty," Dolores said. "I put on my boy clothes again and went downstairs and she said, 'Your father said to be out or he's gonna kill you.' I was on the streets for four years, and I was convicted of a major, violent crime and sent to prison. It saved my life. I spent almost four years in prison happier than ever before. When you're in there, either you're a man, or they'll turn you into a woman. So I was a sister. That was my first experience at being myself one hundred percent." After she was released, Dolores learned that her mother had lied. "She told my father I ran away. When he found out what she'd done, that was their divorce. When I told him about my transition, he said, 'Oh, thank God.'" Dolores spent ten years in therapy before her first hormone shot. Eventually she met Gustaf Prell, a transman who was the love of her life, and they were legally married—under the law, however, she was a man and he was a woman.

When Tyler Holmes was a confused little girl named Serena, she "wished for boy parts," but "didn't really wish to be a boy." She had a brief relationship with a sixteen-year-old, Freddie Johnson, and became pregnant. When their son, Louie, was born, Freddie expressed little interest. But when Louie was two, Freddie's mother began complaining to the Department of Social Services about Serena. Louie's guardian *ad litem*, assigned to look after the child's interests, told Serena to sign something. "I didn't know what it was, and I signed it, and it turned out it was for custody," Tyler said. "I lost my child." When Serena befriended Gustaf Prell and Dolores Martinez soon thereafter, she began to question her allegiance to her own gender. When she was hospitalized for endometriosis, her doctors said it could be treated with an estrogen-based medication, but Serena said that she'd prefer treatment with testosterone, that she really wanted facial hair and a lower voice. She began calling herself Tyler.

One Thursday in 2008, Gustaf, who had always been depressive, went to the emergency room of a local hospital seeking admission because he was suicidal; he was told that no beds were available to a transgender person. He hanged himself two days later, age twenty-seven. Dolores filed a complaint, but the Board of Mental Health found the hospital not at fault. Because transgender people are not a protected class, the ruling stated, the hospital had discretion to refuse them admission if their presence might disturb other patients.

After Gustaf was gone, it seemed natural for Tyler and Dolores to get together. I asked whether the fact that neither of them had made a surgical transition had any bearing on their attraction. Tyler said, "Love and relationships aren't based on what you have underneath your clothes, what pronouns you go by, or the name you use. With Dolores, it's based on the person she is and the way I feel about her, and the person I am and the way she feels about me. Dolores has expressed wanting some form of surgery at some point, but that's her thing as far as when or what she wants." Dolores said, "I see Tyler as a boy with benefits; he straps it on so I can select a size."

In the five years since Tyler relinquished custody, Louie, now seven, has lived with his paternal grandmother. Tyler and Dolores are allowed to see Louie only once a week, for a supervised visit. Tyler said he didn't think Louie had noticed his transition; I felt that Tyler's full beard might have clued Louie in, not to mention Dolores's habit of addressing him with male pronouns. Both Tyler and Dolores were interested in Louie's gendered behavior. Dolores said, "Louie could be like my husband was, where he was a girl one day and a boy the next. He likes My Little Ponies, which we have to sneak in to him because he's not allowed any girl toys. I'm not a doctor, but I think he's genderqueer right now." Tyler said, "He's never said anything about being trans or wanting to be a girl, but I never said anything when I was little." It seemed to me that absent any assertion from Louie that he wanted to be a girl, he was probably not trans. He did, however, do badly with male stereotypes. He inhabited a polarized world with either a terrifying genderlessness or an oppressive genderedness. "He might not know for sure that he's a girl," Tyler said. "He might not know for sure that he's a boy. He might float back and forth from day to day, and that's okay, too. I don't want him to lose twenty-five years of his life like I did."

Perhaps the immutable error of parenthood is that we give our children what we wanted, whether they want it or not. We heal our wounds with the love we wish we'd received, but are often blind to the wounds we inflict. Dolores said, "I want Louie to be comfortable with himself whether he's a male, female, somewhere in the middle. I have a lot more years to fix than a youngster. My life is not what I want for him." Children should be able to be themselves; they also want rules and boundaries, and I feared that Dolores and Tyler's infinitely permissive idea of love might be petrifying to a child. The longing of a child is to be seen, and once the child is seen, he or she wants to be loved for a true self. Dolores and Tyler were full of love unnuanced by seeing. "He's the most beautiful boy that I've ever seen, and probably the most beautiful child on the planet for all I know," Tyler said. "It's cool, because it's almost like I'm transitioning with my son. He has it a little bit better than most trans kids because he has two trans parents. We're not going to let him do it by himself like our parents did. He has people who will go with him." Dolores said, "His transition needs to move forward. I see him living in my yesterday. So hopefully he can learn from my tomorrow."

The debate over gender identity was once framed as a nature-nurture divide; nowadays, it's an intractable-tractable divide, which is equally hard to call. Clearly nature is involved, but the question is whether nurture enables it, whether it can and should disable it. The answers are frustratingly vague. Psychodynamics has proposed a range of contradictory explanations for cross-gender identification; as Amy Bloom wryly pointed out in her book *Normal*, it's either absent fathers and overinvolved mothers, or dominant fathers and submissive mothers; it's parents who encourage cross-gender identification and play, or who forbid and thereby mystify cross-gender identification and play. Some little boys may want to wear dresses because they have brutal fathers who scare them and loving mothers with whom they identify; others may have a condition determined by genetics, brain development, or the uterine environment.

Transitioning is still bound up with the medical and therapeutic communities. In the best cases, this means that responsible professionals can separate the fears and desires of the parents from those of their offspring and distinguish between an immutable imperative and a transient neurosis. That can, however, be daunting. Separating the psychiatric, the endocrine, and the neurocognitive seems almost poignantly old-fashioned. Modern psychiatry seeks the chemical pathways of emotional and thought disorders, but attempts to distinguish mind from brain are still primitive, and a condition as complex as GID must be described from multiple angles at once. Heino Meyer-Bahlburg, who serves on the *DSM* committee, acknowledged that the description of GID "cannot be achieved on a purely scientific basis."

In his own practice, Meyer-Bahlburg believes that transition is best avoided if possible. "It's terrible to mutilate a healthy body and make someone infertile," he said. "Sexual functioning is not terrific even in the best cases and is horrific in the worst. There is some feeling that you're enhancing a disorder rather than treating it." He believes in a centrist treatment. "We try to introduce them to more of their same-sex peers," he said, "and if their fathers have already turned into sissy-boy-hating, distant fathers, as happens in this homophobic country, we try to get them to reengage positively and to develop a relationship.

Many of these children become more comfortable in their birth gender, and even if they don't, they can have a broader circle of friends and experiences." That said, he has also put children on puberty blockers as early as eleven. "Sometimes, I help patients make the change, and sometimes, in a noncoercive fashion, I try to stop them from doing so," he said. "It's only based on my own intuition; I have no algorithm." Edgardo Menvielle said, "Most young children don't come with a claim about their identity. They are brought because they are different in their gender expression. Whether they should transition or not? You're never really sure you're doing the right thing."

Members of the trans community often fear therapists who steer children away from their true selves; parents are more likely to fear that their children will have surgery and come to regret it. It is impossible to know how many people who have transitioned socially but not physically have transitioned back. We do know, however, that as many as one in a hundred people who have had sex-reassignment surgery wish they had not done so.

Danielle Berry, born Dan Bunten, underwent sex-reassignment surgery in 1992 at forty-three in what she later described as a "midlife crisis." She subsequently said, "I'm now concerned that much of what I took as a gender dysfunction might have been nothing more than a neurotic sexual obsession. I was a cross-dresser for all of my sexual life and had always fantasized going femme as an ultimate turn-on. I just wish I would have tried more options before I jumped off the precipice."

The Iraqi-born Sam Hashimi underwent sex-reassignment surgery in England after his wife left him in 1997. "Trudi had never worked a day of her life," he said. "She'd think nothing of spending a few thousand pounds on a dress. I always used to wonder what it would be like to have none of the responsibility I had, to have doors opened for me and all the privileges a woman seems to have." So he became Samantha Kane. But Samantha found "being a woman rather shallow and limiting" and decided she'd made a terrible mistake. She underwent a painful and unsatisfactory "reversal" of her genital surgery and, after adopting the new name Charles, sued the psychiatrist who had supported the surgical transition.

Such stories are unfortunately used to discredit the trans movement as a whole. Cases of profound postsurgical regret make headlines, while much less space is given to people who would have been much happier with a full surgical transition but were never able to achieve one. Mistakes will be made in both directions, and lives can be ruined either way. Some children who are supported in conforming to a chosen gender identity may later feel trapped by it; their parents and doctors may make misguided decisions about hormone blockers, hormones, or surgery. Other children, not supported for transition, live and die in despair. It is terrible to perform unnecessary surgery on a healthy body, but it is also terrible to deny succor to a mind that knows itself.

Far more boys are referred for treatment for GID than girls. However, this does not mean that more natal boys have gender-atypical behavior than natal girls, only that they worry their parents more. Feminism won for women many rights formerly reserved for men. Girls who are aggressive and dominant are often admired; the very word *tomboy* has a measure of fondness built into it—though there is no shortage of insults for assertive women. In contrast, no movement seeks to legitimize stereotypically feminine traits in men. Girls can be masculine; boys are effeminate. Girls in jeans and T-shirts wear "unisex clothing," but boys in skirts are "in drag." Kim Pearson described asking everyone in a parents group who had been a tomboy to raise her hand; hands went up all over the room. She then asked everyone who had been a sissy to raise his hand. No one stirred.

When Scott Earle was a tomboy named Anne-Marie, her parents regarded her toughness as a sign of strength. They were both pediatricians, living in liberal Vermont. "I loved the idea of having a woman unencumbered by limits," Lynn Luginbuhl, Scott's mother, said. Gender irregularities were plentiful in Scott's early life. "As a little girl, Anne-Marie had this beautiful curly blonde hair," Scott's father, Morris, said. "One morning we got up and Anne-Marie, who was eighteen months old, was in her older brother Ben's room, and Ben, maybe five, had cut off all her hair. Ben got in trouble, but later I wondered if Anne-Marie somehow asked for it." Lynn said, "We had this pink, down snowsuit. My mother said to Anne-Marie, age four, 'Oh, you're a beautiful pink lady in that snowsuit.' Anne-Marie refused to put it on. We finally dyed it black, and then she would wear it."

In Anne-Marie's first conversation with other trans people online, when she was fourteen, the name *Scott* emerged, and she realized that was what she wanted to be called. A few months later, her parents returned from a party to find a letter on their dresser: "Dear Mommy and Daddy, I have to be a guy. I'm trans." Morris recalled, "I didn't even know what that word meant. We walked downstairs to the basement where Scott was watching TV, and I said, 'Is there anything that would make us not think you're one of the greatest people we ever met?'"

Lynn called some gay friends for advice, but they knew no more about being trans than she did. "I found a therapist who helped make people less inclined to transition physically," she said. "Scott hated her. I had to come to an understanding that he really was going to live as a guy. We eventually found a therapist who had counseled seventy transgender people, and she felt Scott didn't need to see her because he was so clear. I thought I was raising this strong woman, but most eight-year-old girls do not wear boys' underwear." For Morris, the challenge to accepting Scott's new identity wasn't a conservative belief in an unbreachable wall between maleness and femaleness, but a utopian belief that no natural disparity exists between genders—which made transition pointless. But he didn't fight Scott's wishes. "If there's a snowstorm, you don't spend time trying to get it to go away," he said.

They called their local endocrinologist at the University of Vermont (UVM), where they were both referring physicians, and he said he didn't deal with such cases. Lynn was shocked. "As pediatricians, when we take care of people, we need to leave our opinions at the door," she said. "Our job is to meet people on their terms. This was no different." She eventually found a trans health group in Philadelphia, drove Scott seven hours down, went to the appointment, and drove straight back. In testimony before the Vermont Senate on trans rights, years later, Lynn said, "I think what is hard is when you don't know what to do, or when there is nothing you can do. It was very clear that there were lots of things to do. So we just did them."

Scott, academically advanced, was boarding at St. Paul's, a New England prep school. Lynn drove him back after Christmas break; they stopped at a gas station, and when Scott used the men's room, his mother realized how far along he was. When he came out as trans at a school assembly shortly after his return, he was greeted with support from other students and much of the faculty, but not from the school administration, led by an ostensibly broad-minded Episcopal bishop. He told Lynn that her daughter needed to grow out of this and suggested that Scott might have a better time starting fresh in a new place. "I knew he was just trying to get rid of me," Scott said, so he left.

He met up with trans people on the Internet, then in real life; he dyed his hair blue and got a Mohawk. He said he didn't care about academics, and might not finish his education. Lynn said to him, "Look, we've worked really hard to respect you and let you be who you are, and now we're asking you to finish school and go to college." Scott agreed it was a fair bargain. Lynn suggested that he go to college early and register as a guy. UVM was eager to have him, so in what would have been his junior year of high school, he became a freshman in college.

Morris took Scott to freshman orientation. "He was wearing a T-shirt from some trans event," Morris said. "I was thinking, 'If you want to be a guy, be a guy, but don't go wear this trans shirt and look all weird.' We got to the orientation, and a number of the volunteers said, 'Hey, I went to that conference,' or, 'Great T-shirt.'" Scott had a single room with a private bathroom in a boys' dorm, but he hated the beer drinkers and football players, so he joined the UVM Pride Suite, with a variety of gay undergrads. The following year, he established a seven-person suite for trans people. He went on to start a trans conference at the university, to convince UVM that students should be able to put whatever name they wanted on their student IDs, and to get the designation *transgender* added to housing forms.

I first saw the family soon after Scott began his freshman year. When I went back, two years later, Scott had moved away from a trans identity and toward an exclusively male one—a gay male one. "I still haven't figured out how the person who was my daughter who likes guys is therefore gay," Morris said. In the general population, some men are gay because they are attracted to men, and when they become women, they remain attracted to men. Some men are gay because they are attracted to sameness, and once they become women, they are attracted to women. These are not independent variables; they are components of a complex relationship with one's own and other people's gender. By some estimates, about half of transwomen and a third of transmen are gay or bisexual.

Lynn said, "I asked him lots of questions about how people have sex. He discussed it with me because he was being gracious and I wanted to know. I worry because there are anatomical things that are different, given that he doesn't want bottom surgery, so he's got to meet one hell of a nice guy not to mind. But people have richly varied tastes. During those transition years, I would stop by UVM pretty often for lunch, and we'd talk on the phone quite a bit. In the last year he's been much less forthcoming. He's doing what a normal teenager does." Scott said, "I'm fine being out as gay, but I'm not out as trans except to close friends. For a while, my transition was most of what I thought about and did. I'm no longer interested in making my life like an example. I am probably going to medical school. I know my being out could be important for other medical students who have trans issues. But it's also my life."

Scott's younger brother, Charlie, said he didn't have a hard time with his old friends learning that his sister was now his brother. But he has a hard time telling newer friends that his brother used to be his sister. When those friends come over, Charlie puts away the framed photos of Scott as a little girl. Scott doesn't mind his parents having the photos out, and he doesn't mind Charlie putting them away. Lynn said, "If we get rid of them, we erase his childhood. I had a daughter until Scott turned fourteen. Of course, I didn't have a daughter really, because Scott was Scott the whole time. But also, I did."

I found two models for political engagement among trans people. Some activists were newly affirmed in their gender and eager to claim a loud trans identity; over time, I saw them become comfortable passing, wanting simply to live the gender they had always felt themselves to be. For them, activism had been a form of catharsis. Others had made their transitions quietly and privately, often at a great distance from everyone they knew and loved. Over time, they became comfortable with themselves and worked to spare others the difficulty they had experienced. For them, activism was a mechanism of gratitude. Many activists associated themselves with organizations such as TransYouth Family Allies (TYFA), Gender Spectrum, Mermaids (UK), PFLAG Transgender Network, TransFamily of Cleveland, TransActive, Genderfork, the National Center for Transgender Equality, the Transgender Legal Defense & Education Fund (TLDEF), and the Transkids Purple Rainbow Foundation. Some activists were not themselves trans but had an oblique relationship to the trans community. I was especially drawn to two groups that represent the differing archetypes of support for trans children: Gender Spectrum and TYFA.

Stephanie Brill, who founded Gender Spectrum in 2007, trades richly in nuance—sometimes at the expense of clarity, but always with an acknowledgment that among human experiences gender lies at the pinnacle of complexity. She is versed in gender theory and queer theory and can spin the obscure vocabulary of abstract philosophy into a dazzling array of options for you or for your child. She believes that a just society must have room for boys who like dolls, for heterosexuals who cross-dress at home, for women who are tough at the office and turn kittenish with intimates, for male kids with long hair who want to learn ballet, and for little girls who are interested only in baseball and climbing trees. Kim Pearson and Shannon Garcia, who run TYFA, a group founded in 2006, are equally intelligent, but they are first and foremost mothers of trans kids. Whereas Stephanie Brill radiates intellect, they emanate a Midwestern, everymom warmth. They are large and loud women who can finish each other's jokes. You can call them in the middle of the night, and they'll wake up fast and throw themselves into solving your problem. They can sway a high school principal in a conservative, small town in Middle America by showing that gender variance is a common experience requiring extremely obvious accommodations; they have the kind of courage that makes other people brave.

Stephanie Brill is based in the San Francisco Bay Area, and Gender Spectrum helps liberal families proceed through transition with acuity and self-assurance. Brill encourages parents and patients to explore the many places in the gender middle before they commit to a leap from one side to the other. That is an excellent approach where feasible; it is not feasible in the previously mentioned small towns, where shifting from male to female (or vice versa) is already more than anyone is prepared to entertain. Gender Spectrum is for families pondering the nature of identity; TYFA is for families whose children will kill themselves if they have to live one more day in their natal gender.

Kim Pearson and Shannon Garcia met online in 2006; in January 2007, they set up TYFA, with Amy Guarr, another mom, who is treasurer of the organization, and Jenn Burleton, a transwoman who went on to found TransActive. Ten months later, Amy Guarr's trans son, Ian Benson, took his own life. "It has shaped the way we do things," Kim said. "Because even a kid who's fully supported is still hugely at risk. Children who come out in adolescence know they may lose parents, siblings, friends; they are already at the end of their ropes. So do not ever assume that you have time as a parent to have your own pity party. You can grieve about your child transitioning to another gender, or you can grieve about your child being dead." After the first of Kim and Shannon's workshops that I attended, the two women engaged an anxious father who said, "But what if he changes his mind?" Shannon said, "You just explained how he told you on the changing table at two that he was a girl, and that message hasn't changed in thirteen years. You're worrying about the future. Talk to your kid about today, right now." It took them about ten minutes to bring this man around to an acceptance he had been unable to achieve for over a decade.

While most of her work is with parents, Kim Pearson told me that what she finds hardest is helping trans people to keep their dignity. She described meeting a transwoman, Janice, who introduced herself as "a postoperative transsexual." Kim replied, "Do you view yourself as a woman?" Janice said she did. Kim said, "So I view myself as a woman, and I've never, ever introduced myself by my genitalia. I'm going to challenge you to introduce yourself as a woman, or as a transgender woman, and never to discuss your surgery with a stranger again. Adult trans people say they don't want to be judged by what's under their clothes. Well, then stop introducing yourself by what's under your clothes."

For some families transition is harrowing; for others it is easier; and for some, such as the Pearsons, it's a celebration. Shawn-Dedric Pearson, living in a small town in Arizona, came out officially on May 6, 2006, and a few months later his mother started TransYouth Family Allies, and they boarded a joint bandwagon to change the world.

"I'd faced a lot of expectations of how I should be growing up," Kim said. "I didn't want to do that with my kids. At three, Shawn was going, 'I don't do dresses!' We're like, 'If it's going to be a big deal, we'll switch to pants.'" Nevertheless, her daughter was always unhappy. When Shawn was twelve, she wrote to her parents that she was a lesbian. Things got better for a little while, then they got worse than before. Shawn was failing at school and had constant stomachaches and headaches. "Shawn was staying in a dark room with the covers pulled up," Kim said. "Not eating, or eating constantly. Not sleeping, or sleeping constantly. You could so clearly tell that something horrible was wrong. But we couldn't figure out what."

The Pearsons started family therapy. A few months later, they happened to watch the movie *Transamerica*, and Shawn, then fourteen, knew the answer. A few weeks after that, Kim and Shawn walked into the counselor's office and the dynamic was changed. "I went in with a depressed daughter, and I came out with a happy son," Kim said. "Shawn says, 'I'm not a lesbian. I'm transgender. I'm totally a guy. You know that's who I am.' I said, 'I feel like I've been working on a jigsaw puzzle all of your life, and there were some pieces that never fit. Today, I see those pieces just fitting perfectly. But I have no freaking clue what we do now.' He just blithely says, 'That's okay, Mom. I've got a list. I need a legal name change, I need you to enroll me in school as a boy, and I need to get binders for my chest.'" Kim, who didn't really want to do any of those things, was horrified. "Somewhere in there he said he wanted to get men's shampoo and deodorant and socks," she recalled, "so I said, 'I don't know how to do any of the things you're talking about. But I am really good at shopping. So, what do you say we start there?' He was animated, his face was lighting up. I hadn't seen this kind of spark for years."

When they got home, Shawn found his father, John, relaxing after a long day of work at Home Depot and started showing off his new purchases. Kim took John into their bedroom and explained. John sat staring into space. Kim said, "So, say something." John said, "I don't know what to say." John explained to me, "I went into a cave for twenty-six days. I had to go through a transition myself." After twenty-six days of silence, John made his peace with the idea.

Shawn came out in early June. The therapist cut the family loose in midsummer, and Shawn returned to school on testosterone and with a new name. Kim said, "It was transition at warp speed." Shawn had asked Kim to talk to the school. "I approached it as a medical problem," she said. "If my child was diabetic, you'd make sure he had privacy to give himself shots. We need to look at what restroom he'll use." The school made the nurse's restroom available. Shawn's legal name change hadn't yet come through, and the principal initially refused to alter school records. "I convinced him that the less people knew, the less parents would come to school upset that Shawn was in class with their kids," Kim said.

The family sent around a letter giving everyone the update. The first phone call they had came from one of the people in their community from whom Kim had expected condemnation. "He said, 'Shawn is always welcome in this home. He will always be safe with us,'" Kim recalled. "I started crying. We had prepared ourselves for negative reactions. We really hadn't thought about what it would be like to get a positive one." Kim's work in the computer industry felt increasingly meaningless and had become physically difficult because of fibromyalgia in her hands. "My church is Unity Church," Kim said. "The philosophy is, have faith that things will go as they should. So I had this conversation with the universe. I said, my perfect job would involve travel and public speaking; would use my teaching and course-design skills; I'd be writing. Two weeks later, Shawn came out. Three months later, I was founding TYFA. It was exactly what I asked for."

Soon thereafter, Shawn and Kim headed off to give a presentation at San Diego State University. The car was running low on gas, and Shawn spotted an Indian casino with a gas station. Kim recalled, "I needed to use the restroom. I said, 'I'm taking twenty dollars with me. I'll be back in five minutes.' Put my twenty dollars in a slot machine and hit a ten-thousand-dollar jackpot. That paid for the start-up fees and filing as a nonprofit." Shawn's brother created a website and hosted it on two old computers in his parents' bedroom.

John said, "I never thought I was marrying an activist. I went to hear her in Vegas about a month ago. I always knew Kim was a good communicator. But I was blown away." Kim later wrote to me, "I have found my calling; I have found my purpose; I am using my God-given talents in a way that is satisfying to me and of service to others." She recounted a schedule that involved crisscrossing the country, mostly by car, to do five school trainings in one week, including two full days of driving to do one in Ohio. I wondered whether that one couldn't have been rescheduled. "How can we tell the sixteen-year-old that we can't come?" Kim said. "People say, 'How do you do so much?' I'm like, 'How do you not?'"

Shannon and John Garcia had six boys, or so they thought, in Indiana, in what Shannon has described as "a white-bread neighborhood in a white-bread town in a white-bread state." Their youngest son developed language quickly and at fifteen months said, "I'm not a boy. I'm a girl." Shannon said, "Sure you are," and kept changing the diaper. At two, he asked for a Barbie doll. By the time he was three, Shannon thought he was gay. At four, he entered the Christian preschool his five brothers had attended. At the first parent-teacher meeting, his teacher said, "Your son will not be allowed to play dress-up because boys don't wear skirts." Shannon was outraged. "That was the first time that our son discovered that the way he felt was not acceptable to others outside. Within days, we started to see anxiety."

John, however, was furious with his wife. "It was my fault. I babied him," Shannon said. "He was going to fix it." John confiscated all the girlish toys. He took his son out to the yard, said, "I'm going to butch you up," and gave him a baseball bat. John threw the ball over and over and over, saying, "I want you to hit it." His son stood there with the bat with tears streaming down his face. Shannon said, "It was very ugly in our home. I wanted it fixed, too. But I knew that shaming our son was not the way to do it. I owed it to John to try his way. All that happened is that our child grew to hate him."

The following September, Shannon's son resisted kindergarten with tearful entreaties, saying, "It's too hard to pretend to be a boy all day long." Shannon steeled herself to it. When first grade started, Shannon began bribing him. "If you don't cry all week, I'll buy you a Barbie this weekend," she said. Each week they would choose the bribe, trying to keep it from John. Then one week, the little boy said, "Can I have a quarter instead of a toy?" Shannon asked why. He said, "Because on the way to school, we pass a house with a wishing well. I'm going to ask the bus driver if she'll stop so I can wish I'm a girl."

John kept saying, "You have a penis. That means you're a boy." One day, Shannon noticed that her son had been in the bathroom an awfully long time and pushed the door open. "He had a pair of my best, sharpest sewing scissors poised, ready to cut. Penis in the scissors. I said, 'What are you doing?' He said, 'This doesn't belong here. So I'm going to cut it off.' I said, 'You can't do that.' He said, 'Why not?' I said, 'Because if you ever want to have girl parts, they need that to make them.' I pulled that one right out of my ass. He handed me the scissors and said, 'Okay.'"

The family was preparing to go away to Tennessee for Thanksgiving, and Shannon decided it was a perfect opportunity to experiment. Her husband opposed it; her other five sons hated the idea. Their youngest announced that her new name was Keely. When they set out, Keely was dressed in pink from head to toe, with a barrette taped in her crew cut. "We drive several hours and then stop to eat," Shannon said. "We sit down at the table. My child had never spoken to a stranger, ever. When the waitress gets to Keely, she says, 'And what will you have, pretty girl?' Keely says, 'I'll have chocolate milk, please.' I went to the restroom and I was an absolute puddle of tears on a public bathroom floor. Over the next forty-eight hours, words cannot describe the difference. It was so profound that my husband said, 'I hope you've looked into homeschool options, because she can never go to school as a boy again.'"

They enrolled Keely at a new school and changed the name and gender designation on her educational records. She had previously qualified for services under Title I, a federally funded program for learning-disabled students. Within six months, she was two grade levels ahead in reading, and at grade level for math. "Twelve months later, we went to the doctor for a checkup," Shannon said. "The doctor walked into the exam room and Keely started talking, and I don't think she shut up the whole time we were there. His mouth was hanging open, and he said, 'There is absolutely no way this is the same child that I saw for six years.' She was that profoundly different."

By the time I met Keely, she was seven: beautiful, chatty, and poised beyond her years, with a wicked glint of humor. "I know it was definitely maneuvered by God Himself," Shannon wrote to me afterward. "It was a simple choice for me: a dead son or a living daughter. It really is the choice that most parents with trans kids face. Keely has always been told that she can marry whomever she wants. She told me that she wasn't going to disclose her status to her 'person,' and I told her that it wouldn't be right to withhold that information. I told her that if the person really loved her . . . She finished the sentence, 'Then they won't care!' I said, '*Exactly.*'"

Many parents lag far behind this level of acceptance. More than half of trans people are rejected by their families; even in families with some acceptance, it often comes from only one parent. "In a two-parent family, it's not unusual for one parent to hold the fear and the other to hold the acceptance," Brill said. In her memoir of working with disadvantaged trans kids, Cris Beam writes of the mother of one transgirl, "She told Christina she wished she would just die of AIDS if she was going to act this way." An ostensibly more sophisticated mother wrote in a letter to her trans daughter, "For you to insinuate your man-dressed-as-a-woman self into the whole *process* and *actuality* of being a woman is arrogant and insulting. You discredit and discount not only my own experience of being female but the entire community of women."

In May 2009, a popular radio program out of Sacramento, *Rob, Arnie & Dawn in the Morning*, featured a segment on trans kids. Rob Williams and Arnie States referred to the kids as "idiots" and "freaks," out "for attention," with "a mental disorder that just needs to somehow be gotten out of them." They added, "It makes me sick. 'Mommy, I'm a girl trapped in a boy's body. I want to wear a *dwess*.'" Later they said, "Allowing transgenders to exist, pretty soon it becomes normal to fall in love with animals." One boasted that if his son ever put on high heels, he'd beat him with his own shoe.

Outcry about this broadcast triggered an advertising boycott. Kim Pearson and San Diego transgender activist Autumn Sandeen were invited to appear on the show to discuss the issue. Kim explained that any trans-inclined child whose mother had driven him or her to school while listening to the broadcast would now never broach the subject with her. When the show opened to call-ins, one came from the brother of a transman who had killed himself. Kim warned Williams and States that they had blood on their hands. When the show began, they had made it clear that their apology was required to mollify advertisers; by the end, they were abject.

While wealth and education do not guarantee families of trans kids an easy time, poverty increases the chances that everything will go horribly wrong. Indigence exacerbated the difficulties for Hailey Krueger and Jane Ritter. Each had lived a long secret life. Neither wanted to admit to her mother that she was a lesbian, and both married men. Their hollow marriages were full of lies and abuse and dysfunction. Hailey had dropped out of school in Kansas in the ninth grade; Jane had completed high school in Missouri, but had no professional qualifications. Jane had an adolescent daughter; each had a young son. Hailey was femme, and Jane was butch, and they met in a homeless shelter in Wichita.

Hailey's husband was given to cross-dressing, but only at home and in complete privacy. Soon after marriage, they had a son, whom they named Jayden. "My child was always embarrassed of down there," Hailey said. "He was always trying to hide it, even when he was a baby. He sat down to pee and wiped, like a girl." At five, Jayden declared that his name was Hannah, after Hannah Montana, the Disney character who lives as a normal teenager by day and a rock star by night; that story had resonance for many trans kids I met who were leading a double life.

Jane said, "The first time I met Jayden, in the shelter, age six, I honestly thought it was a girl." After a few months, Hailey and Jane moved out to a trailer with Jayden, and Jane's kids, Bryan and Lillian. "Jayden had just had enough of hiding," Hailey said. "We settled in, and he says, 'Mama, can I put my bra on?' I said, 'Go ahead. No one can see it.'" Jayden told Jane he had something to tell her. "He goes, 'I got a bra on,'" Jane said. "I said, 'Okay.' He was like, 'You're not mad?' I said, 'No, baby, because Mama Jane thinks that everybody needs to be themselves.' His face lit up, and he was so happy." Jane told Bryan and Lillian, "Nobody's going to make no fun." Before long Jayden started introducing himself to other children as Hannah. His father was horrified.

Jane found a job at McDonald's, and Hailey, at Dollar General. They moved into a depressed area of Wichita. By the time Jayden was seven, he was sporting fingernail polish at school. "The school would bring it up, and I'm like, 'Kids will be kids,'" Hailey said. "Then he started wanting to grow his hair out. He wanted a pair of tights, makeup. He cried a lot, wanting to go to school as a girl." As soon as Jayden came home, he'd put on girl clothes. One night, he said to Jane, "I'm so mad at you." Jane said, "Why, baby?" Jayden said, "Because you're able to be who you are. And I can't." Jane said to me, "That just about broke my heart."

The school wanted Jayden in therapy, but Hailey and Jane didn't want him to see someone who would, as Jane put it, "deprogram" him. They had never heard the word *transgender*, had no idea that there were other children like Hannah. They learned of a sixty-five-year-old transwoman, Leona Lambert, who ran a support group. Leona, in turn, introduced them to the Metropolitan Community Church (MCC), the LGBT-positive denomination to which she belonged, and to her pastor, the Reverend Kristina Kohl. MCC was the first public place where Hannah presented herself as a girl.

When Hannah entered first grade, pressure mounted from the school for her to act more like a boy; pressure mounted from Hannah to go to school as a girl. Leona said to Hannah, "For your safety, it's best for you to live a double life right now. They'll beat you up, they'll pick on you. Just fit the norm. Then when you get home, run put on that dress and watch TV. There is no law to protect you in this state." Kristina Kohl said, "All her life, she'll have to make concessions. We all do." Hailey and Jane had three meetings at school to discuss the situation. "I told Jayden, 'If you're purple, and you're the only purple person in this world, I'd love you to death,'" Hailey said. "'But you cannot be Hannah at school.'" Jane said, "Hannah was calling herself a freak. It upset me so bad. I said, 'Hannah, please do not use that word. You are not a freak.'"

Jane's daughter had moved out, but her son was home. Bryan has since been given diagnoses of oppositional defiant disorder—a dysregulated relationship to those in authority—and major depression. At thirteen, he took to attacking his mother. He eventually made a suicide attempt, so Jane contacted Social Services to get him treatment. Bryan complained about his mothers to the social worker and was put into state care. Among his accusations, he said they encouraged his brother to wear dresses.

On February 24, 2009, Jane got Hannah ready for school. "I gave her a hug and a kiss, and I said, 'I got a surprise when you get out of school. We're going to eat pizza and go bowling.'" At one thirty, the social worker who had done Bryan's intake called Hailey. "I've got your child," she said. "You have a court date Tuesday at eight thirty in the morning." The social worker had interviewed Jayden at school and asked what he would wish if he had three wishes. Jayden said, "Change all my boy clothes into girl clothes; me be a girl; my boy body parts be girl body parts." The social worker presented this as evidence that Hailey and Jane had "convinced" their child that he was female. The paperwork noted that Hailey had a female partner, and that her child was therefore subject to "more confusion and social difficulties than other children." The judge ruled that Hannah be placed in a foster family with "healthy parents."

In a little more than a week, Hailey and Jane had lost both children. Kristina became their chief adviser. "Hailey and Jane are educationally challenged; they come out of generational poverty," Kristina told me. "The kids hadn't been to a dentist or a doctor, didn't have shoes that fit. It's not simple. But they love those kids, and Hannah absolutely loves her home." Hannah's foster family would not allow Hannah to use her female name, wear female clothes, or do anything else outside masculine norms. On Hailey and Jane's first supervised visit there, Hannah said, "If I have to be a boy to go home, I will. I'll do anything to go home."

Social and Rehabilitative Services of Kansas (SRS) was now in charge. "SRS dug up some 1950-something psychiatric journal entry about cross-dressers," Kristina told me. "I'm like, 'This has no bearing on the situation we're here to discuss.' But I don't have much clout. I don't know if you can understand how bad it is here." It can be hard to tease the transphobia apart from the homophobia. SRS continued to say in court, "We're not giving this child back to lesbians." SRS finally appointed a therapist, Mia Huntsman, for Hannah and her mothers. They all loved Mia. Hailey said, "We brought Hannah some dresses in therapy because Mia said that she could wear them. Hannah was, 'Oh,

I don't want to do it in case my foster parents find out.' Mia said, 'I'm the therapist, I set guidelines. For your safety, you can do this only in my office, at home, and at church. You can be yourself in these three places.'" On another occasion, Mia said, "I know you want to talk to your mama. I'll leave the room so you can talk." Hannah said, "No, don't do that. I don't want to get in trouble from SRS." Hailey wept openly. "Hannah is that scared," she told me, complaining that Hannah had withdrawn. "She was like a bird being able to fly, okay? Free. Now, even with us, it's like she's caged."

Leona Lambert drove Hailey and Jane to their therapy sessions with Hannah and was eventually allowed to participate. "God, I wish I'd had her guts at that age," Leona said. "Even with being taken away from her moms, seeing her with her little heart broken, I want to trade places with Hannah so bad." Leona showed me her business card, which said FEMALE IMPERSONATOR. I asked her if that was how she thought of herself. She said, "That was the best I could do. I hope Hannah will do better."

Hailey and Jane are allowed to attend Hannah's baseball games. "At the ballpark, she loves my pink sandals," Hailey said. "She says, 'Mama, can I wear those to the picnic table?' I want to just sit there and scream, 'What's it going to hurt for my child to put my flip-flops on and wear them to where she can get her own shoes on?' But they told me no. So I have to abide by that." Following these rules seems like the best way to get Hannah back and may help Hannah get by in Wichita. But it teaches troubling lessons. "In therapy, she said she was tired of the double life," Hailey said. "Then she said, 'But I have to do it because I'm a bad person.'" Mia Huntsman diagnosed her with situational depression. At that point, Hailey said that she was ready to give up, that maybe she and Jane should just have another child and stop trying to get Bryan and Hannah back. It was despair talking, but it was frightening to everyone.

When I met Hailey and Jane, Hannah had been away for seven months. The women saw their child for an hour of therapy and one two-hour supervised home visit each week. They were not allowed to call Hannah, and she was not allowed to call them. It was Hannah's eighth birthday, and Hailey and Jane had done their best to make it festive. "I had a little present," Hailey said, "and I gave it to Hannah and said, 'Here you go, baby boy.' She just looked at me like, 'Mama, do you not accept me anymore?' So the social worker walked out for a second, and Hannah looked at me real quick and said, 'You mean "baby girl"?' I said, 'When these people are around, I can't say that.' I felt so low." Jane said, "How can you just tell this child, 'Okay, here and here you can be yourself, but out here you can't be yourself'? What kind of confusing message are you sending?" Hailey said, "I don't know what I'm supposed to say and what I'm not. My biggest fear is of getting her back and then just losing her again. It will definitely be very dangerous for her and for us if she's herself."

Parents are right to fear for their transgender children. The level of prejudice against them is unimaginable for those who have not encountered the problem. In 2009, the National Center for Transgender Equality and the National Gay and Lesbian Task Force published a large survey of transgender people from every state and territory of the United States, with ethnic distribution roughly comparable to that of the general population. The online distribution of the questionnaire meant that it was skewed toward relatively privileged subjects. Four out of five people surveyed had been harassed or physically or sexually attacked in school, almost half by teachers. Although almost 90 percent had completed at least some college, compared to less than half of the general population, they were twice as likely to be unemployed. One out of ten had been sexually assaulted at work, and almost as many had been physically assaulted at work. A quarter had been fired for gender nonconformity. They experienced poverty at twice the national rate. One out of five had been homeless; a third of that group had been refused entry to a shelter because of their gender. A third had postponed or avoided medical care due to disrespect or discrimination by providers. More than half of trans youth have made a suicide attempt, as opposed to 2 percent of the general population. The rates of substance abuse and depression are staggering. Some 20 to 40 percent of homeless youth are gay or trans, and more than half of trans people of color have supported themselves by streetwalking. One sex worker in a shelter for trans kids in Queens, New York, said, "I like the attention; it makes me feel loved."

Albert Cannon and Roxanne Green knew early on that their son Moses wasn't boyish. At two, he wanted dolls and was much more interested in picking out clothes that would look good on his sister, Shakona, than in toys for himself. In the inner city in Syracuse where they lived, the streets could be tough; Albert worried about his son, but never tried to change him. "God got my kids confused," Albert said. "Shakona more manly than Moses was." Moses insisted on wearing patent leather shoes to school every day and was called a faggot and beaten up all the time. "He could throw a football and could run," Albert said. "Oh my God, could he ever! But he wasn't interested in it." By the time Moses was fourteen, Albert knew what was going on. "I've been sleeping in the living room, and he was in the back with his girlfriends, learning how to tuck it in and seeing if he could look like a woman."

At sixteen, Moses wrote to his parents, "I'm going to buy all girls' clothes and I'm going to become a woman. If you can't accept it, I'm going to kill myself." Roxanne knocked on Moses's bedroom door. "I said, 'Are you sure this is what you want to do? There's a lot of gay-hating people.' He said, 'Mommy, if I'm going to be an embarrassment, I'll just leave.' I said, 'You never can embarrass me.'" Albert was not pleased, but after a few days, he relented. "Ain't no man can tell me they ain't got no feminine in them," he commented. "If they do, they're lying to themselves. But I said, 'Are you sure you're ready for how the world is going to react?' Moses said, 'The question is, is the world ready for me!' I said, 'I'm not even ready for you, babe.'"

Moses took the name Lateisha Latoya Kyesha Green, Teish for short. The girls at school loved the way she dressed; she was suddenly popular. A week after she started dressing, she was jumped and badly beaten, but her determination did not flag. One of the hall monitors told Lateisha that she was going straight to hell because the Bible said so; Roxanne called the principal and reminded him that you cannot preach religion in school. It eventually got to be too much, and Lateisha dropped out. She did hair and got a job as a housekeeper at Motel 7. She was spirited and joyful, but longed for one thing. "Dad," she said to Albert, "I'll never be happy until I become a complete woman." Albert said, "You'll never become a complete woman. But if you mean you want a sex change, I'll help you when I can." Albert began setting money aside and wrote into his will that it was for the surgery. As a bridesmaid in her sister's wedding, Teish wore a red taffeta dress. Albert said, "My sister warned her girls, who were the other bridesmaids, 'You are all in trouble, because Teish is going to outdress you all.'"

At seventeen, Teish liked to "talk to" (in Roxanne's euphemistic phrase) a man who was closeted; when he heard that she had boasted of their relationship, he slashed her face with a knife. "Wow, she was so tough," Albert said. "She wanted to kill him." At home, Teish would sleep between her parents in their bed. "I could keep an eye on her," Roxanne said. "Know she wasn't out with that bastard getting her face cut up." Roxanne and Teish argued constantly, but they also fought for each other fiercely. The Cannon house became the unofficial gathering place for local trans kids. "They tell me they is using drugs to ease the pain," Albert said. "I said, 'The pain ain't going nowhere.' Not that Lateisha didn't try drugs, but she didn't use drugs to escape reality. She had friends who could live here. I never would turn them away. They want to sit down and talk? I'll listen."

Teish had been involved with a number of men, but she didn't fall in love until, at nineteen, she met Dante Haynes, a devastatingly handsome gang member. She soon began referring to him as her fiancé. Dante and Lateisha were together for two and a half years. "So he did experience love as a woman," Albert said. "At least he got that." Roxanne said, "This one wasn't no hush-hush thing. They went everywhere together. Dante always said *she*." Teish had dreams for Dante. "She changed me from doing stupid stuff that I'd probably be in jail for," Dante told me. "I thought I could sell drugs for the rest of my life to get by. She showed me how to feel like you're somebody." Lateisha and Dante broke up; she stayed with her parents. Then on Friday, November 14, 2008, they decided to move back in together. "She was so happy that day," Roxanne said. "It was going to be for the long term."

That evening, Teish's friend Alissa Davis invited her to a party across town. Alissa had said she was pregnant and didn't want the child. She told Teish that she could have it, and Teish was hoping that this plan would work out; she'd already asked Roxanne to help her raise the baby. When Teish got the invitation, she and her brother, Mark, jumped in their father's van and headed over. They didn't know many people at the party. A young man named Dwight DeLee, who had attended school with Teish and Mark, approached the van, saying, "We don't want faggots here." DeLee shot Mark and Teish point-blank as they sat in the van. Mark took a bullet to his shoulder; Teish's bullet went into her chest, then hit the aorta.

"We just skated off," Mark explained to me. "Lateisha's like, her chest hurt, chest hurt. She was like, 'I love you,' then saying to bring her back home, don't take her to the hospital." When the van drove up, Albert was on the porch, and Mark said, "Moses been shot." Albert ran toward the street, calling 911 as he went. He pulled back Teish's shirt, saw no exit wound, and knew it was bad. "She looked at me, smiled," he said. "I knew she wasn't going to make it." Roxanne came running out. "The look she gave me was 'I'm sorry, Mommy. I'm going,'" Roxanne said.

Dante got the call at work. We were talking almost a year after it happened, but Dante took his large head in his hands, and his shoulders bowed. "I seen her that day," he said, "but I didn't get to say good-bye. When they say it gets easier, that's a lie." Albert put an arm around him. Dante picked up his head. "She was an openhearted person," he said. "She loved who she was. She was who she was." Dante remains close to Albert and Roxanne. "That's forever," Dante said. "She would want to see me bettering myself. Working, going to school. She wouldn't want to see me feeling the way I really feel. Someone can shoot me, stab me. I don't care. I mean, I'd be up there with her in heaven. I'd be able to see her again." Albert held out his rough hands as though there were something in them and said, "And I still have the money I was saving for her operation."

DeLee's murder trial was emotionally devastating for everyone. While the rough facts of the case were clear, first-person accounts varied, with witnesses contradicting each other, some recanting under what appeared to be pressure from peers. "There were witnesses who I thought were going to have heart attacks, they were under so much strain and stress," said Michael Silverman, executive director of the Transgender Legal Defense & Education Fund, who worked on the trial. Because DeLee's intent to kill could not be proved, he was found guilty of manslaughter in the first degree rather than murder, but it was manslaughter as a hate crime and he received a twenty-five-year sentence, the maximum for manslaughter. It was the second conviction in the country and the first in New York State to treat the murder of a transgender person as a hate crime.

Months later, the local trans kids were still coming around to see Albert and Roxanne; during the day I spent in Syracuse, two dropped by in a few hours. Albert said, "I'm going to help other kids. Her life maybe was in vain; at least her death won't go in vain." In the corner of their modest living room stood a shrine with Teish's ashes in an urn inscribed with her dates—July 4, 1986–November 14, 2008—and her favorite photo of herself, dressed in red taffeta for her sister's wedding. Every day Roxanne lights two candles and leaves them to burn down. "She wanted to come home to die with us," Albert said. "So she's going to stay at home." Roxanne said, "When I went to get the ashes, I asked, could I look at them? I wanted to see if they'd cremated her with her boots on. Because if so, there would have been some gold stuff in there. She'd have liked that."

Shakona was pregnant when Teish was killed. She named the baby Lateisha.

Severely disabled children, autistic children, schizophrenic children, criminal children—many of these are at greater risk of death than a conventionally healthy child, but parents of trans kids are uniquely poised between two equally terrifying possibilities: if the child is not able to transition, he or she may commit suicide; if the child transitions, he or she may be killed for having done so. The murders of trans people often go unreported; even when a murder is reported, its status as a hate crime often remains unacknowledged. Since 1999, more than four hundred trans people have been murdered in the United States, and Transgender Day of Remembrance puts the rate of fatal hate crimes at more than one a month. Worldwide, a transgender person is murdered every three days.

Commentators have observed that the problem is ubiquitous. The German trans activist Carsten Balzer wrote that such murders "occur in countries with high general murder statistics, such as Brazil, Colombia or Iraq as well as in countries/states with low general murder statistics such as Australia, Germany, Portugal, New Zealand, Singapore, or Spain." Thomas Hammarberg, the Council of Europe's commissioner for human rights, wrote movingly about the murder of a transwoman in Portugal, Gisberta Salce Junior, who was gang-raped and then dumped in a well to die. Data from the first six months of 2009 indicate that about 7 percent of the trans victims murdered worldwide that year were minors. Professionals who support transition are also under attack. Norman Spack told me he had received death threats.

Looking just in the United States in the year 2011, and considering only attacks that were specifically reported as transphobic, the catalog of completed murders is alarming. Krissy Bates was stabbed to death at forty-five in Minneapolis on January 10. Tyra Trent was strangled at twenty-five in Baltimore on February 19. Marcal Camero Tye was shot and then dragged until dead at twenty-five in Forrest City, Arkansas, on March 8. Miss Nate Nate (or Née) Eugene Davis was shot at forty-four in Houston on June 13. Lashai Mclean was shot at twenty-three in Washington, DC, on July 20. Camila Guzman was stabbed repeatedly in the back and neck at thirty-eight in New York City on August 1. Gaurav Gopalan had a subarachnoid hemorrhage due to blunt-impact head trauma at thirty-five in Washington, DC, on September 10. Shelley Hilliard was decapitated, dismembered, and then burned at nineteen in Detroit on November 10. Her mother had to identify her by examining her charred torso at the medical examiner's office.

Anne O'Hara grew up in a small town in Mississippi. Both her parents were addicts, and Anne stole food to feed her sister and brother. "We were dirty," she recalled. "People didn't talk to us." The first person on either side of her family to finish high school, Anne graduated as class salutatorian, then attended Mississippi State University in Starkville. She lived in her car for a year, working at Subway and washing in their bathroom; it took her eight years to get through college, but she made it. She earned a certificate in special education. Anne moved back home, found a job at a school just across the border in Tennessee, and married Clay, a man she'd know all her life who worked in a local plastics factory. When she showed me pictures of their house, she said, "It doesn't look like a lot, but my daddy built it with his own hands, and he built it just for me." Anne set out to change how special education was delivered in rural Tennessee. By the end of a decade, she had succeeded in mainstreaming all of her students from second to fourth grade for science and social studies; some were being invited to parties by nondisabled students.

Anne and Clay, unable to conceive, signed up to adopt. On the day Anne's father died, three boys unknown to Anne were taken into state custody several hundred miles away. Marshall Camacho, Glenn Stevens, and Kerry Adahy had lived with their mother until she was arrested for child abuse. The police had found the children—then age three, four, and five—drugged with their mother's antipsychotics, which she used to sedate them rather than herself; she kept them tied to a pole and fed them nothing but cereal. The state placed the boys with a foster family and enrolled Marshall in the school where Anne taught. "I had Marshall in my classroom for six weeks before he showed his first sign of promise," Anne said. "He told me the name of a letter and its sound, so we threw a popcorn-and-Coke party." A week after the popcorn, Marshall named three letters, then came out with his first coherent sentence: "Where's my party?" Anne assumed that while some of his problems were biological, others were the result of abuse, and she was determined to sort them out. She argued against medication until every behavior management strategy had been tried. "He went from having a fifty-five IQ and being extremely violent and not talking, to a first-grade boy who could read and write with an average IQ," she said. "But he still had horrible moods. So he was diagnosed with bipolar disorder and ADHD and is now medicated for both."

Marshall had been in Anne's class only a few weeks when the social worker in charge of his case told her that the three brothers were to be separated, because Marshall, half Mexican, and Kerry, half Cherokee, looked dark and wouldn't interest white families. Anne said, "What would I need to do to keep them together?" The next day, Friday, she found out she'd need to move to Tennessee, because the foster-care system would not allow the kids to move out of state. The social worker expected Anne to balk; instead, Monday afternoon, Anne and Clay found a new house. They moved in two weeks later, were given the kids, and started adoption proceedings. "A two-year-old will grab everything and rip it in half or drop it or roll it," Anne said. "Nothing is safe. Marshall was doing that at six, but he was angry. So it was just a matter of letting him lick and touch and drop and tear until he got all of that out of his system. It took a year. Glenn had a fascination with putting things in different holes of his body." Kerry had a feminine manner, which was the least of Anne's worries. "Food issues, discipline issues, hygiene issues. I just thought this was one of those. But the other stuff cleared up and this never did. So I just thought, 'Kerry's going to be gay,' which was fine with me. Kerry said, 'I have a girl voice, girl feet, girl hands. Mommy, doesn't my smile look as pretty as a girl's?'"

The boys hid things under their beds and mattresses. If Anne was missing fried chicken or macaroni and cheese, she would go into their room and retrieve it, but objects she would just leave alone. She noticed that Kerry was often hiding girl things, lifted from the houses of his cousins. "You can't attack a child who's taken something like that," Anne said. "I'd say, 'Oh, Alicia lost her such and such, and she would love to have it back.' A few days later, it would be back at Alicia's house. Kerry didn't want to make anyone else sad; he just wanted pretty things." The other kids at school tormented him. In second grade, he stopped doing homework. "Nothing I could do mattered," Anne said. "About a month before the end of school last year, he was sitting on the front porch, with his little knee propped up under his chin, looking out across the field. He said, 'I wish I was a girl.'"

Anne called several local psychologists before finding Darlene Fink in Knoxville, a transgender activist and therapist. After Darlene diagnosed Kerry with GID, Anne spent two solid days researching the subject. "Then we went to Walmart and bought clothes, purses, fake jewelry, and a Barbie doll," Anne said. "Different colors of lip gloss. She was so excited. Then it was 'I want to change my name.' Her first choice was Pearl, from *SpongeBob*. I killed that one. So we went with Kelly." The change was palpable. "She was the child I wanted to raise, the happy one who's comfortable in her own skin."

Clay was angry, and for a couple of weeks he refused Kelly's hugs. Then he told his father, eighty years old, what was going on. Clay's father said, "Don't blame Kelly, or Anne, or yourself. These things happen. I saw it on TV." Clay hugged Kelly that night. Anne's mother, however, said not to think of bringing this child back to Mississippi, and Anne's sister stopped speaking to her. "But it's more complicated," Anne said. "My sister's had to work really hard to have respect in our town and not have people say, 'You were that dirty, poor kid.' Kelly could have made her a topic of gossip and ridicule."

Anne went to tell the principal at school. "I had already talked to two teachers, and after I'd explained for half an hour, they were fine," she said. Anne felt confident; Anne felt beloved. "In our town, people would come over for dinner; they'd invite my kids to birthday parties; I made friends with people on the block. I had a church. I really thought that we were part of the fabric of that community. Well, it turns out, I really didn't even know what that fabric was made out of."

The day after Anne went to the school, the phone calls began. "I didn't recognize the voices," Anne said. "They were going to gut her. They were going to cut off her genitals and treat her like the woman she wanted to be. They were going to snatch her from school or in a parking lot, and I would never see her again. Some of them were going to raise her up right. Some of them were going to kill her." Anne was at a loss. "She's eight," Anne said. "She's the tiniest kid in class." Anne had never thought about the Klan much; they had a rally on the main square once a year that was like a big parade. "I thought they were just a bunch of fools who dressed up in their costumes. It turns out, they're in charge of things." When Anne tried to go to the school the next day, the janitor she'd known ten years wouldn't let her in the building. Her pediatrician asked her to see him in his office. "He had been sitting around the country-club pool, with the other people from the Baptist church. He said, 'People are not talking about *if* they're going to hurt you and Kelly. They're planning *when* and *how* and *what they're going to use* to do it. You have to put your child in a foster home somewhere else, or he's not going to live till the next school year.'" Anne was reeling. She went home, loaded the shotgun, and slept in front of the door. "I'm getting cell phone calls from neighbors saying, 'Anne, there are people parked in front of your house, and they're peeking over the fence.' Of course, they didn't know yet. Those phone calls stopped when the gossip reached them."

Anne met a mother online, Maureen, who said that things were better in the big Southern city where she lived. Anne decided it was as good a destination as any. She sold whatever she could online; Maureen offered to put down the deposit on a trailer for her to rent. "I let it be known I was armed," Anne said, "and that I would kill anyone who stepped on my porch. The phone calls continued and I told them, 'We're no threat to you. We're leaving.' I put the kids in the van with as much stuff as I could and left. Everything fit except the dog." Clay stayed behind because he needed to keep his job. A few days later, he came home to find that a crowd had disemboweled the dog and nailed its remains to a fence. "It was just a message to us not to ever come back," Anne said. "We never will. I'll never see the town I grew up in again. I'll never see my mother or my sister."

Anne began to cry as she recounted all this. Shaking slightly, she said, "I knew I was a lesbian when I was fourteen years old, and I kept that to myself for twenty-one years. I married to fit in and be wanted and keep my home and family and church and everything that was important to me. It wasn't worth it to give all that up to be myself; I preferred to live a lie. I gave it all up in a month for Kelly. That's how important she is. I came out to Clay two days ago." Anne's fear was that Clay would say she and her lesbian ways had done this to Kelly; Clay's fear, as it turned out, was that Anne would think this had happened because he wasn't a good father. "It boiled down to, neither of us is guilty," Anne said. "He just said, 'Well, that explains a lot.' We're better friends now than we've ever been." Anne looked out the window. "It's funny how your priorities change. I've got this happy little girl. All of a sudden, the house my daddy built me doesn't matter. Don't get me wrong. I miss it. But when she gets off that bus and you see this happy little face, you've got the whole world right there. I haven't given up one thing that's worth that."

Daily life remains difficult. For the first week, Anne didn't let the kids outside, in case they'd been followed, and even when we met she wouldn't let them out of viewing distance. Teaching jobs require references, and she didn't want anyone from her new town to be in touch with anyone from the old one, so she couldn't work in her field. Anne had to work with the kids on not blowing Kelly's cover. Marshall and Glenn both complained that they didn't know how they could keep it all a secret, and what if people asked them? So Anne said she was going to do an exercise with them. She told them all to sit together right inside the trailer door while she went outside for a few minutes. Then she walked in, flung open the door, and said, "Hi, kids. I'm Anne O'Hara, and I have a vagina." They all ran away screaming, as she'd known they would. "No one wants to hear that," she said. "It's not secret. It's private. Kelly's anatomy is private, too."

As long as Clay keeps his factory job, they have insurance to pay for the kids' medications. Other than that, his salary pays for his life in Tennessee. Anne is living on the money from selling the lawn mower and the four-wheeler, and on the assistance check she receives for having adopted special-needs children. "We get about nineteen hundred dollars per month," she said. "Living in this trailer, rent and utilities, is nine hundred dollars per month. I spend about a hundred dollars a week on groceries and about twenty-five a week on gas. We have a lot of Tuna Helper, pea soup, bagels, and yogurt. At first, I'd get up in the morning, get them ready for school, and they'd get on the bus, and I'd go to sleep. I'd get up in time to take a shower before they got home. I'd play with them until bed, do their homework, and go back to sleep. I'm awake more than I was. But I haven't put up curtains, and I haven't decorated anything. I don't have the energy."

Anne has another safe place in mind if things fall apart where she is.

She's figured out exactly how she'll move and what she'll do. When I suggested that she talk to school administrators about why she couldn't provide references for a new teaching job, she replied, "I will work at a gas station before I tell anyone my child is transgender." We walked up through the trailer park to meet the school bus. Three exuberant children bounded out and ran to hug Anne. She stood there, so soon after our long, tearful talk, wrapped in all those young arms, and she burst out laughing.

"I don't love my daughter less for mourning over this," she said that evening. "But I miss my mom. I miss my sister. My daddy's grave is back there, and I just have to hope other people are putting flowers on it. I miss my dog. I miss my students. I feel really guilty because I'm still hung up on all this stuff that we left behind. I should just let that go. But it makes me so angry that these people have taken our lives from us." Then Anne smiled again, as though she couldn't really help herself. "You can't grieve all the time when you've got your kids. You see how far they've come, and they reach you right in your heart. That moment when they come off the bus is one of my best moments. My other is when they get up in the morning, and they collide on top of me. So, regret? No. I miss the things that were in the old life. But if I knew this was going to happen, I would still adopt Kelly. I'm the lucky one. Because, honestly, if it weren't for Kelly coming into my life, I would never have entered this bigger, more beautiful world, where I've met you and so many other wonderful people. I would still be married to a man for the next twenty years. I mean, if you just look at it, Kelly has brought more blessings into my life than I could possibly give back to her."

In 1990, Judith Butler published *Gender Trouble*, a book that rocked the idea of the gender binary. In 1999, in a new introduction, she wrote, "One might wonder what use 'opening up possibilities' finally is, but no one who has understood what it is to live in the social world as what is 'impossible,' illegible, unrealizable, unreal, and illegitimate is likely to pose that question." Two decades after the book's publication, those possibilities are open wider even than Butler hoped. When a friend of mine, a professor at a Midwestern university, was pregnant with my goddaughter, one of her students volunteered that she was planning to name her first child Avery because "I just thought Avery is a nice, ungendered name that my kid could keep if he or she ended up a different gender from the one he or she got born as." Norman Spack described similar conversations, calling them "a new era of 'no variant person left behind.'" Playfulness about gender is much more commonplace than it used to be. "To some extent, transgenderism has become a fad," Meyer-Bahlburg said. This observation conformed with my experience. I met people on college campuses who were defining themselves as genderqueer to express revolutionary feelings, or to communicate their individuality; they were gender fluid without being gender dysphoric. This phenomenon may be culturally significant, but it has only a little bit in common with the people who feel they can have no authentic self in their birth gender.

Michele Angello explained that one of her ten-year-old clients says, "I know I'm a boy, but I don't want boy toys. I don't want boy clothes except to go to school." Most of his friends are girls. Angello asked, "What do you imagine for yourself as an adult?" He said, "I'll probably be a dad who sometimes likes to be a girl and sometimes likes to be a boy." Angello explained, "That's drastically different from the nine-year-old male-bodied kid who comes in and says, 'I want to be a mommy when I grow up.'" Such children imagine themselves past convention. The imagining would once have been questioned; now, it is often the convention that is reassessed.

Belonging is one of the things that makes life bearable, and it can be tough to look at a binary world and choose against both sides. A therapist who works with children with various challenges told me that it's much harder to be ambidextrous than it is to be left-handed. Sometimes, idiosyncrasy can be a pose, membership in the smaller club of the anticlub, but often it is a marooned consciousness that occurs not because genderqueer is a cool thing to be, but because neither the duality nor the spectrum fits. Such experiences express the wide vision that lies outside of belonging.

When I met Bridget McCourt in 2009, her son, Matt, was seven and a half and had been dressing as a girl for three years. He had long, beautiful, blond hair and a distinctly boyish manner. When Bridget first agreed to buy him some dresses at Goodwill, she thought they would be just for dress-up, but that was not what Matt had in mind. A few weeks later, it was time to pick out fall clothes. "I let him decide what clothes he wanted," Bridget said. "He went to the girls department and was consistent about wanting girl clothes. I just thought, 'We'll take this day by day.' He pretty clearly says that he is a boy. He's comfortable with his body, but he likes girl things. He's irked by the labeling. I have told him, 'Matt, if I were told I couldn't wear pants, that would feel so limiting to me. So I can understand that you would feel the same way about dresses.'"

Someone who doesn't conform to the stereotypes of his gender, but who identifies with it nonetheless, has no clear path. When I met Matt, he looked like a long-haired boy in a dress. Older trans people who don't appear to inhabit their gender look sad; whenever I saw someone who looked like a middle-aged man in a dress, I felt an ache. In a child, the effect was curiously transfixing, as though he had just imagined himself into being. "For a long while, it was important to him for people to know he was a boy," Bridget said. "At the park, he would come over to me with a kid and say, 'Mom, tell them.' He now realizes that it's just easier to let someone who meets him for five minutes refer to him as *she*." I wondered if Bridget feared for his physical safety. "I worry more about his losing the confidence to be himself," she said. "It would pain me to see him fold inward."

An almost constant tension exists between the accommodations a trans child will make to the norms of the world, and the accommodations the world will make to the norms of a trans child. When Nicole Osman took her daughter, Anneke, to see Santa Claus at a local mall, she was worried that Santa would either look at Anneke and call her a boy, which would be upsetting, or would look at her name and promise her girlish toys, which would be even worse. She tried to explain the possible problem to Anneke, but Anneke said, "Santa knows who I am, and Santa knows what I like." Nicole saw Christmas falling apart. Then she spotted an elf who was keeping the crowd amused while they waited. She took him aside and asked him to get the message to the big guy: Anneke was a girl, and she wanted boy-type toys. Nicole asked me wryly, "Has anyone else you've interviewed had to bribe the elf?"

At four, Anneke said she wanted a short haircut. Nicole suggested a bob, but Anneke wanted a crew cut like her father's. People started mistaking her for a boy. Nicole worried that this would upset Anneke, but Nicole's correcting people was what upset Anneke. At school, Anneke was marginalized by the girls because she wanted to play with trucks and was into soccer, and by the boys because she was a girl. Her father, Ben, was worried. "Since nobody would play with her, I'd show up with a soccer ball at recess, and we would start a game," he said. "One by one, people would join the game. I would slowly pull out, and pretty soon everyone wanted to play with her." Nicole said, "I told her, 'I don't shave my legs; I don't wear makeup; I'm not this princess girl. There's some really amazing, cool girls that are athletic and they like soccer. Then there's a few girls who feel like there's just been a really, really big mistake, that they really should have been born a boy.' There was this long pause, and I was totally expecting her to say, 'Well, I'm one of those cool girls.' She said, 'I think there's been a big mistake.'"

I met Anneke when she was twelve and a half. Her presentation was masculine but she regarded herself as female. Anneke had discovered herself in ice hockey. "At hockey, I'm more masculine," she said. "But sometimes I do feel more of a girl at school, because the boys are weird. I want to pick things from each gender. Lately, I've been thinking about taking testosterone, but still playing hockey with girls and being a girl, but having the deeper voice. It's just a thought." Although Anneke did not want to transition or live as a man, she also didn't want to develop breasts, and she was taking Lupron. "I'm very open to my friends that I am taking a shot, and that's why I'm not going into puberty and all that."

Nicole and Ben had always had somewhat unorthodox arrangements. Nicole worked full-time, while Ben stayed home with Anneke and her little sister. "We've played with those roles a lot," Nicole said. "But the fluidity is challenging. Some days, Anneke goes in the girls' bathroom, some days in the boys' bathroom. That is still so outside the norm." Anneke said, "Everyone's different, right? Other people's way of being different could be being able to skateboard across America or being able to swim for half an hour without stopping. My thing is being different in a gender-fluid way. On the soccer field of life, I'm just not a goalie; I'm a midfielder. I'm me, and that's who I am."

When Vicky and Chet Pearsall took their son out, people usually thought he was a girl. "His dad was an all-American soccer player and professional skier," said Vicky. "Hugh never liked balls. At two, his favorite thing was to wear my red high heels, a towel on his head for hair, and anything he could drape as a sari." As Hugh grew up, Chet tried to set limits. He would tell Hugh that he couldn't go out dressed in girlish clothes, and when Hugh asked why not, Chet said, "You've got a penis." Hugh said, "Well, let's get rid of that." Chet was appalled. Vicky read that most children who want to change gender don't like themselves. Not Hugh. "Hugh thought he was the cat's meow," she said. Vicky and Chet joined a monthly support group. "You'd have a father break down and cry and tell the story of ripping the Barbie doll out of his son's hand, tearing the head off. Everybody came into this group and thought they had this really unique experience with their child, and it was so textbook. The kids did the same exact things." Vicky's concern was how to prevent her child from being traumatized. "I would always ask the trans people who came in to speak to us, 'What did you want to hear from your mom and dad?' They'd start sobbing. I was amazed by the cruelty."

When Hugh was eight, he began to be conscious of other people's take on him. "He started to edit his behavior a lot more," Vicky said. "He's been a happy kid, but there have been times where he has felt really alone, particularly from fourth to sixth grade." At ten, Hugh set up shop as a jeweler, working with semiprecious stones, and quickly found an online market for his creations. Within two years, he had started a business designing handbags as well. "Since about twelve, he's been very conscious of the signals he's sending," Vicky said. "It's not 'Bring it on,' but it's 'I know what I'm doing.' My husband was concerned about his getting beaten up. We enrolled him in tae kwon do classes when he was ten, and this May, he's going to have his black belt." When Hugh was applying to switch schools in ninth grade, before each interview he'd discuss with his mother which bag he should take for his papers—it could be a bag that looked like a briefcase, or it could be something wild. Before one interview, he chose a pink Prada document bag. He was admitted to the school.

By the time I met Vicky, Hugh was fourteen and almost six feet tall, and he was still being mistaken for a girl; it was in his body language and the tilt of his head. Vicky found the idea of surgery upsetting, but would have supported him if he'd gone that way; but he had shown no interest in it. His parents' acceptance of his gender play had not pushed him into transition, any more than their playing ball with him would have turned him into a jock. "When he was little, I just couldn't figure it out," Vicky said. "All we really had to figure out was how to get to the point where we were no longer self-conscious about what who he is says about who we are."

Emmy Werner, one of the founders of the field of positive psychology, has written a great deal about gender roles and their relationship to resilience and has found that resilient children overcome traditional gender roles altogether. "The males can be very assertive, but they're also willing to cry when crying is called for. The women can be very nurturant, but they're also very independent and autonomous. Rearing children in very traditional sex-roles may not be very helpful when it comes to meeting life's emergencies."

In the world of gender, what was progressive two years ago is conservative today; Brill cites as an example a mother in Oakland who filed a complaint alleging that the school's embracing policy toward transgender students didn't specifically address the concerns of gender-fluid children. Some trans people are disturbed by this evolution. Renée Richards, who fought for the right to play professional women's tennis after transitioning in the 1970s, said, "God didn't put us on this earth to have gender diversity. I don't like the kids that are experimenting," and then, "I didn't want to be a trans in the middle of something, a third sex or something that's crazy and freakish and not real." Richards's certainty that God did intend people to be trans the way she is trans, but not the way some other people want to be trans, suggests an intimacy with the Creator that strains credulity. In 2011, the performer Justin Vivian Bond spoke of transitioning without surgery. "I like my penis, and I am keeping it, but I am creating a transbody—a physical record on my body and a medical record that I am a transgender person. I am turned on by people who are genuinely themselves. It's not nature versus nurture. It's nurturing your nature."

When he was still Emma, Eli Rood didn't hate her female body, and she didn't feel that she'd have to kill herself if she couldn't gain access to hormones and surgery. Emma had a good life as a butch lesbian. When she became a man, he was not particularly masculine. Eli has both male and female virtues, and altering his body did not enormously change them. Eli Rood seemed to have transitioned simply because it felt logical; despite a mental health diagnosis of GID, he had taken his gender change as an occasion for clarity.

Emma and her fraternal twin, Kate, grew up in Portland, Oregon. Their mother, Joanna, had become pregnant during a casual relationship and kept her babies. Emma came out as a lesbian; she had a fondness for neckties; she kept a crew cut. She bound her breasts moderately but not tightly and, at five feet seven inches, was read as male about half the time. She started college at fifteen. Joanna said, "I knew she was looking for her tribe, but I missed her. It was harder in some ways to have a child who was so gifted than to have a child who was gender nonconformist."

At her college graduation, Emma came out to her mother and sister as trans. Reviewing it when we were all together, Joanna said, "It seemed like it hurt you, the process of thinking, 'Maybe I'm kind of a freak.' You were a great lesbian; you were good at it. You were very sad about this, and it was very scary." Eli recalled, "I kept wondering, 'Am I really trans?' There was this classic narrative of people who have felt miserable, miserable, miserable, and I wasn't. Finally my therapist said, 'You don't have to be totally miserable to pursue options to make yourself happier.'" In the summer of 2005, age twenty, Eli moved to New York and asked people to use his new name and pronouns. He found a job at the Columbia School of Social Work library, presenting as male. By April 2006, he wanted top surgery. His mother offered to pay half the costs, refinancing her car to do it. Eli grew a beard, as most transmen do to establish their gender beyond discussion. "There have been some testosterone-related emotional and mental changes, but it's hard to gauge what's totally endocrinology, and what's psychosomatic," he said. "I've lost some patience, and I get frustrated more easily. I have more trouble focusing, and my verbal fluency has declined. It took transitioning to realize how much I didn't like my body before. Transition is really a second adolescence. I feel very fortunate in coming at it right on the tail of my first one. I don't regret that first puberty. It contributed to the richness of my experience." He thought for a minute. "If I'd lived earlier, if it had been much, much harder to even think about transitioning, I might not have done it. I didn't choose to have the desire to change. But I did choose to act on it. People make a decision to have chemotherapy or not. People make a decision to take antidepressants or not. That doesn't mean they're not sick with cancer or dangerously sad."

Eli went to the New York City civil court for what should have been a straightforward name change. His request was denied by a judge who said he didn't want to "adjudicate gender." Legally, name changes can be denied only to those who are attempting to evade creditors or who want to dissociate themselves from a criminal record. "People come in all the time and change their name to Bunny Superstar," Eli said. "I was changing mine from Emma to Elliot." The judge wanted medical proof that Eli was changing his sex. He could have supplied it, but was outraged to be asked; the ACLU took the case, and the judge changed the name to Elliot.

Eli's father, absent when he was growing up, always related better to men and, in Eli's view, prefers having a son to a daughter. "He feels qualified to ladle out fatherly advice to a son like, 'Don't go out and get anyone pregnant,'" Eli said. "He actually said that. He was kidding. But it's still kind of weird." Joanna said, "My parents didn't help me much; I educated myself. I was lucky that somehow I had the strength to make myself, and I'm lucky to have produced a child who had the strength to make himself." Eli has struggled with whether to identify as trans or simply as male. "Some people say, 'I'm a man with a transsexual history.' That's a nice turn of phrase. I'm with a woman I've been with for two years. She has dated men and women in the past. There are elements of our relationship that she calls 'lesbionic,' and she says she feels very lucky to have a boyfriend who's familiar with the lesbian landscape. Both of us feel strongly that we're not straight, so we don't have a straight relationship even though I'm a guy and she's a girl." Later, Eli wrote, "I don't feel like my gender has changed much. I'm the same slightly effete masculine person I've been for ages."

The only regret—for all of them—has been Eli's loss of fertility. Joanna took the sea horse as a family symbol because the male sea horse holds his developing offspring in a brood pouch and then gives birth after a labor that can last several days. Kate wrote, "Eli is soon to be rendered infertile by the very treatment that has made possible his visions of himself as a father. So we wait for the day when science might make a sea horse of him." Infertility may be the steepest price of transition; many trans people I met spoke of the longing to have children, but transmen mostly disliked the idea of carrying a pregnancy, and transwomen mostly mourned their inability to do so. They wanted to be fertile in their affirmed gender, and our science is a long way from making that possible; this issue as much as any other defined the limitations of transition.

Early in his transition, Eli wrote on a blog, "I've felt sometimes that the guy who is me—this guy Eli—is out there somewhere, waiting for me to find him, waiting for me to figure out how to become myself. I worry because everything feels unsteady, and I don't know where to look for the guideposts, and I worry that I'll never find him. But someone really important to me once said, 'It's okay. You're strong. And Eli? He'll find you.'"

The International Olympic Committee (IOC) has long required that athletes be screened for gender. The original method was a physical examination; then measurement of hormone levels; then a scan of chromosomes. The reasoning behind such testing is clear. If men and women did not compete separately in athletics, almost all the champions would be men because testosterone strengthens the body. But the testing itself has been fraught with contradictions and problems.

In 2009, the South African runner Caster Semenya was subjected to gender testing after she won gold in the women's 800-meter race of the International Association of Athletics Federations (IAAF) World Championships. IAAF suggested she might have a "rare medical condition" that provided an unfair advantage. Tests revealed that Semenya had internal testes instead of a uterus and ovaries, and a testosterone level three times that of an average genetic female. In the wake of the controversy, the IOC said that women with hyperandrogenism might be disqualified from events. But the idea of a normal level of androgens for women is a fiction; individual levels vary widely. The IOC requires that any irregularities be reviewed by a panel of experts, who decide case by case and in strict confidence. Even before this recent controversy, Arne Ljungqvist, chair of the IOC Medical Commission, said, "There is no scientifically sound lab-based technique that can differentiate between man and woman." Of her humiliating ordeal, Semenya said, "God made me the way I am and I accept myself."

As a human-rights advocate, Shannon Minter spends most of his time in court avoiding ontological questions and focusing on the human stories of the people he represents. In *Kantaras v. Kantaras*, Minter argued on behalf of a transman who was divorcing his wife. The wife was challenging his legal parenthood by attacking his legitimacy as a man—and therefore, by extension, their marriage; Florida does not allow same-sex marriage or adoption. When the case was broadcast on Court TV, Michael Kantaras, who had lived a fully assimilated life, was brutally exposed. An elderly, heterosexual, Republican-appointed judge was called out of retirement to hear the case. Minter called his client's parents as witnesses and saw the judge's thinking changing day by day. "Michael's mom said, 'It is so painful to me to hear anybody refer to Michael, even in the past, as *she*,'" Minter recalled. "Here's this woman that the judge could totally relate to. So he never did it again." The judge eventually wrote, "Transsexualism is a massively complex and difficult problem deserving of the highest respect and sympathy. Being further denied by the courts of the basic fundamental right to marry violates their Constitutional rights and degrades them as human beings."

Minter believes that the unifying challenge for gender activists is to create a society in which gender is disestablished as a legal concept. "Everything short of that is going to entail significant incoherence," he said. "There is no sensible, much less scientifically valid, way to classify people based on race. The Supreme Court has recognized that. We don't put race on birth certificates; race is no longer a legally relevant category except as a self-identification. That must also happen with gender." Minter added that this shouldn't be confused with the somewhat dated feminist ideal of abolishing gender. "People are very attached to their own gender. I certainly am. It's much more like religion. It would be shocking to think that the government could define somebody's religion. It needs to be just as shocking that the government could define someone's gender." Minter's determination comes out of personal history. A man in his fifties who has an extraordinary record of accomplishment and a wide circle of friends, he said, "A week before my father died, he introduced me for the first time to someone else as his *son*, and it meant more to me than anything else that ever happened to me."

In looking at disability, I ran up repeatedly against Peter Singer's eugenic idea that not all human beings are persons; in trans studies, the progressive idea that not all males have male bodies. Though Singer and the trans advocates appear to be at opposite ends of the spectrum, at some level they present the same argument: that changing social mores and advancing science have caused us to question the basic structuring principles of human society. Genesis describes a world born in categories: God made grasses and trees, then whales and fish, then fowl and birds, then cattle and creeping things and beasts, then human beings to have dominion over all the rest. "Male and female he created them," says the verse. In the great creation story, humans and animals occupy categories that can never cross, as do men and women. In the twenty-first century, new arguments are afloat that some human beings are not persons, that some persons are not human beings, that some men are women, that some women are men, that some human beings are persons but are neither women nor men. Globalization has blurred national identity, and intermarriage has compromised racial identity. We like categories and clubs as much as we ever have; it's only that the ones we thought were inviolable turn out not to be, and others that we never imagined are taking their place.

When Carol and Loren McKerrow met, she was runner-up for Miss Texas, and he was completing his training in ophthalmology outside Fort Worth. When they married, he took her home to Helena, Montana. They adopted their son Marc because they thought they were unable to conceive. However, Carol became pregnant with Paul, later Kim, about the time they brought Marc home; Carol gave birth to another son, Todd, a couple of years later. Marc had behavior problems. "Whenever school called," Carol recalled, "it was an awards ceremony, academic or athletic, for Paul, or to tell me Marc had been suspended." While all the anxiety was focused around Marc, Paul was secretly struggling with gender. "I had a paper route when I was ten," Kim remembered. "It was very early. I used to cross-dress because I didn't think anyone would see me. Then I would throw away the clothes and pray that some power could dispel this thing that was making me unlike anyone else I knew of."

Paul became a great athlete and was quarterback on his high school football team. "That was the recipe to be normal, and a way to shut off your brain," Kim said. "If you're uncomfortable with your body, you want to control that body, and sports are a really good way to do it." Paul was valedictorian and class president at Helena High, where he was voted most likely to succeed. "I knew the word *manqué*, as in *artiste manqué*," Kim said. "That was my word, because it just meant, 'Oh, if only you knew.'"

Paul went on to Berkeley and spent his junior year, 1988, abroad. "Everybody else is going to Florence or Paris," Kim said. "I'm going to Norway because I'm just going to hide in a long, dark winter, read

Beckett, drink blackberry tea, and starve. I went thinking, 'I'm going to stop this.' A couple months into it, it was like, 'I can't stop this.'" Some people give a single date for their transition; Kim described hers as happening from 1989 to 1996. She moved to San Francisco and saw old friends and family as little as possible; the only person from her previous life who knew was her brother Todd, who was openly gay. He was easygoing and had come out without much drama, but she kept even him at arm's length. *Kim* was the most generic name she could think of, and she changed her last name to Reed, her old middle name, to make a fresh start. Even so, Kim felt awkward and artificial; it took five years for her to start hormones. "I wasn't sure who I was," Kim said. "I wasn't even sure gender was the gateway. It's awfully complicated, awfully expensive, awfully isolating, and the practical angle alone is very difficult." Today, however, Kim has an unaffected femininity. Once when I was out with her, someone came up to her and said, "My friend is struggling with transitioning. You're so relaxed; how did you learn all these gestures?" Kim said, "When I was making the switch, I was too conscious of how I moved, and it wasn't until I began to forget about it that who I really was started to take over."

In the winter of 1995, Carol's younger sister, Nan, was diagnosed with colon cancer. When Kim, still Paul to the family, would call her aunt, she would talk to her mother, too, but for almost five years, they didn't see each other. When Nan died, however, Carol expected Paul to attend the funeral. Kim, who had been on hormones for over a year, was a pallbearer, with only a ponytail to attract comment. Carol said, "It was a funeral. But he looked *so* sad, and I still had no clue. A month later, Paul called and said, 'Did you ever wonder as I was growing up whether I was comfortable with my own sexual identity?' I said, 'I thought you were the golden child.' He said, 'Well, I've been dressing as a woman.'" Carol was bewildered. "I felt *very* sad, for all that anguish he'd been going through that I didn't even suspect," she said. Kim sent her mother a stack of medical information. "I didn't need to read any pamphlets," Carol said. "For me, it was, 'I love my child; the intelligent, caring, humorous person is still there.' All I wanted to know was, 'Are you happy now? Are you comfortable?'" But she worried about telling Loren.

Kim once said, "When I transitioned, I felt like I had climbed out of a wet suit I had been wearing my entire life. Imagine that magnificent rush, the tactile sensations, as though your body had just woken up. But I also felt like this new person couldn't go home, and I began to dismantle all my connections to Montana. At the time I didn't know how thoroughly all of this saddened me, and to compensate for that, I started to turn my hometown into a place that I didn't really need to go back to." That exile continued even after Loren had been told the news; no one else in the family was to know. Marc had been in a car accident and suffered a traumatic brain injury, which led to even more erratic behavior than he'd previously exhibited, and Kim was afraid of his response. "I felt like I owed it to Marc to tell him, but I thought he would hurt me, and I felt too vulnerable," Kim said. Carol said, "Marc is saying, 'Am I ever going to hear from Paul again?' and it was getting worse and worse. But Kim said, 'When Marc knows, all of Montana knows, and I'm just not ready for it yet.' Kim was right, because Marc wanted something on Paul. Marc wanted to say, 'Well, at least I'm more normal than you turned out to be.'"

Loren had contracted hepatitis in medical school; while Kim was growing into herself, his condition was worsening. He was on a waiting list for a liver transplant, but at sixty-two, he was not given priority. In the summer of 2003, he decided to visit each of his children. Kim had moved to New York, told her parents that she was a lesbian, and started seeing a woman named Claire Jones. Carol and Loren had dinner with Kim and Claire the night they arrived. "I started feeling better about everything," Carol said. "I loved Claire the minute I met her. I was so worried Kim was going to be alone. Claire walked around the corner, and I just breathed a sigh of relief."

Several months later, Loren collapsed and was taken on an emergency flight for treatment in Denver. Kim flew immediately to join her parents. She arrived at the hospital a few hours before her father died, while her brothers were still arranging transport to Colorado. Kim reached Marc on the phone as he was boarding his flight and said, "I've been out of touch. I didn't know how to handle it; but now because of Dad's death, we're all going to be together, and you need to know about me." At the Denver airport, Kim gave Marc her card and said, "Here are my phone numbers. You can call me anytime." At that point, Carol burst into tears—not about Loren, but because Kim and Marc were speaking again. There they all were, displaced in a strange city, bereft of the reason that had brought them there but also more united than they'd been in years. Later that day, Carol, Kim, Marc, and Todd set out for Montana by car. During the long trip, Kim reaffirmed her connection to Marc and tried to answer his many questions. He was bewildered, but not unkind. Whenever there was cell phone reception across the plains of Wyoming, Kim made calls to uncles, aunts, and cousins. "My father has died," Kim recalled. "They're reeling. They're hearing the news about me. And they respond with 'We're just glad to have you back.'"

Carol decided to host a tea party for friends in Helena who could help get the word out about Kim, so she wouldn't need to discuss the matter at the funeral. "My mom, God bless her, just owned it," Kim said. "People couldn't really throw a fit because everyone had the emotional meat tenderizer of my dad's passing forcing them into kindness." Kim was at the airport picking up Claire when the tea party took place. Carol had invited nineteen women and the male pastor from her church. She explained Kim's transition in brief, then said, "I'm not responsible *for* my child and who she's become, but I am responsible *to* her, and she is a wonderful person. I love her. I don't know if you need to know anything else, but that's all I need to know." After a moment of silence as the guests absorbed this information, somebody said, "Amen." Then Carol said, "I'm telling you this now, and I'm not going to speak about it again the rest of the weekend. I'm concentrating on Loren's service, and celebrating his life." When I asked Carol why she hadn't encountered the kind of community hatred that I had seen so many other families battle, she said, "I think it's because of how we had lived our lives up until then." Kim added, "My dad wouldn't grab the bull by the horns like my mom did. A tea party was the last thing he would do. But he would somehow cause things to be such that a tea party would happen. He would delight in the fact that his little nudge had caused everything to fall into place."

Sue O'Leary was one of the guests at the tea party; her son, Tim O'Leary, who had been Paul's closest friend, was in town for the funeral. "There's a viewing of my father's body at the funeral home, and all of my friends who have heard the news are there," Kim said. "I've said I'm not going because I want to keep it about my dad, but I'm really chickening out. Before I know it, Tim and all these guys I knew in high school, essentially the football team, open our front door, and they've got cases of beer under their arms, and Frank Mayo's saying, 'Yeah, I had this dream that we were all fat, bald, and old, and you were a girl.' It was the living room I grew up in, and Claire's sitting on the couch, knocking back cheap beer, and there's a couple more cases outside in a snowbank to keep them cold. This guy has his arm around Claire, and they're laughing, and I was just like, 'This is going to work out just fine.'"

The next day was the funeral. Carol recalled, "I'm not a Bible student at all, but there is one verse everybody knows, John 3:16, and it says, 'God so loved the world that whosoever believeth in Him shall not perish and have everlasting life.' I just really caught on to that *whosoever* and I held on to it that day of the funeral. When people said, 'I see Marc, I see Todd, but I don't see Paul,' I referred them to the friends who had come to my tea party."

As Kim and Claire traveled home from Helena a few days later, Kim decided to make a documentary that would begin with her twentieth high school reunion that fall; Marc had been held back a grade in elementary school, so they graduated in the same class, and both planned to attend. *Prodigal Sons* charts Kim's departure from her geographic community to her identity community, Marc's deterioration and the enormous stress it placed on the family, and Kim's complicated, ambivalent love for her brother. The film is full of the childhood Kim shared with Marc and Todd, including footage shot by her father when she was still Paul, the quarterback. At the film's start, Marc's head injury has fossilized his sense of the past, so that he looks only behind, while Kim's transition has meant that she looks only ahead. As her changing identity and his unchanging identity collide, she enshrines the very history she long wished to abrogate. When Kim appeared on *Oprah* with her mother to promote the film, Oprah played a clip in which Marc accused his mother of trampling the Bible by welcoming Kim. Oprah said, "Well? Do you believe in the Bible?" Carol said, "I believe in my *child.*"

Six months after I met her, Kim called me one night, excitedly, with an invitation. The pastor from her church in Helena was organizing a *Prodigal Sons* weekend: a screening on Friday night, seminars on Saturday to discuss issues raised by the film, and a sermon by Kim on Sunday—all, coincidentally, the weekend of Carol's birthday. I traveled to Montana a few days early. A year earlier, Carol had invited twenty-six people to her house to see the film. "I worried about some of those people, so I told their spouses that I was concerned," she explained. "Since I'd done that, they all felt very proud of saying at the end of the evening, 'See? Everything is fine, Carol. You needn't have worried.'" One of those people was an old friend who had recently lost his wife, and at the end of the screening, he seemed disturbed. Carol asked if he was okay, and he said he was not. "My heart sank," Carol told me. "Then he told me that he had just had no idea that it was so serious with Marc, and how much I had been shouldering." Carol and Don bonded through the conversation, and when I went out to Helena, they had become a couple; two years later, they invited me to their wedding.

At breakfast on the morning of Carol's birthday, I found her furious and mournful. She handed me the *Helena Independent Record,* where a banner headline across the front page blared, "Helena Prodigal Son Returning as Woman," and, below, "Former QB at HHS to present film telling story of sex change." Kim was at a festival in Iceland and wouldn't be arriving until the following day. When Carol and I went to the church to decorate for the festivities, the pastor said she had been in touch with the police to arrange safeguards in case of rioting or attacks. Carol threw up her hands. "The film was going to come here sooner or later, and I didn't want it to just get booked into our local movie house, the Myrna Loy, and have no control over it," she said. "This is the way it should come, at my church, where there is love. But those headlines cheapen it." It is stressful to be stripped bare in front of a small town where you've lived your whole adulthood. Carol is not a show-off, or a lonely person, or a born activist, so she didn't need to tell her story for the reasons that motivate many people. She said, "I know people who have had to look at accounts of their sons being arrested for child pornography, or embezzlement, and Kim has not hurt anyone; in fact, she has helped many people." Nonetheless, she was visibly shaken.

The night of the screening, Plymouth Congregational was packed, with a long waiting list for tickets. I sat next to Carol in the back row, and she cried through much of the film and had to leave the sanctuary twice. When the film ended, Kim stood at the front of the church, and the audience began to applaud. A few people stood up, then a few more, and then it became a standing ovation. When it ended, Kim invited her mother up; Carol had composed her face into a smile by then, and as she walked briskly down the aisle, everyone stood up again, and when Carol arrived at the altar, she and Kim stood with their arms around each other's shoulders while the audience continued cheering. Carol's bravado had transformed the screening into an occasion of triumph. Now, Kim was the one crying. At the reception afterward, I told one of the church ladies that Kim had worried about the conversation the film would provoke, and the lady said, "Our hardest conversations aren't with other people; they're with ourselves. Once she had settled who she was in herself, we were ready to have whatever conversations we needed to make sure she knew this was always home."

On Sunday, the pastor commented that she had never seen more congregants except at Christmas and Easter. The entire McKerrow clan was there; some had had to drive many hours from their farms. The service opened, "We pray today for your blessings on those who are abused for being who they are, and for those who are abusers." Hymns were sung, the parable of the Prodigal Son was read, then Kim came forward. Although the parable is usually interpreted as a story about the father, she said, it is also a story about a son who receives a welcome he would never have dared to expect. She said, "The night before last, when our film was playing in here, I went outside to the columbarium where my father's ashes rest. As I was kneeling there by what I call 'Dad's spot,' I thought of the hours and hours of videotape that he shot lovingly of me during my football games, and how much of the same footage was now being shown inside this sanctuary. Now, it's certainly not the context that any of us expected. But I knew Dad would be proud. And just then, the dusk breeze blew in this waft of sound, and it was strangely familiar to me, and I realized it was the crosstown football game coming from the stadium. The band was playing, and the announcer was bellowing, and all of these old tapes were playing inside here, on the screen, and I knew that new ones were being recorded just a few blocks away. Those recording their new memories to tape should be only so lucky as to be surprised by the last thing that they expected from their loved ones, only so fortunate as to get a chance to welcome them home with radical love. I thought about how all these cycles of lives would continue on, and so many aspects of my life coalesced in that one moment, that one beautiful, stunning, blessed moment, the past and the present, parent and child, male and female: the pain that life sometimes brings, and the soothing love that welcomes it with open arms, after its exhausting journey into a distant country."

That afternoon after the service, Carol and I went for a long walk. I said, "Do you wish that Paul had just been happy to be Paul and had stayed that way?" Carol said, "Well, of course I do. It would have been easier for Paul, and for the rest of us. But the key phrase in there is 'happy to be Paul.' He wasn't, and I am just so glad that he had the courage to do something about it. No, if he had been happy to be Paul, anybody would wish for that, but since he wasn't—I can't imagine the courage that it took. I had somebody say this weekend, 'Carol, Paul died, and I haven't finished mourning that.' I don't feel that. Kim is much more present to people than Paul ever was. Paul was never rude, he just wasn't totally present. We didn't quite have his attention." She laughed, then said with adoring emphasis, "And look what we got! Kim!" And grace seemed to be both the cause and the consequence of her happiness in that emphatic declaration.

As I worked on this chapter, I kept returning in my mind to Tennyson's beautiful tribute to Arthur Henry Hallam, in which he wrote, "And manhood fused with female grace / In such a sort, the child would twine / A trustful hand, unask'd, in thine, / And find his comfort in thy face." Our received notions of masculinity and femininity are a modern conceit. Though Hallam was neither trans nor gay, his magnetism inhered in this blending of strength and gentleness, boldness and compassion. I remember first reading Tennyson's lines when I was a teenager, thinking that he celebrated this friend for the very qualities that most troubled me in myself. I wanted to be something noble, not just a boy who had failed at real masculinity and was making do. I wanted to emulate what was best in my father and mother, in the life of the mind, to which men often stake first claim, and that of the heart, in which women usually have the upper hand. I saw in Tennyson's bracing words an encomium not to an androgynous face, but to the intricate nature of beauty. Masculinity and femininity here seemed not locked in binary competition, but fused in collaboration. Anyone with an open heart should know that the world would have ended long ago without the translators who convey male and female meanings across gender's fierce boundaries. It may be a recent phenomenon for that to be an identity, but what has changed is the characterization of such people— not their eternal merit, not their uncanny, necessary splendor.

I have a great life as a man and have made it all work, but I know that at twelve I'd have chosen to be a woman if it had been an easy and complete transformation. Perhaps that is only because being a woman looked more respectable to me than being a gay man, and twelve is a conformist age. I don't regret not being a woman, any more than I regret not being a tough and easy football hero, or not being born into the British royal family; trans children usually believe they are already members of a different gender, and I never did. Being gay has worked out happily for me in the end, and since one lives in a continuous present, I don't feel the afflictions I have resolved as permanent losses (though my last book was, after all, about depression; my path has had its challenges).

Yet I like to imagine a science-fiction future when gender-bending will not entail surgical procedures, hormone injections, and social disapprobation—a society in which everyone is able to choose his or her own gender at any time. Without physical trauma, such people would be fully of their affirmed gender, with an entirely functioning reproductive system and mind and heart of the self they believe is rightly theirs. If they wish to linger at the middle of a gender spectrum—physically, psychologically, or both—that, too, would be possible. In such a dreamtime, I believe that many people would opt to experience another gender. I've always loved travel, and if someone offered me a trip to the moon, I'd be there in an instant. What trip could be more fascinating and exotic than to know what it truly is to be your own opposite? Or, indeed, to live in some elusive territory to which there is no opposite? I'd plunk down my fortune if there were a round-trip ticket.

At the same time, I know that choice can be burdensome and exhausting and frightening—especially unaccustomed choice. My first book was about a group of Soviet artists, and I was with those artists when they came to the West. I remember one of them bursting into tears in a German supermarket that stocked twenty brands of butter because he couldn't stomach all the decisions the West asked of him. A piece of me thinks that people are not good at choosing, that people who cannot do a competent job of voting in an electoral democracy, who have a record-high divorce rate, who fail to love children born because they didn't organize birth control, would collapse if given full leeway to choose their gender. I likewise believe that choice is the only true luxury, that the striving inherent in decision-making gives decisions value. In modern America, choice is the aspirational currency, and even knowing the weariness selection entails, I like to imagine a future in which we would be able to choose everything. I'd quite possibly choose what I have now—and would love it even more for having done so.

XII

Father

I started this book to forgive my parents and ended it by becoming a parent. Understanding backward liberated me to live forward. I wanted to find out why I had experienced so much pain in my childhood, to understand what was my doing, what was my parents', and what was the world's. I felt I owed it to both my parents and myself to prove that we had been less than half the problem. In retrospect, it seems obvious that my research about parenting was also a means to subdue my anxieties about becoming a parent. But the mind works in mysterious ways, and if this was my secret purpose, it revealed itself only gradually.

I grew up afraid of illness and disability, inclined to avert my gaze from anyone who was too different—despite all the ways I knew myself to be different. This book helped me kill that bigoted impulse, which I had always known to be ugly. The obvious melancholy in the stories I heard should, perhaps, have made me shy away from paternity, but it had the opposite effect. Parenting had challenged these families, but almost none regretted it; they demonstrated that with enough emotional discipline and affective will, one could love anyone. I was comforted by this tutelage in acceptance, the reassurance that difficult love is no less a thing than easy love.

For a long time, children used to make me sad. The origin of my sadness was somewhat obscure to me, but I think it came most from how the absence of children in the lives of gay people had repeatedly been held up to me as my tragedy. Children were the most important thing in the world, and so they were mascots for my failure. My parents had encouraged me to marry a woman and have a family, and the world echoed that imperative. I spent years drifting between relationships with men and relationships with women. I loved some of the women with whom I was intimate, but if children hadn't been part of the equation, I wouldn't have bothered with the other half. The recognition that I was really gay came only when I understood that gayness was a matter not of behavior, but of identity.

When I was coming of age, that identity and being a father seemed incompatible. The unlikely prospect of being a gay parent troubled me then because I thought that growing up with a gay father would make my putative children figures of fun. This perception contained elements of internalized homophobia, but it was also consistent with social reality. I was learning to become militant on my own behalf, but was anxious about implicating others. As a child, I had been teased mercilessly for being different, and I didn't want to foist a version of that experience on anyone else. In the twenty years that followed, social reality changed enough so that I no longer felt those compunctions. It changed largely because other gay people made the leap to having children before I was prepared to do so. Nonetheless, when I more recently expressed a wish for biological children, that wish was repeatedly devalued, often by people who reminded me earnestly that loads of abandoned children needed good homes. I was struck by how regularly these arguments were made by people who had produced biological progeny and had never contemplated adoption. The wish to create a child often struck other people as quaint or self-indulgent.

Since homosexuality does not appear to be transmissible, I was consigning my presumed children to the potential discomfort of coming from a strange place rather than of being a strange thing, and some critics felt that this mitigated the problem. I dislike the implication that since my children were likely to be straight, it was okay for me to produce them. Acceptance of horizontal identity only so long as it never becomes vertical is chauvinism. I would not have been dissuaded from having children if I had known that they were likely to be gay; nor was I dissuaded by the likelihood that they would be straight. Nonetheless, my apprehension about being a gay father far outstripped any concerns that a biological child of mine would be at risk for dyslexia, depression, or the types of cancer from which my mother and grandfather died.

The right to reproduce should be among the inalienable ones. Yet the prejudice against anomalous people is revealed most clearly when members of horizontal identity groups who have the potential to pass on aberrant traits decide to have their own children. Many people are outraged when a disabled or challenged adult produces a disabled or challenged child.

Newscaster and actress Bree Walker was born with ectrodactyly, or lobster-claw syndrome, which results in deformities of the hands and feet. She bore a child with the syndrome, and when she became pregnant again in 1990, she knew that her second child might also inherit the condition. She chose to keep the pregnancy and became the fodder of outrage. "It was shocking to me that anyone would make such negative public assumptions about an unborn child and his ability to cope with the world, regardless of the shape of his hands or feet," Walker said later. She herself has had a successful career and marriage, is telegenic, and has many strengths to pass on. "Is it fair to pass along a genetically disfiguring disease to your child?" one talk-show host asked. "People judge you by your appearance. They judge you by the words that you use. God knows they're going to judge you by the shape of your hands, and the shape of your body, and the shape of your face. They just do." Implicit in many of these criticisms was that Walker had had no right to get pregnant, even that she was morally obligated to abort—no matter how much she wanted her child, or how competent she was to raise it. "I felt that my pregnancy had been terrorized," Walker later said.

The talk shows reduced Walker's children to their disability. As polio survivor and disability activist Bill Holt said, "For anyone to determine that Bree Walker should not have children because of one physical characteristic is to ignore all of the other wonderful things about the woman. Why not say she *should* have lots of children because she has one of the liveliest intellects and prettiest faces on television?" The media condemnation largely failed to acknowledge that veterans of a condition their children may inherit are uniquely qualified to understand the risks and rewards of life with that condition. Their choices are better-informed than our judgments of them.

Some people, however, conceive children as a means of validating their own lives. Joanna Karpasea-Jones, an English disability activist, chose to have five biological children. She did so in part as a means of asserting the social model of disability, saying that within her household, impairments were not disabilities. She and her husband, like most people, wanted biological offspring. "Nor did adoption seem a choice," she wrote, "as then I would never be pregnant or give birth— a thought that was heartbreaking to me." Karpasea-Jones has cerebral palsy caused by premature birth; it is not hereditary. Her partner, however, has hereditary motor and sensory neuropathy, which causes muscle wastage and severe bone deformations. Any biological child would have a fifty-fifty chance of inheriting that condition. "Nearly everyone in our family was disabled anyway: me, my partner, his brother and father, my aunt and uncle," Karpasea-Jones wrote. "If the child was affected, she certainly wouldn't feel the odd one out. Normality is subjective; to us, disability was normal."

The vertical identities within her family doubtless guarantee a sense of belonging, as in a family of dwarfs or deaf people. But her lack of engagement with the likely reality of her children's hurting bodies is distressing. In her extensive writings, she acknowledges that her condition and her partner's have caused them considerable physical pain, which she seems to have been unambivalent about passing on. She subverts her children's bodies to the social model of disability. I have met many proud people with special challenges and seen their happy families. I have also seen pervasive aching, not all of it owing to external circumstances. In fact, Karpasea-Jones's decision was not well received by her own family. "My own mother told me we had been irresponsible to take such a risk and asked me to get an abortion," she wrote. "My partner's mother said that I wouldn't be able to carry a baby to term. I felt pleased when I found myself 11 days overdue without so much as a twinge. That'll show them, I thought." Ego confusion between parents and children is pervasive in every demographic; it's no mean feat to find the difference between helping your children formulate their dreams and trapping them in your own. Karpasea-Jones's children are unlikely to be distressed that they exist, but may well be resentful if they conclude that she bore them in pursuit of an agenda. Yet self-absorbed parents everywhere exploit their children for reflected glory on the soccer field, in the chess club, at the piano. Narcissism is a myopia hardly limited to disability activists.

Deciding whether to have a child is a loaded question for anyone whose genetics are considered suspect. The disability scholar Adrienne Asch wrote in a 1999 essay, "Chronic illness and disability are not equivalent to acute illness or sudden injury. Most people with spina bifida, achondroplasia, Down syndrome, and many other mobility and sensory impairments perceive themselves as healthy, not sick, and describe their conditions as givens of their lives—the equipment with which they meet the world." There is truth in what Asch says, but it is not the whole truth. In 2003, I was sent to interview a young woman named Laura Rothenberg about her cystic fibrosis, and we ended up enjoying a brief friendship that was a function of her illness. Even though both her parents were carriers (CF is a recessive genetic condition), she had a horizontal experience of the illness because neither of them had manifested the disease. She wrote a poignant memoir, *Breathing for a Living*, in which she praised many things inherent in the identity that CF gave her and announced how many things she valued in her life as it had been. Nonetheless, she did not see herself as healthy and would have welcomed a cure—not because she was rejecting this part of herself, but because she wanted to feel good and live long. Her deterioration and death at the age of twenty-two bore little similarity to the experience of a healthy achondroplastic dwarf. Yet, consumed with grief just after her death, her father said to me, "When Laura was conceived, they didn't have an amniocentesis test for CF. But they developed one. If we'd known, Laura would not have been born. I still have the thought, 'My God—she could have been denied life.' What a tragedy that would have been."

Whether to consign someone else to struggle with the extraordinary burdens you have carried is a personal moral issue. Yet all parents make that decision on some scale. Most choose to procreate even though the affluent could conceive children in vitro with donated Superman sperm and Wonder Woman eggs. Asinine people gamely produce asinine children even though stupidity makes life terribly hard; morbidly obese people often produce corpulent children who may be marginalized because of their body weight; depressive parents produce children who may grapple with chronic sadness. The poor have children despite the obvious disadvantages of poverty.

It is not a great leap from choosing to keep a pregnancy despite a prenatal diagnosis to selecting for difference. An article in the *Los Angeles Times* pointed out, "Creating made-to-order babies with genetic defects would seem to be an ethical minefield, but to some parents with disabilities—say, deafness or dwarfism—it just means making babies like them." In a survey of nearly two hundred American clinics that offer preimplantation genetic diagnosis (PGD), a process that has been available for two decades, 3 percent admitted having used the test to select for an embryo with a disability. Dr. Robert J. Stillman, of the Shady Grove Fertility Center, which has offices in Maryland, Virginia, and Pennsylvania, said he had denied requests to select for deafness and dwarfism. "One of the prime dictates of parenting is to make a better world for our children," he said. "Dwarfism and deafness are not the norm."

By what logic does making a better world have to do with hewing to the norm? Michael Bérubé, whose son has Down syndrome, writes, "The question is whether we will maintain a social system that makes allowance for unpredictability, variance, competing moral imperatives, difficult decisions, private decisions, and even perverse decisions." The debate about embryo selection pertains to that most elusive and most socially determined of human rights, which is dignity. In 2008, Britain amended the Human Fertilisation and Embryology Act to make selecting for a disability illegal. People who choose PGD to avoid Down syndrome, for example, would get a full genetic profile and would not be permitted to implant an embryo with any known disability. Deaf activists were horrified. "There is no going around this," wrote one blogger. "We are being devalued, unworthy to be humans simply because we are imperfect."

Sharon Duchesneau and Candace McCullough, lesbian Deaf women, wanted a child, and in 2002 they asked a friend who was fifth-generation deaf to be their sperm donor. They produced two deaf children, Gauvin and Jehanne. They decided to share their experience with a reporter from the *Washington Post*, fomenting an onslaught of attacks much like those on Bree Walker. Fox News ran a story under the headline, "Victims from Birth: Engineering Defects in Helpless Children Crosses the Line." Letters published in the *Post* were similarly hostile. One reader wrote, "That three people (I include the sperm donor) could deliberately deprive another person of a natural faculty is monstrous and cruel and reveals their basic resentment toward people who can hear. There are laws that give access to medical care for children of parents who would deny it on religious grounds. There should be similar protections for children subject to the abuse of being genetically programmed to replicate the disabilities of misguided parents."

Legal scholar John Corvino pointed out that the public rage was rooted in a fundamental metaphysical fallacy. "They could have chosen a different donor," he argued. "Or they could have chosen adoption rather than pregnancy. But neither of those choices would have resulted in Gauvin's having hearing. On the contrary, they would have resulted in his not being born at all." The Deaf activist Patrick Boudreault said, "No one is talking, ever, about deliberately deafening a child born hearing."

Few people would assert that a Deaf married couple should not procreate because of the risk of producing deaf children. Some would stipulate that the line be drawn between what one accepts and what one seeks, arguing that the deaf children of heterosexual deaf parents occur by "natural" process—but love and rules do not mix well, and the concept of *natural* is itself a constantly shifting, unnatural idea often used to veneer prejudice. Those who objected to Duchesneau's and McCullough's choice may also not have understood the life experience of those two women, who are college-educated, professionally successful, apparently happy, socially active, and in a good relationship. The original article explained, "At the same time that many would-be parents are screening out qualities they don't want, many are also selecting for qualities they do want. And in many cases, the aim is to produce not so much a superior baby as a specific baby. A white baby. A black baby.

A boy. A girl. Or a baby that's been even more minutely imagined. 'In most cases,' says Sean Tipton, spokesman for the American Society of Reproductive Medicine, 'what the couples are interested in is someone who physically looks like them.' In this sense Candy and Sharon are like many parents, hoping for a child who will be in their own image."

This is a difficult argument to buck. Sharon said, "It would be nice to have a child who is the same as us." Candy said, "I want to be the same as my child; I want the baby to enjoy what we enjoy." These don't seem like radical statements until you learn they came from deaf people. In an article in *Nature*, Carina Dennis offers further insight into the two women's motives: "Communication and the pursuit of intimacy are central to being human. If you genuinely believe that your children will have at least as rich an emotional life if they cannot hear, and that you will be better able to communicate with them, why not make this choice?" Candy had grown up in a deaf household with uneducated, working-class parents; Sharon had grown up with hearing parents and did not come into herself until she entered the signing world of Gallaudet. Both women looked up to the educated Deaf of Deaf. They felt they had worked to find their version of happiness and could convey it to the next generation. Parents want children who will be able to benefit from what they have to give.

William Saletan, national correspondent at *Slate*, wrote, "Old fear: designer babies. New fear: deformer babies." Of course, "deformer" babies are designer babies, too; they just don't follow the most popular designs. And designer babies aren't going anywhere; they will undoubtedly become increasingly common as technology advances. The very phrase *designer babies* is pejorative, but not so long ago *test-tube babies* was used with disdain, before IVF became standard operating procedure for an aging middle class. In 2006, nearly half the PGD clinics surveyed by the Genetics and Public Policy Center at Johns Hopkins University offered a gender-selection service. In 2007, the Bridge Centre fertility clinic in London screened embryos so a baby wouldn't suffer from a serious squint that afflicted the father, and University College London recently announced the birth of one of the first babies selected to be free of a genetic breast-cancer vulnerability. The Fertility Institutes in Los Angeles declared that they were planning to help couples select for gender, hair color, and eye color, though such a salvo ensued that they suspended the program. Such choices are inevitably the future. How different are they from standard protocols for sperm and egg donors, which screen donors for undesirable hereditary traits and provide information on physical attractiveness, coloring, height, weight, and college entrance test scores? Most people are attracted to others with desirable traits; our very impulse toward sexual congress is a subjective screening process.

A 2004 study conducted at Johns Hopkins notes that the growing debate about reproductive genetic testing has largely been framed by two opposing views: those who see it as "an opportunity to prevent suffering and who oppose limitations on research, technological advance and reproductive choice," and those who "believe that reproductive genetic testing will have adverse ethical and social impacts and who support restrictions on its development and use." In *The Case Against Perfection*, the Harvard philosopher Michael Sandel writes, "Prospective parents remain free to choose whether to use prenatal testing and whether to act on the results. But they are not free to escape the burden of choice that the new technology creates."

Human beings like to fix things; if we learn to control the weather, we will soon be blind to the majesty of hurricanes and intolerant of the implacable silence of a blizzard. Forty years ago, the toxicologist Marc Lappé cautioned, "It would be unthinkable and immoral if in our zeal to 'conquer' genetic defects, we failed to recognize that the 'defectives' we identify and abort are no less human than we." And yet in 2005, the journalist Patricia E. Bauer described in the *Washington Post* the pressures she had had to negotiate when she decided to keep a daughter prenatally diagnosed with Down syndrome. She wrote, "Prenatal testing is making your right to abort a disabled child more like your duty to abort a disabled child." No one should be forced to keep a pregnancy she dreads, and no one should be pressured to terminate a pregnancy she desires. Those who are prepared to love children with horizontal qualities give dignity to them, whether or not they have used prenatal testing. With access to reproductive technologies, we are conjecturing what kind of children will make us happy, and what kind we will make happy. It may be irresponsible to avoid this guesswork, but it is naïve to think it is anything more. Hypothetical love has little in common with love.

Which parents should have children and which children should be born will always be debated. We question the decision of people with HIV to produce kids they may not live to raise; we try to prevent teen pregnancies; we judge whether people with disabilities should pass on those differences. It is possible to sterilize people with opprobrium as well as with a scalpel, and it is almost equally cruel. Educating people on the challenges their children may embody is sensible, but preventing them from having children because we think we know the value of those lives smacks of fascism. It is not happenstance that you need a license to get married, but not to have a child.

The United States has less upward mobility than ever before, and less than most other industrialized nations. A 2011 report from the Brookings Institution said, "American mobility is exceptional; where we stand out is our limited mobility from the bottom." Nearly all the families I met are victims of the beliefs that have spawned that crisis of mobility: the assumption that betterment is a project undertaken by individuals on their own, in which the rest of us need not implicate ourselves. Yet, no one in any of the categories this book explores would have had a better life a half century ago. The dizzying technological advances that threaten many of those identities have coincided with an identity politics that shapes a more tolerant world. We live in an increasingly diverse society, and the lessons in tolerance that come with that diversity have extended even to populations too disenfranchised to make their own claims—a change larger in scope than any that the suffragettes or the civil rights activists envisioned. Disabled people are on television; transgender people hold public office; members of the helping professions are working with criminals, prodigies, and people conceived in rape. Jobs programs exist for people with schizophrenia or autism.

The idea that we live in a shameless time is widely lamented. Why are so many people going on TV to talk about and manifest their idiocy, their pathos, even their cruelty? Why do we embrace rich people who have stolen their fortunes? We may not be ashamed enough of what is authentically reprehensible, but we are likewise increasingly unashamed of what never should have discomfited us in the first place. The opposite of identity politics is embarrassment. We are closer than ever to the rights of life, liberty, and the pursuit of happiness. Fewer and fewer people are mortified by who they truly are.

Extraordinary is a numbers game. You may argue over whether something extraordinary is good or bad, but you cannot viably argue about whether it is extraordinary—and yet the term is endlessly subject to false claims. Ordinary people insist that they are unique, while extraordinary people maintain that they are really just like everyone else. Dull people would like to be thought remarkable, while exceptional people long for the modest comforts of fitting in. Everyone whose baby is typical can recount the incredibly special things his child does, and everyone whose baby is unmistakably peculiar will explain why grave illness or astonishing gifts do not really create a chasm between such offspring and other children. This mutual counterfeiting reflects a larger ambivalence, which is that we long for and resist difference; we aspire to and fear individuality. A child's most challenging differences from his parents, by definition, manifest in areas that are unfamiliar to them. Our tendency to misrepresent children as more or less original than they are reflects our misgivings about the relationship between individuality and happiness.

In 2008, the Associated Press reported that a baby with two faces had been born in a village in northern India. Lali Singh had diprosopus, or craniofacial duplication, a rare condition in which a single head has two noses, two mouths, two pairs of lips, and two pairs of eyes. The director of the hospital where she was born said, "She is leading a normal life with no breathing difficulties." Whatever constitutes a "normal life" in Saini Sunpura, it almost certainly does not include "doing well and being worshipped as the reincarnation of a Hindu goddess of valor, Durga, a fiery deity traditionally depicted with three eyes and many arms." A hundred people a day were flocking to the house to touch Lali's feet, offer money, and receive blessings; the village chief had asked the state government for funds to build her a temple. The article mentions only parenthetically that craniofacial duplication is often linked to serious health complications.

Had Lali been born in Duluth or Wichita or Beijing or Paris, her birth would have been a worrisome situation rather than a cause for celebration. Lali's mother, Sushma, said, "My daughter is fine—like any other child." Her father, Vinod, took Lali to a New Delhi hospital, but turned down the offer of a CAT scan to determine whether her internal organs were normal and did not pursue treatment for her cleft palate, which interfered with her ability to feed. "I don't feel the need of that at this stage as my daughter is behaving like a normal child," he explained. Lali died two months later, mostly of problems that might have been assuaged had she received appropriate early medical care.

The newspaper account of Lali's short life was less surprising to me than it would have been ten years ago because I encountered versions of it again and again in my research. The beauty of this story—the parents' apparently instantaneous acceptance of their unusual offspring—became tragic when they confused the rightness of their child with normality. Lali's parents believed that their love and tolerance defined their daughter, when those qualities really only defined them as loving parents. When broad-mindedness blinds us to our offspring's needs, our love becomes denial. Acknowledging difference need not threaten love; indeed, it can enrich it.

Ideally, profound acceptance allows children to become most fully themselves. Within his or her own family, someone's dwarfism or autism or prodigiousness or transgenderism may be secondary. Such people are ideally, first and foremost, the children of their parents, fully recognized citizens of the tiny nation that is family. Parents need not merely love their children despite their defects but may find the surprising rightness in those imperfections. A wise psychiatrist once said to me, "People want to get better, but they don't want to change." But I would propose that only by allowing people born with horizontal identities *not* to change does one allow them to get better. Any of us can be a better version of himself, but none of us can be someone else.

Mainstreaming, inclusion, deinstitutionalization, the disability rights movement, identity politics—all these forces both emphasize and normalize difference. They focus on securing accommodation of unusual needs, while asserting that our most basic needs are all the same. They aspire to change the world so that more people can feel unremarkable in it. Many of the parents I interviewed were dedicated to extending the optimal conditions they had achieved at home into the larger community, and so they had become activists—some as a life's calling, others merely by agreeing to speak on the record. They did so in hopes that a kinder society would help their children across their life span. An integrated educational system benefits many people with horizontal identities; it likewise helps those who share a classroom with them. Similarly, building a compassionate society benefits not only those who are newly tolerated, but also those who are newly tolerating. Incorporating exceptional people into the social fabric is expensive and time-consuming. The emotional and logistical calisthenics can be draining. Yet if parents often end up grateful for their problematical children, then so, in the end, can we all be grateful for the courage such people may embody, the generosity they may teach us, even the ways they complicate the world.

In common parlance, *diversity* means that clubs should admit racial minorities and that colleges should admit some gay people. Selflessness is not the sole engine in honoring diversity, as is clear when the term indicates a balanced investment strategy or refers to the multiplicity of species in our forests, seas, and wetlands. The town where I went to college was long famous for its elm trees; indeed, it was called the Elm City until Dutch elm disease reached North America and denuded the town's streets and parks. When change happens, monoculture is a problem. In an era of accelerating transformation, when social values are shifting dramatically and the physical environment is altering at a breakneck pace, it is impossible to foretell what will prove adaptive. I am not championing dwarfism or deafness or criminality or gayness as the answer to any pivotal problem. What I do know is that it would be a mistake to turn us all into elms. It can look pretty, the long alleys of matching trees, their noble trunks aligning in symmetrical resemblance, but it is an irresponsible way to plan.

I began work on this book at about the same time I met John, who is now my husband. I had always wanted children, had contemplated having a child with an old friend, had dabbled in research on fertility—but the possibility had lingered in abstraction. John gave me more courage to be extraordinary, and more confidence about being ordinary, but from the stories of these hundreds of exceptional families I gradually understood that those were not incompatible goals, that being anomalous does not deprive anyone of the right or ability to be typical. Emily Perl Kingsley helped get children with Down syndrome on television so that no one else would feel as alone as she had. Neurodiversity and Deaf rights activists claimed the acceptance of aberration as their due. Ruth Schekter said, "Children like ours are not preordained as a gift. They're a gift because that's what we have chosen." Sue Klebold said, "Columbine made me feel more connected to mankind than anything else possibly could have." Anne O'Hara talked about how helping her transgender daughter "has brought more blessings into my life than I could possibly give back to her." Their tenor of persuasive wonder resonated deeply with me.

I had struggled for years with childlessness, and just when I had reconciled myself to that sadness, I began to see its inverse hope and started to figure out how I could be fruitful and multiply. What I couldn't know then was whether I truly *wanted* children, or whether I simply wanted to prove wrong everyone who had pitied my sexual orientation. When you have longed for the moon and are suddenly offered all its silver light, it's hard to remember what you intended to do with it. I had a history of depression. Was I giving up on that cheerless self in favor of some new happiness, or was I going to be stuck with a lot of sadness for which I would need to find new structures? I could not bring children into the world if I could not protect them from my adventures in despair. Knowing that parenting is no sport for perfectionists, I had sought lessons in humility from the families I interviewed. In my anxiety, I also kept remembering something my mother said to me when I was heading off for my road test: that two things in life look incredibly daunting until you realize that almost everyone does them—driving and having children.

I had been unpopular as a child, and children continued to intimidate me. I felt that in their eyes, I was still bad at dodgeball, with a funny gait, and emotionally gauche—that I had retained all the qualities that had made children shun me in my own childhood, qualities I had eventually understood to be aligned with my sexuality. I was still afraid of being called *gay* by children; my secure identity resonated like an insult when spoken by a child. I avoided children because of how *much* they made me feel. Like any powerful feeling, it was hard to read; what was manifest was its strength rather than its nature. I was usually relieved to leave other people's children after a few hours. Would I feel otherwise if I had my own? My persistent dark fantasy was that I would have children and wouldn't like them and would be stuck with them for the rest of my life. My link to my parents had been a source of great joy to me and to them, and I wanted to carry that forward, but much of my desolation had also drawn on the dynamics of my family, where emotions could run so high that it was hard to tell the difference between what happened to me and what happened to them. I had been consumed by being a son; recently emerged from that whale's mouth, I was afraid to be swallowed by being a father. I was also afraid of becoming the oppressor of a child who was different from me, as I had at times felt oppressed.

John already had a biological son when I met him. He and the child's biological mother, Laura, had been coworkers, and Laura had observed him for years before she and her partner, Tammy, asked him to help them have a child. Though not especially close to them, he had agreed, and they signed legal documents in which he forswore paternal rights and they forswore claims to support. He had offered to be in the child's life to the extent he was able, if the child and his mothers so wished, but in deference to Tammy's position as adoptive mother, he had remained largely uninvolved. He did not immediately make a point of introducing me to Tammy and Laura, but a few months after our relationship began, we ran into them with their toddler, Oliver, at the 2001 Minnesota State Fair. Oliver, unable to comprehend *donor dad*, called John *donut dad*, which made everybody laugh. But then who was I? Eighteen months later, they asked John to be their donor again, and Laura subsequently gave birth to Lucy. I was wary of John's connection to this family, and also fascinated. John had fathered *children*, and I looked at them for clues to who he really was. I didn't like them yet, but that was irrelevant to this grip of emotion and biology.

I had been considering the possibility of having my own biological children for some years. In 1999, during a business trip to Texas, I attended a dinner that included my college friend Blaine. Blaine had always been magical to me: reflexively kind, with an acute intelligence that she never shows off, and possessed of timeless grace. She had recently divorced and shortly thereafter lost her mother, and she mentioned that the best tribute she could pay to her happy childhood was to become a mother herself. I said, in a lighthearted way at a table full of other people, that I'd be game to be the father to her child. She countered, brightly, that she might just take me up on the offer. That she might actually want to have a child with me was unimaginable; I suggested it with the rhetorical politesse with which I'd invited new acquaintances in remote countries to stop by for a drink if they ever found themselves in Greenwich Village. When I got home, however, I wrote her a letter and said I knew she'd probably been joking, but that I thought she would be the best mother in the world, and I hoped she'd have a child with someone.

Four years later, Blaine flew to New York in 2003 for my surprise fortieth birthday party. We went out to dinner the following night and realized that we both wanted to follow through with the baby project. I had never been so honored or so alarmed. Our arrangements would be similar to John's with Tammy and Laura in some ways, but different in others; I would be the legal father of a child who would bear my last name. Though our child would live in Texas with Blaine, the relationship would be explicitly paternal.

I wasn't ready to tell John right away, and when I did tell him, he exploded, as I had feared he might. He had been a sperm donor. I would be in an ongoing, profound relationship with Blaine that he feared might lethally triangulate our own. So began the most difficult epoch of our relationship. We talked about it for months—John and I, Blaine and I—and the negotiations escalated to Balkan intensity. It took three years to iron out the details, but John, whose benevolence always triumphs, finally relented, and Blaine and I created a pregnancy, working through an IVF clinic. Blaine, meanwhile, had met her partner, Richard, putting a reasonable if unusual balance in place.

The more curious our arrangements became, the more traditional they started to feel. John had previously proposed that we get married, and I decided to honor the idea, though I was still a leery convert to gay marriage. Marrying was in part my way to reassure John of his centrality as we moved forward with the Blaine plan, but it soon became, more profoundly, a means for me to celebrate his handsomeness, wit, and sense of moral purpose; the fact that my family and friends adored him; and the way he could see the same things in their hearts that I did. We tied the knot on June 30, 2007, at a wedding in the countryside, and I thought how if all my traumas had led me to this day, they were not so bad as they had seemed in the instant. In my wedding toast, I said, "The love that dared not speak its name is now broadcasting." Tammy and Laura and their children came; Oliver served as John's ring-bearer. Blaine, four months pregnant with the child she and I had conceived, came with Richard, and John ventured that we'd had the first gay shotgun wedding.

In October, some complications in the pregnancy emerged, so John and I hurried to Fort Worth a month early for the delivery by Caesarean section on November 5, 2007. I watched the obstetrician pull little Blaine out of the convex surface of her mother's swollen belly and was the first person to hold her. I kept trying on the idea that I was now a father, and I didn't know what to do with it; it was as though I had suddenly been told that I was still myself and also a shooting star. I held the new baby; Blaine held her; Richard held her; John held her. Who were we all to this thrilling creature? Who was she to all of us? How did that alter who we were to one another? Already deep in my research, I knew that every child has a touch of the horizontal and reshapes his or her parents. I scanned my daughter's small face for clues as to who she was, and for hints of whom she would make me become.

John and I headed back to New York ten days later. When we got home, I was preoccupied with my new child, but kept imagining that I was being supportive of something wonderful Blaine had done, rather than being engaged with something I had done. I didn't yet understand that the biological thrill of dawning parenthood was only a ghostly suggestion of the passion that is parenthood itself. I had to separate the relief of having escaped that defining tragedy to which my parents had given so much airtime from the more enormous reality of a new human being for whom I was responsible. I did not want to be so attached to little Blaine that her living in Texas became intolerable; I did not want to be so unattached that she felt neglected. I was just self-aware enough to know that what I wanted of my emotions was irrelevant.

Getting married and having babies are both public events. Like many public things, they reify what they expose. I had had a vision of our life, and suddenly everyone else had a vision of it, too. Implicating others in your reality strengthens it, and we had dragged a large number of friends and family into the process through which love creates a household, a process in which interior truth receives a carapace that protects and sustains it. I was grateful that our friends had celebrated our marriage; I was grateful that John welcomed the daughter he had dreaded; I was grateful, too, that John and Blaine had begun to trust each other. I finally noticed how much Blaine had in common with my own mother—the same ability to find humor in the dailiness of life; the same careful restraint with her own emotions; the same wild imagination hidden from almost everyone by decorous elegance and obdurate reserve; the same intelligent empathy tinged with sadness. I had, like many men, found an echo of my mother to produce my child. Blaine's eighty-six-year-old father, whose values I had thought might be challenged by our arrangements, was delighted, and my father was thrilled.

I soon realized that I wanted to bring up a child at home with John, to be a pledge between us. John's original arrangement with Tammy and Laura had answered a question; the arrangement with Blaine was more intimate; and the prospect of having a child who would live full-time with the two of us was an explosion of everything we'd been taught to expect from life as gay men. I hadn't wanted to get married; then the reality had entranced me. I exacted a child as fair trade, believing John, too, would end up entranced. Because John was less sure about wanting this child than I professed to be, I had to act as cheerleader for the enterprise. I was full of hopeful infatuation with a person who did not yet exist and sure that fatherhood would exalt everything I already cherished about John, but the conversation stalled there. Our love for each other was a prerequisite for a child, but not a reason for one. We could not procreate as a social experiment or a political statement or to make ourselves whole, and I could not be the sole enthusiast in our decision. Then John gave me an antique cradle tied up with a bow for my birthday and said, "If it's a boy, can we call him George, after my grandpa?"

A lawyer laid out the legal advantages of having one woman provide the egg and another the womb, so neither would have a full claim as mother. John had proposed that I be the biological father of this child and said that he might sire the next, if there were one. Like many middle-age couples with fertility issues, we began the blind-dating egg hunt. We flew to San Diego to ingratiate ourselves with our preferred donor agency. Joyful though our decision was, I felt sorry that I would never see what might come of mixing John's genes with my own. I was thankful we could get an egg, regretful that neither of us could produce one; happy we could have a child at all, and sad about the aura of manufacturing that clung to the venture. Without assisted reproductive technology, I would not have the children I have, but it would have been fun to produce them in an ecstatic moment of physical love rather than through draining bureaucracy. It was costly, too, and though the money was well spent, we both rued that economic privilege was the necessary condition of what we preferred to consider an act of love.

My research made me acutely conscious of the quasi-eugenic aspect of the donor search—the ways we were opting for a donor who conformed to our standards of intelligence, character, health, and appearance. For me, these personal decisions had worrisome political overtones. I did not want to devalue the extraordinary lives I had come to respect, yet I couldn't deny that I wanted a child who would be familiar enough so that we could soothe him or her with our mutualities. At the same time, I understood that genetic lineage comes with no guarantees. The catalog of attractive attributes touting each donor made me feel as though we were choosing online a car we would be driving the rest of our lives. Sunroof? Good highway mileage? Red hair? High SAT scores? Grandparents who lived past eighty? The whole quest was absurd, depressing, morally troubling. Yet, the care of choosing the egg donor seemed like one concrete gesture we could make in a time of petrifying abstraction, an iota of knowledge in this vast mystery.

We told Laura and Tammy about our plan, and Laura said to John, "We couldn't have had Oliver and Lucy without you, and we'll never be able to thank you enough for that, but I could be your surrogate to show how much you and Andrew mean to us." It was a gesture of spectacular generosity, and we accepted it. There followed medical screenings of Laura, the egg donor, and me; samples (the bright hospital room, the leatherette briefcase of dated girlie magazines provided by the staff); fertility treatments for Laura; embryo transfers; and ultrasounds. Like many of the families I had met, mine was touched in equal measure by changes in social norms and changes in technology. Their fortunate concurrence was the precondition of our children.

We got pregnant on our second IVF protocol. Although we had been extremely deliberate in egg selection, we ultimately decided not to have amniocentesis. This decision caught me by surprise when I made it with John and Laura. The risk of having a disabled child (highly unlikely according to less invasive but less conclusive tests) no longer seemed frightening enough to risk a miscarriage. I could have imagined terminating if we had received bad amnio results, but I could no longer have done so with the logic that would have guided me before I wrote this book. My research had shattered that clarity, so I succumbed to avoidance.

You never know anyone as admiringly as you do when she is carrying your child, and I marveled at the way Laura wove the life she was building for us into the life she had built for herself. We drew inexorably closer to her and to Tammy and the kids. Oliver and Lucy referred to the yet-to-come baby as their brother. I was shy of their enthusiasm at first, but John and I went to Minneapolis for the late stages of the pregnancy and ended up staying there for more than a month, seeing the four of them almost every day, which gave me a chance to observe how Oliver and Lucy echoed John's wit and gentleness. When they learned that little Blaine called us Daddy and Papa John, they told their mothers they wanted to call us Daddy and Papa, too.

I was not prepared for the idea that all of these children were in various degrees mine, but the sweetness with which John had come to celebrate the Blaines modeled a path to acceptance. Having set out to have two children, I was suddenly contemplating four, and I now believed that I could love them all profoundly, even if I loved them differently. To bring us closer had been part of Laura's purpose in helping us, and it worked. John's insistence that we were all one family made it happen. Without my campaigning, we wouldn't have had little Blaine, or this new child, but without John's optimism, we'd have stayed compartmentalized. That would have been the easier path, and I mistook it for the better one. I taught John a great deal about doing things instead of simply imagining them, and he taught me a great deal about experiencing those things once they were done. By little Blaine, by the imminent baby, by Oliver and Lucy, and by the extraordinary families I'd come to know, I had been changed, and children no longer made me sad.

The day of George's birth—April 9, 2009—was emotionally charged before it began. My awareness of the perils of childbirth outstripped Laura's and John's; I had heard too many stories that started, "The pregnancy seemed to go so well, and then suddenly, when she went into labor . . ." I tried to quell my anxiety, but by the time George's head showed, my palms were damp with fear. Laura had chosen to deliver without pain medication, and I found myself newly in awe. For nine months, I had felt the favor she did us as though someone had offered to carry an increasingly heavy bag of groceries up an increasingly steep staircase, but suddenly I understood that she had made a *life* for us. Seeing her give birth, I witnessed the pain of the final dilation and pushing and felt the radical newness coming out of her. I saw clearly for the first time something wild and heroic in her, an acreage of heart and valor beyond anything male experience had taught me. Then she pushed twice and out George popped, instantly proving the strength of his lungs with a good cry, and wiggling his arms and legs. The obstetrician pronounced him healthy. And then we noticed his umbilical cord, which was knotted.

George had come out at just the right time. If the labor had gone on longer or we had waited a few more days to induce, the knot might have tightened, depriving him of oxygen, destroying his brain, and giving Laura a potentially fatal placental hemorrhage. I looked at that knot the way one often looks at fate—as a thing so nearly missed—and I cut the umbilical cord below the knot, so that danger could be kept far away from our miraculous baby. All I wanted was to hold him and look at him, to try to take from his small and squirming body the transient illusion that he would bring nothing but euphoria into the rest of our lives.

We went through all the semimedicalized and personal rituals that follow a healthy birth. Many photos were taken, and we took off our shirts so he could be on our skin, and we watched him be weighed and measured, and we saw ointments put on his eyes, and we introduced him to Oliver and Lucy. I handed around a box of champagne truffles that Blaine's brother had sent me from London (you can't bring actual champagne into a delivery room), and we called my father and step-mother, my brother, Blaine, and a few others who matter deeply to us. John was instantly enraptured, as I knew he would be, because birth is so mysterious and so much weirder than sorcery or intergalactic war-fare that it humbles you instantly. I had felt it with little Blaine and I felt it again here. This person hadn't existed before, and now he did, and I remember thinking what everyone had always thought, that his coming into the world made up for all the previous losses.

By the time John and I had settled in our hospital room and the nurse had given George his first bath, it was two thirty in the morn-ing, and we all fell blissfully into our beds. I am the heavy sleeper in the family, so I slumbered peacefully while John got up every few hours to check on George and feed him. When I woke up, John had taken George into Laura's room down the hall; Tammy and the kids were there, eating cinnamon rolls, and the air was festive. John said he was going to lie down for a bit and that I should talk to the pediatrician. I'm the one in the family who deals with everything medical, and I thought this was the predictable stuff of day one in George's life—a hearing test, what to do about the hepatitis-B vaccine, and so on. Blithely I sat there eating, helping Oliver and Lucy hold the baby safely, and then the pediatrician came in and said she was concerned.

George had not been drawing his legs up the way that babies are supposed to and was instead holding them out stiff and straight for up to three minutes at a time. She referred to this as "inappropriately high muscle tone" and said that it might reflect brain damage, and that she wanted to order a CAT scan. I asked whether this was unusual, and she said, simply, that it didn't frequently occur at this stage. Laura brightly volunteered that George was going to be fine, and everyone else went on with the cinnamon rolls, and I felt the inside parts of my body that are usually warm go cold, while the parts exposed to the air suddenly seemed to be on fire. The pediatrician calmly explained that the baby's unusual behavior could signal bleeding in the brain, and that such bleeding might resolve itself or might need to be alleviated surgically. She mentioned the knot in the cord and said we needed to be certain that it hadn't had an impact. She noted that his head was unusually large, which could be related to hydrocephalus or the pres-ence of tumors. She added that he was stiffening one leg more than the other, which might mean that he had asymmetrical brain development or a mass in his brain. She was young, and I could tell that this was the steady, competent manner she had learned for the purpose of being honest with people.

From the time George was conceived until that day, I had kept thinking how ironic it would be if, in the midst of writing about exceptional children, I were to produce such a child. I knew, though, that nature is no stranger to irony. Now, I asked how soon the CAT scan could be done, and the pediatrician said she'd set it up as soon as possible, and in her brisk and pleasant way she left the room. I looked at George and knew I loved him by how hard I suddenly tried not to love him. I remembered all the parents who had described spreading the news about their thriving baby and then picking up the phone a day or two later to report a different tale. A rational piece of me was trying to decide under what circumstances I would support whatever heroic measures might be called for. A terrified piece of me was contemplating giving him up into care. My strongest impulse was to hold him tight and not let him go for the tests at all. I wanted him to be well, but I wanted me to be well, too, and even as I formulated that divide, it collapsed, and I saw that one thing could not be true without the other.

I called my father and spoke to my brother and e-mailed a few friends. My brother immediately checked with pediatric neurologists in New York; my father got a physician who is a family friend on the line, and we talked the whole thing through. So many parents had told me how the need to deal with such situations upstages the emotions of them, and I was relieved to settle into problem-solving mode. I would do everything right, which would postpone anguish. I remembered parents saying that they don't tell you at the beginning that your child will need thirty major interventions; they tell you he will need one, and then a little later that he will need one more, and then another—that the gradualism deprives you of volition. I was determined to be awake at each choice to what might come next.

I called the nurses' station to find out when we were having the scan and found out that because of a computer glitch the request had been lost. The pediatric nurse explained that she had to do an arterial blood draw; she drove a needle deep into his wrist. An arterial blood draw? Had any of the five hundred parents I had met mentioned an arterial blood draw? Finally, the news came that we were set for the CAT scan. Alas, our nurse had cycled off, and we were now assigned a pretty young woman with the bedside manner of a flight attendant, her banal friendliness not quite masking an irritable boredom. I asked if she'd assisted at such a procedure before. "A CAT scan on a newborn?" she said. "No, I've never even heard of anyone doing one before." I felt two conflicting guilts: first that I had produced a child who might suffer, and second that despite all the stories I'd heard from parents who found deep meaning in bringing up exceptional children, I didn't want to join their number. Of course, most of those other parents had not opted into their circumstances; I also remembered that valor cannot be achieved on a schedule.

The imaging room was grim, despite touches intended to make it cheerful and friendly; indeed, its cheerful friendliness was part of what made it grim, as though the festive decor would have been unnecessary in less gruesome circumstances. We watched helplessly as George was positioned in the machine. He was more or less asleep and did not stir as his head was locked into place with several blankets wedged next to it and straps fastened across his forehead. They let us stay, wearing big lead aprons, and we tried to comfort George, and I was suddenly aware of how uncomforting I was to someone who had not yet learned to turn to me for comfort.

Back in our room, so recently cozy, we waited. A new nurse came on shift, and I begged her to get the results. The on-call pediatrician phoned radiology. The results weren't in, so we waited some more. Finally, I fought my way past the nurses' station and cornered a newly arrived on-call pediatrician, who told me that the results had been there for an hour. "I think we should talk about this with your husband," he said gravely. We walked back to the room where John was waiting, and I blurted out sweatily, "Is there bleeding in his brain?" and the pediatrician said there was not. Then he launched into what they had been testing for and what each image showed, and he eventually revealed that the scan was completely clear. George was fine. The whole thing was over.

I think all love is one-third projection and one-third acceptance and never more than one-third knowledge and insight. With my children's births, I had projected and accepted so much, so fast. I remembered Sara Hadden's wanting to baptize her son after she found out how severely disabled he was, as a way of formalizing her belief that he was nonetheless a person. I realized that George, who had done nothing more admirable than cry and feed, was richly and permanently human to me, possessed of a soul, and no alteration could change that. The tree doesn't grow far from the apple.

John and I became fathers when gay parenting was a thrillingly new advance. I understood the day George was declared well that hope is not a thing with feathers, but a squalling, pink thing newly arrived, that no other optimism is so great as having a child. Our love for our children is almost entirely situational, yet it is nearly the strongest emotion we know. This book's stories were to my love for my children much as parables are to faith, the concrete narratives that make the greatest abstractions true. I am the parent I am in the wake of this book's epic narratives of resilience.

When I was born, the common view was that nurture decided almost everything. In the decades that followed, the emphasis shifted to nature. In the last twenty years, people have talked more broadly about the intricate ways that nature and nurture propel each other. I was intellectually persuaded by this nuanced integration, but the experience of having my own children has made me wonder if a third element is involved, some unknowable inflection of spirit or divinity. One's children are so specific, and the notion that they wouldn't exist if one hadn't conceived them at the moment one did feels impossible. Most of the parents I interviewed for this book said they would never want other children than the ones they had, which at first seemed surprising given the challenges their children embody. But why does any of us prefer our own children, all of them defective in some regard, to others real or imagined? If some glorious angel descended into my living room and offered to exchange my children for other, better children—brighter, kinder, funnier, more loving, more disciplined, more accomplished—I would clutch the ones I have and, like most parents, pray away the atrocious specter.

Roger Penrose, a British mathematical physicist, asked whether our physical world and the Platonic realm of ideas might be one and the same. He has suggested that the anthropic principle may demonstrate that the universe has a structural need for consciousness—effectively, that the existence of anything proves its inevitability. Counter to the Copernican revolution, the anthropic principle suggests that human beings are not incidental; that our existence is evidence that we had to be; that the comprehensibility of anything is a function of our comprehension as much as the other way around. Subjectivity may be truer than objectivity. The idea has some resonance with parenting. Most of us believe that our children are the children we had to have; we could have had no others. They will never seem to us to be happenstance; we love them because they are our destiny. Even when they are flawed, do wrong, hurt us, die—even then, they are part of the rightness by which we measure our own lives. Indeed, they are the rightness by which we measure life itself, and they bring us to life as profoundly as we do them.

After George arrived, the question arose of how all these relationships might constellate. John and I have complete charge of George; Blaine and I had agreed in advance that we would make the major decisions about little Blaine together; Laura and Tammy have separate parental authority, and we do not set the course for Oliver and Lucy, nor Laura and Tammy for George. The three arrangements are different, and in the same ways most parents try to suppress sibling rivalry, we struggle to avoid situational comparisons. Occasional frictions are sparked by conflicting priorities and boundaries, disparate resources, myriad parenting styles—but they are dwarfed by the reality that it all somehow functions. We have fought hard for the familial relationships into which others stumble, and there is a veteran's peace in our mutual devotion.

It must be easier to lead a life in which you are not constantly invent-ing all the roles, in which there is a script to follow. We have often felt like Christopher Columbus landing for the first time on the wilder shores of love, and while being a pioneer can be thrilling, sometimes one would prefer a place where the roads have already been built and the Internet access is wireless. Most people expect to have children, and certain susceptibilities are attached to that; I had expected not to have children, and the reversal contains stranger ones. We have made many careful, thoughtful decisions, but so much of how we've worked it out wasn't actually rooted in choice. Like other parents, I simply lived my life from day to day, until the unusual became quotidian. I have said that parents do not reproduce, but create. In fact, we also discover. I sometimes think of my life as forty years of toil up some steep hill, and then I joined hands with John, and then with Blaine, and then with Tammy and Laura, and in a different way with everyone else chronicled in this volume. Somehow the lot of us made it to the crest, and when I looked out, I saw all creation spread at my feet. I had no idea, when I was hiking, that this was what I was climbing toward; forty years in the wilderness has never prepared anyone for this view.

John and I sent out birth announcements that included a picture of us with George. One of John's cousins returned her copy with a terse note that began, "Your lifestyle is against our Christian values," and ended, "We wish to have no further contact." Some people scorn the idea of calling five primary parents and four children in three states a family, or fear that the existence of our family somehow undermines theirs. An old friend said to me over lunch one day, "Isn't it wonderful how your father accepts your children?" I pointed out that my children were his grandchildren, and she said, "Yes, but even so." That presump-tive caul of negativity is onerous. Some people are trapped by the belief that love comes in finite quantities, and that our kind of love exhausts the supply upon which they need to draw. I do not accept competitive models of love, only additive ones. My journeys toward a family and this book have taught me that love is a magnifying phenomenon—that every increase in love strengthens all the other love in the world, that much as loving one's family can be a means of loving God, so the love that exists within any family can fortify the love of all families. I espouse reproductive libertarianism, because when everyone has the broadest choice, love itself expands. The affection my family have found in one another is not a better love, but it is another love, and just as species diversity is crucial to sustain the planet, this diversity strengthens the ecosphere of kindness. The road less traveled by, as it turns out, leads to pretty much the same place.

One resolves cognitive dissonance by assimilating what it is too late to change, and in that spirit I wonder whether I would have found as much joy in marriage and children if they had come easily—if I had been straight or had grown up thirty years later in a somewhat more welcoming society. Perhaps I would; perhaps all the complex imagining I've had to do could have been applied to broader endeavors. I believe, however, that the struggle has given me a vision as a parent that I would not have had without it. So much of me had been consecrated to loneliness, and now I am not lonely anymore. Now, children make me happy. A generation ago, this love would have stayed dormant and unrealized. But so, too, would much of the love described in this book, the love of all these parents for children who would once have died young or been put away or lived unacknowledged as fully human. My family is radical for a different reason from most of the others I have chronicled, but all of us are exponents of revolutionary love against the odds.

Pain is the threshold of intimacy, and catastrophe burnishes devotion. I know this, yet I am routinely surprised to discover it. One may be infuriated and depressed by vulnerability and still be drawn to its seductions. While I mostly fell for the friends I adore because they are wise, kind, generous, and fun, I have loved them most acutely when they or I have been most sad, because there is a psychic proximity in desolate times that happiness does not match. My depression hatched an intimacy with my father that I'd never have known if he hadn't helped me through that struggle. As a parent, for all that I relish glee, I know that attachment happens when things turn dark. Parenting is an exercise in safety, and the perpetual menace of danger is what exalts parental love above affection; without the night terrors, the spiking fevers, the litany of bruises and woes, it would be a second-rate entertainment. It took me some time to understand that attention to one's children's needs is the essence of gratification. From that perspective, it made sense that the difficult loves of these pages are so deep. I want more than anything for my children to be happy, and I love them because they are sad, and the erratic project of kneading that sadness into joy is the engine of my life as a father, as a son, as a friend—and as a writer.

For many years, my primary identity was as a historian of sadness. Pictures of despair are widely admired, and perfect bleakness is generally thought to reflect the integrity of the author. But when I've tried to write about happiness, I've had an inverse revelation, which is that you cannot write about it without seeming shallow. Even when one emphasizes the sorrowful or the joyful, one is being honest, just as one is honest when one says that the sky above is blue without getting into the brownness of the earth below. The families I met mostly emphasize the craning art of looking up, but they do so with integrity. I am unabashed by this book's occasional whiff of rapture and reject the idea that beauty is the enemy of truth, or that pain can't be the hare to joy's tortoise.

The realist writer William Dean Howells once wrote to Edith Wharton that "what the American public always wants is a tragedy with a happy ending." The implication of his remark was that we didn't have the stomach for Lear mad upon the heath with no redemption in sight. I would offer a different reading. I would say that it is increasingly our character to seek transformation. Early psychoanalytic models are about accepting life's problems; modern therapies focus on resolving them, eliminating them, or redefining them as something other than problems. Does some artifice creep into this brazen triumphalism? People often affect a happiness they do not feel; people whose neurosis has turned to misery are not only miserable, but also believe that they have failed. But the vital piece of this inclination toward the light is the unshakable belief that catastrophes properly end in resolution, that tragedies are frequently a phase rather than an endgame.

This book seeks the nobility buried in Howells's disparagement. It is predicated on an even more optimistic notion, which is that the happy endings of tragedies have a dignity beyond the happy endings of comedies, that they not only transcend the mawkishness to which Howells alludes, but also produce a contentment more cherished than one untempered by suffering. Sometimes, people end up thankful for what they mourned. You cannot achieve this state by seeking tragedy, but you can keep yourself open more to sorrow's richness than to unmediated despair. Tragedies with happy endings may be sentimental tripe, or they may be the true meaning of love. Insofar as I have written a self-help book, it is a how-to manual for receptivity: a description of how to tolerate what cannot be cured, and an argument that cures are not always appropriate even when they are feasible. As the jagged Alps are to the romantic sublime, so this curious joy is to the character of these families—nearly impossible, terrible, and terribly beautiful.

Given how unimaginable my family would have been fifty years ago, I have no choice but to champion progress; change has been good to me, and I am indebted to it. I hope these stories will contribute to the cataract that is honing the rough surface of the world. Until the planet grows smooth, however, love will continue to toughen under siege; the very threats to love strengthen it even as they suffuse it with pain. In the harsh moments of loss that are my topic here, love manacles a tender heart. I felt something brilliant and terrifying for my son as he lay in that *Star Trek*–like CAT scanner that I had not yet felt for little Blaine, who had not encountered such adversity, or for Oliver and Lucy, who were already themselves when I got to know them. It changed my relationship to them all. Children ensnared me the moment I connected fatherhood with loss, but I am not sure I would have noticed that if I hadn't been immersed in this research. Encountering so much strange love, I fell into its bewitching patterns and saw how splendor can illuminate even the most abject vulnerabilities. I had witnessed and learned the terrifying joy of unbearable responsibility, recognized how it conquers everything else. Sometimes, I had thought the heroic parents in this book were fools, enslaving themselves to a life's journey with their alien children, trying to breed identity out of misery. I was startled to learn that my research had built me a plank, and that I was ready to join them on their ship.

Acknowledgments

A book such as this one is a group enterprise, and I am grateful, first and foremost, to the individuals and families who agreed to be interviewed, in many cases speaking about painful experiences at considerable personal cost. *Far from the Tree* would not exist without them, and neither would the world it documents. I am humbled by their grit, wisdom, generosity, and truthfulness.

The original impetus for this investigation came from an assignment to write about Deaf culture for the *New York Times Magazine*, and I thank Adam Moss and Jack Rosenthal for proposing that topic to me, and Annette Grant for editing my article. I engaged with the question of prodigies when I was assigned to write about Evgeny Kissin for the *New Yorker*, and I am grateful to Tina Brown, Henry Finder, and Charles Michener for encouraging me in that work. Leslie Hawke came to my house one night in 2001 with a screening copy of Lisa Hedley's astonishing film *Dwarfs: Not a Fairy Tale*; from our conversation that night, this book took shape. In 2007, Adam Moss suggested that I write about the neurodiversity movement for *New York*, an assignment that turned out to be pivotal in my evolving understanding of the people I was writing about; Emily Nussbaum was my editor for that story. I thank them both.

I was lucky enough to have guides who helped me enter many of the communities I wished to document. Jackie Roth opened up Deaf culture to me starting in 1994 and arranged many interviews I've included here. I Gede Marsaja and I Gede Primantara were my guides in Desa Kolok. Betty Adelson was my chief adviser on dwarfs, and I thank her for reading and correcting drafts of that chapter. Suzanne Elliott Armstrong and Betsy Goodwin were helpful as I worked on Down syndrome. Daniel M. Geschwind, Thomas Insel, James D. Watson, and Bruce Stillman assisted me incalculably with the science of autism. Jeffrey Lieberman was my tireless guide to the science of schizophrenia, and David Nathan generously spent time discussing the condition and helping me to meet patients. For their tremendous assistance with my schizophrenia research, I thank Colleen Marie Barrett, Bruce M. Cohen, Cathie Cook, and Scott Rauch at McLean Hospital. Kathleen Seidel educated me on many issues around disability and gave me my training in disability rights. I am particularly grateful to Justin Davidson, Siu Li GoGwilt, Charles Hamlen, Sarah Durie Solomon, and Shirley Young for their unflagging support as I worked on the prodigies chapter, and to Susan Ebersole and Robert Sirota for introducing me to students at the Manhattan School of Music. I am grateful to Jesse Dudley for translating for me *Dad's Aspirations Are That High*, by Yuanju Li (2001) (爸爸的心就这么高 : **钢琴天才郎朗和他的父亲** /

Ba ba de xin jiu zhe mo gao: gang qin tian cai Lang Lang he ta de fu qin). I thank Dina Temple-Raston for inviting me to Rwanda and helping me secure interviews with rape survivors there, and Janet Benshoof for sharing her insights from a lifetime devoted to reproductive rights. In connection with the crime chapter, I thank the inspirational Stephen DiMenna, who encouraged me to accompany him to the Hennepin County Home School, where Tom Bezek, Thelma Fricke, Shelley Whelan, and Terry Wise kindly facilitated my interviews with residents and their families. Alex Busansky and Jennifer Trone, of the Commission on Safety and Abuse in America's Prisons, provided terrific background information for that chapter. My work on the trans community relied on the help and support of Matt Foreman, Lisa Mottet, Kim Pearson and her TYFA team, and Rachel Pepper.

I was fortunate to have a sterling research team who obtained and organized vast bodies of information. Over a decade, smart and stalwart Ian Beilin, witty and compelling Stephen Bitterolf, rigorous and loyal Susan Ciampa, conscientious Jonah Engle, free-thinking Edric Mesmer, scrupulous and astute Kari Milchman, gracious and splendid Deborah Pursch, courageous Jacob Shamberg, and brilliantly imaginative Rachel Trocchio variously brought knowledge, coherence, and discernment to my research. Pat Towers edited a sample chapter. I am very grateful to Susan Kittenplan for her excellent edit of the manuscript when it was at its most cumbersome. I thank Eugene Corey for transcribing the earlier interviews, and Sandra Arroyo, Sonia Houmis, Kathleen Vach, and the rest of the team at TruTranscripts for working on the later ones.

I became something of a residency junky while working on this book. I had one stay at the Rockefeller Foundation Bellagio Center, one at the Ucross Foundation, two at the MacDowell Colony, and four at Yaddo. The serenity these institutions afforded me was critical to the book. I would like particularly to thank Pilar Palacia and Darren Walker at the Rockefeller Foundation; Sharon Dynak and Ruthie Salvatore at Ucross; Michelle Aldredge, Nancy Devine, David Macy, Brendan Tapley, and Cheryl Young at MacDowell; and Cathy Clarke, Elaina Richardson, and Candace Wait at Yaddo.

I remain deeply indebted as always to my wise and loyal agent and friend, Andrew Wylie, who has championed my work now for almost a quarter century and has helped me to become the writer I am. I am grateful also to his able deputies, especially Sarah Chalfant, Alexandra Levenberg, and Jeffrey Posternak. I pay tribute to my beloved editor at Scribner, Nan Graham, who reads with a valiant heart and a kind pencil; her signal mix of empathy, enthusiasm, patience, and insight shaped this book from the time when I was only imagining it to the time when I finally completed it. I thank, also, at Scribner Brian Belfiglio, Steve Boldt, Rex Bonomelli, Daniel Burgess, Roz Lippel, Kate Lloyd, Susan Moldow, Greg Mortimer, Carolyn Reidy, Kathleen Rizzo, Kara Watson, and Paul Whitlatch. At Chatto & Windus, I thank Alison Samuel, who bought the book, and Clara Farmer, who saw it through production. I am grateful to Andrew Essex, Ben Freda, Jonathan Hills, Trinity Ray, Eric Rayman, Andres Saavedra, and Eric Schwinn for their help with other aspects of publication.

I thank Cheryl Henson and Ed Finn for giving me the jacket image, and Adam Fuss for creating it; I thank Annie Leibovitz for creating and giving me my author photo.

Every book I've written has been corrected by Katherine Keenum, my freshman writing tutor. Her devotion is profoundly heartening, and her close reading, invaluable.

Kathleen Seidel came on board to organize my bibliography, compile citations, and check facts; she took it upon herself to question prejudices related to identity, disability, medicine, and the law. She was a brilliant *diaskeuast*, and this would have been an entirely different book without her meticulous intelligence, bracing precision, passion for accuracy, and sense of justice.

Alice Truax wrestled multiple drafts of this book to the ground. Her understanding of my purpose was so profound that I felt as though she had climbed inside my mind to make repairs. My method is associative; hers, logical. With infinite patience and skill, she chipped away at great blocks of chaos to reveal the coherence trapped inside them.

Many people helped keep my life running while I was writing this book, and I'd like to thank Sergio Avila, Lorilynn Bauer, Juan and Amalia Fernandez, Ildikó Fülöp, Judy Gutow, Christina Harper, Brenda Hernández-Reynoso, Marsha Johnson, Celso, Miguela, and Olga Mancol, Tatiana Martushev, Heather Nedwell, Jacek Niewinski, Mindy Pollack, Kylee Sallak, Eduardo and Elfi de los Santos, Marie Talentowski, Ester Tolete, Danusia Trevino, and Bechir Zouay.

It is impossible to acknowledge everyone who participated in this work; almost daily, someone said something that helped me understand more clearly my underlying topics of identity and love. Among the glorious people who made helpful introductions or discussed ideas that are central to the book or read and commented on sections of it are Cordelia Anderson, Laura Anderson, Anne Applebaum, Lucy Armstrong, Dorothy Arnsten, Jack Barchas, Nesli Basgoz, Frank Bayley, Cris Beam, Bill and Bunny Beekman, Meica and Miguel de Beistegui, Erika Belsey and Alexi Worth, Mary Bisbee-Beek, Richard Bradley, Susan Brody, Hugo Burnand, Elizabeth Burns, Elizabeth and Blake Cabot, Mario and Ariadne Calvo-Platero, S. Talcott Camp, Thomas Caplan, Christian Caryl, Amy Fine Collins, Cathryn Collins, Robert Couturier, Dana B. Cowin and Barclay Palmer, Rebecca Culley and Peter K. Lee, Mary D'Alton, Meri Nana-Ama Danquah, Cecile David-Weill, Justin Davidson and Ariella Budick, Nick Davis and Jane Mendelsohn, Roland Davis and Margot Norris, Miraj Desai, Freddy Eberstadt, Nenna Eberstadt and Alistair Bruton, Nicholas Rollo David Evans, Melissa Feldman, Lorraine Ferguson, Susannah Fiennes, Adam and Olivia Flatto, Bill Foreman and Reg Barton, Cornelia Foss, Richard A. Friedman and Bob Hughes, Richard C. Friedman, Fran Gallacher, Arlyn Gardner, Rhonda Garelick, Kathleen Gerard, Bernard Gersten and Cora Cahan, Icy Gordon, Ann Gottleib, Philip Gourevich and Larissa MacFarquhar, Geordie and Kathryn Greig, Guo Fang, Melanie and Martin Hall, Han Feng, Amy Harmon, John Hart, Ashton Hawkins and Johnnie Moore, David Hecht, Cheryl Henson and Ed Finn, David Herskovits and Jennifer Egan, Gillie Holme and Camille Massey, Richard Hubbard, Ana Joanes, Lisa Jonas, Maira Kalman, William Kentridge and Anne Stanwix, Terry Kirk, Larry Kramer, Søren Krogh, Mary Krueger and Andreas Saavedra, Roger and Neroli Lacey, Jhumpa Lahiri and Alberto Vourvoulias-Bush, Katherine Lanpher, Paul LeClerc, Michael Lee and Ashutosh Khandekar, Justin Leites, Jeffrey and Rosemarie Lieberman, Jennie Livingston, Betsy de Lotbinière, Kane Loukas and Christina Rieck, Ivana Lowell and Howard Blum, Sue Macartney-Snape, John MacPhee, Jamie Marks, Mary E. Marks, Cleopatra Mathis, Tey Meadow, James Meyer, Juliet Mitchell, Isaac Mizrahi, R. Clayton Mulford, Freda and Christian Murck, John and Nancy Novogrod, Rusty O'Kelley III and John Haskins, Ann Olson, Beatrix Ost and Ludwig Kuttner, Mary Alice Palmer, Harriet Paterson and Rick Cockett, Julie Peters, Alice Playten, Francine du Plessix Gray, Charles and Barbara Prideaux, Dièry Prudent and Mariza Scotch, Deborah and David Pursch, Emily K. Rafferty, Kim Reed and Claire Jones, Maggie Robbins, Paul and Susannah Robinson, Marion Lignana Rosenberg, Robert Rosenkranz and Alexandra K. Munroe, Steven Rosoff and Tànis Allen, Ira Sachs, Eric Saltzman, Phillip and Donna Satow, Christina Schmidt, Lisa Schmitz, John Schneeman, Jill Schuker, Alex Shand, Julie Sheehan, Nicola Shulman, Polly Shulman, Michael Silverman, Dee Smith, Doug Smith, Gordon Smith, Calvin,

Emmett, and Abigail Solomon, David and Sarah Long Solomon, Cindy Spiegel, Moonhawk River Stone, Kerry J. Sulkowicz and Sandra Leong, Ezra Susser, Claudia Swan, Dean Swanson, András Szántó and Alanna Stang, Dina Temple-Raston, Phyllis Toohey, Tara Tooke, Carll Tucker and Jane Bryant Quinn, Susan Wadsworth, Kathryn Walker, Jim and Liz Watson, Caroline Weber, Helen Whitney, Susan Willard, Hope and Grant Winthrop, Jaime Wolf, Micky Wolfson, Doug Wright and Dave Clement, and Larisa Zvezdochetova.

I thank Laura Scher and Tammy Ward for cheering me on as I wrote and for bringing so much joy into my life.

I am forever indebted to Blaine Smith for her exquisite sympathy, generosity, and wisdom; I am grateful to her also for her insights on this book's design.

My stepmother, Sarah Durie Solomon, talked through *Far from the Tree* with me year in and year out, providing copious insights and encouragement. Additionally, she urged me to stay with my father and her for long periods when I needed to write. The time we all had together was magical, and this book would not exist without it.

My father, Howard Solomon, my most loyal reader, pored over a stupefying number of early fragments and later versions of this book. We talked about every interview and idea, and he never wavered in his conviction that the undertaking would succeed. His lifelong devotion was my first experience of the kind of unstinting parenthood I've chronicled here.

I am grateful to Oliver Scher, Lucy Scher, Blaine Solomon, and George Solomon for their patience when my work kept me from fun and games. This book is a tribute to them, but it required their forbearance.

Finally, I thank my husband, John Habich Solomon, who lived with me when I was working and lived without me when I was working. His editing of the manuscript into precision was a great boon; his editing of my life into happiness is the greatest boon I've ever known.

Notes

These notes are presented in compressed form in print and at greater length online at http://www.andrewsolomon.com/far-from-the-tree/footnotes.

A few notes on the notes. First, I allowed everyone I interviewed the choice of being quoted by name or pseudonymously. I have indicated all pseudonyms in the notes. Though I attempted to stay as true as possible to the identities of those who are quoted pseudonymously, I have changed some personal information to protect the privacy of people who wished me to do so.

I have put into these notes citations for all quotations from printed sources; everything else is from personal interviews conducted between 1994 and 2012.

To avoid making this book even longer than it is or festooning it with ellipsis marks, I have condensed some quotations from written material. Where I have done so, the full text appears in the online notes.

Epigraph

See *The Collected Poems of Wallace Stevens* (1990), pages 193–94.

I: Son

1 Winnicott's statement is in the paper "Anxiety associated with insecurity," on page 98 of *Through Paediatrics to Psycho-analysis* (1958).

2 My investigation of Deaf culture resulted in an article, "Defiantly deaf," *New York Times Magazine*, August 29, 1994.

3 The Cochlear corporation website (http://www.cochlear.com) contains numerous instances of the word *miracle*; see also, for example, Aaron and Nechama Parnes's report from the 2007 Cochlear Celebration, "Celebrating the miracle of the cochlear implant," at http://www.hearingpocket.com/celebration1.shtml. For the other side of the story, see Paddy Ladd, *Understanding Deaf Culture: In Search of Deafhood* (2003), page 415: "In the 1990s, genetic engineering has initiated the process of trying to identify 'the deaf gene,' thus bringing within theoretical reach what might be termed the 'final solution'—that of eradicating Deaf people altogether." Harlan Lane likened attempts to eliminate deafness to attempts to eliminate ethnic groups in Paul Davies, "Deaf culture clash," *Wall Street Journal*, April 25, 2005.

3 For more on the ideal age of implantation for cochlear implants, see Chapter II: Deaf in this book.

4 Studies establishing a heightened risk of abuse for children who do not resemble their fathers include Rebecca Burch and George Gallup, "Perceptions of paternal resemblance predict family violence," *Evolution & Human Behavior* 21, no. 6 (November 2000); and Hongli Li and Lei Chang, "Paternal harsh parenting in relation to paternal versus child characteristics: The moderating effect of paternal resemblance belief," *Acta Psychologica Sinica* 39, no. 3 (2007).

5 The theologian John Polkinghorne reported this interpretation in keeping with what he had learned from Dirac. From page 31 of Polkinghorne, *Science and Theology: An Introduction* (1998): "Ask a quantum entity a particle-like question and you will get a particle-like answer; ask a wave-like question and you will get a wave-like answer."

5 "All I know is what I have words for" comes from part 5.6 of Ludwig Wittgenstein, *Tractatus Logico-Philosophicus* (1922): "Die Grenzen meiner Sprache bedeuten die Grenzen meiner Welt." C. K. Ogden translates the sentence as "The limits of my language mean the limits of my world"; that version occurs on page 149 of Ludwig Wittgenstein, *Tractatus Logico-Philosophicus*, translated by C. K. Ogden (1922).

5 From the entry "apple" in *The Oxford Dictionary of Proverbs*, edited by Jennifer Speake (2009): "The apple never falls far from the tree: Apparently of Eastern origin, it is frequently used to assert the continuity of family characteristics. Cf. 16th cent. Ger. *der Apfel fellt nicht gerne weit vom Baume.*"

6 From the opening of Leo Tolstoy, *Anna Karenina*: "Happy families are all alike; each unhappy family is unhappy in its own way." The line is the first in the book and occurs on page 5 of this edition: Leo Tolstoy, *Anna Karenina*, translated by Constance Garnett (2004).

7 Early development of gay children is discussed on pages 16–21 of Richard C. Friedman, *Male Homosexuality: A Contemporary Psychoanalytic Perspective* (1990).

7 For more information on gender-atypical color preference as a predictor of homosexuality, see Vanessa LoBue and Judy S. DeLoache, "Pretty in pink: The early development of gender-stereotyped colour preferences," *British Journal of Developmental Psychology* 29, no. 3 (September 2011).

10 The unforgettable last line, "Wherever they go, and whatever happens to them on the way, in that enchanted place on the top of the Forest a little boy and his Bear will always be playing," occurs on pages 179–80 of A. A. Milne, *The House at Pooh Corner* (1961).

11 See Amos Kamil, "Prep-school predators: The Horace Mann School's secret history of sexual abuse," *New York Times Magazine*, June 6, 2012.

13 The quotation about "wounded, confused people" is from a Facebook post by Peter Lappin.

14 For more information on surrogate partner therapy, see the website of the International Professional Surrogates Association, http://surrogatetherapy.org/.

15 The gay-damning quotation comes from "The homosexual in America," *Time*, January 21, 1966.

16 Hendrik Hertzberg, "The Narcissus survey," *New Yorker*, January 5, 1998.

16 On December 22, 2011, Michigan governor Rick Snyder signed House Bill 4770 (now Public Act 297 of 2011), the Public Employee Domestic Partner Benefit Restriction Act. The text and legislative history of House Bill 4770 can be found on the website of the Michigan legislature, http://www.legislature.mi.gov/mileg .aspx?page=getobject&objectname=2011-HB-4770.

16 On Uganda, see Josh Kron, "Resentment toward the West bolsters Uganda's anti-gay bill," *New York Times*, February 29, 2012; and Clar Ni Chonghaile, "Uganda anti-gay bill resurrected in parliament," *Guardian*, February 8, 2012; see also, three notes down, reference to Scott Lively.

16 The description of torture and murder of gays in Iraq comes from Matt McAllester, "The hunted," *New York*, October 4, 2009.

17 The *This American Life* episode "81 Words" (at http://www.thisamericanlife.org/radio-archives/episode/204/81-Words) is an absorbing account of the removal of homosexuality from the *Diagnostic and Statistical Manual of Mental Disorders*; see also Ronald Bayer, *Homosexuality and American Psychiatry: The Politics of Diagnosis* (1981).

17 The passage references Scott Lively, *Redeeming the Rainbow: A Christian Response to the "Gay" Agenda* (2009). Scott Lively has recently been sued by a Ugandan gay rights group, who have accused him of fomenting persecution of gays in their country; see Laurie Goodstein, "Ugandan gay rights group sues U.S. evangelist," *New York Times*, March 14, 2012.

17 The response of the surrogate-shopper to Ray Blanchard appears in "Fraternal birth order and the maternal immune hypothesis of male homosexuality," *Hormones & Behavior* 40, no. 2 (September 2001), and is described in Alice Domurat Dreger, "Womb gay," *Hastings Center Bioethics Forum*, December 4, 2008.

17 The debate over Maria Iandolo New's administration of dexamethasone to expectant mothers is chronicled in Shari Roan, "Medical treatment carries possible side effect of limiting homosexuality," *Los Angeles Times*, August 15, 2010.

18 For an example of African-American objections to the language of civil rights being used by gay people, see this statement by North Carolina minister Rev. Patrick Wooden, quoted in David Kaufman, "Tensions between black and gay groups rise anew in advance of anti-gay marriage vote in N.C.," *Atlantic*, May 4, 2012: "African-Americans are appalled that their Civil Rights movement has been co-opted by the so-called Civil Rights movement of the homosexuals. It is an insult, it is angering when LGBT groups say there is no difference between being black and being homosexual."

19 "If you bring forth what is within you . . ." is Saying 70 in Elaine H. Pagels, *Beyond Belief: The Secret Gospel of Thomas* (2003), page 53.

19 Maternal infanticide statistics occur on page 42 of James Alan Fox and Marianne W. Zawitz, "Homicide trends in the United States" (2007), in the chart "Homicide Type by Gender, 1976–2005." See also Steven Pinker, "Why they kill their newborns," *New York Times*, November 2, 1997.

19 Parental rejection of visibly disabled children is discussed on pages 152–54 of Meira Weiss, *Conditional Love: Parents' Attitudes Toward Handicapped Children* (1994). For a dated, albeit useful, review of literature on familial adjustment to severe burn scars in children, see Dale W. Wisely, Frank T. Masur, and Sam B. Morgan, "Psychological aspects of severe burn injuries in children," *Health Psychology* 2, no. 1 (Winter 1983).

19 A recent study from the CDC found that the majority of adopted children have significant health problems and disabilities. The report was put together by Matthew D. Bramlett, Laura F. Radel, and Stephen J. Blumberg and published as "The health and well-being of adopted children," *Pediatrics* 119, suppl. 1 (February 1, 2007).

20 The first occurrence of the term *commercial eugenics* appears to occur in M. MacNaughton, "Ethics and reproduction," *American Journal of Obstetrics & Gynecology* 162, no. 4 (April 1990).

20 See Francis Fukuyama, *Our Posthuman Future: Consequences of the Biotechnology Revolution* (2002).

21 Freud explores the polarities of emotion within love and hate in *The Ego and the Id* (1989).

21 See Matt Ridley, *Nature via Nurture: Genes, Experience, and What Makes Us Human* (2003).

22 The Clarence Darrow quotation comes from his closing argument for the defense in the Leopold-Loeb murder trial, republished in *Famous American Jury Speeches* (1925). From page 1050: "I know that one of two things happened to Richard Loeb; that this terrible crime was inherent in his organism, and came from some ancestor, or that it came through his education and his training after he was born."

22 Statistics on the incidence of disability occur on page 25 of Paul T. Jaeger and Cynthia Ann Bowman, *Understanding Disability: Inclusion, Access, Diversity, and Civil Rights* (2005).

22 The quotation by Tobin Siebers occurs on page 176 of *Disability Theory* (2008).

23 The idea that the most effortful years of dealing with a child with special needs are the first decade of his life, when the situation is still novel and confusing; the second decade, because it is adolescence; and the last decade of the parents' life, when they are old and weak and worry acutely about what will happen to their child after they are gone, is described as the U-shaped stress graph—high at the beginning and at the end. See the discussion by Marsha Mailick Seltzer and her colleagues in their chapter, "Midlife and later life parenting of adult children with mental retardation," in *The Parental Experience in Midlife*, edited by Carol Ryff and Marsha Mailick Seltzer (1996), pages 459–532.

23 The quotation from Simon Olshansky ("Most parents who have a mentally defective child . . .") occurs on page 190 of his paper "Chronic sorrow: A response to having a mentally defective child," *Social Casework* 43, no. 4 (1962).

23 Aaron Antonovsky discusses the "sense of coherence" extensively in *Health, Stress, and Coping* (1980).

23 The quotation from Ann Masten (". . . the ordinariness of the phenomenon") occurs on page 227 of her paper "Ordinary magic: Resilience processes in development," *American Psychologist* 56, no. 3 (March 2001).

24 Parents reported deterioration of their health due to caregiving demands in Bryony A. Beresford, "Resources and strategies: How parents cope with the care of a disabled child," *Journal of Child Psychology & Psychiatry* 35, no. 1 (January 1994).

24 The study finding cellular alteration in longtime caretakers is Elissa Epel et al., "Accelerated telomere shortening in response to life stress," *Proceedings of the National Academy of Sciences* 101, no. 49 (December 2004).

24 The statistic that fathers who described a significant caregiving burden died younger than fathers with a lighter caregiving burden appears on page 204 of *Cognitive Coping, Families and Disability*, edited by Ann P. Turnbull, Joan M. Patterson, and Shirley K. Behr (1993), in Tamar Heller's chapter "Self-efficacy coping, active involvement, and caregiver well-being throughout the life course among families of persons with mental retardation," citing B. Farber, L. Rowitz, and I. DeOllos, "Thrivers and nonsurvivors: Elderly parents of retarded offspring" (1987), paper presented at the annual meeting of the American Association on Mental Deficiency, Detroit.

24 The study in which 94 percent of parent-participants reported that they were

getting along as well as most other people is Douglas A. Abbott and William H. Meredith, "Strengths of parents with retarded children," *Family Relations* 35, no. 3 (July 1986).

24 The quotation about increased marital closeness and empathy occurs in Glenn Affleck and Howard Tennen's chapter, "Cognitive adaptation to adversity: Insights from parents of medically fragile infants," in *Cognitive Coping, Families, and Disability*, edited by Ann P. Turnbull, Joan M. Patterson, and Shirley K. Behr (1993), page 138.

24 The study in which participants overwhelmingly reported positive parenting experiences is Allen G. Sandler and Lisa A. Mistretta, "Positive adaptation in parents of adults with disabilities," *Education & Training in Mental Retardation & Developmental Disabilities* 33, no. 2 (June 1998).

24 Glenn Affleck and Howard Tennen compare optimistic and pessimistic parents in the chapter "Cognitive adaptation to adversity: Insights from parents of medically fragile infants," in *Cognitive Coping, Families, and Disability*, edited by Ann P. Turnbull, Joan M. Patterson, and Shirley K. Behr (1993), page 139.

24 See Miguel de Unamono, *The Tragic Sense of Life in Men and Nations* (1977), page 5: "It is not usually our ideas that make us optimists or pessimists, but our optimism or pessimism—of perhaps physiological or pathological origin, the one as well as the other—that makes our ideas."

24 The comparative happiness study is P. Brickman, D. Coates, and R. Janoff-Bulman, "Lottery winners and accident victims: Is happiness relative?," *Journal of Personal & Social Psychology* 36, no. 8 (August 1978); the subject is the central theme of Daniel Gilbert, *Stumbling on Happiness* (2006).

24 See Martha Nibley Beck, *Expecting Adam: A True Story of Birth, Rebirth and Everyday Magic* (1999).

24 The quotation from Clara Claiborne Park (". . . it is still love") occurs on page 267 of *The Siege* (1967).

25 The quotation from the unnamed mother ("This thought runs like a bright golden thread . . .") comes from page 56 of Mrs. Max A. Murray's 1959 article, "Needs of parents of mentally retarded children," reprinted in *Families and Mental Retardation*, edited by Jan Blacher and Bruce L. Baker (2002).

25 Marty Wyngaarden Krauss and Marsha Mailick Seltzer catalog pitfalls and resources for parents of disabled children in "Coping strategies among older mothers of adults with retardation: A life-span developmental perspective," in *Cognitive Coping, Families, and Disability*, edited by Ann P. Turnbull, Joan M. Patterson, and Shirley K. Behr (1993), page 177.

25 See, for example, Kate Scorgie and Dick Sobsey, "Transformational outcomes associated with parenting children who have disabilities," *Mental Retardation* 38, no. 3 (June 2000).

25 See, for example, Robert M. Hodapp and Diane V. Krasner, "Families of children with disabilities: Findings from a national sample of eighth-grade students," *Exceptionality* 5, no. 2 (1995); Rosalyn Roesel and G. Frank Lawlis, "Divorce in families of genetically handicapped/mentally retarded individuals," *American Journal of Family Therapy* 11, no. 1 (Spring 1983); Lawrence J. Shufeit and Stanley R. Wurster, "Frequency of divorce among parents of handicapped children," ERIC Document Reproduction Service no. ED 113 909 (1975); and Don Risdal and George H. S. Singer, "Marital adjustment in parents of children with disabilities: A historical review and meta-analysis," *Research & Practice for Persons with Severe Disabilities* 29, no. 2 (Summer 2004). Risdal and Singer's meta-study

found that "there is a detectable overall negative impact on marital adjustment, but this impact is small and much lower than would be expected given earlier assumptions about the supposed inevitability of damaging impacts of children with disabilities on family well-being."

25 Dubious professionals abound in Jeanne Ann Summers, Shirley K. Behr, and Ann P. Turnbull, "Positive adaptation and coping strengths of families who have children with disabilities," in *Support for Caregiving Families: Enabling Positive Adaptation to Disability*, edited by George H. S. Singer and Larry K. Irvin (1989), page 29.

25 The quotation from the mother exasperated by her encounters with dubious professionals occurs in Janet Vohs, "On belonging: A place to stand, a gift to give," in *Cognitive Coping, Families, and Disability*, edited by Ann P. Turnbull, Joan M. Patterson, and Shirley K. Behr (1993).

26 For an in-depth exploration of institutionalization in the United States and campaigns to marshal support for families' efforts to care for their disabled children at home, see Joseph P. Shapiro, *No Pity: People with Disabilities Forging a New Civil Rights Movement* (1993).

26 Geraldo Rivera's 1972 investigation of conditions at the Willowbrook State School in Staten Island is included in the DVD video documentary *Unforgotten: Twenty-Five Years After Willowbrook* (2008).

26 The quoted description of conditions at Willowbrook comes from John J. O'Connor, "TV: Willowbrook State School, 'the Big Town's leper colony,'" *New York Times*, February 2, 1972.

26 Russell Barton used the term *mental bedsores* on page 7 of *Institutional Neurosis* (1959).

26 The observation about the "highly restrictive manner" in which many families find themselves living is made by Jan Blacher in "Sequential stages of parental adjustment to the birth of a child with handicaps: Fact or artifact?," *Mental Retardation* 22, no. 2 (April 1984).

27 The care of disabled people in preindustrial society is discussed on pages 2–3 of Lennard Davis, *Enforcing Normalcy: Disability, Deafness, and the Body* (1995).

27 Adolf Hitler is quoted on page 33 of *Exploring Disability: A Sociological Introduction*, edited by Colin Barnes, Geof Mercer, and Tom Shakespeare (1999), citing to M. Burleigh, *Death and Deliverance: Euthanasia in Germany, 1900–1945* (1994).

27 For a discussion of compulsory sterilization in Europe and the United States, see pages 34–35 of Richard Lynn, *Eugenics: A Reassessment* (2001).

27 The "Ugly Law" was Section 36034 of the Chicago Municipal Code (repealed 1974). It is discussed at length in Adrienne Phelps Coco, "Diseased, maimed, mutilated: Categorizations of disability and an ugly law in late nineteenth-century Chicago," *Journal of Social History* 44, no. 1 (Fall 2010).

27 The Jim Crow comparison is expounded by Justice Thurgood Marshall in the 1985 Supreme Court decision *City of Cleburne, Texas v. Cleburne Living Center, Inc.*, in which he states of the mentally ill, "A regime of state-mandated segregation and degradation soon emerged that, in its virulence and bigotry, rivaled, and indeed paralleled, the worst excesses of Jim Crow." The decision can be found in its entirety at http://www.law.cornell.edu/supct/html/historics/ USSC_CR_0473_0432_ZX.html.

27 The quotation from Sharon Snyder and David T. Mitchell occurs on page 72 of *Cultural Locations of Disability* (2006).

27 Figures on educational attainment of disabled children and economic status of

disabled adults rely on the discussion on pages 45–49 of Colin Barnes and Geof Mercer, *Disability* (2003).

28 The Royal College of Obstetricians and Gynaecology's proposal to establish guidelines for euthanasia of severely ill preemies is discussed in Peter Zimonjic, "Church supports baby euthanasia," *Times*, November 12, 2006.

28 The full text of the US Rehabilitation Act of 1973 (29 USC § 701) can be found online at http://www.law.cornell.edu/uscode/text/29/701, and the Americans with Disabilities Act (42 USC § 12101) at http://www.law.cornell.edu/usc-cgi/get_external.cgi?type=pubL&target=101-336.

28 Vice President Biden's speech is described in "Biden praises Special Olympic athletes," *Spokesman-Review*, February 19, 2009.

28 For a scholarly discussion of disability law's shrinking protections, see Samuel R. Bagenstos, "The future of disability law," *Yale Law Journal* 114, no. 1 (October 2004). Note also, for example, the US Supreme Court decision in the case *Toyota Motor Manufacturing v. Williams*, 534 U.S. 184 (2002) (full text at http://www.law.cornell.edu/supct/html/00-1089.ZO.html), which mandated a narrow interpretation of what constitutes "substantial limitation" of "major life activities."

28 Erving Goffman, *Stigma: Notes on the Management of Spoiled Identity* (1986).

28 The quotation from Susan Burch occurs on page 7 of *Signs of Resistance: American Deaf Cultural History, 1900 to World War II* (2004).

28 Michael Oliver's statement "Disability has nothing to do with the body, it is a consequence of social oppression" occurs on page 35 of *Understanding Disability: From Theory to Practice* (1996).

29 Figures on changes in life expectancy over time can be found in Laura B. Shrestha, "Life Expectancy in the United States," Congressional Research Service, 2006.

29 The quotation from Ruth Hubbard about abortion for Huntington's disease occurs on page 93 of her essay "Abortion and disability," in *The Disability Studies Reader*, 2nd ed., edited by Lennard Davis (2006).

29 Philip Kitcher is quoted on page 71 of James C. Wilson's essay "(Re)writing the genetic body-text: Disability, textuality, and the Human Genome Project," in *The Disability Studies Reader*, 2nd ed., edited by Lennard Davis (2006).

29 The quotation from Marsha Saxton occurs on pages 110–11 of her essay "Disability rights and selective abortion," in *The Disability Studies Reader*, 2nd ed., edited by Lennard Davis (2006).

29 The quotation from Sharon Snyder and David T. Mitchell occurs on page 31 of their book, *Cultural Locations of Disability* (2006).

29 William Ruddick discusses the "hospitality view" of women in his article "Ways to limit prenatal testing," in *Prenatal Testing and Disability Rights*, edited by Adrienne Asch and Erik Parens (2000).

29 The quotation from Laura Hershey comes from her article "Choosing disability," *Ms.*, July 1994.

30 The quotation from Ruth Hubbard occurs on page 232 of her article "Eugenics: New tools, old ideas," in *Embryos, Ethics, and Women's Rights: Exploring the New Reproductive Technologies*, edited by Elaine Hoffman Baruch, Amadeo F. D'Adamo, and Joni Seager (1988).

30 For criticism of the Human Genome Project, see Mary Jo Iozzio, "Genetic anomaly or genetic diversity: Thinking in the key of disability on the human genome," *Theological Studies* 66, no. 4 (December 2005); and James C. Wilson, "(Re)writing the genetic body-text: Disability, textuality, and the Human Genome Project," in *The Disability Studies Reader*, 2nd ed., edited by Lennard Davis (2006).

713

30 Donna Haraway refers to the "act of canonization" on page 215 of her *Simians, Cyborgs, and Women: The Reinvention of Nature* (1991).

30 Michel Foucault's reference to "a technology of abnormal individuals" occurs on page 61 of *Abnormal: Lectures at the Collège de France, 1974–1975* (2003); his reference to "physical vigor and the moral cleanliness of the social body" occurs on page 54 of *The History of Sexuality*, vol. 1 (1990); his discussion of error occurs on page 22 of his introduction to Georges Canguilhem, *The Normal and the Pathological* (1991).

30 All of the quotations in this passage come from Deborah Kent, "Somewhere a mockingbird," in *Prenatal Testing and Disability Rights*, edited by Erik Parens and Adrienne Asch (2000), pages 57–63.

32 John Hockenberry's view of "Jerry's kids" occurs on page 36 of *Moving Violations: War Zones, Wheelchairs and Declarations of Independence* (1996).

32 Rod Michalko likens helping to name-calling on page 20 of *The Difference That Disability Makes* (2002).

32 Arlene Mayerson discusses the danger of "benevolence" to the disabled in Nancy Gibbs, "Pillow angel ethics," *Time*, January 7, 2007.

32 Results of the happiness study are reported in David Kahneman et al., "Would you be happier if you were richer? A focusing illusion," *Science* 312, no. 5782 (June 30, 2006).

33 The quotation from Steven R. Smith occurs on page 26 of his paper "Social justice and disability: Competing interpretations of the medical and social models," in *Arguing About Disability: Philosophical Perspectives*, edited by Kristjana Kristiansen, Simo Vehmas, and Tom Shakespeare (2009).

34 For more information on the "pro-ana" and "pro-mia" movement, see Virginia Heffernan, "Narrow-minded," *New York Times*, May 25, 2008.

34 The quotation from Lucy Grealy occurs on page 157 of her *Autobiography of a Face* (1994).

35 See Dylan M. Smith et al., "Happily hopeless: Adaptation to a permanent, but not to a temporary, disability," *Health Psychology* 28, no. 6 (November 2009).

35 The failure-to-diagnose suit is described in Rebecca Allison, "Does a cleft palate justify an abortion?," *Guardian*, December 2, 2003.

35 The quotation from the mother of the child with a cleft palate comes from Barry Nelson, "Born with just a little difference," *Northern Echo*, December 2, 2003.

35 The quotation from Bruce Bauer occurs in Eric Zorn, "At 15, Lauren is coming forward for kids like her," *Chicago Tribune*, April 24, 2003.

35 Chris Wallace is profiled in Chris Dufresne, "Amazing feat," *Los Angeles Times*, October 8, 1997.

36 The quotation from Joanne Green comes from her article "The reality of the miracle: What to expect from the first surgery," *Wide Smiles*, 1996.

36 The passage by Alice Domurat Dreger occurs on pages 55–57 of *One of Us: Conjoined Twins and the Future of Normal* (2004). It has been condensed.

36 The French study finding an inverse relationship between tolerance for disability and socioeconomic status is Annick-Camille Dumaret et al., "Adoption and fostering of babies with Down syndrome: A cohort of 593 cases," *Prenatal Diagnosis* 18, no. 5 (May 1998).

36 The American study finding attitudinal differences toward disability among different socioeconomic strata is Elizabeth Lehr Essex et al., "Residential transitions of adults with mental retardation: Predictors of waiting list use and placement," *American Journal of Mental Retardation* 101, no. 6 (May 1997).

36 Studies on racial and socioeconomic disparities in rates of out-of-home placement of disabled children include the above-cited studies by Dumaret and Essex; Jan Blacher, "Placement and its consequences for families with children who have mental retardation," in *When There's No Place Like Home: Options for Children Living Apart from Their Natural Families*, edited by Jan Blacher (1994); Frances Kaplan Grossman, *Brothers and Sisters of Retarded Children: An Exploratory Study* (1972); Robert Hanneman and Jan Blacher, "Predicting placement in families who have children with severe handicaps: A longitudinal analysis," *American Journal on Mental Retardation* 102, no. 4 (January 1998); and Tamar Heller and Alan Factor, "Permanency planning for adults with mental retardation living with family caregivers," *American Journal on Mental Retardation* 96, no. 2 (September 1991).

37 The quotation from Jim Sinclair (". . . this is what we hear when you pray for a cure . . .") occurs in his 1993 essay, "Don't mourn for us," at http://www .jimsinclair.org/dontmourn.htm.

37 The quotation from Aimee Mullins occurs in Susannah Frankel, "Body beautiful," *Guardian*, August 29, 1998.

37 Bill Shannon is profiled in Bill O'Driscoll, "Turning the tables," *Pittsburgh City Paper*, March 29, 2007.

38 See "Oscar Pistorius hopes to have place at London Olympics," British Broadcasting Corporation, March 17, 2012; "Oscar Pistorius: The 'Blade Runner' who is a race away from changing the Olympics," Associated Press/*Washington Post*, May 16, 2012; and Tim Rohan, "Pistorius will be on South Africa's Olympic team," *New York Times*, July 4, 2012.

39 See Adam Doerr, "The wrongful life debate," *Genomics Law Report*, September 22, 2009.

39 The quotation from the French court decision comes from Wim Weber, "France's highest court recognises 'the right not to be born,'" *Lancet* 358, no. 9297 (December 8, 2001); the aftermath is described in Lynn Eaton, "France outlaws the right to sue for being born," *British Medical Journal* 324, no. 7330 (January 19, 2002).

39 See Adam Doerr, "The wrongful life debate," *Genomics Law Report*, September 22, 2009; Ronen Perry, "It's a wonderful life," *Cornell Law Review* 93 (2008); and the decision in *Turpin v. Sortini*, 31 Cal. 3d 220, 643 P.2d 954 (May 3, 1982); that California Supreme Court case pertained to a suit with the deaf child named as plaintiff. The full text of the decision can be found on the Stanford Law School website, http://scocal.stanford.edu/opinion/turpin-v-sortini-30626.

39 *Curlender v. BioScience Laboratories*, 106 Cal. App. 3d 811, 165 Cal. Rptr. 477 (1980). The decision can be found in its entirety at http://law.justia.com/cases/california/calapp3d/106/811.html.

39 The quotation from the wrongful-life lawsuit brought by the parents of a child with Tay-Sachs occurs in the court decision in *Miller v. HCA, Inc.*, 118 S.W. 3d 758 (Tex. 2003). The decision can be read in its entirety on the website of the Supreme Court of Texas, http://www.supreme.courts.state.tx.us/historical/2003/sep/010079.pdf.

42 The quotation from Nigel Andrews comes from his review "Glowing wonder of an Anatolian epiphany," *Financial Times*, March 15, 2012.

42 The quotation about increased growth and maturity in parents of disabled children comes from Richard P. Hastings et al., "Factors related to positive perceptions in mothers of children with intellectual disabilities," *Journal of Applied Research in Intellectual Disabilities* 15, no. 3 (September 2002).

42 See Kate Scorgie and Dick Sobsey, "Transformational outcomes associated with parenting children who have disabilities," *Mental Retardation* 38, no. 3 (June 2000).

42 The study of mothers who saw advantages in their parenting experience is described on page 138 of *Cognitive Coping, Families, and Disability*, edited by Ann P. Turnbull, Joan M. Patterson, and Shirley K. Behr (1993), in Glenn Affleck and Howard Tennen's chapter, "Cognitive adaptation to adversity: Insights from parents of medically fragile infants."

42 The study comparing developmental outcomes in children of mothers who tried to find meaning in their experience is described on page 135 of *Infants in Crisis: How Parents Cope with Newborn Intensive Care and Its Aftermath*, edited by Glenn Affleck, Howard Tennen, and Jonelle Rowe (1991).

44 The quotation from Tobin Siebers about inclusion occurs on page 183 of *Disability Theory* (2008).

45 The quotation from Roy McDonald comes from Danny Hakim, Thomas Kaplan, and Michael Barbaro, "After backing gay marriage, 4 in G.O.P. face voters' verdict," *New York Times*, July 4, 2011; the quotation from Jared Spurbeck comes from his article "NY senator's grandkids made him realize 'gay is OK,'" *Yahoo! News*, June 26, 2011.

45 Personal communication with Doug Wright.

46 See Ann Whitcher-Gentzke, "Dalai Lama brings message of compassion to UB," *UB Reporter*, September 21, 2006.

47 This Western naïveté about nirvana was explained to me by Robert Thurman in 2006.

47 Jalāl al-Dīn Rūmī (Maulana), *The Essential Rumi* (1995), page 142: "Don't turn away. Keep your gaze on the bandaged place. That's where the light enters you."

II: Deaf

49 "I was planning to write on the Deaf": My article "Defiantly deaf" was published in the *New York Times Magazine*, August 29, 1994.

49 Interactions between protesters and Lexington Center for the Deaf administrators were described in David Firestone, "Deaf students protest new school head," *New York Times*, April 27, 1994.

49 An index of state schools for the deaf in the United States can be found on the Laurent Clerc National Deaf Education Center's website, http://clerccenter .gallaudet.edu/Clerc_Center/Information_and_Resources/Info_to_Go/Resources/ Superintendents_of_Schools_for_the_Deaf_Contact_Information.html.

50 Figures on the percentage of deaf children with hearing parents come from Ross E. Mitchell and Michael A. Karchmer, "Chasing the mythical ten percent: Parental hearing status of deaf and hard of hearing students in the United States," *Sign Language Studies* 4, no. 2 (Winter 2004).

51 See St. Augustine, *Contra Julianum*: "We acknowledge, indeed, how much pertains to our own transgressions: from what source of culpability does it come that innocent ones deserve to be born sometimes blind, sometimes deaf, which defect, indeed, hinders faith itself, by the witness of the Apostle, who says, 'Faith comes by hearing (Rom. X, 17).'" This passage is from *Augustini, Sancti Aurelii, Hipponensis Episcopi Traditio Catholica, Saecula IV–V, Opera Omnia, Tomus Decimus, Contra Julianum, Horesis Pelagianea Defensorum, Liber Tertius, Caput IV–10. Excudebatur et venit apud J. P. Migne editorem*, 1865, cited in Ruth E. Bender, *The*

716

Conquest of Deafness: A History of the Long Struggle to Make Possible Normal Living to Those Handicapped by Lack of Normal Hearing (1970), page 27.

51 Education of deaf children by noble families is the subject of Susan Plann, *A Silent Minority: Deaf Education in Spain, 1550–1835* (1997).

51 The history of the deaf in France and the work of the Abbé de l'Épée is the subject of James R. Knowlson, "The idea of gesture as a universal language in the XVIIth and XVIIIth centuries," *Journal of the History of Ideas* 26, no. 4 (October–December 1965); and Anne T. Quartararo, "The perils of assimilation in modern France: The Deaf community, social status, and educational opportunity, 1815–1870," *Journal of Social History* 29, no. 1 (Autumn 1995).

51 See Phyllis Valentine's chapter "Thomas Hopkins Gallaudet: Benevolent paternalism and the origins of the American Asylum," in *Deaf History Unveiled: Interpretations from the New Scholarship*, edited by John Vickrey Van Cleve (1999), pages 53–73.

51 For a detailed history of the Deaf community on Martha's Vineyard, see Nora Ellen Groce, *Everyone Here Spoke Sign Language: Hereditary Deafness on Martha's Vineyard* (1985).

51 The story of Gallaudet University is told in Brian H. Greenwald and John Vickrey Van Cleve, *A Fair Chance in the Race of Life: The Role of Gallaudet University in Deaf History* (2010).

51 Alexander Graham Bell set forth his proposals in "Memoir upon the formation of a deaf variety of the human race," a paper presented to the National Academy of Sciences on November 13, 1883, and published in the 1884 *Memoirs of the National Academy of Sciences*; and in "Historical notes concerning the teaching of speech to the deaf," *Association Review* 2 (February 1900).

51 Thomas Edison's interest in the oralist movement sprang in part from his experience as a hearing-impaired person. Edison served for a time as a member of the Advisory Board of the Volta Bureau, the organization founded by Alexander Graham Bell to promote education in "speech reading, speech and hearing" to the deaf; see John A. Ferrall's article "Floating on the wings of silence with Beethoven, Kitto, and Edison," *Volta Review* 23 (1921), pages 295–96.

51 Bell and the ascendancy of oralism are discussed in Douglas C. Baynton, *Forbidden Signs: American Culture and the Campaign against Sign Language* (1996); Carol Padden and Tom Humphries, *Inside Deaf Culture* (2005); and John Vickrey Van Cleve, *Deaf History Unveiled: Interpretations from the New Scholarship* (1999).

52 The quotation from George Veditz appears in Carol Padden and Tom Humphries, *Deaf in America: Voices from a Culture* (1988), page 36.

52 Patrick Boudreault is an assistant professor at California State University, Northridge. All quotations from Boudreault come from my interview with him in 2008 and subsequent communications.

52 Aristotle's conclusions about the comparative intelligence of the deaf and the blind were set forth in *The History of Animals* and *On Sense and the Sensible*. Aristotle contended that "of persons destitute from birth of either sense, the blind are more intelligent than the deaf and dumb" because "rational discourse is a cause of instruction in virtue of its being audible." These quotations occur at *Sense and Sensibilia* 437a, 3–17, on page 694 of *The Complete Works of Aristotle: The Revised Oxford Translation*, edited by J. Barnes (1984).

52 William Stokoe's *Sign Language Structure: An Outline of the Visual Communication Systems of the American Deaf* was originally published in 1960 by the University of Buffalo's Department of Anthropology and Linguistics and was reprinted in the *Journal of Deaf Studies & Deaf Education* 10, no. 1 (Winter 2005).

52 Hemispheric lateralization and sign language are discussed by Oliver Sacks in *Seeing Voices: A Journey into the World of the Deaf* (1989), pages 93–111; and in Heather P. Knapp and David P. Corina's chapter, "Cognitive and neural representations of language: Insights from sign languages of the deaf," in Kristin A. Lindgren et al., *Signs and Voices: Deaf Culture, Identity, Language, and Arts* (2008), pages 77–89.

52 The effect of left-hemisphere damage on the ability to produce Sign is the subject of Ursula Bellugi et al., "Language, modality, and the brain," in *Brain Development and Cognition*, edited by M. H. Johnson (1993); and Gregory Hickock, Tracy Love-Geffen, and Edward S. Klima, "Role of the left hemisphere in sign language comprehension," *Brain & Language* 82, no. 2 (August 2002).

52 Studies demonstrating that people who learn Sign in adulthood tend to use the visual part of their brain more include Madeleine Keehner and Susan E. Gathercole, "Cognitive adaptations arising from nonnative experience of sign language in hearing adults," *Memory & Cognition* 35, no 4 (June 2007).

53 The *Peter and the Wolf* study—J. Feijoo, "Le foetus, Pierre et le Loup"—originally appeared in *L'Aube des Sens*, edited by E. Herbinet and M. C. Busnel (1981), and was subsequently cited by Marie-Claire Busnel, Carolyn Granier-Deferre, and Jean-Pierre Lecanuet, "Fetal audition," *Annals of the New York Academy of Sciences* 662, Developmental Psychobiology (October 1992).

Japanese acoustics researchers Yoichi Ando and Hiroaki Hattori described babies' prenatal acclimation to airport noise in "Effects of intense noise during fetal life upon postnatal adaptability," *Journal of the Acoustical Society of America* 47, no. 4, pt. 2 (1970).

53 Newborn language preferences are discussed in Jacques Mehler et al., "A precursor of language acquisition in young infants," *Cognition* 29, no. 2 (July 1988); and Christine Moon, Robin Panneton Cooper, and William P. Fifer, "Two-day-olds prefer their native language," *Infant Behavior and Development* 16, no. 4 (October–December 1993).

53 "Declining non-native phoneme perception" has been a major focus of study by infant psychologist Janet F. Werker of the University of Ottawa; her academic reports on the subject include "Cross-language speech perception: Evidence for perceptual reorganization during the first year of life," *Infant Behavior & Development* 25, no. 1 (January–March 2002); and "Infant-directed speech supports phonetic category learning in English and Japanese," *Cognition* 103, no. 1 (April 2007). A less technical description of her work can be found in her article "Becoming a native listener," *American Scientist* 77, no. 1 (January–February 1989).

53 For information on early language development, see Robert J. Ruben, "A time frame of critical/sensitive periods of language development," *Acta Otolaryngologica* 117, no. 2 (March 1997). Early rapidity in the acquisition of sign language is discussed in John D. Bonvillian et al., "Developmental milestones: Sign language acquisition and motor development," *Child Development* 54, no. 6 (December 1983). Studies on the decline in the brain's ability to acquire language over time include Helen Neville and Daphne Bavelier, "Human brain plasticity: Evidence from sensory deprivation and altered language experience," *Progress in Brain Research* 138 (2002); Aaron J. Newman et al., "A critical period for right hemisphere recruitment in American Sign Language processing," *Nature Neuroscience* 5, no. 1 (January 2002); Rachel I. Mayberry et al., "Age of acquisition effects on the functional organization of language in the adult brain," *Brain &*

Language 119, no. 1 (October 2011); and Nils Skotara et al., "The influence of language deprivation in early childhood on L2 processing: An ERP comparison of deaf native signers and deaf signers with a delayed language acquisition," *BMC Neuroscience* 13, no. 44 (provisionally published May 3, 2012).

53 The deaf man who had no language at all until the age of twenty-seven is the subject of Susan Schaller, *A Man without Words* (1995).

53 The estimate of the incidence of hearing impairment in prisoners comes from Katrina Miller, "Population management strategies for deaf and hard-of-hearing offenders," *Corrections Today* 64, no. 7 (December 2002).

53 The rate of vocabulary acquisition of deaf children of hearing parents is reviewed in Raymond D. Kent, editor, *The MIT Encyclopedia of Communication Disorders* (2004), pages 336–37.

54 The Douglas Baynton quotation ("The difficulty of learning spoken English . . . a soundproof glass cubicle") comes from *Forbidden Signs: American Culture and the Campaign against Sign Language* (1996), page 5.

54 The observation that a mother must "impose herself upon his natural play-learning patterns, often against his will" comes from Eugene D. Mindel and McKay Vernon, *They Grow in Silence: The Deaf Child and His Family* (1971), page 58, as cited in Beryl Lieff Benderly, *Dancing Without Music: Deafness in America* (1990), page 51.

54 All quotations from Jackie Roth occurring in this chapter come from multiple interviews and communications with her since 1994.

54 Although it is often thought that IDEA mandates that children with disabilities be educated with their nondisabled peers, the law actually calls for the education of disabled children in such a way as to "ensure their access to the general curriculum to the maximum extent possible," in the "least restrictive environment" possible. See Sultana Qaisar, "IDEA 1997—'Inclusion is the law,'" paper presented at the Annual Convention of the Council for Exceptional Children, Kansas City, Missouri, April 18–21, 2001; and Perry A. Zirkel, "Does Brown v. Board of Education play a prominent role in special education law?," *Journal of Law & Education* 34, no. 2 (April 2005).

54 Statistics on the decline of residential schools come from Ross E. Mitchell and Michael Karchmer, "Demographics of deaf education: More students in more places," *American Annals of the Deaf* 151, no. 2 (2006).

54 Judith Heumann declared that separate education for deaf students was "immoral" in her article "Oberti decision is core of the ED's inclusion position," *Special Educator*, November 2, 1993, page 8, as cited in Jean B. Crockett and James M. Kaufmann, *The Least Restrictive Environment: Its Origins and Interpretations in Special Education* (1999), page 21.

55 Justice Rehnquist's words occur in *Board of Education v. Rowley*, 458 U.S. 176 (1982); the full text of the decision can be found at http://www.law.cornell.edu/supremecourt/text/458/176.

55 Statistics on high school completion, college attendance, and earnings potential of deaf children and young adults come from Bonnie Poitras Tucker, "Deaf culture, cochlear implants, and elective disability," *Hastings Center Report* 28, no. 4 (July 1, 1998).

55 Studies finding superior performance of deaf children of deaf parents compared to deaf children of hearing parents include E. Ross Stuckless and Jack W. Birch, "The influence of early manual communication on the linguistic development of deaf children," *American Annals of the Deaf* 142, no. 3 (July 1997); Kenneth E.

Brasel and Stephen P. Quigley, "Influence of certain language and communication environments in early childhood on the development of language in Deaf individuals," *Journal of Speech & Hearing Research* 20, no. 1 (March 1977); and Kathryn P. Meadow, "Early manual communication in relation to the deaf child's intellectual, social, and communicative functioning," *Journal of Deaf Studies & Deaf Education* 10, no. 4 (July 2005).

55 Helen Keller's observation is famous, but it may also be apocryphal. According to the tireless research librarians at Gallaudet University, this sentence appears to represent a distillation of sentiments expressed in two published sources. See Tom Harrington, "FAQ: Helen Keller Quotes," Gallaudet University Library, 2000, http://www.gallaudet.edu/library/research_help/research_help/frequently_asked_questions/people/helen_keller_quotes.html.

55 The quotation from Lennard Davis appears in *My Sense of Silence: Memoirs of a Childhood with Deafness* (2000), pages 6–8. It has been condensed. "To this day if I sign 'milk,' I feel more milky than if I say the word" occurs on page 6; the rest of the passage occurs two pages later.

56 Figures on the incidence of deafness come from "Quick statistics" on the website of the National Institute on Deafness and Other Communication Disorders, http://www.nidcd.nih.gov/health/statistics/quick.htm.

56 The quotation from Carol Padden and Tom Humphries ("Culture provides a way for Deaf people to reimagine themselves . . .") appears in *Inside Deaf Culture* (2005), page 161.

56 The Gallaudet protests were extensively covered by the mass media; one representative article is Lena Williams, "College for deaf is shut by protest over president," *New York Times*, March 8, 1988. The Deaf President Now! story has since been told in depth in Jack Gannon, *The Week the World Heard Gallaudet* (1989); Katherine A. Jankowski, *Deaf Empowerment: Emergence, Struggle, and Rhetoric* (1997); and John B. Christiansen and Sharon N. Barnartt, *Deaf President Now!: The 1988 Revolution at Gallaudet University* (2003).

57 Gould's resignation was described in David Firestone, "Chief executive to step down at deaf center," *New York Times*, June 22, 1994.

60 This passage is based on my interview with Lewis Merkin in 1994 and subsequent personal communications.

60 All quotations by MJ Bienvenu come from my interviews with her in 1994 and subsequent communications.

60 For more information on the genes and epigenetic influences that contribute to deafness, see Lilach M. Friedman and Karen B. Avraham, "MicroRNAs and epigenetic regulation in the mammalian inner ear: Implications for deafness," *Mammalian Genome* 20, no. 9–10 (September–October 2009); and A. Eliot Shearer et al., "Deafness in the genomics era," *Hearing Research* 282, nos. 1–2 (December 2011).

60 Information on the genetics of deafness can be found in Kathleen S. Arnos and Pandya Arti's chapter, "Advances in the genetics of deafness," in *Oxford Handbook of Deaf Studies, Language, and Education*, edited by Marc Marschark and Patricia Elizabeth Spencer (2003); Mustafa Tekin, Kathleen S. Arnos, and Arti Pandya, "Advances in hereditary deafness," *Lancet* 358 (September 29, 2001); and W. Virginia Norris et al., "Does universal newborn hearing screening identify all children with GJB2 (Connexin 26) deafness?: Penetrance of GJB2 deafness," *Ear & Hearing* 27, no. 6 (December 2006). Also useful are two recent review articles on the practical applications of genetic research: Marina Di Domenico

et al., "Towards gene therapy for deafness," *Journal of Cellular Physiology* 226, no. 10 (October 2011); and Guy P. Richardson, Jacques Boutet de Monvel, and Christine Petit, "How the genetics of deafness illuminates auditory physiology," *Annual Review of Physiology* 73 (March 2011).

61 Connexin 26 mutations on GJB2 were first reported in David P. Kelsell et al., "Connexin 26 mutations in hereditary non-syndromic sensorineural deafness," *Nature* 357, no. 6628 (1997).

61 Syndromal forms of deafness include Usher syndrome, Pendred syndrome, and Waardenburg syndrome; information on all three can be found on the website of the National Institute on Deafness and Other Communication Disorders, http://www.nidcd.nih.gov/health/hearing/Pages/Default.aspx.

61 For authoritative background reading on gap junctions and their role in deafness, see Regina Nickel and Andrew Forge's entry in the *Encyclopedia of Life Sciences* (*ELS*), "Gap junctions and connexins: The molecular genetics of deafness" (2010); and H.-B. Zhao et al., "Gap junctions and cochlear homeostasis," *Journal of Membrane Biology* 209, nos. 2–3 (May 2006).

61 Increases in deafness due to assortative mating are discussed in Kathleen S. Arnos et al., "A comparative analysis of the genetic epidemiology of deafness in the United States in two sets of pedigrees collected more than a century apart," *American Journal of Human Genetics* 83, no. 2 (August 2008); and Walter J. Nance and Michael J. Kearsey, "Relevance of connexin deafness (DFNB1) to human evolution," *American Journal of Human Genetics* 74, no. 6 (June 2004).

61 The Hittites are mentioned in the article by Arnos cited above. An additional, more detailed source is M. Miles, "Hittite deaf men in the 13th century B.C." (2008). Descendants of the Hittites in modern Anatolia continue to possess the 35delG mutation; see Mustafa Tekin, "Genomic architecture of deafness in Turkey reflects its rich past," *International Journal of Modern Anthropology* 2 (2009).

61 The quotation from Nancy Bloch about the discovery of the GJB2 gene appears in Denise Grady, "Gene identified as major cause of deafness in Ashkenazi Jews," *New York Times*, November 19, 1998.

61 The quotation from Humphrey-Dirksen Bauman ("The question of what lives are worth living . . .") comes from *Open Your Eyes: Deaf Studies Talking* (2008), page 14.

61 All quotations from Christina Palmer come from my interview with her in 2008 and subsequent personal communications.

62 The Whorf-Sapir hypothesis was originally proposed by Benjamin Lee Whorf, whose writings have been anthologized in *Language, Thought, and Reality: Selected Writings of Benjamin Lee Whorf* (1956). Chris Swoyer, "The linguistic relativity hypothesis" in *The Stanford Encyclopedia of Philosophy* (2003) provides a convenient summary.

62 I met and interviewed William Stokoe in 1994.

62 The MJ Bienvenu quotation ("We do not want or need to become hearing . . .") comes from her article "Can Deaf people survive 'deafness'?" in *Deaf World: A Historical Reader and Primary Sourcebook*, edited by Lois Bragg (2001), page 318.

62 The Barbara Kannapell quotation ("I believe 'my language is me . . .'") comes from her article "Personal awareness and advocacy in the Deaf community," in *Sign Language and the Deaf Community: Essays in Honor of William C. Stokoe*, edited by Charlotte Baker and Robbin Battison (1980), pages 106–16.

62 The quotation from Carol Padden and Tom Humphries ("Deaf people's bodies have been labeled . . .") comes from *Inside Deaf Culture* (2005), page 6.

62 Edgar L. Lowell's "shepherd/wolf" statement is quoted in Beryl Lieff Benderly, *Dancing without Music: Deafness in America* (1990), page 4.

62 Tom Bertling's "baby talk" reference appears in *A Child Sacrificed to the Deaf Culture* (1994), page 84.

63 Beryl Lieff Benderly's "holy war" comment occurs in *Dancing without Music: Deafness in America* (1990), page xi.

63 The exhibit *History Through Deaf Eyes* is described in Jean Lindquist Bergey and Jack R. Gannon, "Creating a national exhibition on deaf life," *Curator* 41, no. 2 (June 1998); Douglas Baynton, Jack R. Gannon, and Jean Lindquist Bergey, *Through Deaf Eyes: A Photographic History of an American Community* (2001); and "Groundbreaking exhibition charts 'History Through Deaf Eyes,'" *USA Today*, February 2006.

The quotation from Kristen Harmon (now a professor of English at Gallaudet University) comes from her paper "I thought there would be more Helen Keller: History through Deaf eyes and narratives of representation," in *Signs and Voices: Deaf Culture, Identity, Language, and Arts*, edited by Kristin A. Lindgren et al. (2008). It has been condensed.

63 An example of advocacy for the adoption of deaf children by deaf adults can be found in Barbara J. Wheeler, "This child is mine: Deaf parents and their adopted deaf children," in *Deaf World: A Historical Reader and Primary Sourcebook*, edited by Lois Bragg (2001).

63 The quotation about the Moonies is from Edward Dolnick, "Deafness as culture," *Atlantic Monthly*, September 1993.

63 Heppner is quoted in Edward Dolnick, "Deafness as culture," *Atlantic Monthly*, September 1993.

63 The "four stages of deaf identity" were originally enumerated in Neil S. Glickman, "The development of culturally deaf identities," in *Culturally Affirmative Psychotherapy with Deaf Persons*, edited by Neil S. Glickman and M. A. Harvey (1996), as cited in Irene Leigh's chapter, "Who am I?: Deaf identity issues," in *Signs and Voices: Deaf Culture, Identity, Language, and Arts*, edited by Kristin A. Lindgren et al. (2008), pages 25–26.

63 This passage is based on my interviews with Caro Wilson in 2007 and subsequent personal communications.

68 Kristen L. Johnson's dissertation, "Ideology and Practice of Deaf Goodbyes," earned her a PhD from the UCLA Department of Anthropology in 1994. She is currently affiliated with the English Department at Ohio State University.

69 For more information on Bi-Bi education, see Carol LaSasso and Jana Lollis, "Survey of residential and day schools for deaf students in the United States that identify themselves as bilingual-bicultural programs," *Journal of Deaf Studies & Deaf Education* 8, no. 1 (January 2003); and *The Oxford Handbook of Deaf Studies, Language and Education*, edited by Marc Marschark and Patricia Elizabeth Spencer (2003), page 45. A useful resource page for the layperson, "Bilingual bicultural deaf education," can be found on the Rochester Institute of Technology website, http://library.rit.edu/guides/deaf-studies/education/bilingual-bicultural-deaf-education.html.

70 The quotation from Harlan Lane ("The dilemma is that deaf people want access . . .") comes from his article "Do deaf people have a disability?," *Sign Language Studies* 2, no. 4 (Summer 2002), page 375.

70 This passage is based on my interview with Bridget O'Hara in 2010 and subsequent personal communications. Her name and all others in this passage are pseudonyms. Some other identifying details have been changed.

74 The story of the abuse of Catholic boarding-school students in Wisconsin was originally reported by Laurie Goodstein in "Vatican declined to defrock U.S. priest who abused boys," *New York Times*, March 25, 2010; the quotation comes from Goodstein's follow-up article, "For years, deaf boys tried to tell of priest's abuse," *New York Times*, March 27, 2010.

74 The show about sexual abuse in the Deaf community is Terrylene Sacchetti, *In the Now*; it was performed at Deaf Women United and subsequently on a thirty-six-city tour.

74 This passage is based on my interviews with Megan Williams, Michael Shamberg, and Jacob Shamberg in 2008 and subsequent interviews and personal communications. I note in the interests of full disclosure that I employed Jacob to assist me with research for this chapter.

79 This passage is based on my interview with Chris and Barb Montan in 2008 and subsequent personal communications.

82 Writings representing the anti-oralist pole include Humphrey-Dirksen Bauman, "Audism: Exploring the metaphysics of oppression," *Journal of Deaf Studies & Deaf Education* 9, no. 2 (Spring 2004); and Paddy Ladd, *Understanding Deaf Culture: In Search of Deafhood* (2003).

Articles critical of their perspective include two by Jane K. Fernandes and Shirley Shultz Myers: "Inclusive Deaf studies: Barriers and pathways," *Journal of Deaf Studies & Deaf Education* 15, no. 1 (Winter 2010); and "Deaf studies: A critique of the predominant U.S. theoretical direction," *Journal of Deaf Studies & Deaf Education* 15, no. 1 (Winter 2010).

82 Total Communication is described in *Hearing, Mother Father Deaf*, edited by Michele Bishop and Sherry L. Hicks, (2009); and Larry Hawkins and Judy Brawner, "Educating children who are deaf or hard of hearing: Total Communication," *ERIC Digest* 559 (1997). Signed Exact English is the subject of Diane Corcoran Nielsen et al., "The importance of morphemic awareness to reading achievement and the potential of signing morphemes to supporting reading development," *Journal of Deaf Studies & Deaf Education* 16, no. 3 (Summer 2011). On Simultaneous Communication, see Nicholas Schiavetti et al., "The effects of Simultaneous Communication on production and perception of speech," *Journal of Deaf Studies & Deaf Education* 9, no. 3 (June 2004); and Stephanie Tevenal and Miako Villanueva, "Are you getting the message? The effects of SimCom on the message received by deaf, hard of hearing, and hearing students," *Sign Language Studies* 9, no. 3 (Spring 2009). For a comparison of ASL grammar and that of spoken languages, see Ronnie B. Wilbur, "What does the study of signed languages tell us about 'language'?," *Sign Language & Linguistics* 9, nos. 1–2 (2006).

82 Interview with Gary Mowl in 1994.

83 The anecdote about Benjamin Bahan is told in the 2007 film *Through Deaf Eyes* (2007), at 59.19–1.00.24.

83 For a useful resource in this area, see Tom Harrington and Sarah Hamrick, "FAQ: Sign languages of the world by country," on the Gallaudet University website, http://library.gallaudet.edu/Library/Deaf_Research_Help/Frequently_Asked_Questions_%28FAQs%29/Sign_Language/Sign_Languages_of_the_World_by_Country.html.

83 Interview with Clark Denmark in 1994.

83 These sign languages are discussed in Humphrey-Dirksen Bauman, *Open Your Eyes: Deaf Studies Talking* (2008), page 16.

83 Bengkala is the focus of I Gede Marsaja, *Desa Kolok: A Deaf Village and Its Sign Language in Bali, Indonesia* (2008). The first report in the medical literature of the strain of deafness prevalent there is S. Winata et al., "Congenital non-syndromal autosomal recessive deafness in Bengkala, an isolated Balinese village," *Journal of Medical Genetics* 32 (1995). For a general, accessible discussion of syndromic deafness within endogamous communities, see John Travis, "Genes of silence: Scientists track down a slew of mutated genes that cause deafness," *Science News*, January 17, 1998. Additionally, for an opinionated overview of the academic research on the subject, see Annelies Kusters, "Deaf utopias? Reviewing the sociocultural literature on the world's 'Martha's Vineyard situations,'" *Journal of Deaf Studies & Deaf Education* 15, no. 1 (January 2010).

84 These complex webs of relations are the subject of Hildred and Clifford Geertz's oft-cited *Kinship in Bali* (1975).

87 This passage is based on my interviews with Apryl and Raj Chauhan in 2008 and thereafter, and personal communications.

89 Volta originally disclosed the findings of his 1790 experiment to the greater scientific community in a presentation to the Royal Society, "On the electricity excited by the mere contact of conducting substances of different kinds," *Philosophical Transactions of the Royal Society* 90 (1800).

90 Useful general references on the history of cochlear implants include Huw Cooper and Louise Craddock, *Cochlear Implants: A Practical Guide* (2006); the Deafness Research Foundation's "Cochlear implant timeline" at http://www .drf.org/cochlear+timeline; and National Institute on Deafness and Other Communication Disorders, "Cochlear implants" (last updated March 2011), http://www.nidcd.nih.gov/health/hearing/coch.asp. Fan-Gang Zeng et al., "Cochlear implants: System design, integration and evaluation," *IEEE Review of Biomedical Engineering* 1, no. 1 (January 2008), is a recent scholarly review of the state of the science. For discussions of the ethical controversy surrounding implantation, see John B. Christiansen and Irene W. Leigh, *Cochlear Implants in Children: Ethics and Choices* (2002); and Linda R. Komesaroff, *Surgical Consent: Bioethics and Cochlear Implantation* (2007).

90 Figures on the numbers of individuals who have received cochlear implants come from the above-cited National Institute on Deafness and Other Communication Disorders fact sheet on cochlear implants, at http://www.nidcd.nih.gov/health/ hearing/coch.asp; and from Irene W. Leigh et al., "Correlates of psychosocial adjustment in deaf adolescents with and without cochlear implants: A preliminary investigation," *Journal of Deaf Studies & Deaf Education* 14, no. 2 (Spring 2009).

90 Statistics on the proportion of severely hearing-impaired children under the age of three who receive implants come from Kate A. Belzner and Brenda C. Seal, "Children with cochlear implants: A review of demographics and communication outcomes," *American Annals of the Deaf* 154, no. 3 (Summer 2009).

90 Figures on racial and socioeconomic disparity in the distribution of implants come from John B. Christiansen and Irene W. Leigh, *Cochlear Implants in Children: Ethics and Choices* (2002), page 328.

90 Cochlear's CEO made the remark about the as yet untapped market for implants in an interview with Bruce Einhorn, "Listen: The sound of hope," *BusinessWeek*, November 14, 2005.

91 Lorry G. Rubin and Blake Papsin, "Cochlear implants in children: Surgical site infections and prevention and treatment of acute otitis media and meningitis," *Pediatrics* 126, no. 2 (August 2010), indicates that postoperative surgical site

infections occur in up to 12 percent of patients receiving cochlear implants; other complications include acute otitis media and bacterial meningitis. See also Kevin D. Brown et al., "Incidence and indications for revision cochlear implant surgery in adults and children," *Laryngoscope* 119, no. 1 (January 2009): "The revision rate was 7.3% for children and 3.8% for adults." Also, Daniel M. Zeitler, Cameron L. Budenz, and John Thomas Roland Jr., "Revision cochlear implantation," *Current Opinion in Otolaryngology & Head & Neck Surgery* 17, no. 5 (October 2009): "A small but significant percentage (3–8%) of all cochlear implant procedures requires RCI surgery. The most common indication for RCI is hard failure (40–80%), but other common indications include soft failures, wound complications, infection, improper initial placement, and electrode extrusions."

91   The R2-D2 comment is from personal communication.

91   The source of the anecdote about the woman who received a cochlear implant in early adulthood is Abram Katz, "The bionic ear: Cochlear implants: Miracle or an attack on 'deaf culture'?" *New Haven Register*, March 18, 2007.

91   HHS's position on hearing screening for newborns can be found in the National Institute on Deafness and Other Communication Disorders fact sheet "Newborn hearing screening" (last updated February 14, 2011), at http://report.nih.gov/NIHfactsheets/ViewFactSheet.aspx?csid=104.

91   From the National Association of the Deaf's organizational history timeline (http://www.nad.org/nad-history):
     "1999 . . . The NAD successfully co-drafts and pushes for passage of the Walsh Bill (Newborn and Infant Hearing Screening and Intervention Act of 1999)."
     "2003 . . . Newborn and infant hearing screening hits 90%, as an outcome of NAD advocacy efforts."

91   The Australian study demonstrating improvement for children implanted before their first birthday is Shani J. Dettman et al., "Communication development in children who receive the cochlear implant under 12 months," *Ear & Hearing* 28, no. 2 (April 2007).

91   The study finding less progress in development of spoken language by children implanted at the age of four than in those implanted at two is Ann E. Geers, "Speech, language, and reading skills after early cochlear implantation," *Archives of Otolaryngology—Head & Neck Surgery* 130, no. 5 (May 2004).

91   The impact of cochlear implants upon brain plasticity is discussed in James B. Fallon et al., "Cochlear implants and brain plasticity," *Hearing Research* 238, nos. 1–2 (April 2008); and Kevin M. J. Green et al., "Cortical plasticity in the first year after cochlear implantation," *Cochlear Implants International* 9, no. 2 (2008).

92   Recent studies on adolescents implanted as children include Alexandra White et al., "Cochlear implants: The young people's perspective," *Journal of Deaf Studies & Deaf Education* 12, no. 3 (Summer 2007); Lisa S. Davidson et al., "Cochlear implant characteristics and speech perception skills of adolescents with long-term device use," *Otology & Neurology* 31, no. 8 (October 2010); Elena Arisi et al., "Cochlear implantation in adolescents with prelinguistic deafness," *Otolaryngology—Head & Neck Surgery* 142, no. 6 (June 2010); and Mirette B. Habib et al., "Speech production intelligibility of early implanted pediatric cochlear implant users," *International Journal of Pediatric Otorhinolaryngology* 74, no. 8 (August 2010).

92   The study of open speech discrimination in children receiving cochlear implants was conducted by Susan B. Waltzman et al., "Open-set speech perception in congenitally deaf children using cochlear implants," *American Journal of Otology* 18, no. 3 (1997), as cited by Bonnie Poitras Tucker in "Deaf culture, cochlear

implants, and elective disability," *Hastings Center Report* 28, no. 4 (July 1, 1998). A 2004 study had similar findings: Marie-Noëlle Calmels et al., "Speech perception and speech intelligibility in children after cochlear implantation," *International Journal of Pediatric Otorhinolaryngology* 68, no. 3 (March 2004).

92   The survey of parents' perceptions of their implanted children's hearing and verbal comprehension was conducted by Gallaudet Research Institute, *Regional and National Summary Report of Data from the 1999–2000 Annual Survey of Deaf and Hard of Hearing Children and Youth* (2001).

92   The review concluding that implants offer only coarse and degraded versions of sound, and that children with the implant perceive fewer fine distinctions of spoken language than their peers can be found in *Oxford Handbook of Deaf Studies, Language and Education* (2003), page 435.

92   In its brochures "The Reason to Choose AB" and "Hear Your Best," Advanced Bionics prominently quotes from Michael Chorost, author of *Rebuilt: My Journey Back to the Hearing World* (2006): "The Bionic Ear appeared to offer more potential for being upgraded in the future as new and better coding strategies and software became available so that I could conceivably have more and better hearing."

92   Interview with Robert Ruben, 1994.

92   Degrees of deafness and ways of classifying hearing loss are delineated in Richard J. H. Smith et al., "Deafness and hereditary hearing loss overview," *GeneReviews*™ (1999–2012), at http://www.ncbi.nlm.nih.gov/books/NBK1434/.

93   Although NAD's 1993 position paper condemning "invasive surgery on defenseless children" does not appear to have been published on the NAD website, the full text is archived on an Israeli website at http://www.zak.co.il/d/deaf-info/old/ci-opinions.

93   The modification of NAD's position regarding cochlear implants was voted at the NAD's Board of Directors meeting held October 6–7, 2000; see National Association of the Deaf, "NAD position statement on cochlear implants," October 6, 2000. Additional resources on the debate within the Deaf community about cochlear implants: Marie Arana-Ward, "As technology advances, a bitter debate divides the deaf," *Washington Post*, May 11, 1997; Felicity Barringer, "Pride in a soundless world: Deaf oppose a hearing aid," *New York Times*, May 16, 1993; and Brad Byrom, "Deaf culture under siege," *H-Net Reviews*, March 2003.

93   Christina Palmer made this statement directly to me. The "deaf ethnicity hypothesis" is the subject of Richard Clark Eckert, "Toward a theory of deaf ethnos: Deafnicity ≈ D/deaf (Hómaemon • Homóglosson • Homóthreskon)," *Journal of Deaf Studies & Deaf Education* 15, no. 4 (Fall 2010).

93   This passage is based on my interview with Dan, Nancy, and Emma Hessey in 2007 and subsequent communications.

97   Figures for the cost of cochlear implantation come from the Alexander Graham Bell Association's FAQ "The cost of cochlear implants," at http://nc.agbell.org/page.aspx?pid=723. Others estimate the total cost at $50,000 to $100,000; see the University of Miami School of Medicine's "Costs associated with cochlear implants," at http://cochlearimplants.med.miami.edu/implants/08_Costs%20Associated%20with%20Cochlear%20Implants.asp.

97   Figures on cost savings attributable to cochlear implantation come from two studies: André K. Cheng et al., "Cost-utility analysis of the cochlear implant in children," *Journal of the American Medical Association* 274, no. 7 (August 16, 2000); and Jeffrey P. Harris et al., "An outcomes study of cochlear implants in

deaf patients: Audiologic, economic, and quality-of-life changes," *Archives of Otolaryngology—Head & Neck Surgery* 121, no. 4 (April 1995).

97 The quotation from the first mother ("If your child needs glasses . . .") comes from the article "Implants help child emerge from silent world," Associated Press/*Casper Star-Tribune*, April 24, 2006; the second ("If at 20 . . .") comes from Anita Manning, "The changing deaf culture," *USA Today*, May 2, 2000.

97 This passage is based on my interview with Bob Osbrink in 2008 and subsequent communications.

99 The quotation from Rory comes from Arthur Allen, "Sound and fury," *Salon*, May 24, 2000.

100 Teresa Blankmeyer Burke's statement occurs in her essay "Bioethics and the deaf community," in *Signs and Voices: Deaf Culture, Identity, Language, and Arts*, edited by Kristin A. Lindgren et al. (2008), pages 69–70.

100 Paula Garfield and Tomato Lichy describe their feelings about having a deaf daughter in Rebecca Atkinson, "'I hoped our baby would be deaf,'" *Guardian*, March 21, 2006.

101 This passage is based on my interview with Felix, Rachel, and Sharon Feldman in 2008 and subsequent personal communications. All names in this passage are pseudonyms.

103 Harlan Lane likens cochlear implantation to genital surgery on infants with intersex conditions in his paper "Ethnicity, ethics and the deaf-world," *Journal of Deaf Studies & Deaf Education* 10, no. 3 (Summer 2005).

103 See Paddy Ladd, *Understanding Deaf Culture: In Search of Deafhood* (2003), page 415: "In the 1990s, genetic engineering has initiated the process of trying to identify 'the deaf gene,' thus bringing within theoretical reach what might be termed the 'final solution'—that of eradicating Deaf people altogether."

103 Harlan Lane likened attempts to eliminate deafness to attempts to eliminate ethnic groups in Paul Davies, "Deaf culture clash," *Wall Street Journal*, April 25, 2005.

103 John B. Christiansen and Irene W. Leigh report that only half of the parents they surveyed had communicated with deaf adults prior to a decision to implant their children, and that some of those who did were met with hostility for even considering the procedure; see their paper "Children with cochlear implants: Changing parent and deaf community perspectives," *Archives of Otolaryngology—Head & Neck Surgery* 130, no. 5 (May 2004).

103 Gunilla Preisler discusses the Swedish practice of requiring parents of deaf children to learn about deafness from Deaf people in "The psychosocial development of deaf children with cochlear implants," in *Surgical Consent: Bioethics and Cochlear Implantation*, edited by Linda Komesaroff (2007), pages 120–36.

104 Studies describing both the social gains and difficulties faced by young people with cochlear implants include Yael Bat-Chava, Daniela Martin, and Joseph G. Kosciw, "Longitudinal improvements in communication and socialization of deaf children with cochlear implants and hearing aids: Evidence from parental reports," *Journal of Child Psychology & Psychiatry* 46, no. 12 (December 2005); Daniela Martin et al., "Peer relationships of deaf children with cochlear implants: Predictors of peer entry and peer interaction success," *Journal of Deaf Studies & Deaf Education* 16, no. 1 (January 2011); and Renée Punch and Merv Hyde, "Social participation of children and adolescents with cochlear implants: A qualitative analysis of parent, teacher, and child interviews," *Journal of Deaf Studies & Deaf Education* 16, no. 4 (2011).

104 J. William Evans used the phrase *culturally homeless* in "Thoughts on the psychosocial implications of cochlear implantation in children," in *Cochlear Implants in Young Deaf Children*, edited by E. Owens and D. Kessler (1989), page 312, as cited in Harlan Lane, "Cultural and infirmity models of deaf Americans," *Journal of the American Academy of Rehabilitative Audiology* 23 (1990), page 22.

104 References to physical enhancement as "cyborg" occur in Brenda Jo Brueggemann, "Think-between: A deaf studies commonplace book," in *Open Your Eyes: Deaf Studies Talking*, edited by Humphrey-Dirksen Bauman (2008), page 182.

104 The study in which two-thirds of parent-participants reported no resistance by their children to using implants was conducted at the Gallaudet Research Institute and reported in John B. Christiansen and Irene W. Leigh, *Cochlear Implants in Children: Ethics and Choices* (2002), page 168.

104 This passage is based on my interview with Barbara Matusky in 2008 and subsequent communications.

107 Kathryn Woodcock expressed her dissatisfaction with the disapproval of many in the Deaf community of the use of speech and hearing by other Deaf people in "Cochlear implants vs. Deaf culture?" in *Deaf World: A Historical Reader and Primary Sourcebook*, edited by Lois Bragg (2001), page 327.

107 The quotation from Irene Leigh comes from *A Lens on Deaf Identities* (2009), page 21.

107 Quotations from Josh Swiller occur on pages 14–15 and 100–101 of *The Unheard: A Memoir of Deafness and Africa* (2007). His personal website is at http://joshswiller.com. See also Jane Brody's interview with Swiller, "Cochlear implant supports an author's active life," *New York Times*, February 26, 2008.

108 The first paper documenting the finding that sharks regenerate receptive hair cells is Jeffrey T. Corwin, "Postembryonic production and aging in inner ear hair cells in sharks," *Journal of Comparative Neurology* 201, no. 4 (October 1981). Further research is reported by Corwin in "Postembryonic growth of the macula neglecta auditory detector in the ray, *Raja clavata*: Continual increases in hair cell number, neural convergence, and physiological sensitivity," *Journal of Comparative Neurology* 217, no. 3 (July 1983); and in "Perpetual production of hair cells and maturational changes in hair cell ultrastructure accompany postembryonic growth in an amphibian ear," *Proceedings of the National Academy of Science* 82, no. 11 (June 1985).

108 Regeneration of cochlear hair cells in birds was first reported in Douglas A. Cotanche, "Regeneration of hair cell stereociliary bundles in the chick cochlea following severe acoustic trauma," *Hearing Research* 30, nos. 2–3 (1987).

108 Early experiments with the use of retinoic acid to stimulate hair cell regeneration are described in M. W. Kelley et al., "The developing organ of Corti contains retinoic acid and forms supernumerary hair cells in response to exogenous retinoic acid in culture," *Development* 119, no. 4 (December 1993). Retinoic acid and calf serum were administered to rats by Philippe P. Lefebvre et al., "Retinoic acid stimulates regeneration of mammalian auditory hair cells," *Science* 260, no. 108 (April 30, 1993).

108 For an example of work by Staecker's group, see Mark Praetorius et al., "Adenovector-mediated hair cell regeneration is affected by promoter type," *Acta Otolaryngologica* 130, no. 2 (February 2010).

109 Further research on the cultivation of auditory hair cells and their introduction into living organisms is reported in Huawei Li et al., "Generation of hair cells by stepwise differentiation of embryonic stem cells," *Proceedings of the National*

Academy of Sciences 100, no. 23 (November 11, 2003); and Wei Chen et al., "Human fetal auditory stem cells can be expanded in vitro and differentiate into functional auditory neurons and hair cell-like cells," *Stem Cells* 2, no. 5 (May 2009). For a general review on the state of research into hair cell regeneration, see John V. Brigande and Stefan Heller, "Quo vadis, hair cell regeneration?," *Nature Neuroscience* 12, no. 6 (June 2009).

109 Exploring potential gene therapies to promote the growth of auditory hair cells: Samuel P. Gubbels et al., "Functional auditory hair cells produced in the mammalian cochlea by in utero gene transfer," *Nature* 455, no. 7212 (August 27, 2008); and Kohei Kawamoto et al., "Math1 gene transfer generates new cochlear hair cells in mature guinea pigs in vivo," *Journal of Neuroscience* 23, no. 11 (June 2003).

109 The ATOH1 gene figures large in Shinichi Someya et al., "Age-related hearing loss in C57BL/6J mice is mediated by Bak-dependent mitochondrial apoptosis," *Proceedings of the National Academy of Sciences* 106, no. 46 (November 17, 2009).

109 The transduction channel is the focus of Math P. Cuajungco, Christian Grimm, and Stefan Heller, "TRP channels as candidates for hearing and balance abnormalities in vertebrates," *Biochimica et Biophysica Acta (BBA)—Molecular Basis of Disease* 1772, no. 8 (August 2007).

109 Vaccine researcher Stanley A. Plotkin describes the history of rubella in the United States and attempts to staunch it in "Rubella eradication?" *Vaccine* 19, nos. 25–26 (May 2001).

110 Marvin T. Miller is quoted in Monica Davey, "As town for deaf takes shape, debate on isolation re-emerges," *New York Times*, March 21, 2005.

110 The comment that isolationism is no longer fashionable comes from Tom Willard, "*N.Y. Times* reports on proposed signing town," *Deafweekly*, March 23, 2005.

111 Statistics on the number of ASL users come from the Gallaudet University Library; see Tom Harrington, "American Sign Language: Ranking and number of users" (2004), http://libguides.gallaudet.edu/content.php?pid=114804&sid=991835.

111 The 432 percent increase in ASL courses in a decade is documented in Elizabeth B. Welles, "Foreign language enrollments in United States institutions of higher education, Fall 2002," *Profession* (2004).

111 For a representative work promoting teaching sign language to babies, see Joseph Garcia, *Signing with Your Baby: How to Communicate with Infants Before They Can Speak* (2002).

111 The term *Deafhood* was coined by the British Deaf activist Paddy Ladd, author of *Understanding Deaf Culture: In Search of Deafhood* (2003).

111 The quotation from Edna Edith Sayers decrying the trivialization of sign language and its appropriation by hearing persons occurs in *Deaf World: A Historical Reader and Primary Sourcebook*, edited by Lois Bragg (2001), page 116.

111 The passage by Harlan Lane ("The relation of the hearing parent to the young deaf child . . .") occurs in *The Mask of Benevolence* (1992).

112 Jack Wheeler's remarks appear in a Deafness Research Foundation fund-raising brochure, "Let's Talk About Conquering Deafness" (2000).

112 Lawrence Hott and Diane Garey commented that "deafness is almost always one generation thick" in their film, *Through Deaf Eyes* (2007), which is available on DVD from Gallaudet University. The phrase *culture of converts* was first used by Frank Bechter in his essay "The deaf convert culture and its lessons for deaf theory," in *Open Your Eyes* (2008), pages 60–79.

113 From the introduction by Aina Pavolini to Amadou Hampâté Bâ, *The Fortunes of Wangrin* (1999), page ix: "After the independence of Mali in 1960, he formed

part of his country's delegation to the UNESCO General Conference held that year in Paris; it was on this occasion that he made his passionate plea for the preservation of Africa's heritage with the famous statement, 'En Afrique, quand un vieillard meurt, c'est un bibliothèque qui brûle' ('In Africa, when an old person dies, it's a library burning down')."

113 Estimates on the disappearance of languages come from Nicholas Evans, *Dying Words: Endangered Languages and What They Have to Tell Us* (2009); Evans's words come from Nicholas Evans and Stephen C. Levinson, "The myth of language universals: Language diversity and its importance for cognitive science," *Behavioral & Brain Sciences* 32 (2009), page 429.

113 For more commentary on the demise of Sign, see Lou Ann Walker, "Losing the language of silence," *New York*, January 13, 2008.

114 My first book was *The Irony Tower: Soviet Artists in a Time of Glasnost* (1991).

114 Carol Padden's question ("How can two conflicting impulses exist . . .") occurs in *Inside Deaf Culture* (2005), page 163.

III: Dwarfs

115 My primary sources for much of this chapter are Betty M. Adelson, *Dwarfism: Medical and Psychosocial Aspects of Profound Short Stature* (2005) and *The Lives of Dwarfs: Their Journey from Public Curiosity toward Social Liberation* (2005).

115 Proposals for towns for little people are discussed in John Van, "Little people veto a miniaturized village," *Chicago Tribune*, June 16, 1989; and Sharon LaFraniere, "A miniature world magnifies dwarf life," *New York Times*, March 3, 2010.

115 Victor A. McKusick was the founder of the discipline of medical genetics, and the leading investigator in the field of dwarfism among the Amish. For an accessible introduction to both Ellis–van Creveld syndrome and cartilage hair hypoplasia, see his review "Ellis–van Creveld syndrome and the Amish," *Nature Genetics* 24 (March 2000).

115 Because dwarfism is often not apparent at birth and does not always require medical intervention, calculations of incidence based on hospital records are inadequate, and even experts on dwarfism tend to offer figures rather tentatively. The renowned geneticist Dr. Victor McKusick told Betty Adelson in 1983 that he estimated that there were several million people in the world with dwarfism; see Betty M. Adelson, *The Lives of Dwarfs* (2005), pages 128–29. Joan Ablon comments that numbers range from twenty thousand to a hundred thousand, and quotes Charles Scott, a geneticist with a specialty in dwarfism, who estimated numbers at twenty thousand to twenty-five thousand; see Joan Ablon, *Little People in America: The Social Dimension of Dwarfism* (1984). Achondroplasia is said to occur in one in twenty thousand births, so if there is an American population of 318 million people, there should be about sixteen thousand Americans with achondroplasia, and Adelson told me that if you include all forms of skeletal dysplasia, the number approximately doubles, which would indeed give a number around thirty thousand, though she pointed out that this does not include hypopituitary disorders, Turner syndrome, juvenile arthritis, kidney disease, and various iatrogenic conditions, for which there are no precise figures; see Betty M. Adelson, *Dwarfism* (2005), pages 21–23. LPA has a membership of more than six thousand, some of whom are average-statured family members of dwarfs. With all of this in mind, it's impossible to say what proportion of dwarfs belong to LPA, but it seems likely that it is upward of 10 percent.

116 Betty Adelson's statement "The only permissible prejudice in PC America is against dwarfs" and subsequent statements from her, unless otherwise noted, are from correspondence and personal interviews conducted between 2003 and 2012.

116 The quotation from Mary D'Alton (". . . you can fix that, right? . . .") comes from a personal interview in 2010.

116 This passage is based on my interview with Mary Boggs in 2003.

118 William Hay recalled his visit with a general in *Deformity: An Essay* (1754). On page 16, Hay described himself as a hunchback, "scarce five Feet high"— quite possibly a person with diastrophic dysplasia. He was also a member of the House of Commons. With the phrase "a worm and no man," Hay was quoting from the Bible, Psalms 22:6: "But I am a worm, and no man; a reproach of men, and despised of the people." For a recent article about Hay, see "William Hay, M.P. for Seaford (1695–1755)," *Parliamentary History* 29, suppl. s1 (October 2010).

118 Betty Adelson refers to Woody Allen's theory of the essential funniness of the word *dwarf* on page 6 of *Dwarfism: Medical and Psychosocial Aspects of Profound Short Stature* (2005). Allen's fondness for *dwarf* is apparent in *The Complete Prose of Woody Allen* (1991), which contains numerous examples of the word used in a humorous context.

119 For scholarly discussion of modern freak shows, see Michael M. Chemers, "Le freak, c'est chic: The twenty-first century freak show as theatre of transgression," *Modern Drama* 46, no. 2 (Summer 2003); and Brigham A. Fordham, "Dangerous bodies: Freak shows, expression, and exploitation," *UCLA Entertainment Law Review* 14, no. 2 (2007).

119 A post–World Cup dwarf-tossing event in New Zealand eventually led to a pink slip for British rugby player Mike Tindall after paparazzi spied him cavorting there; see Richard White, "Mike Tindall gropes blonde," *Sun*, September 15, 2011; Robert Kitson, "Mike Tindall defended by England after incident at 'dwarf-throwing' bash," *Guardian*, September 15, 2011; and Rebecca English, "After World Cup shame, a £25,000 fine and humiliation for Tindall (and Zara's face says it all)," *Daily Mail*, January 12, 2012. In January 2012, Leopard's Lounge & Broil in Windsor, Ontario, hosted a dwarf-tossing event; see Sonya Bell, "Dwarf-tossing: Controversial event at Windsor strip club draws 1,000 fans," *Toronto Star*, January 29, 2012. At least one adult entertainer bills herself as "the world's smallest porn star"; see Allen Stein, "Stoughton cop resigns after he left beat to see dwarf porn star," *Enterprise News*, July 20, 2010.

119 Barbara Spiegel's recollections come from my interview with her in 2003 and subsequent communications.

119 Statistics on the percentage of skeletal dysplasias attributable to de novo mutations and recessive genes come from Clair A. Francomano, "The genetic basis of dwarfism," *New England Journal of Medicine* 332, no. 1 (January 5, 1995); and William A. Horton et al., "Achondroplasia," *Lancet* 370 (July 14, 2007).

119 For a scholarly review article on pituitary dwarfism, see Kyriaki S. Alatzoglou and Mehul T. Dattani, "Genetic causes and treatment of isolated growth hormone deficiency: An update," *Nature Reviews Endocrinology* 6, no. 10 (October 2010). Psychosocial dwarfism is discussed in Wayne H. Green, Magda Campbell, and Raphael David, "Psychosocial dwarfism: A critical review of the evidence," *Journal of the American Academy of Child Psychiatry* 23, no. 1 (January 1984); and the newspaper article "The little boy who was neglected so badly by his mother that he became a dwarf," *Daily Mail*, August 28, 2010.

119 The quotation from Marie-Hélène Huet comes from pages 6–7 of her book *Monstrous Imagination* (1993).

119 John Mulliken is quoted in Allison K. Jones, "Born different: Surgery can help children with craniofacial anomalies, but it can't heal all of the pain," *Telegram & Gazette*, May 23, 1995.

119 Betty Adelson describes the thoughtless manner in which some doctors have broken the news of a child's achondroplasia to parents on page 160 of *Dwarfism: Medical and Psychosocial Aspects of Profound Short Stature* (2005).

119 The mother's recollection of doctors' attitudes toward her child comes from a Yahoo! discussion group post by Brenda, June 12, 2001.

120 Joan Ablon quotes the mother and father whose doctor told them, "I regret to tell you that your child is a dwarf," on page 17 of *Living with Difference: Families with Dwarf Children* (1988).

120 The quotation from Ginny Sargent ("No matter what we [as dwarfs] feel . . .") comes from a Yahoo! discussion group post, September 4, 2001.

120 Matt Roloff's reminiscence of his parents' lowered expectations of him comes from a personal interview in 2003; he makes a similar statement on page 28 of *Against Tall Odds: Being a David in a Goliath World* (1999).

120 This passage is based on my interview with Amy and Matt Roloff in 2003 and subsequent communications.

120 Descriptions of the Roloff children come from Virginia Heffernan, "The challenges of an oversized world," *New York Times*, March 4, 2006.

121 This passage is based on my interview with Lisa Hedley in 2008 and subsequent personal communications. Her documentary on dwarfism, *Dwarfs: Not a Fairy Tale*, was first broadcast as part of the HBO *American Undercover Sundays* series on April 29, 2001. Though I have kept Lisa's name because of the prominence of her film, her daughter's name, Rose, is a pseudonym.

121 One of the brochures Lisa Hedley was given was John G. Rogers and Joan O. Weiss, "My Child Is a Dwarf" (1977), published by LPA.

121 This quotation from Lisa Hedley ("With one word my husband and I became unwitting members of a community . . .") comes from her article "A child of difference," *New York Times Magazine*, October 12, 1997.

124 The quotation from Barbara Spiegel comes from my interview with her in 2003 and subsequent communications.

124 Alasdair G. W. Hunter reported on his evaluation of the comparative life satisfaction of dwarfs and their parents in "Some psychosocial aspects of nonlethal chondrodysplasias I: Assessment using a life-styles questionnaire," *American Journal of Medical Genetics* 78, no. 1 (June 1998).

125 Study participants tended to rate their achondroplasia as "not serious" in Sarah E. Gollust et al., "Living with achondroplasia in an average-sized world: An assessment of quality of life," *American Journal of Medical Genetics* 120A, no. 4 (August 2003).

125 LPA now explicitly concerns itself with disabling conditions often accompanying short stature and includes disability rights among the organization's advocacy areas. See http://www.lpaonline.org/mc/page.do?sitePageId=84634#Disability.

125 Paul Steven Miller's comment about LPA and disability occurs in chapter 6 of Dan Kennedy, *Little People: Learning to See the World Through My Daughter's Eyes* (2003) at http://littlepeoplethebook.com/online-edition/chapter-06/.

125 Rosemarie Garland Thomson's reference to "exclusionary discourse" occurs on page 6 of *Extraordinary Bodies: Figuring Physical Disability in American Culture and Literature* (1997).

126 The anonymous mother's concerns about the implications and ramifications of physical accommodations come from a personal interview in 2003.

126 Linda Hunt differentiates between dwarfism and disease in her letter in response to Lisa Hedley, "A child of difference," *New York Times Magazine*, November 2, 1997.

126 Joan Ablon describes the history of LPA in "Dwarfism and social identity: Self-help group participation," *Social Science & Medicine* 15B (1981); and Betty Adelson in both *Dwarfism* (2005), pages 187–90, and *The Lives of Dwarfs* (2005), pages 319–21.

126 William Safire discusses words used to describe little people in "On language: Dwarf planet," *New York Times*, September 10, 2006; see also Lynn Harris, "Who you calling a midget?," *Salon*, July 16, 2009.

126 Barnum's most famous performers were the proportionate dwarfs Charles Sherwood Stratton and his wife, Lavinia Bump Warren, known to audiences as "General and Mrs. Tom Thumb." Stratton is author of the extravagantly titled autobiography *Sketch of the Life: Personal Appearance, Character and Manners of Charles S. Stratton, the Man in Miniature, Known as General Tom Thumb, and His Wife, Lavinia Warren Stratton, Including the History of Their Courtship and Marriage, With Some Account of Remarkable Dwarfs, Giants, & Other Human Phenomena, of Ancient and Modern Times, Also, Songs Given at Their Public Levees* (1874). For a brief contemporary account of Stratton's career, see "Giants and dwarfs," *Strand Magazine* 8 (July–December 1894); for a modern analysis, see Michael M. Chemers, "Jumpin' Tom Thumb: Charles Stratton onstage at the American Museum," *Nineteenth Century Theatre & Film* 31 (2004). Lavinia Warren is the subject of Melanie Benjamin's recent novel *The Autobiography of Mrs. Tom Thumb* (2011).

126 The offending article: David Segal, "Financial fraud is focus of attack by prosecutors," *New York Times*, March 11, 2009. The public editor's follow-up: Clark Hoyt, "Consistent, sensitive and weird," *New York Times*, April 18, 2009.

126 Interview with Barbara Spiegel in 2003 and subsequent communications.

126 Betty Adelson's advice about names is quoted by Lynn Harris in "Who you calling a midget?," *Salon*, July 16, 2009.

126 This passage is based on my interview with Dan Kennedy, author of *Little People: Learning to See the World Through My Daughter's Eyes* (2003), in 2003 and subsequent communications.

127 For more information on the association between hearing loss and cognitive skills among dwarfs, see G. Brinkmann et al., "Cognitive skills in achondroplasia," *American Journal of Medical Genetics* 47, no. 5 (October 1993).

128 For authoritative and detailed information on dwarfing conditions, consult the National Organization for Rare Disorders (http://www.rarediseases.org), the National Library of Medicine's Genetics Home Reference (http://ghr.nlm .nih.gov), and the Mayo Clinic (http://www.mayoclinic.com/health/dwarfism/ DS01012).

128 Victor McKusick's estimates are quoted on page 128 of Betty M. Adelson, *The Lives of Dwarfs* (2005), citing Susan Lawrence, "Solving big problems for little people," *Journal of the American Medical Association* 250, no. 3 (March 1983).

128 The genetic mechanism of achondroplasia was first described by Clair A. Francomano et al., "Localization of the achondroplasia gene to the distal 2.5 Mb of human chromosome 4p," *Human Molecular Genetics* 3, no. 5 (May 1994); R. Shiang, et al., "Mutations in the transmembrane domain of FGFR3 cause the

most common genetic form of dwarfism, achondroplasia," *Cell* 78, no. 2 (July 29, 1994); and Gary A. Bellus, "Achondroplasia is defined by recurrent G380R mutations of FGFR3," *American Journal of Human Genetics* 56 (1995), pages 368–73.

128 Achondroplasia prevalence rates come from Sue Thompson, Tom Shakespeare, and Michael J. Wright, "Medical and social aspects of the life course for adults with a skeletal dysplasia: A review of current knowledge," *Disability & Rehabilitation* 30, no. 1 (January 2008).

129 Findings of increased mortality rates in children with achondroplasia come from Jacqueline T. Hecht et al., "Mortality in achondroplasia," *American Journal of Human Genetics* 41 no. 3 (September 1987); and Julia Wynn et al., "Mortality in achondroplasia study: A 42-year follow-up," *American Journal of Medical Genetics* 143A, no. 21 (November 2007).

129 Complications of hydrocephalus are discussed in Glenn L. Keiper Jr. et al., "Achondroplasia and cervicomedullary compression: Prospective evaluation and surgical treatment," *Pediatric Neurosurgery* 31, no. 2 (August 1999).

129 Dwarfism caused by inadequate iodine intake/uptake, known as cretinism, is discussed in Zu-Pei Chen and Basil S. Hetzel, "Cretinism revisited," *Best Practice & Research Clinical Endocrinology & Metabolism* 24, no. 1 (February 2010).

129 For more detailed scholarly resources on physical problems experienced by dwarfs, see Patricia G. Wheeler et al., "Short stature and functional impairment: A systematic review," *Archives of Pediatric & Adolescent Medicine* 158, no. 3 (March 2004).

129 Dental problems in short-statured children are described in Heidrun Kjellberg et al., "Craniofacial morphology, dental occlusion, tooth eruption, and dental maturity in boys of short stature with or without growth hormone deficiency," *European Journal of Oral Sciences* 108, no. 5 (October 2000).

130 Physical activities that create pressure on the spine and increase the risk of developing osteoarthritis are contraindicated for people with bone disorders; see Tracy L. Trotter et al., "Health supervision for children with achondroplasia," *Pediatrics* 116, no. 3 (2005).

130 See Richard Pauli et al., *To Celebrate: Understanding Developmental Differences in Young Children with Achondroplasia* (1991).

130 LPA facilitated its members' participation in a study by Jacqueline T. Hecht et al., "Obesity in achondroplasia," *American Journal of Medical Genetics* 31, no. 3 (November 1988). The problem of monitoring weight gain in children with atypical growth is addressed in Julie Hoover-Fong et al., "Weight for age charts for children with achondroplasia," *American Journal of Medical Genetics Part A* 143A, 19 (October 2007).

130 Useful scholarly articles on medical complications of dwarfism include Steven E. Kopits, "Orthopedic complications of dwarfism," *Clinical Orthopedics & Related Research* 114 (January–February 1976); Dennis C. Stokes et al., "Respiratory complications of achondroplasia," *Journal of Pediatrics* 102, no. 4 (April 1983); Ivor D. Berkowitz et al., "Dwarfs: Pathophysiology and anesthetic implications," *Anesthesiology* 7, no. 4 (October 1990); Cheryl S. Reid et al., "Cervicomedullary compression in young patients with achondroplasia: Value of comprehensive neurologic and respiratory evaluation," *Journal of Pediatrics* 110, no. 4 (1987); Rodney K. Beals and Greg Stanley, "Surgical correction of bowlegs in achondroplasia," *Journal of Pediatric Orthopedics* 14, no. 4 (July 2005); and Elisabeth A. Sisk et al., "Obstructive sleep apnea in children with achondroplasia: Surgical

and anesthetic considerations," *Otolaryngology—Head and Neck Surgery* 120, no. 2 (February 1999).

131 This passage is based on my interview with Leslie Parks in 2003 and subsequent communications.

133 The cliché about cheery children is exemplified by Drash et al., who are regarded as "dated" and too narrowly focused by Thompson et al. See Philip W. Drash, Nancy E. Greenberg, and John Money, "Intelligence and personality in four syndromes of dwarfism," in *Human Growth*, edited by D. B. Cheek (1968), 568–81. Philadelphia: Lea and Febiger, 1968; and Sue Thompson, Tom Shakespeare, and Michael J. Wright, "Medical and social aspects of the life course for adults with a skeletal dysplasia: A review of current knowledge," *Disability & Rehabilitation* 30, no. 1 (January 2008), pages 1–12.

133 Studies by Joan Ablon have concluded that dwarf children often develop bright personalities to compensate for their social challenges; see *Living with Difference* (1988), page 17; and "Personality and stereotype in osteogenesis imperfecta: Behavioral phenotype or response to life's hard challenges?," *American Journal of Medical Genetics* 122A (October 15, 2003).

134 For findings of a relatively contented childhood, see Alasdair G. W. Hunter's three-part report, "Some psychosocial aspects of nonlethal chondrodysplasias," *American Journal of Medical Genetics* 78, no. 1 (June 1998); James S. Brust et al., "Psychiatric aspects of dwarfism," *American Journal of Psychiatry* 133, no. 2 (February 1976); Sarah E. Gollust et al., "Living with achondroplasia in an average-sized world: An assessment of quality of life," *American Journal of Medical Genetics* 120A, no. 4 (August 2003); and M. Apajasalo et al., "Health-related quality of life of patients with genetic skeletal dysplasias," *European Journal of Pediatrics* 157, no. 2 (February 1998).

134 Joan Ablon's comment about overprotectiveness occurs on page 64 of *Living with Difference* (1988).

134 Richard Crandall's words of warning about strollers occur on page 49 of his book *Dwarfism: The Family and Professional Guide* (1994).

134 For the Restricted Growth Association survey, see Tom Shakespeare, Michael Wright, and Sue Thompson, *A Small Matter of Equality: Living with Restricted Growth* (2007); conclusions about parental treatment and eventual emotional adjustment can be found on page 25.

134 A significant incidence of depression in young adults was found in Alasdair G. W. Hunter, "Some psychosocial aspects of nonlethal chondrodysplasias, II: Depression and anxiety," *American Journal of Medical Genetics* 78, no. 1 (June 1998); see also Sue Thompson, Tom Shakespeare, and Michael J. Wright, "Medical and social aspects of the life course for adults with a skeletal dysplasia: A review of current knowledge," *Disability & Rehabilitation* 30, no. 1 (January 2008). Hunter cautiously ventures that "adults who were born to unaffected parents may be at greater risk of depression than those who had an affected parent" (page 12).

135 Joan Ablon describes common emotional experiences associated with LPA membership in chapter 8 of *Little People in America: The Social Dimension of Dwarfism* (1984), "The encounter with LPA."

135 The study finding that dwarfs have lower self-esteem, less education, and lower annual incomes, and are less likely to be married is Sarah E. Gollust et al., "Living with achondroplasia in an average-sized world: An assessment of quality of life," *American Journal of Medical Genetics* 120A, no. 4 (August 2003).

135 The survey finding significant income disparity between people with dwarfism

and their average-size family members is described in Betty Adelson, *Dwarfism: Medical and Psychosocial Aspects of Profound Short Stature* (2005), page 259.

135 Michael Ain describes his job-hunting difficulties in Lisa Abelow Hedley's documentary *Dwarfs: Not a Fairy Tale* (2001).

135 The quotation from Ruth Ricker was recounted to me by Dan Kennedy in 2003.

135 All quotations from John Wolin come from his article "Dwarf like me," *Miami Herald*, January 24, 1993.

135 The LP who described the experience of seeing other dwarfs for the first time was quoted in Ken Wolf, "Big world, little people," *Newsday*, April 20, 1989.

136 This passage is based on my interview with Janet and Beverly Charles in 2003.

137 This passage is based on my interview with Leslye Sneider and Bruce Johnson in 2005 and subsequent communications.

139 Basic sources on dwarf-tossing include Alice Domurat Dreger, "Lavish dwarf entertainment," *Hastings Center Bioethics Forum*, March 25, 2008; and Deborah Schoeneman, "Little people, big biz: Hiring dwarfs for parties a growing trend," *New York Post*, November 8, 2001.

139 The passage of New York's "Dwarf Tossing and Dwarf Bowling Prohibition" (1990 NY Laws 2744) was reported in Elizabeth Kolbert, "On deadline day, Cuomo vetoes 2 bills opposed by Dinkins," *New York Times*, July 24, 1990.

    For more on the French ban and challenge, see the report of the United Nations Human Rights Committee, *Views of the Human Rights Committee under article 5, paragraph 4, of the Optional Protocol to the International Covenant on Civil and Political Rights, Seventy-fifth session, Communication No. 854/1999, submitted by Manuel Wackenheim* (July 15, 2002); and Emma Jane Kirby's BBC report "Appeal for 'dwarf-tossing' thrown out," British Broadcasting Corporation, September 27, 2002.

    The Florida ban and challenge are described in "Dwarf tossing ban challenged," United Press International, November 29, 2001; and "Federal judge throwing dwarf-tossing lawsuit out of court," *Florida Times-Union*, February 26, 2002.

139 Law enforcement crackdowns against dwarf-tossers and bowlers are described in Steven Kreytak, "Tickets issued for dwarf-tossing," *Newsday*, March 11, 2002; and Eddie D'Anna, "Staten Island nightspot cancels dwarf-bowling event for Saturday," *Staten Island Advance*, February 27, 2008.

139 The Fidelity party and SEC penalty are described in Jason Nisse, "SEC probes dwarf-tossing party for Fidelity trader," *Independent*, August 14, 2005; and Jenny Anderson, "Fidelity is fined $8 million over improper gifts," *New York Times*, March 6, 2008.

139 For comparison of dwarf-tossing with contact sports, see Robert W. McGee, "If dwarf tossing is outlawed, only outlaws will toss dwarfs: Is dwarf tossing a victimless crime?," *American Journal of Jurisprudence* 38 (1993). The real-life consequence of the idea that dwarf-tossing is acceptable behavior was most recently demonstrated when a thirty-seven-year-old man with achondroplasia sustained permanent spinal cord damage after being unwillingly tossed by a boor at a British pub, likely inspired by the Mike Tindall escapade; news of the incident inspired a number of dwarf celebrities to speak out in solidarity and concern. See the news reports "Dwarf left paralysed after being thrown by drunken Rugby fan," *Telegraph*, January 12, 2012; "Golden Globes: Peter Dinklage cites Martin Henderson case," *Los Angeles Times*, January 16, 2012; and Alexis Tereszcuk, "The little couple slam dwarf tossing," *Radar Online*, March 20, 2012. See also Angela Van Etten, "Dwarf tossing and exploitation," *Huffington Post*, October 19, 2011.

139 The discussion of Radio City and LPA and the quotations by dwarf actors are all

from Lynn Harris, "Who you calling a midget?," *Salon*, July 16, 2009. For more on the debate about dwarfs as entertainers, see Chris Lydgate, "Dwarf vs. dwarf: The Little People of America want respect—and they're fighting each other to get it," *Willamette Week*, June 30, 1999.

140 Herschel Walker's and Joan Rivers's offensive *Celebrity Apprentice* episode (season 8, episode 6) was broadcast on April 5, 2009. Jimmy Korpai's complaint to the FCC about *Celebrity Apprentice* is described in Lynn Harris, "Who you calling a midget?," *Salon*, July 16, 2009.

140 The first scientific studies on *Homo floresiensis* were Peter Brown et al., "A new small-bodied hominin from the Late Pleistocene of Flores, Indonesia," *Nature* 431, no. 7012 (October 27, 2004); and Michael J. Morwood et al., "Archaeology and age of a new hominin from Flores in eastern Indonesia," *Nature* 431, no. 7012 (October 27, 2004).

140 Alexander Chancellor's commentary occurs in his article "Guide to age," *Guardian*, November 6, 2004.

140 For information on the plight of Pygmies in modern Africa, see *Minorities under Siege: Pygmies Today in Africa* (2006); and African Commission on Human and Peoples' Rights International Work Group for Indigenous Affairs, *Report of the African Commission's Working Group on Indigenous Populations/Communities: Research and information visit to the Republic of Gabon, 15–30 September 2007* (2010).

140 Responses to proposals to ban use of the term *midget* are described by Lynn Harris in "Who you calling a midget?," *Salon*, July 16, 2009.

141 This passage is based on my many interviews with Betty Adelson between 2003 and 2012.

142 Quotations from mothers bereft at Kopits's passing were posted as reader comments at Bertalan Mesko, "Dr. Steven E. Kopits, a modern miracle maker," *Science Roll*, January 27, 2007, http://scienceroll.com/2007/01/27/dr-steven-e -kopits-a-modern-miracle-maker/.

144 For more information on cultural interpretations of physical difference, see David M. Turner, "Introduction: Approaching anomalous bodies," in *Social Histories of Disability and Deformity: Bodies, Images and Experiences*, edited by David M. Turner and Kevin Stagg (2006), pages 1–16.

144 Leviticus 21:16–24 (American Standard Version): "Then the Lord spoke to Moses, saying, 'Speak to Aaron, saying, "No man of your offspring throughout their generations who has a defect shall approach to offer the food of his God. For no one who has a defect shall approach: a blind man, or a lame man, or he who has a disfigured face, or any deformed limb, or a man who has a broken foot or broken hand, or a hunchback or a dwarf, or one who has a defect in his eye or eczema or scabs or crushed testicles. No man among the descendants of Aaron the priest who has a defect is to come near to offer the Lord's offerings by fire; since he has a defect, he shall not come near to offer the food of his God. He may eat the food of his God, both of the most holy and of the holy, only he shall not go in to the veil or come near the altar because he has a defect, so that he will not profane My sanctuaries. For I am the Lord who sanctifies them."' So Moses spoke to Aaron and to his sons and to all the sons of Israel."

144 Martha Undercoffer's comments were made in a Yahoo! discussion group post on September 23, 2002.

145 The quotation from the dwarf who uses an MP3 player to block out unwanted comments occurs on page 29 of Tom Shakespeare, Michael Wright, and Sue Thompson, *A Small Matter of Equality* (2007).

145 This passage is based on my interview with Harry Wieder in 2003 and subsequent communications. His memorial service is described in Susan Dominus, "Remembering the little man who was a big voice for causes," *New York Times*, May 1, 2010.

146 William Safire refers to "cruel folklore" and "Rumpelstiltskins" in "On language: Dwarf planet," *New York Times*, September 10, 2006.

146 Joan Ablon's comment about the magical status of dwarfs occurs on page 6 of *Living with Difference* (1988).

146 Anne Lamott's remark occurs on page 25 of Tom Shakespeare, Michael Wright, and Sue Thompson, *A Small Matter of Equality* (2007).

146 This passage is based on my interview with Taylor, Carlton, and Tracey van Putten in 2008 and subsequent communications.

148 The quotation from the LP about dwarfs' romantic difficulties occurs on page 241 of Betty M. Adelson, *Dwarfism* (2005).

148 John Wolin's remarks occur in his article "Dwarf like me," *Miami Herald*, January 24, 1993.

148 The comment about the sexual incongruity between LPs and APs comes from an LPA chat room, April 15, 2006.

149 The quotation from Harry Wieder comes from my interview with him.

149 Betty Adelson describes attitudes toward mixed-height marriages on pages 57–58 and page 246 of *Dwarfism* (2005).

149 Increased rates of depression in LPs in mixed-height marriages were reported by Alasdair Hunter in "Some psychosocial aspects of nonlethal chondrodysplasias, II: Depression and anxiety," *American Journal of Medical Genetics* 78, no. 1 (June 1998); and "Some psychosocial aspects of nonlethal chondrodysplasias, III: Self-esteem in children and adults," *American Journal of Medical Genetics* 78 (June 1998).

149 On dwarfs' marriage tendencies inside and outside LPA, I've relied on personal communications with Betty Adelson.

149 John Wolin's remarks occur in his article "Dwarf like me," *Miami Herald*, January 24, 1993.

149 For scholarly overviews of reproductive complications and anesthesia in achondroplastic dwarfs, see Judith E. Allanson and Judith G. Hall, "Obstetric and gynecologic problems in women with chondrodystrophies," *Obstetrics & Gynecology* 67, no. 1 (January 1986); and James F. Mayhew et al., "Anaesthesia for the achondroplastic dwarf," *Canadian Anaesthetists' Journal* 33, no. 2 (March 1986).

149 The quotation from the dwarf mother about rudeness from strangers comes from Ellen Highland Fernandez, *The Challenges Facing Dwarf Parents: Preparing for a New Baby* (1989).

149 Betty Adelson's remarks about dwarfs who bear children occur on page 249 of *Dwarfism* (2005).

150 This passage is based on my interviews and other communications with Cheryl, Clinton, and Clinton Brown Jr. between 2003 and 2010.

155 See the previously cited scholarly sources on genetics of dwarfism: Clair A. Francomano, "The genetic basis of dwarfism," *New England Journal of Medicine* 332, no. 1 (January 5, 1995); and William Horton, "Recent milestones in achondroplasia research," *American Journal of Medical Genetics* 140A (2006).

155 For more information on lethal skeletal dysplasias, double heterozygosity, and prenatal diagnosis, see Anne E. Tretter et al., "Antenatal diagnosis of lethal skeletal dysplasias," *American Journal of Medical Genetics* 75, no. 5 (December

1998); Maureen A. Flynn and Richard M. Pauli, "Double heterozygosity in bone growth disorders," *American Journal of Medical Genetics* 121A, no. 3 (2003); and Peter Yeh, "Accuracy of prenatal diagnosis and prediction of lethality for fetal skeletal dysplasias," *Prenatal Diagnosis* 31, no. 5 (May 2011).

155 The discovery of genes responsible for achondroplasia was first reported in Clair A. Francomano et al., "Localization of the achondroplasia gene to the distal 2.5 Mb of human chromosome 4p," *Human Molecular Genetics* 3, no. 5 (May 1994); R. Shiang et al., "Mutations in the transmembrane domain of FGFR3 cause the most common genetic form of dwarfism, achondroplasia," *Cell* 78, no. 2 (July 29, 1994); and Gary A. Bellus, "Achondroplasia is defined by recurrent G380R mutations of FGFR3," *American Journal of Human Genetics* 56 (1995), pages 368–73. The discovery of the gene responsible for diastrophic dysplasia was first reported in Johanna Hästbacka et al., "The diastrophic dysplasia gene encodes a novel sulfate transporter: Positional cloning by fine-structure linkage disequilibrium mapping," *Cell* 78, no. 6 (September 23, 1994); for pseudoachondroplasia, in Jacqueline T. Hecht et al., "Mutations in exon 17B of cartilage oligomeric matrix protein (COMP) cause pseudoachondroplasia," *Nature Genetics* 10, no. 3 (July 1995); and for SED, in Brendan Lee et al., "Identification of the molecular defect in a family with spondyloepiphyseal dysplasia," *Science*, New Series 244, no. 4907 (May 26, 1989).

For background on the genetics and incidence of dwarfism, see Clair A. Francomano, "The genetic basis of dwarfism," *New England Journal of Medicine* 332, no. 1 (January 5, 1995); and R. J. M. Gardner's "A new estimate of the achondroplasia mutation rate," *Clinical Genetics* 11, no. 1 (April 2008).

155 John Wasmuth's remarks about the proper use of prenatal diagnosis are quoted on pages 17–18 of Dan Kennedy's *Little People* (2003).

156 The survey of attitudes toward abortion following prenatal diagnosis of achondroplasia was described in Jen Joynt and Vasugi Ganeshananthan, "Abortion decisions," *Atlantic Monthly*, April 2003.

156 John Richardson refers to couples who wish to screen out average-size fetuses on page 9 of his memoir, *In the Little World: A True Story of Dwarfs, Love, and Trouble* (2001).

156 The quotation from Darshak Sanghavi comes from his article "Wanting babies like themselves, some parents choose genetic defects," *New York Times*, December 5, 2006.

156 Betty Adelson and Joe Stramondo referred to "coercive eugenics" in an unpublished 2005 letter to the editor of the *New York Times*.

156 The anecdote about clinics' refusal to implant dwarf embryos comes from Andy Geller, "Docs' designer defect baby: Disabled by choice," *New York Post*, December 22, 2006.

156 The quotation from Carol Gibson comes from the article "Babies with made-to-order defects?," Associated Press, December 21, 2006.

156 This passage is based on my interview with Ginny Foos in 2003 and subsequent communications.

157 For discussion of potential economic disparity in the burden of disability resulting from the proliferation of prenatal diagnoses of dwarfing conditions, see Amy Harmon, "The problem with an almost-perfect genetic world," *New York Times*, November 20, 2005.

157 Tom Shakespeare's comments about impairment were made on the BBC radio program *Belief*, broadcast on December 30, 2005.

157 The LPA statement was issued in 2005 as "Little People of America on pre-

implantation genetic diagnosis" and can be found on the organization's website, http://data.memberclicks.com/site/lpa/LPA_PGD_Position_Statement_2007.doc.

157 All quotations from Ericka Peasley come from my interview with her in 2009.

157 For more information on Morquio syndrome, see Benedict J. A. Lankester et al., "Morquio syndrome," *Current Orthopaedics* 20, no. 2 (April 2006).

157 Gene therapy for chondrodysplasias is discussed in R. Tracy Ballock, "Chondrodysplasias," *Current Opinion in Orthopedics* 11, no. 5 (October 2000), pages 347–52.

158 The quotation from Virginia Heffernan ("...a cherished inheritance...") comes from her article "The challenges of an oversized world," *New York Times*, March 4, 2006.

158 The following passage is based on my interviews with Monique Duras, Oleg Prigov, and Anatole Prigov in 2004 and 2008 and other communications. Their names are pseudonyms. Some other identifying details have been changed.

160 On geographic differences in preference for limb-lengthening surgery, see P. Bregani et al., "Emotional implications of limb lengthening in adolescents and young adults with achondroplasia," *Life-Span & Disability* 1, no. 2 (July–December 1998).

161 The development of and controversy over limb-lengthening is discussed in David Lawrence Rimoin, "Limb lengthening: Past, present, and future," *Growth, Genetics & Hormones* 7, no. 3 (1991); Eric D. Shirley and Michael C. Ain, "Achondroplasia: Manifestations and treatment," *Journal of the American Academy of Orthopedic Surgeons* 17, no. 4 (April 2009); and Lisa Abelow Hedley, "The seduction of the surgical fix," in *Surgically Shaping Children: Technology, Ethics, and the Pursuit of Normality*, edited by Erik Parens (2006). The technique is described in detail in S. Robert Rozbruch and Svetlana Ilizarov, *Limb Lengthening and Reconstructive Surgery* (2007).

161 Betty Adelson refers to the price of limb-lengthening surgery on page 95 of *Dwarfism* (2005).

162 The controversy within LPA about Dror Paley is described by Betty Adelson on pages 90–94 of *Dwarfism* (2005).

162 For Gillian Mueller's comments on limb-lengthening, see her article "Extended limb-lengthening: Setting the record straight," *LPA Online*, 2002, at http://www .lpaonline.org/library_ellmueller.html.

162 The quotation from the LPA executive about the need to wait until a child is old enough to consider thoughtfully the ramifications of limb-lengthening surgery occurs on pages 170–71 of Dan Kennedy, *Little People* (2003).

162 The therapeutic potential of limb-lengthening is discussed in Hui-Wan Park et al., "Correction of lumbosacral hyperlordosis in achondroplasia," *Clinical Orthopaedics & Related Research* 12, no. 414 (September 2003).

162 The quotation from Dan Kennedy about the benefits of longer arms occurs on page 186 of *Little People* (2003).

162 For more information on complications of limb-lengthening surgery, see Douglas Naudie et al., "Complications of limb-lengthening in children who have an underlying bone disorder," *Journal of Bone & Joint Surgery* 80, no. 1 (January 1998); and Bernardo Vargas Barreto et al., "Complications of Ilizarov leg lengthening," *International Orthopaedics* 31, no. 5 (October 2007).

163 The quotation from Arthur W. Frank about the imperative to "fix" comes from page 18 of his article "Emily's scars: Surgical shapings, technoluxe, and bioethics," *Hastings Center Report* 34, no. 2 (March/April 2004).

163 For more on Nicholas Andry and the history of orthopedic medicine, see Anne Borsay's chapter, "Disciplining disabled bodies: The development of orthopaedic medicine in Britain, c. 1800–1939," in *Social Histories of Disability and Deformity: Bodies, Images and Experiences*, edited by David M. Turner and Kevin Stagg (2006).

164 FDA approval of Humatrope for "unexplained shortness" was reported in Mark Kaufman, "FDA approves wider use of growth hormone," *Washington Post*, July 26, 2003.

164 Growth hormone treatment for short stature is discussed in Carol Hart, "Who's deficient, who's just plain short?" *AAP News* 13, no. 6 (June 1997); Natalie Angier, "Short men, short shrift: Are drugs the answer?" *New York Times*, June 22, 2003; "Standing tall: experts debate the cosmetic use of growth hormones for children," ABC News, June 19, 2003; and Susan Brink, "Is taller better?" and "When average fails to reach parents' expectations," *Los Angeles Times*, January 15, 2007.

164 Studies finding a positive correlation between height and income include Nicola Persico, Andrew Postlewaite, and Dan Silverman, "The effect of adolescent experience on labor market outcomes: The case of height," *Journal of Political Economy* 112, no. 5 (2004); Timothy A. Judge and Daniel M. Cable, "The effect of physical height on workplace success and income," *Journal of Applied Psychology* 89, no. 3 (2004); and Inas Rashad, "Height, health and income in the United States, 1984–2005," W. J. Usery Workplace Research Group Paper Series, Working Paper 2008-3-1. For a summary of the research in layperson's terms, see "Feet, dollars and inches: The intriguing relationship between height and income," *Economist*, April 3, 2008.

164 The quotation from Vitruvius ("For the human body is so designed by nature . . .") occurs on pages 72–73 of *The Ten Books on Architecture* (*De Architectura*) (1960).

164 The quotation from William Safire comes from his article "On language: Dwarf planet," *New York Times*, September 10, 2006.

164 John Richardson's comment on the abiding difference of dwarfs occurs on page 9 of *In the Little World* (2001).

164 This passage is based on my interview with Crissy and Kiki Trapani in 2008.

IV: Down Syndrome

169 Emily Perl Kingsley's inspirational essay "Welcome to Holland" was first featured in Dear Abby's column "A fable for parents of a disabled child," *Chicago Tribune*, November 5, 1989. For information on the concert band piece by Steven Barton, see http://www.c-alanpublications.com/Merchant2/merchant .mvc?Screen=PROD&Store_Code=CAPC&Product_Code=11770; for guitarist Nunzio Rosselli's 2006 CD *Welcome to Holland*, see http://www.cduniverse.com/ productinfo.asp?pid=7245475; for information on other adaptations, see http:// www.gosprout.org/film/prog07/bio.htm. The essay is featured in Jack Canfield, *Chicken Soup for the Soul: Children with Special Needs* (2007), and can also be found all over the Internet.

170 The President's Committee for People with Intellectual Disabilities (at http:// www.acf.hhs.gov/programs/pcpid) is my source for statistics on the number of people and families affected by intellectual disabilities.

170 Down syndrome prevalence estimates come from Jan Marshall Friedman et al., "Racial disparities in median age at death of persons with Down syndrome: United States, 1968–1997," *Morbidity & Mortality Weekly Report* 50, no. 22 (June 8, 2001); Stephanie L. Sherman et al., "Epidemiology of Down syndrome," *Mental*

Retardation & Developmental Disabilities Research Reviews 13, no. 3 (October 2007); and Mikyong Shin et al., "Prevalence of Down syndrome among children and adolescents in 10 regions," *Pediatrics* 124, no. 6 (December 2009).

170 Statistics on the rate of miscarriage in Down syndrome pregnancies come from Joan K. Morris, Nicholas J. Wald, and Hilary C. Watt, "Fetal loss in Down syndrome pregnancies," *Prenatal Diagnosis* 19, no. 2 (February 1999).

170 For general information on health problems associated with DS, see Don C. Van Dyke et al., *Medical and Surgical Care for Children with Down Syndrome* (1995); Paul T. Rogers and Mary Coleman, *Medical Care in Down Syndrome* (1992); and Claudine P. Torfs and Roberta E. Christianson, "Anomalies in Down syndrome individuals in a large population-based registry," *American Journal of Medical Genetics* 77, no. 5 (June 1998).

170 For more information on tumor resistance in Down syndrome, see Henrik Hasle et al., "Risks of leukaemia and solid tumours in individuals with Down's syndrome," *Lancet* 355, no. 9119 (January 15, 2000); Quanhe Yang et al., "Mortality associated with Down's syndrome in the USA from 1983 to 1997: A population-based study," *Lancet* 359, no. 9311 (March 23, 2002); and Kwan-Hyuck Baek et al., "Down's syndrome suppression of tumour growth and the role of the calcineurin inhibitor DSCR1," *Nature* 459 (June 25, 2009).

The decreased risk of arteriosclerosis in Down syndrome is discussed in Arin K. Greene et al., "Risk of vascular anomalies with Down syndrome," *Pediatrics* 121, no. 1 (January 2008), pages 135–40.

171 See Elizabeth H. Aylward et al., "Cerebellar volume in adults with Down syndrome," *Archives of Neurology* 54, no. 2 (February 1997); and Joseph D. Pinter et al., "Neuroanatomy of Down's syndrome: A high-resolution MRI study," *American Journal of Psychiatry* 158, no. 10 (October 2001): 1659–65.

171 The risk of depression in people with Down syndrome is discussed in Dennis Eugene McGuire and Brian A. Chicoine, *Mental Wellness in Adults with Down Syndrome* (2006).

171 Studies demonstrating the existence of Down syndrome in primates include Sunny Luke et al., "Conservation of the Down syndrome critical region in humans and great apes," *Gene* 161, no. 2 (1995); and Harold M. McClure et al., "Autosomal trisomy in a chimpanzee: Resemblance to Down's syndrome," *Science* 165, no. 3897 (September 5, 1969).

171 For more information on the history of prenatal testing, see Cynthia M. Powell, "The current state of prenatal genetic testing in the United States," in *Prenatal Testing and Disability Rights*, edited by Erik Parens and Adrienne Asch (2000).

171 The relative risks incurred in different methods of prenatal testing are discussed in Isabelle C. Bray and David E. Wright, "Estimating the spontaneous loss of Down syndrome fetuses between the times of chorionic villus sampling, amniocentesis and live birth," *Prenatal Diagnosis* 18, no. 10 (October 1998).

171 For more information on the triple screen, see Tim Reynolds, "The triple test as a screening technique for Down syndrome: Reliability and relevance," *International Journal of Women's Health* 9, no. 2 (August 2010); Robert H. Ball et al., "First- and second-trimester evaluation of risk for Down syndrome," *Obstetrics & Gynecology* 110, no. 1 (July 2007); and N. Neely Kazerouni et al., "Triple-marker prenatal screening program for chromosomal defects," *Obstetrics & Gynecology* 114, no. 1 (July 2009).

171 New developments in prenatal screening are the subject of Roni Rabin, "Screen all pregnancies for Down syndrome, doctors say," *New York Times*, January 9, 2007;

and Deborah A. Driscoll and Susan J. Gross, "Screening for fetal aneuploidy and neural tube defects," *Genetic Medicine* 11, no. 11 (November 2009).

171 This passage is based on my interviews with Emily Perl Kingsley in 2004 and 2007, and additional communications.

173 Jason Kingsley and Mitchell Levitz, *Count Us In: Growing Up with Down Syndrome* (1994), page 28.

177 New York State's Residential Habilitation program is described at http://www .opwdd.ny.gov/hp_services_reshab.jsp; other states have similar programs.

179 Jean Marc Gaspard Itard described his efforts to educate a feral child in the early nineteenth century in *De l'Education d'un Homme Sauvage, ou Des Premiers Developpemens Physiques et Moraux du Jeune Sauvage de l'Aveyron* (1801), published in English under the title *The Wild Boy of Aveyron* (1962).

179 Édouard Séguin is quoted on page 9 of the *Handbook of Early Childhood Intervention*, edited by Jack P. Shonkoff and Samuel J. Meisels (2000). For more information on Séguin, and works on the history of mental retardation in the United States, see Édouard Séguin, *Idiocy and Its Treatment by the Physiological Method* (1866); *Mental Retardation in America: A Historical Reader*, edited by Steven Noll and James W. Trent (2004); and James W. Trent Jr., *Inventing the Feeble Mind: A History of Mental Retardation in the United States* (1995).

179 Samuel Gridley Howe's condemnation of disabled individuals was first published in his *Report Made to the Legislature of Massachusetts, upon Idiocy* (1848) and has been anthologized in *Mental Retardation in America: A Historical Reader*, edited by Steven Noll and James W. Trent (2004).

179 John Langdon H. Down's first description of the syndrome now associated with his name was published as "Observations on an ethnic classification of idiots," *London Hospital, Clinical Letters & Reports* 3 (1866), and has more recently been reprinted in *Mental Retardation* 33, no. 1 (February 1995).

179 Seminal documents in the history of the concept of "Mongolism" referenced in this section include John Langdon H. Down's above-cited report; Francis Graham Crookshank, *The Mongol in Our Midst: A Study of Man and His Three Faces* (1924); L. S. Penrose, "On the interaction of heredity and environment in the study of human genetics (with special reference to Mongolian imbecility)," *Journal of Genetics* 25, no. 3 (April 1932); L. S. Penrose, "The blood grouping of Mongolian imbeciles," *Lancet* 219, no. 5660 (February 20, 1932); and L. S. Penrose, "Maternal age, order of birth and developmental abnormalities," *British Journal of Psychiatry* 85, no. 359 (New Series No. 323) (1939).

Contemporary historical analysis of the subject includes Daniel J. Kevles's chapter, "'Mongolian imbecility': Race and its rejection in the understanding of a mental disease," and David Wright's chapter, "Mongols in our midst: John Langdon Down and the ethnic classification of idiocy, 1858–1924," in *Mental Retardation in America: A Historical Reader*, edited by Steven Noll and James W. Trent (2004); and Daniel J. Kevles, *In the Name of Eugenics: Genetics and the Uses of Human Heredity* (1985).

179 The argument that Down's view was progressive is proposed in David Wright, "Mongols in Our Midst: John Langdon Down and the Ethnic Classification of Idiocy, 1858–1924," in Steven Noll and James W. Trent Jr., editors, *Mental Retardation in America: A Historical Reader* (2004), page 102.

179 The replacement of disabled workers in the job market by immigrants and historic classifications of intellectual impairment are both discussed in the introduction to Richard Noll, *Mental Retardation in America* (2004), pages 1–16.

180 Oliver Wendell Holmes declared that "three generations of imbeciles are enough" in *Buck v. Bell*, 274 US 200 (1927).

180 See Jérôme Lejeune et al., "Étude des chromosomes somatiques de neuf enfants mongoliens," *Comptes Rendus Hebdomadaires des Séances de l'Académie des Science* 248, no. 11 (1959). Almost simultaneously, but independently, the gene was found by Patricia Jacobs in England; see Patricia Jacobs et al., "The somatic chromosomes in mongolism," *Lancet* 1, no. 7075 (April 1959).

180 Erik Erikson's institutionalization of his Down syndrome child is described in Lawrence J. Friedman, *Identity's Architect: A Biography of Erik H. Erikson* (1999).

180 See Simon Olshansky, "Chronic sorrow: A response to having a mentally defective child," *Social Casework* 43, no. 4 (1962).

180 The quotation from Albert Solnit and Mary Stark comes from their article "Mourning and the birth of a defective child," *Psychoanalytic Study of the Child* 16 (1961).

181 Arthur Miller and Inge Morath's institutionalization of their son with Down syndrome is described in Suzanna Andrews, "Arthur Miller's missing act," *Vanity Fair*, September 2007.

181 The statement that "a Down's is not a person" was made by Joseph Fletcher in his article (with Bernard Bard) "The right to die," *Atlantic Monthly*, April 1968.

181 See Ann Taylor Allen, "The kindergarten in Germany and the United States, 1840–1914: A comparative perspective," *History of Education* 35, no. 2 (March 2006).

181 For further information on the history and philosophy of Montessori education, see Gerald Lee Gutek, *The Montessori Method: The Origins of an Educational Innovation* (2004).

181 The history of disability service and education organizations (including the Association for Retarded Citizens) and the growth of the disability rights movement are examined in Doris Zames Fleischer and Frieda Zames, *The Disability Rights Movement: From Charity to Confrontation* (2001).

181 The full text of the Social Security Act of 1935 can be found at http://www.ssa.gov/history/35act.html. Matching federal funds for the care of the disabled is authorized in Section 514 (a): "From the sums appropriated therefor and the allotments available under section 512, the Secretary of the Treasury shall pay to each State which has an approved plan for services for crippled children, for each quarter, beginning the quarter commencing July 1, 1935, an amount which shall be used exclusively for carrying out the State plan, equal to one-half of the total sum expended during such quarter for carrying out such plan."

181 John Bowlby's groundbreaking works include *Maternal Care and Mental Health* (1952), *Child Care and the Growth of Love* (1965), and the "Attachment trilogy": *Attachment* (1969), *Separation: Anxiety and Anger* (1973), and *Loss: Sadness and Depression* (1980).

182 The establishment of the President's Panel on Mental Retardation in 1961 is chronicled on pages 83–86 of Edward Shorter, *The Kennedy Family and the Story of Mental Retardation* (2000); see also Fred J. Krause's official history, *President's Committee on Mental Retardation: A Historical Review 1966–1986* (1986), at http://www.acf.hhs.gov/programs/pcpid/docs/gm1966_1986.pdf.

182 See Eunice Kennedy Shriver, "Hope for retarded children," *Saturday Evening Post*, September 22, 1962.

182 See Edward Zigler and Sally J. Styfco, *The Hidden History of Head Start* (2010).

182 The quoted passage comes from §504 of the Rehabilitation Act of 1973. For the full text of the law, see http://www.access-board.gov/enforcement/rehab-act -text/title5.htm; for more information in layperson's language, see the website of the National Dissemination Center for Children with Disabilities, http://nichcy .org/laws/section504.

183 New York State's Statewide Early Intervention Program is described in the booklet *The Early Intervention Program: A Parent's Guide*, at http://www.health.ny.gov/ publications/0532.pdf; the state's comprehensive evaluation and intervention standards are promulgated in Demie Lyons et al., "Down syndrome assessment and intervention for young children (age 0–3): Clinical practice guideline: Report of the recommendations" (2005).

183 For more information on early intervention, see Dante Cicchetti and Marjorie Beeghly, editors, *Children with Down Syndrome: A Developmental Perspective* (1990); Demie Lyons et al., "Down syndrome assessment and intervention for young children (age 0–3): Clinical practice guideline: Report of the recommendations" (2005); Marci J. Hanson, "Twenty-five years after early intervention: A follow-up of children with Down syndrome and their families," *Infants & Young Children* 16, no. 4 (November–December 2003); and Stefani Hines and Forrest Bennett, "Effectiveness of early intervention for children with Down syndrome," *Mental Retardation & Developmental Disabilities Research Reviews* 2, no. 2 (1996).

184 This passage is based on my interview with Elaine Gregoli in 2005.

186 For discussion of the history of reform in the education of disabled children, see Richard A. Villa and Jacqueline Thousand, "Inclusion: Welcoming, valuing, and supporting the diverse learning needs of all students in shared general education environments," in *Down Syndrome: Visions for the 21st Century*, edited by William I. Cohen et al. (2002).

186 IDEA is also known as Public Law 94-142. For more information on this legislation, see US Congress, House Committee on Education and the Workforce, Subcommittee on Education Reform, *Individuals with Disabilities Education Act (IDEA): Guide to Frequently Asked Questions* (2005).

186 Michael Bérubé argues for the universal benefits of inclusion on pages 208–11 of *Life as We Know It* (1996).

187 This passage is based on my interview with Betsy Goodwin in 2004 and subsequent communications.

189 For further discussion of the "Baby Doe" legislation, see Kathryn Moss, "The 'Baby Doe' legislation: Its rise and fall," *Policy Studies Journal* 15, no. 4 (June 1987); and H. Rutherford Turnbull, Doug Guess, and Ann P. Turnbull, "*Vox populi* and Baby Doe," *Mental Retardation* 26, no. 3 (June 1988).

189 Peter Singer condones infanticide of profoundly disabled infants in his essay "Taking life: Humans," on pages 175–217 of *Practical Ethics* (1993); see also his book *Rethinking Life and Death: The Collapse of Our Traditional Ethics* (1994). Disabled individuals respond to Singer's pronouncements about the value of their lives in Not Dead Yet's "NDY Fact Sheet Library: Pete Singer" (at http:// www.notdeadyet.org/docs/singer.html); and Cal Montgomery, "A defense of genocide," *Ragged Edge Magazine*, July–August 1999.

189 The mother whose doctor suggested that she was being "defensive" by expressing satisfaction with her relationship with her Down syndrome child was quoted in Bryony A. Beresford, "Resources and strategies: How parents cope with the care of a disabled child," *Journal of Child Psychology & Psychiatry* 35, no. 1 (January 1994).

189 Marca Bristo's response to Peter Singer's philosophy occurs in Cal Montgomery, "A defense of genocide," *Ragged Edge Magazine*, July–August 1999.

189 The quotation from Adrienne Asch and Erik Parens comes from their essay "The disability rights critique of prenatal genetic testing: Reflections and recommendations," in *Prenatal Testing and Disability Rights* (2000); the quotation that follows comes from Adrienne Asch, "Disability equality and prenatal testing: Contradictory or compatible?," *Florida State University Law Review* 30, no. 2 (Winter 2003).

189 Leon Kass sets forth his objections to prenatal diagnosis in his essay "Implications of prenatal diagnosis for the human right to life," in *Intervention and Reflection: Basic Issues in Medical Ethics*, edited by Ronald Munson (2000).

190 The quotation from Janice McLaughlin ("Mourning the choice a woman is compelled to make . . .") comes from her paper "Screening networks: Shared agendas in feminist and disability movement challenges to antenatal screening and abortion," *Disability & Society* 18, no. 3 (2003).

190 My source for estimates of the numbers of abortions following prenatal diagnosis of Down syndrome, and the numbers of prenatally diagnosed DS babies born annually, is Brian Skotko, "Prenatally diagnosed Down syndrome: Mothers who continued their pregnancies evaluate their health care providers," *American Journal of Obstetrics & Gynecology* 192, no. 3 (March 2005).

190 The quotation from Tierney Temple Fairchild's doctor ("Almost everything you want to happen will happen") occurs on page 81 of Mitchell Zuckoff, *Choosing Naia: A Family's Journey* (2002).

190 The quotation from Tierney Temple Fairchild comes from her article "The choice to be pro-life," *Washington Post*, November 1, 2008; see also her speech "Rising to the occasion: Reflections on choosing Naia," *Leadership Perspectives in Developmental Disability* 3, no. 1 (Spring 2003).

190 Memoirs of parents of children with Down syndrome include Willard Abraham, *Barbara: A Prologue* (1958); Martha Nibley Beck, *Expecting Adam* (1999); Michael Bérubé, *Life as We Know It* (1996); Martha Moraghan Jablow, *Cara* (1982); Danny Mardell, *Danny's Challenge* (2005); Vicki Noble, *Down Is Up for Aaron Eagle* (1993); Greg Palmer, *Adventures in the Mainstream* (2005); Kathryn Lynard Soper, *Gifts: Mothers Reflect on How Children with Down Syndrome Enrich Their Lives* (2007); Mitchell Zuckoff, *Choosing Naia* (2002); and Cynthia S. Kidder and Brian Skotko, *Common Threads: Celebrating Life with Down Syndrome* (2001).

191 This passage is based on my interview with Deirdre Featherstone and Wilson Madden in 2007 and subsequent communications.

194 David Patterson discusses the genetic phenomena that give rise to such a wide variety of manifestations in Down syndrome in his chapter, "Sequencing of chromosome 21/The Human Genome Project," in *Down Syndrome: Visions for the 21st Century*, edited by William I. Cohen et al. (2003).

194 One study finding that people with Down syndrome are generally agreeable is Brigid M. Cahill and Laraine Masters Glidden, "Influence of child diagnosis on family and parental functioning: Down syndrome versus other disabilities," *American Journal on Mental Retardation* 101, no. 2 (September 1996).

194 For more on psychopathology in DS, see Ann Gath and Dianne Gumley, "Retarded children and their siblings," *Journal of Child Psychology & Psychiatry* 28, no. 5 (September 1987); Beverly A. Myers and Siegfried M. Pueschel, "Psychiatric disorders in a population with Down syndrome," *Journal of Nervous & Mental Disease* 179 (1991); Dennis Eugene McGuire and Brian A. Chicoine, *Mental*

Wellness in Adults with Down Syndrome (2006); and Jean A. Rondal et al., editors, *The Adult with Down Syndrome: A New Challenge for Society* (2004).

195 The quoted study, finding that people with Down syndrome experience considerable emotional difficulty, is Elisabeth M. Dykens, "Psychopathology in children with intellectual disability," *Journal of Child Psychology & Psychiatry* 41, no. 4 (May 2000); see also Elisabeth M. Dykens, "Psychiatric and behavioral disorders in persons with Down syndrome," *Mental Retardation & Developmental Disabilities Research Review* 13, no. 3 (October 2007).

195 The sexual abuse of disabled individuals occurs not only at the hands of caretakers and nondisabled predators but also at the hands of other disabled individuals, especially in group settings; see Deborah Tharinger, Connie Burrows Horton, and Susan Millea, "Sexual abuse and exploitation of children and adults with mental retardation and other handicaps," *Child Abuse & Neglect* 14, no. 3 (1990); Eileen M. Furey and Jill J. Niesen, "Sexual abuse of adults with mental retardation by other consumers," *Sexuality & Disability* 12, no. 4 (1994); and Eileen M. Furey, James M. Granfield, and Orv C. Karan, "Sexual abuse and neglect of adults with mental retardation: A comparison of victim characteristics," *Behavioral Interventions* 9, no. 2 (April 1994).

195 Behavioral problems and parenting stress are discussed in R. Stores et al., "Daytime behaviour problems and maternal stress in children with Down's syndrome, their siblings, and non-intellectually disabled and other intellectually disabled peers," *Journal of Intellectual Disability Research* 42, no. 3 (June 1998); and Richard P. Hastings and Tony Brown, "Functional assessment and challenging behaviors: Some future directions," *Journal of the Association for Persons with Severe Handicaps* 25, no. 4 (Winter 2000).

195 For a recent review of progress in gene therapy for Down syndrome, see Cristina Fillat and Xavier Altafaj, "Gene therapy for Down syndrome," *Progress in Brain Research* 197 (2012).

195 The main promoter of multivitamin regimens—aka orthomolecular treatment— and the target of most of the referenced criticism was Henry Turkel (1903– 92), whose treatment incorporated vitamins, antihistamines, and diuretics; see Henry Turkel, "Medical amelioration of Down's syndrome incorporating the orthomolecular approach," *Journal of Orthomolecular Psychiatry* 4, no. 2 (2nd Quarter 1975). Papers critical of supplementation include Len Leshin, "Nutritional supplements for Down syndrome: A highly questionable approach," *Quackwatch*, October 18, 1998, http://www.quackwatch.org/01QuackeryRelatedTopics/down .html; Cornelius Ani, Sally Grantham-McGregor, and David Muller, "Nutritional supplementation in Down syndrome: Theoretical considerations and current status," *Developmental Medicine & Child Neurology* 42, no. 3 (March 2000); Nancy J. Lobaugh et al., "Piracetam therapy does not enhance cognitive functioning in children with Down syndrome," *Archives of Pediatric & Adolescent Medicine* 155, no. 4 (April 2001); W. Carl Cooley, "Nonconventional therapies for Down syndrome: A review and framework for decision making," in *Down Syndrome: Visions for the 21st Century*, edited by William I. Cohen et al. (2002); and Nancy J. Roizen, "Complementary and alternative therapies for Down syndrome," *Mental Retardation & Developmental Disabilities Research Reviews* 11, no. 2 (April 2005). For more information on growth hormone, see Salvador Castells and Krystyna E. Wiesniewski, editors, *Growth Hormone Treatment in Down's Syndrome* (1993).

195 See Rolf R. Olbrisch, "Plastic and aesthetic surgery on children with Down's syndrome," *Aesthetic Plastic Surgery* 9, no. 4 (December 1985); Siegfried M.

Pueschel et al., "Parents' and physicians' perceptions of facial plastic surgery in children with Down syndrome," *Journal of Mental Deficiency Research* 30, no. 1 (March 1986); Siegfried M. Pueschel, "Facial plastic surgery for children with Down syndrome," *Developmental Medicine & Child Neurology* 30, no. 4 (August 1988); and R. B. Jones, "Parental consent to cosmetic facial surgery in Down's syndrome," *Journal of Medical Ethics* 26, no. 2 (April 2000).

195 The National Down Syndrome Society sets forth the organization's position on facial normalization surgery in "Cosmetic surgery for children with Down syndrome," http://www.ndss.org/index.php?option=com_content&view=article&id=153&limitstart=6. Mitchell Zuckoff also discusses the subject in *Choosing Naia: A Family's Journey* (2002).

195 This passage is based on my interview with Michelle Smith in 2004.

198 The percentage of instances of Down syndrome that arise from spontaneous genetic mutation comes from D. Mutton et al., "Cytogenetic and epidemiological findings in Down syndrome, England and Wales 1989 to 1993," *Journal of Medical Genetics* 33, no. 5 (May 1996). For a recent review of DS genetics, see David Patterson, "Genetic mechanisms involved in the phenotype of Down syndrome," *Mental Retardation & Developmental Disabilities Research Reviews* 13, no. 3 (October 2007).

198 For statistics on termination of DS pregnancies I have relied upon Caroline Mansfield et al., "Termination rates after prenatal diagnosis of Down syndrome, spina bifida, anencephaly, and Turner and Klinefelter syndromes: A systematic literature review," *Prenatal Diagnosis* 19, no. 9 (September 1999). Mansfield came up with a 92 percent rate, which has been the standard number for many years. A recent meta-analysis, however, suggests that Mansfield's estimate is inflated, and that the abortion rate is somewhat less than that; see Jaime L. Natoli et al., "Prenatal diagnosis of Down syndrome: A systematic review of termination rates (1995–2011)," *Prenatal Diagnosis* 32, no. 2 (February 2012).

198 Figures on life expectancy in Down syndrome come from David Strauss and Richard K. Eyman, "Mortality of people with mental retardation in California with and without Down syndrome, 1986–1991," *American Journal on Mental Retardation* 100, no. 6 (May 1996); Jan Marshall Friedman et al., "Racial disparities in median age at death of persons with Down syndrome: United States, 1968–1997," *Morbidity & Mortality Weekly Report* 50, no. 22 (June 8, 2001); and Steven M. Day et al., "Mortality and causes of death in persons with Down syndrome in California," *Developmental Medicine & Child Neurology* 47, no. 3 (March 2005).

199 The study finding that more than a quarter of respondents would not choose a cure for DS if one was available was described by Karen Kaplan, "Some Down syndrome parents don't welcome prospect of cure," *Los Angeles Times*, November 22, 2009. Kaplan was quoting and reporting on a paper presented by Angela Inglis, Catriona Hippman, and Jehannine C. Austin, "Views and opinions of parents of individuals with Down syndrome: Prenatal testing and the possibility of a 'cure'?," abstract published in Courtney Sebold, Lyndsay Graham, and Kirsty McWalter, "Presented abstracts from the Twenty-Eighth Annual Education Conference of the National Society of Genetic Counselors (Atlanta, Georgia, November 2009)," *Journal of Genetic Counseling* 18, no. 6 (November 2009).

199 For statistics on DS population trends, I have relied on a report by the US Centers for Disease Control, "Down syndrome cases at birth increased" (2009); Joan K. Morris and Eva Alberman, "Trends in Down's syndrome live births and antenatal diagnoses in England and Wales from 1989 to 2008: Analysis of data from the National Down Syndrome Cytogenetic Register," *British Medical Journal* 339

(2009); and Guido Cocchi et al., "International trends of Down syndrome, 1993–2004: Births in relation to maternal age and terminations of pregnancies," *Birth Defects Research Part A: Clinical and Molecular Teratology* 88, no. 6 (June 2010).

199 Figures on the percentage of children with Down syndrome born to women under thirty-five come from the National Down Syndrome Society. For more on the factors at play in decision-making following prenatal testing, see Miriam Kupperman et al., "Beyond race or ethnicity and socioeconomic status: Predictors of prenatal testing for Down syndrome," *Obstetrics & Gynecology* 107, no. 5 (May 2006).

199 Socioeconomic differences in attitudes toward parenting Down syndrome children are explored in Annick-Camille Dumaret et al., "Adoption and fostering of babies with Down syndrome: A cohort of 593 cases," *Prenatal Diagnosis* 18, no. 5 (May 1998).

199 Predictions that the population of people with DS might double by 2025 come from Jean A. Rondal, "Intersyndrome and intrasyndrome language differences," in Jean A. Rondal et al., *Intellectual Disabilities: Genetics, Behaviour and Inclusion* (2004).

199 The American College of Obstetricians and Gynecologists recommended universal nuchal translucency screening in "Screening for fetal chromosomal abnormalities," *ACOG Practice Bulletin* 77 (January 2007). Press reports on the recommendations include Roni Rabin, "Screen all pregnancies for Down syndrome, doctors say," *New York Times*, January 9, 2007; and Amy Harmon, "The DNA age: Prenatal test puts Down syndrome in hard focus," *New York Times*, May 9, 2007.

199 George Will used the phrase *search and destroy* in his article "Golly, what did Jon do?," *Newsweek*, January 29, 2007.

199 For a study of the impact of parent-to-parent contact on pregnant women's decisions on abortion after prenatal diagnosis of Down syndrome, see Karen L. Lawson and Sheena A. Walls-Ingram, "Selective abortion for Down syndrome: The relation between the quality of intergroup contact, parenting expectations, and willingness to terminate," *Journal of Applied Social Psychology* 40, no. 3 (March 2010). Advocacy for parent education is discussed in Adrienne Asch, "Prenatal diagnosis and selective abortion: A challenge to practice and policy," *American Journal of Public Health* 89, no. 11 (November 1999); Adrienne Asch and Erik Parens, "The disability rights critique of prenatal genetic testing: Reflections and recommendations," *Prenatal Testing and Disability Rights*, edited by Erik Parens and Adrienne Asch (2000); Lynn Gillam, "Prenatal diagnosis and discrimination against the disabled," *Journal of Medical Ethics* 25, no. 2 (April 1999); and Rob Stein, "New safety, new concerns in tests for Down syndrome," *Washington Post*, February 24, 2009.

199 Stephen Quake is quoted in Dan Hurley, "A drug for Down syndrome," *New York Times*, July 29, 2011. Quake's work is also discussed in Jocelyn Kaiser, "Blood test for mom picks up Down syndrome in fetus," *ScienceNOW Daily News*, October 6, 2008; Andrew Pollack, "Blood tests ease search for Down syndrome," *New York Times*, October 6, 2008; and Amy Dockser Marcus, "New prenatal tests offer safer, early screenings," *Wall Street Journal*, June 28, 2011.

199 Babak Khoshnood et al. anticipate an increase in economic stratification of families with Down syndrome children in "Advances in medical technology and creation of disparities: The case of Down syndrome," *American Journal of Public Health* 96, no. 12 (December 2006).

200 Michael Bérubé discusses the long-term ramifications of reductions in support for families with DS children in Amy Harmon, "The problem with an almost-perfect genetic world," *New York Times*, November 20, 2005.

200 The study finding that women who after testing knowingly choose to give birth to a child with Down syndrome are more harshly judged than those who had no opportunity for testing is Karen L. Lawson, "Perceptions of deservedness of social aid as a function of prenatal diagnostic testing," *Journal of Applied Social Psychology* 33, no. 1 (2003). The quotation appears on page 76.

200 The first quotation from Michael Bérubé ("So much depends . . .") occurs on page 78 of *Life as We Know It* (1996); the second comes from Amy Harmon, "The problem with an almost-perfect genetic world," *New York Times*, November 20, 2005.

200 Pharmaceutical advances in the treatment of Down syndrome are discussed in Dan Hurley, "A drug for Down syndrome," *New York Times*, July 29, 2011.

200 The study finding improvement in hippocampal development in mice administered Prozac is Sarah Clark et al., "Fluoxetine rescues deficient neurogenesis in hippocampus of the Ts65Dn mouse model for Down syndrome," *Experimental Neurology* 200, no. 1 (July 2006); for the memantine study, see Albert C. S. Costa et al., "Acute injections of the NMDA receptor antagonist memantine rescue performance deficits of the Ts65Dn mouse model of Down syndrome on a fear conditioning test," *Neuropsychopharmacology* 33, no. 7 (June 2008).

200 The study finding improvement in mice following elevation of norepinephrine levels is Ahmad Salehi et al., "Restoration of norepinephrine-modulated contextual memory in a mouse model of Down syndrome," *Science Translational Medicine* 1, no. 7 (November 2009).

200 See William J. Netzer et al., "Lowering β-amyloid levels rescues learning and memory in a Down syndrome mouse model," *PLoS ONE* 5, no. 6 (2010).

200 Quotations by William Mobley, Craig C. Garner, and Albert Costa come from Dan Hurley, "A drug for Down syndrome," *New York Times*, July 29, 2011.

201 This passage is based on my interview with Angelica Roman-Jiminez in 2007.

203 The quotation from Martha Nibley Beck ("If you'll cast your mind back to high school biology . . .") occurs on pages 327–28 of *Expecting Adam* (1999).

203 The quotation about babyfaceness comes from the study of the pitch of parents' voices: Deborah J. Fidler, "Parental vocalizations and perceived immaturity in Down syndrome," *American Journal on Mental Retardation* 108, no. 6 (November 2003).

204 Fathers' adaptation to Down syndrome is discussed in W. Steven Barnett and Glenna C. Boyce, "Effects of children with Down syndrome on parents' activities," *American Journal on Mental Retardation* 100, no. 2 (September 1995); L. A. Ricci and Robert M. Hodapp, "Fathers of children with Down's syndrome versus other types of intellectual disability: Perceptions, stress and involvement," *Journal of Intellectual Disability Research* 47, nos. 4–5 (May–June 2003); and Jennifer C. Willoughby and Laraine Masters Glidden, "Fathers helping out: Shared child care and marital satisfaction of parents of children with disabilities," *American Journal on Mental Retardation* 99, no. 4 (January 1995).

204 There are a great many studies of the experiences of siblings of disabled children. Researchers focusing on the subject include Brian G. Skotko, Jan Blacher, and Zolinda Stoneman.

204 The quotation from Colgan Leaming comes from her article "My brother is not his disability," *Newsweek Web Exclusive*, June 1, 2006.

205 This passage is based on my interviews with Susan Arnsten, Adam Delli-Bovi,

Teegan Delli-Bovi, and William Walker Russell III in 2007 and subsequent communications. Susan's artwork may be seen at http://fineartamerica.com/profiles/susan-arnstenrussell.html.

207 Exodus 37:9: "The cherubs were with wings spread upwards, sheltering the Ark cover . . . with their faces toward one another."

210 Statistics on the percentage of mentally retarded adults who live with their parents come from Tamar Heller, Alison B. Miller, and Alan Factor, "Adults with mental retardation as supports to their parents: Effects on parental caregiving appraisal," *Mental Retardation* 35, no. 5 (October 1997); see also Clare Ansberry, "Parents devoted to a disabled child confront old age," *Wall Street Journal,* January 7, 2004.

210 The quotation about nurturing and support comes from Arnold Birenbaum and Herbert J. Cohen, "On the importance of helping families," *Mental Retardation* 31, no. 2 (April 1993).

210 The relationship between severity of disability and out-of-home placement is explored in Jan Blacher and Bruce L. Baker, "Out-of-home placement for children with retardation: Family decision making and satisfaction," *Family Relations* 43, no. 1 (January 1994).

210 The fears of siblings following outplacement of a family member are discussed in Frances Kaplan Grossman, *Brothers and Sisters of Retarded Children: An Exploratory Study* (1972).

210 For my discussion of families and placement of children with Down syndrome, I have relied upon the following papers by Bruce L. Baker and Jan Blacher: "Out-of-home placement for children with mental retardation: Dimensions of family involvement," *American Journal on Mental Retardation* 98, no. 3 (November 1993); "For better or worse? Impact of residential placement on families," *Mental Retardation* 40, no. 1 (February 2002); "Family involvement in residential treatment of children with retardation: Is there evidence of detachment?," *Journal of Child Psychology & Psychiatry* 35, no. 3 (March 1994); and "Out-of-home placement for children with retardation: Family decision making and satisfaction," *Family Relations* 43, no. 1 (January 1994).

211 The quotation from the first mother ("I could never put my child in one of *those* places!") occurs on pages 229–30 of Jan Blacher, *When There's No Place Like Home: Options for Children Living Apart from Their Natural Families* (1994); the quotation from the second ("Calling the Regional Center was the scariest phone call I ever made") comes from Jan Blacher and Bruce L. Baker, "Out-of-home placement for children with retardation: Family decision making and satisfaction," *Family Relations* 43, no. 1 (January 1994).

211 For discussion of the appropriateness of young people with Down syndrome leaving the family home at a similar age to typical young people, see Zolinda Stoneman and Phyllis Waldman Berman, editors, *The Effects of Mental Retardation, Disability, and Illness on Sibling Relationships* (1993).

211 Figures for the reduction in numbers and proportion of children and youth living in residential institutions come from K. Charlie Lakin, Lynda Anderson, and Robert Prouty, "Decreases continue in out-of-home residential placements of children and youth with mental retardation," *Mental Retardation* 36, no. 2 (April 1998). According to the State of the States in Developmental Disabilities Project report "Top Ten State Spending on Institutional Care for People with Disabilities" (at http://www.centerforsystemschange.org/view.php?nav_id=54), "Alaska, District of Columbia, Hawaii, Maine, Michigan, New Hampshire, New Mexico, Oregon, Rhode Island, Vermont, and West Virginia no longer fund

state-operated institutions for 16 or more persons," leaving thirty-nine of the fifty states still funding state-operated institutions for sixteen or more persons. The increase in life expectancy of people with Down syndrome and other forms of intellectual disability is discussed in Matthew P. Janicki et al., "Mortality and morbidity among older adults with intellectual disability: Health services considerations," *Disability & Rehabilitation* 21, nos. 5–6 (May–June 1999).

211 Information on the number of institutions visited by families prior to placement, and criteria used in evaluating them, come from Jan Blacher and Bruce L. Baker, "Out-of-home placement for children with retardation: Family decision making and satisfaction," *Family Relations* 43, no. 1 (January 1994).

211 The quotation about abuses in residential facilities for the developmentally disabled in New York State comes from Danny Hakim, "At state-run homes, abuse and impunity," *New York Times*, March 12, 2011.

212 Information on trends in residential placement and statistics on public expenditures for people with intellectual disabilities come from Robert W. Prouty et al., editors, "Residential services for persons with developmental disabilities: Status and trends through 2004," Research and Training Center on Community Living, Institute on Community Integration/UCEDD College of Education and Human Development, University of Minnesota, July 2005; K. Charlie Lakin, Lynda Anderson, and Robert Prouty, "Decreases continue in out-of-home residential placements of children and youth with mental retardation," *Mental Retardation* 36, no. 2 (April 1998); and K. Charlie Lakin, Lynda Anderson, and Robert Prouty, "Change in residential placements for persons with intellectual and developmental disabilities in the USA in the last two decades," *Journal of Intellectual & Developmental Disability* 28, no. 2 (June 2003).

212 Parents describe their adult DS children as a comfort in Tamar Heller, Alison B. Miller, and Alan Factor, "Adults with mental retardation as supports to their parents: Effects on parental caregiving appraisal," *Mental Retardation* 35, no. 5 (October 1997); and Clare Ansberry, "Parents devoted to a disabled child confront old age," *Wall Street Journal*, January 7, 2004. Figures on the numbers of people with DS moved to residential placement after the death of their parents come from Marsha Mailick Seltzer and Marty Wyngaarden Krauss, "Quality of life of adults with mental retardation/developmental disabilities who live with family," *Mental Retardation & Developmental Disabilities Research Reviews* 7, no. 2 (May 2001).

212 The quotation from the father about his DS daughter's dwindling social life comes from a personal communication.

212 The study finding that adults with DS tend to socialize within their parents' network of friends is Marty Wyngaarden Krauss, Marsha Mailick Seltzer, and S. J. Goodman, "Social support networks of adults with mental retardation who live at home," *American Journal on Mental Retardation* 96, no. 4 (January 1992).

213 For more information on People First, see "History of People First," http://www .peoplefirstwv.org/aboutpeoplefirst/history.html. Figures on the number of self-advocacy groups in the United States and the quotation given both come from the "People First Chapter Handbook and Toolkit" (2010), http://www.peoplefirstwv .org/images/PF_of_WV_Chapter_Handbook_final.pdf.

213 See Nigel Hunt, *The World of Nigel Hunt: The Diary of a Mongoloid Youth* (New York: Garrett Publications, 1967).

213 See Jason Kingsley and Mitchell Levitz, *Count Us In: Growing Up with Down Syndrome* (1994).

213 A transcript of Windy Smith's speech at the 2000 Republican National Convention is hosted on the ABC News website at http://abcnews.go.com/ Politics/story?id=123241&page=1. The quotation about "grotesque political theater" comes from Tom Scocca, "Silly in Philly," *Metro Times*, August 9, 2000.

214 For an interview with Chris Burke, see Jobeth McDaniel, "Chris Burke: Then and Now," *Ability Magazine*, February 2007. Burke maintains a personal website at http://www.chrisburke.org; Bobby Brederlow's is at http://www.bobby.de/. Judith Scott is the subject of her sister Joyce Scott's memoir, *EnTWINed* (2006); see also John M. MacGregor, *Metamorphosis: The Fiber Art of Judith Scott: The Outsider Artist and the Experience of Down's Syndrome* (1999). For an interview with Lauren Potter, see Michelle Diament, "Down syndrome takes center stage on Fox's 'Glee,'" *Disability Scoop*, April 12, 2010.

214 For more information on short-term memory and information processing in Down syndrome, see Robert M. Hodapp and Elisabeth M. Dykens's chapter, "Genetic and behavioural aspects: Application to maladaptive behaviour and cognition," in Jean A. Rondal et al., *Intellectual Disabilities: Genetics, Behaviour and Inclusion* (2004).

214 Greg Palmer, *Adventures in the Mainstream: Coming of Age with Down Syndrome* (2005). Ned Palmer's poem appears in the book on page 40; the quotation appears on page 98.

215 The marriage saga of Corky (Chris Burke) and Amanda (Andrea Friedman) begins at season 4, episode 3, "Premarital Syndrome" (originally broadcast on October 4, 1992; see http://www.tvguide.com/tvshows/life-goes-on-1992/episode-3-season -4/premarital-syndrome/202678). For the backstory on this love story, see Howard Rosenberg, "There's more to 'life' than ratings," *Los Angeles Times*, April 18, 1992, and "They'll take romance," *People*, April 6, 1992.

215 This passage is based on my interview with Tom and Karen Robards in 2007 and subsequent communications.

V: Autism

221 My source for historical information on autism prevalence, and autism in general, is Laura Schreibman, *The Science and Fiction of Autism* (2005). On March 30, 2012, the CDC upped its autism prevalence estimates from 1:110 to 1:88; see Jon Baio, "Prevalence of autism spectrum disorders: Autism and Developmental Disabilities Monitoring Network, 14 sites, United States, 2008," *Morbidity & Mortality Weekly Report (MMWR)*, March 30, 2012.

221 The quotation from Eric Kandel comes from my interview with him in 2009. He has spoken about this, also, in Eric Kandel, "Interview: biology of the mind," *Newsweek*, March 27, 2006.

222 According to the Coalition for SafeMinds website at http://safeminds .org, "SafeMinds" stands for "Sensible Action for Ending Mercury-Induced Neurological Disorders."

222 The full text of the Combating Autism Act of 2006 (Public Law 109–416) can be found at http://thomas.loc.gov/cgi-bin/bdquery/z?d109:S843:; the text of the Combating Autism Reauthorization Act of 2011 (Public Law 112–32) can be found at http://thomas.loc.gov/cgi-bin/query/z?c112:H.R.2005:. The role of parent advocacy groups in promoting the bill is described in Ed O'Keefe's report for ABC News, "Congress declares war on autism," broadcast December 6, 2006. Cure Autism Now and Autism Speaks merged in 2007; see Autism Speaks'

February 5, 2007, press release, "Autism Speaks and Cure Autism Now complete merger" (http://www.autismspeaks.org/about-us/press-releases/autism-speaks-and-cure-autism-now-complete-merger).

222 Thomas Insel's remark was a personal communication.

222 The astonishing proliferation of books and films about autism is vividly revealed by WorldCat, a consolidated catalog of library holdings worldwide. A search of the keyword *autism* for 1997 yields 1,221 items; for 2011, 7,486 items.

222 The diagnostic criteria for autism ("299.00 Autistic Disorder"), Asperger syndrome ("299.80 Asperger's Disorder"), and PDD-NOS ("299.80 Pervasive Developmental Disorder Not Otherwise Specified") can be found in *Diagnostic and Statistical Manual of Mental Disorders DSM-IV-TR*, 4th ed. (2000), pages 70–84.

222 For a reliable, basic introduction to autism, see Shannon des Roches Rosa et al., *The Thinking Person's Guide to Autism* (2011).

223 Sources of estimates on the incidence of regression in autism include C. Plauché Johnson et al., "Identification and evaluation of children with autism spectrum disorders," *Pediatrics* 120, no. 5 (November 2007); Gerry A. Stefanatos, "Regression in autistic spectrum disorders," *Neuropsychology Review* 18 (December 2008); Sally J. Rogers, "Developmental regression in autism spectrum disorders," *Mental Retardation & Developmental Disabilities Research Review* 10, no. 2 (May 2004); and Robin L. Hansen, "Regression in autism: Prevalence and associated factors in the CHARGE study," *Ambulatory Pediatrics* 8, no. 1 (January 2008).

223 Emily Perl Kingsley's 1987 essay, "Welcome to Holland," can be found all over the Internet, as well as in Jack Canfield, *Chicken Soup for the Soul: Children with Special Needs* (2007). Susan Rzucidlo's retort, "Welcome to Beirut," also self-published, can be found at http://www.bbbautism.com/beginners_beirut.htm and on a few dozen other websites.

224 My original work on neurodiversity may be found in my article "The autism rights movement," *New York*, May 25, 2008.

224 This passage is based on numerous interviews with Betsy Burns and Jeff Hansen between 2003 and 2012 and other communications.

225 The neurologist was perhaps overly pessimistic to assert that Cece would never talk if she hadn't begun to do so after intensive early intervention; a 2004 paper concluded that 90 percent of autistic children develop functional speech by the age of nine: Catherine Lord et al., "Trajectory of language development in autistic spectrum disorders," in *Developmental Language Disorders: From Phenotypes to Etiologies* (2004).

225 Jim Simons, who has been a leading funder of autism research through the Simons Foundation, noted in a personal communication that when his daughter got a fever, her autism symptoms dissipated and she was able to function better than she usually could. That other bodily conditions might have some impact on the expression of autistic symptoms and might underlie sudden, nonpermanent transformations such as Cece's is a subject of investigation, though there is not enough science yet to make therapeutic use of the idea. For a discussion of the correlation between fever and behavioral improvement, see L. K. Curran et al., "Behaviors associated with fever in children with autism spectrum disorders," *Pediatrics* 120, no. 6 (December 2007); Mark F. Mehler and Dominick P. Purpura, "Autism, fever, epigenetics and the locus coeruleus," *Brain Research Reviews* 59, no. 2 (March 2009); and David Moorman, "Workshop report: Fever and autism," Simons Foundation for Autism Research, April 1, 2010, http://

sfari.org/news-and-opinion/workshop-reports/2010/workshop-report-fever
-and-autism.

226 The first quotation from Elizabeth (Betsy) Burns's 2003 novel, *Tilt: Every Family Spins on Its Own Axis*, occurs on page 96, the second on pages 43–44.

226 Researchers have found a higher-than-average incidence of psychiatric conditions among family members of individuals with autism; e.g., Mohammad Ghaziuddin, "A family history study of Asperger syndrome," *Journal of Autism and Developmental Disorders* 35, no. 2 (2005); and Joseph Piven and Pat Palmer. "Psychiatric disorder and the broad autism phenotype: Evidence from a family study of multiple-incidence autism families," *American Journal of Psychiatry* 156, no. 14 (April 1999).

231 The *Oxford English Dictionary*, 2nd ed. (1989), offers the following passage from Eugen Bleuler's 1913 paper, "Autistic thinking," *American Journal of Insanity* 69 (1913), page 873:
       "When we look more closely we find amongst all normal people many and important instances where thought is divorced both from logic and from reality. I have called these forms of thinking autistic, corresponding to the idea of schizophrenic autismus."

231 The term *childhood schizophrenia* was coined in the 1930s and was loosely used to refer to a wide range of cognitive impairments manifesting in early childhood. Propagators of the term include Lauretta Bender, a child psychiatrist practicing at Bellevue Hospital, who published numerous reports of her clinical observations. For a contemporary expression of concern about the inappropriate application of the term, see Hilde L. Mosse, "The misuse of the diagnosis childhood schizophrenia," *American Journal of Psychiatry* 114, no. 9 (March 1958); Robert F. Asarnow and Joan Rosenbaum Asarnow review the history of the diagnosis in "Childhood-onset schizophrenia: Editors' introduction," *Schizophrenia Bulletin* 20, no. 4 (October 1994).

231 Leo Kanner's seminal 1943 report, "Autistic disturbances of affective contact," is included in an anthology of his papers, *Childhood Psychosis: Initial Studies and New Insights* (1973).

231 In 1943, Kanner noted the supposed coldness of the mothers of autistic children, but left open the possibility that the condition was inborn. See "Autistic disturbances of affective contact," in *Childhood Psychosis: Initial Studies and New Insights* (1973), page 42. By 1949, Kanner had more fully developed his parent-blaming theory; the term *refrigerator* appears twice in his 1949 article "Problems of nosology and psychodynamics in early childhood autism," *American Journal of Orthopsychiatry* 19, no. 3 (July 1949). But Kanner's attributions changed as understanding of the neurological basis of autism evolved. From a remembrance by his colleagues Eric Schopler, Stella Chess, and Leon Eisenberg, "Our memorial to Leo Kanner," *Journal of Autism & Developmental Disorders* 11, no. 3 (September 1981), page 258: "The man credited with the term 'refrigerator mother' explained to the members of the National Society for Autistic Children, at their annual meeting in 1971, that the blame for their child's autism implied by this term was now established as inappropriate and incorrect."

231 Bruno Bettelheim's notorious statement "The precipitating factor in infantile autism is the parent's wish that his child should not exist" occurs on page 125 of *The Empty Fortress: Infantile Autism and the Birth of the Self* (1967).

231 Interview with Isabelle Rapin in 2009.

231 Bernard Rimland posited a biological hypothesis of autism causation in *Infantile Autism: The Syndrome and Its Implications for a Neural Theory of Behavior* (1964).

231 Laura Schreibman, *The Science and Fiction of Autism* (2005), is the source of the refrigerator name-tag anecdote. From pages 84–85: "It is widely rumored that these first attendees wore name tags in the shape of little refrigerators."

231 The quotation from Eustacia Cutler occurs on page 208 of her autobiography, *A Thorn in My Pocket* (2004).

231 Asperger's original paper was published in German during World War II: Hans Asperger, "Die 'autistischen psychopathen' im kindesalter," *Archiv für Psychiatrie & Nervenkrankheiten* (*European Archives of Psychiatry and Clinical Neuroscience*) 117, no. 1 (1944), pages 76–136. Uta Frith translated the paper into English in 1981, giving it the title "'Autistic psychopathy' in childhood"; that translation was later included in the anthology *Autism and Asperger Syndrome* (1991).

232 The *little professor* moniker's first appearance in the professional literature occurs in Hans Asperger, "Die 'autistischen psychopathen' im kindesalter," *Archiv für Psychiatrie & Nervenkrankheiten* (*European Archives of Psychiatry and Clinical Neuroscience*) 117, no. 1 (1944). From page 118: "Die aus einer Kontaktstörung kommende Hilflosigkeit dem praktischen Leben gegenüber, welche den 'Professor' charakterisiert und zu einer unsterblichen Witzblattfigur macht, ist ein Beweis dafür."

232 On proposals for revisions to the *DSM-5* diagnostic criteria for autistic spectrum disorders, see Claudia Wallis, "A powerful identity, a vanishing diagnosis," *New York Times*, November 2, 2009; and Benedict Carey, "New definition of autism will exclude many, study suggests," *New York Times*, January 19, 2012. For scholarly discussions of the *DSM* changes, see Mohammad Ghaziuddin, "Should the DSM V drop Asperger syndrome?" *Journal of Autism & Developmental Disorders* 40, no. 9 (September 2010); and Lorna Wing et al., "Autism spectrum disorders in the DSM-V: Better or worse than the DSM-IV?," *Research in Developmental Disabilities* 32, no. 2 (March–April 2011).

232 All of these anecdotes about social deficits of individuals with Asperger syndrome come from personal communications.

232 Temple Grandin's story first came to widespread attention through the title essay in Oliver Sacks, *An Anthropologist on Mars* (1995), and through her autobiography, *Thinking in Pictures: And Other Reports from My Life with Autism* (1995). She has also been the subject of several television programs, including the 2006 BBC documentary *The Woman Who Thinks Like a Cow*, and the HBO biopic *Temple Grandin*. ASAN organizational website: http://www.autisticadvocacy.org/. For an interview with Ari Ne'eman, see Claudia Kalb, "Erasing autism," *Newsweek*, May 25, 2009.

233 Temple Grandin likened her mind to an Internet search engine in an interview with me in 2004. She had previously used the image in her autobiography, *Thinking in Pictures: And Other Reports from My Life with Autism* (1995), page 31.

233 The quotation from John Elder Robison occurs on page 2 of *Look Me in the Eye: My Life with Asperger's* (2007).

233 This passage is based on my interview with Jennifer Franklin in 2008 and subsequent communications. The quotations from poems are from her book *Persephone's Ransom* (2011).

235 My basic source on ABA is Laura Ellen Schreibman, *The Science and Fiction of Autism* (2005). Works by O. Ivar Lovaas include "Behavioral treatment and normal educational and intellectual functioning in young autistic children," *Journal of Consulting & Clinical Psychology* 55, no. 1 (February 1987); and "The

development of a treatment-research project for developmentally disabled and autistic children," *Journal of Applied Behavior Analysis* 26, no. 4 (Winter 1993).

236 The passage from Scott Sea occurs in his article "Planet autism," *Salon*, September 27, 2003. It has been condensed.

237 Juliet Mitchell's comments are from personal communications. She has written about autism in *Mad Men and Medusas: Reclaiming Hysteria* (2000).

237 For a recent use of the changeling metaphor, see Portia Iversen, *Strange Son: Two Mothers, Two Sons, and the Quest to Unlock the Hidden World of Autism* (2006), pages xii–xiv. For scholarly discussion of changeling myths as a response to disability, see D. L. Ashliman, "Changelings," *Folklore & Mythology Electronic Texts*, University of Pittsburgh, 1997, at http://www.pitt.edu/~dash/changeling.html; and Susan Schoon Eberly, "Fairies and the folklore of disability: Changelings, hybrids and the solitary fairy," *Folklore* 99, no. 1 (1988). For two autistic activists' perspectives, see Amanda Baggs, "The original, literal demons," *Autism Demonized*, February 12, 2006, at http://web.archive.org/web/20060628231956/http://autismdemonized.blogspot.com/; and Ari Ne'eman, "Dueling narratives: Neurotypical and autistic perspectives about the autism spectrum," 2007 SAMLA Convention, Atlanta, Georgia, November 2007, at http://www.cwru.edu/affil/sce/Texts_2007/Ne'eman.html.

237 Martin Luther's assertion that changelings were only soulless pieces of flesh comes from *Werke, Kritische Gesamtausgabe: Tischreden* (1912–21), vol. 5, p. 9, as cited in D. L. Ashliman, "German changeling legends," *Folklore & Mythology Electronic Texts*, University of Pittsburgh, 1997, http://www.pitt.edu/~dash/changeling.html.

237 The quotation from Walter Spitzer comes from his article "The real scandal of the MMR debate," *Daily Mail*, December 20, 2001.

238 Amanda Baggs, *Autism Demonized*, privately published weblog, 2006.

238 This passage is based on my interview with Nancy Corgi in 2007. All names in this passage are pseudonyms.

241 Reviews of language impairment and language development in autism include Morton Ann Gernsbacher, Heather M. Geye, and Susan Ellis Weismer, "The role of language and communication impairments within autism," in *Language Disorders and Developmental Theory*, edited by P. Fletcher and J. F. Miller (2005); and Gerry A. Stefanatos and Ida Sue Baron. "The ontogenesis of language impairment in autism: A neuropsychological perspective," *Neuropsychology Review* 21, no. 3 (September 2011). For discussion on oral-motor function in autism, see Morton Ann Gernsbacher et al., "Infant and toddler oral- and manual-motor skills predict later speech fluency in autism," *Journal of Child Psychology & Psychiatry* 49, no. 1 (2008).

241 Alison Tepper Singer's comments were made in an interview in 2007.

241 The quotations from Micki Bresnahan are from our interview in 2008; the unnamed mother expressed her view about learning Sign in a personal communication in 2008.

242 The quotations from Carly Fleischmann and her father come from two reports: John McKenzie, "Autism breakthrough: Girl's writings explain her behavior and feelings," ABC News, February 19, 2008; and Carly Fleischmann, "You asked, she answered: Carly Fleischmann, 13, talks to our viewers about autism," ABC News, February 20, 2008.

242 The passage about Harry and Laura Slatkin is based on my interview with them in 2008 and subsequent communications.

244 The scene described here appears in *Autism Every Day*.

245 The term *the autisms* was first proposed by Daniel H. Geschwind and Pat Levitt in "Autism spectrum disorders: Developmental disconnection syndromes," *Current Opinion in Neurobiology* 17, no. 1 (February 2007).

245 The "mindblindness" hypothesis was proposed by Simon Baron-Cohen in *Mindblindness: An Essay on Autism and Theory of Mind* (1995).

245 Mirror neuron dysfunction in autism is discussed in Lindsay M. Oberman et al., "EEG evidence for mirror neuron dysfunction in autism spectrum disorders," *Cognitive Brain Research* 24, no. 2 (July 2005); and Lucina Q. Uddin et al., "Neural basis of self and other representation in autism: An fMRI study of self-face recognition," *PLoS ONE* 3, no. 10 (2008).

246 The "weak central coherence" hypothesis is proposed in Uta Frith, *Autism: Explaining the Enigma* (2003).

246 Arousal hypotheses are discussed in Corinne Hutt et al., "Arousal and childhood autism," *Nature* 204 (1964); and Elisabeth A. Tinbergen and Nikolaas Tinbergen, "Early childhood autism: An ethological approach," *Advances in Ethology, Journal of Comparative Ethology*, suppl. no. 10 (1972). Numerous respected autism researchers subsequently challenged Tinbergen regarding his speculations; see, e.g., Bernard Rimland et al., "Autism, stress, and ethology," *Science*, n.s., 188, no. 4187 (May 2, 1975).

246 The quotations by Kamran Nazeer occur on pages 68 and 69 of *Send in the Idiots: Stories from the Other Side of Autism* (2006).

246 John Elder Robison speaks of his fondness for machines on page 12 of *Look Me in the Eye: My Life with Asperger's* (2007).

246 For the report of the Yale face-processing study, see Robert T. Schultz et al., "Abnormal ventral temporal cortical activity during face discrimination among individuals with autism and Asperger syndrome," *Archives of General Psychiatry* 57, no. 4 (April 2000).

246 The Digimon aficionado features in David J. Grelotti et al., "fMRI activation of the fusiform gyrus and amygdala to cartoon characters but not to faces in a boy with autism," *Neuropsychologia* 43, no. 3 (2005).

246 This passage is based on my interview with Bob, Sue, and Ben Lehr in 2008 and subsequent communications.

247 The seminal book on FC is Douglas Biklen's *Communication Unbound: How Facilitated Communication Is Challenging Traditional Views of Autism and Ability/Disability* (1993).

249 For more information on brain development in autism, see Stephen R. Dager et al., "Imaging evidence for pathological brain development in autism spectrum disorders," in *Autism: Current Theories and Evidence* (2008); Martha R. Herbert et al., "Localization of white matter volume increase in autism and developmental language disorder," *Annals of Neurology* 55, no. 4 (April 2004); Eric Courchesne et al., "Evidence of brain overgrowth in the first year of life in autism," *Journal of the American Medical Association* 290, no. 3 (July 2003); Nancy J. Minshew and Timothy A. Keller, "The nature of brain dysfunction in autism: Functional brain imaging studies," *Current Opinion in Neurology* 23, no. 2 (April 2010); and Eric Courchesne et al., "Brain growth across the life span in autism: Age-specific changes in anatomical pathology," *Brain Research* 1380 (March 2011).

250 Useful recent reviews of the state of the science in autism genetics include Judith Miles, "Autism spectrum disorders: A genetics review," *Genetics in Medicine* 13,

no. 4 (April 2011); and Daniel H. Geschwind, "Genetics of autism spectrum disorders," *Trends in Cognitive Sciences* 15, no. 9 (September 2011).

250 Prenatal contributors to autism are discussed in Tara L. Arndt, Christopher J. Stodgell, and Patricia M. Rodier, "The teratology of autism," *International Journal of Developmental Neuroscience* 23, nos. 2–3 (April–May 2005).

250 For more information on the association between paternal age and autism, see Abraham Reichenberg et al., "Advancing paternal age and autism," *Archives of General Psychiatry* 63, no. 9 (September 2006); Rita M. Cantor et al., "Paternal age and autism are associated in a family-based sample," *Molecular Psychiatry* 12 (2007); and Maureen S. Durkin et al., "Advanced parental age and the risk of autism spectrum disorder," *American Journal of Epidemiology* 168, no. 11 (December 2008).

250 The possible contribution of genetic incompatibility to the development of autism is discussed in William G. Johnson et al., "Maternally acting alleles in autism and other neurodevelopmental disorders: The role of HLA-DR4 within the major histocompatibility complex," in *Maternal Influences on Fetal Neurodevelopment*, edited by Andrew W. Zimmerman and Susan L. Connors (2010).

250 For more on assortative mating hypotheses, see Simon Baron-Cohen, "The hyper-systemizing, assortative mating theory of autism," *Progress in Neuropsychopharmacology & Biological Psychiatry* 30, no. 5 (July 2006); and Steve Silberman, "The geek syndrome," *Wired*, December 2001.

250 A new multicenter sibling study has identified mutations in 279 genes occurring only in the autistic subjects; see Stephen Sanders et al., "De novo mutations revealed by whole-exome sequencing are strongly associated with autism," *Nature* 485, no. 7397 (May 10, 2012).

250 Influences on genetic expression are discussed in Isaac N. Pessah and Pamela J. Lein, "Evidence for environmental susceptibility in autism: What we need to know about gene x environment interactions," in *Autism: Current Theories and Evidence*, edited by Andrew Zimmerman (2008).

250 Variable penetrance is the subject of Dan Levy, Michael Wigler et al., "Rare de novo and transmitted copy-number variation in autistic spectrum disorders," *Neuron* 70, no. 5 (June 2011).

250 Figures on autism and genetic concordance in identical twins come from Anthony Bailey et al., "Autism as a strongly genetic disorder: Evidence from a British twin study," *Psychological Medicine* 25 (1995).

251 Studies on the broad autism phenotype, i.e., the manifestation of autistic traits in immediate and extended family members of people with autism, include Nadia Micali et al., "The broad autism phenotype: Findings from an epidemiological survey," *Autism* 8, no. 1 (March 2004); Joseph Piven et al., "Broader autism phenotype: Evidence from a family history study of multiple-incidence autism families," *American Journal of Psychiatry* 154 (February 1997); and Molly Losh et al., "Neuropsychological profile of autism and the broad autism phenotype," *Archives of General Psychiatry* 66, no. 5 (May 2009).

251 For scholarly discussion of the genome-wide incidence of autism-related genes, see Joseph T. Glessner et al., "Autism genome-wide copy number variation reveals ubiquitin and neuronal genes," *Nature* 459 (May 28, 2009).

251 This 20 to 30 percent statistic reflects risk to the sibling over general population risk as established by the CDC. Accepting an autism prevalence that is constantly being recalculated but that is hovering at about one in a hundred, and a risk for siblings is about one in five, we come up with this comparative statistic; see Brett

759

S. Abrahams and Daniel H. Geschwind, "Advances in autism genetics: On the threshold of a new neurobiology," *Nature Review Genetics* 9, no. 5 (May 2008).

251 Interview with Matthew State, 2009.

251 Interview with Thomas Insel, 2010.

251 Interview with Michael Wigler and Jonathan Sebat, 2008.

252 More background on pleiotropism and autism can be found in Annemarie Ploeger et al., "The association between autism and errors in early embryogenesis: What is the causal mechanism?," *Biological Psychiatry* 67, no. 7 (April 2010).

252 For a study linking genes associated with autism and co-morbid conditions, see Daniel B. Campbell et al., "Distinct genetic risk based on association of MET in families with co-occurring autism and gastrointestinal conditions," *Pediatrics* 123, no. 3 (March 2009).

252 Sebat and Wigler's report on their autism genetics research is Jonathan Sebat et al., "Strong association of de novo copy number mutations with autism," *Science* 316, no. 5823 (April 20, 2007).

252 Jonathan Sebat's study of the association between microdeletions and increased head circumference is described in the Simons Foundation press release "Relating copy-number variants to head and brain size in neuropsychiatric disorders," at http://sfari.org/funding/grants/abstracts/relating-copy-number-variants-to -head-and-brain-size-in-neuropsychiatric-disorders.

253 The quotation from Daniel Geschwind comes from a personal interview in 2012. Geschwind's recent papers on the genetics of autism include "Autism: Many genes, common pathways?," *Cell* 135, no. 3 (October 31, 2008); and "The genetics of autistic spectrum disorders," *Trends in Cognitive Sciences* 15, no. 9 (September 2011).

253 For studies of rapamycin's effect on learning, memory deficits, and seizures in mice, see Dan Ehninger et al., "Reversal of learning deficits in a Tsc2+/- mouse model of tuberous sclerosis," *Nature Medicine* 14, no. 8 (August 2008); and L.-H. Zeng et al., "Rapamycin prevents epilepsy in a mouse model of tuberous sclerosis complex," *Annals of Neurology* 63, no. 4 (April 2008).

253 The quotation from Alcino Silva comes from a 2008 UCLA press release, "Drug reverses mental retardation in mice," at http://www.newswise.com/articles/drug -reverses-mental-retardation-in-mice.

253 The role of mGluR receptors in autism is discussed in Mark F. Bear et al., "The mGluR theory of fragile X mental retardation," *Trends in Neurosciences* 27, no. 7 (July 2004); and Randi Hagerman et al., "Fragile X and autism: Intertwined at the molecular level leading to targeted treatments," *Molecular Autism* 1, no. 12 (September 2010). For a study finding amelioration of behavioral abnormalities in genetically engineered mice administered mGluR antagonists, see Zhengyu Cao et al., "Clustered burst firing in FMR1 premutation hippocampal neurons: Amelioration with allopregnanolone," *Human Molecular Genetics* (published online ahead of print, April 6, 2012).

254 For a preliminary report of findings in a clinical trial of drug treatment for Rett syndrome, see Eugenia Ho et al., "Initial study of rh-IGF1 (Mecasermin [DNA] injection) for treatment of Rett syndrome and development of Rett-specific novel biomarkers of cortical and autonomic function (S28.005)," *Neurology* 78, meeting abstracts 1 (April 25, 2012).

254 For discussion of potential drug therapies for fragile X syndrome, see the recent review article by Randi Hagerman et al., "Fragile X syndrome and targeted treatment trials," *Results and Problems in Cell Differentiation* 54 (2012), pages 297–

335. Recruitment efforts are under way for a new fragile X study; see the press release "Clinical trials of three experimental new treatments for Fragile X are accepting participants," FRAXA Research Foundation, March 22, 2012.

254 The quote by Geraldine Dawson comes from her presentation at the Alexandria Summit, "Translating Innovation into New Approaches for Neuroscience," in 2012. Dawson is chief scientific officer for Autism Speaks.

254 For the study finding similar genetic mutations in fragile X and in autism, see Ivan Iossifov et al., "De novo gene disruptions in children on the autistic spectrum," *Neuron* 74, no. 2 (April 2012); and Cold Spring Harbor Laboratory's press release about the study, "A striking link is found between the Fragile-X gene and mutations that cause autism," at http://www.cshl.edu/Article-Wigler/a-striking -link-is-found-between-the-fragile-x-gene-and-mutations-that-cause-autism.

254 Simon Baron-Cohen discusses his "empathizing/systemizing" hypothesis in "The extreme male brain theory of autism," *Trends in Cognitive Science* 6, no. 6 (June 2002); "Autism: The empathizing-systemizing (E-S) theory," *Annals of the New York Academy of Sciences* 1156 (March 2009); and "Empathizing, systemizing, and the extreme male brain theory of autism," *Progress in Brain Research* 186 (2010).

255 The association of high levels of fetal testosterone and autistic traits is discussed in Bonnie Auyeung and Simon Baron-Cohen, "A role for fetal testosterone in human sex differences: Implications for understanding autism," in *Autism: Current Theories and Evidence*, edited by Andrew Zimmerman (2008); and Bonnie Auyeung et al., "Foetal testosterone and autistic traits in 18 to 24-month-old children," *Molecular Autism* 1, no. 11 (July 2010).

255 The study of savants is the lifework of Darold Treffert; for just two of his reports on the subject, see "The savant syndrome in autism," in *Autism: Clinical and Research Issues*, edited by Pasquale J. Accardo et al. (2000); and "The savant syndrome: An extraordinary condition. A synopsis: Past, present, future," *Philosophical Transactions of the Royal Society*, Part B 364, no. 1522 (May 2009). The perfect map of Rome was created by Stephen Wiltshire and is displayed on his website, http://www.stephenwiltshire.co.uk/Rome_Panorama_by_Stephen_ Wiltshire.aspx.

255 Michael Rutter reported on the impact of institutionalization on Romanian orphans in Michael Rutter et al., "Are there biological programming effects for psychological development?: Findings from a study of Romanian adoptees," *Developmental Psychology* 40, no. 1 (2004).

255 Bettelheim's comparison of autistic children to concentration camp inmates occurs on pages 66–78 of *The Empty Fortress* (1972).

255 Margaret Bauman's clinical experiences are discussed in Rachel Zimmerman, "Treating the body vs. the mind," *Wall Street Journal*, February 15, 2005.

255 Statistics on the percentage of autistic individuals with comorbid diagnoses of depression and anxiety were provided by Lonnie Zwaigenbaum at a 2009 presentation at Cold Spring Harbor Laboratory.

Studies establishing a high frequency of comorbid psychiatric problems include Luke Tsai, "Comorbid psychiatric disorders of autistic disorder," *Journal of Autism & Developmental Disorders* 26, no. 2 (April 1996); Christopher Gillberg and E. Billstedt, "Autism and Asperger syndrome: Coexistence with other clinical disorders," *Acta Psychiatrica Scandinavica* 102, no. 5 (November 2000); and Gagan Joshi et al., "The heavy burden of psychiatric comorbidity in youth with autism spectrum disorders: A large comparative study of a psychiatrically referred population," *Journal of Autism & Developmental Disorders* 40, no. 11 (November 2010).

256 The quotation from Kamran Nazeer comes from pages 161–62 of *Send in the Idiots: Stories from the Other Side of Autism* (2006).

256 This passage is based on my interview with John Shestack and Portia Iversen in 2008.

257 The quotation from Daniel Geschwind comes from personal communication in 2011.

257 The quotation from Isabelle Rapin comes from a 2009 presentation at Cold Spring Harbor Laboratory.

257 Laura Schreibman discusses autism diagnostic instruments on page 68 of *The Science and Fiction of Autism* (2005).

257 I have taken the August Bier quotation from Victoria Costello, "Reaching children who live in a world of their own," *Psychology Today*, December 9, 2009.

 The original German is *Eine gute Mutter diagnostiziert oft viel besser wie ein schlechter Arzt* and may be found at http://dgrh.de/75jahredgrh0.html.

258 Interview with Kathleen Seidel in 2008. I note in the interest of full disclosure that I employed Kathleen Seidel to help me with research, citations, and the bibliography for this book starting in 2009.

258 This passage is based on my interview with Icilda Brown in 2005. All names in this passage are pseudonyms.

260 The Autism Society of America's estimates of the incidence of autism come from their organizational website, http://www.autism-society.org/.

260 For recent studies on autism prevalence, see Gillian Baird et al., "Prevalence of disorders of the autism spectrum in a population cohort of children in South Thames: The Special Needs and Autism Project (SNAP)," *Lancet* 368, no. 9531 (July 15, 2006); Michael D. Kogan et al., "Prevalence of parent-reported diagnosis of autism spectrum disorder among children in the US, 2007," *Pediatrics* 124, no. 5 (2009); and Catherine Rice et al., "Changes in autism spectrum disorder prevalence in 4 areas of the United States," *Disability and Health Journal* 3, no. 3 (July 2010).

260 Diagnostic substitution in California is the subject of Lisa A. Croen et al., "The changing prevalence of autism in California," *Journal of Autism and Developmental Disorders* 32, no. 3 (June 2002); see also Marissa King and Peter Bearman, "Diagnostic change and the increased prevalence of autism," *International Journal of Epidemiology* 38, no. 5 (October 2009).

260 Estimates of the lifetime cost of supporting individuals with autism come from Laura Ellen Schreibman, *The Science and Fiction of Autism* (2005), page 71; see also Michael Ganz, "The lifetime distribution of the incremental societal costs of autism," *Archives of Pediatric & Adolescent Medicine* 161, no. 4 (April 2007).

261 The quotation from Steven Hyman comes from a personal communication in 2008.

261 See Marissa King and Peter Bearman, "Diagnostic change and the increased prevalence of autism," *International Journal of Epidemiology* 38, no. 5 (October 2009); and Dorothy V. Bishop et al., "Autism and diagnostic substitution: Evidence from a study of adults with a history of developmental language disorder," *Developmental Medicine & Child Neurology* 50, no. 5 (May 2008).

261 For information on regression in autism, see Sally J. Rogers, "Developmental regression in autism spectrum disorders," *Mental Retardation & Developmental Disabilities Research Reviews* 10, no. 2 (2004); Janet Lainhart et al., "Autism, regression, and the broader autism phenotype," *American Journal of Medical Genetics* 113, no. 3 (December 2002); and Jeremy R. Parr et al., "Early developmental

regression in autism spectrum disorder: Evidence from an international multiplex sample," *Journal of Autism & Developmental Disorders* 41, no. 3 (March 2011). For the idea that regression in autism may be the expression of an unfolding genetic process, see Gerry A. Stefanatos, "Regression in autistic spectrum disorders," *Neuropsychology Review* 18 (December 2008).

261 Eric Fombonne presented this in a talk at UCLA in 2012. It represents work by Judith Miller that reclassified old files using modern diagnostic criteria. Miller showed that prevalence was previously underestimated (i.e., at that time, many children were excluded from studies—as not meeting diagnostic criteria—who would now be included). She will be the first author on a paper that summarizes this work, which is not yet published.

261 Andrew Wakefield first proposed an association between the MMR vaccine and autism in "Ileal-lymphoid-nodular hyperplasia, non-specific colitis, and pervasive developmental disorder in children," *Lancet* 351 (1998).

261 Official figures on measles incidence and deaths in the UK following increasing rejection of the MMR vaccine can be found in the UK Health Protection Agency report "Measles notifications and deaths in England and Wales, 1940–2008" (2010).

261 Thomas Verstraeten et al., "Safety of thimerosal-containing vaccines: A two-phased study of computerized health maintenance organization databases," *Pediatrics* 112, no. 5 (November 2003).

262 The *Lancet*'s apology for the 1998 paper by Andrew Wakefield was announced by editor in chief Richard Horton in "A statement by the editors of The Lancet," *Lancet* 363, no. 9411 (March 2004). The final retraction occurred six years later, after the UK General Medical Council announced the results of its investigation; see Editors of the Lancet, "Retraction—Ileal-lymphoid-nodular hyperplasia, non-specific colitis, and pervasive developmental disorder in children," *Lancet* 375, no. 9713 (February 2010). The story was reported by David Derbyshire, "Lancet was wrong to publish MMR paper, says editor," *Telegraph*, February 21, 2004; Cassandra Jardine, "GMC brands Dr Andrew Wakefield 'dishonest, irresponsible and callous,'" *Telegraph*, January 29, 2010; and David Rose, "Lancet journal retracts Andrew Wakefield MMR scare paper," *Times*, February 3, 2010.

262 For a brief overview of the history of vaccine causation theories of autism, see Stanley Plotkin, Jeffrey S. Gerber, and Paul A. Offit, "Vaccines and autism: A tale of shifting hypotheses," *Clinical Infectious Diseases* 48, no. 4 (February 15, 2009).

262 The 20–50 percent regression estimate comes from Emily Werner and Geraldine Dawson, "Validation of the phenomenon of autistic regression using home videotapes," *Archives of General Psychiatry* 62, no. 8 (August 2005).

262 David Kirby, *Evidence of Harm: Mercury in Vaccines and the Autism Epidemic: A Medical Controversy* (2005).

263 The Wright family conflict was reported in Jane Gross and Stephanie Strom, "Autism debate strains a family and its charity," *New York Times*, June 18, 2007.

263 Jenny McCarthy's books include *Louder Than Words: A Mother's Journey in Healing Autism* (2007) and *Mother Warriors: A Nation of Parents Healing Autism Against All Odds* (2008).

263 The Hannah Poling case is discussed in Paul A. Offit, "Vaccines and autism revisited: The Hannah Poling case," *New England Journal of Medicine* 358, no. 20 (May 15, 2008).

263 The quotation from Lenny Schafer comes from a telephone interview with him in 2008.

264 For an example of papers promoting the hypothesis that autism is associated with environmental metals, see Mary Catherine DeSoto and Robert T. Hitlan, "Sorting out the spinning of autism: Heavy metals and the question of incidence," *Acta Neurobiologiae Experimentalis* 70, no. 2 (2010). In contrast, recent research demonstrates the absence of any association of autism with genes that regulate heavy metals in the body: Sarah E. Owens et al., "Lack of association between autism and four heavy metal regulatory genes," *NeuroToxicology* 32, no. 6 (December 2011).

264 See Yumiko Ikezuki et al., "Determination of bisphenol A concentrations in human biological fluids reveals significant early prenatal exposure," *Human Reproduction* 17, no. 11 (November 2002).

264 The study of twins and environmental factors is Joachim Hallmayer et al., "Genetic heritability and shared environmental factors among twin pairs with autism," *Archives of General Psychiatry* (July 4, 2011).

264 The quotation from Neil Risch comes from Erin Allday, "UCSF, Stanford autism study shows surprises," *San Francisco Chronicle*, July 5, 2011.

264 The quotation from Joseph Coyle comes from Laurie Tarkan, "New study implicates environmental factors in autism," *New York Times*, July 4, 2011.

264 The study finding an increased incidence of autism in children of mothers who used SSRIs during pregnancy is Lisa A. Croen et al., "Antidepressant use during pregnancy and childhood autism spectrum disorders," *Archives of General Psychiatry* 68, no. 11 (November 2011).

264 These results rely on complex models and specific assumptions that may not be met. Joachim Hallmayer's data show a 22 percent rate of concordance among dizygotic twins, and slightly more than 60 percent for monozygotic twins; see Joachim Hallmayer et al., "Genetic heritability and shared environmental factors among twin pairs with autism," *Archives of General Psychiatry* 68, no. 11 (November 2011). A simple and standard means of ascertaining heritability is Falconer's formula, which is $h_b^2 = 2(r_{mz}-r_{dz})$, in which h_b^2 represents general heritability, r_{mz} is monozygotic twin correlation, and r_{dz} is dizygotic twin correlation. This would lead to a heritability estimate of about 70 percent, consistent with previous results. A recent very large study comparing siblings and half siblings supports a ratio of 60 percent or higher; see John N. Constantino et al., "Autism recurrence in half siblings: Strong support for genetic mechanisms of transmission in ASD," *Molecular Psychiatry*, epub ahead of print (February 28, 2012).

264 This passage is based on my interview with Mark Blaxill in 2008.

265 Blaxill is coauthor of Amy S. Holmes, Mark F. Blaxill, and Boyd E. Haley, "Reduced levels of mercury in first baby haircuts of autistic children," *International Journal of Toxicology* 22, no. 4 (July–August 2003); and Martha R. Herbert et al., "Autism and environmental genomics," *NeuroToxicology* 27, no. 5 (September 2006).

266 The reports of the Yale study of the responses of autistic subjects to *Who's Afraid of Virginia Woolf?* are in Ami Klin et al., "Visual fixation patterns during viewing of naturalistic social situations as predictors of social competence in individuals with autism," *Archives of General Psychiatry* 59, no. 9 (September 2002); and Ami Klin et al., "Defining and quantifying the social phenotype in autism," *American Journal of Psychiatry* 159 (June 2002).

266 See page 5 of Catherine Lord and James McGee, *Educating Children with Autism* (2005), in which she explains, "Although there is evidence that interventions lead to improvements, there does not appear to be a clear, direct relationship between any particular intervention and children's progress."

266 The quotation from Bryna Siegel occurs on page 3 of *Helping Children with Autism Learn: Treatment Approaches for Parents and Professionals* (2003).

266 Early reports by Charles B. Ferster on his work in behavioral conditioning include "Positive reinforcement and behavioral deficits of autistic children," *Child Development* 32 (1961); and "The development of performances in autistic children in an automatically controlled environment," *Journal of Chronic Diseases* 13, no. 4 (April 1961).

266 ABA is discussed at length in Laura Schreibman, *The Science and Fiction of Autism* (2005); and Michelle R. Sherer and Laura Schreibman, "Individual behavioral profiles and predictors of treatment effectiveness for children with autism," *Journal of Consulting & Clinical Psychology* 73, no. 3 (June 2005).

266 For a recent, comprehensive literature review on behavioral interventions for autism spectrum conditions, see Maria B. Ospina et al., "Behavioural and developmental interventions for autism spectrum disorder: A clinical systematic review," *PLoS One* 3, no. 11 (November 2008).

266 For more on Floortime, see Stanley I. Greenspan and Serena Weider, *Engaging Autism: Using the Floortime Approach to Help Children Relate, Communicate, and Think* (2006).

266 The AAP has concluded that the efficacy of AIT has not been established; see American Academy of Pediatrics Policy Committee on Children with Disabilities, "Auditory integration training and facilitated communication for autism," *AAP Policy Committee on Children with Disabilities* 102, no. 2 (1998).

267 The Rapid Prompting Method is described in Portia Iversen, *Strange Son: Two Mothers, Two Sons, and the Quest to Unlock the Hidden World of Autism* (2006); and Tito Rajarshi Mukhopadhyay, *The Mind Tree: A Miraculous Child Breaks the Silence of Autism* (2003).

267 Scholarly papers on service animals include Olga Solomon, "What a dog can do: Children with autism and therapy dogs in social interaction," *Ethos* 38, no. 1 (March 2010); and François Martin and Jennifer Farnum, "Animal-assisted therapy for children with pervasive developmental disorders," *Western Journal of Nursing Research* 24, no. 6 (October 2002).

267 The first quote about Kaleb and Chewey comes from Amanda Robert, "School bars autistic child and his service dog, " *Illinois Times*, July 23, 2009; the second is taken from the decision in *Nichelle v. Villa Grove Community Unit School District No. 302, Board of Education 302* (Appellate Court of Illinois, Fourth District, decided August 4, 2010; full text at http://caselaw.findlaw.com/il-court-of-appeals/1537428.html). For more on the outcome of the lawsuit filed by the parents against the school district, see Patrick Yeagle, "Dog fight ends with hall pass," *Illinois Times*, September 9, 2010.

267 For a popular work on the gluten- and casein-free diet, see Karyn Seroussi, *Unraveling the Mystery of Autism and Pervasive Developmental Disorder: A Mother's Story of Research and Recovery* (2000).

267 A recent Cochrane Review paper concluded, "There is no evidence of effect of SSRIs in children and emerging evidence of harm. There is limited evidence of the effectiveness of SSRIs in adults from small studies in which risk of bias is unclear"; see Katrina Williams et al., "Selective serotonin reuptake inhibitors (SSRIs) for autism spectrum disorders (ASD)," *Evidence-Based Child Health: A Cochrane Review Journal* 6, no. 4 (July 2011).

267 Statistics on the prevalence of seizure disorders in people with autism come from the National Institute of Neurological Disorders & Stroke's "Autism Fact

Sheet" (2011), at http://www.ninds.nih.gov/disorders/autism/detail_autism.htm.

267 Psychopharmacological treatments are discussed in Melissa L. McPheeters et al., "A systematic review of medical treatments for children with autism spectrum disorders," *Pediatrics* 127, no. 5 (May 2011).

267 The passage from Kamran Nazeer occurs on page 28 of *Send in the Idiots* (2006).

267 This passage is based on my interview with Bruce Spade in 2007. All names in this passage are pseudonyms.

269 The quotation from Anton Chekhov comes from page 30 of David Mamet's translation of *The Cherry Orchard* (1987). From the original Russian: "Если против какой-нибудь болезни предлагается очень много средств, то это значит, что болезнь неизлечима." http://ilibrary.ru/text/472/p.1/index.html.

269 Barry Kaufman's books include *Son-Rise* (1976) and *Son-Rise: The Miracle Continues* (1995). Although the Option Institute's promotional materials cite anecdotal evidence of the Son-Rise Program's effectiveness, and refer to research soon to be featured in peer-reviewed journals, rigorous evaluations of the program have yet to be published; see Jeremy Parr, "Clinical evidence: Autism," *Clinical Evidence Online* 322 (January 2010). A 2003 survey conducted in the UK found that "involvement led to more drawbacks than benefits for the families over time." A 2006 follow-up concluded that "the programme is not always implemented as it is typically described in the literature," which significantly complicates the task of evaluation; see Katie R. Williams and J. G. Wishart, "The Son-Rise Program intervention for autism: An investigation into family experiences," *Journal of Intellectual Disability Research* 47, nos. 4–5 (May–June 2003); and Katie R. Williams, "The Son-Rise Program intervention for autism: Prerequisites for evaluation," *Autism* 10, no. 1 (January 2006). In March 2010, the UK Advertising Standards Authority ruled that an advertisement for an Option Institute lecture was misleading in that it implied that the Son-Rise Program could cure autism when, in fact, this has never been established; see "ASA adjudication on the Option Institute and Fellowship," issued March 3, 2010, http://www.asa.org.uk/Asa-Action/Adjudications/2010/3/The-Option-Institute-and-Fellowship/TF_ADJ_48181.aspx. For the allegation that the child was never autistic at all, see Bryna Siegel, *The World of the Autistic Child* (1996), pages 330–31. Siegel writes, "I've run across a couple of the professionals who were among those alleged to have diagnosed the boy as autistic, and both remain uncertain that the boy actually was autistic before treatment."

269 For more on Holding Therapy, see Jean Mercer, "Coercive restraint therapies: A dangerous alternative mental health intervention," *Medscape General Medicine* 7, no. 3 (August 9, 2005).

270 Rupert Isaacson, *The Horse Boy: A Father's Quest to Heal His Son* (2009).

270 The dangers of chelation are discussed in Saul Green, "Chelation therapy: Unproven claims and unsound theories," *Quackwatch*, July 24, 2007.

270 Mercury causation hypotheses are discussed in Karin B. Nelson and Margaret L. Bauman, "Thimerosal and Autism?," *Pediatrics* 111, no. 3 (March 2003).

270 The death of an autistic boy during IV chelation is reported in Arla J. Baxter and Edward P. Krenzelok, "Pediatric fatality secondary to EDTA chelation," *Clinical Toxicology* 46, no. 10 (December 2008).

270 For information about the "Lupron protocol" and state medical board disciplinary actions against its promoters, see Trine Tsouderos, "'Miracle drug' called junk

science," *Chicago Tribune*, May 21, 2009; Steve Mills and Patricia Callahan, "Md. autism doctor's license suspended," *Baltimore Sun*, May 4, 2011; Meredith Cohn, "Lupron therapy for autism at center of embattled doctor's case," *Baltimore Sun*, June 16, 2011; Maryland State Board of Physicians, Final Decision and Order in the matter of Mark R. Geier, M.D. (March 22, 2012), at http://www.mbp.state .md.us/BPQAPP/orders/d2425003.222.pdf; Statement of Charges under the Maryland Medical Practice Act in the Matter of David A. Geier (May 16, 2011), at http://www.mbp.state.md.us/BPQAPP/orders/GeierCharge05162011.pdf; and out-of-state suspension notices and orders on the websites of the Medical Board of California, State of Florida Department of Health, Medical Licensing Board of Indiana, Commonwealth Board of Kentucky, New Jersey State Board of Medical Examiners, State Medical Board of Ohio, Virginia Department of Health Professions, and the State of Washington Department of Health Medical Quality Assurance Commission.

270 Melissa L. McPheeters et al., "A systematic review of medical treatments for children with autism spectrum disorders," *Pediatrics* 127, no. 5 (May 2011), discusses alternative as well as conventional treatments.

270 This passage is based on my interview with Amy Wolf in 2004 and subsequent communications. All names in this passage are pseudonyms.

272 The Musashino Higashi Gakuen School's organizational website is at http:// www.musashino-higashi.org, and the Boston Higashi School website is at http:// www.bostonhigashi.org.

273 The study of enhanced abilities in autism is a special focus of Laurent Mottron and his research team at Hôpital Rivière-des-Prairies in Montréal. Reports of their work include M. J. Caron et al., "Cognitive mechanisms, specificity and neural underpinnings of visuospatial peaks in autism," *Brain* 129, no. 7 (July 2006); Laurent Mottron et al., "Enhanced perceptual functioning in autism: An update, and eight principles of autistic perception," *Journal of Autism & Developmental Disorders* 36, no. 1 (January 2006); Robert M. Joseph et al., "Why is visual search superior in autism spectrum disorder?," *Developmental Science* 12, no. 6 (December 2009); and Fabienne Samson et al., "Enhanced visual functioning in autism: An ALE meta-analysis," *Human Brain Mapping* (April 4, 2011).

273 This and subsequent quotations by Joyce Chung come from my interview with her in 2008 and subsequent communications.

273 Thorkil Sonne's innovative business venture is described in David Bornstein, "For some with autism, jobs to match their talents," *New York Times*, June 30, 2011.

273 The quotation from John Elder Robison on being a savant occurs on page 209 of *Look Me in the Eye* (2007).

273 This passage is based on my interviews with Temple Grandin in 2004 and 2008.

274 The following quotations in this passage from Eustacia Cutler come from *A Thorn in My Pocket* (2004), page 38 ("tantrums are hard to handle"); page 106 ("God says be fruitful and multiply"); page 151 ("Adolescence is hard enough for any child"); page 164 ("slowly, with no innate concept"); and page 219 ("despite her extraordinary accomplishments").

274 The next quote ("You have to pull them out of the limbo") is from personal communication with Eustacia Cutler in 2012.

276 The quotation from Jim Sinclair comes from his essay "Don't mourn for us," *Our Voice* 1, no. 3 (1993).

276 The quotation from Jim Sinclair likening the expression *person with autism* to

person with maleness comes from his 1999 essay "Why I dislike 'person-first' language," archived at http://web.archive.org/web/20030527100525/http://web.syr.edu/~jisincla/person_first.htm.

276 The quotation from Isabelle Rapin comes from a 2009 presentation at Cold Spring Harbor Laboratory.

276 The quotation from Alex Plank comes from my interview with him in 2008.

276 Quotations from Ari Ne'eman here and following are from my interview with him in 2008 and subsequent communications.

277 Ari Ne'eman's December 7, 2007, memo to Autistic Self Advocacy Network members, "An urgent call to action: Tell NYU Child Study Center to abandon stereotypes against people with disabilities," can be read in its entirety on the organization's website, http://www.autisticadvocacy.org/modules/smartsection/print.php?itemid=21.

277 For news reports about the ransom notes protest, see Joanne Kaufman, "Campaign on childhood mental illness succeeds at being provocative," *New York Times*, December 14, 2007; Shirley S. Wang, "NYU bows to critics and pulls ransom-note ads," *Wall Street Journal Health Blog*, December 19, 2007; Robin Shulman, "Child study center cancels autism ads," *Washington Post*, December 19, 2007; and Joanne Kaufman, "Ransom-note ads about children's health are canceled," *New York Times*, December 20, 2007. In 2010, a scholarly paper was published about the ransom notes scandal: Joseph F. Kras, "The 'Ransom Notes' affair: When the neurodiversity movement came of age," *Disability Studies Quarterly* 30, no. 1 (January 2010).

278 Ne'eman's appointment to the National Council on Disability was announced in the December 16, 2009, White House press release "President Obama Announces More Key Administration Posts." The ensuing controversy is described in Amy Harmon, "Nominee to disability council is lightning rod for dispute on views of autism," *New York Times*, March 28, 2010.

278 This and subsequent quotations from Judy Singer come from an interview I did with her in 2008.

278 The first published use of the term *neurodiversity* occurs in Harvey Blume, "Neurodiversity," *Atlantic*, September 30, 1998. Judy Singer's first published use of the term *neurodiversity* occurs in her essay "Why can't you be normal for once in your life: From a 'problem with no name' to a new kind of disability," in *Disability Discourse*, edited by M. Corker and S. French (1999).

278 The quotations by Camille Clark come from personal e-mail communications.

279 The quotation from Jim Sinclair ("The ways we relate are *different*") comes from his essay "Don't mourn for us," *Our Voice* 1, no. 3 (1993).

279 The quotation from Gareth Nelson comes from Emine Saner, "It is not a disease, it is a way of life," *Guardian*, August 6, 2007.

279 The quotation from Richard Grinker, author of *Unstrange Minds: Remapping the World of Autism* (2007), comes from my interview with him in 2008.

280 The "baby-eating" image was created by Adriana Gamondes and published as "Pass the Maalox: An AoA Thanksgiving nightmare," *Age of Autism*, November 29, 2009 (removed from the blog, but archived at http://web.archive.org/web/20091202093726/http://www.ageofautism.com/2009/11/pass-the-maalox-an-aoa-thanksgiving-nightmare.html).

281 The quotation from Kit Weintraub ("The fact that my children have an abnormality of development") comes from her 2007 essay, "A mother's perspective," published on the website of the Association for Science in Autism Treatment, http://www.asatonline.org/forum/articles/mother.htm.

281 The quotation from Jonathan Mitchell ("The neurodiverse reach a vulnerable audience") comes from his 2007 essay "Neurodiversity: Just say no," http://www .jonathans-stories.com/non-fiction/neurodiv.html.

282 Newsgroup posts characterizing ideological opponents in insulting terms come from the Evidence of Harm discussion group on Yahoo! and were quoted in Kathleen Seidel's May 2005 letter "Evidence of venom: An open letter to David Kirby," published at http://www.neurodiversity.com/evidence_of_venom.html.

282 The quotation from Sarah Spence comes from personal communication in 2011.

282 Simon Baron-Cohen's statement that "autism is both a disability and a difference" occurs in Emine Saner, "It is not a disease, it is a way of life," *Guardian*, August 6, 2007.

283 The passage from the autistics.org website appears in Amy Harmon, "How about not 'curing' us, some autistics are pleading," *New York Times*, December 20, 2004.

283 *In My Language*, MOV video, directed by Amanda Baggs, privately produced, January 14, 2007, http://www.youtube.com/watch?v=JnylM1hI2jc.

283 The quotation from Jane Meyerding ("If people on the autistic spectrum all came out") comes from her 1998 essay "Thoughts on finding myself differently brained," published online at http://www.planetautism.com/jane/diff.html.

284 The quote by Richard Grinker ("When people pity me for my daughter, I don't understand the sentiment") occurs on page 35 of his book *Unstrange Minds: Remapping the World of Autism* (2007).

284 The quotation from Kate Movius ("Nothing has yielded a 'eureka' moment") comes from her article "Autism: Opening the window," *Los Angeles*, September 2010.

284 For speculation that various historic and literary figures might have been autistic, see Michael Fitzgerald, *The Genesis of Artistic Creativity: Asperger's Syndrome and the Arts* (2005).

285 This passage is based on my interview with Bill, Jae, Chris, and Jessie Davis in 2003, and further interviews with Bill, as well as other communications.

285 Vincent Carbone's method is described in Vincent J. Carbone and Emily J. Sweeney-Kerwin, "Increasing the vocal responses of children with autism and developmental disabilities using manual sign mand training and prompt delay," *Journal of Applied Behavior Analysis* 43, no. 4 (Winter 2010).

289 The Jae Davis Parent Scholarship program is described in Justin Quinn, "Local parents get scholarships to attend conference on autism," *Lancaster Intelligencer-Journal*, July 30, 2004; and "For mother and son, life lessons as death nears: Woman ravaged by cervical cancer prepares autistic son for her passing," *Lancaster Intelligencer-Journal*, August 20, 2003; the Jae Davis Internship Program is mentioned in Maria Coole, "Report recommendations could put Pa. at forefront in autism services," *Lancaster Intelligencer-Journal*, April 23, 2005. In September 2004, the Organization for Autism Research announced the establishment of the Jae Davis Memorial Award; see "OAR Seeks Nominations for Community Service Award in Honor of the Late Jae Davis," at http://www.researchautism .org/news/pressreleases/PR090204.asp.

289 Oliver Sacks, *An Anthropologist on Mars: Seven Paradoxical Tales* (1995).

290 News reports on murders and attempted murders of autistic children and adults by their parents that are described in this section:

Charles-Antoine Blais: Peter Bronson, "For deep-end families, lack of hope can kill," *Cincinnati Enquirer*, October 9, 2005.

Casey Albury: Kevin Norquay, "Autism: Coping with the impossible," *Waikato Times*, July 17, 1998; Paul Chapman, "Mom who strangled autistic child tried to get her to jump off bridge," *Vancouver Sun*, July 11, 1998; and "Murder accused at 'end of her tether,'" *Evening Post*, July 14, 1998.

Pierre Pasquiou: "Suspended jail term for French mother who killed autistic son," *BBC Monitoring International Reports*, March 2, 2001.

James Joseph Cummings: "Man gets five years in prison for killing autistic son," Associated Press, 1999.

Daniel Leubner: "Syracuse: Woman who killed autistic son is freed," *New York Times*, May 12, 2005.

Gabriel Britt: "Man pleads guilty to lesser charge," *Aiken Standard*, August 7, 2003.

Johnny Churchi: Barbara Brown, "Mother begins trial for death of her son," *Hamilton Spectator*, May 5, 2003; and Susan Clairmont, "'Sending you to heaven' said mom," *Hamilton Spectator*, May 6, 2003.

Angelica Auriemma: Nancie L. Katz, "Guilty in autistic's drowning," *New York Daily News*, February 19, 2005. Sentencing information comes from the New York State Department of Corrections and Community Supervision.

Terrance Cottrell: Chris Ayres, "Death of a sacrificial lamb," *The Times*, August 29, 2003.

Jason Dawes: Lisa Miller, "He can't forgive her for killing their son but says spare my wife from a jail cell," *Daily Telegraph*, May 26, 2004.

Patrick Markcrow and Sarah Naylor: Peter Bronson, "For deep-end families, lack of hope can kill," *Cincinnati Enquirer*, October 9, 2005.

Christopher DeGroot: Cammie McGovern, "Autism's parent trap," *New York Times*, June 5, 2006.

Jose Stable: Al Baker and Leslie Kaufman, "Autistic boy is slashed to death and his father is charged," *New York Times*, November 23, 2006.

Brandon Williams: Cheryl Korman, "Judge: Autistic's mom to serve 10 years for 'torture of her vulnerable child,'" *Tucson Citizen*, September 19, 2008.

Jacob Grabe: Paul Shockley, "Grabe gets life in son's murder," *Daily Sentinel*, March 31, 2010.

Son of Zvia Lev: Michael Rotem, "Mother found guilty of killing her autistic son," *Jerusalem Post*, February 22, 1991.

292　The quotation from the president of the Montreal Autism Society comes from Debra J. Saunders, "Children who deserve to die," *San Francisco Chronicle*, September 23, 1997.

292　Laura Slatkin's remark about "that hidden, dark thought" is quoted in Diane Guernsey, "Autism's angels," *Town & Country*, August 1, 2006.

292　The quotation from Cammie McGovern comes from her article "Autism's parent trap," *New York Times*, June 5, 2006.

292　The quotation from Joel Smith comes from the essay "Murder of autistics," published on his weblog, *This Way of Life*, http://www.geocities.com/growingjoel/murder.html.

292　The quotation from Karen McCarron comes from the Associated Press reports "'Autism left me hollow,' says mother accused of murder," *Dispatch-Argus*, June 6, 2007; and "Mom convicted in autistic girl's death," *USA Today*, January 17, 2008.

292　Karen McCarron's friend is quoted in Phil Luciano, "Helping everyone but herself," *Peoria Journal Star*, May 18, 2006.

292　The quotations from Mike McCarron, Katie's grandfather, come from a discussion of Kristina Chew, "I don't have a title for this post about Katherine McCarron's mother," *Autism Vox*, June 8, 2006, at http://archive.blisstree.com/feel/i-dont-have-a-title-for-this-post-about-katherine-mccarrons-mother/comment-page-2/#comments/; and an interview with journalist Phil Luciano, "This was not about autism," *Peoria Journal-Star*, May 24, 2006.

293 Stephen Drake's and Dave Reynolds's remarks occur in Not Dead Yet's June 22, 2006, press release, "Disability advocates call for restraint and responsibility in murder coverage."

293 Heidi Shelton is quoted in Larry Welborn, "Mom who drugged son gets deal," *Orange County Register*, May 4, 2003.

293 John Victor Cronin's wife's comment appears in Nick Henderson, "Attack on wife: Mental health system blamed," *Advertiser*, October 13, 2006.

294 The quotation from Debra Whitson comes from the article "Woman charged with trying to kill son," *Milwaukee Journal Sentinel*, May 14, 1998.

294 Statistics on the percentage of filicides attributed by their perpetrators to "altruism" come from Phillip J. Resnick, "Child murder by parents: A psychiatric review of filicide," *American Journal of Psychiatry* 126, no. 3 (September 1969).

294 For a discussion of the impact of altruistic explanations for filicide, see Dick Sobsey, "Altruistic filicide: Bioethics or criminology?," *Health Ethics Today* 12, no. 1 (Fall/November 2001).

294 Possible motivations for filicide are discussed on page 111 of John E. Douglas et al., *Crime Classification Manual: A Standard System for Investigating and Classifying Violent Crimes* (1992).

VI: Schizophrenia

296 Statistics on suicide risk in schizophrenia come from Maurizio Pompili et al., "Suicide risk in schizophrenia: Learning from the past to change the future," *Annals of General Psychiatry* 6 (March 16, 2007).

296 The quotation from the sister of a schizophrenic man comes from Carole Stone, "First person: Carole Stone on life with her schizophrenic brother," *Guardian*, November 12, 2005.

297 This passage is based on an interview with Kitty and Pamela Watson in 2007 and on subsequent communications. All names in this passage are pseudonyms.

302 Useful general introductions to schizophrenia include Christopher Frith and Eve Johnstone, *Schizophrenia: A Very Short Introduction* (2003); Michael Foster Green, *Schizophrenia Revealed: From Neurons to Social Interactions* (2001); Rachel Miller and Susan E. Mason, *Diagnosis: Schizophrenia* (2002); E. Fuller Torrey, *Surviving Schizophrenia* (2006); and the NIH booklet *Schizophrenia* (2007).

302 The quotation from the schizophrenic woman describing her positive symptoms ("I could find no rest, for horrible images assailed me . . .") occurs on page 37 of Marguerite Sechehaye, *Autobiography of a Schizophrenic Girl: The True Story of "Renee"* (1951).

302 The quotation from the patient describing negative symptoms of schizophrenia ("I am all the time losing . . .") occurs on page 2 of Christopher Frith and Eve Johnstone, *Schizophrenia: A Very Short Introduction* (2003).

302 The quotation from Eric Kandel is from a personal communication in 2009.

302 The poem quoted is Emily Dickinson's "I Felt a Cleaving in My Mind," no. 937 in *The Complete Poems of Emily Dickinson* (1960).

303 The life course of schizophrenia is described in greater detail in Elaine Walker

et al., "Schizophrenia: Etiology and course," *Annual Review of Psychology* 55 (February 2004). See also figure 1 in Jeffrey A. Lieberman et al., "Science and recovery in schizophrenia," *Psychiatric Services* 59 (May 2008).

303 The contribution of hormones to the development of schizophrenia is discussed in Laura W. Harris et al., "Gene expression in the prefrontal cortex during adolescence: Implications for the onset of schizophrenia," *BMC Medical Genomics* 2 (May 2009); and Elaine Walker et al., "Stress and the hypothalamic pituitary adrenal axis in the developmental course of schizophrenia," *Annual Review of Clinical Psychology* 4 (January 2008).

303 For more information on white matter in schizophrenia, see G. Karoutzou et al., "The myelin-pathogenesis puzzle in schizophrenia: A literature review," *Molecular Psychiatry* 13, no. 3 (March 2008); and Yaron Hakak et al., "Genome-wide expression analysis reveals dysregulation of myelination-related genes in chronic schizophrenia," *Proceedings of the National Academy of Sciences* 98, no. 8 (April 2001).

303 The synaptic-pruning hypothesis was originally proposed in I. Feinberg, "Schizophrenia: Caused by a fault in programmed synaptic elimination during adolescence?," *Journal of Psychiatric Research* 17, no. 4 (1983). For a recent review article on the subject, see Gábor Faludi and Károly Mirnics, "Synaptic changes in the brain of subjects with schizophrenia," *International Journal of Developmental Neuroscience* 29, no. 3 (May 2011).

304 Statistics on response to antipsychotics over the short and long term come from Jeffrey A. Lieberman and T. Scott Stroup, "The NIMH-CATIE schizophrenia study: What did we learn?," *American Journal of Psychiatry* 168, no. 8 (August 2011).

304 This passage is based on my interview with Connie and Steve Lieber in 2008 and subsequent communications.

304 Brain & Behavior Research Foundation (formerly NARSAD) website: http://bbrfoundation.org/.

304 Figures on grant-making come from the Brain & Behavior Research Foundation (formerly NARSAD), "Our history" (2011), http://bbrfoundation.org/about/our-history. As of 2012, the most recent NARSAD grant statistics were: total given, $275,947,302.20; total number of grantees, 3,117; total number of grants given, 4,061; total number of institutions, 426; total number of countries (other than the United States), 30.

304 Herbert Pardes made this remark at a NARSAD gala in 2010.

305 Bleuler's invention of the word *schizophrenia* is discussed in Paolo Fusar-Poli and Pierluigi Politi, "Paul Eugen Bleuler and the birth of schizophrenia (1908)," *American Journal of Psychiatry*, 165, no. 11 (2008).

305 Frederick Plum declared that "schizophrenia is the graveyard of neuropathologists" in his paper "Prospects for research on schizophrenia. 3. Neurophysiology: Neuropathological findings," *Neurosciences Research Program Bulletin* 10, no. 4 (November 1972).

305 For more information on the genetics of schizophrenia, see Nancy C. Andreasen, *Brave New Brain* (2001); and Yunjung Kim et al., "Schizophrenia genetics: Where next?," *Schizophrenia Bulletin* 37, no. 3 (May 2011).

305 The most comprehensive study of schizophrenia risk in relatives is the Roscommon (Ireland) Family Study; see Kenneth S. Kendler et al., "The Roscommon Family Study. I. Methods, diagnosis of probands, and risk of schizophrenia in relatives," *Archives of General Psychiatry* 50, no. 7 (July 1993); and numerous subsequent

reports published by Kendler and his colleagues from 1993 to 2001. For a review and synthesis of twin studies discussing the various sorts of environmental influences that might contribute to the differential development of schizophrenia in twins, see Patrick F. Sullivan, Kenneth S. Kendler, and Michael C. Neale, "Schizophrenia as a complex trait: Evidence from a meta-analysis of twin studies," *Archives of General Psychiatry* 60, no. 12 (December 2003).

305 All quotations from Deborah Levy come from my interview with her in 2008 and subsequent communications.

306 Studies on dopamine function in schizophrenia include Anissa Abi-Dargham et al., "Increased baseline occupancy of D2 receptors by dopamine in schizophrenia," *Proceedings of the National Academy of Sciences* 97, no. 14 (July 2000); and Philip Seeman et al., "Dopamine supersensitivity correlates with D2High states, implying many paths to psychosis," *Proceedings of the National Academy of Sciences* 102, no. 9 (March 2005).

306 For more information on hippocampal function in schizophrenia, see Stephan Heckers, "Neuroimaging studies of the hippocampus in schizophrenia," *Hippocampus* 11, no. 5 (2001); and J. Hall et al., "Hippocampal function in schizophrenia and bipolar disorder," *Psychological Medicine* 40, no. 5 (May 2010).

306 Epigenetics of schizophrenia is explored in Karl-Erik Wahlberg et al., "Gene-environment interaction in vulnerability to schizophrenia," *American Journal of Psychiatry* 154, no. 3 (March 1997); and Paul J. Harrison and D. R. Weinberger, "Schizophrenia genes, gene expression, and neuropathology: On the matter of their convergence," *Molecular Psychiatry* 10, no. 1 (January 2005).

306 The question of parasites and schizophrenia, Jaroslav Flegr's hypothesis that schizophrenia is exacerbated by toxoplasmosis, is described in Kathleen McAuliffe, "How your cat is making you crazy," *Atlantic*, March 2012.

306 Copy number variations in schizophrenia are the focus of Daniel F. Levinson et al., "Copy number variants in schizophrenia: Confirmation of five previous findings and new evidence for 3q29 microdeletions and VIPR2 duplications," *American Journal of Psychiatry* 168, no. 3 (March 2011); Jan O. Korbel et al., "The current excitement about copy-number variation: How it relates to gene duplication and protein families," *Current Opinion in Structural Biology* 18, no. 3 (June 2008); and G. Kirov et al., "Support for the involvement of large copy number variants in the pathogenesis of schizophrenia," *Human Molecular Genetics* 18, no. 8 (April 2009). The contribution of paternal age to schizophrenia is discussed in E. Fuller Torrey, "Paternal age as a risk factor for schizophrenia: How important is it?," *Schizophrenia Research* 114, nos. 1–3 (October 2009); and Alan S. Brown, "The environment and susceptibility to schizophrenia," *Progress in Neurobiology* 93, no. 1 (January 2011).

306 For more information on spontaneous mutations and schizophrenia, see Anna C. Need et al., "A genome-wide investigation of SNPs and CNVs in schizophrenia," *PLoS Genetics* 5, no. 2 (February 2009); and Hreinn Stefansson et al., "Large recurrent microdeletions associated with schizophrenia," *Nature* 455, no. 7210 (September 11, 2008).

306 John Krystal's comments come from my interview with him in 2012.

306 The development of transgenic mice that display schizophrenia-associated traits was first described in Takatoshi Hikida et al., "Dominant-negative DISC1 transgenic mice display schizophrenia-associated phenotypes detected by measures translatable to humans," *Proceedings of the National Academy of Sciences of the United States of America* 104, no. 36 (September 4, 2007); and Koko Ishizuka et al., "Evidence that many of the DISC1 isoforms in C57BL/6J mice are also

expressed in 129S6/SvEv mice," *Molecular Psychiatry* 12, no. 10 (October 2007). For a recent review article on transgenic mouse research, see P. Alexander Arguello and Joseph A. Gogos, "Cognition in mouse models of schizophrenia susceptibility genes," *Schizophrenia Bulletin* 36, no. 2 (March 2010).

307 The quotation from Eric Kandel comes from a personal communication. For a review of work by Kandel and his colleagues, see Christoph Kellendonk, Eleanor H. Simpson, and Eric R. Kandel, "Modeling cognitive endophenotypes of schizophrenia in mice," *Trends in Neurosciences* 32, no. 6 (June 2009).

307 Maryellen Walsh's observation ("The history of schizophrenia is the history of blame") occurs on page 154 of her book *Schizophrenia: Straight Talk for Family and Friends* (1985).

307 Frieda Fromm-Reichman introduced the concept of the "schizophrenogenic mother" in her paper "Notes on the development of treatment of schizophrenics by psychoanalytic psychotherapy," *Psychiatry* 11, no. 3 (August 1948); this was followed by the proliferation of the term throughout the scientific literature, e.g., Loren R. Mosher, "Schizophrenogenic communication and family therapy," *Family Processes* 8 (1969).

307 The source of the quotation characterizing the schizophrenic patient as an "unsuccessful mediator" between parents is Murray Bowen et al., "The role of the father in families with a schizophrenic patient," *American Journal of Psychiatry* 115, no. 11 (May 1959).

307 See Gregory Bateson et al., "Toward a theory of schizophrenia," *Behavioral Science* 1, no. 4 (1956).

307 Examples of parent-blaming in the literature of systems-oriented family therapy include Ruth Wilmanns Lidz and Theodore Lidz, "The family environment of schizophrenic patients," *American Journal of Psychiatry* 106 (November 1949); Murray Bowen, Robert H. Dysinger, and Betty Basamania, "The role of the father in families with a schizophrenic patient," *American Journal of Psychiatry* 115, no. 11 (May 1959); and Gregory Bateson et al., "Toward a theory of schizophrenia," *Behavioral Science* 1, no. 4 (1956). For an extended critique of parent-blame theories, see John G. Howells and Waguih R. Guirguis, *The Family and Schizophrenia* (1985).

308 The quotation from Thomas Insel ("blame and shame") comes from a personal communication in 2010.

308 The NAMI finding that 57 percent of respondents believed that schizophrenia is caused by parental behavior is described on page 41 of Peter Wyden, *Conquering Schizophrenia* (1998).

308 In the pop-psychology bestseller *The Secret* (2006), Rhonda Byrne declares unequivocally, "Humans have the power to intentionally think and create their entire life with their mind."

308 "The religion of healthy-mindedness" serves as the title of a chapter in William James, *The Varieties of Religious Experience* (1905). The quotation about "the conquering efficacy of courage, hope, and trust, and a correlative contempt for doubt, fear, worry" appears on page 95.

308 The quotation from Patricia Backlar ("I sometimes felt as though I wore a scarlet letter *S* . . .") occurs on pages 15–16 of her book *The Family Face of Schizophrenia* (1994).

308 The quotation beginning "An entire generation of mental health professionals" occurs on pages 160–61 of Maryellen Walsh, *Schizophrenia: Straight Talk for Family and Friends* (1985).

308 The quotation from E. Fuller Torrey ("Any parent who has raised a child . . .") occurs on page 152 of his book *Surviving Schizophrenia* (2006).

308 This passage is based on my interview with Paul and Freda Smithers in 2008. All names in this passage are pseudonyms.

309 The quotation from John Bunyan ("Let them . . . recover one to his wits that was mad . . .") comes from "The Jerusalem sinner saved, or, good news for the vilest of men," in *The Miscellaneous Works of John Bunyan*, edited by Richard L. Greaves and Robert Sharrock (1979).

309 For a layperson's reference on the history of treatments for schizophrenia, see Robert Whitaker, *Mad in America: Bad Science, Bad Medicine, and the Enduring Mistreatment of the Mentally Ill* (2003). Henry Cotton's theory of "focal infection" (for which tooth-pulling was supposedly a remedy) is described in Richard Noll, "The blood of the insane," *History of Psychiatry* 17, no. 4 (December 2006). For more information on the history of lobotomy, see Joel T. Braslow, "History and evidence-based medicine: Lessons from the history of somatic treatments from the 1900s to the 1950s," *Mental Health Services Research* 1, no. 4 (December 1999).

309 Thorazine is a trademark for chlorpromazine. For more information, see Thomas A. Ban, "Fifty years chlorpromazine: A historical perspective," *Neuropsychiatric Disease & Treatment* 3, no. 4 (August 2007).

309 The quotation from Helen Mayberg ("It's as though you have a house burning down . . .") comes from personal communication in 2011.

310 The quotation from the Russian political prisoner ("One loses his individuality, his mind is dulled . . .") comes from the samizdat publication *Chronicle of Current Events* 18 (March 5, 1971), translated from Russian and cited in John D. LaMothe, *Controlled Offensive Behavior: USSR*, Defense Intelligence Agency Report ST-CS-01-169-72 (1972). Soviet use of psychiatric medication was described in Carl Gershman, "Psychiatric abuse in the Soviet Union," *Society* 21, no. 5 (July 1984).

310 The quotation from Janet Gotkin ("I became alienated from my self . . .") occurs on page 17 of the Committee on the Judiciary report *Drugs in Institutions* (1977), which contains the transcript of hearings held on July 31 and August 18, 1975.

310 The quotation beginning "The muscles of your jawbone go berserk" occurs on pages 35–36 of Jack Henry Abbott, *In the Belly of the Beast* (1981).

310 This passage is based on interviews with Penny, Peter, Doug, and Polly Pease in 2008 and subsequent communications.

313 The McLean schizophrenia genetics study is ongoing; recruitment information is available on their website, http://www.mclean.harvard.edu/research/clinical/study.php?sid=68.

313 For more information on clozapine intoxication, see Carl R. Young, Malcolm B. Bowers Jr., and Carolyn M. Mazure, "Management of the adverse effects of clozapine," *Schizophrenia Bulletin* 24, no. 3 (1998).

313 Foucault's treatise on mental illness is *Madness and Civilization: A History of Insanity in the Age of Reason* (1964).

314 See, for example, Erving Goffman, "The insanity of place," *Psychiatry: Journal of Interpersonal Relations* 32, no. 4 (November 1969).

314 The quotations from R. D. Laing occur on pages 115, 121, and 133 of *The Politics of Experience* (1967).

314 The seminal works of "antipsychiatry" include Erving Goffman's and R. D. Laing's works cited above, as well as Thomas Szasz's books *The Myth of Mental Illness* (1974) and *Insanity: The Idea and Its Consequences* (1987).

314 Figures on the reduction in institutionalized populations come from page 421 of E. Fuller Torrey, *Surviving Schizophrenia* (2006).

314 E. Fuller Torrey's statement "Freedom to be insane is an illusory freedom" occurs on page 34 of his book *Nowhere to Go: The Tragic Odyssey of the Homeless Mentally Ill* (1988).

314 Judge Berel Caesar is quoted on page 160 of Rael Jean Isaac and Virginia C. Armat, *Madness in the Streets: How Psychiatry and the Law Abandoned the Mentally Ill* (1990).

314 The quotations from Ann Braden Johnson ("the myth that mental illness is a myth" and "Bureaucrats who drew up programs . . .") occur on pages 4 and xiv, respectively, of *Out of Bedlam: The Truth About Deinstitutionalization* (1990).

314 Nancy C. Andreasen describes the function of hospitals as communities on page 32 of *The Family Face of Schizophrenia* (1994).

315 The quotation from the frustrated father ("The authorities say it is their choice and their right to live like stray animals . . .") occurs on page 11 of Rael Jean Isaac and Virginia C. Armat, *Madness in the Streets* (1990).

315 This passage is based on my interview with Madeline Grammont in 2008. All names in this passage are pseudonyms.

316 For a large-scale study of schizophrenia risk in twins, see Alastair G. Cardno et al., "Heritability estimates for psychotic disorders: The Maudsley twin psychosis series," *Archives of General Psychiatry* 56, no. 2 (February 1999): 162–68.

316 For a review of enlarged lateral ventricles in schizophrenia, see Danilo Arnone et al., "Magnetic resonance imaging studies in bipolar disorder and schizophrenia," *British Journal of Psychiatry* 195, no. 3 (September 2009).

316 The function of dendritic spines is described in detail in Anissa Abi-Dargham and Holly Moore, "Prefrontal DA transmission at D1 receptors and the pathology of schizophrenia," *Neuroscientist* 9, no. 5 (2003).

316 Temporal lobe function in schizophrenia is discussed in Christos Pantelis et al., "Structural brain imaging evidence for multiple pathological processes at different stages of brain development in schizophrenia," *Schizophrenia Bulletin* 31, no. 3 (July 2005).

316 For more information on synaptic connectivity and frontal lobe function in schizophrenia, see Gábor Faludi and Károly Mirnics, "Synaptic changes in the brain of subjects with schizophrenia," *International Journal of Developmental Neuroscience* 29, no. 3 (May 2011); and Francine M. Benes, "Amygdalocortical circuitry in schizophrenia: From circuits to molecules," *Neuropsychopharmacology* 35, no. 1 (January 2010). Synaptic connectivity in autism is discussed in Carlos A. Pardo and Charles G. Eberhart, "The neurobiology of autism," *Brain Pathology* 17, no. 4 (October 2007).

316 For discussion of the contribution of maternal infection to schizophrenia, see Douglas Fox, "The insanity virus," *Discover*, June 2010; and Alan S. Brown and Ezra S. Susser, "In utero infection and adult schizophrenia," *Mental Retardation & Developmental Disabilities Research Reviews* 8, no. 1 (February 2002).

316 Studies documenting an increase in schizophrenia in offspring of women who experienced the death or life-threatening illness of a close relative during pregnancy include Ali S. Khashan et al., "Higher risk of offspring schizophrenia following antenatal maternal exposure to severe adverse life events," *Archives of General Psychiatry* 65, no. 2 (2008); and Matti O. Huttunen and Pekka Niskanen, "Prenatal loss of father and psychiatric disorders," *Archives of General Psychiatry* 35, no. 4 (1978). Unforeseen mental health consequences of war are documented in Jim van Os and Jean-Paul Selten, "Prenatal exposure to maternal stress and

subsequent schizophrenia: The May 1940 invasion of the Netherlands," *British Journal of Psychiatry* 172, no. 4 (April 1998); and Dolores Malaspina et al., "Acute maternal stress in pregnancy and schizophrenia in offspring: A cohort prospective study," *BMC Psychiatry* 8 (2008). Schizophrenia following famine is discussed in Hans W. Hoek, Alan S. Brown, and Ezra S. Susser, "The Dutch famine and schizophrenia spectrum disorders," *Social Psychiatry & Psychiatric Epidemiology* 33, no. 8 (July 1998); and David St. Clair et al., "Rates of adult schizophrenia following prenatal exposure to the Chinese famine of 1959–1961," *Journal of the American Medical Association* 294, no. 5 (2005).

316 Prenatal stress hormones and dopamine activation in schizophrenia are explored in Alan S. Brown, "The environment and susceptibility to schizophrenia," *Progress in Neurobiology* 93, no. 1 (January 2011); and Dennis K. Kinney et al., "Prenatal stress and risk for autism," *Neuroscience & Biobehavioral Reviews* 32, no. 8 (October 2008).

316 For a recent study finding an increased risk of schizophrenia following traumatic brain injury, see Charlene Molloy et al., "Is traumatic brain injury a risk factor for schizophrenia?: A meta-analysis of case-controlled population-based studies," *Schizophrenia Bulletin* (August 2011).

316 Meta-analyses of studies on increased risk of schizophrenia in immigrant populations include Elizabeth Cantor-Graae and Jean-Paul Selten, "Schizophrenia and migration: A meta-analysis and review," *American Journal of Psychiatry* 162, no. 1 (January 2005); and Jean-Paul Selten, Elizabeth Cantor-Graae, and Rene S. Kahn, "Migration and schizophrenia," *Current Opinion in Psychiatry* 20, no. 2 (March 2007).

316 For studies establishing an association between severity of schizophrenic symptoms and recreational use of cocaine, methamphetamine, and cannabis, see, e.g., Killian A. Welch et al., "The impact of substance use on brain structure in people at high risk of developing schizophrenia," *Schizophrenia Bulletin* 37, no. 5 (September 2011); and P. A. Ringen et al., "The level of illicit drug use is related to symptoms and premorbid functioning in severe mental illness," *Acta Psychiatrica Scandinavica* 118, no. 4 (October 2008).

316 Methamphetamine use and psychosis in postwar Japan are discussed in Hiroshi Suwaki, Susumi Fukui, and Kyohei Konuma, "Methamphetamine abuse in Japan," in *Methamphetamine Abuse: Epidemiologic Issues and Implications*, edited by Marissa J. Miller and Nicholas J. Kozel (1991); and Mitsumoto Sato, Yohtaro Numachi, and Takashi Hamamura, "Relapse of paranoid psychotic state in methamphetamine model of schizophrenia," *Schizophrenia Bulletin* 18, no. 1 (1992).

317 For the Swedish cannabis/schizophrenia study, see Stanley Zammit et al., "Self reported cannabis use as a risk factor for schizophrenia in Swedish conscripts of 1969: Historical cohort study," *British Medical Journal* 325, no. 7374 (November 23, 2002).

317 The quotation from Cyril D'Souza comes from my interview with him in 2007. One of his recent articles that addresses this topic is R. Andrew Sewell, Mohini Ranganathan, and Deepak Cyril D'Souza, "Cannabinoids and psychosis," *International Review of Psychosis* 21, no. 2 (April 2009).

317 Dysregulation of neural transmitters is described in Paul J. Harrison and D. R. Weinberger, "Schizophrenia genes, gene expression, and neuropathology: On the matter of their convergence," *Molecular Psychiatry* 10, no. 1 (January 2005).

317 Studies and review articles by Anissa Abi-Dargham and her colleagues include Anissa Abi-Dargham et al., "Increased baseline occupancy of D2 receptors

by dopamine in schizophrenia," *Proceedings of the National Academy of Sciences* 97, no. 14 (July 2000); Anissa Abi-Dargham and Holly Moore, "Prefrontal DA transmission at D1 receptors and the pathology of schizophrenia," *Neuroscientist* 9, no. 5 (October 2003); Bernard Masri et al., "Antagonism of dopamine D2 receptor/beta-arrestin 2 interaction is a common property of clinically effective antipsychotics," *Proceedings of the National Academy of Sciences* 105, no. 36 (September 9, 2008); Nobumi Miyake et al., "Presynaptic dopamine in schizophrenia," *CNS Neuroscience & Therapeutics* 17, no. 2 (April 2011); and Robert W. Buchanan et al., "Recent advances in the development of novel pharmacological agents for the treatment of cognitive impairments in schizophrenia," *Schizophrenia Bulletin* 33, no. 5 (2007).

317 Elyn Saks credits talk therapy with saving her life in *The Center Cannot Hold: My Journey Through Madness* (2007). Cognitive behavioral therapy for schizophrenia is discussed in Xavier Amador, *I Am Not Sick, I Don't Need Help* (2007); Jennifer Gottlieb and Corinne Cather, "Cognitive behavioral therapy (CBT) for schizophrenia: An in-depth interview with experts," Schizophrenia.com (February 3, 2007); Debbie M. Warman and Aaron T. Beck, "Cognitive behavioral therapy," National Alliance on Mental Illness (2003); Susan R. McGurk et al., "A meta-analysis of cognitive remediation in schizophrenia," *American Journal of Psychiatry* 164, no. 12 (2007); and Sara Tai and Douglas Turkington, "The evolution of cognitive behavior therapy for schizophrenia: Current practice and recent developments," *Schizophrenia Bulletin* 35, no. 5 (2009).

318 The quotation from Jeffrey Lieberman ("There is no better time in the history of mankind to have a mental illness than now . . .") comes from my interview with him in 2008.

318 International Early Psychosis Association website: http://www.iepa.org.au.

318 Thomas McGlashan discusses the potential benefits of early treatment in an article written with Scott Woods, "Early antecedents and detection of schizophrenia: Understanding the clinical implications," *Psychiatric Times* 28, no. 3 (March 2011).

318 Jeffrey Lieberman's comment about the "Humpty-Dumpty situation" comes from the article "A beacon of hope: Prospects for preventing and recovering from mental illness," *NARSAD Research Quarterly* 2, no. 1 (Winter 2009).

318 The quotation from Jack Barchas comes from a personal communication in 2010.

318 Early symptoms of schizophrenia are described in Nancy C. Andreasen, "Schizophrenia: The characteristic symptoms," *Schizophrenia Bulletin* 17, no. 1 (1991); and Tandy J. Miller et al., "The PRIME North America randomized double-blind clinical trial of olanzapine versus placebo in patients at risk of being prodromally symptomatic for psychosis II: Baseline characteristics of the 'prodromal' sample," *Schizophrenia Research* 61, no. 1 (March 2003).

318 Thomas McGlashan and his colleagues reported their findings in Thomas H. McGlashan et al., "Randomized, double-blind trial of olanzapine versus placebo in patients prodromally symptomatic for psychosis," *American Journal of Psychiatry* 163, no. 5 (May 2006); and Keith A. Hawkins et al., "Neuropsychological course in the prodrome and first episode of psychosis: Findings from the PRIME North America double blind treatment study," *Schizophrenia Research* 105, nos. 1–3 (October 2008). McGlashan's assessment of the results as only "marginally significant" comes from Benedict Carey, "Mixed result in drug trial on pretreating schizophrenia," *New York Times*, May 1, 2006.

319 Studies from the UK and Australia finding benefit in cognitive-behavioral therapy include Patrick D. McGorry et al., "Randomized controlled trial of

interventions designed to reduce the risk of progression to first-episode psychosis in a clinical sample with subthreshold symptoms," *Archives of General Psychiatry* 59, no. 10 (October 2002); Mike Startup, M. C. Jackson, and S. Bendix, "North Wales randomized controlled trial of cognitive behaviour therapy for acute schizophrenia spectrum disorders: Outcomes at 6 and 12 months," *Psychological Medicine* 34, no. 3 (April 2004); Mike Startup et al., "North Wales randomized controlled trial of cognitive behaviour therapy for acute schizophrenia spectrum disorders: Two-year follow-up and economic evaluation," *Psychological Medicine* 35, no. 9 (2005); P. Kingsep et al., "Cognitive behavioural group treatment for social anxiety in schizophrenia," *Schizophrenia Research* 63, nos. 1–2 (September 2003); and Andrew Gumley et al., "Early intervention for relapse in schizophrenia: Results of a 12-month randomized controlled trial of cognitive behavioural therapy," *Psychological Medicine* 33, no. 3 (April 2003).

319 For more information on prevention of psychosis by omega-3 fatty acids, see K. Akter et al., "A review of the possible role of the essential fatty acids and fish oils in the aetiology, prevention or pharmacotherapy of schizophrenia," *Journal of Clinical Pharmacy & Therapeutics* (April 19, 2011); Claire B. Irving et al., "Polyunsaturated fatty acid supplementation for schizophrenia: Intervention review," *Cochrane Library* 9 (January 20, 2010); and Max Marshall and John Rathbone, "Early intervention in psychosis," *Cochrane Library* 15, no. 6 (June 2011).

319 The quotation from Thomas McGlashan comes from my interview with him in 2007.

319 The concept of a "psychosis risk syndrome" was first developed by Thomas McGlashan and incorporated into the design of the PRIME study: Keith A. Hawkins et al., "Neuropsychological course in the prodrome and first episode of psychosis: Findings from the PRIME North America double blind treatment study," *Schizophrenia Research* 105, nos. 1–3 (October 2008). McGlashan and his colleagues argue for the establishment of the syndrome as a diagnostic category in Scott W. Woods et al., "The case for including Attenuated Psychotic Symptoms Syndrome in DSM-5 as a psychosis risk syndrome," *Schizophrenia Research* 123, nos. 2–3 (November 2010). Their proposals attracted considerable opposition; see, e.g., Cheryl M. Corcoran, Michael B. First, and Barbara Cornblat, "The psychosis risk syndrome and its proposed inclusion in the DSM-V: A risk-benefit analysis," *Schizophrenia Research* 120 (July 2010); and Allen Frances, "Psychosis risk syndrome: Far too risky," *Australian & New Zealand Journal of Psychiatry* 45, no. 10 (October 2011). For a scholarly review of the controversy, see Barnaby Nelson and Alison R. Yung, "Should a risk syndrome for first episode psychosis be included in the DSM-5?," *Current Opinion in Psychiatry* 24, no. 2 (March 2011); for a journalistic discussion, see Sally Satel, "Prescriptions for psychiatric trouble and the DSM-V," *Wall Street Journal*, February 19, 2010. A report of the decision of the DSM working committee finally to drop the diagnosis is presented in Benedict Carey, "Psychiatry manual drafters back down on diagnoses," *New York Times*, May 8, 2012.

319 The quotation from John Krystal ("What they do in the *DSM* is a fashion question . . .") comes from a personal communication in 2012.

319 The anecdote from Jeffrey Lieberman about an anonymous patient comes from my interview with him in 2007.

320 This passage is based on my interviews with George Clark, Charlotte Clark, Electa Reischer, and Jackie Clark in 2008 and subsequent communications.

324 The quotation from Deborah Levy comes from my interview with her in 2008.

324 The quotation from Larry Davidson and David Stayner ("While perhaps appearing wooden and vacant to others . . .") comes from their paper "Loss, loneliness, and the desire for love: Perspectives on the social lives of people with schizophrenia," *Psychiatric Rehabilitation Journal* 20, no. 3 (Winter 1997).

325 The quotation from Jean Frazier comes from my interview with her in 2008.

325 The quotation from the unnamed mother whose son's therapist proposed a motto is from a personal communication, 2008.

325 This passage is based on my interviews with George, Giuseppe, and Bridget Marcolo in 2008 and subsequent communications. All names in this passage are pseudonyms.

327 For more information on recovery and the recovery movement, see Robert Paul Liberman et al., "Operational criteria and factors related to recovery from schizophrenia," *International Review of Psychiatry* 14, no. 4 (November 2002); Jeffrey A. Lieberman et al., "Science and recovery in schizophrenia," *Psychiatric Services* 59 (May 2008); and Kate Mulligan, "Recovery movement gains influence in mental health programs," *Psychiatric News* 38, no. 1 (January 2003).

328 The quotation from the unnamed mother ("Two years ago, I would have thought he was living a sad, wasted, pointless life . . .") comes from a personal interview in 2009.

328 This passage is based on my interview with Marnie Callahan in 2008. All names in this passage are pseudonyms.

328 The quotation from Jeffrey Lieberman ("The problem is . . .") comes from my interview with him in 2011.

329 Statistics on homelessness among people with schizophrenia occur on page 3 of E. Fuller Torrey, *Out of the Shadows: Confronting America's Mental Illness Crisis* (1997).

329 See the US Department of Health and Human Services, Substance Abuse and Mental Health Services Administration, *Results from the 2008 National Survey on Drug Use and Health: National Findings* (2008).

329 The quotation from Jean Frazier ("The thing that makes me emotionally drained . . .") comes from my interview with her in 2008.

329 Estimates of costs associated with schizophrenia come from Eric Q. Wu et al., "The economic burden of schizophrenia in the United States in 2002," *Journal of Clinical Psychiatry* 66, no. 9 (September 2005).

329 Elevated rates of suicide in schizophrenia are reported in Kahyee Hor and Mark Taylor, "Suicide and schizophrenia: A systematic review of rates and risk factors," *Journal of Psychopharmacology* 24, no. 4 suppl. (November 2010); and Alec Roy and Maurizio Pompili, "Management of schizophrenia with suicide risk," *Psychiatric Clinics of North America* 32, no. 4 (December 2009). See also Maurizio Pompili et al., "Suicide risk in schizophrenia: Learning from the past to change the future," *Annals of General Psychiatry* 6 (March 16, 2007).

329 The anecdote about the feces-eating prisoner who remained uncommitted following a petition to the court occurs on page 142 of E. Fuller Torrey, *Out of the Shadows* (1997).

329 The quotation from Kenneth Duckworth ("It's harder to get into a state hospital than into Harvard Medical School") comes from Deborah Sontag, "A schizophrenic, a slain worker, troubling questions," *New York Times*, June 17, 2011.

330 Figures for the percentage of individuals with schizophrenia who live with

their families rely on Richard S. E. Keefe and Philip D. Harvey, *Understanding Schizophrenia: A Guide to New Research on Causes and Treatment* (1994) (estimating 65 percent, page 173); Agnes B. Hatfield, *Family Education in Mental Illness* (1990) (estimating 65 percent, page 15; the family survey finding that only 3 percent of responders thought their schizophrenic relatives should live in the family home is discussed on pages 16–17); and Ellen Lukens, "Schizophrenia," in *Handbook of Social Work Practice with Vulnerable and Resilient Populations*, 2nd ed., edited by Alex Gitterman (2001) (estimating 50–70 percent, page 288). For more information on living arrangements and parent satisfaction, see Benedicte Lowyck et al., "Can we identify the factors influencing the burden family-members of schizophrenic patients experience?," *International Journal of Psychiatry in Clinical Practice* 5, no. 2 (January 2001).

330 The quotation from Jeffrey Lieberman ("The problem is that people burn out . . .") comes from my interview with him in 2009.

330 The quotation from Ezra Susser ("You have to be really careful . . .") comes from my interview with him in 2008.

330 The referenced WHO study is Dan Chisholm et al., "Schizophrenia treatment in the developing world: An interregional and multinational cost-effectiveness analysis," *Bulletin of the World Health Organization* 86, no. 8 (July 2008). A 1999 study from Nigeria disputes the claim that schizophrenia outcomes are better in developing countries; see Oye Gureje and Rotimi Bamidele, "Thirteen-year social outcome among Nigerian outpatients with schizophrenia," *Social Psychiatry & Psychiatric Epidemiology* 34, no. 3 (March 1999).

330 The quotation from Cyril D'Souza ("It was very difficult for me to understand . . .") comes from my interview with him in 2007.

330 The description of treatment of mental patients in Senegal is based on personal reporting I did there in 2000.

331 The quotation from Esso Leete ("Criticize only constructively . . .") comes from her article "Interpersonal environment: A consumer's personal recollection," in *Surviving Mental Illness: Stress, Coping, and Adaptation*, edited by Agnes B. Hatfield and Harriet P. Lefley (1993).

331 The advice to "approach delusions in a spirit of shared inquiry" is made at East Community's "Family and friends" webpage, http://www.eastcommunity.org/home/ec1/smartlist_12/family_and_friends.html.

331 The quotation from the father ("My loving, bright, amusing son . . .") occurs on page 34 of Raquel E. Gur and Ann Braden Johnson, *If Your Adolescent Has Schizophrenia: An Essential Resource for Parents* (2006); the quotation from the mother ("These kids die but they never get buried") occurs on page 93.

331 The quotation "The sick child inhabits a different world . . ." occurs on page 3 of Nona Dearth and Families of the Mentally Ill Collective, *Families Helping Families: Living with Schizophrenia* (1986).

331 The murder of Malcolm Tate is described on page 79 of E. Fuller Torrey, *Out of the Shadows: Confronting America's Mental Illness Crisis* (1997). A judgment in *Lothell Tate v. State of South Carolina*, affirming Lothell Tate's conviction for the murder of her brother, was issued by the South Carolina Supreme Court on April 13, 1992.

331 This passage is based on my interview with Rosemary Baglio in 2008.

334 Anosognosia is the subject of Xavier Francisco Amador, *I Am Not Sick, I Don't Need Help!* (2007).

334 "That proves you mad, because you know it not" occurs in act 4, scene 3 of

Thomas Dekker's 1604 play, *The Honest Whore*, reissued by Nick Hern Books in 1998.

334 The quotation from Elyn Saks ("We should not be in the business of choosing selves") occurs on page 12 of her book *Refusing Care: Forced Treatment and the Rights of the Mentally Ill* (2002).

335 For more information on IQ and outcomes in schizophrenia, see Janet C. Munro et al., "IQ in childhood psychiatric attendees predicts outcome of later schizophrenia at 21 year follow-up," *Acta Psychiatrica Scandinavica* 106, no. 2 (August 2002); and Maurizio Pompili et al., "Suicide risk in schizophrenia: Learning from the past to change the future," *Annals of General Psychiatry* 6, no. 10 (2007).

335 The quotation from John Krystal ("You have no idea how many people you interact with who are hearing voices . . .") comes from my interview with him in 2012.

335 Linda Bishop is the subject of Rachel Aviv, "God knows where I am: What should happen when patients reject their diagnosis?," *New Yorker*, May 30, 2011.

335 Judi Chamberlin's comment ("If it isn't voluntary, it isn't treatment") occurs in David Davis, "Losing the mind," *Los Angeles Times*, October 26, 2003. Chamberlin is the author of *On Our Own: Patient-Controlled Alternatives to the Mental Health System* (1978).

335 The Mad Pride movement is discussed in Gabrielle Glaser, "'Mad pride' fights a stigma," *New York Times*, May 11, 2008.

336 The quotation from the Asheville Radical Mental Health Collective organizer ("It used to be you were labeled . . .") comes from Gabrielle Glaser, "'Mad pride' fights a stigma," *New York Times*, May 11, 2008.

336 The quotation from David Oaks ("They took a wrecking ball to the cathedral of my mind"), Sally Zinman's praise of Oaks, and the American Psychiatric Association's response come from David Davis, "Losing the mind," *Los Angeles Times*, October 26, 2003.

336 Peter Breggin describes drug-induced improvement in schizophrenics as a "disability, a loss of mental capacity" on page 2 of *Psychiatric Drugs: Hazards to the Brain* (1983).

337 Psychiatric drug "pro-choice" advocates are featured in I. A. Robinson and Astrid Rodrigues, "'Mad Pride' activists say they're unique, not sick," ABC News, August 2, 2009.

337 The quotation from Will Hall occurs on page 3 of his book *Harm Reduction Guide to Coming Off Psychiatric Drugs* (2007).

337 This quotation from Clare Allan ("There seems to be some sort of agreement . . .") and the one that follows ("Rightly or wrongly, the truth was I didn't feel proud . . .") come from her article "Misplaced pride," *Guardian*, September 27, 2006; "According to my doctor, I'm mad . . ." appears in the comments section of that article.

337 The statement "We are a network of people living with . . ." occurs on the Icarus Project website, http://theicarusproject.net/.

338 Alison Jost discusses Mad Pride in her article "Mad pride and the medical model," *Hastings Center Report* 39, no. 4 (July–August 2009).

338 This passage is based on my interview with Walter Forrest in 2008. All names in this passage are pseudonyms.

339 The anecdote about the casting difficulties involved in the production of *One Flew Over the Cuckoo's Nest* occurs on page 38 of Otto F. Wahl, *Media Madness: Public Images of Mental Illness* (1995).

339 The survey finding that 40 percent of landlords immediately rejected mentally

ill applicants for apartments is reported in Joseph M. Alisky and Kenneth A. Iczkowski, "Barriers to housing for deinstitutionalized psychiatric patients," *Hospital & Community Psychiatry* 41, no. 1 (January 1990).

339 For details on the miserable employment prospects of people with schizophrenia, see Eric Q. Wu et al., "The economic burden of schizophrenia in the United States in 2002," *Journal of Clinical Psychiatry* 66, no. 9 (September 2005); and David S. Salkever et al., "Measures and predictors of community-based employment and earnings of persons with schizophrenia in a multisite study," *Psychiatric Services* 58, no. 3 (March 2007).

339 The effectiveness of employment as therapy was noted by Stephen Marder in Mark Moran, "Schizophrenia treatment should focus on recovery, not just symptoms," *Psychiatric News* 39, no. 22 (November 19, 2004). Marder is a coauthor of Robert S. Kern et al., "Psychosocial treatments to promote functional recovery in schizophrenia," *Schizophrenia Bulletin* 35, no. 2 (March 2009).

339 The quotation from James Beck ("Many people can't tolerate working with chronic schizophrenics . . .") occurs on page 97 of Rael Jean Isaac and Virginia C. Armat, *Madness in the Streets* (1990).

340 Statistics on risk of homicide by people with schizophrenia come from Cameron Wallace et al., "Serious criminal offending and mental disorder: Case linkage study," *British Journal of Psychiatry* 172, no. 6 (June 1998).

340 For the 1998 study on violence in psychiatric patients, see Henry J. Steadman et al., "Violence by people discharged from acute psychiatric inpatient facilities and by others in the same neighborhoods," *Archives of General Psychiatry* 55, no. 5 (May 1998).

340 Increased risk of violence to family members of people with schizophrenia is documented in Annika Nordström and Gunnar Kullgren, "Victim relations and victim gender in violent crimes committed by offenders with schizophrenia," *Social Psychiatry & Psychiatric Epidemiology* 38, no. 6 (June 2003); and Annika Nordström, Lars Dahlgren, and Gunnar Kullgren, "Victim relations and factors triggering homicides committed by offenders with schizophrenia," *Journal of Forensic Psychiatry & Psychology* 17, no. 2 (June 2006).

340 The murder of Stephanie Moulton by Deshawn Chappell is discussed in Deborah Sontag, "A schizophrenic, a slain worker, troubling questions," *New York Times*, June 17, 2011; and John Oldham's letter to the editor in response to "How budget cuts affect the mentally ill," *New York Times*, June 25, 2011.

341 Quotations that appear in this account of Jared Loughner's shooting spree and the aftermath come from the following sources: "We have a mentally unstable person in the class . . .": Matthew Lysiak and Lukas I. Alpert, "Gabrielle Giffords shooting: Frightening, twisted shrine in Arizona killer Jared Lee Loughner's yard," *New York Daily News*, January 10, 2011. "It seemed obvious that he had mental problems" and "We don't understand why this happened": Leslie Eaton, Daniel Gilbert, and Ann Zimmerman, "Suspect's downward spiral," *Wall Street Journal*, January 13, 2011. Loughner "rocked back and forth," "experienced delusions, bizarre thoughts . . .": Mark Lacey, "After being removed from court, Loughner is ruled incompetent," *New York Times*, May 25, 2011. "Mr. Loughner has a due process right . . .": Mark Lacey, "Lawyers for defendant in Giffords shooting seem to be searching for illness," *New York Times*, August 16, 2011. "Is it ethical and proper . . .": Mark Lacey, "After being removed from court, Loughner is ruled incompetent," *New York Times*, May 25, 2011.

341 Judicial authorization for continued medication for Jared Loughner is reported

in "Judge allows forced medication for Arizona shooting suspect," *New York Times*, August 28, 2011.

341 Loughner's guilty plea was reported in Fernanda Santos, "Life term for gunman after guilty plea in Tucson killings," *New York Times*, August 7, 2012.

342 The Los Angeles County Jail is described as the facility containing the largest number of schizophrenics in the United States in the article "Treatment not jail: A plan to rebuild community mental health," *Sacramento Bee*, March 17, 1999. For a comprehensive general source on mental health and the criminal justice system, see the Council of State Governments report *Criminal Justice / Mental Health Consensus Project* (2002).

342 Statistics on the total number of people with schizophrenia in jail and on probation come from Paula Ditton, *Mental Health and Treatment of Inmates and Probationers* (1999).

342 Massachusetts statistics come from the most comprehensive available study of mental illness in incarcerated persons: Sasha Abramsky and Jamie Fellner, *Ill-Equipped: U.S. Prisons and Offenders with Mental Illness* (2003).

342 This passage is based on my interviews with Susan Weinreich and Bobbe Evans in 2007 and subsequent communications.

346 The four quotations about voices and delusions come from personal communications.

347 The quotation from Michael Foster Green ("When an illness is viewed as inexplicable and impenetrable . . .") occurs on the first page of his book *Schizophrenia Revealed* (2001).

347 Karl Jaspers uses the phrase *abyss of difference* on page 219 of *General Psychopathology* (1963), as cited by Christopher Frith and Eve Johnstone on page 123 of *Schizophrenia: A Very Short Introduction* (2003).

347 The quotation from Jay Neugeboren ("For paid professionals to act as if Robert were merely a vessel of flesh . . .") occurs on pages 136–39 of his book about Robert's schizophrenia, *Imagining Robert: My Brother, Madness, and Survival* (2003). It has been condensed.

347 Andy Behrman describes his experiences with bipolar disorder in his essay "Mental health recovery: A personal perspective," About.com, December 29, 2011.

348 The quotation from Richard C. Friedman ("The problem in psychiatric diagnosis . . .") comes from personal communication in 2011.

348 This passage is based on my interview with Patricia, Winston, and Sam Fischer in 2008, and subsequent communications. All names in this passage are pseudonyms, except the name of David Nathan.

VII: Disability

355 Elaine Fowler Palencia, *Taking the Train: Poems* (1997), pages 6–7.

356 My definitions of various disability categories come from the National Dissemination Center for Children with Disabilities' FAQ "Severe and/or multiple disabilities," http://www.nichcy.org/Disabilities/Specific/Pages/SevereandorMultipleDisabilities.aspx.

357 "Loving things for reasons" is a line in Richard Wilbur's poem "Winter Spring," which appears on page 453 of his *Collected Poems, 1943–2004* (2004).

357 For basic information on severe disabilities, I have relied upon *Introduction to Persons with Severe Disabilities: Educational and Social Issues*, edited by John J. J. McDonnell et al. (1995); the twenty thousand births per year figure occurs on page 75.

357 This passage is based on my interviews with David and Sara Hadden in 2004 and 2007 and subsequent communications.

363 Quotations from Alan O. Ross come from pages 55–56 and 157 of his book *The Exceptional Child in the Family* (1972).

363 The quotation from Susan Allport ("It is not parent providing care to helpless young . . .") occurs on page 103 of her book *A Natural History of Parenting: A Naturalist Looks at Parenting in the Animal World and Ours* (1997).

363 Sarah Hrdy's observation ("Nurturing has to be teased out, reinforced, maintained . . .") occurs on page 174 of her book *Mother Nature: Maternal Instincts and How They Shape the Human Species* (1999).

364 The characterization of maternal attachment as "transactional, rather than linear and unidirectional" comes from Carol George and Judith Solomon, "Attachment and caregiving: The caregiving behavioral system," in *Handbook of Attachment: Theory, Research, and Clinical Applications*, edited by Jude Cassidy and Phillip R. Shaver (1999), page 659.

364 Carrie Knoll tells the story of her encounter with parents of a child with holoprosencephaly in her article "In parents' eyes, the faintest signs of hope blur the inevitable," *Los Angeles Times*, October 28, 2002.

364 This passage is based on my interview with Louis and Greta Winthrop in 2005. All names in this passage are pseudonyms.

365 Sophia Isako Wong's question (". . . what rewards do parents expect . . .") comes from her article "At home with Down syndrome and gender," *Hypatia* 17, no. 3 (Summer 2002).

365 See Simon Olshansky, "Chronic sorrow: A response to having a mentally defective child," *Social Casework* 43, no. 4 (1962).

365 Sigmund Freud, *Mourning and Melancholia*, vol. 14, *The Standard Edition of the Complete Psychological Works of Sigmund Freud* (1955).

366 The reference to ". . . the deadly pall of tragedy . . ." occurs on page 27 of Jeanne Ann Summers, Shirley K. Behr, and Ann P. Turnbull, "Positive adaptation and coping strengths of families who have children with disabilities," in *Support for Caregiving Families: Enabling Positive Adaptation to Disability*, edited by George H. S. Singer and Larry K. Irvin (1989).

366 Discrepancies between professionals' observations of family stress and family members' actual experience are discussed in Anne E. Kazak and Robert S. Marvin, "Differences, difficulties and adaptation: Stress and social networks in families with a handicapped child," *Family Relations* 33, no. 1 (January 1984).

366 Jerome Groopman's comment about language ("Language is as vital to the physician's art as the stethoscope . . .") occurs in his article "Hurting all over," *New Yorker*, November 13, 2000.

366 This passage is based on my interview with Paul and Cris Donovan in 2007 and subsequent communications.

371 For research finding that social isolation is a risk factor for depression and attachment impairment, see pages 93–95 of *Infants in Crisis: How Parents Cope with Newborn Intensive Care and Its Aftermath*, edited by Glenn Affleck, Howard Tennen, and Jonelle Rowe (1991); see also Glenn Affleck and Howard Tennen, "Appraisal and coping predictors of mother and child outcomes after newborn intensive care," *Journal of Social & Clinical Psychology* 10, no. 4 (1991).

371 The concept of an "internal locus of control" is discussed in Bryony Beresford, "Resources and strategies: How parents cope with the care of a disabled child," *Journal of Child Psychology & Psychiatry* 35, no. 1 (January 1994); and Emmy

Werner and Ruth Smith, *Journeys from Childhood to Midlife: Risk, Resilience, and Recovery* (2001).

372 This passage is based on my interview with Susanna Singer in 2006 and subsequent communications.

374 Cecilia Bartoli's website: http://www.ceciliabartolionline.com.

376 The statistic on the percentage of disabled children who live with parents into adulthood occurs on page 460 of *The Parental Experience in Midlife*, edited by Carol Ryff and Marsha Mailick Seltzer (1996).

376 The modern increase in the life expectancy of disabled people is discussed on page 85 of *Mental Retardation in the Year 2000*, edited by Louis Rowitz (1992); see also Richard K. Eyman et al., "Survival of profoundly disabled people with severe mental retardation," *American Journal of Diseases of Childhood* 147, no. 3 (1993).

376 The role of parental caregiving in providing companionship and a sense of purpose is discussed in Tamar Heller, Alison B. Miller, and Alan Factor, "Adults with mental retardation as supports to their parents: Effects on parental caregiving appraisal," *Mental Retardation* 35, no. 5 (October 1997).

376 This passage is based on my interview with Bill Zirinsky and Ruth Schekter in 2005, and on Bill's articles "Sam's story," *Exceptional Parent*, June 1997; "Saying goodbye to our cherished boy, Sam Zirinsky," *Crazy Wisdom Community Journal*, May–August 2004; "Life with my two little girls," *Crazy Wisdom Community Journal*, January–April 2006; and "If you could see her through my eyes: A journey of love and dying in the fall of 2007," *Crazy Wisdom Community Journal*, January–April 2008.

380 References cited in the paragraph about sibling adjustment: Finding siblings more responsible and tolerant: Sally L. Burton and A. Lee Parks, "Self-esteem, locus of control, and career aspirations of college-age siblings of individuals with disabilities," *Social Work Research* 18, no. 3 (September 1994). Finding siblings more unhappy, but not suffering unduly from psychiatric problems: Naomi Breslau et al., "Siblings of disabled children: Effects of chronic stress in the family," *Archives of General Psychiatry* 44, no. 12 (December 1987). Finding the worse the disability, the better the sibling adjustment: Frances Kaplan Grossman, *Brothers and Sisters of Retarded Children: An Exploratory Study* (1972), especially pages 177–78. Finding siblings were helped by a specific diagnosis: Ann Gath and Dianne Gumley, "Retarded children and their siblings," *Journal of Child Psychology & Psychiatry* 28, no. 5 (September 1987).

381 Allen Shawn describes his experience as the fraternal twin of a profoundly disabled sister in *Twin: A Memoir* (2010).

381 This passage is based on my interviews with John, Eve, and Dylan Morris in 2007 and subsequent communications.

385 The discussion of the Ashley treatment and ensuing controversy is based on my telephone interview with Ashley's father in 2008 and subsequent communications; *The "Ashley Treatment"* weblog established by Ashley's parents at http://ashleytreatment.spaces.live.com, which is the source of all quotations from Ashley's father's writings; Chris Ayres and Chris Lackner, "Father defends decision to stunt disabled girl's growth," *Ottawa Citizen*, January 4, 2007; Elizabeth Cohen's report for CNN "Disability community decries 'Ashley treatment,'" broadcast January 12, 2007; Nancy Gibbs, "Pillow angel ethics," *Time*, January 7, 2007; Ed Pilkington, "Frozen in time: The disabled nine-year-old girl who will remain a child all her life," *Guardian*, January 4, 2007; Geneviève Roberts, "Brain-damaged girl is frozen in time by parents to keep her alive," *Independent*,

January 4, 2007; Sam Howe Verhovek, "Parents defend decision to keep disabled girl small," *Los Angeles Times*, January 3, 2007; the CNN feature "'Pillow angel' parents answer CNN's questions," broadcast March 12, 2008; and the BBC report "Treatment keeps girl child-sized," broadcast January 4, 2007.

387 The quotation from Douglas Diekema comes from the CNN report "Ethicist in Ashley case answers questions," broadcast January 11, 2007.

387 The quotations from Daniel Gunther come from the CNN report "Ethicist in Ashley case answers questions," broadcast January 11, 2007; and from Nancy Gibbs, "Pillow angel ethics," *Time*, January 7, 2007.

387 For the clinical report of the Ashley treatment, see Daniel F. Gunther and Douglas S. Diekema, "Attenuating growth in children with profound developmental disability: A new approach to an old dilemma," *Archives of Pediatric & Adolescent Medicine* 260, no. 10 (October 2006).

387 The quotation from Arthur Caplan comes from his January 5, 2007, opinion piece for MSNBC, "Is 'Peter Pan' treatment a moral choice?"

387 The reference to "surgical mutilation" occurs in a response to the article "The Ashley treatment," on *Burkhart's Blog*, January 6, 2007; "They might as well kill her" occurs in the article "The mistreatment of Ashley X," *Family Voyage*, January 4, 2007.

388 FRIDA's statement was published in a press release on January 10, 2007, http://fridanow.blogspot.com/2007/01/for-immediate-release-january-10-2007.html.

388 Helen Henderson deplored the advent of "designer cripples" in her op-ed piece "Earthly injustice of 'pillow angels,'" *Toronto Star*, June 27, 2009.

388 Julia Epstein's characterization of the Ashley treatment as "terminally infantilizing" occurs in Nancy Gibbs, "Pillow angel ethics," *Time*, January 7, 2007.

388 The two statements by mothers of severely disabled children come from Elizabeth Cohen's report for CNN "Disability community decries 'Ashley treatment,'" broadcast January 12, 2007 (quoting Penny Richards, "Sigh," *Temple University Disability Studies Weblog*, January 5, 2007; and article by "Nufsaid," "The world has gone completely nuts," *Ramblings*, January 4, 2007).

388 The Seattle Growth Attenuation and Ethics Working Group statement comes from Benjamin S. Wilfond et al., "Navigating growth attenuation in children with profound disabilities: Children's interests, family decision-making, and community concerns," *Hastings Center Report* 40, no. 6 (November–December 2010).

389 Norman Fost characterizes public concern about the "Ashley treatment" as intrusive in his article "Offense to third parties?," whereas Eva Feder Kittay characterizes the procedure as discriminatory in "Discrimination against children with cognitive impairments?"; both were published in *Hastings Center Report* 40, no. 6 (November–December 2010).

389 The MSNBC survey was described in the CNN report "'Pillow angel' parents answer CNN's questions," broadcast March 12, 2008.

389 The quotation from Daniel Gunther ("The argument that a beneficial treatment should not be used . . .") occurs in Nancy Gibbs, "Pillow angel ethics," *Time*, January 7, 2007.

389 The quotation from Peter Singer ("What matters in Ashley's life . . .") occurs in his op-ed piece "A convenient truth," *New York Times*, January 26, 2007.

390 I here draw from William Shakespeare's Sonnet 116.

390 The quotations from Anne McDonald come from her article "The other story from a 'pillow angel': Been there. Done that. Preferred to grow," *Seattle Post-Intelligencer*, June 15 2007.

391 The quotation about the uncertainties of prognosis for communication in three-

year-olds comes from a letter by Miriam A. Kalichman published online as "Replies to growth-attenuation therapy: Principles for practice," *Pediatrics* (June 18, 2009).

391 The quotation from Alice Domurat Dreger comes from her article "Attenuated thoughts," *Hastings Center Report* 40, no. 6 (November–December 2010).

392 The quotation from Norman Kunc ("From the age of three until the age of twelve . . .") comes from his interview with Michael F. Giangreco, "The stairs don't go anywhere! A disabled person's reflections on specialized services and their impact on people with disabilities," University of Vermont, September 7, 1996, http://www.normemma.com/articles/arstairs.htm.

393 Examples of references to genocide in the literature of disability include Paddy Ladd and Mary John, "Deaf people as a minority group: The political process," in the 1992 Open University syllabus *Constructing Deafness: Social Construction of Deafness: Deaf People as a Minority Group—the Political Process*; Harlan Lane, "Ethnicity, ethics and the deaf-world," *Journal of Deaf Studies & Deaf Education* 10, no. 3 (Summer 2005); and Bridget Brown's letter to the *Chicago Tribune* and *Time* magazine, *Down Syndrome Development Council Forum* 6, March 2007, page 3.

393 Peter Singer's description of Frank Shann occurs on pages 38–56 of *Rethinking Life and Death: The Collapse of Our Traditional Ethics* (1994); the quotation "If the cortex of the brain is dead . . ." occurs on page 42.

394 Peter Singer's statement "Killing a disabled infant is not morally equivalent to killing a person" occurs on page 191 of *Practical Ethics*, 2nd ed. (1993). Singer's definition of *person* can be found on pages 86–87.

394 Peter Singer's statement beginning "If we compare a severely defective human infant with a nonhuman animal . . ." occurs on page 128 of his article "Sanctity of life or quality of life?," *Pediatrics* 72, no. 1 (July 1983).

394 The story of the Miller family's ordeal comes from the Supreme Court of Texas opinion in *Miller v. HCA, Inc.*, 118 S.W.3d 758 (Tex. 2003), http://www.supreme .courts.state.tx.us/historical/2003/sep/010079.pdf; see also Kris Axtman, "Baby case tests rights of parents," *Christian Science Monitor*, March 27, 2003.

394 See Not Dead Yet et al., "Brief of amici curiae in support of respondents," *Miller v. HCA, Inc.*, Civil Action No. 01-0079 (Supreme Court of Texas, filed March 21, 2002), http://www.notdeadyet.org/docs/millerbrief.html.

394 "Many disability rights advocates believe that the Millers' suit promotes infanticide . . ." comes from Dave Reynolds, "Who has the right to decide when to save the sickest babies?," *Inclusion Daily Express*, June 14, 2002.

395 The quotations from Ellen Wright Clayton ("I think that it is really inappropriate . . .") and George Annas ("The truth is, no one really knows . . .") come from Kris Axtman, "Baby case tests rights of parents," *Christian Science Monitor*, March 27, 2003.

395 The excerpt from the New York Court of Appeals decision in *Becker v. Schwartz*, 46 N.Y.2d 401 (1978), is quoted in Pilar N. Ossorio, "Prenatal genetic testing and the courts," in *Prenatal Testing and Disability Rights*, edited by Adrienne Asch and Erik Parens (2000), page 320.

395 This passage is based on my interview with Julia Hollander in 2006 and subsequent communications, as well as her book *When the Bough Breaks: A Mother's Story* (2008).

396 The quotation from Julia Hollander beginning "In Limbo, the babies have died" comes from her book *When the Bough Breaks: A Mother's Story* (2008), page 22. The quotation beginning "One night in the dark" comes from page 69.

399 All quotations from Tania Beale come from her article with Julia Hollander, "A tale of two mothers," *Guardian*, March 8, 2008.

401 The quotations from Chris Borthwick come from pages 205 and 207 of his article "The proof of the vegetable," *Journal of Medical Ethics* 21, no. 4 (August 1995).

402 For an exploration of the Jewish concept of God in relationship, see Martin Buber, *I and Thou* (2000); e.g., page 49: "Spirit is not in the I, but between I and Thou."

402 The quotation from Maggie Robbins ("Consciousness is not a noun, it's a verb") comes from a personal communication in 2010.

402 For more information on parenting in animals, see Susan Allport, *A Natural History of Parenting: A Naturalist Looks at Parenting in the Animal World and Ours* (1997).

403 The quotations from Annie Leclerc ("the profound taste we have for children") and Daphne de Marneffe ("not only to her recognition . . .") occur on pages 90 and 82, respectively, of Daphne de Marneffe, *Maternal Desire: On Children, Love, and the Inner Life* (2004).

403 The quotation from Sigmund Freud ("parental love, which is so moving and at bottom so childish, is nothing but parental narcissism born again") occurs on page 91 of *On Narcissism: An Introduction* (1981).

403 For Anna Freud's thoughts on the mother-child relationship, see *The Harvard Lectures* (1992), especially Lecture Five (pages 65–78), "Stages of development."

403 See Rozsika Parker, *Torn in Two: The Experience of Maternal Ambivalence* (1995, 2005). The quotation "the Scylla of intrusiveness and the Charybdis of neglect" occurs on page 140, while the quotation about "a sort of sadness" occurs on page 45.

VIII: Prodigies

406 The quotation from Raymond Radiguet ("Child prodigies exist . . .") occurs on pages viii–ix of his novel *Count d'Orgel's Ball* (1989).

406 The statement "A prodigy is a group enterprise" occurs on page 121 of David Henry Feldman and Lynn T. Goldsmith, *Nature's Gambit: Child Prodigies and the Development of Human Potential* (1991).

407 See Steven Mithen, *The Singing Neanderthals: The Origins of Music, Language, Mind and Body* (2006).

407 Psychologist Anne Fernald of Stanford University has conducted pioneering research in the role of singsong "baby talk" in child development; see Anne Fernald, "Four month olds prefer to listen to motherese," *Infant Behavior & Development* 8 (1985); and Anne Fernald and P. Kuhl, "Acoustic determinants of infant preference for motherese speech," *Infant Behavior and Development* 10 (1987).

407 The quotation from John Blacking (music "is there in the body . . .") occurs on page 100 of his book *How Musical Is Man?* (1973).

407 For a cross-cultural study of musical communication of emotion, see Thomas Fritz et al., "Universal recognition of three basic emotions in music," *Current Biology* 19, no. 7 (April 2009).

407 Robert Garfias's identification of music as a "primary means of sustaining a process of socialization" occurs on page 100 of his article "Thoughts on the process of language and music acquisition," in *Music and Child Development: Proceedings of the 1987 Biology of Music Making Conference*, edited by F. Wilson and R. Roehmann (1989).

407 Géza Révész refers to Handel's singing before he could talk on page 7 of *The Psychology of a Musical Prodigy* (1925). The story may, however, be apocryphal;

Handel's earliest biographer, John Mainwaring, does not describe Handel's infancy.

407 Arthur Rubinstein describes his early habit of expressing his desires in song on page 4 of *My Young Years* (1973).

407 The quotation from John Sloboda ("Musical idioms are not languages") occurs on page 106 of his essay "Musical ability," in *Ciba Foundation Symposium 178: The Origins and Development of High Ability* (1993).

407 All quotations from Leon Botstein come from my interview with him in 2010 and subsequent communications.

407 This passage is based on my interviews with Evgeny Kissin, Emilia Kissin, and Anna Pavlovna Kantor in 1996, and on a subsequent interview with Evgeny Kissin in 2008, as well as other communications.

410 Evgeny Kissin's Carnegie Hall debut garnered overwhelmingly positive reviews: see Allan Kozinn, "Recital by Yevgeny Kissin, a young Soviet pianist," *New York Times*, October 2, 1990; Peter Goodman, "Sparks fly from his fingertips," *Newsday*, October 2, 1990; Harold C. Schonberg, "Russian soul gets a new voice at the keyboard," *New York Times*, October 7, 1990; and Michael Walsh and Elizabeth Rudulph, "Evgeny Kissin, new kid," *Time*, October 29, 1990.

411 The quotation from Anne Midgette comes from her review "Kissin is dexterous but lacking in emotion," *Washington Post*, March 2, 2009.

412 This passage is based on my interview with Yefim Bronfman in 2010. For another profile of Bronfman, see Anne Midgette, "A star who plays second fiddle to music," *New York Times*, December 15, 2007. Bronfman is depicted in Philip Roth's novel *The Human Stain* (2000).

412 Peter Kivy discusses Plato's concept of genius throughout the first chapter (pages 1–13) of *The Possessor and the Possessed: Handel, Mozart, Beethoven, and the Idea of Musical Genius* (2001).

412 See Longinus, *On the Sublime*, translated by Thomas R. R. Stebbing (1867), page 4.

412 John Locke's statement "I imagine the minds of children as easily turn'd this or that way, as water it self" occurs on page 2 of his work *Some Thoughts Concerning Education* (1695).

412 Kant's statement "If an author owes a product to his genius, he himself does not know how he came by the ideas for it" occurs on page 175 of *Critique of Judgment* (1987).

412 See E. F. J. Payne's rendition on page 391 of *The World as Will and Representation* (1966), simplified here.

412 See Francis Galton, *Hereditary Genius* (1869).

412 Lewis Terman's research reports include "A new approach to the study of genius," *Psychological Review* 29, no. 4 (1922); *Genetic Studies of Genius*, vol. 1, *Mental and Physical Traits of a Thousand Gifted Children* (1925); and *The Gifted Group at Mid-Life: Thirty-Five Years Follow-Up of the Superior Child* (1959).

413 Scott Barry Kaufman offers a critical review of Terman's work in his article "The truth about the Termites," *Psychology Today*, September 2009.

413 Paul Popenoe's statement "no son of an unskilled laborer has ever become an eminent man of science in the United States" occurs on page 134 of his book *The Child's Heredity* (1929).

413 For in-depth investigations of the contribution of the British and American eugenics movement to the development of Nazi racial policies, see Henry P. David, Jochen Fleischhacker, and Charlotte Hohn, "Abortion and eugenics in Nazi Germany," *Population & Development Review* 13, no. 1 (March 1988);

Timothy Ryback, *Hitler's Private Library* (2010); and Edwin Black, *War Against the Weak: Eugenics and America's Campaign to Create a Master Race* (2004).

413 Alfred Kroeber considers the subject of genius in *Configurations of Culture Growth* (1944).

413 This passage is based on my interviews with Leon Fleisher and Julian Fleisher in 2010 and subsequent communication.

416 The quotation from Daines Barrington occurs on pages 285 and 286 of his "Account of a very remarkable young musician" (1780), reprinted in 2008 by the Mozart Society of America.

416 All quotations from Veda Kaplinsky come from my interview with her in 2010.

416 The Japanese proverb "the ten-year-old prodigy becomes a talented fifteen-year-old on the way to mediocrity at twenty" is cited in "Music: Prodigies' progress," *Time*, June 4, 1973.

416 All quotations from Charles Hamlen come from my interviews with him in 1996 and 2007 and other communications.

417 All quotations from Karen Monroe come from my interview with her in 2007.

417 The quotations from and about Van Cliburn occur on pages 182–83 of Claude Kenneson, *Musical Prodigies: Perilous Journeys, Remarkable Lives* (1993).

417 The increase in the number of piano competitions is chronicled in Michael Johnson, "The dark side of piano competitions," *New York Times*, August 8, 2009.

417 All quotations from Robert Levin come from my interview with him in 2010.

417 This passage is based on my interview with Sue, Joe, and Drew Petersen in 2010 and subsequent communications.

418 All quotations from Miyoko Lotto come from Roberta Hershenson, "Playing piano recitals and skipping fifth grade," *New York Times*, July 9, 2009.

419 All quotations from Justin Davidson come from my interviews with him in 2010 and 2012 and prior and subsequent communication.

420 "Craftsmanship has never stood in the way of genius" is an English-language paraphrase of a sentiment frequently expressed by Pierre-Auguste Renoir, as, for example, in a letter to the painter Henry Mottez, ca. 1910, quoted in Jean Renoir, *Renoir: My Father* (2001), pages 415–16.

420 The quotation from Steven Isserlis ("It should be taught like a mixture of religion and science . . .") comes from my interview with him in 2010.

420 This passage is based on my interviews with Mikhail, Natalie, Misha, and Natasha Paremski in 2007 and prior and subsequent communications.

421 Natasha Paremski's performance of Rachmaninoff's Piano Concerto no. 2 was described as both "fresh" and "raw" by reviewer Anne Midgette in "Pinch-hitting at Caramoor: Young pianist and Rachmaninoff," *New York Times*, June 25, 2007.

422 For more information on absolute pitch, see Daniel J. Levitin and Susan E. Rogers, "Absolute pitch: Perception, coding, and controversies," *Trends in Cognitive Sciences* 9, no.1 (January 2005); and A. Bachem, "Absolute pitch," *Journal of the Acoustical Society of America* 27, no. 6 (1955).

423 The anecdotes about children's manifestation of absolute pitch come from my interview with David A. Ross in 2010, as do all quotations from him.

423 Acquisition of perfect pitch is discussed in Annie H. Takeuchi and Stewart H. Hulse, "Absolute pitch," *Psychological Bulletin* 113, no. 2 (1993); and Diana Deutsch et al., "Absolute pitch among American and Chinese conservatory students," *Journal of the Acoustical Society of America* 199, no. 2 (February 2006).

423 Daniel J. Levitin evaluates the ability of nonmusicians to replicate the opening

pitches of popular songs in "Absolute memory for musical pitch: Evidence from the production of learned melodies," *Perception & Psychophysics* 56, no. 4 (1994).

423 See Nicholas A. Smith and Mark A. Schmuckler, "Dial A440 for absolute pitch: Absolute pitch memory by non-absolute pitch possessors," *Journal of the Acoustical Society of America* 123, no. 4 (April 2008).

423 Both anecdotes about the difficulties encountered in group performance by musicians with absolute pitch come from my interview with David A. Ross.

423 The seminal study on absolute pitch and the planum temporale is Gottfried Schlaug et al., "In vivo evidence of structural brain asymmetry in musicians," *Science*, n.s., 267, no. 5198 (February 3, 1995); see also Julian Paul Keenan, "Absolute pitch and planum temporale," *Neuroimage* 14, no. 6 (December 2001).

423 Thomas Elbert et al. reported the finding of brain enlargement in violin players in "Increased cortical representation of the fingers of the left hand in string players," *Science* 270, no. 5234 (October 13, 1995).

423 For neuroimaging evidence of enhanced motor coordination in musicians, see Burkhard Maess et al., "Musical syntax is processed in Broca's area: An MEG study," *Nature Neuroscience* 4, no. 5 (May 2001); and Vanessa Sluming et al., "Broca's area supports enhanced visuospatial cognition in orchestral musicians," *Journal of Neuroscience* 27, no. 14 (April 4, 2007).

423 This passage is based on my interviews and conversations with Robert, Orna, and Jay Greenberg in 2007 and 2008 and subsequent communication.

424 The quotation from Samuel Zyman ("What would you do if you met an eight-year-old boy who can compose . . .") comes from his article "New music from a very new composer," *Juilliard Journal*, May 2003.

424 Jay's description of his compositional mental process comes from Rebecca Leung, "Prodigy, 12, compared to Mozart," CBS News, February 18, 2009.

424 The quotation from Nancy Andreasen (". . . the creative process is similar in artists and scientists . . .") occurs on page 78 of her book *The Creating Brain: The Neuroscience of Genius* (2005).

424 Jay's description of the mathematical underpinnings of one of his compositions comes from the liner notes to the recording *Symphony No. 5; Quintet for Strings* (2006).

425 "My music does express my feelings . . ." comes from Matthew Gurewitsch, "Early works of a new composer (very early, in fact)," *New York Times*, August 13, 2006.

425 See *The Complete Works of Aristotle*, vol. 2, edited by Jonathan Barnes, translated by E. S. Forster (1984), *Problemata* xxx 1, 953a10–14.

425 For a host of diabolical legends about Paganini, see G. I. C. De Courcy's 1957 biography, *Paganini the Genoese* (repr., 1977); and "Fiddler Paganini's ways: Stories and facts in the great man's life," *New York Times*, July 27, 1891. For a more modern take on the great violinist, see Maiko Kawabata, "Virtuosity, the violin, the devil . . . what really made Paganini 'demonic'?," *Current Musicology*, March 22, 2007.

425 The quotation from Cesare Lombroso occurs on page 333 of his book *The Man of Genius* (1888).

425 The role of dopamine receptors in the creative process is explored in Örjan de Manzano et al., "Thinking outside a less intact box: Thalamic dopamine D2 receptor densities are negatively related to psychometric creativity in healthy individuals," *PLoS One* 5, no. 5 (May 17, 2010).

425 Norman Geschwind refers to "pathologies of superiority" in his paper "The

biology of cerebral dominance: Implications for cognition," *Cognition* 17, no. 3 (August 1984). Geschwind and Albert M. Galaburda are authors of *Cerebral Lateralization* (1987); Daniel Goleman reports on their work in his article "Left vs. right: Brain function tied to hormone in the womb," *New York Times*, September 24, 1985.

426 Pinchas Noy describes preoccupation with music as a defensive strategy in "The development of musical ability," *Psychoanalytic Study of the Child* 23 (1968).

426 Miraca Gross discusses resilience in child prodigies in her essay "Social and emotional issues for exceptional and intellectually gifted students," in Maureen Neihart et al., *The Social and Emotional Development of Gifted Children: What Do We Know?* (2002), pages 19–30.

426 The quotation from Zarin Mehta ("Thank God we don't have such talented children") comes from my interview with him in 2010.

426 The quotation from Elisha Abas ("Sometimes the shoulders of a child are not big enough to handle his genius") comes from Daniel J. Wakin, "Burned out at 14, Israeli concert pianist is back where he 'really belongs,'" *New York Times*, November 2, 2007.

426 All quotations from Joseph Polisi come from my interview with him in 2010.

426 The quotation from Brandenn Bremmer ("America is a society that demands perfection") occurs on page 142 of Alissa Quart, *Hothouse Kids: The Dilemma of the Gifted Child* (2006); the quotation from his parents ("He was born an adult . . .") comes from the news report "Child prodigy's time to 'do something great,' Mom says," *Washington Post*, March 20, 2005.

427 Terence Judd and Michael Rabin are both discussed in Richard Morrison, "The prodigy trap," *Sunday Times*, April 15, 2005.

427 Christiaan Kriens is mentioned in Joyce Maynard, "Prodigy, at 13," *New York Times*, March 4, 1973.

427 The quotation from Julian Whybra about suicide among gifted youth occurs on page 40 of his chapter, "Extension and enrichment programmes," in *Meeting the Social and Emotional Needs of Gifted and Talented Children*, edited by Michael J. Stopper (2000). Nancy Robinson takes issue with the assertion that intellectually gifted children are less hardy than other children on page xiv of her introduction to *The Social and Emotional Development of Gifted Children: What Do We Know?*, edited by Maureen Neihart et al. (2002).

427 All quotations from Robert Sirota come from my interview with him in 2010 and subsequent communications.

427 Jascha Heifetz's quip about the dangers of prodigiousness appears in the liner notes of his 1959 recording of Sibelius's *Violin Concerto* (RCA Victor Red Seal/ BMG Classics).

428 The quotation from Isaac Babel occurs on page 628 of *The Complete Works of Isaac Babel*, translated by Cynthia Ozick (2002). It has been condensed.

428 The quotations from Ruth Slenczynska occur on pages 31, 137, and 232 of her autobiography, *Forbidden Childhood* (1957).

428 The psychologist who examined Ervin Nyiregyházi was Géza Révész; his book is *The Psychology of a Musical Prodigy* (1925).

428 All quotations from Ervin Nyiregyházi come from Kevin Bazzana, *Lost Genius: The Curious and Tragic Story of an Extraordinary Musical Prodigy* (2007): "I was like a calling card," page 44; "By the time I was five . . . ," page 53; "My mother hated me," page 37; and "Whatever obstacles were put in my way, I just gave up," page 41. Nyiregyházi's praise for Hitler is mentioned on page 40: "Perceiving himself

to be emotionally deprived, struggling with the conflicting emotions of youth, he seems, self-defensively, to have projected all of the blame for his anxieties onto his mother, making her the enemy of everything he held dear. She died in the Holocaust, and he was once (while drunk) heard to say that Hitler was a great man because Hitler had killed his mother."

428 This passage is based on my interview with Lorin Hollander in 2007.

429 Mozart originally wrote "Next to God comes Papa" in a March 1778 letter reproduced on page 183 of *The Letters of Wolfgang Amadeus Mozart* (1866); see also Maynard Solomon, *Mozart: A Life* (1996).

429 Paganini's description of abuse by his father ("If he didn't think I was industrious enough . . .") is described on page 13 of G. I. C. de Courcy's 1957 biography, *Paganini the Genoese* (repr., 1977), citing to Julius Max Schottky, *Paganini's Leben und Treiben als Kunstler und als Mensch* (1830).

429 The quotation describing how Clara Wieck's father examined and wrote in her diary occurs on pages 18–20 of Nancy B. Reich, *Clara Schumann: The Artist and the Woman* (1985); the quotation from Robert Schumann occurs on page 64.

429 This passage is based on my interview with Scott Frankel in 2010, and prior and subsequent communications.

431 All quotations in this passage come from an interview by Nikki Murfitt, "The heart-breaking moment I realised my mother had cut me off forever, by violin virtuoso Vanessa-Mae," *Daily Mail*, August 7, 2008.

431 This passage is based on my interview with Nicolas Hodges in 2010 and subsequent communications.

432 The anecdote about Rudolf Serkin was recounted to me in 2009 by Gary Graffman, the sometime director of Curtis, who was with Serkin when he made this remark.

432 The quotation from Yo-Yo Ma occurs on page 265 of Samuel and Sada Applebaum, *The Way They Play*, vol. 13 (1984).

432 The quotation from Thérèse Mahler comes from my interview with her in 2010.

433 The quotation from Hoang Pham comes from my interview with him in 2010.

433 This passage is based on my interview with Ken Noda in 2009 and subsequent communications.

433 Takayo Noda is an accomplished artist and poet; see http://www.takayonoda .com.

436 This passage is based on my interview with Candy Bawcombe in 2010.

439 This passage is based on my interview with David Waterman in 2010 and subsequent communications.

441 This passage is based on my interview with Vikram, Marion, and Solanda Price in 2010. All names in this passage are pseudonyms, and some identifying details have been changed.

443 Mitsuko Uchida's remark about society's bewildering preoccupation with prodigies comes from a personal communication in 2012.

443 The quotation from Janice Nimura ("The child prodigy is the polite version of the carny freak . . .") comes from her article "Prodigies have problems too," *Los Angeles Times*, August 21, 2006.

443 The anecdote about Leonard Bernstein occurs on page 107 of Clifton Fadiman, *The Little, Brown Book of Anecdotes* (1985). In full: "Bernstein's father was criticized for not having given his talented son more encouragement. 'How was I to know he would grow up to be Leonard Bernstein?' he protested." I have heard the anecdote phrased as I have phrased it from other members of the Bernstein family.

443 This passage is based on my interview with Jonathan Floril in 2010.

444 The characterization of Jonathan Floril as "more than a prodigy, not only because of what he performs, but also how he performs" comes from Alfredo Brotons Muñoz, "Más que un prodigio," *Levante EMV*, May 7, 2007. In the original: "Aunque, como luego se explicará, va más allá de eso, de momento no puede escapar a la calificación de prodigio. No sólo por cómo toca, sino por lo que toca."

445 The quotation from Gore Vidal ("Hatred of one parent or the other can make an Ivan the Terrible or a Hemingway: the protective love, however, of two devoted parents can absolutely destroy an artist") occurs on page 34 of his collection of essays *Matters of Fact and Fiction* (1977).

445 For the study finding a threefold increase in early parental loss among eminent people, see Catherine Cox, *The Early Mental Traits of Three Hundred Geniuses* (1926). Eighty-three years later, Dean Keith Simonton and Anna V. Song published a follow-up study, "Eminence, IQ, physical and mental health, and achievement domain: Cox's 282 geniuses revisited," *Psychological Science* 20, no. 4 (April 2009).

445 This passage is based on my interviews with Lang Lang and Lang Guoren in 2005 and 2009 and on other communications. Lang Lang maintains a website at http://www.langlang.com and has published two autobiographies, which I have used as sources: *Lang Lang: Playing with Flying Keys* (2008), with Michael French; and *Journey of a Thousand Miles: My Story* (2008), with David Ritz. I have also consulted David Remnick, "The Olympian: How China's greatest musician will win the Beijing Games," *New Yorker*, August 4, 2008; and made use of *Dad's Aspirations Are That High*, by Yuanju Li (2001) (an unpublished English translation of 爸爸的心就这么高：钢琴天才郎朗和他的父亲 / *Ba ba de xin jiu zhe mo gao: Gang qin tian cai Lang Lang he ta de fu qin*).

448 John von Rhein likened Lang Lang to Liberace in his review "Bend the rules, but don't break the bond," *Chicago Tribune*, August 18, 2002.

448 For Anthony Tommasini's caustic review of Lang Lang's performance, see "A showman revs up the classical genre," *New York Times*, November 10, 2003.

449 The favorable comment by Anthony Tommasini about Lang Lang comes from a 2008 review, "Views back (and forward) on an outdoor stage," *New York Times*, July 17, 2008.

449 Popular books promoting the ten-thousand-hours hypothesis include Malcolm Gladwell, *Outliers: The Story of Success* (2008); Daniel Coyle, *The Talent Code: Greatness Isn't Born, It's Grown* (2009); and Geoff Colvin, *Talent Is Overrated: What Really Separates World-Class Performers from Everybody Else* (2010).

449 For the ten-thousand-hours study and follow-ups, see K. Anders Ericsson, R. T. Krampe, and C. Tesch-Romer, "The role of deliberate practice in the acquisition of expert performance," *Psychological Review* 100 (1993); K. Anders Ericsson, Michael J. Prietula, and Edward T. Cokel, "The making of an expert," *Harvard Business Review*, July–August 2007; and K. Anders Ericsson, Roy W. Roring, and Kiruthiga Nandagopal, "Giftedness and evidence for reproducibly superior performance," *High Ability Studies* 18, no. 1 (June 2007).

450 For the study finding that practice time matters more than talent, see Michael J. A. Howe, Jane W. Davidson, and John A. Sloboda, "Innate talents: Reality or myth?," *Behavioural & Brain Sciences* 21, no. 3 (June 1998).

450 The quotation from David Brooks comes from his article "Genius: The modern view," *New York Times*, May 1, 2009.

450 The quotation from Leopold Auer ("Practice three hours a day if you are any

good . . .") was recalled by his protégé Joseph Szigeti on page 4 of *Szigeti on the Violin* (1979).

450 For the original marshmallow study and follow-up reports, see Walter Mischel, E. B. Ebbesen, and A. R. Zeiss, "Cognitive and attentional mechanisms in delay of gratification," *Journal of Personality & Social Psychology* 21, no. 2 (February 1972); Yuichi Shoda, Walter Mischel, and Philip K. Peake, "The nature of adolescent competencies predicted by preschool delay of gratification," *Journal of Personality & Social Psychology* 54, no. 4 (1988); and Yuichi Shoda, Walter Mischel, and Philip K. Peake, "Predicting adolescent cognitive and self-regulatory competencies from preschool delay of gratification: Identifying diagnostic conditions," *Developmental Psychology* 26, no. 6 (1990).

450 The dramatic difference in SAT scores between children who could delay gratification and those who could not was reported in Yuichi Shoda, Walter Mischel, and Philip K. Peake, "Predicting adolescent cognitive and self-regulatory competencies from preschool delay of gratification: Identifying diagnostic conditions," *Developmental Psychology* 26, no. 6 (1990); and noted in Jonah Lehrer, "Don't! The secret of self-control," *New Yorker*, May 18, 2009.

450 The quotation from Angela L. Duckworth occurs in Jonah Lehrer, "Don't! The secret of self-control," *New Yorker*, May 18, 2009; see also Angela L. Duckworth and Martin E. P. Seligman, "Self-discipline outdoes IQ in predicting academic performance of adolescents," *Psychological Science* 16, no. 12 (December 2005).

450 Ellen Winner refers to the "commonsense myth" that giftedness is "entirely inborn," and the "psychologists' myth" that "giftedness is entirely a matter of hard work" on page 308 of *Gifted Children: Myths and Realities* (1996).

450 The quotation from Edward Rothstein ("The contemporary attack on genius . . .") comes from his article "Connections: myths about genius," *New York Times*, January 5, 2002.

451 The quotation from Yehudi Menuhin ("Maturity, in music and in life, has to be earned by living") occurs on page 22 of his biography *Unfinished Journey* (1977), as cited on page 44 of Claude Kenneson, *Musical Prodigies: Perilous Journeys, Remarkable Lives* (1993).

451 The quotation from Gabriel Kahane comes from my interview with him in 2010.

451 This passage is based on my experience attending Marc Yu's New York debut in 2007, my interview with Chloe and Marc Yu that year, and subsequent communications.

454 A substantial body of research supports the hypothesis that tonal languages such as Chinese enhance musicality in young children; see, e.g., Diana Deutsch et al., "Absolute pitch among students in an American music conservatory: Association with tone language fluency," *Journal of the Acoustical Society of America* 125, no. 4 (April 2009); and Ryan J. Giuliano et al., "Native experience with a tone language enhances pitch discrimination and the timing of neural responses to pitch change," *Frontiers in Psychology* 2, no. 146 (August 2011). The observation about typical Chinese hand shape comes from my interview with Veda Kaplinsky.

454 The quotation from Mihaly Csikszentmihalyi ("One cannot be exceptional and normal at the same time") occurs on page 177 of *Creativity: Flow and the Psychology of Discovery and Invention* (1996).

455 All quotations from Robert Blocker come from my interview with him in 2010.

455 This passage is based on my interview with May Armstrong in 2010.

456 Charles Hamlen told me the story about the tour of Los Alamos in 2007.

457 The quotation from the English journalist ("His playing was so cultured . . .")

comes from Stephen Moss, "At three he was reading the Wall Street Journal," *Guardian*, November 10, 2005.

457 The quotation from Daniel Singal ("The problem is not the pursuit of equality but the bias against excellence that has accompanied it") comes from his article "The other crisis in American education," *Atlantic Monthly*, November 1991.

458 John Cloud's characterization of the No Child Left Behind Act as "radically egalitarian" comes from his article "Are we failing our geniuses?," *Time*, August 16, 2007.

458 For the Templeton report, see Nicolas Colangelo, *A Nation Deceived: How Schools Hold Back America's Brightest Students* (2004).

458 The finding that 80 percent of gifted subjects constantly monitored their behavior to conform to the norms of less gifted children is reported on page 14 of Maureen Neihart et al., *The Social and Emotional Development of Gifted Children* (2002); the finding that 90 percent of subjects did not want to be identified as a "brain" comes from B. Bradford Brown and Laurence Steinberg, "Academic achievement and social acceptance: Skirting the 'brain-nerd' connection," *Education Digest* 55, no. 7 (1990).

458 Miraca Gross presents the findings of her study of sixty gifted students in Australia in *Exceptionally Gifted Children* (1993); her subjects' satisfaction with radical academic acceleration is discussed on pages 26–27.

458 The quotations from Norbert Wiener ("the suffering which grows from belonging half to the adult world and half to the world of the children about him" and "... I was not so much a mixture of child and man ...") occur on pages 117–18 and 106–7 of his autobiography, *Ex-Prodigy: My Childhood and Youth* (1953); see also his sequel, *I Am a Mathematician: The Later Life of a Prodigy* (1956).

459 This passage is based on my interviews with Joshua Bell and Shirley Bell in 2007 and subsequent communications.

462 For an extensive history of sound recording, see David L. Morton Jr., *Sound Recording: The Life Story of a Technology* (2006). Digital reproductions of Thomas Edison's papers documenting the invention of the phonograph can be found on the Rutgers University website http://edison.rutgers.edu/docsamp.htm.

463 This passage is based on my interviews with Conrad Tao and Mingfang Ting in 2010.

465 This passage is based on my interviews with Sylvester, Stephanie, and Christian Sands in 2010 and subsequent communication.

466 The jazzman's term for this sort of exchange is *trading fours*. Oscar Peterson's and Christian's performances may be seen on YouTube at http://www.youtube.com/watch?v=fYpoWD1qmEA.

467 Paul Potts's performance can be viewed at http://www.youtube.com/watch?v=1k08yxu57NA; and Jackie Evancho's at http://www.youtube.com/watch?v=6ar0r02FZng.

467 This passage is based on my interviews with Nico Muhly, Bunny Harvey, and Frank Muhly in 2010–12, and on subsequent communications; see also Rebecca Mead, "Eerily composed: Nico Muhly's sonic magic," *New Yorker*, February 11, 2008.

471 See Alfred Louis Kroeber, *Configurations of Culture Growth* (1944), page 9.

471 The quotation from Isaac Newton comes from a letter he wrote to Robert Hooke, February 15, 1676, and occurs on page 231 of *The Correspondence of Isaac Newton*, vol. 3 (1961).

472 See Lucretius, *On the Nature of Things* (1851).

472 See *Essays of Schopenhauer* (1897), page 153.

472   The quotation from Margaret Mead ("There is in America an appalling waste of first-rate talents . . .") is condensed from a passage on page 213 of her essay "The gifted child in the American culture of today," *Journal of Teacher Education* 5, no. 3 (1954), as cited on page 51 of Jan Davidson, Bob Davidson, and Laura Vanderkam, *Genius Denied: How to Stop Wasting Our Brightest Young Minds* (2004).

472   The quotation from Rhonda Garelick ("crisis in admiration") comes from a personal communication, 2011.

473   This passage is based on my interviews with Jeffrey, Martha, and Gabriel Kahane in 2009 and 2010.

475   The characterization of Gabriel Kahane as a "highbrow polymath" comes from Nate Chinen, "Gabriel Kahane, *Where Are the Arms*," *New York Times*, September 19, 2011.

475   The quotation from Goethe's mother ("Air, fire, water and earth . . .") occurs on page 153 of Bruno Bettelheim, *The Uses of Enchantment* (1976). It has been condensed.

IX: Rape

478   The Stigma Inc. website (http://www.stigmatized.org) is no longer online; an archived version can be viewed at http://web.archive.org/web/20070901030454/www.stigmatized.org/about.htm.

478   Rape as property theft is discussed in the entry "Sexual assault" in *Encyclopedia of Rape*, edited by Merrill D. Smith (2004), pages 224–25.

478   According to *Encyclopedia of Rape*, edited by Merrill D. Smith (2004), pages xiii–xvii, the Code of Hammurabi (c. 1780 BCE) "declared that a virgin was innocent if raped, but that her attacker should be executed. Married women who were raped were considered to be guilty of adultery and could be executed along with their attackers."

478   Rape in ancient Greece is explored in Daniel Ogden, "Rape, adultery and the protection of bloodlines in classical Athens," in *Rape in Antiquity*, edited by Susan Deacy and Karen F. Pierce (1997), pages 25–41.

478   For more information on rape in ancient and seventeenth-century law, see "Ancient law codes," in *Encyclopedia of Rape*, edited by Merrill D. Smith (2004), pages 14–15; and Else L. Hambleton, *Daughters of Eve: Pregnant Brides and Unwed Mothers in Seventeenth-Century Massachusetts* (2004).

478   Rape in classical mythology is discussed in "Art," in *Encyclopedia of Rape* (2004), page 15; and James A. Arieti, "Rape and Livy's view of Roman history," in *Rape in Antiquity*, edited by Susan Deacy and Karen F. Pierce (1997), pages 209–29.

478   See "Rape of the Sabine women," in *Encyclopedia of Rape* (2004), pages 196–97; and Norman Bryson, "Two narratives of rape in the visual arts: Lucretia and the Sabine women," in *Rape: An Historical and Cultural Enquiry*, edited by Sylvana Tomaselli and Roy Porter (1986), pages 152–73.

479   The permissibility of infanticide of rape-conceived children is discussed in John Boswell, *The Kindness of Strangers: The Abandonment of Children in Western Europe from Late Antiquity to the Renaissance* (1998), page 200; see also "Pregnancy," in *Encyclopedia of Rape* (2004), pages 154–55.

479   For more information on Galen's ideas of rape and fertility, see "'Blaming the victim' syndrome" (pages 26–28) and "Pregnancy" (pages 154–55) in *Encyclopedia of Rape* (2004).

479   St. Augustine's discussion of rape and humility is cited on page 251 of Corinne

Saunder, "Classical paradigms of rape in the Middle Ages: Chaucer's Lucretia and Philomena," in *Rape in Antiquity* (1997), edited by Susan Deacy and Karen F. Pierce, citing to Augustine, *City of God Against the Pagans*, vol. 1, edited and translated by George E. McCracken (1957).

479 Rape in seventeenth- to eighteenth-century America is discussed in "Rape in the United States: Eighteenth century," *Encyclopedia of Rape* (2004), pages 179–81; and Else L. Hambleton, *Daughters of Eve: Pregnant Brides and Unwed Mothers in Seventeenth-Century Massachusetts* (2004).

479 The quotation from the *Kingston British Whig* occurs on page 115 of Patrick J. Connor, "The law should be her protector: The criminal prosecution of rape in upper Canada, 1791–1850," in *Sex Without Consent: Rape and Sexual Coercion in America*, edited by Merrill D. Smith (2001), pages 103–35.

479 For more information on the rape of African slaves and disparate treatment of black and white suspects and perpetrators, see the chapter "Slavery" in Susan Brownmiller, *Against Our Will: Men, Women, and Rape* (1975), pages 153–69; the entries "African-Americans" (pages 5–7) and "Slavery" (pages 234–36) in *Encyclopedia of Rape* (2004); Diane Miller Sommerville, "'I was very much wounded': Rape law, children, and the antebellum South," in *Sex Without Consent: Rape and Sexual Coercion in America*, edited by Merrill D. Smith (2001), pages 136–77; and Diana Miller Sommerville, *Rape and Race in the Nineteenth-Century South* (2004).

479 The legal requirement that women resist is discussed in the *Encyclopedia of Rape* entry "Rape in the United States: Nineteenth century," pages 181–83.

479 The experience of rape-conception in the mid-twentieth century is discussed throughout Rickie Solinger, *Wake Up Little Susie: Single Pregnancy and Race before Roe v. Wade* (2000); the quotation from the mother ("If a certain male wanted to get out of being named the true father . . .") occurs on page 73.

479 See the *Encyclopedia of Rape* entry "Freud, Sigmund/Freudian theory," pages 82–83.

480 The quotations from Menachem Amir come from his study *Patterns in Forcible Rape* (1971). From page 254: "Reflected in women is the tendency for passivity and masochism, and a universal desire to be violently possessed and aggressively handled by men"; and page 258: "In a way, the victim is always the cause of the crime."

480 See Susan Brownmiller, *Against Our Will* (1975).

480 Brownmiller's call for "gender free, non-activity-specific" sexual assault laws occurs on page 378 of *Against Our Will* (1975).

480 The historic definition of rape as "an act of sexual intercourse undertaken by a man with a woman, not his wife, against her will and by force" occurs in the *Encyclopedia of Rape* entry "Rape law," page 186. Marital rape and the marital exception are discussed in Diana E. H. Russell, *Rape in Marriage* (1990); David Finkelhor and Kersti Yllö, *License to Rape: Sexual Abuse of Wives* (1985); Jacquelyn C. Campbell and Peggy Alford, "The dark consequences of marital rape," *American Journal of Nursing* 89, no. 7 (July 1989); and the *Encyclopedia of Rape* entries "Hale, Sir Matthew (1609–1676)" (pages 94–95) and "Marital rape" (pages 122–24).

480 Michel Foucault's pronouncement "There is no difference, in principle, between sticking one's fist into someone's face or one's penis into their sex" occurs in his essay "Confinement, psychiatry, prison," in *Politics, Philosophy, Culture: Interviews and Other Writings, 1977–1984* (1988), page 200.

480 For a discussion of state and federal laws on sexual assault in the United States, see the entry "Rape law" in *Encyclopedia of Rape* (2004), pages 186–89.

480 The relative severity of punishment for sexual offenses is discussed in the entry "Rape law" in *Encyclopedia of Rape*, pages 186–89; and Diane E. H. Russell and Rebecca M. Bolen, *The Epidemic of Rape and Child Sexual Abuse in the United States* (2000).

481 Statistics on sexual assault occur on pages 35–36 of Patricia Tjaden and Nancy Thoennes, *Full Report of the Prevalence, Incidence, and Consequences of Violence Against Women: Findings from the National Violence against Women Survey* (2000). The CDC's identification of rape as "one of the most underreported crimes" occurs in the news item "Sexual Assault Awareness Month, April 2005," *Morbidity & Mortality Weekly Report* 54, no. 12 (April 1, 2005), page 311.

481 This passage is based on my interview with Marina James in 2008. All names in this passage are pseudonyms.

484 Wolfgang Jöchle originally argued that fear might induce human ovulation in "Coitus-induced ovulation," *Contraception* 7, no. 6 (1973); and Mary M. Krueger in "Pregnancy as a result of rape," *Journal of Sex Education & Therapy* 14, no. 1 (1988); for a recent review of the subject, see Juan J. Tarín, Toshio Hamatani, and Antonio Cano, "Acute stress may induce ovulation in women," *Reproductive Biology & Endocrinology* 8, no. 53 (2010), pages 1–13.

484 The estimate that as few as 3 percent of female rape victims become pregnant comes from Allen J. Wilcox et al., "Likelihood of conception with a single act of intercourse: Providing benchmark rates for assessment of post-coital contraceptives," *Contraception* 63, no. 4 (April 2001), pages 211–15.

484 Melissa M. Holmes et al. report an increased incidence of pregnancy among rape victims who are regularly abused in "Rape-related pregnancy: Estimates and descriptive characteristics from a national sample of women," *American Journal of Obstetrics & Gynecology* 175, no. 2 (August 1996).

484 The estimate that twenty-five thousand rape-related pregnancies occur annually in the United States comes from Felicia H. Stewart and James Trussell, "Prevention of pregnancy resulting from rape: A neglected preventive health measure," *American Journal of Preventive Medicine* 19 (November 2000); the thirty-two thousand estimate is from Melissa M. Holmes et al., "Rape-related pregnancy: Estimates and descriptive characteristics from a national sample of women," *American Journal of Obstetrics & Gynecology* 175, no. 2 (August 1996).

485 For the 1996 study of child-bearing decisions made by rape victims, see Melissa M. Holmes et al., "Rape-related pregnancy: Estimates and descriptive characteristics from a national sample of women," *American Journal of Obstetrics & Gynecology* 175, no. 2 (August 1996).

485 The quotation from Ana Milena Gil ("Pregnancy born of desire and fed by love . . .") comes from her paper (with Ana Maria Jaramillo and Bertha Ortiz), "Pregnancy resulting from rape: Breaking the silence of multiple crises," *Women's Health Collection*, January 1, 2001.

485 The rape victim's question "If someone shot you, would you walk around with a bullet inside of you?" comes from Natela Cutter, "'Anne Smith': A rape victim found relief in the abortion," *U.S. News & World Report* 124, no. 2 (January 19, 1998).

486 The statement "The baby was innocent . . ." comes from Amy Engeler, "I can't hate this baby," *Redbook* 192, no. 4 (February 1999).

486 All quotations from Joan Kemp come from her article "Abortion: The second rape," *Sisterlife*, Winter 1990.

486 The quotation from Kay Zibolsky ("The baby was part of my healing process . . .") comes from Marie McCullough, "Abortion, rape debate," *Chicago Tribune*, September 26, 1995.

486 The quotation from Kathleen DeZeeuw ("I began to realize that this little life inside me was struggling, too . . .") comes from the film *Children of Rape* (1994).

486 The quotation from Sharon Bailey ("Basically, my feelings were 'It's just you and me, kid'") occurs on page 86 of *Victims and Victors: Speaking Out about Their Pregnancies, Abortions, and Children Resulting from Sexual Assault*, edited by David C. Reardon, Julie Makimaa, and Amy Sobie (2000).

486 The quotation from Kathleen DeZeeuw ("The first time I held him . . .") comes from the film *Children of Rape* (1994).

486 The quotation "I had tried to convince myself . . ." occurs on page 87 of *Victims and Victors: Speaking Out about Their Pregnancies, Abortions, and Children Resulting from Sexual Assault*, edited by David C. Reardon, Julie Makimaa, and Amy Sobie (2000).

486 The passage by Padmasayee Papineni comes from her article "Children of bad memories," *Lancet* 362, no. 9386 (September 6, 2003). It has been condensed.

487 This passage is based on my interview with Brenda Henriques in 2007. All names in this passage are pseudonyms.

489 My primary source on the history of abortion law is Leslie J. Reagan, *When Abortion Was a Crime: Women, Medicine, and Law in the United States, 1867–1973* (1997); and the *Encyclopedia of Rape* entry "Abortion," pages 2–4.

489 The quotations from the American Medical Association come from the organization's position statement "Pregnancy from rape does not justify abortion," *Journal of the American Medical Association* 43 (August 6, 1904), page 413.

489 The rise in illegal abortions during the Great Depression is chronicled in chapter 5 of Leslie J. Reagan, *When Abortion Was a Crime: Women, Medicine, and Law in the United States, 1867–1973* (1997), pages 132–59.

489 The suggestion that offering abortions to unmarried women and widows would result in "lowering of the moral tone" occurs in Frederick J. Taussig's review of *Abortion: Legal or Illegal?* by A. J. Rongy, *Birth Control Review* 17 (June 1933), page 153, as cited in Leslie J. Reagan, *When Abortion Was a Crime: Women, Medicine, and Law in the United States, 1867–1973* (1997), page 142. Taussig's description of social and economic conditions that would justify offering abortions occurs on pages 443–44 of his book *The Prevention and Treatment of Abortion* (1910), as cited in Leslie J. Reagan, *When Abortion Was a Crime: Women, Medicine, and Law in the United States, 1867–1973* (1997), page 142. It has been condensed.

489 The 1938 trial of Aleck Bourne for abortion is described in Leslie J. Reagan, *When Abortion Was a Crime: Women, Medicine, and Law in the United States, 1867–1973* (1997), page 175.

489 Abortion committees are discussed in Leslie J. Reagan, *When Abortion Was a Crime: Women, Medicine, and Law in the United States, 1867–1973* (1997), pages 174–75.

490 The quotation from the pathologizing, victim-blaming social worker ("She became a passive object . . .") occurs on page 133 of Rickie Solinger, *Wake Up Little Susie: Single Pregnancy and Race before Roe vs. Wade* (2000), citing to Marion K. Sanders, "Social work: A profession chases its tail," *Harper's*, March 1957.

490 Early proposals to legalize abortion are discussed in Leslie J. Reagan, *When Abortion Was a Crime: Women, Medicine, and Law in the United States, 1867–1973* (1997), pages 220–21.

490 Coerced relinquishment and maternity homes are central subjects of Rickie Solinger, *Wake Up Little Susie: Single Pregnancy and Rape before Roe v. Wade* (2000) and *Beggars and Choosers: How the Politics of Choice Shapes Adoption, Abortion, and Welfare in the United States* (2001).

490 The quotation from Kathleen Leahy Koch ("I was just someone who had to have a baby for some worthy family . . .") occurs on page 73 of Rickie Solinger, *Beggars and Choosers: How the Politics of Choice Shapes Adoption, Abortion, and Welfare in the United States* (2001).

490 The quotation from Kay Ball ("I was so ashamed and beaten down emotionally . . .") occurs on page 75 of Rickie Solinger, *Beggars and Choosers: How the Politics of Choice Shapes Adoption, Abortion, and Welfare in the United States* (2001).

490 Post-*Roe* abortion politics are explored in William Saletan, "Electoral politics and abortion: Narrowing the message," in *Abortion Wars: A Half Century of Struggle, 1950–2000,* edited by Rickie Solinger (1998); and Saletan's book *Bearing Right: How Conservatives Won the Abortion War* (2003) (results of the poll appear on page 163).

491 Idaho governor Cecil D. Andrus is quoted in Timothy Egan, "Idaho governor vetoes measure intended to test abortion ruling," *New York Times,* March 31, 1990.

491 See William Saletan, *Bearing Right: How Conservatives Won the Abortion War* (2003), page 168 and pages 172–73. See also Michael Baruzzini, "Justice or comfort?: Conservatives and the rape exceptions," *Catholic Lane,* June 16, 2011, at http://catholiclane.com/justice-or-comfort-conservatives-and-the-rape-exception; and the Church of Jesus Christ of Latter Day Saints, "The law of chastity," *Gospel Principles* (2012), at http://www.lds.org/library/display/0,4945,11-1-13-49,00.html.

491 The quotation from the antiabortion advocate ("It would be wrong . . . Two wrongs do not make a right") comes from Bob Ellis, "South Dakota abortion task force studies rape exceptions," *Dakota Voice,* January 20, 2006.

491 Megan Barnett states, "My child is not the exception . . ." in the film *I Love My Baby Who Was Conceived by Rape* (2006).

491 The quotation from John C. Willke ("The woman has been subjected to an ugly trauma") comes from Bob Ellis, "South Dakota abortion task force studies rape exceptions," *Dakota Voice,* January 20, 2006.

491 Rebecca Kiessling's statement "I am not a product of rape, but a child of God" comes from her pamphlet, "Conceived in Rape: A Story of Hope." The sarcastic reply occurs on the January 26, 2009, entry of the *First World Problems* blog, at http://ivytheadventure.livejournal.com/2009/01/26/.

491 The quotation from Joan Raphael-Leff ("an internal foreigner . . .") occurs on page 129 of her paper "Psychotherapy and pregnancy," *Journal of Reproductive & Infant Psychology* 8, no. 2 (April 1990). It has been condensed.

491 The quotation from the rape survivor who characterized her child as "a living, breathing torture mechanism" occurs on page 183 of William Saletan, *Bearing Right* (2003), citing to the Minutes of the Louisiana Senate Committee on Health and Welfare, May 29, 1991.

491 The mother who described the experience of rape-related pregnancy as "entrapment beyond description" is quoted on page 133 of David Finkelhor and Kersti Yllö, *License to Rape* (1985).

492 Joan Kemp describes abortion as a solution "that is imposed by a society that places too much importance on a male lineage" in her article "Abortion: The second rape," *Sisterlife*, Winter 1990.

492 Denise Kalasky describes her abortion experience in her article "Accomplices in incest," *Post-Abortion Review* 2, no. 1 (Winter 1993).

492 David C. Reardon is author of "Rape, incest and abortion: Searching beyond the myths," *Post-Abortion Review* 2, no. 1 (Winter 1994); and coeditor with Julie Makimaa and Amy Sobie of the anthology *Victims and Victors: Speaking Out about Their Pregnancies, Abortions, and Children Resulting from Sexual Assault* (2000). The Elliott Institute website: http://www.afterabortion.info.

492 David Mall and Walter F. Watts first posited the existence of a "postabortion syndrome" in their book, *The Psychological Aspects of Abortion* (1979), a concept further promoted by Joyce Arthur in "Psychological aftereffects of abortion: The rest of the story," *Humanist* 57, no. 2 (March–April 1997). Controversy over the legitimacy of PAS is discussed in Emily Bazelon, "Is there a post-abortion syndrome?," *New York Times Magazine*, January 21, 2007.

492 David Reardon's characterization of abortion as "medical rape" occurs in his article "Rape, incest and abortion: Searching beyond the myths," *Post-Abortion Review* 2, no. 1 (Winter 1994).

492 The quotation from Sandra Mahkorn ("can be lessened with proper support") occurs on page 67 of her chapter, "Pregnancy and sexual assault," in *The Psychological Aspects of Abortion*, edited by David Mall and Walter F. Watts (1979).

492 The quotation from George E. Maloof ("Incestuous pregnancy offers a ray of generosity to the world . . .") occurs on page 98 of his chapter, "The consequences of incest: Giving and taking life," in *The Psychological Aspects of Abortion*, edited by David Mall and Walter F. Watts (1979).

493 Statistics pertaining to the frequent discovery of rape-related pregnancy in the second trimester come from Melissa M. Holmes et al., "Rape-related pregnancy: Estimates and descriptive characteristics from a national sample of women," *American Journal of Obstetrics & Gynecology* 175, no. 2 (August 1996).

493 The quotation from Susan Brison ("Trauma not only haunts the conscious and unconscious mind . . .") occurs on page x of the introduction to her book *Aftermath: Violence and the Remaking of a Self* (2002).

493 Vera Folnegović-Šmalc's description of suicidality among rape victims comes from her chapter, "Psychiatric aspects of the rapes in the war against the republics of Croatia and Bosnia-Herzegovina," in *Mass Rape: The War against Women in Bosnia-Herzegovina*, edited by Andrea Stiglmayer, translated by Marion Faber (1994), pages 174–79.

493 This passage is based on my interview with Melinda Stephenson in 2007 and subsequent communications. All names in this passage are pseudonyms.

496 For a journalistic discussion of evolutionary theories of rape, see Erica Goode, "What provokes a rapist to rape?," *New York Times*, January 15, 2000.

496 The quotation from Jonathan A. Gottschall and Tiffani A. Gottschall occurs on page 10 of their paper "Are per-incident rape-pregnancy rates higher than per-incident consensual pregnancy rates?," *Human Nature: An Interdisciplinary Biosocial Perspective* 14, no. 1 (March 1, 2003).

496 See Randy Thornhill and Craig T. Palmer, *A Natural History of Rape: Biological Bases of Sexual Coercion* (2000).

496 The quotation from Catharine MacKinnon ("Forced pregnancy is familiar . . .") occurs on page 74 of her chapter "Turning rape into pornography: Postmodern

genocide," in *Mass Rape: The War against Women in Bosnia-Herzegovina*, edited by Andrea Stiglmayer, translated by Marion Faber (1994). It has been condensed.

496 Susan Brownmiller's statement "Men began to rape women when they discovered that sexual intercourse led to pregnancy" occurs on page 314 of *Against Our Will* (1975).

496 Mary P. Koss is cited in Erica Goode, "What provokes a rapist to rape? Scientists debate notion of an evolutionary drive," *New York Times*, January 15, 2000.

496 The finding that women who have been raped before the age of eighteen are twice as likely as those who have not to be revictimized in adulthood is reported on page 39 of Patricia Tjaden and Nancy Thoennes, *Full Report of the Prevalence, Incidence, and Consequences of Violence against Women: Findings from the National Violence against Women Survey* (2000).

496 Interview with Lori Michaels, Clarabel Michaels, Ringo Smythe, and Bobby Michaels in 2007. All names in this section are pseudonyms.

500 The mother's statement "My son will never know the details of his conception" occurred in a public discussion, "Children born of rape," on the Adoption.com Forums, archived at http://web.archive.org/web/20070508215233/http://forums .adoption.com/single-parenting/128755-children-born-rape.html.

500 The quotation from Holly van Gulden about secret-keeping comes from her 1998 article "Talking with children about difficult history," at http://www.family -source.com/cache/731451/idx/0.

500 The quotation from the man relieved that his mother was neither a "bad girl" nor a "tramp" occurs on page 103 of *Victims and Victors: Speaking Out about Their Pregnancies, Abortions, and Children Resulting from Sexual Assault*, edited by David C. Reardon, Julie Makimaa, and Amy Sobie (2000).

500 The story of and quotations from Lee Ezell come from the film *Children of Rape* (1994).

500 See Sherrie Eldridge, "Unexpected rejection: The subject no one wants to talk about," *Jewel Among Jewels Adoption News* (Winter 1999).

501 This passage is based on my interview with Lisa Boynton in 2007. All names in this passage are pseudonyms.

503 The horrendous recommendation of euthanasia for children of rape occurred in a blog post by Jenifer Ann Cazador, "Lost souls of polygamy central," *The Wrecking Machine*, April 2008, formerly at http://the-wrecking-machine.blogspot .com/2008/04/lost-souls-of-polygamy-central.html.

503 The quotation from Kathleen DeZeeuw occurs on page 79, and the quotation from Cindy Speltz occurs on pages 97–98, of *Victims and Victors* (2000). The second quotation has been condensed.

503 The quotation from the anti-abortionist conceived in rape and put up for adoption occurs on pages 148–49 of *Victims and Victors* (2000).

503 This passage is based on my interview with Tina Gordon in 2007. All names in this passage are pseudonyms.

506 See Stigma Inc., "Information," at http://web.archive.org/web/20060221101659/ www.stigmatized.org/information.htm.

507 This passage is based on my interview with Emily Barrett in 2008. All names in this passage are pseudonyms.

511 This paragraph relies on Diana E. H. Russell, *Rape in Marriage* (1990). The 14 percent statistic occurs on page xxxii, the story of the Burnhams on pages xvii–xviii.

512 The quotation from Louise McOrmond-Plummer ("The woman raped by her partner was routinely blamed") comes from her article "My story of partner rape" (2006), http://www.aphroditewounded.org/loustory.html; see also Patricia Weiser Easteal and Louise McOrmond-Plummer, *Real Rape, Real Pain: Help for Women Sexually Assaulted by Male Partners* (2006).

512 This passage is based on my interview with Ashley Green in 2007. All names in this passage are pseudonyms.

516 The reference to "coerced childbearing as a weapon in the arsenal of power and control" occurs on page 27 of Anthony Lathrop, "Pregnancy resulting from rape," *Journal of Obstetric, Gynecologic & Neonatal Nursing* 27, no. 1 (January 1998).

516 The quotation from the first woman coerced into bearing children ("He raped me to keep me pregnant all the time") occurs on page 23 of Raquel Kennedy Bergen, *Wife Rape: Understanding the Response of Survivors and Service Providers* (1996); the quotation from the second ("They own you when you have a child by him") occurs on page 219 of Jacquelyn C. Campbell et al., "The influence of abuse on pregnancy intention," *Women's Health Issues* 5, no. 4 (Winter 1995).

517 This passage is based on my interview with Mindy Woods and Larry Foster in 2007. All names in this passage are pseudonyms.

520 This passage is based on my interview with Barbara, Jeffrey, and Pauline Schmitz in 2007. All names in this passage are pseudonyms.

526 Statistics on numbers of war children can be found on page 7 of Kai Grieg, *The War Children of the World* (2001).

526 The quotation from Ruth Seifert ("The rape of women communicates from man to man . . .") occurs on page 59 of her essay "War and rape: A preliminary analysis," in *Mass Rape: The War against Women in Bosnia-Herzegovina*, edited by Andrea Stiglmayer, translated by Marion Faber (1994). It has been condensed.

526 Susan Brownmiller's characterization of wartime rape as an "extracurricular battlefield" occurs on page 182 of her essay, "Making female bodies the battlefield," in *Mass Rape: The War against Women in Bosnia-Herzegovina*, edited by Andrea Stiglmayer, translated by Marion Faber (1994).

526 Books consulted on the Rwandan genocide include Alison Liebhafsky Des Forges, *"Leave None to Tell the Story": Genocide in Rwanda* (1999); Jean Hatzfeld, *Machete Season: The Killers in Rwanda Speak* (2005); Elizabeth Neuffer, *The Key to My Neighbour's House: Seeking Justice in Bosnia and Rwanda* (2002); Binaifer Nowrojee, *Shattered Lives: Sexual Violence during the Rwandan Genocide and Its Aftermath* (1996); Philip Gourevitch, *We Wish to Inform You That Tomorrow We Will Be Killed with Our Families: Stories from Rwanda* (1999); and Jonathan Torgovnik, *Intended Consequences: Rwandan Children Born of Rape* (2009). For journalistic coverage, see Donatella Lorch, "Rape used as a weapon in Rwanda: Future grim for genocide orphans," *Houston Chronicle*, May 15, 1995; Elizabeth Royte, "The outcasts," *New York Times Magazine*, January 19, 1997; Lindsey Hilsum, "Rwanda's time of rape returns to haunt thousands," *Guardian*, February 26, 1995; Lindsey Hilsum, "Don't abandon Rwandan women again," *New York Times*, April 11, 2004; and Emily Wax, "Rwandans are struggling to love children of hate," *Washington Post*, March 28, 2004.

526 The Rwandan proverb "A woman who is not yet battered is not a real woman" is reported on page 20 of Binaifer Nowrojee's report for Human Rights Watch, *Shattered Lives: Sexual Violence during the Rwandan Genocide and Its Aftermath* (1996).

526 The role of Rwandan media in inciting genocide is discussed in Dina Temple-Raston's remarkable book *Justice on the Grass* (Free Press, 2005). See also Russell Smith, "The impact of hate media in Rwanda," BBC News, December 3, 2003.

526 Statistics on wartime rapes in Rwanda are supported by the UN Office for the Coordination of Humanitarian Affairs news report "Our bodies, their battle ground: Gender-based violence in conflict zones," *IRIN News*, September 1, 2004. Estimates of the numbers of wartime rapes and births come from the introduction by Marie Consolée Mukagendo, "The struggles of Rwandan women raising children born of rape," in Jonathan Torgovnik's photo essay, *Intended Consequences: Rwandan Children Born of Rape* (2009).

527 See Padmasayee Papineni, "Children of bad memories," *Lancet* 362, no. 9386 (September 6, 2003).

527 The phrase *living legacy of a time of death* comes from Emily Wax, "Rwandans are struggling to love children of hate," *Washington Post*, March 28, 2004.

527 The quotation from Catherine Bonnet occurs on page 79 of Binaifer Nowrojee's report *Shattered Lives: Sexual Violence during the Rwandan Genocide and Its Aftermath* (1996), citing to Bonnet's paper, "Le viol des femmes survivantes du génocide du Rwanda," in *Rwanda: Un génocide du XXᵉ siècle*, edited by Raymond Verdier, Emmanuel Decaux, and Jean-Pierre Chrétien (1995), page 18.

527 All quotations from Jean Damascene Ndayambaje come from my interview with him in 2004.

527 All quotations from Espérance Mukamana come from my interview with her in 2004.

527 The loaded names chosen by some women are cataloged in Emily Wax, "Rwandans are struggling to love children of hate," *Washington Post*, March 28, 2004.

528 All quotations from Alphonsine Nyirahabimana come from my interview with her in 2004.

528 All quotations from Célestin Kalimba come from my interview with him in 2004.

528 All quotations from Marie Rose Matamura come from my interview with her in 2004.

529 General information sources on rape as a tool of war include Susan Brownmiller, *Against Our Will* (1975); Maria de Bruyn, *Violence, Pregnancy and Abortion: Issues of Women's Rights and Public Health* (2003); and the Global Justice Center report *The Right to an Abortion for Girls and Women Raped in Armed Conflict* (2011). For further information on rape in specific conflicts noted in this passage, see Nayanika Mookherjee, "'Remembering to forget': Public secrecy and memory of sexual violence in the Bangladesh war of 1971," *Journal of the Royal Anthropological Institute* 12, no. 2 (June 2006); Martina Vandenburg and Kelly Askin, "Chechnya: Another battleground for the perpetration of gender based crimes," *Human Rights Review* 2, no. 3 (2001); Michele L. Leiby, "Wartime sexual violence in Guatemala and Peru," *International Studies Quarterly* 53, no. 2 (June 2009); "Comfort women," *Encyclopedia of Rape*, pages 46–48; the Amnesty International report "Liberia: No impunity for rape" (2004); and Louise Taylor's report for Human Rights Watch, "'We'll kill you if you cry': Sexual violence in the Sierra Leone conflict" (2003).

529 The statement "These incidents of rape are clearly aimed to subjugate, humiliate, and terrorize the entire community, not just the women and girls raped by the militias" appears on page 5 of the Human Rights Watch report "Sexual violence and its consequences among displaced persons in Darfur and Chad" (2005).

529 See "Rape of Nanking," *Encyclopedia of Rape*, pages 194–96.

529 Rape as a weapon during the conflict in Bangladesh is discussed in Robert Trumball, "Dacca raising the status of women while aiding rape victims," *New York Times*, May 12, 1972; Aubrey Menen, "The rapes of Bangladesh," *New York Times*, July 23, 1972; and Susan Brownmiller, *Against Our Will* (1976), pages 78–86.

529 The quotation from the Kosovar husband ("If I were normal, I would keep the kid, accept my wife . . .") comes from Helena Smith, "Rape victims' babies pay the price of war," *Observer*, April 16, 2000.

529 The quotation from the Bosnian rape survivor ("It was a hard birth . . .") occurs on page 131 of Alexandra Stiglmayer, "The rapes in Bosnia-Herzegovina," in *Mass Rape: The War against Women in Bosnia-Herzegovina*, edited by Andrea Stiglmayer, translated by Marion Faber (1994).

529 See Helena Smith, "Rape victims' babies pay the price of war," *Observer*, April 16, 2000.

530 This passage is based on my interview with Marianne Mukamana in 2004.

530 The quotation from the East Timorese rape survivor ("I was used like a horse by the Indonesian soldiers . . .") occurs on page 337 of Susan Harris Rimmer, "'Orphans' or veterans?: Justice for children born of war in East Timor," *Texas International Law Journal* 42, no. 2 (Spring 2007), citing to Galuh Wandita et al., "Learning to engender reparations in Timor-Leste: Reaching out to female victims," in *Engendering Reparations: Recognising and Compensating Women Victims of Human Rights Violations*, edited by Ruth Rubio-Marín (2006).

530 The characterization of children of rape as a "symbol of the trauma the nation as a whole went through" occurs on page 16 of Elisabeth Rehn and Ellen Johnson Sirleaf's report to UNIFEM, *Women, War and Peace: The Independent Experts' Assessment on the Impact of Armed Conflict on Women and Women's Role in Peace-Building* (2002).

531 The quotation from Zahra Ismail ("This creates a problem for ensuring fundamental social benefits for children . . .") occurs on page 18 of her dissertation, "Emerging from the shadows: Finding a place for children born of war" (2008).

531 See Robert McKelvey, *The Dust of Life: America's Children Abandoned in Vietnam* (1999).

531 The citizenship status of children conceived in rape during the Bosnian conflict is explored in Joana Daniel's thesis, "No man's child: The war rape orphans" (2003); and "Children born of war rape in Bosnia-Herzegovina and the Convention on the Rights of the Child," in *Born of War: Protecting Children of Sexual Violence Survivors in Conflict Zones*, edited by R. Charli Carpenter (2007), pages 21–39; see also the UNICEF Innocenti Research Centre report, *Birth Registration and Armed Conflict* (2007).

531 The denial of citizenship to offspring of Kuwaiti women raped during the Iraqi occupation is discussed in Kathy Evans, "Kuwait's rape children offer bitter reminder," *Guardian*, July 29, 1993.

531 The quotations from Zahra Ismail about wartime-rape-conceived children as victims occur on pages 13–14 of her dissertation, "Emerging from the shadows: Finding a place for children born of war" (2008).

531 Pursuant to Article 7, part 1, of the UN Convention on the Rights of the Child (full text at http://www2.ohchr.org/english/law/crc.htm), every child "shall be registered immediately after birth and shall have the right from birth to a name, the right to acquire a nationality and, as far as possible, the right to know and be cared for by his or her parents."

531 R. Charli Carpenter discusses UK policy on the adoption of babies from the Balkans in her paper "War's impact on children born of rape and sexual exploitation: Physical, economic and psychosocial dimensions" (presented at the University of Alberta, Edmonton, conference The Impact of War on Children, April 2005).

531 This passage is based on my interview with Marcelline Niyonsenga in 2004.

532 The quotation from Bishop Carlos Belo and Susan Harris Rimmer's commentary occur on page 332 of her paper "'Orphans' or veterans?: Justice for children born of war in East Timor," *Texas International Law Journal* 42, no. 2 (Spring 2007).

533 The technical name for the Helms Amendment is Section 104(f) of the Foreign Assistance Act of 1961, as amended. The full text of the amendment can be found at http://www.law.cornell.edu/uscode/text/22/2151b, and an extensive discussion of its ramifications appears in the Global Justice Center report *The Right to an Abortion for Girls and Women Raped in Armed Conflict* (2011).

533 See the Global Justice Center report *The Right to an Abortion for Girls and Women Raped in Armed Conflict* (2011), page 10.

533 All quotations from Janet Benshoof come from my interview with her in 2011.

533 This passage is based on my interview with Alphonsine Mukamakuza in 2004.

534 The Rome Statute of the International Criminal Court was adopted July 17, 1998, and entered into force on July 1, 2002. For the full text, see United Nations, Treaty Series, vol. 2187, p. 3, http://treaties.un.org/pages/ViewDetails .aspx?src=TREATY&mtdsg_no=XVIII-10&chapter=18&lang=en; see also the website of the Rome Statute of the International Criminal Court, http://untreaty .un.org/cod/icc/index.html.

534 See International Criminal Tribunal for Rwanda, *The prosecutor versus Jean-Paul Akayesu*, Case No. ICTR-96-4-T, Judgment 688, September 2, 1998; a summary of the judgment can be found at http://www.uniurb.it/scipol/pretelli/9%20 Akayesu.pdf.

534 A 2004 report by the Iraq Ministry of Women's Affairs found that more than half of the four hundred rapes reported since the US invasion resulted in the murder of rape survivors by their families; see Yifat Susskind, "The murder of Du'a Aswad," *Madre*, May 22, 2007.

534 The quotation from Susan Harris Rimmer occurs on page 324 of her paper "'Orphans' or veterans?: Justice for children born of war in East Timor," *Texas International Law Journal* 42, no. 2 (Spring 2007).

534 The quotation from Jeanne Muliri Kabekatyo ("We want to make out of these children artisans of peace") comes from Danielle Shapiro, "Mothers in Congo get help in raising children of rape," *Christian Science Monitor*, May 9, 2010.

535 This passage is based on my interview with Christine Uwamahoro in 2004.

X: Crime

538 Popular overestimation of the deterrent effects of incarceration is discussed in Peter W. Greenwood et al., *Diverting Children from a Life of Crime: Measuring Costs and Benefits* (1996).

538 The quotation from Fight Crime: Invest in Kids ("Those on the front lines . . .") occurs on page 2 of the organization's position statement "Investments in children prevent crime and save money" (2003), http://www.fightcrime.org/wp-content/ uploads/sites/default/files/reports/Cost-Bft%20Br%20FINAL%204-30-03.pdf.

538 For the meta-analysis of studies on the correlation between rehabilitation

programs and recidivism, see Mark W. Lipsey and David B. Wilson, "Effective interventions for serious juvenile offenders: A synthesis of research," on pages 313–66 of *Serious and Violent Juvenile Offenders: Risk Factors and Successful Interventions*, edited by Rolf Loeber and David P. Farrington (1998).

538 The quotation from the NIH on the futility of scare tactics to reduce youth crime occurs on page 7 of the report *Preventing Violence and Related Health-Risking Social Behaviors in Adolescents* (2004).

538 Joseph A. Califano's reference to "colleges of criminality" occurs on page 20 of the Columbia University National Center on Addiction and Substance Abuse report *Criminal Neglect: Substance Abuse, Juvenile Justice and the Children Left Behind* (2004).

538 Statistics on rates of rearrest of juveniles after release from prison occur on page 7 of Patrick A. Langan and David J. Levin's report to the Department of Justice, "Recidivism of prisoners released in 1994" (2002).

539 Crime victims' survivors' lack of postexecution satisfaction is explored in Scott Vollum and Dennis R. Longmire, "Covictims of capital murder: Statements of victims' family members and friends made at the time of execution," *Violence & Victims* 22, no. 5 (October 2007); and Thomas J. Mowen and Ryan D. Schroeder, "Not in my name: An investigation of victims' family clemency movements and court appointed closure," *Western Criminology Review* 12, no. 1 (January 2011).

539 This passage is based on my interviews with Cora Nelson, Peter Makya, Jennifer Stiles, Maudy Stiles, Ethan Heinz, and Marcella Smith between 2003 and 2006 and subsequent communications. All names in this passage are pseudonyms.

543 Adolescent weapon-carrying was assessed in the National Longitudinal Study of Adolescent Health, with findings published in multiple reports; see, e.g., Robert W. Blum et al., "The effects of race/ethnicity, income, and family structure on adolescent risk behaviors," *American Journal of Public Health* 90, no. 12 (December 2000); and John Hagan and Holly Foster, "Youth violence and the end of adolescence," *American Sociological Review* 66 (December 2001).

543 See Robert Agnew and Sandra Huguley, "Adolescent violence toward parents," *Journal of Marriage & the Family* 51, no. 3 (August 1989); and Charles W. Peek, Judith L. Fischer, and Jeannie S. Kidwell, "Teenage violence toward parents: A neglected dimension of family violence," *Journal of Marriage & the Family* 47 (1985).

543 Statistics on juvenile arrest rates occur on page 5 of Dean John Champion, *The Juvenile Justice System: Delinquency, Processing, and the Law* (2004).

543 Relative chances of apprehension of juvenile and adult suspects are discussed in Monique M. Matherne and Adrian Thomas, "Family environment as a predictor of adolescent delinquency," *Adolescence* 36, no. 144 (Winter 2001).

543 Jennifer L. Truman, *Criminal Victimization, 2010*, Bureau of Justice Statistics Special Report NCJ 235508 (2011). See also statistics on referrals to court, incarceration, and probation on pages 29–57 of Charles Puzzanchera and Melissa Sickmund's report to the US Department of Justice, *Juvenile Court Statistics 2005* (2008); see also Charles Puzzanchera, *Juvenile Arrests 2007* (2009).

543 The characterization of juvenile detention centers as "an extension of the principal's office" occurs in Sara Rimer, "Unruly students facing arrest, not detention," *New York Times*, January 4, 2004.

543 Statistics on the decline in juvenile murder arrests occur on page 1 of Charles Puzzanchera, *Juvenile Arrests 2007* (2009).

544 Waivers are discussed in chapter 9 (pages 297–342) of Dean John Champion, *The Juvenile Justice System: Delinquency, Processing, and the Law* (2004).

544 For information on the expansion of the waiver system, see *Juvenile Offenders and Victims: 2006 National Report* (2006), pages 113–14; see also Melissa Sickmund, "Juveniles in court," National Report Series Bulletin (June 2003), https://www.ncjrs.gov/html/ojjdp/195420/page4.html, page 4.

544 The US Supreme Court decision outlawing the death penalty in juvenile cases occurred in *Roper v. Simmons*, 543 U.S. 551, decided March 1, 2005, available at http://www.supremecourt.gov/opinions/04pdf/03-633.pdf. For a press report on the case, see David Stout, "Supreme Court bars death penalty for juvenile killers," *New York Times*, March 1, 2005. Statistics on the percentage of juveniles on death row prior to *Roper v. Simmons* come from page 187 of Dean John Champion, *The Juvenile Justice System: Delinquency, Processing, and the Law* (2004).

544 Authoritative modern sources on the history of juvenile crime and juvenile justice in the United States include Dean John Champion, *The Juvenile Justice System: Delinquency, Processing, and the Law* (2004); and Clemens Bartollas, *Voices of Delinquency* (2003). For a nineteenth-century perspective, see Bradford Kinney Pierce, *A Half Century with Juvenile Delinquents: The New York House of Refuge and Its Times* (1869). The tragic story of Thomas Granger was told by William Bradford, governor of the Massachusetts Bay Colony, in his diary, *Of Plymouth Plantation, 1620–1647*, edited by Samuel Eliot Morison (1957), pages 320–21.

545 The quotation from the Society for the Prevention of Pauperism ("Here is one great school of vice and desperation . . .") occurs on pages 37–39 of Bradford Kinney Pierce, *A Half Century with Juvenile Delinquents: The New York House of Refuge and Its Time* (1869); the phrase *simple labor* appears on page 62; a discussion of the organization's proposals can be found on pages 62–74.

545 The quotation from Chicago judge Julian Mack ("The problem for determination by the judge . . .") occurs on pages 119–20 of his article "The juvenile court," *Harvard Law Review* 23 (1909).

545 The quotation from Judge Benjamin Lindsey ("Our laws against crime are as inapplicable to children as they would be to idiots") occurs on page 133 of Ben Lindsey and Harvey O'Higgins, *The Beast* (1970), as cited in Rachel Aviv, "No remorse: Should a teenager be given a life sentence?," *New Yorker*, January 2, 2012.

545 The full text of the Supreme Court decision *In re Gault*, 387 U.S. 1, decided May 15, 1967, can be found on the Cornell University Legal Information Institute website, http://www.law.cornell.edu/supct/html/historics/USSC_CR_0387_0001_ZS.html. The reference to "Kangaroo Court" occurs on pages 27–28 of the decision.

545 The full text of the Juvenile Justice and Delinquency Prevention Act can be found on the US Department of Justice website, http://www.ojjdp.gov/about/ojjjact.txt. For a discussion of the provisions of the act, see pages 36–39 of Dean John Champion, *The Juvenile Justice System: Delinquency, Processing, and the Law* (2004).

545 The US Department of Justice official's lament about the "psychobabble of social workers" comes from Merrill Hartson, "Juvenile court system too soft on criminals, U.S. official says," Associated Press, September 4, 1985.

545 The paucity of treatment programs for court-involved youth is discussed on page 7 of the Columbia University National Center on Addiction and Substance Abuse report *Criminal Neglect: Substance Abuse, Juvenile Justice and the Children Left Behind* (2004).

546 See, for example, Rosemary Sarri and Jeffrey Shook, "Human rights and juvenile justice in the United States," in *Children's Human Rights: Progress and Challenges for Children Worldwide*, edited by Mark Ensalaco and Linda C. Majka (2005).

546   For a discussion of the study finding that only a third of adolescent defendants thought their attorneys were helpful, see page 126 of Thomas Grisso and Robert G. Schwartz, *Youth on Trial: A Developmental Perspective on Juvenile Justice* (2000); juvenile defendants' understanding of the Miranda warning is discussed on page 114.

546   The quotation from Thomas Grisso and Robert G. Schwartz ("The adult-like procedures introduced by the left . . .") occurs on page 31 of their book *Youth on Trial: A Developmental Perspective on Juvenile Justice* (2000).

546   For more information on brain development and delinquent behavior, see Daniel R. Weinberger, "A brain too young for good judgment," *New York Times*, March 10, 2001; and Laurence Steinberg and Elizabeth Cauffman, "Maturity of judgment in adolescence: Psychosocial factors in adolescent decision making," *Law & Human Behavior* 20, no. 3 (June 1996).

546   Statistics on the association of drug and alcohol intoxication and the commission of crimes come from page 11 of the Columbia University National Center on Addiction and Substance Abuse report *Criminal Neglect: Substance Abuse, Juvenile Justice and the Children Left Behind* (2004); rates of drug and alcohol abuse among adolescent criminal defendants from page 2; rates of substance-abuse treatment from page 56. For more detail on the level of substance-abuse treatment in correctional facilities, see the HHS report *Drug and Alcohol Treatment in Juvenile Correctional Facilities: The DASIS Report* (2002).

547   This passage is based on my interview with Sophia and Josiah McFeely in 2004 and subsequent communications. All names in this passage are pseudonyms.

549   Numbers of adolescent defendants with psychiatric diagnoses come from Linda A. Teplin et al., "Psychiatric disorders in youth in juvenile detention," *Archives of General Psychiatry* 59, no. 12 (2002); and page 35 of the Columbia University National Center on Addiction and Substance Abuse report *Criminal Neglect: Substance Abuse, Juvenile Justice and the Children Left Behind* (2004).

549   The proportion of incarcerated adolescents with learning disabilities comes from page 5 of Ronald D. Stephens and June Lane Arnette, "From the courthouse to the schoolhouse: Making successful transitions," *OJJDP: Juvenile Justice Bulletin* NCJ-178900 (2000).

549   For the study of "easy" and "difficult" babies and later court involvement, see Rolf Loeber and Dale F. Hay, "Developmental approaches to aggression and conduct problems," on pages 488–515 of *Development through Life: A Handbook for Clinicians*, edited by Michael Rutter and Dale F. Hay (1994).

549   For the study on the relationship between youthful "troublesomeness" and adolescent offending, see David P. Farrington, "The development of offending and antisocial behaviour from childhood: Key findings from the Cambridge Study in Delinquent Development," *Journal of Child Psychology & Psychiatry* 36, no. 6 (September 1995).

549   An increased risk for offending for those who start young is found in Richard Dembo et al., "Predictors of recidivism to a juvenile assessment center: A three year study," *Journal of Child & Adolescent Substance Abuse* 7, no. 3 (1998); see also Patrick Tolan and Peter Thomas, "The implications of age of onset for delinquency risk II: Longitudinal data," *Journal of Abnormal Child Psychology* 23, no. 2 (April 1995): 157–81.

549   The quotation from Carol Carothers ("It is hard to imagine a worse place . . .") comes from her testimony "Juvenile detention centers: Are they warehousing children with mental illnesses?," on behalf of the National Alliance on Mental

Illness before the Governmental Affairs Committee, United States Senate on Juvenile Detention Centers, July 7, 2004.

550 This passage is based on my interview with Brianna Gandy in 2003. All names in this passage are pseudonyms.

551 This passage is based on my interview with Jackson Simpson, Alexa Simpson, and Jackson's father in 2003. All names in this section are pseudonyms.

552 The description of hellish conditions at the Mississippi juvenile detention center comes from David M. Halbfinger, "Care of juvenile offenders in Mississippi is faulted," *New York Times*, September 1, 2003.

552 The quotation describing filthy, inhumane conditions in a Mississippi detention center comes from the complaint filed in *D.W. et al. v. Harrison County, Mississippi*, Case 1:2009cv00267, US District Court for the Southern District of Mississippi (Complaint filed April 20, 2009; Memorandum of Agreement filed June 24, 2009); see also the Southern Poverty Law Center press release "SPLC sues Mississippi county to stop 'shocking' abuse of children at detention center," April 20, 2009.

552 Stripping and isolation of adolescent female inmates is described in David Halbfinger, "Care of juvenile offenders in Mississippi is faulted," *New York Times*, September 1, 2003.

552 "Blender meals" are described in John Broder, "Dismal California prisons hold juvenile offenders," *New York Times*, February 15, 2004.

552 The characterization of California's juvenile prisons as "a dysfunctional jumble of antiquated facilities" comes from John Broder, "Dismal California prisons hold juvenile offenders," *New York Times*, February 15, 2004.

552 Conditions at the Nevada Youth Training Center are described in Ralph F. Boyd, *Investigation of Nevada Youth Training Center, Elko, Nevada* (2005), as cited on page 20 of the Columbia University National Center on Addiction and Substance Abuse report *Criminal Neglect: Substance Abuse, Juvenile Justice and the Children Left Behind* (2004).

552 The death of a seventeen-year-old inmate and deplorable conditions at the Miami-Dade Regional Juvenile Detention Center are described in the Miami-Dade County Grand Jury report *Investigation into the death of Omar Paisley and the Department of Juvenile Justice, Miami-Dade Regional Juvenile Detention Center*, January 27, 2004.

552 The statement from Joseph Califano ("We have fifty-one different systems of juvenile injustice . . .") occurs on page 20 of the Columbia University National Center on Addiction and Substance Abuse report *Criminal Neglect: Substance Abuse, Juvenile Justice and the Children Left Behind* (2004).

553 All quotations from Home School staff and residents come from interviews and personal communications between 2003 and 2005, and subsequent communications.

553 See Stephen DiMenna's website: http://www.stephendimenna.com/.

555 This passage is based on my interviews with Dashonte Malcolm, Audrey Malcolm, Bishop Forbes, Mother Forbes, and Darius Stewart between 2003 and 2007, and subsequent communications. All names in this passage are pseudonyms.

557 Comprehensive general resources on gangs include James C. Howell et al., "U.S. gang problem trends and seriousness," *National Gang Center Bulletin* 6 (May 2011); and James C. Howell, *Gangs in America's Communities* (2011); for specific background on the Bloods, see the Virginia Fusion Center, *Bloods Street Gang Intelligence Report* (2008).

559 See "Interview with Leslie Van Houten," *CNN Larry King Weekend*, Cable News Network, June 29, 2002.

560 See Suzanne Daley's interview with Aicha el-Wafi, mother of Zacarias Moussaoui, "Mysterious life of a suspect from France," *New York Times*, September 21, 2001.

560 This passage is based on my interview with Dan Patterson in 2004. All names in this passage are pseudonyms.

560 See Lionel Dahmer, *A Father's Story* (1994).

561 The quotation from Lionel Dahmer occurs on pages 127–28 of *A Father's Story* (1994). It has been condensed.

561 See Rachel King, *Capital Consequences: Families of the Condemned Tell Their Stories* (2005). For a summary of King's work and conclusions, see her article "The impact of capital punishment on families of defendants and murder victims," *Judicature* 89, no. 5 (March–April 2006).

561 The story of Dave Herman and his family is told in chapter 7 of Rachel King, *Capital Consequences* (2005), pages 221–45. The quotations from Esther Herman ("I had two very active businesses . . ." and "Dave had been a good person . . .") occur on pages 223 and 231. They have been condensed.

561 This passage is based on my interview with Noel Marsh, Felicity Tompkins, and Steve Tompkins in 2003. All names in this passage are pseudonyms.

563 Studies of aggression in monkeys include Maribeth Champoux et al., "Serotonin transporter gene polymorphism, differential early rearing, and behavior in rhesus monkey neonates," *Molecular Psychiatry* 7, no. 10 (2002); and Allyson Bennett et al., "Early experience and serotonin transporter gene variation interact to influence primate CNS function," *Molecular Psychiatry* 7, no. 1 (2002).

563 See Avshalom Caspi et al., "Role of genotype in the cycle of violence in maltreated children," *Science* 297, no. 5582 (August 2002). For a general review of research in this area, see Terrie E. Moffitt, "Genetic and environmental influences on antisocial behaviors: Evidence from behavioral-genetic research," *Advances in Genetics* 55 (2005).

564 The quotation about the benefits of "a positive family environment" occurs on page 457 of Karol L. Kumpfer and Rose Alvarado, "Family-strengthening approaches for the prevention of youth problem behaviors," *American Psychologist* 58, nos. 6–7 (June–July 2003). It has been condensed.

564 The statement "The parental attachment factor explains delinquency" occurs on page 32 of Jill Leslie Rosenbaum, "Family dysfunction and female delinquency," *Crime & Delinquency* 35, no. 1 (January 1989); see also Joseph H. Rankin and Roger Kern, "Parental attachments and delinquency," *Criminology* 32, no. 4 (November 1994).

564 This passage is based on my interviews with Karina Lopez and Emma Lopez in 2003 and 2004 and subsequent communications. All names in this passage are true except for "Cesar Marengo," which is a pseudonym.

567 The murder of Luis Alberto Anaya and the prosecution of José Monroy Vega, Juan Carlos Ortiz-Mendoza, and Ramiro Montoya Pineda were covered extensively in the *Minneapolis Star Tribune*; see, e.g., Paul Gustafson, "Gang member found not guilty of St. Paul killing," May 6, 2004; "Doubts about witness lead to acquittal in murder case," July 24, 2004; and "Gang member sentenced for shooting death of rival," August 20, 2004. Sureños (also known as Sureños 13) is an alliance of Mexican-American street gangs that originated in Southern California during the 1970s and has since spread throughout the United States. In 2009, the Minnesota Metro Gang Strike Force estimated that Sureños 13 was the region's fastest-

growing gang, with 106 members residing in the Minneapolis/St. Paul area; see Metro Gang Strike Force, "2008 Annual Report" (2009).

568 Statistics on single-parent families come from pages 10–11 of Howard Snyder and Melissa Sickmund, *Juvenile Offenders and Victims* (2006); see also Stephen Demuth and Susan L. Brown, "Family structure, family processes, and adolescent delinquency: The significance of parental absence versus parental gender," *Journal of Research in Crime & Delinquency* 41, no. 1 (February 2004).

568 This passage is based on my interview with Jamaal Carson and Breechelle Carson in 2003. All names in this passage are pseudonyms.

569 The quotation from John Bowlby ("comfortless and unpredictable, and they respond either by shrinking from it or doing battle with it") occurs on page 208 of John Bowlby, Margery Fry, and Mary D. Salter Ainsworth, *Separation: Anxiety and Anger*, vol. 2: *Attachment and Loss* (1973). For further discussion of abuse and neglect as a contributing factor to delinquency, see Frank J. Elgar et al., "Attachment characteristics and behavioural problems in rural and urban juvenile delinquents," *Child Psychiatry & Human Development* 34, no. 1 (Fall 2003). The increased incidence of crimes committed by abused and neglected children is reported on page 3 of Cathy Widom and Michael G. Maxfield, *An Update on the "Cycle of Violence"* (2001).

569 This passage is based on my interview with Huaj Kyuhyun in 2003. All names in this passage are pseudonyms.

570 For discussion of exposure to violence as a risk factor for delinquency, see Cathy Widom and Michael G. Maxfield, *An Update on the "Cycle of Violence"* (2001); Karol L. Kumpfer, *Strengthening America's Families* (1999); Sally Preski and Deborah Shelton, "The role of contextual, child, and parent factors in predicting criminal outcomes in adolescence," *Issues in Mental Health Nursing* 22 (March 2001); and Carolyn Hilarski, "Victimization history as a risk factor for conduct disorder behaviors," *Stress, Trauma & Crisis* 7, no. 1 (January 2004).

570 For the report of the study finding increased risk of engaging in violent behavior in children exposed to violence, see Terence P. Thornberry, *Violent Families and Youth Violence* (1994); additionally, criminologist James C. Howell discusses and analyzes Thornberry's study on pages 113–14 of *Preventing and Reducing Juvenile Delinquency: A Comprehensive Framework* (2003).

570 The quotation from Jess McDonald ("The Child Welfare System is a feeder system for the juvenile justice system") occurs on page 32 of the Columbia University National Center on Addiction and Substance Abuse report *Criminal Neglect: Substance Abuse, Juvenile Justice and the Children Left Behind* (2004).

570 This passage is based on my interview with Ryan Nordstrom and his parents in 2004. All names in this passage are pseudonyms.

570 At least one study has found an association between early exposure to pornography and offending: David L. Burton, George Stuart Leibowitz, and Alan Howard, "Comparison by crime type of juvenile delinquents on pornography exposure: The absence of relationships between exposure to pornography and sexual offense characteristics," *Journal of Forensic Nursing* 6, no. 3 (September 2010).

570 David P. Farrington summarizes a major inquiry into youths' high-risk behavior in "The development of offending and antisocial behaviour from childhood: Key findings from the Cambridge Study in Delinquent Development," *Journal of Child Psychology & Psychiatry* 36, no. 6 (September 1995).

571 See Judith Rich Harris, *The Nurture Assumption: Why Children Turn Out the Way They Do* (1998), especially the discussion of "groupness" on page 128. The

tendency of juveniles to commit crimes in groups is discussed on page 370 of *Child Delinquents: Development, Intervention, and Service Needs*, edited by Rolf Loeber and David P. Farrington (2001).

571 For discussion of the contribution of the social environment to juvenile delinquency, see Kenneth C. Land, "Influence of neighborhood, peer, and family context: Trajectories of delinquent/criminal offending across the life course" (2000).

571 Statistics on the percentage of juvenile crimes committed by females come from page 4 of Charles Puzzanchera, *Juvenile Arrests 2007* (2009).

571 For further discussion of precursors to female offending, see Leslie D. Leve and Patricia Chamberlain, "Female juvenile offenders: Defining an early-onset pathway for delinquency," *Journal of Child & Family Studies* 13, no. 4 (December 2004); and Jill Leslie Rosenbaum, "Family dysfunction and female delinquency," *Crime & Delinquency* 35, no. 1 (January 1989).

571 Statistics on the incidence of childhood sexual abuse among female criminal defendants come from George Calhoun et al., "The neophyte female delinquent: A review of the literature," *Adolescence* 28, no. 110 (Summer 1993); and Margaret A. Zahn et al., "Causes and correlates of girls' delinquency," US Department of Justice (April 2010).

571 Statistics on the percentage of chronic juvenile offenders who are gang members come from James C. Howell's report to the US Office of Juvenile Justice and Delinquency Prevention *Youth Gang Programs and Strategies* (2000).

571 Statistics on gang membership come from the National Youth Gang Center, *National Youth Gang Survey Analysis* (2011), http://www.nationalgangcenter.gov/Survey-Analysis/Measuring-the-Extent-of-Gang-Problems.

571 This passage is based on my interviews with Krishna Mirador, Carol Malloy, and Raul Mirador from 2003 to 2009, and subsequent communications. All names in this passage are pseudonyms.

572 For the Indian court decision finding that Ananda Marga was the intended recipient of the arms drop in the Purulia arms drop case, see *State v. Peter James Gifran von Kalkstein Bleach et al.*, Purulia arms dropping case, Sessions Trial No. 1, Calcutta Court of Session, judgment issued June 1997, http://www.cbi.gov.in/dop/judgements/padc.pdf.

576 As Krishna noted, many gangs started out as neighborhood baseball teams; see Robert Chow, "Barrios' rivalry began with sports, cars," *Orange County Register*, August 6, 1990.

579 See Elizabeth Bishop, "Questions of Travel," *Questions of Travel* (1965).

582 This passage is based on my interview with Tyndall Wilkie in 2003. All names in this passage are pseudonyms.

582 This passage is based on the story of Mitt Ebbetts as recounted to me in 2004 by a member of staff at a juvenile facility. All names in this passage are pseudonyms.

583 An official study found that nearly half of Castington inmates anticipate difficulty finding work after release; see Her Majesty's Young Offender Institution, Castington and Oswald Unit, "Summary of questionnaires and interviews," February 16, 2010, http://www.justice.gov.uk/downloads/publications/inspectorate-reports/hmipris/2010_CASTINGTON_YJB_survey_rps.pdf.

584 The survey of juvenile caseworkers is described on page 387 of Rolf Loeber and David P. Farrington, *Child Delinquents: Development, Intervention, and Service Needs* (2001).

584 Figures on the cost of jailing juveniles come from page 16 of Peter W. Greenwood

et al., RAND Corporation report *Diverting Children from a Life of Crime: Measuring Costs and Benefits* (1996), estimating $21,000/year; and page 32 of Karol Kumpfer, *Strengthening America's Families: Exemplary Parenting and Family Strategies for Delinquency Prevention* (1999), estimating $34,000–$64,000/year.

584 For more information on prison programming and its role in reducing recidivism, see the discussion on pages 210–11 of James C. Howell, *Preventing and Reducing Juvenile Delinquency* (2003); Cole Barton et al., "Generalizing treatment effects of functional family therapy: Three replications," *American Journal of Family Therapy* 13, no. 3 (Fall 1985); and Roger Przybylski's report to the Colorado Division of Criminal Justice, *What Works: Effective Recidivism Reduction and Risk-Focused Prevention Programs* (2008).

584 The quotation from Joseph Califano ("Treatment and accountability . . .") occurs on page 9 of the Columbia University National Center on Addiction and Substance Abuse report *Criminal Neglect: Substance Abuse, Juvenile Justice and the Children Left Behind* (2004).

584 The positive impact of family-based intervention is explored in William Shadish et al., "Effects of family and marital psychotherapies: A meta-analysis," *Journal of Consulting & Clinical Psychology* 61, no. 6 (December 1993).

584 The quotation about the effectiveness of family and group interventions occurs on page 255 of Susan R. Woolfenden, Katrina Williams, and Jennifer K. Peat, "Family and parenting interventions for conduct disorder and delinquency: A meta-analysis of randomized controlled trials," *Archives of Disease in Childhood* 86, no. 4 (April 2002).

584 The effectiveness of prenatal home visits in reducing juvenile crime is discussed on page 90 of the US surgeon general's report *Youth Violence* (2001). For more information on preventive programs, see Peter W. Greenwood et al., *Diverting Children from a Life of Crime: Measuring Costs and Benefit* (1996).

585 Delinquency prevention programs are likened to "the dental model" in Robert Nix, "Preschool intervention programs and the process of changing children's lives," *Prevention & Treatment* 6, no. 1 (December 2003).

585 Recent publications by Alan Kazdin on the parenting of defiant children include *Parent Management Training: Treatment for Oppositional, Aggressive, and Antisocial Behavior in Children and Adolescents* (2005); and Alan E. Kazdin, P. L. Marciano, and M. Whitley, "The therapeutic alliance in cognitive-behavioral treatment of children referred for oppositional, aggressive, and antisocial behavior," *Journal of Consulting and Clinical Psychology* 73, no. 4 (August 2005).

585 For the study concluding that behavioral-communication programs could cut recidivism in half, see Patrick Tolan et al., "Family therapy with delinquents: A critical review of the literature," *Family Processes* 25, no. 4 (December 1986).

585 For the two studies finding significantly reduced recidivism among participants in family therapy, see William H. Quinn and David J. Van Dyke, "A multiple family group intervention for first-time juvenile offenders: Comparisons with probation and dropouts on recidivism," *Journal of Community Psychology* 32, no. 2 (February 2004); and Cole Barton et al., "Generalizing treatment effects of functional family therapy: Three replications," *American Journal of Family Therapy* 13, no. 3 (Fall 1985).

585 Statistics on the increased incidence of arrest for violent crimes in youth from families who had received no early intervention come from Arthur J. Reynolds et al., "Long-term effects of an early childhood intervention on educational

achievement and juvenile arrest," *Journal of the American Medical Association* 285, no. 18 (May 9, 2001).

585 Meager implementation of family therapy by juvenile institutions was found in Karol L. Kumpfer and Rose Alvarado, "Family-strengthening approaches for the prevention of youth problem behaviors," *American Psychologist* 58, nos. 6–7 (June–July 2003), page 457.

585 For demonstrations of the cost savings resulting from expenditures on family education, see Lawrence J. Schweinhart, Helen V. Barnes, and David P. Weikart, *Significant Benefits: The High/Scope Perry Preschool Study through Age 27* (1993). For documentation of even greater savings with later-stage intervention, see Robert Barnoski, *Outcome Evaluation of Washington State's Research-Based Programs for Juvenile Offenders* (2004).

585 Criminologist Peter Greenwood compares costs of the "three strikes" law with parole and parent training in the RAND Corporation report *Diverting Children from a Life of Crime: Measuring Costs and Benefits* (1996); specific figures cited occur on page 25.

586 Estimates of the total cost of the failure to provide adequate preventive services come from page 6 of Lawrence J. Schweinhart et al., *Lifetime Effects: The HighScope Perry Preschool Study through Age 40* (2005).

587 This passage is based on my interviews with Tom and Sue Klebold between 2005 and 2007, and subsequent communications. My sources on the Columbine tragedy include reports in the *Denver Rocky Mountain News* by Lynn Bartels, Dan Luzadder, and Kevin Vaughan (see the bibliography for all titles); David Cullen's articles on *Salon* and his subsequent book, *Columbine* (2009); coverage in the *New York Times* by David Brooks and Judith Warner; Nancy Gibbs and Timothy Roche, "The Columbine tapes," *Time*, December 20, 1999; Michael Paterniti, "Columbine never sleeps," *GQ*, April 2004; Brooks Brown and Rob Merritt, *No Easy Answers: The Truth behind Death at Columbine* (2002); Ralph Larkin, *Comprehending Columbine* (2007); and Susan Klebold, "I will never know why," *O, The Oprah Magazine*, November 2009.

588 Nathan Dykeman said of the Klebolds, "They're in a glass cage," in an ABC *Good Morning America* interview, "More insight on Dylan Klebold," broadcast April 30, 1999.

XI: Transgender

599 The quotation from Richard C. Friedman ("... 'Don't worry—it won't happen to you'") comes from personal communication in 2011.

599 Amy Bloom's observation ("Male is not gay or straight; it's male . . .") occurs on page 18 of her book *Normal: Transsexual CEOs, Crossdressing Cops, and Hermaphrodites with Attitude* (2002).

599 The quotations from Jan Morris ("Transsexualism is not a sexual mode or preference . . ." and "My inner uncertainty . . .") occur on pages 8 and 7 of her memoir, *Conundrum* (2006).

599 These definitions, commonly accepted though occasionally debated, are cataloged on pages 4–6 of Stephanie Brill and Rachel Pepper, *The Transgender Child: A Handbook for Families and Professionals* (2008).

600 The quotation from Aiden Key ("My gender is who I am; my sexuality is who I bounce it off of") comes from my interview with him in 2009.

600 The quotation from the mother ("She's four—I don't think she's got sexual desires yet") comes from a personal interview in 2009.

600 See Richard Green, *The "Sissy Boy Syndrome" and the Development of Homosexuality* (1987).

601 My sources on ENDA and NGLTF advocacy include David Herszenhorn, "House approves broad protections for gay workers," *New York Times*, November 8, 2007; and Rea Carey's November 5, 2009, testimony before the Senate Committee on Health, Education, Labor, and Pensions. (I am a member of the Task Force board of directors, which I joined after I began researching this chapter.)

601 Diagnostic criteria for gender identity disorder appear on pages 576–80 of the *Diagnostic and Statistical Manual of Mental Disorders, DSM-IV-TR*, 4th ed. (2000).

601 Stephanie Brill and Rachel Pepper discuss the emergence of gender-stereotypical behavior in chapter 3 (pages 61–72) of *The Transgender Child* (2008).

601 Unless otherwise specified, all quotations from Stephanie Brill come from my interviews with her in 2009 and subsequent communications.

602 See Simona Giordano, "Lives in a chiaroscuro: Should we suspend the puberty of children with gender identity disorder?," *Journal of Medical Ethics* 34, no. 8 (August 2008).

602 "Official" statistics on incidence of gender reassignment surgery appear on page 579 of the *Diagnostic and Statistical Manual of Mental Disorders, DSM-IV-TR* (2000). I have applied those proportions to American population estimates.

602 Lynn Conway offers her analysis of transgender population statistics in her essay "The numbers don't add; transsexual prevalence," GID Reform Advocates (2008), http://gidreform.org/gid30285.html.

602 The quotation from Barbara Walters ("what's between their legs doesn't match what's between their ears") comes from her ABC News report "Transgender children face unique challenges," *20/20*, April 27, 2007.

602 The National Center for Transgender Equality estimates that between .25 percent and 1 percent of the population is transsexual; see page 1 of the organization's brochure "Understanding Transgender" (2009).

603 The quotation from Holly Devor occurs on page xxvi of *FTM: Female-to-Male Transsexuals in Society* (1997).

603 The word *cisgender* is new enough that it still awaits a place in the *Oxford English Dictionary*, but notable enough to have its own Wikipedia page (http://en.wikipedia.org/wiki/Cisgender); a 1991 article by German sexologist Volkmar Sigusch featured the neologism *zissexuelle*, and *cisgender* can be found in Usenet posts as far back as 1994.

603 This passage is based on my interview with Venessia, Joseph, Josie, and Jade Romero in 2009 and subsequent communications.

604 TransYouth Family Allies website: http://imatyfa.org/. (I am a member of the TYFA board of directors, which I joined after I began researching this chapter.)

606 Josie agreed to be profiled in the 2010 National Geographic documentary *Sex, Lies and Gender* and is featured in Stephanie Innes, "Meet Josie, 9: No secret she's transgender," *Arizona Star*, July 25, 2010.

607 A recent study has established that of the 4,508 genes actively transcribed in the mouse brain, 257 are more highly expressed in males and 355 in females; see Xia Yang et al., "Tissue-specific expression and regulation of sexually dimorphic genes in mice," *Genome Research* 16, no. 8 (August 2006). These numbers are far greater than the numbers of genes involved in the differentiation of the gonads. Given the increased size and complexity of the human brain, it is likely that even

larger numbers of genes are associated with sexually dimorphic processes other than reproduction, including behavior and disposition. For a useful review of current research on genetic and epigenetic contributions to sex differences in behavior, see Irfan A. Qureshi and Mark F. Mehler, "Genetic and epigenetic underpinnings of sex differences in the brain and in neurological and psychiatric disease susceptibility," *Progress in Brain Research* 186 (2010). For further discussion of genetic and biological contributions to gender identity, see Louis Gooren, "The biology of human psychosexual differentiation," *Hormones & Behavior* 50 (2006): 589–601; Dick F. Swaab, "Sexual differentiation of the brain and behavior," *Best Practice & Research Clinical Endocrinology & Metabolism* 21, no. 3 (September 2007); and Lauren Hare et al., "Androgen receptor repeat length polymorphism associated with male-to-female transsexualism," *Biological Psychiatry* 65, no. 1 (January 1, 2009).

607 Unless otherwise specified, all quotations from Norman Spack come from my interview with him in 2009.

607 The possible influence of DES on development of gender dysphoria is discussed on pages 226–71 of Deborah Rudacille, *The Riddle of Gender: Science, Activism and Transgender Rights* (2005); the survey is described on page 17.

607 For more information on endocrine disruptors and differences in gendered behavior, see David Crews and John A. McLachlan, "Epigenetics, evolution, endocrine disruption, health, and disease," *Endocrinology* 147, no. 6 (June 2006). Nicholas Kristof's reports on the subject include "It's time to learn from frogs," *New York Times*, June 27, 2009; and "Chemicals and our health," *New York Times*, July 16, 2009.

608 The quotation from Georges Canguilhem ("Diversity is not disease; the *anomalous* is not the pathological") occurs on page 137 of his book *The Normal and the Pathological* (1991).

608 Diagnostic criteria for gender identity disorder appear on pages 576–80 of the *Diagnostic and Statistical Manual of Mental Disorders, DSM-IV-TR*, 4th ed. (2000). For in-depth discussion of gender-atypical behaviors common to children with GID, see Kenneth J. Zucker and Susan J. Bradley, *Gender Identity Disorder and Psychosexual Problems in Children and Adolescents* (1995); and the chapter "Childhood, interrupted," on pages 192–225 of Deborah Rudacille, *The Riddle of Gender* (2005).

608 Heino Meyer-Bahlburg analyzes the statistical variance of children with GID from gender-typical behavior in his paper "Gender identity disorder of childhood: Introduction," *Journal of the American Academy of Child Psychiatry* 24, no. 6 (November 1985).

608 Figures for the percentage of children with GID whose cross-gender identification persists into adolescence are based on the findings in Richard Green, *The "Sissy Boy Syndrome" and the Development of Homosexuality* (1987); Kelley D. Drummond et al., "A follow-up study of girls with gender identity disorder," *Developmental Psychology* 44, no. 1 (January 2008); and M. S. Wallien and Peggy T. Cohen-Kettenis, "Psychosexual outcome of gender-dysphoric children," *Journal of the American Academy of Child & Adolescent Psychiatry* 47, no. 12 (December 2008).

609 The quotation from Kelly Winters ("Behaviors that would be ordinary or even exemplary . . .") comes from her essay "Issues of GID diagnosis for transsexual women and men" (2007).

609 Gerald Mallon and Teresa DeCrescenzo refer to "the sports corrective" and "the etiquette corrective" on page 58 of *Social Services with Transgendered Youth* (1999);

and on page 230 of their article "Transgender children and youth: A child welfare practice perspective," *Child Welfare* 85, no. 2 (March–April 2006).

609 The quotation from Diane Ehrensaft ("The mental health profession has been consistently doing harm . . .") comes from Lois Wingerson, "Gender identity disorder: Has accepted practice caused harm?," *Psychiatric Times*, May 19, 2009.

609 Deborah Rudacille's observation about GID ("The diagnosis legitimizes the range of hormonal and surgical interventions . . .") occurs on page 216 of *The Riddle of Gender* (2005).

609 The quotation from William Narrow ("The harm of retention is stigma . . .") comes from Susan Jeffrey, "APA 2009: DSM-V on track for 2019, but difficult decisions lie ahead," *Medscape Medical News*, May 26, 2009.

610 Although gender reassignment surgery generally remains ineligible for insurance reimbursement, in November 2011 the Internal Revenue Service dropped its opposition to a 2010 Tax Court ruling allowing a federal tax deduction; see Jonathan Berr, "Sex change surgery is now tax deductible," *Time*, November 10, 2011.

610 All quotations from Michele Angello come from my interview with her in 2009 and subsequent communications.

610 See "AMA policy regarding sexual orientation" (2007), http://www.ama-assn .org/ama/pub/about-ama/our-people/member-groups-sections/glbt-advisory -committee/ama-policy-regarding-sexual-orientation.page.

610 The quotation from Edgardo Menvielle ("The goal is for the child to be well adjusted . . .") comes from Patricia Leigh Brown, "Supporting boys or girls when the line isn't clear," *New York Times*, December 2, 2006.

610 The characterization of Peggy Cohen-Kettenis's work occurs on page 29 of Alice Dreger, "Gender identity disorder in childhood: Inconclusive advice to parents," *Hastings Center Report* 39, no. 1 (January–February 2009).

611 The quotations from Aristotle ("the single cause" as to "why the man is man or the musician musical" is simply "because each thing is inseparable from itself") occur in *Metaphysics*, Book VII, pt. 17, on page 311 of *A New Aristotle Reader* (1987).

611 John Locke's statement "a man is a man" occurs in "Mr. Locke's reply to the Bishop of Worcester," in *The Works of John Locke, Esq., in Three Volumes*, vol. 1 (1727), page 419.

611 This passage is based on my interviews with Bettina and Greg Verdi in 2009 and subsequent communications. All names in this passage are pseudonyms.

613 The quotations in these two paragraphs from the two parents of trans people and the trans son of one of them come from personal interviews conducted between 2007 and 2010.

614 See Richard Green and John Money, *Transsexualism and Sex Reassignment* (1969). Money first publicly referred to the "John/Joan" case in *Man and Woman, Boy and Girl* (1972).

614 David Reimer told his story to John Colapinto, who published it first as "The true story of John/Joan," *Rolling Stone*, December 11, 1997; and three years later in *As Nature Made Him: The Boy Who Was Raised as a Girl* (2000). Colapinto commented on Reimer's death in "Gender gap: What were the real reasons behind David Reimer's suicide?," *Slate*, June 3, 2004.

614 For reports of the Johns Hopkins study, see William G. Reiner and John P. Gearhart, "Discordant sexual identity in some genetic males with cloacal exstrophy assigned to female sex at birth," *New England Journal of Medicine* 350,

no. 4 (January 22, 2004); and William G. Reiner, "Gender identity and sex-of-rearing in children with disorders of sexual differentiation," *Journal of Pediatric Endocrinology & Metabolism* 18, no. 6 (June 2005).

615 The quotation from William G. Reiner ("These children demonstrate . . .") comes from a Johns Hopkins University press release, "Hopkins research shows nature, not nurture, determines gender," May 12, 2000.

615 For the UCLA study of effeminate boys, see George Rekers, O. Ivar Lovaas, and B. Low, "Behavioral treatment of deviant sex role behaviors in a male child," *Journal of Applied Behavioral Analysis* 7 (1974); and Richard Green, *The "Sissy Boy Syndrome" and the Development of Homosexuality* (1987).

615 The incident that ended George Rekers's public career as an academic standard-bearer against homosexuality was first reported by Penn Bullock and Brandon K. Thorp in "Christian right leader George Rekers takes vacation with 'rent boy,'" *Miami New Times*, May 4, 2010.

615 The quotation from Kirk Murphy's sister comes from Scott Bronstein and Jesse Joseph's report for Cable News Network, "Therapy to change 'feminine' boy created a troubled man, family says," broadcast June 10, 2011.

615 See Phyllis Burke, *Gender Shock: Exploding the Myths of Male and Female* (1996).

616 This passage is based on my interview with Tony Ferraiolo and Anne Ferraiolo in 2008 and subsequent communications.

619 Jim Collins Foundation website: http://jimcollinsfoundation.org.

619 Information on the amounts of cross-sex hormones required to effect transition come from my interview with Norman Spack in 2009. For a detailed discussion of hormone treatment, see Wylie C. Hembree et al., "Endocrine treatment of transsexual persons: An Endocrine Society clinical practice guideline," *Journal of Clinical Endocrinology & Metabolism* 94, no. 9 (September 2009); and Louis J. Gooren, Erik J. Giltay, and Mathijs C. Bunck, "Long-term treatment of transsexuals with cross-sex hormones: Extensive personal experience," *Journal of Clinical Endocrinology & Metabolism* 93, no. 1 (January 2008).

620 See World Professional Association for Transgender Health, *Harry Benjamin International Gender Dysphoria Association's Standards of Care for Gender Identity Disorders*, 6th version (2001).

620 The various surgeries associated with gender reassignment are described in exquisite detail in the chapter "Medical and surgical options," on pages 196–211, of Mildred L. Brown and Chloe Ann Rounsley, *True Selves: Understanding Transsexualism* (1996). See also TS Roadmap, http://www.tsroadmap.com/physical/hair/zapidx.html.

621 For a scholarly source on hormone blockers, see Norman Spack, "An endocrine perspective on the care of transgender adolescents," *Journal of Gay & Lesbian Mental Health* 13, no. 4 (October 2009). News coverage of the subject includes Lauren Smiley, "Girl/boy interrupted," *SF Weekly*, July 11, 2007; and Hanna Rosin, "A boy's life," *Atlantic Monthly*, November 2008.

621 Follow-up studies of the Dutch cohort include Peggy T. Cohen-Kettenis and Stephanie H. van Goozen, "Sex reassignment of adolescent transsexuals: A follow-up study," *Journal of the American Academy of Child & Adolescent Psychiatry* 36 (1997); Yolanda L. Smith, Stephanie H. van Goozen, and Peggy T. Cohen-Kettenis, "Adolescents with gender identity disorder who were accepted or rejected for sex reassignment surgery: A prospective follow-up study," *Journal of the American Academy of Child & Adolescent Psychiatry* 40 (2001); and Yolanda L. Smith et al., "Sex reassignment: Outcomes and predictors of treatment for

adolescent and adult transsexuals," *Psychological Medicine* 35 (2005). For a handy summary of this work, see Peggy Cohen-Kettenis, H. A. Delemarre–van de Waal, and L. J. Gooren, "The treatment of adolescent transsexuals: Changing insights," *Journal of Sexual Medicine* 5, no. 8 (August 2008).

622 UK policy on hormone-blocking therapy is discussed in Simona Giordano, "Lives in a chiaroscuro: Should we suspend the puberty of children with gender identity disorder?," *Journal of Medical Ethics* 34, no. 8 (August 2008); Naomi Coleman, "Boys will be girls," *Guardian*, August 20, 2003; and Viv Groskop, "My body is wrong," *Guardian*, August 14, 2008.

622 Domenico Di Ceglie reports that 20 percent of his patients choose not to complete gender reassignment in Lauren Smiley, "Girl/boy interrupted," *SF Weekly*, July 11, 2007.

622 All quotations from Shannon Minter come from my interview with him in 2009 and subsequent communications.

623 This passage is based on my interview with Jennifer Finney Boylan and Hildegarde Boylan in 2007. I have, additionally, drawn some passages from Jennifer Finney Boylan, *She's Not There: A Life in Two Genders* (2003).

625 Alice Domurat Dreger's lament about early transition and sex-role rigidity comes from her article "Trans advocates (at least where genderqueer kids are concerned)," *Stranger (The Queer Issue: You're Doing It Wrong)*, June 21, 2011.

626 The quotation from Just Evelyn ("I knew his life would be difficult and sad . . .") occurs on page 6 of her book, *Mom, I Need to Be a Girl* (1998).

626 The quotation from Aleshia Brevard ("I consciously tried to create a boy child . . .") occurs in her 2001 essay, "The woman I was not born to be," on pages 242–43 of *Sexual Metamorphosis: An Anthology of Transsexual Memoirs*, edited by Jonathan Ames (2005).

626 Cris Beam's account of "Ariel" occurs on page 77 of *Transparent: Love, Family, and Living the T with Transgendered Teenagers* (2007).

626 This passage is based on my interview with Hendrik and Alexia Koos in 2009. All names in this passage are pseudonyms.

627 This passage is based on my interview with Rex and Karen Butt and Cadence Case in 2009, and subsequent communications.

629 This passage is based on my interviews with Jonah and Lily Marx in 2008 and 2009. All names in this passage are pseudonyms and some identifying details have been changed.

631 See the American Psychiatric Association's 2000 "Position statement on therapies focused on attempts to change sexual orientation (reparative or conversion therapies)." See also the American Psychological Association Task Force on Appropriate Therapeutic Responses to Sexual Orientation August 2009 press release, "Insufficient evidence that sexual orientation change efforts work." For the "heated debate" about reparative therapy for trans people, see the next note.

631 Kenneth Zucker's publications include: Kenneth J. Zucker and Susan J. Bradley, *Gender Identity Disorder and Psychosexual Problems in Children and Adolescents* (1995); Susan J. Bradley and Kenneth J. Zucker, "Gender identity disorder: A review of the past 10 years," *Journal of the Academy of Child & Adolescent Psychiatry* 36, no. 7 (July 1997); and Susan J. Bradley and Kenneth J. Zucker, "Children with gender nonconformity: Drs. Bradley and Zucker reply," *Journal of the American Academy of Child & Adolescent Psychiatry* 42, no. 3 (March 2003). For journalistic coverage of Zucker's work, see Alix Spiegel, "Q&A: Therapists on gender identity issues in kids," NPR broadcast, May 7, 2008; and Daniel Goleman, "The wrong

sex: A new definition of childhood pain," *New York Times*, March 22, 1994. Exemplifying criticism of Zucker's position are Simon D. Pickstone-Taylor's letter "Children with gender nonconformity," *Journal of the American Academy of Child & Adolescent Psychiatry* 42, no. 4 (March 2003); Y. Gavriel Ansara and Peter Hegarty, "Cisgenderism in psychology: Pathologising and misgendering children from 1999 to 2008," *Psychology & Sexuality* 2 (2011); and Stephanie Wilkinson, "Drop the Barbie! If you bend gender far enough, does it break?," *Brain, Child: The Magazine for Thinking Mothers* (Fall 2001).

631 Organizational websites: NARTH (National Association for Research and Therapy of Homosexuality), http://www.narth.com/; Catholic Education Resource Center, http://www.catholiceducation.org/. Works published and promoted by CERC and NARTH principals that cite to Zucker's work include Richard Fitzgibbons Jr. and Joseph Nicolosi, "When boys won't be boys: Childhood gender identity disorder," *Lay Witness* (June 2001); Joseph Nicolosi and Linda Ames Nicolosi, *A Parent's Guide to Preventing Homosexuality* (2002); and A. Dean Byrd and the NARTH Scientific Advisory Committee, "Gender identity disorders in childhood and adolescence: A critical inquiry and review of the Kenneth Zucker research" (March 2007). Proponents of reparative therapy also include orthodox Jews, e.g., Susan L. Rosenbluth, "Help for Jewish homosexuals that is consistent with Torah principles," *Jewish Voice & Opinion* 13, no. 4 (December 1999).

631 The mother's description of her experience implementing reparative therapy comes from Alix Spiegel's NPR report "Two families grapple with sons' gender preferences: Psychologists take radically different approaches in therapy," *All Things Considered*, May 7, 2008.

631 For the follow-up study of patients at Zucker's clinic, see Kelley D. Drummond et al., "A follow-up study of girls with gender identity disorder," *Developmental Psychology* 44, no. 1 (January 2008).

632 The mother who doubted that her adult daughter would outlive her is profiled in Hanna Rosin, "A boy's life," *Atlantic Monthly*, November 2008. Rosin reports Zucker's comparison of "young children who believe they are meant to live as the other sex to people who want to amputate healthy limbs, or who believe they are cats, or those with something called ethnic-identity disorder. 'If a five-year-old black kid came into the clinic and said he wanted to be white, would we endorse that?' he told me. 'I don't think so. What we would want to do is say, "What's going on with this kid that's making him feel that it would be better to be white?"'"

632 Zucker's characterization of transgender children as rigid and joyless is quoted in Stephanie Wilkinson, "Drop the Barbie! If you bend gender far enough, does it break?," *Brain, Child: The Magazine for Thinking Mothers* (Fall 2001).

632 Zucker's characterization of belief in the immutability of gender dysphoria as "simple-minded biological reductionism" occurs on page 267 of Susan J. Bradley and Kenneth J. Zucker, "Children with gender nonconformity: Drs. Bradley and Zucker reply," *Journal of the American Academy of Child & Adolescent Psychiatry* 42, no. 3 (March 2003); and as "liberal essentialism" in Alix Spiegel's May 7, 2008, NPR report, "Q&A: Therapists on gender identity issues in kids."

632 Susan Coates's observations about creativity and anxiety in gender-dysphoric youth come from my interview with her in 2008 and subsequent communications.

633 This passage is based on my interview with Dolores Martinez and Tyler Holmes in 2009 and subsequent communications. All names in this passage are pseudonyms.

635 Amy Bloom discusses the contribution of parents to cross-gender identification on page 38 of *Normal: Transsexual CEOs, Crossdressing Cops, and Hermaphrodites with Attitude* (2002).

635 Heino Meyer-Bahlburg contends that GID cannot be categorized "on a purely scientific basis" on page 461 of his article "From mental disorder to iatrogenic hypogonadism: Dilemmas in conceptualizing gender identity variants as psychiatric conditions," *Archives of Sexual Behavior* 39, no. 2 (April 2010).

636 All quotations from Edgardo Menvielle come from my interview with him in 2009 unless otherwise specified.

636 The finding of a 1 percent rate of post-transition dissatisfaction is reported on page 211 of Mildred L. Brown and Chloe Ann Rounsley, *True Selves: Understanding Transsexualism* (1996).

636 Danielle Berry expresses her regret about her "jump off the precipice" in Lynn Conway, "A warning for those considering MtF sex reassignment surgery (SRS)" (2005, revised 2007), at http://ai.eecs.umich.edu/people/conway/TS/Warning.html.

636 The quotation from Sam Hashimi comes from Helen Weathers, "A British tycoon and father of two has been a man and a woman . . . and a man again . . . and knows which sex he'd rather be," *Daily Mail Online*, January 4, 2009.

637 All quotations and anecdotes from Kim Pearson come from my interviews with her between 2007 and 2012.

637 This passage is based on my interviews with Scott Earle, Lynn Luginbuhl, Morris Earle, and Charlie Earle in 2007 and 2008. Though Lynn and Morris were happy to be quoted by name, Scott asked me to use a pseudonym, which I have done; Charlie's name is also a pseudonym.

639 For more on gayness among trans people, see Autumn Sandeen, who said on KRXQ on June 11, 2009, that "fifty-three percent of transgender women identify as lesbian or bisexual, and ten to thirty percent of transmen are gay." For their book in development, *Understanding Transgender Lives*, Brett Genny Beemyn and Sue Rankin at http://www.umass.edu/stonewall/uploads/listWidget/9002/Understanding%20Transgender%20Lives.pdf describe a survey in which "one third of respondents (32%, n = 1,120) reported that their sexual orientation is bisexual, and 30% (n = 1,029) identified as heterosexual. Sixteen percent (n = 567) identified 'Other,' which include but are not limited to 'a mix of asexual, gay, and heterosexual,' 'ambivalent,' 'attracted to genderqueer people,' 'autobisexual,' 'bisexual when dressed in female clothes otherwise heterosexual,' 'pansexual,' 'queer,' and 'transgender lesbian.' Twelve percent identified as lesbian, four percent identified as gay, and five percent identified as asexual. One percent of respondents (n = 26) did not respond to the question."

641 This passage is based on my interview with Kim, John, and Shawn Pearson in 2007 and subsequent communications.

644 This passage is based on my interview with Shannon and Keely Garcia in 2009 and subsequent communications.

645 According to a 2011 survey sponsored by the National Center for Transgender Equality and the National Gay and Lesbian Task Force, "Fifty-seven percent (57%) faced some rejection by their family and 43% were accepted"; see page 101 of Jaime M. Grant et al., *Injustice at Every Turn* (2011).

645 Cris Beam's description of the mother's wish that her transgender child would die of AIDS occurs on page 36 of *Transparent: Love, Family, and Living the T with Transgendered Teenagers* (2007).

645 The excerpt from the outraged mother's letter to her transgender child is taken from pages 175–76 of Mildred L. Brown and Chloe Ann Rounsley, *True Selves* (1996).

646 The transphobic drive-time shock-jock harangue and its aftermath was chronicled in the *Sacramento Bee*; see Carlos Alcalá, "Radio segment on transgender kids raises hackles," *21Q: A Bee Entertainment Blog*, June 2, 2009; Carlos Alcalá, "Under fire, radio host says transgender comments were 'a joke,'" *Sacramento Bee*, June 4, 2009 (source of quotations from the show); Matthew Keys, "Local radio show takes heat, loses advertisers over transgender comments," *Sacramento Press*, June 5, 2009; Bill Lindelof, "Transgender controversy," *Sacramento Bee*, June 9, 2009; Carlos Alcalá, "On-air controversy: Radio show back today with transgender advocates," *Sacramento Bee*, June 11, 2009; and Bill Lindelof, "Broadcasters apologize on air for transgender remarks," *Sacramento Bee*, June 12, 2009.

646 This passage is based on my interview with Hailey Krueger and Jane Ritter in 2009. All names in this passage are pseudonyms.

650 See the National Center for Transgender Equality and the National Gay and Lesbian Task Force study *Injustice at Every Turn: A Report of the National Transgender Discrimination Survey* (2011); and for similar findings among youth, Michael Bochenek and A. Widney Brown's report for Human Rights Watch, *Hatred in the Hallways: Violence and Discrimination against Lesbian, Gay, Bisexual, and Transgender Students in U.S. Schools* (2001).

650 Statistics on homelessness and prostitution among transgender youth come from Nicholas Ray's 2007 report to the National Gay & Lesbian Task Force, "Lesbian, gay, bisexual and transgender youth: An epidemic of homelessness"; and David Kihara, "Giuliani's suppressed report on homeless youth," *Village Voice*, August 24, 1999.

650 The quotation from the transgender sex worker ("I like the attention; it makes me feel loved") comes from Corey Kilgannon, "After working the streets, bunk beds and a Mass," *New York Times*, May 2, 2007.

650 This passage is based on my interview with Albert Cannon, Roxanne Green, and Dante Haynes in 2009.

652 Teish Green's murder and Dwight DeLee's trial were thoroughly chronicled by the *Syracuse Post-Standard*; for an index of all coverage, search http://www.syracuse.com for *Moses Cannon*. Articles consulted for this passage include Matt Michael, "Syracuse man was killed for being gay, police say," *Syracuse Post-Standard*, November 16, 2008; Jim O'Hara, "Syracuse man indicted on hate-crime murder charge," *Syracuse Post-Standard*, April 3, 2009; and Jim O'Hara, "Dwight DeLee gets the maximum in transgender slaying," *Syracuse Post-Standard*, August 18, 2009.

653 The quotation from Michael Silverman about Dwight DeLee's trial comes from my interview with him in 2009.

653 Statistics on murders of transgender people come from Gwendolyn Ann Smith's informational website, Remembering Our Dead, http://www.gender.org/remember. For discussion of proposals to extend hate-crime protection to transgender people, see David Stout, "House votes to expand hate-crime protection," *New York Times*, May 4, 2007. See also http://www.transgenderdor.org/.

654 Carsten Balzer refers to the international incidence of murder of transgender people, and the frequent murder of minors, on pages 156–57 of his report "Preliminary results of Trans Murder Monitoring Project," *Liminalis* 3 (July 2009); on page 157, Balzer cites Thomas Hammarberg's account of the

Portuguese incident in "Discrimination against transgender persons must no longer be tolerated," Office of the Commissioner for Human Rights, 2009.

654 Contemporary news reports on murders of transgender people: Krissy Bates: Abby Simons, "'The killing of one of our own,'" *Minneapolis Star Tribune*, January 22, 2011; and Abby Simons, "Man guilty of murdering transgender victim," *Minneapolis Star Tribune*, November 24, 2011. Tyra Trent: Jessica Anderson, "Vigil remembers transgender murder victim," *Sun*, March 5, 2011. Marcal Camero Tye: Jeannie Nuiss, "FBI may investigate dragging death as hate crime," *Commercial Appeal*, March 20, 2011. Nate Nate: Dale Lezon, "HPD releases suspect sketch in cross-dresser's killing," *Houston Chronicle*, June 14, 2011. Lashai Mclean: Pat Collins, "Transgender person slain in northeast," *NBC Washington*, July 21, 2011. Camila Guzman: Steven Thrasher, "Camila Guzman, transgender murder victim, remembered in East Harlem vigil," *Village Voice*, August 12, 2011. Gaurav Gopalan: Trey Graham, "The final days of Gaurav Gopalan," *Washington City Paper*, September 21, 2011. Shelley Hilliard: Gina Damron, "Mom waits for answers in transgender teen's death," *Detroit Free Press*, November 12, 2011.

654 This passage is based on my interview with Anne O'Hara, Marshall Camacho, Glenn Stevens, and Kerry Adahy in 2009. All names in this passage are pseudonyms.

659 The quotation from Judith Butler ("One might wonder what use 'opening up the possibilities' finally is . . .") occurs on page viii of the revised edition of her book *Gender Trouble: Feminism and the Subversion of Identity* (1999).

660 This passage is based on my interview with Bridget and Matt McCourt in 2009. All names in this passage are pseudonyms.

661 This passage is based on my interview with Nicole, Ben, and Anneke Osman in 2009.

662 This passage is based on my interview with Vicky Pearsall in 2007 and subsequent communications. All names in this passage are pseudonyms.

663 Emmy Werner's comment about children who are gender-flexible comes from an interview with Robin Hughes on the episode "Resilience" of the Australian radio show *Open Mind*, broadcast April 29, 1996.

663 The quotations from Renée Richards disapproving of gender fluidity come from Debra Rosenberg, "Rethinking gender," *Newsweek*, May 21, 2007; and Maureen Dowd, "Between torment and happiness," *New York Times*, April 26, 2011.

664 Justin Vivian Bond's remark about "nurturing your nature" comes from Mike Albo, "The official Justin Bond," *Out*, April 11, 2011.

664 This passage is based on my interview with Eli, Joanna, and Kate Rood in 2007 and subsequent communications, as well as Eli's blog at http://translocative .blogspot.com/.

666 The quotation from Kate Rood ("Eli is soon to be rendered infertile . . .") comes from her article "The sea horse: Our family mascot," *New York Times*, November 2, 2008.

666 The closing quotation from Eli Rood comes from his essay "Not quite a beginning," *Eli's Coming*, February 3, 2006, http://translocative.blogspot .com/2006/02/not-quite-beginning.html.

666 See David Smith, "Gender row athlete Caster Semenya wanted to boycott medal ceremony," *Guardian*, August 21, 2009.

666 IOC Medical Commission chairman Arne Ljungqvist admitted, "There is no scientifically sound lab-based technique that can differentiate between man and woman," in Debra Rosenberg, "Rethinking gender," *Newsweek*, May 21, 2007.

666 Caster Semenya declared, "I accept myself," in the cover story of a September 2009 issue of the South African magazine *YOU*, as reported in the *Independent Online*, September 8, 2009.

667 This passage is based on my interview with Shannon Minter in 2009.

667 The full text of the decision in the case, *In re the marriage of Michael J. Kantaras v. Linda Kantaras* (Case 98-5375CA, Circuit Court of the Sixth Judicial Circuit in and for Pasco County, Florida, February 2003), is available online at http://www .transgenderlaw.org/cases/kantarasopinion.pdf; the quotation from the judge ("Transsexualism is a massively complex and difficult problem deserving of the highest respect and sympathy . . .") occurs on page 774.

668 Genesis 5:2: "Male and female he created them."

668 This passage is based on my interviews with Carol McKerrow, Don Harriot, Kim Reed, and other members of their families in 2009 and subsequent interviews and communications, as well as Kim's film *Prodigal Sons* (2009) and Kim and Carol's appearance on *Oprah* in 2010.

672 See Martin J. Kidston, "Helena prodigal son returning as woman," *Independent Record*, September 24, 2009; see also Kidston's report on the film showing two days later, "250 pack church for transgender documentary," *Independent Record*, September 26, 2009.

674 The lines by Alfred, Lord Tennyson come from "In memoriam A.H.H." (1849), on page 155 of *The Complete Works of Alfred Lord Tennyson* (1891).

675 My book about Russian art is *The Irony Tower: Soviet Artists in a Time of Glasnost* (1991).

XII: Father

679 The quotations from Bree Walker and the talk-show hosts ("It was shocking to me . . ." and "Is it fair . . .") come from Daniel Corone, "Bree Walker blasts KFI's *Baby Talk*," *Los Angeles Times*, August 17, 1991.

679 The second quotation from Bree Walker ("I felt that my pregnancy had been terrorized . . .") comes from Steven A. Holmes, "Radio talk about TV anchor's disability stirs ire in Los Angeles," *New York Times*, August 23, 1991; the third and fourth ("The darkest moment of my life" and "Tossed the coin . . .") come from her interview with ABC News, "Medical mystery: Ectrodactyly," broadcast on January 29, 2007.

679 The quotation from Bill Holt ("For anyone to determine that Bree Walker should not have children . . .") comes from Daniel Corone, "Bree Walker blasts KFI's *Baby Talk*," *Los Angeles Times*, August 17, 1991.

679 All quotations from Joanna Karpasea-Jones come from her article "Daring disabled parenting," *Mothering*, November–December 2007.

680 The quotation from Adrienne Asch ("Chronic illness and disability are not equivalent to acute illness or sudden injury . . .") comes from pages 1650–51 of her article "Prenatal diagnosis and selective abortion: A challenge to practice and policy," *American Journal of Public Health* 89, no. 11 (November 1999). It has been condensed.

680 See Laura Rothenberg, *Breathing for a Living* (2004), and my article "The Amazing Life of Laura," *Glamour*, July 2003.

681 The reference to "made-to-order babies" comes from Lindsey Tanner, "Physicians could make the perfect imperfect baby," *Los Angeles Times*, December 31, 2006.

681 For the survey finding that 3 percent of PGD clinics have selected *for* disability,

see Susannah Baruch, David Kaufman, and Kathy L. Hudson, "Genetic testing of embryos: Practices and perspectives of US in vitro fertilization clinics," *Fertility & Sterility* 89, no. 5 (May 2008).

681 Robert J. Stillman's comment (". . . Dwarfism and deafness are not the norm") occurs in Darshak Sanghavi, "Wanting babies like themselves, some parents choose genetic defects," *New York Times*, December 5, 2006.

681 The quotation from Michael Bérubé ("The question is whether we will maintain a social system that makes allowance for unpredictability . . .") occurs on page 86 of his memoir, *Life as We Know It: A Father, a Family and an Exceptional Child* (1996).

681 The Human Fertilisation and Embryology Act 2008 represented an amendment and updating of legislation enacted in 1990; for the full text, see http://www .legislation.gov.uk/ukpga/2008/22/contents. The controversy over its provisions pertaining to disability was described in Steven D. Emery, Anna Middleton, and Graham H. Turner, "Whose deaf genes are they anyway?: The Deaf community's challenge to legislation on embryo selection," *Sign Language Studies* 10, no. 2 (Winter 2010). The comment by pseudonymous blogger Mishka Zena comes from the post "Eugenics too close to home: Tomato Lichy, U.K. activist," *Endless Pondering*, March 10, 2008, at http://www.mishkazena.com/2008/03/10/eugenics -too-close-to-home-tomato-livy-uk-activist.

682 Sharon Duchesneau and Candace McCullough tell their story in Liz Mundy, "A world of their own," *Washington Post Magazine*, March 31, 2002. For a scholarly article about this case, see Humphrey-Dirksen Bauman, "Designing deaf babies and the question of disability," *Journal of Deaf Studies & Deaf Education* 10, no. 3 (Summer 2005).

682 See Wendy McElroy, "Victims from birth: Engineering defects in helpless children crosses the line," FOX News, April 9, 2002.

682 John Sproston's letter to the editor expressing dismay at Sharon Duchesneau and Candace McCullough's desire to give birth to a deaf child ("That three people could deliberately deprive another person of a natural faculty . . .") was published in the *Washington Post* on June 9, 2004, and is quoted in Judith F. Daar, "ART and the search for perfectionism: On selecting gender, genes, and gametes," *Journal of Gender, Race and Justice* 9, no. 2 (Winter 2005).

682 The quotation from John Corvino ("They could have chosen a different donor . . .") comes from his article "Why Baby Gauvin is not a victim," *Gay & Lesbian Review Worldwide* 9, no. 6 (2002).

682 Patrick Boudreault's comment ("No one is talking, ever, about deliberately deafening a child born hearing") comes from a personal communication in 2008.

683 Sean Tipton's comment about the usual desire of parents to bring forth children who resemble them, and Sharon's and Candy's replies, come from Liza Mundy, "A world of their own," *Washington Post Magazine*, March 31, 2002.

683 Carina Dennis's observation ("Communication and the pursuit of intimacy are central to being human . . .") occurs on page 894 of her article "Genetics: Deaf by design," *Nature* 431 (October 21, 2004).

683 See William Saletan, "Deformer babies: The deliberate crippling of children," *Slate*, September 21, 2006.

683 The Johns Hopkins survey of PGD clinics is described in Susannah Baruch, David Kaufman, and Kathy L. Hudson, "Genetic testing of embryos: Practices and perspectives of US *in vitro* fertilization clinics," *Fertility & Sterility* 89, no. 5 (May 2008).

683 See Gautam Naik, "A baby, please. Blond, freckles, hold the colic: Laboratory techniques that screen for diseases in embryos are now being offered to create designer children," *Wall Street Journal*, February 12, 2009.

683 See the University College London press release "First baby tested for breast cancer form BRCA1 before conception born in U.K.," January 9, 2009; and the CNN report "'Cancer-free' baby born in London," broadcast January 9, 2009.

683 The Los Angeles Fertility Institutes' plans to offer selection for gender, hair, and eye color were described in Gautam Naik, "A baby, please. Blond, freckles, hold the colic: Laboratory techniques that screen for diseases in embryos are now being offered to create designer children," *Wall Street Journal*, February 12, 2009.

684 Results of the Johns Hopkins survey of public opinion regarding genetic testing are reported in Aravinda Chakravarti et al., *Reproductive Genetic Testing: What America Thinks* (2004).

684 See Michael J. Sandel, *The Case Against Perfection* (2007).

684 The quotation from Marc Lappé ("It would be unthinkable and immoral . . .") comes from his pioneering paper on genetic selection, "How much do we want to know about the unborn?," *Hastings Center Report* 3, no. 1 (February 1973).

684 Patricia Bauer's observation that "prenatal testing is making your right to abort a disabled child more like your duty to abort a disabled child" comes from her article "The abortion debate no one wants to have," *Washington Post*, October 18, 2005.

685 The statement "American mobility is exceptional; where we stand out is our limited mobility from the bottom" comes from Scott Winship, "Mobility impaired," *National Review*, November 14, 2011.

686 See Gurinder Osan, "Baby with two faces born in North India," Associated Press/MSNBC, April 9, 2008. All quotations come from this report.

686 Lali's death from a heart attack was reported on the BBC Channel 4 program *Body Shock*, broadcast September 16, 2008.

687 New Haven's arboreal tragedy and the city's recovery efforts are described in Charlotte Libov, "New Haven holding on to 'Elm City' nickname," *New York Times*, April 24, 1988; Bruce Fellman, "The Elm City: Then and now," *Yale Alumni Magazine*, September/October 2006; and David K. Leff, "Remaining elms hint at tree's elegant past," *Hartford Courant*, October 27, 2011.

688 Our journey and that of other gay parents who seek to create a family through assisted reproductive technology is described in Emma Brockes, "Gay parenting: It's complicated," *Guardian*, April 20, 2012. I wrote about our experiences in "Meet my real modern family," *Newsweek*, January 30, 2011.

698 Roger Penrose discusses the anthropic principle on pages 433–34 of *The Emperor's New Mind: Concerning Computers, Minds, and the Laws of Physics* (1989).

701 The quotation from William Dean Howells ("what the American public always wants is a tragedy with a happy ending") occurs on page 147 of Edith Wharton's autobiography, *A Backward Glance* (1934).

701 Compare, for example, the insight-oriented approach advocated by psychologists such as Erik H. Erikson (see his 1959 anthology, *Identity and the Life Cycle*) with the cognitive techniques described by Martin Seligman in *Learned Optimism* (1991).

Bibliography

This bibliography catalogs all sources to which direct citations have been made. Other references influenced my thinking and helped me to understand my subject more clearly, and researchers who assisted me used yet others in compiling notes. A complete bibliography that includes all such titles may be found online at http://www.andrew solomon.com/far-from-the-tree/bibliography.

Abbott, Douglas A., and William H. Meredith. "Strengths of parents with retarded children." *Family Relations* 35, no. 3 (July 1986): 371–75.

Abbott, Jack Henry. *In the Belly of the Beast: Letters from Prison*. New York: Random House, 1981.

Abi-Dargham, Anissa, and Holly Moore. "Prefrontal DA transmission at D1 receptors and the pathology of schizophrenia." *Neuroscientist* 9, no. 5 (2003).

Abi-Dargham, Anissa, et al. "Increased baseline occupancy of D2 receptors by dopamine in schizophrenia." *Proceedings of the National Academy of Sciences* 97, no. 14 (July 2000): 8104–9.

Ablon, Joan. "Dwarfism and social identity: Self-help group participation." *Social Science & Medicine* 15B (1981): 25–30.

———. *Little People in America: The Social Dimension of Dwarfism*. New York: Praeger, 1984.

———. *Living with Difference: Families with Dwarf Children*. New York: Praeger, 1988.

———. "Personality and stereotype in osteogenesis imperfecta: Behavioral phenotype or response to life's hard challenges?" *American Journal of Medical Genetics* 122A (October 15, 2003): 201–14.

Abraham, Willard. *Barbara: A Prologue*. New York: Rinehart, 1958.

Abrahams, Brett S., and Daniel H. Geschwind. "Advances in autism genetics: On the threshold of a new neurobiology." *Nature Review Genetics* 9, no. 5 (May 2008): 341–55.

Abramsky, Sasha, and Jamie Fellner. *Ill-Equipped: U.S. Prisons and Offenders with Mental Illness*. New York: Human Rights Watch, 2003.

Accardo, Pasquale J., Christy Magnusen, and Arnold J. Capute, eds. *Autism: Clinical and Research Issues*. Baltimore: York Press, 2000.

Adelson, Betty M. *Dwarfism: Medical and Psychosocial Aspects of Profound Short Stature*. Baltimore: Johns Hopkins University Press, 2005.

———. *The Lives of Dwarfs: Their Journey from Public Curiosity Toward Social Liberation*. New Brunswick, NJ: Rutgers University Press, 2005.

Adelson, Betty, and Joe Stramondo. Unpublished letter to the editor of the *New York Times*, 2005.

Adoption.com Forums. "Children born of rape." Public discussion. Mesa, AZ: Adoption Media, 2004–06.

Advanced Bionics. "The Reason to Choose AB." Valencia, CA: Advanced Bionics, 2009.

———. "Hear Your Best." Valencia, CA: Advanced Bionics, 2011.

Advertising Standards Authority. "ASA adjudication on the Option Institute and Fellowship." Complaint Reference 104067. London: Advertising Standards Authority, March 3, 2010.

Affleck, Glenn, and Howard Tennen. "Appraisal and coping predictors of mother and child outcomes after newborn intensive care." *Journal of Social & Clinical Psychology* 10, no. 4 (1991): 424–47.

Affleck, Glenn, Howard Tennen, and Jonelle Rowe, eds. *Infants in Crisis: How Parents Cope with Newborn Intensive Care and Its Aftermath*. New York: Springer, 1991.

African Commission on Human and Peoples' Rights International Work Group for Indigenous Affairs. *Report of the African Commission's Working Group on Indigenous Populations/Communities: Research and Information Visit to the Republic of Gabon, 15–30 September 2007*. Copenhagen: International Work Group for Indigenous Affairs, 2010.

Agnew, Robert, and Sandra Huguley. "Adolescent violence toward parents." *Journal of Marriage & the Family* 51, no. 3 (August 1989): 699–711.

Akter, K., et al. "A review of the possible role of the essential fatty acids and fish oils in the aetiology, prevention or pharmacotherapy of schizophrenia." *Journal of Clinical Pharmacy & Therapeutics* 37, no. 2 (April 2012): 132–39.

Alatzoglou, Kyriaki S., and Mehul T. Dattani. "Genetic causes and treatment of isolated growth hormone deficiency: An update." *Nature Reviews Endocrinology* 6, no. 10 (October 2010): 562–76.

Albo, Mike. "The official Justin Bond." *Out*, April 11, 2011.

Alcalá, Carlos. "Radio segment on transgender kids raises hackles." *21Q: A Bee Entertainment Blog*, June 2, 2009. http://www.sacbee.com/static/weblogs/ticket/archives/2009/06/radio-segment-o.html.

———. "Under fire, radio host says transgender comments were 'a joke.'" *Sacramento Bee*, June 4, 2009.

———. "On-air controversy: Radio show back today with transgender advocates." *Sacramento Bee*, June 11, 2009.

Alexander Graham Bell Association. "The cost of cochlear implants." Washington, DC: Alexander Graham Bell Association, 2011. http://nc.agbell.org/page.aspx?pid=723.

Alisky, Joseph M., and Kenneth A. Iczkowski. "Barriers to housing for deinstitutionalized psychiatric patients." *Hospital & Community Psychiatry* 41, no. 1 (January 1990): 93–95.

Allan, Clare. "Misplaced pride." *Guardian*, September 27, 2006.

Allanson, Judith E., and Judith G. Hall. "Obstetric and gynecologic problems in women with chondrodystrophies." *Obstetrics & Gynecology* 67, no. 1 (January 1986): 74–78.

Allday, Erin. "UCSF, Stanford autism study shows surprises." *San Francisco Chronicle*, July 5, 2011.

Allen, Ann Taylor. "The kindergarten in Germany and the United States, 1840–1914: A comparative perspective." *History of Education* 35, no. 2 (March 2006): 173–88.

Allen, Arthur. "Sound and fury." *Salon*, May 24, 2000. http://www.salon.com/health/feature/2000/05/24/cochlear.

Allen, Woody. *The Complete Prose of Woody Allen*. New York: Random House, 1991.

Allison, Rebecca. "Does a cleft palate justify an abortion? Curate wins right to challenge doctors." *Guardian*, December 2, 2003.

Allport, Susan. *A Natural History of Parenting: A Naturalist Looks at Parenting in the Animal World and Ours*. New York: Three Rivers Press, 1997.

Amador, Xavier Francisco. *I Am Not Sick, I Don't Need Help! How to Help Someone with Mental Illness Accept Treatment*. Peconic, NY: Vida Press, 2007.

American Academy of Pediatrics Policy Committee on Children with Disabilities. "Auditory integration training and facilitated communication for autism." *AAP Policy Committee on Children with Disabilities* 102, no. 2 (1998): 431–33.

American College of Obstetricians and Gynecologists. "New recommendations for Down syndrome: Screening should be offered to all pregnant women." Press release. Washington, DC: American College of Obstetricians and Gynecologists, January 2, 2007.

———. "Screening for fetal chromosomal abnormalities." *ACOG Practice Bulletin* 77 (January 2007): 1–11.

American Medical Association. "Pregnancy from rape does not justify abortion." *Journal of the American Medical Association* 43 (August 6, 1904): 413.

———. "AMA policy regarding sexual orientation." Chicago: American Medical Association, 2007.

American Psychiatric Association. "Position statement on therapies focused on attempts to change sexual orientation (reparative or conversion therapies)." Washington, DC: American Psychiatric Association, 2000.

American Psychological Association Task Force on Appropriate Therapeutic Responses to Sexual Orientation. "Insufficient evidence that sexual orientation change efforts work, says APA." Press release. Washington, DC: American Psychological Association, August 5, 2009.

Ames, Jonathan, ed. *Sexual Metamorphosis: An Anthology of Transsexual Memoirs*. New York: Vintage, 2005.

Amir, Menachem. *Patterns in Forcible Rape*. Chicago: University of Chicago Press, 1971.

Amnesty International. "Liberia: No impunity for rape." New York: Amnesty International, 2004.

Anderson, Jenny. "Fidelity is fined $8 million over improper gifts." *New York Times*, March 6, 2008.

Anderson, Jessica. "Vigil remembers transgender murder victim." *Sun*, March 5, 2011.

Ando, Yoichi, and Hiroaki Hattori. "Effects of intense noise during fetal life upon postnatal adaptability (statistical study of the reactions of babies to aircraft noise)." *Journal of the Acoustical Society of America* 47, no. 4, pt. 2 (1970): 1128–30.

Andreasen, Nancy C. "Schizophrenia: The characteristic symptoms." *Schizophrenia Bulletin* 17, no. 1 (1991): 27–49.

———. *Brave New Brain: Conquering Mental Illness in the Era of the Genome*. Oxford and New York: Oxford University Press, 2001.

———. *The Creating Brain: The Neuroscience of Genius*. New York: Dana Press, 2005.

Andrews, Nigel. "Glowing wonder of an Anatolian epiphany." *Financial Times*, March 15, 2012.

Andrews, Suzanna. "Arthur Miller's missing act." *Vanity Fair*, September 2007.

Angier, Natalie. "Short men, short shrift: Are drugs the answer?" *New York Times*, June 22, 2003.

BIBLIOGRAPHY

Ani, Cornelius, Sally Grantham-McGregor, and David Muller. "Nutritional supplementation in Down syndrome: Theoretical considerations and current status." *Developmental Medicine & Child Neurology* 42, no. 3 (March 2000): 207–13.

Anonymous parents of Ashley X. "The 'Ashley treatment.'" Blog. Established January 2, 2007; last updated May 18, 2008. http://ashleytreatment.spaces.live.com.

Ansara, Y. Gavriel, and Peter Hegarty. "Cisgenderism in psychology: Pathologising and misgendering children from 1999 to 2008." *Psychology & Sexuality* 2 (2011): 1–24.

Ansberry, Clare. "Parents devoted to a disabled child confront old age." *Wall Street Journal*, January 7, 2004.

Antonovsky, Aaron. *Health, Stress, and Coping*. San Francisco: Jossey-Bass, 1980.

Apajasalo, M., et al. "Health-related quality of life of patients with genetic skeletal dysplasias." *European Journal of Pediatrics* 157, no. 2 (February 1998): 114–21.

Applebaum, Samuel. *The Way They Play*. Neptune, NJ: Paganiniana Publications, 1984.

Arana-Ward, Marie. "As technology advances, a bitter debate divides the deaf." *Washington Post*, May 11, 1997.

Arguello, P. Alexander, and Joseph A. Gogos. "Cognition in mouse models of schizophrenia susceptibility genes." *Schizophrenia Bulletin* 36, no. 2 (March 2010): 289–300.

Arisi, Elena, et al. "Cochlear implantation in adolescents with prelinguistic deafness." *Archives of Otolaryngology—Head & Neck Surgery* 142, no. 6 (June 2010): 804–8.

Aristotle, and Jonathan Barnes, ed. *The Complete Works of Aristotle: The Revised Oxford Translation*. Oxford and New York: Oxford University Press, 1984.

———. *The New Aristotle Reader*. Princeton, NJ: Princeton University Press, 1987.

Arndt, Tara L., Christopher J. Stodgell, and Patricia M. Rodier. "The teratology of autism." *International Journal of Developmental Neuroscience* 23, nos. 2–3 (April–May 2005): 189–99.

Arnone, Danilo, et al. "Magnetic resonance imaging studies in bipolar disorder and schizophrenia: Meta-analysis." *British Journal of Psychiatry* 195, no. 3 (September 2009): 194–201.

Arnos, S. Kathleen, et al. "A comparative analysis of the genetic epidemiology of deafness in the United States in two sets of pedigrees collected more than a century apart." *American Journal of Human Genetics* 83, no. 2 (August 2008): 200–207.

Arthur, Joyce. "Psychological aftereffects of abortion: The rest of the story." *Humanist* 57, no. 2 (March–April 1997): 7–9.

Asarnow, Robert F., and Joan Rosenbaum Asarnow. "Childhood-onset schizophrenia: Editors' introduction." *Schizophrenia Bulletin* 20, no. 4 (October 1994): 591–97.

Asch, Adrienne. "Prenatal diagnosis and selective abortion: A challenge to practice and policy." *American Journal of Public Health* 89, no. 11 (November 1999): 1649–57.

———. "Disability equality and prenatal testing: Contradictory or compatible?" *Florida State University Law Review* 30, no. 2 (Winter 2003): 315–42.

Ashliman, D. L. "Changelings." *Folklore & Mythology Electronic Texts*. University of Pittsburgh, 1997. http://www.pitt.edu/~dash/changeling.html.

Asperger, Hans. "'Autistic psychopathy' in childhood." Trans. Uta Frith. In *Autism and Asperger Syndrome*, ed. Uta Frith, 37–92. Cambridge: Cambridge University Press, 1991.

Atkinson, Rebecca. "'I hoped our baby would be deaf.'" *Guardian*, March 21, 2006.

Autism Every Day. Documentary film. Directed by Lauren Thierry. New York: Autism Speaks/Milestone Video, 2006.

834

"'Autism left me hollow,' says mother accused of murder." Associated Press, June 6, 2007.

Autism Speaks. "Autism Speaks and Cure Autism Now Complete Merger." Press release. February 5, 2007.

Autistic Self Advocacy Network. "An urgent call to action: Tell NYU Child Study Center to abandon stereotypes against people with disabilities." Washington, DC: Autistic Self Advocacy Network, December 7, 2007. http://www.autistic advocacy.org/modules/smartsection/print.php?itemid=21.

Auyeung, Bonnie, et al. "Foetal testosterone and autistic traits in 18- to 24-month-old children." *Molecular Autism* 1, no. 11 (July 2010): 1–8.

Aviv, Rachel. "God knows where I am: What should happen when patients reject their diagnosis?" *New Yorker*, May 30, 2011.

———. "No remorse: Should a teenager be given a life sentence?" *New Yorker*, January 2, 2012.

Axtman, Kris. "Baby case tests rights of parents." *Christian Science Monitor*, March 27, 2003.

Aylward, Elizabeth H., et al. "Cerebellar volume in adults with Down syndrome." *Archives of Neurology* 54, no. 2 (February 1997): 209–12.

Ayres, Chris. "Death of a sacrificial lamb." *The Times*, August 29, 2003.

Ayres, Chris, and Chris Lackner. "Father defends decision to stunt disabled girl's growth." *Ottawa Citizen*, January 4, 2007.

Bâ, Amadou Hampaté. *The Fortunes of Wangrin*. Introduction by Aina Pavolini Taylor. Bloomington: Indiana University Press, 1999.

Babel, Isaac. *The Complete Works of Isaac Babel*. Trans. Cynthia Ozick. New York: Norton, 2002.

"Babies with made-to-order defects?" Associated Press, December 21, 2006.

Bachem, A. "Absolute pitch." *Journal of the Acoustical Society of America* 27, no. 6 (1955): 1180–85.

Backlar, Patricia. *The Family Face of Schizophrenia: Practical Counsel from America's Leading Experts*. New York: Putnam, 1994.

Baek, Kwan-Hyuck, et al. "Down's syndrome suppression of tumour growth and the role of the calcineurin inhibitor DSCR1." *Nature* 459 (June 25, 2009): 1126–30.

Bagenstos, Samuel R. "The future of disability law." *Yale Law Journal* 114, no. 1 (October 2004): 1–84.

Baggs, Amanda. *Autism Demonized*. February 12, 2006. http://web.archive.org/web/20060628231956/http://autismdemonized.blogspot.com/.

———. "The original, literal demons." *Autism Demonized*, February 12, 2006.

Bailey, Anthony, et al. "Autism as a strongly genetic disorder: Evidence from a British twin study." *Psychological Medicine* 25 (1995): 63–77.

Baio, Jon. "Prevalence of autism spectrum disorders: Autism and Developmental Disabilities Monitoring Network, 14 sites, United States, 2008." *Morbidity & Mortality Weekly Report*, March 30, 2012.

Baird, Gillian, et al. "Prevalence of disorders of the autism spectrum in a population cohort of children in South Thames: The Special Needs and Autism Project (SNAP)." *Lancet* 368, no. 9531 (July 15, 2006): 210–15.

Baker, Al, and Leslie Kaufman. "Autistic boy is slashed to death and his father is charged." *New York Times*, November 23, 2006.

Baker, Bruce L., and Jan Blacher. "Out-of-home placement for children with mental retardation: Dimensions of family involvement." *American Journal on Mental Retardation* 98, no. 3 (November 1993): 368–77.

———. "Out-of-home placement for children with retardation: Family decision making and satisfaction." *Family Relations* 43, no. 1 (January 1994): 10–15.

———. "For better or worse? Impact of residential placement on families." *Mental Retardation* 40, no. 1 (February 2002): 1–13.

Ball, Robert H., et al. "First- and second-trimester evaluation of risk for Down syndrome." *Obstetrics & Gynecology* 110, no. 1 (July 2007): 10–17.

Ballock, R. Tracy. "Chondrodysplasias." *Current Opinion in Orthopedics* 11, no. 5 (October 2000): 347–52.

Balzer, Carsten. "Preliminary results of Trans Murder Monitoring Project." *Liminalis* 3 (July 2009): 147–59.

Ban, Thomas A. "Fifty years chlorpromazine: A historical perspective." *Neuropsychiatric Disease & Treatment* 3, no. 4 (August 2007): 495–500.

Bard, Bernard, and Joseph Fletcher. "The right to die." *Atlantic Monthly*, April 1968.

Barnes, Colin, and Geof Mercer. *Disability*. Cambridge, UK: Polity Press, 2003.

Barnes, Colin, Geof Mercer, and Tom Shakespeare, eds. *Exploring Disability: A Sociological Introduction*. Cambridge, UK: Polity Press, 1999.

Barnett, W. Steven, and Glenna C. Boyce. "Effects of children with Down syndrome on parents' activities." *American Journal on Mental Retardation* 100, no. 2 (September 1995): 115–27.

Barnoski, Robert. *Washington State's Implementation of Functional Family Therapy for Juvenile Offenders: Preliminary Findings*. Olympia: Washington State Institute for Public Policy, 2002.

———. *Outcome Evaluation of Washington State's Research-Based Programs for Juvenile Offenders*. Olympia: Washington State Institute for Public Policy, 2004.

Baron-Cohen, Simon. *Mindblindness: An Essay on Autism and Theory of Mind*. Cambridge, MA: MIT Press, 1995.

———. "The extreme male brain theory of autism." *Trends in Cognitive Science* 6, no. 6 (June 2002): 248–54.

———. "The hyper-systemizing, assortative mating theory of autism." *Progress in Neuropsychopharmacology & Biological Psychiatry* 30, no. 5 (July 2006): 865–72.

———. "Autism: The empathizing-systemizing (E-S) theory." *Annals of the New York Academy of Sciences* 1156 (March 2009): 68–80.

———. "Empathizing, systemizing, and the extreme male brain theory of autism." *Progress in Brain Research* 186 (2010): 167–75.

Barringer, Felicity. "Pride in a soundless world: Deaf oppose a hearing aid." *New York Times*, May 16, 1993.

Barrington, Daines. "Account of a very remarkable young musician." ("Reprinted from the LXth volume of the Philosophical Transactions for the year 1770.") In *Miscellanies*. London: J. Nichols, 1781. Repr., Malden, MA: Mozart Society of America, 2008.

Bartel, Paul. "The art of Susan Weinreich." *Provocateur*, February 1996.

Bartels, Lynn. "Klebold's father to give deposition." *Denver Rocky Mountain News*, July 30, 2003.

———. "Columbine parents outraged: Families of victims lash out at Klebolds' interview comments." *Denver Rocky Mountain News*, May 17, 2004.

Bartollas, Clemens. *Voices of Delinquency*. Boston: Allyn & Bacon, 2003.

Barton, Cole, et al. "Generalizing treatment effects of functional family therapy: Three replications." *American Journal of Family Therapy* 13, no. 3 (Fall 1985): 16–26.

Barton, Russell. *Institutional Neurosis.* Bristol: Wright, 1959.

Baruch, Susannah, David Kaufman, and Kathy L. Hudson. "Genetic testing of embryos: Practices and perspectives of US in vitro fertilization clinics." *Fertility & Sterility* 89, no. 5 (May 2008): 1053–58.

Baruzzini, Michael, "Justice or comfort?: Conservatives and the rape exception." *Catholic Lane,* June 16, 2011, http://catholiclane.com/justice-or-comfort-conservatives-and-the-rape-exception.

Bat-Chava, Yael, Daniela Martin, and Joseph G. Kosciw. "Longitudinal improvements in communication and socialization of deaf children with cochlear implants and hearing aids: Evidence from parental reports." *Journal of Child Psychology & Psychiatry* 46, no. 12 (December 2005): 1287–96.

Bateson, Gregory, et al. "Toward a theory of schizophrenia." *Behavioral Science* 1, no. 4 (1956): 251–64.

Bauer, Patricia. "The abortion debate no one wants to have." *Washington Post,* October 18, 2005.

Bauman, Humphrey-Dirksen. "Audism: Exploring the metaphysics of oppression." *Journal of Deaf Studies & Deaf Education* 9, no. 2 (Spring 2004): 239–46.

———. "Designing deaf babies and the question of disability." *Journal of Deaf Studies & Deaf Education* 10, no. 3 (Summer 2005): 311–15.

———, ed. *Open Your Eyes: Deaf Studies Talking.* Minneapolis: University of Minnesota Press, 2008.

Baxter, Arla J., and Edward P. Krenzelok. "Pediatric fatality secondary to EDTA chelation." *Clinical Toxicology* 46, no. 10 (December 2008): 1083–84.

Bayer, Ronald. *Homosexuality and American Psychiatry: The Politics of Diagnosis.* New York: Basic Books, 1981.

Baynton, Douglas C. *Forbidden Signs: American Culture and the Campaign Against Sign Language.* Chicago: University of Chicago Press, 1996.

Baynton, Douglas, Jack R. Gannon, and Jean Lindquist Bergey. *Through Deaf Eyes: A Photographic History of an American Community.* Washington, DC: Gallaudet University Press, 2001.

Bazelon, Emily. "Is there a post-abortion syndrome?" *New York Times Magazine,* January 21, 2007.

Bazzana, Kevin. *Lost Genius: The Curious and Tragic Story of an Extraordinary Musical Prodigy.* New York: Carroll & Graf, 2007.

Beals, Rodney K., and Greg Stanley. "Surgical correction of bowlegs in achondroplasia." *Journal of Pediatric Orthopedics* 14, no. 4 (July 2005): 245–49.

Beam, Cris. *Transparent: Love, Family, and Living the T with Transgendered Teenagers.* New York: Harcourt, 2007.

Bear, Mark F., Kimberly M. Huber, and Stephen T. Warren. "The mGluR theory of fragile X mental retardation." *Trends in Neurosciences* 27, no. 7 (July 2004): 370–77.

Beck, Martha Nibley. *Expecting Adam: A True Story of Birth, Rebirth and Everyday Magic.* New York: Times Books, 1999.

Beemyn, Brett Genny, and Sue Rankin. *Understanding Transgender Lives.* New York: Columbia University Press, forthcoming.

Behrman, Andy. "Mental health recovery: A personal perspective." About.com, December 29, 2011.

Bell, Alexander Graham. "Memoir upon the formation of a deaf variety of the human race." Paper presented to the National Academy of Sciences, November 13, 1883. *Memoirs of the National Academy of Sciences* (1884): 1–86.

———. "Historical notes concerning the teaching of speech to the deaf." *Association Review* 2 (February 1900): 33–68.

Bell, Sonya. "Dwarf-tossing: Controversial event at Windsor strip club draws 1,000 fans." *Toronto Star,* January 29, 2012.

Belluck, Pam. "Living with love, chaos and Haley." *New York Times,* October 22, 2006.

Bellus, Gary A. "Achondroplasia is defined by recurrent G380R mutations of FGFR3." *American Journal of Human Genetics* 56 (1995): 368–73.

Belzner, Kate A., and Brenda C. Seal. "Children with cochlear implants: A review of demographics and communication outcomes." *American Annals of the Deaf* 154, no. 3 (Summer 2009): 311–33.

Bender, Lauretta. "Childhood schizophrenia." *Nervous Child* 1 (1941): 138–40.

———. "Childhood schizophrenia." *American Journal of Orthopsychiatry* 17, no. 1 (January 1947): 40–56.

Bender, Ruth E. *The Conquest of Deafness: A History of the Long Struggle to Make Possible Normal Living to Those Handicapped by Lack of Normal Hearing.* Cleveland, OH: Press of Case Western Reserve University, 1970.

Benderly, Beryl Lieff. *Dancing Without Music: Deafness in America.* Washington, DC: Gallaudet University Press, 1990.

Benes, Francine M. "Amygdalocortical circuitry in schizophrenia: From circuits to molecules." *Neuropsychopharmacology* 35, no. 1 (January 2010): 239–57.

Benjamin, Melanie. *The Autobiography of Mrs. Tom Thumb: A Novel.* New York: Delacorte, 2011.

Bennett, Allyson, et al. "Early experience and serotonin transporter gene variation interact to influence primate CNS function." *Molecular Psychiatry* 7, no. 1 (2002): 118–22.

Beresford, Bryony A. "Resources and strategies: How parents cope with the care of a disabled child." *Journal of Child Psychology & Psychiatry* 35, no. 1 (January 1994): 171–209.

Bergen, Raquel Kennedy. *Wife Rape: Understanding the Response of Survivors and Service Providers.* Thousand Oaks, CA: Sage Publications, 1996.

———. "Studying wife rape: Reflections on the past, present, and future." *Violence Against Women* 10, no. 12 (December 2004): 1407–16.

Bergen, Raquel Kennedy, and Elizabeth Barnhill. *Marital Rape: New Research and Directions.* Applied Research Forum of the National Network on Violence Against Women. Harrisburg, PA: National Resource Center on Domestic Violence, February 2006.

Bergey, Jean Lindquist, and Jack R. Gannon. "Creating a national exhibition on deaf life." *Curator* 41, no. 2 (June 1998): 82–89.

Berkowitz, Ivor D., et al. "Dwarfs: Pathophysiology and anesthetic implications." *Anesthesiology* 7, no. 4 (October 1990): 739–59.

Berr, Jonathan. "Sex change surgery is now tax deductible." *Time,* November 10, 2011.

Berreby, David. "Up with people: Dwarves meet identity politics." *New Republic,* April 29, 1996.

Bertling, Tom. *A Child Sacrificed to the Deaf Culture.* Wilsonville, OR: Kodiak Media Group, 1994.

Bettelheim, Bruno. *The Empty Fortress: Infantile Autism and the Birth of the Self.* New York: Free Press, 1967.

———. *The Uses of Enchantment: The Meaning and Importance of Fairy Tales.* New York: Knopf, 1976.

Bérubé, Michael. *Life as We Know It: A Father, a Family and an Exceptional Child.* New York: Pantheon, 1996.

"Biden praises Special Olympic athletes." *Spokesman-Review*, February 19, 2009.

Biklen, Douglas. *Communication Unbound: How Facilitated Communication Is Challenging Traditional Views of Autism and Ability/Disability*. New York: Teachers College Press, 1993.

Birenbaum, Arnold, and Herbert J. Cohen. "On the importance of helping families: Policy implications from a national study." *Mental Retardation* 31, no. 2 (April 1993): 67–74.

Bishop, Dorothy V., et al. "Autism and diagnostic substitution: Evidence from a study of adults with a history of developmental language disorder." *Developmental Medicine & Child Neurology* 50, no. 5 (May 2008): 341–45.

Bishop, Elizabeth. *Questions of Travel*. New York: Farrar, Straus & Giroux, 1965.

Bishop, Michele, and Sherry L. Hicks, ed. *Hearing, Mother Father Deaf*. Washington, DC: Gallaudet University Press, 2009.

Blacher, Jan, ed. *Severely Handicapped Young Children and Their Families: Research in Review*. Orlando, FL: Academic Press, 1984.

———. "Sequential stages of parental adjustment to the birth of a child with handicaps: Fact or artifact?" *Mental Retardation* 22, no. 2 (April 1984): 55–68.

———. *When There's No Place Like Home: Options for Children Living Apart from Their Natural Families*. Baltimore: Paul H. Brookes, 1994.

Blacher, Jan, and Bruce L. Baker. "Out-of-home placement for children with retardation: Family decision making and satisfaction." *Family Relations* 43, no. 1 (January 1994): 10–15.

———. "Family involvement in residential treatment of children with retardation: Is there evidence of detachment?" *Journal of Child Psychology & Psychiatry* 35, no. 3 (March 1994): 505–20.

———, eds. *Families and Mental Retardation: The Best of AAMR*. Thousand Oaks, CA: Sage Publications, 2002.

Blacher, Jan, Bruce L. Baker, and Kristin Abbott Feinfield. "Leaving or launching? Continuing family involvement with children and adolescents in placement." *American Journal on Mental Retardation* 104, no. 5 (September 1999): 452–65.

Blacher, Jan, et al. "Depression in Latino mothers of children with mental retardation: A neglected concern." *American Journal on Mental Retardation* 101, no. 5 (September 1997): 483–96.

Black, Edwin. *War Against the Weak: Eugenics and America's Campaign to Create a Master Race*. New York: Thunder's Mouth Press, 2004.

Blacking, John. *How Musical Is Man?* Seattle: University of Washington Press, 1973.

Blanchard, Ray. "Fraternal birth order and the maternal immune hypothesis of male homosexuality." *Hormones & Behavior* 40, no. 2 (September 2001): 105–14.

Bleuler, Eugen P. "Autistic thinking." *American Journal of Insanity* 69 (April 1913): 873.

Bloom, Amy. *Normal: Transsexual CEOs, Crossdressing Cops, and Hermaphrodites with Attitude*. New York: Random House, 2002.

Blum, Robert W., et al. "The effects of race/ethnicity, income, and family structure on adolescent risk behaviors." *American Journal of Public Health* 90, no. 12 (December 2000): 1879–84.

Blume, Harvey. "Neurodiversity." *Atlantic Monthly*, September 30, 1998.

Board of Education v. Rowley. 458 US 176 (1982).

Bochenek, Michael, and A. Widney Brown. *Hatred in the Hallways: Violence and Discrimination Against Lesbian, Gay, Bisexual, and Transgender Students in U.S. Schools*. New York: Human Rights Watch, 2001.

Bonvillian, John D., Michael D. Orlansky, and Lesley Lazin Novack. "Developmental milestones: Sign language acquisition and motor development." *Child Development* 54, no. 6 (December 1983): 1435–45.

Bornstein, David. "For some with autism, jobs to match their talents." *New York Times Opinionator,* June 30, 2011. http://opinionator.blogs.nytimes.com/2011/06/30/putting-the-gifts-of-the-autistic-to-work.

Borthwick, Chris. "The proof of the vegetable." *Journal of Medical Ethics* 21, no. 4 (August 1995): 205–8.

Boswell, John. *The Kindness of Strangers: The Abandonment of Children in Western Europe from Late Antiquity to the Renaissance.* Chicago: University of Chicago Press, 1998.

Boudreault, Patrick, et al. "Deaf adults' reasons for genetic testing depend on cultural affiliation: Results from a prospective, longitudinal genetic counseling and testing study." *Journal of Deaf Studies & Deaf Education* 15, no. 3 (Summer 2010): 209–27.

Bowen, Murray, Robert H. Dysinger, and Betty Basamania. "The role of the father in families with a schizophrenic patient." *American Journal of Psychiatry* 115, no. 11 (May 1959): 1017–20.

Bowlby, John. *Maternal Care and Mental Health.* WHO Monograph Series, no. 2. Geneva: World Health Organization, 1952.

Bowlby, John, Margery Fry, and Mary D. Salter Ainsworth. *Child Care and the Growth of Love.* Baltimore: Penguin Books, 1965.

———. *Separation: Anxiety and Anger.* Vol. 2, *Attachment and Loss.* New York: Basic Books, 1973.

———. *Loss: Sadness and Depression.* Vol. 3, *Attachment and Loss.* New York: Basic Books, 1980.

———. *Attachment.* 2nd ed. Vol. 1, *Attachment and Loss.* New York: Basic Books, 1982.

Boyd, Ralph F. *Investigation of Nevada Youth Training Center, Elko, Nevada.* US Department of Justice, Civil Rights Division, May 2005.

Boylan, Jennifer Finney. *She's Not There: A Life in Two Genders.* New York: Broadway, 2003.

Bradford, William. *Of Plymouth Plantation, 1620–1647.* Ed. Samuel Eliot Morison. New Brunswick, NJ: Rutgers University Press, 1957.

Bradley, Susan J., and Kenneth J. Zucker. "Gender identity disorder: A review of the past 10 years." *Journal of the American Academy of Child & Adolescent Psychiatry* 36, no. 7 (July 1997): 872–80.

———. "Children with gender nonconformity: Drs. Bradley and Zucker reply." *Journal of the American Academy of Child & Adolescent Psychiatry* 42, no. 3 (March 2003): 266–68.

Bragg, Lois, ed. *Deaf World: A Historical Reader and Primary Sourcebook.* New York: New York University Press, 2001.

Bramlett, Matthew D., Laura F. Radel, and Stephen J. Blumberg. "The health and well-being of adopted children." *Pediatrics* 119, suppl. 1 (February 1, 2007): S54–S60.

Brasel, Kenneth E., and Stephen P. Quigley. "Influence of certain language and communication environments in early childhood on the development of language in Deaf individuals." *Journal of Speech & Hearing Research* 20, no. 1 (March 1977): 95–107.

Braslow, Joel T. "History and evidence-based medicine: Lessons from the history of somatic treatments from the 1900s to the 1950s." *Mental Health Services Research* 1, no. 4 (December 1999): 231–40.

Bray, Isabelle C., and David E. Wright. "Estimating the spontaneous loss of Down syndrome fetuses between the times of chorionic villus sampling, amniocentesis and live birth." *Prenatal Diagnosis* 18, no. 10 (October 1998): 1045–54.

Bregani, P., et al. "Emotional implications of limb lengthening in adolescents and young adults with achondroplasia." *Life-Span & Disability* 1, no. 2 (July–December 1998): 6.

Breggin, Peter Roger. *Psychiatric Drugs: Hazards to the Brain.* New York: Springer, 1983.

Breslau, Naomi, et al. "Siblings of disabled children: Effects of chronic stress in the family." *Archives of General Psychiatry* 44, no. 12 (December 1987): 1040–46.

Brickman, P., D. Coates, and R. Janoff-Bulman. "Lottery winners and accident victims: Is happiness relative?" *Journal of Personal & Social Psychology* 36, no. 8 (August 1978): 917–27.

Brigande, John V., and Stefan Heller. "Quo vadis, hair cell regeneration?" *Nature Neuroscience* 12, no. 6 (June 2009): 679–85.

Brill, Stephanie, and Rachel Pepper. *The Transgender Child: A Handbook for Families and Professionals.* San Francisco: Cleis Press, 2008.

Brindley, Madeleine. "Fears over fertilisation and embryology bill clause." *Western Mail*, April 7, 2008.

Brink, Susan. "Is taller better?" *Los Angeles Times*, January 15, 2007.

———. "When average fails to reach parents' expectations." *Los Angeles Times*, January 15, 2007.

Brinkmann, G., et al. "Cognitive skills in achondroplasia." *American Journal of Medical Genetics* 47, no. 5 (October 1993): 800–804.

Brison, Susan J. *Aftermath: Violence and the Remaking of a Self.* Princeton, NJ: Princeton University Press, 2002.

Brocke, Emma. "Gay parenting: It's complicated." *Guardian*, April 20, 2012.

Broder, John M. "Dismal California prisons hold juvenile offenders." *New York Times*, February 15, 2004.

Brody, Jane E. "Cochlear implant supports an author's active life." *New York Times*, February 26, 2008.

Bronson, Peter. "For deep-end families, lack of hope can kill." *Cincinnati Enquirer*, October 9, 2005.

Brooks, David. "The Columbine killers." *New York Times*, April 24, 2004.

———. "Columbine: Parents of a killer." *New York Times*, May 15, 2004.

———. "Genius: The modern view." *New York Times*, May 1, 2009.

Brown, Alan S. "The environment and susceptibility to schizophrenia." *Progress in Neurobiology* 93, no. 1 (January 2011): 23–58.

Brown, Alan S., and Ezra S. Susser. "In utero infection and adult schizophrenia." *Mental Retardation & Developmental Disabilities Research Reviews* 8, no. 1 (February 2002): 51–57.

Brown, B. Bradford, and L. Steinberg. "Academic achievement and social acceptance: Skirting the 'brain-nerd' connection." *Education Digest* 55, no. 7 (1990): 55–60.

Brown, Barbara. "Mother begins trial for death of her son: Johnny Churchi was 13, autistic, and found strangled in his family apartment Oct. 2001." *Hamilton Spectator*, May 5, 2003.

Brown, Brooks, and Rob Merritt. *No Easy Answers: The Truth Behind Death at Columbine.* New York: Lantern Books, 2002.

Brown, Kevin D., et al. "Incidence and indications for revision cochlear implant surgery in adults and children." *Laryngoscope* 119, no. 1 (January 2009): 152–57.

BIBLIOGRAPHY

Brown, Mildred L., and Chloe Ann Rounsley. *True Selves: Understanding Transsexualism*. San Francisco: Jossey-Bass, 1996.

Brown, Patricia Leigh. "Supporting boys or girls when the line isn't clear." *New York Times*, December 2, 2006.

Brown, Peter, et al. "A new small-bodied hominin from the Late Pleistocene of Flores, Indonesia." *Nature* 431, no. 7012 (October 27, 2004): 1055–61.

Brownmiller, Susan. *Against Our Will: Men, Women, and Rape*. New York: Simon & Schuster, 1975.

Brust, James S., et al. "Psychiatric aspects of dwarfism." *American Journal of Psychiatry* 133, no. 2 (February 1976): 160–64.

Buber, Martin. *I and Thou*. New York: Scribner, 2000.

Buchanan, Robert W., et al. "Recent advances in the development of novel pharmacological agents for the treatment of cognitive impairments in schizophrenia." *Schizophrenia Bulletin* 33, no. 5 (2007): 1120–30.

Buck v. Bell. 274 US 200 (1927).

Bullock, Penn, and Brandon K. Thorp. "Christian right leader George Rekers takes vacation with 'rent boy.'" *Miami New Times*, May 4, 2010.

Bunyan, John. *The Miscellaneous Works of John Bunyan*. Ed. Richard L. Greaves and Robert Sharrock. Oxford, UK: Clarendon Press, 1979.

Burch, Rebecca, and George Gallup. "Perceptions of paternal resemblance predict family violence." *Evolution & Human Behavior* 21, no. 6 (November 2000): 429–35.

Burch, Susan. *Signs of Resistance: American Deaf Cultural History, 1900 to World War II*. New York: New York University Press, 2004.

Burke, Phyllis. *Gender Shock: Exploding the Myths of Male and Female*. New York: Anchor, 1996.

Burkhart, Alan. "The Ashley treatment." *Burkhart's Blog*, January 6, 2007. http://alanburkhart.blogspot.com/2007/01/ashley-treatment.html.

Burns, Elizabeth. *Tilt: Every Family Spins on Its Own Axis: A Novel*. Naperville, IL: Sourcebooks, 2003.

Burton, David L., George Stuart Leibowitz, and Alan Howard. "Comparison by crime type of juvenile delinquents on pornography exposure: The absence of relationships between exposure to pornography and sexual offense characteristics." *Journal of Forensic Nursing* 6, no. 3 (September 2010): 121–29.

Burton, Sally L., and A. Lee Parks. "Self-esteem, locus of control, and career aspirations of college-age siblings of individuals with disabilities." *Social Work Research* 18, no. 3 (September 1994): 178–85.

Busnel, Marie-Claire, Carolyn Granier-Deferre, and Jean-Pierre Lecanuet. "Fetal audition." *Annals of the New York Academy of Sciences* 662 (October 1992): 118–34.

Butler, Judith. *Gender Trouble: Feminism and the Subversion of Identity*. London and New York: Routledge, 1999.

Byrd, A. Dean, and the NARTH Scientific Advisory Committee. "Gender identity disorders in childhood and adolescence: A critical inquiry and review of the Kenneth Zucker research." Encino, CA: National Association for Research and Therapy of Homosexuality, March 2007.

Byrne, Rhonda. *The Secret*. New York: Atria Books, 2006.

Byrom, Brad. "Deaf culture under siege." *H-Net Reviews*, March 2003.

Cahill, Brigid M., and Laraine Masters Glidden. "Influence of child diagnosis on family and parental functioning: Down syndrome versus other disabilities." *American Journal on Mental Retardation* 101, no. 2 (September 1996): 149–60.

Calhoun, George, et al. "The neophyte female delinquent: A review of the literature." *Adolescence* 28, no. 110 (Summer 1993): 461–71.

Calmels, Marie-Noëlle, et al. "Speech perception and speech intelligibility in children after cochlear implantation." *International Journal of Pediatric Otorhinolaryngology* 68, no. 3 (March 2004): 347–51.

Campbell, Daniel B., et al. "Distinct genetic risk based on association of MET in families with co-occurring autism and gastrointestinal conditions." *Pediatrics* 123, no. 3 (March 2009): 1018–24.

Campbell, Jacquelyn C., and Peggy Alford. "The dark consequences of marital rape." *American Journal of Nursing* 89, no. 7 (July 1989): 946–49.

Campbell, Jacquelyn C., et al. "The influence of abuse on pregnancy intention." *Women's Health Issues* 5, no. 4 (Winter 1995): 214–22.

Canfield, Jack, et al. *Chicken Soup for the Soul: Children with Special Needs: Stories of Love and Understanding for Those Who Care for Children with Disabilities.* Deerfield Beach, FL: Health Communications, 2007.

Canguilhem, Georges. *The Normal and the Pathological.* Introduction by Michel Foucault. Trans. Carolyn R. Fawcett and Robert S. Cohen. New York: Zone Books, 1991.

Cantor, Rita M., et al. "Paternal age and autism are associated in a family-based sample." *Molecular Psychiatry* 12 (2007): 419–23.

Cantor-Graae, Elizabeth, and Jean-Paul Selten. "Schizophrenia and migration: A meta-analysis and review." *American Journal of Psychiatry* 162, no. 1 (January 2005): 12–24.

Cao, Zhengyu, et al., "Clustered burst firing in FMR1 premutation hippocampal neurons: Amelioration with allopregnanolone." *Human Molecular Genetics* (published online ahead of print, April 6, 2012).

Caplan, Arthur. "Is 'Peter Pan' treatment a moral choice?" MSNBC, January 5, 2007. http://www.msnbc.msn.com/id/16472931/ns/health-health_care/t/peter-pan-treatment-moral-choice/.

Carbone, Vincent J., and Emily J. Sweeney-Kerwin. "Increasing the vocal responses of children with autism and developmental disabilities using manual sign mand training and prompt delay." *Journal of Applied Behavior Analysis* 43, no. 4 (Winter 2010): 705–9.

Cardno, Alastair G., et al. "Heritability estimates for psychotic disorders: The Maudsley twin psychosis series." *Archives of General Psychiatry* 56, no. 2 (February 1999): 162–68.

Carey, Benedict. "Mixed result in drug trial on pretreating schizophrenia." *New York Times*, May 1, 2006.

———. "New definition of autism will exclude many, study suggests." *New York Times*, January 19, 2012.

———. "Psychiatry manual drafters back down on diagnosis." *New York Times*, May 8, 2012.

Carey, Rea. "Testimony of the National Gay and Lesbian Task Force Action Fund, Rea Carey, Executive Director, Committee on Health, Education, Labor, and Pensions, United States Senate, November 5, 2009." Washington, DC: National Gay and Lesbian Task Force Action Fund, 2009.

Caron, M. J., et al. "Cognitive mechanisms, specificity and neural underpinnings of visuospatial peaks in autism." *Brain* 129, no. 7 (July 2006): 1789–802.

Carothers, Carol. "Juvenile detention centers: Are they warehousing children with mental illnesses?" Statement of Carol Carothers on behalf of the National Alliance on Mental Illness before the Governmental Affairs Committee, United States Senate on Juvenile Detention Centers, July 7, 2004. Richmond, VA: National Alliance for Mental Illness, 2004.

Carpenter, R. Charli. "War's impact on children born of rape and sexual exploitation: Physical, economic and psychosocial dimensions." Paper presented at the Impact of War on Children Conference, University of Alberta, Edmonton, April 2005.

———. *Born of War: Protecting Children of Sexual Violence Survivors in Conflict Zones.* Sterling, VA: Kumarian Press, 2007.

Caspi, Avshalom, et al. "Role of genotype in the cycle of violence in maltreated children." *Science* 297, no. 5582 (August 2002): 851–54.

Cassidy, Jude, and Phillip R. Shaver, eds. *Handbook of Attachment: Theory, Research, and Clinical Applications.* New York: Guilford Press, 1999.

Castells, Salvador, and Krystyna E. Wiesniewski, eds. *Growth Hormone Treatment in Down's Syndrome.* New York: John Wiley & Sons, 1993.

Cazador, Jenifer Ann. "Lost souls of polygamy central." *The Wrecking Machine*, April 2008.

Chakravarti, Aravinda, et al. *Reproductive Genetic Testing: What America Thinks.* Washington, DC: Genetics & Public Policy Center, 2004.

Chamberlin, Judi. *On Our Own: Patient-Controlled Alternatives to the Mental Health System.* New York: Hawthorn Books, 1978.

Champion, Dean John. *The Juvenile Justice System: Delinquency, Processing, and the Law.* 4th ed. New Jersey: Pearson Prentice Hall, 2004.

Champoux, Maribeth, et al. "Serotonin transporter gene polymorphism, differential early rearing, and behavior in rhesus monkey neonates." *Molecular Psychiatry* 7, no. 10 (2002): 1058–63.

Chancellor, Alexander. "Guide to age." *Guardian*, November 6, 2004.

Chapman, Paul. "Mom who strangled autistic child tried to get her to jump off bridge." *Vancouver Sun*, July 11, 1998.

Cheek, D. B. *Human Growth.* Philadelphia: Lea and Febiger, 1968.

Chekhov, Anton. *The Cherry Orchard.* Trans. David Mamet. New York: Grove Press, 1987.

Chemers, Michael M. "Le freak, c'est chic: The twenty-first century freak show as theatre of transgression." *Modern Drama* 46, no. 2 (Summer 2003): 285–304.

———. "Jumpin' Tom Thumb: Charles Stratton Onstage at the American Museum." *Nineteenth Century Theatre & Film* 31 (2004): 16–27.

Chen, Wei, et al. "Human fetal auditory stem cells can be expanded in vitro and differentiate into functional auditory neurons and hair cell-like cells." *Stem Cells* 2, no. 5 (May 2009): 1196–1204.

Chen, Zu-Pei, and Basil S. Hetzel. "Cretinism revisited." *Best Practice & Research Clinical Endocrinology & Metabolism* 24, no. 1 (February 2010): 39–50.

Cheng, André K., et al. "Cost-utility analysis of the cochlear implant in children." *Journal of the American Medical Association* 274, no. 7 (August 2000): 850–56.

Chew, Kristina. "I don't have a title for this post about Katherine McCarron's mother." *Autism Vox*, June 8, 2006. http://archive.blisstree.com/feel/i-dont-have-a-title -for-this-post-about-katherine-mccarrons-mother/.

"Child prodigy's time to 'do something great,' Mom says." *Washington Post*, March 20, 2005.

Children of Rape. Documentary film. Featuring Phil Donahue. Princeton, NJ: Films for the Humanities & Sciences, 1994.

Chinen, Nate. "Gabriel Kahane, *Where Are the Arms.*" *New York Times*, September 19, 2011.

Chisholm, Dan, et al. "Schizophrenia treatment in the developing world: An interregional and multinational cost-effectiveness analysis." *Bulletin of the World Health Organization* 86, no. 7 (July 2008): 542–51.

Chorost, Michael. *Rebuilt: My Journey Back to the Hearing World*. New York: Mariner Books, 2006.

Chow, Robert. "Barrios' rivalry began with sports, cars." *Orange County Register*, August 6, 1990.

Christiansen, John B., and Irene W. Leigh. *Cochlear Implants in Children: Ethics and Choices*. Washington, DC: Gallaudet University Press, 2002.

———. "Children with cochlear implants: Changing parent and deaf community perspectives." *Archives of Otolaryngology—Head & Neck Surgery* 130, no. 5 (May 2004): 673–77.

Christiansen, John B., and Sharon N. Barnartt. *Deaf President Now! The 1988 Revolution at Gallaudet University*. Washington, DC: Gallaudet University Press, 2003.

Church of Jesus Christ of Latter Day Saints. "The law of chastity." *Gospel Principles*, 2012, http://www.lds.org/library/display/0,4945,11-1-13-49,00.html.

Cicchetti, Dante, and Marjorie Beeghly, eds. *Children with Down Syndrome: A Developmental Perspective*. Cambridge, UK, and New York: Cambridge University Press, 1990.

City of Cleburne v. Cleburne Living Center. 473 US 432 (1985).

Clairmont, Susan. "'Sending you to heaven' said mom: She put a belt around Johnny's neck and then held a pillow over his face." *Hamilton Spectator*, May 6, 2003.

Clark, Sarah, et al. "Fluoxetine rescues deficient neurogenesis in hippocampus of the Ts65Dn mouse model for Down syndrome." *Experimental Neurology* 200, no. 1 (July 2006): 256–61.

Cloud, John. "Are we failing our geniuses?" *Time*, August 16, 2007.

Cocchi, Guido, et al. "International trends of Down syndrome, 1993–2004: Births in relation to maternal age and terminations of pregnancies." *Birth Defects Research Part A: Clinical & Molecular Teratology* 88, no. 6 (June 2010): 474–79.

Coco, Adrienne Phelps. "Diseased, maimed, mutilated: Categorizations of disability and an ugly law in late nineteenth-century Chicago." *Journal of Social History* 44, no. 1 (Fall 2010): 23–37.

Cohen, Elizabeth. "Disability community decries 'Ashley treatment.'" Cable News Network, January 12, 2007; updated March 12, 2008.

Cohen-Kettenis, Peggy T. "Psychosexual outcome of gender-dysphoric children." *Journal of the American Academy of Child & Adolescent Psychiatry* 47, no. 12 (December 2008): 1413–23.

Cohen-Kettenis, Peggy, H. A. Delemarre–van de Waal, and L. J. Gooren. "The treatment of adolescent transsexuals: Changing insights." *Journal of Sexual Medicine* 5, no. 8 (August 2008): 1892–97.

Cohen-Kettenis, Peggy T., and Stephanie H. van Goozen. "Sex reassignment of adolescent transsexuals: A follow-up study." *Journal of the American Academy of Child & Adolescent Psychiatry* 36, no. 2 (February 1997): 263–71.

Cohn, Meredith. "Lupron therapy for autism at center of embattled doctor's case." *Baltimore Sun*, June 16, 2011.

Colangelo, Nicolas. *A Nation Deceived: How Schools Hold Back America's Brightest Students.* Iowa City: Institute for Research and Policy on Acceleration, University of Iowa, 2004.

Colapinto, John. "The true story of John/Joan." *Rolling Stone*, December 11, 1997.

———. *As Nature Made Him: The Boy Who Was Raised as a Girl.* New York: HarperCollins, 2000.

———. "Gender gap: What were the real reasons behind David Reimer's suicide?" *Slate*, June 3, 2004.

Coleman, Naomi. "Boys will be girls." *Guardian*, August 20, 2003.

Columbia University. National Center on Addiction and Substance Abuse. *Criminal Neglect: Substance Abuse, Juvenile Justice and the Children Left Behind.* New York: National Center on Addiction and Substance Abuse at Columbia University, 2004.

Colvin, Geoff. *Talent Is Overrated: What Really Separates World-Class Performers from Everybody Else.* New York: Portfolio, 2010.

Constantino, John N., et al. "Autism recurrence in half siblings: Strong support for genetic mechanisms of transmission in ASD." *Molecular Psychiatry.* Epub ahead of print, February 28, 2012.

Conway, Lynn. "A warning for those considering MtF sex reassignment surgery (SRS)." Ann Arbor, MI: Lynn Conway, April 9, 2005; updated March 16, 2007. http://ai.eecs.umich.edu/people/conway/TS/Warning.html.

———. "The numbers don't add: Transsexual prevalence." GID Reform Advocates, 2008.

Coole, Maria. "Report recommendations could put Pa. at forefront in autism services." *Lancaster Intelligencer-Journal*, April 23, 2005.

Cooper, Huw, and Louise Craddock. *Cochlear Implants: A Practical Guide.* 2nd ed. London: Whurr, 2006.

Corcoran, Cheryl M., Michael B. First, and Barbara Cornblat. "The psychosis risk syndrome and its proposed inclusion in the DSM-V: A risk-benefit analysis." *Schizophrenia Research* 120 (July 2010).

Cornell, Christoph U., et al. "Research in people with psychosis risk syndrome: A review of the current evidence and future directions." *Journal of Child Psychology & Psychiatry* 51, no. 4 (April 2010): 390–431.

Corone, Daniel. "Bree Walker blasts KFI's *Baby Talk*." *Los Angeles Times*, August 17, 1991.

Corvino, John. "Why Baby Gauvin is not a victim." *Gay & Lesbian Review Worldwide* 9, no. 6 (2002): 25.

Corwin, Jeffrey T. "Postembryonic production and aging in inner ear hair cells in sharks." *Journal of Comparative Neurology* 201, no. 4 (October 1981): 541–43.

———. "Postembryonic growth of the macula neglecta auditory detector in the ray, *Raja clavata*: Continual increases in hair cell number, neural convergence, and physiological sensitivity." *Journal of Comparative Neurology* 217, no. 3 (July 1983): 345–56.

———. "Perpetual production of hair cells and maturational changes in hair cell ultrastructure accompany postembryonic growth in an amphibian ear." *Proceedings of the National Academy of Sciences* 82, no. 11 (June 1985): 3911–15.

Costa, Albert C. S., Jonah J. Scott-McKean, and Melissa R. Stasko. "Acute injections of the NMDA receptor antagonist memantine rescue performance deficits of the Ts65Dn mouse model of Down syndrome on a fear conditioning test." *Neuropsychopharmacology* 33, no. 7 (June 2008): 1624–32.

Costello, Victoria. "Reaching children who live in a world of their own." *Psychology Today*, December 9, 2009.

Cotanche, Douglas A. "Regeneration of hair cell stereociliary bundles in the chick cochlea following severe acoustic trauma." *Hearing Research* 30, nos. 2–3 (1987): 181–95.

Council of State Governments. *Criminal Justice / Mental Health Consensus Project*. New York: Council of State Governments Eastern Regional Conference, 2002.

Courchesne, Eric, et al. "Evidence of brain overgrowth in the first year of life in autism." *Journal of the American Medical Association* 290, no. 3 (July 2003): 337–44.

Courchesne, Eric, Kathleen Campbell, and Stephanie Solso. "Brain growth across the life span in autism: Age-specific changes in anatomical pathology." *Brain Research* 1380 (March 2011): 138–45.

Cox, Catherine. *The Early Mental Traits of Three Hundred Geniuses*. Stanford, CA: Stanford University Press, 1926.

Coyle, Daniel. *The Talent Code: Greatness Isn't Born, It's Grown*. New York: Bantam, 2009.

Crandall, Richard, and Thomas Crosson, eds. *Dwarfism: The Family and Professional Guide*. Irvine, CA: Short Stature Foundation & Information Center, 1994.

Crews, David, and John A. McLachlan. "Epigenetics, evolution, endocrine disruption, health, and disease." *Endocrinology* 147, no. 6 (June 2006): S4–S10.

Crockett, Jean B., and James M. Kaufmann. *The Least Restrictive Environment: Its Origins and Interpretations in Special Education*. London and New York: Routledge, 1999.

Croen, Lisa A., et al. "The changing prevalence of autism in California." *Journal of Autism & Developmental Disorders* 32, no. 3 (June 2002): 207–15.

———. "Antidepressant use during pregnancy and childhood autism spectrum disorders." *Archives of General Psychiatry*. Epub ahead of print, July 4, 2011.

Crookshank, Francis Graham. *The Mongol in Our Midst: A Study of Man and His Three Faces*. New York: Dutton, 1924.

Csikszentmihalyi, Mihaly. *Creativity: Flow and the Psychology of Discovery and Invention*. New York: HarperCollins, 1996.

Cuajungco, Math P., Christian Grimm, and Stefan Heller. "TRP channels as candidates for hearing and balance abnormalities in vertebrates." *Biochimica et Biophysica Acta (BBA)—Molecular Basis of Disease* 1772, no. 8 (August 2007): 1022–27.

Cullen, David. "Inside the Columbine High investigation." *Salon*, September 23, 1999. http://www.salon.com/news/feature/1999/09/23/columbine/index.html.

———. "'Kill mankind. No one should survive.'" *Salon*, September 23, 1999. http://www.salon.com/news/feature/1999/09/23/journal/index.html.

———. *Columbine*. New York: Twelve, 2009.

Curlender v. BioScience Laboratories. 106 Cal. App. 3d 811, 165 Cal. Rptr. 477 (California, 1980).

Curran, L. K., et al. "Behaviors associated with fever in children with autism spectrum disorders." *Pediatrics* 120, no. 6 (December 2007): E1386–E1392.

Cutler, Eustacia. *A Thorn in My Pocket: Temple Grandin's Mother Tells the Family Story*. Arlington, TX: Future Horizons, 2004.

Cutter, Natela. "'Anne Smith': A rape victim found relief in the abortion." *U.S. News & World Report* 124, no. 2 (January 19, 1998): 29–30.

Daar, Judith F. "ART and the search for perfectionism: On selecting gender, genes, and gametes." *Journal of Gender, Race & Justice* 9, no. 2 (Winter 2005): 241–73.

Dahmer, Lionel. *A Father's Story*. New York: William Morrow, 1994.

Daley, Suzanne. "Mysterious life of a suspect from France." *New York Times*, September 21, 2001.

Damron, Gina. "Mom waits for answers in transgender teen's death." *Detroit Free Press*, November 12, 2011.

Daniel, Joana. "No man's child: The war rape orphans." Master's thesis, Ludwig Boltzmann Institute for Human Rights, Vienna, 2003.

D'Anna, Eddie. "Staten Island nightspot cancels dwarf-bowling event for Saturday." *Staten Island Advance*, February 27, 2008.

Darrow, Clarence S. "Closing argument for the defense in the Leopold-Loeb murder trial, Criminal Court of County, Chicago, Illinois, August 22, 23, and 25, 1924." In *Famous American Jury Speeches: Addresses Before Fact-Finding Tribunals*, ed. Frederick C. Hicks, 992–1089. St. Paul, MN: West Publishing, 1925.

Davey, Monica. "As town for deaf takes shape, debate on isolation re-emerges." *New York Times*, March 21, 2005.

David, Henry P., Jochen Fleischhacker, and Charlotte Hohn. "Abortion and eugenics in Nazi Germany." *Population & Development Review* 13, no. 1 (March 1988): 81–112.

Davidson, Jan, Bob Davidson, and Laura Vanderkam. *Genius Denied: How to Stop Wasting Our Brightest Young Minds*. New York: Simon & Schuster, 2004.

Davidson, Larry, and David Stayner. "Loss, loneliness, and the desire for love: Perspectives on the social lives of people with schizophrenia." *Psychiatric Rehabilitation Journal* 20, no. 3 (Winter 1997): 3–12.

Davidson, Lisa S., Ann E. Geers, and Christine A. Brenner. "Cochlear implant characteristics and speech perception skills of adolescents with long-term device use." *Otology & Neurology* 31, no. 8 (October 2010): 1310–14.

Davies, Paul. "Deaf culture clash." *Wall Street Journal*, April 25, 2005.

Davis, David. "Losing the mind." *Los Angeles Times*, October 26, 2003.

Davis, Lennard. *Enforcing Normalcy: Disability, Deafness, and the Body*. London: Verso, 1995.

———. *My Sense of Silence: Memoirs of a Childhood with Deafness*. Urbana: University of Illinois Press, 2000.

Day, Steven M., et al. "Mortality and causes of death in persons with Down syndrome in California." *Developmental Medicine & Child Neurology* 47, no. 3 (March 2005): 171–76.

Deacy, Susan, and Karen F. Pierce, eds. *Rape in Antiquity*. London: Duckworth, 2002.

Deafness Research Foundation. "The cochlear implant timeline." Deafness Research Foundation, 2009.

Dearth, Nona, and Families of the Mentally Ill Collective. *Families Helping Families: Living with Schizophrenia*. New York and London: W. W. Norton, 1986.

de Bruyn, Maria. *Violence, Pregnancy and Abortion: Issues of Women's Rights and Public Health*. 2nd ed. Chapel Hill, NC: Ipas, 2003.

de Courcy, G. I. C. *Paganini the Genoese*. Norman: University of Oklahoma Press, 1957.

Dekker, Thomas. *The Honest Whore*. London: Nick Hern Books, 1998.

de Manzano, Örjan, et al. "Thinking outside a less intact box: Thalamic dopamine D2 receptor densities are negatively related to psychometric creativity in healthy individuals." *PLoS One* 5, no. 5 (May 17, 2010): E10670.

De Marneffe, Daphne. *Maternal Desire: On Children, Love and the Inner*. New York: Little, Brown, 2004.

Dembo, R., et al. "Predictors of recidivism to a juvenile assessment center: A three year study." *Journal of Child & Adolescent Substance Abuse* 7, no. 3 (1998): 57–77.

Demuth, Stephen, and Susan L. Brown. "Family structure, family processes, and adolescent delinquency: The significance of parental absence versus parental gender." *Journal of Research in Crime & Delinquency* 41, no. 1 (February 2004): 58–81.

Dennis, Carina. "Deaf by design." *Nature*, October 20, 2004.

Derbyshire, David. "Lancet was wrong to publish MMR paper, says editor." *Telegraph*, February 21, 2004.

Des Forges, Alison Liebhafsky. *"Leave None to Tell the Story": Genocide in Rwanda*. New York: Human Rights Watch; Paris: International Federation of Human Rights, 1999.

DeSoto, Mary Catherine, and Robert T. Hitlan. "Sorting out the spinning of autism: Heavy metals and the question of incidence." *Acta Neurobiologiae Experimentalis* 70, no. 2 (2010): 165–76.

Dettman, Shani J., et al. "Communication development in children who receive the cochlear implant younger than 12 months: Risks versus benefits." *Ear & Hearing* 28, suppl. no. 2 (April 2007): 11S–18S.

de Unamono, Miguel. *The Tragic Sense of Life in Men and Nations*. Princeton, NJ: Princeton University Press, 1977.

Deutsch, Diana, et al. "Absolute pitch among American and Chinese conservatory students: Prevalence differences, and evidence for a speech-related critical period." *Journal of the Acoustical Society of America* 199, no. 2 (February 2006): 719–22.

———. "Absolute pitch among students in an American music conservatory: Association with tone language fluency." *Journal of the Acoustical Society of America* 125, no. 4 (April 2009): 2398–403.

Devor, Holly. *FTM: Female-to-Male Transsexuals in Society*. Bloomington and Indianapolis: Indiana University Press, 1997.

Diagnostic and Statistical Manual of Mental Disorders, DSM-IV-TR. 4th ed. Arlington, VA: American Psychiatric Association, 2000.

Diament, Michelle. "Down syndrome takes center stage on Fox's 'Glee.'" *Disability Scoop*, April 12, 2010.

Dickinson, Emily. *The Complete Poems of Emily Dickinson*. Boston: Little, Brown, 1960.

Di Domenico, Marina, et al. "Towards gene therapy for deafness." *Journal of Cellular Physiology* 226, no. 10 (October 2011): 2494–99.

Ditton, Paula. *Mental Health and Treatment of Inmates and Probationers*. Washington, DC: US Department of Justice, Office of Justice Programs, Bureau of Justice Statistics, 1999.

Doerr, Adam. "The wrongful life debate." *Genomics Law Report*, September 22, 2009.

Dolnick, Edward. "Deafness as culture." *Atlantic Monthly*, September 1993.

Dominus, Susan. "Remembering the little man who was a big voice for causes." *New York Times*, May 1, 2010.

Douglas, John E., et al. *Crime Classification Manual: A Standard System for Investigating and Classifying Violent Crimes*. San Francisco: Jossey-Bass, 1992.

Dowd, Maureen. "Between torment and happiness." *New York Times*, April 26, 2011.

Down, John Langdon H. "Observations on an ethnic classification of idiots." *London Hospital, Clinical Letters & Reports* 3 (1886): 259–62. Reprinted in *Mental Retardation* 33, no. 1 (February 1995): 54–56.

Drake, Stephen. "Disability advocates call for restraint and responsibility in murder coverage." Press release. Forest Park, IL: Not Dead Yet, June 22, 2006.

Dreger, Alice Domurat. *One of Us: Conjoined Twins and the Future of Normal*. Cambridge, MA: Harvard University Press, 2004.

———. "Lavish dwarf entertainment." *Hastings Center Bioethics Forum*, March 25, 2008.

———. "Womb gay." *Hastings Center Bioethics Forum*, December 4, 2008.

———. "Gender identity disorder in childhood: Inconclusive advice to parents." *Hastings Center Report* 39, no. 1 (January–February 2009): 26–29.

———. "Attenuated thoughts." *Hastings Center Report* 40, no. 6 (November–December 2010): 3.

———. "Trans advocates (at least where genderqueer kids are concerned)." *The Stranger (The Queer Issue: You're Doing It Wrong)*, June 21, 2011.

Dreger, Alice, Ellen K. Feder, and Anne Tamar-Mattis. "Preventing homosexuality (and uppity women) in the womb?" *Hastings Center Bioethics Forum*, June 29, 2010.

Driscoll, Deborah A., and Susan J. Gross. "Screening for fetal aneuploidy and neural tube defects." *Genetic Medicine* 11, no. 11 (November 2009): 818–21.

Drummond, Kelley D., et al. "A follow-up study of girls with gender identity disorder." *Developmental Psychology* 44, no. 1 (January 2008): 34–45.

Duckworth, Angela Lee, and Martin E. P. Seligman. "Self-discipline outdoes IQ in predicting academic performance of adolescents." *Psychological Science* 16, no. 12 (December 2005): 939–44.

Dufresne, Chris. "Amazing feat: Toledo's Wallace began life in pain and braces because of club feet, but his mother's 'miracle' made it a Gump-like success story." *Los Angeles Times*, October 8, 1997.

Dumaret, Annick-Camille, et al. "Adoption and fostering of babies with Down syndrome: A cohort of 593 cases." *Prenatal Diagnosis* 18, no. 5 (May 1998): 437–45.

Durkin, Maureen S., et al. "Advanced parental age and the risk of autism spectrum disorder." *American Journal of Epidemiology* 168, no. 11 (December 2008): 1268–76.

"Dwarf left paralysed after being thrown by drunken Rugby fan." *Telegraph*, January 12, 2012.

"Dwarf tossing ban challenged." United Press International, November 29, 2001.

Dwarfs: Not a Fairy Tale. Documentary film. Produced and directed by Lisa Abelow Hedley and Bonnie Strauss. New York: HBO Home Video, 2001.

D.W., et al. v. Harrison County, Mississippi. Case 1:2009cv00267. US District Court for the Southern District of Mississippi, filed April 20, 2009.

Dykens, Elisabeth M. "Psychopathology in children with intellectual disability." *Journal of Child Psychology & Psychiatry* 41, no. 4 (May 2000): 407–17.

———. "Psychiatric and behavioral disorders in persons with Down syndrome." *Mental Retardation & Developmental Disabilities Research Reviews* 13, no. 3 (October 2007): 272–78.

East Community. "Family and friends." Salem, OR: Early Assessment and Support Team, 2003. http://www.eastcommunity.org/home/ec1/smartlist_12/family_and_friends.html.

Easteal, Patricia Weiser, and Louise McOrmond-Plummer. *Real Rape, Real Pain: Help for Women Sexually Assaulted by Male Partners.* Melbourne, Victoria, Australia: Hybrid, 2006.

Eaton, Leslie, Daniel Gilbert, and Ann Zimmerman. "Suspect's downward spiral." *Wall Street Journal*, January 13, 2011.

Eaton, Lynn. "France outlaws the right to sue for being born." *British Medical Journal* 324, no. 7330 (January 19, 2002): 129.

Eberly, Susan Schoon. "Fairies and the folklore of disability: Changelings, hybrids and the solitary fairy." *Folklore* 99, no. 1 (1988): 58–77.

Eckert, Richard Clark. "Toward a theory of deaf ethnos: Deafnicity ≈ D/deaf (Hómaemon • Homóglosson • Homóthreskon)." *Journal of Deaf Studies & Deaf Education* 15, no. 4 (Fall 2010): 317–33.

Egan, Timothy. "Idaho governor vetoes measure intended to test abortion ruling." *New York Times*, March 31, 1990.

Egley, Arlen, Jr., James C. Howell, and John P. Moore. "Highlights of the 2008 National Youth Gang Survey." Washington, DC: US Department of Justice, Office of Justice Programs, Office of Juvenile Justice & Delinquency Prevention, March 2010.

Ehninger, Dan, et al. "Reversal of learning deficits in a Tsc2+/- mouse model of tuberous sclerosis." *Nature Medicine* 14, no. 8 (August 2008): 843–48.

"81 Words." Radio broadcast. Ira Glass and Alix Spiegel, correspondents. *This American Life*, WBEZ Chicago/National Public Radio, January 18, 2002. http://www .thisamericanlife.org/radio-archives/episode/204/81-Words.

Einhorn, Bruce. "Listen: The sound of hope." *BusinessWeek*, November 14, 2005.

Elbert, Thomas, et al. "Increased cortical representation of the fingers of the left hand in string players." *Science* 270, no. 5234 (October 13, 1995): 305–7.

Eldridge, Sherrie. "Unexpected rejection: The subject no one wants to talk about." *Jewel Among Jewels Adoption News*, Winter 1999.

Elgar, Frank J., et al. "Attachment characteristics and behavioural problems in rural and urban juvenile delinquents." *Child Psychiatry & Human Development* 34, no. 1 (Fall 2003): 35–48.

Ellis, Bob. "South Dakota abortion task force studies rape exceptions." *Dakota Voice*, January 20, 2006.

———. "Rape and the abortion question: Should children conceived of rape be treated differently than other children?" *Dakota Voice*, August 2, 2006.

Emery, Steven D., Anna Middleton, and Graham H. Turner. "Whose deaf genes are they anyway?: The Deaf community's challenge to legislation on embryo selection." *Sign Language Studies* 10, no. 2 (Winter 2010): 155–69.

Engeler, Amy. "I can't hate this baby." *Redbook* 192, no. 4 (February 1999): 108–12.

English, Rebecca. "After World Cup shame, a £25,000 fine and humiliation for Tindall (and Zara's face says it all)." *Daily Mail*, January 12, 2012.

Ensalaco, Mark, and Linda C. Majka, eds. *Children's Human Rights: Progress and Challenges for Children Worldwide*. New York: Rowman & Littlefield, 2005.

Epel, Elissa, et al. "Accelerated telomere shortening in response to life stress." *Proceedings of the National Academy of Sciences* 101, no. 49 (December 2004): 17312–15.

Ericsson, K. Anders, Ralph T. Krampe, and Clemens Tesch-Romer. "The role of deliberate practice in the acquisition of expert performance." *Psychological Review* 100 (1993): 363–406.

Ericsson, K. Anders, Michael J. Prietula, and Edward T. Cokel. "The making of an expert." *Harvard Business Review*, July–August 2007.

Ericsson, K. Anders, Roy W. Roring, and Kiruthiga Nandagopal. "Giftedness and evidence for reproducibly superior performance." *High Ability Studies* 18, no. 1 (June 2007): 3–56.

Erikson, Erik. *Identity and the Life Cycle: Selected Papers*. New York: International Universities Press, 1959.

Essex, Elizabeth Lehr, et al. "Residential transitions of adults with mental retardation: Predictors of waiting list use and placement." *American Journal of Mental Retardation* 101, no. 6 (May 1997): 613–29.

"Ethicist in Ashley case answers questions." Television news report. Amy Burkholder, correspondent. Cable News Network, January 11, 2007. http://www.cnn .com/2007/HEALTH/01/11/ashley.ethicist/index.html.

Evans, Kathy. "Kuwait's rape children offer bitter reminder." *Guardian*, July 29, 1993.

Evans, Nicholas. *Dying Words: Endangered Languages and What They Have to Tell Us.* New York: Wiley-Blackwell, 2009.

Evans, Nicholas, and Stephen C. Levinson. "The myth of language universals: Language diversity and its importance for cognitive science." *Behavioral & Brain Sciences* 32 (2009): 429–92.

Evelyn, Just. *"Mom, I Need to Be a Girl!"* Imperial Beach, CA: Walter Trook, 1998.

Eyman, Richard K., et al. "Survival of profoundly disabled people with severe mental retardation." *American Journal of Diseases of Childhood* 147, no. 3 (March 1993): 329–36.

Fadiman, Clifton. *The Little, Brown Book of Anecdotes.* New York: Little, Brown, 1985.

Fairchild, Tierney. "Rising to the occasion: Reflections on choosing Naia." *Leadership Perspectives in Developmental Disability* 3, no. 1 (Spring 2003). Waltham: Developmental Disabilities Leadership Forum, Shriver School of the University of Massachusetts Medical School, 2003.

———. "The choice to be pro-life." *Washington Post*, November 1, 2008.

Fallon, James B., Dexter R. F. Irvine, and Robert K. Shepherd. "Cochlear implants and brain plasticity." *Hearing Research* 238, nos. 1–2 (April 2008): 110–17.

Faludi, Gábor, and Károly Mirnics. "Synaptic changes in the brain of subjects with schizophrenia." *International Journal of Developmental Neuroscience* 29, no. 3 (May 2011): 305–9.

Farrington, David P. "The development of offending and antisocial behaviour from childhood: Key findings from the Cambridge Study in Delinquent Development." *Journal of Child Psychology & Psychiatry* 36, no. 6 (September 1995): 929–64.

"Federal judge throwing dwarf-tossing lawsuit out of court." *Florida Times-Union*, February 26, 2002.

"Feet, dollars and inches: The intriguing relationship between height and income." *Economist*, April 3, 2008.

Feinberg, Irving. "Schizophrenia: Caused by a fault in programmed synaptic elimination during adolescence?" *Journal of Psychiatric Research* 17, no. 4 (1982–83): 319–34.

Feldman, David Henry, and Lynn T. Goldsmith. *Nature's Gambit: Child Prodigies and the Development of Human Potential.* New York: Teachers College Press, 1991.

Fellman, Bruce. "The Elm City: Then and now." *Yale Alumni Magazine*, September/October 2006.

Feminist Response in Disability Activism. "Feminist Response in Disability Activism (FRIDA) to lead 'Ashley Treatment Action' at the American Medical Association Headquarters." Press release, January 10, 2007. http://fridanow.blogspot.com /2007/01/for-immediate-release-january-10-2007.html.

Fernald, Anne. "Four month olds prefer to listen to motherese." *Infant Behavior & Development* 8 (1985): 181–95.

Fernald, Anne, and Patricia Kuhl. "Acoustic determinants of infant preference for motherese speech." *Infant Behavior & Development* 10 (1987): 279–93.

Fernandes, Jane K., and Shirley Shultz Myers. "Inclusive Deaf studies: Barriers and pathways." *Journal of Deaf Studies & Deaf Education* 15, no. 1 (Winter 2010): 17–29.

Fernandez, Ellen Highland. *The Challenges Facing Dwarf Parents: Preparing for a New Baby.* Tamarac, FL: Distinctive Publishing, 1989.

Ferrall, John A. "Floating on the wings of silence with Beethoven, Kitto, and Edison." *Volta Review* 23 (1921): 295–96.

Ferster, Charles B. "Positive reinforcement and behavioral deficits of autistic children." *Child Development* 32 (1961): 437–56.

Ferster, Charles B., and Marian K. DeMyer. "The development of performances in autistic children in an automatically controlled environment." *Journal of Chronic Diseases* 13, no. 4 (April 1961): 312–14.

"Fiddler Paganini's ways: Stories and facts in the great man's life." *New York Times*, July 27, 1891.

Fidler, Deborah J. "Parental vocalizations and perceived immaturity in Down syndrome." *American Journal on Mental Retardation* 108, no. 6 (November 2003): 425–34.

Fight Crime: Invest in Kids. "Investments in children prevent crime and save money." Washington, DC: Fight Crime: Invest in Kids, 2005. http://www.fightcrime.org /reports/CostBenefit.pdf.

Fillat, Cristina, and Xavier Altafaj. "Gene therapy for Down syndrome." *Progress in Brain Research* 197 (2012): 237–47.

Finkelhor, David, and Kersti Yllö. *License to Rape: Sexual Abuse of Wives*. New York: Holt, Rinehart & Winston, 1985.

Firestone, David. "Deaf students protest new school head." *New York Times*, April 27, 1994.

———. "Chief executive to step down at deaf center." *New York Times*, June 22, 1994.

Fitzgerald, Michael. *The Genesis of Artistic Creativity: Asperger's Syndrome and the Arts*. London: Jessica Kingsley Publishers, 2005.

Fitzgibbons, Richard, Jr., and Joseph Nicolosi. "When boys won't be boys: Childhood Gender Identity Disorder." *Lay Witness*, June 2001.

Fleischer, Doris Zames, and Frieda Zames. *The Disability Rights Movement: From Charity to Confrontation*. Philadelphia: Temple University Press, 2001.

Fleischmann, Carly. "You asked, she answered: Carly Fleischmann, 13, talks to our viewers about autism." ABC News, February 20, 2008. http://abcnews.go.com/ Health/story?id=4320297.

Flynn, Maureen A., and Richard M. Pauli. "Double heterozygosity in bone growth disorders: Four new observations and review." *American Journal of Medical Genetics* 121A, no. 3 (2003): 193–208.

Fost, Norman. "Offense to third parties?" *Hastings Center Report* 40, no. 6 (November–December 2010): 30.

Foucault, Michel. *Madness and Civilization: A History of Insanity in the Age of Reason*. New York: Vintage, 1988.

———. *Politics, Philosophy, Culture: Interviews and Other Writings, 1977–1984*. London: Routledge, 1988.

———. *The History of Sexuality, Vol. 1: An Introduction*. New York: Vintage, 1990.

———. *Abnormal: Lectures at the Collège de France, 1974–1975*. London: Verso, 2003.

Fox, Douglas. "The insanity virus." *Discover*, June 2010.

Fox, James Alan. *Uniform Crime Reports: Supplementary Homicide Reports, 1976–1994*. Data from Federal Bureau of Investigation Uniform Crime Reporting Program. Ann Arbor: Institute for Social Research, University of Michigan, 1996.

Fox, James Alan, and Marianne W. Zawitz. "Homicide trends in the United States." Washington, DC: US Department of Justice, Bureau of Justice Statistics, 2007.

Frances, Allen. "Psychosis risk syndrome: Far too risky." *Australian & New Zealand Journal of Psychiatry* 45, no. 10 (October 2011).

Francomano, Clair A. "The genetic basis of dwarfism." *New England Journal of Medicine* 332, no. 1 (January 5, 1995): 58–59.

Francomano, Clair A., et al. "Localization of the achondroplasia gene to the distal 2.5 Mb of human chromosome 4p." *Human Molecular Genetics* 3, no. 5 (May 1994): 787–92.

Frank, Arthur W. "Emily's scars: Surgical shapings, technoluxe, and bioethics." *Hastings Center Report* 34, no. 2 (March/April 2004): 18–29.

Frankel, Susannah. "Body beautiful: Alexander McQueen asked some of fashion's leading designers to dress people with physical disabilities. His aim? Not to change the world, but to challenge our perceptions of beauty." *Guardian*, August 29, 1998.

Frankfurt, Harry G. *The Reasons of Love*. Princeton, NJ: Princeton University Press, 2004.

Franklin, Jennifer. *Persephone's Ransom*. Georgetown, KY: Finishing Line Press, 2011.

FRAXA Research Foundation. "Clinical trials of three experimental new treatments for Fragile X are accepting participants." Press release, March 22, 2012.

Freud, Anna. *The Harvard Lectures*. Madison, CT: International Universities Press, 1992.

Freud, Sigmund. *Mourning and Melancholia*. In *The Standard Edition of the Complete Psychological Works of Sigmund Freud*. Trans. Joan Riviere. Ed. James Strachey. Vol. 14, *1914–1916*. London: Hogarth Press, 1955.

———. *On Narcissism: An Introduction*. In *The Standard Edition of the Complete Psychological Works of Sigmund Freud*. Trans. Joan Riviere. Ed. James Strachey. Vol. 14, *1914–1916*. London: Hogarth Press, 1955.

———. *The Ego and the Id*. In *The Standard Edition of the Complete Psychological Works of Sigmund Freud*. Trans. Joan Riviere. Ed. James Strachey. Vol. 19, *1923–1925*. New York: Norton, 1960, 1989.

Friedman, Alfred S., et al. *Psychotherapy for the Whole Family: Case Histories, Techniques, and Concepts of Family Therapy of Schizophrenia in the Home and Clinic*. New York: Springer, 1965.

Friedman, Jan Marshall, S. A. Rasmussen, and Q. Yang. "Racial disparities in median age at death of persons with Down syndrome: United States, 1968–1997." *Morbidity & Mortality Weekly Report* 50, no. 22 (June 8, 2001): 463–65.

Friedman, Lawrence J. *Identity's Architect: A Biography of Erik H. Erikson*. London: Free Association Books, 1999.

Friedman, Lilach M., and Karen B. Avraham. "MicroRNAs and epigenetic regulation in the mammalian inner ear: Implications for deafness." *Mammalian Genome* 20, nos. 9–10 (September–October 2009): 581–603.

Friedman, Richard C. *Male Homosexuality: A Contemporary Psychoanalytic Perspective*. New Haven, CT: Yale University Press, 1990.

Frith, Christopher, and Eve Johnstone. *Schizophrenia: A Very Short Introduction*. Oxford, UK, and New York: Oxford University Press, 2003.

Frith, Uta, ed. *Autism and Asperger Syndrome*. Cambridge, UK: Cambridge University Press, 1991.

———. *Autism: Explaining the Enigma*. 2nd ed. Oxford, UK, and Malden, MA: Blackwell, 2003.

Fritz, Thomas, et al. "Universal recognition of three basic emotions in music." *Current Biology* 19, no. 7 (April 2009): 573–76.

Fromm-Reichmann, Frieda. "Notes on the development of treatment of schizophrenics by psychoanalytic psychotherapy." *Psychiatry* 11, no. 3 (August 1948): 263–73.

Fukuyama, Francis. *Our Posthuman Future: Consequences of the Biotechnology Revolution*. New York: Farrar, Straus & Giroux, 2002.

Furey, Eileen M., James M. Granfield, and Orv C. Karan. "Sexual abuse and neglect of adults with mental retardation: A comparison of victim characteristics." *Behavioral Interventions* 9, no. 2 (April 1994): 75–86.

Furey, Eileen M., and Jill J. Niesen. "Sexual abuse of adults with mental retardation by other consumers." *Sexuality & Disability* 12, no. 4 (1994): 285–95.

Fusar-Poli, Paolo, and Pierluigi Politi. "Paul Eugen Bleuler and the birth of schizophrenia (1908)." *American Journal of Psychiatry* 165, no. 11 (2008): 1407.

Gallaudet Research Institute. *Regional and National Summary Report of Data from the 1999–2000 Annual Survey of Deaf and Hard of Hearing Children and Youth.* Washington, DC: Gallaudet University Press, 2001.

Galton, Francis. *Hereditary Genius.* London: Macmillan, 1869.

Gannon, Jack. *The Week the World Heard Gallaudet.* Washington, DC: Gallaudet University Press, 1989.

Ganz, Michael. "The lifetime distribution of the incremental societal costs of autism." *Archives of Pediatric & Adolescent Medicine* 161, no. 4 (April 2007): 343–49.

Garcia, Joseph. *Signing with Your Baby: How to Communicate with Infants Before They Can Speak.* Seattle: Northlight Communications, 2002.

Gardner, R. J. M. "A new estimate of the achondroplasia mutation rate." *Clinical Genetics* 11, no. 1 (April 2008): 31–38.

Garfias, Robert. "Thoughts on the process of language and music acquisition." *Music and Child Development: Proceedings of the 1987 Biology of Music Making Conference.* Ed. F. Wilson and R. Roehmann. St. Louis: MMB Music, 1989.

Gath, Ann, and Dianne Gumley. "Retarded children and their siblings." *Journal of Child Psychology & Psychiatry* 28, no. 5 (September 1987): 715–30.

Geers, Ann E. "Speech, language, and reading skills after early cochlear implantation." *Archives of Otolaryngology—Head & Neck Surgery* 130, no. 5 (May 2004): 634–38.

Geertz, Hildred, and Clifford Geertz. *Kinship in Bali.* Chicago: University of Chicago Press, 1975.

Geller, Andy. "Docs' designer defect baby: Disabled by choice." *New York Post,* December 22, 2006.

Gernsbacher, Morton Ann, et al. "Infant and toddler oral- and manual-motor skills predict later speech fluency in autism." *Journal of Child Psychology & Psychiatry* 49, no. 1 (2008): 43–50.

Gernsbacher, Morton Ann, Heather M. Geye, and Susan Ellis Weismer. "The role of language and communication impairments within autism." In *Language Disorders and Developmental Theory*, ed. P. Fletcher and J. F. Miller, 73–93. Amsterdam, Netherlands: John Benjamins, 2005.

Gershman, Carl. "Psychiatric abuse in the Soviet Union." *Society* 21, no. 5 (July 1984): 54–59.

Geschwind, Daniel H. "Autism: Many genes, common pathways?" *Cell* 135, no. 3 (October 31, 2008): 391–95.

———. "The genetics of autism spectrum disorders." *Trends in Cognitive Sciences* 15, no. 9 (September 2011): 409–16.

Geschwind, Daniel H., and Pat Levitt. "Autism spectrum disorders: Developmental disconnection syndromes." *Current Opinion in Neurobiology* 17, no. 1 (February 2007): 103–11.

Geschwind, Norman. "The biology of cerebral dominance: Implications for cognition." *Cognition* 17, no. 3 (August 1984): 193–208.

Geschwind, Norman, and Albert M. Galaburda. *Cerebral Lateralization.* Cambridge, MA: MIT Press, 1987.

Ghaziuddin, Mohammad. "A family history study of Asperger syndrome." *Journal of Autism & Developmental Disorders* 35, no. 2 (2005): 177–82.

———. "Should the DSM V drop Asperger syndrome?" *Journal of Autism & Developmental Disorders* 40, no. 9 (September 2010): 1146–48.

"Giants and dwarfs." *Strand Magazine* 8 (July–December 1894): 432–38.

Gibbs, Nancy. "Pillow angel ethics." *Time*, January 7, 2007.

Gibbs, Nancy, and Timothy Roche. "The Columbine tapes." *Time*, December 20, 1999.

Gil, Ana Milena, Ana Maria Jaramillo, and Bertha Ortiz. "Pregnancy resulting from rape: Breaking the silence of multiple crises." *Women's Health Collection*, January 1, 2001.

Gilbert, Daniel. *Stumbling on Happiness.* New York: Knopf, 2006.

Gillam, Lynn. "Prenatal diagnosis and discrimination against the disabled." *Journal of Medical Ethics* 25, no. 2 (April 1999): 163–71.

Gillberg, Christopher, and E. Billstedt. "Autism and Asperger syndrome: Coexistence with other clinical disorders." *Acta Psychiatrica Scandinavica* 102, no. 5 (November 2000): 321–30.

Giordano, Simona. "Lives in a chiaroscuro: Should we suspend the puberty of children with gender identity disorder?" *Journal of Medical Ethics* 34, no. 8 (August 2008): 580–85.

Giuliano, Ryan J., et al. "Native experience with a tone language enhances pitch discrimination and the timing of neural responses to pitch change." *Frontiers in Psychology* 2, no. 146 (August 2011): 1–12.

Gladwell, Malcolm. *Outliers: The Story of Success.* New York: Little, Brown, 2008.

Glascher, Jan, et al. "Lesion mapping of cognitive abilities linked to intelligence." *Neuron* 61, no. 5 (March 2009): 681–91.

Glaser, Gabrielle. "'Mad pride' fights a stigma." *New York Times*, May 11, 2008.

Glessner, Joseph T., et al. "Autism genome-wide copy number variation reveals ubiquitin and neuronal genes." *Nature* 459 (May 28, 2009): 569–73.

Global Justice Center. *The Right to an Abortion for Girls and Women Raped in Armed Conflict.* New York: Global Justice Center, 2011.

Goffman, Erving. "The insanity of place." *Psychiatry: Journal of Interpersonal Relations* 32, no. 4 (November 1969): 357–87.

———. *Stigma: Notes on the Management of Spoiled Identity (1963).* New York: Simon & Schuster, 1986.

"Golden Globes: Peter Dinklage cites Martin Henderson case." *Los Angeles Times*, January 16, 2012.

Goleman, Daniel. "Left vs. right: Brain function tied to hormone in the womb." *New York Times*, September 24, 1985.

———. "The wrong sex: A new definition of childhood pain." *New York Times*, March 22, 1994.

Gollust, Sarah E., et al. "Living with achondroplasia in an average-sized world: An assessment of quality of life." *American Journal of Medical Genetics* 120A, no. 4 (August 2003): 447–58.

Goode, Erica. "What provokes a rapist to rape?: Scientists debate notion of an evolutionary drive." *New York Times*, January 15, 2000.

Goodman, Peter. "Sparks fly from his fingertips." *Newsday*, October 2, 1990.

Goodstein, Laurie. "Vatican declined to defrock U.S. priest who abused boys." *New York Times*, March 25, 2010.

———. "Words of a victim." *New York Times*, March 26, 2010.

Goodstein, Laurie, and David Callender. "For years, deaf boys tried to tell of priest's abuse." *New York Times*, March 27, 2010.

Gooren, Louis. "The biology of human psychosexual differentiation." *Hormones & Behavior* 50 (2006): 589–601.

Gooren, Louis J., Erik J. Giltay, and Mathijs C. Bunck. "Long-term treatment of transsexuals with cross-sex hormones: Extensive personal experience." *Journal of Clinical Endocrinology & Metabolism* 93, no. 1 (January 2008): 19–25.

Gotkin, Janet, and Paul Gotkin. *Too Much Anger, Too Many Tears: A Personal Triumph over Psychiatry*. New York: HarperPerennial, 1992.

Gottlieb, Jennifer, and Corinne Cather. "Cognitive behavioral therapy (CBT) for schizophrenia: An in-depth interview with experts." San Francisco: Schizophrenia.com, February 3, 2007.

Gottschall, Jonathan A., and Tiffani A. Gottschall. "Are per-incident rape-pregnancy rates higher than per-incident consensual pregnancy rates?" *Human Nature: An Interdisciplinary Biosocial Perspective* 14, no. 1 (March 1, 2003): 1–20.

Gourevich, Philip. *We Wish to Inform You That Tomorrow We Will Be Killed with Our Families: Stories from Rwanda*. New York: Picador, 1999.

Grady, Denise. "Gene identified as major cause of deafness in Ashkenazi Jews." *New York Times*, November 19, 1998.

Graham, Trey. "The final days of Gaurav Gopalan." *Washington City Paper*, September 21, 2011.

Grandin, Temple. *Thinking in Pictures: And Other Reports from My Life with Autism*. New York: Doubleday, 1995.

Grant, Jaime M., et al. *Injustice at Every Turn: A Report of the National Transgender Discrimination Survey*. New York: National Center for Transgender Equality, 2011.

Grealy, Lucy. *Autobiography of a Face*. Boston: Houghton Mifflin, 1994.

Green, Joanne. "The reality of the miracle: What to expect from the first surgery." Wide Smiles, 1996.

Green, Kevin M.J., et al. "Cortical plasticity in the first year after cochlear implantation." *Cochlear Implants International* 9, no. 2 (2008): 103–17.

Green, Michael Foster. *Schizophrenia Revealed: From Neurons to Social Interactions*. New York and London: W. W. Norton, 2001.

Green, Richard. *The "Sissy Boy" Syndrome and the Development of Homosexuality*. New Haven, CT: Yale University Press, 1987.

Green, Richard, and John Money. *Transsexualism and Sex Reassignment*. Baltimore: Johns Hopkins University Press, 1969.

Green, Saul. "Chelation therapy: Unproven claims and unsound theories." *Quackwatch*, July 24, 2007. http://www.quackwatch.org/01QuackeryRelatedTopics/chelation.html.

Green, Wayne H., Magda Campbell, and Raphael David. "Psychosocial dwarfism: A critical review of the evidence." *Journal of the American Academy of Child Psychiatry* 23, no. 1 (January 1984): 39–48.

Greene, Arin K., et al. "Risk of vascular anomalies with Down syndrome." *Pediatrics* 121, no. 1 (January 2008): 135–40.

Greenspan, Stanley I., and Serena Weider. *Engaging Autism: Using the Floortime Approach to Help Children Relate, Communicate, and Think*. New York: Da Capo, 2006.

Greenwald, Brian H., and John Vickrey Van Cleve, eds. *A Fair Chance in the Race of Life: The Role of Gallaudet University in Deaf History*. Washington, DC: Gallaudet University Press, 2010.

Greenwood, Peter W., et al. *Diverting Children from a Life of Crime: Measuring Costs and Benefits*. Santa Monica, CA: RAND, 1996.

Grelotti, David J., et al. "fMRI activation of the fusiform gyrus and amygdala to cartoon characters but not to faces in a boy with autism." *Neuropsychologia* 43, no. 3 (February 2005): 373–85.

Grieg, Kai. *The War Children of the World*. Bergen, Norway: War and Children Identity Project, 2001.

Grinker, Roy Richard. *Unstrange Minds: Remapping the World of Autism*. New York: Basic Books, 2007.

Grisso, Thomas, and Robert G. Schwartz, eds. *Youth on Trial: A Developmental Perspective on Juvenile Justice*. Chicago: University of Chicago Press, 2000.

Groce, Nora Ellen. *Everyone Here Spoke Sign Language: Hereditary Deafness on Martha's Vineyard*. Cambridge, MA: Harvard University Press, 1985.

Groopman, Jerome. "Hurting all over." *New Yorker*, November 13, 2000.

Groskop, Viv. "My body is wrong." *Guardian*, August 14, 2008.

Gross, Jane, and Stephanie Strom. "Autism debate strains a family and its charity." *New York Times*, June 18, 2007.

Gross, Miraca. *Exceptionally Gifted Children*. London and New York: Routledge, 1993.

Grossman, Frances Kaplan. *Brothers and Sisters of Retarded Children: An Exploratory Study*. Syracuse, NY: Syracuse University Press, 1972.

"Groundbreaking exhibition charts 'History Through Deaf Eyes.'" *USA Today*, February 2006.

Gubbels, Samuel P., et al. "Functional auditory hair cells produced in the mammalian cochlea by in utero gene transfer." *Nature* 455, no. 7212 (August 27, 2008): 537–41.

Guernsey, Diane. "Autism's angels." *Town & Country*, August 1, 2006.

Gumley, Andrew, et al. "Early intervention for relapse in schizophrenia: Results of a 12-month randomized controlled trial of cognitive behavioural therapy." *Psychological Medicine* 33, no. 3 (April 2003): 419–31.

Gunther, Daniel F., and Douglas S. Diekema. "Attenuating growth in children with profound developmental disability: A new approach to an old dilemma." *Archives of Pediatric & Adolescent Medicine* 260, no. 10 (October 2006): 1013–17.

Gur, Raquel E., and Ann Braden Johnson. *If Your Adolescent Has Schizophrenia: An Essential Resource for Parents*. Oxford, UK, and New York: Oxford University Press, 2006.

Gureje, Oye, and Rotimi Bamidele. "Thirteen-year social outcome among Nigerian outpatients with schizophrenia." *Social Psychiatry & Psychiatric Epidemiology* 34, no. 3 (March 1999): 147–51.

Gurewitsch, Matthew. "Early works of a new composer (very early, in fact)." *New York Times*, August 13, 2006.

Gustafson, Paul. "Gang member found not guilty of St. Paul killing." *Minneapolis Star Tribune*, May 6, 2004.

———. "Doubts about witness lead to acquittal in murder case." *Minneapolis Star Tribune*, July 24, 2004.

———. "Gang member sentenced for shooting death of rival." *Minneapolis Star Tribune*, August 20, 2004.

Gutek, Gerald Lee. *The Montessori Method: The Origins of an Educational Innovation: Including an Abridged and Annotated Edition of Maria Montessori's The Montessori Method*. Lanham, MD: Rowman & Littlefield, 2004.

Habib, Mirette B., et al. "Speech production intelligibility of early implanted pediatric cochlear implant users." *International Journal of Pediatric Otorhinolaryngology* 74, no. 8 (August 2010): 855–59.

Hagan, John, and Holly Foster. "Youth violence and the end of adolescence." *American Sociological Review* 66 (December 2001): 874–99.

Hagerman, Randi, et al. "Fragile X syndrome and targeted treatment trials." *Results & Problems in Cell Differentiation* 54 (2012): 297–335.

Hagerman, Randi, Gry Hoem, and Paul Hagerman. "Fragile X and autism: Intertwined at the molecular level leading to targeted treatments." *Molecular Autism* 1, no. 12 (September 2010): 1–14.

Hakak, Yaron, et al. "Genome-wide expression analysis reveals dysregulation of myelination-related genes in chronic schizophrenia." *Proceedings of the National Academy of Sciences* 98, no. 8 (April 2001): 4746–51.

Hakim, Danny. "At state-run homes, abuse and impunity." *New York Times*, March 12, 2011.

Hakim, Danny, Thomas Kaplan, and Michael Barbaro. "After backing gay marriage, 4 in G.O.P. face voters' verdict." *New York Times*, July 4, 2011.

Halbfinger, David M. "Care of juvenile offenders in Mississippi is faulted." *New York Times*, September 1, 2003.

Hall, Jeremy, et al. "Hippocampal function in schizophrenia and bipolar disorder." *Psychological Medicine* 40, no. 5 (May 2010): 761–70.

Hall, Will. *Harm Reduction Guide to Coming Off Psychiatric Drugs*. New York and Northampton, MA: Icarus Project & Freedom Center, 2007.

Hallmayer, Joachim, et al. "Genetic heritability and shared environmental factors among twin pairs with autism." *Archives of General Psychiatry* 68, no. 11 (November 2011): 1095–102.

Hambleton, Else L. *Daughters of Eve: Pregnant Brides and Unwed Mothers in Seventeenth-Century Massachusetts*. London and New York: Routledge, 2004.

Hammarberg, Thomas. "Discrimination against transgender persons must no longer be tolerated." Strasbourg, France: Council of Europe, Office of the Commissioner for Human Rights, 2009.

Hanneman, Robert, and Jan Blacher. "Predicting placement in families who have children with severe handicaps: A longitudinal analysis." *American Journal on Mental Retardation* 102, no. 4 (January 1998): 392–408.

Hansen, Robin L. "Regression in autism: Prevalence and associated factors in the CHARGE study." *Ambulatory Pediatrics* 8, no. 1 (January 2008): 25–31.

Hanson, Marci J. *Teaching Your Down's Syndrome Infant: A Guide for Parents*. Baltimore: University Park Press, 1977.

———. "Twenty-five years after early intervention: A follow-up of children with Down syndrome and their families." *Infants & Young Children* 16, no. 4 (November–December 2003): 354–65.

Haraway, Donna. *Simians, Cyborgs, and Women: The Reinvention of Nature*. New York: Routledge, 1991.

Hare, Lauren, et al. "Androgen receptor repeat length polymorphism associated with male-to-female transsexualism." *Biological Psychiatry* 65, no. 1 (January 2009): 93–96.

Harmon, Amy. "How about not 'curing' us, some autistics are pleading." *New York Times*, December 20, 2004.

———. "The problem with an almost-perfect genetic world." *New York Times*, November 20, 2005.

———. "The DNA age: Prenatal test puts Down syndrome in hard focus." *New York Times*, May 9, 2007.

———. "Nominee to disability council is lightning rod for dispute on views of autism." *New York Times*, March 28, 2010.

Harrington, Tom. "FAQ: Helen Keller quotes." Washington, DC: Gallaudet University Library, 2000. http://www.gallaudet.edu/library/research_help/research_help/frequently_asked_questions/people/helen_keller_quotes.html.

———. "American Sign Language: Ranking and number of users." Washington, DC: Gallaudet University Library, 2004. http://libguides.gallaudet.edu/content.php?pid=114804&sid=991835.

Harrington, Tom, and Sarah Hamrick. "FAQ: Sign languages of the world by country." Washington, DC: Gallaudet University Library, no date. http://library.gallaudet.edu/Library/Deaf_Research_Help/Frequently_Asked_Questions_%28FAQs%29/Sign_Language/Sign_Languages_of_the_World_by_Country.html.

Harris, Jeffrey P., John P. Anderson, and Robert Novak. "An outcomes study of cochlear implants in deaf patients: Audiologic, economic, and quality-of-life changes." *Archives of Otolaryngology—Head & Neck Surgery* 121, no. 4 (April 1995): 398–404.

Harris, Judith Rich. *The Nurture Assumption: Why Children Turn Out the Way They Do.* New York: Free Press, 1998.

Harris, Laura W., et al. "Gene expression in the prefrontal cortex during adolescence: Implications for the onset of schizophrenia." *BMC Medical Genomics* 2 (May 2009): 28.

Harris, Lynn. "Who you calling a 'midget'?" *Salon*, July 16, 2009. http://www.salon.com/life/feature/2009/07/16/m_word/index.html.

Harrison, Paul J. "Schizophrenia susceptibility genes and neurodevelopment." *Biological Psychiatry* 61, no. 10 (2007): 1119–20.

Harrison, Paul J., and Daniel R. Weinberger. "Schizophrenia genes, gene expression, and neuropathology: On the matter of their convergence." *Molecular Psychiatry* 10, no. 1 (January 2005): 40–68.

Hart, Carol. "Who's deficient, who's just plain short? Despite advances, growth hormone decision tough." *AAP News* 13, no. 6 (June 1997): 14–15.

Hartson, Merrill. "Juvenile court system too soft on criminals, U.S. official says." Associated Press, September 4, 1985.

Hasle, H., I. H. Clemmensen, and M. Mikkelsen. "Risks of leukaemia and solid tumors in individuals with Down's syndrome." *Lancet* 355 (2000): 165–69.

Hästbacka, Johanna, et al. "The diastrophic dysplasia gene encodes a novel sulfate transporter: Positional cloning by fine-structure linkage disequilibrium mapping." *Cell* 78, no. 6 (September 23, 1994): 1073–87.

Hastings, Richard P., and Tony Brown. "Functional assessment and challenging behaviors: Some future directions." *Journal of the Association for Persons with Severe Handicaps* 25, no. 4 (Winter 2000): 229–40.

Hastings, Richard P., et al. "Factors related to positive perceptions in mothers of children with intellectual disabilities." *Journal of Applied Research in Intellectual Disabilities* 15, no. 3 (September 2002): 269–75.

Hatfield, Agnes B., and Harriet P. Lefley. *Surviving Mental Illness: Stress, Coping, and Adaptation.* New York: Guilford Press, 1993.

Hatzfeld, Jean. *Machete Season: The Killers in Rwanda Speak.* New York: Farrar, Straus & Giroux, 2005.

Hawkins, Keith A., et al. "Neuropsychological course in the prodrome and first episode of psychosis: Findings from the PRIME North America Double Blind Treatment Study." *Schizophrenia Research* 105, nos. 1–3 (October 2008): 1–9.

Hawkins, Larry, and Judy Brawner. "Educating children who are deaf or hard of hearing: Total Communication." ERIC Digest 559. Reston, VA: ERIC Clearinghouse on Disabilities and Gifted Education, Council for Exceptional Children, 1997.

Hay, William. *Deformity: An Essay.* London: Printed for R. and J. Dodsley, and sold by M. Cooper, 1754.

Hecht, Jacqueline T., et al. "Mortality in achondroplasia." *American Journal of Human Genetics* 41, no. 3 (September 1987): 454–64.

———. "Obesity in achondroplasia." *American Journal of Medical Genetics* 31, no. 3 (November 1988): 597–602.

———. "Mutations in exon 17B of cartilage oligomeric matrix protein (COMP) cause pseudoachondroplasia." *Nature Genetics* 10, no. 3 (July 1995): 325–29.

Heckers, Stephan. "Neuroimaging studies of the hippocampus in schizophrenia." *Hippocampus* 11, no. 5 (October 2001): 520–28.

Hedley, Lisa Abelow. "A child of difference." *New York Times Magazine,* October 12, 1997.

Heffernan, Virginia. "The challenges of a oversized world." *New York Times,* March 4, 2006.

———. "Narrow-minded." *New York Times,* May 25, 2008.

Heller, Tamar, and Alan Factor. "Permanency planning for adults with mental retardation living with family caregivers." *American Journal on Mental Retardation* 96, no. 2 (September 1991): 163–76.

Heller, Tamar, Alison B. Miller, and Alan Factor. "Adults with mental retardation as supports to their parents: Effects on parental caregiving appraisal." *Mental Retardation* 35, no. 5 (October 1997): 338–46.

Hembree, Wylie C., et al. "Endocrine treatment of transsexual persons: An Endocrine Society clinical practice guideline." *Journal of Clinical Endocrinology & Metabolism* 94, no. 9 (September 2009): 3132–54.

Henderson, Helen. "Earthly injustice of 'pillow angels.'" *Toronto Star,* June 27, 2009.

Henderson, Nick. "Attack on wife: Mental health system blamed; man avoids jail after 'tragic' case." *Advertiser,* October 13, 2006.

Herbert, Martha R., et al. "Localization of white matter volume increase in autism and developmental language disorder." *Annals of Neurology* 55, no. 4 (April 2004): 530–40.

———. "Autism and environmental genomics." *NeuroToxicology* 27, no. 5 (September 2006): 671–84.

Her Majesty's Young Offender Institution. HMYOI Castington and Oswald Unit. "Summary of questionnaires and interviews." Acklington, Northumberland: HMYOI Castington and Oswald Unit, February 16, 2010.

Hershenson, Roberta. "Playing piano recitals and skipping fifth grade." *New York Times,* July 9, 2009.

Hershey, Laura. "Choosing disability." *Ms. Magazine,* July 1994.

Herszenhorn, David M. "House approves broad protections for gay workers." *New York Times,* November 8, 2007.

Hertzberg, Hendrik. "The Narcissus survey." *New Yorker,* January 5, 1998.

Hickock, Gregory, et al. "Discourse deficits following right hemisphere damage in deaf signers." *Brain & Language* 66 (1999): 233–48.

Hickock, Gregory, Tracy Love-Geffen, and Edward S. Klima. "Role of the left hemisphere in sign language comprehension." *Brain & Language* 82, no. 2 (August 2002): 167–78.

Hikida, Takatoshi, et al. "Dominant-negative DISC1 transgenic mice display schizophrenia-associated phenotypes detected by measures translatable to humans." *Proceedings of the National Academy of Sciences* 104, no. 36 (September 4, 2007): 14501–6.

Hilarski, Carolyn. "Victimization history as a risk factor for conduct disorder behaviors: Exploring connections in a national sample of youth." *Stress, Trauma & Crisis* 7 (2004): 47–59.

Hilsum, Lindsey. "Rwanda's time of rape returns to haunt thousands." *Guardian,* February 26, 1995.

———. "Don't abandon Rwandan women again." *New York Times*, April 11, 2004.

Hines, Stefani, and Forrest Bennett. "Effectiveness of early intervention for children with Down syndrome." *Mental Retardation & Developmental Disabilities Research Reviews* 2, no. 2 (1996): 96–101.

Ho, Eugenia, et al. "Initial study of rh-IGF1 (Mecasermin [DNA] injection) for treatment of Rett syndrome and development of Rett-specific novel biomarkers of cortical and autonomic function (S28.005)." *Neurology* 78, meeting abstracts 1 (April 25, 2012).

Hockenberry, John. *Moving Violations: War Zones, Wheelchairs and Declarations of Independence*. New York: Hyperion, 1996.

Hodapp, Robert M., and Diane V. Krasner. "Families of children with disabilities: Findings from a national sample of eighth-grade students." *Exceptionality* 5, no. 2 (1995): 71–81.

Hoek, Hans W., Alan S. Brown, and Ezra S. Susser. "The Dutch famine and schizophrenia spectrum disorders." *Social Psychiatry & Psychiatric Epidemiology* 33, no. 8 (July 1998): 373–79.

Hoffman Baruch, Elaine, Amadeo F. D'Adamo, and Joni Seager Jr., eds. *Embryos, Ethics and Women's Rights: Exploring the New Reproductive Technologies*. New York: Harrington Park Press, 1988.

Hollander, Julia. "'Why is there no one to help us?'" *Guardian*, May 28, 2003.

———. *When the Bough Breaks: A Mother's Story*. London: John Murray, 2008.

———. "'I had to give my baby away'—a mother's moving story of caring for her disabled child." *Daily Mail*, March 1, 2008.

———. "A tale of two mothers." *Guardian*, March 8, 2008.

Holmes, Amy S., Mark F. Blaxill, and Boyd E. Haley. "Reduced levels of mercury in first baby haircuts of autistic children." *International Journal of Toxicology* 22, no. 4 (July–August 2003): 277–85.

Holmes, Melissa M., et al. "Rape-related pregnancy: Estimates and descriptive characteristics from a national sample of women." *American Journal of Obstetrics & Gynecology* 175, no. 2 (August 1996): 320–25.

Holmes, Steven A. "Radio talk about TV anchor's disability stirs ire in Los Angeles." *New York Times*, August 23, 1991.

"The homosexual in America." *Time*, January 21, 1966.

Hoover-Fong, Julie E., et al. "Weight for age charts for children with achondroplasia." *American Journal of Medical Genetics Part A* 143A, no. 19 (October 2007): 2227–35.

Hor, Kahyee, and Mark Taylor. "Suicide and schizophrenia: A systematic review of rates and risk factors." *Journal of Psychopharmacology* 24, no. 4 suppl. (November 2010): 81–90.

Horton, Richard. "A statement by the editors of The Lancet." *Lancet* 363, no. 9411 (March 2004): 820–21.

Horton, William. "Recent milestones in achondroplasia research." *American Journal of Medical Genetics* 140A (2006): 166–69.

Horton, William A., Judith G. Hall, and Jacqueline T. Hecht. "Achondroplasia." *Lancet* 370 (July 14, 2007): 162–72.

Howe, Michael J. A., Jane W. Davidson, and John A. Sloboda. "Innate talents: Reality or myth?" *Behavioural & Brain Sciences* 21, no. 3 (June 1998): 399–442.

Howe, Samuel Gridley. *Report Made to the Legislature of Massachusetts, Upon Idiocy*. Boston: Coolidge & Wiley, 1848.

Howell, James C. *Youth Gang Programs and Strategies*. Washington, DC: US Office of Juvenile Justice and Delinquency Prevention, 2000.

———. *Preventing and Reducing Juvenile Delinquency: A Comprehensive Framework.* Thousand Oaks, CA: Sage Publications, 2003.

———. *Gangs in America's Communities.* Thousand Oaks, CA: Sage Publications, 2011.

Howell, James C., et al. "U.S. gang problem trends and seriousness." *National Gang Center Bulletin* 6 (May 201R1): 1–23.

Howells, John G., and Waguih R. Guirguis. *The Family and Schizophrenia.* Madison, CT: International Universities Press, 1985.

Hoyt, Clark. "Consistent, sensitive and weird." *New York Times,* April 18, 2009.

Hrdy, Sarah Blaffer. *Mother Nature: Maternal Instincts and How They Shape the Human Species.* New York: Ballantine Books, 1999.

Huet, Marie-Hélène. *Monstrous Imagination.* Cambridge, MA: Harvard University Press, 1993.

Human Rights Watch. "Sexual violence and its consequences among displaced persons in Darfur and Chad." New York: Human Rights Watch, 2005.

Hunt, Linda. Letter in response to "A child of difference" by Lisa Abelow Hedley (October 12, 1997). *New York Times Magazine,* November 2, 1997.

Hunt, Nigel. *The World of Nigel Hunt: The Diary of a Mongoloid Youth.* New York: Garrett Publications, 1967.

Hunter, Alasdair G. W. "Some psychosocial aspects of nonlethal chondrodysplasias, I: Assessment using a life-styles questionnaire." *American Journal of Medical Genetics* 78, no. 1 (June 1998): 1–8.

———. "Some psychosocial aspects of nonlethal chondrodysplasias, II: Depression and anxiety." *American Journal of Medical Genetics* 78, no. 1 (June 1998): 9–12.

———. "Some psychosocial aspects of nonlethal chondrodysplasias, III: Self-esteem in children and adults." *American Journal of Medical Genetics* 78 (June 1998): 13–16.

Hurley, Dan. "A drug for Down syndrome." *New York Times,* July 29, 2011.

Hutt, Corinne, et al. "Arousal and childhood autism." *Nature* 204 (November 28, 1964): 908–9.

Huttunen, Matti O., and Pekka Niskanen. "Prenatal loss of father and psychiatric disorders." *Archives of General Psychiatry* 35, no. 4 (1978): 429–31.

Ikezuki, Yumiko, et al. "Determination of bisphenol A concentrations in human biological fluids reveals significant early prenatal exposure." *Human Reproduction* 17, no. 11 (November 2002): 2839–41.

"I Love My Baby Who Was Conceived by Rape." Documentary film. Sioux Falls, SD: Vote Yes For Life, 2006.

"Implants help child emerge from silent world." *Casper Star-Tribune,* April 24, 2006.

Inglis, Angela, Catriona Hippman, and Jehannine C. Austin. "Views and opinions of parents of individuals with Down syndrome: Prenatal testing and the possibility of a 'cure'?" Abstract in Courtney Sebold, Lyndsay Graham, and Kirsty McWalter. "Presented abstracts from the Twenty-Eighth Annual Education Conference of the National Society of Genetic Counselors (Atlanta, Georgia, November 2009)." *Journal of Genetic Counseling* 18, no. 6 (November 2009): 622–91.

In My Language. Documentary film. Directed by Amanda Baggs. Privately produced, January 14, 2007. http://www.youtube.com/watch?v=JnylM1hI2jc.

Innes, Stephanie. "Meet Josie, 9: No secret she's transgender." *Arizona Star,* July 25, 2010.

In re the marriage of Michael J. Kantaras v. Linda Kantaras. Case no. 98-5375CA, Circuit Court of the Sixth Judicial Circuit in and for Pasco County, Florida, February 2003.

"Interview with Leslie Van Houten." Television news report. Larry King, correspondent. *Larry King Weekend,* Cable News Network, June 29, 2002. http://transcripts.cnn.com/TRANSCRIPTS/0206/29/lklw.00.html.

Iossifov, Ivan, et al. "De novo gene disruptions in children on the autistic spectrum." *Neuron* 74, no. 2 (April 2012): 285–99.

Iozzio, Mary Jo. "Genetic anomaly or genetic diversity: Thinking in the key of disability on the human genome." *Theological Studies* 66, no. 4 (December 2005): 862–81.

Irving, Claire B., Roger Mumby-Croft, and L. A. Joy. "Polyunsaturated fatty acid supplementation for schizophrenia: Intervention review." *Cochrane Library* 9 (January 20, 2010): 1–64.

Isaac, Rael Jean, and Virginia Armat. *Madness in the Streets: How Psychiatry and the Law Abandoned the Mentally Ill*. New York: Free Press, 1990.

Isaacson, Rupert. *The Horse Boy: A Father's Quest to Heal His Son*. New York: Little, Brown, 2009.

Ishizuka, Koko, et al. "Evidence that many of the DISC1 isoforms in C57BL/6J mice are also expressed in 129S6/SvEv mice." *Molecular Psychiatry* 12, no. 10 (October 2007): 897–99.

Ismail, Zahra. "Emerging from the shadows: Finding a place for children born of war." Thesis, European University Center for Peace Studies, Stadtschlaining, Austria, 2008.

Itard, Jean Marc Gaspard. *The Wild Boy of Aveyron*. Trans. George and Muriel Humphrey. New York: Meredith, 1962.

Iversen, Portia. *Strange Son: Two Mothers, Two Sons, and the Quest to Unlock the Hidden World of Autism*. New York: Riverhead Books, 2006.

Jablow, Martha Moraghan. *Cara: Growing with a Retarded Child*. Philadelphia: Temple University Press, 1982.

Jacobs, Patricia, et al. "The somatic chromosomes in mongolism." *Lancet* 1, no. 7075 (April 1959): 710.

Jaeger, Paul T., and Cynthia Ann Bowman. *Understanding Disability: Inclusion, Access, Diversity, and Civil Rights*. Westport, CT: Praeger, 2005.

Jalāl al-Dīn Rūmī (Maulana). *The Essential Rumi*. Versions by Coleman Barks and John Moyne. New York: HarperCollins, 1995.

James, William. *The Varieties of Religious Experience: A Study in Human Nature*. London: Longmans, Green, 1905.

Janicki, Matthew P., et al. "Mortality and morbidity among older adults with intellectual disability: Health services considerations." *Disability & Rehabilitation* 21, nos. 5–6 (May–June 1999): 284–94.

Jankowski, Katherine A. *Deaf Empowerment: Emergence, Struggle, and Rhetoric*. Washington, DC: Gallaudet University Press, 1997.

Jardine, Cassandra. "I love my baby, but I had to give her up." *Telegraph*, May 19, 2004.

———. "GMC brands Dr Andrew Wakefield 'dishonest, irresponsible and callous.'" *Telegraph*, January 29, 2010.

Jeffrey, Susan. "APA 2009: DSM-V on track for 2019, but difficult decisions lie ahead." *Medscape Medical News*, May 26, 2009.

Jöchle, Wolfgang. "Coitus-induced ovulation." *Contraception* 7, no. 6 (1973): 527–64.

Johns Hopkins Medical Institution. "Hopkins research shows nature, not nurture, determines gender." Press release, May 12, 2000.

Johnson, Ann Braden. *Out of Bedlam: The Truth About Deinstitutionalization*. New York: Basic Books, 1990.

Johnson, C. Plauché, Scott M. Meyers, and the Council on Children with Disabilities. "Identification and evaluation of children with autism spectrum disorders." *Pediatrics* 120, no. 5 (November 2007): 1183–215.

Johnson, Kristen L. *Ideology and Practice of Deaf Goodbyes.* PhD dissertation, Department of Anthropology, University of California at Los Angeles, 1994.

Johnson, M. H., ed. *Brain Development and Cognition.* Cambridge, MA: Blackwell, 1993.

Johnson, Michael. "The dark side of piano competitions." *New York Times,* August 8, 2009.

Jones, Allison K. "Born different: Surgery can help children with craniofacial anomalies, but it can't heal all of the pain." *Telegram & Gazette,* May 23, 1995.

Jones, R. B. "Parental consent to cosmetic facial surgery in Down's syndrome." *Journal of Medical Ethics* 26, no. 2 (April 2000): 101–42.

Joseph, Robert M., et al. "Why is visual search superior in autism spectrum disorder?" *Developmental Science* 12, no. 6 (December 2009): 1083–96.

Joshi, Gagan, et al. "The heavy burden of psychiatric comorbidity in youth with autism spectrum disorders: A large comparative study of a psychiatrically referred population." *Journal of Autism & Developmental Disorders* 40, no. 11 (November 2010): 1361–70.

Jost, Alison. "Mad pride and the medical model." *Hastings Center Report* 39, no. 4 (July–August 2009): 49.

Joynt, Jen, and Vasugi Ganeshananthan. "Abortion decisions." *Atlantic Monthly,* April 2003.

Judge, Timothy A., and Daniel M. Cable. "The effect of physical height on workplace success and income: Preliminary test of a theoretical model." *Journal of Applied Psychology* 89, no. 3 (2004): 428–41.

"Judge allows forced medication for Arizona shooting suspect." *New York Times,* August 28, 2011.

Kahneman, David, et al. "Would you be happier if you were richer? A focusing illusion." *Science* 312 (June 30, 2006): 1908–10.

Kaiser, Jocelyn. "Blood test for mom picks up Down syndrome in fetus." *ScienceNOW Daily News,* October 6, 2008.

Kalasky, Denise (pseud.). "Accomplices in incest." *Post-Abortion Review* 2, no. 1 (Winter 1993).

Kalb, Claudia. "Erasing autism." *Newsweek,* May 25, 2009.

Kalichman, Miriam A. "Replies to growth-attenuation therapy: Principles for practice." Letter to the editor. *Pediatrics,* June 18, 2009. http://pediatrics.aappublications.org/content/123/6/1556/reply.

Kamil, Amos. "Prep-school predators: The Horace Mann School's secret history of sexual abuse." *New York Times Magazine,* June 6, 2012.

Kandel, Eric. "Interview: Biology of the mind." *Newsweek,* March 27, 2006.

Kanner, Leo. "Autistic disturbances of affective contact." *Nervous Child* 2 (1943): 217–50. Reprinted in Leo Kanner. *Childhood Psychosis: Initial Studies and New Insights,* New York: Wiley, 1973, 1–43.

———. "Problems of nosology and psychodynamics in early childhood autism." *American Journal of Orthopsychiatry* 19, no. 3 (July 1949): 416–26.

———. *Childhood Psychosis: Initial Studies and New Insights.* Washington, DC: V. H. Winston & Sons, 1973.

Kanner, Leo, and Leon Eisenberg. "Early infantile autism, 1943–1955." *American Journal of Orthopsychiatry* 26 (1956): 55–65. Reprinted in Leo Kanner, *Childhood Psychosis: Initial Studies and New Insights,* New York: Wiley, 1973, 91–103.

Kant, Emmanuel. *Critique of Judgment.* Trans. Werner S. Pluhar. Indianapolis, IN: Hackett Publishing, 1987.

Kaplan, Karen. "Some Down syndrome parents don't welcome prospect of cure." *Los Angeles Times*, November 22, 2009.

Karoutzou, G., H. M. Emrich, and D. E. Dietrich. "The myelin-pathogenesis puzzle in schizophrenia: A literature review." *Molecular Psychiatry* 13, no. 3 (March 2008): 245–60.

Karpasea-Jones, Joanna. "Daring dis-abled parenting." *Mothering*, November–December 2007.

Katz, Abram. "The bionic ear: Cochlear implants: Miracle or an attack on 'deaf culture'?" *New Haven Register*, March 18, 2007.

Katz, Nancie L. "Guilty in autistic's drowning." *New York Daily News*, February 19, 2005.

Kaufman, Barry. *Son-Rise*. New York: Harper & Row, 1976.

———. *Son-Rise: The Miracle Continues*. Tiburon, CA: H. J. Kramer, 1995.

Kaufman, David. "Tensions between black and gay groups rise anew in advance of anti-gay marriage vote in N.C." *Atlantic Monthly*, May 4, 2012.

Kaufman, Joanne. "Campaign on childhood mental illness succeeds at being provocative." *New York Times*, December 14, 2007.

———. "Ransom-note ads about children's health are canceled." *New York Times*, December 20, 2007.

Kaufman, Marc. "FDA approves wider use of growth hormone." *Washington Post*, July 26, 2003.

Kaufman, Scott Barry. "The truth about the Termites." *Psychology Today*, September 2009.

Kawabata, Maik. "Virtuosity, the violin, the devil . . . what really made Paganini 'demonic'?" *Current Musicology*, March 22, 2007.

Kawamoto, Kohei, et al. "Math1 gene transfer generates new cochlear hair cells in mature guinea pigs in vivo." *Journal of Neuroscience* 23, no. 11 (June 2003): 4395–400.

Kazak, Anne E., and Robert S. Marvin. "Differences, difficulties and adaptation: Stress and social networks in families with a handicapped child." *Family Relations* 33, no. 1 (January 1984): 67–77.

Kazdin, Alan E. "Treatment of antisocial behavior in children: Current status and future directions." *Psychological Bulletin* 102 (September 1987): 187–203.

———. *Parent Management Training: Treatment for Oppositional, Aggressive, and Antisocial Behavior in Children and Adolescents*. Oxford, UK, and New York: Oxford University Press, 2005.

Kazdin, E., L. Marciano, and M. Whitley. "The therapeutic alliance in cognitive-behavioral treatment of children referred for oppositional, aggressive, and antisocial behavior." *Journal of Consulting and Clinical Psychology* 73, no. 4 (August 2005).

Kazerouni, N. Neely, et al. "Triple-marker prenatal screening program for chromosomal defects." *Obstetrics & Gynecology* 114, no. 1 (July 2009): 50–58.

Keehner, Madeleine, and Susan E. Gathercole. "Cognitive adaptations arising from nonnative experience of sign language in hearing adults." *Memory & Cognition* 35, no. 4 (June 2007): 752–61.

Keenan, Julian Paul, et al. "Absolute pitch and planum temporale." *Neuroimage* 14, no. 6 (December 2001): 1402–8.

Keiper, Glenn L., Jr., Bernadette Koch, and Kerry R. Crone. "Achondroplasia and cervicomedullary compression: Prospective evaluation and surgical treatment." *Pediatric Neurosurgery* 31, no. 2 (August 1999): 78–83.

Kellendonk, Christoph, Eleanor H. Simpson, and Eric R. Kandel. "Modeling cognitive endophenotypes of schizophrenia in mice." *Trends in Neurosciences* 32, no. 6 (June 2009): 347–58.

Kelley, Matthew W., et al. "The developing organ of Corti contains retinoic acid and forms supernumerary hair cells in response to exogenous retinoic acid in culture." *Development* 119, no. 4 (December 1993): 1041–53.

Kelsell, David P., et al. "Connexin 26 mutations in hereditary non-syndromic sensorineural deafness." *Nature* 357, no. 6628 (1997): 80–83.

Kemp, Joan. "Abortion: The second rape." *Sisterlife*, Winter 1990.

Kendler, Kenneth S., et al. "The Roscommon Family Study. I. Methods, diagnosis of probands, and risk of schizophrenia in relatives." *Archives of General Psychiatry* 50, no. 7 (July 1993): 527–40.

Kennedy, Dan. *Little People: Learning to See the World Through My Daughter's Eyes.* Emmaus, PA: Rodale, 2003.

Kenneson, Claude, ed. *Musical Prodigies: Perilous Journeys, Remarkable Lives.* New York: Amadeus Press, 1993.

Kenney, Susan. "A marshmallow and a song." *General Music Today* 22, no. 2 (January 2009): 27–29.

Kent, Raymond D., ed. *The MIT Encyclopedia of Communication Disorders.* Cambridge, MA: MIT Press, 2004.

Kern, Robert S., et al. "Psychosocial treatments to promote functional recovery in schizophrenia." *Schizophrenia Bulletin* 35, no. 2 (March 2009): 347–61.

Kevles, Daniel J. *In the Name of Eugenics: Genetics and the Uses of Human Heredity.* New York: Knopf, 1985.

Keys, Matthew. "Local radio show takes heat, loses advertisers over transgender comments." *Sacramento Press*, June 5, 2009.

Khashan, Ali S., et al. "Higher risk of offspring schizophrenia following antenatal maternal exposure to severe adverse life events." *Archives of General Psychiatry* 65, no. 2 (2008): 146–52.

Khoshnood, Babak, et al. "Advances in medical technology and creation of disparities: The case of Down syndrome." *American Journal of Public Health* 96, no. 12 (December 2006): 2139–44.

Kidder, Cynthia S., and Brian Skotko. *Common Threads: Celebrating Life with Down Syndrome.* Rochester Hills, MI: Band of Angels Press, 2001.

Kidston, Martin J. "Helena prodigal son returning as woman." *Independent Record*, September 24, 2009.

———. "250 pack church for transgender documentary." *Independent Record*, September 26, 2009.

Kiessling, Rebecca. "Conceived in Rape: A Story of Hope." Snowflake, AZ: Heritage House, no date.

Kihara, David. "Giuliani's suppressed report on homeless youth." *Village Voice*, August 17, 1999.

Kilgannon, Corey. "After working the streets, bunk beds and a Mass." *New York Times*, May 2, 2007.

Kim, Yunjung, et al. "Schizophrenia genetics: Where next?" *Schizophrenia Bulletin* 37, no. 3 (May 2011): 456–63.

King, Marissa, and Peter Bearman. "Diagnostic change and the increased prevalence of autism." *International Journal of Epidemiology* 38, no. 5 (October 2009): 1224–34.

King, Rachel. *Don't Kill in Our Names: Families of Murder Victims Speak Out Against the Death Penalty.* New Brunswick, NJ: Rutgers University Press, 2003.

———. *Capital Consequences: Families of the Condemned Tell Their Stories.* New Brunswick, NJ: Rutgers University Press, 2005.

————. "The impact of capital punishment on families of defendants and murder victims." *Judicature* 89, no. 5 (March–April 2006): 292–96.

Kingsep, Patrick, Paula Nathan, and David Castle. "Cognitive behavioural group treatment for social anxiety in schizophrenia." *Schizophrenia Research* 63, nos. 1–2 (September 2003): 121–29.

Kingsley, Emily Perl. "Welcome to Holland." Essay, privately published, 1987.

Kingsley, Jason, and Mitchell Levitz. *Count Us In: Growing Up with Down Syndrome.* New York: Harcourt, Brace, 1994.

Kinney, Dennis K., et al. "Prenatal stress and risk for autism." *Neuroscience & Biobehavioral Reviews* 32, no. 8 (October 2008): 1519–32.

Kirby, David. *Evidence of Harm: Mercury in Vaccines and the Autism Epidemic.* New York: St. Martin's Press, 2005.

Kirby, Emma Jane. "Appeal for 'dwarf-tossing' thrown out." British Broadcasting Corporation, September 27, 2002.

Kirov, G., et al. "Support for the involvement of large copy number variants in the pathogenesis of schizophrenia." *Human Molecular Genetics* 18, no. 8 (April 2009): 1497–503.

Kitson, Robert. "Mike Tindall defended by England after incident at 'dwarf-throwing' bash." *Guardian*, September 15, 2011.

Kittay, Eva Feder. "Discrimination against children with cognitive impairments?" *Hastings Center Report* 40, no. 6 (November–December 2010): 32.

Kivy, Peter. *The Possessor and the Possessed: Handel, Mozart, Beethoven, and the Idea of Musical Genius.* New Haven, CT: Yale University Press, 2001.

Kjellberg, Heidrun, Martin Beiring, and Kerstin Albertsson Wikland. "Craniofacial morphology, dental occlusion, tooth eruption, and dental maturity in boys of short stature with or without growth hormone deficiency." *European Journal of Oral Sciences* 108, no. 5 (October 2000): 359–67.

Klebold, Susan. "I will never know why." *O, The Oprah Magazine*, November 2009.

Klin, Ami, et al. "Defining and quantifying the social phenotype in autism." *American Journal of Psychiatry* 159, no. 6 (June 2002): 895–908.

————. "Visual fixation patterns during viewing of naturalistic social situations as predictors of social competence in individuals with autism." *Archives of General Psychiatry* 59, no. 9 (September 2002): 809–16.

Knoll, Carrie. "In parents' eyes, the faintest signs of hope blur the inevitable." *Los Angeles Times*, October 28, 2002.

Knowlson, James R. "The idea of gesture as a universal language in the XVIIth and XVIIIth centuries." *Journal of the History of Ideas* 26, no. 4 (October–December 1965): 495–508.

Kogan, Michael D., et al. "Prevalence of parent-reported diagnosis of autism spectrum disorder among children in the U.S., 2007." *Pediatrics* 124, no. 5 (November 2009): 1395–403.

Kolbert, Elizabeth. "On deadline day, Cuomo vetoes 2 bills opposed by Dinkins." *New York Times*, July 24, 1990.

Komesaroff, Linda R. *Surgical Consent: Bioethics and Cochlear Implantation.* Washington, DC: Gallaudet University Press, 2007.

Kopits, Steven E. "Orthopedic complications of dwarfism." *Clinical Orthopedics & Related Research* 114 (January–February 1976): 153–79.

Korbel, Jan O., et al. "The current excitement about copy-number variation: How it relates to gene duplication and protein families." *Current Opinion in Structural Biology* 18, no. 3 (June 2008): 366–74.

Korman, Cheryl. "Judge: Autistic's mom to serve 10 years for 'torture of her vulnerable child.'" *Tucson Citizen*, September 19, 2008.

Kozinn, Allen. "Recital by Yevgeny Kissin, a young Soviet pianist." *New York Times*, October 2, 1990.

Kras, Joseph F. "The 'Ransom Notes' affair: When the neurodiversity movement came of age." *Disability Studies Quarterly* 30, no. 1 (January 2010).

Krauss, Marty Wyngaarden, Marsha Mailick Seltzer, and S. J. Goodman. "Social support networks of adults with mental retardation who live at home." *American Journal on Mental Retardation* 96, no. 4 (January 1992): 432–41.

Kreytak, Steven. "Tickets issued for dwarf-tossing." *Newsday*, March 11, 2002.

Kristiansen, Kristjana, Simo Vehmas, and Tom Shakespeare, eds. *Arguing About Disability: Philosophical Perspectives*. London and New York: Routledge, 2009.

Kristof, Nicholas. "It's time to learn from frogs." *New York Times*, June 27, 2009.

———. "Chemicals and our health." *New York Times*, July 16, 2009.

Kroeber, Alfred Louis. *Configurations of Culture Growth*. Berkeley: University of California Press, 1944.

Kron, Josh. "Resentment toward the West bolsters Uganda's anti-gay bill." *New York Times*, February 29, 2012.

Krueger, Mary M. "Pregnancy as a result of rape." *Journal of Sex Education & Therapy* 14, no. 1 (1988): 23–27.

Kumpfer, Karol L. *Strengthening America's Families: Exemplary Parenting and Family Strategies for Delinquency Prevention*. Washington, DC: US Department of Justice, Office of Juvenile Justice and Delinquency Prevention, 1999.

Kumpfer, Karol L., and Rose Alvarado. "Family-strengthening approaches for the prevention of youth problem behaviors." *American Psychologist* 58, nos. 6–7 (June–July 2003): 457–65.

Kunc, Norman, and Michael F. Giangreco. "The stairs don't go anywhere! A disabled person's reflections on specialized services and their impact on people with disabilities." Burlington: University of Vermont, September 7, 1995.

Kupperman, Miriam, et al. "Beyond race or ethnicity and socioeconomic status: Predictors of prenatal testing for Down syndrome." *Obstetrics & Gynecology* 107, no. 5 (May 2006): 1087–97.

Kusters, Annelies. "Deaf utopias? Reviewing the sociocultural literature on the world's 'Martha's Vineyard situations.'" *Journal of Deaf Studies & Deaf Education* 15, no. 1 (January 2010): 3–16.

Lacey, Mark. "After being removed from court, Loughner is ruled incompetent." *New York Times*, May 25, 2011.

———. "Lawyers for defendant in Giffords shooting seem to be searching for illness." *New York Times*, August 16, 2011.

Ladd, Paddy. *Understanding Deaf Culture: In Search of Deafhood*. Clevedon, Avon, UK: Multilingual Matters, 2003.

Ladd, Paddy, and Mary John. *Constructing Deafness: Social Constructions of Deafness: Deaf People as a Minority Group—the Political Process*. Milton Keynes, Buckinghamshire, UK: Open University, 1992.

LaFraniere, Sharon. "A miniature world magnifies dwarf life." *New York Times*, March 3, 2010.

Laing, Ronald David. *The Divided Self*. New York: Pantheon, 1960.

———. *The Politics of Experience*. New York: Pantheon, 1967.

———. *The Politics of the Family and Other Essays*. New York: Pantheon, 1971.

Laing, Ronald David, and A. Esterson. *Sanity, Madness and the Family*. New York: Basic Books, 1964.

Lainhart, Janet, et al. "Autism, regression, and the broader autism phenotype." *American Journal of Medical Genetics* 113, no. 3 (December 2002): 231–37.

Lakin, K. Charlie, Lynda Anderson, and Robert Prouty. "Decreases continue in out-of-home residential placements of children and youth with mental retardation." *Mental Retardation* 36, no. 2 (April 1998): 165–67.

———. "Change in residential placements for persons with intellectual and developmental disabilities in the USA in the last two decades." *Journal of Intellectual & Developmental Disability* 28, no. 2 (June 2003): 205–10.

LaMothe, John D. *Controlled Offensive Behavior: USSR*. Report ST-CS-01-169-72. Washington, DC: Defense Intelligence Agency, 1972.

Lancet, editors of. "Retraction—ileal-lymphoid-nodular hyperplasia, non-specific colitis, and pervasive developmental disorder in children." *Lancet* 375, no. 9713 (February 2010): 445.

Land, Kenneth C. "Influence of neighborhood, peer, and family context: Trajectories of delinquent/criminal offending across the life course." Durham, NC: Department of Sociology, Duke University, 2000.

Lane, Harlan. "Cultural and infirmity models of deaf Americans." *Journal of the American Academy of Rehabilitative Audiology* 23 (1990): 11–26.

———. *The Mask of Benevolence: Disabling the Deaf Community*. New York: Alfred A. Knopf, 1992.

———. "Do deaf people have a disability?" *Sign Language Studies* 2, no. 4 (Summer 2002): 356–79.

———. "Ethnicity, ethics and the deaf-world." *Journal of Deaf Studies & Deaf Education* 10, no. 3 (Summer 2005): 291–310.

Langan, Patrick A., and David J. Levin. "Recidivism of prisoners released in 1994." Bureau of Justice Statistics Special Report NCJ 193427. Washington, DC: US Department of Justice, Bureau of Justice Statistics, 2002.

Lang Lang and David Ritz. *Journey of a Thousand Miles: My Story*. New York: Spiegel & Grau, 2008.

Lang Lang and Michael French. *Lang Lang: Playing with Flying Keys*. New York: Delacorte Press, 2008.

Lang Lang and Yuanju Liu / 刘元举, 刘元举著. *Ba ba de xin jiu zhe mo gao: Gang qin tian cai Lang Lang he ta de fu qin* (Dad's Aspirations Are So High) / 爸爸的心就这么高: 钢琴天才郎朗和他的父亲. Beijing: 作家出版社 (Zuo jia chu ban she), 2001. Private translation.

Lankester, Benedict J. A., et al. "Morquio syndrome." *Current Orthopaedics* 20, no. 2 (April 2006): 128–31.

Lappé, Marc. "How much do we want to know about the unborn?" *Hastings Center Report* 3, no. 1 (February 1973): 8–9.

Larkin, Ralph. *Comprehending Columbine*. Philadelphia: Temple University Press, 2007.

LaSasso, Carol, and Jana Lollis. "Survey of residential and day schools for deaf students in the United States that identify themselves as bilingual-bicultural programs." *Journal of Deaf Studies & Deaf Education* 8, no. 1 (January 2003): 79–91.

Lathrop, Anthony. "Pregnancy resulting from rape." *Journal of Obstetric, Gynecologic & Neonatal Nursing* 27, no. 1 (January 1998): 25–31.

Lawrence, Susan. "Solving big problems for little people." *Journal of the American Medical Association* 250, no. 3 (July 15, 1983): 323–30.

Lawson, Karen L. "Perceptions of deservedness of social aid as a function of prenatal diagnostic testing." *Journal of Applied Social Psychology* 33, no. 1 (January 2003): 76–90.

Lawson, Karen L., and Sheena A. Walls-Ingram. "Selective abortion for Down syndrome: The relation between the quality of intergroup contact, parenting expectations, and willingness to terminate." *Journal of Applied Social Psychology* 40, no. 3 (March 2010): 554–78.

Leaming, Colgan. "My brother is not his disability." *Newsweek Web Exclusive*, June 1, 2006. http://www.thedailybeast.com/newsweek/2006/05/31/my-brother-is-not -his-disability.html.

Lee, Brendan, et al. "Identification of the molecular defect in a family with spondyloepiphyseal dysplasia." *Science*, n.s., 244, no. 4907 (May 26, 1989): 978–80.

Leete, Esso. "The treatment of schizophrenia: A patient's perspective." *Hospital & Community Psychiatry* 38, no. 5 (May 1987): 486–91.

———. "How I perceive and manage my illness." *Schizophrenia Bulletin* 15, no. 2 (1989): 197–200.

Lefebvre, Philippe P., et al. "Retinoic acid stimulates regeneration of mammalian auditory hair cells." *Science* 260, no. 108 (April 30, 1993): 692–95.

Leff, David K. "Remaining elms hint at tree's elegant past." *Hartford Courant*, October 27, 2011.

Lehrer, Jonah. "Don't! The secret of self-control." *New Yorker*, May 18, 2005.

Leiby, Michele L. "Wartime sexual violence in Guatemala and Peru." *International Studies Quarterly* 53, no. 2 (June 2009): 445–68.

Leigh, Irene. *A Lens on Deaf Identities*. Oxford and New York: Oxford University Press, 2009.

Leigh, Irene W., et al. "Correlates of psychosocial adjustment in deaf adolescents with and without cochlear implants: A preliminary investigation." *Journal of Deaf Studies & Deaf Education* 14, no. 2 (Spring 2009): 244–59.

Lejeune, Jérôme, et al. "Étude des chromosomes somatiques de neuf enfants mongoliens." *Comptes rendus hebdomadaires des séances de l'Académie des sciences* 248, no. 11 (1959): 1721–22.

Leshin, Len. "Nutritional supplements for Down syndrome: A highly questionable approach." *Quackwatch*, October 18, 1998. http://www.quackwatch.org/01 QuackeryRelatedTopics/down.html.

Leung, Rebecca. "Prodigy, 12, compared to Mozart." CBS News, February 18, 2009. http://www.cbsnews.com/2100-18560_162-657713.html.

Leve, Leslie D., and Patricia Chamberlain. "Female juvenile offenders: Defining an early-onset pathway for delinquency." *Journal of Child & Family Studies* 13, no. 4 (December 2004): 439–52.

Levinson, Douglas F., et al. "Copy number variants in schizophrenia: Confirmation of five previous findings and new evidence for 3q29 microdeletions and VIPR2 duplications." *American Journal of Psychiatry* 168, no. 3 (March 2011): 302–16.

Levitin, Daniel J. "Absolute memory for musical pitch: Evidence from the production of learned melodies." *Perception & Psychophysics* 56, no. 4 (1994): 414–23.

———. *This Is Your Brain on Music: The Science of a Human Obsession*. New York: Dutton, 2006.

Levitin, Daniel J., and Susan E. Rogers. "Absolute pitch: Perception, coding, and controversies." *Trends in Cognitive Sciences* 9, no. 1 (January 2005): 26–33.

Levy, Dan, et al. "Rare de novo and transmitted copy-number variation in autistic spectrum disorders." *Neuron* 70, no. 5 (June 2011): 886–97.

Lezon, Dale. "HPD releases suspect sketch in cross-dresser's killing." *Houston Chronicle*, June 14, 2011.

Li, Hongli, and Lei Chang. "Paternal harsh parenting in relation to paternal versus child characteristics: The moderating effect of paternal resemblance belief." *Acta Psychologica Sinica*, 39, no. 3 (2007): 495–501.

Li, Huawei, et al. "Generation of hair cells by stepwise differentiation of embryonic stem cells." *Proceedings of the National Academy of Sciences* 100, no. 23 (November 11, 2003): 13495–500.

Liberman, Robert Paul, et al. "Operational criteria and factors related to recovery from schizophrenia." *International Review of Psychiatry* 14, no. 4 (November 2002): 256–72.

Libov, Charlotte. "New Haven holding on to 'Elm City' nickname." *New York Times*, April 24, 1988.

Lidz, Ruth Wilmanns, and Theodore Lidz. "The family environment of schizophrenic patients." *American Journal of Psychiatry* 106 (November 1949): 332–45.

Lieberman, Jeffrey A. "A beacon of hope: Prospects for preventing and recovering from mental illness." *NARSAD Research Quarterly* 2, no. 1 (Winter 2009): 23–26.

Lieberman, Jeffrey A., and T. Scott Stroup. "The NIMH-CATIE schizophrenia study: What did we learn?" *American Journal of Psychiatry* 168, no. 8 (August 2011): 770–75.

Lieberman, Jeffrey A., et al. "Science and recovery in schizophrenia." *Psychiatric Services* 59 (May 2008): 487–96.

Life Goes On: The Complete First Season. Television series. Directed by Michael Braverman. Performances by Bill Smitrovich, Patti LuPone, Kellie Martin, Chris Burke. Burbank, CA: Warner Home Video, 2006 (originally broadcast 1989–90).

Lindelof, Bill. "Transgender controversy: Radio hosts to respond to critics on air Thursday: Letter from DJ says remarks were 'hateful.'" *Sacramento Bee*, June 9, 2009.

———. "Broadcasters apologize on air for transgender remarks." *Sacramento Bee*, June 12, 2009.

Lindgren, Kristin A., Doreen DeLuca, and Donna Jo Napoli, eds. *Signs and Voices: Deaf Culture, Identity, Language, and Arts*. Washington, DC: Gallaudet University Press, 2008.

"The little boy who was neglected so badly by his mother that he became a dwarf." *Daily Mail*, August 28, 2010.

Little People of America. "Little People of America on pre-implantation genetic diagnosis." Tustin, CA: Little People of America, 2005.

Lively, Scott. *Redeeming the Rainbow: A Christian Response to the "Gay" Agenda*. Springfield, MA: MassResistance, 2009.

Lobaugh, Nancy J., et al. "Piracetam therapy does not enhance cognitive functioning in children with Down syndrome." *Archives of Pediatric & Adolescent Medicine* 155, no. 4 (April 2001): 442–48.

LoBue, Vanessa, and Judy S. DeLoache. "Pretty in pink: The early development of gender-stereotyped colour preferences." *British Journal of Developmental Psychology* 29, no. 3 (September 2011): 656–67.

Locke, John. *Some Thoughts Concerning Education*. Cambridge, UK: Printed for A. & J. Churchill, 1695.

———. *The Works of John Locke, Esq., in Three Volumes*. London: Printed for Arthur Bettesworth et al., 1727.

Loeber, Rolf, and David P. Farrington, eds. *Serious and Violent Juvenile Offenders: Risk Factors and Successful Interventions.* Thousand Oaks, CA: Sage Publications, 1998.

———, eds. *Child Delinquents: Development, Intervention, and Service Needs.* Thousand Oaks, CA: Sage Publications, 2001.

Loeber, Rolf, and Dale F. Hay. "Developmental approaches to aggression and conduct problems." In *Development Through Life: A Handbook for Clinicians,* ed. Michael Rutter and Dale F. Hay, 488–515. Oxford, UK: Blackwell Scientific Publications, 1994.

Lombroso, Cesare. *The Man of Genius.* London: Walter Scott Publishing, 1888.

Longinus. *On the Sublime.* Trans. Thomas R. R. Stebbing. Oxford, UK: Shrimpton, 1867.

Lorch, Donatella. "Rape used as a weapon in Rwanda: Future grim for genocide orphans." *Houston Chronicle,* May 15, 1995.

Lord, Catherine, et al. "Trajectory of language development in autistic spectrum disorders." In *Developmental Language Disorders: From Phenotypes to Etiologies,* ed. Mabel L. Rice and Steven F. Warren, 7–30. New York: Taylor & Francis, 2004.

Lord, Catherine, and James McGee, eds. *Educating Children with Autism.* Washington, DC: National Academies Press, 2001.

Losh, Molly, et al. "Neuropsychological profile of autism and the broad autism phenotype." *Archives of General Psychiatry* 66, no. 5 (May 2009): 518–26.

Lothell Tate v. State of South Carolina. South Carolina Supreme Court, April 13, 1992.

Louise. "My story of partner rape." Minneapolis, MN: Aphrodite Wounded/Pandora's Aquarium, 2006.

Lovaas, O. Ivar. "Behavioral treatment and normal educational and intellectual functioning in young autistic children." *Journal of Consulting & Clinical Psychology* 55, no. 1 (February 1987): 3–9.

———. "The development of a treatment-research project for developmentally disabled and autistic children." *Journal of Applied Behavior Analysis* 26, no. 4 (Winter 1993): 617–30.

Lovaas, O. Ivar, Benson Schaeffer, and James Q. Simmons. "Building social behavior in autistic children by use of electric shock." *Journal of Experimental Research in Personality* 1 (1965): 99–105.

Lowyck, Benedicte, et al. "Can we identify the factors influencing the burden family-members of schizophrenic patients experience?" *International Journal of Psychiatry in Clinical Practice* 5 (2001): 89–96.

Luciano, Phil. "Case doesn't make sense." *Peoria Journal Star,* May 17, 2006.

———. "Helping everyone but herself." *Peoria Journal Star,* May 18, 2006.

———. "'This was not about autism.'" *Peoria Journal Star,* May 24, 2006.

Lucretius. *On the Nature of Things.* London: H. G. Bohn, 1851.

Luke, Sunny, Swati Gandhi, and Ram S. Verma. "Conservation of the Down syndrome critical region in humans and great apes." *Gene* 161, no. 2 (1995): 283–85.

Luzadder, Dan, and Kevin Vaughan. "Journey into madness." *Denver Rocky Mountain News,* December 12, 1999.

———. "Amassing the facts: Bonded by tragedy, officers probe far, wide for answers." *Denver Rocky Mountain News,* December 13, 1999.

———. "Biggest question of all: Detectives still can't fathom teen-age killers' hatred." *Denver Rocky Mountain News,* December 14, 1999.

Lydgate, Chris. "Dwarf vs. dwarf: The Little People of America want respect—and they're fighting each other to get it." *Willamette Week,* June 30, 1999.

Lynn, Richard. *Eugenics: A Reassessment.* Westport, CT: Praeger, 2001.

873

Lyons, Demie, et al. *Clinical Practice Guideline: Report of the Recommendations: Down Syndrome Assessment and Intervention for Young Children (Age 0–3 Years).* Albany: New York State Department of Health, 2005.

Lysiak, Matthew, and Lukas I. Alpert. "Gabrielle Giffords shooting: Frightening, twisted shrine in Arizona killer Jared Lee Loughner's yard." *New York Daily News,* January 10, 2011.

MacGregor, John M. *Metamorphosis: The Fiber Art of Judith Scott: The Outsider Artist and the Experience of Down's Syndrome.* Oakland, CA: Creative Growth Art Center, 1999.

Mack, Julian. "The juvenile court." *Harvard Law Review* 23 (1909): 104–22.

MacNaughton, M. "Ethics and reproduction." *American Journal of Obstetrics & Gynecology* 162, no. 4 (April 1990): 879–82.

"'Mad Pride' activists say they're unique, not sick." Television news report. I. A. Robinson and Astrid Rodrigues, correspondents. ABC News, August 2, 2009. http://abcnews.go.com/Health/story?id=8382903.

Maess, Burkhard, et al. "Musical syntax is processed in Broca's area: An MEG study." *Nature Neuroscience* 4, no. 5 (May 2001): 540–45.

Mainwaring, George. *Memoirs of the Life of the Late George Frederic Handel.* New York: Da Capo, 1980.

Malaspina, Dolores, et al. "Acute maternal stress in pregnancy and schizophrenia in offspring: A cohort prospective study." *BMC Psychiatry* 8 (2008): 71.

Mall, David, and Walter F. Watts, eds. *The Psychological Aspects of Abortion.* Washington, DC: University Publications of America, 1979.

Mallon, Gerald P. *Social Services with Transgendered Youth.* Binghamton, NY: Harrington Park Press, 1999.

Mallon, Gerald P., and Teresa DeCrescenzo. "Transgender children and youth: A child welfare practice perspective." *Child Welfare* 85, no. 2 (March–April 2006): 215–42.

"Man gets five years in prison for killing autistic son." Associated Press, September 8, 1999.

Manning, Anita. "The changing deaf culture." *USA Today,* May 2, 2000.

"Man pleads guilty to lesser charge." *Aiken Standard,* August 7, 2003.

Mansfield, Caroline, Suellen Hopfer, and Theresa M. Marteau. "Termination rates after prenatal diagnosis of Down syndrome, spina bifida, anencephaly, and Turner and Klinefelter syndromes: A systematic literature review." *Prenatal Diagnosis* 19, no. 9 (September 1999): 108–12.

———. "New prenatal tests offer safer, early screenings." *Wall Street Journal,* June 28, 2011.

Mardell, Danny. *Danny's Challenge: The True Story of a Father Learning to Love His Son.* London: Short Books, 2005.

Marsaja, I Gede. *Desa Kolok: A Deaf Village and Its Sign Language in Bali, Indonesia.* Nijmegen, Netherlands: Ishara Press, 2008.

Marschark, Marc, and Patricia Elizabeth Spencer, eds. *Oxford Handbook of Deaf Studies, Language & Education.* Oxford, UK, and New York: Oxford University Press, 2003.

Marshall, Max, and John Rathbone. "Early intervention in psychosis." *Cochrane Library* 15, no. 6 (June 2011): 1–161.

Martin, Daniela, et al. "Peer relationships of deaf children with cochlear implants: Predictors of peer entry and peer interaction success." *Journal of Deaf Studies & Deaf Education* 16, no. 1 (January 2011): 108–20.

Martin, François, and Jennifer Farnum. "Animal-assisted therapy for children with pervasive developmental disorders." *Western Journal of Nursing Research* 24, no. 6 (October 2002): 657–70.

Masri, Bernard, et al. "Antagonism of dopamine D2 receptor/beta-arrestin 2 interaction is a common property of clinically effective antipsychotics." *Proceedings of the National Academy of Sciences* 105, no. 36 (September 9, 2008): 13656–61.

Masten, Ann S. "Ordinary magic: Resilience processes in development." *American Psychologist* 56, no. 3 (March 2001): 227–38.

Matherne, Monique M., and Adrian Thomas. "Family environment as a predictor of adolescent delinquency." *Adolescence* 36, no. 144 (Winter 2001): 655–64.

Mayberry, Rachel I., et al. "Age of acquisition effects on the functional organization of language in the adult brain." *Brain & Language* 119, no. 1 (October 2011): 16–29.

Mayhew, James F., et al. "Anaesthesia for the achondroplastic dwarf." *Canadian Anaesthetists' Journal* 33, no. 2 (March 1986): 216–21.

Maynard, Joyce. "Prodigy, at 13." *New York Times*, March 4, 1973.

McAllester, Matt. "The hunted." *New York*, October 4, 2009.

McAuliffe, Kathleen. "How your cat is making you crazy." *Atlantic*, March 2012.

McCarthy, Jenny. *Louder Than Words: A Mother's Journey in Healing Autism.* New York: Dutton Adult, 2007.

———. *Mother Warriors: A Nation of Parents Healing Autism Against All Odds.* New York: Dutton Adult, 2008.

McClure, Harold M., et al. "Autosomal trisomy in a chimpanzee: Resemblance to Down's syndrome." *Science* 165, no. 3897 (September 5, 1969): 1010–13.

McCullough, Marie. "Abortion, rape debate." *Chicago Tribune*, September 26, 1995.

McDaniel, Jobeth. "Chris Burke: Then and now." *Ability Magazine*, February 2007.

McDonald, Anne. "The other story from a 'pillow angel': Been there. Done that. Preferred to grow." *Seattle Post-Intelligencer,* June 15, 2007.

McDonnell, John J. J., et al. *Introduction to Persons with Severe Disabilities: Educational and Social Issues.* New York: Allyn & Bacon, 1995.

McElroy, Wendy. "Victims from birth: Engineering defects in helpless children crosses the line." FOX News, April 9, 2002. http://www.foxnews.com/story/0,2933,49849,00.html.

McGee, Robert W. "If dwarf tossing is outlawed, only outlaws will toss dwarfs: Is dwarf tossing a victimless crime?" *American Journal of Jurisprudence* 38 (1993): 335–58.

McGlashan, Thomas H., et al. "Randomized, double-blind trial of olanzapine versus placebo in patients prodromally symptomatic for psychosis." *American Journal of Psychiatry* 163, no. 5 (May 2006): 790–99.

McGlashan, Thomas H., and Ralph E. Hoffman. "Schizophrenia as a disorder of developmentally reduced synaptic connectivity." *Archives of General Psychiatry* 57, no. 7 (July 2000): 637–48.

McGlashan, Thomas, and Scott Woods. "Early antecedents and detection of schizophrenia: Understanding the clinical implications." *Psychiatric Times* 28, no. 3 (March 2011).

McGorry, Patrick D., et al. "Randomized controlled trial of interventions designed to reduce the risk of progression to first-episode psychosis in a clinical sample with subthreshold symptoms." *Archives of General Psychiatry* 59, no. 10 (October 2002): 921–28.

McGovern, Cammie. "Autism's parent trap." *New York Times*, June 5, 2006.

McGuire, Dennis Eugene, and Brian A. Chicoine. *Mental Wellness in Adults with Down Syndrome: A Guide to Emotional and Behavioral Strengths and Challenges*. Bethesda, MD: Woodbine House, 2006.

McGurk, Susan R., et al. "A meta-analysis of cognitive remediation in schizophrenia." *American Journal of Psychiatry* 164, no. 12 (2007): 1791–802.

McKelvey, Robert. *The Dust of Life: America's Children Abandoned in Vietnam*. Seattle: University of Washington Press, 1999.

McKenzie, John. "Autism breakthrough: Girl's writings explain her behavior and feelings." ABC News, February 19, 2008. http://abcnews.go.com/Health/story?id=4311223.

McKusick, Victor Almon. "Ellis–van Creveld syndrome and the Amish." *Nature Genetics* 24 (March 2000): 203–4.

McKusick, Victor Almon, et al. "Dwarfism in the Amish: The Ellis–van Creveld syndrome." *Bulletin of the Johns Hopkins Hospital* 115 (1964): 307–36.

McLaughlin, Janice. "Screening networks: Shared agendas in feminist and disability movement challenges to antenatal screening and abortion." *Disability & Society* 18, no. 3 (2003): 297–310.

McPheeters, Melissa L., et al. "A systematic review of medical treatments for children with autism spectrum disorders." *Pediatrics* 127, no. 5 (May 2011): E1312–E1321.

Mead, Margaret. "The gifted child in the American culture of today." *Journal of Teacher Education* 5, no. 3 (1954): 211–14.

Mead, Rebecca. "Eerily composed: Nico Muhly's sonic magic." *New Yorker*, February 11, 2008.

Meadow, Kathryn P. "Early manual communication in relation to the deaf child's intellectual, social, and communicative functioning." *Journal of Deaf Studies & Deaf Education* 10, no. 4 (Fall 2005): 321–29.

"Medical mystery: Ectrodactyly." Interview with Bree Walker. Jim Jensen, correspondent. ABC News, January 29, 2007. http://abcnews.go.com/Health/story?id=2832319.

Mehler, Jacques, et al. "A precursor of language acquisition in young infants." *Cognition* 29, no. 2 (July 1988): 143–78.

Mehler, Mark F., and Dominick P. Purpura. "Autism, fever, epigenetics and the locus coeruleus." *Brain Research Reviews* 59, no. 2 (March 2009): 388–92.

Menen, Aubrey. "The rapes of Bangladesh." *New York Times*, July 23, 1972.

Menuhin, Yehudi. *Unfinished Journey*. New York: Knopf, 1977.

Menvielle, Edgardo J. "Parents struggling with their child's gender issues." *Brown University's Child & Adolescent Behavior Letter* 20, no. 7 (July 2004): 2–4.

Menvielle, Edgardo J., Ellen Perrin, and Catherine Tuerk. "To the beat of a different drummer: The gender-variant child." *Contemporary Pediatrics* 22, no. 2 (May 2005): 38–46.

Mercer, David. "Mom convicted in autistic girl's death." Associated Press, January 17, 2008.

Mercer, Jean. "Coercive restraint therapies: A dangerous alternative mental health intervention." *Medscape General Medicine* 7, no. 3 (August 9, 2005): 3.

Mesko, Bertalan. "Dr. Steven E. Kopits, a modern miracle maker." *Science Roll*, January 27, 2007. http://scienceroll.com/2007/01/27/dr-steven-e-kopits-a-modern-miracle-maker.

Metro Gang Strike Force. *2008 Annual Report*. Report 09-0568. New Brighton, MN: Metro Gang Strike Force, 2009.

Meyer-Bahlburg, Heino F. L. "Gender identity disorder of childhood: Introduction." *Journal of the American Academy of Child Psychiatry* 24, no. 6 (November 1985): 681–83.

———. "From mental disorder to iatrogenic hypogonadism: Dilemmas in conceptualizing gender identity variants as psychiatric conditions." *Archives of Sexual Behavior* 39, no. 2 (April 2010): 461–76.

Meyerding, Jane. "Thoughts on finding myself differently brained." Privately published, 1998. http://www.planetautism.com/jane/diff.html.

Miami-Dade County Grand Jury. *Investigation into the Death of Omar Paisley and the Department of Juvenile Justice Miami-Dade Regional Juvenile Detention Center.* Miami: Circuit Court of the Eleventh Judicial Circuit of Florida in and for the County of Miami-Dade, January 27, 2004.

Micali, Nadia, et al. "The broad autism phenotype: Findings from an epidemiological survey." *Autism* 8, no. 1 (March 2004): 21–37.

Michael, Matt. "Syracuse man was killed for being gay, police say." *Syracuse Post-Standard,* November 16, 2008.

Michalko, Rod. *The Difference That Disability Makes.* Philadelphia: Temple University Press, 2002.

Michigan Legislature. House Bill 4770 (now Public Act 297 of 2011), the Public Employee Domestic Partner Benefit Restriction Act. Effective December 22, 2011. http://www.legislature.mi.gov/mileg.aspx?page=getobject&objectname =2011-HB-4770.

Midgette, Anne. "Pinch-hitting at Caramoor: Young pianist and Rachmaninoff." *New York Times,* June 25, 2007.

———. "A star who plays second fiddle to music." *New York Times,* December 15, 2007.

———. "Kissin is dexetrous but lacking in emotion." *Washington Post,* March 2, 2009.

Miles, Judith. "Autism spectrum disorders: A genetics review." *Genetics in Medicine* 13, no. 4 (April 2011): 273–362.

Miles, M. "Hittite deaf men in the 13th century B.C." Stockholm, Sweden: Independent Living Institute, 2008.

Miller, Alice. *Prisoners of Childhood: The Drama of the Gifted Child.* New York: Basic Books, 1981.

Miller, Katrina. "Population management strategies for deaf and hard-of-hearing offenders." *Corrections Today* 64, no. 7 (December 2002): 90–95.

Miller, Lisa. "He can't forgive her for killing their son but says spare my wife from a jail cell." *Daily Telegraph,* May 26, 2004.

Miller, Rachel, and Susan Elizabeth Mason. *Diagnosis Schizophrenia: A Comprehensive Resource for Patients, Families, and Helping Professionals.* New York: Columbia University Press, 2002.

Miller, Tandy J., et al. "The PRIME North America randomized double-blind clinical trial of olanzapine versus placebo in patients at risk of being prodromally symptomatic for psychosis II: Baseline characteristics of the 'prodromal' sample." *Schizophrenia Research* 61, no. 1 (March 2003): 19–30.

Miller v. HCA, Inc. 118 S.W.3d 758 (Texas, 2003).

Mills, Steve, and Patricia Callahan. "Md. autism doctor's license suspended." *Baltimore Sun,* May 4, 2011.

Milne, A. A. *The House at Pooh Corner.* New York: Dutton, 1961

Minorities Under Siege: Pygmies Today in Africa. Nairobi: IRIN News Service, April 2006.

Minshew, Nancy J., and Timothy A. Keller. "The nature of brain dysfunction in autism: Functional brain imaging studies." *Current Opinion in Neurology* 23, no. 2 (April 2010): 124–30.

Mischel, Walter, E. B. Ebbesen, and A. R. Zeiss. "Cognitive and attentional mechanisms in delay of gratification." *Journal of Personality & Social Psychology* 21, no. 2 (February 1972): 204–18.

Mischel, Walter, Yuichi Shoda, and Philip K. Peake. "The nature of adolescent competencies predicted by preschool delay of gratification." *Journal of Personality & Social Psychology* 54, no. 4 (April 1988): 687–96.

"The mistreatment of Ashley X." *Family Voyage*, January 4, 2007. http://thefamily voyage.blogspot.com/2007/01/mistreatment-of-ashley-x.html.

Mitchell, Jonathan. "Neurodiversity: Just say no." Los Angeles: Jonathan Mitchell, 2007. http://www.jonathans-stories.com/non-fiction/neurodiv.html.

Mitchell, Juliet. *Mad Men and Medusas: Reclaiming Hysteria.* New York: Basic Books, 2000.

Mitchell, Ross E., and Michael A. Karchmer. "Chasing the mythical ten percent: Parental hearing status of deaf and hard of hearing students in the United States." *Sign Language Studies* 4, no. 2 (Winter 2004): 138–63.

———. "Demographics of deaf education: More students in more places." *American Annals of the Deaf* 151, no. 2 (2006): 95–104.

Mithen, Steven. *The Singing Neanderthals: The Origins of Music, Language, Mind and Body.* Boston: Harvard University Press, 2006.

Miyake, Nobumi, et al. "Presynaptic dopamine in schizophrenia." *CNS Neuroscience & Therapeutics* 17, no. 2 (April 2011): 104–9.

Moffitt, Terrie E. "Genetic and environmental influences on antisocial behaviors: Evidence from behavioral-genetic research." *Advances in Genetics* 55 (2005): 41–104.

Molloy, Charlene, et al. "Is traumatic brain injury a risk factor for schizophrenia? A meta-analysis of case-controlled population-based studies." *Schizophrenia Bulletin* (August 2011): epub ahead of print.

Money, John, and Anke Ehrhardt. *Man and Woman, Boy and Girl.* Baltimore: Johns Hopkins University Press, 1972.

Montgomery, Cal. "A defense of genocide." *Ragged Edge Magazine*, July–August 1999. http://www.raggededgemagazine.com/0799/b799ps.htm.

Mookherjee, Nayanika. "'Remembering to forget': Public secrecy and memory of sexual violence in the Bangladesh war of 1971." *Journal of the Royal Anthropological Institute* 12, no. 2 (June 2006): 433–50.

Moon, Christine, Robin Panneton Cooper, and William P. Fifer. "Two-day-olds prefer their native language." *Infant Behavior & Development* 16, no. 4 (October–December 1993): 495–500.

Moorman, David. "Workshop report: Fever and autism." New York: Simons Foundation for Autism Research, April 1, 2010.

Moran, Mark. "Schizophrenia treatment should focus on recovery, not just symptoms." *Psychiatric News* 39, no. 22 (November 19, 2004): 24.

"More insight on Dylan Klebold." Interview with Nathan Dykeman. Charles Gibson, correspondent. *Good Morning America*, ABC News, April 30, 1999.

Morris, Jan. *Conundrum.* New York: New York Review of Books, 2006.

Morris, Joan K., and Eva Alberman. "Trends in Down's syndrome live births and antenatal diagnoses in England and Wales from 1989 to 2008: Analysis of data from the National Down Syndrome Cytogenetic Register." *British Medical Journal* 339 (2009): B3794.

Morris, Joan K., N. J. Wald, and H. C. Watt. "Fetal loss in Down syndrome pregnancies." *Prenatal Diagnosis* 19, no. 2 (1999): 142–45.

Morrison, Richard. "The prodigy trap." *Sunday Times*, April 15, 2005.

Morton, David L., Jr. *Sound Recording: The Life Story of a Technology.* Baltimore: Johns Hopkins University Press, 2006.

Morwood, Michael J., et al. "Archaeology and age of a new hominin from Flores in eastern Indonesia." *Nature* 431, no. 7012 (October 27, 2004): 1087–91.

Mosher, Loren R. "Schizophrenogenic communication and family therapy." *Family Processes* 8, no. 1 (March 1969): 43–63.

Moss, Kathryn. "The 'Baby Doe' legislation: Its rise and fall." *Policy Studies Journal* 15, no. 4 (June 1987): 629–51.

Moss, Stephen. "At three he was reading the Wall Street Journal." *Guardian*, November 10, 2005.

Mosse, Hilde L. "The misuse of the diagnosis childhood schizophrenia." *American Journal of Psychiatry* 114, no. 9 (March 1958): 791–94.

Mottron, Laurent, et al. "Enhanced perceptual functioning in autism: An update, and eight principles of autistic perception." *Journal of Autism & Developmental Disorders* 36, no. 1 (January 2006): 27–43.

Movius, Kate. "Autism: Opening the window." *Los Angeles*, September 2010.

Mowen, Thomas J., and Ryan D. Schroeder. "Not in my name: An investigation of victims' family clemency movements and court appointed closure." *Western Criminology Review* 12, no. 1 (January 2011): 65–81.

Mozart, Wolfgang Amadeus. *The Letters of Wolfgang Amadeus Mozart.* London: Hurd & Houghton, 1866.

Mueller, Gillian. "Extended limb-lengthening: Setting the record straight." *LPA Online*, 2002. http://www.lpaonline.org/library_ellmueller.html.

Mukhopadhyay, Tito Rajarshi. *The Mind Tree: A Miraculous Child Breaks the Silence of Autism.* New York: Arcade, 2003.

Mulligan, Kate. "Recovery movement gains influence in mental health programs." *Psychiatric News* 38, no. 1 (January 2003): 10.

Mundy, Liza. "A world of their own." *Washington Post Magazine*, March 31, 2002.

Muñoz, Alfredo Brotons. "Más que un prodigio." *Levante EMV,* May 7, 2007.

Munro, Janet C., et al. "IQ in childhood psychiatric attendees predicts outcome of later schizophrenia at 21 year follow-up." *Acta Psychiatrica Scandinavica* 106, no. 2 (August 2002): 139–42.

Munson, Ronald, ed. *Intervention and Reflection: Basic Issues in Medical Ethics.* Belmont, CA: Wadsworth, 2000.

"Murder accused at 'end of her tether.'" *Evening Post*, July 14, 1998.

Murfitt, Nikki. "The heart-breaking moment I realised my mother had cut me off forever, by violin virtuoso Vanessa-Mae." *Daily Mail*, August 7, 2008.

Murray, Mrs. Max A. "Needs of parents of mentally retarded children." *American Journal of Mental Deficiency* 63 (1959): 1078–88.

"Music: Prodigies' progress." *Time*, June 4, 1973.

Mutton, David, et al. "Cytogenetic and epidemiological findings in Down syndrome, England and Wales, 1989 to 1993." *Journal of Medical Genetics* 33, no. 5 (May 1996): 387–94.

Myers, Beverly A., and Siegfried M. Pueschel. "Psychiatric disorders in a population with Down syndrome." *Journal of Nervous & Mental Disease* 179 (1991): 609–13.

Myers, Shirley Shultz, and Jane K. Fernandes. "Deaf studies: A critique of the predominant U.S. theoretical direction." *Journal of Deaf Studies & Deaf Education* 15, no. 1 (Winter 2010): 30–49.

Naik, Gautam. "A baby, please. Blond, freckles, hold the colic: Laboratory techniques that screen for diseases in embryos are now being offered to create designer children." *Wall Street Journal*, February 12, 2009.

Nance, Walter J., and Michael J. Kearsey. "Relevance of connexin deafness (DFNB1) to human evolution." *American Journal of Human Genetics* 74, no. 6 (June 2004): 1081–87.

National Association of the Deaf. "NAD position statement on cochlear implants." Silver Spring, MD: National Association of the Deaf, 1993.

———. "NAD position statement on cochlear implants." Silver Spring, MD: National Association of the Deaf, 2000.

National Center for Transgender Equality. "Understanding Transgender: Frequently Asked Questions About Transgender People." Washington, DC: National Center for Transgender Equality, 2009.

National Dissemination Center for Children with Disabilities. "Severe and/or multiple disabilities." Washington, DC: National Dissemination Center for Children with Disabilities, no date. http://www.nichcy.org/Disabilities/Specific/Pages/SevereandorMultipleDisabilities.aspx.

National Down Syndrome Society. "Cosmetic surgery for children with Down syndrome." Position paper. New York: National Down Syndrome Society, no date. http://www.ndss.org/index.php?option=com_content&view=article&id=153&limitstart=6.

National Youth Gang Center. *National Youth Gang Survey Analysis.* Tallahassee, FL: National Gang Center, 2011.

Natoli, Jaime L., et al. "Prenatal diagnosis of Down syndrome: A systematic review of termination rates (1995–2011)." *Prenatal Diagnosis* 32, no. 2 (February 2012): 142–53.

Naudie, Douglas, et al. "Complications of limb-lengthening in children who have an underlying bone disorder." *Journal of Bone & Joint Surgery* 80, no. 1 (January 1998): 18–24.

Nazeer, Kamran (pseud. Emran Mian). *Send in the Idiots: Stories from the Other Side of Autism.* London: Bloomsbury, 2006.

Need, Anna C., et al. "A genome-wide investigation of SNPs and CNVs in schizophrenia." *PLoS Genetics* 5, no. 2 (February 2009): e1000373.

Ne'eman, Ari. "Dueling narratives: Neurotypical and autistic perspectives about the autism spectrum." 2007 SAMLA Convention, Atlanta, GA, November 2007. http://www.cwru.edu/affil/sce/Texts_2007/Ne'eman.html.

Neihart, Maureen, et al. *The Social and Emotional Development of Gifted Children: What Do We Know?* Waco, TX: Prufrock Press, 2002.

Nelson, Barnaby, and Alison R. Yung. "Should a risk syndrome for first episode psychosis be included in the DSM-5?" *Current Opinion in Psychiatry* 24, no. 2 (March 2011).

Nelson, Barry. "Born with just a little difference." *Northern Echo*, December 2, 2003.

Nelson, Karin B., and Margaret L. Bauman. "Thimerosal and autism?" *Pediatrics* 111, no. 3 (March 2003): 674–79.

Netzer, William J., et al. "Lowering β-amyloid levels rescues learning and memory in a Down syndrome mouse model." *PLoS One* 5, no. 6 (2010): E10943.

Neuffer, Elizabeth. *The Key to My Neighbour's House: Seeking Justice in Bosnia and Rwanda.* London: Bloomsbury, 2002.

Neugeboren, Jay. *Imagining Robert: My Brother, Madness, and Survival: A Memoir.* New Brunswick, NJ: Rutgers University Press, 2003.

Neville, Helen, and Daphne Bavelier. "Human brain plasticity: Evidence from sensory deprivation and altered language experience." *Progress in Brain Research* 138 (2002): 177–88.

Newman, Aaron J., et al. "A critical period for right hemisphere recruitment in American Sign Language processing." *Nature Neuroscience* 5, no. 1 (January 2002): 76–80.

Newton, Isaac. *The Correspondence of Isaac Newton*. Vol. 3. Cambridge, UK: Cambridge University Press, 1961.

New York State Department of Health, Division of Family Health, Bureau of Early Intervention. *The Early Intervention Program: A Parent's Guide*. Albany: New York State Department of Health, no date.

Nichelle v. Villa Grove Community Unit School District No. 302, Board of Education 302. Appellate Court of Illinois, Fourth District, decided August 4, 2010. http://caselaw.findlaw.com/il-court-of-appeals/1537428.html.

Ni Chonghaile, Clar. "Uganda anti-gay bill resurrected in parliament." *Guardian*, February 8, 2012.

Nickel, Regina, and Andrew Forge. "Gap junctions and connexins: The molecular genetics of deafness." In *Encyclopedia of Life Sciences (ELS)*. Chichester, UK: John Wiley & Sons, 2010.

Nicolosi, Joseph, and Linda Ames Nicolosi. *A Parent's Guide to Preventing Homosexuality*. Downer's Grove, IL: InterVarsity Press, 2002.

Nielsen, Diane Corcoran, Barbara Luetke, and Deborah S. Stryker. "The importance of morphemic awareness to reading achievement and the potential of signing morphemes to supporting reading development." *Journal of Deaf Studies & Deaf Education* 16, no. 3 (Summer 2011): 275–88.

Nimura, Janice P. "Prodigies have problems too." *Los Angeles Times*, August 21, 2006.

Nisse, Jason. "SEC probes dwarf-tossing party for Fidelity trader." *Independent*, August 14, 2005.

Nix, Robert L. "Preschool intervention programs and the process of changing children's lives." *Prevention & Treatment* 6, no. 1 (December 2003): Article 33.

Noble, Vicki. *Down Is Up for Aaron Eagle: A Mother's Spiritual Journey with Down Syndrome*. New York: HarperCollins, 1993.

Noll, Richard. "The blood of the insane." *History of Psychiatry* 17, no. 4 (December 2006): 395–418.

Noll, Steven, and James W. Trent Jr., eds. *Mental Retardation in America: A Historical Reader*. New York: New York University Press, 2004.

Nordström, Annika, Lars Dahlgren, and Gunnar Kullgren. "Victim relations and factors triggering homicides committed by offenders with schizophrenia." *Journal of Forensic Psychiatry & Psychology* 17, no. 2 (June 2006): 192–203.

Nordström, Annika, and Gunnar Kullgren. "Victim relations and victim gender in violent crimes committed by offenders with schizophrenia." *Social Psychiatry & Psychiatric Epidemiology* 38, no. 6 (June 2003): 326–30.

Norquay, Kevin. "Autism: Coping with the impossible." *Waikato Times*, July 17, 1998.

Norris, W. Virginia, et al. "Does universal newborn hearing screening identify all children with GJB2 (Connexin 26) deafness?: Penetrance of GJB2 deafness." *Ear & Hearing* 27, no. 6 (December 2006): 732–41.

Not Dead Yet. "NDY Fact Sheet Library: Pete Singer." http://www.notdeadyet.org/docs/singer.html.

Not Dead Yet, et al. "Brief of amici curiae in support of respondents." *Miller v. HCA, Inc.* Civil Action No. 01-0079 (Supreme Court of Texas, filed March 21, 2002). http://www.notdeadyet.org/docs/millerbrief.html.

Nowrojee, Binaifer. *Shattered Lives: Sexual Violence During the Rwandan Genocide and Its Aftermath*. New York: Human Rights Watch, 1996.

Noy, Pinchas. "The development of musical ability." *Psychoanalytic Study of the Child* 23 (1968): 332–47.

Nuiss, Jeannie. "FBI may investigate dragging death as hate crime." *Commercial Appeal*, March 20, 2011.

Oberman, Lindsay M., et al. "EEG evidence for mirror neuron dysfunction in autism spectrum disorders." *Cognitive Brain Research* 24, no. 2 (July 2005): 190–98.

Oberti v. Board of Education of Borough of Clementon School District. 995 F.2d 1204 (Third Circuit Court of Appeals, May 28, 1993).

O'Connor, John J. "TV: Willowbrook State School, 'the Big Town's leper colony.'" *New York Times*, February 2, 1972.

O'Driscoll, Bill. "Turning the tables." *Pittsburgh City Paper*, March 29, 2007.

Oestreich, James. "The violin odyssey of an all-American boy: Joshua Bell, a prodigy who became a star, takes on some unusual projects." *New York Times*, August 31, 1998.

Office of the President. "President Obama announces more key administration posts." Press release, December 16, 2009.

Offit, Paul A. *Autism's False Prophets: Bad Science, Risky Medicine, and the Search for a Cure*. New York: Columbia University Press, 2008.

———. "Vaccines and autism: The Hannah Poling case." *New England Journal of Medicine* 358, no. 20 (May 15, 2008): 2089–91.

O'Hara, Jim. "Syracuse man indicted on hate-crime murder charge." *Syracuse Post-Standard*, April 3, 2009.

———. "Dwight DeLee gets the maximum in transgender slaying." *Syracuse Post-Standard*, August 18, 2009.

O'Keefe, Ed. "Congress declares war on autism." ABC News, December 6, 2006. http://abcnews.go.com/Health/story?id=2708925.

Olbrisch, Rolf R. "Plastic and aesthetic surgery on children with Down's syndrome." *Aesthetic Plastic Surgery* 9, no. 4 (December 1985): 241–48.

Oldham, John, et al. "How budget cuts affect the mentally ill." Letter to the editor. *New York Times*, June 25, 2011.

Oliver, Michael. *Understanding Disability: From Theory to Practice*. New York: St. Martin's, 1996.

Olshansky, Simon. "Chronic sorrow: A response to having a mentally defective child." *Social Casework* 43, no. 4 (1962): 190–94.

Ordoñez, Anna E., and Nitin Gogtay. "Phenomenology and neurobiology of childhood onset schizophrenia." *Current Psychiatry Reviews* 2, no. 4 (November 2006): 463–72.

Osan, Gurinder. "Baby with two faces born in North India." Associated Press, April 9, 2008.

"Oscar Pistorius hopes to have place at London Olympics." British Broadcasting Corporation, March 17, 2012.

"Oscar Pistorius: the 'Blade Runner' who is a race away from changing the Olympics." Associated Press, May 15, 2012.

Ospina, Maria B., et al. "Behavioural and developmental interventions for autism spectrum disorder: A clinical systematic review." *PLoS One* 3, no. 11 (November 2008): E3755.

Owens, Sarah E., et al. "Lack of association between autism and four heavy metal regulatory genes." *NeuroToxicology* 32, no. 6 (December 2011): 769–75.

Padden, Carol, and Tom Humphries. *Deaf in America: Voices from a Culture*. Cambridge, MA: Harvard University Press, 1988.

———. *Inside Deaf Culture*. Cambridge, MA: Harvard University Press, 2005.

Pagels, Elaine H. *Beyond Belief: The Secret Gospel of Thomas*. New York: Random House, 2003.

Palencia, Elaine Fowler. *Taking the Train: Poems*. Middletown, KY: Grex Press, 1997.

Palmer, Greg. *Adventures in the Mainstream: Coming of Age with Down Syndrome*. Bethesda, MD: Woodbine House, 2005.

Pantelis, Christos, et al. "Structural brain imaging evidence for multiple pathological processes at different stages of brain development in schizophrenia." *Schizophrenia Bulletin* 31, no. 3 (July 2005): 672–96.

Papineni, Padmasayee. "Children of bad memories." *Lancet* 362, no. 9386 (September 6, 2003): 825–26.

Pardo, Carlos A., and Charles G. Eberhart. "The neurobiology of autism." *Brain Pathology* 17, no. 4 (October 2007): 434–47.

Parens, Erik, ed. *Surgically Shaping Children: Technology, Ethics, and the Pursuit of Normality*. Baltimore: Johns Hopkins University Press, 2006.

Parens, Erik, and Adrienne Asch, eds. *Prenatal Testing and Disability Rights*. Washington, DC: Georgetown University Press, 2000.

Park, Clara Claiborne. *The Siege*. New York: Harcourt, Brace & World, 1967.

Park, Hui-Wan, et al. "Correction of lumbosacral hyperlordosis in achondroplasia." *Clinical Orthopaedics & Related Research* 12, no. 414 (September 2003): 242–49.

Parker, Rozsika. *Torn in Two: The Experience of Maternal Ambivalence*. London: Virago, 1995, 2005.

Parnes, Aaron, and Nechama Parnes. "Celebrating the miracle of the cochlear implant: Recount of Cochlear Celebration 2007." Brooklyn, NY: Hearing Pocket, 2007. http://www.hearingpocket.com/celebration1.shtml.

Parr, Jeremy R. "Clinical evidence: Autism." *Clinical Evidence Online* 322 (January 2010).

Parr, Jeremy R., et al. "Early developmental regression in autism spectrum disorder: Evidence from an international multiplex sample." *Journal of Autism & Developmental Disorders* 41, no. 3 (March 2011): 332–40.

Paterniti, Michael. "Columbine never sleeps." *GQ*, April 2004.

Patterson, David. "Genetic mechanisms involved in the phenotype of Down syndrome." *Mental Retardation & Developmental Disabilities Research Reviews* 13, no. 3 (October 2007): 199–206.

Pauli, Richard M., et al. *To Celebrate: Understanding Developmental Differences in Young Children with Achondroplasia*. Madison: Midwest Regional Bone Dysplasia Clinic, University of Wisconsin, Madison, 1991.

Peek, Charles W., Judith L. Fischer, and Jeannie S. Kidwell. "Teenage violence toward parents: A neglected dimension of family violence." *Journal of Marriage & the Family* 47 (1985): 1051–58.

Penrose, L. S. "The blood grouping of Mongolian imbeciles." *Lancet* 219, no. 5660 (February 20, 1932): 394–95.

———. "On the interaction of heredity and environment in the study of human genetics (with special reference to Mongolian imbecility)." *Journal of Genetics* 25, no. 3 (April 1932): 407–22.

———. "Maternal age, order of birth and developmental abnormalities." *British Journal of Psychiatry* 85, n.s., 323, no. 359 (1939): 1141–50.

Penrose, Roger. *The Emperor's New Mind: Concerning Computers, Minds, and the Laws of Physics*. Oxford, UK: Oxford University Press, 1989.

People First. *People First Chapter Handbook and Toolkit*. Parkersburg: People First of West Virginia, 2010.

Peres, Judy. "In South Dakota, abortion the issue: Referendum on ban roils low-key state." *Chicago Tribune*, October 21, 2006.

Peretz, Isabelle, and Robert J. Zatorre. "Brain organization for music processing." *Annual Review of Psychology* 56 (February 2005): 89–114.

Perry, Ronen. "It's a wonderful life." *Cornell Law Review* 93 (2008): 329–99.

Persico, Nicola, Andrew Postlewaite, and Dan Silverman. "The effect of adolescent experience on labor market outcomes: The case of height." *Journal of Political Economy* 112, no. 5 (2004): 1019–53.

Pickstone-Taylor, Simon. "Children with gender nonconformity: Author's reply." *Journal of the American Academy of Child & Adolescent Psychiatry* 42, no. 3 (March 2003): 266–68.

Pierce, Bradford Kinney. *A Half Century with Juvenile Delinquents: The New York House of Refuge and Its Times*. New York: D. Appleton, 1869.

Pilkington, Ed. "Frozen in time: The disabled nine-year-old girl who will remain a child all her life." *Guardian*, January 4, 2007.

"'Pillow angel' parents answer CNN's questions." Television news report. Cable News Network, March 12, 2008. http://www.cnn.com/2008/HEALTH/conditions/03/12/pillow.QA/index.html.

Pinker, Steven. "Why they kill their newborns." *New York Times*, November 2, 1997.

Pinter, Joseph D., et al. "Neuroanatomy of Down's syndrome: A high-resolution MRI study." *American Journal of Psychiatry* 158, no. 10 (October 2001): 1659–65.

Piven, Joseph, et al. "Broader autism phenotype: Evidence from a family history study of multiple-incidence autism families." *American Journal of Psychiatry* 154 (February 1997): 185–90.

Piven, Joseph, and Pat Palmer. "Psychiatric disorder and the broad autism phenotype: Evidence from a family study of multiple-incidence autism families." *American Journal of Psychiatry* 156, no. 14 (April 1999): 557–63.

Plann, Susan. *A Silent Minority: Deaf Education in Spain, 1550–1835*. Berkeley: University of California Press, 1997.

Ploeger, Annemarie, et al. "The association between autism and errors in early embryogenesis: What is the causal mechanism?" *Biological Psychiatry* 67, no. 7 (April 2010): 601–7.

Plotkin, Stanley A. "Rubella eradication?" *Vaccine* 19, no. 25–26 (May 2001): 3311–19.

Plotkin, Stanley, Jeffrey S. Gerber, and Paul A. Offit. "Vaccines and autism: A tale of shifting hypotheses." *Clinical Infectious Diseases* 48, no. 4 (February 15, 2009): 456–61.

Plum, Frederick. "Prospects for research on schizophrenia. 3. Neurophysiology: Neuropathological findings." *Neurosciences Research Program Bulletin* 10, no. 4 (November 1972): 384–88.

Pollack, Andrew. "Blood tests ease search for Down syndrome." *New York Times*, October 6, 2008.

Pompili, Maurizio, et al. "Suicide risk in schizophrenia: Learning from the past to change the future." *Annals of General Psychiatry* 6 (March 16, 2007): 10.

Popenoe, Paul. *The Child's Heredity*. Baltimore: Williams & Wilkins, 1930.

Praetorius, Mark, et al. "Adenovector-mediated hair cell regeneration is affected by promoter type." *Acta Otolaryngologica* 130, no. 2 (February 2010): 215–22.

Preski, Sally, and Deborah Shelton. "The role of contextual, child, and parent factors in predicting criminal outcomes in adolescence." *Issues in Mental Health Nursing* 22 (March 2001): 197–205.

Prodigal Sons. Documentary film. Directed by Kim Reed. Produced by Humanities Montana, Catherine S. Campbell, and Montana Human Rights Network. Helena, MT: Big Sky Film Productions, 2009.

Prouty, Robert W., et al., eds. "Residential services for persons with developmental disabilities: Status and trends through 2004." Research and Training Center on Community Living Institute on Community Integration/UCEDD College of Education and Human Development, University of Minnesota, July 2005.

Przybylski, Roger. *What Works: Effective Recidivism Reduction and Risk-Focused Prevention Programs.* Denver: Colorado Division of Criminal Justice, 2008.

Pueschel, Siegfried M., L. A. Monteiro, and Marji Erickson. "Parents' and physicians' perceptions of facial plastic surgery in children with Down syndrome." *Journal of Mental Deficiency Research* 30, no. 1 (March 1986): 71–79.

———. "Facial plastic surgery for children with Down syndrome." *Developmental Medicine & Child Neurology* 30, no. 4 (August 1988): 540–43.

Punch, Renée, and Merv Hyde. "Social participation of children and adolescents with cochlear implants: A qualitative analysis of parent, teacher, and child interviews." *Journal of Deaf Studies & Deaf Education* 16, no. 4 (Fall 2011): 474–93.

Puzzanchera, Charles. *Juvenile Arrests 2007.* OJJDP: Juvenile Justice Bulletin NCJ-225344. Washington, DC: US Department of Justice, Office of Justice Programs, Office of Juvenile Justice and Delinquency Prevention, April 2009.

Puzzanchera, Charles, and Melissa Sickmund. *Juvenile Court Statistics 2005.* OJJDP: Juvenile Justice Bulletin NCJ-224619. Washington, DC: Bureau of Justice Assistance, Office of Juvenile Justice and Delinquency Prevention, 2008.

Qaisar, Sultana. "IDEA 1997—'Inclusion is the law.'" Paper presented at the Annual Convention of the Council for Exceptional Children, Kansas City, MO, April 18–21, 2001.

"Q&A: Therapists on gender identity issues in kids." Radio interview with Dr. Ken Zucker and Dr. Diane Ehrensaft. Alix Spiegel, correspondent. Washington, DC: National Public Radio, May 7, 2008. http://www.npr.org/templates/story/story.php?storyId=90229789.

Quart, Alissa. *Hothouse Kids: The Dilemma of the Gifted Child.* New York: Penguin, 2006.

Quartararo, Anne T. "The perils of assimilation in modern France: The Deaf community, social status, and educational opportunity, 1815–1870." *Journal of Social History* 29, no. 1 (Autumn 1995): 5–23.

Quinn, Justin. "For mother and son, life lessons as death nears: Woman ravaged by cervical cancer prepares autistic son for her passing." *Lancaster Intelligencer Journal,* August 20, 2003.

———. "Local parents get scholarships to attend conference on autism." *Lancaster Intelligencer Journal,* July 30, 2004.

Quinn, William H., and David J. Van Dyke. "A multiple family group intervention for first-time juvenile offenders: Comparisons with probation and dropouts on recidivism." *Journal of Community Psychology* 32, no. 2 (February 2004): 177–200.

Qureshi, Irfan A., and Mark F. Mehler. "Genetic and epigenetic underpinnings of sex differences in the brain and in neurological and psychiatric disease susceptibility." *Progress in Brain Research* 186 (2010): 77–95.

Rabin, Roni. "Screen all pregnancies for Down syndrome, doctors say." *New York Times,* January 9, 2007.

Radiguet, Raymond. *Count d'Orgel's Ball.* Trans. Annapaola Cancogni. Introduction by Jean Cocteau. New York: New York Review Books, 1989.

Raine, Adrian. "Biosocial studies of antisocial and violent behavior in children and adults: A review." *Journal of Abnormal Child Psychology* 30, no. 4 (August 2002): 311–26.

Rankin, Joseph H., and Roger Kern. "Parental attachments and delinquency." *Criminology* 32, no. 4 (November 1994): 495–515.

Raphael-Leff, Joan. "Psychotherapy and pregnancy." *Journal of Reproductive & Infant Psychology* 8, no. 2 (April 1990): 119–35.

Rapoport, Judith L., and Nitin Gogtay. "Childhood onset schizophrenia: Support for a progressive neurodevelopmental disorder." *International Journal of Developmental Neuroscience* 29, no. 3 (May 2011): 251–58.

Rashad, Inas. "Height, health and income in the United States, 1984–2005." *W. J. Usery Workplace Research Group Paper Series*. Working Paper 2008-3-1. Atlanta: Andrew Young School of Policy Studies, Georgia State University, 2008.

Ray, Nicholas. "Lesbian, gay, bisexual and transgender youth: An epidemic of homelessness." Washington, DC: National Gay & Lesbian Task Force, January 30, 2007.

Reagan, Leslie J. *When Abortion Was a Crime: Women, Medicine, and Law in the United States, 1867–1973*. Berkeley: University of California Press, 1997.

Reardon, David C. "Rape, incest and abortion: Searching beyond the myths." *Post-Abortion Review* 2, no. 1 (Winter 1994).

Reardon, David C., Julie Makimaa, and Amy Sobie, eds. *Victims and Victors: Speaking Out About Their Pregnancies, Abortions, and Children Resulting from Sexual Assault*. Springfield, IL: Acorn Books, 2000.

Rehn, Elisabeth, and Ellen Johnson Sirleaf. *Women, War and Peace: The Independent Experts' Assessment on the Impact of Armed Conflict on Women and Women's Role in Peace-Building*. New York: UNIFEM, 2002.

Reich, Nancy B. *Clara Schumann: The Artist and the Woman*. Ithaca, NY: Cornell University Press, 1985.

Reichenberg, Abraham, et al. "Advancing paternal age and autism." *Archives of General Psychiatry* 63, no. 9 (September 2006): 1026–32.

Reid, Cheryl S., et al. "Cervicomedullary compression in young patients with achondroplasia: Value of comprehensive neurologic and respiratory evaluation." *Journal of Pediatrics* 110, no. 4 (April 1987): 522–30.

Reiner, William G. "Gender identity and sex-of-rearing in children with disorders of sexual differentiation." *Journal of Pediatric Endocrinology & Metabolism* 18, no. 6 (June 2005): 549–53.

Reiner, William G., and John P. Gearhart. "Discordant sexual identity in some genetic males with cloacal exstrophy assigned to female sex at birth." *New England Journal of Medicine* 350, no. 4 (January 22, 2004): 333–41.

Rekers, George A., and O. Ivar Lovaas. "Behavioral treatment of deviant sex-role behaviors in a male child." *Journal of Applied Behavior Analysis* 7, no. 2 (Summer 1974): 173–90.

Remnick, David. "The Olympian: How China's greatest musician will win the Beijing Games." *New Yorker*, August 4, 2008.

Renoir, Jean. *Renoir: My Father*. New York: New York Review of Books, 2001.

"Resilience." Radio broadcast. Robin Hughes, correspondent. Interviews with Henry Szeps and Emmy Werner. *Open Mind*, Radio National, Australian Broadcasting Corporation, April 29, 1996. http://www.abc.net.au/rn/talks/8.30/helthrpt/hstories/hr290401.htm.

Resnick, Phillip J. "Child murder by parents: A psychiatric review of filicide." *American Journal of Psychiatry* 126, no. 3 (September 1969): 73–82.

Révész, Géza. *The Psychology of a Musical Prodigy.* New York: Harcourt, Brace, 1925.

Reynolds, Arthur J., et al. "Long-term effects of an early childhood intervention on educational achievement and juvenile arrest: A 15-year follow-up of low-income children in public school." *Journal of the American Medical Association* 285, no. 18 (May 9, 2001): 2339–46.

Reynolds, Dave. "Who has the right to decide when to save the sickest babies?" *Inclusion Daily Express,* June 14, 2002. http://www.inclusiondaily.com/news/advocacy/sidneymiller.htm.

———. "Sidney Miller 'wrongful life' case overturned by state Supreme Court." *Inclusion Daily Express,* October 1, 2003. http://www.inclusiondaily.com/archives/03/10/01.htm.

Reynolds, Tim. "The triple test as a screening technique for Down syndrome: Reliability and relevance." *International Journal of Women's Health* 9, no. 2 (August 2010): 83–88.

Ricci, L. A., and Robert M. Hodapp. "Fathers of children with Down's syndrome versus other types of intellectual disability: Perceptions, stress and involvement." *Journal of Intellectual Disability Research* 47, nos. 4–5 (May–June 2003): 273–84.

Rice, Catherine, et al. "Changes in autism spectrum disorder prevalence in four areas of the United States." *Disability & Health Journal* 3, no. 3 (July 2010): 186–201.

Richardson, Guy P., Jacques Boutet de Monvel, and Christine Petit. "How the genetics of deafness illuminates auditory physiology." *Annual Review of Physiology* 73 (March 2011): 311–34.

Richardson, John. *In the Little World: A True Story of Dwarfs, Love, and Trouble.* New York: HarperCollins, 2001.

Ridley, Matt. *Nature via Nurture: Genes, Experience, and What Makes Us Human.* New York: HarperCollins, 2003.

Rimer, Sara. "Unruly students facing arrest, not detention." *New York Times,* January 4, 2004.

Rimland, Bernard. *Infantile Autism: The Syndrome and Its Implications for a Neural Theory of Behavior.* New York: Appleton-Century-Crofts, 1964.

Rimland, Bernard, et al. "Autism, stress, and ethology." *Science,* n.s., 188, no. 4187 (May 2, 1975): 401–2.

Rimmer, Susan Harris. "'Orphans' or veterans? Justice for children born of war in East Timor." *Texas International Law Journal* 42, no. 2 (Spring 2007): 323–44.

Rimoin, David Lawrence. "Limb lengthening: Past, present, and future." *Growth, Genetics & Hormones* 7, no. 3 (1991): 4–6.

Ringen, P. A., et al. "The level of illicit drug use is related to symptoms and premorbid functioning in severe mental illness." *Acta Psychiatrica Scandinavica* 118, no. 4 (October 2008): 297–304.

Risdal, Don, and George H. S. Singer. "Marital adjustment in parents of children with disabilities: A historical review and meta-analysis." *Research & Practice for Persons with Severe Disabilities* 29, no. 2 (Summer 2004): 95–103.

Roan, Shari. "Medical treatment carries possible side effect of limiting homosexuality." *Los Angeles Times,* August 15, 2010.

Robert, Amanda. "School bars autistic child and his service dog." *Illinois Times,* July 23, 2009.

Roberts, Geneviève. "Brain-damaged girl is frozen in time by parents to keep her alive." *Independent,* January 4, 2007.

Robison, John Elder. *Look Me in the Eye: My Life with Asperger's.* New York: Crown, 2007.

Rochester Institute of Technology. "Bilingual bicultural deaf education." Rochester, NY: Rochester Institute of Technology, no date. http://library.rit.edu/guides/deaf-studies/education/bilingual-bicultural-deaf-education.html.

Roesel, Rosalyn, and G. Frank Lawlis. "Divorce in families of genetically handicapped/mentally retarded individuals." *American Journal of Family Therapy* 11, no. 1 (Spring 1983): 45–50.

Rogers, John G., and Joan O. Weiss. *My Child Is a Dwarf.* Owatonna, MN: Little People of America Foundation, 1977.

Rogers, Paul T., and Mary Coleman. *Medical Care in Down Syndrome: A Preventive Medicine Approach.* New York: Marcel Dekker, 1992.

Rogers, Sally J. "Developmental regression in autism spectrum disorders." *Mental Retardation & Developmental Disabilities Research Review* 10, no. 2 (May 2004): 139–43.

Rohan, Tim. "Oscar Pistorius fails to meet qualifying time for Olympics." *New York Times,* June 29, 2012.

———. "Pistorius will be on South Africa's Olympic team." *New York Times,* July 4, 2012.

Roizen, Nancy J. "Complementary and alternative therapies for Down syndrome." *Mental Retardation & Developmental Disabilities Research Reviews* 11, no. 2 (April 2005): 149–55.

Roloff, Matt. *Against Tall Odds: Being a David in a Goliath World.* Sisters, OR: Multnomah Publishers, 1999.

Rondal, Jean A., Alberto Rasore-Quartino, and Salvatore Soresi, eds. *The Adult with Down Syndrome: A New Challenge for Society.* London: Whurr, 2004.

Rondal, Jean A., et al. *Intellectual Disabilities: Genetics, Behaviour and Inclusion.* London: Whurr, 2004.

Rood, Eli. "Not quite a beginning." *Eli's Coming,* February 3, 2006. http://translocative.blogspot.com/2006/02/not-quite-beginning.html.

Rood, Kate. "The sea horse: Our family mascot." *New York Times,* November 2, 2008.

Rosa, Shannon des Roches, et al. *The Thinking Person's Guide to Autism.* New York: Deadwood City Publishing, 2011.

Rose, David. "Lancet journal retracts Andrew Wakefield MMR scare paper." *The Times,* February 3, 2010.

Rosenbaum, Jill Leslie. "Family dysfunction and female delinquency." *Crime & Delinquency* 35, no. 1 (January 1989): 31–44.

Rosenberg, Debra. "Rethinking gender." *Newsweek,* May 21, 2007.

Rosenberg, Howard. "There's more to 'Life' than ratings." *Los Angeles Times,* April 18, 1992.

Rosenbluth, Susan L. "Help for Jewish homosexuals that is consistent with Torah principles." *Jewish Voice & Opinion* 13, no. 4 (December 1999).

Rosin, Hanna. "A boy's life." *Atlantic Monthly,* November 2008.

Ross, Alan O. *The Exceptional Child in the Family: Helping Parents of Exceptional Children.* 5th printing. New York & London: Grune & Stratton, 1972.

Rotem, Michael. "Mother found guilty of killing her autistic son." *Jerusalem Post,* February 22, 1991.

———. "Mother who killed autistic son sent to prison for one year." *Jerusalem Post,* March 22, 1991.

Roth, Philip. *The Human Stain.* Boston: Houghton Mifflin, 2000.

Rothenberg, Laura. *Breathing for a Living: A Memoir.* New York: Hyperion, 2003.

Rothstein, Edward. "Connections: Myths about genius." *New York Times,* January 5, 2002.

Rowitz, Louis, ed. *Mental Retardation in the Year 2000.* New York: Springer, 1992.

Roy, Alec, and Maurizio Pompili. "Management of schizophrenia with suicide risk." *Psychiatric Clinics of North America* 32, no. 4 (December 2009): 863–83.

Royte, Elizabeth. "The outcasts." *New York Times Magazine,* January 19, 1997.

Rozbruch, S. Robert, and Svetlana Ilizarov. *Limb Lengthening and Reconstructive Surgery.* Boca Raton, FL: CRC Press, 2007.

Ruben, Robert J. "A time frame of critical/sensitive periods of language development." *Acta Otolaryngologica* 117, no. 2 (March 1997): 202–5.

Rubin, Lorry G., and Blake Papsin. "Cochlear implants in children: Surgical site infections and prevention and treatment of acute otitis media and meningitis." *Pediatrics* 126, no. 2 (August 2010): 381–91.

Rubinstein, Arthur. *My Young Years.* New York: Knopf, 1973.

Rudacille, Deborah. *The Riddle of Gender: Science, Activism and Transgender Rights.* New York: Pantheon, 2005.

Russell, Diana E. H. *Rape in Marriage.* Bloomington and Indianapolis: Indiana University Press, 1990.

Russell, Diane E. H., and Rebecca M. Bolen. *The Epidemic of Rape and Child Sexual Abuse in the United States.* Thousand Oaks, CA: Sage Publications, 2000.

Rutter, Michael, et al. "Are there biological programming effects for psychological development? Findings from a study of Romanian adoptees." *Developmental Psychology* 40, no. 1 (2004): 81–94.

Ryback, Timothy. *Hitler's Private Library.* New York: Random House, 2010.

Ryff, Carol, and Marsha Mailick Seltzer, eds. *The Parental Experience in Midlife.* Chicago: University of Chicago Press, 1996.

Rzucidlo, Susan F. "Welcome to Beirut." Privately published, no date. http://www.bbbautism.com/beginners_beirut.htm.

Sacks, Oliver. *Seeing Voices: A Journey into the World of the Deaf.* Berkeley: University of California Press, 1989.

———. *An Anthropologist on Mars: Seven Paradoxical Tales.* New York: Alfred A. Knopf, 1995.

Safire, William. "On language: Dwarf planet." *New York Times,* September 10, 2006.

St. Clair, David, et al. "Rates of adult schizophrenia following prenatal exposure to the Chinese famine of 1959–1961." *Journal of the American Medical Association* 294, no. 5 (2005): 557–62.

Saks, Elyn R. *Refusing Care: Forced Treatment and the Rights of the Mentally Ill.* Chicago: University of Chicago Press, 2002.

———. *The Center Cannot Hold: My Journey Through Madness.* New York: Hyperion, 2007.

Salehi, Ahmad, et al. "Restoration of norepinephrine-modulated contextual memory in a mouse model of Down syndrome." *Science Translational Medicine* 1, no. 7 (November 2009): 7ra17.

Saletan, William. *Bearing Right: How Conservatives Won the Abortion War.* Berkeley: University of California Press, 2003.

———. "Deformer babies: The deliberate crippling of children." *Slate,* September 21, 2006. http://www.slate.com/id/2149854.

Salkever, David S., et al. "Measures and predictors of community-based employment and earnings of persons with schizophrenia in a multisite study." *Psychiatric Services* 58, no. 3 (March 2007): 315–24.

Samson, Fabienne, et al. "Enhanced visual functioning in autism: An ALE meta-analysis." *Human Brain Mapping* (April 4, 2011): epub ahead of print.

Sandel, Michael J. "The case against perfection." *Atlantic Monthly,* April 2004.

———. *The Case Against Perfection: Ethics in the Age of Genetic Engineering*. Cambridge, MA: Harvard University Press, 2009.

Sanders, Stephen, et al. "De novo mutations revealed by whole-exome sequencing are strongly associated with autism." *Nature* 485, no. 7397 (May 10, 2012): 237–41.

Sandler, Allen G., and Lisa A. Mistretta. "Positive adaptation in parents of adults with disabilities." *Education & Training in Mental Retardation & Developmental Disabilities* 33, no. 2 (June 1998): 123–30.

Saner, Emine. "It is not a disease, it is a way of life." *Guardian*, August 7, 2007.

Sanghavi, Darshak. "Wanting babies like themselves, some parents choose genetic defects." *New York Times*, December 5, 2006.

Santos, Fernanda. "Life term for gunman after guilty plea in Tucson killings." *New York Times*, August 7, 2012.

Sara, Sally. "For people with Down syndrome, longer life has complications." *New York Times*, June 1, 2008.

Satel, Sally. "Prescriptions for psychiatric trouble and the DSM-V." *Wall Street Journal*, February 19, 2010.

Sato, Mitsumoto, Yohtaro Numachi, and Takashi Hamamura. "Relapse of paranoid psychotic state in metamphetamine model of schizophrenia." *Schizophrenia Bulletin* 18, no. 1 (1992): 115–22.

Saunders, Debra J. "Children who deserve to die." *San Francisco Chronicle*, September 23, 1997.

Schaller, Susan. *A Man Without Words*. Berkeley: University of California Press, 1995.

Schiavetti, Nicholas, Robert L. Whitehead, and Dale Evan Metz. "The effects of Simultaneous Communication on production and perception of speech." *Journal of Deaf Studies & Deaf Education* 9, no. 3 (June 2004): 286–304.

Schlaug, Gottfried, et al. "In vivo evidence of structural brain asymmetry in musicians." *Science*, n.s., 267, no. 5198 (February 3, 1995): 699–701.

Schoeneman, Deborah. "Little people, big biz: Hiring dwarfs for parties a growing trend." *New York Post*, November 8, 2001.

Schonberg, Harold C. "Russian soul gets a new voice at the keyboard." *New York Times*, October 7, 1990.

Schopenhauer, Arthur. *Essays of Schopenhauer*. London and New York: Walter Scott, 1897.

———. *The World as Will and Representation*. Trans. E. F. J. Payne. New York: Dover, 1958.

Schopler, Eric, Stella Chess, and Leon Eisenberg. "Our memorial to Leo Kanner." *Journal of Autism & Developmental Disorders* 11, no. 3 (September 1981): 257–69.

Schreibman, Laura Ellen. *The Science and Fiction of Autism*. Cambridge, MA: Harvard University Press, 2005.

Schultz, Robert T., et al. "Abnormal ventral temporal cortical activity during face discrimination among individuals with autism and Asperger syndrome." *Archives of General Psychiatry* 57, no. 4 (April 2000): 331–40.

Schweinhart, Lawrence J., Helen V. Barnes, and David P Weikart. *Significant Benefits: The High/Scope Perry Preschool Study Through Age 27*. Ypsilanti, MI: High Scope Press, 1993.

Schweinhart, Lawrence J., et al. *Lifetime Effects: The HighScope Perry Preschool Study Through Age 40*. Ypsilanti, MI: High Scope Press, 2005.

Scocca, Tom. "Silly in Philly." *Metro Times*, August 9, 2000. http://www2.metrotimes.com/archives/story.asp?id=277

Scorgie, Kate, and Dick Sobsey. "Transformational outcomes associated with parenting children who have disabilities." *Mental Retardation* 38, no. 3 (June 2000): 195–206.

Scott, Joyce. *EnTWINed*. Oakland, CA: Judith Scott Foundation, 2006.

Sea, Scott. "Planet autism." *Salon*, September 27, 2003. http://dir.salon.com/story/mwt/feature/2003/09/27/autism/index.html.

Sebat, Jonathan. "Relating copy-number variants to head and brain size in neuropsychiatric disorders." Press release. New York: Simons Foundation Autism Research Initiative, no date. http://sfari.org/funding/grants/abstracts/relating-copy-number-variants-to-head-and-brain-size-in-neuropsychiatric-disorders.

Sebat, Jonathan, et al. "Strong association of de novo copy number mutations with autism." *Science* 316, no. 5823 (April 20, 2007): 445–49.

Sechehaye, Marguerite. *Autobiography of a Schizophrenic Girl: The True Story of "Renee."* New York: Grune & Stratton, 1951.

Seeman, Philip, et al. "Dopamine supersensitivity correlates with D2^{High} states, implying many paths to psychosis." *Proceedings of the National Academy of Sciences* 102, no. 9 (March 2005): 3513–18.

Segal, David. "Financial fraud is focus of attack by prosecutors." *New York Times*, March 11, 2009.

Séguin, Édouard. *Idiocy and Its Treatment by the Physiological Method*. Originally published in 1866. Reprint, New York: Columbia University Educational Reprints, 1907.

Seidel, Kathleen. "Evidence of venom: An open letter to David Kirby." Neurodiversity.com, May 2005. http://www.neurodiversity.com/evidence_of_venom.html.

Seligman, Martin E. P. *Learned Optimism*. New York: Knopf, 1991.

Selten, Jean-Paul, Elizabeth Cantor-Graae, and Rene S. Kahn. "Migration and schizophrenia." *Current Opinion in Psychiatry* 20, no. 2 (March 2007): 111–15.

Seltzer, Marsha Mailick, and Marty Wyngaarden Krauss. "Quality of life of adults with mental retardation/developmental disabilities who live with family." *Mental Retardation & Developmental Disabilities Research Reviews* 7, no. 2 (May 2001): 105–14.

"Semenya: I accept myself." *Independent Online*, September 8, 2009.

Seroussi, Karyn. *Unraveling the Mystery of Autism and Pervasive Developmental Disorder: A Mother's Story of Research and Recovery*. New York: Simon & Schuster, 2000.

Sessions, Laura. "New study questions teen risk factors." *Washington Post*, November 30, 2000.

Sewell, R. Andrew, Mohini Ranganathan, and Deepak Cyril D'Souza. "Cannabinoids and psychosis." *International Review of Psychosis* 21, no. 2 (April 2009): 152–62.

Sex, Lies and Gender. Documentary film. Directed by David Elisco. Washington, DC: National Geographic Television, 2010.

Shadish, William R., et al. "Effects of family and marital psychotherapies: A meta-analysis." *Journal of Consulting & Clinical Psychology* 61, no. 6 (December 1993): 992–1002.

Shakespeare, Tom, Michael Wright, and Sue Thompson. *A Small Matter of Equality: Living with Restricted Growth*. Yeovil, Somerset, UK: Restricted Growth Association, May 2007.

Shapiro, Danielle. "Mothers in Congo get help in raising children of rape." *Christian Science Monitor*, May 9, 2010.

Shapiro, Joseph P. *No Pity: People with Disabilities Forging a New Civil Rights Movement*. New York: Times Books, 1993.

Shawn, Allen. *Twin: A Memoir*. New York: Viking, 2010.

Shearer, A. Eliot, et al. "Deafness in the genomics era." *Hearing Research* 282, nos. 1–2 (December 2011): 1–9.

Sherer, Michelle R., and Laura Schreibman. "Individual behavioral profiles and predictors of treatment effectiveness for children with autism." *Journal of Consulting & Clinical Psychology* 73, no. 3 (June 2005): 525–38.

Sherman, Stephanie L., et al. "Epidemiology of Down syndrome." *Mental Retardation & Developmental Disabilities Research Reviews* 13, no. 3 (October 2007): 221–27.

Shiang, R., et al. "Mutations in the transmembrane domain of FGFR3 cause the most common genetic form of dwarfism, achondroplasia." *Cell* 78, no. 2 (July 29, 1994): 335–42.

Shin, Mikyong, et al. "Prevalence of Down syndrome among children and adolescents in 10 regions." *Pediatrics* 124, no. 6 (December 2009): 1565–71.

Shirley, Eric D., and Michael C. Ain. "Achondroplasia: Manifestations and treatment." *Journal of the American Academy of Orthopedic Surgeons* 17, no. 4 (April 2009): 231–41.

Shockley, Paul. "Grabe gets life in son's murder." *Daily Sentinel*, March 31, 2010.

Shoda, Yuichi, Walter Mischel, and Philip K. Peake. "The nature of adolescent competencies predicted by preschool delay of gratification." *Journal of Personality & Social Psychology* 54, no. 4 (1988): 687–96.

———. "Predicting adolescent cognitive and self-regulatory competencies from preschool delay of gratification: Identifying diagnostic conditions." *Developmental Psychology* 26, no. 6 (1990): 978–86.

Shonkoff, Jack P., and Samuel J. Meisels, eds. *Handbook of Early Childhood Intervention.* Cambridge, UK: Cambridge University Press, 2000.

Shorter, Edward. *The Kennedy Family and the Story of Mental Retardation.* Philadelphia: Temple University Press, 2000.

Shrestha, Laura B. "Life expectancy in the United States." Washington, DC: Congressional Research Service, 2006.

Shriver, Eunice Kennedy. "Hope for retarded children." *Saturday Evening Post,* September 22, 1962.

Shufeit, Lawrence J., and Stanley R. Wurster. "Frequency of divorce among parents of handicapped children." ERIC Document Reproduction Service No. ED 113 909. Washington, DC: National Institute of Education, 1975.

Shulman, Robin. "Child study center cancels autism ads." *Washington Post,* December 19, 2007.

Sickmund, Melissa. "Juveniles in court." National Report Series Bulletin. Rockville, MD: Office of Juvenile Justice and Delinquency Prevention, June 2003.

Siebers, Tobin. *Disability Theory.* Ann Arbor: University of Michigan Press, 2008.

Siegel, Bryna. *The World of the Autistic Child.* New York: Oxford University Press, 1996.

———. *Helping Children with Autism Learn: Treatment Approaches for Parents and Professionals.* Oxford, UK, and New York: Oxford University Press, 2003.

Silberman, Steve. "The geek syndrome." *Wired,* December 2001.

Simons, Abby. "'The killing of one of our own': More than 200 honored Krissy Bates, hours after a Blaine man was charged in her killing." *Minneapolis Star Tribune,* January 22, 2011.

———. "Man guilty of murdering transgender victim." *Minneapolis Star Tribune,* November 24, 2011.

Simonton, Dean Keith, and Anna V. Song. "Eminence, IQ, physical and mental health, and achievement domain: Cox's 282 geniuses revisited." *Psychological Science* 20, no. 4 (April 2009): 429–34.

Sinclair, Jim. "Don't mourn for us." *Our Voice* 1, no. 3. Syracuse, NY: Autism Network International, 1993. http://www.autreat.com/dont_mourn.html.

————. "Why I dislike 'person-first' language." Syracuse, NY: Jim Sinclair, 1999. http://web.archive.org/web/20030527100525/http://web.syr.edu/~jisincla/person_first.htm.

Singal, Daniel. "The other crisis in American education." *Atlantic Monthly*, November 1991.

Singer, George H. S., and Larry K. Irvin, eds. *Support for Caregiving Families: Enabling Positive Adaptation to Disability*. Baltimore: Paul H. Brookes, 1989.

Singer, Judy. "Why can't you be normal for once in your life: From a 'problem with no name' to a new kind of disability." In *Disability Discourse*, eds. M. Corker and S. French. Maidenhead, UK: Open University Press, 1999.

Singer, Peter. "Sanctity of life or quality of life?" *Pediatrics* 72, no. 1 (July 1983): 128–29.

————. *Practical Ethics*. 2nd ed. Cambridge, UK: Cambridge University Press, 1993.

————. *Rethinking Life and Death: The Collapse of Our Traditional Ethics*. New York: St. Martin's Griffin, 1994.

————. "A convenient truth." *New York Times*, January 26, 2007.

Sisk, Elisabeth A., et al. "Obstructive sleep apnea in children with achondroplasia: Surgical and anesthetic considerations." *Archives of Otolaryngology—Head & Neck Surgery* 120, no. 2 (February 1999): 248–54.

Skotara, Nils, et al. "The influence of language deprivation in early childhood on L2 processing: An ERP comparison of deaf native signers and deaf signers with a delayed language acquisition." *BMC Neuroscience* 13, no. 44 (provisionally published May 3, 2012).

Skotko, Brian. "Mothers of children with Down syndrome reflect on their postnatal support." *Pediatrics* 115, no. 1 (January 2005): 64–77.

————. "Prenatally diagnosed Down syndrome: Mothers who continued their pregnancies evaluate their health care providers." *American Journal of Obstetrics & Gynecology* 192, no. 3 (March 2005): 670–77.

Skotko, Brian, and Susan P. Levine. "What the other children are thinking: Brothers and sisters of persons with Down syndrome." *American Journal of Medical Genetics, Part C: Seminars in Medical Genetics* 142C, no. 3 (August 2006): 180–86.

Slenczynska, Ruth, and Louis Biancolli. *Forbidden Childhood*. New York: Doubleday, 1957.

Sloboda, John. "Musical ability." In *Ciba Foundation Symposium 178: The Origins and Development of High Ability*, 106–18. New York: John Wiley & Sons, 1993.

Sluming, Vanessa, et al. "Broca's area supports enhanced visuospatial cognition in orchestral musicians." *Journal of Neuroscience* 27, no. 14 (April 4, 2007): 3799–806.

Smiley, Lauren. "Girl/boy interrupted: A new treatment for transgender kids puts puberty on hold so that they won't develop into their biological sex." *SF Weekly*, July 11, 2007.

Smith, David. "Gender row athlete Caster Semenya wanted to boycott medal ceremony." *Guardian*, August 21, 2009.

Smith, Dylan M., et al. "Happily hopeless: Adaptation to a permanent, but not to a temporary, disability." *Health Psychology* 28, no. 6 (November 2009): 787–91.

Smith, Gwendolyn Ann. *Remembering Our Dead*. Informational website. Gender Education & Advocacy, 2005. http://www.gender.org/remember.

Smith, Helena. "Rape victims' babies pay the price of war." *Observer*, April 16, 2000.

Smith, Joel. "Murder of autistics." *This Way of Life*, no date. http://www.geocities.com/growingjoel/murder.html.

Smith, Merrill D. *Sex Without Consent: Rape and Sexual Coercion in America*. New York: New York University Press, 2001.

————, ed. *Encyclopedia of Rape*. Westport, CT: Greenwood Press, 2004.

Smith, Nicholas A., and Mark A. Schmuckler. "Dial A440 for absolute pitch: Absolute pitch memory by non-absolute pitch possessors." *Journal of the Acoustical Society of America* 123, no. 4 (April 2008): 77–84.

Smith, Richard J. H., et al. "Deafness and hereditary hearing loss overview." *GeneReviews* (Internet) (1999–2012): 1–22.

Smith, Russell. "The impact of hate media in Rwanda." BBC News, December 3, 2003. http://news.bbc.co.uk/2/hi/africa/3257748.stm.

Smith, Yolanda L. S., Stephanie H. M. van Goozen, and Peggy T. Cohen-Kettenis. "Adolescents with gender identity disorder who were accepted or rejected for sex reassignment surgery: A prospective follow-up study." *Journal of the American Academy of Child & Adolescent Psychiatry* 40, no. 4 (April 2001): 472–81.

Smith, Yolanda L. S., et al. "Sex reassignment: Outcomes and predictors of treatment for adolescent and adult transsexuals." *Psychological Medicine* 35, no. 1 (January 2005): 89–99.

Snyder, Howard, and Melissa Sickmund. *Juvenile Offenders and Victims: 2006 National Report.* Bureau of Justice Statistics Special Report NCJ 212906. Washington, DC: US Department of Justice, Office of Justice Programs, Office of Juvenile Justice & Delinquency Prevention, 2006.

Snyder, Sharon, and David T. Mitchell. *Cultural Locations of Disability.* Chicago: University of Chicago Press, 2006.

Sobsey, Dick. "Altruistic filicide: Bioethics or criminology?" *Health Ethics Today* 12, no. 1 (November 2001): 9–11.

Solinger, Rickie, ed. *Abortion Wars: A Half Century of Struggle, 1950–2000.* Berkeley: University of California Press, 1998.

———. *Wake Up Little Susie: Single Pregnancy and Race Before Roe v. Wade.* London and New York: Routledge, 2000.

———. *Beggars and Choosers: How the Politics of Choice Shapes Adoption, Abortion, and Welfare in the United States.* New York: Hill & Wang, 2001.

Solnit, Albert J., and Mary H. Stark. "Mourning and the birth of a defective child." *Psychoanalytic Study of the Child* 16 (1961): 523–37.

Solomon, Andrew. *The Irony Tower: Soviet Artists in a Time of Glasnost.* New York: Knopf, 1991.

———. "Defiantly deaf." *New York Times Magazine*, August 29, 1994.

———. "Questions of genius." *New Yorker*, August 26, 1996.

———. "The amazing life of Laura." *Glamour*, July 2003.

———. "The pursuit of happiness." *Allure*, September 2004.

———. "The autism rights movement." *New York*, May 25, 2008.

———. "Meet my real modern family." *Newsweek*, January 30, 2011.

Solomon, Maynard. *Mozart: A Life.* New York: HarperCollins, 1996.

Solomon, Olga. "What a dog can do: Children with autism and therapy dogs in social interaction." *Ethos* 38, no. 1 (March 2010): 143–66.

Someya, Shinichi, et al. "Age-related hearing loss in C57BL/6J mice is mediated by Bak-dependent mitochondrial apoptosis." *Proceedings of the National Academy of Sciences* 106, no. 46 (November 17, 2009): 19432–37.

Sommerville, Diane Miller. *Rape and Race in the Nineteenth-Century South.* Chapel Hill: University of North Carolina Press, 2004.

Sontag, Deborah. "A schizophrenic, a slain worker, troubling questions." *New York Times*, June 17, 2011.

Soper, Kathryn Lynard. *Gifts: Mothers Reflect on How Children with Down Syndrome Enrich Their Lives.* Bethesda, MD: Woodbine House, 2007.

Southern Poverty Law Center. "SPLC sues Mississippi county to stop 'shocking' abuse of children at detention center." Press release. Montgomery, AL: Southern Poverty Law Center, April 20, 2009. http://www.splcenter.org/get-informed/ news/splc-sues-mississippi-county-to-stop-shocking-abuse-of-children-at -detention-cente.

Spack, Norman. "An endocrine perspective on the care of transgender adolescents." *Journal of Gay & Lesbian Mental Health* 13, no. 4 (October 2009): 309–19.

Speake, Jennifer, ed. *The Oxford Dictionary of Proverbs.* Oxford, UK, and New York: Oxford University Press, 2009.

Spitzer, Walter. "The real scandal of the MMR debate." *Daily Mail,* December 20, 2001.

Spurbeck, Jared. "NY senator's grandkids made him realize 'gay is OK.'" *Yahoo! News,* June 26, 2011.

"Standing tall: Experts debate the cosmetic use of growth hormones for children." Television news report. Jamie Cohen, correspondent. ABC News, June 19, 2003. http://abcnews.go.com/Health/story?id=116731.

Startup, Mike, M. C. Jackson, and S. Bendix. "North Wales randomized controlled trial of cognitive behaviour therapy for acute schizophrenia spectrum disorders: Outcomes at 6 and 12 months." *Psychological Medicine* 34, no. 3 (April 2004): 413–422.

Startup, Mike, et al. "North Wales randomized controlled trial of cognitive behaviour therapy for acute schizophrenia spectrum disorders: Two-year follow-up and economic evaluation." *Psychological Medicine* 35, no. 9 (2005): 1307–16.

State v. Peter James Gifran von Kalkstein Bleach et al. (Purulia arms dropping case). Sessions Trial No. 1, Calcutta Court of Session, judgment issued June 1997.

Steadman, Henry J., et al. "Violence by people discharged from acute psychiatric inpatient facilities and by others in the same neighborhoods." *Archives of General Psychiatry* 55, no. 5 (May 1998): 393–401.

Stefanatos, Gerry A. "Regression in autistic spectrum disorders." *Neuropsychology Review* 18 (December 2008): 305–19.

Stefanatos, Gerry A., and Ida Sue Baron. "The ontogenesis of language impairment in autism: A neuropsychological perspective." *Neuropsychology Review* 21, no. 3 (September 2011): 252–70.

Stefansson, Hreinn, et al. "Large recurrent microdeletions associated with schizophrenia." *Nature* 455, no. 7210 (September 11, 2008): 232–36.

Stein, Allen. "Stoughton cop resigns after he left beat to see dwarf porn star." *Enterprise News,* July 20, 2010.

Stein, Rob. "New safety, new concerns in tests for Down syndrome." *Washington Post,* February 24, 2009.

Steinberg, Laurence, and Elizabeth Cauffman. "Maturity of judgment in adolescence: Psychosocial factors in adolescent decision making." *Law & Human Behavior* 20, no. 3 (June 1996): 249–72.

Stephens, Ronald D., and June Lane Arnette. "From the courthouse to the schoolhouse: Making successful transitions." OJJDP: Juvenile Justice Bulletin NCJ-178900. Washington, DC: US Department of Justice, Office of Justice Programs, Office of Juvenile Justice & Delinquency Prevention, 2000.

Stevens, Wallace. *The Collected Poems of Wallace Stevens.* New York: Vintage, 1990.

Stewart, Felicia H., and James Trussell. "Prevention of pregnancy resulting from rape: A neglected preventive health measure." *American Journal of Preventive Medicine* 19, no. 4 (November 2000): 228–29.

Stiglmayer, Alexandra, ed. *Mass Rape: The War Against Women in Bosnia-Herzegovina.* Trans. Marion Faber. Lincoln: University of Nebraska Press, 1994.

Stokes, Dennis C., et al. "Respiratory complications of achondroplasia." *Journal of Pediatrics* 102, no. 4 (April 1983): 534–41.

Stokoe, William. *Sign Language Structure: An Outline of the Visual Communication Systems of the American Deaf.* Studies in Linguistics, Occasional Papers, No. 8. Buffalo, NY: University of Buffalo Department of Anthropology and Linguistics, 1960. Reprinted in *Journal of Deaf Studies & Deaf Education* 10, no. 1 (Winter 2005): 3–37.

Stone, Carole. "First person: Carole Stone on life with her schizophrenic brother." *Guardian,* November 12, 2005.

Stoneman, Zolinda. "Supporting positive sibling relationships during childhood." *Mental Retardation & Developmental Disability Research Reviews* 7, no. 2 (May 2001): 134–42.

Stoneman, Zolinda, and Phyllis Waldman Berman, eds. *The Effects of Mental Retardation, Disability, and Illness on Sibling Relationships.* Baltimore: Paul H. Brookes, 1993.

Stoneman, Zolinda, and John M. Crapps. "Mentally retarded individuals in family care homes: Relationships with the family-of-origin." *American Journal on Mental Retardation* 94, no. 4 (January 1990): 420–30.

Stoneman, Zolinda, et al. "Childcare responsibilities, peer relations, and sibling conflict: Older siblings of mentally retarded children." *American Journal on Mental Retardation* 93, no. 2 (September 1988): 174–83.

———. "Ascribed role relations between children with mental retardation and their younger siblings." *American Journal on Mental Retardation* 95, no. 5 (March 1991): 537–50.

Stopper, Michael J., ed. *Meeting the Social and Emotional Needs of Gifted and Talented Children.* London: David Fulton, 2000.

Stores, R., et al. "Daytime behaviour problems and maternal stress in children with Down's syndrome, their siblings, and non-intellectually disabled and other intellectually disabled peers." *Journal of Intellectual Disability Research* 42, no. 3 (June 1998): 228–37.

Stout, David. "Supreme Court bars death penalty for juvenile killers." *New York Times,* March 1, 2005.

———. "House votes to expand hate-crime protection." *New York Times,* May 4, 2007.

Stratton, Charles Sherwood. *Sketch of the Life: Personal Appearance, Character and Manners of Charles S. Stratton, the Man in Miniature, Known as General Tom Thumb, and His Wife, Lavinia Warren Stratton, Including the History of Their Courtship and Marriage, With Some Account of Remarkable Dwarfs, Giants, & Other Human Phenomena, of Ancient and Modern Times, Also, Songs Given at Their Public Levees.* New York: Samuel Booth, 1874.

Strauss, David, and Richard K. Eyman. "Mortality of people with mental retardation in California with and without Down syndrome, 1986–1991." *American Journal on Mental Retardation* 100, no. 6 (May 1996): 643–51.

Stuckless, E. Ross, and Jack W. Birch. "The influence of early manual communication on the linguistic development of deaf children." *American Annals of the Deaf* 142, no. 3 (July 1997): 71–79.

Sullivan, Patrick F., Kenneth S. Kendler, and Michael C. Neale. "Schizophrenia as a complex trait: Evidence from a meta-analysis of twin studies." *Archives of General Psychiatry* 60, no. 12 (December 2003): 1187–92.

Summers, Carl R., K. R. White, and M. Summers. "Siblings of children with a disability: A review and analysis of the empirical literature." *Journal of Social Behavior & Personality* 9, no. 5 (1994): 169–84.

"Suspended jail term for French mother who killed autistic son." *BBC Monitoring International Reports*, March 2, 2001.

Susser, Ezra S., and Shang P. Lin. "Schizophrenia after prenatal exposure to the Dutch Hunger Winter of 1944–1945." *Archives of General Psychiatry* 49, no. 12 (December 1992): 983–88.

Susskind, Yifat. "The murder of Du'a Aswad." *Madre*, May 22, 2007.

Suwaki, Hiroshi, Susumi Fukui, and Kyohei Konuma. "Methamphetamine abuse in Japan." In *Methamphetamine Abuse: Epidemiologic Issues and Implications*, ed. Marissa J. Miller and Nicholas J. Kozel, 84–98. Research Monograph 115. Washington, DC: National Institute on Drug Abuse, 1991.

Swaab, Dick F. "Sexual differentiation of the brain and behavior." *Best Practice & Research Clinical Endocrinology & Metabolism* 21, no. 3 (September 2007): 431–44.

Swiller, Josh. *The Unheard: A Memoir of Deafness and Africa*. New York: Macmillan, 2007.

Swoyer, Chris. "The linguistic relativity hypothesis." In *The Stanford Encyclopedia of Philosophy*, ed. Edward N. Zalta. Stanford, CA: Stanford University, 2003.

"Syracuse: Woman who killed autistic son is freed." *New York Times*, May 12, 2005.

Szasz, Thomas Stephen. *The Myth of Mental Illness: Foundations of a Theory of Personal Conduct*. New York: Harper & Row, 1974.

———. *Insanity: The Idea and Its Consequences*. New York: Wiley, 1987.

Szigeti, Joseph. *Szigeti on the Violin*. New York: Dover, 1979.

Tai, Sara, and Douglas Turkington. "The evolution of cognitive behavior therapy for schizophrenia: Current practice and recent developments." *Schizophrenia Bulletin* 35, no. 5 (September 2009): 865–73.

Takeuchi, Annie H., and Stewart H. Hulse. "Absolute pitch." *Psychological Bulletin* 113, no. 2 (1993): 345–61.

Tanner, Lindsey. "Physicians could make the perfect imperfect baby." *Los Angeles Times*, December 31, 2006.

Tarín, Juan J., Toshio Hamatani, and Antonio Cano. "Acute stress may induce ovulation in women." *Reproductive Biology & Endocrinology* 8 (May 26, 2010): 53.

Tarkan, Laurie. "New study implicates environmental factors in autism." *New York Times*, July 4, 2011.

Taylor, Louise. "'We'll kill you if you cry': Sexual violence in the Sierra Leone conflict." New York: Human Rights Watch, 2003.

Taylor, William, and Clive Jones. "William Hay, M.P. for Seaford (1695–1755)." *Parliamentary History* 29, suppl. s1 (October 2010): lxi–lxxxvii.

Tekin, Mustafa. "Genomic architecture of deafness in Turkey reflects its rich past." *International Journal of Modern Anthropology* (2009): 39–51.

Tekin, Mustafa, Kathleen S. Arnos, and Arti Pandya. "Advances in hereditary deafness." *Lancet* 358 (September 29, 2001): 1082–90.

Temple Grandin. Feature film. Santa Monica, CA: HBO Films, 2010.

Temple-Raston, Dina. *Justice on the Grass*. New York: Free Press, 2005.

Tennyson, Alfred. *The Complete Works of Alfred Lord Tennyson*. London: Frederick Stokes, 1891.

Teplin, Linda A., et al. "Psychiatric disorders in youth in juvenile detention." *Archives of General Psychiatry* 59, no. 12 (2002): 1133–43.

Tereszcuk, Alexis. "The little couple slam dwarf tossing." *Radar Online*, March 20, 2012.

Terman, Lewis M. "A new approach to the study of genius." *Psychological Review*, 29, no. 4 (1922): 310–18.

———. *Genetic Studies of Genius*. Vol. 1. *Mental and Physical Traits of a Thousand Gifted Children*. Stanford, CA: Stanford University Press, 1926.

———. *The Gifted Group at Mid-Life: Thirty-Five Years Follow-Up of the Superior Child*. Stanford, CA: Stanford University Press, 1959.

Tevenal, Stephanie, and Miako Villanueva. "Are you getting the message? The effects of SimCom on the message received by deaf, hard of hearing, and hearing students." *Sign Language Studies* 9, no. 3 (Spring 2009): 266–86.

Tharinger, Deborah, Connie Burrows Horton, and Susan Millea. "Sexual abuse and exploitation of children and adults with mental retardation and other handicaps." *Child Abuse & Neglect* 14, no. 3 (1990): 301–12.

"Therapy to change 'feminine' boy created a troubled man, family says." Television news report. Scott Bronstein and Jessi Joseph, correspondents. Cable News Network, June 8, 2011. http://edition.cnn.com/2011/US/06/07/sissy.boy.experiment/.

Thompson, Sue, Tom Shakespeare, and Michael J. Wright. "Medical and social aspects of the life course for adults with a skeletal dysplasia: A review of current knowledge." *Disability & Rehabilitation* 30, no. 1 (January 2008): 1–12.

Thomson, Rosemarie Garland. *Extraordinary Bodies: Figuring Physical Disability in American Culture and Literature*. New York: Columbia University Press, 1997.

Thornberry, Terence P. *Violent Families and Youth Violence*. Fact Sheet 21. Washington, DC: US Department of Justice, Office of Justice Programs, Office of Juvenile Justice and Delinquency Prevention, 1994.

Thornhill, Randy, and Craig T. Palmer. *A Natural History of Rape: Biological Bases of Sexual Coercion*. Cambridge, MA: MIT Press, 2000.

Thrasher, Steven. "Camila Guzman, transgender murder victim, remembered in East Harlem vigil." *Village Voice*, August 12, 2011.

Through Deaf Eyes. Documentary film. Directed by Lawrence Hott and Diane Garey. Washington, DC: WETA-TV/Florentine Films/Hott Productions in association with Gallaudet University, 2007.

Tinbergen, Elisabeth A., and Nikolaas Tinbergen. "Early childhood autism: An ethological approach." *Advances in Ethology, Journal of Comparative Ethology*, suppl. no. 10 (1972): 1–53.

Tjaden, Patricia, and Nancy Thoennes. *Full Report of the Prevalence, Incidence, and Consequences of Violence Against Women: Findings from the National Violence Against Women Survey*. Report NCJ 183781. Washington, DC: National Institute of Justice, 2000.

Tolan, Patrick, ed. *Multi-Systemic Structural-Strategic Interventions for Child and Adolescent Behavior Problems*. New York: Haworth, 1990.

Tolan, Patrick, et al. "Family therapy with delinquents: A critical review of the literature." *Family Processes* 25, no. 4 (December 1986): 619–50.

Tolan, Patrick, and Peter Thomas. "The implications of age of onset for delinquency risk II: Longitudinal data." *Journal of Abnormal Child Psychology* 23, no. 2 (April 1995): 157–81.

Tolstoy, Leo. *Anna Karenina*. Trans. Constance Garnett. New York: Spark Educational Publishing, 2004.

Tomaselli, Sylvana, and Roy Porter, eds. *Rape: An Historical and Cultural Enquiry*. Oxford, UK: Blackwell, 1986.

Tommasini, Anthony. "A showman revs up the classical genre." *New York Times*, November 10, 2003.

———. "Views back (and forward) on an outdoor stage." *New York Times*, July 17, 2008.

Toppo, Greg. "10 years later, the real story behind Columbine." *USA Today*, April 14, 2009.

Torgovnik, Johnathan. *Nowhere to Go: The Tragic Odyssey of the Homeless Mentally Ill.* New York: Harper and Row, 1988.

———. *Out of the Shadows: Confronting America's Mental Illness Crisis.* New York: Wiley, 1997.

———. *Surviving Schizophrenia: A Manual for Families, Patients and Providers.* 5th ed. New York: HarperCollins, 2006.

———. *Intended Consequences: Rwandan Children Born of Rape.* New York: Aperture, 2009.

Torrey, E. Fuller, et al. "Paternal age as a risk factor for schizophrenia: How important is it?" *Schizophrenia Research* 114, nos. 1–3 (October 2009): 1–5.

Toyota Motor Manufacturing v. Williams. 534 US 184 (2002).

"Transgender children face unique challenges." Television news report. Produced by Joneil Adriano. Barbara Walters, correspondent. *20/20*, ABC News, April 27, 2007. http://abcnews.go.com/2020/story?id=3091754.

"Transgender person slain in northeast." Television news report. Pat Collins, correspondent. NBC Washington, July 21, 2011. http://www.nbcwashington.com/news/local/Transgender-Person-Slain-in-Northeast-125919853.html.

Travis, John. "Genes of silence: Scientists track down a slew of mutated genes that cause deafness." *Science News*, January 17, 1998.

"Treatment keeps girl child-sized." Television news report. BBC News, January 4, 2007. http://news.bbc.co.uk/2/hi/americas/6229799.stm.

"Treatment not jail: A plan to rebuild community mental health." *Sacramento Bee*, March 17, 1999.

Treffert, Darold A. "The savant syndrome: An extraordinary condition." *Philosophical Transactions of the Royal Society*, pt. B 364, no. 1522 (May 2009): 1351–57.

Trent, James W., Jr. *Inventing the Feeble Mind: A History of Mental Retardation in the United States.* Berkeley: University of California Press, 1995.

Tretter, Anne E., et al. "Antenatal diagnosis of lethal skeletal dysplasias." *American Journal of Medical Genetics* 75, no. 5 (December 1998): 518–22.

Trotter, Tracy L., Judith G. Hall, and the American Academy of Pediatrics Committee on Genetics. "Health supervision for children with achondroplasia." *Pediatrics* 116, no. 3 (2005): 771–83.

Truman, Jennifer L. *Criminal Victimization, 2010.* Bureau of Justice Statistics Special Report NCJ 235508. Washington, DC: US Department of Justice, Bureau of Justice Statistics, 2011.

Trumball, Robert. "Dacca raising the status of women while aiding rape victims." *New York Times*, May 12, 1972.

Tsai, Luke. "Comorbid psychiatric disorders of autistic disorder." *Journal of Autism & Developmental Disorders* 26, no. 2 (April 1996): 159–63.

Tsouderos, Trine. "'Miracle drug' called junk science." *Chicago Tribune*, May 21, 2009.

Tucker, Bonnie Poitras. "Deaf culture, cochlear implants, and elective disability." *Hastings Center Report* 28, no. 4 (July 1, 1998): 6–14.

Turkel, Henry. "Medical amelioration of Down's syndrome incorporating the orthomolecular approach." *Journal of Orthomolecular Psychiatry* 4, no. 2 (2nd quarter 1975): 102–15.

Turnbull, Ann P., Joan M. Patterson, and Shirley K. Behr, eds. *Cognitive Coping, Families, and Disability.* Baltimore: Paul H. Brookes, 1993.

Turnbull, H. Rutherford, III, Doug Guess, and Anne P. Turnbull. "Vox populi and Baby Doe." *Mental Retardation* 26, no. 3 (June 1988): 127–32.

Turner, David M., and Kevin Stagg, eds. *Social Histories of Disability and Deformity: Bodies, Images and Experiences.* London and New York: Routledge, 2006.

Turpin v. Sortini, 31. Cal.3d 220, 643 P.2d 954 (California, 1982).

"Two families grapple with sons' gender preferences: Psychologists take radically different approaches in therapy." Radio broadcast. Alix Spiegel, correspondent. *All Things Considered*, National Public Radio, May 7, 2008. http://www.npr.org/templates/story/story.php?storyId=90247842.

Uddin, Lucina Q., et al. "Neural basis of self and other representation in autism: An fMRI study of self-face recognition." *PLoS One* 3, no. 10 (2008): E3526.

UK Health Protection Agency. "Measles notifications and deaths in England and Wales, 1940–2008." London: Health Protection Agency, 2010.

UK Parliament. "Human Fertilisation and Embryology Act 2008." Enacted November 13, 2008. http://www.opsi.gov.uk/acts/acts2008/ukpga_20080022_en_1.

Unforgotten: Twenty-Five Years After Willowbrook. Documentary film. Directed by Danny Fisher. Includes "Willowbrook: The last great disgrace," documentary film by Geraldo Rivera for ABC News (1972). New York: City Lights Pictures, 2008.

UNICEF Innocenti Research Centre. *Birth Registration and Armed Conflict.* Siena: Innocenti Research Centre, 2007.

United Nations Human Rights Committee. *Views of the Human Rights Committee Under Article 5, Paragraph 4, of the Optional Protocol to the International Covenant on Civil and Political Rights, Seventy-Fifth Session, Communication No. 854/1999, Submitted by Manuel Wackenheim.* Geneva: United Nations Human Rights Committee, July 15, 2002.

United Nations Office for the Coordination of Humanitarian Affairs. "Our bodies, their battleground: Gender-based violence in conflict zones." *IRIN News*, September 1, 2004.

University College of London. "First baby tested for breast cancer form BRCA1 before conception born in U.K." Press release, January 9, 2009.

University of California, Los Angeles. "Drug reverses mental retardation in mice." Press release. Los Angeles: University of California Health Sciences Center, June 20, 2008. http://www.newswise.com/articles/view/541960.

University of Miami School of Medicine. "Costs associated with cochlear implants." Miami: University of Miami, 2009. http://cochlearimplants.med.miami.edu/implants/08_Costs%20Associated%20with%20Cochlear%20Implants.asp.

US Congress. Americans with Disabilities Act (42 USC § 12101). http://www.law.cornell.edu/usc-cgi/get_external.cgi?type=pubL&target=101-336.

———. US Rehabilitation Act of 1973 (29 USC § 701). http://www.law.cornell.edu/uscode/text/29/701.

———. Senate Committee on the Judiciary. *Drugs in Institutions.* Hearings Before the Subcommittee to Investigate Juvenile Delinquency of the Committee on the Judiciary, July 31 and August 18, 1975. Washington, DC: US Government Printing Office, 1977.

———. House Committee on Education and the Workforce. Subcommittee on Education Reform. *Individuals with Disabilities Education Act (IDEA): Guide to Frequently Asked Questions.* Washington, DC: US Government Printing Office, February 2005.

US Department of Health and Human Services, Agency for Healthcare Research and Quality. *Preventing Violence and Related Health-Risking Social Behaviors in Adolescents.* National Institutes of Health State-of-the-Science Conference Statement, October 13–15, 2004. Rockville, MD: Agency for Healthcare Research and Quality, 2004.

US Department of Health and Human Services, Centers for Disease Control and Prevention. "Sexual Assault Awareness Month, April 2005." *Morbidity & Mortality Weekly Report* 54, no. 12 (April 1, 2005): 311.

———. "Down syndrome cases at birth increased." Atlanta, GA: US Centers for Disease Control and Prevention, 2009. http://www.cdc.gov/features/dsdownsyndrome/.

US Department of Health and Human Services, National Institute of Mental Health. *Schizophrenia.* NIH Publication No. 06-3517. Washington, DC: National Institute of Mental Health, 2007. http://www.nimh.nih.gov/publicat/schizoph.cfm.

US Department of Health and Human Services, National Institute of Neurological Disorders and Stroke. *Autism Fact Sheet.* NIH Publication No. 09-1877. Bethesda, MD: National Institute of Neurological Disorders and Stroke, April 2009.

———. *Newborn Hearing Screening.* Washington, DC: National Institutes of Health, 2010.

———. "Quick statistics." Bethesda, MD: National Institute on Deafness and Other Communication Disorders, 2010.

US Department of Health and Human Services, Office of the Surgeon General. *Youth Violence: A Report of the Surgeon General.* Washington, DC: Office of the Surgeon General, 2001.

US Department of Health and Human Services, Substance Abuse and Mental Health Services Administration. *Drug and Alcohol Treatment in Juvenile Correctional Facilities: The DASIS Report.* Rockville, MD: Substance Abuse and Mental Health Services Administration, 2002.

———. *Results from the 2008 National Survey on Drug Use and Health: National Findings.* Rockville, MD: Substance Abuse and Mental Health Services Administration, 2008.

Van, John. "Little people veto a miniaturized village." *Chicago Tribune,* June 16, 1989.

Van Buren, Abigail. "A fable for parents of a disabled child." *Chicago Tribune,* November 5, 1989.

Vandenburg, Martina, and Kelly Askin. "Chechnya: Another battleground for the perpetration of gender based crimes." *Human Rights Review* 2, no. 3 (April 2001): 140–49.

Van Dyke, Don C., et al., eds. *Medical and Surgical Care for Children with Down Syndrome: A Guide for Parents.* Bethesda, MD: Woodbine House, 1995.

Van Etten, Angela Muir. "Dwarf tossing and exploitation." *Huffington Post,* October 19, 2011. http://www.huffingtonpost.com/angela-van-etten/dwarf-tossing-b_1020953.html.

van Gulden, Holly. "Talking with children about difficult history." Oakland, CA: Pact, An Adoption Alliance, 1998. http://www.pactadopt.org/press/articles/diffhis.html.

van Os, Jim, and Jean-Paul Selten. "Prenatal exposure to maternal stress and subsequent schizophrenia: The May 1940 invasion of The Netherlands." *British Journal of Psychiatry* 172, no. 4 (April 1998): 324–26.

Vargas Barreto, Bernardo, et al. "Complications of Ilizarov leg lengthening: A comparative study between patients with leg length discrepancy and short stature." *International Orthopaedics* 31, no. 5 (October 2007): 587–91.

Vaughan, Kevin. "Questions for killers' families: In suit, Rohrboughs seeking to interview Harrises, Klebolds." *Denver Rocky Mountain News,* October 12, 2004.

Vaughan, Kevin, and Jeff Kass. "Columbine cover-up alleged: Released reports conclude officials hid damaging evidence." *Denver Rocky Mountain News,* September 16, 2004.

Verhovek, Sam Howe. "Parents defend decision to keep disabled girl small." *Los Angeles Times,* January 3, 2007.

Verstraeten, Thomas, et al. "Safety of thimerosal-containing vaccines: A two-phased study of computerized health maintenance organization databases." *Pediatrics* 112, no. 5 (November 2003): 1039–48.

Vickrey Van Cleve, John, ed. *Deaf History Unveiled: Interpretations from the New Scholarship.* Washington, DC: Gallaudet University Press, 1999.

Vidal, Gore. *Matters of Fact and Fiction.* London: Heinemann, 1977.

Virginia Fusion Center. *Bloods Street Gang Intelligence Report.* Richmond, VA: Commonwealth of Virginia Department of State Police, November 2008.

Vitruvius. *The Ten Books on Architecture (De Architectura).* New York: Dover, 1960.

Vollum, Scott, and Dennis R. Longmire. "Covictims of capital murder: Statements of victims' family members and friends made at the time of execution." *Violence & Victims* 22, no. 5 (October 2007): 601–19.

Volta, Alessandro. "On the electricity excited by the mere contact of conducting substances of different kinds." *Philosophical Transactions of the Royal Society* 90 (1800): 403–31.

von Rhein, John. "Bend the rules, but don't break the bond." *Chicago Tribune,* August 18, 2002.

Wahl, Otto F. *Media Madness: Public Images of Mental Illness.* New Brunswick, NJ: Rutgers University Press, 1995.

Wahlberg, Karl-Erik, et al. "Gene-environment interaction in vulnerability to schizophrenia: Findings from the Finnish Adoptive Family Study of Schizophrenia." *American Journal of Psychiatry* 154, no. 3 (March 1997): 355–62.

Wakefield, Andrew J., et al. "Ileal-lymphoid-nodular hyperplasia, non-specific colitis, and pervasive developmental disorder in children." *Lancet* 351, no. 9103 (February 28, 1998): 637–41.

Wakin, Daniel J. "Burned out at 14, Israeli concert pianist is back where he 'really belongs.'" *New York Times,* November 2, 2007.

Walker, Elaine, et al. "Schizophrenia: Etiology and course." *Annual Review of Psychology* 55 (February 2004): 401–30.

Walker, Elaine, Vijay Mittal, and Kevin Tessner. "Stress and the hypothalamic pituitary adrenal axis in the developmental course of schizophrenia." *Annual Review of Clinical Psychology* 4 (January 2008): 189–216.

Walker, Lou Ann. "Losing the language of silence." *New York Magazine,* January 13, 2008.

Wallace, Cameron, et al. "Serious criminal offending and mental disorder: Case linkage study." *British Journal of Psychiatry* 172, no. 6 (June 1998): 477–84.

Wallis, Claudia. "A powerful identity, a vanishing diagnosis." *New York Times,* November 2, 2009.

Walsh, Maryellen. *Schizophrenia: Straight Talk for Family and Friends.* New York: Quill/ William Morrow, 1985.

Walsh, Michael, and Elizabeth Rudulph. "Evgeni Kissin, new kid." *Time*, October 29, 1990.

Waltzman, Susan B., et al. "Open-set speech perception in congenitally deaf children using cochlear implants." *American Journal of Otology* 18, no. 3 (1997): 342–49.

Wang, Shirley S. "NYU bows to critics and pulls ransom-note ads." *Wall Street Journal Health Blog*, December 19, 2007. http://blogs.wsj.com/health/2007/12/19/nyu -bows-to-critics-and-pulls-ransom-note-ads/.

Warman, Debbie M., and Aaron T. Beck. "Cognitive behavioral therapy." Arlington, VA: National Alliance on Mental Illness, 2003. http://www.nami.org/ Template.cfm?Section=About_Treatments_and_Supports&template=/ ContentManagement/ContentDisplay.cfm&ContentID=7952.

Warner, Judith. "The Columbine syndrome." *New York Times*, August 4, 2007.

Wax, Emily. "Rwandans are struggling to love children of hate." *Washington Post*, March 28, 2004.

Weathers, Helen. "A British tycoon and father of two has been a man and a woman . . . and a man again . . . and knows which sex he'd rather be." *Daily Mail Online*, January 4, 2009.

Weber, Wim. "France's highest court recognizes 'the right not to be born.'" *Lancet* 358, no. 9297 (December 8, 2001): 1972.

Weinberger, Daniel R. "A brain too young for good judgment." *New York Times*, March 10, 2001.

Weinreich, Susan. "Reflections on a childhood before the onset of schizophrenia." *Mental Health News*, Fall 2005.

Weintraub, Kit. "A mother's perspective." Crosswicks, NJ: Association for Science in Autism Treatment, 2007. http://www.asatonline.org/forum/articles/mother.htm.

Weiss, Meira. *Conditional Love: Parents' Attitudes Toward Handicapped Children*. Westport, CT: Bergin & Garvey, 1994.

Welborn, Larry. "Mom who drugged son gets deal: She pleads guilty to child endangerment for giving boy pills during suicide try." *Orange County Register*, May 24, 2003.

Welch, Killian A., et al. "The impact of substance use on brain structure in people at high risk of developing schizophrenia." *Schizophrenia Bulletin* 37, no. 5 (September 2011): 1066–76.

Welles, Elizabeth B. "Foreign language enrollments in United States institutions of higher education, Fall 2002." *Profession* (2004): 128–53.

Werker, Janet F. "Becoming a native listener." *American Scientist* 77, no. 1 (January– February 1989): 54–59.

———. "Infant-directed speech supports phonetic category learning in English and Japanese." *Cognition* 103, no. 1 (April 2007): 147–62.

Werker, Janet F., and Richard C. Tees. "Cross-language speech perception: Evidence for perceptual reorganization during the first year of life." *Infant Behavior & Development* 25, no. 1 (January–March 2002): 121–33.

Werner, Emily, and Geraldine Dawson. "Validation of the phenomenon of autistic regression using home videotapes." *Archives of General Psychiatry* 62, no. 8 (August 2005): 889–95.

Werner, Emmy, and Ruth Smith. *Journeys from Childhood to Midlife: Risk, Resilience, and Recovery*. Ithaca, NY: Cornell University Press, 2001.

Wharton, Edith. *A Backward Glance*. New York: D. Appleton-Century, 1934.

Wheeler, Alexandra, et al. "Cochlear implants: The young people's perspective." *Journal of Deaf Studies & Deaf Education* 12, no. 3 (Summer 2007): 303–16.

BIBLIOGRAPHY

Wheeler, John. "Let's Talk About Conquering Deafness. Join the Dialogue: Introduction." Washington, DC: Deafness Research Foundation, 2000.

Wheeler, Patricia G., et al. "Short stature and functional impairment: A systematic review." *Archives of Pediatric & Adolescent Medicine* 158, no. 3 (March 2004): 236–43.

Whitaker, Robert. *Mad in America: Bad Science, Bad Medicine, and the Enduring Mistreatment of the Mentally Ill.* Cambridge, MA: Perseus, 2002.

Whitcher-Gentzke, Ann. "Dalai Lama brings message of compassion to UB." *UB Reporter,* September 21, 2006.

White, Richard. "Mike Tindall gropes blonde." *Sun,* September 15, 2011.

Whorf, Benjamin Lee. *Language, Thought, and Reality: Selected Writings of Benjamin Lee Whorf.* Cambridge, MA: MIT Press, 1956.

Widom, Cathy. *The Cycle of Violence.* National Institute of Justice, Research in Brief, NCJ 136607. Washington, DC: US Department of Justice, Office of Justice Programs, National Institute of Justice, September 1992.

Widom, Cathy, and Michael G. Maxfield. *An Update on the "Cycle of Violence."* National Institute of Justice, Research in Brief, NCJ 184894. Washington, DC: US Department of Justice, Office of Justice Programs, National Institute of Justice, February 2001.

Wiener, Norbert. *Ex-Prodigy: My Childhood and Youth.* New York: Simon & Schuster, 1953.

———. *I Am a Mathematician: The Later Life of a Prodigy.* Garden City, NY: Doubleday, 1956.

Wilbur, Richard. *Collected Poems 1943–2004.* Orlando, FL: Harcourt, 2004.

Wilbur, Ronnie B. "What does the study of signed languages tell us about 'language'?" *Sign Language & Linguistics* 9, nos. 1–2 (2006): 5–32.

Wilcox, Allen J., et al. "Likelihood of conception with a single act of intercourse: Providing benchmark rates for assessment of post-coital contraceptives." *Contraception* 63, no. 4 (April 2001): 211–15.

Wilfond, Benjamin S., et al. "Navigating growth attenuation in children with profound disabilities: Children's interests, family decision-making, and community concerns." *Hastings Center Report* 40, no. 6 (November–December 2010): 27–40.

Wilkinson, Stephanie. "Drop the Barbie! If you bend gender far enough, does it break?" *Brain, Child: The Magazine for Thinking Mothers,* Fall 2001.

Will, George. "Golly, what did Jon do?" *Newsweek,* January 29, 2007.

Willard, Tom. "N.Y. Times reports on proposed signing town." *DeafWeekly,* March 23, 2005.

Williams, Katie R. "The Son-Rise Program intervention for autism: Prerequisites for evaluation." *Autism* 10, no. 1 (January 2006): 86–102.

Williams, Katie R., and J. G. Wishart. "The Son-Rise Program intervention for autism: An investigation into family experiences." *Journal of Intellectual Disability Research* 47, nos. 4–5 (May–June 2003): 291–99.

Williams, Katrina, et al. "Selective serotonin reuptake inhibitors (SSRIs) for autism spectrum disorders (ASD)." *Evidence-Based Child Health: A Cochrane Review Journal* 6, no. 4 (July 2011): 1044–78.

Williams, Lena. "College for deaf is shut by protest over president." *New York Times,* March 8, 1988.

Willoughby, Jennifer C., and Laraine Masters Glidden. "Fathers helping out: Shared child care and marital satisfaction of parents of children with disabilities." *American Journal on Mental Retardation* 99, no. 4 (January 1995): 399–406.

Winata, Sunaryana, et al. "Congenital non-syndromal autosomal recessive deafness in Bengkala, an isolated Balinese village." *Journal of Medical Genetics* 32 (1995): 336–43.

Wing, Lorna, Judith Gould, Christopher Gillberg. "Autism spectrum disorders in the DSM-V: Better or worse than the DSM-IV?" *Research in Developmental Disabilities* 32, no. 2 (March–April 2011): 768–73.

Wingerson, Lois. "Gender identity disorder: Has accepted practice caused harm?" *Psychiatric Times*, May 19, 2009.

Winner, Ellen. *Gifted Children: Myths and Realities*. New York: Basic Books, 1996.

Winnicott, Donald Woods. *Through Paediatrics to Psycho-Analysis*. London: Hogarth Press, 1958, 1975.

———. *The Child, the Family, and the Outside World*. Reading, MA: Addison-Wesley, 1987.

Winship, Scott. "Mobility impaired." *National Review*, November 14, 2011.

Winters, Kelly. "Issues of GID diagnosis for transsexual women and men." San Diego, CA: GID Reform Advocates, September 30, 2007.

Wisely, Dale W., Frank T. Masur, and Sam B. Morgan. "Psychological aspects of severe burn injuries in children." *Health Psychology* 2, no. 1 (Winter 1983): 45–72.

Wittgenstein, Ludwig. *Tractatus Logico-Philosophicus*. Trans. C. K. Ogden. London: Routledge & Kegan Paul, 1922.

Wolf, Ken. "Big world, little people." *Newsday*, April 20, 1989.

Wolin, John. "Dwarf like me." *Miami Herald*, January 24, 1993.

The Woman Who Thinks Like a Cow. Documentary film. Directed by Emma Sutton. Interviews with Temple Grandin, Eustacia Cutler, Chloe Silverman, Douglas Hare, Bernard Rimland, Nancy Minshew, Francesca Happe. *Horizon*, originally broadcast June 8, 2006. London: British Broadcasting Corporation, 2006.

Wong, Sophia Isako. "At home with Down syndrome and gender." *Hypatia* 17, no. 3 (Summer 2002): 89–119.

Woods, Scott W., et al. "The case for including Attenuated Psychotic Symptoms Syndrome in DSM-5 as a psychosis risk syndrome." *Schizophrenia Research* 123, nos. 2–3 (November 2010).

Woolfenden, Susan R., Katrina Williams, and Jennifer K. Peat. "Family and parenting interventions for conduct disorder and delinquency: A meta-analysis of randomized controlled trials." *Archives of Disease in Childhood* 86, no. 4 (April 2002): 251–56.

World Professional Association for Transgender Health. *Harry Benjamin International Gender Dysphoria Association's Standards of Care for Gender Identity Disorders*. 6th version. Minneapolis: World Professional Association for Transgender Health, 2001. http://www.wpath.org/Documents2/socv6.pdf.

Writers Reading at Sweetwaters Anthology. Ann Arbor, MI: Word'n Woman Press, 2007.

Wu, Eric Q., et al. "The economic burden of schizophrenia in the United States in 2002." *Journal of Clinical Psychiatry* 66, no. 9 (September 2005): 1122–29.

Wyden, Peter. *Conquering Schizophrenia: A Father, His Son, and a Medical Breakthrough*. New York: Alfred A. Knopf, 1998.

Wynn, Julia, et al. "Mortality in achondroplasia study: A 42-year follow-up." *American Journal of Medical Genetics* 143A, no. 21 (November 2007): 2502–11.

Yang, Quanhe, et al. "Mortality associated with Down's syndrome in the U.S.A. from 1983 to 1997: A population-based study." *Lancet* 359 (2002): 1019–25.

Yang, Xia, et al. "Tissue-specific expression and regulation of sexually dimorphic genes in mice." *Genome Research* 16, no. 8 (August 2006): 995–1004.

Bibliography

Yeagle, Patrick. "Dog fight ends with hall pass." *Illinois Times,* September 9, 2010.

Yeh, Peter. "Accuracy of prenatal diagnosis and prediction of lethality for fetal skeletal dysplasias." *Prenatal Diagnosis* 31, no. 5 (May 2011): 515–18.

Young, Carl R., Malcolm B. Bowers Jr., and Carolyn M. Mazure. "Management of the adverse effects of clozapine." *Schizophrenia Bulletin* 24, no. 3 (1998): 381–90.

Zahn, Margaret A., et al. "Causes and correlates of girls' delinquency." US Department of Justice, Office of Justice Programs, Office of Juvenile Justice & Delinquency Prevention, April 2010.

Zammit, Stanley, et al. "Self reported cannabis use as a risk factor for schizophrenia in Swedish conscripts of 1969: Historical cohort study." *British Medical Journal* 325, no. 7374 (November 23, 2002): 1199.

Zeitler, Daniel M., Cameron L. Budenz, and John Thomas Roland Jr. "Revision cochlear implantation." *Current Opinion in Otolaryngology & Head & Neck Surgery* 17, no. 5 (October 2009): 334–38.

Zena, Mishka (pseud. Elizabeth Gillespie). "Eugenics too close to home: Tomato Lichy, U.K. activist." *Endless Pondering,* March 10, 2008. http://www.mishkazena .com/2008/03/10/eugenics-too-close-to-home-tomato-livy-uk-activist.

Zeng, Fan-Gang, et al. "Cochlear implants: System design, integration and evaluation." *IEEE Review of Biomedical Engineering* 1, no. 1 (January 2008): 115–42.

Zeng, Ling-Hui, et al. "Rapamycin prevents epilepsy in a mouse model of tuberous sclerosis complex." *Annals of Neurology* 63, no. 4 (April 2008): 444–53.

Zhao, Hong-Bo, et al. "Gap junctions and cochlear homeostasis." *Journal of Membrane Biology* 209, nos. 2–3 (May 2006): 177–86.

Zigler, Edward, and Sally J. Styfco. *The Hidden History of Head Start.* Oxford, UK, and New York: Oxford University Press, 2010.

Zimmerman, Andrew W. *Autism: Current Theories and Evidence.* Totowa, NJ: Humana Press, 2008.

Zimmerman, Andrew W., and Susan L. Connors, eds. *Maternal Influences on Fetal Neurodevelopment.* New York: Springer, 2010.

Zimmerman, Rachel. "Treating the body vs. the mind." *Wall Street Journal,* February 15, 2005.

Zimonjic, Peter. "Church supports baby euthanasia." *The Times,* November 12, 2006.

Zirinsky, William. "Sam's story." *Exceptional Parent,* June 1997.

———. "Saying goodbye to our cherished boy, Sam Zirinsky." *Crazy Wisdom Community Journal,* May–August 2004.

———. "Life with my two little girls." *Crazy Wisdom Community Journal,* January–April 2006.

———. "If you could see her through my eyes: A journey of love and dying in the fall of 2007." *Crazy Wisdom Community Journal,* January–April 2008.

Zirkel, Perry A. "Does *Brown v. Board of Education* play a prominent role in special education law?" *Journal of Law & Education* 34, no. 2 (April 2005).

Zorn, Eric. "At 15, Lauren is coming forward for kids like her." *Chicago Tribune,* April 24, 2003.

Zucker, Kenneth J., and Susan J. Bradley. *Gender Identity Disorder and Psychosexual Problems in Children and Adolescents.* New York: Guilford Press, 1995.

Zuckoff, Mitchell. *Choosing Naia: A Family's Journey.* Boston: Beacon Press, 2002.

Zyman, Samuel. "New music from a very new composer." *Juilliard Journal,* May 2003.

Permissions

Index

About the Author

Andrew Solomon's last book, *The Noonday Demon: An Atlas of Depression* (Scribner, 2001), won the 2001 National Book Award for Nonfiction, was a finalist for the 2002 Pulitzer Prize, and was included in the *Times* of London's list of one hundred best books of the decade. A *New York Times* bestseller in both hardcover and paperback editions, *The Noonday Demon* has also been a bestseller in seven foreign countries, and has been published in twenty-four languages. It was named a Notable Book by both the *New York Times* and the American Library Association, and received the Books for a Better Life Award from the National Multiple Sclerosis Society, the 2002 Ken Book Award from the National Alliance on Mental Illness of New York City, Mind Book of the Year, the Lambda Literary Award for Autobiography/Memoir, and Quality Paperback Book Club's New Visions Award. Following publication of *The Noonday Demon*, Solomon was honored with the Dr. Albert J. Solnit Memorial Award from Fellowship Place, the Voice of Mental Health Award from the Jed Foundation and the National Mental Health Association (now Mental Health America), the PRISM Award from the National Depressive and Manic-Depressive Association, the Erasing the Stigma Leadership Award from Didi Hirsch Mental Health Services, the Charles T. Rubey L.O.S.S. Award from the Karla Smith Foundation, and the Silvano Arieti Award from the William Alanson White Institute.

A native New Yorker, Andrew Solomon attended the Horace Mann School, graduating cum laude in 1981. He received a bachelor of arts degree in English from Yale University in 1985, graduating magna cum laude, and later earned a master's degree in English at Jesus College, Cambridge. While at Cambridge, he received the top first-class degree in English in his year, the only foreign student ever to be so honored, as well as the University writing prize. He is currently pursuing a PhD in psychology at Cambridge University.

In 1988, Solomon began his study of Russian artists, which culminated with the publication of *The Irony Tower: Soviet Artists in a Time of Glasnost* (Knopf, 1991). He was asked in 1993 to consult with members of the National Security Council on Russian affairs. His first novel, *A Stone Boat* (Faber, 1994), the story of a man's shifting identity as he watches his mother battle cancer, was a national bestseller and runner-up for the *Los Angeles Times* First Fiction prize; it has since been published in five languages.

From 1993 to 2001, Solomon was a contributing writer for the *New York Times Magazine*, writing on a wide range of subjects; he has also written periodically for the *New Yorker*. Such journalism has spanned many topics, including depression, Soviet artists, the cultural rebirth of Afghanistan, and Libyan politics. He has authored essays for many anthologies and books of criticism, and his work has been featured on National Public Radio's *Moth Radio Hour*.

Solomon is an activist and philanthropist in LGBT rights, mental health, education, and the arts. His articles on gay marriage have appeared in the *New Yorker, Newsweek*, the *Advocate*, and *Anderson Cooper 360°*.

He has lectured widely and is a Lecturer in Psychiatry at Weill Cornell Medical College; Special Adviser on Lesbian, Gay, Bisexual, and Transgender Mental Health at the Yale Department of Psychiatry; a director of the University of Michigan Depression Center, Columbia Psychiatry, and Cold Spring Harbor Laboratory; a member of the Board of Visitors of Columbia University Medical School and the Depression and Bipolar Support Alliance. In 2008, Solomon received the Society of Biological Psychiatry's Humanitarian Award for his contributions to the field of mental health, and in 2010, the Brain & Behavior Research Foundation's Productive Lives Award. He is also a fellow of Berkeley College at Yale University and a member of the New York Institute for the Humanities and the Council on Foreign Relations.

He lives with his husband and son in New York and London and is a dual national.